95TH YEAR

WISDEN

CRICKET  *ALMANACK*

EDITED BY NO[...]

PUBLISHED BY SPORTING HANDBOOKS LTD
AT THIRTEEN BEDFORD SQUARE LONDON WC1 FOR
THE PROPRIETORS JOHN WISDEN AND CO LTD
IN TWO EDITIONS, LIMP LINSON COVERS AT SIXTEEN
SHILLINGS NET, CLOTH BOARDS BINDING AT
EIGHTEEN SHILLINGS AND SIXPENCE NET

a

PREFACE

Regular readers of *Wisden* will find that this 95th Edition follows the pattern of its predecessors and presents mainly a record of the first-class game over the past year. I am greatly indebted to Lord Birkett, who only a few weeks before his elevation to the peerage kindly responded to my invitation to write on "The Love of Cricket." Over the past ten years Lord Birkett has produced many masterpieces on cricket in the shape of after-dinner speeches and now we have the privilege of enabling a much wider circle of cricket lovers to enjoy his eloquence.

To mark the retirement of Denis Compton, who hopes to play a few more times as an amateur, Neville Cardus provides a pen-picture which is followed by a comprehensive statistical survey of Compton's remarkable career compiled by W. S. Conder. I have to thank E. M. Wellings for paying tribute to several other players who have given up active participation in the game, and as usual he has written extensively on Public Schools Cricket. Charles Bray welcomes the New Zealand team to England by telling the story of the development of the game there and James Coldham writes of the "Ups and Downs of Northamptonshire."

The Five Cricketers of the Year caused me considerable thought, so numerous were the candidates. In the end I felt that the deeds of three Surrey players, P. J. Loader, A. J. McIntyre and M. J. Stewart, and two of the West Indies team, C. L. Walcott and O. G. Smith, entitled them to preference.

Besides those already mentioned I thank the following for their help and advice: H. S. Altham (Dates), G. A. Copinger (Records), T. L. Goodman (Australia), N. S. Curnow (South Africa), C. A. Anderson (West Indies), A. G. Wiren (New Zealand), S. K. Gurunathan (India), M. Salim-ur-Rehman and Ghulam Mustafa Khan (Pakistan), H. Vaidyasekera (Ceylon), Donald King (Canada), C. Venables (Oxford), P. Piggott (Cambridge), Frank Crompton (Minor Counties), John Arlott (Books), H. E. Richards (Nottingham), A. Bannister, L. N. Bailey (London), Robert Paterson (Stirlingshire), Derek Scott (Dublin), A. W. T. Langford (*The Cricketer*), R. Aird and S. C. Griffith (M.C.C.) and the secretaries of all the first-class and second-class counties.

Finally, I acknowledge the vast amount of work that is done year by year by my colleagues at the Cricket Reporting Agency, namely my partners, E. Eden and Harry Gee, and these members of the staff: Leslie Smith, F. L. Belson, H. E. Abel, P. F. Brincklow, A. W. Williamson, G. A. White and P. M. Voller.

NORMAN PRESTON

CRICKET REPORTING AGENCY,
85, FLEET STREET, LONDON, E.C.4.
February, 1958.

TABLE OF MAIN CONTENTS

(A complete Index appears on the following pages)

*a**

INDEX

NOTE:—r. = runs: w. = wickets.   * signifies "Not out."

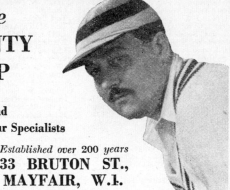

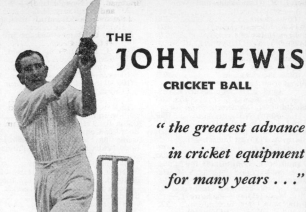

Index

c

[*Sport and General*]

For years former Test players have met at Lord's for the current series. Here is a group with Mr. Robert Menzies, Premier of Australia. *Standing:* G. Duckworth, L. E. G. Ames, A. E. R. Gilligan, N. Haig, R. E. S. Wyatt, Ian Peebles, E. W. Clark. *Seated:* G. Gunn, F. E. Woolley, R. Menzies, Sir Pelham Warner, W. Rhodes, S. F. Barnes, C. P. Mead.

TEST CRICKET AT EDGBASTON AGAIN

[*Central Press*

A section of the new arena at Edgbaston where Test cricket was seen again after an interval of twenty-eight years. Warwickshire, under their enterprising officials, notably Mr. Leslie Deakins, the secretary, are still improving the accommodation with the object of making Edgbaston the best and most comfortable Test ground in England.

ENGLAND'S RECORD PARTNERSHIP

[*Central Press*]

An incident in the first Test at Edgbaston during the long stand of 411 by P. B. H. May (285 not out) and M. C. Cowdrey (154). It was the highest partnership ever made for England and the third highest for any side in the history of Test cricket. S. Ramadhin, the bowler, sent down 774 balls, the most delivered by a bowler in a Test.

ENGLAND TEAM AT TRENT BRIDGE, 1957

[*Central Press*]

Two brothers appeared in the England team for the first time since A. Hearne and G. G. Hearne played in South Africa in 1892. *Standing*: P. E. Richardson, D. V. Smith, T. W. Graveney, M. C. Cowdrey, D. W. Richardson, F. S. Trueman. *Seated*: J. B. Statham, T. E. Bailey, P. B. H. May

1957 WEST INDIES TEAM IN ENGLAND

[Sport and General]

Standing: W. Ferguson (scorer). A. Ganteaume, N. Asgarali, F. C. M. Alexander, G. Sobe's, W. Hall, T. Dewdney, B. H. Pairaudeau, R. Gilchrist, O. G. Smith, Rohan Kanhai. *Seated:* T. N. Peirce (manager), S. Ramadhin, D. Atkinson, F. M. Worrell, J. D. C. Goddard (captain), C. L. Walcott, E. D. Weekes, A. L. Valentine, C. de Caires (manager).

SURREY—COUNTY CHAMPIONS FOR SIXTH SUCCESSIVE YEAR

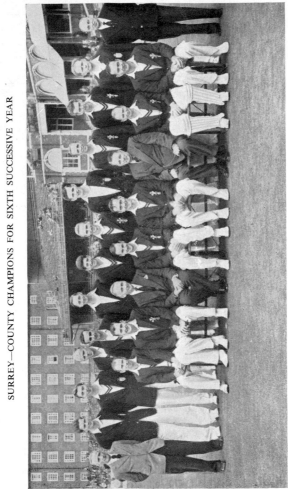

[*Central Press*

Standing: H. Strudwick (scorer), D. Sydenham, M. D. Willett, G. A. R. Lock, B. Constable, R. C. E. Pratt, K. F. Barrington, M. J. Stewart, D. Gibson, T. H. Clark, P. J. Loader, D. F. Cox, A. Sandham (coach). *Seated:* D. G. W. Fletcher, J. C. Laker, Lord Tedder (President), P. B. H. May (captain), A. V. Bedser (vice-captain), B. K. Castor (secretary), A. J. McIntyre, E. A. Bedser.

[*Central Press*

One of the features of Surrey's success has been their brilliant close-fielding. The five men in this picture claimed 293 victims last summer. McIntyre, the wicket-keeper, who has just caught Dawkes (Derbyshire) helped in 60 dismissals; Lock, the bowler, 63; Stewart 77; May 29 and Barrington 64.

[*Central Press*

P. J. LOADER (Surrey)

FIVE CRICKETERS OF THE YEAR

A. J. W. McINTYRE (Surrey)

[*Central Press*

FIVE CRICKETERS OF THE YEAR

[*Central Pres*

M. J. STEWART (Surrey)

O. G. SMITH (West Indies)

[*Sport and General*]

[Sport and General

C. L. WALCOTT (West Indies)

FIVE CRICKETERS OF THE YEAR

C. L. WALCOTT

One of the pillars of West Indies cricket in the last ten years has been CLYDE LEOPOLD WALCOTT, the brilliant all-rounder who was born at Bridgetown on January 17, 1926. When in 1951 *Wisden* paid tribute to F. M. Worrell and Everton Weekes, the Editor remarked in his preface: "My only regret was that room could not be found for C. L. Walcott."

Now the opportunity is taken to include the third member of the famous "W" triumvirate, all of whom first saw the light of day in that lovely sunny island of Barbados. All were born cricketers. Walcott grew up in a cricket atmosphere; his father and two uncles played club cricket and were keen enthusiasts.

As far back as he can remember Walcott had a bat in his hand and he has always played cricket because he loves the game and it gives him immense enjoyment. With his upright style and general command, he gives the impression that he was coached during his early development, but he says that is not so. There are no coaches in Barbados. All he can remember is receiving some advice from the games master at Combermere School, where he was in the first team with Worrell at the age of twelve. The same year he went to Harrison College, the only Public School in the island, and it was at that time that he decided to take up wicket-keeping because he could not get runs and the college needed a stumper. Walcott filled the vacancy.

That such a small island as Barbados—area 166 square miles; population 228,000—should turn out so many excellent cricketers is because everything there is right for cricket. Everyone plays on perfect turf pitches; young batsmen can make their strokes confidently and bowlers must be accurate in length and direction.

Walcott progressed so rapidly in this environment that on his sixteenth birthday he made his first-class debut for Barbados. It was against Trinidad at Bridgetown. He went in first and was dismissed for eight and nought. He played with his elder brother, Keith, for Barbados and the Spartan club at a time when E. A. V. Williams and J. E. D. Sealy were coming to the fore.

Standing six feet two inches and turning the scales at fifteen stone (now he is slightly heavier), Walcott has a commanding presence on and off the field. Modest and quietly spoken, he remains completely unspoiled despite all the publicity he has received for his wonderful achievements. His powerful physique enables him to drive with tremendous force. He has a peerless off-drive and a dazzling square cut, and is no less adept with the pull and hook, so that on his day he is rarely lost for a stroke. In addition, he is an accomplished slip-fielder and in his younger days he was the Test wicket-keeper as well as a really good fast-medium bowler.

When West Indies resumed Test cricket after the war with the visit of the M.C.C. under G. O. Allen in 1947–48, Walcott had already placed his name among the records. Two seasons earlier he made 314 not out on the mat at Trinidad, establishing with his schoolmate Worrell (255 not out) the world's highest partnership of 574 for Barbados. The following season those figures were surpassed by V. S. Hazare and Gul Mahomed, the present holders; they put on 577 for Baroda against Holkar at Baroda.

Walcott signalised his first appearance against M.C.C. by hitting 120 for Barbados, but although he played in all four Tests his highest score in seven innings was 45. He had no regular place in the batting order; instead he was a valuable member of the side by virtue of his safe wicket-keeping.

West Indies broke fresh ground in 1948–49 when they visited India and astonished their hosts by their batting strength. Six of the side shared eleven centuries in the five Tests and Walcott, the wicket-keeper, claimed two. Next came the tour of England in 1950 when West Indies, winning three of the four Tests, firmly established themselves among the great cricketing powers. As many as thirty-seven centuries were hit for them and Walcott and Weekes, seven each, shared the honours. It was Walcott's 168 not out at Lord's which turned the scales and brought them their first Test victory in England—a day followers of West Indies cricket will long remember. To get that innings in its true perspective one should mention that at that time it approached within a single the highest score by a West Indies player in Tests in England—169 not out by George Headley in 1933.

And so to Australia in 1951–52. That journey was full of hope. Some said it was for the Championship of the World, but against the shock, bumping attack of Lindwall and Miller, West Indies suffered a set-back. They won only one of the five Tests and Walcott, although gladly relieved of the job of wicket-keeper, figured among the failures. Nevertheless, he soon benefited by abandoning his position behind the stumps and when the side moved on to New Zealand he hit three centuries in the four matches, including one in the Tests.

Back in his own islands, Walcott proceeded to perform such remarkable feats that he challenged Hutton for the title of the world's best batsman. India, England and Australia, in turn, toured the Caribbean and all their bowlers suffered from his merciless punishment. In five Tests against Hutton's team Walcott scored 698 runs, average 87.25, including three centuries, with 220 at Bridgetown, the highest in all his 38 international engagements.

Facing Australia in 1955–56, Walcott performed feats achieved by no other player in history when both at Port of Spain and

Kingston he hit a century in each innings of the two Tests. Lindwall, Miller, Johnson, Archer, Benaud and Johnston all tasted the full fury of his devastating hitting. His aggregate of 827 was the highest for West Indies in any rubber, and yet he was on the losing side, for Australia won comfortably, gaining three victories with two matches drawn.

Walcott had hit twelve hundreds in his last twelve Tests. Small wonder he was appointed vice-captain for the tour of England last summer, but he found the conditions vastly changed from 1950. No longer were the pitches at Lord's, Leeds and The Oval discouraging to bowlers. Unfortunately he strained a leg muscle when batting beautifully in the first Test at Birmingham and for some weeks laboured under a big handicap, but against the counties in May and August he looked as good as ever. Indeed, he finished fifth in the full season's averages with only May, Worrell, Cowdrey and Graveney above him.

Walcott is a great favourite in Lancashire where he played for Enfield from 1951 to 1954. Since then he has gone to live in British Guiana, where he is coaching their young players as well as playing for the Colony.—N. P.

O. G. SMITH

There is no finer sight than that of a player thoroughly enjoying his cricket. Such a man is O'NEILL GORDON SMITH, whose infectious enthusiasm and huge grin make him such an outstanding personality. With players like Walcott, Worrell, Weekes and Ramadhin in the West Indies side which toured England in 1957 it might not have been easy for a newcomer to capture the limelight, yet Smith did just that and more. Indeed, he scored more runs on the tour than any of the three "W's," became the first man in the side to reach 1,000 runs, took valuable wickets when the regular bowlers had been subdued and did his utmost to raise the drooping spirits of his side by magnificent fielding. Everywhere he went Smith won hosts of admirers by his approach to the game and there was no more popular player anywhere during the season.

To the world at large, Smith is known as "Collie," although few people know the origin of the nickname. It came when he was only four years of age. His parents used to call him by the pet name of "Carl." As it happened his "best friend" in those days was another "Carl" and the two youngsters found that whenever 'Carl' was called they did not know who was wanted. Smith's grandmother decided to change the "Carl" to "Carlie." From there it was an easy step to the present "Collie."

Born at Kingston, Jamaica, on May 5, 1933, Smith first became interested in cricket when about seven years old. Like the majority of youngsters in the West Indies he was keen to join in the street games played with cloth balls and he recalls plenty of spankings for staying out late with the bigger boys.

At his first elementary school at St. Albans, Jamaica, Smith made the side when nine years of age, although the majority of the team were nearer 15. Such were his talents that he became captain before he was 12. In those days Smith followed the inclinations of most youngsters—to bowl as fast as possible and to hit the ball out of sight. He eventually found that fast bowling did not suit him, but to this day he has not lost his ambition to hit sixes.

Figures meant nothing to Smith. In fact, he has little interest in them now. He had never heard of a "hat-trick," averages were something beyond his comprehension and the tactics of the game were a nuisance, interfering with his desire to get on with the game. For this reason he did not like the role of captain.

Eventually he moved to Kingston College and after a year with the Under-15 team played for the Seniors. Apart from his school cricket he used to turn out regularly for a club known as Boys' Town and it was here that he first came to the notice of the Jamaican authorities.

Smith did not see his first first-class match until 1948 when M.C.C. visited West Indies. There he came under the spell of Jim Laker and was so impressed by his ability that he decided to give up fast bowling and concentrate on off-spin. He soon became known as "Jim" by his colleagues at Boys' Town.

In 1949 his club won the Junior Cup and Smith received a bat for the best cricketer in the team. Part of his reward was one day's coaching from Jack Mercer, the former Glamorgan bowler and present coach at Northamptonshire. Apart from that and a little guidance from Major Knibbs, a well-known umpire in West Indies, Smith received no coaching and, perhaps fortunately for his future, no one attempted to alter his style.

Always a brilliant fieldsman, Smith first received big cricket atmosphere when acting as twelfth man for Jamaica while still playing for Boys' Town. Indeed, he achieved the rare distinction of being appointed emergency Test fieldsman for West Indies, both in 1953 against India and 1954 against England before he ever appeared in a first-class match.

He eventually made the Jamaican side in 1955 and played in only two games before being chosen against the Australians. His innings of 169 in the opening match of the tour against an attack comprising Lindwall, Miller, Johnston, Davidson, Johnson and Benaud showed that West Indies had found a new star. Jamaica were 81 for five before Smith and A. P. Binns added 277. This innings earned Smith a place in the first Test and again he showed tremendous form, scoring 104 in the second innings and joining the small list of players who had hit a century on his Test debut.

Success was sweet, but like most cricketers Smith soon had cause to realise how uncertain it could be. In the second Test he failed to score in either innings and was dropped for the next game. He returned for the fourth and fifth Tests without doing anything exceptional.

Early the following year Smith toured New Zealand with the West Indies side and played in all four Tests. Although his batting did not come up to expectations he showed improved skill with his off-breaks and took 13 Test wickets for 18.53 runs each. His experience against Lindwall, Miller and the other Australian bowlers was a turning-point in Smith's career. Miller, in particular, worried him by his controlled swing and on the trip to New Zealand he had time to think. He came to the conclusion that there was more to cricket than he imagined and for the first time realised that the game had science. The result brought a slight change in his methods. He began to eliminate the more dangerous strokes and tried to stop the "head-up, eye-off-the-ball" swings which so often had brought his downfall.

This naturally led to Smith developing into a much more mature cricketer and although he retained his boyish enthusiasm and occasionally forgot his lessons in his exuberance, he became harder to dismiss. The England bowlers twice discovered this. At Birmingham he made 161 and became the only batsman to hit a century on his first appearance both against England and Australia. He followed with 168 in the third Test at Nottingham, an innings which went a considerable way towards saving the match. His other century during the tour, against Derbyshire at Chesterfield, was a typically aggressive innings which brought spectators to their feet. Smith's style naturally attracted interest among Lancashire League clubs and during the season he accepted an engagement to play for Burnley in 1958.—L. S.

A. J. W. McINTYRE

One of the main reasons for Surrey's record run of six County Championships has been the superb close to the wicket fielding. Four players last season accounted for no fewer than 264 wickets. In the centre of all this snapping up of what to many other counties would not even be chances was ARTHUR JOHN WILLIAM McINTYRE for ten years regular wicket-keeper to the County Champions.

Competent and consistent, McIntyre has missed most of the big honours of the game through being contemporary with Godfrey Evans whose sustained brilliance has made him always first choice for England since the first season after the war. McIntyre has only three England caps, two received when Evans was injured and one in his own right—as a batsman against Australia at Brisbane in 1950—but for years he has been to more than one

Selection Committee the keeper in the shadow team for home Tests.

As an all-rounder McIntyre must hold a unique record among cricketers. He was awarded his Surrey second eleven cap as a leg-spin bowler, his first eleven cap as a batsman and yet he has made his name in cricket as a wicket-keeper.

McIntyre was born on May 14, 1918, within a quarter of a mile of famous Kennington Oval where he was to become such a popular figure. At the age of eight he was playing cricket at Kennington Road School, and he pays tribute to the help and encouragement he received from the masters at the school as he developed his batting and leg-spin bowling. On all possible occasions he would slip along to The Oval to watch his idol of those days, Jack Hobbs.

At school he was called upon occasionally to keep wicket and it was as a keeper that he was chosen to play for London Schools. Contemporary with Denis Compton, who is only nine days younger, they played together at Lord's on one occasion for London Schools. They had a century partnership, which was broken in the expected manner—Compton ran out McIntyre. "He learned that very early in his career!" cracks "Mac," as he is known among his colleagues.

Although his name had been put before the Surrey club as a promising young player, McIntyre took a job outside cricket on leaving school because he did not fancy having to sell score-cards. He kept that job for eighteen months, playing cricket with the firm's side, and then answered a call to The Oval where he joined the ground staff in 1936—and was put in charge of the cycle shed!

After two years he made his first appearance in the Surrey team but his career as a batsman-bowler was cut short in 1939 by the war and by December of that year he was in the Army. He saw service in North Africa and took part in the Anzio landings in Italy where he was wounded. Among cricketers in Italy at the time were the Bedser twins, Rhodes of Derbyshire, Hill of Hampshire, Tom Dollery, Tom Pritchard and Arthur Wellard.

When the war in Europe ended cricket became a favourite recreation of the troops and McIntyre, then a sergeant in the A.P.T.C., was soon keeping wicket for the Central Mediterranean Force. It was on the suggestion of the Bedser twins, who pointed out his height of 5 ft. 5½ in. was rather against him being a bowler, that McIntyre wrote to the then Surrey secretary, Mr. A. F. Davey, asking if he might be considered as a wicket-keeper.

When county cricket was resumed in 1946, Mobey was the regular Surrey wicket-keeper; McIntyre kept his place as a batsman-bowler and was awarded his county cap. With the help of that great Surrey wicket-keeper, Herbert Strudwick, who made special journeys from his home at Shoreham to Wandsworth to give him coaching lessons, McIntyre improved his work behind the stumps and on the retirement of Mobey at the end of the 1946 season McIntyre became the Surrey keeper.

That 1947 season was the first time he had kept to Alec Bedser and Laker and he recalls a match against Essex at Chelmsford that year when there were no fewer than 33 extras in the Essex second innings. At the end of the second day the match looked a foregone conclusion for Essex. Surrey, set to get 340 to win, had lost five wickets for 125 and the dry dusty wicket was all against batting. Thanks to McIntyre, who made 70 and shared a fine sixth wicket stand with E. R. T. Holmes (65 not out), Surrey turned pending defeat into victory by two wickets.

Two years later McIntyre had his best season behind the stumps with 94 victims and in 1950 he made his first appearance for England playing against West Indies at The Oval because Evans was suffering from a broken thumb. His good form earned him a place in the M.C.C. team for Australia and New Zealand that winter, during which he made his one Test appearance at Brisbane.

His big year was 1955 when his benefit raised £8,500 and he also won the 100 guineas prize for wicket-keeping. That same year he played against South Africa at Leeds, and would no doubt have kept his place for The Oval game if he had been completely fit for Evans was still out of action.

McIntyre has always been a useful batsman in the middle of the order for Surrey where his aggressiveness has brought him more than 10,000 runs. He passed that milestone during last summer. Of his quick scoring McIntyre recalls the match against Nottinghamshire at Trent Bridge in 1955 when he scored 189 runs for once out. In the first innings he made 110, taking only 108 minutes over his century, helping K. F. Barrington in a stand of 177. In the second innings he made 79 not out, which included four 6's and nine 4's, and helped Peter May put on 149 runs in 57 minutes.

A damaged hand kept McIntyre out of nearly half the 1956 season and it seemed he might lose his place in the side, but he came back in his old form, and as long as he maintains that standard he will be an indispensable unit in Surrey's wonderful fielding combination.—L. N. B.

P. J. LOADER

The initial "P" in the name of PETER JAMES LOADER might well represent "perseverance," so prominent a part did this sterling quality play in his advance from club to county and Test match cricket. Last season he reached the peak of his achievements and earned fame by performing the hat-trick in the fourth Test match with the West Indies—a feat never previously accomplished by an England player in a home Test. In five successive years he helped substantially in the carrying off by Surrey of the County

Championship. His pace, ability to make the ball "move" late in its flight, and his skill in disguising the occasional slower delivery placed him in the forefront of present-day fast bowlers.

Born at Wallington, Surrey, on October 25, 1929, Loader first displayed an interest in cricket around the age of seven when, at the local Grammar School, he engaged in the "pick-up" type of matches in which the majority of boys at small schools take part. Like most youngsters learning to bowl, he felt the irresistible urge for speed, and though receiving no coaching, developed sufficient skill over the years to be chosen to assist Beddington C.C. when 15. With this club he profited from the advice of G. M. ("Gillie") Reay, the former Surrey amateur fast bowler, and at length attracted the attention of the county authorities. A game for Beddington with Surrey Club and Ground was followed by an invitation to assist the Club and Ground team.

Not until 1951 did the opportunity occur for him to play in a first-class match for the county, and then the absence of A. V. Bedser, on Test match duty, and W. S. Surridge, whose father had just died, provided it. In the two Kent innings in this game Loader, still an amateur, dismissed only three batsmen, and those at a cost of 96 runs; but he bowled well enough to impress his possibilities upon those in charge of affairs at The Oval, and the following year he accepted a position on the professional staff. Coaching by Andrew Sandham, and the ever-ready hints and help of Alec Bedser, brought a steady improvement in the young bowler. To begin with, Loader found his first team appearances limited, but he did a lot of capital work in the Minor Counties side. Still, in his first season in the paid ranks he appeared in six first-class matches and took 28 wickets, average 22.07.

In 1953 he took part in fifteen Championship fixtures, and his tally of wickets in all first-class engagements shot up to 80 at 18.28 runs each. Between July 8 and July 17 he enjoyed such a phenomenal spate of success that in three matches he took 34 wickets, average 7.97. At Birmingham he dismissed eight batsmen—seven of them bowled—in the first Warwickshire innings for 72 runs; he followed with nine for 28—the other man was run out—in Kent's first innings at Blackheath; eight for 21 v. Worcestershire at The Oval and six for 70 on the opening day of the meeting with Gloucestershire at Bristol.

A visit to India during the winter with the Commonwealth team captained by B. A. Barnett, the former Australia wicketkeeper, helped to build up Loader's somewhat slight physique, and in 1954 he disposed of 109 batsmen, average 14.57. That season he distinguished himself by taking seven wickets for 37 in the Gentlemen's first innings at Lord's, a feat which gained the special commendation of such celebrities as Sir Pelham Warner and C. B. Fry and paved the way to his selection by England for the last Test match with Pakistan. England lost that Test, so suffering their first reverse at home for three years, but this was by no means the fault of Loader. As proof of this, he was chosen by the Cricket Writers' Club as the best young player of the year. Next winter he was a member of the M.C.C. team which toured Australasia and though, with J. B. Statham and F. H. Tyson, the other fast bowlers, in such devastating form, he was not chosen for a Test, he did well enough in the other games, taking 41 wickets for less than 20 runs apiece.

Upon his return, he maintained that standard of excellence, securing 96 wickets, average 17.65, and when Tyson stood down through indisposition, deputising with success in the fourth Test with South Africa. A cracked bone in a leg caused him to withdraw from the M.C.C. touring team to Pakistan at the season's end, but the summer of 1956 brought him a greater measure of effectiveness, his wickets increasing to 124 and their cost falling to 15.69. Yet, with competition still so strong, he did not appear in any of the Tests with Australia.

For England in South Africa the next winter, Loader took nine wickets in four Test matches for something over 32 runs each, but these figures did nothing like justice to his bowling, and last season he gave evidence of the fact by making his record 133 wickets at 15.47. On seven occasions he dismissed five or more men in an innings, but the feat which naturally afforded him the greatest satisfaction was his six wickets for 36 in the first West Indies innings of the fourth Test at Leeds. He completed a rout of the touring team by disposing of J. D. Goddard, S. Ramadhin and R. Gilchrist with following balls. This performance assured his choice for the final Test, but with the pitch favouring spin-bowlers, he sent down only ten overs in the match for 14 runs and one wicket.

From an early age, Loader was troubled by asthma and he was deemed unfit for National Service; but happily this distressing complaint diminished with the passing years till, around the age of 21, it disappeared altogether. Now he can look forward to a long career and additional laurels. Besides his bowling, he is a keen, safe fieldsman in the deep. His batting methods are of the forthright type expected from No. 11.—E. E.

M. J. STEWART

MICHAEL JAMES STEWART, of Surrey, who created a world first-class record for a fielder other than a wicket-keeper when he made seven catches in an innings against Northamptonshire, at Northampton, on June 7, 1957, was born at Herne Hill, London, on September 16, 1932.

From the time as a toddler when he learned from his father the use of a bat and ball, Stewart showed equal liking for hitting

C

the ball or catching it. Through School, Services and County
Cricket he developed these particular branches of his ability, and
it was no wonder that fielding brought him his first great distinction. The occasion, curiously, almost passed Stewart by, for
he did not realise as he took catch after catch off the Northamptonshire batsmen that a record lay, literally, within his grasp. Even
after he had held his seventh catch—at short-leg off Kelleher, a
former Surrey colleague—Stewart had no idea that he had made
cricket history. Not until a *Wisden* reporter asked him at the end
of his innings whether he knew he had broken a record was he
aware of the fact. The ball, suitably mounted and inscribed—a
gift to Stewart from Surrey—now bears witness that the feat was
indeed performed.

From his young days Stewart took naturally to cricket. He
played his first organised games at Dulwich Hamlet school, then
went to Alleyn's School where he held his place for four years in
the first eleven and captained the side in his last two seasons.
At Alleyn's, Stewart came under the influence of G. R. Charnley,
master-in-charge of cricket, to whom he owns indebtedness for
early coaching and for his first introduction to Surrey as a member
of their Young Amateurs team. In his schooldays, Stewart was a
forcing batsman going in number three or four, a splendid fielder
and a fairly competent off-spin bowler. Selection for the two big
Public Schools' games at Lord's—Southern Schools v. The Rest
and Combined Services v. Public Schools—in 1949 and 1950 were
the landmarks of his school career. Never before had a boy from
Alleyn's been chosen for the Public Schools.

National Service, in the Royal Engineers, followed. Torn
between the desires to proceed to a University and to make sport
his living, Stewart had his mind made up for him when B. H.
Valentine, the former Kent captain, playing in a match with him,
asked whether he would like to come to Kent after leaving the
Army. Stewart had long toyed with the idea of becoming a professional cricketer and he told Valentine that he would be pleased
to throw in his lot with Kent if Surrey had no objections. Officials
of the two counties informally discussed the matter, and after Stewart
had appeared for The Army against The R.A.F. at Lord's, Surrey
decided to offer him a position on the playing staff for season 1953,
the year of his demobilisation.

His career as a professional cricketer was one of gradual but
marked progress. He found his feet by averaging just over 41 in
18 innings in Minor Counties' matches in 1953. Surrey promoted
him to the county eleven in 1954, and he demonstrated his potentialities in no uncertain manner by scoring 301 runs in his first
four innings. He began with 52 and 6 against Gloucestershire,
then he hit 109 against the Pakistan touring team and followed
this noteworthy effort by taking 134 off Essex. His first full season,

1955, yielded him a thousand runs and his county cap. The following season his aggregate went past fifteen hundred runs—including his highest score, 166 against Essex—and last summer he scored 1,801 runs, average 36.75. His safe catching, as well as his attractive batting, proved a valuable factor in Surrey's record run of Championship successes. In 1955 he held 52 catches in all first-class matches, and last summer he took 77—one short of the record standing to the credit of W. R. Hammond.

Stewart's agility and enthusiasm as a fielder sprung from imitation and admiration of Constantine. Stewart, as a youngster, watched the famous West Indies' all-rounder whenever he could, and then, in his local park, dived and jumped for catches in the style of his hero. A cover-point at school, Stewart, under the guidance and discipline of Stuart Surridge who insisted on fielding excellence, graduated to positions close to the wicket. Although quite happy in any place except slip he prefers forward short-leg and short square-leg. Instinctive reaction to the movement of a batsman is the keynote of his fearless fielding only a few yards from the stumps. Confidence in the technique of the Surrey bowlers enables Stewart to stand his ground within dangerous range of the bat, and when he achieved his record performance he said that Lock, Laker and A. Bedser, off whom he made the catches, were so accurate that all were comfortably held although he was so close. A modest understatement was his added comment: "The ball just seemed to keep coming to me."

His promotion to opening batsman occurred when he played for Surrey II. Sandham, the Surrey coach who gave him much useful advice, saw his worth as a number one, and Surridge did not hestitate to put him in first against Pakistan after he had made fifty, as number four, on his debut against Gloucestershire. Cultivation of the hook—a stroke which rarely costs him his wicket—and pull has made Stewart a strong on-side player, but he does not neglect his off-side shots. He drives forcefully with good placement and employs the cut, square and late. One of his early faults was his impetuosity, but he has managed to rectify the failing to a large extent without losing his urge to hit. His first four seasons with Surrey brought him twelve centuries—one of them, 155 not out, made when he shared a first-wicket partnership of 255 with R. C. E. Pratt against Cambridge University in 1956.

Stewart's other sport, Soccer, has given him enjoyment first as an amateur with Wimbledon, Hendon and Corinthian-Casuals, and now as a professional with Charlton Athletic. He gained an Amateur International cap as an inside-forward for England against France in 1956. With ordinary luck and freedom from injury Stewart should continue to advance at both games. The cricket writers voted him the best young player of 1957 by a two-thirds majority.—H. G.

THE LOVE OF CRICKET

By The Rt. Hon. Lord Birkett, P.C.

It is one of life's little ironies that if you would write about the summer game for *Wisden* you must do it in the depth of winter. Your words will not be read until the winter is past and the rain is over and gone and the time of the singing of birds is come; but you write them when the winds blow and the rains fall and the clouds lie very near to the earth. It is perhaps just as well that this is so, for in winter the love of cricket can be a rampart to the mind. Memory can bring back the sunlit fields, and Imagination can conjure up in anticipation the joys that belong to the English spring, and cricket played between the showers. At any rate it is so with me, and though the love of cricket has been sung ever since James Love set down his opening line more than two hundred years ago—

"*Hail, Cricket! glorious, manly British game!*"—

and though the songs and the writings are in four thousand volumes in the British Museum, the theme never grows old, and will no doubt continue to be sung long after we are all gathered to the pavilion of a better world and gaze out on Elysian swards.

I have assumed, of course, that all who read these words are genuine lovers of cricket, for otherwise all that I have written is vanity and vexation of spirit; my words are intended for those who are of the household of faith, and even in that house there are many mansions. The great John Selden who came from the Inner Temple, I am glad to think, and gave us the famous *Table Talk*, reminded us some centuries ago that whilst all men are "equally given to their pleasures, one man's pleasure lies one way and another's another." What makes one man a lover of cricket with a passionate intensity, and at the same time makes another equally good man quite indifferent to it, is past all finding out. "One man's meat is another man's poison" has been true in all ages and is now proverbial. It applies to the major as well as to the minor pleasures of life, and only one thing is certain and that is—

"*Never lad that trod on leather
Lived to feast his heart with all.*"

But the lovers of cricket make up a very great company, and a delightfully mixed one. Over the past two hundred years the poets and the prose writers have been chanting the love of cricket until there is no human experience, grave or slight, that has gone unrecorded. Think of the ecstasy with which Norman Gale celebrated the feat of bowling three curates with three consecutive balls—

> *"I bowled three sanctified souls*
> *With three consecutive balls!*
> *What do I care if Blondin trod*
> *Over Niagara falls?"*

And think of the grave John Nyren compiling the only true cricket classic we possess, and creating one of the immortal books of the world because of the unquenchable love of cricket it breathes in every word and line.

John Nyren with the help of Cowden Clarke, or Cowden Clarke with the help of John Nyren (the mystery will never be solved), produced *The Cricketers of my Time* but the genius of the book extends far beyond the playing of the game, and makes immortal the men of Hambledon who played at Broadhalfpenny Down and Windmill Down in the remote Hampshire countryside. Because of Nyren, Harris and Beldham are as real as Grace, and with the cheering hosts who watched them play, crying "Tich and Turn," as Silver Billy ran, they still stir the imagination with delight.

Today most people love the game of cricket because they play it. Happy indeed are they. They fill the schools, and the Universities, and the Clubs, and the Village sides, and even the streets where the three chalk marks on the wall serve as wickets. For the most part they are young men and women rejoicing in their youth; but there are some who no longer can be counted young, who find their names getting nearer and nearer to the Byes in the batting order as the years pass. Saturday afternoon for such as these is still the great day of the week, and the cricket pitch what the Bat and the Ball Inn was to Nyren, "a little Heaven below."

After all, the great W. G. made 69 runs in the last match he ever played, and was then not out; and he was 66 years of age. At the age of 48, when playing against Somerset, he was c Palairet b Woods for 186, having batted for four hours fifty minutes, and went on to take six Somerset wickets for 64 runs in 48 overs.

No doubt those who love cricket because they play it love also the setting of the game, and find this particular love to grow and develop with the years. They love their own ground set in our incomparable English countryside; they love the companionship of their fellow players, this, too, growing stronger as time passes, and memories accumulate of fine and gallant stands in critical moments, and of wonderful loyalties displayed; they love the long days in the sun, and the curious charm that belongs to a May day of showers; they love the moments, fielding at the boundary's edge, when they have time to see the great white clouds overhead as miracles of beauty; and they savour with keen pleasure all the joys that belong to the best months of the year, and which the summer brings to the true cricketer. Cricket has imperishable memories and indestructible traditions, and the lover of cricket enters into them and makes them his own.

The window of the room where I write these words commands a distant view of the Chiltern Hills and the long sweep of the Misbourne valley. Today, as I write, the familiar scene is almost blotted out with dark low-lying ominous clouds, and the rain beats on my roof with a fierce insistence. Yet down there in the valley, lying close to a beautiful old town, is a cricket field of a singular beauty that I know well. It was once part of a vast park and is set amidst noble trees with the Mansion on the hill-top still to be seen. There is a small pavilion with a little white verandah, and a flag pole where the club colours fly when a match is being played, and attractive wooden benches are set at intervals round the lovely turf. It will be a desolate scene this morning, I know, although I cannot see it, yet here in this book-lined room I can recall this ground, sunlit and radiant, as I have so often seen it, and as it will soon be again. But if you would know how deep and universal is the love of cricket you must know that one of the great highways to the north passes the very edge of the ground. From April to October, when matches are being played, and the white figures of the players can be seen through the trees, then the cars come to a stop at the side of the road, and the occupants watch, if only for a few overs, and enjoy a few moments in this essentially English scene.

Farther up the valley is another lovely ground which adjoins the railway. And there, whenever a match is being played, and a train passes, the passengers crowd to the windows in the hope (usually vain!) of seeing at least one ball bowled, or one run made, or a catch taken. (Curious how often when a train passes it is the end of an over or a wicket has fallen a few moments before!)

It was a sure instinct which made J. M. Barrie picture the dead returning to old and familiar scenes, and the Englishmen dropping out on the endless march to lean over the gate to watch the cricket on a village ground. It was the same instinct that led T. C. P. Wilson to write his lovely but little-known verse of the war heroes who were making the same endless and eternal march, who suddenly exclaimed in recognition—

> *"God! but it's England,"* then they said,
> *"And there's a cricket field."*

But many lovers of cricket turn to the great contests staged at Lord's and The Oval and the great grounds whose names have power to evoke the most fragrant memories. It has long been remarked how certain words can stir the emotions in the most remarkable way. To the cricket lover LORD'S is such a word. Lord's belongs to the whole cricketing world as does no other place. It is not only filled with memories of Grace and Hobbs and a thousand more, but it belongs to Bradman and Victor Trumper and Learie Constantine and George Headley and Nourse, too, and that great company of men from almost every nation under heaven, where English is spoken.

Lord's holds very special memories for all those who were ever there and in whatever capacity. For myself, I think of Bradman coming out of the shade of the pavilion on a June Saturday night more than twenty years ago, before the applauding thousands, and driving Verity for three successive fours off the first three balls he received. It was thrilling beyond all telling. I have seen Bradman make his double centuries, but that moment of mastery on the greatest ground in the world on that June night remains in the memory for ever. He made 36 runs only, and the experts say that he didn't make them very well; but for me it was an innings of beauty and power in an unforgettable setting. And a hundred great moments come to the mind unbidden when the talk is of the love of cricket.

The first sight of MacLaren at Old Trafford; Hammond and Paynter in their noble stand at Lord's in 1938; Denis Compton coming out of the pavilion to a perfect storm of shrill, schoolboy cheering; Jack Hobbs at the wicket or at cover point; Frank Woolley standing up to the fearsome attack of Gregory and McDonald; the fielding of Jack Fingleton; Pellew racing along the boundary, as Clem Hill must have done when he caught Lilley in the most famous Test match of all; Patsy Hendren running between the wickets with his scampering, twinkling feet; Peter May, Tom Graveney, Colin Cowdrey, all visibly in the great tradition; David Sheppard standing firm in a crisis; and a great host of cricketers of every rank and clime. Some lovers of cricket love to read the annals of the game; and some find pleasure in just watching cricket wherever it is played, with a preference perhaps for the lovely little ground tucked away in the countryside.

But to all lovers of cricket there is a kind of music in the sound of the great names, the sound of Grace and Hobbs, the sound of Trent Bridge and Old Trafford; but the greatest music of all is the sound of the bat against the ball. Mr. Ratcliff Ellis expressed this idea to perfection in his lines—

> *"The merry click of bat against the ball,*
> *The expectant hush, the cheering that proclaims*
> *Skill of the greatest of all English games;*
> *Flutter of flags, the branches of the trees*
> *Swaying beneath the gentle summer breeze;*
> *No sweeter music in the world is found*
> *Than that upon an English cricket ground."*

NOTES BY THE EDITOR

ENGLAND REIGN SUPREME

The summer of 1957 brought more glory to England as well as to Surrey under the captaincy of Peter May. Happily the weather was not so unkind as in the previous year, but again many matches were spoiled by rain, especially in the popular holiday month of August when the county treasurers look forward to big attendances.

May's Distinction

May's achievements as captain are without parallel. Never before has the same man led England through a series of Test matches and his county to the top of the Championship in the same year. Lord Hawke, captain of Yorkshire, led England on tour, but not at home. F. S. Jackson led England but not his county, Yorkshire. A. W. Carr provides the nearest approach to May. In 1929 he captained the successful Nottinghamshire side when they won the Championship for the first time since 1907, and he also captained England against South Africa at Manchester and The Oval, but not through the whole series.

The youthful May appears to thrive on responsibility. He made 285 not out—the highest score of his career—in the first Test at Edgbaston at a time when England were in desperate need of runs, and once again he finished top of the final averages, having scored 2,347 runs in 41 innings at 61.76. Confidence and determination to achieve his purpose, in addition to personal charm and ability, show May a born leader.

England's Advance

Since that notable day at Melbourne in February 1951 when England under F. R. Brown rose from the depths of despondency and beat Australia for the first time since 1938, the old country has not lost a single Test series.

Clearly England stand at the top of the cricket world. Rarely has our prestige been so high. There are some who aver that England never possessed a better side, but in making comparisons one must remember that conditions have changed. Pitches are certainly very different in this country and in Australia compared with twenty years ago and at home the duration of matches has been extended. Tactics, too, have changed with a leaning on occasion towards defensive bowling.

The tale of success is illustrated in the following table:

Season	Opponents	Pld.	Won	Lost	Drn.	Captain
1950–51	New Zealand	2	1	0	1	F. R. Brown
1951	South Africa	5	3	1	1	F. R. Brown
1951–52	India	5	1	1	3	N. Howard
1952	India	4	3	0	1	L. Hutton
1953	Australia	5	1	0	4	L. Hutton
1953–54	West Indies	5	2	2	1	L. Hutton
1954	Pakistan	4	1	1	2	L. Hutton (2) D. S. Sheppard (2)
1954–55	Australia	5	3	1	1	L. Hutton
1954–55	New Zealand	2	2	0	0	L. Hutton
1955	South Africa	5	3	2	0	P. B. H. May
1956	Australia	5	2	1	2	P. B. H. May
1956–57	South Africa	5	2	2	1	P. B. H. May
1957	West Indies	5	3	0	2	P. B. H. May
	Totals	57	27	11	19	

All-Round Strength

For all-round ability I would say that A. P. F. Chapman's 1928–29 Australia team had no superior in thirty years. Look at the batting order: J. B. Hobbs, H. Sutcliffe, W. R. Hammond, D. R. Jardine, A. P. F. Chapman, E. Hendren, H. Larwood, G. Geary, M. W. Tate, G. Duckworth, J. C. White. Three batsmen: M. Leyland 137 and 53 not out, C. P. Mead 8 and 72, and E. Tyldesley 31 and 21 each had to be content to appear in only one Test.

The reasons for England's present success are surely the possession of a grand captain; a fine array of bowlers suited to all types of pitches and the way these men have been so brilliantly supported in the field. It is an old adage that bowling and fielding win matches and in this respect the present England team can be said to be second to none. Moreover, England have not depended on one or two individuals. Adequate reserves have been available when first choices have withdrawn.

West Indies, after their wonderful performances of 1950, were expected to offer a stiff challenge. The slender margin which generally exists between success and failure when International teams are in conflict was clearly in evidence during the first Test at Edgbaston. When Ramadhin caused the England batsmen to flounder and was responsible for the side being dismissed for 186 on a perfect pitch, it seemed that West Indies had gained the ascendancy, especially when they replied with a total of 474.

At that juncture England were saved by May and Cowdrey,

the very men who often stood fast during the previous tour of Australia. These two brilliant University players took part in a stand of 411, the highest ever recorded for their country, and so England not only avoided disaster in that match, but went on to outplay the team from the Caribbean. West Indies never had a second chance after they failed to press home their initial advantage at Edgbaston.

New Zealand's Task

What of the future? This summer England receive New Zealand who, since they succeeded in drawing all four three-day Tests when they were last here in 1949, now face a stiffer programme of five five-day matches. The deeds of Sir Edmund Hillary at Everest and the South Pole have stirred the world and brought fresh lustre to New Zealand. May their cricketers show the same determination in their difficult task. We remember with admiration the names of Lowry, Dempster, Donnelly and Sutcliffe. A country which has produced such great players may well acquit themselves creditably in the year 1958.

Meanwhile England will be concerned in finding the men to visit Australia and New Zealand next winter for the purpose of retaining the Ashes which were retrieved in 1953. The batting, it appears, will be built round four main pillars, May, Cowdrey, Richardson and Graveney. There will be a concentrated search for opening batsmen. An obvious choice would have been the Rev. David Sheppard, whom all cricketers will wish success in his new appointment as first Warden of the Mayflower Family Settlement in East London.

Future Test Stars?

Likely candidates are M. J. Stewart and T. H. Clark, the Surrey opening pair, M. Hallam (Leicestershire) and two left-handers, D. V. Smith (Sussex) and W. B. Stott (Yorkshire). For the middle order, J. M. Parks (Sussex), D. W. Richardson (Worcestershire), M. J. K. Smith (Warwickshire), D. J. Insole (Essex), K. F. Barrington (Surrey) and E. R. Dexter, the Cambridge captain, may command attention.

Dexter, who is only 21, has a flair for most games. A magnificent stroke-player, he could develop into an all-rounder like Keith Miller, whom he resembles when in the act of bowling. Dexter caused something like a sensation when, on a drying pitch at Lord's, he took five wickets for eight runs for Gentlemen v. Players. On the other hand, as captain also of Cambridge University golf, he may play himself into the Walker Cup team.

Coming to the specialist bowlers, the accent must be on speed. In the past the teams with successful opening bowlers have won the day in Australia. I refer to Barnes and Foster in 1911–12, Larwood and Tate 1928–29, Larwood and Voce 1932–33, and Statham and Tyson 1954–55. Similarly Australia thrived when Gregory and McDonald, and Lindwall and Miller were in their prime. England can still have Statham, Tyson, Loader and Bailey of the last combination in Australia, and pressing for places will be Trueman, Moss and Dexter.

The ideal spin-bowling trio would be Laker, Lock and Wardle, provided all are fit. Australian crowds have never seen Laker and Lock, who have wrought such destruction on responsive English pitches. The years have taken toll of both men. Laker is frequently troubled by the condition of his worn spinning-finger and Lock has been compelled to undergo a knee operation of the same kind that was previously performed on Denis Compton.

Evans Retains His Youthful Skill

For ten years Godfrey Evans has excelled behind the stumps and at the age of 37 he still retains his youthful skill and enthusiasm. He needs to make only five more Test appearances to pass the record number of 85 held by the incomparable W. R. Hammond. A great inspiration to his colleagues, Evans has no equal in the world as a wicket-keeper who, as a race, are renowned for longevity. Herbert Strudwick kept for England when 46 and the noted Australian, W. A. Oldfield, was in his fortieth year before he retired.

At the age of 40, A. J. McIntyre is still generally regarded as second only to Evans among active English wicket-keepers. A second choice will be needed for Australia and no doubt M.C.C. would like to follow their usual custom and give a chance to a younger man. Possibles are J. T. Murray (Middlesex), G. Millman and K. V. Andrew. Murray performed the stumpers' double by scoring over 1,000 runs and helping in 100 dismissals, but one doubts whether he is better than Millman, who did well in his first season with Nottinghamshire, or Andrew, Evans' understudy four winters ago.

The arrival of Graveney as a prolific run-getter in Test cricket was one of the most satisfactory features of last summer. After being left out at Edgbaston, he failed at Lord's, but in their wisdom the selectors did not cast him aside. In two brilliant displays, he hit 258 at Trent Bridge and 164 at The Oval. The best and most attractive of professional batsmen, he should continue to delight his admirers, for he reached his thirtieth birthday only last June.

Surrey's Six Championships

Surrey again dominated the County Championship. There was no question about their superiority. Peter May took over the captaincy from Stuart Surridge and, by the middle of August,

Surrey claimed the title for the sixth successive year. While May deserved all the praise showered on him for his double feat in so successfully leading both his country and his county, he was the first to pay tribute to his able henchman, Alec Bedser.

For the first time in their history, Surrey gave an official appointment to a professional when they chose Alec Bedser as vice-captain. With May missing many county matches, Surrey were fortunate to possess such an able deputy leader as Bedser. Paying him the warmest of tributes, May said: "Alec has been splendid in every direction. He remains tremendously keen and has bowled as well as ever. He and I have run the show, including team-selection. As an example of our co-operation, I quote the case of Ken Barrington. When Stuart Surridge retired, we started the season minus a slip-fielder. We decided to try Barrington, and it was important for the side for him to be a success. He settled down immediately and took well over fifty catches. Apart from Alec, I do not single out any individuals because we remain essentially a team. Our success is based very much on the fact that we all play for Surrey and not for ourselves."

The way Surrey have monopolised the Championship since 1952 should be an incentive to their sixteen rivals. Much of the glamour of any contest disappears when year after year the same side remains on top, but Surrey have always been a dynamic and entertaining force since Surridge took control of their fortunes. Peter May is firmly convinced they will make it seven in 1958.

Experimental Laws

The summer of 1957 saw the introduction of several experimental Laws which were confined in the main to county cricket. One, the standardisation of boundaries to 75 yards from the middle of the pitch, was acclaimed a great success by the players though it did not bring about any overall improvement in the tempo of the game. The award of bonus points to the side which leads and scores the faster in the first innings proved an interesting innovation, but whether it will survive together with the limitation of the on-side field remains to be seen. All the experiments will be continued for at least one more season, but the crux of the matter still remains with the players.

The following resolution framed by Surrey in the spring of 1957 shows the way: "The attention of all players should be drawn in the most emphatic manner to the concern generally felt at the defensive tactics employed both by batsmen and bowlers. It is felt that the fundamental cause of this outlook lies not in the game itself, for which little or no legislation is needed, but in the approach by many players, in particular the captains."

Pad Play

If our legislators could check the excessive use of pads and devise means to compel batsmen to rely upon their bats, they would remove an annoying modern practice. The closing stages of the Edgbaston Test provided a notable instance and, seen as it was by thousands of T.V. viewers, showed the game of cricket in an adverse light.

Fast True Pitches

When three Test matches ran little more than half their allotted span and the public, having booked accommodation for the fourth day and, at Headingley, also for the fifth day, paid £17,000 without seeing a ball bowled, it was time that the Board of Control considered the state of the pitches prepared for International matches at the six Test centres. During the winter the Board decided to issue an "edict"—their official term—to the effect that all Test pitches must be fast and true. It seems extraordinary when one considers the care which is taken to provide the right conditions for the contestants at Wimbledon, Wentworth and other outdoor sports centres, that cricket, as far as pitches are concerned, should have departed from its high standard of the Golden Era when Test matches in England used to be restricted to three days and yet produced definite results.

Honours for Cricketers

Personalities in the cricket world were honoured in various ways during the year. Their many friends and admirers will wish to congratulate Lord Monckton, President of M.C.C., and Lord Birkett on their elevation to the peerage. H. S. Altham, M.C.C. Treasurer, Hampshire President and Chairman of M.C.C. Youth Cricket Association, became C.B.E., and very recently Denis Compton, too, was made C.B.E. A noted cricket journalist, Alderman J. H. Morgan, became Lord Mayor of Cardiff. Jack Morgan has followed Glamorgan as a professional cricket writer since their entry into the County Championship in 1921, recording their great and their lesser moments. No one was more delighted than he when Glamorgan won the Championship in 1948, and the following year he told the story of Glamorgan's March of Progress in *Wisden*. During his year of office, Glamorgan presented him with a Glamorgan County player's tie and the Chief Citizen of the capital of Wales became the first sportsman to be made an honorary playing member of the club.

DENIS COMPTON: THE CAVALIER

By NEVILLE CARDUS

Denis Compton counts amongst those cricketers who changed a game of competitive and technical interest to sportsmen into a highly individual art that appealed to and fascinated thousands of men and women and boys and girls, none of whom possessed a specialist clue, none of whom could enter into the fine points of expert skill. He lifted cricket into an atmosphere of freedom of personal expression. The score-board seldom told you more than half the truth about what he was doing on the field of play. In an age increasingly becoming standardised, with efficiency the aim at the expense of impulse—for impulse is always a risk—Compton went his unburdened way, a law to himself.

Most cricketers, even some of the greatest, need the evidence of the score-board to demonstrate their gifts over by over; if they are not scoring, if they are compelled by steady bowling or by force of adverse circumstances to fall back on the textbook, they are certain, in such moments, to wear out the patience of all who are not vehemently partisans, or students of academic zeal and watchfulness.

Even a Sir Leonard Hutton or a Peter May needs to do well to convince the lay onlooker that he is really worth watching for hours. Compton fascinated all lovers of cricket, informed or uninformed, whether he was making runs or not, or whether he was taking wickets or not.

In fact, whenever Compton seemed seriously in trouble and under the necessity to work hard he was then even a more arresting spectacle than usual. As we watched him groping and lunging and running out of his ground before the ball was released, we were more than ever aware that here was no merely talented cricketer; here was one under the sway and in the thrall of incalculable genius. For it is certain that Compton often was as much in the dark as the rest of us as to why and how he came by his own personal achievements, how he added to a fundamentally sound technical foundation an unpredictable inspiration, as though grace descended on him.

Once in Australia he ran into a new bowler of curious variations of spin; I think the bowler was Iverson. Compton was momentarily visited by one of his moods of eccentric fallibility. He played forward as though sightless; he played back as though wanting to play forward. He apparently didn't quite know where he was or with what he was coping. At the other end of the wicket a comparative newcomer was batting steadily, but runs were not being scored quickly enough. So the young novice approached Compton between overs for instructions. "You go on just as you are," was Denis's advice. "You're playing well. I'll get on with the antics."

At his greatest—which is really to say most days in a season— he made batting look as easy and as much a natural part of him as the way he walked or talked. Versatility of stroke-play; swift yet, paradoxically, leisurely footwork; drives that were given a lovely lightness of touch by wristy flexion at the last second; strokes that were born almost before the bowler himself had seen the ball's length—all these were the signs of the Master. Yet the word "Master" in all its pontifical use was not applied to him but, in his period, reserved for Sir Leonard. The reason is that Compton's cricket always looked young, fresh and spontaneous. The resonant term "Master" implies a certain air of age and pompousness, a Mandarin authority and poise.

When cricket was begun again, after the Hitler war, Compton in his wonderful years of 1946–1947 expressed by his cricket the renewed life and hopes of a land and nation that had come out of the dark abyss. In a period still sore and shabby and rationed, Compton spread his happy favours everywhere. The crowd sat in the sun, liberated from anxiety and privation. The strain of long years of affliction fell from all shoulders as Compton set the ball rolling or speeding or rippling right and left, as he leaned to it and swept it from the off round the leg boundary, as he danced forward or danced backwards, his hair tousled beyond the pacifying power of any cream or unguent whatsoever . . . yes, the crowd sunned themselves as much in Compton's batting as in the beneficial rays coming from the blue sky. Men and women, boys and girls, cheered him to his century, and ran every one of his runs with him.

As I say, his batting was founded on sound first principles— nose on the ball, the body near to the line. But he was perpetually rendering acquired science and logic more and more flexible. He was a born improviser. Once a beautiful spinner from Douglas Wright baffled him all the way. He anticipated a leg-break, but it was a "googly" when it pitched. To adjust his future physical system at the prompting of instinct working swift as lightning, Compton had to perform a contortion of muscles which sent him sprawling chest-flat on the wicket. But he was in time to sweep the ball to the long-leg boundary.

It is not enough to remember his brilliance only, his winged victories, his moments of animation and fluent effortless control. He has, in the face of dire need, played defensively with as tenaciously and as severely a principled skill as Hutton commanded at his dourest. Compton's 184 for England at Trent Bridge in 1948 must go down in history among the most heroically Spartan innings ever played. . . . England batted a second time 344 behind, and lost Washbrook and Edrich for 39. Compton and Hutton then staved away disaster until 150 was reached, and Hutton was bowled.

In a dreadful light Compton defended with terrific self-restraint against Miller at his fiercest. It is possible the match might have been snatched by him from the burning. Alas, at the crisis, a vicious "bumper" from Miller rose shoulder high. Compton instinctively hooked, thought better of it too late, slipped on the greasy turf, and fell on his wicket. For six hours and fifty minutes he mingled defence and offence in proportion. He did not, merely because his back was to the wall, spare the occasional loose ball. At Manchester, in the same rubber of 1948, Compton again showed us that there was stern stuff about him, the ironside breastplate as well as the Cavalier plume. He was knocked out by Lindwall. Stitches were sewn into his skull and, after a rest, he came back when England's score was 119 for five. He scored 145 not out in five hours twenty minutes.

These two superbly heroic innings, in the face of odds, may be taken as symbolical of a life and career not all sunshine and light heart, although Compton has lavished plenty of both on us. Nature was generous with him at his cradle; she gave him nearly everything. Then in his prime and heyday she snatched away his mainspring, she crippled him with many summers of his genius still to come.

In his fortieth year he is as young at heart and as richly endowed in batsmanship as at any time of his life. There are ample fruits in his cornucopia yet—if it were not for "that knee"! Still, we mustn't be greedy. He has shared the fruits of the full and refreshing cornucopia generously with us. He will never be forgotten for his precious gifts of nature and skill, which statistics have no power to indicate let alone voice. Perhaps there is more of him to come. It is hard to believe that nature is any readier than we ordinary mortals are to see him at last reposing with the authentic "Old Masters." Whatever his future, our hearts won't let him go. Thank you, Denis!

DENIS COMPTON

BORN MAY 23, 1918

Statistics by W. S. CONDER

BATTING (All First-Class Matches)

Season	Inns.	Not Outs	Runs	100's	50's	Highest Inns.	Average	Catches
1936	32	3	1004	1	8	100*	34.62	10
1937	46	4	1980	3	16	177	47.14	27
1938	47	6	1868	5	8	180*	45.56	35
1939	50	6	2468	8	11	214*	56.09	11
In India 1944–5 ...	13	2	990	5	2	249*	90.00	5
In India 1945–6 ...	4	0	316	2	1	124	79.00	1
1946	45	6	2403	10	10	235	61.61	24
M.C.C. in Australia 1946–7	25	3	1432	5	8	163	65.09	9
M.C.C. in New Zealand 1946–7 .	6	1	228	0	1	97*	45.60	2
1947	50	8	3816	18	12	246	90.85	31
1948	47	7	2451	9	8	252*	61.27	30
M.C.C. in South Africa 1948–9 ...	26	5	1781	8	4	300	84.80	24
1949	56	4	2530	9	11	182	48.65	28
1950	23	2	957	2	4	144	45.57	7
M.C.C. in Australia 1950–1	21	5	882	4	2	142	55.12	11
M.C.C. in New Zealand 1950–1 .	5	0	213	0	2	79	42.60	4
1951	40	6	2193	8	9	172	64.50	25
1952	54	6	1880	4	10	132	39.16	26
1953	47	5	1659	4	12	143*	39.50	24
M.C.C. in West Indies 1953–4	14	1	630	1	4	133	48.46	7
1954	28	2	1524	4	9	278	58.61	17
M.C.C. in Australia 1954–5	16	2	799	3	3	182	57.07	3
1955	36	1	1209	2	6	158	34.54	12
1956	21	1	705	2	3	110	35.25	13
M.C.C. in South Africa 1956–7...	22	1	792	2	5	131	37.71	7
1957	45	0	1554	3	9	143	34.53	17
Totals ...	819	87	38264	122	178	300	52.27	410

AGGREGATES

	Inns.	Not Outs	Runs	100's	50's	Highest Inns.	Average
In England............	667	67	30201	92	146	278	50.33
In Australia..........	62	10	3113	12	13	182	59.86
In West Indies	14	1	630	1	4	133	48.46
In South Africa	48	6	2573	10	9	300	61.26
In India	17	2	1306	7	3	249*	87.06
In New Zealand	11	1	441	0	3	97*	44.10
Totals	819	87	38264	122	178	300	52.27

TEST MATCHES

	Tests	Inns.	Not Outs	Runs	100's	50's	Highest Inns.	Average
Australia	28	51	8	1842	5	9	184	42.83
South Africa ...	24	42	1	2205	7	11	208	53.78
New Zealand ...	8	11	0	510	2	2	116	46.36
West Indies	9	14	2	592	2	2	133	49.33
India...........	5	8	4	205	0	2	71*	51.25
Pakistan	4	5	0	453	1	2	278	90.60
Totals	78	131	15	5807	17	28	278	50.06

COUNTY CHAMPIONSHIP MATCHES

	Inns.	Not Outs	Runs	100's	50's	Highest Inns.	Average
1936	31	3	989	1	8	100*	35.32
1937	32	2	1345	2	10	177	44.83
1938	27	3	1195	3	4	180*	49.79
1939	34	4	1853	6	8	214*	61.76
1946	34	4	1840	8	7	235	61.33
1947	28	7	2033	11	5	178	96.80
1948	25	5	1236	4	4	252*	61.80
1949	39	4	1773	5	10	182	50.65
1950	16	2	795	2	4	144	56.78
1951	24	3	1150	4	5	172	54.76
1952	41	2	1439	3	9	130	36.89
1953	28	3	1098	4	7	143*	43.92
1954	21	2	1029	3	7	117	54.15
1955	20	1	590	1	3	150	31.05
1956	13	0	405	2	1	110	31.15
1957	37	0	1404	3	9	143	37.94
Totals	450	45	20174	62	101	252*	49.81

TEST MATCHES

	Inns.	Not Outs	Runs	100's	50's	Highest Inns.	Average
1937 (v. New Zealand) ...	1	0	65	0	1	65	65.00
1938 (v. Australia)	6	1	214	1	1	102	42.80
1939 (v. West Indies)	5	2	189	1	0	120	63.00
1946 (v. India)	4	2	146	0	2	71*	73.00
1946–7 (v. Australia)	10	1	459	2	2	147	51.00
1946–7 (v. New Zealand) .	1	0	38	0	0	38	38.00
1947 (v. South Africa) ...	8	0	753	4	2	208	94.12
1948 (v. Australia)	10	1	562	2	2	184	62.44
1948–9 (v. South Africa) .	9	1	406	1	2	114*	50.75
1949 (v. New Zealand) ...	6	0	300	2	0	116	50.00
1950 (v. West Indies)	2	0	55	0	0	44	27.50
1950–1 (v. Australia)	8	1	53	0	0	23	7.57
1950–1 (v. New Zealand) .	3	0	107	0	1	79	35.66
1951 (v. South Africa) ...	6	0	312	1	2	112	52.00
1952 (v. India)	4	2	59	0	0	35*	29.50
1953 (v. Australia)	8	1	234	0	2	61	33.42
1953–4 (v. West Indies) ..	7	0	348	1	2	133	49.71
1954 (v. Pakistan)	5	0	453	1	2	278	90.60
1954–5 (v. Australia)	7	2	191	0	1	84	38.20
1955 (v. South Africa) ...	9	0	492	1	3	158	54.66
1956 (v. Australia)	2	1	129	0	1	94	129.00
1956–7 (v. South Africa) .	10	0	242	0	2	64	24.20
Totals	131	15	5807	17	28	278	50.06

Signifies not out.

FOR MIDDLESEX AGAINST TEAMS IN ENGLAND

	Inns.	Not Outs	Runs	100's	50's	Highest Inns.	Average
Derbyshire..........	15	4	810	2	6	214	73.63
Essex	31	4	1693	5	10	181	62.70
Glamorgan	11	1	213	0	2	75	21.30
Gloucestershire	27	2	1159	2	5	177	46.36
Hampshire...........	33	3	1228	4	7	143	40.93
Kent	33	0	1564	5	8	168	47.39
Lancashire	31	0	1368	7	4	179	44.12
Leicestershire	17	3	944	3	5	151	67.42
Northamptonshire	28	4	1742	7	10	147	72.58
Nottinghamshire	25	2	594	1	3	111	25.82
Somerset	26	3	1248	4	2	252*	54.26
Surrey	50	7	2068	6	9	235	48.07
Sussex	42	5	2000	7	9	182	54.05
Warwickshire	22	0	994	2	5	172	45.18
Worcestershire	24	5	1513	5	9	143	79.63
Yorkshire	35	2	1036	2	7	122	31.39
Oxford University	3	1	173	1	0	158	86.50
Cambridge University.	3	0	277	1	1	202	92.33
Australia	7	2	208	0	3	65	41.60
South Africa	5	1	244	1	0	154	61.00
West Indies	6	0	128	0	0	38	21.33
New Zealand	3	0	165	1	0	148	55.00
India...............	2	0	86	0	1	70	43.00
Rest of England......	1	0	246	1	0	246	246.00
Totals	480	49	21701	67	106	252*	50.35

FOR OTHER TEAMS IN ENGLAND

	Inns.	Not Outs	Runs	100's	50's	Highest Inns.	Average
M.C.C.							
v. Cambridge University	4	0	199	0	2	85	49.75
v. Oxford University ..	5	0	288	1	2	116	57.60
v. Surrey	14	0	412	2	1	123	29.42
v. Yorkshire	9	0	409	1	3	127	45.44
v. Australians	6	1	128	0	0	45	25.60
v. Indians	2	1	64	0	0	36	64.00
v. New Zealand	1	0	63	0	1	63	63.00
v. South Africans	5	0	307	1	1	147	61.40
v. West Indians	1	0	115	1	0	115	115.00
South	5	1	140	0	1	70	35.00
England XI	9	0	384	1	2	132	42.66
England v. Rest	3	0	14	0	0	14	4.66
Rest v. England XI	2	0	108	1	0	108	54.00
South of England	9	1	507	1	4	101	63.37
Players	25	3	889	1	4	150	40.40
M.C.C. S. African XI..	2	1	260	2	0	135	260.00
Sir P. Warner's XI ...	1	0	50	0	1	50	50.00
Rest of England	2	0	61	0	0	41	30.50
L. E. G. Ames' XI	2	0	30	0	0	24	15.00
T. N. Pearce's XI							
v. South Africans	2	0	54	0	0	27	27.00
v. Australians	2	0	55	0	0	45	27.50
Totals	111	8	4537	12	22	150	44.04

FOR M.C.C. TOURING TEAMS (EXCLUDING TESTS)

	Inns.	Not Outs	Runs	100's	50's	Highest Inns.	Average
In Australia	37	6	2410	10	10	182	77.74
In South Africa	29	5	1925	9	5	300	80.20
In West Indies	7	1	282	0	2	90*	47.00
In New Zealand	7	1	296	0	2	97*	49.33
Totals	80	13	4913	19	19	300	73.32

FOR TEAMS IN INDIA

	Inns.	Not Outs	Runs	100's	50's	Highest Inns.	Average
Europeans	4	1	301	1	2	124	100.33
Service's XI	3	0	245	2	0	120	81.66
Bengal Governor's XI	2	0	149	1	0	123	74.50
C. K. Nayudu's XI	2	0	138	1	0	100	69.00
Holkar	4	1	372	1	1	249*	124.00
East Zone	2	0	101	1	0	101	50.50
Totals	17	2	1306	7	3	249*	87.06

MODE OF DISMISSAL

Bowled	190
Caught	383
Lbw	75
Run Out	26
Stumped	50
Hit Wicket	8
Totals	732

BATTING ON ENGLISH GROUNDS

Ground	Inns.	Not Outs	Runs	100's	50's	Highest Inns.	Average
Birmingham	9	0	317	0	4	75	35.22
Bournemouth	6	2	289	2	1	115	72.25
Bradford	1	0	40	0	0	40	40.00
Brentwood	2	1	60	0	0	34	60.00
Bristol	10	2	224	0	1	57	28.00
Cambridge	3	0	277	1	1	202	92.33
Canterbury	11	0	552	2	3	106	50.18
Chelmsford	6	1	289	0	3	87	57.80
Colchester	6	1	376	1	4	113	75.20
Derby	7	1	321	1	3	100*	53.50
Dover	2	0	9	0	0	5	4.50
Folkestone	4	0	79	0	1	50	19.75
Frome	2	1	133	1	0	103*	133.00
Glastonbury	2	0	150	1	0	110	75.00
Gloucester	3	0	157	0	1	82	52.33
Hastings	17	1	840	2	5	132	52.50
Hove	21	1	824	2	4	121	41.20
Kettering	1	0	59	0	1	59	59.00
Kidderminster	2	0	130	0	1	82	65.00
Kingston-on-Thames	4	0	45	0	0	25	11.25
Leeds	17	1	611	1	4	114	38.18
Leicester	8	2	517	2	2	151	86.16
Leyton	2	0	130	1	0	109	65.00
Lord's	372	33	16511	47	79	252	48.70
Maidstone	3	0	325	1	2	142	108.33
Manchester	24	3	1439	7	6	158	68.52

Ground	Inns.	Not Outs	Runs	100's	50's	Highest Inns.	Average
Northampton	7	3	431	3	0	111*	107.75
Nottingham	19	0	1182	6	2	278	62.21
The Oval	49	9	2080	4	12	246	52.00
Oxford	3	1	173	1	0	158	86.50
Peterborough	2	0	102	1	0	100	51.00
Portsmouth	4	0	116	0	1	52	29.00
Scarborough	14	1	643	3	1	135	49.46
Sheffield	4	0	180	1	0	122	45.00
Southampton	2	0	61	0	1	53	30.50
Southend	2	0	20	0	0	12	10.00
Swansea	3	1	78	0	1	67*	39.00
Taunton	3	0	52	0	0	42	17.33
Tunbridge Wells	1	0	14	0	0	14	14.00
Weston-super-Mare ..	1	0	49	0	0	49	49.00
Worcester	8	2	316	1	2	101*	52.66
Totals	667	67	30201	92	146	278	50.33

BATTING ON AUSTRALIAN GROUNDS

Ground	Inns.	Not Outs	Runs	100's	50's	Highest Inns.	Average
Adelaide	10	2	701	4	1	182	87.62
Brisbane............	11	1	312	1	2	110	31.20
Hobart.............	5	1	302	1	1	124	75.50
Launceston	4	0	375	2	1	163	93.75
Melbourne..........	17	2	528	2	1	143	35.20
Perth	3	1	239	1	1	106	119.50
Sydney	12	3	656	1	6	115	72.88
Totals	62	10	3113	12	13	182	59.86

BATTING ON SOUTH AFRICAN GROUNDS

Ground	Inns.	Not Outs	Runs	100's	50's	Highest Inns.	Average
Benoni	2	1	371	1	1	300	371.00
Bulawayo	3	1	134	0	1	60	67.00
Bloemfontein	1	0	32	0	0	32	32.00
Capetown	9	2	535	2	4	125	76.42
Durban	6	0	250	1	1	106	41.66
Johannesburg	12	0	547	2	2	131	45.58
Kimberley	1	1	150	1	0	150*	
Pietermaritzburg.....	4	0	263	2	0	141	65.75
Port Elizabeth.......	7	1	240	1	0	108	40.00
Pretoria	2	0	17	0	0	15	8.50
Salisbury	1	0	34	0	0	34	34.00
Totals	48	6	2573	10	9	300	61.26

BATTING IN INDIA

Ground	Inns.	Not Outs	Runs	100's	50's	Highest Inns.	Average
Bombay	10	2	844	4	2	249*	105.50
Calcutta	5	0	359	3	0	123	71.80
Indore	1	0	22	0	0	22	22.00
Madras	1	0	81	0	1	81	81.00
Totals	17	2	1306	7	3	249*	87.06

BATTING ON NEW ZEALAND GROUNDS

Ground	Inns.	Not Outs	Runs	100's	50's	Highest Inns.	Average
Auckland	2	1	175	0	2	97*	175.00
Christchurch	2	0	117	0	1	79	58.50
Dunedin.............	3	0	62	0	0	28	20.66
Wellington...........	4	0	87	0	0	32	21.75
Totals	11	1	441	0	3	97*	44.10

BATTING IN WEST INDIES

Ground	Inns.	Not Outs	Runs	100's	50's	Highest Inns.	Average
Jamaica	5	0	148	0	1	56	29.60
Barbados	4	0	162	0	1	93	40.50
British Guiana	2	0	82	0	1	64	41.00
Trinidad.............	3	1	238	1	1	133	119.00
Totals	14	1	630	1	4	133	48.46

FOR M.C.C. TOURING TEAMS IN AUSTRALIA

	Inns.	Not Outs	Runs	100's	50's	Highest Inns.	Average
v. Australia	25	4	703	2	3	147	33.47
v. Australian XI	4	0	184	1	0	115	46.00
v. Combined XI	5	0	421	2	1	142	84.20
v. New South Wales ..	5	3	276	0	3	92	138.00
v. Queensland	5	0	275	1	2	110	55.00
v. South Australia	4	0	368	2	1	182	92.00
v. Tasmania	5	1	354	1	2	163	88.50
v. Victoria	7	1	391	2	1	143	65.16
v. Western Australia ..	2	1	141	1	0	106	141.00
Totals	62	10	3113	12	13	182	59.86

FOR M.C.C. TOURING TEAMS IN NEW ZEALAND

	Inns.	Not Outs	Runs	100's	50's	Highest Inns.	Average
v. New Zealand	4	0	145	0	1	79	36.25
v. Auckland	2	1	175	0	2	97*	175.00
v. Otago.............	3	0	62	0	0	28	20.66
v. Wellington	2	0	59	0	0	32	29.50
Totals	11	1	441	0	3	97*	44.10

FOR M.C.C. TOURING TEAMS IN SOUTH AFRICA

	Inns.	Not Outs	Runs	100's	50's	Highest Inns.	Average
v. Cape Province	1	0	121	1	0	121	121.00
v. Combined Universities	2	0	176	1	1	125	88.00
v. Eastern Province ...	3	1	144	1	0	108	72.00
v. Griqualand West ..	1	1	150	1	0	150*	—
v. Natal	4	0	222	2	0	106	55.50
v. A Natal XI	2	0	156	1	0	141	78.00

	Inns.	Not Outs	Runs	100's	50's	Highest Inns.	Average
v. N.E. Transvaal.....	2	1	371	1	1	300	371.00
v. Orange Free State ..	1	0	32	0	0	32	32.00
v. Rhodesia	4	1	168	0	1	60	56.00
v. South Africa	19	1	648	1	4	114	36.00
v. A South African XI	2	0	17	0	0	15	8.50
v. Transvaal	5	0	304	1	2	131	60.80
v. Western Province...	2	1	64	0	0	34	64.00
Totals	48	6	2573	10	9	300	61.26

TEST MATCH HUNDREDS (17)

v. Australia (5).
    184   at Nottingham, 1948.
    147   at Adelaide, 1946–7.
    145*   at Manchester, 1948.
    103*   at Adelaide, 1946–7.
    102   at Nottingham, 1938.

v. South Africa (7).
    208   at Lord's, 1947.
    163   at Nottingham, 1947.
    158   at Manchester, 1955.
    115   at Manchester, 1947.
    114   at Johannesburg, 1948–9.
    112   at Nottingham, 1951.
    113   at The Oval, 1947.

v West Indies (2).
    133   at Port of Spain, 1954.
    120   at Lord's, 1939.

v. New Zealand (2).
    116   at Lord's, 1949.
    114   at Leeds, 1949.

v. Pakistan (1).
    278   at Nottingham, 1954.

FULL LIST OF HUNDREDS—122

1936 (1)

100*   Middlesex v. Northamptonshire, at Northampton.

1937 (3)

177   Middlesex v. Gloucestershire, at Lord's.
116   M.C.C. v. Oxford University, at Lord's.
111   Middlesex v. Nottinghamshire, at Nottingham.

1938 (5)

180*   Middlesex v. Essex, at Lord's.
163   Middlesex v. Gloucestershire, at Lord's.
134   Middlesex v. Lancashire, at Manchester.
102   England v. Australia, at Nottingham (FIRST TEST).
100   M.C.C. v. Surrey, at Lord's.

1939 (8)

214* Middlesex v. Derbyshire, at Lord's.
181   Middlesex v. Essex, at Lord's.
143   Middlesex v. Hampshire, at Lord's.
120   England v. West Indies, at Lord's (FIRST TEST).
115   M.C.C. v. West Indies, at Lord's.
115   Middlesex v. Lancashire, at Manchester.
111* Middlesex v. Northamptonshire, at Northampton.
103* Middlesex v. Somerset, at Frome.

1944–5 (5)

249* Holkar v. Bombay, at Bombay.
123† Bengal Governor's XII v. Stuart's XII, at Calcutta.
120   Services XI v. C.C. of India, at Bombay.
109   Services XI v. Governor's XI, at Calcutta.
100   C. K. Nayudu's XI v. C.C. of India, at Bombay.

1945–6 (2)

124   Europeans v. Hindus, at Bombay.
101   East Zone v. Australian Services, at Calcutta.

1946 (10)

235   Middlesex v. Surrey, at Lord's.
202   Middlesex v. Cambridge University, at Cambridge.
147* Middlesex v. Northamptonshire, at Lord's.
142   Middlesex v. Kent, at Maidstone.
124   Middlesex v. Lancashire, at Manchester.
122   Middlesex v. Warwickshire, at Lord's.
121   Middlesex v. Sussex, at Hove.
115   Middlesex v. Hampshire, at Bournemouth.
103   An England XI v. The Rest, at Lord's.
100   Middlesex v. Lancashire, at Manchester.

1946–7 (5)

163   M.C.C. v. Tasmania, at Launceston.
147 ⎫
103* ⎬ England v. Australia, at Adelaide (FOURTH TEST).
143   M.C.C. v. Victoria, at Melbourne.
124   M.C.C. v. Combined XI, at Hobart.

1947 (18)

246   Champion County v. The Rest, at The Oval.
208   England v. South Africa, at Lord's (SECOND TEST).
178   Middlesex v. Surrey, at Lord's.
168   Middlesex v. Kent, at Lord's.
163   England v. South Africa, at Nottingham (FIRST TEST).
154   Middlesex v. South Africa, at Lord's.
151   Middlesex v. Leicestershire, at Leicester.
139   Middlesex v. Lancashire, at Lord's.
137*   Middlesex v. Surrey, at Lord's.
129   Middlesex v. Essex, at Lord's.
115   England v. South Africa, at Manchester (THIRD TEST).
113   England v. South Africa, at The Oval (FIFTH TEST).
112   Middlesex v. Worcestershire, at Lord's.
110   Middlesex v. Northamptonshire, at Northampton.
110   Middlesex v. Sussex, at Lord's.
106   Middlesex v. Kent, at Canterbury.
101   South of England v. South Africa, at Hastings.
100*   Middlesex v. Sussex, at Hove.

† *This twelve-a side match was recognised as first-class by the India Cricket Board of Control.*

1948 (9)

252* Middlesex v. Somerset, at Lord's.
184 England v. Australia, at Nottingham (FIRST TEST).
145* England v. Australia, at Manchester (THIRD TEST).
145 Middlesex v. Kent, at Lord's.
135 ⎫
⎬ M.C.C. South African Team v. H. D. G. Leveson Gower's XI, at Scarborough.
125* ⎭
123* Middlesex v. Surrey, at The Oval.
123 M.C.C. v. Surrey, at Lord's.
100* Middlesex v. Derbyshire, at Derby.

1948–9 (8)

300 M.C.C. v. North-Eastern Transvaal, at Benoni.
150* M.C.C. v. Griqualand West, at Kimberley.
141 M.C.C. v. A Natal XI, at Pietermaritzburg.
125 M.C.C. v. Combined Universities, at Cape Town.
121 M.C.C. v. Cape Province, at Cape Town.
114 England v. South Africa, at Johannesburg (SECOND TEST).
108 M.C.C. v. Eastern Province, at Port Elizabeth.
106 M.C.C. v. Natal, at Durban.

1949 (9)

182 Middlesex v. Sussex, at Lord's.
179 Middlesex v. Lancashire, at Lord's.
148 Middlesex v. New Zealanders, at Lord's.
140 Middlesex v. Northamptonshire, at Lord's.
127 M.C.C. v. Yorkshire, at Scarborough.
122 Middlesex v. Yorkshire, at Sheffield.
116 England v. New Zealand, at Lord's (SECOND TEST).
114 England v. New Zealand, at Leeds (FIRST TEST).
102* Middlesex v. Hampshire, at Bournemouth.

1950 (2)

144 Middlesex v. Somerset, at Lord's.
115* Middlesex v. Surrey, at The Oval.

1950–1 (4)

142 M.C.C. v. Combined XI, at Launceston.
115 M.C.C. v. Australian XI, at Sydney.
107 M.C.C. v. Victoria, at Melbourne.
106 M.C.C. v. Western Australia, at Perth.

1951 (8)

172 Middlesex v. Warwickshire, at Lord's.
169 Middlesex v. Sussex, at Lord's.
158 Middlesex v. Oxford University, at Oxford.
150 Players v. Gentlemen, at Lord's.
147 M.C.C. v. South Africans, at Lord's.
113 Middlesex v. Leicestershire, at Lord's.
113 Middlesex v. Essex, at Colchester.
112 England v. South Africa, at Nottingham (FIRST TEST).

1952 (4)

132 An England XI v. India, at Hastings.
130 Middlesex v. Worcestershire, at Lord's.
109* Middlesex v. Leicestershire, at Leicester.
107 Middlesex v. Northamptonshire, at Lord's

1953 (4)

143* Middlesex v. Sussex, at Lord's.
113 Middlesex v. Surrey, at Lord's.
109 Middlesex v. Yorkshire, at Lord's.
100 Middlesex v. Northamptonshire, at Peterborough.

1953–4 (1)

133　　England v. West Indies, at Port of Spain (Fourth Test).

1954 (4)

278　　England v. Pakistan, at Nottingham (Second Test).
117　　Middlesex v. Hampshire, at Lord's.
113　　Middlesex v. Worcestershire, at Lord's.
101*　Middlesex v. Worcestershire, at Worcester.

1954–5 (3)

182　　M.C.C. v. South Australia, at Adelaide.
113　　M.C.C. v. South Australia, at Adelaide.
110　　M.C.C. v. Queensland, at Brisbane.

1955 (2)

158　　England v. South Africa, at Manchester (Third Test).
150　　Middlesex v. Sussex, at Lord's.

1956 (2)

110　　Middlesex v. Somerset, at Glastonbury.
101　　Middlesex v. Kent, at Lord's.

1956–7 (2)

131　　M.C.C. v. Transvaal, at Johannesburg.
101　　M.C.C. v. Natal, at Pietermaritzburg.

1957 (3)

143　　Middlesex v. Worcestershire, at Lord's.
109　　Middlesex v. Essex, at Leyton.
104　　Middlesex v. Lancashire, at Manchester.

* Signifies not out.

BOWLING

Season	Overs	Maidens	Runs	Wickets	Average
1936	66.5	8	259	10	25.90
1937	126	18	476	11	43.27
1938	130	18	504	16	31.50
1939	172.5	25	626	22	28.45
In India					
1944–5	91.4	11	331	5	66.20
1945–6	9	1	44	0	—
1946	197.5	34	584	20	29.20
M.C.C. in Australia					
1946–7	83.2	11	311	6	51.83
M.C.C. in New Zealand					
1946–7	24.4	7	53	11	4.81
1947	635.4	118	2053	73	28.12
1948	645.3	127	2058	62	33.19
M.C.C. in South Africa					
1948–9	275.4	40	1051	30	35.03
1949	740.4	125	2386	73	32.68
1950	227.2	47	710	14	50.71
M.C.C. in Australia					
1950–1	84.4	7	415	11	37.72
M.C.C. in New Zealand					
1950–1	25	4	75	0	—
1951	434.1	59	1403	48	29.22
1952	662.1	92	2201	77	28.58
1953	318.3	47	1095	31	35.32

Season	Overs	Maidens	Runs	Wickets	Average
M.C.C. in West Indies					
1953–4	81.4	16	325	6	54.16
1954	253.5	35	819	26	31.50
M.C.C. in Australia					
1954–5	16	1	101	2	50.50
1955	130	18	511	8	63.88
1956	85	17	264	10	26.40
M.C.C. in South Africa					
1956–7	16.2	1	73	3	24.33
1957	286.2	59	939	38	24.71
Totals	5171.5	946	19667	613	32.08
and	648.1 eight-ball overs				

COUNTY CHAMPIONSHIP MATCHES

Season	Overs	Maidens	Runs	Wickets	Average
1936	65.5	8	258	8	32.25
1937	69	11	237	8	29.62
1938	55	10	194	8	24.25
1939	127.5	20	445	15	29.66
1946	157.2	30	457	16	28.56
1947	442.3	82	1440	57	25.26
1948	528.3	114	1541	50	30.82
1949	647.1	119	2003	60	33.38
1950	170	35	504	10	50.40
1951	337.5	45	1062	42	25.28
1952	590.1	85	1916	74	25.89
1953	253	44	776	27	28.74
1954	240.5	33	783	25	31.32
1955	127	18	488	8	61.00
1956	70	14	208	5	41.60
1957	268.2	55	838	35	23.94
Totals	4022.3	723	13150	448	29.35
and	127.5 eight-ball overs				

TEST MATCHES

Season	Overs	Maidens	Runs	Wickets	Average
1937 (v. New Zealand)	6	0	34	2	17.00
1939 (v. West Indies)	8	1	28	0	—
1946 (v. India)	12	1	38	0	—
1946–7 (v. Australia)	16.2	0	78	0	—
1947 (v. South Africa)	103	29	263	5	52.60
1948 (v. Australia)	37	6	156	1	156.00
1948–9 (v. South Africa)	98.2	20	308	7	44.00
1949 (v. New Zealand)	33	2	126	5	25.20
1950 (v. West Indies)	7	2	21	0	—
1950–1 (v. Australia)	11.6	1	43	1	43.00
1950–1 (v. New Zealand)	6	0	31	0	—
1951 (v. South Africa)	13	1	45	0	—
1952 (v. India)	9	1	30	0	—
1953 (v. Australia)	3	0	21	1	21.00
1953–4 (v. West Indies)	27.4	3	144	2	72.00
1954 (v. Pakistan)	13	2	36	1	36.00
1956–7 (v. South Africa)	3	1	8	0	—
Totals	269.4	70	1410	25	56.40
and	137.2 eight-ball overs				

BOWLING SUMMARY

IN ENGLAND

	Overs	Maidens	Runs	Wickets	Average
Middlesex (County Championship)	4022.3	723	13150	448	29.35
and	127.5 eight-ball overs				
Middlesex (Other Matches)	201.4	27	915	27	33.88
and	12 eight-ball overs				
Tests (v. Australia)	40	6	177	2	88.50
Tests (v. South Africa)	116	30	308	5	61.60
Tests (v. New Zealand)	39	2	160	7	22.85
Tests (v. India)	21	2	68	0	—
Tests (v. Pakistan)	13	2	36	1	36.00
Tests (v. West Indies)	7	3	49	0	—
and	8 eight-ball overs				
Gentlemen v. Players...........	54.1	6	207	9	23.00
M.C.C..........................	217	26	911	24	37.95
and	25 eight-ball overs				
Other First-Class Matches	208.3	20	907	16	56.68
Totals	4939.5	847	16888	539	31.33
and	172.5 eight-ball overs				

IN AUSTRALIA

	Overs	Maidens	Runs	Wickets	Average
Tests	28	1	121	1	121.00
Other First-Class Matches	155.6	18	706	18	39.22

IN NEW ZEALAND

Tests	6	0	31	0	—
Other First-Class Matches	43.4	11	97	11	8.81

IN SOUTH AFRICA

Tests	101.2	21	316	7	45.14
Other First-Class Matches	190.4	20	808	26	31.07

IN WEST INDIES

Tests	27.4	3	144	2	72.00
Other First-Class Matches	54	13	181	4	45.25

IN INDIA

Other First-Class Matches	100.4	12	375	5	75.00
Totals	5171.5	946	19667	613	32.08
and	648.1 eight-ball overs				

Denis Compton's 613 wickets have been captured as follows:—

Bowled	132
Caught	317
Leg-before-wicket..........	105
Stumped	54
Hit Wicket	5
	613

NOTABLE ACHIEVEMENTS

Denis Compton, Middlesex cricketer, Arsenal footballer, played in 78 Tests for England. His aggregate of 5,807 runs has been surpassed in Tests only by W. R. Hammond, 7,249; D. G. Bradman, 6,996; and L. Hutton, 6,971.

Highest Aggregate for One Season: 3,816 runs in 1947.

Most Hundreds in One Season: Eighteen in 1947.

Fastest Triple Century: 300 out of 399 in 181 minutes for M.C.C. against N.E. Transvaal, Benoni, 1948–49.

Century on First Test Appearance: Compton scored 65 on his Test debut against New Zealand at The Oval, 1937, but he hit a century on his first Test appearance against Australia, South Africa and West Indies.

Highest English Third Wicket Stand: 424 with W. J. Edrich for Middlesex against Somerset at Lord's, 1948.

Four Hundreds in Succession: during M.C.C. tour in Australia, 1946–47.

Three times he has hit two separate hundreds in a match, including England v. Australia, at Adelaide, 1946–47.

On three occasions he has taken ten or more wickets in a match.

His best bowling figures in a match: eleven for 47 runs for M.C.C. v. Auckland, 1946–47.

Compton took twelve wickets for 174 runs and made 137 not out for Middlesex against Surrey at The Oval, 1947.

Many of Compton's fine innings in his later years were achieved when he was severely troubled by his right knee. He first felt discomfort in 1947, and in 1950 an operation was performed when a small piece of bone was removed from the knee. In November 1955 an even more serious operation took place when the knee cap was removed. A series of minor operations followed to improve flexion of the knee. He returned to first-class cricket in June 1956, and seven weeks later played for England against Australia in the final Test, hitting a brilliant 94 at The Oval.

GOOGLY BOWLERS AND CAPTAINS RETIRE

By E. M. WELLINGS

Among the several illustrious players who retired from county cricket after 1957 were D. V. P. Wright, E. Hollies and B. Dooland, who together have taken more than 5,000 wickets. The remaining googly-type bowlers of any standing in English first-class cricket could afterwards be counted on the fingers of one hand—Goonesena, Jenkins and Greenhough, with the left-handers Tribe and, when so minded, Wardle. Moreover, among others retiring was J. T. Ikin for whom googly bowling was a secondary role.

The strategical and tactical changes in big cricket since the war have almost driven such bowlers out of the county game. In an age when field strategy is based on giving nothing away the googly bowler, who trades runs for wickets, has lost his popularity. County captains attend meetings at which they pay lip service to the need for encouraging attacking cricket. But, when they return to their counties, they discard venturesome batsmen and turn their backs on bowlers liable to give runs away, however great their wicket-taking potential may be.

Googly bowling is now out of favour, but none studying the performances of Wright, Hollies and Dooland can doubt that it will rise again. Wright, with his remarkable set of seven hat-tricks, used to take his wickets in fewer overs than any other contemporary bowler. The next change of strategy may well revive a demand for those who take wickets quickly.

Wright was the most controversial bowler of his period, regarded by some as an expensive luxury. There were times when he was costly, and his Test record was not remarkable. Others, and I number myself among them, regard Wright as a magnificent bowler. He bowled leg-breaks and googlies at a pace not attempted by his rivals, and there were occasions when he was quite unplayable. At such times, unfortunately, he was liable to beat bat, wicket, stumper and everything and thus often missed his due reward.

Wright's Test record is a faulty guide. He began on the too-perfect pitches of the 'thirties against an Australian batting side containing Bradman, McCabe, Brown, Fingleton and Hassett. Even then he was unlucky. When at last he found a favourable pitch at Leeds in 1938 and took three wickets so quickly that a remarkable win for England was in prospect, a missed catch in the slips allowed Hassett to play the match-winning innings. Again at Sydney in 1947 Wright had his chance. Once more a vital catch was dropped off his bowling, for Bradman escaped when only two and stayed to make sure that Australia would win.

Having begun handicapped on batsmen's pitches before the

war, Wright afterwards suffered from playing in a wretchedly weak English bowling side. His only worthwhile support was provided by Bedser, and he was not then the great bowler he afterwards became. Wright, then, was not only unlucky in often missing the just reward for superb bowling but unlucky also in his period. Wright played in 34 Tests and had two tours each in Australia and South Africa. There has been no touring cricketer more dependable than Wright both on and off the field, and it was fitting that he should have been among the first professionals to be officially appointed captain of a county side.

Hollies also rose to the captaincy of his county. His first-class career for Warwickshire dates back to 1932, the same year that Wright first played for Kent. Whereas Wright was a speedy bowler with vicious spin, Hollies rolled up slower and more insidiously artful balls. There has perhaps never been an English googly bowler with such control of length and direction. In that he and Wright provided another contrast. They differed greatly, too, in their approach to the wicket. Before reducing his run Wright was electrifying with bounds and leaps; Hollies bobbed gently towards the crease.

Hollies has the distinction, if that is the right word, of having taken more wickets in first-class cricket than he made runs. Yet in one of his 13 Tests he saved England with his bat, for against South Africa at Nottingham in 1947 he and J. W. Martin put on 51 for the last wicket. The season of 1946 was his greatest. His 184 wickets then cost only 15.6 each, and against Nottinghamshire he took all ten wickets for 49, bowling seven of his opponents and having three others lbw. It may be that the M.C.C. selectors erred in not then including him in their team for Australia. It was not until 1950, when he was too old to adapt his methods to Australian conditions, that he toured there. Between the two tours he bowled one particular googly at The Oval in 1948 which will long be quoted. Bradman came to play his final Test innings, and Hollies, with that now famous delivery, bowled him second ball for nought.

The third googly bowler to leave county cricket was Dooland, a South Australian who suffered from lack of encouragement in a time of Australian plenty just after the war. In their more recent lean period his country must often have regretted the discouraging treatment which drove him into English cricket. In that he began in the northern league game and finally had five seasons with Nottinghamshire. In the 1946–47 season Dooland looked a better bowler each time he opposed the M.C.C. touring team. He played in two Tests and bowled excellently, but he was surprisingly omitted from the 1948 touring team. As a result he was lost to Australian cricket for a decade, during which their spin bowling became progressively weaker and weaker.

When Dooland returned to his own country aged 33 after the

1957 season, he was a genuine all-rounder, who had either done the double or come close to it in each of his county seasons. On two occasions he played for the Players at Lord's, and none can question that his absence during the past ten years has been Test cricket's loss.

Ikin, who has suffered much in recent years from back and stomach trouble, has been one of the disappointments of post-war cricket. He was thrust forward at the start of the period, when there were gaps in all teams. It was perhaps his misfortune to be made to fill one of them in the Test team before he was sufficiently mature. Yet his start was promising enough. After beginning against India he went to Australia in 1946 and overcame the handicap of inexperience with considerable success in the first three Tests. His first in Australia was on the wickedly sticky pitch at Brisbane, but with his 32 he shared with Hammond the distinction of being England's top scorer in the match.

In the next two Tests Ikin also scored well, but subsequently he achieved little in big matches, and his record in 18 Tests was modest. He lacked neither the necessary temperament nor courage, for he was ever ready to interpose himself between his wicket and the fastest bowling. It may be that he lacked ambition. There were certainly the qualities in his rugged left-handed batting that make for success in the highest circles, and in addition to being a useful right-arm bowler he was among the greatest fielders at short-leg and in the gully.

Three county captains retired in 1957, and they included E. D. R. Eagar who had led Hampshire in every post-war season. Figures alone cannot tell the story of Eagar's part in the cricket of that period. He was a Gloucestershire man who gave everything to Hampshire as their captain-secretary. None has done more for that county, and none has made more sacrifice for any county.

In a period when the expression county amateur has concealed many a super-professional Eagar was too busy working for his adopted county to give thought to himself. He sacrificed any chance of a more financially rewarding career and also his own batting. In earlier days with Oxford and Gloucestershire Eagar was a bold, attacking batsman. The need in Hampshire was for someone more stubborn, and he did his best to become a solid number four. The damage to his cricket was obvious, though he still achieved much as a batsman for Hampshire, and in the field he averaged more than a catch a match. It was, however, off the field that Eagar achieved most. While other counties turned to football pools for revenue Hampshire existed on the tireless work of their captain. He toiled round the year to popularise the county's cricket, built up the membership to previously unimagined heights and persuaded more people than ever before to pay at the gates. As secretary he continues at that work.

The other retiring captains were C. H. Palmer and W. H. H. Sutcliffe. Palmer, like Eagar, was a cricket migrant. He made his name as a graceful stroke-making batsman with Worcestershire before becoming Leicestershire's secretary-captain. Those who saw his beautiful 85 at Worcester in the first match of the 1948 Australian touring team will number Palmer among the post-war disappointments. At his best he looked a Test class player, and several less able by far than Palmer batted several times for England. He played in only one Test, and it may be that he should have been given more chances.

In addition to his batting Palmer was a valuable medium-paced bowler, and as such he made his greatest impact on recent cricket. In the middle of Surrey's all-conquering run as champions Palmer took eight of their wickets at Leicester in 1955, while their innings crashed from 42 for one to 67 for nine and while not a single run was scored off him.

Unlike most of his predecessors Sutcliffe took over the Yorkshire captaincy at a time of a cricket slump in the county. He thus had to tackle a difficult task of reformation so unusual in Yorkshire that none existed there able to advise him from first-hand knowledge. He did not manage to restore the side to its more familiar position, but he himself always set a personal example of resolute batsmanship and played some doughty innings.

Another retiring cricketer was F. W. Stocks after 12 years of sound left-handed batting and useful right-arm bowling for Nottinghamshire. There are remarkable features about his career, for he started in 1946 with a century in his first match and with a wicket from his initial delivery. In the same season he played in a Test trial, his only representative match, and he had the unusual distinction of making his highest score, 171 in 1956, against an Australian touring team.

Finally, late in the year, another Australian exile and one of the period's oustanding left-handed batsmen, Livingston of Northamptonshire, announced his departure. And a season saddened by such losses threatened still greater sadness until Denis Compton revised his intentions from total to partial retirement.

CAREER FIGURES

	Runs	Highest Inns.	Average	Runs	Wickets	Average
B. Dooland	6907	115*	24.32	21370	987	21.65
E. D. R. Eagar	12175	158*	21.93	1465	31	47.25
W. E. Hollies	1671	47	5.00	48656	2323	20.94
J. T. Ikin	17637	192	36.74	10159	332	30.59
L. Livingston........	15174	210	45.16	28	2	14.00
C. H. Palmer	17118	201	31.93	8846	351	25.20
F. W. Stocks	11397	171	29.60	9794	223	43.91
W. H. H. Sutcliffe...	7418	181	26.21	334	15	22.26
D. V. P. Wright	5907	84*	12.35	49305	2056	23.98

* Signifies not out.

D

STORY OF NEW ZEALAND CRICKET

By Charles Bray

A Yorkshireman, James Cook, discovered New Zealand in 1769, but there is no evidence that this distinguished son of the "broad acres" was an ardent cricketer or that he introduced the game to the natives of his newly-discovered land. More likely it came with the arrival of the military as it did in South Africa. In 1840 New Zealand was declared a Crown Colony. By that time cricket had made its appearance in both the North and South islands.

Nineteen years passed, however, before any definite competitive spirit appeared. In 1859 Auckland sent by slow coastal steamer (there was no other means of communication) a challenge to Wellington to play a cricket match. It took a long time for the challenge to reach its destination, a long time for Wellington to make up their minds and still more delay for the reply to get back to Auckland. Weeks went by. Then unannounced the Auckland team arrived in Wellington. The local lads were caught on the hop. Some of their best players, so history tells us, were up country and could not be contacted. Yet the match had to be played. Auckland went home cock-a-hoop having won by four wickets.

Three years later Wellington challenged Auckland to a return encounter. The match was duly played and again Wellington lost. But the foundations, upon which New Zealand was to build her Test cricket, had been well and truly laid. It was destined to be a hard uphill fight. There were, however, men of steel in this thinly-populated new country. The greater the difficulties the more determined were these early pioneers to place New Zealand on the cricket map of the world. One called Shadrach Jones of Dunedin took the first step. He was personally responsible for bringing Parr's All-England XI touring Australia in 1864 to New Zealand and it cost him £5,000. He didn't care. The ice was broken.

In 1876 Lillywhite's All-England team played eight matches, winning six and drawing two. In 1881–82 Shaw and Shrewsbury's English XI had seven games, five of which they won. Between those two visits the first Australian team sailed the Tasman sea, and played seven matches before going to England. A tremendous fillip was given to New Zealand cricket when Canterbury beat that side which included such illustrious names as Spofforth, Murdoch, Boyle, Garrett, Bannerman and Horan.

Those sturdy pioneers were now reaping some reward for their labours. Before the end of the century four more representative Australian teams toured New Zealand. Tasmania sent a side. So did Fiji and several came from Australian States. In 1902–3 Sir Pelham Warner skippered a team from England known as Lord

Hawke's XI and in 1906–7 came the first M.C.C. side led by Captain Wynyard.

Lord Plunket was Governor of New Zealand at this time and it was in 1906 that he presented a challenge trophy (The Plunket Shield) to be competed for by the provinces. The four major associations are Auckland, Wellington, Canterbury and Otago, and each plays the other usually around Christmas because it is as well to remember that cricket in New Zealand always has been and still is strictly amateur apart from the odd professional coach.

Landmarks in the Dominion's cricket history now became frequent. After the First World War there was a gap, but in 1922–23 A. C. MacLaren led an M.C.C. side which included such brilliant players as A. P. F. Chapman, the Hon. F. S. Calthorpe, Tom Lowry, a New Zealander then up at Cambridge who was later to captain his country on two tours of England, Tich Freeman and Dick Tyldesley. The two professionals were a great success and a great attraction. So was the young Percy Chapman and the burly Tom Lowry who rather indiscreetly hit 130 in the third match at Wellington.

The year 1927 was a red-letter one in New Zealand's cricket history. It saw their first visit to England as a cricketing country. Tom Lowry led the team. They were not accorded Test match status but did sufficiently well to warrant official recognition for the side which followed four years later.

The first Lowry team played 26 first-class matches, won seven, lost five and drew 14. The team included names subsequently to become famous not only in New Zealand but wherever the game was played: C. S. Dempster; Charles Dacre; Roger Blunt; J. E. Mills; M. L. Page, later to captain his country; K. C. James, a great little wicket-keeper, and W. E. Merritt, a spin bowler of international class. Merritt, only 18, took 169 wickets in all matches. At the end of the tour Dacre signed as professional for Gloucestershire. Later Merritt went to Lancashire league, Blunt took up a business appointment in Nottingham, James qualified for Northamptonshire and Dempster for Leicestershire.

In this his first visit, C. S. Dempster showed his remarkable skill with the bat. He made 1,430 runs, average 44.68, and was second in the bowling averages although bowling was not one of his recognised accomplishments. Six of the New Zealanders scored over a thousand runs on that tour. The bowling was weak. The fielding, appalling at first, improved tremendously under the stern direction of the captain.

Harold Gilligan, who has been New Zealand's representative in England for many years, took the next M.C.C. side to the Dominion in the winter of 1929–30. They opened with five matches in Australia, but the main purpose of the tour was to play in New Zealand. This was an even stronger side than the previous one.

Gilligan had with him such brilliant amateurs as K. S. Duleep-sinhji, E. W. Dawson, G. B. Legge, M. J. Turnbull and M. J. C. Allom and six of the leading professionals of the day—F. E. Woolley, E. H. Bowley, M. S. Nichols, T. S. Worthington, F. Barratt and W. L. Cornford. The three Tests originally arranged were increased to four but only the first produced a definite result, England winning by eight wickets.

This was a famous match. Batting first, New Zealand lost three wickets for 15 runs to Nichols and then Allom, bowling in his first Test, took four wickets in five balls, including the hat-trick. Duleepsinhji, who prior to the first Test could not make a run, suddenly hit form and in six Test innings scored 358 runs, twice not out, for an average of 89.75. In the second Test Dempster and Mills made centuries for New Zealand in the first innings. Frank Woolley achieved the remarkable bowling figures of seven for 76 in an innings of 440 runs.

A year later (1931) New Zealand undertook their second tour of England and this time with Test match status, but only one Test was allotted them. They did so well in their opening matches— a strong M.C.C. team was defeated by an innings and 122 runs— and made such a brilliant recovery to save the first Test at Lord's that two more Tests were arranged. The Lord's game is still regarded as the most famous in New Zealand cricket history. It was their first Test match abroad. It was at headquarters and it ended in New Zealand striving for victory after being 230 runs behind on the first innings. Heroes of the fight-back were Dempster (120), Blunt (96), Page (104) and the skipper Tom Lowry, who made 34 with an injured hand. England, set to get 240 to win in two hours twenty minutes, never tried to get the runs.

In the second Test at The Oval New Zealand took a thrashing, Herbert Sutcliffe, Hammond and Duleepsinhji making hundreds which enabled Jardine to declare at 416 for four wickets. The tourists were unable to reach 200 in either innings. The third Test at Old Trafford was washed out, play being possible only on the third day.

Of the 32 first-class matches, New Zealand won six, lost only three, the other 23 being drawn. The strength of the batting and the comparative weakness of the bowling was undoubtedly the reason for the high number of drawn games. Dempster, Blunt, Mills, Lowry, Vivian and Weir all made over a thousand runs. No bowler took a hundred wickets although Merritt came within one of that feat, but the average cost was 26.48 runs apiece.

I have reason to remember this New Zealand tour. In their first match against Essex, Dempster made a double century. I dropped him in the slips when he was 46. Jack O'Connor made 129 (remember the figure) in our first innings. In the second match against my county Tom Lowry made 129 before he was caught on the boundary by me, a catch which caused some controversy because I could not say whether I was over the boundary line when I caught the ball. The umpire consulted the crowd and eventually gave Lowry out. It has remained a subject of good-natured banter between us ever since. To complete the coincidence of 129 I made exactly that score in our second innings.

The winter of 1932 recorded another landmark in New Zealand cricket history. So impressive had been Tom Lowry's 1931 side that when D. R. Jardine took his famous "body-line" team to Australia, New Zealand was included in the tour; two Tests were played and both drawn. Walter Hammond was then in his prime. He made 227 at Christchurch and 336 not out at Auckland—then the record individual Test score. The precedent established by Jardine's team was continued. It is now the normal practice for the England team to cross to New Zealand after the end of each Australian tour.

G. O. Allen's team of 1936–37 did not play any Tests in New Zealand because the Dominion was sending a team to England the following summer. This time Lowry came as manager but played in a number of matches. M. L. Page was the captain with H. G. Vivian vice-captain.

Three Tests were played and again it was made apparent that three days were not enough to ensure definite results. Two of the three were drawn, England winning the Manchester match by 130 runs. The third Test is historic in that Denis Compton made his debut. He scored 65 before being run out unluckily. A hard drive from Hardstaff cannoned off the bowler's hand into the stumps with Compton out of his ground. The record of M. L. Page's side was on a par with the previous New Zealand touring team. Out of the 32 first-class matches, nine were won, nine were lost and 14 drawn. Again the side was top-heavy in batting. Two brilliant young batsmen made their appearance, W. M. Wallace, aged 20, and M. P. Donnelly, 19. They finished first and second in the team's batting averages. The tall W. A. Hadlee was also a most promising performer. John Cowie was the pick of the bowlers, taking over a hundred wickets, the first New Zealander to accomplish that feat on an England tour.

The Second World War hit this young cricketing country as hard if not harder than any other. But when W. R. Hammond's M.C.C. team returned after playing four matches, including one Test in New Zealand after the 1946–47 Australian tour, they brought back glowing accounts of a young left-hander named Sutcliffe. He had hit two hundreds, 197 and 128, in one match against the tourists for Otago and scored 58 in the only Test. W. A. Hadlee showed that he had developed into a class batsman and it was no surprise when he was chosen to lead the 1949 team to England.

This was unquestionably New Zealand's best team. They drew all four Tests with England. Thirteen of the 32 first-class matches were won. The only defeat was by Oxford University. Under the genial managership of Mr. J. H. Phillipps and the efficient captaincy of W. A. Hadlee so popular did the tourists become that not only did the receipts cover the £25,000 expenses but a net profit of £15,000 was taken back to New Zealand. Martin Donnelly and Bert Sutcliffe had a superb season both making over 2,000 runs. Sutcliffe scored seven centuries, Donnelly five. V. J. Scott and W. M. Wallace also hit five hundreds each and J. R. Reid four. The batting was immensely strong. A pity the bowling was not as good. Cowie was affected by minor strains and therefore did not repeat his success of 1937. He was now 37. Age was beginning to tell.

A young fast bowler, J. A. Hayes, tore a muscle so badly half-way through the tour that he was unable to play again. The bulk of the bowling fell on the tubby, cheerful T. B. Burtt, slow left-arm immaculate length, good flight, who attacked the off-stump so accurately that he constantly tied down the opposing batsmen. Burtt took 128 wickets for an average of 22.88.

This side did not achieve the long-coveted first victory over England but they did well enough for New Zealand to shed the mantle of "the poor relation" of international cricket and to warrant a full Test programme with the home country in future.

It was therefore a profound disappointment when Sir Leonard Hutton's Ashes winning team went on to New Zealand in 1955 to find that first-class cricket in the Dominion had suffered an astonishing set-back. Bert Sutcliffe was only a shadow of his former self. Hadlee, Wallace, Donnelly, Scott, Cowie and Burtt had all left the international arena. None of similar calibre had been discovered to fill the gaps. The result was that the M.C.C. won all four matches. The two Tests must have been bitterly disappointing for New Zealand. The first they lost by eight wickets and the second went against them by an innings and 20 runs in three days. England achieved a world's record by dismissing New Zealand in the second innings for 26, the lowest total in Test cricket.

Since that disaster, however, New Zealand have registered their first Test victory. It was against the West Indies at Auckland in March 1956 by 190 runs. The fact that New Zealand had lost the first three Tests did not lessen the joy in winning their first victory in 26 years of Test cricket.

So to 1958. This will be New Zealand's fifth official visit to England. For the first time they will play five Tests of five days' duration. We look forward to having them here again and wish them a happy and prosperous tour.

UPS AND DOWNS OF NORTHAMPTONSHIRE

By JAMES D. COLDHAM

Northamptonshire County Cricket Club grew naturally out of the Northampton Town Club which was formed in 1820 and by 1850 was the most powerful in the county. Some of the members were drawn from outlying districts, and in the latter year the local Press began referring loosely to this Town Club as "Northamptonshire." The venue was the Northampton Race Course, an expanse of 120 acres and for generations a public right-of-way, jealously guarded by the Freemen and townspeople.

In the 'seventies representative cricket was at a low ebb and, as the outcome of a discussion on July 3, 1878, during the annual North versus South Northants match at Kettering, a Public Meeting at the George Hotel, Kettering, on July 31 considered "the best means of placing the County Club on a footing of equality with other counties." As it was realised that "Northamptonshire" had never been properly organised and was really a town club supported by few of the gentry, a Committee was elected *representing all parts of the County*, the Earl Spencer remaining President. Other notable officials were Sir Herewald Wake, a member of M.C.C., the Hon. and Rev. J. Marsham of the eminent Kent family, and Mr. Fred Tebbutt, proprietor of a shoe business and energetic Honorary Secretary, who arranged more ambitious fixtures.

From 1881 until 1885, of thirty-five matches eighteen were won and eight lost. Essex and M.C.C. were defeated; the first game (in 1884) at Wellingborough School saw Warwickshire worsted by an innings. Eighteen of Northamptonshire met the Australians in 1880 and two years later the County played them (with the aid of Alfred Shaw) on equal terms; both ventures were lost.

Tom Bowley, Joe Potter and Tom Alley secured 458 wickets. A schoolmaster, G. J. Gulliver, hit the first century, 103, off M.C.C. at Lord's in 1884; and five brothers Kingston batted zestfully. Eight of them appeared between 1874 and 1909.

New County Ground

As a small body of Freemen claimed that they possessed the freehold of the Race Course, the expansion of County Cricket there was impossible. Once a brewer's dray was driven deliberately across the pitch prepared by the Yorkshire-born groundsman, who gave the driver a good thrashing and asked the Committee for a small rise in pay.

In 1885 a ploughed field of ten acres of Abington Parish was purchased from Sir R. Loyd Lindsay (afterwards Lord Wantage) by the new "Northamptonshire County Cricket and Recreation Grounds Company, Ltd.," Sir Herewald Wake and Mr. Joseph Hill, Squire of Wollaston, advancing £2,000 for the site. The first match at the present County Ground was on May 14, 16, 1886, when Surrey Club and Ground won by six wickets.

Northamptonshire did not flourish as the best professionals were lured to more prosperous counties, Arthur Mold, for instance, joining Lancashire and playing for England; the membership was about 300; the County families remained aloof; finance was always a worry.

The Minor Counties Championship

Wellingborough School and the local Leagues produced some talented players, and in 1896 a rebuilt side entered the Minor Counties Championship. Between 1899 and 1904 they enjoyed substantial success, twice winning the title outright and twice tying for first place. No matches were lost between July 1898 and July 1901.

The genial Reptonian, Tom Horton, was captain and he was assured of class batting from the impetuous C. J. T. Pool, more solidity from W. H. Kingston, and ballast down to number eleven. Besides scoring prolifically, G. J. Thompson and W. East carried the attack. From 1898 until 1904 ninety-one games brought them 964 wickets. Thompson was the greatest all-rounder ever produced by Northamptonshire; East was a capable and accurate medium pacer and dour batsman.

George Thompson

An Old Wellingburian, George Thompson, first appeared in 1895 at the age of seventeen, and bowled and batted the County into first-class cricket. With his complete double circle of the arm action, he was above medium pace and brought the ball off the ground with plenty of life and spin. His length was superb. As a batsman he tended to be over-cautious, but when conditions warranted he would hit hard and often. Close in he held many catches. In Minor County days he scored 5,174 runs, average 35.93, and took 751 wickets at 14.01 runs each; and from 1905 until 1922 his figures were 8,322 runs, average 23.57, and 1,078 wickets at 18.88 runs each. The first Northants player to represent England against Australia—at Birmingham in 1909—Thompson came second to Hobbs with an average of 33.37 in the Tests in South Africa that winter, besides taking 23 wickets.

Promotion came in 1905, and no one worked harder for it than the open-handed and enthusiastic President, Lord Lilford, and the Honorary Secretary, the gifted Mr. A. J. Darnell, a household name in Law, Politics and Sport.

During the first four seasons irresolute and unenterprising batting were the bane, excepting such as C. J. T. Pool's 166 at Worcester, Dr. H. C. Pretty's 200 in as many minutes at Chesterfield, and Thompson's not out 103 at Fenner's after Cambridge had routed them for 57 and replied with 405, all in 1906. Top class spinners were specially feared. In 1907 Blythe of Kent took seventeen wickets in one day; and when at Ashley Down the County sank to a new low—12 all out—before Gloucestershire's Dennett, a telegram to the captain, E. M. Crosse, read: "Bring the Boys Home—Mother."

Thompson and East virtually monopolised the attack until 1908 when W. "Bumper" Wells, who could make the ball fly disagreeably, earned a regular place. They commanded respect. At The Oval in 1906 Surrey were dismissed on a plumb pitch for 96; the same year Thompson secured fifteen for 167 against Leicestershire at Northampton. It was heartening to beat Lancashire by one wicket at Northampton; and Northants did *not* finish last in those years.

New Blood

Composed almost entirely of local men, the team received an enlivening "shot in the arm" from outside. Fresh natives like the Denton twins, J. S. and W. H., both sound run-getters, F. "Fanny" Walden, a mighty atom of cricket and soccer, and stout W. A. Buswell, a cheerful 'keeper, were joined by four bold batsmen, R. A. Haywood and C. N. Woolley from Kent, John Seymour from Sussex and versatile S. G. Smith, the outstanding West Indian all-rounder who was, moreover, the first high-class left-hander Northamptonshire possessed.

Halcyon Days

After a poor start in 1909, eight of nine consecutive matches were won, the bowling of Smith and Thompson, who each took a hundred wickets and were admirably contrasted, being supported by increasingly offensive batting and lively fielding. Despite a drop from seventh to tenth place in 1910, S. G. Smith notched a thousand runs; at Sheffield, Yorkshire were beaten for the first time by five wickets, G. A. T. Vials contributing a sparkling 100. With Gloucestershire at Northampton 1,391 runs were scored for thirty-six wickets, including a mighty 204 by Smith. At Portsmouth, Northants were in dire straits until Smith and Thompson added 232. In 1911 only once was a total of 300 exceeded against the attack; and the batting advanced in all the rightful qualities. Against Gloucestershire at home Thompson and Haywood hit 222 in two and a half hours; the same pair put on 236 at Dewsbury. East's seven for 11 at the expense of Lancashire compensated somewhat for two collapses. Kent, however, were overcome at

Tonbridge by 135 runs, Thompson securing twelve wickets; and everyone pulled well to beat Yorkshire at Northampton by 44 runs.

In the wet 1912 Northants finished a close second to Yorkshire. Ten matches were won and one lost out of eighteen. A reasonable assumption is that if rain had not curtailed play on August 7, Yorkshire (103 and 105 for seven wickets) could have been beaten by Lancashire (347) and Northants (211 for eight wickets declared) could have upset Leicestershire (96 and 96 for six wickets)—and Northamptonshire would have displaced Yorkshire! The success was due to the determination of the captain, Vials, the collective power resulting from constant association—only twelve appeared in the County matches—and excellent, well-varied bowling. Vials headed the batting with an average of 28.26; Smith took 84 wickets at 12.15 runs each and Thompson 106 at 14.59 each.

Rumpus at Lord's

All was not well with County Cricket and early in 1913 A. J. Darnell, a pioneer of the Saturday start, proposed to the Advisory Committee of M.C.C. that matches be restricted to two days and there be a system of promotion and relegation. Lord Hawke, who favoured a smaller Championship, complained that Northamptonshire were taking too much of a lead. After a rumpus at Lord's, Lord Harris stilled the troubled waters and Mr. Darnell apologised for having unintentionally caused antipathy—and a few days later Yorkshire were beaten at Leeds by 20 runs, Smith (the new captain) and Thompson collecting eighteen wickets.

Northants finished fourth, winning thirteen games. Batsmen made great strides, four reaching four figures—Haywood 1,453, Smith 1,424, W. H. Denton 1,055 and J. S. Denton 1,007—and Thompson mustered 902 runs. Between them, Thompson and Smith secured 255 wickets. At Bristol, 516 was compiled in little over five hours, this orgy being led by Smith and Haywood, who in two hours added 216 for the third partnership. At Leyton, W. H. Denton carried out his bat for a solid 230. At Horsham, Thompson and Smith, who each took ten wickets, bowled unchanged.

S. G. Smith's "swan-song" in 1914 brought him 1,193 runs, average 41.13, and 99 wickets at 16.63 runs apiece. Again, his chief helper was Thompson. Despite a fall to ninth place, the County continued strongly all round. Against Sussex at Brighton their 557 for six wickets, declared, remains the highest ever; Smith stole the honours with 177, adding 180 with Thompson. Fifty-five matches had been won in six great years, but financially the club was as certain of instability as the Liberal Party was of power.

In 1919 S. G. Smith was domiciled in New Zealand and Thompson wounded and ill; the head and the right arm were gone.

Under a succession of captains the County struggled. 1921 found Haywood glorious with 1,909 runs, average 42.42, including eight centuries; it was a severe blow when he departed that autumn. Financial losses resulted in two general meetings battling over Reconstruction; V. W. C. Jupp of Sussex and England was appointed Secretary and Stephen Schilizzi emerged as a benefactor of the practical "Cricket is a business" School.

In February 1923 a prominent local agriculturalist, Alfred Cockerill, who had spent £10,000 in acquiring the County Ground, gave it to the club to be preserved for sport for ever; a unique gift. That year, however, Northants finished last for the first time.

Jupp the Cornerstone

V. W. C. Jupp was qualified in 1924. The following summer he scored 1,143 runs and took 110 wickets; it was the cornerstone of the most successful season between the wars when nine encounters brought victory and eleventh place was attained. The short, broad and increasingly rotund Jupp threw himself into the fight against odds. Secretary for eleven years, captain for six, a nimble-footed batsman on all sorts of wickets and a grand adaptable off- and leg-spinner, he scored 13,635 runs, average 30.44, and collected 1,078 wickets, average 22.31; six times he achieved the "double" for the County before he gave up in 1938.

In the 'twenties other remarkable exponents included Woolley, by now reliant on economy of effort at number one; "Fanny" Walden, at his best when the need was greatest; A. P. R. Hawtin, a stylish and confident stroke-maker; Ben Bellamy, second best wicket-keeper-batsman in the country; "Bumper" Wells, veteran fast bowler and hard hitter; length specialist A. E. Thomas, "the William Attewell of Northants cricket"; two class batsmen in H. F. Bagnall and W. W. Timms; and E. W. "Nobby" Clark, a fast left-hander with a beautiful action who touched a peak that few others of his generation reached. Eighteen seasons brought him 1,097 wickets at 21.31 runs apiece, and eight appearances for England.

The measure of the weakness was revealed to the full against Yorkshire, although Jupp, Wells, Thomas and Clark sometimes bowled wonderfully well against the strongest county.

The Arrival of Bakewell

In 1930 the Australians were spun out at Northampton for 93, but Northants finished at the foot of the table. Things became worse, and although, in September 1931, a Special General Meeting assented to the continuance of the club, thorough-going retrenchment was advocated.

Northants commenced 1933 by overwhelming West Indies by an innings and 62 runs; though they finished disappointingly, A. H.

Bakewell shone brightly. He became the first to reach 2,000 in all matches in a season, which included 246 against Nottinghamshire at Northampton and 257 against Glamorgan at Swansea in successive innings. A great future was being forecast for him. Making his debut in 1928, he impressed immediately with his brilliancy at short-leg; later his stroke-play won him his place for England. A better batsman than he looked, in an effort of 30 he would produce every stroke in the game, his off-driving being particularly exhilarating. Returning from Chesterfield after the last match of 1936, in which he batted superbly for 241 not out, Bakewell was injured in a tragic car smash; his career was finished and Northants, who would soon be bereft of Jupp and Clark, could ill-afford to lose him.

Snowden's Feats

A. W. Snowden, an amateur opening batsman from Peterborough, made his debut against New Zealand in 1931 at the age of 17; he scored his first fifty against India and his maiden century against Australia. He captained the county at the age of 18 and before he was 21 he and Bakewell achieved a feat which was then without parallel by compiling two opening stands of over 100 on the same day against Warwickshire at Edgbaston. Unfortunately business claimed him soon after he came of age.

Between May 1935 and May 1939, 101 matches failed to produce a victory. It was a shocking patch, but several players epitomised "Courage": J. E. Timms, a well-equipped and defiant cavalier batsman and relisher of any fight with high-bouncing bowlers; young Dennis Brookes, already looking an England batsman with his upstanding stance and style of purest simplicity; R. J. Partridge, swinging the new ball appreciably and spurred on by his thankless task; New Zealander, K. C. James, maintaining his international reputation behind the stumps; and a born leader, R. P. Nelson, the powerful left-handed Cambridge Blue, taking charge in 1938 and bringing the County finally out of the slough of despond in May 1939, when Leicestershire were vanquished at Northampton by an innings and 193 runs.

R. P. Nelson was killed, alas, in 1940; but Northamptonshire's Elder Statesman, A. P. R. Hawtin, and an enthusiastic captain, P. E. Murray Willis, kept the club in the news. Matches were played *each* war summer, and this shire which had finished seventeenth eight times between 1919 and 1939 did more for the game than any other.

The opening match in 1946 was appropriately at Lord's with Middlesex; at the close the Middlesex last pair were together and 23 runs were needed. There was a heightened tone about Northamptonshire's cricket; subsequent results disappointed. One recalls pleasurably the opening stands of Brookes and Percy Davis;

left-handed Barron, so full of promise; the comeback of "Nobby" Clark, for five overs the fastest in the land; Timms at cover; and slow left-hander Vincent Broderick, a young England hope; but few matches ended in their favour. A strong leader was required.

F. R. Brown Era

In 1949 F. R. Brown of Cambridge, Surrey and England, who was living at Daventry, took the reins, and a "New Look" transformed the County. He understood the game thoroughly; at his elbow were a revitalised Executive and a playing staff rich in numbers and prowess. Winning ten matches in 1949, Northants jumped to sixth place; in 1952 they finished eighth. Skipper from 1949 to 1953, Brown, when freed from representative calls, scored with his pugnacious approach 4,331 runs, average 30.94, and took 391 wickets, average 23.23, while reshaping the seam, leg-break and googly departments. His right-hand man was the Yorkshireman Brookes; when at Headingly in 1953 Yorkshire were defeated for the first time for forty years, he was both acting-captain and century-maker. These years saw two pre-war Lancastrians in Norman Oldfield, overflowing with neat strokes and scorer in 1949 of 2,192 runs, average 49.81, and Albert Nutter, a hostile opening bowler; F. Jakeman who, by fierce left-handed hitting in 1951, made 558 runs in four consecutive innings before dismissal, including 258 not out off Essex at Northampton; Frank Tyson, the fastest bowler in the country; Australians "Jock" Livingston, a left-handed batsman and ubiquitous fieldsman of sheer delight, and George Tribe of Herculean all-round feats; and Desmond Barrick, who hits the ball harder than most.

Notable Personalities

As captain since 1954 the quiet, knowledgeable and shrewd Brookes has proved even more successful than Brown. No longer is the Northampton pitch easy paced and a nightmare to all bowlers alike; decisive results have increased. Since 1955, Surrey have been beaten four times; and Northants rose from seventh in 1954 and 1955 to fourth in 1956, and to second in 1957—the most successful campaign in their history, with 218 points from 28 matches, of which 15 were won. The battery of left-handed spinners, including one Tribe who accomplished the "double" for the sixth successive year, and the "Typhoon" that did *not* fizzle out into a gentle zephyr, together with a grand 'keeper in Andrew who created a new Northants record (68 victims), were the men-of-the-season. The potential is tremendous; the best has not yet been seen of the Cambridge Blue, Raman Subba Row, who in 1955 broke fresh ground in hitting 260 not out against Lancashire at Northampton, and several young bowlers who may well beat Tribe's record of 175 wickets taken the same year. Through it all remains Dennis Brookes, who first appeared in 1934, and is the sheet-anchor in a side of quick scorers. No one has amassed more runs for the county: 26,075, average 36.52, which includes 257 off Gloucestershire at Bristol in 1949; or more centuries: 63; or more runs in a season: 2,198, average 51.11 in 1952.

No reference to Northamptonshire cricket would be complete without mention of Leo Bullimer who was for 51 years the county scorer until retiring in 1950. His efforts in raising funds did much to keep Northamptonshire going during some of their worst financial crises.

A Controversy

Why do Northamptonshire engage so many players from outside (especially from overseas)? The answer is plain. A small county without either the population or resources of Yorkshire, Northamptonshire, nevertheless, possess a public with the palate for good cricket—and cricketers. Therefore, while talent scouts comb the county and trials are held regularly, experts from elsewhere are encouraged to become specially registered. Financial backing? That go-ahead modern firm, British Timken, is prepared to offer winter employment, something that redounds to the honour and skill of the present-day professional; and there is a football competition, organised by the county's eleven-year-old Supporters Club which, whatever else one may think of it, makes football serve the needs of cricket. The county have 2,000 members; 63,000 odd if one includes those who support this competition.

Heading for the title of "Champion County," Northamptonshire consider they are doing a real service to English cricket by making so many excellent craftsmen available for our delectation.

(*Statistics for the first-class years have been taken from compilations by either Mr. C. Smith or the author and published in the "Northamptonshire Year Book."*)

M.C.C. EXAMINE AMATEUR STATUS

BROKEN TIME EXPENSES PROPOSED

During the winter a Special Committee appointed by M.C.C. conducted a thorough inquiry into various aspects of the position of the amateur player in the framework of present-day first-class cricket. Their report is given here in full and, provided the recommendations are approved by the County Clubs, many financial problems which have confronted leading amateurs should be resolved.

The Duke of Norfolk, President of M.C.C., emphasised when issuing the report that there was no intent to delve into the past and that any final decisions would not be retrospective. At the same time he made it clear that it was intended to stop indirect payments to amateurs by Supporters' Clubs or other organisations.

These are problems confined almost entirely to English first-class cricket which demands that the regular player devotes all four summer months to the game. Down the years the amateur has generally proved himself a great asset in this set-up. The experienced professionals who were consulted by the Committee were unanimous that they did not wish to see his disappearance from the game.

*In the circumstances the Committee have taken a reasonable course, though many lovers of the game will not welcome this open acknowledgment that certain broken-time expenses are necessary to enable amateurs to take part in major overseas tours.—*EDITOR.

This Committee was established by M.C.C. after consultation with, and with the approval of, the Counties, to examine the problems of Amateur Status in the light of present-day conditions.

1. Committee Procedure

The Committee held five meetings between October 9, 1957, and January 15, 1958: between its second and third meetings the President and three other of its members held a full and free discussion on certain aspects of the question with leading professional cricketers whom they had invited to meet them at Lord's.

2. General

The Committee were agreed that the following reasons prompted the inquiry:—

    (i) The wish to eliminate any major anomaly in relation to amateur status in first-class cricket and at the same time to safeguard the interests of the professional.

    (ii) The wish to preserve in first-class cricket the leadership and general approach to the game traditionally associated with the Amateur player.

    (iii) The wish to ensure that the leading Amateurs are not prevented by the hard facts of present-day economics from accepting invitations to accompany major M.C.C. Touring Teams.

    In reviewing their field the Committee agreed in principle that no close parallel could usefully be drawn between first-class cricket and other fields of sport because:—

        (a) In no other sport had Amateurs and Professionals been so long, so continuously, so widely, and so closely associated.

        (b) No other sport made such great and continuous demands on the players' time.

3. Distinction between Amateur and Professional

    (i) The Committee accepted as basic to the problem that, whereas some fifty years ago many Amateurs could afford to, and did, play first-class cricket entirely at their own expense, this was no longer the case.

    (ii) The Committee rejected any solution of the problem on the lines of abolishing the distinction between Amateur and Professional and regarding them all alike as "cricketers." They considered that the distinctive status of the amateur cricketer was not obsolete, was of great value to the game and should be preserved.

The Professionals whom they had consulted supported these views. They did, however, emphasise the urgency of resolving certain anomalies existing in present practice.

4. Definition of Amateur Status

The Committee unanimously agreed that:—

(i) Any cricketer carrying out full-time administrative duties with a County Club should continue to be regarded as an Amateur.

(ii) Any cricketer directly or indirectly paid for *playing* cricket by a County Cricket Club or any associated organisation should be regarded as a Professional.

In this connection the Committee considered the problem of the pseudo Assistant Secretary, who might, in fact, be paid for playing cricket under the umbrella of his nominal secretarial duties. They felt that it was impossible to legislate for these cases under any general formula and that they must be examined individually by machinery created for the purpose: see para. 7 (ii).

5. Amateurs writing, broadcasting and advertising

The Committee reviewed the question of Amateurs writing cricket books, contributing to the Press, broadcasting and appearing on television programmes and were unanimously agreed that no restrictions were necessary, other than those imposed by the M.C.C. in the case of official overseas tours, the Board of Control in the case of Test and Trial matches at home, and County Clubs in the case of their own players.

On the question of advertising by Amateurs, there was divergence of view amongst the Professionals consulted.

The opinion of the Committee was that advertising of this nature was not a new development. It was, in fact, open only to one or two quite exceptional players at any time and should be open to Amateurs and Professionals alike, subject to review from time to time, and subject to it not infringing the general restrictions in relation to tours, Test Matches, etc., already mentioned.

6. Expenses and Allowances

(a) *At Home*

Whilst recognising that Amateurs were fully entitled to the repayment of genuine out-of-pocket expenses incurred whilst playing, and that the Counties themselves must be the final judge of such claims, the Committee were disturbed by the apparent over-liberal interpretation of the word "expenses" in certain cases that had come to their notice.

In the view of the Committee, expense allowances must be restricted to those expenses actually incurred during a match, including meals during travelling and gratuities, with an additional amount to cover special cost of laundry and of the upkeep of cricket equipment.

The Committee suggested that the M.C.C. should ask the Advisory County Cricket Committee to give urgent consideration to this matter with a view to establishing a formula for such allowances.

(b) *On Major M.C.C. Overseas Tours*

(i) The Committee were agreed that, while maintaining the status of the Amateur on M.C.C. Overseas Tours, all players should as far as possible receive equal treatment in the matter of expenses and that these expenses should be assessed on the basis of experience of recent tours.

This proposal meets the views expressed during the discussion with the Professionals.

(ii) Despite fears expressed by the Professionals, and also by members of the Committee, that the introduction of broken-time payments for Amateurs during tours might lead to similar payments by the Counties in the case of first-class cricket in England, the Committee were agreed that a clear distinction can and should be drawn between the money-earning position of an Amateur out of England for some months during a tour, and of one playing cricket in England during the season.

From the first the Committee were agreed that in the case of major Overseas Tours, the M.C.C. should be represented by the strongest possible team, and that without some financial aid to offset the loss of earnings certain Amateurs might well not be available in the years to come.

They reached the conclusion that the M.C.C. should accept the principle of compensation to Amateurs for loss of earnings during major overseas tours and felt that a graded system of broken-time payment was the most realistic method of dealing with the problem.

(iii) The Committee were agreed that such compensation for loss of earnings should be granted on the following general conditions:—

(a) Only those Amateurs making application for compensation to receive more than the allowance for expenses.

(b) In every case such compensation for loss of earnings should be substantially below the payment made to professionals on any tour.

(c) Such rules as may be laid down by the M.C.C. should be regarded as rigid, and not open to *ad hoc* alterations to meet any special case.

(d) Each application for compensation should be fully examined and a decision reached on the facts as found.

7. Determination of Status

(i) The Committee were agreed that a satisfactory solution of the problems of Amateur Status could only be reached with the goodwill and co-operation of County Committees: they were confident that this would be forthcoming.

(ii) The Committee recommended that the M.C.C. should inform the Advisory County Cricket Committee that, if invited, they would set up a Standing Committee to examine and report on any doubtful case of status.

They suggested that such a Standing Committee might consist of a Chairman and two members drawn from the M.C.C. Committee with two additional members from County Clubs nominated annually by the Advisory County Cricket Committee. This Committee should be empowered to examine any case of payment, including expenses, made directly or indirectly to an Amateur by a County Club or any associated organisation.

Should their decision not be accepted by the County and player concerned, the Standing Committee shall bring the case before the Advisory County Cricket Committee whose recommendations will be submitted to the M.C.C. for confirmation.

Reports of the Standing Committee shall at all times remain confidential.

The members of the Special Committee were: The Duke of Norfolk (Chairman), H. S. Altham, G. O. Allen, M. J. C. Allom, Col. R. J. de C. Barber, F. R. Brown, E. D. R. Eagar, C. A. F. Hastilow, C. G. Howard, D. J. Insole, P. B. H. May, C. H. Palmer, Col. R. S. Rait Kerr, A. B. Sellers, Rev. D. S. Shepherd. R. Aird (Secretary).

The report was due for discussion at the Advisory County Cricket Committee's meeting on March 11, 1958, and then if any or all these proposals were adopted they needed confirmation by the M.C.C. full Committee to become effective.

The results of these two meetings, as far as Wisden is concerned, await publication until the 1959 edition.

DATES IN CRICKET HISTORY

By H. S. ALTHAM

1300   First probable reference to cricket: in the wardrobe accounts of King Edward I: locality Newenden, Kent.

1550(c.) Cricket played at "The Free School" at Guildford.

1595   G. Florio's Italian-English Dictionary mentions cricket.

1611   A reference to cricket in John Bullokar's "England Expositor."

1622   At Boxmoor in Sussex six parishioners were prosecuted for playing cricket in the churchyard on Sunday.

1647   Probable reference to cricket being played by Winchester Scholars on St. Catherine's Hill, in a Latin Poem by Robert Matthew.

1654   Seven parishioners of Eltham fined for playing cricket on the Lord's Day.

1665(c.) John Churchill, Duke of Marlborough, playing cricket at old St. Paul's School.

1676   First reference to cricket outside England, played by the Navy at Aleppo.

1677   First reference to a definite match "in Sussex."

1694   2/6 paid for a Wagger [sic] about the Cricket Match at Lewis [sic].
       First mention of cricket at Oxford University.

1706   First full description of a cricket match: in a Latin Poem written by William Goldwin of Eton, and King's, Cambridge.

1710   First reference to cricket at the University: Cambridge.

1719   First "County Match": Kent v. London.

1727   Articles of Agreement governing the conduct of matches between the teams of the second Duke of Richmond and Mr. Brodrick of Peperharow.
       First mention of cricket at Oxford University.

1729   Date of earliest surviving bat: inscribed "J. C." (John Chitty) 1729. This bat is in the Pavilion at The Oval.

1743   Picture of a match by Francis Hayman, now at Lord's.

1744   June 18. The first great match of which the full score is preserved: Kent v. All-England on the Artillery Ground, Finsbury, which has continued ever since to be the ground of the H.A.C. This match, which was won by Kent by one wicket, was described in full by James Love in his "Cricket: a Heroic Poem" published the same year.
       The first known issue of the Laws of Cricket: these, undoubtedly a recension of a far earlier code, were drawn up by the London Club of which Frederick Louis, Prince of Wales and father of George III, was President.

First recorded charge for admission: 2d. to the Artillery Ground.

1750(*c.*) Foundation of the Hambledon Club: they played first on Broadhalfpenny and then on Windmill Down, often defeated All England, and lasted till 1796. Their great players, immortalised in Nyren (see 1833), evolved a new and much advanced technique.

1751 Old Etonians play the Gentlemen of England. Cricket mentioned as far north as Durham and Yorkshire.

1760 "Winchester beat Eton" in Port Meadow, Oxford.

1771 Sheffield play Nottingham.

1772 Picture of boys playing cricket at Harrow School.

1774 "Batts" advertised for sale by maker, William Staples of Sevenoaks.

1775 First recorded century: 136 by John Small, sen., for Hambledon v. Surrey.

1776 Earliest known score-cards, printed by Pratt, scorer to the Vine Club, Sevenoaks.

1780 Duke of Penshurst (established 1760) manufacture the first six-seamed ball and present it to the Prince of Wales, afterwards George IV. Farington, in his diary of 1811, says that the Duke family had then been making cricket balls for 250 years.

1787 First match, Middlesex v. Essex, on Thomas Lord's first ground, on the site of Dorset Square.
Formation of M.C.C. by members of the White Conduit Club.

1788 June 27. M.C.C. play their first match at Lord's.
First revision of the Laws by M.C.C., dated May 30.

1791 Publication of the first record of match scores by Samuel Britcher: these subsequently covered the chief matches till 1805.

1796 A match between Eton and Westminster at Hounslow: first recorded school match, played in defiance of Dr. Heath, Headmaster of Eton, who flogged the whole eleven on their return; Eton lost by 66 runs.

1800 Publication of first book on cricket technique, by Thomas Boxall.

1800? A match between Eton and Harrow.

1803 William Pitt refers to cricket in introducing his Defence Act.

1805 Eton play Harrow at Lord's and win by an innings. Lord Byron, the poet, was in the Harrow XI.

1806 First Gentlemen v. Players match at Lord's.

1807 First mention of the "straight-armed" (i.e. round-arm) bowling, by John Willes of Kent.

1809 Lord's second ground opened at "North Bank."

1810 Lowest score ever recorded in a first-class match: 6 by "The Bs" v. England at Lord's.

1814 Lord's third ground opened on present site: the original turf of the first ground was transplanted at each move.

1817 First two separate centuries: 107 and 157 by William Lambert for Sussex v. Epsom at Lord's.

1820 First recorded score of 200: 278 by William Ward for M.C.C. v. Norfolk at Lord's, a record for that ground for 105 years.

1821 First century in Gentlemen v. Players: 113 not out by Thomas Beagley.

1822 John Willes "no-balled" for throwing, i.e. round-arm bowling.

1825 First Harrow v. Winchester match. Winchester won.

1826 First recorded century in a school match, 146 not out by W. Meyrick for Winchester v. Harrow.
First Eton v. Winchester match. Winchester won.

1827 First University match; drawn. The captains were Charles Wordsworth, Oxford, and Herbert Jenner, Cambridge.
The three Experimental Matches between Sussex and England to try out the new (round-arm) bowling, now perfected by William Lillywhite and James Broadbridge of Sussex.

1828 M.C.C. authorise the bowler to raise his hand level with the elbow.

1833 John Nyren writes his "Young Cricketer's Tutor" and "The Cricketers of my Time": this is the *locus classicus* for the early history and personalities of the game.

1835 M.C.C. adopt a revised Code of the Laws on May 20.

1836 First North v. South match: for many years recognised as the greatest match of the season.
Sussex County Cricket Club formed, the earliest County Club properly so constituted.

1838 Opening of the Trent Bridge Ground, Nottingham, by William Clarke.
Printing of score-cards for Gentlemen v. Players at Brighton.

1841 The Duke of Wellington issues an order that a cricket ground is to be made as an adjunct to every military barracks.

1842 The Canterbury Week and "The Old Stagers" instituted.

1845 Cricket ceased to be "unlawful."
Surrey County Cricket Club established, and first match on The Oval.
I Zingari formed.

1846 "The All-England Eleven," organised by William Clarke, began its great missionary work of playing matches, against odds, all over the country. The eleven was subsequently managed by George Parr. An admirable lithograph of the team, from a drawing by the famous Kent batsman, N. Felix, was published in 1847.

Last match played for the single wicket championship: A. Mynn v. N. Felix.

Fenner's Ground, Cambridge, opened: leased by C.U.C.C. from 1873: freehold purchased 1892.

The Telegraph Score Board introduced at Lord's.

Score-cards first sold at Lord's.

1848 July 18, W. G. Grace born.

1849 First Yorkshire v. Lancashire match.

1850 J. Wisden bowls all ten batsmen in one innings, North v. South.

1051 Oxford University C.C. rents The Magdalen Ground, Cowley, for a University Ground: they migrated to their present quarters in "The Parks" in 1881.

1852 The United All-England XI formed, in rivalry to the All-England XI. Secretaries: Wisden and Dean.

1854 Last of the "Public Schools Weeks" (Eton, Harrow, Winchester) at Lord's.

1850–55(*c.*) About this time the mowing machine began to be used on cricket grounds.

1855 W. Clarke takes 476 wickets in a season.

Bramall Lane Ground, Sheffield. opened.

1857 The Cricketers Fund Friendly Society instituted.

For ten years the great match between the A.E.E. and the U.A.E.E. was played in its support. From 1884, until his death, Lord Harris was its president, and the society has done invaluable work for professional cricketers and their dependants.

1858 First recorded instance of a hat being given to the bowler for taking three wickets with consecutive balls.

1862 In a match at The Oval, England v. Surrey, Edgar Willsher of Kent was no-balled by John Lillywhite for having his hand higher than his shoulder. Willsher left the field, and the game was suspended for the day. Next day another umpire replaced Lillywhite, who refused to reconsider his view. This led to the change in the law in 1864.

Publication of Vols. 1–4 of "Scores and Biographies," compiled by Arthur Haygarth. This work recorded the full scores of all discoverable matches from 1744 onwards.

1863 Yorkshire County Cricket Club formed.

1864 "Overhand bowling" authorised: June 10.

Middlesex C.C.C. formed: they first played on the Cattle Market ground, Islington, migrating later to Prince's ground, Chelsea, and finally to Lord's in 1877.

Lancashire C.C.C. formed.

W. G. Grace's first appearance in big cricket: two days before his sixteenth birthday he scored 170 and 56 not out for South Wales Club v. Gentlemen of Sussex.

First issue of "Wisden's Cricketers' Almanack."

1865 Practice nets first used at Lord's.

1867 Culmination of long period of rivalry and ill-feeling between professionals of North and South, and of the two "All-England" XI's: these two great matches abandoned this year.

1868 Visit to England of a team of Australian aborigines, managed by Charles Lawrence.

1870 The heavy roller first used at Lord's: the great general improvement of pitches begins with this innovation.

1871 W. G. Grace's greatest year: the first batsman to reach 2,000 runs in a season (2,739): no other batsman achieved this until A. E. Stoddart and William Gunn did so in 1893. "W.G." played in three benefit matches for three of the best-known old professionals and with much, for the beneficiaries, depending on his success, he scored 189 not out, 268, and 217.

1872 First experiment, at Lord's, in covering the pitch before the start of a match.

1873 The "County Championship" is generally reckoned to date from this year, as it was for this season that county qualification rules were first framed: first "champions," Notts. But "Lillywhite's Companion" uses the term "Champion County" in 1869.
First recorded instance of 1,000 runs and 100 wickets in a season, by W. G. Grace.

1876 W. G. Grace established the following records:—
(1) First score of 300 in first-class cricket: 344 for M.C.C. v. Kent at Canterbury. His next two scores were 177 for Glos. v. Notts, and 318 not out for Glos. v. Yorks.
(2) He also scored 400 not out for All-England XI v. XXII of Grimsby.

1878 Visit of first Australian team to England: D. W. Gregory captain. Australian cricket establishes its reputation by their sensational defeat in a single day and by nine wickets over a very strong M.C.C. XI.

1880 First Test Match in England: England beats Australia by five wickets. W. G. Grace 152, W. L. Murdoch 153 not out.

1882 First Australian victory in a Test Match in England, by seven runs at The Oval: a spectator dies from excitement.
Tradition of "The Ashes" established by "obituary notice" to English cricket in the *Sporting Times*.

1884 A completely revised Code of the Laws adopted by M.C.C. on April 21.

1884–5 First series of five Test Matches in Australia. England wins three.

1888–9 Present Lord's pavilion built.

1890 The first "Board of Control" established in South Africa.

1892 Instructions to umpires issued by M.C.C.

1895 First 1,000 runs in May: W. G. Grace, at the age of 47, in 22 days. He also scored his 100th century.

1898 Board of Control set up to administer Test Matches played in England.

1899 First series of five Test Matches in England: Australia won the only finished game, at Lord's, by ten wickets.
For the first time a single Selection Committee picked the teams for all the "Tests": hitherto they had been chosen by M.C.C. for matches at Lord's and for matches elsewhere by the County Committee of the ground concerned.
First score of 300 by an Australian in England: 300 not out by Victor Trumper, then on his first tour, v. Sussex at Brighton.
Record individual score: 628 not out by A. E. J. Collins for Clark's v. North Town, a junior house match at Clifton College.
The "Mound Stand" built at Lord's.

1902 Easter classes for boys instituted at Lord's.

1903 Abortive agitation for wider wickets and "Timeless Tests."
First representative Public Schools' XI play M.C.C. at Lord's.

1905 Australian Board of Control set up.

1909 Imperial Cricket Conference constituted: M.C.C., Australia and South Africa the original members.

1911 Warwickshire champions: first county to be so outside the "big nine" who had originated the championship.
The last instance of a genuine "double blue" in the University match: D. C. Collins played for Cambridge v. Oxford this year and next year rowed bow in the University Boat Race.

1912 The first and the only Triangular Tournament in England.
First "Trial Matches" for the "Tests."
First "Test Match" in England for which more than three days were allowed: the last match at The Oval, as the rubber depended on it, was to be played to a finish; it lasted four days and was won by England.

1926 India, New Zealand and West Indies admitted to the Imperial Cricket Conference.

1930 Four-day "Test Matches" in England.

1932-3 The "body-line" controversy during the M.C.C. tour in Australia.

1935 M.C.C. condemn "body-line" bowling and issue instructions to umpires against its future practice.

1937 M.C.C. appoint a County Cricket Commission to examine and report on the state of county cricket.

1938 Test Matches at Lord's televised for the first time.

1941 Centenary of Tom Brown's Match: M.C.C. v. Rugby School.
1944 Flying bomb passes low over Lord's during Army v. R.A.F. match.
     M.C.C. select Committee to report on the post-war resumption of first-class cricket.
1945 Australian Services XI tour England: the "Victory Tests."
1947 Major revision of the Laws of Cricket.
1948 First Five-day Test Matches in England.
1949 Election of 26 professional cricketers to Honorary Life Membership of M.C.C.
1952 M.C.C. Youth Cricket Association established to help all boys to get more and better cricket.
     Pakistan admitted to Imperial Cricket Conference.
1956 J. C. Laker took 19 wickets in one match, England v. Australia.
1957 Special Committee appointed by M.C.C. to review the conduct of the game and future Welfare of First-class cricket issued their report.

DATES IN THE EVOLUTION OF THE LAWS

The Pitch

The 22 yards laid down in the laws of 1744 has never varied: it may well have originated from the width of the Saxon acre-strip or the mediaeval measure of the gad $= 5\frac{1}{2}$ yards. It is identical with the length of the agricultural chain.

The Popping Crease

The 46 inches between the creases, laid down in 1744, represent the old English unit of the cloth yard, 45 inches, plus 2 half-inches to the middle of each crease.

1819. The 46 inches between creases increased to 48 inches.

The Bowling Crease

1902. The length of the bowling crease, which since 1774 had been 3 feet on either side of the wicket, increased to 4 feet. Both creases were originally cut in the turf; whitewash was not used till the 1830's, at Lord's not till the early 'sixties.

Sweeping and Rolling

1788. Originally the pitch was left untouched during a match, but in 1788 by mutual consent the pitch could be rolled, watered, covered and mown during a match
1793. Sawdust was authorised in the laws.
1849. The pitch could be swept and rolled before each innings at the request of either side.
1860. The rolling between the innings to be solely at the request of the side batting next.

1883. Rolling permitted for 10 minutes before the start of play on each day.

1913. Covering the bowler's footholds and the batsmen's standing ground authorised.

1931. Period of rolling reduced to 7 minutes.

The Wicket

Year	Stumps	Height	Bails	Breadth
c. 1700	2	22 inches	1	6 inches
c. 1775	3	22 inches	1	6 inches
1785	3	22 inches	2 or 1	6 inches
1798	3	24 inches	2 or 1	7 inches
c. 1819	3	26 inches	2	7 inches
c. 1823	3	27 inches	2	8 inches
1931	3	28 inches	2	9 inches

The Bat

No dimensions specified in original laws, when the bat was curved and much longer in the handle.

1774. Width of bat limited to $4\frac{1}{4}$ inches.

1835. Length of bat limited to 38 inches.

1836. Dark's bats were sold by Sadd of Cambridge for 8s. 6d.

1853–4. Cane handles were invented by Nixon.

1880. Rubber handle-covers patented.

Early bats were very heavy: the bat with which William Ward made his record score of 278 in 1820 weighed 4 lb. 2 oz.

The Ball

1744. "Between 5 and 6 ounces."

1774. Between $5\frac{1}{2}$ and $5\frac{3}{4}$ ounces.

1838. Circumference to be between 9 and $9\frac{1}{4}$ inches.

1927. Circumference to be between $8\frac{13}{16}$ and 9 inches.

Pads

Circa 1800. A player named Robinson experiments with boards strapped to his legs. He is "laughed out of his invention."

Circa 1836. Pads invented by (?) H. Daubeny of Oxford.

1880. Skeleton pads advertised for sale in *Wisden*.

Gloves

c. 1827. Tubular gloves produced by Daniel Day: no doubt in reaction to the new round-arm bowling.

c. 1850. Wicket-keeping "gauntlets" first appeared.

The Over

1744. 4 balls.

1887. 6 balls introduced in Australia.

1889. 5 balls.

1900.   6 balls.

1918.   8 balls used experimentally in Australia.

1922.   8 balls authorised for Australia. (Since then 8 balls to the over has always been the rule in Australia, excepting in two Test series with England, i.e. 1928–29 and 1932–33 when the 6-ball over was in force.)

1939.   8 balls used experimentally in first-class matches.

1946.   6 balls.

1947.   At the request of either captain the final over of a match must be completed, even though time has been reached.

No-ball

c. 1809.   "Foot over crease," the only no-ball.

1816.   First attempt to legislate against "throwing": the hand to be below the elbow.

1835.   The hand not to be above the shoulder.

1864.   Revised to present form.

1884.   The "absolutely satisfied" clause inserted in the no-ball law.

1899.   "*Either* umpire . . . shall call no-ball."

1947.   The back foot, at the moment of delivery, need not be "grounded" though it must be behind the bowling crease.

Declaration

1889.   First authorised, but only on the third day.

1900.   Any time after lunch on the second day.

1910.   At any time on the second day.

1957.   At any time.

Follow-on

1787.   First recorded instance.

1835.   Compulsory after a deficit of a hundred.

1854–1894.   After a deficit of 80 runs.

1894.   Compulsory after a deficit of a hundred and twenty.

1900.   Optional after a deficit of a hundred and fifty.

Handled Ball

1797.   First recorded.

Toss

1744.   Toss confers choice of pitch and innings.

1774.   Visiting side to have the choice of pitch and innings.

c. 1809.   Umpires to select pitch, and toss to give choice of innings.

L.B.W.

1744.   No mention.

1774.   If, *with design*, the striker prevents the ball hitting the wicket with his leg.

1788.   "Design" clause omitted, and ball must pitch straight.

1795.   First recorded.

c. 1821. Ball need not pitch straight, but must be "delivered straight."

1839. Reverts to 1788.

1901. Very strong move to alter law by omitting "pitch straight" clause, but two-thirds majority necessary for any alteration of laws not secured in M.C.C. meeting.

1937. Altered to present law, after a two seasons' trial.

Stumped

1744. First recorded.

Scoring

1827. Wides first recorded as such.

1829. No-balls to be scored as such, and a run debited: first recorded thus, 1830.

1836. The bowler to be credited by name with the wickets caught and stumped.

1840. Bowling analysis first kept in M.C.C. score-book.

1844. Wides to be "run for."

1848. Leg-byes first recorded as such.

Boundaries

1884. First mentioned in the laws, though operative, with varying allowances, long before.

1910. Advisory County Cricket Committee recommended allowance of six runs for hits over the boundary, hitherto for hits out of the ground only.

Experimental Championship Rules

1957. On-side fielders limited to five, with not more than two behind the popping crease. Maximum boundary of 75 yards from centre of pitch. Two bonus points to side leading on first innings provided it scored the faster.

CRICKET OVERSEAS

Europe

1777. A print showing a cricket match at Belle Isle, France.

1810. Crawfurd's "Light Division" play cricket at Lisbon.

1815. June 12: a match played by the officers of the Brigade of Guards near Brussels, visited by the Duke of Wellington.

1820. Near Naples, Eton beat "The World."

1829. An English cricket club near Paris.

1830. A good cricket ground near Geneva.

1846. An English XI plays a match at Calais.

1856. First mention of cricket in Holland.

1857. A cricket club at Balta Liman on the Bosphorus.

1863. Paris Cricket Club formed.
1864. Match between Boulogne and Barnsley Cricket Clubs.
1865. A cricket week at Hamburg.
1866. Cricket known to be played in Denmark.
1867. M.C.C. send a team to Paris.
1892. Visit of first Dutch team to England.
1921. First tour of Free Foresters to Holland.
1922. M.C.C. visit Denmark.
1923. M.C.C. XI v. Army of the Rhine.
1926. First Danish XI to visit England.

Australia

1803–4. Reputed introduction of cricket by officers of regiments stationed at Sydney.
1830. First printed account of a match.
1832. First club formed in Tasmania, Hobart.
1845. Melbourne Cricket Club formed.
1846. First recorded games in Western Australia and South Australia.
1851. First Inter-Colonial match: Tasmania v. Victoria at Launceston.
1856. First Inter-State match. N.S.W. v. Victoria at Melbourne.
1861–2. First visit of an English team, captained by H. H. Stephenson. This was a business speculation financed by Messrs. Spiers and Pond, the caterers, who cleared over £11,000. All matches were against odds. At the end of the tour, Charles Lawrence, the Surrey professional, stayed at Sydney as coach.
1863–4. Second English team under George Parr; all matches against odds. William Caffyn stays as professional at Melbourne.
1876–7. First Test Match: England v. Australia, at Melbourne. Australia won by 45 runs. Charles Bannerman 165, the first Test Match century.
1873. Adelaide Oval opened.
1892–3. Sheffield Shield Inter-State competition instituted.
1910–11. First visit of a South African team.
1930–1. First visit of a West Indian team.
1931–2. Visit of South Africans: Bradman averages 201 in Test Matches.

New Zealand

1848. Cricket clubs existing at Dunedin and Wellington.
1860. First Inter-Provincial match, Wellington v. Auckland.
1864. George Parr's team visits New Zealand from Australia.
1878. First Australian team to England visits New Zealand.
1894. Formation of New Zealand Cricket Council, as a governing body for the game in that country.

1906–7. Institution of the Plunket Shield Competition. First visit of M.C.C. side to New Zealand, under Captain E. G. Wynyard. Two Representative Matches played, of which each side won one.

Africa

1808. A match advertised to be played at Cape Town between officers of the Artillery Mess and officers of the Colony "for a thousand dollars a side."

1842. Cricket played at Wynberg, Cape Colony, and first known century in Africa: 110 by Mr. Taylor for Civilians v Military.

1843. Port Elizabeth Cricket Club formed.

1843–4. Cricket played by military teams at Pietermaritzberg, Natal.

1863. First cricket club in Transvaal.

1875. "Champion Bat" competition established in Cape Colony.

1888–9. First visit of an English team, captain C. A. Smith. In the two "Tests" played England won easily.

1889–90. Currie Cup Tournament established.

1894. First visit of South African team to England.

1902–3. Darling's Australian team visits South Africa on way home from England. Trumper's batting a revelation to the South Africans.

1905. First M.C.C. team, captain P. F. Warner, visits South Africa. South African cricket finally established in reputation by winning four out of the five Test Matches. This was really the triumph of the "googly" on matting, as bowled by Vogler, White, Faulkner and Schwartz.

1910–11. Visit of South African XI to Australia: sensational batting by Faulkner and Trumper.

1935. South Africa, under H. F. Wade, gain their first Test victory in England, and win the rubber.

1938–9. M.C.C. in South Africa: turf wickets now almost universal. With England leading by one up, the fifth Test Match was to be played to a finish; it lasted ten days, and then, to enable the England team to catch their boat, had to be abandoned. Set to make 696 in their last innings, England had made 654 for five wickets.

America

North America

1737. First mention of cricket in the United States, in Georgia.

1751. A match recorded between New York and a London XI, played "according to the London method," i.e. presumably in accordance with the 1744 rules.

1790.   A cricket club existed at Boston.

1844.   First match between Canada and the U.S.A.

1859.   First touring team to leave England (captain, George Parr) visited the U.S.A. and Canada. Their matches drew large crowds, and, together with their general experiences on the tour, were well described by their scorer, Fred Lillywhite, in the first book in the long catalogue of "touring literature."

1878.   The Australian team visits America on their way back from England.

1880.   First team from America, a Canadian XI, visits England: a modest team with a modest programme.

1884.   A Philadelphian team visits England.

1896.   Haverford College play English Public Schools.

1903.   Kent visit Canada.

1905.   First M.C.C. team to visit U.S.A. and Canada. Captain, E. W. Mann.

South America

1842.   There was a club at Rio, Brazil.

1861.   Buenos Aires Cricket Club established.

1891–2.   First North v. South of Argentina match.

1912.   Visit of M.C.C. team to the Argentine, under the captaincy of Lord Hawke.

West Indies

1842.   Trinidad Cricket Club already "of very long standing."

1863.   Kingston Cricket Club formed in Jamaica.

1886.   A West Indies team tours in Canada and U.S.A.

1887.   An American team toured the West Indies.

1891.   First Triangular Tournament between Barbados, Trinidad and Demerara.

1895.   First visit of an English team; captain, R. S. Lucas.

1900.   First West Indies team to tour England.

1901.   First matches of an English touring team against the Combined West Indies. West Indies win two out of three.

1906.   Second West Indies tour in England: S. G. Smith scores 1,000 runs and takes 100 wickets.

1911.   First M.C.C. team to visit West Indies.

1928.   First Test Matches in England. England won all three.

1930–31.   First West Indies team to tour Australia.

1950.   West Indies under J. D. Goddard gain their first Test victory in England and win the rubber.

1954–55.   First Australian team visited West Indies; were first visiting side to win Test rubber in Caribbean.

India

1792.   Calcutta Cricket Club formed.

1804.   First century in India: 102 by Robert Vansittart for Old Etonians v. The Rest.

1848. Parsees form the Oriental Cricket Club.
1866. Hindus form the Bombay Cricket Club.
1883. First Mohammedan Club.
1886. Parsee team visits England.
1889–90. First English team visits India; captain, G. F. Vernon.
1911. First Indian team visits England.
1932. First Test Match v. India in England.
1947–48. First Indian team to tour Australia.
1949 First Commonwealth team to tour India.
1951–52. India, at Madras, gain their first Test victory over England.

Pakistan

1952. Pakistan visit India on first tour and play their first Test matches.

Fiji

1874. First recorded match, Levuka v. H.M.S. *Pearl*.
1895. Fijian team visits New Zealand.
1905. Australian team visits Fiji en route for England.

CRICKET DRESS

Eighteenth Century

Three-cornered or jockey hats, often with silver or gold lace; shirts, generally frilled; nankeen breeches, silk stockings, buckled shoes. The Hambledon Club has sky-blue coats with buttons engraved "C.C." The first uniform of the M.C.C. was in azure blue.

1800–1850

From about 1810–15 trousers begin to replace breeches, though Eton and Harrow still wore the latter in 1830. Tall "beaver" hats, in black or white, became the rule. Shirts no longer frilled, but now worn with rather high collars and spreading bow ties; singlets instead of shirts not uncommon. Wide braces often seen, especially on professionals. Black "Oxford" shoes universal. Belts, with metal clasps, for the waist.

Towards the end of this period the tall hat began to give place to a soft and full flannel cap, generally white, or, less commonly, to a straw hat, often rather of a haymaker's shape. Short, white flannel jackets, mentioned as early as 1812, began to appear as forerunners of "the blazer"; T. Lockyer, the Surrey cricketer, is thought to have been the first to wear "a cricket coat."

1850–1880

Under the lead of I Zingari (established 1845) Club cricket colours begin to appear, often as ribbons round the white bowler hats now replacing the tall and straw hats of the previous two decades. Club caps date from about 1850, but Eton may have sported their light blue caps as early as 1831 and the Rugby XI were "habited alike" in 1843. The Winchester XI first wore their blue caps in 1851 and Harrow their striped caps in 1852. The Cambridge "blue" seems to date from 1861, the Oxford "blue" certainly from 1863. Coloured shirts became common as uniform, e.g. a pattern of coloured spots, stripes or checks on a white ground: the All-England XI wore white shirts with pink spots.

The Oxford and Cambridge XI's for many years wore dark and light blue shirts. The Harlequins, founded 1852, originally wore blue trousers. Rugby School now present sole survival of the coloured shirt.

The term "blazer" is said to have been first applied to the scarlet coats adopted by the Lady Margaret Boat Club (St. John's College, Cambridge) as early as 1862, or possibly from the coats worn by the crew at the "Captain's Gig" of H.M.S. *Blazer, c.* 1850. The coloured cricket blazer seems to have appeared at about the same time: the Oxford XI of 1863 wore blue blazers. Shaw and Shrewsbury's team to Australia in 1884–85 wore blazers and caps to match.

Shoes progressively gave place to boots, either brown or white with brown straps.

1880–1895

Coloured shirts disappear. White shirts, with starched or semi-starched fronts, the rule. Ties not so common, but small bow ties in low turned-down starched collars common enough, White buckskin boots were first worn about 1882, but they only gradually superseded the old brown and brown-and-white type. The modern "sweater," probably an evolution from the old "singlet," came in during this period.

1895 to date

Very little change. About the end of the century came soft white hats, in felt or linen, possibly on an Australian model, and in the last twenty years appeared rubber-soled boots, even now worn by some bowlers in dry weather; also sleeveless sweaters.

Umpires' white coats seem first to have been worn in 1861, but as late as 1882 the old uniform of the tall hat or "billycock" and black coat was by no means uncommon.

TEST CRICKETERS
FULL LIST FROM 1877 TO SEPTEMBER 1957

Here is a complete record of all appearances by cricketers in Test matches. The following lists have been compiled on a home and abroad basis, appearances abroad being printed in *italics*.

Abbreviations.—E: England. A: Australia. SA: South Africa. WI: West Indies. NZ: New Zealand. In: India. P: Pakistan.

All appearances are placed in this order of seniority. Hence, any England cricketer playing against Australia in England has that achievement recorded first and the remainder of his appearances at home (if any) are set down before passing to matches abroad. To denote English professionals, initials are given in brackets. The figures immediately following each name represent the total number of appearances in *all* Tests.

Where the season embraces two different years, the first year is given, i.e. 1876 indicates 1876–77.

ENGLAND

Abel (R.) 13: v A 1888 (3) 1896 (3) 1902 (2); *v A 1891 (3)*; *v SA 1888 (2)*

Absolom C. 1: *v A 1878*

Allen, G. O. 25: v A 1930 (1) 1934 (2); v WI 1933 (1); v NZ 1931 (3); v In 1936 (3); *v A 1932 (5) 1936 (5)*; *v WI 1947 (3)*; *v NZ 1932 (2)*

Allom, M. J. C. 5: *v SA 1930 (1)*; *v NZ 1929 (4)*

Ames (L. E. G.) 47: v A 1934 (5) 1938 (2); v SA 1929 (1) 1935 (4); v WI 1933 (3); v NZ 1931 (3) 1937 (3); v In 1932 (1); *v A 1932 (5) 1936 (5)*; *v SA 1938 (5)*; *v WI 1929 (4)*; *1934 (4)*; *v NZ 1932 (2)*

Andrew (K. V.) 1: *v A 1954*

Appleyard (R.) 9: v A 1956 (1); v SA 1955 (1); v P 1954 (1); *v A 1954 (4)*; *v NZ 1954 (2)*.

Archer A. G. 1: *v SA 1898*

Armitage (T) 2: *v A 1876 (2)*

Arnold (E. G.) 10: v A 1905 (4); v SA 1907 (2); *v A 1903 (4)*

Arnold (J.) 1: v NZ 1931

Astill (W. E.) 9: *v SA 1927 (5)*; *v WI 1929 (4)*

Attewell (W.) 10: v A 1890 (1); *v A 1884 (5) 1887 (1) 1891 (3)*

Bailey, T. E. 52: v A 1953 (5) 1956 (4); v SA 1951 (2) 1955 (5); v WI 1950 (2) 1957 (4); v NZ 1949 (4), v P 1954 (3); *v A 1950 (4) 1954 (5)*; *v SA 1956 (5)*; *v WI 1953 (5)*; *v NZ 1950 (2) 1954 (2)*.

Bakewell (A. H.) 6: v SA 1935 (2); v WI 1933 (1); v NZ 1931 (2); *v In 1933 (1)*

Barber (W.) 2: v SA 1935 (2)

Barlow (R. G.) 17: v A 1882 (1) 1884 (3) 1886 (3); *v A 1881 (4) 1882 (4) 1886 (2)*

Barnes (S. F.) 27: v A 1902 (1) 1909 (3) 1912 (3); v SA 1912 (3); *v A 1901 (3) 1907 (5) 1911 (5)*; *v SA 1913 (4)*

Barnes (W.) 21: v A 1880 (1) 1882 (1) 1884 (2) 1886 (2) 1888 (3) 1890 (2); *v A 1882 (4) 1884 (5) 1886 (1)*

Barnett (C. J.) 20: v A 1938 (3); 1948 (1); v SA 1947 (3); v WI 1933 (1); v NZ 1937 (3); v In 1936 (1); *v A 1936 (5)*; *v In 1933 (3)*

Barratt (F.) 5: v SA 1929 (1); *v NZ 1929 (4)*

Barrington (K.) 2: v SA 1955 (2)

Barton (V.) 1: *v SA 1891*

Bates (W.) 15: *v A 1881 (4) 1882 (4) 1884 (5) 1886 (2)*

Bean (G.) 3: *v A 1891 (3)*

Bedser (A. V.) 51: v A 1948 (5) 1953 (5); v SA 1947 (2) 1951 (5) 1955 (1); v WI 1950 (3); v NZ 1949 (2); v In 1946 (3) 1952 (4); v P 1954 (2); *v A 1946 (5) 1950 (5) 1954 (1)*; *v SA 1948 (5)*; *v NZ 1947 (1) 1950 (2)*

E

Berry (R.) 2: v WI 1950 (2)
Bird, M. C. 10: *v SA 1909 (5) 1913 (5)*
Bligh, Hon. Ivo. 4: *v A 1882 (4)*
Blythe (C.) 19: v A 1905 (1) 1909 (2); v SA 1907 (3); *v A 1901 (5) 1907 (1); v SA 1905 (5) 1909 (2)*
Board (J. H.) 6: *v SA 1898 (2) 1905 (4)*
Booth (M. W.) 2: *v SA 1913 (2)*
Bosanquet, B. J. T. 7: v A 1905 (3); *v A 1903 (4)*
Bowden, M. P. 2: *v SA 1888 (2)*
Bowes (W. E.) 15: v A 1934 (3) 1938 (2); v SA 1935 (4); v WI 1939 (2); v In 1932 (1); 1946 (1); *v A 1932 (1); v NZ 1932 (1)*
Bowley (E. H.) 5: v SA 1929 (2); *v NZ 1929 (3)*
Bradley, W. M. 2: v A 1899 (2)
Braund (L. C.) 23: v A 1902 (5); v SA 1907 (3); *v A 1901 (5) 1903 (5) 1907 (5)*
Brearley, W. 4: v A 1905 (2) 1909 (1); v SA 1912 (1)
Brennan, D. V. 2: v SA 1951 (2)
Briggs (John) 33: v A 1886 (3) 1888 (3) 1893 (2) 1896 (1) 1899 (1); *v A 1884 (5) 1886 (2) 1887 (1) 1891 (3) 1894 (5); 1897 (5); v SA 1888 (2)*
Brockwell (W.) 7: v A 1893 (1) 1899 (1); *v A 1894 (5)*
Bromley-Davenport, R. H. 4: *v SA 1895 (3) 1898 (1)*
Brookes, (D.) 1: *v WI 1947*
Brown, F. R. 22: v A 1953 (1); v SA 1951 (5); v WI 1950 (1); v NZ 1931 (2) 1937 (1) 1949 (2); v In 1932 (1); *v A 1950 (5); v NZ 1932 (2) 1950 (2)*
Brown (G.) 7: v A 1921 (3); *v SA 1922 (4)*
Brown (J. T.) 8: v A 1896 (2) 1899 (1); *v A 1894 (5)*
Buckenham (C. P.) 4: *v SA 1909 (4)*
Butler (H. J.) 2: v SA 1947 (1); *v WI 1947 (1)*
Butt (H. R.) 3: *v SA 1895 (3)*

Calthorpe, Hon. F. S. G. 4: *v WI 1929 (4)*
Carr, A. W. 11: v A 1926 (4); v SA 1929 (2); *v SA 1922 (5)*
Carr, D. B. 2: *v In 1951 (2)*
Carr, D. W. 1: v A 1909
Chapman, A. P. F. 26: v A 1926 (4) 1930 (4); v SA 1924 (2); v WI 1928 (3); *v A 1924 (4) 1928 (4); v SA 1930 (5)*
Charlwood (H.) 2: *v A 1876 (2)*
Chatterton (W.) 1: *v SA 1891*
Christopherson, S. 1: v A 1884
Clark (E. W.) 8: v A 1934 (2); v SA 1929 (1); v WI 1933 (2); *v In 1933 (3)*
Clay, J. C. 1: v SA 1935
Close (D. B.) 5: v SA 1955 (1); v WI 1957 (2); v NZ 1949 (1); *v A 1950 (1)*
Compton (D.) 78: v A 1938 (4) 1948 (5) 1953 (5) 1956 (1); v SA 1947 (5) 1951 (4) 1955 (5); v WI 1939 (3) 1950 (1); v NZ 1937 (1) 1949 (4); v In 1946 (3) 1952 (2); v P 1954 (4); *v A 1946 (5) 1950 (4) 1954 (4); v SA 1948 (5) 1956 (5); v WI 1953 (5); v NZ 1947 (1) 1950 (2)*
Cook (C.) 1: v SA 1947
Copson (W.) 3: v SA 1947 (1); v WI 1939 (2)
Cornford (W.) 4: *v NZ 1929 (4)*
Coventry, Hon. C. J. 2: *v SA 1888 (2)*
Cowdrey, M. C. 23: v A 1956 (5); v SA 1955 (1); v WI 1957 (5); *v A 1954 (5); v SA 1956 (5); v NZ 1954 (2)*
Coxon (A.) 1: v A 1948
Cranston, J. 1: v A 1890
Cranston, K. 8: v A 1948 (1); v SA 1947 (3); *v WI 1947 (4)*
Crapp (J. F.) 7: v A 1948 (3); *v SA 1948 (4)*
Crawford, J. N. 12: v SA 1907 (2); *v A 1907 (5); v SA 1905 (5)*
Cuttell, (W. R.) 2: *v SA 1898 (2)*

Dawson, E. W. 5: *v SA 1927 (1); v NZ 1929 (4)*
Dean (H.) 3: v A 1912 (2); v SA 1912 (1)
Denton (D.) 11: v A 1905 (1); *v SA 1905 (5) 1909 (5)*
Dewes, J. G. 5: v A 1948 (1); v WI 1950 (2); *v A 1950 (2)*
Dipper (A. E.) 1: v A 1921

Doggart, G. H. G. 2: v WI 1950 (2)
Dollery (H. E.) 4: v A 1948 (2); v SA 1947; v WI 1950 (1)
Dolphin (A.) 1: *v A 1920*
Douglas, J. W. H. T. 23: v A 1912 (1) 1921 (5); v SA 1924 (1); *v A 1911 (5) 1920 (5) 1924 (1); v SA 1913 (5)*
Druce, N. F. 5: *v A 1897 (5)*
Ducat (A.) 1: v A 1921
Duckworth (G.) 24: v A 1930 (5); v SA 1924 (1) 1929 (4) 1935 (1); v WI 1928 (1); v In 1936 (3); *v A 1928 (5); v SA 1930 (3); v NZ 1932 (1)*
Duleepsinhji, K. S. 12: v A 1930 (4); v SA 1929 (1); v NZ 1931 (3); *v NZ 1929 (4)*
Durston (T. J.) 1: v A 1921

Edrich, W. J. 39: v A 1938 (4) 1948 (5) 1953 (3); v SA 1947 (4); v WI 1950 (2); v NZ 1949 (4); v In 1946 (1); v P 1954 (1); *v A 1946 (5) 1954 (4); v SA 1938 (5); v NZ 1947 (1)*
Elliott (H.) 4: v WI 1928 (1); *v SA 1927 (1); v In 1933 (2)*
Emmett (G. M.) 1: v A 1948
Emmett (T.) 7: *v A 1876 (2) 1878 (1) 1881 (4)*
Evans, A. J. 1: v A 1921
Evans (T. G.) 81: v A 1948 (5) 1953 (5) 1956 (5); v SA 1947 (5) 1951 (3) 1955 (3); v WI 1950 (3) 1957 (5); v NZ 1949 (4); v In 1946 (1) 1952 (4); v P 1954 (4); *v A 1946 (4) 1950 (5) 1954 (4); v SA 1948 (3) 1956 (5); v WI 1947 (4) 1953 (4); v NZ 1947 (1) 1950 (2) 1954 (2)*

Fagg (A. E.) 5: v WI 1939 (1); v In 1936 (2); *v A 1936 (2)*
Fane, F. L. 14: *v A 1907 (4); v SA 1905 (5) 1909 (5)*
Farnes, K. 15: v A 1934 (2) 1938 (4); *v A 1936 (2); v SA 1938 (5); v WI 1934 (2)*
Farrimond (W.) 4: v SA 1935 (1); *v SA 1930 (2); v WI 1934 (1)*
Fender, P. G. H. 13: v A 1921 (2) 1929 (1); *v A 1920 (3); v SA 1922 (5)*
Ferris, J. J. 1: *v SA 1891*
Fielder, (A.) 6: *v A 1903 (2) 1907 (4)*
Fishlock (L. B.) 4: v In 1936 (2) 1946 (1); *v A 1946 (1)*
Flowers (W.) 8: v A 1893 (1); *v A 1884 (5) 1886 (2)*
Ford, F. G. J. 5: *v A 1894 (5)*
Foster, F. R. 11: v A 1912 (3); v SA 1912 (3); *v A 1911 (5)*
Foster, R. E. 8: v SA 1907 (3); *v A 1903 (5)*
Fothergill (A. J.) 2: *v SA 1888 (2)*
Freeman (A. P.) 12: v SA 1929 (3); v WI 1928 (3); *v A 1924 (2); v SA 1927 (4)*
Fry, C. B. 26: v A 1899 (5) 1902 (3) 1905 (4) 1909 (3) 1912 (3); v SA 1907 (3) 1912 (3); *v SA 1895 (2)*

Gay, L. H. 1: *v A 1894*
Geary (G.) 14: v A 1926 (2) 1930 (1) 1934 (2); v SA 1924 (1) 1929 (2); *v A 1928 (4); v SA 1927 (2)*
Gibb, P. A. 8: v In 1946 (2); *v A 1946 (1); v SA 1938 (5)*
Gilligan, A. E. R. 11: v SA 1924 (4); *v A 1924 (5); v SA 1922 (2)*
Gilligan, A. H. H. 4: *v NZ 1929 (4)*
Gimblett (H.) 3: v WI 1939 (1); v In 1936 (2)
Gladwin (C.) 8: v SA 1947 (2); v NZ 1949 (1); *v SA 1948 (5)*
Goddard (T. W.) 8: v A 1930 (1); v WI 1939 (2); v NZ 1937 (2); *v SA 1938 (3)*
Gover (A. R.) 4: v NZ 1937 (2); v In 1936 (1) 1946 (1)
Grace, E. M. 1: v A 1880
Grace, G. F. 1: v A 1880
Grace, W. G. 22: v A 1880 (1) 1882 (1) 1884 (3) 1886 (3) 1888 (3) 1890 (2) 1893 (2) 1896 (3) 1899 (1); *v A 1891 (3)*
Graveney (T. W.) 37: v A 1953 (3) 1956 (2); v SA 1951 (1) 1955 (5); v WI 1957 (4); v In 1952 (4); v P 1954 (3); *v A 1954 (2); v In 1951 (4); v WI 1953 (5); v NZ 1954 (2)*
Greenwood (A.) 2: *v A 1876 (2)*
Grieve, B. A. F. 2: *v SA 1888 (2)*
Griffith, S. C. 3: *v SA 1948 (2); v WI 1947 (1)*

Gunn (G.) 15: v A 1909 (1); *v A 1907 (5) 1911 (5)*; *v WI 1929 (4)*
Gunn (J.) 6: v A 1905 (1); *v A 1901 (5)*
Gunn (W.) 11: v A 1888 (2) 1890 (2) 1893 (3) 1896 (1) 1899 (1); *v A 1886 (2)*

Haig, N. E. 5: v A 1921 (1); *v WI 1929 (4)*
Haigh (S.) 11: v A 1905 (2) 1909 (1); 1912 (1); *v SA 1898 (2) 1905 (5)*
Hallows (C.) 2: v A 1921 (1); v WI 1928 (1)
Hammond, W. R. 85: v A 1930 (5) 1934 (5) 1938 (4); v SA 1929 (4) 1935 (5);
    v WI 1928 (3) 1933 (3) 1939 (3); v NZ 1931 (3) 1937 (3); v In 1932 (1) 1936 (2)
    1946 (3); *v A 1928 (5) 1932 (5) 1936 (5) 1946 (4)*; *v SA 1927 (5) 1930 (5)
    1938 (5)*; *v NZ 1932 (2) 1947 (1)*; *v WI 1934 (4)*
Hardinge (H. T. W.) 1: v A 1921
Hardstaff (J.) 5: *v A 1907 (5)*
Hardstaff (J., Jnr.) 23: v A 1938 (2) 1948 (1); v SA 1935 (1); v WI 1939 (3); v NZ
    1937 (3); v In 1936 (2) 1946 (2); *v A 1936 (5) 1946 (1)*; *v WI 1947 (3)*
Harris, Lord 4: v A 1880 (1) 1884 (2); *v A 1878 (1)*
Hartley, J. C. 2: *v SA 1905 (2)*
Hawke, Lord 5: *v SA 1895 (3) 1898 (2)*
Hayes (E. G.) 5: v A 1909 (1); v SA 1912 (1); *v SA 1905 (3)*
Hayward (T. W.) 35: v A 1896 (2) 1899 (5) 1902 (1) 1905 (5) 1909 (1); v SA
    1907 (3); *v A 1897 (5) 1901 (5)*; *1903 (5) v SA 1895 (3)*
Hearne (A.) 1: *v SA 1891*
Hearne (F.) 2: *v SA 1888 (2)*
Hearne (G. G.) 1: *v SA 1891*
Hearne (J. T.) 12: v A 1896 (3) 1899 (3); *v A 1897 (5)*; *v SA 1891 (1)*
Hearne (J. W.) 24: v A 1912 (3) 1921 (1) 1926 (1); v SA 1912 (2) 1924 (3);
    v A 1911 (5) 1920 (2) 1924 (4); *v SA 1913 (3)*
Hendren (E.) 51: v A 1921 (2) 1926 (5) 1930 (2) 1934 (4); v SA 1924 (5) 1929 (4)
    v WI 1928 (1); *v A 1920 (5) 1924 (5) 1928 (5)*; *v SA 1930 (5)*; *v WI 1929 (4)
    1934 (4)*
Heseltine, C. 2: *v SA 1895 (2)*
Hill (A.) 2: *v A 1876 (2)*
Hill, A. J. L. 3: *v SA 1895 (3)*
Hilton (M. J.) 4: v SA 1951 (1); v WI 1950 (1); *v In 1951 (2)*
Hirst (G. H.) 24: v A 1899 (1) 1902 (4) 1905 (3) 1909 (4); v SA 1907 (3);
    v A 1897 (4) 1903 (5)
Hitch (J. W.) 7: v A 1912 (1) 1921 (1); v SA 1912 (1); *v A 1911 (3) 1920 (1)*
Hobbs (J. B.) 61: v A 1909 (3) 1912 (3) 1921 (1) 1926 (5) 1930 (5); v SA 1912 (3)
    1924 (4) 1929 (1); v WI 1928 (2); *v A 1907 (4) 1911 (5) 1920 (5) 1924 (5)
    1928 (5)*; *v SA 1909 (5) 1913 (5)*
Hollies (E.) 13: v A 1948 (1); v SA 1947 (3); v WI 1950 (2); v NZ 1949 (4);
    v WI 1934 (3)
Holmes, E. R. T. 5: v SA 1935 (1); *v WI 1934 (4)*
Holmes (P.) 7: v A 1921 (1); v In 1932 (1); *v SA 1927 (5)*
Hone, L. 1: *v A 1878*
Hopwood (J. L.) 2: v A 1934 (2)
Hornby, A. N. 3: v A 1882 (1) 1884 (1); *v A 1878 (1)*
Howard, N. D. 4: *v In 1951 (4)*
Howorth (R.) 5: v SA 1947; *v WI 1947 (4)*
Howell (H.) 5: v A 1921 (1); v SA 1924 (1); *v A 1920 (3)*
Humphries (J.) 3: *v A 1907 (3)*
Hunter (J.) 5: *v A 1884 (5)*
Hutchings, K. L. 7: v A 1909 (2); *v A 1907 (5)*
Hutton (L.) 79: v A 1938 (3) 1948 (4) 1953 (5); v SA 1947 (5) 1951 (5); v WI
    1939 (3) 1950 (3); v NZ 1937 (3) 1949 (4); v In 1946 (3) 1952 (4); v P
    1954 (2); *v A 1946 (5) 1950 (5) 1954 (5)*; *v SA 1938 (4) 1948 (5)*; *v WI 1947 (2)
    1953 (5)*; *v NZ 1950 (2) 1954 (2)*

Iddon (J.) 5: v SA 1935 (1); *v WI 1934 (4)*
Ikin (J. T.) 18: v SA 1951 (3) 1954 (1); v In 1946 (2); 1952 (2); *v A 1946 (5)*; *v NZ
    1947 (1)*; *v WI 1947 (4)*
Insole, D. J. 9: v A 1956 (1); v SA 1955 (1); v WI 1950 (1) 1957 (1); *v SA 1956 (5)*

Jackson, (L.) 1: v NZ 1949
Jackson, Rt. Hon. Sir F. S. 20: v A 1893 (2) 1896 (3) 1899 (5) 1902 (5) 1905 (5)
Jardine, D. R. 22: v WI 1928 (2) 1933 (2); v NZ 1931 (3); v In 1932 (1);
v A 1928 (5) 1932 (5); *v NZ 1932 (1)*; *v In 1933 (3)*
Jenkins (R. O.) 9: v WI 1950 (2); v In 1952 (2); *v SA 1948 (5)*
Jessop, G. L. 18: v A 1899 (1) 1902 (4) 1905 (1) 1909 (2); v SA 1907 (3) 1912 (2);
v A 1901 (5)
Jones, A. O. 12: v A 1899 (1) 1905 (2) 1909 (2); *v A 1901 (5) 1907 (2)*
Jupp (H.) 2: *v A 1876 (2)*
Jupp, V. W. C. 8: v A 1921 (2); v WI 1928 (2); *v SA 1922 (4)*

Keeton (W. W.) 2: v A 1934 (1); v WI 1939 (1)
Kennedy (A. S.) 5: *v SA 1922 (5)*
Kenyon (D.) 8: v A 1953 (2); v SA 1955 (3); *v In 1951 (3)*
Killick, E. T. 2: v SA 1929 (2)
Kilner (R.) 9: v A 1926 (4); v SA 1924 (2); *v A 1924 (3)*
King (J. H.) 1: v A 1909
Kinneir (S. P.) 1: *v A 1911*
Knight (A. E.) 3: *v A 1903 (3)*
Knight, D. J. 2: v A 1921 (2)
Knox, N. A. 2: v SA 1907 (2)

Laker (J. C.) 38: v A 1948 (3) 1953 (3) 1956 (5); v SA 1951 (2) 1955 (1); v WI
1950 (1) 1957 (4); v NZ 1949 (1); v In 1952 (4); v P 1954 (1); *v SA 1956 (5)*;
v WI 1947 (4) 1953 (4)
Langridge (James) 8: v SA 1935 (1); v WI 1933 (2); v In 1936 (1) 1946 (1);
v In 1933 (3)
Larwood (H.) 21: v A 1926 (2) 1930 (3); v SA 1929 (3); v WI 1928 (2); v NZ
1931 (1); *v A 1928 (5) 1932 (5)*
Leadbeater (E) 2: *v In 1951 (2)*
Lee (H. W.) 1: *v SA 1930*
Lees (W.) 5: *v SA 1905 (5)*
Legge, G. B. 5: *v SA 1927 (1)*; *v NZ 1929 (4)*
Leslie, C. F. H. 4: *v A 1882 (4)*
Leveson Gower, H. D. G. 3: *v SA 1909 (3)*
Levett, W. H. V. 1: *v In 1933*
Leyland (M.) 41: v A 1930 (3) 1934 (5) 1938 (1); v SA 1929 (5) 1935 (4);
v WI 1928 (1) 1933 (1); v In 1936 (2); *v A 1928 (1) 1932 (5) 1936 (5)*;
v SA 1930 (5); *v WI 1934 (3)*
Lilley (A. A.) 35: v A 1896 (3) 1899 (4) 1902 (5) 1905 (5) 1909 (5); v SA 1907 (3);
v A 1901 (5) 1903 (5)
Lillywhite (Jas. Jnr.) 2: *v A 1876 (2)*
Loader (P. J.) 8: v SA 1955 (1); v WI 1957 (2); v P 1954 (1); *v SA 1956 (4)*
Lock (G. A. R.) 20: v A 1953 (2) 1956 (4); v SA 1955 (3); v WI 1957 (3); v In
1952 (2); *v SA 1956 (1)*; *v WI 1953 (5)*
Lockwood (W. H.) 12: v A 1893 (2) 1899 (1) 1902 (4); *v A 1894 (5)*
Lohmann (G. A.) 18: v A 1886 (3) 1888 (3) 1890 (2) 1896 (1); *v A 1886 (2)
1887 (1) 1891 (3)*; *v SA 1895 (3)*
Lowson (F. A.) 7: v SA 1951 (2) 1955 (1); *v In 1951 (4)*
Lucas, A. P. 5: v A 1880 (1) 1882 (1) 1884 (2); *v A 1878 (1)*
Lyttelton, Rt. Hon. A. 4: v A 1880 (1) 1882 (1) 1884 (2)

Macaulay (G. G.) 8: v A 1926 (1); v SA 1924 (1); v WI 1933 (2); *v SA 1922 (4)*
MacBryan, J. C. W. 1: v SA 1924
McConnon (J.) 2: v P 1954 (2)
McGahey, C. P. 2: *v A 1901 (2)*
MacGregor, G. 8: v A 1890 (2) 1893 (3); *v A 1891 (3)*
McIntyre (A. J.) 3: v SA 1955 (1); v WI 1950 (1); *v A 1950 (1)*
MacKinnon, F. A. 1: *v A 1878*
MacLaren, A. C. 35: v A 1896 (2) 1899 (4) 1902 (5) 1905 (4) 1909 (5); *v A 1894 ( )
1897 (5) 1901 (5)*
McMaster, J. E. P. 1: *v SA 1888*
Makepeace (H.) 4: *v A 1920 (4)*
Mann, F. G. 7: v NZ 1949 (2); *v SA 1948 (5)*

Mann, F. T. 5: *v SA 1922 (5)*
Marriott, C. S. 1: v WI 1933
Martin (F.) 2: v A 1890 (1); *v SA 1891 (1)*
Martin, J. W. 1: v SA 1947
Mason, J. R. 5: *v A 1897 (5)*
Matthews (A. D. G.) 1: v NZ 1937
May, P. B. H. 44: v A 1953 (2) 1956 (5); v SA 1951 (2) 1955 (5); v WI 1957 (5); v In 1952 (4); v P 1954 (4); *v A 1954 (5)*; *v SA 1956 (5)*; *v WI 1953 (5)*; *v NZ 1954 (2)*
Mead (C. P.) 17: v A 1921 (2); *v A 1911 (4) 1928 (1)*; *v SA 1913 (5) 1922 (5)*
Mead (W.) 1: v A 1899
Midwinter (W. E.) 4: *v A 1881 (4)*
Miller, A. M. 1: *v SA 1895*
Milligan, F. W. 2: *v SA 1898 (2)*
Mitchell (A.) 6: v SA 1935 (2); v In 1936 (1); *v In 1933 (3)*
Mitchell, F. 2: *v SA 1898 (2)*
Mitchell (T. B.) 5: v A 1934 (2); v SA 1935 (1) *v A 1932 (1)*; *v NZ 1932 (1)*
Mitchell-Innes, N. S. 1: v SA 1935
Mold (A.) 3: v A 1893 (3)
Moon, L. J. 4: *v SA 1905 (4)*
Morley (F.) 4: v A 1880 (1); *v A 1882 (3)*
Moss (A. E.) 2: v A 1956 (1); *v WI 1953 (1)*
Murdoch, W. L. 1: *v SA 1891*

Newham (W.) 1: *v A 1887*
Nichols (M. S.) 14: v A 1930 (1); v SA 1935 (4); v WI 1933 (1) 1939 (1) *v NZ 1929 (4)*; *v In 1933 (3)*

Oakman (A. S. M.) 2: v A 1956 (2)
O'Brien, Sir T. C. 5: v A 1884 (1) 1888 (1); *v SA 1895 (3)*
O'Connor (J.) 4: v SA 1929 (1); *v WI 1929 (3)*
Oldfield (N.) 1: v WI 1939

Paine (G. A. E.) 4: *v WI 1934 (4)*
Palairet, L. C. H. 2: v A 1902 (2)
Palmer, C. H. 1: *v WI 1953*
Parker (C. W. L.) 1: v A 1921
Parkhouse (W. G. A.) 5: v WI 1950 (2); *v A 1950 (2)*; *v NZ 1950 (1)*
Parkin (C. H.) 10: v A 1921 (4); v SA 1924 (1); *v A 1920 (5)*
Parks (J. H.) 1: v NZ 1937
Parks (J. M.) 1: v P 1954
Pataudi, Nawab of 3: v A 1934 (1); *v A 1932 (2)*
Paynter (E.) 20: v A 1938 (4); v WI 1939 (2); v NZ 1931 (1) 1937 (2); v In 1932 (1); *v A 1932 (3)*; *v SA 1938 (5)*; *v NZ 1932 (2)*
Peate (E.) 9: v A 1882 (1) 1884 (3) 1886 (1); *v A 1881 (4)*
Peebles, I. A. R. 13: v A 1930 (2); v NZ 1931 (3); *v SA 1927 (4) 1930 (4)*
Peel (R.) 20: v A 1888 (3) 1890 (1) 1893 (1) 1896 (1); *v A 1884 (5) 1887 (1) 1891 (3) 1894 (5)*
Penn, F. 1: v A 1880
Perks (R. T. D.) 2: v WI 1939 (1); *v SA 1938 (1)*
Philipson, H. 5: *v A 1891 (1) 1894 (4)*
Pilling (R.) 8: v A 1884 (1) 1886 (1) 1888 (1); *v A 1881 (4) 1887 (1)*
Place (W.) 3: *v WI 1947 (3)*
Pollard (R.) 4: v A 1948 (2); v In 1946 (1); *v NZ 1947 (1)*
Poole (C. J.) 3: *v In 1951 (3)*
Pope (G. H.) 1: v SA 1947
Pougher (A. D.) 1: *v SA 1891*
Price (W. F.) 1: v A 1938

Quaife (W. G.) 7: v A 1899 (2); *v A 1901 (5)*

Ranjitsinhji, K. S. 15: v A 1896 (2) 1899 (5) 1902 (3); *v A 1897 (5)*
Read, H. D. 1: v SA 1935

Read (J. M.) 17: v A 1882 (1) 1890 (2) 1893 (1); *v A 1884 (5) 1886 (2) 1887 (1) 1891 (3)*; *v SA 1888 (2)*

Read, W. W. 18: v A 1884 (2) 1886 (3) 1888 (3) 1890 (2) 1893 (2); *v A 1882 (4) 1887 (1)*; *v SA 1891 (1)*

Relf (A. E.) 13: v A 1909 (1); *v A 1903 (2)*; *v SA 1905 (5) 1913 (5)*

Rhodes (W.) 58: v A 1899 (3) 1902 (5) 1905 (4) 1909 (4) 1912 (3) 1921 (1) 1926 (1); v SA 1912 (3); *v A 1903 (5) 1907 (5) 1911 (5) 1920 (5)*; *v SA 1909 (5) 1913 (5)*; *v WI 1929 (4)*

Richardson (D. W.) 1: v WI 1957

Richardson, P. E. 15: v A 1956 (5); v WI 1957 (5); *v SA 1956 (5)*

Richardson (T.) 14: v A 1893 (1) 1896 (3); *v A 1894 (5) 1897 (5)*

Richmond (T. L.) 1: v A 1921

Ridgway (F.) 5: *v In 1951(5)*

Robertson (J. D.) 11: v SA 1947 (1); v NZ 1949 (1); *v WI 1947 (4)*; *v In 1951 (5)*

Robins, R. W. V. 19: v A 1930 (2); v SA 1929 (1) 1935 (3); v WI 1933 (?); v NZ 1931 (1) 1937 (3); v In 1932 (1) 1936 (2); *v A 1936 (4)*

Root (C. F.) 3: v A 1926 (3)

Royle, V. P. F. A. 1: *v A 1878*

Russell (A. C.) 10: v A. 1921 (2); *v A 1920 (4)*; *v SA 1922 (4)*

Sandham (A.) 14: v A 1921 (1); v SA 1924 (2); *v A 1924 (2)*; *v SA 1922 (5)*; *v WI 1929 (4)*

Schultz, S. S. 1: *v A 1878*

Scotton (W. H.) 15: v A 1884 (1) 1886 (3); *v A 1881 (4) 1884 (5) 1886 (2)*

Selby (J.) 6: *v A 1876 (2) 1881 (4)*

Shackleton (D.) 3: v SA 1951 (1); v WI 1950 (1); *v In 1951 (1)*

Sharp (J.) 3: v A 1909 (3)

Sharpe (J. W.) 3: v A 1890 (1); *v A 1891 (2)*

Shaw (A.) 7: v A 1880 (1); *v A 1876 (2) 1881 (4)*

Sheppard, Rev. D. S. 12: v A 1956 (2); v WI 1950 (1) 1957 (2); v In 1952 (2); v P 1954 (2); *v A 1950 (2)*; *v NZ 1950 (1)*

Sherwin (M.) 3: v A 1888 (1); *v A 1886 (2)*

Shrewsbury (A.) 23: v A 1884 (3) 1886 (3) 1890 (2) 1893 (3); *v A 1881 (4) 1884 (5) 1886 (2) 1887 (1)*

Shuter, J. 1: v A 1888

Sims (J. M.) 4: v SA 1935 (1); v In 1936 (1); *v A 1936 (2)*

Simpson, R. T. 27: v A 1953 (3); v SA 1951 (3); v WI 1950 (3); v NZ 1949 (2); v In 1952 (2); v P 1954 (3); *v A 1950 (5) 1954 (1)*; *v SA 1948 (1)*; *v NZ 1950 (2) 1954 (2)*

Simpson-Hayward, G. H. 5: *v SA 1909 (5)*

Sinfield (R. A.) 1: v A 1938

Smailes (T. F.) 1: v In 1946 (1)

Smith, C. A. 1: *v SA 1888*

Smith (C. I. J.) 5: v NZ 1937 (1); *v WI 1934 (4)*

Smith (D.) 2: v SA 1935 (2)

Smith (D. V.) 3: v WI 1957 (3)

Smith (E. J.) 11: v A 1912 (3); v SA 1912 (3); *v A 1911 (4)*; *v SA 1913 (1)*

Smith (H.) 1: v WI 1928

Smith (T. P. B.) 4: v In 1946 (1); *v A 1946 (2)*; *v NZ 1947 (1)*

Smithson (G. A.) 2: *v WI 1947 (2)*

Southerton (J.) 2: *v A 1876 (2)*

Spooner, R. H. 10: v A 1905 (2) 1909 (2) 1912 (3); v SA 1912 (3)

Spooner (R. T.) 7: v SA 1955 (1); *v In 1951 (5)*; *v WI 1953 (1)*

Stanyforth, R. T. 4: *v SA 1927 (4)*

Staples (S. J.) 3: *v SA 1927 (3)*

Statham (J. B.) 38: v A 1953 (1) 1956 (3); v SA 1951 (2) 1955 (4); v WI 1957 (3); v P 1954 (4); *v A 1954 (5)*; *v SA 1956 (4)*; *v NZ 1950 (1) 1954 (2)*; *v WI 1953 (4)*; *v In 1951 (5)*

Steel, A. G. 13: v A 1880 (1) 1882 (1) 1884 (3) 1886 (3) 1888 (1); *v A 1882 (4)*

Stevens, G. T. S. 10: v A 1926 (2); *v SA 1922 (1) 1927 (5)*; *v WI 1929 (2)*

Stoddart, A. E. 16: v A 1893 (3) 1896 (3); *v A 1887 (1) 1891 (3) 1894 (5) 1897 (2)*

Storer (W.) 6: v A 1899 (1); *v A 1897 (5)*

Street (G.) 1: *v SA 1922*

Strudwick (H.) 28: v A 1921 (2) 1926 (5); v SA 1924 (1); *v A 1911 (1) 1920 (4) 1924 (5); v SA 1909 (5) 1913 (5)*

Studd, C. T. 5: v A 1882 (1); *v A 1882 (4)*

Studd, G. B. 4: *v A 1882 (4)*

Sugg (F. H.) 2: v A 1888 (2)

Sutcliffe (H.) 54: v A 1926 (5) 1930 (4) 1934 (4); v SA 1924 (5) 1929 (5) 1935 (2); v WI 1928 (3) 1933 (2); v NZ 1931 (2); v In 1932 (1); *v A 1924 (5) 1928 (4) 1932 (5); v SA 1927 (5); v NZ 1932 (2)*

Tate (F. W.) 1: v A 1902

Tate (M. W.) 39: v A 1926 (5) 1930 (5); v SA 1924 (5) 1929 (5) 1935 (1); v WI 1928 (3); v NZ 1931 (1); *v A 1924 (5) 1928 (5); v SA 1930 (5); v NZ 1932 (1)*

Tattersall (R.) 16: v A 1953 (1); v SA 1951 (5); v P 1954 (1); *v A 1950 (2); v NZ 1950 (2); v In 1951 (5)*

Tennyson, Lord, 9: v A 1921 (4); *v SA 1913 (5)*

Thompson (G. J.) 6: v A 1909 (1); *v SA 1909 (5)*

Titmus (F. J.) 2: v SA 1955 (2)

Townsend, C. L. 2: v A 1899 (2)

Townsend, D. C. H. 3: *v WI 1934 (3)*

Townsend (L. F.) 4: *v WI 1929 (1); v In 1933 (3)*

Tremlett (M. F.) 3: *v WI 1947 (3)*

Trott (A. E.) 2: *v SA 1898 (2)*

Trueman (F. S.) 16: v A 1953 (1) 1956 (2); v SA 1955 (1); v WI 1957 (5); v In 1952 (4); *v WI 1953 (3)*

Tufnell, N. C. 1: *v SA 1909*

Turnbull, M. J. 9: v WI 1933 (2); v In 1936 (1); *v SA 1930 (5); v NZ 1929 (1); v SA 1927 (5)*

Tyldesley (E.) 14: v A 1921 (3) 1926 (1); v SA 1924 (1); v WI 198 2(3); *v A 1928 (1); v SA 1927 (5)*

Tyldesley (J. T.) 31: v A 1899 (2) 1902 (5) 1905 (5) 1909 (4); v SA 1907 (3); *v A 1901 (5) 1903 (5); v SA 1898 (2)*

Tyldesley (R.) 7: v A 1930 (2); v SA 1924 (4); *v A 1924 (1)*

Tylecote, E. F. S. 6: v A 1886 (2); *v A 1882 (4*

Tyler (E. J.) 1: *v SA 1895*

Tyson (F. H.) 13: v A 1956 (1); v SA 1955 (2); v P 1954 (1); *v A 1954 (5); v SA 1956 (2); v NZ 1954 (2)*

Ulyett (G.) 25: v A 1882 (1) 1884 (3) 1886 (3) 1888 (2) 1890 (1); *v A 1876 (2) 1878 (1) 1881 (4) 1884 (5) 1887 (1); v SA 1888 (2)*

Valentine, B. H. 7: v SA 1938 (5); v In 1933 (2)

Verity (H.) 40: v A 1934 (5) 1938 (4); v SA 1935 (4); v WI 1933 (2) 1939 (1); v NZ 1931 (2) 1937 (1); v In 1936 (3); *v A 1932 (4) 1936 (5); v SA 1938 (5); v NZ 1932 (1); v In 1933 (3)*

Vernon G. F. 1: *v A 1882*

Vine (J.) 2: *v A 1911 (2)*

Voce (W.) 27: v NZ 1931 (1) 1937 (1); v In 1932 (1) 1936 (1) 1946 (1); *v A 1932 (4) 1936 (5) 1946 (2); v SA 1930 (5); v NZ 1932 (2); v WI 1929 (4)*

Waddington (A.) 2: *v A 1920 (2)*

Wainwright (E.) 5: v A 1893 (1); *v A 1897 (4)*

Walters, C. F. 11: v A 1934 (5); v WI 1933 (3); *v In 1933 (3)*

Ward (A.) 7: v A 1893 (2); *v A 1894 (5)*

Wardle (J. H.) 28: v A 1953 (3) 1956 (1); v SA 1951 (2) 1955 (3); v WI 1950 (1) 1957 (1); v P 1954 (4); *v A 1954 (4); v SA 1956 (4); v WI 1947 (1) 1953 (2); v NZ 1954 (2)*

Warner, Sir Pelham, 15: v A 1909 (1); 1912 (1); v SA 1912 (1); *v A 1903 (5); v SA 1898 (2) 1905 (5)*

Warr, J. J. 2: *v A 1950 (2)*

Warren, (A. R.) 1: v A 1905

Washbrook (C.) 37: v A 1948 (4) 1956 (3); v SA 1947 (5); v WI 1950 (2); v NZ 1937 (1) 1949 (2); v In 1946 (3); *v A 1946 (5) 1951 (5); v SA 1948 (5); v NZ 1947 (1) 1951 (1)*

Watkins (A.) 15: v A 1948 (1); v NZ 1949 (1); v In 1952 (3); *v SA 1948 (5); v In 1951 (5)*

Watson (W.) 17: v A 1953 (3) 1956 (2); v SA 1951 (5) 1955 (1); v In 1952 (1); *v WI 1953 (5)*

Webbe, A. J. 1: *v A 1878*
Wellard (A. W.) 2: v A 1938 (1); v NZ 1937 (1)
Wharton (A.) 1: v NZ 1949
White, J. C. 15: v A 1921 (1) 1930 (1); v SA 1929 (3); v WI 1928 (1); *v A 1928 (5); v SA 1930 (4)*
Whysall (W. W.) 4: v A 1930 (1); *v A 1924 (3)*
Wilkinson (L. L.) 3: *v SA 1938 (3)*
Wilson, C. E. M. 2: *v SA 1898 (2)*
Wilson, E. R. 1: *v A 1920*
Wood (A.) 4: v A 1938 (1); v WI 1939 (3)
Wood, G. E. C. 3: v SA 1924 (3)
Wood (H.) 4: v A 1888 (1); *v SA 1888 (2) 1891 (1)*
Wood (R.) 1: *v A 1886*
Woods, S. M. J. 3: *v SA 1895 (3)*
Woolley (F. E.) 64: v A 1909 (1) 1912 (3) 1921 (5) 1926 (5) 1930 (2) 1934 (1);
    v SA 1912 (3) 1924 (5) 1929 (3); v NZ 1931 (1); v In 1932 (1); *v A 1911 (5) 1920 (5) 1924 (5); v SA 1909 (5) 1913 (5) 1922 (5); v NZ 1929 (4)*
Worthington (T. S.) 9: v In 1936 (2); *v A 1936 (3); v NZ 1929 (4)*
Wright, C. W. 3: *v SA 1895 (3)*
Wright (D. V. P.) 34: v A 1938 (3) 1948 (1); v SA 1947 (4); v WI 1939 (3) 1950 (1);
    v NZ 1949 (1); v In 1946 (2); *v A 1946 (5) 1950 (5); v SA 1938 (3) 1948 (3); v NZ 1947 (1) 1950 (2)*
Wynyard, E. G. 3: v A 1896 (1); *v SA 1905 (2)*
Wyatt, R. E. S. 40: v A 1930 (1) 1934 (4); v SA 1929 (2) 1935 (5); v WI 1933 (2);
    v In 1936 (1); *v A 1932 (5) 1936 (2); v SA 1927 (5) 1930 (5); v NZ 1932 (2); v WI 1929 (2) 1934 (4)*

Yardley, N. W. D. 20: v A 1948 (5); v SA 1947 (5); v WI 1950 (3); *v A 1946 (5); v SA 1938 (1); v NZ 1947 (1)*
Young (H.) 2: v A 1899 (2)
Young (J. A.) 8: v A 1948 (3); v SA 1947 (1); v NZ 1949 (2); *v SA 1948 (2)*
Young, R. A. 2: *v A 1907 (2)*

AUSTRALIA

a'Beckett, E. L. 4: v E 1928 (2) v SA 1931 (1); *v E 1930 (1)*
Alexander, G. 2: v E 1884 (1); *v E 1880 (1)*
Alexander, H. H. 1: v E 1932
Allan, F. E. 1: v E 1878
Allen, R. 1: v E 1886
Andrews, T. J. E. 16: v E 1924 (3); *v E 1921 (5) 1926 (5); v SA 1921 (3)*
Archer, K. A. 5: v E 1950 (3); v WI 1951 (2)
Archer, R. G. 19: v E 1954 (4); v SA 1952 (1); *v E 1953 (3) 1956 (5); v WI 1955 (5); v P 1956 (1)*
Armstrong, W. W. 50: v E 1901 (4) 1903 (3) 1907 (5) 1911 (5) 1920 (5); v SA 1910 (5); *v E 1902 (5) 1905 (5) 1909 (5) 1921 (5); v SA 1902 (3)*

Badcock, C. L. 7: v E 1936 (3); *v E 1938 (4)*
Bannerman, A. C. 28: v E 1878 (1) 1881 (3) 1882 (4) 1884 (4) 1886 (1) 1887 (1) 1891 (3); *v E 1880 (1) 1882 (1) 1884 (3) 1888 (3) 1893 (3)*
Bannerman, C. 3: v E 1876 (2) 1878 (1)
Bardsley, W. 41: v E 1911 (4) 1920 (5) 1924 (3); v SA 1910 (5); *v E 1909 (5) 1912 (3) 1921 (5) 1926 (5); v SA 1912 (3) 1921 (3)*
Barnes, S. G. 13: v E 1946 (4); v In 1947 (3); *v E 1938 (1) 1948 (4); v NZ 1946 (1)*
Barnett, B. A. 4: *v E 1938 (4)*
Barrett, J. E. 2: *v E 1890 (2)*
Benaud, R. 27: v E 1954 (5); v SA 1952 (4); v WI 1951 (1); *v E 1953 (3) 1956 (5); v WI 1955 (5); v In 1956 (3); v P 1956 (1)*
Blackham, J. McC. 35: v E 1876 (2) 1878 (1) 1881 (4) 1882 (4) 1884 (2) 1886 (1) 1887 (1) 1891 (3) 1894 (1); *v E 1880 (1) 1882 (1) 1884 (3) 1886 (3) 1888 (3) 1890 (2) 1893 (3)*
Blackie, D. J. 3: v E 1928 (3)

Bonnor, G. J. 17: v E 1882 (4) 1884 (3); *v E 1880 (1) 1882 (1) 1884 (3) 1886 (2) 1888 (3)*

Boyle, H. F. 12: v E 1878 (1) 1881 (4) 1882 (1) 1884 (1); *v E 1880 (1) 1882 (1) 1884 (3)*

Bradman, D. G. 52: v E 1928 (4) 1932 (4) 1936 (5) 1946 (5); v SA 1931 (5); v WI 1930 (5); v In 1947 (5); *v E 1930 (5) 1934 (5) 1938 (4) 1948 (5)*

Bromley, E. H. 2: v E 1932 (1); *v E 1934 (1)*

Brown, W. A. 22: v E 1936 (2); v In 1947 (3); *v E 1934 (5) 1938 (4) 1948 (2); v SA 1935 (5); v NZ 1946 (1)*

Bruce, W. 14: v E 1884 (2) 1891 (3) 1894 (4); *v E 1886 (2) 1893 (3)*

Burn, K. E. 2: *v E 1890 (2)*

Burge, P. 8: v E. 1954 (1); *v E 1956 (3); v WI 1955 (1); v In 1956 (3)*

Burke, J. W. 14: v E 1950 (2) 1954 (2); v WI 1951 (1); *v E 1956 (5); v In 1956 (3); v P 1956 (1)*

Burton, F. J. 2: v E 1886 (1) 1887 (1)

Callaway, S. T. 3: v E 1891 (2) 1894 (1)

Carkeek, W. 6: v E 1912 (3); v SA 1912 (3)

Carter, H. 28: v E 1907 (5) 1911 (5) 1920 (2); v SA 1910 (5); *v E 1909 (5) 1921 (4); v SA 1921 (2)*

Charlton, P. C. 2: *v E 1890 (2)*

Chipperfield, A. G. 14: v E 1936 (3); *v E 1934 (5) 1938 (1); v SA 1935 (5)*

Collins, H. L. 19: v E 1920 (5) 1924 (5); *v E 1921 (3) 1926 (3); v SA 1921 (3)*

Coningham, A. 1: v E 1894

Cooper, B. B. 1: v E 1876

Cooper, W. H. 2: v E 1881 (1) 1884 (1)

Cottam, J. 1: v E 1886

Cotter, A. 21: v E 1903 (2) 1907 (2) 1911 (4); v SA 1910 (5); *v E 1905 (3) 1909 (5)*

Coulthard, G. 1: v E 1881

Craig, I. D. 6: v S.A. 1952 (1); *v E 1956 (2); v In 1956 (2); v P 1956 (1)*

Crawford, P. 4: v E 1956; v In 1956 (3)

Darling, J. 34: v E 1894 (5) 1897 (3) 1901 (3); *v E 1896 (3) 1899 (5) 1902 (5) 1905 (5); v SA 1902 (3)*

Darling, L. S. 12: v E 1932 (2) 1936 (1); *v E 1934 (4); v SA 1935 (5)*

Davidson, A. K. 12: v E 1954 (3); *v E 1953 (5) 1956 (2); v In 1956 (1); v P 1956 (1)*

de Courcy, J. H. 3: *v E 1953 (3)*

Donnan, H. 5: v E 1891 (2); *v E 1896 (3)*

Dooland, B. 3: v E 1946 (2); v In 1947 (1)

Duff, R. A. 22: v E 1901 (4) 1903 (5); *v E 1902 (5) 1905 (5); v SA 1902 (3)*

Eady, C. J. 2: v E 1901 (1); *v E 1896 (1)*

Ebeling, H. I. 1: *v E 1934*

Edwards, J. D. 3: *v E 1888 (3)*

Emery, S. H. 4: *v E 1912 (2); v SA 1912 (2)*

Evans, E. 6: v E 1881 (2) 1882 (1) 1884 (1); *v E 1886 (2)*

Fairfax, A. 10: v E 1928 (1); v WI 1930 (5); *v E 1930 (4)*

Favell, L. 6: v E 1954 (4); *v WI 1955 (2)*

Ferris, J. J. 8: v E 1886 (2) 1887 (1); *v E 1888 (3) 1890 (2)*

Fingleton, J. H. 18: v E 1932 (3) 1936 (5); v SA 1931 (1); *v E 1938 (4); v SA 1935 (5)*

Fleetwood-Smith, L. O.'B. 10: v E 1936 (3); *v E 1938 (4); v SA 1935 (3)*

Freer, F. 1: v E 1946

Garrett, T. W. 19: v E 1876 (2) 1878 (1) 1881 (3) 1882 (3) 1884 (3) 1886 (2) 1887 (1); *v E 1882 (1) 1886 (3)*

Gehrs, D. R. A. 6: v E 1903 (1); v SA 1910 (4); *v E 1905 (1)*

Giffen G. 31: v E 1881 (3) 1882 (4) 1884 (3) 1891 (3) 1894 (5); *v E 1882 (1) 1884 (3) 1886 (3) 1893 (3) 1896 (3)*

Giffen, W. F. 3: v E 1886 (1) 1891 (2)

Graham, H. 6: v E 1894 (2); *v E 1893 (3) 1896 (1)*

Gregory, D. W. 3: v E 1876 (2) 1878 (1)

Gregory, E. J. 1: v E 1876

Gregory, J. M. 24: v E 1920 (5) 1924 (5) 1928 (1); *v E 1921 (5) 1926 (5); v SA 1921 (3)*

Gregory, R. 2: v E 1936 (2)

Gregory, S. E. 58: v E 1891 (1) 1894 (5) 1897 (5) 1901 (5) 1903 (4) 1907 (2) 1911 (1); *v E 1890 (2) 1893 (3) 1896 (3) 1899 (5) 1902 (5) 1905 (3) 1909 (5) 1912 (3); v SA 1902 (3) 1912 (3)*

Grimmett, C. V. 37: v E 1924 (1) 1928 (5) 1932 (3); v SA 1931 (5); v WI 1930 (5); *v E 1926 (3) 1930 (5) 1934 (5); v SA 1935 (5)*

Groube, T. U. 1: *v E 1880*

Hamence, R. A. 3: v E 1946 (1); v In 1947 (2)

Harry, J. 1: v E 1894

Hartigan, R. J. 2: v E 1907 (2)

Hartkopf, A. E. V. 1: v E 1924

Harvey, M. 1: v E 1946

Harvey, R. N. 48: v E 1950 (5) 1954 (5); v SA 1952 (5); v WI 1951 (5); v In 1947 (2); *v E 1948 (2) 1953 (5) 1956 (5); v SA 1949 (5); v WI 1955 (5); v In 1956 (3); v P 1956 (1)*

Hassett, A. L. 43: v E 1946 (5) 1950 (5); v SA 1952 (5); v WI 1951 (4); v In 1947 (4); *v E 1938 (4) 1948 (5) 1953 (5); v SA 1949 (5); v NZ 1946 (1)*

Hazlitt, G. 9: v E 1907 (2) 1911 (1); *v E 1912 (3); v SA 1912 (3)*

Hendry, H. L. 11: v E 1924 (1) 1928 (4); *v E 1921 (4); v SA1 912 (2)*

Hill, Clem, 49: v E 1897 (5) 1901 (5) 1903 (5) 1907 (5) 1911 (5); v SA 1910 (5); *v E 1896 (3) 1899 (3) 1902 (5) 1905 (5); v SA 1902 (3)*

Hill, J. C. 3: *v E 1953 (2); v WI 1955 (1)*

Hodges, J. 2: v E 1876 (2)

Hole, G. 18: v E 1950 (1) 1954 (3); v SA 1952 (4); v WI 1951 (5); *v E 1953 (5)*

Hopkins, A. J. 20: v E 1901 (2) 1903 (5); *v E 1902 (5) 1905 (3) 1909 (2); v SA 1902 (3)*

Horan, T. 15: v E 1876 (1) 1878 (1) 1881 (4) 1882 (4) 1884 (4); *v E 1882 (1)*

Hordern, H. V. 7: v E 1911 (5); v SA 1910 (2)

Hornibrook, P. M. 6: v E 1928 (1); *v E 1930 (5)*

Howell, W. P. 18: v E 1897 (3) 1901 (4) 1903 (3); *v E 1899 (5) 1902 (1), v SA 1902 (2)*

Hunt, W. A. 1: v SA 1931

Hurwood, A. 2: v WI 1930 (2)

Iredale, F. A. 14: v E 1894 (5) 1897 (4); *v E 1896 (2) 1899 (3)*

Ironmonger, H. 14: v E 1928 (2) 1932 (4); v SA 1931 (4); v WI 1930 (4)

Iverson, J. 5: v E 1950 (5)

Jackson, A. A. 8: v E 1928 (2); v WI 1930 (4); *v E 1930 (2)*

Jarvis, A. H. 11: v E 1884 (3) 1894 (4); *v E 1886 (2) 1888 (2)*

Jennings, C. B. 6: *v E 1912 (3); v SA 1912 (3)*

Johnson, I. W. 45: v E 1946 (4) 1950 (5) 1954 (4); v SA 1952 (1); v WI 1951 (4); v In 1947 (4); *v E 1948 (4) 1956 (5); v SA 1949 (5); v WI 1955 (5); v NZ 1946 (1); v In 1956 (2); v P 1956 (1)*

Johnson, L. 1: v In 1947

Johnston, W. A. 40: v E 1950 (5) 1954 (4); v SA 1952 (5); v WI 1951 (5); v In 1947 (4); *v E 1948 (5) 1953 (3); v SA 1949 (5); v WI 1955 (4)*

Jones, E. 19: v E 1894 (1) 1897 (5) 1901 (2); *v E 1896 (3) 1899 (5) 1902 (2); v SA 1902 (1)*

Jones, S. P. 12: v E 1881 (2) 1884 (4) 1886 (1) 1887 (1); *v E 1882 (1) 1886 (3)*

Kelleway, C. E. 26: v E 1911 (4) 1920 (5) 1924 (5) 1928 (1); v SA 1910 (5); *v E 1912 (3); v SA 1912 (3)*

Kelly, J. J. 36: v E 1897 (5) 1901 (5) 1903 (5); *v E 1896 (3) 1899 (5) 1902 (5) 1905 (5); v SA 1902 (3)*

Kelly, T. J. D. 2: v E 1876 (1) 1878 (1)

Kendall, T. 2: v E 1876 (2)

Kippax, A. F. 22: v E 1924 (1) 1928 (5) 1932 (1); v SA 1931 (4); v WI 1930 (5); *v E 1930 (5) 1934 (1)*

Laver, F. 15: v E 1901 (1) 1903 (1); *v E 1899 (4) 1905 (5) 1909 (4)*

Langley, G. 26: v E 1954 (2); v SA 1952 (5); v WI 1951 (5); *v E 1953 (4) 1956 (3)*; *v WI 1955 (4)*; *v In 1956 (2)*; *v P 1956 (1)*

Lee, P. K. 2: v E 1932 (1); v SA 1931 (1)

Lindwall, R. 55: v E 1946 (4) 1950 (5) 1954 (4); v SA 1952 (4); v WI 1951 (5); v In 1947 (5); *v E 1948 (5) 1953 (5) 1956 (4)*; *v SA 1949 (4)*; *v WI 1955 (5)*; *v NZ 1946 (1)*; *v In 1956 (3)*; *v P 1956 (1)*

Love, H. S. 1: v E 1932

Loxton, S. J. 12: v E 1950 (3); v In 1947 (1); *v E 1948 (3)*; *v SA 1949 (5)*

Lyons, J. J. 14: v E 1886 (1) 1891 (3) 1894 (3) 1897 (1); *v E 1888 (1) 1890 (2) 1893 (3)*

Macartney, C. G. 35: v E 1907 (5) 1911 (1) 1920 (2); v SA 1910 (4); *v E 1909 (5) 1912 (3) 1921 (5) 1926 (5)*; *v SA 1912 (3) 1921 (2)*

Mackay, K. 6: *v E 1956 (3)*; *v In 1956 (3)*

Maddocks, L. 7: v E 1954 (3); *v E 1956 (2)*; *v WI 1955 (1)*; *v In 1956 (1)*

Mailey, A. A. 21: v E 1920 (5) 1924 (5); *v E 1921 (3) 1926 (5)*; *v SA 1921 (3)*

Marr, P. 1: v E 1884

Massie, H. H. 9: v E 1881 (4) 1882 (3) 1884 (1); *v E 1882 (1)*

Matthews, T. J. 8: v E 1911 (2); *v E 1912 (3)*; *v SA 1912 (3)*

Mayne, E. R. 4: *v E 1912 (1)*; *v SA 1912 (1) 1921 (2)*

McAlister, P. A. 8: v E 1903 (2) 1907 (4); *v E 1909 (2)*

McCabe, S. J. 39: v E 1932 (5) 1936 (5); v SA 1931 (5); v WI 1930 (5); *v E 1930 (5) 1934 (5) 1938 (4)*; *v SA 1935 (5)*

McCool, C. 14: v E 1946 (5); v In 1947 (3); *v SA 1949 (5)*; *v NZ 1946 (1)*

McCormick, E. L. 12: v E 1936 (4); *v E 1938 (3)*; *v SA 1935 (5)*

McDonald, C. C. (21): v E 1954 (2); v SA 1952 (5); v WI 1951 (1); *v E 1956 (5)*; *v WI 1955 (5)*; *v In 1956 (2)*; *v P 1956 (1)*

McDonald, E. A. 11: v E 1920 (3); *v E 1921 (5)*; *v SA 1921 (3)*

McDonnell, P. S. 19: v E 1881 (4) 1882 (3) 1884 (2) 1886 (2) 1887 (1); *v E 1880 (1) 1884 (3) 1888 (3)*

McLaren, J. W. 1: v E 1911

McLeod, C. E. 17: v E 1894 (1) 1897 (5) 1901 (2) 1903 (3); *v E 1899 (1) 1905 (5)*

McLeod, R. W. 6: v E 1891 (3); *v E 1893 (3)*

Meuleman, K. 1: *v NZ 1946*

Midwinter, W. E. 8: v E 1876 (2) 1882 (1) 1886 (2); *v E 1884 (3)*

Miller, K. R. 55: v E 1946 (5) 1950 (5) 1954 (4); v SA 1952 (4); v WI 1951 (5); v In 1947 (5); *v E 1948 (5) 1953 (5) 1956 (5)*; *v SA 1949 (5)*; *v WI 1955 (5)*; *v NZ 1946 (1)*; *v P 1956 (1)*.

M'Ilwraith, J. 1: *v E 1886*

Minnett, R. B. 9: v E 1911 (5); *v E 1912 (1)*; *v SA 1912 (3)*

M'Kibbin, T. R. 5: v E 1894 (1) 1897 (2); *v E 1896 (2)*

Moroney, J. 7: v E 1950 (1); v WI 1951 (1); *v SA 1949 (5)*

Morris, A. R. 46: v E 1946 (5) 1950 (5) 1954 (4); v SA 1952 (5); v WI 1951 (4); v In 1947 (4); *v E 1948 (5) 1953 (5)*; *v SA 1949 (5)*; *v WI 1955 (4)*.

Morris, S. 1: v E 1884

Moses, H. 6: v E 1886 (2) 1887 (1) 1891 (2) 1894 (1)

Moule, W. H. 1: *v E 1880*

M'Shane, P. G. 3: v E 1884 (1) 1886 (1) 1887 (1)

Murdoch, W. L. 18: v E 1876 (1) 1878 (1) 1881 (4) 1882 (4) 1884 (1); *v E 1880 (1) 1882 (1) 1884 (3) 1890 (2*

Musgrove, H. 1: v E 1884

Nagel, L. E. 1: v E 1932

Nash, L. J. 2: v E 1936 (1); v SA 1931 (1)

Nitschke, H. C. 2: v SA 1931 (2)

Noble, M. A. 42: v E 1897 (4) 1901 (5) 1903 (5) 1907 (5); *v E 1899 (5) 1902 (5) 1905 (5) 1909 (5)*; *v SA 1902 (3)*

Noblet, G. 3: v SA 1952 (1); v WI 1951 (1); *v SA 1949 (1)*

Nothling, O. E. 1: v E 1928

O'Brien, L. P. 5: v E 1932 (2) 1936 (1); *v SA 1935 (2)*

O'Connor, J. A. 4: v E 1907 (3); *v E 1909 (1)*

Oldfield, W. A. 54: v E 1920 (3) 1924 (5) 1928 (5) 1932 (4) 1936 (5); v SA 1931 (5);
    v WI 1930 (5); *v E 1921 (1) 1926 (5) 1930 (5) 1934 (5); v SA 1921 (1) 1935 (5)*
O'Reilly, W. J. 27: v E 1932 (5) 1936 (5); v SA 1931 (2); *v E 1934 (5) 1938 (4);*
    v SA 1935 (5); v NZ 1946 (1)
Oxenham, R. K. 7: v E 1928 (3); v SA 1931 (1); v WI 1930 (3)

Palmer, G. E. 17: v E 1881 (4) 1882 (4) 1884 (2); *v E 1880 (1) 1884 (3) 1886 (3)*
Park, R. L. 1: v E 1920
Pellew, C. E. 10: v E 1920 (4); *v E 1921 (5); v SA 1921 (1)*
Ponsford, W. H. 29: v E 1924 (5) 1928 (2) 1932 (3); v SA 1931 (4); v WI 1930 (5)
    v E 1926 (2) 1930 (4) 1934 (4)
Pope, R. 1: v E 1884

Ransford, V. S. 20: v E 1907 (5) 1911 (5); v SA 1910 (5); *v E 1909 (5)*
Reedman, J. C. 1: v E 1894
Richardson, A. J. 9: v E 1924 (4); *v E 1926 (5)*
Richardson, V. Y. 19: v E 1924 (3) 1928 (2) 1932 (5); *v E 1930 (4); v SA 1935 (5)*
Rigg, K. E. 8: v E 1936 (3); v SA 1931 (4); v WI 1930 (1)
Ring, D. 13: v SA 1952 (5); v WI 1951 (5); v In 1947 (1); *v E 1948 (1) 1953 (1)*
Robertson, W. R. 1: v E 1884
Robinson, R. 1: v E 1936
Rutherford, J. 1: *v I 1956*
Ryder, J. S. 20: v E 1920 (5) 1924 (3) 1928 (5); *v E 1926 (4); v SA 1921 (3)*

Saggers, R. A. 6: *v E 1948 (1); v SA 1949 (5)*
Saunders, J. V. 14: v E 1901 (1) 1903 (2) 1907 (5); *v E 1902 (4); v SA 1902 (2)*
Scott, H. J. H. 8: v E 1884 (2); *v E 1884 (3) 1886 (3)*
Sievers, M. 3: v E 1936 (3)
Slight, J. 1: *v E 1880*
Smith, D. 2: *v E 1912 (2)*
Spofforth, F. R. 18: v E 1876 (1) 1878 (1) 1881 (1) 1882 (4) 1884 (3) 1886 (1);
    v E 1882 (1) 1884 (3) 1886 (3)

Tallon, D. 21: v E 1946 (5) 1950 (5); v In 1947 (5); *v E 1948 (4) 1953 (1);*
    v NZ 1946 (1)
Taylor, J. M. 20: v E 1920 (5) 1924 (5); *v E 1921 (5) 1926 (3); v SA 1921 (2)*
Thompson, N. 2: v E 1876 (2)
Thoms, G. 1: v WI 1951
Thurlow, H. M. 1: v SA 1931
Toshack, E. 12: v E 1946 (5); v In 1947 (2); *v E 1948 (4); v NZ 1946 (1)*
Travers, J. F. 1: v E 1901
Tribe, G. 3: v E 1946 (3)
Trott, A. E. 3: v E 1894 (3)
Trott, G. H. S. 24: v E 1891 (3) 1894 (5) 1897 (5); *v E 1888 (3) 1890 (2) 1893 (3)*
    1896 (3)
Trumble, H. 32: v E 1894 (1) 1897 (5) 1901 (5) 1903 (4); *v E 1890 (2) 1893 (3)*
    1896 (3) 1899 (5) 1902 (3): v SA 1902 (1)
Trumble, J. W. 7: v E 1884 (4); *v E 1886 (3)*
Trumper, V. T. 48: v E 1901 (5) 1903 (5) 1907 (5) 1911 (5); v SA 1910 (5);
    v E 1899 (5) 1902 (5) 1905 (5) 1909 (5); v SA 1902 (3)
Turner, C. T. B. 17: v E 1886 (2) 1887 (1) 1891 (3) 1894 (3); *v E 1888 (3) 1890 (2)*
    1893 (3)

Waite, M. G. 2: *v E 1938 (2)*
Wall, T. W. 18: v E 1928 (1) 1932 (4); v SA 1931 (3); v WI 1930 (1); *v E 1930 (5)*
    1934 (4)
Walters, F. H. 1: v E 1884
Ward, F. 4: v E 1936 (3); *v E 1938 (1)*
Watson, W. 4: v E 1954 (1); *v WI 1955 (3)*
Whitty, W. J. 14: v E 1911 (2); v SA 1910 (5); *v E 1909 (1) 1912 (3); v SA 1912 (3)*
Wilson, J. 1: *v In 1956*
Woodfull, W. M. 35: v E 1928 (5) 1932 (5); v SA 1931 (5); v WI 1930 (5);
    v E 1926 (5) 1930 (5) 1934 (5)
Woods, S. M. J. 3: v *E 1888 (3)*
Worrall, J. 11: v E 1884 (1) 1887 (1) 1894 (1) 1897 (1); *v E 1888 (3) 1899 (4)*

SOUTH AFRICA

Adcock, N. A. T. 14: v E 1956 (5); v NZ 1953 (5); *v E 1955 (4)*
Anderson, J. H. 1: v A 1902
Ashley, W. H. 1: v E 1888

Balaskas, X. C. 9: v E 1930 (2) 1938 (1); v A 1935 (3); *v E 1935 (1)*; *v NZ 1931 (2)*
Baumgartner, H. V. 1: v E 1913
Beaumont, R. 5: v E 1913 (2); *v E 1912 (1)*; *v A 1912 (2)*
Begbie, D. W. 5: v E 1948 (3); v A 1949 (2)
Bell, A. J. 16: v E 1930 (3); *v E 1929 (3) 1935 (3)*; *v A 1931 (5)*; *v NZ 1931 (2)*
Bisset, M. 3: v E 1898 (2) 1909 (1)
Bissett, G. F. 4: v E 1927 (4)
Blanckenberg, J. M. 18: v E 1913 (5) 1922 (5); v A 1921 (3); *v E 1924 (5)*
Bock, E. G. 1: v A 1935
Bond, G. E. 1: v E 1938
Brann, W. H. 3: v E 1922 (3)
Briscoe, A. W. 2: v E 1938 (1); v A 1935 (1)
Brown, L. S. 2: *v A 1931 (1)*; *v NZ 1931 (1)*
Buys, I. D. 1: v E 1922

Cameron, H. B. 26: v E 1927 (5) 1930 (5); *v E 1929 (4) 1935 (5)*; *v A 1931 (5)*; *v NZ 1931 (2)*
Campbell, T. 5: v E 1909 (4); *v E 1912 (1)*
Carter, C. P. 10: v E 1913 (2); v A 1921 (3); *v E 1912 (2) 1924 (3)*
Catterall, R. H. 24: v E 1922 (5) 1927 (5) 1930 (4); *v E 1924 (5) 1929 (5)*
Chapman, H. W. 2: v E 1913 (1); v A 1921 (1)
Cheetham, J. E. 24: v E 1948 (1); v A 1949 (3); v NZ 1953 (5); *v E 1951 (5) 1955 (3)*; *v A 1952 (5)*; *v NZ 1952 (2)*
Christy, J. A. J. 10: v E 1930 (1); *v E 1929 (2)*; *v A 1931 (5)*; *v NZ 1931 (2)*
Chubb, G. W. A. 5: *v E 1951 (5)*
Cochran, J. A. K. 1: v E 1930
Coen, S. K. 2: v E 1927 (2)
Commaille, J. M. 12: v E 1909 (5) 1927 (2); *v E 1924 (5)*
Conyngham, D. P. 1: v E 1922
Cook, F. J. 1: v E 1895
Cooper, A. H. C. 1: v E 1913
Cox, J. L. 3: v E 1913 (3)
Cripps, G. 1: v E 1891
Curnow, S. H. 7: v E 1930 (3); *v A 1931 (4)*
Crisp, R. J. 9: v A 1935 (4); *v E 1935 (5)*

Dalton, E. L. 15: v E 1930 (1) 1938 (4); v A 1935 (1); *v E 1929 (1) 1935 (4)*; *v A 1931 (2)*; *v NZ 1931 (2)*
Davies, E. Q. 5: v E 1938 (3); v A 1935 (2)
Dawson, O. C. 9: v E 1948 (4); *v E 1947 (5)*
Deane, H. G. 17: v E 1927 (5) 1930 (2); *v E 1924 (5) 1929 (5)*
Dixon, C. D. 1: v E 1913
Dower, R. R. 1: v E 1898
Draper, R. 2: v A 1949 (2)
Duckworth, C. A. R. 2: v E 1956 (2)
Duminy, J. P. 3: v E 1927 (2); *v E 1929 (1)*
Dunell, O. R. 2: v E 1888 (2)
Du Toit, J. F. 1: v E 1891
Dyer, D. V. 3: *v E 1947 (3)*

Endean, W. R. 23: v E 1956 (5); v NZ 1953 (5); *v E 1951 (1) 1955 (5)*; *v A 1952 (5)*; *v NZ 1952 (2)*

Faulkner, G. A. 25: v E 1905 (5) 1909 (5); *v E 1907 (3) 1912 (3) 1924 (1)*; *v A 1910 (5) 1912 (3)*
Fichardt, C. G. 2: v E 1891 (1) 1895 (1)
Finlason, C. E. 1: v E 1888
Floquet, C. E. 1: v E 1909

Francis, H. H. 2: v E 1898 (2)
Francois, C. M. 5: v E 1922 (5)
Frank, C. N. 3: v A 1921 (3)
Frank, W. H. B. 1: v E 1895
Fuller, E. R. H. 6: *v E 1955 (2); v A 1952 (2); v NZ 1952 (2)*
Fullerton, G. M. 7: v A 1949 (2); *v E 1947 (2) 1951 (3)*
Funston, K. J. 13: v E 1956 (3); v NZ 1953 (3); *v A 1952 (5); v NZ 1952 (2)*

Gleeson, R. A. 1: v E 1895
Glover, G. K. 1: v E 1895
Goddard, T. L. 10: v E 1956 (5); *v E 1955 (5)*
Gordon, N. 5: v E 1938 (5)
Graham, R. 2: v E 1898 (2)
Grieveson, R. E. 2: v E 1938 (2)

Hall, A. E. 7: v E 1922 (4) 1927 (2) 1930 (1)
Halliwell, E. A. 8: v E 1891 (1) 1895 (3) 1898 (1); v A 1902 (3)
Hands, P. A. M. 7: v E 1913 (5); v A 1921 (1); *v E 1924 (1)*
Hands, R. H. M. 1: v E 1913
Hanley, M. A. 1: v E 1948
Harris, T. A. 3: v E 1948 (1); *v E 1947 (2)*
Hartigan, G. P. D. 5: v E 1912 (3); *v E 1912 (1); v A 1912 (1)*
Harvey, R. L. 2: v A 1935 (2)
Hathorn, M. 12: v E 1905 (5); v A 1902 (3); *v E 1907 (3); v A 1910 (1)*
Hearne, F. 4: v E 1891 (1) 1895 (3)
Hearne, G. A. L. 3: v E 1922 (2): *v F 1924 (1)*
Heine, P. 9: v E 1956 (5); *v E 1955 (4)*
Hime, C. F. W. 1: v E 1895
Hutchinson, P. 2: v E 1888 (2)

Innes, A. R. 2: v E 1888 (2)
Ironside, D. E. J. 3: v NZ 1953 (3)

Johnson, C. L. 1: v E 1895
Jones, P. S. T. 1: v A 1902

Keith, H. J. 8: v E 1956 (3); *v E 1955 (4); v A 1952 (1)*
Kempis, G. A. 1: v E 1888
Kotze, J. J. 3: v A 1902 (2) *v E 1907 (1)*
Kuys, F. 1: v E 1898

Langton, A. B. C. 15: v E 1938 (5); v A 1935 (5); *v E 1935 (5)*
Le Roux, F. le S. 1: v E 1913
Lewis, P. T. 1: v E 1913
Lindsay, J. D. 3: *v E 1947 (3)*
Lindsay, N. V. 1: v A 1921
Ling, W. V. S. 6: v E 1922 (3); v A 1921 (3)
Llewellyn, C. B. 15: v E 1895 (1) 1898 (1); v A 1902 (3); *v E 1912 (3); v A 1910 (5) 1912 (2)*
Lundie, E. B. 1: v E 1913

Mann, N. B. F. 19: v E 1948 (5); v A 1949 (5); *v E 1947 (5) 1951 (4)*
Mansell, P. N. F. 13: *v E 1951 (2) 1955 (4); v A 1952 (5); v NZ 1952 (2)*
Markham, L. A. 1: v E 1948
Marx, W. F. E. 3: v A 1921 (3)
McCarthy, C. N. 15: v E 1948 (5); v A 1949 (5); *v F 1951 (5)*
McGlew, D. J. 19: v E 1956 (1); v NZ 1953 (5); *v E 1951 (2) 1955 (5); v A 1952 (4); v NZ 1952 (2)*
McLean, R. A. 24: v E 1956 (5); v NZ 1953 (4); *v E 1951 (3) 1955 (5); v A 1952 (5); v NZ 1952 (2)*
McMillan, Q. 13: v E 1930 (5); *v E 1929 (2); v A 1931 (4); v NZ 1931 (2)*
Meintjes, D. J. 2: v E 1922 (2)
Melle, M. G. 7: v A 1949 (2); *v E 1951 (1); v A 1952 (4)*

Melville, A. 11: v E 1938 (5) 1948 (1); *v E 1947* (5)
Middleton, J. 6: v E 1895 (2) 1898 (2) ; v A 1902 (2)
Mills, C. 1: v E 1891
Milton, W. H. 3: v E 1888 (2) 1891 (1)
Mitchell, B. 42: v E 1930 (5) 1938 (5) 1948 (5); v A 1935 (5); *v E 1929 (5) 1935 (5) 1947 (5)*; *v A 1931 (5)*; *v NZ 1931 (2)*
Mitchell, F. 3: *v E 1912 (1)*; *v A 1912* (2)
Morkel, D. P. B. 16: v E 1927 (5); *v E 1929* (5); *v A 1931* (5); *v NZ 1931 (1)*
Murray, A. R. A. 10: v NZ 1953 (4); *v A 1952* (4); *v NZ 1952* (2)

Nel, J. 5: v A 1949 (5)
Newberry, C. 4: v E 1913 (4)
Newson, E. S. 3: v E 1930 (1) 1938 (2)
Nicholson, F. 4: v A 1935 (4)
Nicolson, J. F. W. 3: v E 1927 (3)
Norton, N. O. 1: v E 1909
Nourse, A. D. 45: v E 1905 (5) 1909 (5) 1913 (5) 1922 (5); v A 1902 (3) 1921 (3); *v E 1907 (3) 1912 (3) 1924 (5)*; *v A 1910 (5) 1912 (3)*
Nourse, Jnr., A. D. 34: v E 1938 (5) 1948 (5); v A 1935 (5) 1949 (5); *v E 1935 (4) 1947 (5) 1951 (5)*
Nupen, E. P. 17: v E 1922 (4) 1927 (5) 1930 (3); v A 1921 (2) 1935 (1); *v E 1924* (2)

Ochse, A. E. 2: v E 1888 (2)
Ochse, A. L. 3: v E 1927 (1); *v E 1929* (2)
Owen-Smith, H. G. 5: *v E 1929* (5)

Palm, A. W. 1: v E 1927
Parker, G. M. 2: *v E 1924* (2)
Parkin, D. C. 1: v E 1891
Pearse, O. C. 3: *v A 1910* (3)
Pegler, S. J. 16: v E 1909 (1); *v E 1912 (3) 1924 (5)*; *v A 1910 (4) 1912 (3)*
Pithey, A. J. 3: v E 1956 (3)
Plimsoll, J. B. 1: *v E 1947*
Poore, R. M. 3: v E 1895 (3)
Powell, A. W. 1: v E 1898
Prince, C. F. 1: v E 1898
Promnitz, H. L. E. 2: v E 1927 (2)

Quinn, N. A. 12: v E 1930 (1); *v E 1929* (4); *v A 1931* (5); *v NZ 1931* (2)

Reid, N. 1: v A 1921
Richards, A. 1: v E 1895
Richards, W. H. 1: v E 1888
Robertson, J. B. 3: v A 1935 (3)
Routledge, T. 4: v E 1891 (1) 1895 (3)
Rowan, A. M. B. 15: v E 1948 (5); *v E 1947 (5) 1951 (5)*
Rowan, E. A. B. 26: v E 1938 (4) 1948 (4); v A 1935 (3) 1949 (5); *v E 1935 (5) 1951 (5)*
Rowe, G. A. 5: v E 1895 (2) 1898 (2); v A 1902 (1)

Samuelson, S. V. 1: v E 1909
Schwarz, R. O. 20: v E 1905 (5) 1909 (4); *v E 1907 (3) 1912 (1)*: *v A 1910 (5) 1912 (2)*
Seccull, A. W. 1: v E 1895
Shalders, W. A. 12: v E 1898 (1) 1905 (5); v A 1902 (3); *v E 1907* (3)
Shepstone, G. H. 2: v E 1895 (1) 1898 (1)
Sherwell, P. W. 13: v E 1905 (5); *v E 1907 (3)*; *v A 1910* (5)
Siedle, I. J. 18: v E 1927 (1) 1930 (5); v A 1935 (5); *v E 1929 (3) 1935 (4)*
Sinclair, J. H. 25: v E 1895 (3) 1898 (2) 1905 (5) 1909 (4); v A 1902 (3); *v E 1907 (3)*; *v A 1910 (5)*
Smith, C. J. E. 3; v A 1902 (3)
Smith, F. W. 3: v E 1888 (2) 1895 (1)
Smith, V. I. 8: v A 1949 (3); *v E 1947 (4) 1955 (1)*

Snooke, S. D. 1: v E 1907
Snooke, S. J. 26: v E 1905 (5) 1909 (5) 1922 (3); *v E 1907 (3) 1912 (3)*; *v A 1910 (5) 1912 (2)*
Solomon, W. R. 1: v E 1898
Stewart, R. B. 1: v E 1888
Stricker, L. A. 13: v E 1909 (4); *v E 1912 (2)*; *v A 1910 (5) 1912 (2)*
Susskind, M. J. 5: *v E 1924 (5)*

Taberer, H. M. 1: v A 1902
Tancred, A. B. 2: v E 1888 (2)
Tancred, L. J. 14: v E 1905 (5) 1913 (1); v A 1902 (3); *v E 1907 (1) 1912 (2)*; *v A 1912 (2)*
Tancred, V. M. 1: v E 1898
Tapscott, L. E. 2: v E 1922 (2)
Tapscott, L. G. 1: v E 1913

Tayfield, H. J. 27: v E 1956 (5); v A 1949 (5); v NZ 1953 (5); *v E 1955 (5)*; *v A 1952 (5)*; *v NZ 1952 (2)*
Taylor, A. I. 1: v E 1956
Taylor, D. 2: v E 1913 (2)
Taylor, H. W. 42: v E 1913 (5) 1922 (5) 1927 (5) 1930 (4); v A 1921 (3); *v E 1912 (3) 1924 (5) 1929 (3)*; *v A 1912 (3) 1931 (5)*; *v NZ 1931 (1)*
Theunissen, N. H. 1: v E 1888
Thornton, G. 1: v A 1902
Tomlinson, D. S. 1: *v E 1935*
Tuckett, L. 9: v E 1948 (4); *v E 1947 (5)*
Tuckett, L. R. 1: v E 1913

Van der Bijl, P. G. 5: v E 1938 (5)
Van der Merwe, E. A. 2: v A 1935 (1); *v E 1929 (1)*
Van Ryneveld, C. B. 15: v E 1956 (5); v NZ 1953 (5); *v E 1951 (5)*
Viljoen, K. G. 27: v E 1930 (3) 1938 (4) 1948 (2); v A 1935 (4); *v E 1935 (4) 1947 (5)*; *v A 1931 (4)*; *v NZ 1931 (1)*
Vincent, C. L. 25: v E 1927 (5) 1930 (5); *v E 1929 (4)*; *1935 (4)*; *v A 1931 (5)*; *v NZ 1931 (2)*
Vintcent, C. H. 3: v E 1888 (2) 1891 (1)
Vogler, A. E. 15: v E 1905 (5) 1909 (5); *v E 1907 (3)*; *v A 1910 (2)*

Wade, H. F. 10: v A 1935 (5); *v E 1935 (5)*
Wade, W. W. 11: v E 1938 (3) 1948 (5); v A 1949 (3)
Waite, J. H. B. 26: v E 1956 (5); v NZ 1953 (5); *v E 1951 (4) 1955 (5)*; *v A 1952 (5)*; *v NZ 1952 (2)*
Ward, T. A. 23: v E 1913 (5) 1922 (5); v A 1921 (3); *v E 1912 (2) 1924 (5)*; *v A 1912 (3)*
Watkins, J. C. 15: v E 1956 (2); v A 1949 (3); v NZ 1953 (3); *v A 1952 (5)*; *v NZ 1952 (2)*
Westcott, R. J. 3: v NZ 1953 (3)
White, G. C. 17: v E 1905 (5) 1909 (4); *v E 1907 (3) 1912 (2)*; *v A 1912 (3)*
Willoughby, J. T. I. 2: v E 1895 (2)
Wimble, C. S. 1: v E 1891
Winslow, P. 5: v A 1949 (2); *v E 1955 (3)*
Wynne, O. E. 6: v E 1948 (3); v A 1949 (3)

Zulch, J. W. 16: v E 1909 (5) 1913 (3); v A 1921 (3); *v A 1910 (5)*

WEST INDIES

Achong, E. 6: v E 1929 (1) 1934 (2); *v E 1933 (3)*
Alexander, F. C. M. 2: *v E 1957 (2)*
Asgarali, N. 2: *v E 1957 (2)*
Atkinson, D. 21: v E 1953 (4); v A 1955 (4); *v E 1957 (2)*; *v A 1951 (2)*; *v NZ 1951 (1) 1955 (4)*; *v In 1948 (4)*

Barrow, I. 11: v E 1929 (1) 1934 (1); *v E 1933 (3) 1939 (1)*; *v A 1930 (5)*
Bartlett, E. L. 5: *v E 1928 (1)*; *v A 1930 (4)*

Betancourt, N. 1: v E 1929
Binns, A. P. 5: v A 1955 (1); v In 1952 (1); *v NZ 1955 (3)*
Birkett, L. S. 4: *v A 1930 (4)*
Browne, C. R. 4: *v F 1929 (2); v E 1928 (2)*
Butler, L. 1: v A 1955

Caires, F. I. de 3: v E 1929 (3)
Cameron, F. J. 5: *v In 1948 (5)*
Cameron, J. H. 2: *v E 1939 (2)*
Carew, G. 4: v E 1934 (1) 1947 (2); *v In 1948 (1)*
Challenor, G. 3: *v E 1928 (3)*
Christiani, C. M. 4: v E 1934 (4)
Christiani, R. J. 22: v E 1947 (4) 1953 (1); v In 1952 (2); *v E 1950 (4); v A 1951 (5); v NZ 1951 (1); v In 1948 (5)*
Clarke, C. B. 3: *v E 1939 (3)*
Constantine, L. N. 18: v E 1929 (3) 1934 (3); *v E 1928 (3) 1933 (1) 1939 (3); v A 1930 (5)*
Cosra, O. C. da, 5: v E 1929 (1) 1934 (1); *v E 1933 (3)*

Depeiza, C. 5: v A 1955 (3); *v NZ 1955 (2)*
Dewdney, T. 6: v A 1955 (2); *v E 1957 (1); v NZ 1955 (3)*

Ferguson, W. 8: v E 1947 (4) 1953 (1); *v In 1948 (3)*
Fernandes, M. P. 2: v E 1929 (1); *v E 1928 (1)*
Francis, G. N. 10: v E 1929 (1); *v E 1928 (3) 1933 (1); v A 1930 (5)*
Frederick M.: 1 v E 1953
Fuller, R. L. 1: v E 1934
Furlonge, H. 3: v A 1955 (1); *v NZ 1955 (2)*

Ganteaume, A. 1: v E 1947
Gaskin, B. 2: v E 1947 (2)
Gibbs, G. 1: v A 1955
Gilchrist, R. 4: *v E 1957 (4)*
Gladstone, G. 1: v E 1929
Goddard, J. D. 27: v E 1947 (4); *v E 1950 (4) 1957 (5); v A 1951 (4); v NZ 1951 (2) 1955 (3); v In 1948 (5)*
Gomez, G. E. 29: v E 1947 (4) 1953 (4); v In 1952 (4); *v E 1939 (2) 1950 (4); v A 1951 (5); v NZ 1951 (1); v In 1948 (5)*
Grant, G. C. 12: v E 1934 (4); *v E 1933 (3); v A 1930 (5)*
Grant, R. S. 7: v E 1934 (4); *v E 1939 (3)*
Grell, M. 1: v E 1929
Griffith, H. C. 13: v E 1929 (3); *v E 1928 (3) 1933 (2); v A 1930 (5)*
Guillen, S. C. 5: *v A 1951 (3); v NZ 1951 (2)*

Headley, G. 22: v E 1929 (4) 1934 (4) 1947 (1) 1953 (1); *v E 1933 (3) 1939 (3); v A 1930 (5); v In 1948 (1)*
Hoad, E. L. G. 4: v E 1929 (1); *v E 1928 (1) 1933 (2)*
Holt, J. K. 10: v E 1953 (5); v A 1955 (5)
Hunte, E. 2: v E 1929 (2)
Hunte, R. L. 1: v E 1929
Hylton, L. G. 6: v E 1934 (4); *v E 1939 (2)*

Johnson, H. H. 3: v E 1947 (1); *v E 1950 (2)*
Johnson, T. 1: *v E 1939*
Jones, C. M. 4: v E 1929 (1) 1934 (3)
Jones, P. E. 9: v E 1947 (1); *v E 1950 (2); v A 1951 (1); v In 1948 (5)*

Kanhai, Rohan 5: *v E 1957 (5)*
Kentish, E. 2: v E 1947 (1) 1953 (1)
King, F. 14: v E 1953 (3); v A 1955 (4); v In 1952 (5); *v NZ 1955 (2)*

Legall, R. 4: v In 1952 (4)

McWatt, C. A. 6: v E 1953 (5), v A 1955 (1)
Marshall, N. 1: v A 1955
Marshall, R. E. 4: *v A 1951 (2); v NZ 1951 (2)*

Martin, F. R. 9: v E 1929 (1); *v E 1928 (3)*; *v A 1930 (5)*
Martindale, E. A. 10: v E 1934 (4); *v E 1933 (3) 1939 (3)*
Merry, C. A. 2: *v E 1933 (2)*
Miller, R. 1: v In 1952
Moodie, G. H. 1: v E 1934

Neblett, J. 1: v E 1934
Nunes, R. K. 4: v E 1929 (1); *v E 1928 (3)*

Pairaudeau, B. H. 13: v E 1953 (2); v In 1952 (5); *v E 1957 (2)*; *v NZ 1955 (4)*
Passalaique, C. 1: v E 1929
Pierre, L. R. 1: v E 1947

Rae, A. F. 15: v In 1952 (2); *v E 1950 (4)*; *v A 1951 (3)*; *v NZ 1951 (1)*; *v In 1948 (5)*

Ramadhin, S. 33: v E 1953 (5); v A 1955 (4); v In 1952 (4); *v E 1950 (4) 1957 (5);
    v A 1951 (5); v NZ 1951 (2) 1955 (4)*
Rickards, K. 2: v E 1947 (1); *v A 1951 (1)*
Roach, C. A. 16: v E 1929 (4) 1934 (1); *v E 1928 (3) 1933 (3)*; *v A 1930 (5)*
Roberts, A. 1: *v NZ 1955*

St. Hill, E. 2: v E 1929 (2)
St. Hill, W. H. 3: v E 1929 (1); *v E 1928 (2)*
Scott, A. P. H. 1: v In 1952
Scott, O. C. 8: v E 1929 (1); *v E 1928 (2)*; *v A 1930 (5)*
Sealey, B. J. 1: *v E 1933*
Sealy, J. E. D. 11: v E 1929 (2) 1934 (4); *v E 1939 (3)*; *v A 1930 (2)*
Small, J. A. 3: v E 1929 (1); *v E 1928 (2)*
Smith, O. G. 13: v A 1955 (4); *v E 1957 (5)*; *v NZ 1955 (4)*
Sobers, G. 14: v E 1953 (1); v A 1955 (4); *v E 1957 (5)*; *v NZ 1955 (4)*
Stollmeyer, J. B. 32: v E 1947 (2) 1953 (5); v A 1955 (2); v In 1952 (5); *v E 1939
    (3) 1950 (4); v A 1951 (5); v NZ 1951 (1); v In 1948 (4)*
Stollmeyer, V. H. 1: *v E 1939*

Trim, J. 4: v E 1947 (1); *v A 1951 (1)*; *v In 1948 (2)*

Valentine, A. L. 28: v E 1953 (3); v A 1955 (3); v In 1952 (5); *v E 1950 (4) 1957
    (2); v A 1951 (5); v NZ 1951 (2) 1955 (4)*
Valentine, V. A. 2: *v E 1933 (2)*

Walcott, C. L. 38: v E 1947 (4) 1953 (5); v A 1955 (5); v In 1952 (5); *v E 1950
    (4) 1957 (5); v A 1951 (3); v NZ 1951 (2); v In 1948 (5)*
Walcott, L. A. 1: v E 1929
Weekes, E. 43: v E 1947 (4) 1953 (4); v A 1955 (5); v In 1952 (5); *v E 1950 (4)
    1957 (5); v A 1951 (5); v NZ 1951 (2) 1955 (4); v In 1948 (5)*
Weekes, K. H. 2: *v E 1939 (2)*
Wight, C. V. 2: v E 1929 (*1*); *v E 1928 (1)*
Wight, L. 1: v In 1952
Wiles, C. A. 1: *v E 1933*
Williams, E. A. V. 4: v E 1947 (3); *v E 1939 (1)*
Wishart, K. L. 1: v E 1934
Worrell, F. M. 32: v E 1947 (3) 1953 (4); v A 1955 (4); v In 1952 (5); *v E 1950 (4)
    1957 (5); v A 1951 (5); v NZ 1951 (2)*

NEW ZEALAND

Alabaster, J. C. 6: v WI 1955 (1); *v In 1955 (4)*; *v P 1955 (1)*
Allcott, C. F. W. 6: v E 1929 (2); v SA 1931 (1); *v E 1931 (3)*
Anderson, W. M. 1: v A 1946

Badcock, F. T. 7: v E 1929 (3) 1932 (2); v SA 1931 (2)

Barber, R. T. 1: v WI 1955
Beard, D. D. 4: v WI 1951 (2) 1955 (2)
Beck, J. E. F. 8: v WI 1955 (4); *v SA 1953 (4)*
Bell, W. 2: *v SA 1953 (2)*
Blair, R. W. 9: v E 1955 (1); v SA 1952 (2); v WI 1955 (2); *v SA 1953 (2)*
Blunt, R. C. 9: v E 1929 (4); v SA 1931 (2); *v E 1931 (3)*
Burke, C. C. 1: v A 1946
Burtt, T. B. 10: v E 1947 (1) 1950 (2); v SA 1952 (1); v WI 1951 (2); *v E 1949 (4)*
Butterfield, L. A. 1: v A 1946

Cave, H. B. 17: v E 1955 (2); v WI 1955 (3); *v E 1949 (4)*; *v In 1955 (5)*; *v P 1955 (3)*
Chapple, M. E. 8: v E 1955 (1); v SA 1952 (1); v WI 1955 (1); *v SA 1953 (5)*
Cleverley, D. C. 2: v SA 1931 (1); v A 1946 (1)
Colquhoun, I. A. 2: v E 1955 (2)
Cowie, J. 9: v E 1947 (1); v A 1946 (1); *v E 1937 (3) 1949 (4)*
Cresswell, G. F. 3: v E 1950 (2); *v E 1949 (1)*
Cromb, I. B. 5: v SA 1931 (2); *v E 1931 (3)*

Dempster, C. S. 10: v E 1929 (4) 1932 (2); v SA 1931 (2); *v E 1931 (2)*
Dempster, E. W. 5: v SA 1952 (1); *v SA 1953 (4)*
Dickinson, G. R. 3: v E 1929 (2); v SA 1931 (1)
Dunning, J. A. 4: v E 1932 (1); *v E 1937 (3)*
Donnelly, M. P. 7: *v E 1937 (3) 1949 (4)*

Emery, R. W. G. 2: v WI 1951 (2)

Fisher, F. E. 1: v SA 1952
Foley, H. 1: v E 1929
Freeman, D. L. 2: v E 1932 (2)

Gallichan, N. M. 1: *v E 1937*
Guillen, S. C. 3: v WI 1955 (3)
Guy, J. W. 8: v WI 1955 (2); *v In 1955 (5)*; *v P 1955 (1)*

Hadlee, W. A. 11: v E 1947 (1) 1950 (2); v A 1946 (1); *v E 1937 (3) 1949 (4)*
Harford, N. S. 4: *v In 1955 (2)*; *v P 1955 (2)*
Harris, P. G. 3: *v In 1955 (1)*; *v P 1955 (2)*
Hayes, J. A. 11: v E 1950 (2) 1955 (1); v WI 1951 (2); *v In 1955 (5)*; *v P 1955 (1)*
Henderson, M. 1; v E 1929

James, K. C. 11: v E 1929 (4) 1932 (2); v SA 1931 (2); *v E 1931 (3)*

Kerr, J. L. 7: v E 1932 (2); v SA 1931 (1); *v E 1931 (2) 1937 (2)*

Leggat, I. B. 1: *v SA 1953*
Leggat, J. G. 9: v E 1955 (1); v SA 1952 (1); v WI 1951 (1) 1955 (1); *v In 1955 (3)*;
  v P 1955 (2)
Lissette, A. F. 2; v WI 1955 (2)
Lowry, T. C. 7: v E 1929 (4); *v E 1931 (3)*

MacGibbon, A. R. 21: v E 1950 (2) 1955 (2); v SA 1952 (1); v WI 1955 (3); *v
  SA 1953 (5)*; *v In 1955 (5)*; *v P 1955 (3)*
McGirr, H. M. 2: v E 1929 (2)
McGregor, S. N. 13: v E 1955 (2); v WI 1955 (4); *v In 1955 (4)*; *v P 1955 (3)*
McLeod, E. A. 1: v E 1929
McMahon, T. G. 5: v WI 1955 (1); *v In 1955 (3)*; *v P 1955 (1)*
McRae, D. A. N. 1: v A 1946
Maloney, D. A. R. 3: *v E 1937 (3)*
Matheson, A. M. 2: v E 1929 (1); *v E 1931 (1)*
Merritt, W. E. 6: v E 1929 (4); *v E 1931 (2)*
Meuli, E. M. 1: v SA 1952
Miller, L. S. M. 9: v SA 1952 (2); v WI 1955 (3); *v SA 1953 (4)*

Mills, J. W. E. 7: v E 1929 (3) 1932 (1); *v E 1931 (3)*
Moir, A. M. 13: v E 1950 (2) 1955 (2); v SA 1952 (1); v WI 1951 (2) 1955 (1); *v In 1955 (2); v P 1955 (3)*
Mooney, F. L. H. 14: v E 1950 (2); v SA 1952 (2); v WI 1951 (2); *v E 1949 (3); v SA 1953 (5)*

Newman, J. 3: v E 1932 (2); v SA 1931 (1)

Overton, G. W. F. 3: *v SA 1953 (3)*

Page, M. L. 14: v E 1929 (4) 1932 (2); v SA 1931 (2); *v E 1931 (3) 1937* (3)
Petrie, E. C. 4: *v In 1955 (2); v P 1955 (2)*
Poore, M. B. 14: v E 1955 (1); v SA 1952 (1); *v SA 1953 (5); v In 1955 (4); v P 1955 (3)*

Rabone, G. O. 12: v E 1955 (2); v SA 1952 (1); v WI (1951 (2); *v E 1949 (4); v SA 1953 (3)*
Reid, J. R. 27: v E 1950 (2) 1955 (2); v SA 1952 (2); v WI 1951 (2) 1955 (4); *v E 1949 (2); v SA 1953 (5); v In 1955 (5); v P 1955 (3)*
Roberts, A. W. 5: v E 1929 (1); v SA 1931 (2); *v E 1937 (2)*
Rowe, C. G. 1: v A 1946

Scott, R. H. 1: v E 1947
Scott, V. J. 10: v E 1947 (1) 1950 (2); v A 1946 (1); v WI 1951 (2); *v E 1949 (4)*
Sinclair, I. M. 2: v WI 1955 (2)
Smith, D. 1: v E 1932
Smith, F. B. 4: v E 1947 (1); v WI 1951 (1); *v E 1949 (2)*
Snedden, C. A. 1: v E 1947
Sutcliffe, B. 28: v E 1947 (1) 1950 (2) 1955 (2); v SA 1952 (2); v WI 1951 (2) 1955 (2); *v E 1949 (4); v SA 1953 (5); v In 1955 (5); v P 1955 (3)*

Taylor, D. D. 3: v E 1947 (1); v WI 1955 (2)
Tindill, E. W. 5: v E 1947 (1); v A 1946 (1); *v E 1937 (3)*

Vivian, H. G. 7: v E 1932 (1); v SA 1931 (1); *v E 1931 (2) 1937 (3)*

Wallace, W. M. 13: v E 1947 (1) 1950 (2); v A 1946 (1); v SA 1952 (2); *v E 1937 (3) 1949 (4)*
Watt, L. A. 1: v E 1955
Weir, G. L. 11: v E 1929 (3) 1932 (2); v SA 1931 (2); *v E 1931 (3) 1937 (1)*
Whitelaw, D. 2: v E 1932 (2)

INDIA

Adhikari, H. R. 20: v E 1951 (3); v A 1956 (2); v WI 1948 (5); v P 1952 (2); *E 1952 (3); v A 1947 (5).*
Ali, S. Nazir, 2: v E 1933 (1); *v E 1932 (1)*
Ali, S. Wazir, 7: v E 1933 (3); *v E 1932 (1) 1936 (3)*
Amarnath, L. 24: v E 1933 (3) 1951 (3); v WI 1948 (5); v P 1952 (5); *v E 1946 (3); v A 1947 (5)*
Amar Singh 7: v E 1933 (3); *v E 1932 (1) 1936 (3)*
Amir Elahi 1: *v A 1947*
Apte, M. L. 7: v P 1952 (2); *v WI 1952 (5)*

Banerjee, S. N. 1: v WI 1948
Banerjee, Sunil, 1: v WI 1948
Bhandari, P. 3: v A 1956 (1); v NZ 1955 (1); *v P 1954 (1).*

Chowdhury, N. 2: v E 1951 (1); **v WI 1948 (1)**
Colah, S. H. M. 2: v E 1933 (1); *v E 1932 (1)*
Contractor, N. J. 5: v A 1956 (1); v NZ 1955 (4)

Dani, H. T. 1: v P 1952
Divecha, R. V. 5: v E 1951 (2); v P 1952 (1); *v E 1952 (2)*

Gadkari, C. V. 6: *v WI 1952 (3); v P 1954 (3)*
Gaekwad, D. K. 5: v P 1952 (2); *v E 1952 (1); v WI 1952 (2)*
Gaekwad, H. G. 1: v P 1952
Ghorpade, J. M. 4: v A 1956 (1); v NZ 1955 (1); *v WI 1952 (2)*.
Ghulam Ahmed 20: v E 1951 (2); v A 1956 (2); v WI 1948 (3); v NZ 1955 (1); v P 1952 (4); *v E 1952 (4); v P 1954 (4)*
Gopalan, M. 1: v E 1933
Gopinath, C. D. 7: v E 1951 (3); v P. 1952 (1); *v E 1952 (1); v P 1954 (2)*
Gul Mahomed 8: v P 1952 (2); *v E 1946 (1); v A 1947 (5)*
Gupte, S. P. 20: v E 1951 (1); v A 1956 (3); v NZ 1955 (5); v P 1952 (2); *v WI 1952 (5); v P 1954 (5)*

Hafeez, A. 3: *v E 1946 (3)*
Hazare, V. S. 30: v E 1951 (5); v WI 1948 (5); v P 1952 (3); *v E 1946 (3) 1952 (4); v A 1947 (5); v WI 1952 (5)*
Hindlekar, D. D. 4: *v E 1936 (1) 1946 (3)*
Hussain, Dilawar, 3: v E 1933 (2); *v E 1936 (1)*

Ibrahim, K. C. 4: v WI 1948 **(4)**
Irani, J. K. 2: *v A 1947 (2)*

Jai, L. P. 1: v E 1933
Jamshedji, R. J. 1: v E 1933
Jahangir Khan, M. 4: *v E 1932 (1) 1936 (3)*
Jilani, M. Baqa, 1: *v E 1936*
Joshi, P. G. 6: v E 1951 (2); v P 1952 (1); *v WI 1952 (3)*

Kardar, A. H., *see* Hafeez
Kishenchand G. 5: v P 1952 (1); *v A 1947 (4)*
Kripal Singh 6: v A 1956 (2); v NZ 1955 (4)

Lall Singh 1: *v E 1932*

Maka, E. S. 2: v P 1952 (1); *v WI 1952 (1)*
Mankad, V. 42: v E 1951 (5); v A 1956 (3); v WI 1948 (5); v NZ 1955 (4); v P 1952 (4); *v E 1946 (3) 1952 (3); v A 1947 (5); v WI 1952 (5); v P 1954 (5)*
Manjrekar, V. L. 26: v E 1951 (2); v A 1956 (3); v NZ 1955 (5); v P 1952 (3); *v E 1952 (4); v WI 1952 (4); v P 1954 (5)*
Mantri, M. K. 4: v E 1951 (1); *v E 1952 (2); v P 1954 (1)*
Meherhomji, K. R. 1: *v E 1936*
Mehra, V. 2: v NZ 1955 (2)
Merchant, V. M. 10; v E 1933 (3) 1951 (1); *v E 1936 (3) 1946 (3)*
Modi, R. S. 10: v E 1951 (1); v WI 1948 (5); v P 1952 (1); *v E 1946 (3)*
Mushtaq Ali 11: v E 1933 (2) 1951 (1); v WI 1948 (3); *v E 1936 (3) 1946 (2)*

Naoomal Jeoomal 3: v E 1933 (2); *v E 1932 (1)*
Nadkarni, R. G. 1: v NZ 1955
Navle, J. G. 2: v E 1933 (1); *v E 1932 (1)*
Nayudu, C. K. 7: v E 1933 (3); *v E 1932 (1) 1936 (3)*
Nayudu, C. S. 11: v E 1933 (2) 1951 (1); *v E 1936 (2) 1946 (2); v A 1947 (4)*
Nissar. Mahomed 6: v E 1933 (2); *v E 1932 (1) 1936 (3)*
Nyalchand, K. 1: v P 1952

Palia, P. E. 2: *v E 1932 (1) 1936 (1)*
Patankar, C. T. 1: v NZ 1955
Pataudi, Nawab of, 3: *v E 1946 (3)*
Patel, J. S. 4: v A 1956 (2); v NZ 1955 (1); *v P 1954 (1)*
Patil, S. R.: 1 v NZ 1955
Patiala, Yuvraj of. 1: v E 1933

Phadkar, D. G. 30: v E 1951 (4); v A 1956 (1); v WI 1948 (4); v NZ 1955 (4); v P 1952 (2); *v E 1952 (4)*; *v A 1947 (4)*; *v WI 1952 (4)*; *v P 1954 (3)*
Punjabi, P. L. 5: *v P 1954 (5)*

Rai Singh 1: *v A 1947*
Rajindernath, V. 1: v P 1952
Ramaswami, C. 2: *v E 1936 (2)*
Ramchand, G. S. 25: v A 1956 (3); v NZ 1955 (5); v P 1952 (3); *v E 1952 (4)*; *v WI 1952 (5)*; *v P 1954 (5)*
Ramji, L. 1: v E 1933
Rangachari, C. 4: v WI 1948 (2); *v A 1947 (2)*
Rangnekar, K. M. 3: *v A 1947 (3)*
Rege, M. 1: v WI 1948
Roy, P. 27: v E 1951 (5); v A 1956 (3); v NZ 1955 (3); v P 1952 (3); *v E 1952 (4)*: *v WI 1952 (4)*; *v P 1954 (5)*]

Sarwate, C. T. 9: v E 1951 (1); v WI 1948 (2); *v E 1946 (1)*; *v A 1947 (5)*
Sen, P. 14: v E 1951 (2); v WI 1948 (5); v P 1952 (2); *v E 1952 (2)*; *v A 1947* **(3)**
Shinde, S. G. 7: v E 1951 (3) v WI 1948 (1); *v E 1946 (1) 1952 (2)*
Shodhan, D. H. 3: v P 1952 (1); *v WI 1952 (2)*
Sohoni, S. W. 4: v E 1951 (1): *v E 1946 (2)*; *v A 1947 (1)*
Sunderram, G. 2: v NZ 1955 (2)
Swamy, V (1): v NZ 1955

Tamhane, N. S. 12: v A 1956 (3); v NZ 1955 (4); *v P 1954 (5)*
Tarpore, K. 1: v WI 1948

Umrigar, P. R. 33: v E 1951 (5); v A 1956 (3); v WI 1948 (1); v NZ 1955 (5); v P 1952 (5); *v E 1952 (4)*; *v WI 1952 (5)*, *v P 1954 (5)*

Vizianagram, Maharaj Sir Vijaya, 3: *v E 1936* **(3)**

Note.—Hafeez, on going later to Oxford University, took his correct name, Kardar.

PAKISTAN

Agha Saadat Ali 1: v NZ 1955
Alim-ud-Din 12: v A 1956 (1); v NZ 1955 (3); v In 1954 (5); *v E 1954 (3)*
Amir Elahi 5: *v In 1952 (5)*
Anwar Hussain 4: *v In 1952 (4)*

Fazal Mahmood 16: v A 1956 1); v NZ 1955 (2); v In 1954 (4); *v E 1954 (4)*; *v In 1952 (5)*

Ghazali, M. E. Z. 2: *v E 1954 (2)*
Gul Mahomed 1: v A 1956

Hanif Mohammad 18: v A 1956 (1): v NZ 1955 (3); v In 1954 (5); *v E 1954 (4)*; *v In 1952 (5)*

Imtiaz Ahmed 18: v A 1956 (1); v NZ 1955 (3); v In 1954 (5); *v E 1954 (4); v In 1952 (5)*
Israr Ali 2: *v In 1952 (2)*

Kardar, A. H. 18: v A 1956 (1); v NZ 1955 (3); v In 1954 (5); *v E 1954 (4)*; *v In 1952 (5)*
Khalid Hassan 1: *v E 1954*
Khalid Wazir 2: *v E 1954 (2)*
Khan Mohammad 11: v A 1956 (1); v NZ 1955 (3); v In 1954 (4); *v E 1954 (2)*; *v In 1952 (1)*

Mahmood Hussain 12: v NZ 1955 (1); v In 1954 (5); *v E 1954 (2)*; *v In 1952 (4)*
Maqsood Ahmed 16: v NZ 1955 (2); v In 1954 (5); *v E 1954 (4)*; *v In 1952 (5)*
Mathias, W. 1: v NZ 1955
Miran Bux 2: v In 1954 (2)
Mohammad Aslam 1: *v E 1954*

Nazar Mohammad 5: *v In 1952 (5)*

Shuja-ud-Din 11: v NZ 1955 (3); v In 1954 (5); *v E 1954 (3)*

Wallis Mathias 2: v NZ 1955 (1); v A 1956 (1)
Waqar Hassan 18: v A 1956 (1); v NZ 1955 (3); v In 1954 (5); *v E 1954 (4)*; *v In 1952(5)*
Wazir Mohammad 10: v A 1956 (1); v NZ 1955 (1); v In 1954 (5); *v E 1954 (2)*; *v In 1952 (1)*

Zulfiqar Ahmed 9: v A 1956 (1); v NZ 1955 (3); *v E 1954 (2); v In 1952 (3)*

Twelve cricketers have appeared for two countries in Test Matches, namely:

W. E. Midwinter, for England v. Australia and for Australia v. England; J. J. Ferris, W. L. Murdoch, A. E. Trott and S. M. J. Woods, for Australia v. England and for England v. South Africa; F. Mitchell played for England v. South Africa and for South Africa v. England and v. Australia; F. Hearne played for England v. South Africa and for South Africa v. England; Nawab of Pataudi played for England v. Australia and for India v. England; A. H. Kardar (Hafeez) played for India v England and for Pakistan v England, India, Australia and New Zealand; Amir Elahi played for India v. Australia and for Pakistan v India; S. Guillen played for West Indies against Australia and New Zealand and for New Zealand against West Indies; Gul Mahomed played for India against England, Australia and Pakistan and for Pakistan against Australia.

CRICKET RECORDS

AMENDED BY G. A. COPINGER TO SEPTEMBER 1957

Unless otherwise stated, all records, apart from Throwing the Cricket Ball, apply only to first-class cricket.

* denotes "not out" or an unfinished partnership.

(A), (S.A.), (W.I.), (N.Z.), (I) or (P) indicates either the nationality of the player, or the country in which the record was made.

INDEX

BATTING

BOWLING AND FIELDING

THE SIDES

TEST MATCH RECORDS

INDIVIDUAL SCORES OF 300 OR MORE

452*	D. G. Bradman, New South Wales v. Queensland, at Sydney ..	1929–30
443*	B. B. Nimbalkar, Maharashtra v. Western India States, at Poona	1948–49
437	W. H. Ponsford, Victoria v. Queensland, at Melbourne ..	1927–28
429	W. H. Ponsford, Victoria v. Tasmania, at Melbourne	1922–23
424	A. C. MacLaren, Lancashire v. Somerset, at Taunton	1895
385	B. Sutcliffe, Otago v. Canterbury, at Christchurch	1952–53
383	C. W. Gregory, New South Wales v. Queensland, at Brisbane ..	1906–07
369	D. G. Bradman, South Australia v. Tasmania, at Adelaide ..	1935–36
365*	C. Hill, South Australia v. New South Wales, at Adelaide ..	1900–01
364†	L. Hutton, England v. Australia, at The Oval	1938
359*	V. M. Merchant, Bombay v. Maharashtra, at Bombay ..	1943–44
357*	R. Abel, Surrey v. Somerset, at The Oval	1899
357	D. G. Bradman, South Australia v. Victoria, at Melbourne ..	1935–36
355	B. Sutcliffe, Otago v. Auckland, at Dunedin	1949–50
352	W. H. Ponsford, Victoria v. New South Wales, at Melbourne ..	1926–27
345	C. G. Macartney, Australia v. Nottinghamshire, at Nottingham	1921
344*	G. Headley, All Jamaica v. Lord Tennyson's Team, at Kingston	1931–32
344	W. G. Grace, M.C.C. v. Kent, at Canterbury	1876
343*	P. A. Perrin, Essex v. Derbyshire, at Chesterfield	1904
341	G. H. Hirst, Yorkshire v. Leicestershire, at Leicester ..	1905
340*	D. G. Bradman, New South Wales v. Victoria, at Sydney ..	1928–29
338*	R. C. Blunt, Otago v. Canterbury, at Christchurch	1931–32
338	W. W. Read, Surrey v. Oxford University, at The Oval ..	1888
336*	W. H. Ponsford, Victoria v. South Australia, at Melbourne ..	1927–28
336*	W. R. Hammond, England v. New Zealand, at Auckland ..	1932–33
334	D. G. Bradman, Australia v. England, at Leeds	1930

† Hutton batted 13 hours 20 minutes—the longest innings in first-class cricket.

333	K. S. Duleepsinhji, Sussex v. Northamptonshire, at Hove	..	1930
332	W. H. Ashdown, Kent v. Essex, at Brentwood		1934
331*	J. D. Robertson, Middlesex v. Worcestershire, at Worcester	..	1949
325*	H. L. Hendry, Victoria v. New Zealand, at Melbourne	..	1925–26
325	C. L. Badcock, South Australia v. Victoria, at Adelaide	..	1935–36
325	A. Sandham, England v. West Indies, at Kingston	..	1929–30
324	J. B. Stollmeyer, Trinidad v. British Guiana, at Port of Spain	..	1946–47
322	E. Paynter, Lancashire v. Sussex, at Hove		1937
321	W. L. Murdoch, New South Wales v. Victoria, at Sydney	..	1881–82
319	Gul Mahomed, Baroda v. Holkar, at Baroda	..	1946–7
318*	W. G. Grace, Gloucestershire v. Yorkshire, at Cheltenham	..	1876
317	W. R. Hammond, Gloucestershire v. Notts, at Gloucester	..	1936
316*	V. S. Hazare, Maharashtra v. Baroda, at Poona	..	1939–40
316*	J. B. Hobbs, Surrey v. Middlesex, at Lord's		1926
316	R. H. Moore, Hampshire v. Warwickshire, at Bournemouth		1937
315*	T. Hayward, Surrey v. Lancashire, at The Oval	..	1898
315*	P. Holmes, Yorkshire v. Middlesex, at Lord's	..	1925
315*	A. F. Kippax, New South Wales v. Queensland, at Sydney	..	1927–28
314*	C. L. Walcott, Barbados v. Trinidad, at Port of Spain	..	1945–46
313	H. Sutcliffe, Yorkshire v. Essex, at Leyton	..	1932
312*	W. W. Keeton, Nottinghamshire v. Middlesex, at The Oval‡		1939
311	J. T. Brown, Yorkshire v. Sussex, at Sheffield	..	1897
310	H. Gimblett, Somerset v. Sussex, at Eastbourne	..	1948
309	V. S. Hazare, The Rest v. Hindus, at Brabourne Stadium	..	1943–44
308*	F. M. Worrell, Barbados v. Trinidad, at Bridgetown	..	1943–44
306*	A. Ducat, Surrey v. Oxford University, at The Oval	..	1919
306*	F. A. B. Rowan, Transvaal v. Natal, at Johannesburg	..	1939–40
305*	F. E. Woolley, M.C.C. v. Tasmania, at Hobart	..	1911–12
305*	F. R. Foster, Warwickshire v. Worcestershire, at Dudley	..	1914
305*	W. H. Ashdown, Kent v. Derbyshire, at Dover	..	1935
304*	P. H. Tarilton, Barbados v. Trinidad, at Bridgetown	..	1919–20
304*	A. D. Nourse, sen., Natal v. Transvaal, at Johannesburg	..	1919–20
304*	E. D. Weekes, West Indies v. Cambridge University, at Cambridge		1950
304	R. M. Poore, Hampshire v. Somerset, at Taunton	..	1899
304	D. G. Bradman, Australia v. England, at Leeds	..	1934
303*	W. W. Armstrong, Australia v. Somerset, at Bath	..	1905
302*	P. Holmes, Yorkshire v. Hampshire, at Portsmouth	..	1920
302*	W. R. Hammond, Gloucestershire v. Glamorgan, at Bristol	..	1934
302	W. R. Hammond, Gloucestershire v. Glamorgan, at Newport	..	1939
301	W. G. Grace, Gloucestershire v. Sussex, at Bristol	..	1896
301*	E. Hendren, Middlesex v. Worcestershire, at Dudley		1933
300*	Imtiaz Ahmed, Prime Minister's XI v. Commonwealth XI, at Bombay	..	1950–51
300*	V. T. Trumper, Australia v. Sussex, at Hove	..	1899
300*	F. Watson, Lancashire v. Surrey, at Manchester	..	1928
300	J. T. Brown, Yorkshire v. Derbyshire, at Chesterfield	..	1898
300	D. C. S. Compton, M.C.C. v. N.E. Transvaal, at Benoni	..	1948–49

HIGHEST FOR TEAMS

INDIVIDUAL SCORES

FOR ENGLISH TEAMS IN AUSTRALIA

305*	F. E. Woolley, M.C.C. v. Tasmania, at Hobart	..	..	1911–12
287	R. E. Foster, England v. Australia, at Sydney	..	..	1903–04

AGAINST AUSTRALIANS IN ENGLAND

364	L. Hutton, for England v. Australia, at The Oval (in any match)	1938
219	A. Sandham, for Surrey, at The Oval (record for any county) ..	1934

FOR AUSTRALIAN TEAMS IN ENGLAND

345	C. G. Macartney, v. Nottinghamshire, at Nottingham	..	..	1921
334	D. G. Bradman, Australia v. England, at Leeds ..	..	..	1930

AGAINST ENGLISH TEAMS IN AUSTRALIA

280 A. J. Richardson, South Australia v. M.C.C., at Adelaide .. 1922–23
270 D. G. Bradman, Australia v. England, at Melbourne (in any
     home Test) 1936–37

FOR EACH FIRST-CLASS COUNTY

Derbyshire	..	274 G. Davidson, v. Lancashire, at Manchester	.. 1896
Essex	..	343* P. A. Perrin, v. Derbyshire, at Chesterfield	.. 1904
Glamorgan	..	287* E. Davies, v. Gloucestershire, at Newport	.. 1939
Gloucestershire	..	318* W. G. Grace, v. Yorkshire, at Cheltenham	.. 1876
Hampshire	..	316 R. H. Moore, v. Warwickshire, at Bournemouth	.. 1937
Kent	..	332 W. H. Ashdown, v. Essex, at Brentwood	.. 1934
Lancashire	..	424 A. C. MacLaren, v. Somerset, at Taunton	.. 1895
Leicestershire	..	252* S. Coe, v. Northamptonshire, at Leicester	.. 1914
Middlesex	..	331* J. D. Robertson, v. Worcestershire, at Worcester	.. 1949
Northamptonshire	..	260* R. Subba Row, v. Lancashire, at Northampton	.. 1955
Nottinghamshire	..	312* W. W. Keeton, v. Middlesex, at The Oval‡	.. 1939
Somerset	..	310 H. Gimblett, v. Sussex, at Eastbourne	.. 1948
Surrey	..	357* R. Abel, v. Somerset, at The Oval	.. 1899
Sussex	..	333 K. S. Duleepsinhji, v. Northants, at Hove	.. 1930
Warwickshire	..	305* F. R. Foster, v. Worcestershire, at Dudley	.. 1914
Worcestershire	..	276 F. L. Bowley, v. Hampshire, at Dudley	.. 1914
Yorkshire	..	341 G. H. Hirst, v. Leicestershire, at Leicester	.. 1905

‡ On this date Eton played Harrow at Lord's.

HIGHEST IN A MINOR COUNTY MATCH

323* F. E. Lacey, Hampshire v. Norfolk, at Southampton 1887

HIGHEST IN MINOR COUNTIES CHAMPIONSHIP

282 F. Garnet, Berkshire v. Wiltshire, at Reading 1908
254 H. E. Morgan, Glamorgan v. Monmouthshire, at Cardiff .. 1901
253* G. J. Whittaker, Surrey II v. Gloucestershire II, at The Oval .. 1950
253 A. Booth, Lancashire II v. Lincolnshire II, at Grimsby .. 1950
252 †J. A. Deed, Kent II v. Surrey II, at The Oval 1924
† On debut.

HIGHEST IN AN IMPORTANT SCHOOL MATCH IN ENGLAND

278 J. L. Guise, Winchester v. Eton, at Eton 1921

HIGHEST IN OTHER MATCHES

628* A. E. J. Collins, Clarke's House v. North Town, at Clifton College.
     (A Junior House match. His innings of 6 hours 50 minutes was
     spread over five afternoons) 1899
566 C. J. Eady, Break-o'-Day v. Wellington, at Hobart .. 1901–02
506* J. C. Sharp, Melbourne G.S. v. Geelong Coll., at Melbourne .. 1914–15
485 A. E. Stoddart, Hampstead v. Stoics, at Hampstead .. 1886
466* G. T. S. Stevens, Beta v. Lambda (University College School House
     Match), at Neasden 1919
459 J. A. Prout, Wesley Coll. v. Geelong Coll., at Geelong .. 1908–09
438 W. W. Armstrong, Melbourne v. Melbourne University, at
     Melbourne 1903–04
419* J. S. Carrick, West of Scotland v. Priory Park, at Chichester .. 1885
417* J. Worrall, Carlton v. Melbourne University .. 1895–96
415* W. N. Roe, Emmanuel College, L.V.C. v. Caius College L.V.C.,
     at Cambridge 1881
412* M. I. Yusef, Government Indian School v. Star Club, at Bulawayo 1936–37
404* E. F. S. Tylecote, Classical v. Modern, at Clifton College .. 1868
402* A. H. Du Boulay, School of Military Engineering v. Royal Navy
     and Royal Marines, at Chatham 1907

HUNDRED ON DEBUT IN ENGLAND

(The following list does not include instances of players who have previously appeared in first-class cricket outside England.)

114	F. H. Bacon, Hampshire v. Warwickshire, at Birmingham ..	1894
107*	G. Barker, Essex v. Canadians, at Clacton	1954
116*	B. L. Bisgood, Somerset v. Worcestershire, at Worcester ..	1907
107*	H. O. Bloomfield, Surrey v. Northamptonshire, at Northampton..	1921
124	G. J. Bryan, Kent v. Nottinghamshire, at Nottingham ..	†1920
100	J. F. Byrne, Warwickshire v. Leicestershire, at Birmingham	1897
118	A. P. F. Chapman, Cambridge University v. Essex, at Cambridge	1920
101*	S. H. Day, Kent v. Gloucestershire, at Cheltenham ..	†1897
176	F. C. de Saram, Oxford University v. Gloucestershire, at Oxford	1934
108	E. W. Dillon, London County v. Worcestershire, at Crystal Palace	1900
215*	G. H. G. Doggart, Cambridge University v. Lancashire, at Cambridge	1948
137	C. H. M. Ebden, Camb. U. v. Leveson Gower's XI, at Cambridge	1902
108	A. Fairbairn, Middlesex v. Somerset, at Taunton	†‡1947
123	H. Gimblett, Somerset v. Essex, at Frome	1935
101	P. M. Hall, Oxford University v. Free Foresters, at Oxford ..	1919
121	C. P. Hamilton, Army v. West Indies, at Aldershot ..	1933
156	M. N. Harbottle, Army v. Oxford University, at Camberley ..	1938
124	P. Hearn, Kent v. Warwickshire, at Gillingham	1947
101	K. A. Higgs, Sussex v. Worcestershire, at Hove	1920
103*	A. L. Hilder, Kent v. Essex, at Gravesend	†1924
158*	J. H. Human, Camb. U. v. Leveson Gower's XI, at Eastbourne ..	1932
111*	C. F. H. Leslie, Oxford U., v. M.C.C. and Ground, at Oxford	1881
108	A. C. MacLaren, Lancashire v. Sussex, at Hove ..	1890
144	F. W. Marlow, Sussex v. M.C.C. and Ground, at Lord's ..	1891
124	N. Miller, Surrey v. Sussex, at Hove	1899
100*	W. Murray Wood, Oxford University v. Gloucestershire, at Oxford	1936
164	M. Nichol, Worcestershire v. West Indies, at Worcester ..	1928
101	C. A. L. Payne, M.C.C. and Ground v. Derbyshire, at Lord's ..	1905
138*	F. B. Pinch, Glamorgan v. Worcestershire, at Swansea ..	1921
124	H. C. Pretty, Surrey v. Nottinghamshire, at The Oval ..	1899
149	H. R. J. Rhys, Free Foresters v. Cambridge U., at Cambridge	1929
195*	J. Ricketts, Lancashire v. Surrey, at The Oval	1867
137	J. G. C. Scott, Sussex v. Oxford University, at Eastbourne ..	1907
135	J. K. E. Slack, Cambridge University v. Middlesex, at Cambridge..	1954
141	F. W. Stocks, Nottinghamshire v. Kent, at Nottingham ..	1946
110	Hon. L. H. Tennyson, M.C.C. and Ground v. Oxford U., at Lord's	†1913
103	A. H. Trevor, Sussex v. Kent, at Hove	†1880
125	G. S. Tuck, Royal Navy v. New Zealanders, at Portsmouth ..	1927
100*	C. Tyson, Yorkshire v. Hampshire, at Southampton ..	1921
102	I. D. Walker, Middlesex v. Surrey at The Oval	1862
131*	R. Whitehead, Lancashire v. Nottinghamshire, at Manchester ..	1908
117*	E. R. Wilson, A. J. Webbe's XI v. Cambridge U., at Cambridge	1899
124	L. Winslow, Sussex v. Gloucestershire, at Hove	1875

A number of players abroad have also made a century on a first appearance.

The highest innings on debut was hit by W. F. E. Marx when he made 240 for Transvaal against Griqualand West at Johannesburg in 1920-21.

The following feats stand alone for a cricketer making two separate hundreds on debut: A. R. Morris, New South Wales, 148 and 111 against Queensland in 1940-41, and N. J. Contractor, Gujerat, 152 and 102 not out against Baroda in 1952-53.

† In second innings. S. H. Day, schoolboy at Malvern, aged 18.
‡ A. Fairbairn (Middlesex) in 1947 scored centuries in the second innings of his first two matches in first-class cricket: 108 Middlesex v. Somerset, at Taunton; 110* Middlesex v. Nottinghamshire, at Nottingham.

MOST INDIVIDUAL HUNDREDS

(35 OR MORE)

	Hundreds Total	Abr'd	100th 100		Hundreds Total	Abr'd	100th 100
J. B. Hobbs ...	197	22	1923	W. G. Grace ..	126	1	1895
E. Hendren	170	19	1928	D. C. S. Compton	122	30	1952
W. R. Hammond	167	33	1935	D. G. Bradman	117	76	1947–8
C. P. Mead	153	8	1927	A. Sandham ..	107	20	1935
H. Sutcliffe	149	14	1932	T. Hayward ...	104	4	1913
F. E. Woolley ..	145	10	1929	L. E. G. Ames ..	102	13	1950
L. Hutton	129	24	1951	E. Tyldesley ..	102	8	1934

J. W. Hearne	96	A. E. Dipper......	53	James Langridge ..	42
C. B. Fry	94	G. L. Jessop	53	H. W. Parks	42
J. T. Tyldesley ...	86	James Seymour ...	53	T. F. Shepherd ...	42
W. J. Edrich	85	E. H. Bowley	52	V. T. Trumper	42
R. E. S. Wyatt ...	85	A. Ducat	52	J. Gunn	41
J. Hardstaff, junr...	83	D. Kenyon	51	K. R. Miller	41
M. Leyland	80	W. W. Whysall....	51	A. D. Nourse, junr.	41
John Langridge ..	76	G. Cox, junr.....	50	J. H. Parks	41
H. T. W. Hardinge	75	H. E. Dollery	50	W. H. Ashdown ...	39
C. Washbrook ...	75	H. Gimblett	50	W. A. Brown	39
R. Abel	74	V. S. Hazare	50	R. J. Gregory	39
J. O'Connor	72	F. Watson	50	W. R. D. Payton..	39
W. G. Quaife	72	K. S. Duleepsinhji	49	F. Bowley	38
K. S. Ranjitsinhji..	72	W. M. Woodfull ..	49	J. F. Crapp	38
A. C. Russell	71	C. J. Barnett	48	A. D. Nourse, senr.	38
D. Denton	69	W. Gunn	48	N. Oldfield	38
T. W. Graveney ..	68	E. G. Hayes	48	Rev. J. H. Parsons..	38
D. Brookes	67	C. G. Macartney..	48	W. W. Read	38
P. Holmes	67	A. C. Maclaren ..	47	J. Sharp	38
J. D. Robertson ..	67	W. H. Ponsford ..	47	Rev. D. S. Sheppard	38
P. A. Perrin	66	R. N. Harvey	46	L. J. Todd	38
P. B. H. May	63	J. Iddon	46	J. Arnold	37
G. Gunn	62	A. R. Morris	46	G. Brown	37
G. H. Hirst	60	W. W. Armstrong ..	45	H. W. Lee	37
P. F. Warner	60	L. G. Berry	45	M. A. Noble	37
A. L. Hassett	59	A. W. Carr	45	E. Oldroyd	37
A. Shrewsbury ...	59	C. Hill	45	H. S. Squires	37
A. E. Fagg	58	E. Paynter	45	C. J. B. Wood ...	37
W. Rhodes	58	H. H. I. Gibbons..	44	N. F. Armstrong ..	36
L. B. Fishlock ...	56	D. J. Insole	44	W. Place	36
C. Hallows	55	A. Mitchell	44	C. S. Dempster....	35
W. W. Keeton ...	54	A. F. Kippax	43	G. M. Emmett	35
R. T. Simpson ...	54	H. Makepeace ...	43	D. R. Jardine	35
W. Bardsley	53	V. M. Merchant ..	43	B. H. Valentine ...	35

In all cricket J. B. Hobbs hit 244 hundreds and W. G. Grace hit 217.

TWO SEPARATE HUNDREDS IN A MATCH

Seven Times: W. R. HAMMOND.

Six Times: J. B. HOBBS.

Five Times: C. B. FRY.

Four Times: D. G. BRADMAN, L. B. FISHLOCK, H. T. W. HARDINGE, E. HENDREN, G. L. JESSOP, P. A. PERRIN, B. SUTCLIFFE, H. SUTCLIFFE.

Three Times: L. E. G. AMES, D. C. S. COMPTON, D. DENTON, K. S. DULEEPSINHJI, R. E. FOSTER, W. G. GRACE, T. W. GRAVENEY, G. GUNN, T. HAYWARD, V. S. HAZARE, L. HUTTON, C. P. MEAD, A. C. RUSSELL, J. T. TYLDESLEY.

Twice: B. J. T. BOSANQUET, M. C. COWDREY, C. C. DACRE, G. M. EMMETT, A. E. FAGG, H. GIMBLETT, C. HALLOWS, R. HAMENCE, A. L. HASSETT, G. HEADLEY, J. H. KING, A. F. KIPPAX, JOHN LANGRIDGE, H. W. LEE, E. LESTER, G. C. B. LLEWELLYN, C. G. MACARTNEY, P. B. H. MAY, A. R. MORRIS, E. PAYNTER, W. RHODES, JAS. SEYMOUR, E. TYLDESLEY, C. L. WALCOTT, W. W. WHYSALL.

W. Lambert scored 107 and 157 for Sussex v. Epsom at Lord's in 1817 and it was not until W. G. Grace made 130 and 102* for South of the Thames v. North of the Thames at Canterbury in 1868 that the feat was repeated.

A. E. Fagg alone has scored two double hundreds in the same match; 244 and 202* for Kent v. Essex at Colchester, 1938.

W. L. Foster, 140 and 172*, and R. E. Foster, 134 and 101*, at Worcester against Hampshire in July 1899, set up a record by brothers both scoring two separate hundreds in the same first-class match. This remains unequalled.

G. Gunn, 183 and G. V. Gunn, 100* for Notts. v. Warwickshire at Birmingham in 1931, provide the only instance of father and son each hitting a century in the same innings of a first-class match.

Most Recent Instances

In 1954–55:—

110	and 103	M. C. Cowdrey	M.C.C. v. New South Wales, at Sydney.
126	and 110	C. L. Walcott	West Indies v. Australia, at Trinidad.
155	and 110	C. L. Walcott	West Indies v. Australia, at Kingston.

In 1955:—

121*	and 105	J. M. Allan	Kent v. Northamptonshire, at Northampton.
115*	and 103*	M. C. Cowdrey	Kent v. Essex, at Gillingham.
111	and 118	D. J. Insole	Essex v. Kent, at Gillingham.
121	and 117*	D. M. Young	Glos. v. Northants, at Kettering.

In 1956:—

138	and 125*	J. W. Burke	Australians v. Somerset at Taunton.

In 1956–57:—

153	and 120	T. W. Graveney	C. G. Howard's XI v. C.C. of India President's XI, at Bombay.
112	and 114	L. Favell	South Australia v. New South Wales, at Sydney.
110	and 100	C. Pinch	South Australia v. Western Australia, at Perth.

In 1957:—

106	and 101*	T. W. Graveney	Glos. v. Warwickshire, at Birmingham.
101	and 100*	J. M. Parks	Sussex v. Worcestershire, at Worcester.

TWO SEPARATE HUNDREDS IN A TEST MATCH

Twice in one Series: C. L. Walcott v. Australia (1954–55).

Twice: H. Sutcliffe v. Australia (1924–25), South Africa (1929).
         G. Headley v. England (1929–30 and 1939).

Once: W. Bardsley v. England (1909).
        A. C. Russell v. South Africa (1922–23).
        W. R. Hammond v. Australia (1928–29).
        E. Paynter v. South Africa (1938–39).
        D. C. S. Compton v. Australia (1946–47).
        A. R. Morris v. England (1946–47).
        A. Melville v. England (1947).
        B. Mitchell v. England (1947).
        D. G. Bradman v. India (1947–48).
        V. S. Hazare v. Australia (1947–48).
        E. Weekes v. India (1948–49).
        J. R. Moroney v. South Africa (1949–50).

BATSMEN WHO HAVE SCORED 30,000 RUNS

	Career	Runs	Inns.	Times Not Out	Highest Inns.	100's	Average.
J. B. Hobbs	1905–34	61237	1315	106	316*	197	50.65
F. E. Woolley	1906–38	58969	1532	85	305*	145	40.75
E. Hendren	1907–38	57610	1300	166	301*	170	50.80
C. P. Mead	1905–36	55060	1335	185	280*	153	47.87
W. G. Grace	1865–1908	54896	1493	105	344	126	39.55
W. R. Hammond ..	1920–51	50493	1004	104	336*	167	56.10
H. Sutcliffe	1919–45	50135	1087	123	313	149	52.00
T. Hayward........	1893–1914	43518	1137	96	315	104	41.80
A. Sandham	1911–37	41284	1002	81	325	107	44.82
L. Hutton	1934–57	40051	812	91	364	129	55.54
W. Rhodes	1898–1930	39797	1532	236	267*	58	30.70
R. E. S. Wyatt	1923–57	39404	1141	157	232	85	40.04
E. Tyldesley	1909–36	38874	961	106	256*	102	45.46
D. C. S. Compton..	1936–57	38264	819	87	300	122	52.27
J. T. Tyldesley	1895–1923	37809	991	62	295*	86	40.69
J. W. Hearne	1909–35	37250	1024	116	285	96	41.02
L. E. G. Ames	1926–51	37245	950	95	295	102	43.56
D. Denton	1894–1920	36520	1164	70	221	69	33.38
W. J. Edrich	1934–57	36306	934	89	267*	85	42.96
G. H. Hirst	1889–1929	36203	1215	152	341	60	34.05
W. G. Quaife	1894–1928	36050	1204	186	255*	72	35.41
G. Gunn	1902–32	35190	1062	82	220	62	35.90
John Langridge	1928–55	34380	984	66	250*	76	37.45
M. Leyland	1920–48	33660	932	101	263	80	40.50
H. T. W. Hardinge .	1902–33	33519	1021	103	263*	75	36.51
R. Abel	1881–1904	32621	991	73	357*	74	35.53
C. Washbrook	1933–57	31931	822	93	251*	75	43.79
J. Hardstaff, junr. ..	1930–55	31841	812	94	266	83	44.34
James Langridge....	1924–53	31716	1058	157	167	42	35.20
C. B. Fry	1892–1921	30886	658	43	258*	94	50.22
P. Holmes	1913–35	30574	810	84	315	67	42.11
L. G. Berry	1924–51	30188	1048	57	232	45	30.46

1,000 RUNS IN A SEASON

(OVERSEAS TOURS INCLUDED)

28 Times: W. G. GRACE 2,000 (6); F. E. WOOLLEY 3,000 (1), 2,000 (12).

27 Times: C. P. MEAD 3,000 (2), 2,000 (9).

26 Times: J. B. HOBBS 3,000 (1), 2,000 (16).

25 Times: E. HENDREN 3,000 (3), 2,000 (12); W. G. QUAIFE 2,000 (1).

24 Times: H. SUTCLIFFE 3,000 (3), 2,000 (12).

21 Times: D. DENTON 2,000 (5); W. R. HAMMOND 3,000 (3), 2,000 (9), W. RHODES 2,000 (2).

20 Times: G. GUNN; T. HAYWARD 3,000 (2), 2,000 (8); James LANGRIDGE 2,000 (1); A. SANDHAM 2,000 (8).

19 Times: J. W. HEARNE 2,000 (4); G. H. HIRST 2,000 (3): E. TYLDESLEY 3,000 (1), 2,000 (5); J. T. TYLDESLEY 3,000 (1), 2,000 (4); C. WASHBROOK 2,000 (2).

18 Times: L. G. BERRY 2,000 (1); H. T. W. HARDINGE 2,000 (4); P. A. PERRIN; R. E. S. WYATT 2,000 (5).

17 Times: L. E. G. AMES 3,000 (1), 2,000 (5); D. C. S. COMPTON 3,000 (1), 2,000 (5); L. HUTTON 3,000 (1), 2,000 (8); JOHN LANGRIDGE 2,000 (11); M. LEYLAND 2,000 (3).

16 Times: D. G. BRADMAN 2,000 (4); EMRYS DAVIES 2,000 (1); E. G. HAYES 2,000 (2); J. O'CONNOR 2,000 (4); JAMES SEYMOUR 2,000 (1).

15 Times: E. H. BOWLEY 2,000 (4); D. BROOKES 2,000 (6); A. E. DIPPER 2,000 (5); H. E. DOLLERY 2,000 (2); W. J. EDRICH 3,000 (1), 2,000 (8); P. HOLMES 2,000 (7).

FOUR HUNDREDS OR MORE IN SUCCESSION
Six in Succession

C. B. FRY: in 1901.   D. G. BRADMAN: in 1938 39.

Five in Succession

E. WEEKES: in 1955–56.

Four In Succession

J. B. HOBBS: 1920, 1925.	JOHN LANGRIDGE: 1949.
H. SUTCLIFFE: 1931, 1939.	C. G. MACARTNEY: 1921.
D. G. BRADMAN: 1931–32 (A.).	P. B. H. MAY: 1956–57.
D. C. S. COMPTON: 1946–47.	V. M. MERCHANT: 1941–42.
K. S. DULEEPSINGHJI: 1931.	A. MITCHELL: 1933.
C. B. FRY: 1911.	NAWAB OF PATAUDI: 1931.
W. R. HAMMOND: 1936–37.	E. TYLDESLEY: 1926.
T. HAYWARD: 1906.	W. W. WHYSALL: 1930.
H. T. W. HARDINGE: 1913.	F. E. WOOLLEY: 1929.

Five Hundreds in Successive Test Innings

E. Weekes (West Indies), 141 v. England, 1947–48; 128, 194, 162 and 101 v. India, 1948–49.

Four Hundreds in Successive Test Innings

J. H. Fingleton (Australia), 112, 108, 118 in South Africa, 1935–36, and 100 v. England in Australia, 1936–37.

A. Melville (South Africa), 103 v. England in South Africa, 1938–39, 189, 104* and 117 in England, 1947.

MOST HUNDREDS IN A SEASON

Eighteen: D. C. S. Compton, in 1947. These included six centuries against the South Africans in which matches his average was 84.78. His aggregate for the season was 3,816, also a record.

Sixteen: J. B. Hobbs, in 1925, when aged 42, played 16 three-figure innings in first-class matches. It was during this season that he exceeded the number of hundreds obtained in first-class cricket by W. G. Grace.

Fifteen: W. R. Hammond, in 1938.

Fourteen: H. Sutcliffe, in 1932.

Thirteen: D. G. Bradman in 1938, C. B. Fry in 1901, W. R. Hammond in 1933 and 1937, T. Hayward in 1906. E. Hendren in 1923, 1927 and 1928, C. P Mead in 1928, and H. Sutcliffe in 1928 and 1931.

FAST SCORING

E. Alletson, for Notts v. Sussex, at Brighton, in 1911, scored 189 out of 227 runs obtained whilst at the wicket in ninety minutes.

D. Compton, for M.C.C. v. N.E. Transvaal, at Benoni, in 1948–49, scored 300 out of 399 in 181 minutes.

P. H. G. Fender, for Surrey v. Northamptonshire, at Northampton, in 1920, scored 113* out of 171 in forty-two minutes. He reached 50 in nineteen minutes and 100 in thirty-five minutes. Fender and H. A. Peach added 171 in forty-two minutes

F

G. L. Jessop, for Gloucestershire v. Yorkshire, at Harrogate, in 1897, scored 101 out of 118 in forty minutes.

G. L. Jessop, for Gentlemen of South v. Players of South, at Hastings, in 1907, scored 191 runs out of 234 in ninety minutes. He reached 50 in twenty-four minutes, 100 in forty-two, and 150 in sixty-three.

C. I. J. Smith, in June 1938, made 69 in twenty minutes for Middlesex against Sussex at Lord's, and ten days later against Gloucestershire at Bristol he scored 66 in eighteen minutes—the first 50 coming in the record time of eleven minutes.

For Auckland v. Otago, at Dunedin in 1936–37, P. E. Whitelaw and W. N. Carson added 445 runs for the third wicket in 268 minutes—a world's record

Worcestershire, set to make 131 in forty minutes against Nottinghamshire at Worcester in 1951, hit off the runs in thirty-five minutes for the loss of D. Kenyon's wicket. The other batsmen were G. Dews and R. O. Jenkins.

Kent scored 219 in seventy-one minutes when beating Gloucestershire at Dover, 1937. They averaged nine runs an over.

F. R. Santall (201) scored 173 out of 230 in 116 minutes before lunch on the third day for Warwickshire v. Northants at Northampton, 1933.

F. R. Brown made 168 out of 206 in 125 minutes for Surrey v. Kent, Blackheath, 1932. He advanced from 100 to 150 in fifteen minutes.

H. Sutcliffe (194) and M. Leyland (45) hit 102 off six consecutive overs for Yorkshire v. Essex, Scarborough, 1932.

J. B. Hobbs (47) and J. N. Crawford (48) made 98 without loss in thirty-two minutes at The Oval, 1919, after Kent left Surrey to get 95 in forty-two minutes.

RECORD HIT

The Rev. W. Fellows, while at practice on the Christchurch Ground at Oxford in 1856, drove a ball bowled by Charles Rogers 175 yards from hit to pitch.

MOST PERSONAL SIXES IN AN INNINGS

11	C. K. Nayudu (153)	Hindus v. M.C.C., at Bombay	1926–27
11	C. J. Barnett (194)	Gloucestershire v. Somerset, at Bath	1934
11	R. Benaud (135)	Australians v. T. N. Pearce's XI, at Scarborough	1953

MOST RUNS SCORED OFF ONE OVER

34	E. Alletson	off E. H. Killick, Notts v. Sussex, at Hove (including two no-balls)	1911
32	C. Smart	off G. Hill, Glamorgan v. Hampshire, at Cardiff	1935
31	A. W. Wellard	off F. E. Woolley, Somerset v. Kent, at Wells (including five 6's)	1938
30	D. G. Bradman	off A. P. Freeman, Australians v. England XI, at Folkestone	1934
30	H. B. Cameron	off H. Verity, South Africans v. Yorkshire, at Sheffield	1935
30	A. W. Wellard	off T. R. Armstrong, Somerset v. Derbyshire, at Wells (five 6's)	1936
30	P. L. Winslow	off J. T. Ikin, South Africans v. Lancashire, at Manchester	1955
28	J. H. de Courcy	off W. T. Greensmith, Australians v. Essex, at Southend	1953
28	H. L. Hazell	off H. Verity, Somerset v. Yorkshire, at Bath	1936
28	G. L. Jessop	off L. C. Braund, Gloucestershire v. Somerset, at Bristol	1904
28	G. L. Jessop	off R. D. Burrows, Gloucestershire v. Worcestershire, at Stourbridge	1910
28	J. E. McConnon	off N. I. Thomson, Glamorgan v. Sussex, at Cardiff	1955

(All the above instances refer to six-ball overs.)

300 RUNS IN ONE DAY

345	C. G. Macartney	Australians v. Notts	Nottingham	1921
338*	R. C. Blunt	Otago v. Canterbury	Christchurch	1931–32
334	W. H. Ponsford	Victoria v. New South Wales	Melbourne	1926–27
333	K. S. Duleepsinhji	Sussex v. Northamptonshire	Hove	1930
331*	J. D. Robertson	Middlesex v. Worcestershire	Worcester	1949
322	E. Paynter	Lancashire v. Sussex	Hove	1937
318	C. W. Gregory	New South Wales v. Queensland (completed innings 383)	Brisbane	1906–7
316	R. H. Moore	Hampshire v. Warwickshire	Bournemouth	1937
309	D. G. Bradman	Australia v. England (completed innings 334)	Leeds	1930
307	W. H. Ashdown	Kent v. Essex (completed innings 332)	Brentwood	1934
306	A. Ducat	Surrey v. Oxford University	The Oval	1919
305	F. R. Foster	Warwickshire v. Worcestershire	Dudley	1914

HIGHEST PARTNERSHIPS

577	V. Hazare (288) and Gul Mahomed (319), fourth wicket for Baroda v. Holkar, at Baroda	1946–47
574	F. M. Worrell (255*) and C. L. Walcott (314*), fourth wicket for Barbados v. Trinidad, at Port of Spain	1945–46
555	P. Holmes (224*) and H. Sutcliffe (313), first wicket, Yorkshire v. Essex, at Leyton ..	1932
554	J. T. Brown (300) and J. Tunnicliffe (243), first wicket, Yorkshire v. Derbyshire, at Chesterfield	1898
502	F. M. Worrell (308*) and J. D. Goddard (218*), fourth wicket, Barbados v. Trinidad, at Bridgetown	1943–44
490	E. H. Bowley (283) and John Langridge (195), first wicket, Sussex v. Middlesex, at Hove	1933
487	G. Headley (344*) and C. C. Passailaigue (261*), sixth wicket, Jamaica v. Lord Tennyson's XI, at Kingston	1931–32
456	E. R. Mayne (209) and W. H. Ponsford (248), first wicket, Victoria v. Queensland, at Melbourne	1923–24
455	B. B. Nimbalkar (443*) and K. V. Bhandarkar (205), second wicket for Maharashtra v. Western India States, at Poona	1948–49
451	D. G. Bradman (244) and W. H. Ponsford (266), second wicket, 5th Test, Australia v. England, at Kennington Oval ..	1934

PARTNERSHIPS FOR FIRST WICKET

555	P. Holmes and H. Sutcliffe, Yorkshire v. Essex, at Leyton ..	1932
554	J. T. Brown and J. Tunnicliffe, Yorkshire v. Derbyshire, at Chesterfield ..	1898
490	E. H. Bowley and John Langridge, Sussex v. Middlesex, at Hove	1933
456	E. R. Mayne and W. H. Ponsford, Victoria v. Queensland, at Melbourne	1923–24
428	J. B. Hobbs and A. Sandham, Surrey v. Oxford U., at The Oval	1926
424	J. F. W. Nicolson and I. J. Siedle, Natal v. Orange Free State, at Bloemfontein	1926–27
413	V. Mankad and P. Roy, India v. New Zealand, at Madras (World Test Record) ..	1955–56
391	A. O. Jones and A. Shrewsbury, Notts v. Glos., at Bristol	1899
390	L. Wight and G. Gibbs, British Guiana v. Barbados, at Georgetown ..	1951–52
380	H. Whitehead and C. J. B. Wood, Leicestershire v. Worcestershire, at Worcester ..	1906
379	R. Abel and W. Brockwell, Surrey v. Hampshire, at The Oval ..	1897

378	J. T. Brown and J. Tunnicliffe, Yorkshire v. Sussex, at Sheffield ..	1897
375	W. H. Ponsford and W. M. Woodfull, Victoria v. New South Wales, at Melbourne	1926–27
373	B. Sutcliffe and L. A. Watt, Otago v. Auckland, at Auckland ..	1950–51
368	A. C. MacLaren and R. H. Spooner, Lancashire v. Gloucestershire, at Liverpool	1903
368	E. H. Bowley and J. H. Parks, Sussex v. Glos., at Hove ..	1929
364	R. Abel and D. L. A. Jephson, Surrey v. Derbyshire, at The Oval	1900
361	N. Oldfield and V. Broderick, Northamptonshire v. Scotland, at Peterborough	1953
359	L. Hutton and C. Washbrook, England v. South Africa, at Johannesburg	1948–49
355	A. F. Rae and J. B. Stollmeyer, West Indies v. Sussex, at Hove ..	1950
352	T. Hayward and J. B. Hobbs, Surrey v. Warwickshire, at The Oval ..	1909
350	C. Washbrook and W. Place, Lancashire v. Sussex, at Manchester (unbroken) ..	1947

FIRST-WICKET HUNDREDS IN BOTH INNINGS

B. Sutcliffe and D. D. Taylor, for Auckland v. Canterbury in 1948–49, scored for the first wicket 220 in the first innings and 286 in the second innings. This is the only instance of two double century opening stands in the same match.

T. Hayward and J. B. Hobbs in 1907 accomplished a performance without parallel by scoring over 100 together for the first wicket of Surrey four times in one week: 106 and 125 v. Cambridge University, at The Oval, and 147 and 105 v. Middlesex, at Lord's.

L. Hutton and C. Washbrook, in three consecutive innings which they opened together for England in Test Matches with Australia in 1946–47, made 138 in the second innings at Melbourne, and 137 and 100 at Adelaide. They also opened with 168 and 129 at Leeds in 1948.

J. B. Hobbs and H. Sutcliffe, in three consecutive innings which they opened together for England in Test matches with Australia in 1924–25, made 157 and 110 at Sydney and 283 at Melbourne. On 26 occasions—15 times in Test matches—Hobbs and Sutcliffe took part in a three-figure first wicket partnership. Seven of these stands exceeded 200.

P. Holmes and H. Sutcliffe made 100 or more runs for the first wicket of Yorkshire on sixty-nine occasions; J. B. Hobbs and A. Sandham of Surrey on sixty-three; W. W. Keeton and C. B. Harris of Notts on forty-six; T. Hayward and J. B. Hobbs of Surrey on forty; G. Gunn and W. W. Whysall of Notts on forty; C. B. Fry and J. Vine of Sussex on thirty-three; E. Davies and A. H. Dyson of Glamorgan on thirty-two; and A. O. Jones and J. Iremonger of Notts on twenty-four.

J. Douglas and A. E. Stoddart in 1896 scored over 150 runs for the first wicket of Middlesex three times within a fortnight. In 1901, J. Iremonger and A. O. Jones obtained over 100 for the first wicket of Nottinghamshire four times within eight days, scoring 134 and 144* v. Surrey at The Oval, 238 v. Essex at Leyton, and 119 v. Derbyshire at Welbeck.

J. W. Lee and F. S. Lee, brothers, in 1934, for Somerset, scored over 100 runs thrice in succession in the County Championship.

W. G. Grace and A. E. Stoddart in three consecutive innings against the Australians in 1893 made over 100 runs for each opening partnership.

In consecutive innings for Lancashire in 1928 C. Hallows and F. Watson opened with 200, 202, 107, 118: reached three figures twelve times, 200 four times.

J. B. Hobbs during his career, which extended from 1905 to 1934, helped to make 100 or more for the first wicket in first-class cricket 166 times—15 of them in 1926, when in consecutive innings he helped to make 428, 182, 106 and 123 before a wicket fell. As many as 117 of the 166 stands were made for Surrey.

In the period 1919–1939 inclusive, H. Sutcliffe shared in 145 first wicket partnerships of 100 runs or more.

WICKET RECORDS FOR ALL COUNTRIES

Best First Wicket Stands

English	..	555	P. Holmes (224*) and H. Sutcliffe (313), Yorkshire v. Essex, at Leyton 1932
Australian	..	456	W. H. Ponsford (248) and E. R. Mayne (209), Victoria v. Queensland, at Melbourne .. 1923–24
South African	..	424	J. F. W. Nicolson (252*) and I. J. Siedle (174), Natal v. Orange Free State, at Bloemfontein 1926–27
Indian	..	413	V. Mankad (231) and P. Roy (173), India v. New Zealand, at Madras 1955–56
West Indian	..	390	L. Wight (262*) and G. Gibbs (216), British Guiana v. Barbados, at Georgetown .. 1951–52
New Zealand	..	373	B. Sutcliffe (275) and L. A. Watt (96), Otago v. Auckland, at Auckland 1950–51
Pakistan	..	248	Nazar Mohammad (105) and Hanif Mohammad (135), Pakistan v. South Zone, at Hyderabad (Dn) 1952–53

Best Second Wicket Stands

Indian	..	455	B. B. Nimbalkar (443*) and K. V. Bhandakar (205), Maharashtra v. W.I. States, at Poona 1948–49
Australian	..	451	D. G. Bradman (244) and W. H. Ponsford (266), Australia v. England, at The Oval .. 1934
English	..	429	J. G. Dewes (204*) and G. H. G. Doggart (219*), Cambridge U. v. Essex, at Cambridge 1949
South African	..	305	S. K. Coen (165) and J. M. M. Commaille (186), Orange Free State v. Natal, at Bloemfontein 1926–27
New Zealand	..	301	C. S. Dempster (180) and C. F. W. Allcott (131), N. Z'drs. v. Warwicks., at Birmingham 1927
West Indian	..	295	J. B. Stollmeyer (261) and K. B. Trestrail (161) Trinidad v. Jamaica, at Port of Spain 1949–50
Pakistan	..	269	Nazar Mohammad (170) and Murawwat Hussain (100), Pakistan v. Ceylon, at Ceylon Oval 1948–49

Best Third Wicket Stands

New Zealand	..	445	P. E. Whitelaw (195) and W. N. Carson (290), Auckland v. Otago, at Dunedin .. 1936–37
West Indian	..	434	J. B. Stollmeyer (324) and G. E. Gomez (190), Trinidad v. British Guiana, at Port of Spain 1946–47
English	..	424	D. C. S. Compton (252*) and W. J. Edrich (168*), Middlesex v. Somerset, at Lord's .. 1948
Indian	..	410	L. Amarnath (262) and R. S. Modi (156), Indians v. The Rest, at Calcutta .. 1946–47
Australian	..	389	S. J. McCabe (192) and W. H. Ponsford (281*), Australians v. M.C.C., at Lord's .. 1934
South African	..	319	A. Melville (189) and A. D. Nourse, junr. (149), South Africa v. England, at Nottingham 1947
Pakistan	..	273	Hanif Mohammad (174) and V. L. Manjrekar (108), Hassan Mahmood XI v. Air Vice-Marshal XI, at Karachi 1953–54

Best Fourth Wicket Stands

Indian	..	577	V. S. Hazare (288) and Gul Mahomed (319), Baroda v. Holkar, at Baroda .. 1946–47
West Indian	..	574	F. M. Worrell (255*) and C. L. Walcott (314*), Barbados v. Trinidad, at Port of Spain 1945–46
English	..	448	R. Abel (193) and T. Hayward (273), Surrey v. Yorkshire, at The Oval .. 1899
Australian	..	424	I. S. Lee (258) and S. O. Quin (210), Victoria v. Tasmania, at Melbourne 1933–34

South African..	342	E. A. B. Rowan (196) and P. J. M. Gibb (203), Transvaal v. N.E. Transvaal, at Johannesburg	1952–53
New Zealand ..	324	W. M. Wallace (197) and J. R. Reid (188*), N. Z'drs. v. Camb. U., at Cambridge ..	1949
Pakistan	255	Hanif Mohammad (230*) and Raees Mohammad (118*), Karachi v. Sind, at Karachi ..	1954–55

Best Fifth Wicket Stands

Australian	..	405	D. G. Bradman (234) and S. G. Barnes (234), Australia v. England, at Sydney	1946–47
English..	..	393	E. G. Arnold (200*) and W. B. Burns (196), Worcs. v. Warwicks., at Birmingham ..	1909
Indian ..	..	360	Uday Merchant (217) and M. N. Raiji (170), Bombay v. Hyderabad, at Bombay ..	1947–48
South African ..		327	A. W. Briscoe (191) and H. B. Cameron (182), Transvaal v. Griqualand West, at Jo'burg..	1934–35
New Zealand ..		266	B. Sutcliffe (355) and W. S. Haig (67), Otago v. Auckland, at Dunedin	1949–50
West Indian ..		283	N. L. Bonitto (207) and A. P. Binns (157), Jamaica v. British Guiana, at Georgetown..	1951–52
Pakistan	..	192	Waqar Hassan (123) and Wazir Mohammad (87), Pakistan v. Surrey, at The Oval ..	1954

Best Sixth Wicket Stands

West Indian ..		487	G. Headley (344*) and C. C. Passailaigue (261*), Jamaica v. Lord Tennyson's XI, at Kingston	1931–32
Australian	..	428	W. W. Armstrong (172*) and M. A. Noble (284), Australians v. Sussex, at Hove ..	1902
English..	..	411	R. M. Poore (304) and E. G. Wynyard (225), Hampshire v. Somerset, at Taunton ..	1899
Indian ..	..	371	V. M. Merchant (359*) and R. S. Modi (168), Bombay v. Maharashtra, at Bombay ..	1943–44
South African ..		244	J. M. M. Commaille (132*) and A. W. Palm (106*), Western Province v. Griqualand West, at Johannesburg	1923–24
New Zealand ..		184	D. C. Collins (85) and H. M. McGirr (117), Wellington v. Otago, at Dunedin ..	1923–24
Pakistan	..	171	Imtiaz Ahmed (120) and Wazir Mohammad (45), Pakistan v. Nagpur, at Nagpur ..	1952–53

Best Seventh Wicket Stands

West Indian ..		347	D. Atkinson (219) and C. Depeiza (112), West Indies v. Australia, at Bridgetown ..	1954–55
English..	..	344	K. S. Ranjitsinhji (230) and W. Newham (153), Sussex v. Essex, at Leyton	1902
Australian	..	335	C. W. Andrews (253) and E. C. Bensted (155), Queensland v New South Wales, at Sydney	1934–35
Pakistan	..	308	Waqar Hassan (189) and Imtiaz Ahmed (209), Pakistan v. New Zealand, at Lahore ..	1955–56
South African ..		299	B. Mitchell (159) and A. Melville (153), Transvaal v. Griqualand West, at Kimberley	1946–47
Indian ..	..	274	K. C. Ibrahim (250) and K. M. Rangnekar (138), Bijapur XI v. Bengal XI, at Bombay..	1942–43
New Zealand ..		265	J. L. Powell (164) and N. Doreen (105*), Canterbury v. Otago, at Christchurch ..	1929–30

Best Eighth Wicket Stands

Australian	..	433	A. Sims (184*) and V. T. Trumper (293), An Australian XI v. Canterbury, at Christchurch	1913–14

English..	..	292	Lord Hawke (166) and R. Peel (210*), York-shire v. Warwickshire, at Birmingham	1896
West Indian	..	255	E. A. V. Williams (131*) and E. A. Martindale (134), Barbados v. Trinidad, at Bridgetown	1935–36
Indian ..		236	C. T. Sarwate (235) and R. P. Singh (88), Holkar v. Delhi and Dis., at New Delhi	1949–50
South African ..		222	D. P. B. Morkel (114) and S. S. L. Steyn (261*), Western Province v. Border, at Cape Town	1929–30
New Zealand ..		190	J. E. Mills (104*) and C. F. W. Allcott (102*), New Zealanders v. Civil Service, at Chiswick	1927
Pakistan		121	Ismail Ibrahim (32) and Maqsood Ahmed (90), Karachi Blues v. Karachi Whites, at Karachi	1956–57

Best Ninth Wicket Stands

English..		283	J. Chapman (165) and A. R. Warren (123), Derbyshire v. Warwickshire, at Blackwell ..	1910
Indian ..		245	V. S. Hazare (316*) and N. D. Nagarwalla (98), Maharashtra v. Baroda, at Poona	1939–40
New Zealand		239	H. B. Cave (118) and I. B. Leggat (142*), Central Districts v. Otago, at Dunedin	1952–53
Australian		232	C. Hill (365*) and E. Walkley (53), South Australia v. N.S.W., at Adelaide	1900–01
South African ..		221	N. V. Lindsay (160*) and G. R. McCubbin (97), Transvaal v. Rhodesia, at Bulawayo ..	1922–23
Pakistan		140	Mushtaq Mohammad (87) and Alidul Dyer (45), Karachi Whites v. Hyderabad, at Hyderabad	1956–57
West Indian	..	134	W. Hall (77) and F. C. M. Alexander (36), E. Weekes's XI v. C. L. Walcott's XI, at Port of Spain	1956–57

Best Tenth Wicket Stands

Australian	..	307	A. F. Kippax (260*), and J. E. H. Hooker (62) New South Wales v. Victoria, at Melbourne	1928–29
Indian ..		249	C. T. Sarwate (124*) and S. N. Banerjee (121), Indians v. Surrey, at The Oval	1946
English..		235	A. Fielder (112*) and F. E. Woolley (185), Kent v. Worcestershire, at Stourbridge	1909
New Zealand		184	R. C. Blunt (338*) and W. Hawkesworth (21), Otago v. Canterbury, at Christchurch	1931–32
West Indian		138	E. L. G. Hoad (149*) and H. C. Griffith (84), West Indies v. Sussex, at Hove	1933
South African ..		129	F. Caulfield (56*) and L. R. Tuckett (70), Orange Free State v. Western Province, at Bloemfontein	1925–26
Pakistan		104	Zulfiqar Ahmed (63*) and Amir Elahi (47), Pakistan v. India, at Madras	1952–53

(All the English record wicket partnerships were made in the County Championship with the exception of the second, for which the best county stand is: 398, W. Gunn (196) and A. Shrewsbury (267), Notts v. Sussex, at Nottingham, 1890.)

HIGHEST AGGREGATES IN A SEASON: OVER 3,000

		Inns.		Times Not Out		Runs		Highest Score		No. of 100's		Average
1947	D. C. S. Compton	50	..	8	..	3816	..	246	..	18	..	90.85
1947	W. J. Edrich	52	..	8	..	3539	..	267*	..	12	..	80.43
1906	T. Hayward	61	..	8	..	3518	..	219	..	13	..	66.37
1949	L. Hutton	56	..	6	..	3429	..	269*	..	12	..	68.58
1928	F. E. Woolley	59	..	4	..	3352	..	198	..	12	..	60.94
1932	H. Sutcliffe	52	..	7	..	3336	..	313	..	14	..	74.13
1933	W. R. Hammond	54	..	5	..	3323	..	264	..	13	..	67.81

		Inns.	Times Not Out	Runs	Highest Score	No. of 100's	Average
1928	E. Hendren	54	7	3311	209*	13	70.44
1901	R. Abel	68	8	3309	247	7	55.15
1937	W. R. Hammond	55	5	3252	217	13	65.04
1933	E. Hendren	65	9	3186	301*	11	56.89
1921	C. P. Mead	52	6	3179	280*	10	69.10
1904	T. Hayward	63	5	3170	205	11	54.65
1899	K. S. Ranjitsinhji	58	8	3159	197	8	63.18
1901	C. B. Fry	43	3	3147	244	13	78.67
1900	K. S. Ranjitsinhji	40	5	3065	275	11	87.57
1933	L. E. G. Ames .	57	5	3058	295	9	58.80
1901	J. T. Tyldesley .	60	5	3041	221	9	55.29
1928	C. P. Mead	50	10	3027	180	13	75.67
1925	J. B. Hobbs ...	48	5	3024	266*	16	70.32
1928	E. Tyldesley ...	48	10	3024	242	10	79.57
1938	W. R. Hammond	42	2	3011	271	15	75.27
1923	E. Hendren	51	12	3010	200*	13	77.17
1931	H. Sutcliffe ...	42	11	3006	230	13	96.96
1937	J. H. Parks ...	63	4	3003	168	11	50.89
1928	H. Sutcliffe ...	44	5	3002	228	13	76.97

W. G. Grace scored 2,739 runs in 1871 when every stroke was run out. He made ten centuries and twice exceeded 200, with an average of 78·25 all first-class matches and the over was four balls.

LARGEST AGGREGATES OUTSIDE ENGLAND

		Inns.	Not out	Runs	Highest Score	No. of 100's	Average
In Australia							
1928–29	D. G. Bradman	24	6	1690	340*	7	93.88
In South Africa							
1948–49	D. C. S. Compton	26	5	1781	300	8	84.80
In West Indies							
1929–30	E. Hendren	18	5	1765	254	6	135.76
In India							
1926–27	A. Sandham	33	4	1977	150	8	68.17

1,000 RUNS IN MAY

Three batsmen have scored 1,000 runs in May, and three others—D. G. Bradman twice—have made 1,000 runs before June. Their innings-by-innings records are as follows:—

	Runs	Average
W. G. GRACE, May 9 to May 30, 1895 (22 days): 13, 103, 18, 25, 288, 52, 257, 73*, 18, 169 .. .. .. "W.G." was within two months of completing his 47th year.	1016	112.88
W. R. HAMMOND, May 7 to May 31, 1927 (25 days): 27, 135, 108, 128, 17, 11, 99, 187, 4, 30, 83, 7, 192, 14 .. Hammond scored his 1,000th run on May 28, thus equalling "W.G.'s" record of 22 days.	1042	74.42
C. HALLOWS, May 5 to May 31, 1928 (27 days): 100, 101, 51*, 123, 101*, 22, 74, 104, 58, 34*, 232	1000	125.00
T. HAYWARD, April 16 to May 31, 1900: 120*, 55, 108, 131*, 55, 193, 120, 5, 6, 3, 40, 146, 92 .. Hayward scored 120 not out on April 16.	1074	97.63
D. G. BRADMAN, April 30 to May 31, 1930: 236, 185*, 78, 9, 48*, 66, 4, 44, 252*, 32, 47* .. .. .. On April 30 Bradman scored 75 not out.	1001	143.00

D. G. BRADMAN, April 30 to May 31, 1938:
258, 58, 137, 278, 2, 143, 145*, 5, 30* 1056 150.85
    Bradman scored 258 on April 30, and his 1,000th run on May 27.
W. J. EDRICH, April 30 to May 31, 1938:
104, 37, 115, 63, 20*, 182, 71, 31, 53*, 45, 15, 245, 0, 9, 20* .. 1010 84.16
    Edrich scored 21 not out on April 30. All his runs were scored at Lord's.

1,000 RUNS IN TWO SEPARATE MONTHS

L. Hutton, by scoring 1,294 in June 1949, made more runs in a single month than anyone else. The previous best was by W. R. Hammond, 1,281, in August 1936. Hutton also made 1,050 in August 1949, and thus joined C. B. Fry, K. S. Ranjitsinhji and H. Sutcliffe, who scored over 1,000 in each of two months in the same season.

BOWLING AND FIELDING RECORDS
Four Wickets With Consecutive Balls

J. Wells, Kent v. Sussex, at Brighton	1862
G. Ulyett, England v. New South Wales, at Sydney	1878–79
G. Nash, Lancashire v. Somerset, at Manchester	1882
J. B. Hide, Sussex v. M.C.C. and Ground, at Lord's	1890
F. Shacklock, Notts v. Somerset, at Nottingham	1893
A. Downes, Otago v. Auckland, at Dunedin	1893–94
F. Martin, M.C.C. and Ground v. Derbyshire, at Lord's ..	1895
A. Mold, Lancashire v. Notts, at Nottingham	1895
W. Brearley, Lancashire v. Somerset, at Manchester	1905
(Not all in same innings)	
S. Haigh, M.C.C. v. Army XI, at Pretoria	1905–06
†A. E. Trott, Middlesex v. Somerset, at Lord's	1907
(It was Trott's benefit match and he did the hat-trick also in the same innings)	
F. A. Tarrant, Middlesex v. Gloucestershire, at Bristol ..	1907
A. Drake, Yorkshire v. Derbyshire, at Chesterfield	1914
S. G. Smith, Northamptonshire v. Warwickshire, at Edgbaston ..	1914
H. A. Peach, Surrey v. Sussex, at The Oval	1924
A. F. Borland, Natal v. Griqualand West, at Kimberley ..	1926–27
J. E. H. Hooker, New South Wales v. Victoria, at Sydney ..	1928–29
(Not all in same innings)	
R. Tyldesley, Lancashire v. Derbyshire, at Derby	1929
(Not all in same innings)	
R. J. Crisp, Western Province v. Griqualand West, at Johannesburg ..	1931–32
R. J. Crisp, Western Province v. Natal, at Durban	1933–34
A. R. Gover, Surrey v. Worcestershire, at Worcester	1935
W. H. Copson, Derbyshire v. Warwickshire, at Derby ..	1937
W. A. Henderson, North-Eastern Transvaal v. Orange Free State at Bloemfontein	1937–38
F. Ridgway, Kent v. Derbyshire, at Folkestone	1951
A. K. Walker, Notts v. Leicestershire, at Leicester	1956

(Walker dismissed Firth with the last ball of the first innings and Lester, Tompkin and Smithson with the first three balls of the second innings, a feat without parallel.)

†Trott's double performance is without parallel in important cricket.

In their match with England at The Oval in 1863, Surrey lost four wickets in the course of a four-ball over from G. Bennett. From his first H. H. Stephenson was stumped, from his second W. Caffyn was run out, E. Dowson was bowled by his third, and G. Griffiths was caught off his fourth.

Double Hat-Trick

Besides Trott's performance, which is given in the preceding section, the following instances are recorded of players having performed the hat-trick twice in the same match:—

A. Shaw, Notts v. Gloucestershire, at Trent Bridge, 1884.
T. J. Matthews, Australia v. South Africa, at Manchester, 1912.
C. W. L. Parker, Gloucestershire v. Middlesex, at Bristol, 1924.
R. O. Jenkins, Worcestershire v. Surrey, at Worcester, 1949.

Most Hat-Tricks

SEVEN TIMES
D. V. P. Wright.

SIX TIMES
T. W. Goddard.
C. W. L. Parker.

FIVE TIMES
S. Haigh.
V. W. C. Jupp.
A. E. G. Rhodes.
F. A. Tarrant.

FOUR TIMES
J. T. Hearne.
J. C. Laker.
G. G. Macaulay.

THREE TIMES
H. J. Butler.
W. H. Copson.
R. J. Crisp.
J. W. H. T. Douglas.
A. P. Freeman.
G. Giffen.
J. W. Hearne.

A. Hill.
R. O. Jenkins.
A. S. Kennedy.
G. A. R. Lock.
W. H. Lockwood.
E. A. McDonald.
T. J. Matthews.
T. L. Pritchard.
T. Richardson.
A. Shaw.
F. R. Spofforth.
M. W. Tate.
H. Trumble.

TEN WICKETS IN ONE INNINGS

	O.	M.	R.		
W. Clarke (Notts)	....			v. Leicester., at Nottingham	1845
E. Hinkly (Kent)	....			v. England, at Lord's	1848
J. Wisden (North)	....			v. South, at Lord's	1850
V. E. Walker (England)	43		74	v. Surrey, at The Oval	1859
E. M. Grace (M.C.C.)	.....			v. Gents. of Kent, at Canterbury	1862
V. E. Walker (Middlesex)	44.2		104	v. Lancashire, at Manchester	1865
G. Wootton (All England)	..			v. Yorkshire, at Sheffield	1865
W. Hickton (Lancashire)	36.2	19	46	v. Hampshire, at Manchester	1870
S. E. Butler (Oxford)	24.1	11	38	v. Cambridge, at Lord's	1871
Jas. Lillywhite (South)	60.2	22	129	v. North, at Canterbury	1872
A. Shaw (M.C.C.)	36.2	8	73	v. North, at Lord's	1874
E. Barratt (Players)	29	11	43	v. Australians, at The Oval	1878
G. Giffen (Fourth Aust. XI)	26	10	66	v. The Rest, at Sydney	1883–84
W. G. Grace (M.C.C.)	36.2	17	49	v. Oxford U., at Oxford	1886
G. Burton (Middlesex)	52.3	25	59	v. Surrey, at The Oval	1888
A. E. Moss (Canterbury)	21.3		28	v. Wellington, at Christchurch	1889–90
S. M. J. Woods (Cambridge U.)	31	6	69	v. Thornton's XI, at Cambridge	1890
T. Richardson (Surrey)	15.3	3	45	v. Essex, at The Oval	1894
H. Pickett (Essex)	27	11	32	v. Leicester., at Leyton	1895
E. J. Tyler (Somerset)	34.3	15	49	v. Surrey, at Taunton	1895
W. P. Howell (Australians)	23.2	14	28	v. Surrey, at The Oval	1899
C. H. G. Bland (Sussex)	25.2	0	48	v. Kent, at Tonbridge	1899
J. Briggs (Lancashire)	28.5	7	55	v. Worcester., at Manchester	1900
A. E. Trott (Middlesex)	14.2	5	42	v. Somerset, at Taunton	1900
A. Fielder (Players)	24.5	1	90	v. Gentlemen, at Lord's	1906
G. Dennett (Gloucester.)	19.4	7	26	v. Essex, at Bristol	1906
A. E. E. Vogler (Eastern Prov.)	12	2	40	v. Griq. West, at Johannesburg	1906–07
C. Blythe (Kent)	16	7	30	v. Northants, at Northampton	1907

	O.	M.	R.		
A. Drake (Yorkshire)	8.5	0	35	v. Somerset, at Weston	1914
W. Bestwick (Derbyshire) ..	19	2	40	v. Glamorgan, at Cardiff ..	1921
A. A. Mailey (Australians) ..	28.4	5	66	v. Glos., at Cheltenham	1921
C. W. L. Parker (Gloucester.)	40.3	13	79	v. Somerset, at Bristol	1921
T. Rushby (Surrey)	17.5	4	43	v. Somerset, at Taunton ...	1921
J. C. White (Somerset)	42.2	11	76	v. Worcester., at Worcester.	1921
G. C. Collins (Kent)	19.3	4	65	v. Notts, at Dover	1922
H. Howell (Warwicks.)	25.1	5	51	v. Yorkshire, at Birmingham	1923
A. S. Kennedy (Players)	22.4	10	37	v. Gentlemen, at The Oval ..	1927
G. O. Allen (Middlesex)	25.3	10	40	v. Lancashire, at Lord's ...	1929
A. P. Freeman (Kent)	42	9	131	v. Lancashire, at Maidstone	1929
G. Geary (Leicester.)	16.2	8	18	v. Glamorgan, at Pontypridd	1929
C. V. Grimmett (Australians)	22.3	8	37	v. Yorkshire, at Sheffield...	1930
A. P. Freeman (Kent)	30.4	8	53	v. Essex, at Southend	1930
H. Verity (Yorkshire)	18.4	6	36	v. Warwicks., at Leeds	1931
A. P. Freeman (Kent)	36.1	9	79	v. Lancashire, at Manchester	1931
V. W. C. Jupp (Northants) ..	39	6	127	v. Kent, at Tunbridge Wells	1932
H. Verity (Yorkshire)	19.4	16	10	v. Notts, at Leeds	1932
T. W. Wall (Sth. Australia)..	12.4	2	36	v. N.S.W., at Sydney	1932–33
T. B. Mitchell (Derbyshire)..	19.1	4	64	v. Leicester., at Leicester ...	1935
J. Mercer (Glamorgan)	26	10	51	v. Worcester., at Worcester.	1936
T. W. Goddard (Gloucester.)	28.4	4	113	v. Worcester., at Cheltenham	1937
T. F. Smailes (Yorkshire) ..	17.1	5	47	v. Derbyshire, at Sheffield..	1939
E. A. Watts (Surrey)	24.1	8	67	v. Warwicks., at Birmingham	1939
W. E. Hollies (Warwicks.) ..	20.4	4	49	v. Notts, at Birmingham	1946
J. M. Sims (East)	18.4	2	90	v. West, at Kingston	1948
T. E. Bailey (Essex)	39.4	9	90	v. Lancs., at Clacton	1949
J. K. Graveney (Gloucester.)	18.4	2	66	v. Derby., at Chesterfield...	1949
R. Berry (Lancashire)	36.2	9	102	v. Worcester., at Blackpool .	1953
S. Gupte (Bombay)	24.2	7	78	v. Comb.XI, at Bombay 1954–5	
J. C. Laker (Surrey)........	46	18	88	v. Australians, at The Oval ..	1956
J. C. Laker (England)	51.2	23	53	v. Australia, at Manchester	1956
G. A. R. Lock (Surrey).....	29.1	18	54	v. Kent, at Blackheath	1956
K. Smales (Notts)	41.3	20	66	v. Gloucestershire, at Stroud	1956

NINETEEN WICKETS IN A MATCH

J. C. Laker, England v. Australia at Manchester, for 90 runs 1956

SEVENTEEN WICKETS IN A MATCH

F. P. Fenner, Cambridge Town Club v. The University, at Cambridge	1844
W. Mycroft, for 103 runs, Derbyshire v. Hampshire, at Southampton	1876
W. G. Grace, for 89 runs, Gloucestershire v. Notts, at Cheltenham ..	1877
G. Giffen, for 201 runs, South Australia v. Victoria, at Adelaide	1885–86
C. T. B. Turner, for 50 runs, Australians v. An England Eleven, at Hastings	1888
W. Mead, for 205 runs, Essex v. Australians, at Leyton	1893
W. Mead, for 119 runs, Essex v. Hampshire, at Southampton	1895
W. P. Howell, for 54 runs, Australians v. Western Province, at Cape Town	1902–03
W. Brearley, for 137 runs, Lancashire v. Somerset, at Manchester	1905
C. Blythe, for 48 runs, Kent v. Northants, at Northampton	1907
H. Dean, for 91 runs, Lancashire v. Yorkshire, at Liverpool	1913
S. F. Barnes, for 159 runs, England v. South Africa, at Johannesburg	1913–14
A. P. Freeman, for 67 runs, Kent v. Sussex, at Brighton	1922
F. C. L. Matthews, for 89 runs, Notts v. Northants, at Nottingham	1923

C. W. L. Parker, for 56 runs, Gloucestershire v. Essex, at Gloucester　　1925
G. R. Cox, for 106 runs, Sussex v. Warwickshire, at Horsham　　..　1926
A. P. Freeman, for 92 runs, Kent v. Warwickshire, at Folkestone　　..　1932
H. Verity, for 91 runs, Yorkshire v. Essex, at Leyton　　..　　..　1933
J. C. Clay, for 212 runs, Glamorgan v. Worcestershire, at Swansea　　..　1937
T. W. Goddard, for 106 runs, Gloucestershire v. Kent, at Bristol　　..　1939

REMARKABLE ANALYSES

(Also see Ten Wickets in One Innings on preceding pages)

	O.	M.	R.	W.		
H. Verity (Yorkshire)	19.4	16	10	10	v. Notts, at Leeds	1932
G. Geary (Leicestershire)	16.2	8	18	10	v. Glamorgan, at Ponty-pridd	1929
A. E. Vogler (Eastern Province)	12	2	26	10	v. Griqualand West, at Johannesburg	1906
A. P. Freeman (Kent)	10	4	11	9	v. Sussex, at Brighton	1922
H. Verity (Yorkshire)	6.3	3	12	9	v. Kent, at Sheffield	1936
C. T. B. Turner (Australia)	17.1	10	15	9	v. An England XI, at Stoke	1888
F. R. Spofforth (Australia)	15.2	7	18	9	v. Oxford University, at Oxford	1886
A. Rowan (Transvaal)	15.4	7	19	9	v. Australians, at Johannesburg	1949–50
W. G. Grace (M.C.C.)	35.1	25	20	9	v. Notts, at Lord's	1885
J. C. Laker (England)	14	12	2	8	v. The Rest, at Bradford	1950
D. Shackleton (Hampshire)	11.1	7	4	8	v. Somerset, at Weston	1955
E. Peate (Yorkshire)	16	11	5	8	v. Surrey, at Holbeck	1883
G. A. Lohmann (England)	9.4	5	7	8	v. South Africa, at Port Elizabeth	1896
C. H. Palmer (Leic.)	14	12	7	8	v. Surrey, at Leicester	1955
J. E. D. Sealy (Barbados)	6.7	2	8	8	v. Trinidad, at Bridge-town	1942
M. G. Melle (Transvaal)	12	7	8	8	v. Griqualand West, at Johannesburg	1950–51
G. Dennett (Gloucestershire)	6	1	9	8	v. Northants, at Gloucester	1907
G. Freeman (Yorkshire)	13	8	11	8	v. Lancashire, at Holbeck	1868
J. Briggs (English XI)	14.2	5	11	8	v. South Africa XI, at Cape Town	1889
A. Kennedy (Hampshire)	13	7	11	8	v. Glamorgan, at Cardiff	1921
W. Copson (Derbyshire)	8.2	2	11	8	v. Warwickshire, at Derby	1937
R. Peel (Yorkshire)	20.2	13	12	8	v. Notts, at Sheffield	1888
R. W. Norden (Transvaal)	12	8	12	8	v. Rhodesia, at Johannesburg	1905
C. W. L. Parker (Gloucestershire)	17	10	12	8	v. Essex, at Gloucester	1925
W. H. R. Andrews (Somerset)	6.4	2	12	8	v. Surrey, at The Oval	1937
F. R. Spofforth (Australia)	8.3	6	3	7	v. An England XI, at Birmingham	1884
W. A. Henderson (N.E. Transvaal)	9.3	7	4	7	v. Orange Free State, at Bloemfontein	1937–38
F. Morley (M.C.C.)	22	18	6	7	v. Oxford University, at Oxford	1877
A. Waddington (Yorkshire)	7	4	6	7	v. Sussex, at Hull	1922
R. Tyldesley (Lancashire)	14	12	6	7	v. Northants, at Liverpool	1924
F. Morley (Notts)	10.2	7	7	7	v. Derbyshire, at Nottingham	1879
A. Shaw (Notts)	41.2	36	7	7	v. M.C.C., at Lord's	1875

	O.	M.	R.	W.		
L. T. Driffield (Cambridge)..	6.4	3	7	7 v. M.C.C., at Cambridge	1900
J. Bailey (Hampshire)	7	3	7	7 v. Notts, at Southampton	1932
G. Geary (Leicestershire) ...	13.3	8	7	7 v. Warwickshire, at Hinckley..........	1936
L. Cook (Lancashire)	14	9	8	7 v. Derbyshire, at Chesterfield	1920
G. R. Cox (Sussex)	16	9	8	7 v. Derbyshire, at Hove..	1920
A. Kennedy (Hampshire) ...	10	7	8	7 v. Warwickshire, at Portsmouth	1927
James Langridge (Sussex) ..	11.5	7	8	7 v. Gloucestershire, at Cheltenham	1932
C. Blythe (Kent)	7.5	3	9	7 v. Leicestershire, at Leicester	1912
T. Emmett (Yorkshire)	9.3	6	9	7 v. Sussex, at Hove	1870
G. G. Macaulay (Yorkshire).	14	7	9	7 v. Northants, at Kettering	1933
F. Morley (Notts)	22	15	9	7 v. Kent, at Town Malling	1878
F. Morley (Notts)	19.2	12	9	7 v. Surrey, at The Oval ..	1880
H. Verity (Yorkshire)	6	1	9	7 v. Sussex, at Hove	1939
F. E. Woolley (Kent)	6.3	3	9	7 v. Surrey, at The Oval ..	1911
V. I. Smith (South Africans).	4.5	3	1	6 v. Derbyshire, at Derby .	1947
S. Cosstick (Victoria)	21.1	20	1	6 v. Tasmania, at Melbourne	1868–69
F. E. Field (Warwickshire)..	8.4	7	2	6 v. Worcestershire, at Dudley	1914
T. Wass (Notts)	4.4	3	3	6 v. M.C.C., at Lord's....	1907
A. Penn (Kent)	13.3	11	3	6 v. Sussex, at Tunbridge Wells...........	1878
R. G. Barlow (Lancashire)..	10.1	9	3	6 v. Derbyshire, at Derby.	1881
G. G. Macaulay (Yorkshire).	7	4	3	6 v. Derbyshire, at Hull ..	1921
J. Cowie (New Zealand) ...	8	5	3	6 v. Ireland, at Dublin ...	1937
A. D. Pougher (M.C.C.) ...	3	3	0	5 v. Australians, at Lord's.	1896
G. R. Cox (Sussex)	6	6	0	5 v. Somerset, at Weston-super-Mare	1921
R. Tyldesley (Lancashire) ...	4	4	0	5 v. Leicestershire, at Manchester	1924
P. T. Mills (Gloucestershire).	6.4	6	0	5 v. Somerset, at Bristol ..	1928
F. W. Tate (Sussex)	4	3	1	5 v. Kent, at Tonbridge...	1888
D. Ashby (Canterbury)	15.2	13	2	5 v. Auckland, at Auckland	1877–78
E. H. Killick (Sussex)	6.1	4	2	5 v. Hampshire, at Chichester	1907
E. R. H. Toshack (Australia)	2.3	1	2	5 v. India, at Brisbane ...	1947–48
G. A. R. Lock (Surrey).....	5.3	4	2	5 v. Worcestershire, at The Oval	1954

Sixteen or More Wickets in a Day

17 C. Blythe, Kent v. Northants, at Northampton (for 48 runs) .. 1907
17 H. Verity, Yorkshire v. Essex, at Leyton (for 91 runs) 1933
17 T. W. Goddard, Gloucestershire v. Kent, at Bristol (for 106 runs) 1939
16 T. Emmett, Yorkshire v. Cambridgeshire, at Hunslet (for 38 runs) 1869
16 J. Southerton, South v. North, at Lord's (for 52 runs) .. 1875
16 T. Wass, Nottinghamshire v. Lancashire, at Liverpool (for 69 runs) 1906
16 A. E. E. Vogler, Eastern Province v. Griqualand West, at Johannesburg (for 38 runs) 1906
16 T. Wass, Nottinghamshire v. Essex, at Nottingham (for 103 runs) 1908
16 J. C. White, Somerset v. Worcestershire, at Bath (for 83 runs) .. 1919

200 OR MORE WICKETS IN A SEASON

			Overs	Maidens	Runs	Wickets	Average
	1928	A. P. Freeman ...	1976.1	423	5489	304	18.05
	1933	A. P. Freeman ...	2039	651	4549	298	15.26
(2)	1895	T. Richardson ...	1690.1	463	4170	290	14.37
(1)	1888	C. T. B. Turner**	2427.2	1127	3307	283	11.68
	1931	A. P. Freeman	1618	360	4307	276	15.60
	1930	A. P. Freeman ...	1914.3	472	4632	275	16.84
(2)	1897	T. Richardson	1603.4	495	3945	273	14.45
	1929	A. P. Freeman ...	1670.5	381	4879	267	18.27
	1900	W. Rhodes	1553	455	3606	261	13.81
(2)	1896	J. T. Hearne	2003.1	818	3670	257	14.28
	1932	A. P. Freeman ...	1565.5	404	4149	253	16.39
	1901	W. Rhodes	1565	505	3797	251	15.12
	1937	T. W. Goddard ...	1478.1	359	4158	248	16.76
	1910	W. C. Smith	1423.3	420	3225	247	13.05
(2)	1896	T. Richardson	1656.2	526	4015	246	16.32
(2)	1899	A. E. Trott	1772.4	587	4086	239	!7.09
	1947	T. W. Goddard ...	1451.2	344	4119	238	17.30
	1925	M. W. Tate	1694.3	472	3415	228	14.97
(2)	1898	J. T. Hearne	1802.2	781	3120	222	14.05
	1925	C. W. L. Parker ..	1512.3	478	3311	222	14.91
(2)	1890	G. A. Lohmann .	1759.1	737	2998	220	13.62
	1923	M. W. Tate	1608.5	331	3061	219	13.97
	1925	C. F. Root	1493.2	416	3770	219	17.21
	1931	C. W. L. Parker ..	1320.4	386	3125	219	14.26
(1)	1884	F. R. Spofforth***	1625	672	2732	218	12.53
	1936	H. Verity	1289.3	463	2847	216	13.18
(2)	1955	G. A. R. Lock ...	1408.4	497	3109	216	14.39
	1909	C. Blythe	1273.5	343	3128	215	14.54
(1)	1882	E. Peate	1853.1	868	2466	214	11.52
(2)	1895	A. Mold	1629	598	3400	213	15.96
	1902	W. Rhodes	1306.3	405	2801	213	13.15
	1926	C. W. L. Parker .	1739.5	556	3920	213	18.40
(2)	1893	J. T. Hearne	1741.4	667	3492	212	16.47
	1935	A. P. Freeman .	1503.2	320	4562	212	21.51
	1957	G. A. R. Lock ...	1194.1	449	2550	212	12.02
	1900	A. E. Trott......	1547.1	363	4923	211	23.33
	1925	G. G. Macaulay .	1338.2	307	3268	211	15.48
	1935	H. Verity	1279.2	453	3032	211	14.36
(1)	1870	J. Southerton ...	1863.2	696	3069	210	14.61
(1)	1888	G. A. Lohmann .	1649.1	783	2280	209	10.90
	1923	C. H. Parkin .	1356.2	356	3543	209	16.94
	1906	G. H. Hirst	1306.1	271	3434	208	16.50
(2)	1894	A. Mold	1288.3	456	2548	207	12.30
	1922	C. W. L. Parker .	1294.5	445	2712	206	13.16
	1922	A. Kennedy	1346.4	366	3444	205	16.80
	1924	M. W. Tate	1469.5	465	2818	205	13.74
	1925	E. A. McDonald ..	1249.4	282	3828	205	18.67
	1934	A. P. Freeman .	1744.4	440	4753	205	23.18
	1924	C. W. L. Parker .	1303.5	411	2913	204	14.27
(2)	1889	G. A. Lohmann .	1614.1	646	2714	202	13.43
	1937	H. Verity	1386.2	487	3168	202	15.68
(1)	1878	A. Shaw	2630	—	2203	201	10.96
	1907	G. E. Dennett ...	1216.2	305	3227	201	16.05
	1937	A. R. Gover	1219.4	191	3816	201	18.98
	1924	C. H. Parkin .	1162.5	357	2735	200	13.67
	1935	T. W. Goddard .	1553	384	4073	200	20.36
	1936	A. R. Gover	1159.2	185	3547	200	17.73
(3)	1939	T. W. Goddard .	819	139	2973	200	14.86
	1951	R. Appleyard	1313.2	391	2829	200	14.14

(1) *Indicates 4-ball;* (2) *5-ball: and* (3) *8-ball overs. All others were 6-ball overs.*

** Exclusive of matches not reckoned as first-class.
*** Including Smokers v. Non-Smokers, at Lord's, and all matches of the Australians' tour.

In four consecutive seasons (1928–31), A. P. Freeman took 1,122 wickets, and in eight consecutive seasons (1928–35), 2,090 wickets. In each of these eight seasons he took over 200 wickets.

T. Richardson took 1,005 wickets in four consecutive seasons (1894–97).

In 1896, J. T. Hearne took his 100th wicket as early as June 12th. In 1931, C. W. L. Parker did the same and A. P. Freeman obtained his 100th wicket a day later.

BOWLERS WHO HAVE TAKEN 2,000 WICKETS

	Career	Wickets	Runs	Average
W. Rhodes	1898–1930	4187	69993	16.71
A. P. Freeman	1914–36	3776	69577	18.42
C. W. L. Parker	1903–35	3278	63821	19.46
J. T. Hearne	1888–1923	3061	54342	17.75
T. W. Goddard	1922–52	2979	59116	19.84
A. S. Kennedy	1907–36	2874	61044	21.24
W. G. Grace	1865–1908	2876	51545	17.92
M. W. Tate	1912–37	2783	50544	18.16
G. H. Hirst	1889–1919	2739	51300	18.72
C. Blythe	1899 1914	2506	42136	16.81
W. E. Astill	1906–39	2431	57784	23.76
J. C. White	1909–37	2356	43759	18.57
W. E. Hollies	1932–57	2323	48656	20.94
R. T. D. Perks	1930–55	2233	53770	24.07
J. Briggs	1879–1900	2221	35390	15.93
G. E. Dennett	1903–26	2147	42568	19.82
T. Richardson	1892–1905	2105	38794	18.42
A. Shaw	1864–97	2072	24827	11.97
F. E. Woolley	1906–38	2068	41066	19 85
G. Geary	1912–39	2063	41339	22.03
D. V. P. Wright	1932–57	2056	49309	23.98
J. Newman	1906–30	2032	51211	25 20
S. Haigh	1895–1913	2012	32091	15.94

BOWLERS WHO HAVE TAKEN 100 WICKETS IN A SEASON EIGHT TIMES OR MORE

23 Times: W. RHODES 200 wickets (3).

17 Times: A. P. FREEMAN 300 wickets (1), 200 wickets (7).

16 Times: T. W. GODDARD 200 wickets (4); C. W. L. PARKER 200 wickets (5); R. T. D. PERKS.

15 Times: J. T. HEARNE 200 wickets (3); G. H. HIRST 200 wickets (1); A. S. KENNEDY 200 wickets (1).

14 Times: C. BLYTHE 200 wickets (1); W. E. HOLLIES; M. W. TATE 200 wickets (3); J. C. WHITE.

12 Times: J. BRIGGS; G. E. DENNETT 200 wickets (1).

11 Times: A. V. BEDSER; G. GEARY; C. GLADWIN; S. HAIGH; M. S. NICHOLS; A. E. RELF.

10 Times: W. ATTEWELL; W. G. GRACE; V. W. C. JUPP; J. C. LAKER; G. MACAULAY 200 wickets (1); W. MEAD; T. B. MITCHELL; T. RICHARDSON 200 wickets (3); R. TYLDESLEY; J. H. WARDLE; T. WASS; D. V. P. WRIGHT.

9 Times: W. E. ASTILL; W. E. BOWES; R. HOWORTH; J. MERCER; A. MOLD 200 wickets (2); J. NEWMAN; C. F. ROOT 200 wickets (1); D. SHACKLETON; J. SOUTHERTON 200 wickets (1); H. VERITY 200 wickets (3).

8 Times: H. DEAN; A. R. GOVER 200 wickets (2); H. LARWOOD; G. A. LOHMANN 200 wickets (3); R. PEEL; A. SHAW; J. M. SIMS; F. A. TARRANT, R. TATTERSALL; G. J. THOMPSON; A. W. WELLARD; F. E. WOOLLEY; J. A. YOUNG.

ALL-ROUND CRICKET

2,000 RUNS AND 200 WICKETS IN A SEASON

1906 G. H. Hirst 2,385 runs and 208 wickets

3,000 RUNS AND 100 WICKETS IN A SEASON

1937 J. H. Parks 3,003 runs and 101 wickets.

2,000 RUNS AND 100 WICKETS IN A SEASON

		Runs	Wickets			Runs	Wickets
1873	W. G. Grace	2139	106	1914	J. W. Hearne	2116	123
1876	W. G. Grace	2622	129	1914	F. E. Woolley	2272	125
1899	C. L. Townsend	2440	101	1920	J. W. Hearne	2148	142
1900	G. L. Jessop	2210	104	1921	V. W. C. Jupp	2169	121
1904	G. H. Hirst	2501	132	1921	F. E. Woolley	2101	167
1905	G. H. Hirst	2266	110	1922	F. E. Woolley	2022	163
1909	W. Rhodes	2094	141	1923	F. E. Woolley	2091	101
1911	W. Rhodes	2261	117	1933	L. Townsend	2268	100
1911	F. A. Tarrant	2030	111	1937	E. Davies	2012	103
1913	J. W. Hearne	2036	124	1937	Jas. Langridge	2082	101

1,000 RUNS AND 200 WICKETS IN A SEASON

		Runs	Wickets			Runs	Wickets
1899	A. E. Trott	1175	239	1923	M. W. Tate	1168	219
1900	A. E. Trott	1337	211	1924	M. W. Tate	1419	205
1922	A. S. Kennedy	1129	205	1925	M. W. Tate	1290	228

The double feat of scoring 1,000 runs and taking 100 wickets in one season of first-class cricket has been accomplished 266 times as follows:—

SIXTEEN
W. Rhodes

FOURTEEN
G. H. Hirst

TEN
V. W. C. Jupp

NINE
W. E. Astill

EIGHT
W. G. Grace
M. S. Nichols
A. E. Relf
F. A. Tarrant
M. W. Tate
F. E. Woolley

SIX
P. G. H. Fender
Jas. Langridge
G. E. Tribe

FIVE
J. W. H. T. Douglas
J. W. Hearne
A. S. Kennedy
J. Newman

FOUR
E. G. Arnold
T. E. Bailey
J. Gunn
R. Kilner

THREE
W. W. Armstrong (Australia)
L. C. Braund
G. Giffen (Australia)
N. E. Haig
R. Howorth
C. B. Llewellyn
Ray Smith
S. G. Smith
F. J. Titmus
L. Townsend
A. W. Wellard

TWO
W. H. R. Andrews
F. R. Brown

D. B. Close
J. N. Crawford
E. Davies
B. Dooland
F. R. Foster
G. Goonesena
J. L. Hopwood
R. O. Jenkins
G. L. Jessop
W. H. Lockwood
S. H. Martin
J. H. Parks
G. H. Pope
R. A. Sinfield
C. T. Studd
G. J. Thompson
C. L. Townsend
A. E. Trott
A. J. Watkins
J. C. White

ONE

J. Bailey

F. Barratt
M. W. Booth
B. J. T. Bosanquet
W. Brockwell
V. Broderick
Hon. F. S. G. Calthorpe
H. L. Collins (Australia)
L. N. Constantine (West-Indies)
J. A. Cuffe
W. R. Cuttell
G. Davidson
A. Drake
G. A. Faulkner (South Africa)
W. Flowers
A. E. R. Gilligan
J. M. Gregory (Australia)
S. Haigh
J. Hallows
T. Hayward
M. J. Horton
R. Illingworth

F. S. Jackson
V. E. Jackson
E. H. Killick
J. H. King
V. Mankad (India)
J. R. Mason
B. L. Muncer
G. E. Palmer (Australia)
F. Pearson
R. Peel
R. W. V. Robins
C. F. Root
H. L. Simms
T. F. Smailes
T. P. B. Smith
L. J. Todd
H. Trumble (Australia)
J. Vine
E. Wainwright
J. E. Walsh
A. F. Wensley
W. Wooller

T. E. Bailey, B. Dooland, G. Goonesena, R. Illingworth, F. J. Titmus and G. E. Tribe accomplished this feat in 1957.

L. E. G. Ames, in 1928 scored 1,919 runs and obtained 121 wickets while keeping wicket. In 1929 his aggregates were 1,795 runs and 127 wickets, and in 1932, 2,482 runs and 100 wickets.

J. T. Murray, in 1957, scored 1,025 runs and obtained 104 wickets while keeping wicket.

CENTURY AND HAT-TRICK

1885 W. E. Roller, Surrey v. Sussex, at The Oval, 204 and 4 for 28 including hat-trick.
1927 R. E. S. Wyatt, M.C.C. v. Ceylon, at Colombo, 124 and 5 for 39 including hat-trick.
1928 L. N. Constantine, West Indies v. Northamptonshire, at Northampton, 7 for 45 including hat-trick, 107 (five 6's) and 6 for 67.
1937 Emrys Davies, Glamorgan v. Leicestershire, at Leicester, 139 and 4 for 27 and 3 for 31 including hat-trick.

WICKET-KEEPING FEATS

Most Dismissals:	H. Strudwick (1902–27)	1,493
Most Catches:	H. Strudwick (1902–27)	1,235
Most Stumpings:	L. E. G. Ames (1926–38)	413

12 wickets in match, ct. 8, st. 4, E. Pooley, Surrey v. Sussex, at The Oval 1868
12 wickets in match, ct. 9, st. 3, D. Tallon, Queensland v. New South Wales, at Sydney 1933–39
10 wickets in match, all ct., A. E. Wilson, Gloucestershire v. Hampshire, at Portsmouth 1953
10 wickets in match, ct. 5, st. 5, H. Phillips, Sussex v. Surrey, at The Oval 1872
10 wickets in match, ct. 2, st. 8, E. Pooley, Surrey v. Kent, at The Oval 1878
10 wickets in match, ct. 9, st. 1, T. W. Oates, Nottinghamshire v. Middlesex, at Nottingham 1906

10 wickets in match, ct. 1, st. 9, F. H. Huish, Kent v. Surrey, at The
   Oval   1911
10 wickets in match, ct. 9, st. 1, J. C. Hubble, Kent v. Gloucestershire,
   at Cheltenham   1923
10 wickets in match, ct. 8, st. 2, H. Elliott, Derbyshire v. Lancashire,
   at Manchester   1935
10 wickets in match, ct. 7, st. 3, P. Corrall, Leicestershire v. Sussex,
   at Hove   1936
7 wickets in innings, ct. 4, st. 3, E. J. Smith, Warwickshire v. Derby-
   shire, at Edgbaston   1926
7 wickets in innings, ct. 6, st. 1, W. Farrimond, Lancashire v. Kent,
   at Manchester   1930
7 wickets in innings, ct. 7, W. F. Price, Middlesex v. Yorkshire, at
   Lord's   1937
7 wickets in innings, ct. 3, st. 4, D. Tallon, Queensland v. Victoria, at
   Brisbane   1938–39
7 wickets in innings, ct. 7, R. Saggers, N.S.W. v. Queensland and
   Victoria Combined, at Brisbane   1940–41
7 wickets in innings, ct. 1, st. 6, H. Yarnold, Worcestershire v. Scot-
   land, at Broughty Ferry   1951
7 wickets in innings, ct. 4, st 3, J. Brown, Scotland v. Ireland, at Dublin   1957

   Three men stumped off successive balls, W. H. Brain, Gloucestershire
v. Somerset, at Cheltenham, 1893. (The bowler thus credited with the hat-trick
was C. L. Townsend.)

   A. Wood kept wicket for Yorkshire in 222 consecutive County Championship matches (1928–1935).

127 wickets in a season, ct. 79, st. 48, L. E. G. Ames, of Kent   1929
121 wickets in a season, ct. 69, st. 52, L. E. G. Ames, of Kent   1928
110 wickets in a season, ct. 62, st. 48, H. Yarnold, of Worcestershire   ..   1949
107 wickets in a season, ct. 77, st. 30, G. Duckworth, of Lancashire   ..   1928
104 wickets in a season, ct. 82, st. 22, J. T. Murray, of Middlesex   ..   1957
102 wickets in a season, ct. 70, st. 32, F. H. Huish, of Kent   1913
100 wickets in a season, ct. 36, st. 64, L. E. G. Ames, of Kent   1932
100 wickets in a season, ct. 62, st. 38, F. H. Huish, of Kent   1911

MOST CATCHES

In a Career

913   F. E. Woolley   871   W. G. Grace

In a Season

78	W. R. Hammond	1928	64	K. F. Barrington	1957
77	M. J. Stewart	1957	64	J. Tunnicliffe	1904
70	J. Tunnicliffe	1901	63	K. Grieves	1950
69	John Langridge	1955	63	G. A. R. Lock	1957
65	W. R. Hammond	1925	63	C. A. Milton	1956
65	J. Tunnicliffe	1895			

In a Match

10   W. R. Hammond, Gloucestershire v. Surrey, Cheltenham   1928
 8   W. B. Burns, Worcestershire v. Yorkshire, Bradford   1907
 8   A. H. Bakewell, Northamptonshire v. Essex, Leyton   1928
 8   W. R. Hammond, Gloucestershire v. Worcestershire, Cheltenham ..   1932
 8   K. Grieves, Lancashire v. Sussex, Manchester..   1951
 8   C. A. Milton, Gloucestershire v. Sussex, Hove..   1952

In an Innings

 7   M. J. Stewart, Surrey v. Northamptonshire, Northampton   1957

THROWING THE CRICKET BALL

140 yards 2 feet, R. Percival, on the Durham Sand Racecourse ..	1884
140 yards 9 inches, Ross Mackenzie, at Toronto	1872

W. F. Forbes, on March 16th, 1876, threw 132 yards at the Eton College Sports. He was then 18 years of age.

William Yardley, while a boy at Rugby, threw 100 yards with his right hand and 78 with his left.

Charles Arnold, of Cambridge, once threw 112 yards with the wind and 108 against. W. H. Game, at The Oval, in 1875, threw the ball 111 yards and then back the same distance. W. G. Grace threw 109 yards one way and back 105, and George Millyard 108 with the wind and 103 against. At The Oval in 1868, W. G. Grace made three successive throws of 116, 117 and 118 yards, and then threw back over 100 yards. D. G. Foster (Warwickshire) has thrown 133 yards, and in 1930 he made a Danish record with 120.1 metres—about 130 yards.

GREAT TOTALS

1107	Victoria v. New South Wales, at Melbourne	1926–27
1059	Victoria v. Tasmania, at Melbourne	1922–23
918	New South Wales v. South Australia, at Sydney	1900–01
912	(eight wkts., dec.), Holkar v. Mysore, at Indore ..	1945–46
903	(seven wkts.), England v. Australia, at The Oval ..	1938
887	Yorkshire v. Warwickshire, at Edgbaston	1896
849	England v. West Indies, at Kingston	1929–30
843	Australians v. Oxford and Cambridge Universities Past and Present, at Portsmouth	1893

HIGHEST FOR EACH FIRST-CLASS COUNTY

Derbyshire ..	645 v. Hampshire, at Derby	1898
Essex	692 v. Somerset, at Taunton	1895
Glamorgan ..	587 (eight wickets) v. Derbyshire, at Cardiff ..	1951
Gloucestershire ..	653 (six wickets) v. Glamorgan, at Bristol ..	1928
Hampshire ..	672 (seven wickets) v. Somerset, at Taunton ..	1899
Kent	803 (four wickets) v. Essex, at Brentwood ..	1934
Lancashire..	801 v. Somerset, at Taunton	1895
Leicestershire ..	701 (four wickets) v. Worcestershire, at Worcester..	1906
Middlesex ..	642 (three wickets) v. Hampshire, at Southampton..	1923
Northamptonshire	557 (six wickets) v. Sussex, at Hove	1914
Nottinghamshire ..	739 (seven wickets) v. Leicestershire, at Nottingham	1903
Somerset ..	675 (nine wickets) v. Hampshire, at Bath ..	1924
Surrey	811 v. Somerset, at The Oval	1899
Sussex	705 (eight wickets) v. Surrey, at Hastings ..	1902
Warwickshire ..	657 (six wickets), v. Hampshire, at Edgbaston ..	1899
Worcestershire ..	633 v. Warwickshire, at Worcester	1906
Yorkshire ..	887 v. Warwickshire, at Edgbaston	1896

SMALL TOTALS

12	Oxford University v. M.C.C. and Ground, at Oxford	†1877
12	Northamptonshire v. Gloucestershire, at Gloucester	1907
13	Nottinghamshire v. Yorkshire, at Nottingham	1901
15	M.C.C. v. Surrey, at Lord's	1839
15	Victoria v. M.C.C., at Melbourne	†1903–04
15	Northamptonshire v. Yorkshire, at Northampton	†1908
15	Hampshire v. Warwickshire, at Edgbaston	1922
	(Following-on, Hampshire scored 521 and won by 155 runs)	

† Signifies that one man was absent.

16	M.C.C. and Ground v. Surrey, at Lord's	..	..	..	..	1872
16	Derbyshire v. Notts, at Nottingham	..				1879
16	Surrey v. Nottinghamshire, at the Oval	..	..			1880
16	Warwickshire v. Kent, at Tonbridge	..				1913
16	Trinidad v. Barbados, at Bridgetown	..				1941–42
17	Gloucestershire v. Australians, at Cheltenham	..				1896
18	Kent v. Sussex, at Gravesend	..				†1867
18	Australians v. M.C.C. and Ground, at Lord's					†1896
19	Sussex v. Surrey, at Godalming					1830
19	Sussex v. Nottinghamshire, at Hove	..				†1873
19	M.C.C. and Ground v. Australians, at Lord's					1878

† Signifies that one man was absent.

LOWEST FOR EACH COUNTY

Derbyshire	..	..	16 v. Nottinghamshire, at Nottingham	..	..	1879
Essex	..	..	30 v. Yorkshire, at Leyton ..	..	..	1901
Glamorgan	..	..	22 v. Lancashire, at Liverpool	..	..	1924
Gloucestershire	..	..	17 v. Australians, at Cheltenham	..	..	1896
Hampshire	..	..	15 v. Warwickshire, at Birmingham	..	..	1922
Kent	..	..	18 v. Sussex, at Gravesend	..	..	1867
Lancashire	..	..	25 v. Derbyshire, at Manchester	..	..	1871
Leicestershire	..	..	25 v. Kent, at Leicester	..	..	1912
Middlesex	..	..	20 v. M.C.C., at Lord's	..	..	1864
Northamptonshire	..		12 v. Gloucestershire, at Gloucester	..	..	1907
Nottinghamshire	..		13 v. Yorkshire, at Nottingham	..	..	1901
Somerset	..	..	25 v. Gloucestershire, at Bristol	..	..	1947
Surrey	..	..	16 v. Nottinghamshire, at The Oval	..	..	1880
Sussex	..	..	19 v. Nottinghamshire, at Hove	..	..	1873
Warwickshire	..	..	16 v. Kent, at Tonbridge	..	..	1913
Worcestershire	..		24 v. Yorkshire, at Huddersfield	..	..	1903
Yorkshire	..	..	26 v. Surrey, at The Oval	..	..	1909

HIGHEST AGGREGATES

2376 for 38 wickets, Maharashtra v. Bombay, at Poona	..	..	1948–49
2078 for 40 wickets, Bombay v. Holkar, at Bombay	..	..	1944–45
1981 for 35 wickets, England v. South Africa, at Durban	..	1938–39
1929 for 39 wickets, New South Wales v. South Australia, at Sydney..	1925–26

IN ENGLAND

1723 for 31 wickets, England v. Australia, at Leeds	..	..	1948
1601 for 29 wickets, England v. Australia, at Lord's	..	..	1930
1502 for 28 wickets, M.C.C. v. New Zealand, at Lord's	..	..	1927
1496 for 24 wickets, England v. Australia, at Nottingham	..	..	1938
1494 for 37 wickets, England v. Australia, at The Oval..	..	..	1934
1492 for 33 wickets, Worcestershire v. Oxford University, at Worcester	1904
1477 for 32 wickets, Hampshire v. Oxford University, at Southampton	1913
1477 for 33 wickets, England v. South Africa, at The Oval	..	..	1947
1475 for 27 wickets, Northamptonshire v. Surrey, at Northampton	..	1920

HEAVY SCORING IN FOURTH INNINGS

654 (five wickets), England v. South Africa, at Durban 1938–39
(After being set 696 to win. The match was left drawn on the tenth day.)

604 Maharashtra v. Bombay, at Poona 1948–49

576 (eight wickets), Trinidad v. Barbados, at Port of Spain 1946
(After being set 672 to win. Match drawn on fifth day.)

572 New South Wales v. South Australia, at Sydney 1907–08
(After being set 593 to win)

518 Victoria v. Queensland, at Brisbane 1926–27
(When set 753 to win)

507 (seven wickets), Cambridge University v. M.C.C. and Ground, at Lord's 1896
502 (six wickets), Middlesex v. Nottinghamshire, at Trent Bridge .. 1925
    (Game won by an unfinished stand of 271: county record)
502 (eight wickets), Players v. Gentlemen, at Lord's 1900
    (Unless otherwise stated, the side making the runs won the match.)

BIGGEST VICTORIES

Yorkshire (555 for one wkt., dec.) beat Essex at Leyton on June 15, 16 17, 1932, by an innings and 313 runs. Holmes and Sutcliffe made 555, the world's highest first-wicket partnership.

Middlesex (464 for one wkt., dec.) beat Essex at Leyton on May 23, 25, 26, 1914, by an innings and 56 runs.

The only instance in first-class cricket of a side winning without having a batsman dismissed in either innings occurred when Lancashire beat Leicestershire at Manchester in 1956 by ten wickets. A. Wharton and J. Dyson were the two men concerned.

Victoria (1,059) beat Tasmania by an innings and 666 runs at Melbourne, 1922–23.

Victoria (1,107) beat New South Wales by an innings and 656 runs at Melbourne, 1926–27.

New South Wales (918) beat South Australia by an innings and 605 runs at Sydney, 1900–01.

England (903 for seven wkts., dec.) beat Australia by an innings and 579 runs at The Oval in 1938.

England (521 and 342 for eight wkts., dec.) beat Australia by 675 runs at Brisbane in 1928–29.

Surrey (698) beat Sussex by an innings and 485 runs at The Oval in 1888.

Australians (675) beat Nottinghamshire by an innings and 517 runs at Nottingham in 1921. In their previous game they defeated Northamptonshire by an innings and 484 runs.

SCORERS OF 1,500 RUNS IN TESTS

ENGLAND

	Tests	Inns.	Not Outs	Runs	Highest Score	100's	Average
W. R. Hammond ..	85	140	16	7249	336*	22	58.45
L. Hutton	79	138	15	6971	364	19	56.67
D. C. S. Compton ..	78	131	15	5807	278	17	50.60
J. B. Hobbs	61	102	7	5410	211	15	56.94
H. Sutcliffe	54	84	9	4555	194	16	60.73
E. Hendren	51	83	9	3525	205*	7	47.63
F. E. Woolley	64	98	7	3283	154	5	36.07
P. B. H. May ....:	44	71	5	3095	285*	8	40.89
M. Leyland	41	65	5	2764	187	9	46.06
C. Washbrook	37	66	6	2569	195	6	42.81
W. J. Edrich	39	63	2	2440	219	6	40.00
L. E. G. Ames	47	72	12	2434	149	8	40.56
W. Rhodes	58	98	21	2325	179	2	30.19
T. G. Evans	81	120	14	2311	104	2	21.80
T. W. Graveney ...	37	59	9	2103	258	4	42.06
T. E. Bailey	52	77	13	2051	134*	1	32.04
T. Hayward	35	60	2	1999	137	3	34.46
A. C. Maclaren	35	61	4	1931	140	5	33.87
R. E. S. Wyatt	40	64	6	1839	149	2	31.70
J. T. Tyldesley	31	55	1	1661	138	4	30.75
J. Hardstaff, junr. ..	23	38	3	1636	205*	4	46.74
E. Paynter	20	31	5	1540	243	4	59.23

* Signifies not out.

AUSTRALIA

	Tests	Inns.	Not Outs	Runs	Highest Score	100's	Average
D. G. Bradman	52	80	10	6996	334	29	99.94
R. N. Harvey	48	83	6	4222	205	16	54.83
A. R. Morris........	46	79	3	3533	206	12	46.48
C. Hill	49	89	3	3402	191	7	39 55
V. Trumper	48	89	8	3163	214*	8	39.04
A. L. Hassett	43	69	3	3073	198*	10	46.56
K. R. Miller	55	87	7	2958	147	7	36.97
W. W. Armstrong ..	50	84	10	2873	159*	6	38.82
S. J. McCabe	39	62	5	2748	232	6	48.21
W. Bardsley	41	66	5	2469	193*	6	40.47
W. M. Woodfull ...	35	54	4	2300	161	7	46.00
S. E. Gregory	58	100	7	2282	201	4	24.53
C. G. Macartney ...	35	55	4	2132	170	7	41.80
W. H. Ponsford ...	29	48	4	2122	266	7	48.22
M. A. Noble	42	73	7	1997	133	1	30.25
J. Darling	34	60	2	1657	178	3	28.56
W. A. Brown	22	35	1	1592	206*	4	46.82

SOUTH AFRICA

	Tests	Inns.	Not Outs	Runs	Highest Score	100's	Average
B. Mitchell	42	80	9	3471	189*	8	48.88
A. D. Nourse, junr.	34	52	7	2960	231	9	53.81
H. W. Taylor	42	76	4	2936	176	7	40.77
A. D. Nourse, senr.	45	83	8	2234	111	1	29.78
E. A. B. Rowan ...	26	50	5	1965	236	3	43.66
G. A. Faulkner	25	47	4	1754	204	4	40.79
R. H. Catterall	24	43	2	1555	120	3	37.92

WEST INDIES

	Tests	Inns.	Not Outs	Runs	Highest Score	100's	Average
E. Weekes	43	73	4	4000	207	14	57.97
C. L. Walcott	38	66	6	3329	220	14	55.48
F. M. Worrell	32	57	5	2691	261	8	51.75
G. A. Headley	22	40	4	2190	270	10	60.83
J. B. Stollmeyer	32	56	5	2159	160	4	42.33

INDIA

	Tests	Inns.	Not Outs	Runs	Highest Score	100's	Average
V. S. Hazare	30	52	6	2192	164*	8	47.65
V. Mankad	42	69	5	2084	231	5	32.56
P. R. Umrigar	33	50	5	1931	223	6	42.91
P. Roy	27	48	4	1642	173	5	37.31

NEW ZEALAND

	Tests	Inns.	Not Outs	Runs	Highest Score	100's	Average
B. Sutcliffe........	28	51	4	2140	230*	4	45.53

Signifies not out.

BOWLERS WITH 75 WICKETS IN TESTS

ENGLAND

	Tests	Runs	Wickets	Average
A. V. Bedser	51	5876	236	24.89
S. F. Barnes	27	3106	189	16.43
J. C. Laker	38	3608	161	22.40
M. W. Tate	39	4051	155	26.13
H. Verity	40	3510	144	24.37
W. Rhodes	58	3425	127	26.96
J. B. Statham	38	3094	123	25.15
T. E. Bailey	52	3504	121	28.95
J. Briggs	33	2094	118	17.74
G. A. Lohmann	18	1205	112	10.75

	Tests	Runs	Wickets	Average
D. V. P. Wright	34	4224	108	39.11
R. Peel	20	1715	102	16.81
J. H. Wardle	28	2080	102	20.39
C. Blythe	19	1863	100	18.63
W. Voce	27	2733	98	27.88
T. Richardson.............	14	2220	88	25.22
W. R. Hammond	85	3127	83	37.67
F. E. Woolley	64	2815	83	33.91
G. O. Allen	25	2379	81	29.37
H. Larwood	21	2216	78	28.41

AUSTRALIA

	Tests	Runs	Wickets	Average
C. V. Grimmett	37	5231	216	24.21
R. R. Lindwall	55	4704	212	22.18
K. R. Miller	55	3905	170	22.97
W. A. Johnston.............	40	3825	160	23.90
W. J. O'Reilly.............	27	3254	144	22.59
H. Trumble	32	3072	141	21.78
M. A. Noble	42	3027	121	25.01
I. W. Johnson	45	3182	109	29.19
G. Giffen	31	2791	103	27.09
C. T. B. Turner	17	1670	101	16.53
A. A. Mailey...............	21	3358	99	33.91
F. R. Spofforth.............	18	1731	94	18.41
A. Cotter	21	2549	89	28.64
W. W. Armstrong	50	2923	87	33.59
J. M. Gregory	24	2648	85	31.15
J. V. Saunders	14	1797	79	22.74
G. E. Palmer.............	17	1678	78	21.51

SOUTH AFRICA

	Tests	Runs	Wickets	Average
H. J. Tayfield	27	3312	141	23.48
C. L. Vincent	25	2631	84	31.32
G. A. Faulkner.............	25	2180	82	26.58

WEST INDIES

	Tests	Runs	Wickets	Average
S. Ramadhin	33	3736	127	29.41
A. L. Valentine.............	28	3444	120	28.70

INDIA

	Tests	Runs	Wickets	Average
V. Mankad	42	4973	158	**31.47**
S. Gupte	21	2386	95	25.11

MOST WICKETS IN A TEST

19/90	J. C. Laker, England v. Australia, Manchester	.. ..	1956
17/159	S. F. Barnes, England v. South Africa, Johannesburg ..	..	1913–14
15/28	J. Briggs, England v. South Africa, Cape Town	..	1888–89
15/45	G. A. Lohmann, England v. South Africa, Port Elizabeth	..	1895–96
15/99	C. Blythe, England v. South Africa, Leeds	.. ..	1907
15/104	H. Verity, England v. Australia, Lord's ..	.. ..	1934
15/124	W. Rhodes, England v. Australia, Melbourne	.. ..	1903–04
14/90	F. R. Spofforth, Australia v. England, Oval	.. ..	1882
14/99	A. V. Bedser, England v. Australia, Nottingham	.. ..	1953
14/144	S. F. Barnes, England v. South Africa, Durban	.. ..	1913–14
14/199	C. V. Grimmett, Australia v. South Africa, Adelaide ..	..	1931–32

The best for South Africa is 13/165 by H. Tayfield against Australia at Melbourne, 1952–53.

MOST BALLS BOWLED IN A TEST MATCH

S. Ramadhin (West Indies) sent down 774 balls in 129 overs against England at Birmingham, 1957. It was the most delivered by any bowler in a Test, beating

H. Verity's 766 for England against South Africa at Durban, 1939. In this match
Ramadhin also bowled most balls (588) in any single first-class innings, including
Tests. The highest number of balls bowled by one man in a first-class match is
917 by C. S. Nayudu for Holkar v. Bombay, 1944–45. It should be noted that
six balls were bowled to the over in the Australia v. England Test series of 1928–29
and 1932–33 when the eight-ball over was otherwise in force in Australia.

WICKET-KEEPING FEATS

MOST VICTIMS IN A TEST CAREER

202 in 81 matches	T. G. Evans (England).	
130 in 54 matches	W. A. Oldfield (Australia).	

MOST VICTIMS IN A TEST SERIES

23 (16 c 7 s)	J. H. B. Waite	South Africa v. New Zealand	..	1953–54
21 (16 c 5 s)	G. R. Langley	Australia v. West Indies	.. ..	1951–52
21 (13 c 8 s)	R. A. Saggers	Australia v. South Africa	.. ..	1949–50
21 (15 c 6 s)	H. Strudwick	England v. South Africa	.. ..	1913–14

MOST VICTIMS IN A TEST INNINGS

5 (1 c 4 s)	W. A. Oldfield, Australia v. England, at Melbourne	.. 1924–25
5 (2 c 3 s)	G. R. Langley, Australia v. West Indies, at Georgetown	1954–55
5 (all c)	G. R. Langley, Australia v. West Indies, at Kingston	.. 1954–55

MOST VICTIMS IN ONE TEST

9 (8 c 1 s)	G. R. Langley, Australia v. England, at Lord's ..	.. 1956
8 (6 c 2 s)	L. E. G. Ames, England v. West Indies, at The Oval	1933
8 (all c)	J. J. Kelly, Australia v. England, at Sydney	.. 1901–02
8 (all c)	G. R. Langley, Australia v. West Indies, at Kingston	.. 1954–55

SLOW INDIVIDUAL TEST BATTING

18 in 180 minutes—G. O. Rabone, New Zealand v. England, Dunedin.	1954–55
19 not out in 150 minutes—W. L. Murdoch, Aust. v. Engl., Melbourne	1882–83
31 in 266 minutes—K. Mackay, Australia v. England, Lord's ..	1956
34 in 225 minutes—W. H. Scotton, England v. Australia, Oval	.. 1886
38 in 260 minutes—T. E. Bailey, England v. Australia, Leeds ..	1953
41 in 240 minutes—A. C. Bannerman, Australia v. England, Melbourne	1891–92
40 in 295 minutes—H. L. Collins, Australia v. England, Manchester ..	1921
71 in 255 minutes—T. E. Bailey, England v. Australia, Lord's ..	1953
82 in 360 minutes—W. H. Scotton, England v. Australia Adelaide	.. 1884–85
117 in 530 minutes—P. E. Richardson, England v. South Africa, Johannesburg (He took 490 minutes to reach 100)	1956–57

SMALLEST TEST TOTALS IN ONE FULL DAY'S PLAY

95　At Karachi, October 1956, Australia 80 all out; Pakistan 15 for two wickets.

117　At Madras, October 1956, India 117 for five wickets v. Australia.

122　At Port Elizabeth, March 1957. England's last wicket fell after first twenty
　　　minutes without addition. South Africa then made 122 for seven wickets
　　　in five and a half hours.

125　At Dunedin, March 1955, New Zealand 125 all out v. England.

128　At Barbados, February 9, 1954. England added only 128 v. West Indies.

ENGLAND v. AUSTRALIA

SUMMARY OF RESULTS

Season	Visiting Captain	Won by England	Won by Australia	Drawn	Total
1876–77	J. Lillywhite (E.)	1	1	0	2
1878–79	Lord Harris ....(E.)	0	1	0	1
1880	W. L. Murdoch ....(A.)	1	0	0	1
1881–82	A. Shaw ....(E.)	0	2	2	4
1882	W. L. Murdoch ....(A.)	0	1	0	1
1882–83	Hon. Ivo. Bligh ....(E.)	2	2	0	4
1884	W. L. Murdoch ....(A.)	1	0	2	3
1884–85	A. Shrewsbury ....(E.)	3	2	0	5
1886	H. J. H. Scott ......(A.)	3	0	0	3
1886–87	A. Shrewsbury ......(E.)	2	0	0	2
1887–88	W. W. Read........(E.)	1	0	0	1
1888	P. S. McDonnell ....(A.)	2	1	0	3
1890*	W. L. Murdoch ....(A.)	2	0	0	2
1891–92	W. G. Grace ....(E.)	1	2	0	3
1893	J. McC. Blackham ..(A.)	1	0	2	3
1894–95	A. E. Stoddart ......(E.)	3	2	0	5
1896	G. H. S. Trott ......(A.)	2	1	0	3
1897–98	A. E. Stoddart ......(E.)	1	4	0	5
1899	J. Darling ....(A.)	0	1	4	5
1901–2	A. C. MacLaren ....(E.)	1	4	0	5
1902	J. Darling ....(A.)	1	2	2	5
1903–4	P. E. Warner ....(E.)	3	2	0	5
1905	J. Darling ....(A.)	2	0	3	5
1907–8	A. O. Jones ....(E.)	1	4	0	5
1909	M. A. Noble ....(A.)	1	2	2	5
1911–12	J. W. H. T. Douglas..(E.)	4	1	0	5
1912	S. E. Gregory ......(A.)	1	0	2	3
1920–21	J. W. H. T. Douglas.(E.)	0	5	0	5
1921	W. W. Armstrong ...(A.)	0	3	2	5
1924–25	A. E. R. Gilligan ....(E.)	1	4	0	5
1926	H. L. Collins ....(A.)	1	0	4	5
1928–29	A. P. F. Chapman ...(E.)	4	1	0	5
1930	W. M. Woodfull ....(A.)	1	2	2	5
1932–33	D. R. Jardine........(E.)	4	1	0	5
1934	W. M. Woodfull ....(A.)	1	2	2	5
1936–37	G. O. Allen ....(E.)	2	3	0	5
1938*	D. G. Bradman ....(A.)	1	1	2	4
1946–47	W. R. Hammond ....(E.)	0	3	2	5
1948	D. G. Bradman ....(A.)	0	4	1	5
1950–51	F. R. Brown........(E.)	1	4	0	5
1953	A. L. Hassett ......(A.)	1	0	4	5
1954–55	L. Hutton ....(E.)	3	1	1	5
1956	I. W. Johnson ......(A.)	2	1	2	5
	In Australia................	38	49	5	92
	In England	24	21	36	81
	Totals	62	70	41	173

* The match at Manchester was abandoned without a ball bowled.

HIGHEST TOTALS FOR AN INNINGS

By England		By Australia	
627 (7 wkts.), The Oval ..	1938	729 (6 wkts.), Lord's	1930
903 (8 wkts.), Nottingham	1938	701 .. The Oval	1934
658 .. Sydney	1928–29	695 .. The Oval	1930
636 (9 wkts.), Manchester	1934	659 (8 wkts.), Sydney	1946–47
		645 .. Brisbane	1946–47
		604 .. Melbourne	1936–37
		601 (8 wkts.), Brisbane ...	1954–55

SMALLEST TOTALS FOR AN INNINGS

36 .. Australia .. Edgbaston 1902	44 .. Australia .. The Oval 1896
42 .. Australia .. Sydney 1887–88	45 .. England .. Sydney 1886–87

RECORD PARTNERSHIP FOR EACH WICKET

By England

323 for 1st	J. B. Hobbs and W. Rhodes, at Melbourne	1911–12
382 for 2nd	L. Hutton and M. Leyland, at The Oval	1938
262 for 3rd	W. R. Hammond and D R. Jardine, at Adelaide ..	1928–29
222 for 4th	W. R. Hammond and E. Paynter, at Lord's ..	1938
206 for 5th	E. Paynter and D. Compton, at Nottingham ..	1938
215 for 6th	L. Hutton and J. Hardstaff, at The Oval ..	1938
143 for 7th	J. Vine and F. E. Woolley, at Sydney	1911–12
124 for 8th	E. Hendren and H. Larwood, at Brisbane ..	1928–29
151 for 9th	W. W. Read and W. H. Scotton, at The Oval ..	1884
130 for 10th	R. E. Foster and W. Rhodes, at Sydney	1903–04

By Australia

180 for 1st	W. Bardsley and S. E. Gregory, at The Oval ..	1909
451 for 2nd	W. H. Ponsford and D. G. Bradman, at The Oval ..	1934
276 for 3rd	D. G. Bradman and A. L. Hassett, at Brisbane ..	1946–47
388 for 4th	W. H. Ponsford and D. G. Bradman, at Leeds ..	1934
405 for 5th	S. G. Barnes and D. G. Bradman, at Sydney ..	1946–47
346 for 6th	D. G. Bradman and J. H. Fingleton, at Melbourne ..	1936–37
165 for 7th	C. Hill and H. Trumble, at Melbourne ..	1897–98
243 for 8th	C. Hill and R. J. Hartigan, at Adelaide ..	1907–08
154 for 9th	J. McC. Blackham and S. E. Gregory, at Sydney ..	1894–95
127 for 10th	J. M. Taylor and A. A. Mailey, at Sydney	1924–25

HUNDRED ON DEBUT IN ENGLAND–AUSTRALIA TESTS

For England

152	W.G.Grace,atThe Oval	1880	173 K. S. Duleepsinhji, Lord's	1930
154*	K.S.Ranjitsinhji,Manchester	1896	102 Nawab of Pataudi, Sydney	1932–33
287	R. E. Foster, Sydney ..	1903–04	100 L. Hutton, Nottingham	1938
119	G. Gunn, Sydney	1907–08		
115	H. Sutcliffe, Sydney ..	1924–25	102 D. C. S. Compton, Nottingham	1938
137	M. Leyland, Melbourne	1928–29	109 W. Watson, Lord's	1953

For Australia

165*	C. Bannerman, Melbourne (Retired.) ..	1876–77	104 H. L. Collins, Sydney..	1920–21
			110 W. H. Ponsford, Sydney	1924–25
107	H. Graham, Lord's ..	1893	164 A. A. Jackson, Adelaide	1928–29
104	R. A. Duff, Melbourne	1901–02	112 R. N. Harvey, Leeds..	1948
116	R. J. Hartigan, Adelaide	1907–08	101* J. Burke, Adelaide ..	1950–51

Signifies not out.

INDIVIDUAL HUNDREDS IN THE MATCHES 1876-1955

FOR ENGLAND (121)

132*	R. Abel, Sydney	1891–2	119 J. B. Hobbs, Lord's	1926
120	L. E. G. Ames, Lord's	1934	100 J. B. Hobbs, The Oval	1926
134	W. Barnes, Adelaide	1884–5	142 J. B. Hobbs, Melbourne	1928–9
129	C. J. Barnett, Adelaide	1936–7	126 K. L. Hutchings, Melbourne	1907–8
126	C. J. Barnett, Nottingham	1938	100 L. Hutton, Nottingham	1938
103*	L. C. Braund, Adelaide	1901–2	364 L. Hutton, The Oval	1938
102	L. C. Braund, Sydney	1903–4	122* L. Hutton, Sydney	1946–7
121	J. Briggs, Melbourne	1884–5	156* L. Hutton, Adelaide	1950–1
140	J. T. Brown, Melbourne	1894–5	145 L. Hutton, Lord's	1953
121	A. P. F. Chapman, Lord's	1930	103 Hon. F. S. Jackson, The Oval	1893
102	D. C. S. Compton, Nottingham	1938	118 Hon. F. S. Jackson, The Oval	1899
147 103*	D. C. S. Compton, Adelaide	1946–7	128 Hon. F. S. Jackson, Manchester	1902
184	D. C. S. Compton, Nottingham	1948	144* Hon. F. S. Jackson, Leeds	1905
145*	D. C. S. Compton, Manchester	1948	113 Hon. F. S. Jackson, Manchester	1905
102	M. C. Cowdrey, Melbourne	1954–5	104 G. L. Jessop, The Oval	1902
173	K. S. Duleepsinhji, Lord's	1930	137 M. Leyland, Melbourne	1928–9
119	W. J. Edrich, Sydney	1946–7	109 M. Leyland, Lord's	1934
111	W. J. Edrich, Leeds	1948	153 M. Leyland, Manchester	1934
287	R. E. Foster, Sydney	1903–4	110 M. Leyland, The Oval	1934
144	C. B. Fry, The Oval	1905	126 M. Leyland, Brisbane	1936–7
152	W. G. Grace, The Oval	1880	111* M. Leyland, Melbourne	1936–7
170	W. G. Grace, The Oval	1886	187 M. Leyland, The Oval	1938
111	T. W. Graveney, Sydney	1954–5	130 A. C. MacLaren, Melbourne	1894–5
119	G. Gunn, Sydney	1907–8	109 A. C. MacLaren, Sydney	1897–8
122*	G. Gunn, Sydney	1907–8	124 A. C. MacLaren, Adelaide	1897–8
102*	W. Gunn, Manchester	1893	116 A. C. MacLaren, Sydney	1901–2
251	W. R. Hammond, Sydney	1928–9	140 A. C. MacLaren, Nottingham	1905
200	W. R. Hammond, Melbourne	1928–9	117 H. Makepeace, Melbourne	1920–1
119* 177	W. R. Hammond, Adelaide	1928–9	102 P. B. H. May, Sydney	1954–5
113	W. R. Hammond, Leeds	1930	101 P. B. H. May, Leeds	1956
112	W. R. Hammond, Sydney	1932–3	182* C. P. Mead, The Oval	1921
101	W. R. Hammond, Sydney	1932–3	102 Nawab of Pataudi, Sydney	1932–3
231*	W. R. Hammond, Sydney	1936–7	216* E. Paynter, Nottingham	1938
240	W. R. Hammond, Lord's	1938	154* K. S. Ranjitsinhji, Manchester	1896
169*	J. Hardstaff, junr., The Oval	1938	175 K. S. Ranjitsinhji, Sydney	1897–8
130	T. Hayward, Manchester	1899	117 W. W. Read, The Oval	1884
137	T. Hayward, The Oval	1899	179 W. Rhodes, Melbourne	1911–12
114	J. W. Hearne, Melbourne	1911–12	104 P. E. Richardson, Manchester	1956
127*	E. Hendren, Lord's	1926	135* A. C. Russell, Adelaide	1920–1
169	E. Hendren, Brisbane	1928–9	101 A. C. Russell, Manchester	1921
132	E. Hendren, Manchester	1934	102* A. C. Russell, The Oval	1921
126*	J. B. Hobbs, Melbourne	1911–12	105 J. Sharp, The Oval	1909
187	J. B. Hobbs, Adelaide	1911–12	113 Rev. D. S. Sheppard, Manchester	1956
178	J. B. Hobbs, Melbourne	1911–12	105* A. Shrewsbury, Melbourne	1884–5
107	J. B. Hobbs, Lord's	1912		
122	J. B. Hobbs, Melbourne	1920–1		
123	J. B. Hobbs, Adelaide	1920–1		
115	J. B. Hobbs, Sydney	1924–5		
154	J. B. Hobbs, Melbourne	1924–5		
119	J. B. Hobbs, Adelaide	1924–5		

* *Signifies not out.*

164	A. Shrewsbury, Lord's..	1886
106	A. Shrewsbury, Lord's..	1893
156*	R. T. Simpson, Melbourne	1950-1
135*	A. G. Steel, Sydney	1882-3
148	A. G. Steel, Lord's	1884
134	A. E. Stoddart, Adelaide	1891-2
173	A. E. Stoddart, Melbourne	1894-5
115	H. Sutcliffe, Sydney	1924-5
176 \ 127 }	H. Sutcliffe, Melbourne.	1924-5
143	H. Sutcliffe, Melbourne.	1924-5
161	H. Sutcliffe, The Oval ..	1926
135	H. Sutcliffe, Melbourne.	1928-9
161	H. Sutcliffe, The Oval ..	1930
194	H. Sutcliffe, Sydney	1932-3
138	J. T. Tyldesley, Edgbaston	1902
100	J. T. Tyldesley, Leeds...	1905
112*	J. T. Tyldesley, The Oval	1905
149	G. Ulyett, Melbourne ..	1881-2
117	A. Ward, Sydney	1894-5
109	W. Watson, Lord's	1953
112	C. Washbrook, Melbourne	1946-7
143	C. Washbrook, Leeds...	1948
133*	F. E. Woolley, Sydney..	1911-12
123	F. E. Woolley, Sydney..	1924-5

Note.—In consecutive innings in 1928–29 W. R. Hammond scored 251 at Sydney, 200 and 32 at Melbourne, and 119* and 177 at Adelaide.

FOR AUSTRALIA (129)

133*	W. W. Armstrong, Melbourne	1907-8
158	W. W. Armstrong, Sydney............	1920-1
121	W. W. Armstrong, Adelaide	1920-1
123*	W. W. Armstrong, Melbourne	1920-1
118	C. L. Badcock, Melbourne	1936-7
165*	C. Bannerman, Melbourne	1876-7
136 \ 130 }	W. Bardsley, The Oval..	1909
193*	W. Bardsley, Lord's	1926
234	S. G. Barnes, Sydney ...	1946-7
141	S. G. Barnes, Lord's....	1948
128	G. J. Bonnor, Sydney...	1884-5
112	D. G. Bradman, Melbourne	1928-9
123	D. G. Bradman, Melbourne	1928-9
131	D. G. Bradman, Nottingham	1930
254	D. G. Bradman, Lord's.	1930
334	D. G. Bradman, Leeds..	1930
232	D. G. Bradman, The Oval	1930
103*	D. G. Bradman, Melbourne	1932-3
304	D. G. Bradman, Leeds..	1934
244	D. G. Bradman, The Oval	1934
270	D. G. Bradman, Melbourne	1936-7
212	D. G. Bradman, Adelaide	1936-7
169	D. G. Bradman, Melbourne	1936-7
144*	D. G. Bradman, Nottingham	1938
102*	D. G. Bradman, Lord's..	1938
103	D. G. Bradman, Leeds...	1938
187	D. G. Bradman, Brisbane	1946-7
234	D. G. Bradman, Sydney.	1946-7
138	D. G. Bradman, Nottingham	1948
173*	D. G. Bradman, Leeds..	1948
105	W. A. Brown, Lord's...	1934
133	W. A. Brown, Nottingham	1938
206*	W. A. Brown, Lord's...	1938
101*	J. Burke, Adelaide	1950-1
104	H. L. Collins. Sydney..	1920-1
162	H. L. Collins, Adelaide..	1920-1
114	H. L. Collins, Sydney...	1924-5
101	J. Darling, Sydney	1897-8
178	J. Darling, Adelaide ..	1897-8
160	J. Darling, Sydney	1897-8
104	R. A. Duff. Melbourne..	1901-2
146	R. A. Duff, The Oval...	1905
100	J. H. Fingleton, Brisbane	1936-7
136	J. H. Fingleton, Melbourne	1936-7
161	G. Giffen, Sydney	1894-5
107	H. Graham, Lord's.....	1893
105	H. Graham, Sydney	1894-5
100	J. M. Gregory, Melbourne	1920-1
201	S. E. Gregory, Sydney...	1894-5
103	S. E. Gregory, Lord's...	1896
117	S. E. Gregory, The Oval	1899
112	S. E. Gregory, Adelaide.	1903-4
116	R. J. Hartigan, Adelaide	1907-8
112	R. N. Harvey, Leeds....	1948
122	R. N. Harvey, Manchester	1953
162	R. N. Harvey, Brisbane.	1954-5
128	A. L. Hassett, Brisbane.	1946-7
137	A. L. Hassett, Nottingham	1948
115	A. L. Hassett, Nottingham	1953
104	A. L. Hassett, Lord's ..	1953
112	H. L. Hendry, Sydney..	1928-9
188	C. Hill, Melbourne	1897-8
135	C. Hill, Lord's	1899
119	C. Hill, Sheffield	1902
160	C. Hill, Adelaide	1907-8
124	T. Horan, Melbourne...	1881-2
140	F. A. Iredale, Adelaide..	1894-5
108	F. A. Iredale, Manchester	1896

* *Signifies not out.*

164	A. A. Jackson, Adelaide.	1928–9
147	C. Kelleway, Adelaide..	1920–1
100	A. F. Kippax, Melbourne	1928–9
100	R. Lindwall, Melbourne.	1946–7
134	J. J. Lyons, Sydney.....	1891–2
170	C. G. Macartney, Sydney	1920–1
115	C. G. Macartney, Leeds.	1921
133*	C. G. Macartney, Lord's	1926
151	C. G. Macartney, Leeds.	1926
109	C. G. Macartney, Manchester.............	1926
187*	S. J. McCabe, Sydney...	1932–3
137	S. J. McCabe, Manchester.............	1934
112	S. J. McCabe, Melbourne	1936–7
232	S. J. McCabe, Nottingham	1938
104*	C. McCool, Melbourne..	1946–7
147	P. S. McDonnell, Sydney	1881–2
103	P. S. McDonnell, The Oval	1884
124	P. S. McDonnell, Adelaide	1884–5
112	C. E. McLeod, Melbourne	1897–8
141*	K. R. Miller, Adelaide..	1946–7
145*	K. R. Miller, Sydney...	1950–1
109	K. R. Miller, Lord's ...	1953
155	A. R. Morris, Melbourne	1946–7
122 124* }	A. R. Morris, Adelaide	1946–7
105	A. R. Morris, Lord's ...	1948
182	A. R. Morris, Leeds....	1948
196	A. R. Morris, The Oval.	1948
206	A. R. Morris, Adelaide.	1950–1
153	A. R. Morris, Brisbane..	1954–5

153*	W. L. Murdoch, The Oval	1880
211	W. L. Murdoch, The Oval	1884
133	M. A. Noble, Sydney...	1903–4
116	C. E. Pellew, Melbourne	1920–1
104	C. E. Pellew, Adelaide..	1920–1
110	W. H. Ponsford, Sydney	1924–5
128	W. H. Ponsford, Melbourne	1924–5
110	W. H. Ponsford, Leeds.	1930
181	W. H. Ponsford, Leeds..	1934
266	W. H. Ponsford, The Oval	1934
143*	V. S. Ransford, Lord's..	1909
100	A. J. Richardson, Leeds.	1926
138	V. Y. Richardson, Melbourne	1924–5
201*	J. Ryder, Adelaide	1924–5
112	J. Ryder, Melbourne ...	1928–9
102	H. J. H. Scott, The Oval	1884
108	J. M. Taylor, Sydney...	1924–5
143	G. H. S. Trott, Lord's..	1896
135*	V. T. Trumper, Lord's..	1899
104	V. T. Trumper, Manchester	1902
185*	V. T. Trumper, Sydney..	1903–4
113	V. T. Trumper, Adelaide	1903–4
166	V. T. Trumper, Sydney..	1907–8
113	V. T. Trumper, Sydney..	1911–12
141	W. M. Woodfull, Leeds.	1926
117	W. M. Woodfull, Manchester	1926
111	W. M. Woodfull, Sydney	1928–9
107	W. M. Woodfull, Melbourne	1928–9
102	W. M. Woodfull, Melbourne	1928–9
155	W. M. Woodfull, Lord's	1930

D. G. Bradman's scores in 1930 were 8 and 131 at Nottingham, 254 and 1 at Lord's, 334 at Leeds, 14 at Manchester, and 232 at The Oval.

D. G. Bradman scored a hundred in six consecutive Test Matches v. England —three in 1936–37 and three in 1938.

No right-handed batsman has obtained two 100's for Australia in a Test Match against England. H. Sutcliffe, in his first two games for England, scored 59 and 115 at Sydney and 176 and 127 at Melbourne in 1924–25. In the latter match, which lasted into the seventh day, he was on the field throughout except for 86 minutes, namely 27 hours 52 minutes.

C. Hill made 98 and 97 at Adelaide in 1901–02, and F. E. Woolley 95 and 93 at Lord's in 1921.

C. G. Macartney in 1926, Sutcliffe (H.) in 1924–25 and A. Morris in 1946–47 made three hundreds in consecutive innings.

J. B. Hobbs and H. Sutcliffe shared in eleven first-wicket three-figure partnerships.

L. Hutton and C. Washbrook have twice made three-figure stands in each innings, at Adelaide in 1946–47 and at Leeds in 1948.

H. Sutcliffe, during his highest score of 194, v. Australia in 1932–33, took part in three stands each exceeding 100, viz. 112 with R. E. S. Wyatt for the first wicket, 188 with W. R. Hammond for the second wicket, and 123 with

* Signifies not out.

the Nawab of Pataudi for the third wicket. In 1903–04 R. E. Foster, in his historic innings of 287, added 192 for the fifth wicket with L. C. Braund, 115 for the ninth with A. E. Relf, and 130 for the tenth with W. Rhodes.

When L. Hutton scored 364 at The Oval in 1938 he added 382 for the second wicket with M. Leyland, 135 for the third wicket with W. R. Hammond and 215 for the sixth wicket with J. Hardstaff, junr.

D. C. S. Compton and A. Morris at Adelaide in 1946–47 provide the only instance of a player on each side hitting two separate hundreds in a Test match.

MOST RUNS IN A RUBBER

For England—905, average 113.12, by W. R. Hammond, 1928–29.
For Australia—974, average 139.14, by D. G. Bradman, 1930.

MOST WICKETS IN A RUBBER

For England—46, for 9.60 runs each, in 1956, by J. C. Laker.
For England—39, for 17.48 runs each, in 1953, by A. V. Bedser.
For England—38, for 23.18 runs each, in 1924–25, by M. W. Tate.
For Australia—36, for 26.27 runs each, in 1920–21, by A. A. Mailey.

MOST WICKETS IN A MATCH

For England—19, for 90 runs, J. C. Laker, at Manchester, 1956.
For England—15, for 124 runs, W. Rhodes, at Melbourne, 1903–04.
For England—15, for 104 runs, H. Verity, at Lord's, 1934.
For Australia—14, for 90 runs, F. R. Spofforth, at The Oval, 1882.

THE HAT-TRICK

FOR ENGLAND			FOR AUSTRALIA		
W. Bates	Melbourne	1882–83	F. R. Spofforth	Melbourne	1878–79
J. Briggs.......	Sydney ...	1891–92	H. Trumble	Melbourne	1901–02
J. T. Hearne ...	Leeds.....	1899	H. Trumble	Melbourne	1903–04

WICKET-KEEPING

W. A. Oldfield in Tests v. England dismissed 90 men: 59 caught, 31 stumped.
A. A. Lilley dismissed 84 Australians.

SCORERS OF OVER 2,000 RUNS

	Innings		Not out		Runs		Highest Innings		Average
D. G. Bradman	63	..	7	..	5028	..	334	..	89.78
J. B. Hobbs............	71	..	4	..	3636	..	187	..	54.26
W. R. Hammond	58	..	3	..	2852	..	251	..	51.85
H. Sutcliffe	46	..	5	..	2741	..	194	..	66.85
C. Hill	76	..	1	..	2660	..	188	..	35.46
L. Hutton	49	..	6	..	2428	..	364	..	56.46
V. T. Trumper	74	..	5	..	2263	..	185*	..	32.79
S. E Gregory	92	..	7	..	2193	..	201	..	25.80
W. W. Armstrong	71	..	9	..	2172	..	158	..	35.03
A. R. Morris..........	43	..	2	..	2080	..	206	..	50.73

* Signifies not out.

ENGLAND v. SOUTH AFRICA
SUMMARY OF RESULTS

Season	Visiting Captain	Won by England	Won by South Africa	Drawn	Total
1888–89	C. A. Smith ....(E.)	2	0	0	2
1891–92	W. W. Read ....(E.)	1	0	0	1
1895–96	Lord Hawke ....(E.)	3	0	0	3
1898–99	Lord Hawke ....(E.)	2	0	0	2
1905–06	P. F. Warner ....(E.)	1	4	0	5
1907	P. W. Sherwell ....(S.A.)	1	0	2	3
1909–10	H. D. G. Leveson Gower (E.)	2	3	0	5
1912	F. Mitchell ....(S.A.)	3	0	0	3
1913–14	J. W. H. T. Douglas ....(E.)	4	0	1	5
1922–23	F. T. Mann ....(E.)	2	1	2	5
1924	H. W. Taylor ....(S.A.)	3	0	2	5
1927–28	Capt. R. T. Stanyforth..(E.)	2	2	1	5
1929	H. G. Deane ....(S.A.)	2	0	3	5
1930–31	A. P. F. Chapman ......(E.)	0	1	4	5
1935	H. F. Wade ....(S.A.)	0	1	4	5
1938–39	W. R. Hammond ....(E.)	1	0	4	5
1947	A. Melville ....(S.A.)	3	0	2	5
1948–49	F. G. Mann ....(E.)	2	0	3	5
1951	A. D. Nourse ....(S.A.)	3	1	1	5
1955	J. E. Cheetham .....(S.A.)	3	2	0	5
1956–57	P. B. H. May ....(E.)	2	2	1	5
	In South Africa	24	13	16	53
	In England	18	4	14	36
	Totals	42	17	30	89

HIGHEST TOTALS

By England			By South Africa		
654 for 5	Durban	1938–39	538 ..	Leeds............	1951
608 ..	Johannesburg....	1948–49	533 ..	Nottingham.....	1947
559 for 9 dec.	Cape Town ..	1938–39	530 ..	Durban	1938–39
554 for 8	Lord's	1947	521 for 8	Manchester ...	1955
551 ..	Nottingham	1947	513 for 8	Cape Town......	1930–31
534 for 6	The Oval	1935	500 ..	Leeds	1955
531 for 2	Lord's...........	1924	492 for 8	The Oval.........	1929

SMALLEST TOTALS

By England			By South Africa		
76 ..	Leeds...........	1907	30 ..	Port Elizabeth	1895–96
			30 ..	Edgbaston	1924
			35 ..	Cape Town......	1898–99

RECORD PARTNERSHIPS FOR EACH WICKET
By England

359 for 1st	L. Hutton and C. Washbrook, at Johannesburg ..	1948–49
280 for 2nd	P. A. Gibb and W. J. Edrich, at Durban	1938–39
370 for 3rd	W. J. Edrich and D. C. S. Compton, at Lord's ..	1947
197 for 4th	W. R. Hammond and L. E. G. Ames, at Cape Town ..	1938–39
237 for 5th	D. C. S. Compton and N. W. D. Yardley, at Nottingham..	1947
156 for 6th	C. P. Mead and F. T. Mann, at Durban ..	1922–23
115 for 7th	M. C. Bird and J. W. H. T. Douglas, at Durban ..	1913–14
154 for 8th	H. R. Bromley-Davenport and C. W. Wright, at Johannesburg	1895–96
71 for 9th	H. Wood and J. T. Hearne, at Cape Town	1891–92
92 for 10th	A. C. Russell and A. E. R. Gilligan, at Durban	1922–23

By South Africa

260 for 1st   I. J. Siedle and B. Mitchell, at Cape Town   1930–31
198 for 2nd   E. A. B. Rowan and C. B. van Ryneveld, at Leeds   ..   1951
319 for 3rd   A. Melville and A. D. Nourse, junr., at Nottingham ..   1947
214 for 4th   H. W. Taylor and H. G. Deane, at The Oval   1929
136 for 5th   H. B. Cameron and R. H. Catterall, at Durban   1927–28
171 for 6th   P. L. Winslow and J. H. B. Waite at Manchester   ..   1955
123 for 7th   H. G. Deane and E. P. Nupen, at Durban   1927–28
109 for 8th   B. Mitchell and L. Tuckett, at The Oval   1947
137 for 9th   E. L. Dalton and A. B. C. Langton, at The Oval   ..   1935
103 for 10th H. G. Owen-Smith and A. J. Bell, at Leeds   ..   1929

HUNDRED ON DEBUT IN ENGLAND–S. AFRICA TESTS

For England

104 L. C. Braund Lord's 1907	138 P. B. H. May Leeds 1951
163 D. C. S. Compton	117 and 100 E. Paynter
Nottingham 1947	Jo'burg 1938–39
119 J.W.H.T.Douglas Durban1913–14	119 R. H. Spooner Lord's 1912
106 P. A. Gibb Jo'burg 1938–39	132†P. F. Warner Jo'burg 1898–99

† Carried his bat through the second innings.

No instance for South Africa. The highest scores by South African batsmen in the series are as follows: 93* by A. D. Nourse, sen., at Johannesburg in 1905–06 and 90 by P. N. F. Mansell at Leeds, 1951.

INDIVIDUAL HUNDREDS IN THE MATCHES

For England (77)

120	R. Abel, Cape Town ...	1888–9	138* W. R. Hammond, Birmingham	1929
148*	L. E. G. Ames, The Oval	1935	136* W. R. Hammond, Durban	1930–1
115	L. E. G. Ames, Cape Town.........	1938–9	101* W. R. Hammond, The Oval	1929
104	L. C. Braund, Lord's...	1907	181 W. R. Hammond, Cape Town..............	1938–9
208	D. C. S. Compton, Lord's	1947	120 W. R. Hammond, Durban..............	1938–9
163	D. C. S. Compton, Nottingham	1947	140 W. R. Hammond, Durban..............	1938–9
115	D. C. S. Compton, Manchester..............	1947	122 T. Hayward, Johannesburg..............	1895–6
113	D. C. S. Compton, The Oval	1947	132 E. Hendren, Leeds......	1924
114	D. C. S. Compton, Johannesburg........	1948–9	142 E. Hendren, The Oval..	1924
114	D. C. S. Compton, Nottingham	1951	124 A. J. L. Hill, Cape Town	1895–6
158	D. C. S. Compton, Manchester............	1955	187 J. B. Hobbs, Cape Town	1909–10
101	M. C. Cowdrey, Cape Town..............	1956–7	211 J. B. Hobbs, Lord's	1924
104	D. Denton, Johannesburg	1909–10	100 L. Hutton, Leeds	1947
119	J. W. H. T. Douglas, Durban 1913–14		158 L. Hutton, Johannesburg	1948–9
219	W. J. Edrich, Durban...	1938–9	123 L. Hutton, Johannesburg	1948–9
191	W. J. Edrich, Manchester	1947	100 L. Hutton, Leeds.......	1951
189	W. J. Edrich, Lord's....	1947	110* D. J. Insole, Durban....	1956–7
143	F. L. Fane, Johannesburg	1905–6	102 M. Leyland, Lord's.....	1929
			161 M. Leyland, The Oval..	1935
129	C. B. Fry, The Oval....	1907	136* F. G. Mann, Port Elizabeth	1948–9
106	P. A. Gibb, Johannesburg	1938–9	138 P. B. H. May, Leeds....	1951
120	P. A. Gibb, Durban....	1938–9	112 P. B. H. May, Lord's...	1955
			117 P. B. H. May, Manchester.............	1955

* Signifies not out.

102	C. P. Mead, Johannesburgh 1913–14	
117	C. P. Mead, Port Elizabeth 1913–14	
181	C. P. Mead, Durban... 1922–3	
117 100 }	E. Paynter, Johannesburg 1938–9	
243	E. Paynter, Durban.... 1938–9	
152	W. Rhodes, Johannesburg 1913–14	
117	P. E. Richardson, Johannesburg 1956–7	
108	R. W. V. Robins, Manchester.............. 1935	
140 111 }	A. C. Russell, Durban.. 1922–3	
137	R. T. Simpson, Nottingham 1951	
119	R. H. Spooner, Lord's.. 1912	
122	H. Sutcliffe, Lord's..... 1924	
102	H. Sutcliffe, Johannesburg 1927–8	
114	H. Sutcliffe, Birmingham 1929	
100	H. Sutcliffe, Lord's..... 1929	
104 109* }	H. Sutcliffe, The Oval.. 1929	

100*	M. W. Tate, Lord's	1929
122	E. Tyldesley, Johannesburg...............	1927–8
100	E. Tyldesley, Durban ..	1927–8
112	J. T. Tyldesley, Cape Town..............	1898–9
112	B. H. Valentine, Cape Town..............	1938–9
132*	P. F. Warner, Johannesburg..............	1898–9
195	C. Washbrook, Johannesburg	1948–9
111	A. Watkins, Johannesburg...............	1948–9
134*	H. Wood, Cape Town..	1891–2
115*	F. E. Woolley, Johannesburg...............	1922–3
134*	F. E. Woolley, Lord's...	1924
154	F. E. Woolley, Manchester..............	1929
113	R. E. S. Wyatt, Manchester	1929
149	R. E. S. Wyatt, Nottingham	1935

FOR SOUTH AFRICA (50)

125	P. G. Van der Byl, Durban 1938–9	
120	R. H. Catterall, Birmingham 1924	
120	R. H. Catterall, Lord's.. 1924	
119	R. H. Catterall, Durban 1927–8	
117	E. L. Dalton, The Oval.. 1935	
102	E. L. Dalton, Johannesburg............... 1938–9	
116*	W. R. Endean, Leeds.... 1955	
123	G. A. Faulkner, Johannesburg 1909–10	
102	M. Hathorn, Johannesburg............... 1905–6	
104*	D. J. McGlew, Manchester.............. 1955	
133	D.J. McGlew, Leeds..... 1955	
142	R. A. McLean, Lord's.. 1955	
100	R. A. McLean, Durban. 1956–7	
103	A. Melville, Durban.... 1938–9	
189 104* }	A. Melville, Nottingham 1947	
117	A. Melville, Lord's 1947	
123	B. Mitchell, Cape Town 1930–1	
164*	B. Mitchell, Lord's..... 1935	
128	B. Mitchell, The Oval... 1935	
109	B. Mitchell, Durban.... 1938–9	
120 189* }	B. Mitchell, The Oval.. 1947	
120	B. Mitchell, Cape Town. 1948–9	
120	A. D. Nourse, junr., Cape Town 1938–9	
103	A. D. Nourse, junr., Durban 1938–9	

149	A. D. Nourse, junr., Nottingham	1947
115	A. D. Nourse, junr., Manchester	1947
129*	A. D. Nourse, junr., Johannesburg.........	1948–9
112	A. D. Nourse, junr., Cape Town	1948–9
208	A. D. Nourse, junr., Nottingham	1951
129	H. G. Owen-Smith, Leeds...............	1929
156*	E. A. B. Rowan, Johannesburg.............	1948–9
236	E. A. B. Rowan, Leeds..	1951
115	P. W. Sherwell, Lord's..	1907
141	I. J. Siedle, Cape Town.	1930–1
106	J. H. Sinclair, Cape Town	1898–9
109	H. W. Taylor, Durban..	1913–14
176	H. W. Taylor, Johannesburg...............	1922–3
101	H. W. Taylor, Johannesburg...............	1922–3
102	H. W. Taylor, Durban..	1922–3
101	H. W. Taylor, Johannesburg...............	1927–8
121	H. W. Taylor, The Oval	1929
117	H. W. Taylor, Cape Town..............	1930–1
124	K. J. Viljoen, Manchester	1935
125	W. W. Wade, Port Elizabeth	1948–9

* Signifies not out.

G

113 J. H. B. Waite, Man-
    chester 1955
147 G. C. White, Johannes-
    burg................. 1905–6

118 G. C. White, Durban...1909–10
108 P. L. Winslow, Man-
    chester.............. 1955

A. Melville, B. Mitchell, E. Paynter, A. C. Russell and H. Sutcliffe are the only players who have made two separate hundreds in a match in these Tests.

HIGHEST RUN AGGREGATES BY A BATSMAN IN A RUBBER

England in England .... 753 (av. 94.12) D. C. S. Compton ... 1947
England in South Africa ..... 653 (av. 81.62) E. Paynter 1938–39
South Africa in England ..... 621 (av. 69.00) A. D. Nourse, junr... 1947
South Africa in South Africa.. 582 (av. 64.66) H. W. Taylor 1922–23

HIGHEST WICKET AGGREGATES BY A BOWLER IN A RUBBER

England in England .... 34 (av. 8.29) S. F. Barnes 1912
England in South Africa ..... 49 (av. 10.93) S. F. Barnes 1913–14
South Africa in England ..... 26 (av. 21.84) H. J. Tayfield 1955
South Africa in South Africa.. 36 (av. 21.75) A. E. E. Vogler 1909–10

HIGHEST MATCH AGGREGATES

1,981 for 35 wkts., at Durban 1938–39
1,477 for 33 wkts., at The Oval   1947
1,458 for 31 wkts., at Nottingham   1947

LOWEST MATCH AGGREGATES

378 for 30 wkts., at The Oval 1912
382 for 30 wkts., at Cape Town   1888–89

HAT-TRICK

G. A. Lohmann
    Port Elizabeth 1895–96

T. W. Goddard
    Johannesburg 1938–39

At Leeds in 1947 K. Cranston finished South Africa's second innings by taking 4 wickets in one over of six balls for no runs, but this did not include the hat-trick.

ENGLAND v. WEST INDIES
SUMMARY OF RESULTS

Season	Visiting Captain	Won by England	Won by West Indies	Drawn	Total
1928	R. K. Nunes ....(W.I.)	3	0	0	3
1929–30	F. S. G. Calthorpe .....(E.)	1	1	2	4
1933	G. C. Grant...........(W.I.)	2	0	1	3
1934–35	R. E. S. Wyatt ....(E.)	1	2	1	4
1939	R. S. Grant ....(W.I.)	1	0	2	3
1947–48	G. O. Allen ....(E.)	0	2	2	4
1950	J. D. Goddard ....(W.I.)	1	3	0	4
1953–54	L. Hutton ....(E.)	2	2	1	5
1957	J. D. Goddard ......(W.I.)	3	0	2	5
	In West Indies	4	7	6	17
	In England	10	3	5	18
	Totals	14	10	11	35

HIGHEST TOTALS FOR AN INNINGS

By England			By West Indies		
849	..	Kingston 1930	681	..	(8 wkts.), Port of Spain 1954
619	..	(6 wkts.), Nottingham 1957	558	..	Nottingham 1950
585	..	(4 wkts.), Birmingham 1957	535	..	(7 wkts.), Kingston . . 1935
537	..	Port of Spain 1954	503	..	The Oval 1950

LOWEST TOTALS FOR AN INNINGS

By England			By West Indies		
103	..	Kingston 1935	97	..	Lord's 1933
103	..	The Oval 1950	89	..	The Oval (1st inns.).. 1957
			86	..	The Oval (2nd inns.). 1957

INDIVIDUAL HUNDREDS IN THE MATCHES

For England (35)

105	L. E. G. Ames, Port of Spain 1930
146	L. E. G. Ames, Kingston.. 1930
126	L. E. G. Ames, Kingston.. 1935
107†	A. H. Bakewell, The Oval 1933
120†	D. C. S. Compton, Lord's. 1939
133	D. C. S. Compton, Port of Spain 1954
154†	M. C. Cowdrey, Birmingham 1957
152	M. C. Cowdrey, Lord's . . . 1957
104	T. G. Evans, Manchester . . 1950
258	T. W. Graveney, Nottingham 1957
164	T. W. Graveney, The Oval 1957
140†	S. C. Griffith, Port of Spain 1948
138	W. R. Hammond, The Oval 1939
205*	E. Hendren, Port of Spain. 1930
123	E. Hendren, Georgetown.. 1930
159	J. B. Hobbs, The Oval 1928
196†	L. Hutton, Lord's 1939
165*	L. Hutton, The Oval 1939
202*	L. Hutton, The Oval 1950
169	L. Hutton, Georgetown . . . 1954
205	L. Hutton, Kingston 1954
127	D. R. Jardine, Manchester 1933
135	P. B. H. May, Port of Spain 1954
285*	P. B. H. May, Birmingham 1957
104	P. B. H. May, Nottingham 1957
107	W. Place, Kingston 1948
126	P. E. Richardson, Nottingham 1957
107	P. E. Richardson, The Oval 1957
133	J. D. Robertson, Port of Spain 1948
152†	A. Sandham, Bridgetown . 1930
325	A. Sandham, Kingston 1930
122†	E. Tyldesley, Lord's 1928
114†	C. Washbrook, Lord's 1950
102	C. Washbrook, Nottingham 1950
116†	W. Watson, Kingston 1954

For West Indies (31)

105	I. Barrow, Manchester . . . 1933
107	G. Carew, Port of Spain . . 1948
112†	A. Ganteaume, Port of Spain 1948
176†	G. A. Headley, Bridgetown 1930
114 / 112	G. A. Headley, Georgetown 1930
223	G. A. Headley, Kingston.. 1930
169*	G. A. Headley, Manchester 1933
270*	G. A. Headley, Kingston.. 1935
106 / 107	G. A. Headley, Lord's 1939
166	J. K. Holt, Bridgetown 1954
106	A. F. Rae, Lord's 1950
109	A. F. Rae, The Oval 1950
122	C. A. Roach, Bridgetown . 1930
209	C. A. Roach, Georgetown. 1930
161†	O. G. Smith, Birmingham. 1957
168	O. G. Smith, Nottingham. 1957
168*	C. L. Walcott, Lord's 1950
220	C. L. Walcott, Bridgetown 1954
124	C. L. Walcott, Port of Spain 1954
116	C. L. Walcott, Kingston . . 1954
141	E. Weekes, Kingston 1948
129	E. Weekes, Nottingham . . . 1950
206	E. Weekes, Port of Spain . . 1954
137	K. H. Weekes, The Oval . . 1939
131*	F. M. Worrell, Georgetown 1948
261	F. M. Worrell, Nottingham 1950
138	F. M. Worrell, The Oval . . 1950
167	F. M. Worrell, Port of Spain 1954
191*	F. M. Worrell, Nottingham 1957

† *Signifies hundred on debut in England–West Indies Test. S. C. Griffith provides the only instance of a player hitting his maiden century in first-class cricket in his FIRST Test.*

HAT-TRICK

P. J. Loader, Leeds............ 1957

RECORD PARTNERSHIPS FOR EACH WICKET

By England

212 for 1st	C. Washbrook and R. T. Simpson, at Nottingham ..	1950
266 for 2nd	P. E. Richardson and T. W. Graveney, at Nottingham	1957
264 for 3rd	L. Hutton and W. R. Hammond, at The Oval ..	1939
411 for 4th	P. B. H. May and M. C. Cowdrey, at Birmingham ..	1957
110 for 5th	D. C. S. Compton and T. W. Graveney, at Port of Spain	1953–54
161 for 6th	T. E. Bailey and T. G. Evans, at Manchester ..	1950
174 for 7th	M. C. Cowdrey and T. G. Evans, at Lord's ..	1957
95 for 8th	C. J. Barnett and M. S. Nichols, at The Oval ..	1933
62 for 9th	E. R. T. Holmes and W. F. Farrimond, at Port of Spain	1934–35
56 for 10th	J. C. Laker and H. J. Butler, at Port of Spain ..	1947–48

By West Indies

173 for 1st	G. Carew and A. G. Ganteaume, at Port of Spain ..	1947–48
228 for 2nd	R. K. Nunes and G. Headley, at Kingston ..	1929–30
338 for 3rd	E. D. Weekes and F. M. Worrell, at Port of Spain ..	1953–54
283 for 4th	F. M. Worrell and E. D. Weekes, at Nottingham ..	1950
163 for 5th	V. H. Stollmeyer and K. H. Weekes, at The Oval ..	1939
211 for 6th	C. L. Walcott and G. E. Gomez, at Lord's ..	1950
147 for 7th	G. Headley and R. S. Grant, at Kingston ..	1934–35
99 for 8th	C. A. McWatt and J. K. Holt, at Georgetown ..	1953–54
33 for 9th	C. R. Browne and E. St. Hill, at Georgetown ..	1929–30
55 for 10th	F. M. Worrell and S. Ramadhin, at Nottingham ..	1957

ENGLAND v. NEW ZEALAND
SUMMARY OF RESULTS

Season	Visiting Captain	Won by England	Won by New Zealand	Drawn	Total
1929–30	A. H. H. Gilligan ....(E.)	1	0	3	4
1931	T. C. Lowry ......(N.Z.)	1	0	2	3
1932–33	D. R. Jardine ....(E.)	0	0	2	2
1937	M. L. Page ....(N.Z.)	1	0	2	3
1946–47	W. R. Hammond ....(E.)	0	0	1	1
1949	W. A. Hadlee ......(N.Z.)	0	0	4	4
1950–51	F. R. Brown ....(E.)	1	0	1	2
1954–55	L. Hutton ....(E.)	2	0	0	2
	In New Zealand	4	0	7	11
	In England	2	0	8	10
	Totals	6	0	15	21

HIGHEST TOTALS FOR AN INNINGS

By England	By New Zealand
560 (8 wkts., dec.) Christ-church 1932–33	484 Lord's 1949
550 Christchurch 1950–51	469 (9 wkts., dec.), Lord's.. 1931
548 (7 wkts., dec.), Auckland 1932–33	440 Wellington 1929–30
540 Auckland 1929–30	

LOWEST TOTALS FOR AN INNINGS

By England	By New Zealand
181 Christchurch 1929–30	26 Auckland 1954–55
	112 Christchurch 1929–30

Signifies not out.

INDIVIDUAL HUNDREDS IN THE MATCHES
For England (25)

122† G. O. Allen, Lord's 1931	336* W. R. Hammond, Auckland 1933
137† L. E. G. Ames, Lord's.... 1931	140 W. R. Hammond, Lord's.. 1937
103 L. E. G. Ames, Christchurch 1933	114† J. Hardstaff, Lord's 1937
134* T. E. Bailey, Christchurch. 1951	103 J. Hardstaff, The Oval.... 1937
109 E. H. Bowley, Auckland .. 1930	100 L. Hutton, Manchester... 1937
114 D. C. S. Compton, Leeds.. 1949	101 L. Hutton, Leeds 1949
116 D. C. S. Compton, Lord's. 1949	206 L. Hutton, The Oval 1949
117 K. S. Duleepsinhji, Auckland 1930	196 G. B. Legge, Auckland ... 1930
	121† J. D. Robertson, Lord's... 1949
109 K. S. Duleepsinhji, The Oval 1931	103† R. T. Simpson, Manchester 1949
	117† H. Sutcliffe, The Oval..... 1931
100 W. J. Edrich, The Oval... 1949	109* H. Sutcliffe, Manchester... 1931
100* W. R. Hammond, The Oval 1931	103* C. Washbrook, Leeds..... 1949
227 W. R. Hammond, Christchurch 1933	

For New Zealand (8)

136 C. S. Dempster, Wellington 1930	117† J. W. E. Mills, Wellington. 1930
120 C. S. Dempster, Lord's.... 1931	101 M. L. Page, Lord's....... 1931
206 M. P. Donnelly, Lord's... 1949	101 B. Sutcliffe, Manchester.. 1949
116 W. A. Hadlee, Christchurch 1947	116 B. Sutcliffe, Christchurch.. 1951

† *Signifies hundred on first appearance in England–N.Z. Tests.*

RECORD PARTNERSHIPS FOR EACH WICKET
For England

147 for 1st	L. Hutton (206) and R. T. Simpson (68), at The Oval ..	1949
218 for 2nd	L. Hutton (206) and W. J. Edrich (100), at The Oval ..	1949
245 for 3rd	W. R. Hammond (140) and J. Hardstaff (114), at Lord's	1937
125 for 4th	J. Hardstaff (103) and D. C. S. Compton (65), at The Oval	1937
242 for 5th	W. R. Hammond (227) and L. E. G. Ames (103), at Christchurch	1932–33
189 for 6th	D. C. S. Compton (116) and T. E. Bailey (93), at Lord's	1949
108 for 7th	F. R. Brown (74) and W. Voce (66), at Christchurch ..	1932–33
246 for 8th	L. E. G. Ames (137) and G. O. Allen (122), at Lord's ..	1931
117 for 9th	T. E. Bailey (134*) and D. V. P. Wright (45), at Christchurch	1950–51
28 for 10th	F. H. Tyson (27*) and J. B. Statham (13), at Auckland	1954–55

For New Zealand

276 for 1st	C. S. Dempster (136) and J. E. Mills (117), at Wellington	1929–30
131 for 2nd	B. Sutcliffe (116) and J. R. Reid (50), at Christchurch ..	1950–51
118 for 3rd	C. S. Dempster (120) and M. L. Page (104), at Lord's ..	1931
142 for 4th	M. L. Page (104) and R. C. Blunt (96), at Lord's	1931
120 for 5th	F. B. Smith (96) and M. P. Donnelly (64), at Leeds ..	1949
99 for 6th	W. A. Hadlee (93) and M. L. Page (33), at Manchester	1937
100 for 7th	T. C. Lowry (80) and H. M. McGirr (51), at Auckland	1929–30
104 for 8th	A. W. Roberts (66*) and D. A. P. Moloney (64), at Lord's	1937
63 for 9th	T. C. Lowry (34) and C. F. W. Allcott (20*), at Lord's	1931
57 for 10th	F. L. H. Mooney (46) and J. Cowie (26*), at Leeds ..	1949

HIGHEST AGGREGATES IN A RUBBER

	Year	Tests	Inns.	Total	Highest Inns.	Not Outs	100's	Aver.
W. R. Hammond (E.).	1932–33	2	2	563	336*	1	2	563.00
L. Hutton (E.)	1949	4	6	469	206	0	2	78.16
M. P. Donnelly (N.Z.)	1949	4	6	462	206	0	1	77.00
B. Sutcliffe (N.Z.).....	1949	4	7	423	101	0	1	60.42

HIGHEST INDIVIDUAL SCORES

For England		For New Zealand	
336* W. R. Hammond, at Auckland	1932–33	206 M. P. Donnelly, at Lord's	1949
227 W. R. Hammond, at Christchurch	1932–33		
206 L. Hutton, at The Oval	1949		
196 G. B. Legge, at Auckland	1930		

SCORERS OF 500 RUNS IN TESTS

For England

	Years	Tests	Inns.	Total	Highest Inns.	Not Outs	100's	Aver.
W. R. Hammond.	1931–47	9	11	1015	336*	2	4	112.77
L. Hutton	1937–55	11	17	777	206	0	3	45.71
K. S. Duleepsinhji	1929–31	7	10	558	117	2	2	69.75
D. C. S. Compton	1937–51	8	11	510	116	0	2	46.36

For New Zealand

	Years	Tests	Inns.	Total	Highest Inns.	Not Outs	100's	Aver.
B. Sutcliffe.......	1947–55	9	15	787	116	0	2	52.47
C. S. Dempster...	1929–33	8	11	619	136	4	2	88.43
M. P. Donnelly...	1937–49	7	12	582	206	1	1	52.91
W. A. Hadlee....	1937–51	10	17	534	116	1	1	33.38

BEST BOWLING FEATS

For England

7 for 76	F. E. Woolley, at Wellington	..				1929–30
6 for 29	T. W. Goddard, at Manchester	..	..	..	..	1937
6 for 34	W. E. Bowes, at Auckland	..	..	..	..	1932–33
6 for 44	R. Tattersall, at Wellington	..				1950–51
5 for 14	G. O. Allen, at The Oval	..	..	..	..	1931
5 for 38	M. J. C. Allom at Christchurch	..				1929–30
5 for 48	D. V. P. Wright, at Wellington	..				1950–51
4 for 7	R. Appleyard, at Auckland	..				1954–55
4 for 16	F. Tyson, at Dunedin	..				1954–55
4 for 24	J. B. Statham, at Dunedin	..				1954–55
4 for 28	M. S. Nichols, at Christchurch	..				1929–30
4 for 28	J. B. Statham, at Auckland	..				1954–55

For New Zealand

6 for 67	J. Cowie, at Manchester	..				1937
6 for 83	J. Cowie, at Christchurch	..	..	..	..	1946–47
5 for 62	A. N. Moir, at Auckland	..	..	..	..	1954–55
4 for 36	J. R. Reid, at Dunedin	..	..	..	..	1954–55

HIGHEST NUMBER OF WICKETS IN A SERIES

For England

	Year	Tests	Inns.	O.	M.	R.	W.	Aver.
T. E. Bailey	1949	4	7	158	22	599	16	37.43
M. J. C. Allom ...	1929–30	4	6	99	23	194	13	14.92
F. E. Woolley	1929–30	4	4	101.3	26	261	13	20.07
I. A. R. Peebles ...	1931	3	4	102.4	16	325	13	25.00
J. B. Statham	1954–55	2	4	58.4	23	91	12	7.58
F. H. Tyson	1954–55	2	4	49	18	90	11	8.18

For New Zealand

	Year	Tests	Inns.	O.	M.	R.	W.	Aver.
J. Cowie..........	1937	3	6	139.5	30	395	19	20.78
T. R. Burtt	1949	4	6	195.3	50	568	17	33.41
J. Cowie..........	1949	4	5	147.1	23	451	14	32.21

TEN WICKETS IN A TEST

10 for 140   J. Cowie for New Zealand at Manchester (only instance) .. 1937

MOST WICKETS IN THESE TESTS

FOR ENGLAND

	Years	Tests	Inns.	O.	M.	R.	W.	Aver.
T. E. Bailey	1949–55	8	13	246.4	45	773	25	30.92

FOR NEW ZEALAND

J. Cowie.........	1937–49	8	12	317	57	929	39	23.82
T. R. Burtt	1947–51	7	10	306.5	98	804	23	34.95

HAT-TRICK

M. J. C. Allom, in his first Test match, England v. New Zealand at Christchurch in 1929–30, dismissed T. C. Lowry, K. C. James and F. T. Badcock with consecutive balls and took four wickets in five balls.

ENGLAND v. INDIA

SUMMARY OF RESULTS

Season	Visiting Captain	Won by England	Won by India	Drawn	Total
1932	C. K. Nayudu ....(I.)	1	0	0	1
1933–34	D. R. Jardine ....(E.)	2	0	1	3
1936	Maharaj of Vizianagram..(I.)	2	0	1	3
1946	Nawab of Pataudi ......(I.)	1	0	2	3
1951–52	N. D. Howard ....(E.)	1	1	3	5
1952	V. S. Hazare ....(I.)	3	0	1	4
	In England	7	0	4	11
	In India	3	1	4	8
	Totals	10	1	8	19

HIGHEST TOTALS FOR AN INNINGS

BY ENGLAND

571 ..	(8 wkts.), Manchester..	1936
537 ..	Lord's	1952
471 ..	(8 wkts.), The Oval ...	1936
456 ..	Bombay	1951–52
438 ..	Bombay	1933–34

BY INDIA

485 ..	(9 wkts.), Bombay ..	1951–52
457 ..	(9 wkts.), Madras ...	1951–52
418 ..	New Delhi	1951–52

LOWEST TOTALS FOR AN INNINGS

BY ENGLAND

134 ..	Lord's	1936

BY INDIA

58 ..	Manchester	1952
82 ..	Manchester	1952
93 ..	Lord's	1936
98 ..	The Oval	1952

* *Signifies not out.*

INDIVIDUAL HUNDREDS IN THE MATCHES

FOR ENGLAND (12)

104	T. G. Evans, Lord's	1952
175†	T. W. Graveney, Bombay	1951–2
167	W. R. Hammond, Manchester..............	1936
217	W. R. Hammond, The Oval	1936
205*	J. Hardstaff, junr., Lord's	1946
150	L. Hutton, Lord's	1952
104	L. Hutton, Manchester..	1952
119	D. S. Sheppard, The Oval	1952
136†	B. H. Valentine, Bombay	1933–4
102	C. F. Walters, Madras..	1933–4
138*†	A. J. Watkins, New Delhi	1951–2
128	T. S. Worthington, The Oval	1936

FOR INDIA (13)

118†	L. Amarnath, Bombay..	1933–4
164*	V. S. Hazare, New Delhi	1951–2
155	V. S. Hazare, Bombay..	1951–2
114	V. M. Merchant, Manchester..............	1936
128	V. M. Merchant, The Oval	1946
154	V. M. Merchant, New Delhi	1951–2
133	V. L. Manjrekar, Leeds..	1952
184	V. Mankad, Lord's	1952
112	Mushtaq Ali, Manchester	1936
115	D. G. Phadkar, Calcutta	1951–2
140	P. Roy, Bombay	1951–2
111	P. Roy, Madras........	1951–2
130*	P. R. Umrigar, Madras..	1951–2

† *Signifies hundred on debut in England–India Tests.*

ENGLAND v. PAKISTAN

	Date of First Match	Won by England	Won by Pakistan	Drawn	Total
In England	1954	1	1	2	4

HIGHEST TOTALS:—England, 558 for 6, Nottingham, 1954.
Pakistan, 272, Nottingham, 1954.

LOWEST TOTALS:—England, 130, The Oval, 1954.
Pakistan, 87, Lord's, 1954.

INDIVIDUAL HUNDREDS IN THE MATCHES

FOR ENGLAND (2)

278	D. C. S. Compton, Nottingham	..	..	1954
101	R. T. Simpson, Nottingham	..	..	1954

AUSTRALIA v. SOUTH AFRICA
SUMMARY OF RESULTS

Season	Visiting Captain	Won by Australia	Won by S. Africa	Drawn	Total
1902–03	J. Darling ....(A.)	2	0	1	3
1910–11	P. W. Sherwell ....(S.A.)	4	1	0	5
1912	S. E. Gregory ....(A.) } F. Mitchell ....(S.A.)	2	0	1	3
1921–22	H. L. Collins...........(A.)	1	0	2	3
1931–32	H. B. Cameron ....(S.A.)	5	0	0	5
1935–36	V. Y. Richardson ......(A.)	4	0	1	5
1949–50	A. L. Hassett ....(A.)	4	0	1	5
1952–53	J. E. Cheetham ....(S.A.)	2	2	1	5
	In South Africa	11	0	5	16
	In Australia....................	11	3	1	15
	In England	2	0	1	3
	Totals	24	3	7	34

HIGHEST TOTALS FOR AN INNINGS

By Australia			By South Africa		
578	..	Melbourne....... 1910–11	506	..	Melbourne 1910–11
554	..	Melbourne....... 1931–32	491	..	Johannesburg..... 1935–36
549 for 7		Port Elizabeth ... 1949–50	482	..	Adelaide 1910–11
530	..	Adelaide 1952–53	472 for 8		Johannesburg .. 1921–22
528	..	Sydney 1910–11			
526 for 7		Cape Town 1949–50			
520	..	Melbourne....... 1952–53			
513	..	Adelaide 1931–32			

SMALLEST TOTALS FOR AN INNINGS

By Australia			By South Africa		
75	..	Durban 1949–50	36 & 45†		Melbourne 1931–32
153	..	Melbourne 1931–32	80	..	Melbourne 1910–11
175	..	Johannesburg 1902–03	85	..	Johannesburg..... 1902–03

† The aggregate of 81 (12 extras) for two innings is the smallest in Test cricket.

INDIVIDUAL HUNDREDS IN THE MATCHES

For Australia (47)

159* W. W. Armstrong, Johannesburg 1902–3	205 R. N. Harvey, Melbourne 1952–53
132 W. W. Armstrong, Melbourne................1910 11	112 A. L. Hassett, Johannesburg.............1949–50
132 W. Bardsley, Sydney....1910–11	167 A. L. Hassett, Port Elizabeth 1949–50
121 W. Bardsley, Manchester 1912	163 A. L. Hassett, Adelaide.1952–53
164 W. Bardsley, Lord's.... 1912	142 C. Hill, Johannesburg... 1902–3
226 D. G. Bradman, Brisbane 1931–2	191 C. Hill, Sydney 1910–11
112 D. G. Bradman, Sydney 1931–2	100 C. Hill, Melbourne 1910–11
167 D. G. Bradman, Melbourne 1931–2	114 C. E. Kelleway, Manchester.............. 1912
299* D. G. Bradman, Adelaide 1931–2	102 C. E. Kelleway, Lord's.. 1912
121 W. A. Brown, Cape Town................ 1935–6	101 S. J. Loxton, Johannesburg.............1949–50
109 A. G. Chipperfield, Durban 1935–6	137 C. G. Macartney, Sydney1910–11
203 H. L. Collins, Johannesburg............. 1921–2	116 C. G. Macartney, Durban 1921–2
112 J. H. Fingleton Cape Town 1935–6	149 S. J. McCabe, Durban.. 1935–6
108 J. H. Fingleton, Johannesburg 1935–6	189* S. J. McCabe, Johannesburg.............1935–6
118 J. H. Fingleton, Durban 1935–6	154 C. McDonald, Adelaide 1952–53
119 J. M. Gregory, Johannesburg.............1921–2	111 A. R. Morris, Johannesburg.............1949–50
178 R. N. Harvey, Cape Town..............1949–50	157 A. R. Morris, Port Elizabeth 1949–50
151 R. N Harvey, Durban..1949–50	118 } J. R. Moroney, Johannesburg 1949–50
116 R. N. Harvey, Port Elizabeth 1949–50	101* }
100 R. N. Harvey, Johannesburg..............1949–50	127 K. E. Rigg, Sydney..... 1931–2
109 R. N. Harvey, Brisbane.1952–53	142 J. S. Ryder, Cape Town 1921–2
190 R. N. Harvey, Sydney...1952–53	159 V. T. Trumper, Melbourne 1910–11
116 R. N. Harvey, Adelaide.1952–53	214* V. T. Trumper, Adelaide 1910–11
	161 W. M. Woodfull, Melbourne.............. 1931–2

* *Signifies not out.*

For South Africa (15)

162* W. R. Endean, Melbourne 1952–53	231 A. D. Nourse, junr., Johannesburg....... 1935–6
204 G. A. Faulkner, Melbourne............1910–11	114 A. D. Nourse, junr., Cape Town.........1949–50
115 G. A. Faulkner, Adelaide 1910–11	143 E. A. B. Rowan, Durban 1949–50
122* G. A. Faulkner, Manchester............. 1912	101 J. H. Sinclair, Johannesburg............... 1902–3
152 C. N. Frank, Johannesburg............... 1921–2	104 J. H. Sinclair, Cape Town 1902–3
	103 S. J. Snooke, Adelaide..1910–11
111 A. D. Nourse, senr., Johannesburg........ 1921–2	111 K. G. Viljoen, Melbourne 1931–2
	105 J. W. Zulch, Adelaide...1910–11
	150 J. W. Zulch, Sydney....1910–11

HUNDRED ON DEBUT IN AUSTRALIA–S. AFRICA TESTS

142 .. C. Hill, Johannesburg 1902–03	127 .. K. E. Rigg, Sydney.. 1931–32
132 .. W. Bardsley, Sydney 1910–11	109 .. A. G. Chipperfield, Durban 1935–36
226 .. D. G. Bradman, Brisbane 1931–32	112 .. A. L. Hassett, Johannesburg...... 1949–50
	101 .. S. J. Loxton, Johannesburg..... 1949–50

No instance for South Africa.

MOST WICKETS IN A RUBBER

44, for 14.59 runs each, by C. V. Grimmett for Australia in 1935–36.
30, for 28.10 runs each, by H. Tayfield for South Africa in 1952–53.

HAT-TRICKS

T. J. Matthews (Australia), twice on the same afternoon in separate innings against South Africa at Manchester, 1912. A feat without parallel in Test cricket.

AUSTRALIA v. NEW ZEALAND

One match has been played, at Wellington, where Australia beat New Zealand by an innings and 103 runs in March 1946. No centuries were scored.

AUSTRALIA v. WEST INDIES
SUMMARY OF RESULTS

Season	Visiting Captain	Won by Australia	Won by W. Indies	Drawn	Total
1930–31	G. C. Grant..........(W.I.)	4	1	0	5
1951–52	J. D. Goddard ....(W.I.)	4	1	0	5
1954–55	I. W. Johnson ....(A.)	3	0	2	5
	In Australia...................	8	2	0	10
	In West Indies	3	0	2	5
	Totals	11	2	2	15

* Signifies not out.

HIGHEST TOTALS FOR AN INNINGS

By Australia			By West Indies		
758–8	Kingston	1954–5	510	Bridgetown	1954–5
668	Bridgetown	1954–5			
600–9	Port of Spain	1954–5			
558	Brisbane	1930–1			
515–9	Kingston	1954–5			

INDIVIDUAL HUNDREDS IN THE MATCHES

For Australia (20)

128	R. G. Archer, Kingston	1954–5	110	C. C. McDonald, Port of Spain	1954–5
121	R. Benaud, Kingston	1954–5	127	C. C. McDonald, Kingston	1954–5
223	D. G. Bradman, Brisbane	1930–1	129	K. R. Miller, Sydney	1951–2
152	D. G. Bradman, Melbourne	1930–1	147	K. R. Miller, Kingston	1954–5
133	R. N. Harvey, Kingston	1954–5	137	K. R. Miller, Bridgetown	1954–5
133	R. N. Harvey, Port of Spain	1954–5	109	K. R. Miller, Kingston	1954–5
204	R. N. Harvey, Kingston	1954–5	111	A. R. Morris, Port of Spain	1954–5
132	A. L. Hassett, Sydney	1951–2	183	W. H. Ponsford, Sydney	1930–1
102	A. L. Hassett, Melbourne	1951–2	109	W. H. Ponsford, Brisbane	1930–1
146†	A. F. Kippax, Adelaide	1930–1			
118	R. R. Lindwall, Bridgetown	1954–5			

For West Indies (14)

219	D. Atkinson, Bridgetown	1954–5	126	C. L. Walcott, Port of Spain	1954–5
122	C. Depeiza, Bridgetown	1954–5	110		
102*	G. A. Headley, Brisbane	1930–1	155	C. L. Walcott, Kingston	1954–5
105	G. A. Headley, Sydney	1930–1	110		
123*	F. R. Martin, Sydney	1930–1	139	E. Weekes, Port of Spain	1954–5
104†	O. G. Smith, Kingston	1954–5	108	F. M. Worrell, Melbourne	1951–2
104	J. B. Stollmeyer, Sydney	1951–2			
108	C. L. Walcott, Kingston	1954–5			

† *Signifies hundred on debut in Australia–W. Indies Tests.*

AUSTRALIA v. INDIA

	Date of First Match	Won by Australia	Won by India	Drawn	Total
In Australia	1947–48	4	0	1	5
In India	1956–57	2	0	1	3
Totals		6	0	2	8

HIGHEST TOTALS FOR AN INNINGS

By Australia			By India		
674	Adelaide	1947–48	381	Adelaide	1947–48
575	(8 wkts., dec.), Melbourne	1947–48			

* *Signifies not out.*

LOWEST TOTALS FOR AN INNINGS

By Australia		By India	
107 Sydney	1947–48	58 Brisbane	1947–48
		67 Melbourne	1947–48

INDIVIDUAL HUNDREDS IN THE MATCHES

For Australia (10)

112 S. G. Barnes, Adelaide.. 1947–8
201 D. G. Bradman, Adelaide 1947–8
185† D. G. Bradman, Brisbane 1947–8
132 ⎫ D. G. Bradman, Mel-
127*⎭ bourne 1947–8
161 J. W. Burke, Bombay, ...1956–7
153 R. N. Harvey, Melbourne 1947–8
140 R. N. Harvey, Bombay ..1956–7
198* A. L. Hassett, Adelaide. 1947–8
100* A. R. Morris, Melbourne 1947–8

For India (6)

145 ⎫ V. S. Hazare, Adelaide.. 1947–8
116 ⎭
116 V. Mankad, Melbourne. 1947–8
111 V. Mankad, Melbourne. 1947–8
123 D. Phadkar, Adelaide... 1947–8
109 G. S. Ramchand, Bombay 1956–7

† *Signifies hundred on debut in Australia–India Tests.*

AUSTRALIA v. PAKISTAN

One match has been played, at Karachi, where Pakistan beat Australia by nine wickets in October 1956. No centuries were scored.

SOUTH AFRICA v. NEW ZEALAND

	Date of First Match	Won by South Africa	Won by New Zealand	Drawn	Total
In New Zealand ..	1931–32	3	0	1	4
In South Africa ...	1953–54	4	0	1	5
Totals		7	0	2	9

Highest Totals:—South Africa, 524 for 8, Wellington, 1952–53.
New Zealand, 505, Cape Town, 1953–54.

Lowest Totals:—South Africa, 146, Johannesburg, 1953–54.
New Zealand, 79, Johannesburg, 1953–54.

INDIVIDUAL HUNDREDS IN THE MATCHES

For South Africa (7)

122* X. Balaskas, Wellington 1931–2
103† J. A. J. Christy, Christchurch 1931–2
116 W. R. Endean, Auckland 1952–3
255*†D. J. McGlew, Wellington 1952–3
101 R. A. McLean, Durban. 1953–4
113† B. Mitchell, Christ-
church 1931–2
109† A. R. A. Murray, Wellington 1952–3

For New Zealand (3)

107 G. O. Rabone, Durban.. 1953–4
135 J. R. Reid, Cape Town.. 1953–4
100† H. G. Vivian, Wellington 1931–2

† *Signifies hundred on debut in South Africa–New Zealand Tests.*

D. J. McGlew provides the only instance of a player being on the field throughout a Test.

* *Signifies not out.*

WEST INDIES v. NEW ZEALAND

	Date of First Match	Won by West Indies	Won by New Zealand	Drawn	Total
In New Zealand ..	1951–52	4	1	1	6

HIGHEST TOTALS FOR AN INNINGS

By West Indies	By New Zealand
546 for 6 Auckland 1951–52	236 Christchurch......... 1951–52

WEST INDIES LOWEST-EVER TEST TOTAL

77 v. New Zealand at Auckland, 1955–56.

E. Weekes scored 123, 103 and 156 in three successive Tests in 1956.

J. B. Stollmeyer (152), C. L. Walcott (115) and F. M. Worrell (100) have also scored hundreds for West Indies. No instance for N.Z.

WEST INDIES v. INDIA

	Date of First Match	Won by India	Won by West Indies	Drawn	Total
In India	1948–49	0	1	4	5
In West Indies....	1952–53	0	1	4	5
Totals		0	2	8	10

HIGHEST TOTALS:—India, 454, at New Delhi, 1948; 444 at Kingston, 1953. West Indies, 631, at New Delhi, 1948; 629 (for six wickets, dec.), at Bombay, 1948.

LOWEST TOTALS:—India, 129, at Bridgetown, 1953; West Indies, 228, at Bridgetown, 1953.

INDIVIDUAL HUNDREDS IN THE MATCHES

For India (10)

114*†H. R. Adhikari, New Delhi 1948–9	112 R. S. Modi, Bombay... 1948–9
163* M. L. Apte, Port of Spain 1952–3	106† Mushtaq Ali, Calcutta.. 1948–9
134* V. S. Hazare, Bombay.. 1948–9	150 P. Roy, Kingston 1952–3
122 V. S. Hazare, Bombay.. 1948–9	130 P. R. Umrigar, Port of Spain 1952–3
118 V. L. Manjrekar, Kingston 1952–3	117 P. R. Umrigar, Kingston 1952–3

For West Indies (19)

107† R. J. Christiani, New Delhi 1948–9	108 C. L. Walcott, Calcutta.. 1948–9
101† G. E. Gomez, New Delhi 1948–9	125 C. L. Walcott, Georgetown 1952–3
115† B. Pairaudeau, Port of Spain 1952–3	118 C. L. Walcott, Kingston 1952–3
104 A. F. Rae, Bombay ... 1948–9	128† E. Weekes, New Delhi .. 1948–9
109 A. F. Rae, Madras.... 1948–9	194 E. Weekes, Bombay 1948–9
160 J. B. Stollmeyer, Madras 1948–9	162 } E. Weekes, Calcutta 1948–9
104* J. B. Stollmeyer, Port of Spain 1952–3	101
152† C. L. Walcott, New Delhi 1948–9	207 E. Weekes, Port of Spain 1952–3
	161 E. Weekes, Port of Spain 1952–3
	109 E. Weekes, Kingston ... 1952–3
	237 F. M. Worrell, Kingston 1952–3

† *Signifies hundred on debut in West Indies–India Tests.*

* *Signifies not out.*

INDIA v. NEW ZEALAND

	Date of First Match	Won by India	Won by New Zealand	Drawn	Total
In India	1955–56	2	0	3	5

HIGHEST TOTALS:—India 537 (for three wickets, dec.), Madras, 531 (for seven wickets, dec.), New Delhi. New Zealand 450 (for two wickets, dec.), New Delhi.

LOWEST TOTALS:—India 132, Calcutta. New Zealand 136, Bombay.

INDIVIDUAL HUNDREDS IN THE MATCHES

FOR INDIA (9)		FOR NEW ZEALAND (5)	
177	V. L. Manjrekar, New Delhi	102	J. W. Guy, Hyderabad
118	V. L. Manjrekar, Hyderabad	120	J. R. Reid, Calcutta
231	V. Mankad, Madras	119*	J. R. Reid, New Delhi
223	V. Mankad, Bombay	230*	B. Sutcliffe, New Delhi
106*	G. S. Ramchand, Calcutta	137*	B. Sutcliffe, Hyderabad
173	P. Roy, Madras		
100	P. Roy, Calcutta		
100*	Kripal Singh, Hyderabad		
223	P. R. Umrigar, Hyderabad		

INDIA v. PAKISTAN

	Date of First Match	Won by India	Won by Pakistan	Drawn	Total
In India	1952–53	2	1	2	5
In Pakistan	1954–55	0	0	5	5
Totals		2	1	7	10

HIGHEST TOTALS:—India, 397, Calcutta, 1952–53. Pakistan, 344, Madras, 1952–53.

LOWEST TOTALS:—India, 106, Lucknow, 1952–53. Pakistan, 150, Delhi, 1952–53.

INDIVIDUAL HUNDREDS IN THE MATCHES

FOR INDIA (4)			FOR PAKISTAN (3)		
146*	V. S. Hazare, Bombay..	1952–3	103*	Alim-ud-Din, Karachi..	1954–5
110†	D. S. Shodhan, Calcutta	1952–3	142	Hanif Mohammad, Bahawalpur..............	1954–5
102	P. R. Umrigar, Bombay	1952–3	124*	Nazar Mohammed, Lucknow	1952–3
108	P. R. Umrigar, Peshawar	1954–5			

† *Signifies hundred on debut in India–Pakistan Tests.*

PAKISTAN v. NEW ZEALAND

	Date of First Match	Won by Pakistan	Won by New Zealand	Drawn	Total
In Pakistan	1955–56	2	0	1	3

HIGHEST TOTALS:—Pakistan 561, Lahore. New Zealand 348, Lahore.

LOWEST TOTALS:—Pakistan 289, Karachi. New Zealand 70, Dacca.

Imtiaz Ahmed (209), Hanif Mohammed (103) and Waqar Hassan (189) have scored hundreds for Pakistan, and S. N. McGregor (111) for New Zealand.

* *Signifies not out.*

YOUNGEST TEST PLAYERS

16 years 352 days	Khalid Hassan	Pakistan v. England, at Nottingham, 1954.
17 years 122 days	J. E. D. Sealy	West Indies v. England, at Kensington Oval, Barbados, 1929–30.
17 years 239 days	I. D. Craig	Australia v. South Africa, at Melbourne, 1952–53.
17 years 245 days	G. Sobers	West Indies v. England, at Kingston, 1953–54.
17 years 300 days	Hanif Mohammed	Pakistan v. India, at New Delhi, 1952–53.
18 years 44 days	Khalid Wazir	Pakistan v. England, at Lord's, 1954.
18 years 105 days	J. B. Stollmeyer	West Indies v. England, at Lord's, 1939.
18 years 140 days	D. B. Close	England v. New Zealand, at Manchester, 1949.
18 years 197 days	D. L. Freeman	New Zealand v. England, at Christchurch, 1932–33
18 years 232 days	T. W. Garrett	Australia v. England, at Melbourne, 1876–77.
18 years 267 days	H. G. Vivian	New Zealand v. England, at Manchester, 1931.

OLDEST PLAYERS ON TEST DEBUT

49 years 119 days	J. Southerton	England v. Australia, Melbourne, 1876–77.
46 years 273 days	D. J. Blackie	Australia v. England, Sydney, 1928–29.
41 years 337 days	E. R. Wilson	England v. Australia, Sydney, 1920–21.
41 years 275 days	H. Ironmonger	Australia v. England, Brisbane, 1928–29.
41 years 28 days	R. J. Jamshedji	India v. England, Bombay, 1933.
40 years 346 days	C. A. Wiles	West Indies v. England, Manchester, 1933.
40 years 110 days	H. W. Lee	England v. South Africa, Johannesburg, 1930–31.
40 years 56 days	G. W. A. Chubb	South Africa v. England, Nottingham, 1951.
40 years 37 days	G. Ramaswami	India v. England, Manchester, 1936.
39 years 361 days	G. Challoner	West Indies v. England, Lord's, 1928.
39 years 360 days	A. Wood	England v. Australia, The Oval, 1938.

GENTLEMEN v. PLAYERS

The highest individual scores are:—

266*	..	J. B. Hobbs	Scarboro' 1925	215	..	W. G. Grace	The Oval 1870
247	..	R. Abel	The Oval 1901	203	..	T. Hayward	The Oval 1904
241	..	L. Hutton	Scarboro' 1953	201	..	L. E. G. Ames	Folkestone 1933
232*	..	C. B. Fry	Lord's 1903	195	..	R. Abel	The Oval 1899
223	..	C. P. Mead	Scarboro' 1911	194*	..	E. Hendren	The Oval 1932
217	..	W. G. Grace	Brighton 1871				

W. G. Grace played no fewer than fifteen three-figure innings for Gentlemen v. Players. On his fifty-eighth birthday—at The Oval in July 1906—he scored 74.

J. B. Hobbs in all matches under this title scored 16 three-figure innings, and had an aggregate of 4,052 runs with an average of 54.75.

The match dates back to 1806.

* *Signifies not out.*

OXFORD v. CAMBRIDGE

Largest totals

503	..	Oxford	1900	432‡	..	Cambridge	1936
457	..	Oxford	1946	431	..	Cambridge	1932
453†	..	Oxford	1931	425	..	Cambridge	1938

† For eight wickets.   ‡ For nine wickets.

Smallest totals

32	..	Oxford	1878	42	..	Oxford	1890
39	..	Cambridge	1858	47	..	Cambridge	1838

Highest individual scores

238*	..	Nawab of Pataudi (O.)	1931	193	..	D.C.H. Townsend (O.)	1934
211	..	G. Goonesena (C.)	1957	172*	..	J. F. Marsh (C.)	1904
201*	..	M. J. K. Smith (O.)	1954	171	..	R. E. Foster (O.)	1900
201	..	A. Ratcliffe (C.)	1931	170	..	M. Howell (O.)	1919

A. P. F. Chapman and M. P. Donnelly enjoy the following distinction: Chapman scored a century at Lord's in the University match (102*, 1922); for Gentlemen v. Players (160, 1922), (108, 1926); and for England v. Australia (121, 1930). M. P. Donnelly scored a century at Lord's in the University match (142, 1946), for Gentlemen v. Players (162*, 1947); and for New Zealand v. England (206, 1949).

A. Ratcliffe's 201 for Cambridge remained a record for the match for only one day, being beaten by the Nawab of Pataudi's 238* for Oxford next day.

M. J. K. Smith (Oxford) is the only player who has scored three hundreds: 201* in 1954, 104 in 1955 and 117 in 1956. His aggregate, 477, surpassed the previous best, 457, by the Nawab of Pataudi, 1929–31.

The following players have scored two hundreds: W. Yardley (Cambridge) 100 in 1870 and 130 in 1872; H. J. Enthoven (Cambridge) 104 in 1924 and 129 in 1925; The Nawab of Pataudi (Oxford) 106 in 1929 and 238 not out in 1931; A. Ratcliffe (Cambridge) 201 in 1931 and 124 in 1932; D. R. W. Silk (Cambridge) 116* in 1953 and 118 in 1954.

F. C. Cobden, in the Oxford and Cambridge match in 1870, performed the hat-trick by taking the last three wickets and won an extraordinary game for Cambridge by two runs. The feat is without parallel in first-class cricket. Cobden obtained the last three wickets of Oxford in each innings—a curious coincidence. Other hat-tricks, all for Cambridge, have been credited to A. G. Steel (1879), P. H. Morton (1880), J. F. Ireland (1911), and R. G. H. Lowe (1926).

S. E. Butler, in the 1871 match, took all ten wickets in the Cambridge first innings. The feat is unique in University matches. He bowled 24 overs and a ball. In the follow-on he took 5 wickets for 57, making 15 for 95 runs in the match.

P. R. Le Couteur scored 160 and took eleven Cambridge wickets for 66 runs in 1910—the best all-round performance in the history of the match.

Of the 113 matches played, Cambridge have won 49 and Oxford 42. The remaining twenty-two games have been drawn. The match dates back to 1827.

TIE MATCHES IN FIRST-CLASS CRICKET

There have been sixteen since the first World War:—

Somerset v. Sussex, at Taunton 1919
(The last Sussex batsman not allowed to bat under Law 45.)

* *Signifies not out.*

Orange Free State v. Eastern Province, at Bloemfontein 1925–26
    (Eastern Province had two wickets to fall.)
Essex v. Somerset, at Chelmsford 1926
    (Essex had one man to go in, and the M.C.C. ruled that the game
    should rank as a tie. The ninth wicket fell half a minute before time.)
Gloucestershire v. Australians, at Bristol 1930
Victoria v. M.C.C., at Melbourne 1932–33
    (Victoria's third wicket fell to the last ball of the match when one
    run was needed to win.)
Somerset v. Worcestershire, at Kidderminster 1939
Southern Punjab v. Baroda, at Patiala 1945–46
Essex v. Northamptonshire, at Ilford 1947
Hampshire v. Lancashire, at Bournemouth 1947
D. G. Bradman's XI v. A. L. Hassett's XI, at Melbourne (Bradman's
    Testimonial) 1948–49
Hampshire v. Kent, at Southampton 1950
Sussex v. Warwickshire, at Hove 1952
Essex v. Lancashire, at Brentwood 1952
Northamptonshire v. Middlesex, at Peterborough 1953
Yorkshire v. Leicestershire, at Huddersfield 1954
Sussex v. Hampshire, Eastbourne 1955

Note.—Beginning in 1948 a tie has been recognised only when the scores
are level with all the wickets down in the fourth innings. This ruling applies to
all grades of Cricket, and in the case of a one-day match to the second innings,
provided that the match has not been brought to a further conclusion

FIRST-CLASS MATCHES BEGUN AND FINISHED
IN ONE DAY

The most notable instances during the nineteenth and present centuries are:—

The B's v. England, at Lord's, June 13 1831
Cambridge University v. M.C.C. and Ground, at Cambridge, May 18 .. 1837
M.C.C. and Ground v. Cambridge University, at Lord's, June 19 .. 1848
Gentlemen of Kent v. Gentlemen of England, at Lord's, July 1 .. 1850
North v. South, at Lord's, July 15 1850
M.C.C. and Ground v. Sussex, at Lord's, June 2 1856
Surrey v. Sussex, at The Oval, July 16 1857
Kent v. England, at Lord's, July 5 1858
M.C.C. and Ground v. Oxford University, at Lord's, June 18 .. 1863
North of Thames v. South of Thames, at Lord's, July 8 1863
M.C.C. and Ground v. Surrey, at Lord's, May 14 1872
Middlesex v. Oxford University, at Prince's, June 18 1874
North v. South, at Lord's, May 17 1875
M.C.C. and Ground v. Oxford University, at Oxford, May 24 .. 1877
M.C.C. and Ground v. Australians, at Lord's, May 27 1878
M.C.C. and Ground v. Oxford University, at Oxford, May 28 .. 1880
An England XI v. Australians, at Aston Lower Grounds, Birmingham,
    May 26 1884
M.C.C. and Ground v. Lancashire, at Lord's, May 18 1886
North v. South, at Lord's, May 30 1887
Lancashire v. Surrey, at Manchester, August 2 1888
M.C.C. and Ground v. Notts, at Lord's, June 1 1891
Lancashire v. Somerset, at Old Trafford, August 9 1892
M.C.C. and Ground v. Sussex, at Lord's, May 2 1894
Lancashire v. Somerset, at Old Trafford, July 17 1894
Yorkshire v. Somerset, at Huddersfield, July 19 1894
Leicestershire v. Surrey, at Leicester, June 10 1897
Hampshire v. Yorkshire, at Southampton, May 27 (H. Baldwin's benefit) 1898
Middlesex v. Somerset, at Lord's, May 23 (W. Flower's benefit) .. 1899
Yorkshire v. Worcestershire, at Bradford, May 7 1900
M.C.C. and Ground v. London County, at Lord's, May 20 1903

Transvaal v. Orange Free State, at Johannesburg	1906
Middlesex v. Gentlemen of Philadelphia, at Lord's, July 20 ..	1908
Gloucestershire v. Middlesex, at Bristol, August 26	1909
Kent v. Sussex, at Tonbridge, June 21	1919
Lancashire v. Somerset, at Manchester, May 21	1925
Madras v. Mysore, at Madras, November 4	1934
Ireland v. New Zealanders, at Dublin, September 11	1937
Derbyshire v. Somerset, at Chesterfield, June 11	1947
Lancashire v. Sussex, at Manchester, July 12	1950
Surrey v. Warwickshire, at The Oval, May 16	1953
Somerset v. Lancashire, at Bath, June 6 (H. T. F. Buse's benefit) ..	1953

LARGE ATTENDANCES AND GATE RECEIPTS

933,513 persons (exclusive of about 10,000 who watched the last day's play of the Fifth Test free of charge) were present at the five Test matches between England and Australia in 1936–37, receipts amounting to £A90,909. The Third Test at Melbourne broke the records for attendances and receipts: 350,534 persons were present, and the receipts amounted to £A30,124. In this match, the records for one day's play were also broken—87,798 and £A7,405 on January 4th.

£200,194, record receipts for any series, was paid by the 549,650 people who attended the five Tests between England and Australia in England, 1953.

£57,716 is the largest sum of money taken at any cricket match in the world when England met Australia at Lord's, 1953. The attendance, 137,915, at that match remains the highest for Lord's.

With increased prices for admission after the 1939–45 war, the Third Test at Melbourne in 1946–47 established a new Australian record for receipts— £A44,063. The attendance figures were 343,675. The full figures for the five Tests in 1946–47 were 846,263; receipts £A115,858.

£A47,933 is the largest sum of money taken at any match in Australia when England played at Melbourne in the Third Test, 1954–55. The attendance at that match was 300,270. The full figures for the five Tests in 1954–55 were 707,510; receipts, £A119,059.

Over 158,000 persons were present during the five days of the England v. Australia match at Leeds, and the total receipts were £34,000 .... **1948**

116,000 people (receipts £26,000) were present during the four days of the England v. South Africa Test at Leeds. Both the attendance and receipts were records for any Test between the two countries **1951**

£31,032, which was taken at Leeds in the five days, constituted a new record for receipts for any match between England and South Africa. The total attendance was 113,500 .. .. **1955**

Just under 115,000 persons were present during the four days of the England v. Australia match, at Lord's **1930**

99,614 people were present at the Fourth Test Match at Leeds (over in three days). (75,614 paid: receipts £14,189) **1938**

Over 80,000 persons watched the play, Surrey v. Yorkshire, at The Oval, (Lees' benefit—£2,300—66,923 paid for admission) .. ..July **1906**

78,792 persons watched the play, Yorkshire v. Lancashire, at Leeds, (Hirst's benefit—£3,703) .. ..August, **1904**

78,617 persons were present at the match between Lancashire and Yorkshire, at Manchester **1926**

About 76,000 watched the play in the Surrey v. Kent match at The Oval **1920**

BEST BENEFITS

£14,000	C. Washbrook, Lancashire v. Australians	1948
£12,866	A. V. Bedser, Surrey v. Yorkshire	1953
£12,200	D. C. S. Compton, Middlesex v. Sussex	1949
£9,713	L. Hutton, Yorkshire v. Middlesex	1950

£8,600	A. J. McIntyre, Surrey v. Yorkshire	..	..	..	..	1955
£8,083	W. E. Bowes, Yorkshire v. Middlesex	..	..	..	..	1947
£8,000	R. Pollard, Lancashire v. Derbyshire	..	..	..	..	1949

The following figures were records at the respective date of each match:

| £4,016 | R. Kilner, Yorkshire v. Middlesex | .. | .. | .. | .. | 1925 |
| £3,703 | G. H. Hirst, Yorkshire v. Lancashire | .. | .. | .. | .. | 1904 |

Sir Donald Bradman received £A10,000 from his Testimonial match, D. G. Bradman's XI v. A. L. Hassett's XI, 1948–49.

W. G. Grace was given three Testimonials which raised £1,458, £2,377 and £5,000, a total of £8,835.

Hedley Verity's Memorial Fund in 1945 yielded £8,233.

LORD'S CRICKET GROUND

Lord's and the M.C.C. were founded in 1787. The Club has enjoyed an uninterrupted career since that date, but there have been three grounds known as Lord's. The first (1787–1810) was situated where Dorset Square now is; the second (1809–13), at North Bank, had to be abandoned owing to the cutting of the Regent's Canal; and the third, opened in 1814, is that where the game is played to-day. It was not until 1886 that the freehold of Lord's was secured by the M.C.C. The present pavilion was erected in 1890 at a cost of £21,000.

THE LARGEST INDIVIDUAL SCORES MADE AT LORD'S ARE:—

316*	J. B. Hobbs, Surrey v. Middlesex	..	..	..	..	1926
315*	P. Holmes, Yorkshire v. Middlesex	..	..	..	..	1925
281*	W. H. Ponsford, Australians v. M.C.C.	..	..	..	..	1934
278	W. Ward, M.C.C. v. Norfolk (with E. H. Budd, T. Vigne and F. Ladbroke)	..	..	..	..	1820
278	D. G. Bradman, Australians v. M.C.C.	..	..	..	..	1938
277*	E. Hendren, Middlesex v. Kent	..	..	..	..	1922

THE GREATEST TOTALS OBTAINED THERE ARE:—

FIRST-CLASS MATCHES

729	(six wickets), Australia v. England	..	..	..	..	1930
665	West Indies v. Middlesex ..	..	..	..	..	1939
612	(eight wickets), Middlesex v. Nottinghamshire ..	..	..	..	1921
610	(five wickets), Australians v. Gentlemen of England	..	..	..	1948
609	(eight wickets), Cambridge University v. M.C.C. and Ground	..	..	1913
608	(seven wickets), Middlesex v. Hampshire	..	..	..	..	1919
607	M.C.C. and Ground v. Cambridge University ..	..	..	..	1902

MINOR MATCH

| 735 | (nine wickets), M.C.C. and Ground v. Wiltshire | .. | .. | .. | 1888 |

BIGGEST HIT AT LORD'S

The only known instance of a batsman hitting a ball over the present pavilion at Lord's occurred when A. E. Trott, appearing for M.C.C. against Australians at Lord's, July 31, August 1, 2, 1899, drove M. A. Noble so far and high that the ball struck a chimney pot and fell behind the building.

Signifies not out.

CHAMPION COUNTY SINCE INSTITUTION OF
CHAMPIONSHIP

1873 {	Gloucestershire	1898	Yorkshire
	Nottinghamshire	1899	Surrey
1874	Derbyshire	1900	Yorkshire
1875	Nottinghamshire	1901	Yorkshire
1876	Gloucestershire	1902	Yorkshire
1877	Gloucestershire	1903	Middlesex
1878	Middlesex	1904	Lancashire
1879 {	Nottinghamshire	1905	Yorkshire
	Lancashire	1906	Kent
1880	Nottinghamshire	1907	Nottinghamshire
1881	Lancashire	1908	Yorkshire
1882 {	Nottinghamshire	1909	Kent
	Lancashire	1910	Kent
1883	Nottinghamshire	1911	Warwickshire
1884	Nottinghamshire	1912	Yorkshire
1885	Nottinghamshire	1913	Kent
1886	Nottinghamshire	1914	Surrey
1887	Surrey	1915 {	No competition
1888	Surrey	to	owing to the
1889 {	Surrey	1918	War
	Lancashire	1919	Yorkshire
	Nottinghamshire	1920	Middlesex
1890	Surrey	1921	Middlesex
1891	Surrey	1922	Yorkshire
1892	Surrey	1923	Yorkshire
1893	Yorkshire	1924	Yorkshire
1894	Surrey	1925	Yorkshire
1895	Surrey	1926	Lancashire
1896	Yorkshire	1927	Lancashire
1897	Lancashire	1928	Lancashire

1929	Nottinghamshire
1930	Lancashire
1931	Yorkshire
1932	Yorkshire
1933	Yorkshire
1934	Lancashire
1935	Yorkshire
1936	Derbyshire
1937	Yorkshire
1938	Yorkshire
1939	Yorkshire
1940 {	No competition
to	owing to the
1945	War
1946	Yorkshire
1947	Middlesex
1948	Glamorgan
1949 {	Middlesex
	Yorkshire
1950 {	Lancashire
	Surrey
1951	Warwickshire
1952	Surrey
1953	Surrey
1954	Surrey
1955	Surrey
1956	Surrey
1957	Surrey

The Championship has been won outright as follows:—Yorkshire 22 times Surrey 15, Lancashire 8, Nottinghamshire 8, Middlesex 5, Kent 4, Derbyshire 2, Gloucestershire 2, Warwickshire 2, Glamorgan 1.

Six times, 1873, 1879, 1882, 1889, 1949, 1950, the Championship was shared as follows: Nottinghamshire 4, Lancashire 4, Gloucestershire 1, Middlesex 1, Surrey 2, Yorkshire 1.

POINTS GAINED BY CHAMPIONS FROM 1946

Year	Champions	Played	Won	Points
1946	Yorkshire	26	17	216
1947	Middlesex	26	19	236
1948	Glamorgan	26	13	172
1949 {	Middlesex	26	14	192
	Yorkshire	26	14	192
1950 {	Lancashire	28	16	220
	Surrey	28	17	220
1951	Warwickshire	28	16	216
1952	Surrey	28	20	256
1953	Surrey	28	13	184
1954	Surrey	28	15	208
1955	Surrey	28	23	284
1956	Surrey	28	15	200
1957	Surrey	28	21	312

Note: Yorkshire hold the record number of wins in one season, i.e. 25 out of 32 Championship matches in 1923.

MATCH RESULTS IN THE COUNTY CHAMPIONSHIP

	Won	Lost	Drawn	Tie	Total
Derbyshire	340	548	424	0	1312
Essex	341	428	511	3	1283
Glamorgan	171	304	326	0	801
Gloucestershire	490	615	448	0	1553
Hampshire	334	507	475	3	1319
Kent	641	521	437	2	1601
Lancashire	754	303	649	3	1709
Leicestershire	246	539	461	1	1247
Middlesex	567	389	468	2	1426
Northamptonshire	212	443	357	2	1014
Nottinghamshire	539	349	645	0	1533
Somerset	278	611	361	3	1253
Surrey	762	372	585	3	1722
Sussex	494	584	571	3	1652
Warwickshire	335	388	527	1	1251
Worcestershire	253	518	419	1	1191
Yorkshire	916	254	616	1	1787
	7673	7673	8280	28	23654

11,827 matches have been played in the County Championship of which 7,687 have been finished and 4,140 unfinished.

DATES OF FORMATION OF COUNTY CLUBS NOW FIRST-CLASS

Derbyshire, 1870; Essex, 1864–65 (dissolved in 1866) and re-formed in 1876 and 1886; Glamorgan, 1888–89; Gloucestershire, 1871; Hampshire, 1863; Kent, 1859 and re-formed 1870; Lancashire, 1864; Leicestershire, 1873; Middlesex, 1864; Northamptonshire, about 1843 and re-formed 1878; Nottinghamshire, 1859; Somerset, 1875 and re-organised 1885; Surrey, 1845; Sussex, 1836 and re-formed 1839 and 1857; Warwickshire, 1863–64 and re-formed 1882; Worcestershire, 1865; and Yorkshire, 1863.

CONSTITUTION OF COUNTY CHAMPIONSHIP

When the County Championship was first formed in 1873—the authorities in April having agreed that no cricketer should play for more than one county during the same season—the following counties were considered first-class:— Derbyshire, Gloucestershire, Kent, Lancashire, Middlesex, Notts, Surrey, Sussex and Yorkshire. In 1887 Derbyshire fell out. For 1891 Somerset were promoted. There was a further extension in 1894, as Essex, Derbyshire, Leicestershire and Warwickshire were admitted to the group. Hampshire were added in 1895. Worcestershire, who came in for 1899, have since played regularly except for 1919, the first season after the First World War. Northamptonshire were raised for 1905 and Glamorgan were adopted in 1921.

THE MINOR COUNTIES CHAMPIONSHIP

1895	Norfolk	1924	Berkshire
	Durham	1925	Buckinghamshire
	Worcestershire	1926	Durham
1896	Worcestershire	1927	Staffordshire
1897	Worcestershire	1928	Berkshire
1898	Worcestershire	1929	Oxfordshire
1899	Northamptonshire	1930	Durham
	Buckinghamshire	1931	Leicestershire Second XI
1900	Glamorgan	1932	Buckinghamshire
	Durham	1933	Undecided
	Northamptonshire	1934	Lancashire Second XI
1901	Durham	1935	Middlesex Second XI
1902	Wiltshire	1936	Hertfordshire
1903	Northamptonshire	1937	Lancashire Second XI
1904	Northamptonshire	1938	Buckinghamshire
1905	Norfolk	1939	Surrey Second XI
1906	Staffordshire	1946	Suffolk
1907	Lancashire Second XI	1947	Yorkshire Second XI
1908	Staffordshire	1948	Lancashire Second XI
1909	Wiltshire	1949	Lancashire Second XI
1910	Norfolk	1950	Surrey Second XI
1911	Staffordshire	1951	Kent Second XI
1912	In abeyance	1952	Buckinghamshire
1913	Norfolk	1953	Berkshire
1920	Staffordshire	1954	Surrey Second XI
1921	Staffordshire	1955	Surrey Second XI
1922	Buckinghamshire	1956	Kent Second XI
1923	Buckinghamshire	1957	Yorkshire Second XI

FEATURES OF 1957

Double Hundreds

285*   P. B. H. May (England v. West Indies, at Birmingham).
258   T. W. Graveney (England v. West Indies, at Nottingham).
224   K. Grieves (Lancashire v. Cambridge University, at Cambridge).
219*   G. Sobers (West Indies v. Nottinghamshire, at Nottingham).
211   G. Goonesena (Cambridge University v. Oxford University, at Lord's).
201*   J. D. Robertson (Middlesex v. Essex, at Lord's).
200*   D. Kenyon (Worcestershire v. Nottinghamshire, at Worcester).

Two Hundreds in a Match

106 and 101*   T. W. Graveney (Gloucestershire v. Warwickshire, at Birmingham).
101 and 100*   J. M. Parks (Sussex v. Worcestershire, at Worcester).

First to 1,000 Runs

T. W. Graveney (Gloucestershire), June 12.

First to 2,000 Runs

P. B. H. May (Surrey), August 16.

Stands Over 250

411 for fourth wicket by P. B. H. May and M. C. Cowdrey (England v. West Indies, at Birmingham).
289 for seventh wicket by G. Goonesena and G. W. Cook (Cambridge University v. Oxford University, at Lord's).
266 for second wicket by P. E. Richardson and T. W. Graveney (England v. West Indies, at Nottingham).

The Double

B. Dooland (Nottinghamshire), 1,604 runs; 141 wickets (August 13).
G. Goonesena (Cambridge Univ. and Notts), 1,156 runs; 110 wickets (August 27).
G. E. Tribe (Northamptonshire), 1,181 runs; 140 wickets (August 30).
R. Illingworth (Yorkshire), 1,213 runs; 106 wickets (September 6).
F. J. Titmus (Middlesex), 1,056 runs; 106 wickets (September 6).
T. E. Bailey (Essex), 1,322 runs; 104 wickets (September 10).

200 Wickets

G. A. R. Lock (Surrey), September 10, alone accomplished this feat.

First to 100 Wickets

G. A. R. Lock (Surrey), July 6.

Nine Wickets in an Innings

F. Fee (Ireland v. Scotland, at Dublin), 9 for 26.
D. J. Halfyard (Kent v. Glamorgan, at Neath), 9 for 39.
R. Illingworth (Yorkshire v. Worcestershire, at Worcester), 9 for 42.

Hat-Tricks

L. Coldwell (Worcestershire v. Leicestershire, at Stourbridge).
T. Dewdney (West Indies v. Hampshire, at Southampton).
D. J. Halfyard (Kent v. Worcestershire, at Folkestone).
P. J. Loader (Surrey) (England v. West Indies, at Leeds).

Wicket-Keeping

J. Brown (Scotland v. Ireland, at Dublin) equalled the record of seven victims in an innings, 3 stumped, 4 caught.

J. T. Murray (Middlesex) completed rare double of scoring 1,025 runs and claiming 104 victims, 82 caught, 22 stumped. L. E. G. Ames (Kent) is the only other wicket-keeper to accomplish this. He did it three times.

Fielding

M. J. Stewart (Surrey v. Northamptonshire, at Northampton) held seven catches in an innings and established a record for a fieldsman, other than a wicket-keeper, in one innings.

Totals Over 500

619 for 6, declared (England v. West Indies, at Nottingham).
583 for 4, declared (England v. West Indies, at Birmingham).

Totals Under 50

29   Middlesex v. Derbyshire, at Chesterfield.
31   Glamorgan v. Surrey, at The Oval.
39   Gloucestershire v. Hampshire, at Bournemouth.
41   Leicestershire v. Somerset, at Leicester.
43   Kent v. Middlesex, at Dover.
43   Leicestershire v. Essex, at Brentwood.

Note.—There were 31 instances of a side being dismissed for 75 or less.

Most Balls Bowled in a Test

S. Ramadhin (West Indies v. England, at Birmingham) bowled 588 balls in an innings, a record number for any match, and 774 balls in the game, the most in any Test.

Four Test Wickets to Successive Balls

An exceptional Test incident occured at the end of West Indies first innings at Leeds, where F. S. Trueman dismissed O. G. Smith with the last ball of an over and P. J. Loader performed the hat-trick with the first three balls of the following over.

The "County" Cups

(*Excluding Festival Matches, Champion County v. The Rest and games outside England and Wales*)

Batting: Fastest Hundred—R. E. Marshall (Hampshire v. Kent, at Southampton); in 66 minutes.
Bowling: Best Performance—D. J. Halfyard (Kent v. Glamorgan, at Neath), 9 for 39.
Fielding: Most Catches—M. J. Stewart (Surrey), 75.
Wicket-keeping: Most victims—J. T. Murray (Middlesex), 94 (79 catches, 15 stumpings).
Special Award for Best Performance of Season—To P. B. H. May and M. C. Cowdrey for sharing a stand of 411 for the fourth wicket for England against West Indies, at Birmingham, the highest partnership ever made for England.

FIRST CLASS AVERAGES, 1957

BATTING

(Qualification: 8 innings, average 10.00)

† *Denotes a left-handed batsman.*   * *Signifies not out.*

	Innings	Not Outs	Runs	Highest Innings	Average
P. B. H. May (*Surrey*)	41	3	2347	285*	61.76
M. C. Cowdrey (*Kent*)	43	6	1917	165	51.81
T. W. Graveney (*Gloucestershire*)	53	5	2361	258	49.18
J. M. Parks (*Sussex*)	55	6	2171	132*	44.30
F. A. Lowson (*Yorkshire*)	19	2	752	154	44.23
C. A. Milton (*Gloucestershire*)	31	9	943	89	42.86
†D. V. Smith (*Sussex*)	54	5	2088	166	42.61
D. R. W. Silk (*Somerset*)	16	3	526	79	40.46
†W. Watson (*Yorkshire*)	39	2	1462	162	39.51
D. J. Insole (*Essex*)	49	5	1725	150*	39.20
K. F. Barrington (*Surrey*)	53	11	1642	136	39.09
T. E. Bailey (*Essex*)	42	8	1322	132	38.88
†C. J. Poole (*Nottinghamshire*)	46	6	1535	110*	38.37
D. Kenyon (*Worcestershire*)	62	3	2231	200*	37.81
J. D. Robertson (*Middlesex*)	59	2	2155	201*	37.80
C. D. Melville (*Oxford Univ.*)	21	2	715	142	37.63
†A. Wharton (*Lancashire*)	53	3	1853	164	37.06
E. R. Dexter (*Cambridge Univ*)	43	2	1511	185	36.85
D. F. Cox (*Surrey*)	8	4	147	54	36.75
M. J. Stewart (*Surrey*)	54	5	1801	147*	36.75
M. J. K. Smith (*Warwickshire*)	63	5	2125	127	36.63
†R. C. Wilson (*Kent*)	51	1	1831	157	36.62
†S. E. Leary (*Kent*)	44	10	1231	108	36.20
W. G. A. Parkhouse (*Glamorgan*)	50	4	1642	133	35.69
F. C. Gardner (*Warwickshire*)	57	9	1706	163	35.54
D. C. S. Compton (*Middlesex*)	45	0	1554	143	34.53
M. R. Hallam (*Leicestershire*)	62	2	2068	176	34.46
†W. B. Stott (*Yorkshire*)	42	1	1362	181	33.21
T. H. Clark (*Surrey*)	52	4	1570	99	32.70
†D. W. Richardson (*Worcester*)	63	7	1830	169	32.67
†P. E. Richardson (*Worcester*)	55	0	1795	126	32.63
R. E. Marshall (*Hampshire*)	59	1	1888	163	32.55
B. Constable (*Surrey*)	47	5	1357	107	32.30
†D. B. Close (*Yorkshire*)	56	4	1666	120	32.03
A. B. D. Parsons (*Cbd. Services*)	8	1	223	52	31.85
D. M. Young (*Gloucestershire*)	53	1	1653	114	31.78
R. G. Broadbent (*Worcester*)	49	7	1331	77*	31.69
A. Hamer (*Derbyshire*)	54	1	1678	138	31.66
C. L. McCool (*Somerset*)	58	4	1678	100*	31.07
†K. G. Suttle (*Sussex*)	55	2	1640	165	30.94
D. G. W. Fletcher (*Surrey*)	28	5	708	101	30.78
†A. J. Watkins (*Glamorgan*)	45	6	1199	140	30.74
J. Kelly (*Derbyshire*)	54	4	1535	127	30.70
Rev. D. S. Sheppard (*Sussex*)	18	2	490	117	30.62
J. R. Gray (*Hampshire*)	60	5	1683	124	30.60
D. B. Carr (*Derbyshire*)	49	4	1368	141	30.40
N. F. Horner (*Warwickshire*)	54	3	1545	152	30.29
D. Brookes (*Northants*)	55	3	1574	148*	30.26
†L. Livingston (*Northants*)	39	1	1150	95	30.26
W. J. Stewart (*Warwickshire*)	31	0	924	104	29.80
K. Grieves (*Lancashire*)	48	6	1242	224	29.57

	Innings	Not Outs	Runs	Highest Innings	Average
†G. Pullar (*Lancashire*)	42	3	1146	138	29.38
A. H. Phebey (*Kent*)	55	1	1576	111	29.18
†R. W. Barber (*Cambridge Univ.*)	26	4	637	106	28.95
D. W. Barrick (*Northants*)	54	7	1356	122	28.85
R. Jowett (*Oxford Univ.*)	19	2	489	122	28.76
K. Taylor (*Yorkshire*)	29	2	776	140*	28.74
B. L. Reynolds (*Northants*)	48	5	1235	169	28.72
G. W. Cook (*Cambridge Univ.*) .	35	6	831	111*	28.65
B. Dooland (*Nottinghamshire*)..	59	3	1604	115*	28.64
G. M. Emmett (*Gloucestershire*)	59	0	1690	170	28.64
P. Arnold (*Northamptonshire*) ..	34	3	886	86	28.58
R. Illingworth (*Yorkshire*)	52	9	1213	97	28.20
R. B. Nicholls (*Gloucestershire*).	52	2	1404	84	28.08
M. F. Tremlett (*Somerset*)	57	4	1488	144	28.07
K. Ibadulla (*Warwickshire*)	33	11	613	54	27.86
H. Horton (*Hampshire*).........	55	4	1404	114*	27.52
L. J. Lenham (*Sussex*).........	54	3	1401	130	27.47
G. Dews (*Worcestershire*)	56	2	1479	115	27.38
†A. C. D. Ingleby-Mackenzie (*Hampshire*)...............	51	6	1230	109*	27.33
A. Townsend (*Warwickshire*)...	47	3	1201	154	27.29
H. L. Johnson (*Derbyshire*)	35	9	707	88*	27.19
P. B. Wight (*Somerset*)	52	3	1328	88	27.10
G. Goonesena (*Nottinghamshire*)	48	5	1156	211	26.88
†J. V. Wilson (*Yorkshire*).......	55	7	1287	132	26.81
D. C. Morgan (*Derbyshire*)	47	12	937	64*	26.77
T. C. Dodds (*Essex*)	44	1	1151	97	26.76
I. M. McLachlan (*Cambridge U.*)	24	1	613	101	26.65
B. Hedges (*Glamorgan*)	55	5	1315	139	26.30
†W. E. Jones (*Glamorgan*)......	30	3	708	69*	26.22
†R. C. E. Pratt (*Surrey*)........	16	6	262	76*	26.20
J. P. Fellows-Smith (*Northants*)	24	1	600	109	26.08
†F. W. Stocks (*Nottinghamshire*)	22	1	544	103*	25.90
†J. F. Pretlove (*Kent*)...........	50	4	1191	101	25.89
T. G. Evans (*Kent*)	42	5	953	84*	25.75
C. Washbrook (*Lancashire*) ...	40	3	950	94	25.67
†W. E. Alley (*Somerset*)........	62	2	1540	108	25.66
J. P. Springall (*Nottinghamshire*)	27	1	667	83	25.65
C. H. Palmer (*Leicestershire*)..	60	4	1436	117	25.64
†G. E. Tribe (*Northamptonshire*)	53	6	1181	101	25.12
†N. Hill (*Nottinghamshire*)......	30	2	705	119	25.17
H. M. Barnard (*Hampshire*) ...	36	4	800	86	25.00
R. H. E. Chisholm (*Scotland*)..	9	1	200	61*	25.00
†R. Subba Row (*Northants*).....	10	1	224	70	24.88
D. Barr (*Scotland*)	9	2	174	43	24.85
J. D. Clay (*Nottinghamshire*)...	42	0	1044	86	24.85
G. Barker (*Essex*)	57	0	1416	117	24.84
†J. T. Ikin (*Lancashire*)	53	4	1197	141*	24.42
M. A. Eagar (*Gloucestershire*)..	33	1	756	99	23.62
Rev. J. Aitchison (*Scotland*)....	9	0	212	53	23.55
†S. Singh (*Warwickshire*)	39	8	729	68*	23.51
A. J. McIntyre (*Surrey*)........	40	8	747	96	23.34
R. M. James (*Cambridge Univ.*).	29	1	652	168	23.28
M. Winfield (*Nottinghamshire*)..	18	0	419	74	23.27
G. P. S. Delisle (*Middlesex*) ...	32	4	648	130	23.14
I. M. Gibson (*Oxford Univ.*)...	26	4	508	100*	23.09
M. Hill (*Nottinghamshire*)......	48	1	1081	95	23.00
M. J. Horton (*Worcestershire*)..	52	4	1103	93	22.97
W. J. Edrich (*Middlesex*)......	54	2	1192	77	22.92
D. J. Foreman (*Sussex*)........	34	3	708	61	22.83
G. H. G. Doggart (*Sussex*).....	18	0	408	84	22.66

	Innings	Not Outs	Runs	Highest Innings	Average
L. N. Devereux (*Glamorgan*)...	53	7	1039	108*	22.58
C. Lee (*Derbyshire*)	54	2	1172	83	22.53
J. Pettiford (*Kent*)	38	6	719	59	22.46
P. I. Pieris (*Cambridge Univ.*)...	19	3	359	55*	22.43
G. Potter (*Sussex*)	21	4	381	78	22.41
M. Kasippillai (*Cambridge U.*) .	11	2	201	62*	22.33
†R. T. Spooner (*Warwickshire*) .	38	4	757	118	22.26
G. G. Atkinson (*Somerset*).....	19	2	377	53	22.17
†R. Gale (*Middlesex*)..........	57	0	1260	126	22.10
A. W. H. Rayment (*Hampshire*)	30	0	659	80	21.96
R. J. Giles (*Nottinghamshire*)..	24	0	527	101	21.95
†B. Taylor (*Essex*)...........	63	3	1311	105	21.85
L. A. Savill (*Essex*)	38	3	762	89	21.77
A. C. Walton (*Middlesex*)......	44	0	956	95	21.72
†A. Lightfoot (*Northamptonshire*)	9	0	192	49	21.33
D. J. Green (*Cambridge Univ.*)..	36	2	723	75	21.26
G. A. Edrich (*Lancashire*)......	18	0	374	72	20.77
J. D. Currie (*Oxford Univ.*) ..	8	0	164	38	20.50
A. C. Revill (*Derbyshire*)......	44	1	876	86	20.37
J. van Geloven (*Leicestershire*)..	47	3	895	63	20.34
W. H. H. Sutcliffe (*Yorkshire*)..	51	9	854	75	20.33
A. R. B. Neame (*Kent*)........	9	0	182	69	20.22
T. W. Cartwright (*Warwickshire*)	32	2	606	84	20.20
C. W. Leach (*Warwickshire*)...	24	2	443	67	20.13
R. O. Jenkins (*Worcestershire*)..	33	10	462	60	20.08
J. A. D. Hobbs (*Oxford Univ.*)..	30	1	581	95	20.03
F. J. Titmus (*Middlesex*)......	56	3	1056	70	19.92
E. A. Bedser (*Surrey*).........	41	5	717	65	19.91
J. T. Murray (*Middlesex*)......	57	5	1025	120	19.71
J. Bond (*Lancashire*).........	32	1	608	72	19.61
J. M. Kumleben (*Oxford Univ.*)	16	1	294	100	19.60
C. S. Smith (*Lancashire*)......	45	7	744	103*	19.57
F. H. Tyson (*Northamptonshire*)	42	12	587	70*	19.56
H. W. Stephenson (*Somerset*)..	57	6	982	104*	19.25
J. Dyson (*Lancashire*).........	36	2	649	88	19.08
K. E. Palmer (*Somerset*).......	37	6	591	56*	19.06
G. O. Dawkes (*Derbyshire*)....	48	7	778	75	18.97
D. Hawkins (*Gloucestershire*)...	32	4	529	106	18.89
R. Collins (*Lancashire*)........	21	2	358	54	18.84
P. Walker (*Glamorgan*)........	33	1	603	60	18.84
L. R. Gardner (*Leicestershire*)..	53	5	901	82	18.77
J. M. Kemsley (*Scotland*)......	8	0	149	103	18.62
R. T. Webb (*Sussex*)	23	6	315	35	18.52
G. Lester (*Leicestershire*)......	56	2	999	73	18.50
A. K. Walker (*Nottinghamshire*)	28	4	437	73	18.20
P. J. Sainsbury (*Hampshire*)....	44	8	652	94	18.11
R. Booth (*Worcestershire*).....	49	6	774	68*	18.00
G. A. R. Lock (*Surrey*).......	32	6	464	46	17.84
L. Pickles (*Somerset*).........	28	3	444	70	17.76
W. T. Greensmith (*Essex*).....	46	9	657	61	17.75
D. O. Baldry (*Middlesex*)......	26	0	461	61	17.73
R. G. Woodcock (*Oxford Univ.*)	27	5	390	57	17.72
D. Bennett (*Middlesex*)	51	11	699	51*	17.47
L. C. Dudman (*Scotland*)	9	0	157	48	17.44
R. A. Diment (*Leicestershire*)..	32	0	554	67	17.31
L. Outschoorn (*Worcestershire*)..	40	2	658	115	17.31
E. J. Martin (*Nottinghamshire*)..	15	1	242	38	17.28
M. D. Scott (*Oxford Univ.*).....	26	4	380	52	17.27
†M. Bear (*Essex*)	45	4	698	123	17.02
J. E. McConnon (*Glamorgan*)..	46	3	730	52	16.97
R. Ralph (*Essex*)	48	12	586	66	16.27

	Innings	Not Outs	Runs	Highest Innings	Average
A. E. Fagg (*Kent*)	20	2	290	45*	16.11
R. Bowman (*Oxford Univ.*)....	22	5	271	75	15.94
A. L. Dixon (*Kent*)	32	2	477	73	15.90
R. T. Simpson (*Nottinghamshire*)	20	0	318	113	15.90
A. S. Brown (*Gloucestershire*) ..	33	8	397	45	15.88
A. Jepson (*Nottinghamshire*)...	47	8	615	61	15.76
G. Millman (*Nottinghamshire*)..	42	7	549	58	15.68
†J. H. Wardle (*Yorkshire*)......	42	7	546	64	15.60
A. Wolton (*Warwickshire*).....	17	0	263	48	15.47
D. E. V. Padgett (*Yorkshire*) ..	31	1	462	48	15.40
†D. G. Ufton (*Kent*)	20	1	290	55	15.26
†W. Knightley-Smith (*Gloucs.*)...	19	0	285	55	15.00
F. S. Trueman (*Yorkshire*).....	41	14	405	63	15.00
†J. S. Manning (*Northamptonshire*)	41	4	553	132	14.94
D. J. Ward (*Glamorgan*)	17	4	194	31*	14.92
G. Smith (*Essex*)	29	0	428	64	14.75
K. J. Poole (*Nottinghamshire*)...	12	1	161	32	14.63
D. A. Stripp (*Sussex*)	8	2	87	32*	14.50
W. Wooller (*Glamorgan*)	39	5	493	55	14.50
D. Shackleton (*Hampshire*) ...	41	7	492	64	14.47
K. V. Andrew (*Northants*)......	45	12	476	76	14.42
A. E. James (*Sussex*)...........	43	4	562	52	14.41
N. I. Thomson (*Sussex*)......	41	4	530	59	14.32
M. D. Willett (*Surrey*)	8	1	99	26	14.14
K. Smales (*Nottinghamshire*) ...	30	11	265	63*	13.94
J. Pressdee (*Glamorgan*)	18	3	205	32	13.66
C. Gladwin (*Derbyshire*)	36	17	259	21*	13.63
R. J. Etheridge (*Gloucestershire*)	18	6	161	38	13.41
L. Harrison (*Hampshire*).......	41	8	440	79	13.33
D. Carpenter (*Gloucestershire*) ..	21	0	273	48	13.00
M. J. Cowan (*Yorkshire*)......	13	9	52	19*	13.00
R. Appleyard (*Yorkshire*)......	22	8	179	63	12.78
D. J. Shepherd (*Glamorgan*) ...	44	22	281	53	12.77
D. R. Smith (*Gloucestershire*) ..	47	10	466	63*	12.59
W. Davies (*Glamorgan*).........	23	0	285	58	12.39
S. H. Cosh (*Scotland*)	8	0	99	38	12.37
J. C. Laker (*Surrey*)	28	11	210	44	12.35
V. H. D. Cannings (*Hampshire*)	25	11	172	33*	12.28
H. R. A. Kelleher (*Northants*)...	25	12	158	25	12.15
J. G. Lomax (*Somerset*)	29	0	351	36	12.10
J. Mortimore (*Gloucestershire*)..	31	0	373	47	12.03
R. W. C. Pitman (*Hampshire*)...	14	1	154	28	11.84
A. V. Bedser (*Surrey*)	24	13	130	17*	11.81
†J. B. Statham (*Lancashire*)	33	5	321	53	11.46
J. J. Warr (*Middlesex*).........	46	14	355	40*	11.09
K. C. Preston (*Essex*)	43	5	421	40	11.07
E. D. R. Eagar (*Hampshire*) ...	27	3	263	29	10.95
M. Hickman (*Leicestershire*)...	14	0	152	38	10.85
B. J. Meyer (*Gloucestershire*)...	13	3	107	30*	10.70
H. G. Davies (*Glamorgan*)	38	3	372	39	10.62
†V. S. Munden (*Leicestershire*)..	20	3	180	26*	10.58
G. Smith (*Kent*)	17	4	137	32	10.53
B. D. Wells (*Gloucestershire*) ...	27	5	224	47	10.18
E. Rowe (*Nottinghamshire*)	8	7	10	5*	10.00
B. T. Swift (*Cambridge Univ.*)..	23	7	160	25	10.00

BOWLING

(Qualification: 10 wickets in 10 innings)

† *Denotes a left-arm bowler.*

	Overs	Maidens	Runs	Wickets	Average
†G. A. R. Lock (*Surrey*)	1194.1	449	2550	212	12.02
†V. Broderick (*Northants*)	130.3	52	236	17	13.88
J. B. Statham (*Lancashire*)	896.4	251	1895	126	15.03
J. C. Laker (*Surrey*)	1016.5	393	1921	126	15.24
E. A. Bedser (*Surrey*)	548.5	178	1188	77	15.42
P. J. Loader (*Surrey*)	878.2	217	2058	133	15.47
D. Shackleton (*Hampshire*)	1217.3	447	2429	155	15.67
†C. W. Leach (*Warwickshire*)	155.2	58	305	19	16.05
G. Smith (*Kent*)	389.1	109	923	57	16.19
L. Jackson (*Derbyshire*)	1048.2	355	2295	141	16.27
†M. J. H. Allen (*Northants*)	626	248	1277	78	16.37
A. V. Bedser (*Surrey*)	1032.4	267	2170	131	16.56
T. E. Bailey (*Essex*)	738.3	207	1771	104	17.02
F. S. Trueman (*Yorkshire*)	842.2	184	2303	135	17.05
D. Pickles (*Yorkshire*)	238.4	53	651	37	17.59
K. Ibadulla (*Warwickshire*)	546.5	213	966	54	17.88
A. E. Moss (*Middlesex*)	761.5	180	2055	114	18.02
R. Tattersall (*Lancashire*)	1141.1	399	2434	135	18.02
C. Gladwin (*Derbyshire*)	909.5	351	2021	110	18.37
R. Illingworth (*Yorkshire*)	829.2	289	1951	106	18.40
D. J. Shepherd (*Glamorgan*)	882.1	265	2213	119	18.59
†G. F. Tribe (*Northants*)	932.2	242	2620	140	18.71
W. E. Hollies (*Warwickshire*)	1228.4	409	2501	132	18.94
J. Mortimore (*Gloucestershire*)	670.2	246	1468	76	19.31
J. E. McConnon (*Glamorgan*)	698.5	184	1914	99	19.33
J. Savage (*Leicestershire*)	551	161	1557	80	19.46
B. Lobb (*Somerset*)	812.2	169	2143	110	19.48
†R. J. Hurst (*Middlesex*)	640.3	235	1564	80	19.55
F. J. Titmus (*Middlesex*)	812.4	227	2093	106	19.74
N. I. Thomson (*Sussex*)	970	307	2197	111	19.79
W. E. Alley (*Somerset*)	572.4	144	1412	71	19.88
C. S. Smith (*Lancashire*)	721.1	154	1812	91	19.91
†J. S. Manning (*Northants*)	936.5	336	2175	109	19.95
†J. H. Wardle (*Yorkshire*)	1048.5	404	2281	114	20.00
T. Greenhough (*Lancashire*)	526.5	142	1380	68	20.29
K. C. Preston (*Essex*)	1126.2	270	2850	140	20.35
L. N. Devereux (*Glamorgan*)	256.2	77	618	30	20.60
R. Appleyard (*Yorkshire*)	613.5	152	1568	74	21.18
B. Langford (*Somerset*)	616.2	203	1422	67	21.22
D. R. Smith (*Gloucestershire*)	910.3	212	2265	106	21.36
D. J. Halfyard (*Kent*)	922.4	242	2502	117	21.38
F. H. Tyson (*Northants*)	769.5	161	2169	101	21.47
P. B. Wight (*Somerset*)	77	23	237	11	21.54
J. T. Ikin (*Lancashire*)	111.1	34	262	12	21.83
R. Ralph (*Essex*)	844.5	197	2245	102	22.00
J. D. Bannister (*Warwickshire*)	641.3	173	1618	73	22.16
C. H. Palmer (*Leicestershire*)	441	180	933	42	22.21
R. K. Platt (*Yorkshire*)	225	64	578	26	22.23
†M. J. Hilton (*Lancashire*)	611	227	1432	64	22.37
B. Boshier (*Leicestershire*)	445.4	83	1283	57	22.50
K. J. Aldridge (*Worcestershire*)	311.1	68	889	39	22.79
E. R. Dexter (*Cambridge Univ.*)	210.2	48	639	28	22.82
J. Dyson (*Lancashire*)	207.5	76	465	18	25.83
†C. Cook (*Gloucestershire*)	1068.3	403	2195	96	22.86
D. V. P. Wright (*Kent*)	286.3	93	871	38	22.92

	Overs	Maidens	Runs	Wickets	Average
D. C. Morgan (*Derbyshire*) ..	916	312	2166	94	23.04
J. J. Warr (*Middlesex*).......	806.3	191	2055	89	23.08
†J. W. McMahon (*Somerset*)..	791.1	247	1987	86	23.10
B. Dooland (*Nottinghamshire*)	1334	419	3273	141	23.21
G. Goonesena (*Cambridge U.*)	863.2	194	2559	110	23.26
J. A. Bailey (*Essex*)	555.1	154	1445	61	23.68
V. H. D. Cannings (*Warwick.*)	626.4	210	1377	58	23.74
D. Bennett (*Middlesex*)	545	99	1558	65	23.96
†P. Walker (*Glamorgan*)	357.3	94	871	36	24.19
S. S. Griffiths (*Warwickshire*)	280	58	678	28	24.21
F. Ridgway (*Kent*)	495.1	99	1512	62	24.38
†P. J. Sainsbury (*Hampshire*)..	691.3	268	1396	57	24.49
D. B. Close (*Yorkshire*).......	287	92	787	32	24.59
†D. C. S. Compton (*Middlesex*)	286.2	59	939	38	24.71
S. E. Leary (*Kent*)...........	84.1	13	348	14	24.85
J. C. T. Page (*Kent*)..........	682.4	227	1738	69	25.18
J. Flavell (*Worcestershire*)	841.5	139	2581	101	25.55
C. T. Spencer (*Leicestershire*)	792.3	141	2344	91	25.75
D. L. Bates (*Sussex*)	745	156	2128	82	25.95
J. Pettiford (*Kent*)	105	28	313	12	26.08
R. O. Jenkins (*Worcestershire*)	334.4	67	1071	41	26.12
L. Coldwell (*Worcestershire*)..	665	154	1862	71	26.22
A. Brown (*Kent*).............	237.3	46	710	27	26.29
J. Hilton (*Somerset*)	309.5	83	763	29	26.31
D. J. Insole (*Essex*)	149.2	34	395	15	26.33
A. S. Brown (*Gloucestershire*)	389.3	103	1011	38	26.60
†R. C. Smith (*Leicestershire*)..	408.3	151	933	35	26.65
†R. V. Bell (*Sussex*)...........	288	87	830	31	26.77
C. L. McCool (*Somerset*)....	382.5	72	1181	44	26.84
H. R. A. Kelleher (*Northants*)	478.2	138	1184	44	26.90
B. D. Wells (*Gloucestershire*)..	772.5	239	1779	66	26.95
M. Heath (*Hampshire*)	720.4	171	2057	76	27.06
R. G. Marlar (*Sussex*)........	914.2	227	2625	97	27.06
A. Townsend (*Warwickshire*)	307.1	65	761	28	27.17
I. M. Gibson (*Oxford Univ.*)..	86.4	19	301	11	27.36
H. D. Davies (*Glamorgan*)	411.3	73	1426	52	27.42
E. Smith (*Derbyshire*)	754.4	246	1968	71	27.71
†R. Berry (*Worcestershire*)	1083	422	2422	87	27.83
R. M. James (*Cambridge U.*)..	158.1	41	446	16	27.87
A. E. James (*Sussex*)	650	226	1534	55	27.89
†V. S. Munden (*Leicestershire*)	224	90	533	19	28.05
W. T. Greensmith (*Essex*)....	620.1	133	1775	63	28.17
O. S. Wheatley (*Camb. Univ.*)	588	141	1636	58	28.20
M. D. Burden (*Hampshire*) ...	569.4	167	1580	56	28.21
†M. J. Cowan (*Yorkshire*).....	449.5	89	1297	45	28.82
R. W. Barber (*Camb. Univ.*)..	91.2	21	319	11	29.00
†K. G. Suttle (*Sussex*)	477.4	161	1073	37	29.00
R. G. Carter (*Warwickshire*) ..	681.4	154	2041	70	29.15
A. Jepson (*Nottinghamshire*)..	764	184	1992	68	29.29
M. J. Horton (*Worcestershire*)	965.3	343	2256	75	30.08
R. Bowman (*Oxford Univ.*)...	422.5	80	1326	44	30.13
S. Singh (*Warwickshire*)	478.5	176	1033	34	30.38
J. G. Lomax (*Somerset*)......	128.3	18	397	13	30.53
A. Wharton (*Lancashire*)	349.4	86	953	31	30.74
J. van Geloven (*Leicestershire*)	183	42	493	16	30.81
†C. S. Matthews (*Notts*)	306.5	64	879	28	31.39
D. Hawkins (*Gloucestershire*)	93.2	29	315	10	31.50
†J. M. Allan (*Kent*)	161	51	474	15	31.60
†D. V. Smith (*Sussex*)	462.5	146	1244	39	31.89
G. E. Lambert (*Gloucester*) ...	283	53	871	27	32.25
†R. G. Woodcock (*Oxford U.*)	415	108	1139	35	32.54
†I. M. King (*Essex*)..........	535.5	197	1146	34	33.70

	Overs	Maidens	Runs	Wickets	Average
W. Wooller (*Glamorgan*)	314.4	83	862	25	34.48
J. R. Gray (*Hampshire*)	346	102	855	24	35.62
K. E. Palmer (*Somerset*)	115.5	15	394	11	35.81
R. Jowett (*Oxford Univ.*)	142	25	432	12	36.00
R. W. Wilson (*Oxford Univ.*)	433	101	1203	33	36.45
†D. B. Carr (*Derbyshire*)	274	70	937	25	37.48
†A. J. Watkins (*Glamorgan*) ...	415.2	108	951	26	36.57
†A. K. Walker (*Notts*)	431.4	104	1223	33	37.06
G. W. Cook (*Camb. Univ.*) ...	426.1	116	1228	30	40.93
K. Smales (*Nottinghamshire*) ..	558.5	176	1539	37	41.59
P. I. Pieris (*Cambridge Univ.*)	319	81	910	20	45.50
M. Morgan (*Nottinghamshire*)	286.4	77	807	17	47.47
A. L. Dixon (*Kent*)	272.3	69	834	17	49.05

The following also took 10 wickets, but bowled in fewer than 10 innings:—

F. Fee (*Ireland*)	43	19	60	12	5.00
C. J. M. Kenny (*F. Foresters*)	36.5	7	96	10	9.60
D. Gibson (*Surrey*)	102	18	265	17	15.58
D. Livingstone (*Scotland*) ..	152.5	43	322	18	17.88
T. E. Dickinson (*Somerset*)..	122.4	24	321	17	18.88
R. S. Thresher (*Kent*)	103.2	27	303	14	21.64
D. Hall (*Derbyshire*)	86.3	19	287	12	23.91
S. V. M. Clube (*Oxford Univ.*)	102	15	299	12	24.91
G. H. Chesterton (*Worcester*)	162.2	41	454	18	25.22
E. Leadbeater (*Warwickshire*)	114	36	289	10	28.90
M Ryan (*Yorkshire*)........	94	19	293	10	29.30
†J. Goodwin (*Leicestershire*) ..	182.5	28	576	19	30.31
A. W. H. Rayment (*Hants*)...	90	17	338	10	33.80

INDIVIDUAL SCORES OF 100 AND OVER

There were 230 individual three-figure innings in first-class cricket in 1957, 41 more than in 1956. The list includes 149 hit in County Championship matches and 62 in other first-class games, but not the 19 by members of the West Indies team which can be found in their own section.

T. W. Graveney (8):
258 Eng. v. W. Indies: Nottingham.
164 Eng. v. W. Indies: Oval.
134 Glos. v. Somerset: Bristol.
122 Glos. v Warwickshire: Bristol.
111* Glos. v. Worcs: Bristol.
106 } Glos. v. War: Birmingham.
101* }
101* Glos. v. Middlesex: Lord's.

P. B. H. May (7):
285* Eng. v. W. Indies: Birmingham.
151 Surrey v. M.C.C.: Lord's.
125 Surrey v. Yorks: Oval.
119 T. N. Pearce's XI v. W. Indies: Scarborough.
117 Surrey v. Sussex: Oval.
104 Eng. v. W. Indies: Nottingham.
100 Surrey v. Lancs: Manchester.

K. F. Barrington (6):
136 Champion County v. Rest: Scarborough.
129* Surrey v. Essex: Clacton.
124* Surrey v. Glos: Oval.
110* Surrey v. Comb. Services: Oval.
103* Surrey v. W. Indies: Oval.
101 Surrey v. War: Birmingham.

M. R. Hallam (6):
176 Leics. v. Kent: Leicester.
152 Leics. v. Notts: Nottingham.
151 Leics. v. Somerset: Taunton.
146 Leics. v. Sussex: Hove.
139 M.C.C. v. Oxford U: Lord's.
118 Leics. v. Oxford U: Oxford.

* *Signifies not out.*

D. Kenyon (6):
200* Worcs. v. Notts: Worcester.
175 Worcs. v. Derby: Derby.
123 Worcs. v. Sussex: Eastbourne.
119 Worcs. v. Oxford U: Oxford.
119 Worcs. v. Sussex: Worcester.
115 Worcs. v. Glos: Bristol.

M. C. Cowdrey (5):
165 Kent v Notts: Nottingham.
154 Eng. v. W. Indies: Birmingham.
152 Eng. v. W. Indies: Lord's.
143 L. E. G. Ames's XI v. W. Indies: Hastings.
100 An England XI v. Commonwealth XI: Hastings.

D. W. Richardson (5):
169 Worcs. v. Derby: Dudley.
115 Worcs. v. Essex: Worcester.
113 Worcs. v. Middlesex: Lord's.
110 Worcs. v. Somerset: Taunton.
101* Worcs. v. Glos: Bristol.

D. V. Smith (5):
166 Sussex v. Glos: Hove.
149 Sussex v. Middlesex: Lord's.
147* Sussex v. W. Indies: Hove.
117 Sussex v Glam: Swansea.
102 Players v. Gents: Lord's.

A. Wharton (5):
164 Lancs. v. M.C.C.: Manchester.
114 Lancs. v. Worcs: Blackpool.
106 Lancs. v. Oxford U: Oxford.
103 Lancs. v. Glos: Bristol.
102 Lancs. v. Yorks: Sheffield.

D. Brookes (4):
148* Northants v. Worcs: Worcester.
135* Northants v. Leics: Northm.
103 Northants v. Lancs: Blackpool.
100 Northants v. Surrey: Oval.

D. B. Close (4):
120 Yorks. v. Derby: Chesterfield.
108* M.C.C. v. W. Indies: Lord's.
108 Yorks. v. Derby: Bradford.
103 Yorks. v. Sussex: Hove.

A. Hamer (4):
138 Derby v. Sussex: Derby.
134 Derby v. Worcs: Dudley.
112* Derby v. Surrey: Oval.
104 Derby v. Lancs: Liverpool.

D. J. Insole (4):
150* Essex v. Worcs: Worcester.
140 Essex v. Northants: Westcliff.
115 Essex v. Surrey: Clacton.
106 Essex v. Glam: Ilford.

J. Kelly (4):
127 Derby v. Leics: Chesterfield.
113 Derby v Glos: Gloucester.

J. Kelly—*contd.*
109* Derby v. Glam: Chesterfield.
106 Derby v Yorks: Chesterfield.

R. E. Marshall (4):
163 Hants v. Glam: Portsmouth.
111 Hants v. Surrey: Portsmouth.
107 Hants v. Notts: Cowes.
103 Hants v. Kent: Southampton.

J. M. Parks (4):
132* M.C.C. v. Lancs: Manchester.
124 Sussex v. Cam. U: Cambridge.
101 ⎫
100* ⎭ Sussex v. Worcs: Worcester.

P. E. Richardson (4):
126 Eng. v. W. Indies: Nottingham.
116 Worcs. v. Derby: Derby.
108 Worcs. v. Glos: Bristol.
107 England v. W. Indies: Oval.

J. D. Robertson (4):
201* Middx. v. Essex: Lord's.
119 Middx. v. Sussex: Lord's.
105* Middx. v. Camb. U: Cambridge.
104 Middx. v. Worcs: Lord's.

M. J. Stewart (4):
147* Surrey v. W. Indies: Oval.
140 Surrey v. War: Birmingham.
114* Surrey v. Comb. Services: Oval.
103 Surrey v. War: Oval.

W. Watson (4):
162 Yorks. v. Northants: Harrogate.
134 Yorks. v. Scotland: Paisley.
116 Yorks. v. War: Birmingham.
102 Yorks. v. Worcs: Scarborough.

G. Barker (3):
117 Essex v. Middx: Leyton.
107 Essex v Sussex: Colchester.
100 Essex v. Notts: Southend.

D. C. S. Compton (3):
143 Middx. v. Worcs: Lord's.
109 Middx. v. Essex: Leyton.
104 Middx. v. Lancs: Manchester.

B. Constable (3):
107 Surrey v. Glos: Oval.
105 Surrey v. Essex: Clacton.
100 Surrey v. Oxford U: Guildford.

F. C. Gardner (3):
163 War. v. Glos: Birmingham.
126 War. v. Sussex: Eastbourne.
110 War. v. Oxford U: Oxford.

J. R. Gray (3):
124 Hants v. Camb. U: Bournemouth.
115 Hants v. War: Southampton.
103* Hants v. Derby: Portsmouth.

H. Horton (3):
114* Hants v. Notts: Cowes.
106 Hants v. Notts: Nottingham.
106 Hants v. War: Coventry.

S. E. Leary (3):
108 Kent v. Hants: Southampton.
102* Kent v Camb. U: Cambridge.
100* Kent v. Sussex: Hastings.

F. A. Lowson (3):
154 Yorks. v. Camb. U: Cambridge.
116 Yorks. v. Middx: Lord's.
100 Yorks. v. Glam: Sheffield.

C. H. Palmer (3):
117 Leics. v. Yorks: Leicester.
103 Leics. v. Essex: Leicester.
102* Leics. v. Essex: Brentwood.

G. Pullar (3):
138 Lancs. v. Hants: Manchester.
137 Lancs. v. Notts: Manchester.
121 Lancs. v. Scotland: Manchester.

M. J. K. Smith (3):
127 War. v. Yorks: Birmingham.
110 War. v. Middx: Birmingham.
104* War. v. Derby: Derby.

W. B. Stott (3):
181 Yorks. v. Essex: Sheffield.
139 Yorks. v. Leics: Hull.
114 Yorks. v. Notts: Nottingham.

R. C. Wilson (3):
157 Kent v. Leics: Gravesend.
146 Kent v. Somerset: Taunton.
102 Kent v. Glos: Maidstone.

T. E. Bailey (2):
132 Essex v. Worcs: Leyton.
102* Essex v. Glam: Ilford.

G. W. Cook (2):
111* Camb. U. v. Oxford U: Lord's.
111 Camb. U. v. Lancs: Liverpool.

E. R. Dexter (2):
185 Camb. U. v. Lancs: Cambridge.
100* Camb. U. v. Essex: Cambridge.

G. M. Emmett (2):
170 Glos. v. Glam: Swansea.
114 An Eng. XI v. Comm. XI: Torquay.

B. L. Hedges (2):
139 Glam. v. Notts: Llanelly.
128 Glam. v. Leics: Coalville.

R. Jowett (2):
122 Oxford U. v. D. R. Jardine's XI: Eastbourne.
103 Oxford U. v. Free Foresters: Oxford.

C. D. Melville (2):
142 Oxford U. v. Leics: Oxford.
140* Oxford U. v. Hants: Oxford.

W. G. A. Parkhouse (2):
133 Glam. v. Kent: Neath.
118 Glam. v. Derby: Chesterfield.

A. H. Phebey (2):
111 Kent v. Worcs: Folkestone.
100* Kent v Camb. U: Cambridge.

B. L. Reynolds (?):
169 Northants v. Essex: Westcliff.
157* Northants v. Glos: Northm.

F. W. Stocks (2):
103* Notts v. Worcs: Worcester.
101 Notts v. Somerset: Nottingham.

K. G. Suttle (2):
165 Sussex v. Kent: Hastings.
103 Sussex v. Worcs: Worcester

M. F. Tremlett (2):
144 Somerset v. Leics: Taunton.
106 Somerset v. Sussex: Weston.

A. J. Watkins (2):
140 Glam. v. Hants: Portsmouth.
115* Glam. v. Sussex: Swansea.

The following forty-seven each played one three-figure innings:—

W. E. Alley, 108, Somerset v. Worcs., Worcester.

R. W. Barber, 106, Cambridge U. v. Hants, Bournemouth; D. W. Barrick, 122, Northants v. West Indies, Northampton; M. Bear, 123, Essex v. Glos., Romford.

D. B. Carr, 141, Derby v. Leics., Chesterfield; G. Cox, 100*, Sussex v. Somerset, Hove; I. D. Craig, 127, Free Foresters v. Cambridge U., Cambridge.

G. P. S. Delisle, 130, Middlesex v. Cambridge U., Cambridge; L. N. Devereux, 108*, Glam. v. Lancs., Manchester; G. Dews, 115, Worcs., v. Leics., Stourbridge; B. Dooland, 115*, Notts v. Sussex, Worthing.

J. P. Fellows-Smith, 109, Northants v. Sussex, Hove; D. G. W. Fletcher, 101, Surrey v. Essex, Oval.

H

R. Gale, 126, Middlesex v. Sussex, Lord's; I. Gibson, 100*, Oxford U. v. Glos.
Oxford; R. J. Giles, 101, Notts v. Hants, Cowes; G. Goonesena, 211,
Cambridge U. v. Oxford U., Lord's; K. Grieves, 224, Lancs. v. Cambridge U.,
Cambridge.

D. G. Hawkins, 106, Glos. v. Sussex, Hove; N. Hill, 119, Notts v. War., Nottingham; N. F. Horner, 152, War. v. Derby, Derby.

J. T. Ikin, 141*, Lancs., v. Worcs., Worcester; A. C. D. Ingleby-Mackenzie,
109*, Hants v. Cambridge U., Bournemouth.

R. M. James, 168, Cambridge U. v. Glos., Bristol.

J. M. Kemsley, 103, Scotland v. M.C.C., Aberdeen; J. M. Kumleben, 100,
Oxford U. v. Yorks., Oxford.

L. J. Lenham, 130, Sussex v. Derby, Hove.

C. L. McCool, 100*, Somerset v. Glos., Taunton; I. M. McLachlan, 101, Cambridge
U. v. Essex, Cambridge; J. S. Manning, 132, Northants v. Yorks., Harrogate;
J. T. Murray, 120, Middlesex v. Notts, Nottingham.

L. Outschoorn, 115, Worcs. v. Hants. Worcester.

C. J. Poole, 110*, Notts v. Glos., Nottingham; J. F. Pretlove, 101, Kent v. Leics.,
Gravesend.

Rev. D. S. Sheppard, 117, Sussex v. Yorks., Hove; R. T. Simpson, 113, Notts v.
Middlesex, Nottingham; C. S. Smith, 103*, Cambridge U. v. War.,
Birmingham; R. T. Spooner, 118, War., v. Glam., Cardiff; H. W. Stephenson,
104*, Somerset v. Kent, Taunton; W. J. Stewart, 104, War. v. Leics.,
Birmingham.

B. Taylor, 105, Essex v. Northants, Wellingborough; K. A. Taylor, 140*, Yorks.
v. Notts, Nottingham; A. Townsend, 154, War. v. Worcs., Dudley; G. E.
Tribe. 101, Northants v. West Indies, Northampton.

R. H. Willson, 113*, Sussex v. Somerset, Hove; J. V. Wilson, 132, Yorks. v.
Oxford U., Oxford.

D. M. Young, 114, Glos. v. Lancs., Bristol.

FIELDING STATISTICS IN 1957

104 J. T. Murray (82c, 22s)	41 J. Jordan (28c. 13s)	26 J. Bond
83 B. Taylor (68c, 15s)	39 G. Dews	26 D. Mantell (24c, 2s)
80 R. Booth (60c, 20s)	37 D. B. Close	26 F. J. Titmus
77 H. W. Stephenson (55c, 22s)	36 F. S. Trueman	25 B. Dooland
	36 R. T. Webb (29c, 7s)	25 R. J. Etheridge (17c, 8s)
77 M. J. Stewart	35 T. W. Graveney	
71 K. V. Andrew (54c, 17s)	35 K. C. Preston	25 J. T. Ikin
	35 A. J. Watkins	24 T. E. Bailey
69 J. G. Binks (55c, 14s)	34 W. J. Edrich	24 D. J. Insole
68 G. O. Dawkes (63c, 5s)	34 M. R. Hallam	24 J. M. Parks
	34 C. T. Spencer	24 M. D. Scott (16c, 8s)
64 K. F. Barrington	34 A. Townsend	24 P. Walker
63 G. A. R. Lock	33 M. C. Cowdrey	23 D. Foreman
63 R. T. Spooner (51c, 12s)	33 C. L. McCool (32c, 1s)	23 C. Lee
	32 K. Grieves	23 W. G. A. Parkhouse
60 A. J. McIntyre (51c, 9s)	32 S. E. Leary	23 J. F. Pretlove (21c, 2s)
	32 A. Wharton	21 H. M. Barnard
60 G. Millman (38c, 22s)	31 W. Wooller	21 T. W. Cartwright
56 J. Firth (51c, 5s)	30 M. H. J. Allen	21 J. R. Gray
56 P. J. Sainsbury	30 R. C. Wilson	21 D. W. Richardson
55 T. G. Evans (47c, 8s)	29 I. M. King	21 D. V. Smith
53 J. V. Wilson	29 P. B. H. May	20 G. H. G. Doggart
48 H. G. Davies (40c, 8s)	29 R. Ralph	20 E. B. Lewis (16c, 4s)
47 L. Harrison (42c, 5s)	29 K. Suttle	20 L. Livingston
47 B. T. Swift (37c, 10s)	27 C. A. Milton	20 A. H. Phebey
44 D. B. Carr	27 D. G. Ufton	20 M. F. Tremlett
42 D. C. Morgan	27 A. Wilson (24c, 3s)	20 G. E. Tribe

WEST INDIES IN ENGLAND, 1957

The change in the balance of cricket power among the members of the Imperial Cricket Conference during the last seven years was reflected in the outcome of the five Tests played by West Indies in England last summer. Far from repeating their success of 1950, when they won the rubber by three matches to one, they were thrice beaten by an innings in less than three days and escaped only narrowly in the other two matches that were drawn.

This bare summary paints a gloomy picture of the doings of the 1957 West Indies team and, while the players were naturally disappointed with their lack of success in the Tests, one might well attribute the failure to England's undeniable strength. The West Indies certainly found England a much tougher proposition than was the case seven years earlier, while they themselves, though still possessing plenty of talent, were not so well blended nor so well served in some vital departments.

Yet the overall results of the tour showed little change from those of 1950. Then the first-class victories numbered 17, including the three Test wins; now, minus any Test wins, they showed 14 victories. West Indies, beaten three times in 1950—by England, M.C.C. and Warwickshire again had to acknowledge three defeats, all by England.

Compared with the all-conquering side of 1950, this one lacked three essentials; reliable opening batsmen, a good spin combination and a first-class wicket-keeper. Indeed, the fielding as a whole fell far behind the high standard set by England, the returns from the outfield being particularly erratic.

None of the four recognised opening batsmen, Pairaudeau, Ganteaume, Asgarali and Rohan Kanhai, came up to expectations and consequently Worrell went in first in each of the last three Tests, being partnered by Sobers at Nottingham and at Leeds, and by Asgarali at The Oval.

Much was expected from the three famous "W's," Worrell, Weekes and Walcott, but with the side rarely receiving a sound start, none of them proved such prolific scorers as on their first visit when, incidentally, the pitches generally were more to their liking. Then the number of first-class centuries totalled 34 compared with 19 on this latest tour. Still, all three enjoyed their days of triumph, especially Worrell who touched true greatness at Nottingham where, after a noble spell of bowling, he carried his bat through the first innings for 191.

Weekes had to wait until the last first-class match of the tour at Scarborough for his solitary century, whereas in 1950 he reached three figures seven times, including a triple century at Cambridge and four double centuries. The fall in Weekes' aggregate from 2,310 runs to 1,096 could be partly attributed to sinus trouble and

a broken finger he suffered in the third week in June during the Lord's
Test. Despite his mishap he went on to play a glorious innings of 90
in that match, but the injury troubled him to the end of the tour.

Walcott, too, laboured under a handicap. He pulled a leg
muscle in the first Test at Birmingham at a time when he appeared
to be in his best form and, if he did not dominate any of the big
matches, he finished fifth in the season's first-class averages.

The biggest disappointment was the failure of the two spin
bowlers, Ramadhin and Valentine, to repeat the havoc they wrought
in the 1950 Tests. Though there appeared to be little falling-off in
Ramadhin's ability to deceive batsmen with his mixed right-arm
spin, the fact remained that whereas in 1950 this pair were responsible for the fall of 59 England wickets in four Tests, Ramadhin
claimed only 14 victims in five Tests in 1957 and the slow left-
hander, Valentine, could not manage even one wicket. Valentine
seemed to lose all faith in himself when he faced an England batsman. His control of length simply vanished and he sent down no
more than 26 overs in two Test appearances.

Ramadhin was seen at his best on the opening day of the
Test series at Edgbaston—a day the England batsmen are not
likely to forget. On a perfect pitch he took seven wickets for
49—his best Test performance—causing England to be put out for
186. Then the rubber seemed within the West Indies' grasp,
especially when they gained a first innings lead of 288. But there
followed a record English Test stand of 411 by May and Cowdrey
and, with two members of the attack (Worrell and Gilchrist)
off injured, Ramadhin was compelled to bowl 98 overs while
taking only two more wickets and conceding 179 runs. Altogether
he delivered more balls than any other bowler in any single innings
or in a whole Test match. Never again did Ramadhin worry the
England batsmen and though the circumstances were exceptional
with two men laid low, it did appear that the West Indies sacrificed
their ace bowler at Birmingham in much the same way as they did
to Australia on a similar occasion at Brisbane in 1951.

That only four centuries were hit against West Indies by the
Counties indicated that the side possessed much bowling ability.
Indeed, the party of 17 players contained plenty of natural as well
as tried talent. As in 1950, John Goddard came as captain, this
time having Walcott as vice-captain, but when late in the tour
neither was available, Worrell showed unmistaken gifts of
leadership.

Of the seven newcomers to England as cricket tourists—some
had enjoyed League experience and Alexander kept wicket for two
years at Cambridge—Smith, Sobers, Kanhai and Gilchrist were
particularly impressive. Smith had already scored a century on
debut against Australia and not only did he repeat the feat with
161 in his first match against England at Edgbaston, but he also

hit 168 in a glorious match-saving effort at Trent Bridge. As Smith was also a brilliant fielder and no mean off-spinner, besides always being a joyful character, he won many admirers. More about Smith and also Walcott will be found earlier in the Almanack, where both figure among the Five Cricketers of the Year.

To Sobers, a tall left-handed all-rounder, fell the distinction of hitting the highest score of the tour—219 not out against Nottinghamshire at Trent Bridge. Sobers undoubtedly was a very fine stroke-player who should go far. Rohan Kanhai, 21 years old and the youngest member of the party, came primarily as a batsman and in this respect he too could make a name for himself, but when, in order to strengthen the run-getting powers of the side, he was pressed into service as wicket-keeper in the first three Tests, he was little more than a stopper.

The side had three specialist seam bowlers in Gilchrist, Hall and Dewdney, and if none approached the skill of Worrell, Gilchrist was menacing by virtue of his genuine pace and ability to produce a bouncer as venomous as any sent down by the opposition.

Of nine bowlers who performed more or less regularly, Denis Atkinson, a former West Indies captain, took 55 wickets at an average cost of 22.45 runs. He came to the front in the opening first-class engagement at Worcester where, finding an ideal surface for his off-cutters, he took ten wickets for 62, but later he was overworked and a strained shoulder kept him out of many matches.

When things were going right for them, this West Indies team, like their predecessors, provided rare entertainment. Hailed on arrival as the gay "Calypso" cricketers from the Caribbean, they possibly became careless in their efforts to play attractive cricket. More determination was necessary, but for many of the youngsters the experience gained on such a long and arduous tour, which produced so many pitches of very different character, should be invaluable.

One could not always understand the reasons for some team selections. For instance, England relied mainly on Statham, Trueman and Bailey to bowl on the pacy Lord's pitch, but West Indies decided to call up Valentine, who had been omitted from the previous Test, instead of giving a chance to Dewdney or Hall.

Goddard himself did not enjoy a successful tour, though his resolute defence was invaluable in averting defeat in the two drawn Tests. The uncertainty of the early batting was always a problem, and on top of this he had key men either out of form or beset by injury. Finally he, too, was put out of action by influenza at the end of the first day of the last Test.

For all his troubles, Goddard returned home knowing that his side had been well received by the cricket public of Great

Britain. Both on and off the field the players were extremely popular. Everybody liked them and their approach to the game.—N. P.

WEST INDIES RESULTS

Test Matches.—Played 5, Lost 3, Drawn 2.

First-Class Matches.—Played 31, Won 14, Lost 3, Drawn 13, Abandoned 1.

All Matches.—Played 35, Won 16, Lost 3, Drawn 15, Abandoned 1.

Wins.—Worcestershire, Northamptonshire, Oxford University, Essex, Gloucestershire, Glamorgan (2), Sussex, Derbyshire, Ireland, Surrey, Lancashire, Leicestershire, Kent, L. E. G. Ames' XI, Minor Counties.

Draws.—England (2), E. W. Swanton's XI, Cambridge University, M.C.C., Yorkshire, Nottinghamshire, Surrey, Ireland, Hampshire, Somerset, Middlesex, Warwickshire, Lancashire, T. N. Pearce's XI.

Losses.—England (3).

TEST MATCH AVERAGES
ENGLAND
BATTING

	Matches	Inns.	Not Outs	Runs	Highest Inns.	Average
T. W. Graveney	4	5	1	472	258	118.00
P. B. H. May	5	6	1	489	285*	97.80
F. S. Trueman	5	4	3	89	36*	89.00
M. C. Cowdrey	5	6	0	435	154	72.50
P. E. Richardson	5	7	0	411	126	58.71
Rev. D. S. Sheppard	2	2	0	108	68	54.00
T. G. Evans	5	6	2	201	82	50.25
D. B. Close	2	3	0	89	42	29.66
G. A. R. Lock	3	3	0	37	20	12.33
J. B. Statham	3	2	0	20	13	10.00
J. C. Laker	4	3	1	18	10*	9.00
D. V. Smith	3	4	1	25	16*	8.33
T. E. Bailey	4	4	1	5	3*	1.66
P. J. Loader	2	2	0	1	1	0.50

Also batted: D. J. Insole 20, 0; D. W. Richardson 33; J. H. Wardle 11.

* Signifies not out.

BOWLING

	Overs	Maidens	Runs	Wickets	Average
P. J. Loader	44.3	17	100	10	10.00
G. A. R. Lock	114.2	59	163	15	10.86
F. S. Trueman	173.3	34	455	22	20.68
T. E. Bailey	117	37	277	12	23.08
J. C. Laker	246.2	99	448	18	24.88
J. B. Statham	158.1	37	433	13	33.30
D. V. Smith	45	13	97	1	97.00

Also bowled: D. B. Close 2—1—8—0; T. W. Graveney 5—2—14— 0; J. H. Wardle 22—5—53—1.

WEST INDIES

BATTING

	Matches	Inns.	Not Outs	Runs	Highest Inns.	Average
O. G. Smith	5	10	0	396	168	39.60
F. M. Worrell	5	10	1	350	191*	38.88
G. Sobers	5	10	0	320	66	32.00
C. L. Walcott	5	10	1	247	90	27.44
Rohan Kanhai	5	10	1	206	47	22.88
E. D. Weekes	5	10	0	195	90	19.50
D. Atkinson	2	4	1	55	46	18.33
J. D. Goddard	5	8	1	112	61	16.00
N. Asgarali	2	4	0	62	29	15.50
S. Ramadhin	5	9	1	47	19	5.87
B. H. Pairaudeau	2	4	0	20	7	5.00
R. Gilchrist	4	7	2	22	11*	4.40
F. C. M. Alexander	2	4	1	11	11	3.66
A. L. Valentine.........	2	4	2	4	2*	2.00

Also batted: T. Dewdney 0, 1.

* Signifies not out.

BOWLING

	Overs	Maidens	Runs	Wickets	Average
F. M. Worrell	128.2	25	343	10	34.30
S. Ramadhin	261.3	78	547	14	39.07
O. G. Smith	89	14	223	5	44.60
R. Gilchrist	152.3	19	466	10	46.60
J. D. Goddard	58	18	128	2	64.00
G. Sobers	135	24	355	5	70.10
D. Atkinson	125.4	39	267	2	133.50
A. L. Valentine..........	26	4	88	0	—

Also bowled: C. L. Walcott 1—0—4—0.
T. Dewdney 15—2—43—1.

HUNDREDS

The following hundreds were hit in the Test matches:—

For ENGLAND (8):

M. C. Cowdrey (2): 154 at Birmingham (First Test).
152 at Lord's (Second Test).

T. W. Graveney (2): 258 at Nottingham (Third Test).
164 at The Oval (Fifth Test).

P. B. H. May (2): 285* at Birmingham (First Test).
104 at Nottingham (Third Test).

P. E. Richardson (2): 126 at Nottingham (Third Test).
107 at The Oval (Fifth Test).

For WEST INDIES (3):

O. G. Smith (2): 168 at Nottingham (Third Test).
161 at Birmingham (First Test).

F. M. Worrell (1): 191* at Nottingham (Third Test).

WEST INDIES—FIRST-CLASS AVERAGES
BATTING
† *Denotes left-handed batsman.*

	Matches	Inns.	Not Outs	Runs	Highest Inns.	Average
F. M. Worrell	20	34	9	1470	191*	58.80
C. L. Walcott	21	36	5	1414	131	45.61
†G. Sobers	25	44	6	1644	219*	43.26
O. G. Smith	26	45	9	1483	168	41.19
Rohan Kanhai	22	39	4	1093	95	31.22
N. Asgarali	21	37	3	1011	130*	29.73
E. D. Weekes	23	40	1	1096	105	28.10
A. Ganteaume	19	32	3	800	92	27.58
B. H. Pairaudeau	18	33	0	781	163	23.66
F. C. M. Alexander ...	20	30	10	387	83	19.35
D. Atkinson	16	23	4	324	101*	17.05
†J. D. Goddard	17	21	4	243	61	14.29
W. Hall	15	16	3	178	22	13.69
R. Gilchrist	15	16	5	67	20	6.09
S. Ramadhin	20	22	4	105	28	5.83
T. Dewdney	16	18	7	49	22*	4.45
A. L. Valentine........	16	11	6	19	7	3.80

* *Signifies not out.*

BOWLING
† Denotes left-arm bowler.

	Overs	Maidens	Runs	Wickets	Average
S. Ramadhin	937.1	361	1664	119	13.98
†A. L. Valentine...........	513	160	1180	60	19.66
J. D. Goddard	91	31	173	8	21.62
D. Atkinson	605.1	201	1235	55	22.45
†F. M. Worrell	406.5	94	949	39	24.33
T. Dewdney	317.4	45	974	36	27.05
O. G. Smith	405.3	136	920	34	27.05
†G. Sobers	477.3	145	1172	37	31.67
R. Gilchrist	394.2	54	1176	37	31.78
W. Hall	292	47	906	27	33.55
N. Asgarali	76	24	201	5	40.20

Also bowled: A. Ganteaume 3—0—20—0; C. L. Walcott 8—2—28—0; E. D. Weekes 6—0—32—1.

NOTE.—J. D. Goddard also played for M.C.C. v. Yorkshire, scoring 5 and 4, and bowling 5—1—15—0.

WEST INDIES—HUNDREDS
The following nineteen three-figure innings, all in first-class matches, were played for West Indies:—

F. M. Worrell (4):
    191*   v. England at Nottingham (Third Test).
    135   v. Sussex at Hove.
    107*   v. Northamptonshire at Northampton.
    104   v. Leicestershire at Leicester.

O. G. Smith (3):
    168   v. England at Nottingham (Third Test).
    161   v. England at Birmingham (First Test).
    133   v. Derbyshire at Chesterfield.

G. Sobers (3):
    219*   v. Nottinghamshire at Nottingham.
    104   v. Somerset at Taunton.
    101*   v. M.C.C. at Lord's.

C. L. Walcott (3):
  131   v. Kent at Canterbury.
  117   v. M.C.C. at Lord's.
  115   v. Nottinghamshire at Nottingham.

N. Asgarali (2):
  130* v. Nottinghamshire at Nottingham.
  120* v. Kent at Canterbury.

B. H. Pairaudeau (2):
  163   v. Hampshire at Southampton.
  127   v. Cambridge University at Cambridge.

D. Atkinson (1):
  101* v. Gloucestershire at Bristol.

E. D. Weekes (1):
  105   v. T. N. Pearce's XI at Scarborough.

HUNDREDS AGAINST WEST INDIES

The following fifteen three-figure innings, all in first-class matches, were played against the West Indies:—

M. C. Cowdrey (3):
  154 for England at Birmingham (First Test).
  152 for England at Lord's (Second Test).
  143 for L. E. G. Ames' XI at Hastings.

P. B. H. May (3):
  285* for England at Birmingham (First Test).
  119 for T. N. Pearce's XI at Scarborough.
  104 for England at Nottingham (Third Test).

T. W. Graveney (2):
  258 for England at Nottingham (Third Test).
  164 for England at The Oval (Fifth Test).

P. E. Richardson (2):
  126 for England at Nottingham (Third Test).
  107 for England at The Oval (Fifth Test).

D. Barrick (1):
  122 for Northamptonshire at Northampton.

D. B. Close (1):
  108* for M.C.C. at Lord's.

D. V. Smith (1):
  147 for Sussex at Hove.

M. J. Stewart (1):
  147* for Surrey at The Oval.

G. E. Tribe (1):
  101 for Northamptonshire at Northampton.

* Signifies not out.

WEST INDIES—FIELDING

F. C. M. Alexander (41 caught, 7 stumped) 48, C. L. Walcott 28, G. Sobers 26, Rohan Kanhai (20 caught, 5 stumped) 25, E. D. Weekes 17, O. G. Smith 13, J. D. Goddard 13, A. Ganteaume 11, N. Asgarali 11, F. M. Worrell 10, B. H. Pairaudeau 7, D. Atkinson 6, A. L. Valentine 4, R. Gilchrist 3, W. Hall 3, T. Dewdney 2, S. Ramadhin 2.

F. W. SWANTON'S XI v. WEST INDIES

At Eastbourne, April 25, 26. Drawn. A bitter north-east wind made conditions most unpleasant for this reunion match between old friends. Mr. Swanton's team had all played cricket in the Caribbean and both sides showed plenty of enterprise. The left-handed Sobers spent only two hours hitting a century and Asgarali, Pairaudeau, Walcott and Worrell also displayed splendid form. Hubert Doggart had the misfortune to crack a thumb joint while fielding. Stewart ensured that Swanton's side would make an adequate reply for he hooked and pulled freely and there was some breezy hitting by Graveney and Ingleby-Mackenzie.

West Indies: 368 for six wickets, dec. (G. Sobers 110 not out, N. Asgarali 77, C. L. Walcott 60, F. M. Worrell 40, J. D. Goddard 38 not out, B. H. Pairaudeau (35) and 69 for three wickets; E. W. Swanton's XI: 244 for eight wickets, dec. (M. J. Stewart 93, T. W. Graveney 40, A. C. D. Ingleby-Mackenzie 33).

WORCESTERSHIRE v. WEST INDIES

At Worcester, May 1, 2. West Indies won by an innings and 77 runs, the match being completed by four o'clock on the second day. Slow bowlers held the mastery almost throughout. Berry was given his County cap for taking six of the nine West Indies wickets which fell; next day Atkinson took ten wickets for 62, being almost unplayable with his pacy off-breaks. Valentine, six for 33, gave him admirable support. Rarely can a match have begun so strangely. Ganteaume and Asgarali hit ten 4's in the first 50 runs and twelve of the first eighteen overs were maidens. Smith showed his punishing power, hitting three 6's and seven 4's before falling to a running catch in the deep. The pitch deteriorated so quickly that West Indies dismissed the county twice on the second day in the space of only four hours. Brilliant close to the wicket fielding by Walcott and Sobers, each of whom held four catches, helped West Indies to their speedy success—their first in six visits to Worcester.

West Indies

A. Ganteaume hit wkt b Berry ...	40
N. Asgarali st Booth b Berry	35
C. L. Walcott c Berry b Flavell ...	33
F. M. Worrell st Booth b Berry...	38
G. Sobers b Horton ·············	0
O. G. Smith c Outschoorn b Berry	68
D. Atkinson c Richardson, D. W. b Berry	0

J. D. Goddard c Booth b Flavell ·	27
F. C. M. Alexander not out	31
A. L. Valentine lbw b Berry	7
T. Dewdney not out	2
B 6, l-b 3	9

1/71 2/92 3/140   (9 wkts., dec.) 290
4/140 5/168 6/168 7/220 8/263 9/270

Worcestershire

D. Kenyon c Walcott b Valentine.......	26	— c Sobers b Worrell	0
P. E. Richardson c and b Worrell.......	18	— c and b Worrell	10
L. Outschoorn c Sobers b Worrell ...	0	— b Atkinson	21
D. W. Richardson c Walcott b Atkinson	1	— c Walcott b Atkinson ...	20
G. Dews b Atkinson	4	— b Atkinson	12
M. J. Horton c Sobers b Atkinson ...	0	— b Valentine...........	1
R. O. Jenkins c Walcott b Valentine ...	3	— c Smith b Valentine	28
R. Booth c and b Atkinson	19	— c Ganteaume b Atkinson ...	29
J. Flavell c Sobers b Valentine	0	— not out	6
R. Berry not out	0	— c Smith b Atkinson	0
K. J. Aldridge b Atkinson	1	— b Valentine...........	0
B 8	8	B 3, l-b 3	6

1/26 2/26 3/31 4/53 5/53 6/57 7/78   80   1/1 2/32 3/34 4/61 5/66   133
8/78 9/79   6/68 7/127 8/127 9/127

Worcestershire Bowling

	O.	M.	R.	W.
Flavell	25	4	65	2
Aldridge.......	26	11	48	0
Berry	44	16	105	6
Horton	23	9	49	1
Jenkins	2	0	14	0

West Indies Bowling

	O.	M.	R.	W.	O.	M.	R.	W.
Dewdney	5	0	16	0	3	1	19	0
Worrell	9	1	20	2	5	1	14	2
Atkinson	11.1	4	25	5	17	7	37	5
Valentine	7	3	11	3	16.1	5	22	3
Smith					8	4	18	0
Sobers					6	1	17	0

Umpires: F. S. Lee and E. Davies.

NORTHAMPTONSHIRE v. WEST INDIES

At Northampton, May 4, 6, 7. West Indies won by four wickets. They allowed a commanding position to slip and eventually had to struggle for victory. After losing two wickets cheaply, West Indies recovered through a stand of 135 in two hours by Asgarali and Weekes, followed by a fifth wicket partnership of 109 between Worrell and Sobers. Worrell, missed when seven, cut and drove splendidly in scoring his first hundred of the tour. Northamptonshire collapsed before clever bowling by Ramadhin and Valentine on a pitch which took a fair amount of spin all through. Following on 237 behind, Northamptonshire lost three wickets for 53 before Barrick and Tribe held up the West Indies for three and a half hours and added 179. Tribe's 101—the first century for the county against any West Indies side—included two 6's and fifteen 4's. Barrick, last out, stayed just over six hours and hit seventeen 4's in 122. Needing 96, West Indies broke down, but won with forty-three minutes to spare.

West Indies

N. Asgarali b Tribe	86	— b Tribe	23
B. H. Pairaudeau lbw b Kelleher	2	— lbw b Tribe	27
Rohan Kanhai b Kelleher	2	— c Livingston b Broderick	4
E. D. Weekes c Kelleher b Allen	81	— c Andrew b Broderick	0
F. M. Worrell not out	107	— run out	11
G. S. Sobers c Barrick b Broderick	36	— not out	17
O. G. Smith b Fellows-Smith	1	— c Allen b Broderick	2
J. D. Goddard c Fellows-Smith b Broderick	2	— not out	11
S. Ramadhin not out	2		
B 6, n-b 3	9	L-b 1	1

1/2 2/13 3/148 4/195 (7 wkts., dec.) 328
5/304 6/315 7/326

1/49 2/54 3/54 (6 wkts.) 96
4/65 5/65 6/78

A. L. Valentine and R. Gilchrist did not bat.

Northamptonshire

D. Brookes lbw b Valentine	20	— b Ramadhin	15
B. Reynolds b Ramadhin	1	— b Worrell	2
L. Livingston c Kanhai b Valentine	20	— lbw b Valentine	27
D. Barrick b Ramadhin	0	— c Goddard b Sobers	122
G. E. Tribe c Kanhai b Valentine	2	— c Goddard b Valentine	101
V. Broderick c Weekes b Ramadhin	9	— b Ramadhin	6
J. P. Fellows-Smith b Ramadhin	25	— st Kanhai b Ramadhin	16
F. H. Tyson b Ramadhin	0	— run out	0
M. H. J. Allen c Sobers b Valentine	4	— lbw b Smith	11
K. V. Andrew not out	2	— b Sobers	0
H. R. A. Kelleher b Valentine	8	— not out	5
		B 19, l-b 8	27

1/15 2/23 3/24 4/37 5/46 6/60 7/76 91
8/81 9/81

1/8 2/49 3/53 4/232 332
5/249 6/272 7/273 8/320
9/321

Northamptonshire Bowling

	O.	M.	R.	W.	O.	M.	R.	W.
Tyson	16	3	55	0	4	0	13	0
Kelleher	23	7	49	2	3	0	8	0
Allen	19	6	38	1	4	1	14	0
Tribe	22	4	63	1	14	4	43	2
Broderick	16	2	63	2	9	3	17	3
Fellows-Smith	17	7	51	1				

West Indies Bowling

	O.	M.	R.	W.	O.	M.	R.	W.
Gilchrist	5	1	8	0	10	1	42	0
Worrell	7	2	7	0	19	7	39	1
Ramadhin	19	10	20	5	61	27	88	3
Valentine	16.5	5	56	5	38	13	78	2
				Sobers	19.1	7	28	2
				Smith	18	10	30	1

Umpires: A. E. Pothecary and W. F. Price.

OXFORD UNIVERSITY v. WEST INDIES

At Oxford (Christ Church Ground), May 8, 9, 10. West Indies won by an innings and 90 runs. Their third successive victory was mainly due to more clever bowling by Ramadhin whose skill on rain-affected turf brought him the remarkable match analysis of thirteen wickets for 47 runs. In the first innings, he perplexed his rivals by varied spin, flight and pace, and in the second, after a day lost through rain, he again did much as he pleased. Walton alone batted confidently for the University. Ganteaume, Kanhai, Walcott (nine 4's), Sobers (twelve 4's) and Smith (two 6's) all gave attractive displays of stroke-making for the West Indies who won convincingly despite the weather's interference with play.

Oxford University

I. Gibson c Smith b Dewdney	6	— lbw b Ramadhin 14
J. A. D. Hobbs c Sobers b Atkinson	11	— c Kanhai b Ramadhin 12
A. C. Walton b Ramadhin	64	— c and b Atkinson 19
C. D. Melville b Atkinson	1	— b Ramadhin 0
M. A. Eagar b Ramadhin	3	— b Smith 1
J. D. Currie lbw b Ramadhin	6	— st Kanhai b Ramadhin ... 11
M. D. Scott st Kanhai b Ramadhin	4	— c Walcott b Atkinson ... 1
R. G. Woodcock not out	7	— b Ramadhin 0
J. A. Bailey b Ramadhin	0	— b Ramadhin 4
S. V. C. Clube b Ramadhin	0	— not out 9
J. R. Phillips b Atkinson	5	— b Ramadhin 0
B 8, l-b 3, n-b 1	12	B 6, l-b 5, n-b 2 13

1/9 2/45 3/53 4/64 5/85 6/91 7/108   **119**   1/31 2/36 3/38 4/45 5/66   **84**
8/108 9/108   6/66 7/66 8/70 9/84

West Indies

A. Ganteaume c Melville b Clube	60	O. G. Smith not out 30
B. H. Pairaudeau c Bailey b Clube	10	B 2, l-b 2, w 1 5
C. L. Walcott c Currie b Clube	58	
E. D. Weekes c Melville b Clube	2	
Rohan Kanhai c Scott b Melville	61	1/44 2/120 3/131 (5 wkts., dec.) 293
G. Sobers not out	67	4/132 5/246

D. Atkinson, S. Ramadhin, W. Hall and T. Dewdney did not bat.

West Indies Bowling

	O.	M.	R.	W.	O.	M.	R.	W.
Hall	7	3	10	0	3	0	8	0
Dewdney	6	2	13	1	2	0	5	0
Atkinson	23.4	11	44	3	16	9	10	2
Sobers	11	4	22	0				
Ramadhin	13	7	18	6	23	8	29	7
				Smith	7	3	19	1

Oxford Bowling

Bailey	16	4	41	0
Phillips	18	4	51	0
Clube	27	3	79	4
Gibson	7	1	32	0
Woodcock	17	3	53	0
Melville	11	1	32	1

Umpires: D. Hendren and J. S. Buller.

ESSEX v. WEST INDIES

At Ilford, May 11, 13, 14. West Indies won by four wickets. After being in grave danger of defeat when they lost their first four wickets in the second innings for 15 runs, West Indies made a splendid recovery on a rain-damaged pitch and ran out comfortable winners. Even on the first day the bowlers could always extract a little lift from of the turf, and Atkinson bowled his medium-paced off-breaks splendidly. Yet the Essex batsmen resisted tenaciously, particularly Barker and the left-handed Taylor who shared a second wicket stand of 83. Week-end rain, followed by showers on Monday morning, enlivened the turf and twenty wickets fell in the day for 204 runs. West Indies lost the last eight wickets of their first innings for 71, Walcott alone coping successfully with the hostility of Bailey, who often made the ball fly. Essex, too, found the medium pace off-turn of Atkinson and Goddard difficult in such conditions, and in the last twenty-five minutes West Indies, needing 204 to win, lost their opening pair for 12. Two more wickets tumbled for three runs on the last morning, but Walcott and Weekes, watchful against the good balls and quick to punish the bad, checked the collapse with a stand of 63. Weekes and Worrell added 47, and with Bailey tiring and lacking adequate support, the remaining 79 runs came in fifty-five minutes through free hitting by Worrell and Smith.

Essex

G. Barker c Walcott b Atkinson	34	—	c Weekes b Atkinson	22
L. Savill c Asgarali b Worrell	0	—	b Valentine	13
B. Taylor c Asgarali b Atkinson	58	—	c Asgarali b Atkinson	22
D. J. Insole c Alexander b Gilchrist	14	—	lbw b Goddard	17
T. E. Bailey c Smith b Atkinson	21	—	c Walcott b Goddard	21
M. Bear st Alexander b Atkinson	17	—	c and b Goddard	0
G. Smith c Asgarali b Atkinson	10	—	c Walcott b Goddard	7
B. Knight b Atkinson	6	—	c Alexander b Goddard	0
R. Ralph b Atkinson	19	—	c Asgarali b Atkinson	1
K. C. Preston c Ganteaume b Atkinson	6	—	c Weekes b Atkinson	7
I. King not out	0	—	not out	4
B 7, w 4, n-b 1	12		B 5, l-b 2	7

1/0 2/83 3/102 4/120 5/141 6/153   197   1/36 2/36 3/62 4/92 5/93   121
7/160 8/177 9/191   6/100 7/102 8/103 9/117

West Indies

N. Asgarali b Ralph	11	—	c Bear b Preston	1
A. Ganteaume c Bailey b Preston	1	—	lbw b Bailey	7
C. L. Walcott c Taylor b Bailey	50	—	c King b Preston	29
E. D. Weekes c and b Bailey	7	—	lbw b Bailey	59
F. M. Worrell c Ralph b Bailey	0	—	not out	61
O. G. Smith c Preston b Bailey	7	—	not out	40
D. Atkinson b Ralph	0			
J. D. Goddard not out	8	—	c King b Bailey	7
F. C. M. Alexander c Ralph b Bailey	7	—	b Preston	0
A. L. Valentine b Bailey	6			
R. Gilchrist b Preston	4			
B 8, l-b 6	14			

1/1 2/42 3/66 4/68 5/82 6/85 7/85   115   1/4 2/12 3/15   (6 wkts.) 204
8/98 9/110   4/15 5/78 6/125

West Indies Bowling

	O.	M.	R.	W.		O.	M.	R.	W.
Gilchrist	19	4	45	1	....	8	1	14	0
Worrell	14	2	37	1	....	5	2	6	0
Atkinson	35.2	14	58	8	....	28.5	11	55	4
Valentine	3	1	6	0	....	10	3	19	1
Smith	17	3	39	0					
Goddard					....	15	5	20	5

Essex Bowling

	O.	M.	R.	W.		O.	M.	R.	W.
Bailey	23	7	37	6	....	27	12	69	3
Preston	15.3	3	42	2	....	21.5	6	57	3
Ralph	10	4	14	2	....	13	2	54	0
King	2	1	8	0	....	2	0	10	0
Knight					....	1	0	14	0

Umpires: T. J. Bartley and John Langridge.

CAMBRIDGE UNIVERSITY v. WEST INDIES

At Cambridge, May 15, 16, 17. Drawn. Cambridge forced an honourable draw, finishing 117 ahead after facing first innings arrears of 141. A fourth wicket partnership of 60 in an hour and a quarter by Green and Dexter helped them to recover when they batted first on a placid pitch. Subsequently, Goonesena gave a flourish to the final phase of the innings, but the University attack was handicapped before lunch on the second day when indisposition caused his absence. Pairaudeau and Walcott gained complete control and their second wicket stand reached 205 before Walcott was out to a spectacular tumbling catch behind the bowler. Pairaudeau, with wristy cuts and drives, made his 100 in three hours forty minutes. Smith and Worrell punished the tired attack with 89 in an hour. The University's hopes of saving the game took an early blow when Davies was out, but resolute innings by Cook, Green, Dexter and Goonesena who, promoting himself, passed 50 for the second time, enabled them to save the match comfortably.

Cambridge University

J. T. Davies b Ramadhin	23	— c Alexander b Hall	1
G. W. Cook b Hall	13	— b Ramadhin	35
D. J. Green c Walcott b Smith	46	— c Walcott b Smith	64
I. McLachlan b Ramadhin	0	— lbw b Ramadhin	14
E. R. Dexter lbw b Ramadhin	46	— c Walcott b Hall	37
R. M. James lbw b Ramadhin	1	— c Smith b Dewdney	14
G. Goonesena c Sobers b Ramadhin	55	— b Smith	69
C. S. Smith c Sobers b Hall	6	— c Alexander b Dewdney	2
J. R. Rutherford b Sobers	8	— b Hall	1
B. T. Swift c and b Sobers	8	— not out	6
O. S. Wheatley not out	4	— b Dewdney	0
B 9, l-b 3, n-b 3	15	B 10, l-b 3, n-b 2	15

1/24 2/64 3/64 4/124 5/125 6/140   225   1/7 2/68 3/148 4/185   258
7/184 8/198 9/218   5/205 6/243 7/243 8/251 9/251

West Indies

N. Asgarali c Swift b Goonesena	17	W. Hall b James	0
B. H. Pairaudeau b Smith	127	A. Ganteaume not out	7
C. L. Walcott c Goonesena b Rutherford	86	B 2, l-b 2, w 1, n-b 5	10
G. S. Sobers lbw b Smith	15		
O. G. Smith not out	55	1/26 2/231 3/243 (6 wkts., dec.) 366
F. M. Worrell c James b Wheatley	49	4/258 5/347 6/352

F. C. M. Alexander, S. Ramadhin and T. Dewdney did not bat.

West Indies Bowling

	O.	M.	R.	W.		O.	M.	R.	W.
Hall	18	2	39	2	....	19	5	49	3
Dewdney	9	0	35	0	....	13.4	7	17	3
Worrell	11	6	15	0					
Ramadhin	37	17	70	5	....	30	5	84	2
Sobers	25.2	10	38	2	....	10	3	27	0
Smith	13	8	13	1	....	30	15	53	2
Walcott					....	3	1	13	0

Cambridge Bowling

	O.	M.	R.	W.
Smith	24	3	78	2
Wheatley	18	4	54	1
Goonesena	14	2	43	1
Cook	27	4	97	0
James	17	3	53	1
Rutherford	9	3	31	1

Umpires: F. S. Lee and H. Palmer.

M.C.C. v. WEST INDIES

At Lord's, May 18, 20, 21. Drawn. Rain cut so deeply into the game on the first day, when West Indies made 147 for three wickets, that there never existed much hope of a definite result. Apart from Moss, the M.C.C. bowlers caused the West Indies batsmen little anxiety. Walcott (two 6's and sixteen 4's) gave an impressive display lasting four and a half hours, and at times the left-handed Sobers (eighteen 4's) hit very strongly. In the absence of Ramadhin, the West Indies bowling suffered severely from Close who was so lame from a blow he received on the left foot when in the field that he needed Clark as a runner. Despite his handicap, Close drove and hooked to such effect that he made his 108 out of 157 in two hours twenty minutes with one 6 and fifteen 4's as his chief strokes. This fine display gained him his place in the first Test. Close rested on the last day when Worrell turned the game by taking five wickets for 22 with the new ball. Worrell hit the middle stump three times. Finally, Pairaudeau, Walcott and Weekes batted well against some more excellent bowling by Moss.

West Indies

N. Asgarali c Murray b Moss	12	— c Murray b Tyson	6
B. H. Pairaudeau b Moss	11	— c Murray b Tyson	66
C. L. Walcott c Sheppard b Tyson	117	— lbw b Hilton	49
E. D. Weekes c Cowdrey b Moss	30	— not out	49
F. M. Worrell c Insole b Moss	24		
G. Sobers not out	101		
Rohan Kanhai c Murray b Close	9	— not out	18
D. Atkinson not out	13		
B 11, l-b 8, w 1	20	B 5	5

1/20 2/23 3/107   (6 wkts., dec.) 337   1/27 2/93 3/125   (3 wkts.) 193
4/153 5/241 6/278

J. D. Goddard, A. L. Valentine and R. Gilchrist did not bat.

M.C.C.

D. B. Close retired hurt	108	F. H. Tyson b Worrell	5
T. H. Clark b Worrell	14	M. J. Hilton b Valentine	4
Rev. D. S. Sheppard c Atkinson b Valentine	13	D. J. Shepherd not out	0
T. W. Graveney c and b Valentine	42	A. E. Moss lbw b Worrell	4
M. C. Cowdrey c Gilchrist b Worrell	45	B 9, l-b 4	13
D. J. Insole b Worrell	22	1/44 2/75 3/195 4/244 5/267	284
J. T. Murray c and b Worrell	14	6/273 7/278 8/280 9/284	

M.C.C. Bowling

	O.	M.	R.	W.		O.	M.	R.	W.
Tyson	21	3	57	1	....	11	0	67	2
Moss	31	12	75	4	....	12	4	19	0
Hilton	21	3	78	0	....	13	3	41	1
Shepherd	21	3	49	0	....	9	1	51	0
Close	13	0	58	1					
Clark						2	0	2	0
Insole						1	0	8	0

West Indies Bowling

	O.	M.	R.	W.
Gilchrist	13	0	46	0
Worrell	29.3	7	71	6
Valentine	22	8	47	3
Atkinson	29	6	89	0
Sobers	4	2	18	0

Umpires: C. S. Elliott and John Langridge.

YORKSHIRE v. WEST INDIES

At Sheffield, May 22, 23, 24. Drawn. West Indies dictated the course of the game almost throughout and but for the fact that Goddard, with the first Test six days ahead, was concerned mainly with maintaining his unbeaten record, they would probably have won comfortably. As it was, Yorkshire held two wickets in hand at the close. Sobers helped West Indies to a commanding position with two innings full of powerful drives, and Ramadhin took the honours in attack. The confused look on Padgett's face when his wicket went down in the first innings and the bowling of Close and Illingworth round their legs later were indicative of the concealed spin of this slow bowler. In all he took ten for 68 on a pitch generally favouring batsmen. Yorkshire's first innings threatened to disintegrate completely with seven wickets down for 78 runs. Then Wardle, hitting the few indifferent deliveries hard but otherwise curbing his natural attacking tendencies, and Sutcliffe brought respectability to the total. Wilson, who batted two hours for 27, and Padgett, now more composed, did most to save the county after Goddard's safety-first declaration left them to score 301 runs in three and a half hours to win. Trueman presented few difficulties on his first encounter with the touring team.

West Indies

A. Ganteaume lbw b Wardle	29	—	c Binks b Illingworth	30
B. H. Pairaudeau b Platt	2	—	c Close b Illingworth	25
G. Sobers b Wardle	56	—	b Platt	72
E. D. Weekes c Wilson b Illingworth	19	—	b Platt	53
Rohan Kanhai lbw b Close	39	—	lbw b Platt	21
O. G. Smith b Illingworth	22	—	not out	36
D. Atkinson b Illingworth	19	—	b Trueman	8
J. D. Goddard c Binks b Wardle	13			
F. C. M. Alexander b Wardle	0	—	not out	8
W. Hall b Wardle	1			
S. Ramadhin not out	1			
L-b 4, n-b 3	7		B 14, l-b 3, n-b 2	19

1/15 2/60 3/61 4/112 5/155 6/155   190   1/55 2/56   (6 wkts., dec.) 272
7/176 8/177 9/189   3/155 4/211 5/227 6/242

Yorkshire

D. B. Close c Sobers b Ramadhin	24	— b Ramadhin		22
K. Taylor lbw b Atkinson	9	— b Atkinson		0
J. V. Wilson c Alexander b Ramadhin	25	— lbw b Smith		27
R. Illingworth b Ramadhin	6	— b Ramadhin		0
J. G. Binks b Ramadhin	0	— b Ramadhin		11
W. Watson b Hall	11	— b Atkinson		5
D. E. V. Padgett b Ramadhin	0	— b Ramadhin		38
W. H. H. Sutcliffe b Hall	17	— b Hall		17
J. H. Wardle c Kanhai b Ramadhin	64	— not out		9
F. S. Trueman c Alexander b Hall	0	— not out		0
R. K. Platt not out	2			
L-b 1, n-b 3	4	B 10, l-b 2		12

1/30 2/43 3/59 4/59 5/78 6/78 7/78 162 1/0 2/40 3/44 (8 wkts.) 141
8/132 9/160   4/52 5/82 6/119 7/123 8/141

Yorkshire Bowling

	O.	M.	R.	W.		O.	M.	R.	W.
Trueman	14	4	40	0	....	21	2	76	1
Platt	9	1	24	1	....	16	5	36	3
Illingworth	23	9	51	3	....	28	7	70	2
Wardle	24	9	46	5	....	23	6	47	0
Close	7	3	22	1	....	5	0	24	0

West Indies Bowling

	O.	M.	R.	W.		O.	M.	R.	W.
Hall	20	7	44	3	....	11	1	27	1
Atkinson	25	9	42	1	....	14	5	15	2
Ramadhin	32.3	15	47	6	....	28	18	21	4
Smith	8	3	25	0	....	8	4	22	1
Sobers						24	13	44	0

Umpires: T. J. Bartley and T. W. Spencer.

NOTTINGHAMSHIRE v. WEST INDIES

At Nottingham, May 25, 27, 28. Drawn. Played on a typically easy-paced Trent Bridge pitch, this game never looked like providing a definite result. The sight of boundaries flowing off the bat lost its appeal long before the end and, altogether, 1,207 runs were scored while only sixteen wickets fell. Jepson provided short-lived excitement by twice splitting the West Indies opening pair in his first over but, well as Dooland bowled, Nottinghamshire could not follow up these heartening successes. Sobers batted throughout the first day for the first double-century of his career. He hit thirty-six 4's, eleven of them in his second 50. Walcott, in splendid form, hit majestically off the back foot and, though Weekes was less punishing than expected, Smith struck out with tremendous power in each innings. In the second, Asgarali redeemed his first innings failure by scoring his first century of the tour and Kanhai, who had not impressed behind the wicket, showed himself a far better batsman. In the absence of Ramadhin, the touring team were hardly more successful than Nottinghamshire with the ball. Hall bowled well in his first burst and Valentine kept going nobly, but Nottinghamshire had no trouble in compiling the highest score so far against the tourists.

West Indies

N. Asgarali b Jepson	4	— not out	130
G. Sobers not out	219	— b Jepson	0
C. L. Walcott c Clay b Smales	115		
E. D. Weekes lbw b Dooland	68		
O. G. Smith not out	67	— not out	46
Rohan Kanhai did not bat	—	— c Rowe b M. Hill	95
D. Atkinson did not bat	—	— c Rowe b M. Hill	24
B 3, l-b 13	16	L-b 3	3

1/4 2/197 3/372   (3 wkts., dec.) 489   1/1 2/206 3/248   (3 wkts.) 298
J. D. Goddard, W. Hall, A. L. Valentine and T. Dewdney did not bat.

Nottinghamshire

R. Giles b Hall	9	A. Jepson b Dewdney	54
J. D. Clay lbw b Smith	67	T. Atkinson b Smith	6
H. M. Winfield c Weekes b Atkinson	21	E. J. Rowe b Valentine	0
M. Hill b Valentine	50	B 14, l-b 11, w 1, n-b 7	33
N. Hill b Valentine	46		
B. Dooland c Kanhai b Sobers	46		
J. Kelly c Sobers b Hall	25	1/13 2/65 3/142 4/174 5/258	420
K. Smales not out	63	6/266 7/317 8/396 9/413	

Nottinghamshire Bowling

	O.	M.	R.	W.	O.	M.	R.	W.
Jepson	21	2	70	1	7	2	21	1
Atkinson	24	2	112	0	12	2	46	0
Dooland	38	12	95	1	11	6	21	0
Smales	31	6	130	1	14	1	60	0
Kelly	11	0	66	0	12	2	48	0
M. Hill					8	0	60	2
N. Hill					3	0	26	0
Clay					1	0	13	0

West Indies Bowling

	O.	M.	R.	W.
Hall	25	7	48	2
Dewdney	15	1	42	1
Valentine	54	16	116	3
Atkinson	46	11	97	1
Asgarali	6	2	19	0
Smith	21	9	37	2
Goddard	5	3	5	0
Sobers	10	4	23	1

Umpires: J. F. Crapp and A. Skelding.

ENGLAND v. WEST INDIES

First Test Match

At Birmingham, May 30, 31, June 1, 3, 4. Drawn. The return of Test cricket to Edgbaston after an interval of 28 years produced one of the most remarkable matches of all time. Blessed with fine weather throughout, although the last day turned cold, the contest was notable for some excellent personal performances and a wonderful recovery by England who seemed on the brink of defeat when they began their second innings 288 behind. In the end, West Indies had their backs to the wall and had to fight strenuously to ward off disaster.

Among the records set, the following were most notable:—

(1) May and Cowdrey put on 411 together, a Test record for the fourth wicket: the highest stand ever made for England and the third highest for

any side in the history of Test cricket. It fell 40 short of the highest—451 by Bradman and Ponsford for the Australian second wicket against England at The Oval in 1934. Roy and Mankad made an opening stand of 413 for India against New Zealand at Madras in 1955–56.

(2) May's 285 not out was the best score by an England captain, surpassing Hammond's 240 against Australia at Lord's in 1938. England's best against West Indies is 325 by Sandham at Kingston in 1930.

(3) May's 285 not out was his highest in first-class cricket and the highest individual score in all post-war Test cricket, beating Compton's 278 v. Pakistan at Nottingham in 1954.

(4) Cowdrey's 154 was his highest score in Test cricket and his first Test century in England.

(5) Ramadhin, in his marathon performance, bowled 774 balls, the most delivered by a bowler in a Test, beating Verity's 766 against South Africa at Durban in 1939. He also bowled most balls (588) in any single first class innings, including Tests, beating his colleague Valentine who sent down 552 balls in the second innings against England at Nottingham in 1950. The highest number of balls ever bowled by one man in a first-class match was 917 by C. S. Nayudu for Holkar v. Bombay in 1944–45.

(6) O. G. Smith gained the distinction of hitting a century on his first appearance against England, a feat he had previously accomplished on his first appearance against Australia at Kingston, Jamaica, in 1954–55. Denis Compton hit hundreds on debut against Australia, South Africa and West Indies.

England were fortunate when May won the toss for the twelfth time in sixteen matches. From the original thirteen players selected, they left out Graveney and Wardle and West Indies omitted Valentine.

Seldom can England have given such a disappointing exhibition on a perfect pitch. In four hours the whole side were dismissed for 186 and Ramadhin, with seven wickets for 49, had achieved his best performance in Test cricket.

Ramadhin kept his opponents guessing by his peculiar flick of the right wrist. None could tell his intention, whether he was attempting off spin or leg spin. As usual, he kept his shirt sleeves buttoned at the wrists and it was difficult to see how the ball left his right hand. He acquired very little spin and the majority of his wickets were taken with straight balls.

Gilchrist, a wiry, long-armed fast bowler, provided a contrast to Ramadhin. After lunch he bowled without relief for an hour and fifty minutes, maintaining a fiery pace for seventeen overs.

West Indies lost Pairaudeau to a yorker in Trueman's second over, but Rohan Kanhai and Walcott took command and saw the total to 83 for one wicket by the close of the first day. Early the next day, Walcott, stealing a single, pulled a leg muscle so severely that he collapsed and fainted. Soon he was compelled to have Pairaudeau as a runner and later in the innings Pairaudeau also acted as runner for Worrell. Further ill-luck overtook West Indies at another stage when Gilchrist went lame so that neither he nor Worrell could take part in the attack.

The second day produced an unfinished stand of 119 by O. G. Smith and Worrell. When Statham removed Kanhai with the first ball of the day, and later Walcott went for 90 and Sobers for 53. England were holding their own.

A wonderful slip catch by Bailey, who flung himself to his left and held with both hands a vicious cut, dismissed Sobers. Walcott showed much patience in an innings of four hours twenty minutes, but his punishing powers were revealed in the shape of eleven 4's. By mid-afternoon half the West Indies wickets had gone for 197. They were no more than 11 ahead and Trueman and Statham had the new ball. Here began the long stand by Smith and Worrell. Often each was beaten by the two pace bowlers, but they survived, taking the score to 316 for five wickets.

A record attendance for Edgbaston of 32,000 people saw the cricket on Saturday and still West Indies held the mastery. Indeed, the England bowlers toiled from 3.20 p.m. on Friday until 1.30 p.m. on Saturday before they managed to break the Smith–Worrell partnership of 190 made in five hours.

Pairaudeau occupied an abnormal amount of time in the middle for a man who scored only a single. He spent three and a quarter hours as runner for Walcott and then five hours for Worrell.

Even after Statham bowled Worrell with the last ball before lunch England had to wait another eighty-five minutes for their next success. Altogether Smith stayed six hours and fifty-two minutes for his 161, being eighth out at 469. He hit one 6 and eighteen 4's and scored quite quickly after completing his hundred.

When England batted a second time, West Indies had Hall and Asgarali as substitutes for Walcott and Worrell; later Alexander appeared for Gilchrist, who began the bowling with Atkinson. Ninety minutes elapsed before Ramadhin caused more consternation by deceiving Richardson and then bowling Insole in the next over.

Fortunately for England, Close, despite a blow on the left hand, defended resolutely and he and May raised the score to 102 for two wickets at the close of the third day.

Monday was memorable for the feat of May in batting all day and, excepting the first twenty minutes, Cowdrey was with him the whole time. It was a tremendous struggle. Both found the answer to Ramadhin by playing forward to him. His analysis for the day read: 48 overs, 20 maidens, 74 runs, 0 wickets. At the close England were 378 for three wickets; May 193, Cowdrey 78. While May took four hours ten minutes to reach three figures, Cowdrey, avoiding all risks, completed 50 out of 160 in three hours forty minutes.

As the wonderful partnership ripened on the last day many new cricket records were established. With the position still critical, defence remained the prime objective. Just after one o'clock Cowdrey completed his century in seven and three-quarter hours and thereupon he changed his tactics, driving and cutting powerfully so that his third fifty came in fifty-five minutes.

At length, Asgarali caught Cowdrey at long on. The stand had lasted eight hours twenty minutes, Cowdrey having hit sixteen 4's and 63 singles. In the next half-hour May and Evans put on 59 more runs before May declared. Beginning his match-saving effort at 5.40 p.m. on Saturday, May batted till 3.20 p.m. on Tuesday, and helped to change the total from 65 for two wickets to 583 for four. No man could have done more for England than the captain, whose record innings of 285 not out lasted five minutes short of ten hours. May hit two 6's, twenty-five 4's and 111 singles. The perfect stylist and excelling with the cover drive, he made very few false strokes for such a long stay.

Both Ramadhin and Atkinson bowled tirelessly. West Indies used only two balls throughout the innings, the first being changed after 96 overs so that 162 overs were bowled with the second.

After their gruelling time in the field, West Indies, set to make 296 in two hours twenty minutes, lost Kanhai and Pairaudeau to Trueman for only nine runs. Then with the fielders clustered round the batsmen, Laker and Lock ran riot, seven wickets going for 68 runs, but Goddard, the captain, defended solidly for forty minutes, constantly putting his pads to the ball, and Atkinson was there for the final seven minutes.

No doubt May could have declared when Cowdrey left, but having seen his side out of trouble he was not prepared to give West Indies the slightest chance of success. Attendance 64,968; receipts £29,496.—N.P.

England

P. E. Richardson c Walcott b Ramadhin.	47	— c sub b Ramadhin	34
D. B. Close c Rohan Kanhai b Gilchrist..	15	— c Weekes b Gilchrist	42
D. J. Insole b Ramadhin	20	— b Ramadhin	0
P. B. H. May c Weekes b Ramadhin ...	30	— not out	285
M. C. Cowdrey c Gilchrist b Ramadhin..	4	— c sub b Smith	154
T. E. Bailey b Ramadhin	1		
G. A. R. Lock b Ramadhin	0		
T. G. Evans b Gilchrist	14	— not out	29
J. C. Laker b Ramadhin	7		
F. S. Trueman not out	29		
J. B. Statham b Atkinson	13		
B 3, l-b 3	6	B 23, l-b 16	39

1/32 2/61 3/104 4/115 5/116 6/118   186   1/63 2/65   (4 wkts., dec.) 583
7/121 8/130 9/150   3/113 4/524

West Indies

Rohan Kanhai lbw b Statham	42	—	c Close b Trueman	1
B. H. Pairaudeau b Trueman	1	—	b Trueman	7
C. L. Walcott c Evans b Laker	90	—	c Lock b Laker	1
E. D. Weekes b Trueman	9	—	c Trueman b Lock	33
G. Sobers c Bailey b Statham	53	—	c Cowdrey b Lock	14
O. G. Smith lbw b Laker	161	—	lbw b Laker	5
F. M. Worrell b Statham	81	—	c May b Lock	0
J. D. Goddard c Lock b Laker	24	—	c May b Lock	0
D. Atkinson c Statham b Laker	1	—	not out	0
S. Ramadhin not out	5	—	not out	4
R. Gilchrist run out	0			
B 1, l-b 6	7		B 7	7

1/1 2/83 3/120 4/183 5/197 6/387   474   1/1 2/9 3/25   (7 wkts.)   72
7/466 8/469 9/474   4/27 5/43 6/66 7/68

West Indies Bowling

	O.	M.	R.	W.	O.	M.	R.	W.
Worrell	9	1	27	0				
Gilchrist	27	4	74	2	26	2	67	1
Ramadhin	31	16	49	7	98	35	179	2
Atkinson	12.4	3	30	1	72	29	137	0
Sobers					30	4	77	0
Smith					26	4	72	1
Goddard					6	2	12	0

England Bowling

	O.	M.	R.	W.	O.	M.	R.	W.
Statham	39	4	114	3	2	0	6	0
Trueman	30	4	99	2	5	3	7	2
Bailey	34	11	80	0				
Laker	54	17	119	4	24	20	13	2
Lock	34.4	15	55	0	27	19	31	3
Close					2	1	8	0

Umpires: E. Davies and C. S. Elliott.

GLOUCESTERSHIRE v. WEST INDIES

At Bristol, June 5, 6, 7. West Indies won by 154 runs. There were fine fast-bowling performances by Smith, of Gloucestershire, and Dewdney in the first innings, but the crowd were really roused by the brilliant batting of Atkinson and Emmett, the rival captains, on the last day. Atkinson showed skill and very pleasing style in driving while making a century in two hours, yet Emmett surpassed him. Setting an example of enterprise when his side were left to make 331 at nearly 100 an hour, Emmett drove superbly. He also cut and pulled the fast bowlers audaciously and scored 91, including twelve 4's and a 6, out of 111 in sixty-seven minutes. Emmett's colleagues could not follow his lead and with Sobers and Smith combining variations of flight, pace and spin the rest of the Gloucestershire batting broke down. In the West Indies second innings Weekes played many off-side strokes in his best style. The notable point about the fast bowling of both sides was its accuracy of direction. Gloucestershire's Smith clean-bowled five of his six victims on the first day—a feat which earned him his cap—and Dewdney hit the middle stump each time in taking five wickets next day.

West Indies

A. Ganteaume b Smith	47	— lbw b Lambert	8
N. Asgarali b Cook	25	— b Smith	15
B. H. Pairaudeau b Smith	8	— b Smith	9
E. D. Weekes c Knightley-Smith b Wells	56	— c Graveney b Lambert	73
G. Sobers b Smith	0	— c Meyer b Cook	17
O. G. Smith c Meyer b Smith	0	— lbw b Smith	10
D. Atkinson c Nicholls b Cook	35	— not out	101
F. C. M. Alexander not out	32	— b Lambert	52
W. Hall lbw b Wells	22	— not out	12
A. L. Valentine b Smith	0		
T. Dewdney b Smith	0		
B 7, l-b 9	16	B 2, l-b 9, n-b 1	12

1/58 2/79 3/86 4/96 5/100 6/182   241   1/20 2/33 (7 wkts., dec.) 309
7/182 8/236 9/241   3/46 4/109 5/140 6/142
                                                       7/285

Gloucestershire

G. M. Emmett c Atkinson b Hall	0	— b Sobers	91
D. M. Young b Dewdney	48	— b Atkinson	15
W. Knightley-Smith b Dewdney	25	— b Smith	11
T. W. Graveney c Alexander b Smith	48	— c and b Dewdney	14
R. B. Nicholls c Asgarali b Smith	46	— c and b Sobers	6
D. Hawkins b Sobers	1	— c Smith b Sobers	1
B. J. Meyer b Dewdney	13	— c Asgarali b Sobers	0
G. E. Lambert b Dewdney	6	— b Smith	12
D. R. Smith not out	17	— c Pairaudeau b Smith	12
C. Cook b Dewdney	5	— b Sobers	4
B. D. Wells c Pairaudeau b Hall	6	— not out	0
B 4, n-b 1	5	B 8, l-b 2	10

1/0 2/71 3/78 4/161 5/162 6/174   220   1/71 2/111 3/126 4/138   176
7/192 8/193 9/209   5/144 6/144 7/146 8/171
                                                       9/176

Gloucestershire Bowling

	O.	M.	R.	W.		O.	M.	R.	W.
Lambert	13	3	54	0	....	25	3	92	3
Smith	26	4	72	6	....	29	7	105	3
Wells	30	8	57	2	....	15	4	40	0
Cook	26	8	42	2	....	21	5	60	1

West Indies Bowling

	O.	M.	R.	W.		O.	M.	R.	W.
Hall	19	4	68	2	....	5	0	24	0
Dewdney	20	3	69	5	....	11	2	47	1
Valentine	8	3	13	0					
Smith	21	9	22	2	....	8.3	4	15	3
Sobers	19	10	28	1	....	17	7	39	5
Atkinson	4	1	6	0	....	5	1	29	1
Asgarali	4	2	9	0	....	2	0	12	0

Umpires: J. S. Buller and H. G. Baldwin.

GLAMORGAN v. WEST INDIES

At Cardiff, June 8, 10. West Indies won by five wickets after absorbing cricket. The pitch gave the spin bowlers a chance almost from the start and Ramadhin on the one side and McConnon and Shepherd on the other made full use of the conditions. Only Kanhai, with 46 and 52, scored more than 30 runs in any one innings. Alexander, the wicket-keeper, as well as the Glamorgan batsmen seemed confused by Ramadhin's concealed spin and extras in the first innings equalled the top score. Apart from Kanhai, the West Indies batsmen were equally perplexed on the first day and top-class fielding assured that none received a second chance. Watkins dismissed Kanhai and Sobers with superb catches close to the wicket. Consequently, West Indies were still 51 behind with one wicket left at the close. Glamorgan, losing some of their keenness in the field temporarily, allowed Hall and Dewdney to add another 32 on Monday morning; runs which were of vital importance in such a low-scoring game. Glamorgan faltered for a second time against Ramadhin, who, with a match analysis of eleven for 70, took his total number of wickets to 58 in six games. West Indies needed only 97 to win and Kanhai and Sobers began confidently enough with 39 in as many minutes, but with Sobers out at that total and Asgarali and Weekes falling to more excellent catches close to the wicket the 15,000 spectators who were crammed into Arms Park watched the tense cricket in silence. Victory for the county seemed a distinct possibility when Kanhai's fine innings ended, but Ganteaume, dropped to the middle of the order, and Goddard guided West Indies home, though not without many anxious moments.

Glamorgan

W. G. A. Parkhouse lbw b Atkinson	28	— c Asgarali b Ramadhin	14
W. G. Davies lbw b Ramadhin	7	— b Atkinson	9
B. Hedges c Alexander b Ramadhin	3	— b Ramadhin	4
L. N. Devereux b Atkinson	10	— b Ramadhin	2
A. J. Watkins b Ramadhin	16	— lbw b Sobers	16
J. Pressdee b Ramadhin	5	— not out	14
W. Wooller run out	25	— b Sobers	0
J. E. McConnon c Alexander b Ramadhin	1	— b Ramadhin	1
H. D. Davies b Sobers	0	— c Alexander b Ramadhin	5
D. L. Evans not out	4	— run out	0
D. J. Shepherd b Sobers	11	— b Ramadhin	10
B 23, l-b 5	28	L-b 2	2

1/33 2/43 3/63 4/64 5/81 6/108   138
7/110 8/113 9/126

1/23 2/29 3/31 4/31 5/54   77
6/54 7/55 8/65 9/65

West Indies

Rohan Kanhai c Watkins b McConnon	46	— b McConnon	52
A. Ganteaume lbw b Shepherd	3	— not out	10
N. Asgarali c Evans b McConnon	4	— c Wooller b McConnon	2
E. D. Weekes b McConnon	0	— c Watkins b McConnon	1
G. Sobers c Watkins b McConnon	15	— c and b Devereux	13
D. Atkinson c W. G. Davies b McConnon	0	— c Devereux b Shepherd	3
J. D. Goddard b Shepherd	0	— not out	15
F. C. M. Alexander b Shepherd	3		
S. Ramadhin c W. G. Davies b McConnon	4		
W. Hall c Pressdee b H. D. Davies	20		
T. Dewdney not out	5		
B 11, l-b 8	19	B 4	4

1/18 2/53 3/53 4/70 5/70 6/72 7/72   119
8/81 9/83

1/39 2/47 3/49   (5 wkts.) 100
4/62 5/72

West Indies Bowling

	O.	M.	R.	W.	O.	M.	R.	W.
Dewdney	4	2	8	0	2	1	3	0
Hall	2	0	5	0	2	1	2	0
Atkinson	23	7	48	2	19	12	23	1
Ramadhin	31	19	31	5	25	14	39	6
Sobers	10	4	18	2	7	2	8	2

Glamorgan Bowling

H. D. Davies ..	7.5	1	25	1	....	1	0	4	0
Watkins	2	1	2	0	....	1	0	4	0
Shepherd	22	10	23	3	....	16	5	38	1
McConnon	17	4	50	6	....	15.1	4	37	3
Devereux					....	7	2	13	1

Umpires: D. Davies and J. F. Crapp.

SURREY v. WEST INDIES

At The Oval, June 12, 13, 14. Drawn. Although May and Lock were absent and a strained back prevented Laker from bowling at a critical time on the last afternoon, Surrey took the honours. West Indies began well, but with McIntyre, Laker, Loader and Alec Bedser hitting well the last four Surrey wickets put on 81. Splendid batting by Weekes and Sobers placed the touring team in a favourable position by lunch time on the second day when the total reached 184 for three wickets, but Laker removed the two menacing batsmen. Thereupon, Surrey claimed the new ball and, with Loader dismissing four men for five runs, the last seven wickets collapsed for the addition of 36 to the interval score. Then came a splendid innings by Stewart who, if slow on Thursday evening, hit strongly the next day, particularly to leg, and with one 6 and twenty-two 4's he made his not out 147 in four and three-quarter hours. West Indies were handicapped through the inability of Ramadhin to bowl. They wanted 261 at 74 an hour, but half the side fell for 87 before Smith (two 6's and twelve 4's) gave a breezy display for one hour fifty minutes. He and Pairaudeau added 81, but in the last fifteen minutes both were dismissed along with Goddard so that on Hall and Dewdney rested the final responsibility for saving the side. With only two wickets left, West Indies finished 82 behind.

Surrey

T. H. Clark c Sobers b Hall	12	— b Sobers	36
M. J. Stewart b Dewdney	13	— not out	147
B. Constable run out	43	— c Sobers b Smith	14
K. Barrington c Goddard b Ramadhin..	26	— run out	2
D. G. W. Fletcher c Weekes b Sobers	22	— lbw b Dewdney	21
R. C. E. Pratt c Sobers b Ramadhin	5	— b Dewdney	17
E. A. Bedser c Sobers b Hall	6	— lbw b Dewdney	11
A. J. McIntyre c Weekes b Sobers	24	— not out	14
J. C. Laker c Weekes b Sobers	24		
P. J. Loader c Sobers b Atkinson	16		
A. V. Bedser not out	12		
B 1, l-b 1, n-b 5	7	B 1, l-b 1, n-b 6	8

1/13 2/55 3/91 4/111 5/125 6/129   210   1/42 2/80   (6 wkts., dec.) 270
7/143 8/171 9/188   3/87 4/135 5/198 6/218

West Indies

N. Asgarali b Laker	24	— c Pratt b E. Bedser	31
Rohan Kanhai b Loader	10	— c Barrington b Loader	2
B. H. Pairaudeau b Laker	17	— b E. Bedser	26
E. D. Weekes c Stewart b Laker	64	— c Stewart b Clark	8
G. Sobers c and b Laker	71	— run out	17
O. G. Smith lbw b A. Bedser	17	— c Pratt b E. Bedser	84
D. Atkinson c McIntyre b Loader	8	— b E. Bedser	0
J. D. Goddard b Loader	4	— lbw b Loader	0
W. Hall b Loader	0	— not out	8
T. Dewdney not out	0	— not out	0
S. Ramadhin b Loader	1		
B 2, l-b 2	4	B 1, w 1	2

1/15 2/51 3/58 4/188 5/191 6/205   220   1/4 2/30 3/42   (8 wkts.) 178
7/219 8/219 9/219   4/87 5/87 6/618 7/170 8/170

West Indies Bowling

	O.	M.	R.	W.		O.	M.	R.	W
Dewdney	10	2	30	1	....	13	0	62	3
Hall	15	1	37	2	....	18	4	62	0
Atkinson	23.3	4	72	1	....	26	9	41	0
Ramadhin	20	11	24	2					
Sobers	19	5	40	3	....	28	14	51	1
Smith						11	1	46	1

Surrey Bowling

	O.	M.	R.	W.		O.	M.	R.	W
Loader	25.1	7	57	5	....	11	2	30	2
A. Bedser......	28	4	59	1	....	12	3	17	0
Laker	24	9	48	4	....	9	4	17	0
E. Bedser	15	3	52	0	....	13	5	30	4
Clark						15	2	42	1
Barrington						4	1	20	0

Umpires: P. A. Gibb and N. Oldfield.

SUSSEX v. WEST INDIES

At Hove, June 15, 17, 18. West Indies won by 235 runs, an encouraging result on the eve of the second Test. Marlar, the Sussex captain, surprisingly put them in to bat on a true pitch in blazing sunshine which lasted throughout the match. Two wickets fell for 40 to the pace of Bates, but afterwards the West Indies batsmen did much as they pleased. Walcott and Worrell, both playing for the first time since the Edgbaston Test, regained their form quickly, sharing a stand of 99. Worrell batted four hours, hitting two 6's and nineteen 4's. Smith, the Sussex left-handed opening batsman, chosen for England over the week-end, dominated their first innings, carrying his bat after four and a quarter hours and hitting two 6's and eighteen 4's. Had Valentine, in much better form, not dropped a return from Smith when 24, Sussex would have been in dire trouble. As it was they comfortably saved the follow-on, only to receive severe punishment from the touring batsmen in their second innings. In two hours before lunch on the last day, they added 200 before the declaration. This time Smith fell early, and although Lenham hit hard for a time and Foreman defended well, Valentine was too much for most of the other batsmen.

West Indies

A. Ganteaume lbw b Bates	1	— c Smith b Marlar	75
N. Asgarali c Foreman b Bates	20	— run out	99
C. L. Walcott c Mantell b Bell	67		
F. M. Worrell b Bates..................	135		
J. D. Goddard c Foreman b Bates	37		
G. Sobers run out	16	— not out	52
O. G. Smith c Bates b Marlar	21	— c Bell b Marlar	50
F. C. M. Alexander not out	26		
W. Hall b Marlar.....................	21		
R. Gilchrist not out	0		
B 3, l-b 3, n-b 3	9	B 5, l-b 3	8

1/2 2/40 3/139 4/265   (8 wkts., dec.) 353   1/164 2/191 (3 wkts. dec.) 284
5/266 6/286 7/323 8/353   3/284

A. L. Valentine did not bat.

Sussex

L. J. Lenham c Alexander b Hall	12	— c sub b Valentine	44
D. V. Smith not out	147	— b Gilchrist	9
K. G. Suttle b Valentine	20	— c Goddard b Smith	11
J. M. Parks c Alexander b Valentine	6	— c Hall b Valentine	13
D. J. Foreman c Walcott b Valentine	4	— c Goddard b Valentine	36
R. J. Langridge c Walcott b Smith	9	— c Goddard b Sobers	6
R. G. Marlar c Worrell b Smith	0	— c Goddard b Valentine	0
D. N. Mantell b Valentine	2	— c Smith b Valentine	9
A. E. James run out	28	— b Valentine	12
R. V. Bell run out	3	— b Smith	0
D. L. Bates c Walcott b Smith	8	— not out	0
B 13, l-b 3, n-b 1	17	B 5, n-b 1	6

1/25 2/62 3/70 4/108 5/139 6/139   256   1/22 2/51 3/67 4/83   146
7/154 8/232 9/242   5/107 6/136 7/136 8/141
                                                                 9/141

Sussex Bowling

	O.	M.	R.	W.		O.	M.	R.	W.
Bates	24	4	53	4	....	16	3	39	0
James	35	10	101	0	....	4	1	7	0
Smith	7	1	23	0					
Marlar	22	2	71	2	....	24.4	3	98	2
Bell	20	3	70	1	....	14	4	50	0
Suttle	5	2	11	0	....	16	3	66	0
Parks	3	0	15	0	....	6	1	16	0

West Indies Bowling

	O.	M.	R.	W.		O.	M.	R.	W.
Gilchrist	15	2	47	0	....	12	5	26	1
Hall	12	0	48	1	....	4	0	11	0
Valentine	32	8	86	4	....	27.5	7	64	6
Smith	17.3	5	41	3	....	19	9	26	2
Sobers	2	0	6	0	....	6	3	7	1
Goddard	7	3	11	0	....	2	0	6	0

Umpires: L. H. Gray and A. Skelding.

ENGLAND v. WEST INDIES

Second Test Match

At Lord's, June 20, 21, 22. England won by an innings and 36 runs with over two days to spare. They were vastly superior in the field and possessed a much better balanced side for the occasion. The Lord's pitches throughout the season had shown themselves to be eminently suited to fast and fast-medium bowling, but whereas the England selectors realised this, West Indies did not, or at least chose to ignore the facts. They went into the match with only one bowler of real pace and preferred to recall Valentine who was given only three overs in England's total of 424.

The England selectors made three changes from the side which drew at Edgbaston, bringing in Graveney, Smith and Wardle for Insole, Laker and Lock. Lock declared himself unfit for selection, and Laker, after being one of the original twelve named, withdrew because of back trouble. The selectors sent for Tattersall of Lancashire, but did not require him, deciding to rely on Wardle as the sole spin bowler and to go all out for speed. This also enabled them to include an additional batsman. Smith, the Sussex left-hander, made his Test debut, as did Asgarali for West Indies. Pairaudeau and Atkinson stood down for Asgarali and Valentine.

West Indies won the toss, but broke down so badly on a lively pitch that all the advantage they gained from batting first was lost. Trueman struck an early blow by getting Asgarali leg before to a yorker, but the real trouble for West Indies began when Bailey appeared.

In his 50th Test Match, Bailey had rarely bowled better. Moving the ball either way off the seam and making an occasional ball lift, he completely demoralised the batsmen and West Indies were dismissed in under four hours. Bailey's seven for 44 was the best performance by any bowler against West Indies in a Test in England.

Rohan Kanhai, who batted an hour and a half, was one of the few batsmen who shaped well.

England also began badly, and while still fresh Gilchrist and Worrell gave the batsmen many awkward moments. When Gilchrist dismissed Graveney and May in one over, England were 34 for three, but they recovered through a splendid stand of 95 in eighty-five minutes between Richardson and Cowdrey. They were severe on Ramadhin and Valentine, who were given short spells to rest Gilchrist and Worrell. Gilchrist returned and broke the partnership by bowling Richardson, whose fine aggressive innings, lasting a little over two hours, contained eleven 4's.

England finished the first day seven ahead with six wickets in hand, but they could scarcely have expected to gain the substantial lead they eventually enjoyed. Friday was a most unhappy day for West Indies. Their fielding went to pieces, the bowling was collared and three wickets were lost cheaply before the close. They began well enough, Bailey being bowled without addition to the overnight score of 134, but from that moment everything went wrong.

Close received a "life" when four and Cowdrey was missed at the wicket when 47. Not only did they add 58 for the sixth wicket, but they took the fire out of Gilchrist and Worrell and paved the way for the rest of the onslaught. Cowdrey, never at fault again, took complete control, helped by five dropped catches, made the most of his luck. They put on 174 in five minutes under two hours, the highest seventh wicket partnership in England's Test history. Evans made 82 in that time, hitting eleven 4's.

Cowdrey did not last much longer, batting altogether five hours twenty minutes for 152, his second successive score over 150 in the series. Perfectly timed cover drives and square cuts brought him the majority of his fourteen 4's. The later batsmen made merry and Trueman on-drove Ramadhin for three 6's in one over.

England were all out just on tea time for 424, a lead of 297, nine more than that gained by West Indies in the first Test. West Indies missed no fewer than twelve chances in the innings and could blame only themselves for this unenviable position. In the last hour and fifty minutes on the second day they lost Kanhai, Smith and Walcott for 45 and practically any hope of saving the match had gone. Asgarali, who pulled muscles at the back of both legs, did not open the innings, but went in at the fall of the second wicket with a runner.

A crowd of over 30,000 saw West Indies fight gallantly on Saturday, but their task was hopeless. The ball often rose nastily, particularly at the nursery end where all through the match the faster bowlers were able to exploit a peculiar ridge. Several of the West Indies players received nasty knocks and Weekes, the most unfortunate in this respect, cracked a bone on a finger of his right hand.

Asgarali, still limping, stayed an hour on the third morning, but the first real check to England's bowlers came when Sobers and Weekes put on 100 in ninety-five minutes for the fifth wicket. Both batted extremely well and Weekes showed by far his best form of the tour. He attacked the bowling with a succession of powerful strokes and even his finger injury failed to disturb him. Sobers stayed nearly four hours, but once he left the end was in sight. Worrell never settled down and Weekes fell at 233 after hitting as many as sixteen 4's in his 90 made in two and three-quarter hours. It was a superb innings by a talented player.

The match ended ten minutes after tea and England, by an overwhelming margin, were one up in the series. Bailey, in the match, took eleven wickets, equalling C. S. Marriott and W. Voce for the highest number of wickets obtained in any Test against West Indies. Attendance 98,985, receipts £43,976.—L.S.

West Indies

N. Asgarali lbw b Trueman	0	— c Trueman b Wardle	26
Rohan Kanhai c Cowdrey b Bailey	34	— c Bailey b Statham	0
C. L. Walcott lbw b Bailey	14	— c Trueman b Bailey	21
G. Sobers c May b Statham	17	— c May b Bailey	66
E. D. Weekes c Evans b Bailey	13	— c Evans b Bailey	90
F. M. Worrell c Close b Bailey	12	— c Evans b Trueman	10
O. G. Smith c Graveney b Bailey	25	— lbw b Statham	5
J. D. Goddard c Cowdrey b Bailey	1	— c Evans b Trueman	21
S. Ramadhin b Trueman	0	— c Statham b Bailey	0
R. Gilchrist c and b Bailey	4	— not out	11
A. L. Valentine not out	0	— b Statham	1
B 2, l-b 1, w 4	7	B 4, l-b 6	10

1/7 2/34 3/55 4/79 5/85 6/118 7/120   127   1/0 2/17 3/32 4/80 5/180   261
8/123 9/127   6/203 7/233 8/241 9/256

England

P. E. Richardson b Gilchrist	76	J. H. Wardle c Sobers b Ramadhin	11
D. V. Smith lbw b Worrell	8	F. S. Trueman not out	36
T. W. Graveney lbw b Gilchrist	0	J. B. Statham b Gilchrist	7
P. B. H. May c Kanhai b Gilchrist	0	B 7, l-b 11, w 1	19
M. C. Cowdrey c Walcott b Sobers	152		
T. E. Bailey b Worrell	1		
D. B. Close c Kanhai b Goddard	32	1/25 2/34 3/34 4/129 5/134	424
T. G. Evans b Sobers	82	6/192 7/366 8/379 9/387	

England Bowling

	O.	M.	R.	W.		O.	M.	R.	W.
Statham	18	3	46	1	....	29.1	9	71	3
Trueman	12.3	2	30	2	....	23	5	73	2
Bailey	21	8	44	7	....	22	6	54	4
					Wardle	22	5	53	1

West Indies Bowling

	O.	M.	R.	W.
Worrell	42	7	114	2
Gilchrist	36.3	7	115	4
Ramadhin	22	5	83	1
Valentine	3	0	20	0
Goddard	13	1	45	1
Sobers	7	0	28	2

Umpires: D. Davies and C. S. Elliott.

DERBYSHIRE v. WEST INDIES

At Chesterfield, June 29, July 1, 2. West Indies won by 173 runs. The touring side triumphed comfortably enough in the end, but the first two days brought a succession of thrills for a record total of 22,000 spectators. These began when West Indies, having decided to risk batting first on a typically "green" Chesterfield pitch, ran into trouble against Jackson and Gladwin. After three-quarters of an hour six wickets were down for 41 but a stubborn stand between Alexander and Dewdney enabled West Indies to equal their previous lowest total, made against Essex. The pitch was easier when Derbyshire batted, but after reaching 72 for two by tea they cracked against excellent fast bowling by Gilchrist who gained his best figures of the tour. West Indies were clearly bent on retrieving their batting reputations in the second innings but only Smith fully succeeded. While his colleagues again struggled to find strokes to suit the lively conditions, Smith struck out gloriously for just over three hours. His zest and happy enthusiasm brought him four soaring straight 6's and a standing ovation from the crowd when he walked in. Any hopes Derbyshire possessed of making the 291 required to win vanished when Gilchrist and Dewdney whipped out three batsmen by sheer speed on the second evening. Carr fought valiantly on the last morning but his colleagues were unable to counter the flight and spin of Ramadhin.

West Indies

A. Ganteaume c Dawkes b Jackson	....	4	— b Jackson	51
B. Pairaudeau c Jackson b Gladwin	....	0	— c and b Morgan	9
C. L. Walcott c Carr b Gladwin	....	4	— c and b Morgan	31
Rohan Kanhai run out		24	— b Jackson	24
F. M. Worrell b Morgan	....	17	— lbw b Morgan	9
O. G. Smith b Gladwin		0	— run out	133
D. Atkinson b Gladwin		0	— c Carr b Gladwin	5
F. C. M. Alexander b Jackson	....	26	— b Jackson	14
S. Ramadhin c Hamer b Morgan	....	2	— c Johnson b Morgan	28
T. Dewdney not out	....	22	— lbw b Jackson	1
R. Gilchrist run out		12	— not out	1
L-b 3, n-b 1	....	4	B 8, n-b 1	9

1/0 2/8 3/8 4/39 5/41 6/41 7/57   115   1/30 2/52 3/114 4/180   315
8/63 9/92   5/226 6/244 7/268 8/269
                                                     9/309

Derbyshire

A. Hamer c Walcott b Gilchrist	....	16	— c Walcott b Dewdney	7
C. Lee c Walcott b Atkinson	....	27	— b Gilchrist	0
J. Kelly b Gilchrist	....	23	— b Ramadhin	1
A. C. Revill b Dewdney	....	8	— c Alexander b Dewdney	10
D. B. Carr b Gilchrist	....	21	— b Atkinson	57
G. O. Dawkes b Ramadhin	....	14	— c and b Atkinson	16
H. L. Johnson c Smith b Atkinson	...	1	— c Alexander b Ramadhin	3
D. C. Morgan c Alexander b Gilchrist	...	7	— lbw b Ramadhin	1
E. Smith c Alexander b Dewdney	...	5	— not out	9
C. Gladwin not out		11	— b Gilchrist	2
L. Jackson b Gilchrist	....	0	— b Ramadhin	5
B 4, l-b 1, n-b 2	....	7	B 4, l-b 1, n-b 1	6

1/19 2/54 3/73 4/95 5/98 6/112   140   1/12 2/13 3/24 4/67 5/78   117
7/117 8/131 9/140   6/98 7/100 8/101 9/112

Derbyshire Bowling

	O.	M.	R.	W.	O.	M.	R.	W.
Jackson	11.4	2	33	2	28	9	64	4
Gladwin	17	7	37	4	23	6	80	1
Morgan	11	1	41	2	15	3	47	4
Smith	1	1	0	0	17	2	75	0
Carr					7	1	40	0

West Indies Bowling

	O.	M.	R.	W.	O.	M.	R.	W.
Gilchrist	15.5	1	41	5	8	0	27	2
Worrell	7	3	12	0				
Dewdney	14	0	41	2	6	1	16	2
Atkinson	18	5	30	2	19	6	37	2
Ramadhin	17	12	9	1	18.2	6	31	4

Umpires: H. Elliott and P. Corrall.

ENGLAND v. WEST INDIES
Third Test Match

At Nottingham, July 4, 5, 6, 8, 9. Drawn. This match will be remembered mainly for the feats of Graveney, Worrell and O. G. Smith. The Gloucestershire batsman, after so many disappointing Test displays, made 258, his highest score in first-class cricket, and Worrell and Smith clearly saved West Indies by brilliant and determined centuries. There were two other hundreds—by Peter Richardson and May—and Goddard played a match-saving defensive innings for West Indies on the last day.

For most of the five days bowlers experienced a lean time in a heat-wave. Only nine wickets fell on the first three days while 914 runs were scored. Thunderstorms on Saturday evening and on Sunday drenched the ground, but the pitch was firm when West Indies resumed their first innings promptly to time on Monday. They broke down before Trueman, but following on 247 behind, kept England in the field until after tea on Tuesday. England wanted 121 in the final hour, a task that proved impossible.

Two factors told against England. They dropped Lock from their original twelve which left them with only four front-line bowlers who were reduced to three when Bailey ricked his back. Secondly, having shown the highest standard of ground fielding, England later missed at least five possible chances when West Indies were struggling to avoid defeat.

As usual when batsmen shine at Trent Bridge the pitch came in for a deal of mixed criticism. It was a beauty and remained in perfect order to the end. No doubt, it benefited from the week-end rain which it readily absorbed. With West Indies collapsing, it was rolled twice before lunch on Monday so that not even in the later stages did it become dusty or responsive to spin.

England were fortunate to win the toss in such excellent conditions, but they suffered an early reverse when D. V. Smith nibbled at a short ball in Worrell's third over. Then came Graveney at 11.45 p.m. on Friday and he was not dismissed until 2.20 p.m. on Saturday, during which time he not only hit his first Test century in twenty-two appearances in England but went on to score 258.

Except when he opened his score in lofting Worrell close to backward short leg, Graveney rarely looked in trouble. He drove with tremendous power, making the fullest use of his height. Fourth out at 510, he batted for seven hours fifty-five minutes and altogether hit thirty 4's.

Richardson, who excelled with the cut and pull, made his 126 (ten 4's) in four hours forty minutes, his stand of 266 with Graveney being the highest for England's second wicket against West Indies. The bowling was thoroughly mastered when May joined Graveney and the crowd greatly enjoyed seeing these two artists together.

The end of the first day found England 360 for two wickets; Graveney 188, May 40. The two batsmen continued in the same vein until O. G. Smith, in only his sixth over of the innings, dismissed May leg-before at 487. The England captain scored his faultless 104 (fourteen 4's) in just over three hours.

Whereas Ramadhin and Valentine were innocuous, Smith also disposed of Graveney so that in eleven overs he claimed two wickets for only 14 when over 500 runs were on the board. It was at this stage that Derek Richardson began his first innings as an England player. Staying seventy minutes, he left no doubt as to his promise. Later, when Cowdrey and Evans were punishing the tired bowlers, Ramadhin limped off the field with a strained leg muscle.

West Indies had toiled manfully for ten hours when May declared at the tea interval. They wanted 470 to avoid a follow-on and introduced a new pair of opening batsmen in Worrell and the tall left-handed Sobers. Both rose to the occasion and at the close of the second day West Indies were 59 for no wicket.

Worrell went on to bat all through Saturday, waging a remorseless battle with his colleagues against some splendid bowling and excellent fielding. Laker, in particular, served England admirably. Laker broke the opening stand at 87, after Sobers had defended carefully for two and three-quarter hours, and just before lunch he held a high return from Walcott with the left hand, but another three hours passed before England gained their next success, during which time Kanhai helped Worrell to put on 129.

For the first five hours on Saturday West Indies averaged no more than 30 runs an hour compared with England's steady 60 earlier in the match, but in the last hour Weekes took command with Worrell and they added 66, so that West Indies finished the third day 295 for three wickets; Worrell 145, Weekes 33.

The game underwent a big transformation on Monday. West Indies broke down so badly that they lost twelve wickets in less than six hours. Anxiety over the week-end rain rather than the wiles of Trueman, Statham and Laker—well as these three bowled—caused their downfall. The collapse began when Weekes, trying to hook the third ball of the day, was a shade too soon and it went off the back of a glove on to his wicket. Worrell proceeded to demonstrate that the bowling could be dealt with efficiently, but the loss of Weekes seemed to demoralise the other players and England captured the last seven first innings wickets for the addition of only 77 to Saturday's total. Trueman never made the ball lift or fly in a manner to cause alarm, but he did the main damage in the first hour when in seven overs he took five wickets for 11 runs—a very fine piece of sustained hostile bowling.

Ramadhin, who had Valentine as runner, stayed forty-five minutes while the last wicket put on 55. So Worrell carried his bat through an innings lasting just over nine and a half hours for 191 including twenty-six 4's. He was a tired man, but again opened with Sobers only to fall at the end of another hour to a very fine ball that moved in late. Worrell was on the field continuously from 11.30 a.m. on Thursday until 3.0 p.m. on Monday altogether twenty and a half hours, probably the longest time any cricketer has endured.

When the first five West Indies second innings wickets fell for only 89, England seemed to be galloping to victory, but O. G. Smith, aided in turn by Atkinson and Goddard, applied the brake. Smith played a great innings for his side. Occasionally he indulged in carefree strokes, but for the most part he disciplined himself to the urgency of the occasion. He might well have gone during the last hour on Monday for when only 44 he was dropped on the square-leg boundary off Laker by Pressdee of Glamorgan who was acting substitute for Bailey.

But for that mistake England ought to have won with plenty of time to spare, but West Indies were still in a precarious position at the end of the fourth day when their score stood at 175 for five wickets; Smith 67, Atkinson 36.

With victory almost in sight, England saw their advantage gradually slip away as West Indies fought magnificently for a draw. Above everything else stood out the wonderful innings by O. G. Smith. He surpassed his 161 of the Edgbaston Test and, staying seven hours, was eighth out at 352 having hit three 6's and ten 4's. Just after midday, when Trueman and Statham took the new ball, Atkinson's superb effort of two and a half hours ended in a catch to Evans.

Nearly five and a half hours remained for play, and West Indies had only four wickets left when Goddard, their captain, arrived. He survived an early chance, when only six, off Statham to Evans, and later, when 47, was dropped twice in the same over off Laker by Trueman and Bailey. Unperturbed by these incidents, the left-handed Goddard batted heroically for three hours forty minutes while he and Smith added 154, a record for the West Indies' seventh wicket against England.

Even after Goddard left, England needed another half-hour to finish the innings, for Ramadhin was missed by Graveney at slip. With Bailey taking little part in the attack an abnormal amount of work fell on Trueman, Statham and Laker. All responded nobly.

With only 16 overs bowled in the final hour, England needed to average over seven runs an over and at no time did they look like accomplishing the task. They still wanted 57 when the umpires called time. Attendance 61,167, receipts £30,239.—N.P.

England

P. E. Richardson c Walcott b Atkinson	126	— c Kanhai b Gilchrist	11
D. V. Smith c Kanhai b Worrell	1	— not out	16
T. W. Graveney b Smith	258	— not out	28
P. B. H. May lbw b Smith	104		
M. C. Cowdrey run out	55		
D. W. Richardson b Sobers	33		
T. G. Evans not out	26		
T. E. Bailey not out	3		
B 1, l-b 10, w 1, n-b 1	13	B 7, l-b 2	9

1/14 2/280 3/487   (6 wkts., dec.) 619   1/13   (1 wkt.) 64
4/510 5/573 6/609

J. C. Laker, F. S. Trueman and J. B. Statham did not bat.

West Indies

F. M. Worrell not out		191	— b Statham		16
G. Sobers b Laker		47	— lbw b Trueman		9
C. L. Walcott c and b Laker		17	— c Evans b Laker		7
Rohan Kanhai c Evans b Bailey		42	— c Evans b Trueman		28
E. D. Weekes b Trueman		33	— b Statham		3
O. G. Smith c Evans b Trueman		2	— b Trueman		168
D. Atkinson c Evans b Trueman		4	— c Evans b Statham		46
J. D. Goddard c May b Trueman		0	— c Evans b Statham		61
R. Gilchrist c D. Richardson b Laker		1	— b Statham		0
A. L. Valentine b Trueman		1	— not out		2
S. Ramadhin b Statham		19	— b Trueman		15
B 5, l-b 10		15	B 2, l-b 10		12

1/87 2/120 3/229 4/295 5/297 6/305   **372**   1/22 2/30 3/39 4/56 5/89   **367**
7/305 8/314 9/317   6/194 7/348 8/352 9/365

West Indies Bowling

	O.	M.	R.	W.	O.	M.	R.	W.
Worrell	21	4	79	1	7	1	27	0
Gilchrist	29	3	118	0	7	0	21	1
Atkinson	40	7	99	1	1	0	1	0
Ramadhin	38	5	95	0				
Valentine	23	4	68	0				
Sobers	21	6	60	1				
Goddard	15	5	26	0	1	0	2	0
Smith	25	5	61	2				
Walcott					1	0	4	0

England Bowling

	O.	M.	R.	W.	O.	M.	R.	W.
Statham	28.4	9	78	1	41.2	12	118	5
Trueman	20	8	63	5	35	5	80	4
Laker	62	27	101	3	43	14	98	1
Bailey	28	9	77	1	12	3	22	0
Smith	12	1	38	0	12	5	23	0
Graveney					5	2	14	0

Umpires: F. S. Lee and J. S. Buller.

IRELAND v. WEST INDIES

At Belfast, July 10, 11. Drawn. Irresolute batting caused Ireland to be dismissed for 119. Their top scorers, Eagar and Finlay, both making their first appearances, hit hard but the remainder were easy prey for Valentine and Atkinson, the last seven wickets falling for 38. Steady play by Ganteaume and Asgarali gave West Indies a comfortable start, but Kenny, medium-fast, and Huey, spin, restricted the touring team's lead to 79. Unfortunately less than an hour's play proved possible on the second day when the match was abandoned at 2.30 p.m.

Ireland

R. O'Brien b Hall	11		A. E. Marks c Walcott b Valentine	1
S. F. Bergin c Alexander b Atkinson	13		S. S. J. Huey c Walcott b Valentine	1
M. A. Eagar c Hall b Valentine	41		C. J. M. Kenny b Atkinson	0
L. A. Warke c Sobers b Valentine	9		F. Fee b Atkinson	0
J. S. Pollock st Alexander b Valentine	3		B 2, l-b 3, n-b 6	11
J. A. Duffy c Sobers b Valentine	0		1/18 2/61 3/81 4/86 5/87 6/102	**119**
A. Finlay not out	29		7/108 8/110 9/119	

West Indies

A Ganteaume c Duffy b Huey ...	31
N. Asgarali c Finlay b Huey ...	49
F. C. M. Alexander b Warke	26
B. H. Pairaudeau c Warke b Huey	0
C. L. Walcott b Kenny	29
G. Sobers b Kenny	21
Rohan Kanhai c O'Brien b Huey..	17
D. Atkinson not out............	12
W. Hall c Pollock b Huey	0
T. Dewdney b Kenny	0
A. L. Valentine c and b Kenny ...	0
B 11, l-b 2	13

1/77 2/94 3/94 4/135 5/153   198
6/171 7/193 8/193 9/198

West Indies Bowling

	O.	M.	R.	W.
Dewdney	7	5	6	0
Hall	5	2	9	1
Atkinson.....	22	5	39	3
Valentine	18	9	38	6
Sobers	10	4	16	0

Ireland Bowling

	O.	M.	R.	W.
Warke	11	1	44	1
Kenny	24	4	68	4
Fee	11	2	27	0
Huey	21	6	46	5

Umpires: W. M. Finlay and W. A. McCallan.

IRELAND v. WEST INDIES

At Dublin, July 12. West Indies 140 for seven wickets, declared (B. Pairaudeau 37, N. Asgarali 36, F. Fee four wickets for 61), beat Ireland 61 (G. Sobers five wickets for 43, N. Asgarali three for 14 and O. G. Smith two for 4) in a one-day match by 79 runs.

HAMPSHIRE v. WEST INDIES

At Southampton, July 13, 15, 16. Drawn. The three Hampshire seam bowlers, Shackleton, Heath and Gray, surprised West Indies on the first day when they dismissed them for 110 on a pitch which encouraged swing. With Gray also shaping splendidly with the bat, Hampshire enjoyed a lead of 17 with half their wickets in hand at the close on Saturday. Subsequently West Indies made a fine recovery. With Dewdney performing the hat-trick, Hampshire could add only 32 more runs and then Pairaudeau proceeded to make 163, the highest score of his career. Showing excellent style, he hit two 6's and twenty-nine 4's in a dazzling display which occupied him four hours and ten minutes. With Weekes and Walcott taking part in three-figure stands with Pairaudeau and Worrell completing a charming fifty, West Indies were able to set Hampshire to score 339 in five hours. Unfortunately, only seven more overs proved possible before rain brought a grand match to a premature conclusion.

West Indies

N. Asgarali run out	34	— lbw b Shackleton	5
A. Ganteaume lbw b Heath	0	— b Shackleton	4
B. H. Pairaudeau b Heath	3	— b Shackleton	163
E. D. Weekes b Gray	12	— lbw b Shackleton	62
C. L. Walcott st Harrison b Gray......	4	— b Shackleton	34
G. Sobers not out	37	— c Eagar b Burden	11
O. G. Smith lbw b Shackleton......	9	— lbw b Shackleton	1
F. M. Worrell lbw b Heath	8	— not out	56
F. C. M. Alexander b Shackleton.......	1	— b Shackleton	22
W. Hall b Heath	0	— b Heath	20
T. Dewdney c Eagar b Shackleton	1	— b Heath	0
L-b 1	1	B 4, l-b 4, n-b 1.......	9

1/11 2/23 3/42 4/52 5/54 6/64 7/81   110
8/86 9/91

1/4 2/31 3/163 4/265   387
5/282 6/288 7/288 8/352
9/387

I

Hampshire

R. E. Marshall b Worrell	11	—	not out	18
J. R. Gray c Sobers b Dewdney	83	—	not out	23
H. Horton b Dewdney	8			
E. D. R. Eagar b Sobers	14			
H. M. Barnard lbw b Sobers	0			
A. C. D. Ingleby-Mackenzie c Alexander b Hall	16			
P. J. Sainsbury not out	13			
L. Harrison b Sobers	5			
D. Shackleton c Alexander b Dewdney	0			
M. Heath b Dewdney	0			
M. D. Burden c Alexander b Dewdney	0			
B 3, l-b 2, n-b 4	9		N-b 2	2

1/32 2/55 3/82 4/82 5/113 6/149   **159**   (No wkt.) **43**
7/154 8/159 9/159

Hampshire Bowling

	O.	M.	R.	W.		O.	M.	R.	W.
Shackleton	18.5	10	31	3	....	37	11	103	7
Heath	21	4	58	4	....	30.4	9	114	2
Gray	13	6	20	2	....	9	1	46	0
Sainsbury						13	4	29	0
Burden						20	4	86	1

West Indies Bowling

	O.	M.	R.	W.		O.	M.	R.	W.
Hall	10	2	31	1	....	3	0	9	0
Worrell	16	2	41	1					
Dewdney	19.3	2	38	5	....	4	0	32	0
Sobers	18	9	40	3					

Umpires: A. E. Pothecary and L. H. Gray.

SOMERSET v. WEST INDIES

At Taunton, July 17, 18, 19. Drawn. With rain restricting cricket on the first two days to two and three-quarter hours even a full ration on Friday could not produce a definite result. In the absence of Tremlett who rested because of his poor form with the bat, Stephenson captained Somerset for the first time and he agreed with Goddard to protect the pitch from rain, but it was green and grassy enough to give the fast bowlers help during the little play that took place on Wednesday and Thursday. Lobb and Alley each took five wickets and although Gilchrist replied similarly for the West Indies, Somerset, whose last five wickets put on 76 first thing Friday, gained a first innings lead of 36. Sobers enlivened the closing stages with a grand display of driving and hitting to leg. Batting just under two and a half hours on a docile pitch he made his 104, which included two 6's and fifteen 4's, out of 176. Walcott also enjoyed some useful practice during a stand of 110 with Sobers and scored his first fifty in ten innings.

West Indies

B. H. Pairaudeau c Alley b Lobb	16	—	c Stephenson b Harris	16
Rohan Kanhai c Greetham b Lobb	6	—	lbw b Lobb	0
C. L. Walcott b Lobb	14	—	st Stephenson b McMahon	61
G. Sobers b Alley	13	—	st Stephenson b Palmer	104
E. D. Weekes c McMahon b Lobb	12	—	c and b Harris	18
D. Atkinson c Stephenson b Alley	3	—	c and b Harris	26
F. C. M. Alexander b Alley	2	—	not out	5
J. D. Goddard b Alley	0			
W. Hall b Lobb	8	—	not out	15
R. Gilchrist b Alley	0			
A. L. Valentine not out	1			
L-b 3	3		L-b 8, w 1	9

1/20 2/29 3/50 4/52 5/62 6/68   **78**   1/0 2/33   (6 wkts., dec.) **254**
7/68 8/68 9/76   3/143 4/209 5/227 6/234

Somerset

L. Pickles b Gilchrist	0	J. Harris not out	16
W. E. Alley c Goddard b Gilchrist	11	B. Langford c Goddard b Atkinson	6
G. M. Tripp b Gilchrist	8	J. W. McMahon b Gilchrist	0
C. L. McCool b Hall	0	B. Lobb b Atkinson	13
C. Greetham c Kanhai b Gilchrist	5	L-b 11, n-b 3	14
K. E. Palmer run out	23		
H. W. Stephenson c Valentine b Atkinson	18	1/7 2/18 3/23 4/27 5/36 6/72 7/87 8/96 9/101	114

Somerset Bowling

	O.	M.	R.	W.	O.	M.	R.	W.
Lobb	16.1	3	37	5	10	2	21	1
Alley	16	6	38	5	8	1	31	0
Harris					17	3	59	3
Palmer					12	0	35	1
Langford					9	0	53	0
McMahon					11	1	41	1
McCool					1	0	5	0

West Indies Bowling

	O.	M.	R.	W.
Gilchrist	17	5	33	5
Hall	7	0	33	1
Atkinson	10	3	34	3

Umpires: H. G. Baldwin and R. S. Lay.

MIDDLESEX v. WEST INDIES

At Lord's, July 20, 22, 23. Drawn. Although rain cut the first day's play to two and three-quarter hours the match had an exciting finish, with Middlesex just failing to win. Left to score 182 at 66 an hour, the tourists lost Ganteaume and Asgarali for 10 runs, and despite Worrell's masterful stroke-play they were 108 for five when Edrich claimed the extra half-hour. Compton beat Worrell with a sharply spinning ball; Hall, after hitting Compton for 6, 6, 1, 4, 4, was stumped; Ramadhin was eighth out with ten minutes left, but Alexander and Dewdney managed to hold out. Middlesex, victims of clever medium-pace bowling by Worrell—whose first-innings figures were five for 15 at one stage—were indebted to their fast bowlers and to Edrich and Robertson, their opening pair, for a splendid recovery. These batsmen, with confident, varied strokes, scored 92 in seventy-five minutes in the second innings. Worrell, who made 127 for once out, stood head and shoulders above his colleagues for soundness against the pace bowlers and for skilful technique generally. Bennett, for Middlesex, displayed his all-round ability. Ramadhin, used sparingly, took five for 23 in the match. In the first innings he dismissed Bennett and Warr in a maiden over.

Middlesex

W. J. Edrich c and b Worrell	19	— c Ramadhin b Atkinson	58
J. D. Robertson c Hall b Worrell	26	— c Hall b Ramadhin	45
A. C. Walton b Hall	3	— run out	9
D. O. Baldry c Atkinson b Worrell	4	— b Dewdney	0
D. C. S. Compton c Smith b Worrell	2	— b Atkinson	25
F. J. Titmus c Smith b Worrell	16	— c Kanhai b Atkinson	9
J. T. Murray b Dewdney	14	— b Ramadhin	7
D. Bennett c Walcott b Ramadhin	16	— not out	41
J. J. Warr lbw b Ramadhin	23	— c Alexander b Dewdney	4
R. J. Hurst c Alexander b Dewdney	0	— c Walcott b Dewdney	10
A. E. Moss not out	2	— c Smith b Ramadhin	2
B 4, l-b 13, n-b 2	19	L-b 2, n-b 1	3

1/40 2/49 3/49 4/55 5/70 6/77 7/93 8/137 9/138	144	1/92 2/114 3/114 4/114 5/135 6/152 7/161 8/170 9/192	213

West Indies

A. Ganteaume lbw b Warr	10	— c Edrich b Warr	8
Rohan Kanhai c Warr b Moss	6	— lbw b Bennett	11
N. Asgarali b Moss	0	— b Moss	0
O. C. Smith lbw b Bennett	36	— c Murray b Bennett	0
C. L. Walcott b Warr	17	— c Edrich b Moss	18
F. M. Worrell not out	66	— b Compton	61
D. Atkinson lbw b Bennett	0		
F. C. M. Alexander b Titmus	14	— not out	15
W. Hall b Warr	9	— st Murray b Compton	22
T. Dewdney b Bennett	6	— not out	2
S. Ramadhin b Bennett	1	— b Hurst	3
L-b 11	11	B 1, l-b 2	3

1/7 2/7 3/25 4/53 5/89 6/89   176   1/9 2/10 3/41   (8 wkts.) 143
7/135 8/156 9/168   4/41 5/86 6/108 7/130
     8/133

West Indies Bowling

	O.	M.	R.	W.		O.	M.	R.	W.
Hall	13	3	43	1	....	5	1	26	0
Worrell	22	6	34	5	....	12	5	30	0
Atkinson	12	7	13	0	....	27	6	71	3
Dewdney	16.5	5	28	2	....	24	4	67	3
Ramadhin	6	3	7	2	....	19	6	16	3

Middlesex Bowling

	O.	M.	R.	W.		O.	M.	R.	W.
Moss	13	6	28	2	....	11	2	35	2
Warr	15	4	52	3	....	10	2	41	1
Bennett	9.1	0	39	4	....	7	1	22	2
Hurst	3	1	9	0	....	9	6	5	1
Baldry	4	0	19	0					
Titmus	3	0	18	1	....	6	3	4	0
Compton					....	8	4	33	2

Umpires: W. F. Price and W. Place.

ENGLAND v. WEST INDIES
Fourth Test Match

At Leeds, July 25, 26, 27. England won by an innings and five runs, the match being all over by a quarter to three on Saturday afternoon. This hollow victory gave England the rubber and brought personal distinction to Loader who, in taking nine wickets for 86 runs, performed the hat-trick when the West Indies last four first innings wickets were taken in four balls. Trueman bowled O. G. Smith with the last ball of an over and then Loader removed Goddard, Ramadhin and Gilchrist.

It was only the second hat-trick accomplished by an Englishman in a home Test, the first being by J. T. Hearne against Australia and also at Leeds in 1899. At Manchester, in 1912, T. J. Matthews did the hat-trick twice on the same afternoon for Australia and South Africa in the first match of the Triangular tournament.

Loader, who had not played in the first three Tests, received his chance because Statham was injured and could not be considered for selection. When Bailey dropped out with a split hand, D. W. Richardson was added to the party and he duly became twelfth man. West Indies intended to include Dewdney but an abcess in the mouth put him in hospital and so Pairaudeau completed the eleven which included Alexander for the first time. Atkinson also was unfit.

A heavy overcast sky and stiff cross breeze made the conditions ideal for seam bowling on a well-marled pitch but few people could have anticipated such a poor batting performance by West Indies after Goddard had won the toss.

Forty minutes passed while Worrell and the left-handed Sobers played cautiously against the accurate attack of Trueman and Loader who had eight fielders behind the striker.

May was just preparing for his first bowling change when Sobers turned Loader sharply and Lock, diving to his right, brought off an amazing catch at leg-slip. England appeared to have missed a great chance of dismissing Worrell cheaply when Richardson, by a brilliant pick-up at cover, cut off a sizzling drive which left Worrell stranded in mid-pitch, but in his excitement Richardson sent his return high above Evans's head.

Smith, the Sussex left-arm bowler, put in a very steady spell from the pavilion end and when Loader returned at the opposite end his late swing accounted for both Worrell and Weekes in the same over, the latter also being deceived by a subtle decrease of pace.

With three men out for 42, West Indies were in a bad position, but Rohan Kanhai and Walcott made a stubborn stand, raising the total to 112 for three at tea. Kanhai was treated to a very heavy dose of short-pitched balls by Trueman, but despite a painful blow on the back of the left hand which required strapping the young batsman faced up bravely to the rough treatment.

Laker broke the stand soon after the interval when for the third successive time in the series he deceived Walcott, Cowdrey holding a sharp slip catch. More resistance came from Kanhai and O. G. Smith in an appalling light and it was no surprise when, immediately Smith appealed to them, the umpires stopped the proceedings for nearly half an hour.

Again Laker effected a separation by getting Kanhai, who had defied England for nearly four hours, leg-before. Loader and Trueman took the new ball and in less than three overs the remaining five wickets fell. Trueman hit Pairaudeau's off-stump and bowled Smith round his legs via the pads in one over before Loader completed the rout with his hat-trick.

Worrell struck back for West Indies with a fine ball that swung across the left-handed D. V. Smith and took his off-stump so that England finished the day 11 for one. On Friday, Worrell bowled superbly and achieved his best performance with the ball by finishing with seven wickets for 70 runs. Valentine, Atkinson, Gomez and Ramadhin were the only other West Indies bowlers who had taken as many as seven wickets in a Test innings.

A grey morning and occasional light showers made the conditions unpleasant for both sides. West Indies faced the handicap of bowling with a wet ball, which the umpires dried, but the turf recovered so well that no sawdust was required. Richardson left to the third ball of the morning, caught by the new Test wicket-keeper, and Graveney, after a few challenging strokes, was undisputably bowled by Gilchrist, who sent his middle stump flying. At this stage West Indies stood all square for England's first three wickets—like theirs—had gone for 42, but determined batting by May, Cowdrey and Sheppard turned the scales.

Sobers put in a very good spell of left-arm slow bowling, maintaining the attack from the Kirkstall end from 12.35 p.m. until 3.45 p.m., when the new ball was taken. During this period Sobers's analysis read 28—8—65—1, his solitary prize being May's wicket. May's quest for runs led to his undoing. He was using the cut and drive freely to pierce Sobers's packed off-side field when, essaying a cut, he gave Alexander his second catch of the day. May hit nine 4's.

The May–Cowdrey stand yielded 94 and Cowdrey and Sheppard followed with one of 91. Whereas Cowdrey never became fluent and hit only four 4's, Sheppard introduced a touch of sparkle to the cricket. Occasionally his timing lacked precision but he treated everyone to a fine variety of strokes. Beginning with four boundaries Sheppard swept to his 50 in ninety-five minutes and when seventh out at 264 he had made his 68 (ten 4's) in two hours twenty-five minutes compared with three hours forty minutes taken by Cowdrey over the same score and two hours thirty-five minutes by May for 69.

West Indies were at the cross-roads when Worrell took the second new ball at 3.45 p.m. with England 179 for four wickets. From that point he bowled without relief to the end of the innings on the stroke of 6.30 p.m., his only respite coming from a ten minutes' break for rain and when another shower caused the tea interval to extend to half an hour. During that period Worrell's figures were 22.2—7—42—5. Actually the last five wickets fell for 52 runs, but England gained a valuable lead of 137 runs.

The introduction of Alexander as wicket-keeper brought a noticeable improvement in the West Indies fielding although their returns still fell a long way below the England standard. Rarely, indeed, have England proved so efficient in this vital part of the game and in this match particularly their splendid work went a long way towards keeping their opponents in subjection.

In fact the dramatic breakdown in the second innings came after another wonderful effort by Lock and again at the expense of Sobers. As patient methods failed them in their first innings West Indies seldom wasted a scoring opportunity when they batted a second time. During the innings they despatched the ball to the boundary nineteen times but the final result was the same. Sobers hooked and drove with such skill that he scored 20 from the first four overs. He saw Cowdrey dispose of Worrell with an excellent right-handed slip catch and then he himself was run out by Lock who, fielding between deep point and cover, swooped down on a peerless off-drive and, turning swiftly, landed the ball at the top of the stumps with Sobers helpless in the middle of the pitch.

After that incident, Walcott alone offered real resistance and by lunch time seven wickets were down for 108. Another half-hour sufficed to finish the match and give England their first rubber against West Indies since 1939.

Evans distinguished himself by not conceding a bye and in catching O. G. Smith he raised his number of dismissals in eighty Tests to 200, a figure far in excess of his nearest rival, the Australian, W. A. Oldfield, who claimed 130 victims in fifty-four Tests.

Although only 66,629 people were present during the three days, the receipts amounted to £27,100, including £20,600 taken in advance bookings, some for the fourth and fifth days. Attendance, 54,903; receipts, £28,164.—N. P.

West Indies

F. M. Worrell b Loader	29	—	c Cowdrey b Trueman		7
G. Sobers c Lock b Loader	4	—	run out		29
Rohan Kanhai lbw b Laker	47	—	lbw b Loader		0
E. D. Weekes b Loader	0	—	c Cowdrey b Trueman		14
C. L. Walcott c Cowdrey b Laker	38	—	c Sheppard b Loader		35
O. G. Smith b Trueman	15	—	c Evans b Smith		8
B. H. Pairaudeau b Trueman	6	—	c Trueman b Loader		6
J. D. Goddard b Loader	1	—	c Loader b Lock		4
F. C. M. Alexander not out	0	—	b Laker		11
S. Ramadhin c Trueman b Loader	0	—	run out		6
R. Gilchrist b Loader	0	—	not out		6
L-b 2	2		L-b 5, n-b 1		6

1/16 2/42 3/42 4/112 5/125 6/139   142   1/40 2/40 3/49 4/56 5/71   132
7/142 8/142 9/142   6/92 7/103 8/112 9/122

England

P. E. Richardson c Alexander b Worrell	10	G. A. R. Lock b Gilchrist		20
D. V. Smith b Worrell	0	J. C. Laker c Alexander b Worrell		1
T. W. Graveney b Gilchrist	22	F. S. Trueman not out		2
P. B. H. May c Alexander b Sobers	69	P. J. Loader c Pairaudeau b Worrell		1
M. C. Cowdrey c Weekes b Worrell	68	B 2, l-b 5, w 1		8
Rev. D. S. Sheppard c Walcott b Worrell	68			
T. G. Evans b Worrell	10			

1/1 2/12 3/42 4/136 5/227   279
6/239 7/264 8/272 9/278

England Bowling

	O.	M.	R.	W.		O.	M.	R.	W.
Trueman	17	4	33	2	....	11	0	42	2
Loader	20.3	9	36	6	....	14	2	50	3
Smith	17	6	24	0	....	4	1	12	1
Laker	17	4	24	2	....	6.2	1	16	1
Lock	14	6	23	0	....	1	0	6	1

West Indies Bowling

	O.	M.	R.	W.
Worrell	38.2	9	70	7
Gilchrist	27	3	71	2
Sobers	33	8	79	1
Ramadhin	19	5	34	0
Smith	8	1	17	0

Umpires: D. Davies and J. S. Buller.

SURREY v. WEST INDIES

At The Oval, July 31, August 1, 2. West Indies won by seven wickets—a splendid performance after being 70 behind on first innings. In view of their first innings failure, their chances of success appeared slender when May declared and set them 270 to get in five hours twenty minutes; but the pitch became increasingly easy and they triumphed with twenty-eight minutes to spare. Ganteaume, missed when 19, stayed nearly two and a half hours and Sobers helped him add 70. Then Worrell (thirteen 4's) and Walcott (eight 4's), both driving hard, carried their side to victory in an unbroken stand of 137 in an hour and three-quarters. They began carefully, so that for some time a draw looked in prospect, but after Surrey took the new ball the last 90 runs came inside an hour. A third wicket partnership of 119 by Stewart (eleven 4's) and May (ten 4's) saved Surrey from rout against the spin bowling of Valentine and Ramadhin on the opening day. Apart from Sobers, Walcott and Worrell, the West Indies fared disastrously in reply, particularly against the varied pace of Lock, who also held four brilliant catches. Surrey again began badly, but Constable, let off early in his innings, and Barrington, missed when 61, mastered the bowling, putting on 156 without being parted.

Surrey

T. H. Clark c Asgarali b Gilchrist	4	— b Ramadhin	15
M. J. Stewart b Ramadhin	78	— c Sobers b Ramadhin	16
B. Constable c Sobers b Gilchrist	0	— not out	58
P. B. H. May c Alexander b Valentine	73	— c Sobers b Valentine	6
K. F. Barrington c Smith b Ramadhin	24	— not out	103
E. A. Bedser lbw b Ramadhin	1		
A. J. McIntyre c Alexander b Valentine	2		
G. A. R. Lock b Valentine	0		
J. C. Laker c Alexander b Valentine	9		
P. J. Loader b Valentine	12		
A. V. Bedser not out	5		
B 1, l-b 1	2	B 1	1

1/10 2/10 3/129 4/165 5/171 6/178   210   1/31 2/32   (3 wkts., dec.) 199
7/180 8/190 9/205   3/43

West Indies

N. Asgarali c Lock b Loader	1	— c Barrington b Lock	15
A. Ganteaume c Lock b A. Bedser	3	— b A. Bedser	53
G. Sobers b Laker	39	— c and b A. Bedser	48
E. D. Weekes c Barrington b Loader	1		
C. L. Walcott c Lock b Laker	47	— not out	59
F. M. Worrell c McIntyre b Lock	31	— not out	84
O. G. Smith c Clark b E. Bedser	16		
F. C. M. Alexander c and b Lock	0		
S. Ramadhin c Constable b Lock	0		
R. Gilchrist c McIntyre b Lock	0		
A. L. Valentine not out	0		
B 2	2	B 3, l-b 7, n-b 1	11

1/5 2/7 3/9 4/76 5/111 6/130 7/130   140   1/30 2/100   (3 wkts.) 270
8/130 9/140   3/133

West Indies Bowling

	O.	M.	R.	W.		O.	M.	R.	W.
Worrell	11	2	43	0	....	4	1	11	0
Gilchrist.......	10	2	28	2	....	10	2	21	0
Asgarali	10	2	26	0					
Sobers	4	1	9	0	....	9	1	24	0
Ramadhin	27	11	55	3	....	26	7	56	2
Valentine	16.1	1	47	5	....	27	8	63	1
Smith						5	0	23	0

Surrey Bowling

	O.	M.	R.	W.		O.	M.	R.	W.
Loader	14	4	21	2	....	11	5	29	0
A. Bedser......	8	4	8	1	....	21	2	83	2
Lock	26	12	46	4	....	31	10	70	1
Laker	27	8	39	2	....	22	6	43	0
E. Bedser......	10.1	3	24	1	....	7	1	23	0
Barrington						3	0	11	0

Umpires: A. R. Coleman and D. J. Wood.

GLAMORGAN v. WEST INDIES

At Swansea, August 3, 5, 6. West Indies won by six wickets, repeating their Whitsuntide success at Cardiff. They established a mastery on the first day when 18,000 people saw some effective slow bowling by Ramadhin and Valentine which resulted in Glamorgan being dismissed for 141, West Indies replying with a score of 180 for three wickets. Ganteaume (one 6 and fourteen 4's) and Worrell (one 6 and thirteen 4's) engaged in a sparkling stand of 111 and Smith hit well before the tail collapsed, the last five wickets falling for 39 runs. Parkhouse, like Devereux in the first innings, gave a cautious batting display but Glamorgan were again baffled by Ramadhin's mixed spin and he finished with eleven wickets for 131 runs, being greatly assisted by Alexander's smart wicket-keeping. West Indies needed only 66 and though McConnon bowled his off-spinners effectively the touring team were never in danger.

Glamorgan

W. G. A. Parkhouse c Weekes b Worrell	2	— c Alexander b Smith.......	60
B. Hedges c Ganteaume b Hall	0	— st Alexander b Ramadhin ..	20
L. N. Devereux b Ramadhin	58	— lbw b Ramadhin	4
W. E. Jones b Hall	4	— st Alexander b Ramadhin..	1
D. J. Ward lbw b Ramadhin	1	— b Worrell	19
P. Walker c Weekes b Valentine	34	— c Weekes b Valentine	17
J. E. McConnon b Ramadhin	9	— st Alexander b Ramadhin..	12
W. Wooller not out	24	— lbw b Ramadhin	12
D. L. Evans c Alexander b Valentine ..	4	— b Ramadhin	0
D. J. Shepherd c Alexander b Valentine..	2	— not out	22
F. Clarke b Ramadhin	0	— b Ramadhin	0
L-b 3	3	B 3, l-b 7, w 1	11

1/2 2/6 3/18 4/25 5/94 6/104 7/109   141   1/28 2/34 3/46 4/98   178
8/126 9/132   5/130 6/130 7/146 8/151
                                              9/172

West Indies

B. H. Pairaudeau b Clarke	25	— c Jones b McConnon	22
A. Ganteaume c Evans b Clarke	92	— c Walker b McConnon	16
G. Sobers c Parkhouse b McConnon	0	— c Walker b McConnon	13
E. D. Weekes b Shepherd	4	— lbw b McConnon	7
F. M. Worrell c and b McConnon	69	— not out	0
O. G. Smith c and b Walker	44	— not out	6
J. D. Goddard run out	7		
F. C. M. Alexander c Wooller b Walker	1		
W. Hall b Walker	6		
S. Ramadhin b McConnon	1		
A. L. Valentine not out	0		
B 1, l-b 3, n-b 1	5	L-b 2	2

1/40 2/51 3/70 4/181 5/213 6/242   254   1/36 2/52 3/55   (4 wkts.) 66
7/246 8/253 9/254   4/60

West Indies Bowling

	O.	M.	R.	W.		O.	M.	R.	W.
Worrell	5	2	4	1	....	18	8	24	1
Hall	6	0	24	2	....	2	0	6	0
Ramadhin	32.1	12	64	4	....	46	19	67	7
Valentine	32	16	37	3	....	29	11	53	1
Sobers	9	4	9	0	....	2	1	4	0
Smith					....	9	2	13	1

Glamorgan Bowling

	O.	M.	R.	W.		O.	M.	R.	W.
Clarke	17	3	58	2	....	1	0	3	0
Walker	10	2	28	3	....	1	0	8	0
McConnon	26.1	3	94	3	....	7.4	3	20	4
Shepherd	14	3	44	1	....	8	3	33	0
Devereux	3	0	12	0					
Jones	3	0	13	0					

Umpires: A. E. Pothecary and E. Davies.

WARWICKSHIRE v. WEST INDIES

At Birmingham, August 7, 8, 9. Drawn. Warwickshire, the only county to beat West Indies in 1950, were making a great effort to repeat that performance when rain ruined the final stages by preventing play on the last day. A bold innings of 98 by Horner who hit eleven 4's gave Warwickshire a fine start, but they broke down before Ramadhin, the last seven wickets falling for 19 runs. Rohan Kanhai also showed the value of enterprising methods and with one 6 and eleven 4's as his chief strokes he made 74 out of 112 in eighty-five minutes. On the second morning, Gilchrist, with 2, 4, 4, 4, 6, punished his fellow-countryman, Griffiths, for 20 off five consecutive deliveries, but Hollies bowled his leg breaks with such effect that West Indies' lead was confined to 28. Then Stewart and Smith by skilful batting and quick running between the wickets made a valuable third wicket stand of 82 for the county, but Ramadhin trapped both. The game had reached an intriguing position by Thursday evening when the weather intervened.

Warwickshire

F. C. Gardner b Ramadhin	19	—	b Ramadhin	18
N. F. Horner lbw b Ramadhin	98	—	b Gilchrist	7
W. J. Stewart c Kanhai b Valentine	20	—	lbw b Ramadhin	58
M. J. K. Smith b Valentine	29	—	lbw b Ramadhin	50
T. W. Cartwright lbw b Ramadhin	3	—	b Gilchrist	24
C. W. Leach b Ramadhin	0	—	lbw b Gilchrist	15
S. Singh c Smith b Valentine	4	—	not out	19
R. T. Spooner b Ramadhin	0	—	not out	2
J. D. Bannister b Ramadhin	0			
S. S. Griffiths b Ramadhin	0			
W. E. Hollies not out	4			
B 4, l-b 2, n-b 1	7		B 4, l-b 5, n-b 2	11

1/49 2/92 3/163 4/175 5/175 6/176   **184**   1/19 2/49 3/131   (6 wkts.) **204**
7/176 8/176 9/176   4/140 5/177 6/197

West Indies

A. Ganteaume lbw b Bannister	0	T. Dewdney b Hollies	1
N. Asgarali lbw b Hollies	10	S. Ramadhin c Spooner b Griffiths	3
Rohan Kanhai b Singh	74	R. Gilchrist b Hollies	20
O. G. Smith c and b Hollies	5	A. L. Valentine not out	1
C. L. Walcott b Griffiths	49	B 4, l-b 7	11
E. D. Weekes lbw b Singh	8		
B. H. Pairaudeau c Cartwright b Hollies	30	1/0 2/68 3/78 4/112 5/134 **212**	
		6/167 7/174 8/191 9/211	

West Indies Bowling

	O.	M.	R.	W.	O.	M.	R.	W.
Dewdney	7	0	22	0	12	4	28	0
Gilchrist	17	4	52	0	16	1	38	3
Ramadhin	28	12	43	7	35	10	54	3
Valentine	18.4	6	48	3	31	11	61	0
Smith	4	0	12	0	6	1	12	0

Warwickshire Bowling

	O.	M.	R.	W.
Bannister	9	2	31	1
Griffiths	16	1	73	2
Hollies	26	5	55	5
Singh	9	2	42	2

Umpires: W. E. Phillipson and N. Oldfield.

LANCASHIRE v. WEST INDIES

At Manchester, August 10, 12, 13. West Indies won by nine wickets. They gave a most pleasing display, especially on the first day when under conditions far different from those they enjoy in the Caribbean they hit four 6's and forty-four 4's while making 317 for five wickets. Asgarali and Sobers set the pace with a brisk stand of 167, the best for the second wicket during the tour; later Worrell and Smith put on 126. Lancashire cut a sorry figure on Monday against an efficient attack but following on 238 behind they gave a different display. Ikin and Pullar led the recovery with some confident batting and Grieves and Bond following their example the county resumed on Friday only 31 behind with five wickets in hand. As Bond and Whiteley left quickly on resuming, an early finish seemed certain, but Bowman, the Oxford Blue, making his first county appearance as deputy for Statham, hit one 6 and six 4's in a determined effort that also inspired Heys, the wicket-keeper. He helped himself to one 6 and seven 4's so that West Indies did not complete their task until three o'clock.

West Indies

N. Asgarali c Bond b Greenhough	84	— not out	46
B. H. Pairaudeau c Bond b Smith	4	— c Grieves b Bowman	6
G. Sobers b Whiteley	86		
Rohan Kanhai c Heys b Whiteley	10		
F. M. Worrell c Smith b Whiteley	59		
O. G. Smith not out	67		
C. L. Walcott not out	4	— not out	38
B 1, l-b 1, n-b 1	3	N-b 1	1

1/7 2/174 3/184 4/184   (5 wkts., dec.) 317   1/12   (1 wkt.) 91
5/310

F. C. M. Alexander, J. D. Goddard, W. Hall and A. L. Valentine did not bat.

Lancashire

C. S. Smith b Hall	0	— b Smith	13
J. T. Ikin b Worrell	2	— c Sobers b Goddard	46
G. Pullar b Hall	13	— b Sobers	41
C. Washbrook c Asgarali b Worrell	10	— c Alexander b Valentine	3
K. Grieves c Walcott b Valentine	20	— c Alexander b Worrell	48
J. D. Bond c Goddard b Smith	12	— c Alexander b Hall	33
P. Whiteley not out	12	— run out	5
R. Bowman c Pairaudeau b Smith	7	— c Pairaudeau b Smith	55
T. Greenhough st Alexander b Valentine	0	— b Hall	2
W. Heys c Alexander b Valentine	0	— lbw b Valentine	46
R. Tattersall c Kanhai b Smith	1	— not out	5
L-b 1, n b 1	2	B 18, l-b 4, n-b 8	30

1/2 2/2 3/20 4/26 5/59 6/59 7/66   79   1/52 2/88 3/104 4/130   327
8/70 9/70   5/196 6/214 7/231 8/253
                                              9/298

Lancashire Bowling

	O.	M.	R.	W.		O.	M.	R.	W.
Smith	15	4	45	1	....	3	1	12	0
Bowman	17	2	65	0	....	4	0	15	1
Tattersall	25	3	70	0	....	3	1	4	0
Whiteley	25	8	70	3	....	5	0	25	0
Greenhough	20	5	60	1	....	9	3	17	0
Ikin	1	0	4	0	....	2.3	0	12	0
Washbrook						2	0	5	0

West Indies Bowling

	O.	M.	R.	W.		O.	M.	R.	W.
Worrell	10	1	26	2	....	18	2	42	1
Hall	9	1	27	2	....	21	2	51	2
Smith	8.3	5	10	3	....	27	12	69	2
Valentine	9	5	14	3	....	45	14	108	2
Asgarali						7	5	4	0
Goddard						4	2	3	1
Sobers						11	3	20	1

Umpires: J. F. Crapp and H. G. Baldwin.

YORKSHIRE v. WEST INDIES

At Bradford, August 14, 15, 16. Abandoned without a ball bowled.

Yorkshire (from): W. B. Stott, W. Watson, J. V. Wilson, D. B. Close, D. E. V. Padgett, R. Illingworth, J. H. Wardle, F. S. Trueman, J. G. Binks, R. Appleyard, D. Pickles and J. B. Bolus.

West Indies: A. Ganteaume, N. Asgarali, B. H. Pairaudeau, C. L. Walcott,

F. M. Worrell, G. Sobers, S. Ramadhin, A. L. Valentine, F. C. M. Alexander, Rohan Kanhai and T. Dewdney.

Umpires: P. A. Gibb and W. E. Phillipson.

LEICESTERSHIRE v. WEST INDIES

At Leicester August 17, 19, 20. West Indies won by an innings and 212 runs. Leicestershire offered little resistance. Their two innings occupied only five hours and, excluding a good opening spell by Spencer and Boshier, the attack presented few problems. Palmer won the toss for the twelfth successive time but on a damp pitch of negligible help to the West Indies bowlers the response was deplorable. Gardner apart, the batsmen showed a strange lack of determination. Despite the early loss of Ganteaume and Sobers, West Indies always looked capable of a big total. Consequently, Palmer resorted to numerous "donkey-drops." These brought the wickets of Asgarali, Kanhai and Worrell. Kanhai needed eight for a century when he gave an easy catch trying to hook this strange type of delivery. Worrell, who scored 241 not out on his visit to Grace Road in 1950, hit four 6's and ten 4's in an exhilarating 104 made out of 158 in one and three-quarter hours before, attempting a similar stroke, he stepped back on to his stumps. Facing a deficit of 286, Leicestershire collapsed a second time on a pitch still of easy pace. They succumbed to the left-arm spinners of Valentine, who took six of the first eight wickets for eight runs. Valentine broke his nose when struck by a ball in the nets prior to the start of the last day and did not resume.

Leicestershire

G. Lester c Worrell b Atkinson	3	— c Worrell b Atkinson		13
M. R. Hallam c Alexander b Dewdney	1	— b Dewdney		3
J. van Geloven b Dewdney	2	— c Kanhai b Valentine		20
C. H. Palmer c Sobers b Dewdney	10	— c Worrell b Valentine		3
L. R. Gardner run out	21	— c and b Valentine		0
R. A. Diment c Kanhai b Ramadhin	22	— c Worrell b Valentine		1
J. Firth c Ganteaume b Valentine	2	— lbw b Valentine		8
R. C. Smith b Ramadhin	0	— lbw b Sobers		4
J. S. Savage not out	5	— c Alexander b Valentine		2
C. T. Spencer c Ganteaume b Ramadhin		— not out		13
B. S. Boshier b Valentine	1	— run out		0
L-b 1	1	B 4, l-b 3		7
	—			—
	75			74

1/2 2/4 3/16 4/16 5/56 6/61 7/64 8/64 9/74

1/8 2/34 3/34 4/38 5/40 6/40 7/42 8/59 9/62

West Indies

A. Ganteaume lbw b Spencer	5	F. M. Worrell hit wkt b Palmer	104
N. Asgarali c Diment b Palmer	38	D. Atkinson not out	0
G. Sobers c Lester b Boshier	0	B 11, l-b 8	19
Rohan Kanhai c Spencer b Palmer	92		
F. C. M. Alexander c Smith b Palmer	83		—
E. D. Weekes b Spencer	20	(7 wkts., dec.)	361

S. Ramadhin, T. Dewdney and A. L. Valentine did not bat.

1/10 2/13 3/77 4/158 5/202 6/360 7/361

West Indies Bowling

	O.	M.	R.	W.	O.	M.	R.	W.
Worrell	5	1	6	0	7	2	9	0
Dewdney	12	4	14	3	11.5	1	33	1
Atkinson	11	5	10	1	11	4	12	1
Valentine	14.4	4	32	2	13	8	8	6
Ramadhin	11	6	12	3	2	0	4	0
Sobers					4	3	1	1

Leicestershire Bowling

	O.	M.	R.	W.
Spencer	23	6	53	2
Boshier	22	2	95	1
Smith	35	11	104	0
Savage	7	1	29	0
Palmer	25.1	12	40	4
van Geloven ...	8	0	21	0

Umpires: R. S. Lay and D. J. Wood.

ENGLAND v. WEST INDIES
Fifth Test Match

At The Oval, August 22, 23, 24. England won by an innings and 237 runs and confirmed their overwhelming superiority over West Indies. The match ended at half-past two on Saturday, the third time in the series that a game had ended inside three days. Dismissed for the two lowest totals they had ever recorded in a Test against England, West Indies gave a most disappointing all-round display.

The Oval presented a strange sight before the match began. The outfield was lush green and in perfect order, but the pitch itself, unusually red-brown, and resembled in colour a matting strip. Apparently the heavy rain of the previous week hindered the preparation and much of the dressing remained on top, where it caked. As a result, whenever the ball pitched on the first day a cloud of dust arose as the surface cracked and throughout the match slow bowlers were able to turn the ball appreciably. The dust was not so noticeable on the second and third days, but the ball continued to turn, although not until the West Indies' second innings did it spin quickly enough to be really awkward. Like other touring teams before under similar circumstances, West Indies found Lock and Laker far too good for them.

England made one change from the side successful at Leeds, Bailey returning for Smith. Influenza prevented Gilchrist playing for West Indies and injuries deprived them of two of their best spin bowlers, Atkinson and Valentine. Dewdney played his first Test against England, he and Asgarali replacing Gilchrist and Pairaudeau. At the end of the first day Goddard, the captain, developed influenza and could not bat in either innings.

Richardson and Sheppard formed a new opening pair when May won the toss and for the first time in the series a right-hander, Sheppard, began the innings. Richardson's previous partners were the left-handers, Close and Smith.

With the game half an hour old Goddard realised the pitch was far more suitable to spin than speed and he brought on Ramadhin and Sobers. Although turning the ball slowly, they failed to unsettle the batsmen and Richardson and Sheppard shared the best opening stand of the series. They stayed two and a half hours for 92 before Sheppard returned a catch to Goddard, the best of the bowlers.

A second wicket did not fall until just before half-past five, Richardson and Graveney adding 146 in two and a half hours of splendid stroke-play. Richardson, sound in defence and adept at stealing sharp singles, batted five hours for 107. A breakdown followed Richardson's departure, May, Cowdrey and Bailey being out for the addition of 18, but nothing could disturb Graveney, who drove superbly and finished the day with 113. Next morning Evans hit powerfully and scored 40 of the 66 added for the sixth wicket in fifty-five minutes. Lock and Trueman gave more good support to Graveney who was eventually ninth out for 164 after an innings of almost five and a half hours. He hit seventeen 4's and his only mistake came when at 153 he offered a hard chance to extra cover.

England were all out at lunch time for 412, their fourth total over 400 in the series. Rain held up play for thirty-five minutes after West Indies had scored five without loss. It did not affect the pitch but almost immediately after the game was resumed Worrell gave a catch to short leg.

England had to fight hard for the next success. May soon brought on Laker and Lock and although it was obvious that West Indies faced a hard struggle, Asgarali and Sobers defended resolutely and were content to wait for the occasional loose ball. It seemed that West Indies intended to fight all the way, but after a second interruption, because of bad light, there came an astonishing collapse.

It began when Asgarali gave a catch to slip. Then in the next thirty-three minutes seven more wickets fell for 21 runs and with Goddard absent West Indies were all out just before the close for 89. There seemed no definite policy by the West Indies batsmen who could not decide whether to defend or attack. Walcott, Smith and then Sobers, who had batted so well, were out to reckless strokes and the others were thoroughly beaten. After the break for light Lock took five wickets for ten runs in 31 balls and Laker claimed three for 15. Lock finished the innings by taking four wickets in seven balls.

West Indies followed on 323 behind on the third morning and fared no better. They changed their batting order, Kanhai going in first with Asgarali. He was soon out to Trueman. Then Laker and Lock carried on the devastation of the first innings.

Once more Sobers made a defiant effort but he and Walcott were the only men to reach double figures and in two hours twenty minutes the innings was completed. Sobers remained an hour and forty minutes and was top scorer in each innings. Weekes, completely out of form, failed to score in the match.

Lock accomplished his best Test performance in taking six wickets for 20 in the second innings and eleven for 48 in the match. Only once previously had West Indies been dismissed for under 100 by England, at Lord's in 1933 when they made 97. Attendance, 63,128; receipts, £30,833.—L. S.

England

P. E. Richardson b Smith	107	
Rev. D. S. Sheppard c and b Goddard	40	
T. W. Graveney b Ramadhin	164	
P. B. H. May c Worrell b Smith	1	
M. C. Cowdrey b Ramadhin	2	
T. E. Bailey run out	0	
T. G. Evans c Weekes b Dewdney	40	
G. A. R. Lock c Alexander b Sobers	17	
F. S. Trueman b Ramadhin	22	
J. C. Laker not out	10	
P. J. Loader lbw b Ramadhin	0	
B 1, l-b 8	9	

1/92 2/238 3/242 4/255 5/256 412
6/322 7/366 8/399 9/412

West Indies

F. M. Worrell c Lock b Loader	4	—	c Cowdrey b Lock	0
N. Asgarali c Cowdrey b Lock	29	—	b Lock	7
G. Sobers b Lock	39	—	b Lock	42
C. L. Walcott b Laker	5	—	not out	19
E. D. Weekes c Trueman b Laker	0	—	b Lock	0
O. G. Smith c May b Laker	7	—	c Sheppard b Lock	0
Rohan Kanhai not out	4	—	c Evans b Trueman	8
F. C. M. Alexander b Lock	0	—	b Laker	0
T. Dewdney b Lock	0	—	st Evans b Lock	1
S. Ramadhin c Trueman b Lock	0	—	b Laker	2
J. D. Goddard absent ill	0	—	absent ill	0
N-b 1	1		B 4, l-b 2, n-b 1	7

1/7 2/68 3/73 4/73 5/85 6/89 89
7/89 8/89 9/89

1/10 2/39 3/43 4/69 5/69 86
6/69 7/70 8/75 9/86

West Indies Bowling

	O.	M.	R.	W.	O.	M.	R.	W.
Worrell	11	3	26	0				
Dewdney	15	2	43	1				
Ramadhin	53.3	12	107	4				
Sobers	44	6	111	1				
Goddard	23	10	43	1				
Smith	30	4	73	2				

England Bowling

	O.	M.	R.	W.	O.	M.	R.	W.
Trueman	5	1	9	0	5	2	19	1
Loader	7	4	12	1	3	2	2	0
Laker	23	12	39	3	17	4	38	2
Lock	21.4	12	28	5	16	7	20	6

Umpires: E. Davies and F. S. Lee.

KENT v. WEST INDIES

At Canterbury, August 28, 29, 30. West Indies won by seven wickets with twelve minutes to spare. Kent gave such a consistent display of batting on the first day that they punished the West Indies bowling more severely than any other county excepting Nottinghamshire. When the touring team lost four men for 70, Kent hopes rose, but Walcott, the captain, swung the game the other way with a wonderful display of driving. Hitting one 6 and twenty-two 4's in his 131, he dominated a fifth wicket stand of 206 with Asgarali who also played soundly for 120 not out. Finally, Kent set them to make 165 in one and three-quarter hours. Walcott and Smith tackled this task so well that they knocked off the last 100 runs in only thirty-eight minutes, the stand being notable for the sprinting between the wickets of Smith who at times nearly overlapped his partner.

Kent

A. H. Phebey lbw b Gilchrist	42	— c Kanhai b Hall	7
R. C. Wilson run out	30	— st Kanhai b Ramadhin	41
J. Pettiford b Ramadhin	45	— c Walcott b Ramadhin	18
M. C. Cowdrey c Walcott b Smith	54	— not out	27
J. F. Pretlove st Kanhai b Ramadhin	45	— not out	7
T. G. Evans c Asgarali b Ramadhin	71	— b Hall	26
A. L. Dixon not out	27	— c Walcott b Ramadhin	2
D. J. Halfyard c Weekes b Gilchrist	14	— c Kanhai b Ramadhin	0
F. Ridgway b Gilchrist	4	— lbw b Ramadhin	36
A. Brown lbw b Ramadhin	0		
J. C. T. Page b Ramadhin	0		
B 10, l-b 10, n-b 3	23	L-b 1, n-b 3	4

1/75 2/87 3/179 4/195 5/308 6/309   355   1/29 2/52   (7 wkts., dec.) 168
7/342 8/350 9/351   3/63 4/74 5/74 6/120 7/139

West Indies

G. Sobers b Ridgway	13	— c Phebey b Halfyard	36
B. H. Pairaudeau c Evans b Brown	23	— st Evans b Page	17
Rohan Kanhai c Wilson b Halfyard	20	— lbw b Ridgway	12
E. D. Weekes c Ridgway b Page	8		
C. L. Walcott c Phebey b Brown	131	— not out	48
N. Asgarali not out	120		
A. Ganteaume not out	35		
O. G. Smith (did not bat)		— not out	50
B 1, l-b 3, w 2, n-b 3	9	B 1, n-b 1	2

1/35 2/52 3/66   (5 wkts., dec.) 359   1/16 2/61 3/65   (3 wkts.) 165
4/70 5/276

W. Hall, S. Ramadhin and R. Gilchrist did not bat.

West Indies Bowling

	O.	M.	R.	W.	O.	M.	R.	W.
Gilchrist	20	4	52	3				
Hall	16	2	91	0	12	0	45	2
Sobers	22	7	61	0	14	1	60	0
Ramadhin	37.5	11	83	5	16	3	51	5
Smith	14	3	34	1				
Walcott	4	1	11	0				
Asgarali					9	4	8	0

Kent Bowling

	O.	M.	R.	W.		O.	M.	R.	W.
Ridgway	18	4	54	1	....	10	1	51	1
Halfyard	38	9	89	1	....	9	0	64	1
Brown	18	5	61	2	....	3	0	12	0
Page	23	9	59	1	....	3	0	36	1
Pettiford	20	5	61	0					
Dixon	2	0	14	0					
Cowdrey	5	2	12	0					

Umpires: W. F. Price and P. A. Gibb.

L. E. G. AMES'S XI v. WEST INDIES

At Hastings, August 31, September 2, 3. West Indies won by four wickets.
Worrell sent Ames's team in to bat on a green pitch and bowled so effectively
that four men were out for 67. Then Cowdrey led a recovery. Always at ease,
he hit hard all round in a stay of three hours ten minutes, scoring sixteen 4's.
Dewes, Dooland and Bennett helped him in valuable stands. Despite a brilliant
display by Smith, who made 79, including six 6's and eight 4's, in seventy-seven
minutes and a more restrained innings by Kanhai, the West Indies finished 31
behind on first innings. Good work by Robertson and Barrick and brisk hitting
by the tail-end batsmen left the West Indies to get 270 in about four hours. Only
16 runs came in the first thirty-five minutes, but from that point the total rose
rapidly and the touring side won with three-quarters of an hour in hand. Kanhai,
hitting one 6 and seventeen 4's, and Ganteaume, who helped him add 136 for the
second wicket, bore a big part in the success. In this innings Murray, of Middlesex,
completed the wicket-keeper's "double" of 1,000 runs and 100 wickets in a season
previously achieved only by Ames.

L. E. G. Ames's XI

J. D. Robertson b Worrell	9	— c Pairaudeau b Asgarali	43
J. T. Murray b Worrell	12	— b Gilchrist	12
D. W. Barrick b Worrell	12	— c Alexander b Sobers	59
M. C. Cowdrey run out	143	— c Ganteaume b Ramadhin	4
D. C. S. Compton b Gilchrist	6	— c Ganteaume b Sobers	24
J. G. Dewes b Worrell	24	— c Sobers b Worrell	1
B. Dooland b Gilchrist	50	— b Ramadhin	5
D. Bennett c Pairaudeau b Dewdney	43	— b Sobers	3
G. E. Tribe b Dewdney	10	— c Sobers b Ramadhin	26
J. S. Manning not out	7	— c Alexander b Ramadhin	25
A. E. Moss (did not bat)		— not out	26
B 1, l-b 5	6	B 9, l-b 1	10

1/22 2/29 3/54 4/67   (9 wkts., dec.) 322   1/3 2/30 3/105 4/121   238
5/130 6/218 7/277 8/293 9/322   5/126 6/167 7/177 8/182
                                                     9/187

West Indies

N. Asgarali st Murray b Tribe	25	— c Manning b Moss	17
A. Ganteaume c Murray b Bennett	40	— c Murray b Bennett	60
G. Sobers c Murray b Moss	31	— st Murray b Tribe	21
O. G. Smith c Dewes b Compton	79	— b Bennett	11
Rohan Kanhai not out	71	— st Murray b Tribe	91
F. M. Worrell b Manning	1	— not out	27
B. H. Pairaudeau c Dooland b Manning	12	— b Tribe	26
F. C. M. Alexander st Murray b Tribe	2	— not out	13
R. Gilchrist b Dooland	5		
T. Dewdney b Dooland	2		
S. Ramadhin st Murray b Dooland	11		
B 2, l-b 7, w 1, n-b 2	12	B 4	4

1/55 2/96 3/107 4/214 5/216 6/244   291   1/25 2/161   (6 wkts.) 270
7/261 8/267 9/269   3/193 4/195 5/206 6/244

West Indies Bowling

	O.	M.	R.	W.	O.	M.	R.	W.
Worrell	26	5	73	4	 9	1	19	1
Dewdney	20.5	0	98	2	 9	1	32	0
Gilchrist	16	0	76	2	 5	0	21	1
Ramadhin	5	1	25	0	.... 9.5	2	47	4
Smith	5	0	39	0				
Asgarali	4	2	5	0	 13	4	46	1
Sobers					 10	0	63	3

L. E. G. Ames's XI Bowling

	O.	M.	R.	W.	O.	M.	R.	W.
Moss	15	3	42	1	 11	2	25	1
Bennett	16	2	50	1	 11	3	23	2
Dooland	7.5	3	21	3	 14	1	79	0
Compton	7	0	40	1	 2	0	11	0
Tribe	20	3	90	2	 21	3	80	3
Manning	12	3	33	2	 7	1	37	0
Cowdrey					 2	0	9	0

Umpires: F. S. Lee and A. E. Pothecary.

LANCASHIRE v. WEST INDIES

At Blackpool, September 4, 5, 6. Drawn. With the start delayed until four o'clock on the opening day and the weather generally proving unpleasant there was never much chance of a definite result and the attendance figures were small. Pairaudeau survived an anxious time when facing Statham and the new ball, but Lancashire, too, struggled for runs, having to thank Statham for gaining a narrow lead of two runs. Washbrook, the Lancashire captain, needing 85 to complete his 1,000 runs for the season, retired with a wrenched calf muscle when 35. A charming stand of 110 by Worrell and Weekes provided the best entertainment, Worrell hitting one 6 and thirteen 4's before he declared when needing only five for a century. Lancashire wanted 180 in ninety minutes and though Wharton shaped confidently the task proved beyond their power.

West Indies

A. Ganteaume b Tattersall	24	— lbw b Statham 2
B. H. Pairaudeau b Statham	59	— hit wkt b Smith 0
Rohan Kanhai b Smith	0	— c Barber b Statham 19
F. M. Worrell lbw b Smith	8	— not out 95
E. D. Weekes c Tattersall b Bowman	30	— c Wharton b Ikin 50
O. G. Smith c Statham b Bowman	4	— c and b Ikin 2
F. C. M. Alexander lbw b Tattersall	5	— not out 1
D. Atkinson b Tattersall	24	
W. Hall b Statham	14	
T. Dewdney b Tattersall	4	
S. Ramadhin not out	1	
L-b 1	1	B 5, l-b 2, n-b 5 12

1/71 2/72 3/84 4/97 5/115 6/120   174   1/2 2/8 (5 wkts., dec.) 181
7/142 8/169 9/171   3/27 4/137 5/149

Lancashire

R. W. Barber c Alexander b Ramadhin..	9	—	c Kanhai b Atkinson	......	25
A. Wharton c Weekes b Atkinson	 17	—	not out	......	60
G. Pullar b Worrell	37	—	b Atkinson	......	5
C. Washbrook retired hurt	 35				
J. T. Ikin c Alexander b Smith	 10	—	not out	......	8
J. D. Bond lbw b Smith	4				
C. S. Smith b Atkinson	2				
R. Bowman c Ganteaume b Atkinson	... 5				
W. Heys run out	9				
J. B. Statham not out	27				
R. Tattersall c Ramadhin b Smith	 8				
B 8, l-b 5	13		B 9, l-b 1	......	10

1/26 2/26 3/88 4/103 5/115 6/122   176   1/72 2/78   (2 wkts.) 108
7/125 8/161 9/176

Lancashire Bowling

	O.	M.	R.	W.		O.	M.	R.	W.
Statham	19	5	43	2	....	11	1	19	2
Smith	12	4	28	2	....	13	3	54	1
Bowman	11	4	43	2	....	9	3	19	0
Tattersall	18.2	8	58	4	....	18	4	41	0
Ikin	1	0	1	0	....	7	1	25	2
Wharton						3	1	11	0

West Indies Bowling

	O.	M.	R.	W.		O.	M.	R.	W.
Worrell	9	0	23	1					
Dewdney	4	0	16	0	....	7	0	25	0
Ramadhin	21	11	22	1					
Atkinson	20	4	56	3	....	5	1	14	2
Smith	23	10	46	3					
Hall						8	1	38	0
Ganteaume						3	0	20	0
Weekes						1	0	1	0

Umpires: T. W. Spencer and P. Corrall.

T. N. PEARCE'S XI v. WEST INDIES

At Scarborough, September 7, 9, 10. Drawn. Despite three declarations so much time was lost through rain that a definite result was not achieved. So West Indies finished their first-class engagements undefeated except in three Tests. As usual at Scarborough, there was plenty of attractive batting. May hit three 6's and fifteen 4's in a fine exhibition. One of his 6's from Smith sailed out of the ground to the left of the pavilion. For West Indies, Weekes made his only century of the tour. He claimed only one 6 and nine 4's, but batted so well that he scored his 105 out of 174 in two and a quarter hours. Although 32 behind, Walcott declared on the last morning when only one hour's cricket was possible before lunch, Pearce's side scoring 70. In the next forty-five minutes they added 116, thanks to some boisterous hitting by Graveney, Tribe and Evans. This enabled May to leave West Indies to get 219 in just under two and a half hours. They fell into trouble and when eight wickets were down with ten minutes left were grateful to Kanhai and Gilchrist for playing out time. Bailey completed the double when he disposed of Dewdney during the exciting last half-hour.

T. N. Pearce's XI

P. E. Richardson c Valentine b Asgarali	32	— c and b Gilchrist	21
D. B. Close lbw b Sobers	50	— b Valentine	21
T. W. Graveney run out	16	— not out	46
P. B. H. May st Alexander b Asgarali	119	— c Ganteaume b Weekes	8
D. W. Richardson c Ganteaume b Valentine	37	— c Ganteaume b Valentine	3
T. E. Bailey b Gilchrist	31	— c Walcott b Sobers	7
G. E. Tribe c Weekes b Asgarali	2	— b Valentine	22
T. G. Evans c Kanhai b Asgarali	1	— c Dewdney b Sobers	46
F. H. Tyson not out	30		
J. H. Wardle st Alexander b Sobers	6		
F. S. Trueman not out	21		
B 4, l-b 6	10	L-b 11, n-b 1	12

1/67 2/103 3/103 4/223 (9 wkts., dec.) 355
5/272 6/278 7/282 8/326 9/333

1/45 2/57 (7 wkts., dec.) 186
3/72 4/75 5/144 6/159 7/186

West Indies

A. Ganteaume c Bailey b Tribe	75	— lbw b Tyson	0
N. Asgarali b Tyson	1	— lbw b Tyson	8
G. Sobers b Tribe	39	— b Tribe	49
E. D. Weekes c Wardle b Trueman	105	— c May b Bailey	12
O. G. Smith c D. Richardson b Wardle	29	— c Close b Wardle	39
Rohan Kanhai lbw b Trueman	44	— not out	24
C. L. Walcott c Evans b Trueman	0	— c Close b Wardle	4
F. C. M. Alexander not out	11	— st Evans b Tribe	2
T. Dewdney not out	0	— c Evans b Bailey	2
R. Gilchrist (did not bat)		— not out	3
B 11, l-b 4, w 4	19	B 7, n-b 1	8

1/2 2/95 3/179 4/225 (7 wkts., dec.) 323
5/282 6/282 7/317

1/0 2/25 3/47 (8 wkts.) 151
4/108 5/116 6/126 7/137
8/145

A. L. Valentine did not bat.

West Indies Bowling

	O.	M.	R.	W.		O.	M.	R.	W.
Dewdney	13	0	45	0	....	8	0	30	0
Gilchrist	19	2	69	1	....	6	0	24	1
Asgarali	21	3	72	4					
Sobers	19	2	93	2	....	3	0	19	2
Smith	8	2	33	0					
Valentine	7	0	33	1	....	9.4	0	70	3
Weekes						5	0	31	1

T. N. Pearce's XI Bowling

	O.	M.	R.	W.		O.	M.	R.	W.
Trueman	12	4	39	3					
Tyson	20	1	61	1	....	5	2	7	2
Bailey	9	3	25	0	....	13	2	38	2
Wardle	23	10	59	1	....	18	2	60	2
Tribe	22	3	58	2	....	13	3	38	2
Graveney	12	0	62	0					

Umpires: A. Skelding and D. Davies.

MINOR COUNTIES v. WEST INDIES

At Newcastle-on-Tyne, September 14, 16. West Indies won this two-day match by an innings and 103 runs. Owing to the bitterly cold weather no more than 2,500 people attended the Jesmond ground on Saturday when a stand of 266 in only one and three-quarter hours between Sobers and Kanhai provided rare entertainment. They began by adding 160 in the hour before lunch, but when they left Ryan, the Yorkshire seam bowler, kept a fine length and finished with six wickets for 97. Worrell, the West Indies captain, called on ten bowlers, but in the end it was the two famous spinners, Ramadhin and Valentine, who routed the opposition after a heartening opening stand by Padgett and the local player, Shaw.

West Indies

N. Asgarali c Cherry-Downes b Ryan	29
B. H. Pairaudeau b Cherry-Downes	0
G. Sobers c Rhodes b Cherry-Downes	151
Rohan Kanhai c Shaw b Ryan	146
O. G. Smith b Rhodes	26
W. Hall c Padgett b Ryan	20
F. M. Worrell b Ryan	3
R. Gilchrist c Padgett b Rhodes	12
A. Ganteaume c Padgett b Ryan	15
A. L. Valentine not out	5
S. Ramadhin c Smithson b Ryan	0
B 18, l-b 8, n-b 1	27

1/0 2/57 3/323 4/332 5/363   **434**
6/372 7/389 8/415 9/434

Minor Counties

D. E. V. Padgett (*Yorkshire*) c Gilchrist b Valentine	37	— b Hall	6
P. H. Shaw (*Northumberland*) b Sobers	72	— c Ganteaume b Hall	10
J. R. Thompson (*Wiltshire*) b Ramadhin	10	— b Ramadhin	9
R. W. Smithson (*Northumberland*) c Asgarali b Pairaudeau	24	— lbw b Ramadhin	37
D. M. Haynes (*Staffordshire*) b Ramadhin	29	— c Ganteaume b Valentine	11
D. Allen (*Gloucestershire*) lbw b Valentine	0	— c Ganteaume b Valentine	18
H. J. Rhodes (*Derbyshire*) b Valentine	0	— c Worrell b Ramadhin	1
M. Ryan (*Yorkshire*) b Ramadhin	1	— b Ramadhin	0
J. G. Fox (*Durham*) b Ramadhin	2	— b Ramadhin	23
H. M. A. Cherry-Downes (*Lincolnshire*) c Ganteaume b Ramadhin	0	— not out	15
M. Youll (*Warwickshire*) not out	0	— run out	1
B 11, l-b 2, w 1	14	B 8, w 2, n-b 1	11

1/70 2/90 3/132 4/178 5/183 6/183   **189**   1/14 2/19 3/40 4/67 5/95   **142**
7/184 8/188 9/188   6/99 7/99 8/99 9/101

Minor Counties Bowling

	O.	M.	R.	W.	O.	M.	R.	W.
Rhodes	18	3	97	2				
Cherry-Downes	21	2	143	2				
Ryan	19.3	2	97	6				
Allan	3	1	37	0				
Youll	3	0	33	0				

West Indies Bowling

	O.	M.	R.	W.	O.	M.	R.	W.
Hall	5	0	14	0	8	2	15	2
Ramadhin	18.5	8	21	5	22.3	8	58	5
Worrell	14	4	35	0				
Gilchrist	3	0	15	0	6	1	16	0
Valentine	22	11	23	3	21	8	42	2
Pairaudeau	7	2	26	1				
Kanhai	11	5	14	0				
Smith	6	1	8	0				
Asgarali	4	1	12	0				
Sobers	5	2	7	1				

Umpires: S. H. Moore and R. E. Rushworth.

THE MARYLEBONE CRICKET CLUB

M.C.C. held their 170th Annual Meeting at Lord's on May 1 when the Duke of Norfolk was nominated President-Designate in succession to Viscount Monckton of Brenchley, the appointment to take effect from October 1, 1957.

G. C. Newman, The Earl of Rosebery, F. G. Mann, Major M. F. S. Jewell, G. O. Allen and E. R. T. Holmes retired by rotation from the Committee. The vacancies were filled by the retiring President, G. C. Newman, Sir William Worsley, G. O. Shelmerdine and Rev. D. S. Sheppard.

G. C. Newman, in 1956, was elected an additional member of the Committee for one year and was eligible for re-election in the ordinary way for a further period of three years. G. O. Allen, as Chairman of the Cricket Sub-Committee, was appointed to serve as an additional member of the M.C.C. Committee for a further period of three years.

The deaths of 135 members occurred during the preceding year, and special mention was made in the report of Captain C. B. Fry, the great all-round athlete, Sir Home Gordon, Lord Belper and E. H. Leaf.

Membership

On December 31, 1956, the Club consisted of 7,845 members, including 37 Honorary Life Members and 298 Life Members. Members paying the Abroad List subscription numbered 332.

Associate Membership

Not more than 750 Associate Members were to be elected in 1957 as the new "A" Stand would only be partially built in time for the season.

Finance

The accounts for the year ended December 31, 1956, showed an excess of expenditure over income of £2,278 19s. 6d.

Cricket

Tribute was paid in the report to England's success in the Test series against the Australian team captained by I. W. Johnson, particular reference being made to the consistent batting of P. B. H. May, the England captain, the superb catching of the team and the outstanding performance of J. C. Laker in taking 46 wickets and 19 in the Fourth Test Match at Old Trafford. This series and that in South Africa during the winter, when the England team under P. B. H. May shared honours in the rubber, were both financially successful.

Special Committee Report

In view of the decline in gates at county matches and in the belief that this was in some measure due to the tempo of cricket, the Committee appointed a Special Committee to examine this and other aspects of the county game and to formulate proposals for stimulating interest and support. The Special Committee's report was passed to the counties without amendment or comment so that discussion at the Advisory County Cricket Committee would not be prejudiced.

Youth Cricket

The Committee congratulated H. P. Crabtree on the award to him of the M.B.E. in recognition of his work for Youth Cricket, and recorded appreciation of the invaluable service rendered to the M.C.C. Youth Cricket Association by its Secretary, Vice-Admiral E. G. N. Rushbrooke.

Building and Works

The Committee reported that the new "A" Stand, which was expected to be completed in time for 1958 season, would have a seating capacity of approximately 2,900. The top tier would contain a new Press Box with seats for at least 105 pressmen, besides accommodation for television commentators.

M.C.C. RESULTS

First-Class Matches—Played 8, Won 2, Drawn 4, Lost 2
Other Matches—Played 141, Won 62, Drawn 52, Lost 24,
Abandoned 3

April 24, 25 Wisbech	Wisbech Town	278 for 6* and 223 for 4*	Won by five wickets
	M.C.C.	267 for 8* and 236 for 5	

*Innings declared closed.

M.C.C. v. YORKSHIRE

At Lord's, April 27, 29, 30. M.C.C. won by two runs. They recovered well after appearing likely to be defeated inside two days. When they batted first M.C.C. were always struggling against the lively in-swing attack of Trueman and Platt, the latter taking the last four wickets in less than four overs at a cost of eight runs. Yorkshire established a lead of 70 largely through the skilled stroke-play of Close who received sound help from another left-hander, Wilson, in a second wicket partnership of 73. M.C.C. made such a poor start to their second innings that, with five wickets down, they stood only 20 ahead but the combined efforts of Graveney, Palmer and Murray enabled them to set the county to get 147 on a pitch showing signs of wear. Yorkshire passed 100 with five wickets intact but a collapse followed and though Illingworth batted bravely in a bid to regain the ground lost, he finally mistimed an off-side stroke and gave Bennett a simple return catch.

M.C.C.

M. R. Hallam c Lowson b Cowan	29	—	st Binks b Platt	6
D. V. Smith c Lowson b Trueman	13	—	c Binks b Cowan	15
M. J. K. Smith b Trueman	0	—	c Binks b Platt	0
T. W. Graveney c and b Cowan	18	—	b Platt	55
D. W. Barrick c Close b Platt	2	—	c Padgett b Trueman	32
J. D. Goddard b Trueman	5	—	b Cowan	4
C. H. Palmer b Platt	24	—	c Lowson b Cowan	42
D. Bennett not out	7	—	b Platt	1
J. T. Murray b Platt	0	—	c Lowson b Trueman	46
M. J. Hilton b Platt	0	—	b Trueman	3
A. E. Moss c Padgett b Platt	0	—	not out	1
B 8, l-b 1, n-b 2	11		B 4, l-b 6, n-b 1	11

1/17 2/17 3/56 4/63 5/65 6/89   109
7/99 8/101 9/109

1/17 2/23 3/25 4/81 5/90   216
6/123 7/133 8/192 9/216

Yorkshire

F. A. Lowson lbw b Moss	0	—	c Murray b Bennett	20
D. B. Close c Goddard b Hilton	42	—	c Murray b Moss	5
J. V. Wilson b Moss	30	—	c Hallam b Moss	19
D. E. V. Padgett b Bennett	26	—	lbw b D. Smith	33
W. Watson c Hallam b D. Smith	42	—	c Hallam b Bennett	11
W. H. H. Sutcliffe, c D. Smith b Hilton	28	—	c Murray b Bennett	5
R. Illingworth b Moss	0	—	c and b Bennett	46
F. S. Trueman b D. Smith	0	—	b D. Smith	2
J. G. Binks not out	0	—	c Hallam b D. Smith	0
R. K. Platt lbw b D. Smith	0	—	b Bennett	1
M. J. Cowan (did not bat)	—	—	not out	0
B 9, l-b 2	11		L-b 1, n-b 1	2

1/0 2/73 3/94 4/116   (9 wkts., dec.) 179
5/167 6/179 7/179 8/179 9/179

1/11 2/33 3/50 4/66 5/80   144
6/112 7/116 8/122 9/139

Yorkshire Bowling

	O.	M.	R.	W.	O.	M.	R.	W.
Trueman	13	2	30	3	15.5	1	53	3
Cowan	10	2	25	2	21	3	68	3
Platt	16.5	4	43	5	23	7	53	4
Illingworth					8	2	19	0
Close					7	2	12	0

M.C.C. Bowling

	O.	M.	R.	W.	O.	M.	R.	W.
Moss	15	4	41	3	27	8	75	2
Bennett	14	2	45	1	22.1	7	42	5
Hilton	13	1	50	2				
D. Smith	8.4	4	17	3	21	11	25	3
Goddard	5	1	15	0				

Umpires: A. Thompson and B. L. Muncer.

M.C.C. v. SURREY

At Lord's, May 1, 2, 3. Surrey won by 238 runs and were in command from the start against an M.C.C. team of medium strength. May began his innings with a typical cover drive for four and gave a delightful display of free hitting. He scored his last 50 in forty minutes and hit twenty-four boundaries. M.C.C. started their reply confidently, then collapsed against the combined spin attack of Laker and Lock and finished 169 behind. Clark, who gave a return catch off a full toss when one short of a century, showed commendable enterprise for the second time in the match after May declined to enforce the follow-on. Hallam apart, M.C.C. again batted poorly on the last day, when Lock took advantage of a dry and helpful pitch. His left-arm deliveries did not turn unduly but they lifted sufficiently off a length to cause hurried strokes.

Surrey

M. J. Stewart c Taylor b Bennett	11	— c Warr b Gray 28
T. H. Clark c Hallam b Bennett	62	— c and b Greensmith 99
B. Constable c Taylor b Bennett	2	— b Greensmith 11
P. B. H. May c Smith b Gray	151	
K. F. Barrington c Taylor b Bennett	5	— c Palmer b Marlar 4
E. A. Bedser c Taylor b Smith	3	— lbw b Greensmith 1
A. J. McIntyre b Bennett	42	— b Smith 21
G. A. R. Lock c Smith b Gray	34	— not out 18
J. C. Laker not out	0	
P. J. Loader (did not bat)		— not out 14
B 5, l-b 3	8	L-b 3 3

1/40 2/46 3/113 4/123   (8 wkts., dec.) 318
5/138 6/223 7/310 8/318
A. V. Bedser did not bat.

1/57 2/104   (6 wkts., dec.) 199
3/109 4/130 5/163 6/175

M.C.C.

M. Hallam c Lock b Laker	37	— hit wkt b Loader 58
D. V. Smith c Stewart b Laker	18	— c sub b Lock 19
J. R. Gray run out	50	— c Constable b Lock 1
J. M. Parks c McIntyre b E. Bedser	29	— c Barrington b Lock 5
G. M. Emmett run out	0	— lbw b Lock 6
C. H. Palmer c and b Lock	3	— c McIntyre b Loader 1
D. Bennett c Lock b Laker	0	— lbw b Lock 8
B. Taylor not out	0	— c E. Bedser b Loader 10
W. T. Greensmith c Barrington b Lock	1	— c Barrington b Lock 4
J. J. Warr c A. Bedser b Lock	0	— not out 8
R. G. Marlar st McIntyre b Laker	0	— st McIntyre b Lock 1
B 8, l-b 2, n-b 1	11	B 4, l-b 3, n-b 2 9

1/55 2/72 3/128 4/128 5/138   149
6/140 7/140 8/145 9/145

1/46 2/58 3/68 4/76 5/87   130
6/103 7/107 8/111 9/129

M.C.C. Bowling

	O.	M.	R.	W.	O.	M.	R.	W.
Warr	22	2	72	0	10	0	48	0
Bennett	27	5	83	5	6	1	23	0
Smith	17	4	59	1	6	1	15	1
Gray	11	1	47	2	9	2	19	1
Marlar	5	1	14	0	9	3	32	1
Palmer	6	3	12	0				
Greensmith	6	0	23	0	14	0	59	3

Surrey Bowling

	O.	M.	R.	W.	O.	M.	R.	W.
Loader	15	2	46	0	18	6	40	3
A. Bedser	18	3	34	0	8	0	24	0
Laker	19.3	0	27	4				
Lock	14	8	15	3	25.2	9	47	7
E. Bedser	8	2	16	1	9	5	10	0

Umpires: H. P. Sharp and G. D. Morton.

May 11 Motspur Park	B.B.C. M.C.C.	231 for 8* 125 for 8	Drawn

At Lord's, May 18, 20, 21. M.C.C. drew with WEST INDIES. (See WEST INDIES section.)

May 23 Repton	Repton School M.C.C.	211 for 6* 211 for 8	Drawn
May 25 Framlingham	M.C.C. Framlingham College	180 for 8* 167	Won by 13 runs
May 25 Rugby	Rugby School M.C.C.	115 116 for 1	Won by nine wickets
May 28 Malvern	M.C.C. Malvern College	284 for 6* 237 for 7	Drawn
May 28 Cricklewood	University College Sch. M.C.C.	54 56 for 1	Won by nine wickets
May 28 Winchester	Winchester College M.C.C.	219 for 5* 205 for 3	Drawn
May 29 Highgate	Highgate School M.C.C.	142 143 for 5	Won by five wickets
May 29 South Croydon	M.C.C. Whitgift School	194 for 4* 104	Won by 90 runs

M.C.C. v. CLUB CRICKET CONFERENCE

At Lord's, May 29, 30. Drawn. M.C.C. 214 (S. E. Leary 66, R. S. Thresher four for 39) and 140 for four wickets, dec. (R. Illingworth 61 not out); Club Cricket Conference 146 for eight wickets, dec., and 206 for six wickets (G. Atkins 62).

May 30 Harrow	M.C.C. Harrow School	208 for 9* 212 for 5	Lost by five wickets
May 31 Brentwood	M.C.C. Brentwood School	216 for 6* 148 for 8	Drawn
May 31 Wellington	M.C.C. Wrekin	194 for 7* 131 for 9	Drawn

* Innings declared closed.

June 1 Berkhamsted	M.C.C. Berkhamsted School	226 for 4* 185	Won by 41 runs
June 1 Cheltenham	Cheltenham College M.C.C.	243 for 7* 247 for 8	Won by two wickets
June 1 Cambridge	M.C.C. Leys School	224 for 6* 146 for 5	Drawn
June 1 Radley	Radley College M.C.C.	216 for 6* 188 for 9	Drawn
June 1 Shrewsbury	M.C.C. Shrewsbury School	146 91	Won by 55 runs
June 4 Dulwich	Alleyn's School M.C.C.	77 80 for 4	Won by six wickets
June 4 Shoreham	Lancing College M.C.C.	223 for 3* 124 for 6	Drawn
June 4 Oxford	M.C.C. St. Edward's School	180 for 8* 154 for 8	Drawn

At Manchester, June 5, 6, 7. M.C.C. drew with LANCASHIRE. (See LANCASHIRE section.)

June 5 Northwood	M.C.C. Merchant Taylors' Sch.	229 for 4* 107	Won by 122 runs
June 5 Catford	M.C.C. St. Dunstan's College	246 for 6* 104	Won by 142 runs
June 5 Stonyhurst	Stonyhurst College M.C.C.	176 177 for 3	Won by seven wickets
June 6 Godalming	M.C.C. Charterhouse School	192 151 for 8	Drawn
June 6 Mill Hill	M.C.C. Mill Hill School	190 for 6* 135 for 5	Drawn
June 8 Elstree	M.C.C. Aldenham School	148 101 for 9	Drawn
June 8 Haileybury	Haileybury and I.S.C. M.C.C.	198 for 7* 77 for 5	Drawn
June 8 Oundle	M.C.C. Oundle	196 34 for 1	Drawn
June 8 Motspur Park	University of London M.C.C.	207 208 for 7	Won by three wickets
June 8 Worksop	Worksop College M.C.C.	128 129 for 2	Won by eight wickets

* Innings declared closed.

M.C.C. v. OXFORD UNIVERSITY

At Lord's, June 26, 27, 28. M.C.C. won by 129 runs. They were stronger in all departments than the University whose attack, though steady, was not hostile enough to keep keen rivals subdued. Hallam, of Leicestershire, a splendid driver, and Pollock, the Irish batsman, excelled for M.C.C. Melville, who hit thirteen 4's in 84, gave the best display for Oxford in the first innings, but the University batsmen were nonplussed in the second by the skilful leg-break bowling of Dr. C. B. Clarke, the former West Indies Test player. G. E. Gomez, another former West Indies Test cricketer, showed good form with bat and ball for M.C.C.

M.C.C.

M. R. Hallam c Scott b Melville	139	— b Bowman	5
D. E. Blake c Hobbs b Bowman	2	— c Scott b Bowman	76
G. P. S. Delisle b Jowett	38	— lbw b Woodcock	67
G. E. Gomez b Wilson	31	— b Wilson	31
M. H. Stevenson run out	14	— c Scott b Wilson	28
J. S. Pollock st Scott b Woodcock	82	— b Wilson	14
P. Cranmer c Eagar b Woodcock	27	— b Wilson	6
Dr. C. B. Clarke c Walton b Woodcock	7	— not out	0
C. T. Spencer c Hobbs b Bowman	4		
R. J. Hurst lbw b Woodcock	9		
G. C. Wilson not out	3		
B 5	5	B 3, l-b 2	5

1/23 2/105 3/183 4/219 5/232 6/280   361   1/6 2/124   (7 wkts., dec.) 232
7/310 8/317 9/336   3/181 4/185 5/218 6/225
                                      7/232

Oxford University

J. A. D. Hobbs b Spencer	10	— run out	10
I. Gibson c Hallam b Spencer	0	— c and b Spencer	14
A. C. Walton b Spencer	34	— lbw b Spencer	5
C. D. Melville lbw b Clarke	84	— c Blake b Clarke	36
M. A. Eagar b Spencer	5	— lbw b Clarke	30
J. M. Kumleben lbw b Clarke	12	— b Clarke	40
R. L. Jowett c and b Wilson	56	— st Blake b Clarke	10
R. G. Woodcock c Hallam b Gomez	33	— not out	25
M. D. Scott c Wilson b Spencer	14	— b Clarke	0
R. W. Wilson c Hallam b Gomez	1	— c Hallam b Hurst	3
R. Bowman not out	4	— c Delisle b Clarke	25
B 5, l-b 6, n-b 2	13		

1/8 2/23 3/77 4/83 5/109 6/190   266   1/16 2/21 3/40 4/76 5/115   198
7/231 8/258 9/260   6/137 7/158 8/158 9/167

Oxford Bowling

	O.	M.	R.	W.		O.	M.	R.	W.
Bowman	22	3	88	2	....	19	3	53	2
Melville	11	0	50	1	....	4	1	13	0
Jowett	5	0	20	1	....	9	0	64	0
Wilson	22	3	91	1	....	24.3	5	75	4
Woodcock	26	5	86	4	....	6	0	22	1
Gibson	3	0	21	0					

M.C.C. Bowling

	O.	M.	R.	W.		O.	M.	R.	W.
Spencer	27	11	57	5	....	13	2	56	2
Wilson	17	1	80	1	....	5	0	22	0
Gomez	6	2	9	2	....	9	3	24	0
Clarke	24	7	74	2	....	21.3	7	60	6
Hurst	18	7	33	0	....	11	3	36	1

Umpires: H. P. Sharp and A. Thompson.

M.C.C. v. CAMBRIDGE UNIVERSITY

At Lord's, July 3, 4, 5. Drawn. Cambridge deservedly shared honours, but found little to encourage them for the University Match. Dexter drove well in the first innings, but he often seemed troubled by spin, and his colleagues found the cleverly varied medium-fast deliveries of Morgan—the Guy's Hospital cricket captain and a Blue of 1954—too accurate for ready scoring. Wells, of Gloucestershire, hit four 6's in making 47 in half an hour for M.C.C. Greensmith, of Essex, batted attractively in the second innings; then he and Wells used spin and flight to such good effect that Cambridge, who were left to score 201 in two and three-quarter hours, lost six wickets for 102. Pieris and Smith, however, stood firm for the last thirty-five minutes, including fifteen of the extra half-hour, before Davies, the M.C.C. captain, who formerly played for Cambridge and Kent, gave up the contest as a draw.

M.C.C.

G. Barker c Swift b Pieris	6	— b Goonesena	55
R. A. Gale c McLachlan b Wheatley	11	— b Wheatley	19
W. Knightley-Smith c McLachlan b Dexter	33	— lbw b Wheatley	0
D. O. Baldry c Swift b Wheatley	7	— c Green b Pieris	15
J. G. W. Davies c McLachlan b Smith	16	— c Green b Smith	5
S. Singh c Cook b Smith	10	— b Smith	6
W. T. Greensmith lbw b Wheatley	3	— not out	61
G. C. Downton c Smith b Dexter	12	— c Goonesena b James	20
B. D. Wells c Pieris b James	47	— b James	2
M. N. Morgan c Swift b Dexter	9	— c Goonesena b Smith	0
H. W. Tilly not out	2	— c Green b Wheatley	8
B 10, l-b 6, w 3, n-b 1	20	B 19, l-b 9, n-b 1, w 1	30
	176		**221**

1/14 2/21 3/31 4/55 5/75 6/79 7/110
8/136 9/168

1/25 2/27 3/66 4/73 5/79
6/129 7/193 8/201 9/212

Cambridge University

R. W. Barber c Tilly b Morgan	4	— c Downton b Wells	45
I. McLachlan c Downton b Morgan	14	— c Downton b Wells	19
D. J. Green run out	20	— c Downton b Wells	0
E. R. Dexter c Gale b Greensmith	60	— lbw b Greensmith	3
R. M. James c Davies b Wells	34	— c Downton b Greensmith	4
G. Goonesena run out	2	— b Greensmith	21
G. W. Cook b Singh	18		
P. I. Pieris b Tilly	32	— not out	9
C. S. Smith c Gale b Morgan	11	— not out	7
B. T. Swift c Gale b Morgan	0		
O. S. Wheatley not out	1		
N-b 1	1	B 8, l-b 1, n-b 2	11
	197	(6 wkts.)	**119**

1/11 2/28 3/58 4/129 5/132 6/136
7/169 8/195 9/196

1/52 2/60 3/65
4/69 5/98 6/102

Cambridge Bowling

	O.	M.	R.	W.		O.	M.	R.	W.
Smith	14	5	29	2	....	15	4	40	3
Wheatley	14	4	23	3	....	17	5	35	3
Pieris	17	7	28	1	....	15	3	45	1
Dexter	7	2	26	3					
James	7.4	1	50	1	....	12	4	17	2
Goonesena					...	20	5	37	1
Cook					....	6	1	17	0

M.C.C. Bowling

	O.	M.	R.	W.		O.	M.	R.	W.
Tilly	22	4	41	1	....	11	1	21	0
Morgan	17.5	7	39	4	....	6	1	16	0
Baldry	7	1	31	0					
Singh	10	2	22	1	....	2	2	0	0
Greensmith	14	3	41	1	....	17	2	59	3
Wells	10	2	21	1	....	19	14	12	3
Davies	1	0	1	0	....	1	1	0	0

Umpires: W. Harrington and G. D. Morton.

M.C.C. v. R.M.A. (Sandhurst)

At Lord's, May 22. Drawn.   M.C.C. 247 for five wickets, declared (M. P. Murray 112, A. R. B. Neame 83; R. H. Whitty four for 52); R.M.A. Sandhurst 202 for four wickets (D. S. Williams 112 not out).

June 10 Taunton	M.C.C. Queen's College	215 for 5* 58	Won by 157 runs
June 11 Wellington	Wellington School M.C.C.	147 148 for 4	Won by six wickets
June 12 Tiverton	Blundell's School M.C.C.	207 174	Lost by 33 runs
June 13 Blandford	M.C.C. Bryanston School	185 111	Won by 74 runs
June 14 Devizes	M.C.C. Dauntsey's School	274 for 4* 151 for 4	Drawn
June 15 Bath	M.C.C. Prior Park College	241 for 4* 244 for 0	Lost by ten wickets
June 10 Windsor	Beaumont College M.C.C.	7 for 0 —	Drawn (rain)
June 11 Bishop's Stortford	Bishop's Stortford Coll. M.C.C.	160 for 9* 161 for 3	Won by seven wickets
June 11 Cranleigh	M.C.C. Cranleigh School	199 72	Won by 127 runs
June 11 Eastbourne	Eastbourne College M.C.C.	240 for 9* 169 for 8	Drawn
June 12 Chigwell	M.C.C. Chigwell School	180 113	Won by 67 runs
June 12 Horsham	M.C.C. Christ's Hospital	197 166	Won by 31 runs
June 12 Stamford	M.C.C. Stamford School	239 for 5* 72	Won by 167 runs
June 13 Canterbury	King's School M.C.C.	205 for 8* 186 for 6	Drawn
June 13 Sedbergh	M.C.C. Sedbergh School	203 204 for 7	Lost by three wickets
June 13 Vincent Square	M.C.C. Westminster School	266 108	Won by 158 runs
June 14 Weybridge	M.C.C. St. George's College	226 for 7* 136	Won by 90 runs
June 15 Dulwich	Dulwich College M.C.C.	188 for 6* 189 for 7	Won by three wickets
June 15 Eton	M.C.C. Eton College	247 for 7* 155 for 6	Drawn
June 15 Holt	Gresham's School M.C.C.	132 133 for 5	Won by five wickets
June 15 Edgware	M.C.C. Maurice	229 for 7* 110 for 7	Drawn
June 17 Beddington	M.C.C. Beddington	175 176 for 6	Lost by four wickets
June 18 Ampleforth	M.C.C. Ampleforth College	159 161 for 4	Lost by six wickets

June 18 Bedford	Bedford School M.C.C.	267 for 8* 238 for 9	Drawn
June 18 Banbury	Bloxham School M.C.C.	83 84 for 1	Won by nine wickets
June 19 Lee	M.C.C. City of London School	202 for 1* 163 for 4	Drawn
June 19 Mill Hill	M.C.C. Haberdashers' School	247 for 7* 101	Won by 146 runs
June 19 York	St. Peter's School M.C.C.	312 for 4* 177	Lost by 135 runs
June 20 Settle	Giggleswick School M.C.C.	72 73 for 0	Won by ten wickets
June 26 Epsom	Epsom College M.C.C.	153 154 for 7	Won by three wickets
June 26 Burton Court	M.C.C. Household Brigade	219 for 9* 153	Won by 66 runs
June 26 Monkton Combe	M.C.C. Monkton Combe Sch.	247 for 5* 222 for 8	Drawn
June 26 Reading	Oratory School M.C.C.	195 197 for 4	Won by six wickets
June 27 Brighton	M.C.C. Brighton College	132 134 for 5	Lost by five wickets
June 27 Uttoxeter	Denstone College M.C.C.	236 for 9* 201 for 5	Drawn
June 27 Bath	M.C.C. Downside School	156 158 for 2	Lost by eight wickets
June 27 Leatherhead	M.C.C. St. John's School	195 for 7* 94	Won by 101 runs
June 28 Oxted	M.C.C. Oxted	203 for 9* 121	Won by 82 runs
June 28 Woodford Green	M.C.C. Woodford Wells	260 203 for 8	Drawn
June 29 Wimborne	M.C.C. Canford School	271 for 5* 178 for 8	Drawn
June 29 Felsted	M.C.C. Felsted School	275 for 6* 178	Won by 97 runs
June 29 Stowe	Stowe School M.C.C.	145 146 for 9	Won by one wicket
June 29 Wellingborough	M.C.C. Wellingborough School	246 for 8* 89	Won by 157 runs
July 2 Nottingham	M.C.C. Nottingham High Sch.	248 for 3* 153 for 7	Drawn
July 3 Fleetwood	M.C.C. Rossall School	158 for 9* 51 for 7	Drawn

At Aberdeen, July 3, 4, 5. M.C.C. drew with SCOTLAND.

July 4 Cranbrook	Cranbrook School M.C.C.	140 128 for 8	Drawn
July 4 Snaresbrook	M.C.C. Forest School	231 for 4* 130	Won by 101 runs

July 4 Weston-sup.-Mare	Weston-super-Mare M.C.C.	176 for 8* 143 for 7	Drawn
July 5 Byfleet	Byfleet M.C.C.	142 118	Lost by 24 runs
July 6 Bushey	M.C.C. Bushey	185 105	Won by 80 runs
July 6 Woolhampton	M.C.C. Douai School	206 for 7* 140 for 8	Drawn
July 6 Weybridge	M.C.C. Oatlands Park	157 133	Won by 24 runs
July 6 Winchmore Hill	Winchmore Hill M.C.C.	255 for 7* 136	Lost by 119 runs
July 8 St. Bees	M.C.C. St. Bees School	229 for 3* 129 for 9	Drawn
July 9 Rusholme	Manchester G.S. M.C.C.	76 77 for 5	Won by five wickets
July 9 Sutton Valence	M.C.C. Sutton Valence School	234 for 7* 191	Won by 43 runs
July 10 Beckenham	Cyphers M.C.C.	218 for 8* 219 for 2	Won by eight wickets
July 10 Twickenham	M.C.C. Exiles	126 for 7* —	Drawn (rain)
July 11 Bradfield	M.C.C. Bradfield College	240 for 4* 69 for 2	Drawn (rain)
July 11 Chiswick	M.C.C. Civil Service Crus.	200 for 6* 75 for 2	Drawn (rain)
July 11 New Beckenham	M.C.C. Nat. Provincial Bank	231 for 4* 131 for 4	Drawn (rain)
July 11 Southgate	M.C.C. Southgate	232 for 5* 135 for 5	Drawn (rain)
July 12 Taunton	M.C.C. Taunton School	148 151 for 4	Lost by six wickets
July 13 Dover	M.C.C. Dover College	214 110	Won by 104 runs
July 13 Hornsey	M.C.C. Hornsey	209 162 for 5	Drawn
July 13 Cranwell	R.A.F. College M.C.C.	183 176	Lost by 7 runs
July 13 Sherborne	M.C.C. Sherborne School	155 for 5* 48 for 2	Drawn (rain)
July 13 Chislehurst	M.C.C. West Kent	123 126 for 8	Lost by two wickets
July 15 Beckenham	Beckenham M.C.C.	204 for 9* 208 for 4	Won by six wickets
July 15 Richmond	Richmond M.C.C.	206 for 7* 142	Lost by 64 runs
July 16 Sutton	Sutton M.C.C.	165 83 for 7	Drawn
July 17 Woodford Green	M.C.C. Bancroft's School	170 for 8* 101 for 8	Drawn

July 17 Edgbaston	Midlands C.C.C. M.C.C.	226 for 5* 6 for 0	Drawn (rain)
July 18 Hampton Wick	M.C.C. Hampton Wick Royal	161 157	Won by 4 runs
July 19 Isleworth	M.C.C. Nigerian C.A. XI	163 for 1* 167 for 7	Lost by three wickets
July 20 Wimbledon	King's College School M.C.C.	131 121 for 9	Drawn
July 20 Middleton-on-Sea	M.C.C. Middleton	— —	Abandoned (rain)
July 20 Oakham	Oakham School M.C.C.	157 for 3* 158 for 7	Won by three wickets
July 20 West Kensington	St. Paul's School M.C.C.	102 103 for 7	Won by three wickets
July 23 Roehampton	M.C.C. Bank of England	123 126 for 6	Lost by four wickets
July 23 Clifton	M.C.C. Clifton College	112 113 for 5	Lost by five wickets
July 23 Kingston-on- Thames	M.C.C. Kingston Grammar School	143 103	Won by 40 runs
July 24 Hurlingham	M.C.C. Lords and Commons	221 for 9* 147 for 9	Drawn
July 24 Reading	M.C.C. Reading School	147 87	Won by 60 runs
July 24 Colwyn Bay	M.C.C. Rydal School	70 71 for 0	Lost by ten wickets
July 25 Hampton-on- Thames	M.C.C. Hampton Grammar School	171 for 5* 166	Won by 5 runs
July 25 Liverpool	M.C.C. Liverpool College	146 91	Won by 55 runs
July 25 Tonbridge	M.C.C. Tonbridge School	197 147	Won by 50 runs
July 26, 27 Aldershot	Aldershot Services M.C.C.	353 for 7* and 80 for 5* 256 for 7* and 157 for 6	Drawn
July 27 City Road	M.C.C. H.A.C.	172 for 5* 85 for 6	Drawn
July 27 Marlborough	M.C.C. Marlborough College	107 113 for 5	Lost by five wickets
July 27 Rugby	Rugby C.C. M.C.C.	111 12 for 0	Drawn (rain)
July 27 Crowthorne	M.C.C. Wellington College	115 117 for 4	Lost by six wickets
July 31 Buxton	M.C.C. Buxton	214 for 8* 80	Won by 134 runs
July 31 Guildford	M.C.C. Guildford	143 147 for 7	Lost by three wickets
August 3 Lindfield	M.C.C. Lindfield	188 121	Won by 67 runs

August 5 Sevenoaks	Sevenoaks Vine M.C.C.	216 for 3* 174	Lost by 42 runs
August 5 Wimbledon	M.C.C. Wimbledon	235 for 8* 27	Won by 208 runs
August 7 Chichester	M.C.C. Chichester Priory Pk.	177 179 for 9	Lost by one wicket
August 8 East Grinstead	M.C.C. East Grinstead	277 for 3* 95	Won by 182 runs
August 9 Thames Ditton	M.C.C. Thames Ditton	— —	Abandoned (rain)
August 10 Banstead	M.C.C. Banstead	105 —	Drawn (rain)
August 10 Blackheath	Blackheath M.C.C.	131 105 for 2	Drawn (rain)
August 10 Brighton	M.C.C. Brighton & Hove	101 for 2 —	Drawn (rain)
August 12 Horsham	M.C.C. Horsham	179 —	Drawn (rain)
August 14 Trent Bridge	Notts Amateur M.C.C.	176 for 6* 179 for 0	Won by ten wickets
August 16 Buckhurst Hill	M.C.C. Buckhurst Hill	— —	Abandoned (rain)
August 16 Maidstone	Mote M.C.C.	216 for 6* 221 for 7	Won by three wickets

M.C.C. v. DE FLAMINGOS

At Lord's, August 21. M.C.C. won by 123 runs. M.C.C. 237 (A. C. Walton 82, C. Bakker three for 31, M. Maas three for 56); De Flamingos 114 (Maas 26, O. J. Wait five for 34).

M.C.C. v. IRELAND

At Lord's, August 22, 23. M.C.C. won by seven wickets. Ireland 92 (Wells five for 11) and 264 (L. A. Warke 101, R. O'Brien 62); M.C.C. 279 for five wickets, declared (J. G. Dewes 143) and 78 for three wickets.

August 24 Beaconsfield	M.C.C. Beaconsfield	242 157	Won by 85 runs
August 27 Shanklin, I. of W.	M.C.C. Isle of Wight C.A.	173 for 8* 95	Won by 78 runs

M.C.C. YOUNG PROFESSIONALS v. LONDON FEDERATION OF BOYS' CLUBS

At Lord's, August 27. Drawn. M.C.C. Young Professionals 247 for five wickets, declared (Stark 120, Lever 61 not out); London Federation of Boys' Clubs 139 for nine wickets (B. Timson 49, Kent four for 35).

M.C.C. YOUNG PROFESSIONALS v. ENGLISH SCHOOLS CRICKET ASSOCIATION

At Lord's, August 31. English Schools C.A. won by one wicket. M.C.C. Young Professionals 175 (Stark 79, J. Rushton seven for 52); English Schools C.A. 176 for nine wickets (A. Harvey 60, Mitchell four for 33, Shepherd four for 55).

At Scarborough, August 31, September 2, 3. M.C.C. lost to YORKSHIRE by eight wickets.

K

OTHER MATCHES AT LORD'S

June 20, 21, 22. ENGLAND beat WEST INDIES in the Second Test Match by an innings and 36 runs. (See WEST INDIES section.)

OXFORD v. CAMBRIDGE

July 6, 8, 9. Cambridge won by an innings and 186 runs. The margin was their biggest since the series began in 1827. Other records were the score of 211 by Goonesena, the Light Blues' captain—the highest individual innings by a Cambridge man in the University Match—and the Cambridge seventh wicket stand by Goonesena and Cook of 289, which was the highest for any wicket by either side in the series. This stand was also the highest for the seventh wicket by Cambridge in any match.

Oxford, for all their enthusiasm, were outplayed. Most of their batting was below standard and the bowling lacked the hostility and craft necessary to break the grip of Goonesena and Cook. Wheatley bowled finely on the first day and inflicted damaging blows from which Oxford never recovered, but Goonesena, by reason of his splendid batting and his bowling in the second innings, was the match winner.

The weather was cloudy and close when Walton decided that Oxford should bat, but doubts about taking first innings on a green pitch must soon have assailed him. Hobbs left without a run on the board. Walton was run out, off a leg-bye, at 12, Gibson and Eagar both fell at slip at 16, and when Melville was bowled playing back, half the side were out for 33 in ninety minutes. There was no recovery. Wheatley, who captured three of the first four wickets at a cost of four runs in seven overs, took two more and finished with the remarkable analysis of 15–8–15–5. His accuracy and liveliness at medium-fast pace, allied with the ability to make the ball move sufficiently off the pitch to worry uncertain batsmen, accounted for his effectiveness. Wilson and Bailey, the Oxford last-wicket pair, showed courage and no little skill in scoring quite readily in conditions which defeated their colleagues. Pieris, a steady medium-pace bowler, played his part in the dismissal of Oxford in just under three hours by taking two wickets with consecutive balls, and Swift, an Australian, held three smart catches behind the wicket.

Cambridge batted when the pitch had lost its greenness, but despite attractive stroke-play by Barber and Green they lost four men, including Dexter who looked none too happy against spin, before taking the lead. The wholehearted medium-fast bowling of Bowman and the leg-spin bowling of Gibson kept the Light Blues watchful, and at the end of the first day Cambridge, with five men out for 108, were 16 in front.

Goonesena, 17 not out at that point, held the stage on Monday when Oxford toiled until after tea with the reward of only two more wickets. Variations of the drive, crisp cuts and powerful pulls showed the Cambridge captain to advantage against fast and slow bowlers. He spent four hours over his first hundred—reached with an off-drive which Walton touched but failed to hold—but then he scored so freely that the rest of his runs came in an hour and a half. Caught at mid-wicket attempting a pull, Goonesena hit one 6, one 5 and twenty-one 4's in his grand innings which fell only 27 short of the Nawab of Pataudi's record individual score by any player in the University Match.

Cook, Goonesena's partner in the big stand which lasted three and three-quarter hours, excelled with off-side strokes, the cut being his favourite, and he had hit thirteen boundaries in 111 when his captain declared upon dismissal.

Oxford, to their credit, never relaxed their fielding efforts during a tiring day, and in the last hour Gibson and Hobbs safely cleared 44 of the huge first innings arrears of 332.

There was a different story to tell on the last, overcast, day which commenced with an early setback for Oxford when Smith, fast and hostile, knocked down Hobbs' off-stump. Goonesena gained Cambridge a big advantage in tempting his rival captain forward and having him stumped, but although Oxford had five men out for 118 at lunch the saving of the game, with rain threatening, was not improbable. Gibson, then 61, seemed thoroughly set, but the news that Woodcock, who had retired after a rap on the glove, would not return because of broken bones in his left hand, sent the Dark Blues' hopes tumbling.

Drizzle started and bad light brought a halt for twenty minutes, but the running out of Gibson at 123, after three and a half hours of defiant and pleasing batting, heralded the end. Bowman, seventh out at the same total, was Swift's fifth victim of the match and seven runs later Smith sent Wilson's off-stump flying.

The umpires ordered another stoppage for bad light at twenty minutes past three when the score stood at 141 for eight, but the threat of heavy rain did not materialise and when cricket was resumed just after four o'clock Goonesena, appropriately, brought the match to an end by clean-bowling Scott.

The Cambridge captain and his men received the ovation they deserved as they left the field.

Oxford University

I. M. Gibson c Barber b Wheatley (Manchester G.S. and Brasenose)	8	— run out	63
J. A. D. Hobbs lbw b Wheatley (Liverpool College and St. Peter's)	0	— b Smith	19
A. C. Walton run out (Radley and Lincoln)	4	— st Swift b Goonesena	7
C. D. Melville b Pieris (Michaelhouse, S.A., and Trinity)	9	— lbw b Smith	6
M. A. Eagar c Dexter b Wheatley (Rugby and Worcester)	0	— lbw b Smith	2
R. G. Woodcock c Swift b Wheatley (Worcester R.G.S. and Keble)	11	— retired hurt	5
R. L. Jowett c Swift b Pieris (Bradford G.S. and Magdalen)	0	— lbw b Goonesena	0
M. D. Scott c Swift b Smith (Winchester and Worcester)	0	— b Goonesena	22
R. Bowman b Goonesena (Fettes and University)	17	— c Swift b Goonesena	0
R. W. Wilson not out (Warwick and Brasenose)	17	— b Smith	6
J. A. Bailey b Wheatley (Christ's Hospital and University)	21	— not out	4
B 3, l-b 1, n-b 1	5	B 8, l-b 3, n-b 1	12

1/0 2/12 3/16 4/16 5/33 6/33 7/36   92   1/56 2/82 3/89 4/93 5/104   146
8/44 9/60   6/123 7/123 8/130 9/146

Cambridge University

R. W. Barber lbw b Woodcock (Ruthin and Magdalene)	36	G. Goonesena c Jowett b Woodcock (Colombo and Queen's)	211
I. M. McLachlan b Bowman (St. Peter's, Adelaide, and Jesus)	11	C. S. Smith lbw b Gibson (William Hulme G.S. and Christ's)	8
D. J. Green c Gibson b Bowman (Burton G.S. and Christ's)	20	G. W. Cook not out (Dulwich and Queen's)	111
E. R. Dexter b Gibson (Radley and Jesus)	7	L-b 3, w 1, n-b 1	5
R. M. James lbw b Gibson (St. John's, Leatherhead, and Trinity)	15		(7 wkts., dec.) 424

1/20 2/67 3/67   (7 wkts., dec.) 424
4/80 5/97 6/135 7/424

P. I. Pieris (St. Thomas, Colombo and Queen's), B. T. Swift (St. Peter's, Adelaide and Caius) and O. S. Wheatley (King Edward's, Birmingham, and Caius) did not bat.

Cambridge Bowling

	O.	M.	R.	W.		O.	M.	R.	W.
Smith	12	3	26	1	....	30	13	42	4
Wheatley	15	8	15	5	....	13	4	17	0
Pieris	14	4	31	2	....	7	4	16	0
Dexter	1	0	3	0					
Goonesena	5	2	12	1	....	17.2	6	40	4
Barber						4	0	19	0

Oxford Bowling

	O.	M.	R.	W.
Bailey	36	5	146	0
Bowman	39	10	101	2
Melville	4	0	12	0
Woodcock	13.5	2	40	2
Gibson	17	4	48	3
Wilson	22	11	51	0
Jowett	6	0	21	0

Umpires: H. G. Baldwin and T. W. Spencer.

OXFORD v. CAMBRIDGE

From 1827 to 1957 the Universities played 113 matches, Cambridge winning 49, Oxford 42, and 22 being drawn.

The Universities did not play official matches in the war years 1915 to 1918 and 1940 to 1945. Results since the first world war:—

1919	Oxford won by 45	1936	Cambridge won by eight wickets
1920	Drawn	1937	Oxford won by seven wickets
1921	Cambridge won by inns. and 24	1938	Drawn
1922	Cambridge won by inns. and 100	1939	Oxford won by 45
1923	Oxford won by inns. and 100	1940 to 1945	No official matches
1924	Cambridge won by nine wickets	1946	Oxford won by six wickets
1925	Drawn	1947	Drawn
1926	Cambridge won by 24	1948	Oxford won by inns. and 8
1927	Cambridge won by 116	1949	Cambridge won by seven wickets
1928	Drawn	1950	Drawn
1929	Drawn	1951	Oxford won by 21
1930	Cambridge won by 205	1952	Drawn
1931	Oxford won by eight wickets	1953	Cambridge won by two wickets
1932	Drawn	1954	Drawn
1933	Drawn	1955	Drawn
1934	Drawn	1956	Drawn
1935	Cambridge won by 195	1957	Cambridge won by inns. and 186

Sixty-nine three-figure innings have been played in the University matches. For those scored before 1919 see 1940 *Wisden*. Those subsequent to 1919 include the four highest as shown here:—

238*	..	Nawab of Pataudi	..	1931	Oxford
211	..	G. Goonesena ..	..	1957	Cambridge
201*	..	M. J. K. Smith	..	1954	Oxford
201	..	A. Ratcliffe	..	1931	Cambridge
193	..	D. C. H. Townsend	..	1934	Oxford
170	..	M. Howell	..	1919	Oxford
167	..	B. W. Hone	..	1932	Oxford
157	..	D. R. Wilcox ..	..	1932	Cambridge
149	..	J. T. Morgan	..	1929	Cambridge
146	..	R. O'Brien	..	1956	Cambridge

Signifies not out.

145*	..	H. E. Webb	..	1948	Oxford
142	..	M. P. Donnelly	..	1946	Oxford
136	..	E. T. Killick ..	..	1930	Cambridge
135	..	H. A. Pawson ..	..	1947	Oxford
129	..	H. J. Enthoven	..	1925	Cambridge
127	..	D. S. Sheppard	..	1952	Cambridge
124	..	A. K. Judd ..	..	1927	Cambridge
124	..	A. T. Ratcliffe	..	1932	Cambridge
122	..	P. A. Gibb ..	..	1938	Cambridge
121	..	J. N. Grover ..	..	1937	Oxford
118	..	H. Ashton ..	..	1921	Cambridge
118	..	D. R. W. Silk ..	..	1954	Cambridge
117	..	M. J. K. Smith	..	1956	Oxford
116*	..	D. R. W. Silk ..	..	1953	Cambridge
116	..	M. C. Cowdrey	..	1953	Oxford
115	..	A. W. Allen ..	..	1934	Cambridge
114	..	J. F. Pretlove	..	1955	Cambridge
113	..	E. R. T. Holmes	..	1927	Oxford
111*	..	G. W. Cook ..	..	1957	Cambridge
109	..	C. H. Taylor ..	..	1923	Oxford
108	..	F. G. H. Chalk	..	1934	Oxford
106	..	Nawab of Pataudi	..	1929	Oxford
104	..	H. J. Enthoven	..	1924	Cambridge
104	..	M. J. K. Smith	..	1955	Oxford
102*	..	A. P. F. Chapman	..	1922	Cambridge
101*	..	R. W. V. Robins	..	1928	Cambridge
101	..	N. W. D. Yardley	..	1937	Cambridge
100	..	P. J. Dickinson	..	1939	Cambridge

* *Signifies not out.*

For other particulars see Records.

ETON v. HARROW

July 12, 13. Drawn. Although rain spoiled the match, interfering with play on both days, there were some excellent individual performances with honours going to Eton. Vargas, stylish and forceful, was Harrow's best batsman. After the ruined first day on which Harrow scored 101 for four, he and his colleagues played into the hands of Lane-Fox, a clever slow left-arm bowler, in justifiably forcing the pace in an effort to obtain a decision on the first innings. Clegg, a fine stroke-player who drove powerfully, and Burrows, another aggressive batsman, placed Eton in a strong position by tea when they wanted only five more runs for the lead with five wickets in hand. Rain caused a hold-up, but Eton managed to go ahead before a downpour finished the game. Burrows took out his bat for a splendid 68. A road accident some weeks earlier kept H. C. Blofield, the Eton captain, out of the match, and in his absence the College was led by E. J. Lane-Fox.

Harrow

N. F. Nicholson c and b Fellows..	29	P. W. Faith c Burrow b Fellows..	9
A. J. Anderson c and b Scott.....	24	M. J. H. Weedon b Lane-Fox....	2
A. B. Cable b Ayer.............	5	B. S. Raper not out	0
J. D. C. Vargas c Leonard b Lane-Fox	50	B 5, l-b 5, n-b 4 w 2	16
D. R. J. Foster c Baskervyle-Clegg b Duning	19		
J. B. Lockett c Ayer b Lane-Fox..	29	1/37 2/61 3/67 (9 wkts., dec.)	183
L. J. Champniss c Leonard b Lane-Fox	0	4/94 5/152 6/152 7/175 8/183 9/183	

P. E. d'Abo did not bat.

Eton

W. G. A. Clegg c Weedon b Raper	77	T. Pilkington b d'Abo 5
J. Baskervyle-Clegg b Champniss..	18	R. Fellows not out 8
E. J. Lane-Fox c and b Faith......	9	B 15, l-b 3, w 1 19
A. R. B. Burrows not out	68	
J. W. Leonard b Raper	0	1/69 2/88 3/153 4/155 (6 wkts.) 204
P. Baring b Weedon	0	5/158 6/204

E. J. R. Scott, M. L. Dunning and J. D. Ayer did not bat.

Eton Bowling

	O.	M.	R.	W.
Scott	15	2	35	1
Pilkington.....	10	0	21	0
Fellows	27.1	10	55	2
Ayer	3	0	8	1
Lane-Fox	17	10	14	4
Dunning	12	3	34	1

Harrow Bowling

	O.	M.	R.	W.
Raper	15	7	34	2
Weedon	14	4	25	1
d'Abo	21	4	55	1
Champniss	21	6	45	1
Faith	6	1	26	1

Umpires: A. Thompson and G. D. Morton.

ETON v. HARROW MATCHES

Of the 122 matches played Eton have won 46, Harrow 38 and 38 have been drawn. This is the generally published record, but Harrow men object very strongly to the first game in 1805 being treated as a regular contest between the two schools, contending that it is no more correct to count that one than the fixture in 1857 which has been rejected.

The matches played during the war years 1915–1918 and 1940–1945 are not reckoned as belonging to the regular series.

Results since the first world war:—

1919	Eton won by 202 runs	1935	Drawn
1920	Eton won by nine wickets	1936	Drawn
1921	Eton won by seven wickets	1937	Eton won by seven wickets
1922	Drawn	1938	Drawn
1923	Drawn	1939	Harrow won by eight wickets
1924	Drawn	1946	Drawn
1925	Drawn	1947	Drawn
1926	Drawn	1948	Drawn
1927	Drawn	1949	Eton won by seven wickets
1928	Eton won by 28 runs	1950	Drawn
1929	Drawn	1951	Drawn
1930	Eton won by eight wickets	1952	Harrow won by seven wickets
1931	Eton won by inns. and 16 runs	1953	Eton won by ten wickets
1932	Drawn	1954	Harrow won by nine wickets
1933	Drawn	1955	Eton won by 38 runs
1934	Drawn	1956	Drawn
		1957	Drawn

For other particulars see Records.

Forty three-figure innings have been played in matches between these two schools. Those since 1918:—

159 E. W. Dawson	(in 1923), Eton	104 R. Pulbrook	(in 1932), Harrow
158 I. Akers-Douglas	(in 1928), Eton	103 L. G. Crawley	(in 1921), Harrow
153 N. S. Hotchkin	(in 1931), Eton	103 T. Hare	(in 1947), Eton
135 J. Atkinson-Clark	(in 1930), Eton	102*P. H. Stewart-Brown	(in 1923), Harrow
115 E. Crutchley	(in 1939), Harrow	102 R. V. C. Robins	(in 1953), Eton
112 A. W. Allen	(in 1931), Eton	100 R. H. Cobbold	(in 1923), Eton
111 R. A. Holt	(in 1937), Harrow	100*P. V. F. Cazalet	(in 1926), Eton
109 K. F. H. Hale	(in 1929), Eton	100 A. N. A. Boyd	(in 1934), Eton
109 N. S. Hotchkin	(in 1932), Eton	100*P. M. Studd	(in 1935), Harrow
107 W. N. Coles	(in 1946), Eton	100 S. D. D. Sainsbury	(in 1947), Eton

In 1904, D. C. Boles, of Eton, making 183, set up a new record for the match, beating the 152 obtained in 1841 by Emilius Bayley, afterwards the Rev. Sir John Robert Laurie, Eton. M. C. Bird, Harrow, in 1907, scored 100 not out and 131, the only batsman who has made two 100's in the match. N. S. Hotchkin, Eton, played the following innings: 1931, 153; 1932, 109 and 96; 1933, 88 and 12.

* Signifies not out.

GENTLEMEN v. PLAYERS

July 17, 18, 19. Drawn. The Players, set to make 291 in three and three-quarter hours, looked likely to succeed when they needed 91 in the last hour with seven wickets in hand, but in the event they had to fight to play out time. Sheppard, in only his second first-class game of the summer, quickly settled down with Peter Richardson after a delayed start. Further rain curtailed the first day to two hours' play, and after another delay on the second day, wickets tumbled on a lifting pitch. Trueman, Laker and Hollies caused the last nine wickets of the Gentlemen to fall for 71 runs, but the amateur fast-medium bowlers, Warr, Smith and Dexter, were even more effective. Dexter, the Cambridge Blue, who had previously taken only 18 wickets in first-class cricket, gave particular trouble, and the Players, with nine wickets down, declared at their lowest score for well over a hundred years. Then the pitch rolled out easier, and aggressive batting by Insole, who hit Laker for 20 in one over, enabled May to declare. Smith, who batted two and a quarter hours and hit thirteen 4's, and Gardner laid a sound foundation with a stand of 145, but Dexter again brought about a collapse of the middle batting, and in the end Trueman and Hollies were left to play out the last ten minutes. Denis Compton captained the Players in his last season as a professional.

Gentlemen

P. E. Richardson hit wkt b Trueman	47	— c Evans b Hollies	13
Rev. D. S. Sheppard c Smith b Trueman	55	— c Compton b Trueman	24
D. J. Insole c Trueman b Tyson	21	— not out	79
P. B. H. May c Graveney b Trueman	5	— c Trueman b Laker	8
M. C. Cowdrey b Trueman	6	— lbw b Hollies	8
E. R. Dexter b Laker	13	— st Evans b Smith	13
G. Goonesena b Hollies	6		
C. S. Smith c Compton b Hollies	0		
J. J. Warr st Evans b Laker	0	— st Evans b Laker	13
R. G. Marlar run out	4		
E. B. Lewis not out	9		
B 2, l-b 1	3	B 4, l-b 5	9
	169	(6 wkts., dec.)	**167**

1/87 2/113 3/131 4/131 5/138 6/152
7/156 8/156 9/156

1/34 2/41
3/79 4/87 5/110 6/167

Players

D. V. Smith c Richardson b Dexter	....	19	— c May b Goonesena	102
T. H. Clark c Goonesena b Smith	......	0	— b Smith	 10
F. C. Gardner b Smith	....	0	— c Lewis b Goonesena	 48
T. W. Graveney c Goonesena b Warr	..	6	— run out	 24
D. C. S. Compton c Cowdrey b Dexter	.	6	— c Lewis b Dexter	 26
D. W. Richardson c Lewis b Dexter	....	0	— lbw b Dexter	 2
T. G. Evans c Smith b Dexter	......	7	— c May b Dexter	 4
F. H. Tyson c Goonesena b Dexter	....	0	— b Smith	 2
J. C. Laker c May b Warr	....	7	— c Lewis b Warr	 5
F. S. Trueman not out	....	1	— not out	 3
W. E. Hollies (did not bat)	....	—	— not out	 1
			B 6, l-b 7, w 1, n-b 1 ..	15

1/0 2/0 3/11 4/24 5/30   (9 wkts., dec.) 46   1/11 2/156   (9 wkts.) 242
6/33 7/33 8/38 9/46   3/169 4/207 5/217 6/225
                                                7/225 8/230 9/234

Players Bowling

	O.	M.	R.	W.	O.	M.	R.	W.
Trueman	18	8	38	4	 10	2	25	1
Tyson	15	4	51	1	 9	1	37	0
Hollies	18	6	39	2	 10	1	26	2
Laker	18	6	38	2	 18	5	54	2
Smith					2.5	0	16	1

Gentlemen Bowling

	O.	M.	R.	W.	O.	M.	R.	W.
Warr	10.2	4	23	2	20	7	63	1
Smith	5	1	15	2	16	7	31	2
Dexter	5	2	8	5	12	2	47	3
Marlar					3	0	25	0
Goonesena					13	2	61	2

Umpires: A. E. Pothecary and W. F. Price.

HUNDREDS FOR GENTLEMEN AND PLAYERS AT LORD'S

GENTLEMEN

102*	W. Ward	1825	124	D. J. Knight	1919
134*	W. G. Grace	1868	101	P. G. H. Fender	1921
109	W. G. Grace	1870	160	A. P. F. Chapman	1922
112	W. G. Grace	1872	122	G. T. S. Stevens	1923
163	W. G. Grace	1873	120	M. D. Lyon	1923
152	W. G. Grace	1875	129	G. T. S. Stevens	1925
169	W. G. Grace	1876	108	A. P. F. Chapman	1926
103	A. W. Ridley	1876	123	D. R. Jardine	1927
107	A. P. Lucas	1882	125 103* }	K. S. Duleepsinhji	1930
100	C. T. Studd	1882			
107	E. F. S. Tylecote	1883	165	Nawab of Pataudi	1932
118	W. G. Grace	1895	132	K. S. Duleepsinhji	1932
104	C. B. Fry	1899	104*	R. E. S. Wyatt	1934
102* 136 }	R. E. Foster	1900	175*	H. T. Bartlett	1938
			162*	M. P. Donnelly	1947
126	C. B. Fry	1901	122	F. R. Brown	1950
232*	C. B. Fry	1903	119*	P. B. H. May	1951
168*	A. C. MacLaren	1903	127	C. H. Palmer	1952
121	K. S. Ranjitsinhji	1904	117	R. T. Simpson	1953
114	R. H. Spooner	1906	154	C. H. Palmer	1955

PLAYERS

113*	T. Beagley	1821	154*	J. B. Hobbs	1911
100	J. Saunders	1827	113	J. B. Hobbs	1919
132	Thomas Hayward	1860	108	C. P. Mead	1921
112*	Thomas Hayward	1863	140	J. B. Hobbs	1922
122*	Thomas Hearne	1866	162	A. C. Russell	1922
102	Richard Daft	1872	118	J. B. Hobbs	1924
111	Arthur Shrewsbury	1887	113	R. Kilner	1924
130*	W. Barnes	1889	140	J. B. Hobbs	1925
103	W. Gunn	1892	163	J. B. Hobbs	1926
116*	T. W. Hayward	1896	131	E. Tyldesley	1926
125	Arthur Shrewsbury	1897	107	H. Sutcliffe	1926
139	W. Gunn	1898	161*	J. B. Hobbs	1931
163	J. T. Brown	1900	110	W. R. Hammond	1932
111	T W. Hayward	1900	120	A. Mitchell	1934
140	J. T. Tyldesley	1901	105	C. Washbrook	1946
141	L. C. Braund	1902	101	C. Washbrook	1947
100	W. H. Lockwood	1902	132*	L. Hutton	1948
139	A. E. Knight	1903	123	H. E. Dollery	1950
104 109* }	J. H. King	1904	150	D. C. S. Compton	1951
			115	M. Tompkin	1955
123*	T. W. Hayward	1905	102	D. V. Smith	1957
146*	T. W. Hayward	1907			

* *Signifies not out.*

RESULTS AT LORD'S

Since 1806, 132 matches have been played at Lord's. Gentlemen have won 41, Players 67, with 24 drawn.

Results since 1919:—

1919	Drawn	1936	Drawn
1920	Players won by seven wickets	1937	Players won by eight wickets
1921	Players won by nine wickets	1938	Gentlemen won by 133 runs
1922	Drawn	1939	Players won by 160 runs
1923	Drawn	1946	Players won by innings and 140 runs
1924	Players won by innings and 231 runs	1947	Drawn
1925	Drawn	1948	Players won by seven wickets
1926	Drawn	1949	Players won by four wickets
1927	Drawn	1950	Drawn
1928	Players won by nine wickets	1951	Players won by 21 runs
1929	Players won by seven wickets	1952	Players won by two runs
1930	Drawn	1953	Gentlemen won by 95 runs
1931	Drawn	1954	Players won by 49 runs
1932	Drawn	1955	Players won by 20 runs
1933	Players won by ten wickets	1956	Drawn
1934	Gentlemen won by seven wickets	1957	Drawn
1935	Players won by nine wickets		

BEAUMONT v. ORATORY

July 27. Beaumont won by six wickets. Oratory 158 (M. Hasslacher 72, H. Stevens four for 24); Beaumont 159 for four wickets (B. L. Baker 53).

CLIFTON v. TONBRIDGE

July 29, 30. Clifton won by 100 runs. Stronger in all departments they well deserved success. Bernard, their captain, played a notable part in the victory with a century that was full of attractive forcing strokes and came in just over two hours. Prideaux, the Tonbridge captain, drove powerfully when his side were set to make 272, but although he hit fourteen 4's in 89 his effort was in vain.

Cottrell, lively and accurate, made a valuable contribution to Clifton's win. His dismissal of the Tonbridge opening pair in the first over of the first innings without a run scored gave his team a mastery which they never relaxed.

Clifton

J. R. Bernard c Rylands b Evans	18	— c Evans b Page	104
D. J. Carter b Page	1	— b Meredith	19
M. F. King b Giles	14	— run out	37
C. J. U. Coates b Evans	12	— st Smith b Hudson	0
C. H. Pickwoad lbw b Hudson	15	— b Page	0
J. Cottrell c Evans b Giles	9	— st Smith b Hudson	10
R. W. Mathias c Prideaux b Meredith	12	— b Page	6
G. I. Arthurs b Meredith	16	— not out	24
T. D. Holloway c Giles b Meredith	13	— c Smith b Hudson	5
J. M. Cleese not out	13	— not out	13
M. H. Filer run out	5		
B 9, l-b 1, n-b 1	11	B 3, l-b 4, w 2	9

1/14 2/24 3/38 4/56 5/75 6/81   **139**
7/102 8/105 9/126

1/64 2/168   **(8 wkts., dec.) 227**
3/168 4/168 5/168 6/175
7/185 8/203

Tonbridge

M. S. Connell b Cottrell	0	— lbw b Bernard	9
J. H. Foskett c Pickwoad b Cottrell	24	— c King b Filer	13
R. M. Prideaux c Pickwoad b Cottrell	0	— c Pickwoad b Cottrell	89
J. H. M. MacKinnon b Bernard	8	— st Pickwoad b Mathias	2
P. D. Rylands c Coates b Bernard	4	— b Mathias	14
A. B. E. Hudson b Cottrell	6	— c and b Mathias	5
R. H. C. Page b Filer	5	— c Holloway b Mathias	2
R. M. Giles lbw b Bernard	15	— lbw b Arthurs	21
D. J. Evans st Pickwoad b Mathias	10	— b Cottrell	4
P. Meredith c Cleese b Arthurs	9	— not out	8
M. G. M. Smith not out	10	— c Pickwoad b Cottrell	1
B 3, l-b 1	4	L-b 3	3

1/0 2/0 3/13 4/25 5/36 6/55 7/63   **95**
8/68 9/74

1/16 2/26 3/46 4/52 5/56   **171**
6/116 7/127 8/146 9/154

Tonbridge Bowling

	O.	M.	R.	W.	O.	M.	R.	W.
Meredith	17	6	33	3	12	3	42	1
Page	8	4	18	1	20	6	69	3
Evans	10	2	27	2	8	0	44	0
Hudson	9	3	22	1	17	3	49	3
Giles	9	1	28	2	6	1	14	0

Clifton Bowling

	O.	M.	R.	W.	O.	M.	R.	W.
Cottrell	16	3	28	4	17.1	3	41	3
Bernard	16	6	28	3	8	1	22	1
Filer	8	4	12	1	14	4	38	1
Mathias	6	2	22	1	17	6	28	4
Arthurs	1.4	0	1	1	10	6	11	1
Cleese					9	2	28	0

Umpires: W. Harrington and H. Sharp.

CLIFTON V. TONBRIDGE RESULTS

First played at Lord's in 1914, Clifton winning by nine wickets.
Of 33 matches played at Lord's from 1919, Tonbridge have won 14, Clifton 8 10 drawn, one abandoned.

RUGBY v. MARLBOROUGH

July 31, August 1. Drawn. Defensive, rather than forcing, batting and steady bowling were the keynotes in a game which ended disappointingly. Marlborough did not accept a challenge to make 218 at 70 runs an hour, and though Rugby used eight bowlers they failed to dispose of dour rivals of whom Pyemont was soundest. Colville was Rugby's best batsman.

Rugby

M. F. Attenborough c Goodfellow b Morris	22	— c Flecker b Bell	23
T. B. L. Coghlan b Compton	0	— c Bell b Compton	20
P. D. Snell b Bell	40	— lbw b Reiss	9
P. R. Colville c Marr b Bell	68	— not out	57
P. C. H. Faure lbw b Reiss	2	— lbw b Bell	0
M. C. L. Coghlan c Pyemont b Bell	42	— run out	14
J. L. Cuthbertson b Morris	21		
H. M. Fox lbw b Bell	4		
S. J. Y. Robinson b Morris	3	— not out	13
J. O. Trumper run out	11		
R. W. J. Gemmell not out	6		
B 11, l-b 5, w 1	17	B 6, l-b 1	7

1/1 2/57 3/95 4/118 5/186 6/195   236   1/23 2/30   (5 wkts., dec.) 143
7/208 8/211 9/222   3/35 4/87 5/115

Marlborough

A. Goodfellow b T. Coghlan	14	b Cuthbertson	13
J. W. Flecker b Cuthbertson	9	— b Gemmell	17
P. Pyemont c and b A. Coghlan	38	— not out	50
C. A. Morris c T. Coghlan b A. Coghlan	27	— st Morgan b Trumper	13
B. A. C. Marr c A. Coghlan b Cuthbertson	34	— c Colville b A. Coghlan	8
J. J. Hall-Smith c and b Trumper	4	— not out	14
J. C. Pison lbw b A. Coghlan	1		
P. L. Bell b A. Coghlan	1		
C. R. Reiss b Cuthbertson	1		
D. P. de C. Morgan not out	3		
F. H. Compton c and b A. Coghlan	4		
B 18, l-b 5, n-b 1	24	B 1, n-b 1	2

1/27 2/35 3/96 4/104 5/125 6/130   162   1/20 2/34   (4 wkts.) 117
7/144 8/152 9/153   3/54 4/69

Marlborough Bowling

	O.	M.	R.	W.		O.	M.	R.	W.
Compton	14	1	47	1		15	4	51	1
Bell	22	4	49	4		14	3	30	2
Morris	11.4	2	38	3		1	0	4	0
Goodfellow	7	1	30	0					
Reiss	20	3	55	1		19	3	51	1

Rugby Bowling

	O.	M.	R.	W.		O.	M.	R.	W.
T. Coghlan	22	3	44	1		14	4	38	0
Gemmell	5	2	9	0		8	3	20	1
Cuthbertson	21	11	28	3		9	6	8	1
Robinson	5	0	15	0		2	0	4	0
A. Coghlan	20.4	5	37	5		16	6	28	1
Trumper	1	0	5	1		11	3	16	1
Colville						0.2	0	1	0
Attenborough						2	2	0	0

Umpires: H. Sharp and A. Thompson.

RUGBY v. MARLBOROUGH RESULTS

Of 98 matches, Rugby have won 42 and Marlborough 29; 26 drawn, one abandoned. The match was first played in 1855. All matches, excepting the following, were played at Lord's: Oval—1857, 1863, 1867; Middlesex Ground, Islington—1864; Rugby—1868, 1915, 1917; Marlborough—1870, 1916, 1918, 1944. No match took place in 1858, 1859 and 1861 owing to the weakness of Marlborough cricket in those early years, and in 1940 and 1947 when Rugby were unable to play.

CHELTENHAM v. HAILEYBURY AND I.S.C.

August 2, 3. Cheltenham won by 89 runs. Their first school victory for three years was well deserved by good all-round work. Terdre batted vigorously and Lynch Staunton proved his worth with bat and ball. Haileybury failed to make the best use of Ledger's clever off-break bowling. Haileybury never looked capable of scoring 241 in three hours for victory.

Cheltenham

P. W. F. Stutchbury b Roberts	0	— c Golding b Roberts	13
C. M. Brain c Roberts b Ledger	16	— b Ledger	27
R. C. H. Terdre st Golding b Ledger	56	— b Ledger	65
R. K. O. Carey b Roberts	15	— lbw b Ledger	14
G. L. Prain b Roberts	46	— c and b Ledger	19
C. R. Purvis b Ledger	3	— b Roberts	11
T. G. Lynch Staunton not out	58		
B. Lowe c Crichton b Roberts	24	— not out	7
C. G. Hoole b Roberts	0	— c Smith b Ledger	0
A. F. Benke not out	6		
B 1, l-b 8, w 5	14	B 3, w 1	4

1/0 2/72 3/91 4/99   (8 wkts., dec.) 238
5/108 6/169 7/224 8/229

1/34 2/54   (7 wkts., dec.) 160
3/100 4/131 5/152 6/160
7/160

A. J. Boddy did not bat.

Haileybury and I.S.C.

J. G. Lofting c Benke b Lynch Staunton	33	— c Benke b Boddy	41
M. Higginbottom c Lynch Staunton b Lowe	0	— b Lynch Staunton	1
D. Moeller b Lowe	25	— b Benke	29
P. J. Parsons c Lynch Staunton b Boddy	12	— lbw b Lynch Staunton	10
D. A. Crichton st Brain b Boddy	11	— b Hoole	5
I. A. McDonald c Terdre b Benke	23	— b Benke	3
I. N. Smith c Hoole b Lynch Staunton	26	— c Brain b Lynch Staunton	7
A. G. Roberts lbw b Lowe	15	— b Lowe	7
C. J. Ledger b Benke	0	— c Brain b Benke	21
J. E. Denison lbw b Benke	0	— c Benke b Lowe	12
R. W. Golding not out	1	— not out	0
B 11, l-b 1	12	B 12, l-b 2, w 1	15

1/5 2/47 3/72 4/74 5/85 6/142   158
7/142 8/142 9/142

1/6 2/60 3/84 4/89 5/93   151
6/105 7/105 8/133 9/147

Haileybury and I.S.C. Bowling

	O.	M.	R.	W.		O.	M.	R.	W.
Roberts	26	7	48	5	....	13	1	50	2
Smith	10	2	37	0	....	4	1	9	0
Moeller	8	1	16	0					
McDonald	8	1	34	0	....	2	0	7	0
Ledger	22	5	44	3	....	17.3	2	43	5
Denison	7	0	30	0	....	3	0	29	0
Parsons	7	4	15	0	....	4	1	18	0

Cheltenham Bowling

	O.	M.	R.	W.	O.	M.	R.	W.
Lowe	14.5	2	37	3	10.5	3	34	2
Hoole	5	0	22	0	6	3	6	1
Benke	14	2	40	3	18	6	46	3
Lynch Staunton	16	6	31	2	14	7	21	3
Boddy	7	2	16	2	12	3	28	1
Prain					4	3	1	0

Umpires: B. L. Muncer and A. Thompson.

CHELTENHAM v. HAILEYBURY RESULTS

Of the 60 matches played from 1893, Haileybury have won 19 and Cheltenham 18; 22 drawn, one abandoned.

SOUTHERN SCHOOLS v. THE REST

August 5, 6. Drawn. The splendid batting of Drybrough, of Highgate, overshadowed other performances. Particularly powerful in his off-driving and skilful in cutting, Drybrough scored 128 in three hours in Southern Schools' first innings and hit sixteen 4's. The Rest, for whom Luckin, Kirby and Cook batted well, set their opponents to make 157 in two hours, but although Owen-Hughes bowled cleverly and quickly gained wickets Southern Schools were not troubled to draw. Pataudi made some pleasing strokes. Allom, 6 ft. 10½ in. in height, and son of M. J. C. Allom, the former Surrey and England player, bowled at a good pace for Southern Schools.

The Rest

R. A. C. Luckin b Allom	41	— c and b Pickering	49
P. J. Kippax c Sharman b Clarke	21	— lbw b Drybrough	24
D. Kirby b Allom	51	— run out	22
G. Atkins c Sharman b Allom	7	— b Potter	35
H. E. Cook c Barnard b Allom	84	— c and b Allom	1
D. M. Green b Sharman	16	— b Potter	3
D. C. Eldridge b Drybrough	19	— not out	0
M. K. S. Shatrushalysinghi not out	4	— c and b Allom	0
B 13, l-b 3	16	B 4	4

1/37 2/104 3/123 (7 wkts., dec.) 259
4/126 5/162 6/232 7/259

1/77 2/77 (7 wkts., dec.) 138
3/128 4/129 5/137 6/138
7/138

C. D. R. Barker, H. G. Owen-Hughes and A. W. M. Bain did not bat.

Southern Schools

J. R. Bernard c Cook b Barker	0	— lbw b Owen-Hughes	10
G. J. Sharman lbw b Green	50	— not out	13
A. R. Day run out	3	— c and b Owen-Hughes	10
R. W. Lewis c Barker b Bain	4	— b Owen-Hughes	8
C. D. Drybrough not out	128	— c Cook b Owen-Hughes	12
Nawab of Pataudi c Cook b Barker	11	— not out	27
A. T. C. Allom b Green	5		
C. J. A. Clarke b Barker	33		
B 7, w 1	8		

1/0 2/9 3/15 4/152 (7 wkts., dec.) 242
5/187 6/196 7/242

1/19 2/20 3/38 (4 wkts.) 80
4/47

D. J. Pickering, I. P. Morton and I. C. Potter did not bat.

Southern Schools Bowling

	O.	M.	R.	W.		O.	M	R.	W.
Clarke	17	4	43	1	....	7	3	8	0
Allom	22.3	6	45	4	....	10.4	1	32	2
Bernard	2	0	10	0					
Potter	18	6	38	0	....	14	6	31	2
Pickering	15	7	38	0	....	12	3	31	1
Sharman	18	0	42	1	....	3	1	7	0
Drybrough	5	2	27	1	....	6	2	25	1

Rest Bowling

	O.	M.	R.	W.		O.	M	R.	W.
Barker	23	4	67	3	....	10	1	26	0
Bain	9	4	12	1					
Shatrushalysinghi	8	1	25	0					
Eldridge	11	2	36	0					
Owen-Hughes	11	1	40	0	....	11	1	43	4
Kippax	5	0	32	0	....	2	0	10	0
Green	7	2	22	0					
Atkins	3	2	1	0					

Umpires: H. P. Sharp and W. Harrington.

COMBINED SERVICES v. PUBLIC SCHOOLS

August 7, 8. Drawn. An interesting game, which ended with Public Schools needing only nine runs for victory, produced much excellent batting. Subba Row drove powerfully for his 127 made in two and a half hours, and Sharpe and Shirreff, the Combined Services captain, showed attractive stroke-play. Pataudi was forceful and stylish for Public Schools, and Cook and Allom used the long handle effectively.

Combined Services

A. B. D. Parsons run out	8	— b Potter	0
P. J. Sharpe c Luckin b Drybrough	80	— c Luckin b Green	60
M. L. Y. Ainsworth c Drybrough b Potter	1	— b Owen-Hughes	0
R. Subba Row c Allom b Owen-Hughes	127	— not out	8
C. A. Atkinson b Allom	4	— not out	10
A. C. Shirreff not out	71		
W. J. Foster not out	16	— b Potter	13
M. D. Fenner (did not bat)		— st Cook b Green	26
B 10, l-b 6, w 2	18	L-b 7	7

1/39 2/49 3/135   (5 wkts., dec.) 325   1/0 2/30   (5 wkts., dec.) 124
4/160 5/276   3/31 4/99 5/107

G. H. Hill, K. B. Standring and B. Knight did not bat.

Public Schools

E. A. G. Luckin c Fenner b Standring	5	— c Fenner b Standring	12
G. J. Sharman b Standring	10	— run out	41
D. K rby c Hill b Shirreff	40	— b Hill	36
C. D. Drybrough b Knight	8	— c and b Hill	20
Nawab of Pataudi b Hill	71	— c Subba Row b Shirreff	2
G. Atkins c Fenner b Atkinson	10	— not out	14
M. S. Cook not out	79	— not out	17
A. T. C. Allom run out	55	— c Fenner b Shirreff	0
H. G. Owen-Hughes (did not bat)		— c Sharpe b Knight	9
B 5, w 1, n-b 1	7	L-b 4, n-b 1	5

1/18 2/19 3/43 4/78   (7 wkts., dec.) 285   1/18 2/83 3/107   (7 wkts.) 156
5/125 6/176 7/283   4/110 5/116 6/116 7/130

D. M. Green and I. C. Potter did not bat.

Public Schools Bowling

	O.	M.	R.	W.		O.	M.	R.	W.
Owen-Hughes ..	17	0	107	1	....	8	0	26	1
Potter	8	2	26	1	....	10	3	29	2
Allom	23	5	85	1	....	2	0	15	0
Green	10	1	55	0	....	4	0	28	2
Drybrough	10	1	31	1	....	4	1	19	0
Sharman	1	0	3	0					

Combined Services Bowling

	O.	M.	R.	W.		O.	M.	R.	W.
Knight	22	7	50	1	....	12	1	47	1
Standring	25	11	46	2	....	12	0	48	1
Subba Row ...	13	3	31	0	....	1	0	6	0
Shirreff	12.2	4	45	1	....	6	2	15	2
Ainsworth	4	0	13	0					
Hill	11	3	32	1	....	6	0	35	2
Atkinson	9	4	13	1					
Foster.........	5	0	37	0					
Parsons	2	0	11	0					

Umpires: B. L. Muncer and G. D. Morton.

ROYAL NAVY v. THE ARMY

August 9, 10. Drawn. Royal Navy 85 (D. Goodson five for 39); The Army 37 for two.

THE ARMY v. R.A.F.

August 12, 13. Abandoned without a ball bowled.

THE COUNTY CHAMPIONSHIP IN 1957

A change of captaincy made no difference to Surrey's domination of the Championship. After winning the title five times under W. S. Surridge, they made it six in succession with P. B. H. May in charge. From 1887 to 1892 Surrey were Champions six times running, but they had to share the honour with Lancashire and Nottinghamshire in 1899. Surrey therefore became the first county to win the Championship outright in six consecutive years.

In some quarters a feeling grew that Surrey might have to fight harder for the honour in 1957 but this proved completely wrong and their success was easier than in the five previous years. The second county, Northamptonshire, finished as many as 94 points behind and the Surrey total of 312 points was the highest since 1950 when all counties started playing 28 matches. It must be remembered, however, that last season the system of scoring was changed. Bonus points were added so that the maximum a county could obtain from a match became 14 instead of 12. Surrey won 21 of their games and obtained bonus points from 24 matches.

Surrey went into first place on June 11 and as the season progressed they drew farther and farther away. It soon became obvious that no one could catch them and by August 16 the Championship had been decided. Since the last war only Warwickshire, in 1951, had won the title so early, also on August 16.

At first Lancashire looked like being strong challengers to Surrey. They began by winning their first five games and at the end of May were top of the table. They fell away so badly that from May 28 to June 21 not another point was gained. A good finish with three victories in their last five games helped them finish sixth.

Derbyshire took over first place for a week at the start of June, but they, too, found the pace too hot and eventually Northamptonshire became Surrey's closest rivals without ever threatening to overhaul them. Not since 1912 had Northamptonshire finished as high as second place.

Yorkshire, who looked a strong side at times, but lacked consistency, were third, a rise of four places compared with 1956. Others who made good advances were Derbyshire, who moved from eighth to fourth place, Essex, from eleventh to fifth and Somerset, fifteenth to eighth. Bad declines came from Worcestershire, ninth to sixteenth, Nottinghamshire, eighth to fifteenth, Hampshire, sixth to thirteenth and Gloucestershire, third to twelfth.

Without being particularly brilliant, the weather was a considerable improvement on that of the previous season. Only nine games ended without a decision on first innings compared with 20 in 1956.

FINAL POSITIONS

Points Awarded	Pld. —	Won 12	Lost —	Drn. —	No Desn. —	First Inns. Lead in Match Lost 2	First Inns. Lead in Drn. 2	Bonus Pts. 2	Pts. —
Surrey (1)	28	21	3	3	1	3	3	48	312
Northamptonshire (4)	28	15	2	10	1	0	8	22	218
Yorkshire (7)	28	13	1	11	0	0	5	24	190
Derbyshire (12)......	28	10	8	9	1	2	4	30	162
Essex (11)	28	11	6	10	1	0	5	16	158
Lancashire (2).......	28	10	8	8	2	2	4	24	156
Middlesex (5)	28	10	12	3	3	2	1	22	148
Somerset (15)	28	9	14	5	0	3	2	20	138
Glamorgan (13)	28	10	9	8	1	0	2	12	136
Sussex (9)	28	8	9	9	2	2	6	24	136
Warwickshire (14) ...	28	9	7	11	1	0	5	16	134
Gloucestershire (3) ..	28	8	13	6	1	1	5	24	132
Hampshire (6).......	28	7	12	8	1	1	5	20	116
Kent (16)	28	6	13	9	0	2	3	8	90
Nottinghamshire (8)..	28	5	13	9	1	3	4	14	88
Worcestershire (9) ...	28	4	9	14	1	1	4	8	72
Leicestershire (17) ...	28	2	16	9	1	2	5	2	40

Worcestershire's record includes six points awarded when they batted in fourth innings of drawn match with Sussex and the final scores were equal.

(Figures in brackets indicate 1956 positions.)

SCORING IN THE COUNTY CHAMPIONSHIP

The scheme for scoring in the County Championship was as follows:—

(a) In cases (b) to (f) below, if the side leading on the first innings has scored the faster in the first innings (to be judged by runs per over), it shall score a further 2 points.

(b) Should a match be finished the winning side to score 12 points.

(c) Should a match be finished and the scores be equal (a "Tie") each side to score 6 points.

(d) Should the scores be equal in a drawn match the side batting in the fourth innings to score 6 points in all (whether or not it has first innings lead) and the opponents to score no points, except they will retain such first innings points as they may already have gained.

(e) Should a match be finished, the side which leads on the first innings, if it loses the match, to score 2 points. If the scores on the first innings are equal, the side which loses the match to score 1 point.

(f) Should a match not be finished the side which leads on the first innings to score 2 points (subject to (c) above).

(g) Should a match not be finished and the scores of the first innings be equal, each side to score 1 point (subject to (c) above).

(h) Even should there be no play for any reason, or no result obtained on the first innings, every match shall be included in the table of results as a "match played"; in these cases neither side to score points.

(i) If there is no play in the first two-thirds (measured by playing hours) of a match, and it is not carried to a further conclusion than that of the first innings, the side which leads on the first innings shall score 8 points.

(j) The side which has the highest aggregate on points gained at the end of the season shall be the Champion County.

COUNTY CHAMPIONSHIP STATISTICS FOR 1957

County	FOR			AGAINST		
	Runs	Wickets	Average	Runs	Wickets	Average
Derbyshire.......	9666	413	23.40	9619	442	21.76
Essex	9718	425	22.86	9550	425	22.47
Glamorgan	8999	417	21.58	9187	406	22.62
Gloucestershire...	9534	428	22.27	9719	415	23.41
Hampshire.......	8908	420	21.20	9337	414	22.55
Kent	9909	448	22.11	10054	422	23.82
Lancashire.......	8364	412	20.30	8244	434	18.99
Leicestershire	8115	481	16.87	8479	337	25.16
Middlesex	9761	444	21.98	9126	433	21.07
Northamptonshire	9517	383	24.84	8881	462	19.22
Nottinghamshire .	10850	481	22.55	11007	379	29.04
Somerset	9179	456	20.12	9799	422	23.22
Surrey	8942	306	29.22	7758	535	14.50
Sussex	10234	436	23.47	10670	407	26.21
Warwickshire	10250	429	23.89	10185	428	23.79
Worcestershire ...	10297	415	24.81	10884	371	29.33
Yorkshire	9122	364	25.06	8866	426	20.81
	161365	7158	22.54	161365	7158	22.54

DERBYSHIRE

President—THE DUKE OF DEVONSHIRE

Secretary—W. T. TAYLOR, County Cricket Ground, Nottingham Road, Derby

Captain—D. B. CARR

L. Jackson   County Badge   D. C. Morgan

Derbyshire, severely criticised within the county in 1956 when they finished twelfth, responded by playing so much better that they rose to fourth place in the final Championship Table. The fine weather of May and June suited the team, and of the first twelve games seven were won and only two lost. At the beginning of June they headed the Championship, but the wetter second half of the season produced only three wins in sixteen Championship games. This emphasised two weaknesses. Several batsmen were ineffective on damp turf and the side lacked spin bowlers to take advantage of turning pitches. Perhaps the most pleasing feature of the season was a marked improvement in team-work and enterprise. D. B. Carr, the captain, who enjoyed a considerably more successful season with the bat, led his team capably.

Derbyshire owed much to the excellent all-round form of Morgan, who might well have completed the "double" if the weather had remained fine. He bowled medium-fast effectively in support of Gladwin and Jackson, batted with enterprise, and in addition held 43 catches, a record for the county apart from wicket-keepers.

Hamer, Kelly, Carr and Lee all comfortably exceeded 1,000 runs, with Kelly in particular batting much above his 1956 form. He gave freer rein to his stroke-play, and hit 500 more runs at a considerably increased scoring rate. Hamer displayed soundness, and his feat of carrying his bat for 112 not out in a total of 208 against Surrey at The Oval was one of the best innings in the

Championship. Kelly and Carr set up a third wicket partnership record for the county by making 246 against Leicestershire at Chesterfield. Revill fell below expectations, and was not re-engaged, but Johnson, a hard hitter, improved. Dawkes maintained a high standard of wicket-keeping, and, on occasions, made runs usefully.

Gladwin and Jackson, in his benefit year, yet again proved themselves one of the best opening bowling combinations in the country and they benefited from Morgan's better support. Gladwin passed Mitchell's record of 1,483 first-class wickets for the county, and Jackson exceeded 1,000 wickets. Rhodes, the promising young fast-medium bowler, underwent a shoulder operation early in the summer, and suffered ill-health afterwards. Smith's off-break bowling disappointed, for he showed a lack of flight, and Carr, able to turn his left-arm slows considerably, should perhaps have used himself more often to augment the spin attack.

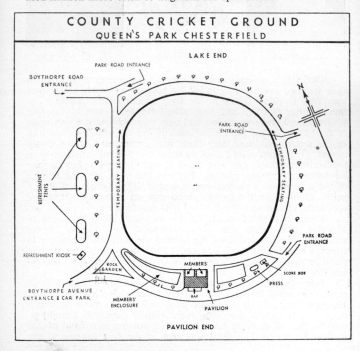

COUNTY CRICKET GROUND
QUEEN'S PARK CHESTERFIELD

LAKE END

PARK ROAD ENTRANCE

BOYTHORPE ROAD ENTRANCE

PARK ROAD ENTRANCE

N

TEMPORARY SEATING

TEMPORARY SEATING

REFRESHMENT TENTS

PARK ROAD ENTRANCE

REFRESHMENT KIOSK

ROCK GARDEN

MEMBERS'

SCORE BOX

PRESS

BOYTHORPE AVENUE ENTRANCE & CAR PARK

MEMBERS' ENCLOSURE

BAR

PAVILION

PAVILION END

DERBYSHIRE RESULTS

All First-Class Matches—Played 30, *Won* 11, *Lost* 9, *Drawn* 10
County Championship Matches—Played 28, *Won* 10, *Lost* 8,
Drawn 9, *No Decision* 1

COUNTY CHAMPIONSHIP AVERAGES
BATTING

	Birthplace	Mtchs.	Inns.	Not Outs	Runs	100's	Highest Inns.	Aver.
A. Hamer	*Huddersfield*	28	50	1	1593	4	138	32.51
J. Kelly	*Bacup*	28	50	4	1483	4	127	32.23
D. C. Morgan..	*Middlesex*	28	44	12	917	0	64*	28.65
H. L. Johnson..	*Barbados*	19	32	8	670	0	88*	27.91
D. B. Carr.....	*Wiesbaden*	27	44	3	1132	1	141	27.60
C. Lee	*Rotherham*	28	50	2	1103	0	83	22.97
I. M. Gibson..	*Glossop*	6	10	3	150	0	66*	21.42
A. C. Revill....	*Bolsover*	23	40	1	757	0	86	19.41
G. O. Dawkes..	*Leicester*	28	4	6	736	0	75	19.36
K. Mohan	*Glossop*	4	6	1	66	0	24*	13.20
C. Gladwin	*Doe Lea*	27	30	14	206	0	21	12.87
D. J. Green ...	*Burton-on-Trent*	4	6	0	73	0	50	12.16
D. J. Short.....	*Chesterfield*	3	5	0	49	0	22	9.80
E. Smith	*Grassover*	25	35	9	233	0	31*	8.96
H. J. Rhodes.	*Hadfield*	3	5	0	32	0	12	6.40
L. Jackson	*Whitwell*	25	29	3	89	0	24	3.42

Also batted: D. Hall (*Derby*) 0*.

* Signifies not out.

BOWLING

	Overs	Maidens	Runs	Wickets	Average
L. Jackson	944 .4	320	2071	129	16.05
C. Gladwin	839.5	334	1793	99	18.11
D. C. Morgan	851	287	2021	84	24.05
H. J. Rhodes...........	72.5	15	211	8	26.37
E. Smith	692	222	1806	68	26.55
I. M. Gibson	34	8	115	3	28.33
D. Hall	48	9	166	5	33.20
D. B. Carr	257	67	843	24	35.12
H. L. Johnson	9.1	0	41	1	41.00
A. C. Revill	73.4	21	248	6	41.33

Also bowled: A. Hamer 2—0—13—0; J. Kelly 1—0—5—0; C. Lee 7—1—22—0; K. Mohan 5—2—14—0.

Amateurs.—D. B. Carr, I. M. Gibson, D. J. Green, D. J. Short.

At Bradford, May 4, 6. DERBYSHIRE lost to YORKSHIRE by nine wickets.

At Leicester, May 11, 13. DERBYSHIRE beat LEICESTERSHIRE by an innings and 132 runs.

DERBYSHIRE v. ROYAL AIR FORCE

At Chesterfield, May 15, 16, 17. Drawn. Derbyshire 330 for seven wickets, dec. (C. Lee 135, D. B. Carr 56); Royal Air Force 139 (E. Smith six for 30) and 400 (G. Atkinson 111, R. Subba Row 85, P. Parfitt 69, Carr four for 50). (Not a First-Class match.)

DERBYSHIRE v. ESSEX

At Burton-on-Trent, May 18, 20. Derbyshire won by an innings and seven runs, taking 14 points. Essex, weakened by injuries and the absence of Insole, playing for M.C.C., fared badly after Bailey, acting as captain, decided to bat on a rain-affected pitch. Jackson, Gladwin and Morgan, the pace bowlers, found the conditions much to their liking. Bailey looked likely to dismiss Derbyshire almost as cheaply, but Revill, making aggressive strokes, and Johnson added 92 for the sixth wicket and ensured a useful lead. Jackson's persistent pace and accuracy brought defeat on the second day for Essex, whose chances were diminished by a mishap to Bailey. He retired after being struck on the right hand by Morgan, and an X-ray showed a cracked knuckle bone.

Essex

G. Barker c Carr b Gladwin	1	— c Johnson b Morgan	23
G. W. Horrex c Dawkes b Gladwin	20	— c Carr b Gladwin	0
B. Taylor c Carr b Gladwin	0	— c Kelly b Jackson	5
G. Smith c Revill b Gladwin	1	— c Dawkes b Jackson	9
T. E. Bailey c Revill b Jackson	2	— retired hurt	11
M. Bear c Dawkes b Morgan	13	— lbw b Jackson	30
B. Knight lbw b Jackson	0	— b Jackson	9
A. Durley c Morgan b Jackson	0	— c Dawkes b Jackson	16
R. Ralph c Carr b Morgan	15	— b Jackson	8
K. C. Preston b Gladwin	20	— lbw b Jackson	0
I. King not out	8	— not out	0
		B 1	1

1/5 2/7 3/8 4/11 5/33 6/37 7/37 8/38   80   1/4 2/13 3/31 4/50 5/63   112
9/64 (1.50 an over)   6/101 7/111 8/111 9/112

Derbyshire

A. Hamer c King b Bailey	2	E. Smith run out	0
C. Lee c Taylor b Bailey	11	C. Gladwin c Taylor b Bailey	5
J. Kelly c Ralph b Preston	24	L. Jackson b Bailey	0
A. C. Revill b Bailey	86	B 4, l-b 5, w 1, n-b 1	11
D. B. Carr c Barker b Bailey	2		
G. O. Dawkes c Smith b Bailey	4		
H. L. Johnson c Taylor b Ralph	41	1/2 2/27 3/75 4/79 5/85 6/177 199
D. C. Morgan not out	13	7/181 8/181 9/195 (2.88 an over)

Derbyshire Bowling

	O.	M.	R.	W.	O.	M.	R.	W.
Jackson	19	7	32	3	.... 23.3	11	38	7
Gladwin	23	14	24	5	 22	13	40	1
Morgan	9.3	2	24	2	 14	4	32	1
Smith	1	1	0	0	 2	1	1	0

Essex Bowling

	O.	M.	R.	W.
Bailey	30.5	12	61	7
Preston	27	2	85	1
Ralph	9	0	38	1
Knight	2	0	4	0

Umpires: L. H. Gray and D. Davies.

DERBYSHIRE v. YORKSHIRE
(L. Jackson's Benefit)

At Burton-on-Trent, May 25, 27, 28. Derbyshire won by 84 runs, taking 14 points. Jackson, with eleven wickes for 114 runs in his benefit match, helped in a notable victory. Kelly, batting four and a half hours, Lee and Carr all showed confidence on the first day, but Yorkshire batted unimpressively, apart from a brilliant innings by Close, who hit three 6's and sixteen 4's. Carr and Dawkes severely punished the bowling before Carr declared Derbyshire's second innings, and Jackson rounded off a most pleasing match for himself by taking the last Yorkshire wicket with seven minutes left for play.

Derbyshire

A. Hamer b Platt	8	— lbw b Trueman	13
C. Lee c Trueman b Illingworth	39	— c Watson b Platt	2
J. Kelly c Watson b Wardle	106	— c Binks b Trueman	0
A. C. Revill c Close b Illingworth	9	— b Platt	15
D. B. Carr c Binks b Illingworth	40	— not out	92
G. O. Dawkes c Watson b Trueman	28	— b Trueman	75
H. L. Johnson c Taylor b Trueman	2	— not out	31
D. C. Morgan c Wilson b Taylor	21		
E. Smith c Sutcliffe b Wardle	16		
C. Gladwin not out	8		
L. Jackson b Trueman	1		
B 9, l-b 5	14	B 2, l-b 1	3

1/12 2/57 3/67 4/152 5/198 6/204   **292**   1/4 2/11   (5 wkts., dec.) **231**
7/242 8/277 9/291 (2.75 an over)   3/30 4/36 5/146

Yorkshire

D. B. Close st Dawkes b Smith	120	— b Jackson	11
K. Taylor b Jackson	20	— c Morgan b Jackson	5
J. V. Wilson b Gladwin	7	— c Hamer b Carr	40
R. Illingworth b Jackson	16	— c Dawkes b Jackson	44
W. Watson c Jackson b Gladwin	0	— b Revill	50
D. E. V. Padgett run out	2	— c Morgan b Carr	15
W. H. H. Sutcliffe c and b Gladwin	6	— not out	40
J. G. Binks c Lee b Jackson	2	— c Gladwin b Jackson	9
J. H. Wardle b Jackson	22	— c Morgan b Carr	0
F. S. Trueman b Jackson	2	— lbw b Jackson	0
R. K. Platt not out	1	— c Johnson b Jackson	17
B 1	1	B 4, l-b 5	9

1/65 2/107 3/145 4/149 5/161 6/165   **199**   1/13 2/20 3/97 4/107   **240**
7/173 8/175 9/188 (2.21 an over)   5/108 6/148 7/202 8/215
                                    9/215

Yorkshire Bowling

	O.	M.	R.	W.		O.	M.	R.	W.
Trueman	23.1	3	68	3	....	22	0	103	3
Platt	25	4	87	1	....	21	8	55	2
Taylor	19	7	31	1					
Illingworth	19	5	51	3	....	3	0	18	0
Wardle	17	7	30	2	....	9	3	27	0
Close	3	0	11	0	....	6	2	25	0

Derbyshire Bowling

	O.	M.	R.	W.		O.	M.	R.	W.
Jackson	28.4	7	51	5	....	29	11	63	6
Gladwin	29	7	57	3	....	13	2	42	0
Morgan	17	3	51	0	....	4	0	16	0
Smith	14	7	35	1	....	14	7	33	0
Carr	1	0	4	0	....	22	3	63	3
Revill					....	8	4	14	1

Umpires: T. W. Spencer and J. S. Buller.

DERBYSHIRE v. SUSSEX

At Derby, May 29, 30, 31. Derbyshire won by 197 runs, taking 14 points. Showing excellent form, Derbyshire were on top throughout the match. Hamer showing splendid concentration, laid the foundations of success with a solid innings in which he hit one 6 and ten 4's. Only Parks and Foreman showed much ability to resist a strong Derbyshire attack, and bright batting by Lee and Kelly enabled Derbyshire to declare for a second time. Jackson, Morgan and Carr, well supported in the field, saw that Sussex found no opportunity to recover.

Derbyshire

A. Hamer lbw b Smith	138	— lbw b Thomson	28
C. Lee b Bates	1	— c Smith b James	51
J. Kelly c Webb b Bates	36	— lbw b Thomson	62
A. C. Revill b Thomson	14	— b James	0
D. B. Carr b James	31	— c Webb b Thomson	14
G. O. Dawkes c Foreman b Smith	19	— c Webb b James	29
H. L. Johnson c Webb b Thomson	22	— not out	11
D. C. Morgan c Potter b Thomson	27	— not out	2
E. Smith c Suttle b Thomson	15		
C. Gladwin not out	4		
B 21, l-b 3	24	B 4, l-b 1	5

1/17 2/94 3/117 4/241   (9 wkts., dec.) 331
5/243 6/276 7/285 8/322 9/331 (3.15
an over)

1/72 2/94   (6 wkts., dec.) 202
3/100 4/133 5/188 6/190

L. Jackson did not bat.

Sussex

D. V. Smith c Dawkes b Jackson	13	— c Morgan b Jackson	3
L. J. Lenham c Dawkes b Jackson	4	— c Dawkes b Morgan	7
K. G. Suttle c Lee b Jackson	15	— c Revill b Jackson	18
J. M. Parks lbw b Smith	57	— c Dawkes b Jackson	20
G. Potter c Lee b Johnson	10	— c Revill b Morgan	12
D. J. Foreman c Kelly b Smith	50	— hit wkt b Morgan	28
N. I. Thomson c Gladwin b Smith	29	— c Revill b Morgan	0
R. T. Webb b Morgan	0	— c Morgan b Carr	21
A. E. James not out	24	— not out	4
D. L. Bates c and b James	5	— c Dawkes b Carr	6
R. G. Marlar c Johnson b Gladwin	4	— b Carr	0
L-b 1	1	L-b 5	5

1/8 2/21 3/62 4/94 5/102 6/166 7/174   212
8/182 9/207 (2.58 an over)

1/3 2/24 3/38 4/56 5/71   124
6/71 7/110 8/124 9/124

Sussex Bowling

	O.	M.	R.	W.		O.	M.	R.	W.
Bates	25	5	90	2	....	10	0	34	0
Thomson	30.3	8	68	4	....	28	5	87	3
James	25	5	79	1	....	20.5	2	72	3
Smith	21	6	57	2	....	3	1	4	0
Suttle	2	1	4	0					
Marlar	1	0	9	0					

Derbyshire Bowling

	O.	M.	R.	W.		O.	M.	R.	W.
Jackson	22	8	35	4	....	14	9	19	3
Gladwin	18.4	9	45	1	...	12	8	13	0
Morgan	19	7	43	1	...	17	5	39	4
Carr	5	1	27	0	....	6	1	30	3
Johnson	1	0	1	1					
Smith	16	4	60	3	....	9	1	18	0

Umpires: J. F. Crapp and W. Place.

At Liverpool, June 1, 3. DERBYSHIRE beat LANCASHIRE by an innings and 66 runs.

At Lord's, June 5, 6, 7. DERBYSHIRE beat MIDDLESEX by 163 runs.

At Birmingham, June 8, 10, 11. DERBYSHIRE lost to WARWICKSHIRE by nine wickets.

At Cambridge, June 12, 13, 14. DERBYSHIRE beat CAMBRIDGE UNIVERSITY by six wickets.

DERBYSHIRE v. WORCESTERSHIRE

At Derby, June 15, 17, 18. Drawn, Worcestershire taking four points. They held the upper hand from the start when, on a pitch much favouring batsmen, Peter Richardson and Kenyon began with a stand of 175. Richardson completed his century before lunch and was able to declare before the close of the first day. Derbyshire replied with consistent batting, but Berry, the left-arm slow bowler, brought about a late collapse. Peter Richardson again batted splendidly before declaring a second time, and they had taken eight Derbyshire wickets when fifty minutes remained for play. Then Smith and Gladwin gamely played out time.

Worcestershire

D. Kenyon b Morgan	175	— c Dawkes b Jackson	21
P. E. Richardson c Carr b Smith	116	— c Revill b Morgan	80
G. Dews c Morgan b Jackson	21	— lbw b Smith	40
D. W. Richardson c Dawkes b Morgan	20	— not out	28
L. Outschoorn b Gladwin	23		
R. G. Broadbent not out	27	— not out	17
R. Booth b Gladwin	13		
J. Flavell b Gladwin	4		
R. Berry not out	2		
B 1, l-b 1	2	B 4, n-b 1	5

1/175 2/226 3/273 (7 wkts., dec.) 403   1/30 2/105 (3 wkts., dec.) 191
4/348 5/356 6/387 7/391 (3.69 an over)   3/149

L. Coldwell and J. Aldridge did not bat.

Derbyshire

A. Hamer b Aldridge	68	— b Coldwell	90
C. Lee c Flavell b Berry	43	— c Booth b Flavell	2
J. Kelly c Booth b Coldwell	1	— c Dews b Aldridge	0
A. C. Revill c Broadbent b Coldwell	56	— c and b Flavell	24
D. B. Carr b Berry	71	— b Aldridge	51
G. O. Dawkes not out	33	— c Dews b Berry	1
H. L. Johnson lbw b Berry	0	— c D. Richardson b Aldridge	11
D. C. Morgan c Booth b Coldwell	1	— run out	0
E. Smith c Dews b Berry	1	— not out	13
C. Gladwin c sub b Flavell	2	— not out	19
L. Jackson b Berry	0		
B 6, l-b 5, n-b 1	12	B 12, l-b 5	17

1/94 2/107 3/130 4/200 5/259 6/259   288   1/7 2/123 3/160 (8 wkts.) 228
7/260 8/263 9/287 (2.71 an over)   4/183 5/183 6/183 7/184
8/184

Derbyshire Bowling

	O.	M.	R.	W.		O.	M.	R.	W.
Jackson	23	4	88	1	....	15	0	50	1
Gladwin	32	7	98	3	....	10	5	29	0
Morgan	32	5	112	2	....	8	0	38	1
Smith	16	2	60	1	....	10	0	69	1
Carr	4	0	32	0					
Johnson	1	0	3	0					
Revill	1	0	8	0					

Worcestershire Bowling

	O.	M.	R.	W.		O.	M.	R.	W.
Flavell	18	6	58	1	....	22	2	89	2
Aldridge	18	3	51	1	....	13	2	54	3
Coldwell	27	5	90	3	....	10	3	29	1
Berry	39.5	14	71	5	....	13	6	35	1
P. Richardson	3	0	6	0	....	1	0	4	0

Umpires: T. J. Bartley and P. Corrall.

DERBYSHIRE v. GLAMORGAN

At Chesterfield, June 19, 20, 21. Drawn, Derbyshire taking four points. In another high-scoring match Hamer and Kelly gave Derbyshire a good start with a big second wicket stand, and Carr and Johnson hit freely before Carr declared. Parkhouse, however, replied with a sound century for Glamorgan, but their tail failed. Then Kelly hit a hundred in two and a half hours before a second Derbyshire declaration, but after the rapid fall of two wickets, Glamorgan played out time safely.

Derbyshire

A. Hamer c Walker b H. D. Davies	 77	— c Walker b H. D. Davies..	27
C. Lee c Walker b H. D. Davies	 10	— b H. D. Davies	0
J. M. Kelly c Parkhouse b H. D. Davies..	66	— not out	109
A. C. Revill c and b Shepherd	 19	— c Devereux b Jones	36
D. B. Carr b Walker	55		
G. O. Dawkes c Watkins b Shepherd	 20	— not out	23
H. L. Johnson st H. G. Davies b Devereux	53		
D. C. Morgan run out	 30		
E. Smith not out	 16		
L-b 12, n-b 4, w 1	 17	B 2, l-b 1, w 1	4

1/14 2/148 3/176 4/187 (8 wkts., dec.) 363   1/3 2/53 (3 wkts., dec.) 199
5/221 6/295 7/333 8/363 (3.10 an over)   3/158

C. Gladwin and L. Jackson did not bat.

Glamorgan

W. G. A. Parkhouse run out	118	— lbw b Jackson	15
W. G. Davies b Smith	 14		
B. Hedges c Morgan b Jackson	 43	— c Dawkes b Jackson	0
W. E. Jones c Dawkes b Smith	 14	— not out	69
A. J. Watkins c Revill b Gladwin	 44		
L. N. Devereux c Dawkes b Gladwin	.. 6	— not out	37
P. Walker run out	 48		
H. G. Davies c Dawkes b Jackson	 27		
J. E. McConnon b Smith	 3		
H. D. Davies c Morgan b Gladwin	 1		
D. J. Shepherd not out	 9		
B 8, l-b 2, w 1, n-b 4	 15	B 4, w 2	6

1/72 2/156 3/183 4/209 5/221 6/292 342   1/3 2/28 (2 wkts.) 127
7/298 8/319 9/323 (2.44 an over)

Glamorgan Bowling

	O.	M.	R.	W.		O.	M.	R.	W.
H. D. Davies...	30	5	118	3	....	15	1	51	2
Watkins	20	4	52	0					
W. G. Davies..	8	2	22	0					
Shepherd	16.4	2	61	2	....	8	2	23	0
McConnon	14	2	25	0	....	11	0	34	0
Walker	18	2	48	1	....	20	4	49	0
Devereux	10	2	20	1					
Jones						8	0	38	1

Derbyshire Bowling

	O.	M.	R.	W.		O.	M.	R.	W.
Jackson	28	4	80	3	....	6	1	29	2
Gladwin	29	11	45	3	....	5	2	10	0
Morgan	27	9	61	0	....	2	0	2	0
Smith	47	20	101	3	....	5	3	6	0
Carr	8	0	34	0	....	8	1	36	0
Johnson	1	0	6	0	....	2	0	11	0
Revill						6	1	22	0
Kelly						1	0	5	0

Umpires: N. Oldfield and W. E. Phillipson.

At Bath, June 22, 24, 25. DERBYSHIRE beat SOMERSET by nine wickets.

At Dudley, June 26, 27, 28. DERBYSHIRE lost to WORCESTERSHIRE by two wickets.

At Chesterfield, June 29, July 1, 2. DERBYSHIRE lost to WEST INDIES by 173 runs.
(See WEST INDIES section.)

DERBYSHIRE v. SURREY

At Derby, July 3, 4, 5. Surrey won by eight wickets, taking 14 points. Put in to bat on a green pitch, Derbyshire never mastered a hostile attack, although Lee and Carr batted sturdily in a fourth wicket stand of 79. Surrey looked likely to build a substantial lead, but good off-spin bowling by Smith restricted their advantage to 14. The Bedser twins, bowling on their birthday, were too much for the batsmen when Derbyshire went in again, Eric Bedser being especially effective with his off-breaks. With plenty of time to spare, Surrey found little difficulty in hitting off the 140 runs for victory.

Derbyshire

A. Hamer c Cox b Loader	2	— b E. Bedser	13
C. Lee c Barrington b A. Bedser	51	— st McIntyre b A. Bedser	45
J. Kelly c Cox b Loader	2	— c Fletcher b E. Bedser	16
A. C. Revill c Fletcher b Loader	2	— c and b E. Bedser	2
D. B. Carr c McIntyre b Cox	52	— c Pratt b E. Bedser	1
G. O. Dawkes b E. Bedser	1	— c Barrington b A. Bedser	8
H. L. Johnson c Barrington b E. Bedser	13	— c Barrington b E. Bedser	0
D. C. Morgan b E. Bedser	3	— not out	31
E. Smith not out	1	— b Loader	12
C. Gladwin c Constable b Cox	1	— c McIntyre b Loader	21
L. Jackson c Stewart b Loader	16	— b Loader	0
B 1, l-b 1	2	B 1, l-b 3	4

1/2 2/12 3/16 4/95 5/104 6/121   146   1/27 2/70 3/73 4/79 5/81   153
7/125 8/128 9/129 (1.97 an over)   6/82 7/96 8/113 9/151

Surrey

T. H. Clark c sub b Smith	57	— c Morgan b Smith 46
M. J. Stewart c Morgan b Jackson	4	
B. Constable c Jackson b Smith	45	— c Morgan b Jackson 9
K. F. Barrington c Dawkes b Jackson	1	— not out 27
D. G. W. Fletcher c Johnson b Carr	11	— not out 51
D. F. Cox b Morgan	9	
R. C. E. Pratt not out	20	
E. A. Bedser st Dawkes b Smith	4	
A. J. McIntyre b Carr	6	
P. J. Loader b Smith	1	
A. V. Bedser c Lee b Smith	0	
L-b 2	2	B 5, l-b 2 7

1/11 2/106 3/107 4/109 5/121 6/141   160   1/76 2/90   (2 wkts.) 140
7/148 8/159 9/160 (2.28 an over)

Surrey Bowling

	O.	M.	R.	W.		O.	M.	R.	W.
Loader	15.1	4	26	4	....	17.5	2	46	3
A. Bedser	23	4	45	1	....	25	6	43	2
Cox	12	2	29	2	....	2	0	5	0
E. Bedser	23	4	41	3	....	24	4	55	5
Pratt	1	0	3	0					

Derbyshire Bowling

	O.	M.	R.	W.		O.	M.	R.	W.
Jackson	24	12	41	2	....	15	3	40	1
Gladwin	11	4	29	0					
Morgan	8	3	18	1	....	13.3	4	23	0
Smith	21.4	4	60	5	....	15	4	35	1
Carr	5	0	10	2	....	13	5	27	0
					Revill	1	0	7	0
					Hamer	1	0	1	0

Umpires: P. Corrall and J. Wood.

At Gloucester, July 6, 8, 9. DERBYSHIRE beat GLOUCESTERSHIRE by two wickets.

At The Oval, July 10, 11, 12. DERBYSHIRE drew with SURREY.

At Nottingham, July 13, 15, 16. DERBYSHIRE drew with NOTTINGHAMSHIRE.

DERBYSHIRE v. MIDDLESEX

At Chesterfield, July 17, 18, 19. Derbyshire won by an innings and 22 runs, taking 14 points. Middlesex, sent in by Carr, were dismissed in their second innings for the lowest total in first-class cricket for three years, and they looked likely to be out for the lowest score for fifty years when their seventh, eighth and ninth wickets all fell at 13, but Bennett and Moss more than doubled the score. In both innings Gladwin, with accurate fast-medium bowling, was the main source of trouble to Middlesex, and he received good support from Morgan, Smith and Jackson. A damp pitch was helpful throughout to bowlers. Derbyshire, too, found conditions difficult; they owed much to a lively seventh wicket stand of 50 between Dawkes and Morgan for their useful lead of 51.

Middlesex

J. D. Robertson c Dawkes b Gladwin ...	38	— lbw b Jackson	0
R. A. Gale c Kelly b Smith	8	— c Dawkes b Gladwin	4
D. O. Baldry lbw b Morgan	4	— b Gladwin	1
W. J. Edrich c Revill b Gladwin	10	— c Carr b Gladwin	0
G. P. S. Delisle b Morgan	0	— b Jackson	6
F. J. Titmus c Carr b Smith	22	— c Morgan b Gladwin	0
J. T. Murray c Dawkes b Gladwin	1	— c and b Gladwin	0
D. Bennett c Dawkes b Gladwin	13	— not out	14
H. W. Tilly c Jackson b Gladwin	0	— lbw b Jackson	0
R. J. Hurst c Carr b Gladwin	2	— run out	0
A. E. Moss not out	0	— c Hamer b Morgan........	2
B 4	4	L-b 2	2

1/24 2/34 3/55 4/62 5/86 6/86 7/93   102   1/0 2/1 3/1 4/1 5/9   29
8/93 9/99 (1.37 an over)   6/9 7/13 8/13 9/13

Derbyshire

A. Hamer b Moss	5		E. Smith c Murray b Tilly	0
C. Lee c and b Titmus	33		C. Gladwin not out	5
J. M. Kelly b Tilly	23		L. Jackson c Titmus b Hurst.....	0
A. C. Revill b Hurst	17		B 4, l-b 5	9
D. B. Carr c Murray b Tilly	4			
D. J. Green c Edrich b Hurst	1			
G. O. Dawkes c Gale b Tilly.....	28		1/12 2/53 3/82 4/82 5/87 6/87	153
D. C. Morgan c Bennett b Hurst..	28		7/137 8/143 9/149 (3.00 an over)	

Derbyshire Bowling

	O.	M.	R.	W.	O.	M.	R.	W.
Jackson	6	4	4	0	11	6	7	3
Gladwin	25.2	14	23	6	14	8	18	5
Morgan	19	5	42	2	4.2	3	2	1
Smith	17	6	29	2	1	1	0	0

Middlesex Bowling

	O.	M.	R.	W.
Moss	5	2	12	1
Bennett	2	0	4	0
Titmus	10	0	33	1
Hurst	21.1	10	50	4
Tilly	13	4	45	4

Umpires: W. F. Phillipson and A. Skelding.

DERBYSHIRE v. LANCASHIRE

At Derby, July 20, 22, 23. Drawn, Derbyshire taking two points. Washbrook's decision that Lancashire should bat, after he won the toss, was difficult, for the pitch had absorbed much rain. In the circumstances Lancashire did well to score 184 brightly on the first day against a lively attack. Hamer again provided the backbone of the Derbyshire batting against varied bowling, and the last pair were together before the first innings lead, but not bonus points, was obtained. Morgan bowled especially well in the Lancashire second innings, which Rhodes brought to a summary end by taking three wickets in six balls. After the early loss of four wickets on the treacherous pitch, Derbyshire gave up the attempt to score 139 in one hour fifty minutes.

Lancashire

A. Wharton c Carr b Jackson	54	— b Morgan	18
J. Dyson lbw b Jackson	9	— b Smith	8
J. T. Ikin c Dawkes b Jackson	2	— c Carr b Smith	6
C. Washbrook lbw b Morgan	26	— lbw b Morgan	28
K. Grieves b Rhodes	35	— c Carr b Morgan	3
J. D. Bond b Morgan	5	— b Jackson	40
C. S. Smith c Dawkes b Morgan	32	— c Smith b Morgan	19
M. J. Hilton c Hamer b Smith	6	— not out	10
T. W. Greenhough lbw b Smith	4	— c Carr b Rhodes	3
A. Wilson run out	0	— b Rhodes	0
R. Tattersall not out	2	— c Carr b Rhodes	0
B 3, l-b 6	9	B 2, l-b 4	6

1/21 2/27 3/80 4/106 5/121 6/141   184   1/20 2/34 3/34 4/49 5/80   141
7/167 8/177 9/178 (2.42 an over)   6/122 7/128 8/141 9/141

Derbyshire

A. Hamer c Wilson b Smith	57	— run out	7
C. Lee c Smith b Dyson	23	— c Greenhough b Tattersall	11
J. Kelly b Tattersall	11	— not out	17
A. C. Revill c Hilton b Tattersall	19	— b Greenhough	9
D. B. Carr run out	3	— not out	9
D. J. Green lbw b Tattersall	0		
G. O. Dawkes c Ikin b Greenhough	21	— c Washbrook b Smith	1
D. C. Morgan c Wharton b Smith	22		
H. J. Rhodes c Wharton b Smith	10		
E. Smith not out	11		
L. Jackson st Wilson b Tattersall	3		
B 2, l-b 3, n-b 2	7	L-b 3, n-b 2	5

1/36 2/61 3/87 4/92 5/95 6/129   187   1/8 2/17   (4 wkts.)   59
7/162 8/163 9/183 (1.92 an over)   3/29 4/41

Derbyshire Bowling

	O.	M.	R.	W.	O.	M.	R.	W.
Jackson	20	8	48	3	20	8	23	1
Rhodes	20	4	53	1	5.5	2	11	3
Morgan	23.3	9	44	3	29	16	33	4
Smith	12	4	30	2	26	13	50	2
Carr					3	1	18	0

Lancashire Bowling

	O.	M.	R.	W.	O.	M.	R.	W.
Smith	20	5	24	3	7	1	15	1
Wharton	5	2	4	0	4	1	11	0
Tattersall	30.5	13	70	4	5	2	3	1
Hilton	26	9	53	0	7	3	9	0
Dyson	11	3	23	1	5	3	4	0
Greenhough	4	1	6	1	8	5	8	1
Ikin					2	1	4	0

Umpires: John Langridge and C. A. Coleman.

DERBYSHIRE v. NOTTINGHAMSHIRE

At Ilkeston, July 27, 29, 30. Drawn, Derbyshire taking four points. Despite a steady effort by Springall, Nottinghamshire lost six men for 113 before Vowles, making his first Championship appearance, rallied his side with a fine display. Millman gave him good support and then a dashing half-century by the acting captain Jepson, enabled the visitors to stay in the whole of the first day. Derbyshire proved more consistent with the bat, and they also made a late rally when, thanks to some enterprising hitting by Gibson, the Cambridge Blue, he and Smith, in an unfinished stand of 58, saw them ahead before Gladwin declared. On the last day, Nottinghamshire made a great bid for victory. After steady batting by N. Hill and a venturesome effort by Poole they set Derbyshire to score 232 in two hours fifty minutes. An opening stand of 91 by Hamer and Lee put Derbyshire in a promising position, but effective bowling by Vowles and Matthews caused a breakdown so that when only three wickets were left and 53 runs were still required in the last half-hour Derbyshire played for a draw.

Nottinghamshire

J. D. Clay b Gladwin	10	— lbw b Morgan	48
J. D. Springall b Gibson	63	— c Dawkes b Jackson	0
N. Hill c Gibson b Jackson	0	— c Jackson b Smith	52
M. Hill b Morgan	16	— lbw b Smith	23
C. J. Poole b Gladwin	16	— c Dawkes b Jackson	65
B. Dooland c Revill b Gladwin	5	— c Lee b Gladwin	27
R. Vowles c Johnson b Jackson	54	— not out	1
G. Millman c Kelly b Morgan	25	— c Dawkes b Jackson	5
A. Jepson b Morgan	50	— b Jackson	11
C. S. Mathews c Hamer b Morgan	4		
M. Morgan not out	8		
L-b 1	1		

1/19 2/20 3/56 4/97 5/109 6/113   252   1/1 2/83   (8 wkts., dec.) 234
7/171 8/204 9/235 (2.54 an over)   3/125 4/126 5/217 6/217
                                          7/228 8/234

Derbyshire

A. Hamer c Dooland b Morgan	54	— c Dooland b Morgan	58
C. Lee c Matthews b Jepson	19	— c Poole b Vowles	43
J. M. Kelly b Morgan	34	— c Poole b Vowles	28
A. C. Revill b Morgan	13	— st Millman b Vowles	0
I. Gibson not out	66	— b Matthews	21
D. C. Morgan c Millman b Matthews	32	— b Matthews	22
H. L. Johnson c Millman b Matthews	6	— not out	12
G. O. Dawkes c Millman b Matthews	7	— b Matthews	2
E. Smith not out	19	— not out	6
B 1, l-b 4	5	B 1, l-b 2	3

1/37 2/102 3/117 4/126   (7 wkts., dec.) 255   1/91 2/106   (7 wkts.) 195
5/174 6/185 7/197 (2.57 an over)   3/108 4/137 5/168 6/177
                                       7/179

C. Gladwin and L. Jackson did not bat.

Derbyshire Bowling

	O.	M.	R.	W.	O.	M.	R.	W.
Jackson	29	8	78	2	17.2	6	69	4
Gladwin	30	11	61	3	14	4	40	1
Morgan	21.1	3	63	4	16	4	45	1
Smith	9	2	18	0	18	5	48	2
Gibson	10	1	31	1	5	0	32	0

Nottinghamshire Bowling

	O.	M.	R.	W.	O.	M.	R.	W.
Jepson	24	8	51	1	12	3	34	0
Matthews	21	9	52	3	16	3	49	3
Dooland	27	7	84	0	4	3	22	0
Vowles	8	2	17	0	8	0	47	3
Morgan	19	5	46	3	12	2	40	1

Umpires: R. S. Lay and N. Oldfield.

DERBYSHIRE v. LEICESTERSHIRE

At Chesterfield, July 31, August 1. Derbyshire won by an innings and 123 runs, taking 14 points. Apart from the early stages of the first day when Hallam, who hit eleven 4's, batted splendidly, Leicestershire struggled throughout. They found Derbyshire's fast-medium bowlers, Jackson, Gladwin and Morgan, in good form. Kelly and Carr emphasised Derbyshire's superiority by adding 246, a new third-wicket record for the county. After Carr declared, Leicestershire collapsed badly on a pitch still good for batsmen, nobody showing much resolution against the seam bowlers.

Leicestershire

G. Lester c Carr b Gladwin	15	— c Dawkes b Gladwin	0
M. R. Hallam st Dawkes b Morgan	95	— c Morgan b Jackson	5
J. van Geloven b Gladwin	34	— lbw b Jackson	19
C. H. Palmer c Morgan b Smith	0	— c Gibson b Morgan	13
L. R. Gardner lbw b Jackson	4	— c Mohan b Jackson	6
P Munden c Gibson b Jackson	0	— c Kelly b Jackson	4
J. Firth lbw b Jackson	0	— b Jackson	11
J. Savage b Gibson	22	— b Morgan	1
R. Smith b Morgan	1	— not out	3
C. T. Spencer run out	3	— b Jackson	0
B. Boshier not out	0	— b Morgan	18
B 1, l-b 1	2	L-b 6	6

1/22 2/119 3/120 4/131 5/137 6/149   176
7/149 8/159 9/168 (2.31 an over)

1/5 2/7 3/36 4/47 5/49   86
6/60 7/65 8/67 9/67

Derbyshire

A. Hamer lbw b Savage	21	D. C. Morgan not out	57
C. Lee b Spencer	5	L-b 6, n-b 3	9
J. M. Kelly c Boshier b Smith	127		
D. B. Carr c Palmer b Smith	141		
I. M. Gibson b Savage	1	1/14 2/40 3/286 (5 wkts., dec.) 385
K. F. Mohan not out	24	4/296 5/304 (3.08 an over)

G. O. Dawkes, E. Smith, C. Gladwin and L. Jackson did not bat.

Derbyshire Bowling

	O.	M.	R.	W.	O.	M.	R.	W.
Jackson	18	5	72	3	18	4	37	6
Gladwin	14	8	20	2	7	3	13	1
Morgan	15	8	22	2	13.2	7	30	3
Gibson	7.4	5	11	1				
Smith	17	3	38	1				
Carr	3	0	11	0				
Mohan	1	1	0	0				

Leicestershire Bowling

	O.	M.	R.	W.
Spencer	21	3	95	1
Boshier	17	0	73	0
Savage	29	4	85	2
Palmer	14	8	18	0
Smith	33	9	72	2
van Geloven	8	1	22	0
Lester	3	0	11	0

Umpires: J. S. Buller and T. W. Spencer.

DERBYSHIRE v. WARWICKSHIRE

At Derby, August 3, 5, 6. Drawn, Derbyshire taking four points. Fielding four pace bowlers, Derbyshire accomplished a good performance in dismissing Warwickshire for a moderate first innings total and consistent batting enabled them to take four points comfortably. Then Horner and Smith mastered the Derbyshire attack in a third wicket stand of 182 which completely changed the course of the game and enabled Warwickshire to declare 293 ahead. Rain on the last morning produced a lifting pitch and only dogged defence enabled Derbyshire to survive against hostile pace bowling by Bannister and Griffiths.

Warwickshire

F. C. Gardner c Dawkes b Jackson	36	lbw b Jackson	0
N. F. Horner lbw b Jackson	9	— c Morgan b Hall	152
T. W. Cartwright b Jackson	0	— c Dawkes b Gladwin	14
M. J. K. Smith c Dawkes b Hall	19	— not out	104
A. Townsend c Dawkes b Gladwin	36	— not out	51
C. W. Leach c Carr b Hall	67		
S. Singh c Dawkes b Gladwin	0		
E. B. Lewis c Dawkes b Morgan	0		
J. D. Bannister c Lee b Hall	26		
S. S. Griffiths c Jackson b Gibson	2		
W. E. Hollies not out	0		
L-b 1	1	L-b 4	4

1/19 2/19 3/59 4/65 5/122 6/122   196   1/4 2/43   (3 wkts., dec.) 325
7/137 8/190 9/196 (2.72 an over)   3/225

Derbyshire

A. Hamer c Townsend b Bannister	15	— c Singh b Bannister	3
C. Lee c Gardner b Hollies	54	— c Horner b Bannister	37
J. M. Kelly c Lewis b Bannister	24	— b Townsend	10
D. B. Carr c Leach b Bannister	24	— c Leach b Townsend	5
I. M. Gibson c Lewis b Bannister	24	— lbw b Bannister	1
K. Mohan c Gardner b Bannister	16	— b Griffiths	15
D. C. Morgan c Lewis b Hollies	33	— lbw b Bannister	17
G. O. Dawkes b Bannister	23	— not out	6
C. Gladwin lbw b Bannister	1	— not out	0
L. Jackson c Gardner b Hollies	24		
D. Hall not out	0		
B 7, l-b 6, n-b 1	14	B 4	4

1/15 2/76 3/101 4/103 5/133 6/156   228   1/3 2/29 3/35   (7 wkts.) 98
7/192 8/197 9/228 (3.45 an over)   4/56 5/57 6/85 7/97

Derbyshire Bowling

	O.	M.	R.	W.	O.	M.	R.	W.
Jackson	17	2	58	3	4	3	1	1
Gladwin	18	8	45	2	29	6	84	1
Hall	22	3	61	3	20	5	81	1
Morgan	11	2	25	1	20	4	65	0
Gibson	4.2	2	6	1	5	0	16	0
Mohan					4	1	14	0
Carr					4	0	26	0
Lee					6	0	22	0
Hamer					1	0	12	0

L

Warwickshire Bowling

	O.	M.	R.	W.	O.	M.	R.	W.
Griffiths	19	3	68	0	18	5	38	1
Bannister	26.3	5	88	7	21.4	10	23	4
Cartwright	9	0	28	0	4	2	6	0
Hollies	10	2	26	3	6	4	6	0
Singh	1	0	4	0	2	2	0	0
Townsend					8	1	21	2

Umpires: A. Skelding and J. F. Crapp.

At Pontypridd, August 7, 8, 9. DERBYSHIRE drew with GLAMORGAN.

At Portsmouth, August 10, 12, 13. DERBYSHIRE drew with HAMPSHIRE.

DERBYSHIRE v. KENT

At Derby, August 14, 15, 16. Kent won by an innings and 50 runs, taking 14 points. On a rain-affected pitch, the Kent pace bowlers proved more effective than those of Derbyshire. After a delayed start Ridgway, Halfyard and Brown bowled with life and accuracy, and Morgan alone of the Derbyshire batsmen distinguished himself. Kent batted solidly but slowly in building up their substantial first innings lead, but their tactics were justified when Derbyshire suffered another collapse. Again only Morgan resisted strongly against Ridgway and Halfyard, who bowled unchanged.

Derbyshire

A. Hamer lbw b Ridgway	4	—	c Evans b Ridgway		3
C. Lee b Ridgway	7	—	b Ridgway		2
J. M. Kelly c Ridgway b Brown	5	—	b Ridgway		17
A. C. Revill c Evans b Brown	11	—	c Wilson b Ridgway		15
D. B. Carr b Pettiford	20	—	lbw b Ridgway		8
I. M. Gibson b Ridgway	1	—	c Ridgway b Halfyard		1
D. C. Morgan not out	38	—	not out		23
G. O. Dawkes b Halfyard	6	—	c Evans b Halfyard		6
E. Smith c Ridgway b Halfyard	0	—	b Halfyard		1
C. Gladwin b Halfyard	1	—	c and b Ridgway		6
L. Jackson c Pettiford b Halfyard	0	—	c Evans b Halfyard		2
B 4, l-b 1	5				

1/6 2/13 3/21 4/34 5/45 6/85 7/96   98   1/3 2/6 3/32 4/45 5/46   84
8/96 9/98 (2.00 an over)   6/46 7/56 8/64 9/79

Kent

A. H. Phebey run out	13	F. Ridgway b Morgan		3
R. C. Wilson b Gladwin	20	D. J. Halfyard not out		15
J. Pettiford lbw b Jackson	11	L-b 8		8
M. C. Cowdrey c Carr b Gladwin	51			
J. F. Pretlove c and b Morgan	39	1/24 2/30 3/70 (7 wkts., dec.)		232
G. W. Cook not out	51	4/123 5/167 6/199 7/202		
T. G. Evans c Jackson b Morgan	21	(2.03 an over)		

A. Brown and J. C. T. Page did not bat.

Kent Bowling

	O.	M.	R.	W.	O.	M.	R.	W.
Ridgway	11	4	17	3	16	1	53	6
Halfyard	16.4	6	33	4	15.1	5	31	4
Brown	12	1	35	2				
Page	2	1	1	0				
Pettiford	7	3	7	1				

Derbyshire Bowling

	O.	M.	R.	W.
Jackson	33	16	37	1
Gladwin	30	14	56	2
Morgan	31	14	68	3
Smith	16	2	55	0
Revill	4	2	8	0

Umpires: H. Elliott and N. Oldfield.

DERBYSHIRE v. SOMERSET

At Chesterfield, August 17, 19, 20. Somerset won by an innings and 21 runs, taking 12 points. They possessed the bowlers to take advantage of a pitch which always took spin, and also batted with splendid consistency. Despite solid work by Lee and good stroke-play on the part of Carr and Dawkes, Derbyshire never mastered the attack after being sent in to bat. Silk, Tremlett, Alley and Stephenson all scored readily but Somerset narrowly failed to add bonus points to their first innings points, Stephenson being caught on the boundary when a six would have given his side the higher scoring rate. Wight, with his off-spinners, achieved the best bowling figures of his career to date when Derbyshire batted a second time.

Derbyshire

A. Hamer c Palmer b Alley	11	—	b Langford	23
C. Lee b Langford	33	—	b Palmer	0
J. M. Kelly c Stephenson b Palmer	16	—	c Tremlett b Wight	9
D. B. Carr c Stephenson b Langford	47	—	b Wight	11
D. C. Morgan c McCool b Palmer	11	—	c Tremlett b Wight	10
D. J. Short b Palmer	19	—	b Wight	8
H. L. Johnson b Dickinson	4	—	c Dickinson b Wight	13
G. O. Dawkes not out	41	—	c Wight b Langford	13
E. Smith lbw b McCool	4	—	b Palmer	11
C. Gladwin c Tremlett b McCool	0	—	not out	2
L. Jackson c Palmer b McCool	6	—	st Stephenson b Wight ...	4
W 2	2		B 8, l-b 7, w 2	17

1/23 2/52 3/81 4/100 5/134 6/137   192   1/4 2/22 3/45 4/58 5/66   121
7/154 8/159 9/163 (2.63 an over)   6/82 7/87 8/106 9/113

Somerset

D. R. W. Silk c Morgan b Gladwin	73	B. Langford c and b Smith	1
G. G. Atkinson c Kelly b Jackson	24	B. Lobb b Morgan	0
P. B. Wight run out	3	T. E. Dickinson not out	4
M. F. Tremlett b Jackson	81	B 1, l-b 1, w 1, n-b 1	4
C. L. McCool b Jackson	30		
W. E. Alley c Johnson b Smith...	48		
K. E. Palmer c Carr b Morgan....	24	1/56 2/59 3/180 4/190 5/238	334
H. W. Stephenson c Hamer b Morgan.................	42	6/272 7/302 8/304 9/305 (2.60 an over)	

Somerset Bowling

	O.	M.	R.	W.		O.	M.	R.	W.
Dickinson	12	2	23	1	....	7	2	7	0
Lobb	9	2	21	0	....	4	0	15	0
Alley..........	12	4	25	1					
Langford	14	4	31	2	....	19	6	29	2
Palmer	17	2	57	3	....	8	3	10	2
McCool	8.4	0	33	3	....	2	0	7	0
Atkinson......						4	1	7	0
Wight						11	7	29	6

Derbyshire Bowling

	O.	M.	R.	W.
Jackson	31	10	67	3
Gladwin	30	15	55	1
Morgan	32	9	77	3
Smith	29	8	106	2
Carr	6	2	25	0

Umpires: P. A. Gibb and N. Oldfield.

At Northampton, August 21, 22, 23. DERBYSHIRE lost to NORTHAMPTONSHIRE by 135 runs.

DERBYSHIRE v. NORTHAMPTONSHIRE

At Buxton, August 24, 26, 27. No decision. Play was confined to six and a quarter hours on the first day, heavy rain making further cricket out of the question. On slowly drying turf, Derbyshire's varied attack of swing and spin gave considerable trouble, and Northamptonshire owed much to the sound batting of Brookes for their modest total. Derbyshire collapsed before the left-arm spin of Manning and Allen, but determined batting by Morgan and Johnson put them into a position to challenge for first innings points.

Northamptonshire

D. Brookes c Carr b Morgan	55
P. Arnold c Morgan b Gladwin	0
R. Subba Row c Dawkes b Hall	0
D. W. Barrick c Lee b Morgan	20
B. L. Reynolds c and b Gladwin	0
A. Lightfoot c and b Smith	19
G. E. Tribe c Johnson b Smith	14
J. S. Manning b Smith	8

K. V. Andrew c Smith b Carr	7
F. H. Tyson not out	0
M. H. J. Allen lbw b Smith	0
L-b 8	8

1/10 2/17 3/55 4/56 5/88 6/104 **131**
7/120 8/131 9/131 (1.89 an over)

Derbyshire

A. Hamer b Lightfoot	0
C. Lee c Barrick b Allen	27
J. M. Kelly lbw b Manning	2
D. B. Carr c Tribe b Manning	0
D. C. Morgan not out	38
J. D. Short c Andrew b Manning	0

| H. L. Johnson not out | 23 |
| B 4, l-b 1 | 5 |

1/7 2/25 3/29 4/29   (5 wkts.) **95**
5/29 (1.85 an over)

G. O. Dawkes, E. Smith, C. Gladwin and D. Hall did not bat.

Derbyshire Bowling

	O.	M.	R.	W.
Hall	6	1	24	1
Gladwin	19	8	29	2
Morgan	23	12	37	2
Smith	14.5	4	26	4
Carr	6	4	7	1

Northamptonshire Bowling

	O.	M.	R.	W.
Tyson	9.2	4	25	0
Lightfoot	4	2	9	1
Manning	16	10	17	3
Allen	18	9	26	1
Tribe	5	1	13	0

Umpires: J. F. Crapp and H. G. Baldwin.

At Hove, August 31, September 2, 3. DERBYSHIRE lost to SUSSEX by four runs.

ESSEX

President—HUBERT ASHTON
Secretary—T. E. BAILEY, 60, London Road, Chelmsford
Captain—D. J. INSOLE

L. H. R. Ralph   County Badge   T. C. Dodds

Essex enjoyed their best season for 18 years, for not since 1939 had they won as many as eleven Championship matches. Winding up the summer in a blaze of glory when inflicting upon Surrey one of the only three defeats suffered by the Champions, they rose from eleventh to fifth place in the table.

For the second year in succession Trevor Bailey headed both the batting and bowling averages and for the fourth time he achieved the "cricketers' double"; but once again the chief run-getter for the county was the captain, Insole, who hit four centuries and on two other occasions fell narrowly short of three figures. Insole bore a prominent part in the win over Surrey at Clacton, scoring 115 in splendid style when Essex required 253 for victory. Dodds, out of the first six matches through back trouble, and Barker, the opening batsmen, each exceeded 1,000 runs, but they experienced varying fortune. When at his best, Barker batted extremely well, but though obtaining three centuries he was dismissed without scoring seven times. While Taylor and Bear, the left-handers, each hit a century and occasional good innings came from Savill, Ralph and Greensmith, none of them could be termed reliable.

A large share of the credit for the advance of Essex attached to the fast-medium bowling of Ralph, who, as a regular member of the team, achieved 100 wickets for the first time. With such analyses as five for 22 v. Warwickshire at Birmingham; six for 33 and four for 53 v. Somerset and five for 29 v. Sussex, both at Colchester, he increased the number of his victims in Championship engagements by 53 compared with 1956 and reduced their cost by over five runs each. During last winter he became a professional.

He did much to make up for the absence at four Test matches of Trevor Bailey, who maintained his usual fire and distinguished himself at Romford by dismissing fourteen Hampshire batsmen for 81 runs beside scoring 130 runs for once out.

Preston, if lacking his speed of earlier years, bowled with marked accuracy, meeting with special success against Lancashire, and he attained 100 wickets for the first time. After the University match J. A. Bailey accomplished useful work, but the slow bowlers met with little reward. Greensmith's leg-breaks became less effective and more expensive and King, the left-hander secured from Warwickshire, while able to keep down runs and fielding admirably, lacked penetrative power.

The return after twenty-four years to Leyton for a week's cricket proved a considerable success and Dodds, who took his benefit there, profited accordingly.

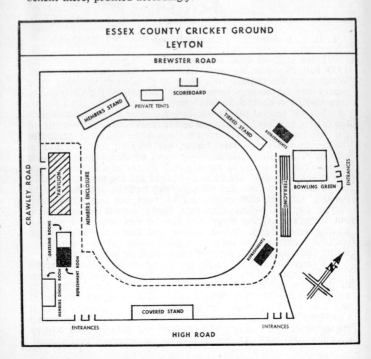

ESSEX RESULTS

All First-Class Matches—Played 31, *Won* 12, *Lost* 7, *Drawn* 12

County Championship Matches—Played 28, *Won* 11, *Lost* 6,
Drawn 10, *No Decision* 1

COUNTY CHAMPIONSHIP AVERAGES
BATTING

	Birthplace	Mtchs.	Inns.	Not Outs	Runs	100's	Highest Inns.	Aver.
T. E. Bailey ...	*Westcliff*	17	28	6	1094	2	132	49.72
D. J. Insole....	*Clapton*	22	38	4	1501	4	150*	44.14
E. Palmer	*Romford*	4	8	5	39	0	11*	39.00
T. C. Dodds...	*Bedford*	24	42	1	1059	0	97	25.82
G. Barker	*Leeds*	28	49	0	1199	3	117	24.46
S. C. Eve......	*Stepney*	2	3	1	48	0	22*	24.00
L. H. Savill....	*Brentwood*	20	32	3	689	0	89	23.75
B. Taylor	*West Ham*	28	49	1	961	1	105	20.02
M. Bear	*Brentwood*	24	39	3	651	1	123	18.08
W. T. Greensmith	*Middlesbrough*	25	39	7	550	0	61	17.18
R. Ralph	*East Ham*	28	43	11	522	0	66	16.31
G. Smith	*Braintree*	14	24	0	341	0	59	14.20
K. C. Preston ..	*Goodmayes*	28	39	4	389	0	40	11.11
I. M. King.....	*Leeds*	25	33	18	127	0	33	8.46
G. W. Horrex..	*Ilford*	4	7	0	41	0	20	5.85
J. A. Bailey....	*Brixton*	8	7	1	29	0	15	4.83
A. Durley	*Ilford*	5	8	0	38	0	16	4.75

Also batted: B. Knight (*Chesterfield*) 0, 9; R. E. Evans (*East Ham*) 4, 0.

* *Signifies not out.*

BOWLING

	Overs	Maidens	Runs	Wickets	Average
T. E. Bailey	442.1	127	1020	70	14.57
R. Ralph	768.5	180	2033	96	21.17
K. C. Preston	1013	237	2585	119	21.72
J. A. Bailey	191.2	42	535	24	22.29
D. J. Insole	133.1	34	318	13	24.46
W. T. Greensmith......	514.2	113	1411	52	27.13
E. Palmer	72	20	225	7	32.14
I. M. King.............	457.5	174	945	27	35.00

Also bowled: G. Barker 2—0—2—0; M. Bear 5—0—7—0; B. Knight 2—0—4—0; G. Smith 13—2—37—0.

Amateurs.—J. A. Bailey, T. E. Bailey, R. E. Evans, S. C. Eve, G. W. Horrex, D. J. Insole, E. Palmer, R. Ralph.

At Cambridge, May 4, 6, 7. ESSEX drew with CAMBRIDGE UNIVERSITY.

At Southampton, May 8, 9, 10. ESSEX beat HAMPSHIRE by 152 runs.

At Ilford, May 11, 13, 14. ESSEX lost to WEST INDIES by four wickets. (See WEST INDIES section.)

ESSEX v. GLAMORGAN

At Ilford, May 15, 16, 17. Drawn, Essex taking four points. After establishing a commanding position, they failed because of unimpressive bowling to force home the advantage. On the opening day, on a good batting pitch, Glamorgan showed little resolution against the lively bowling of Bailey and Ralph. Essex, by contrast, batted with enterprise and assurance. Barker and Insole added 154 for the third wicket and Bailey, much more free than usual, received good support from two young players, Bear and Smith. A storm left Glamorgan to bat on a damp pitch in their second innings, but Wooller and Davies stayed together over three hours before the first wicket fell. The Essex bowling lacked accuracy, and Glamorgan, batting nearly six hours, easily saved the game.

Glamorgan

W. Wooller run out	2	— c Smith b Ralph	39
W. G. Davies c Ralph b Insole	14	— b Ralph	41
B. Hedges c King b Ralph	25	— not out	57
L. N. Devereux b Bailey	18	— c Taylor b Bailey	15
A. J. Watkins c Barker b Bailey	31	— c Bailey b Preston	5
J. Pressdee c Preston b Bailey	1	— lbw b Bailey	11
D. J. Ward c Taylor b Ralph	4	— not out	23
J. E. McConnon b Ralph	15		
H. G. Davies b Preston	28		
H. D. Davies st Taylor b Preston	5		
D. J. Shepherd not out	0		
L-b 2, w 1	3	B 25, l-b 1, w 1, n-b 4 ..	31

1/2 2/43 3/43 4/91 5/94 6/97 7/103   146   1/92 2/92 3/128   (5 wkts.) 222
8/135 9/146 (2.28 an over)   4/145 5/164

Essex

G. Barker b H. D. Davies	98	G. Smith lbw b Shepherd	26
G. W. Horrex b Wooller	2	R. Ralph not out	4
B. Taylor b McConnon	13		
D. J. Insole lbw b Pressdee	106		
T. E. Bailey not out	102	L-b 5, n-b 2	7
S. C. Eve b Shepherd	4		
M. Bear c H. G. Davies b H. D. Davies	34	1/3 2/38 3/192 (7 wkts., dec.) 396	

4/239 5/246 6/340 7/386 (3.32 an over)

K. C. Preston and I. M. King did not bat.

Essex Bowling

	O.	M.	R.	W.		O.	M.	R.	W.
Bailey	23	9	40	3	....	28	15	52	2
Preston	7	0	25	2	....	38	16	64	1
Ralph	20.1	7	54	3	....	20	10	34	2
Insole	7	3	14	1					
King	7	4	10	0	....	23	13	23	0
Smith						10	2	18	0

Glamorgan Bowling

	O.	M.	R.	W.
H. D. Davies ..	19	3	82	2
Watkins	29	8	62	0
Wooller	23	6	80	1
McConnon	11	1	35	1
Shepherd	21	4	59	2
W. G. Davies ..	4	0	21	0
Pressdee	12.2	0	50	1

Umpires: T. J. Bartley and John Langridge.

At Burton, May 18, 20. Essex lost to Derbyshire by an innings and seven runs.

ESSEX v. HAMPSHIRE

At Romford, May 25, 27, 28. Essex won by 46 runs, taking 12 points. Bailey dominated the game to a remarkable degree, and earned an ovation from the players of both teams, as well as the spectators, at the finish. Although suffering from a cracked knuckle bone in the right hand, he scored nearly half his side's runs for once out, took fourteen wickets for 81 runs with lively fast-medium bowling, and was on the field for all but one and a half hours of the match. The Hampshire seam bowlers, Shackleton, Cannings and Heath, used a green pitch well and runs were always hard-earned. Apart from Taylor, Bailey received little batting support in the first innings, but found more solid partners in the second after Essex lost three wickets without a run scored. Only Barnard, Ingleby-Mackenzie and Gray resisted at all effectively during the two Hampshire innings.

Essex

G. Barker lbw b Cannings	5	— b Shackleton	0
R. E. Evans b Shackleton	4	— b Cannings	0
B. Taylor lbw b Heath	35	— run out	17
D. J. Insole b Heath	14	— b Shackleton	0
T. E. Bailey b Heath	59	— not out	71
M. Bear b Cannings	2	— c Sainsbury b Shackleton	1
G. Smith c Harrison b Shackleton	5	— lbw b Shackleton	4
A. Durley b Heath	4	— c Eagar b Cannings	11
R. Ralph b Sainsbury	1	— b Sainsbury	16
K. C. Preston b Sainsbury	1	— b Shackleton	0
I. M. King not out	0	— c Eagar b Heath	9
		B 5, l-b 7	12

1/9 2/9 3/40 4/87 5/94 6/105 7/117 8/118 9/120 (1.62 an over) **130**

1/0 2/0 3/0 4/38 5/44 6/48 7/75 8/105 9/112 **141**

Hampshire

R. E. Marshall b Bailey	4	— c Taylor b Bailey	6
J. R. Gray lbw b Bailey	2	— c King b Bailey	40
H. Horton run out	1	— c Taylor b Bailey	7
P. J. Sainsbury b Ralph	5	— lbw b Preston	3
H. M. Barnard c King b Insole	26	— b Bailey	15
A. C. D. Ingleby-Mackenzie not out	37	— c Taylor b Bailey	23
L. Harrison b Insole	8	— b Bailey	5
E. D. R. Eagar c Taylor b Bailey	0	— c Insole b King	3
D. Shackleton lbw b Bailey	5	— not out	7
V. H. D. Cannings b Bailey	7	— b Bailey	2
M. Heath c Insole b Bailey	0	— c Taylor b Bailey	0
	B 4, l-b 10	14	B 4, l-b 1	5

1/5 2/8 3/9 4/27 5/72 6/82 7/83 8/89 9/109 (2.31 an over) **109**

1/6 2/26 3/34 4/62 5/95 6/100 7/103 8/103 9/116 **116**

Hampshire Bowling

	O.	M.	R.	W.	O.	M.	R.	W.
Shackleton	16	6	37	2	26	6	47	5
Cannings	16	10	15	2	27	14	30	2
Sainsbury	24	10	41	2	4	3	4	1
Heath	24.2	9	37	4	18.4	1	48	1

Essex Bowling

	O.	M.	R.	W.	O.	M.	R.	W.
Bailey	17	5	32	6	23.5	7	49	8
Preston	14	5	30	0	17	6	31	1
Ralph	9	2	19	1	8	1	21	0
Insole	7	1	14	2	4	1	3	0
King					6	3	7	1

Umpires: P. Corrall and N. Oldfield.

ESSEX v. GLOUCESTERSHIRE

At Romford, May 29, 30, 31. Essex, taking 14 points, beat Gloucestershire by six wickets. Even though Essex were without Insole and Bailey, and Gloucestershire without Graveney, the game did not lack interest. Dodds, captaining Essex for the first time, failed to register personal success on his first appearance of the season after back trouble, but he handled his bowlers well. Seam bowlers held the upper hand most of the time on a rather green pitch, but bat mastered ball when Bear, the young Essex left-hander who drove attractively, scored his maiden century. He defied Gloucestershire for over four hours. Essex, left to make 55 to win, lost three men for 16 but in the end won easily. Two newcomers to Championship cricket gave promising displays. Meyer kept wicket smartly and batted soundly for Gloucestershire, and Palmer, a medium-fast right-hand bowler who wore spectacles, bowled some splendid overs for Essex.

Gloucestershire

D. M. Young b Preston	24	—	lbw b Ralph	28
D. Carpenter c Smith b Preston	1	—	b Preston	2
W. Knightley-Smith c King b Palmer	36	—	c Taylor b Preston	37
R. B. Nicholls b Palmer	9	—	c Taylor b Ralph	8
G. M. Emmett c Taylor b Ralph	37	—	c Smith b Ralph	0
D. Hawkins st Taylor b King	14	—	b Preston	15
B. J. Meyer not out	18	—	not out	30
G. E. Lambert c Taylor b Ralph	0	—	st Taylor b King	21
D. R. Smith b Ralph	2	—	b King	0
C. Cook run out	0	—	c Preston b King	13
B. D. Wells b Ralph	12	—	b King	10
B 11, l-b 2, w 2	15		B 23, l-b 4, w 1	28

1/9 2/60 3/77 4/84 5/132 6/142　　　168
7/142 8/144 9/145 (2.50 an over)

1/24 2/60 3/75 4/79　　　192
5/97 6/112 7/158 8/158
9/178

Essex

T. C. Dodds c Nicholls b Lambert	0	—	c and b Smith	1
G. Barker c Carpenter b Lambert	9	—	c Hawkins b Lambert	6
B. Taylor lbw b Lambert	14	—	lbw b Wells	20
G. Smith run out	8	—	b Lambert	1
S. C. Eve b Smith	22	—	not out	22
M. Bear c Meyer b Wells	123	—	not out	2
W. T. Greensmith c Lambert b Wells	16			
R. Ralph lbw b Wells	30			
K. C. Preston c Young b Smith	33			
I. M. King c and b Cook	33			
E. Palmer not out	9			
L-b 6, n-b 3	9		L-b 2, w 1	3

1/0 2/16 3/27 4/53 5/58 6/90 7/171　　　306
8/242 9/294 (2.97 an over)

1/7 2/7 3/16 4/46 (4 wkts.)　　　55

Essex Bowling

	O.	M.	R.	W.	O.	M.	R.	W.
Preston	18	4	50	2	32	10	71	3
Palmer	15	6	35	2	3	0	13	0
Ralph	13.3	6	34	4	22	8	42	3
King	20	10	34	1	11.4	4	25	4
Greensmith					9	4	13	0

Gloucestershire Bowling

	O.	M.	R.	W.		O.	M.	R.	W.
Lambert	26	2	98	3	...	9	2	22	2
Smith	35	5	97	2	...	4	1	14	1
Wells	32	10	64	3	...	6	3	8	1
Cook	9.1	2	38	1	...	2	1	5	0
Emmett						0.4	0	3	0

Umpires: P. Corrall and N. Oldfield.

At The Oval, June 1, 3. ESSEX lost to SURREY by an innings and 87 runs.

At Worcester, June 8, 10, 11. ESSEX drew with WORCESTERSHIRE.

ESSEX v. LANCASHIRE

At Brentwood, June 12, 13, 14. Essex won by seven wickets, taking 14 points. A stand of 62 for the seventh wicket by Hilton and Jordan saved Lancashire from failure on the opening day when the pitch favoured seam bowlers and the accurate Preston achieved considerable success. Thanks to a partnership of 62 by Barker and Taylor, Essex went ahead with six wickets in hand, but rash batting by the later men restricted their lead to 34. With the exception of Ikin, who obtained 50 of 79 added with Edrich, Lancashire displayed much care in the second innings. Edrich stayed over four and a half hours for 72 and, last out, just failed to become the first Lancashireman to carry his bat since 1951. Left to score 143 in four hours on a worn pitch, Essex achieved the task in half that time. Dodds hit ten 4's in eighty minutes and Taylor (nine 4's) and Bailey scored the last 68 without being parted.

Lancashire

G. A. Edrich c Taylor b Ralph	31	—	b Preston	72
A. Wharton c Taylor b Preston	1	—	c Taylor b Bailey	20
J. T. Ikin c Bailey b Ralph	22	—	run out	50
K. Grieves c Bailey b Preston	13	—	lbw b Bailey	1
G. Pullar b Bailey	23	—	b Bailey	4
R. Collins b Ralph	8	—	c Insole b Greensmith	10
M. J. Hilton b Preston	43	—	lbw b Greensmith	9
J. Jordan lbw b King	23	—	b Preston	5
J. B. Statham c Ralph b Preston	7	—	b Preston	0
R. Tattersall not out	0	—	c Taylor b Greensmith	0
T. Greenhough b Preston	0	—	not out	4
B 2, l-b 3, n-b 1	6		N-b 1	1

1/1 2/45 3/58 4/90 5/90 6/104   177
7/166 8/170 9/177 (2.29 an over)

1/22 2/101 3/102 4/106   176
5/123 6/138 7/143 8/143
9/151

Essex

T. C. Dodds c Collins b Statham	4	—	c Grieves b Hilton	58
G. Barker b Statham	40	—	b Tattersall	10
B. Taylor c Statham b Hilton	34	—	not out	51
R. Ralph c Edrich b Hilton	27			
D. J. Insole b Greenhough	36	—	c Jordan b Hilton	0
T. E. Bailey c Statham b Tattersall	34	—	not out	23
M. Bear b Greenhough	0			
G. Smith c Edrich b Tattersall	3			
W. T. Greensmith lbw b Greenhough	5			
K. C. Preston b Wharton	14			
I. M. King not out	2			
B 5, l-b 5, n-b 2	12		L-b 1, n-b 1	2

1/9 2/76 3/95 4/133 5/180 6/184   211
7/188 8/188 9/194 (2.57 an over)

1/39 2/76 3/76   (3 wkts.) 144

Essex Bowling

	O.	M.	R.	W.		O.	M.	R.	W.
Bailey	20	8	38	1	....	26	4	53	3
Preston	21.2	7	35	5	....	13.5	4	36	3
Ralph	22	5	54	3	....	8	3	10	0
King	7	2	16	1	....	9	2	16	0
Greensmith	3	0	16	0	....	27	7	60	3
Insole	4	1	12	0					

Lancashire Bowling

	O.	M.	R.	W.		O.	M.	R.	W.
Statham	22	6	39	2	....	10	2	28	0
Wharton	4.3	1	12	1	....	4	1	11	0
Tattersall	22	10	43	2	....	7	3	24	1
Hilton	11	3	39	2	....	13.5	1	52	2
Greenhough	21	7	66	3	....	4	0	27	0
Ikin	1	1	0	0					

Umpires: R. S. Lay and T. W. Spencer.

ESSEX v. LEICESTERSHIRE

At Brentwood, June 15, 17, 18. Essex won by 181 runs, taking 12 points to two by Leicestershire. On a very fast pitch, Boshier, bowling at a fine pace, proved too much for most of the Essex batsmen on the first day and he achieved the best analysis of his career. Insole, missed when one, played pluckily for ninety minutes and valuable runs came from Ralph and Preston. A partial breakdown followed an opening stand of 92 by Lester and Hallam for Leicestershire, but Palmer (fourteen 4's) drove well for just over three hours. Dodds (eleven 4's) drove fiercely for Essex who cleared arrears of 113 with two men out. Solid batting ensued, Greensmith and Smith adding 93. Leicestershire, needing 227 to win, were dismissed on a worn pitch in seventy-five minutes. Bailey proved specially effective, taking his first four wickets in the course of eight balls for four runs.

Essex

T. C. Dodds c and b Spencer	1	—	run out	57
G. Barker b Spencer	5	—	b Palmer	44
B. Taylor c Firth b Boshier	10	—	c Firth b Boshier	31
D. J. Insole c and b Boshier	65	—	c Hallam b Munden	43
T. E. Bailey c Firth b Boshier	0	—	c Firth b Munden	5
M. Bear c Spencer b Boshier	8	—	st Firth b Palmer	13
G. Smith c Hallam b Boshier	0	—	c Palmer b van Geloven	59
W. T. Greensmith lbw b Boshier	1	—	lbw b van Geloven	40
R. Ralph c Firth b Boshier	31	—	not out	17
K. C. Preston c Palmer b Boshier	25	—	c Diment b Boshier	6
I. M. King not out	2	—	not out	5
L-b 1	1		B 6, l-b 12, n-b 1	19

1/4 2/7 3/31 4/43 5/67 6/67 7/73   149
8/100 9/138 (3.82 an over)

1/88 2/130   (9 wkts., dec.) 339
3/139 4/164 5/193 6/211
7/304 8/311 9/324

Leicestershire

G. Lester c Taylor b Ralph	67	— c Greensmith b Bailey	1
M. R. Hallam b Greensmith	39	— c Ralph b Bailey	4
L. R. Gardner c King b Preston	14	— lbw b Preston	13
C. H. Palmer not out	102	— c Taylor b Bailey	0
R. A. Diment c Ralph b Greensmith	0	— c King b Bailey	4
J. van Geloven b Greensmith	1	— c Greensmith b Preston	8
V. S. Munden c Insole b Preston	8	— b Bailey	0
J. Firth b Preston	12	— c Ralph b Preston	9
C. T. Spencer c Bailey b King	13	— c King b Bailey	1
J. S. Savage c Barker b Greensmith	0	— not out	4
B. S. Boshier run out	0	— b Preston	0
B 1, l-b 1, w 1, n-b 3	6	N-b 1	1

1/92 2/120 3/120 4/127 5/135 6/181 262
7/206 8/236 9/237 (2.51 an over)

1/5 2/5 3/5 4/9 5/30 45
6/31 7/37 8/41 9/45

Leicestershire Bowling

	O.	M.	R.	W.		O.	M.	R.	W.
Spencer	17	1	93	2	....	27	1	61	0
Boshier	19.2	4	45	8	....	31	6	71	2
Palmer	3	0	10	0	....	13	2	25	2
Munden						26	7	85	2
Savage						20	8	58	0
van Geloven						8	4	15	2
Lester						2	0	5	0

Essex Bowling

	O.	M.	R.	W.		O.	M.	R.	W.
Bailey	11	3	15	0	....	10	1	28	6
Preston	29	6	83	3	....	9.2	4	16	4
Ralph	18	4	59	1					
Greensmith	32.5	9	85	4					
King	13	5	14	1					

Umpires: R. S. Lay and T. W. Spencer.

At Bath, June 19, 20, 21. ESSEX lost to SOMERSET by seven wickets.

At Stroud, June 22, 24, 25. ESSEX beat GLOUCESTERSHIRE by innings and 21 runs.

ESSEX v. NORTHAMPTONSHIRE

At Westcliff, June 26, 27, 28. Drawn, Essex taking four points. Sent in to bat on a well-grassed pitch, they lost two wickets cheaply, but Insole, despite much physical punishment from the fast deliveries of Tyson, drove skilfully for four and three-quarter hours, hitting eighteen 4's. Savill, his best partner, helped him add 114. Northamptonshire collapsed against the seam bowling of Bailey and Ralph, but when they followed on 178 behind Reynolds led the way in a recovery. Batting six hours and giving only one sharp chance, Reynolds hit twenty-three 4's in the highest innings of his career. Livingston and Fellows-Smith shared with him in stands of 142 and 92. Essex, requiring 244 to win, lost six men for 108, but Bailey (seventeen 4's) made the game safe with a brisk innings.

Essex

T. C. Dodds c Tribe b Kelleher	34	— c Fellows-Smith b Tyson	..	29
G. Barker c Andrew b Tyson	1	— c Allen b Tyson		0
B. Taylor c Andrew b Tyson	32	— b Tyson		0
D. J. Insole c Brookes b Kelleher	140	— c Tribe b Tyson		20
T. E. Bailey c Reynolds b Tyson	22	— lbw b Allen		79
L. Savill c Livingston b Tyson	41	— c Andrew b Kelleher		0
M. Bear c Kelleher b Tyson	1	— c Andrew b Tyson		0
W. T. Greensmith c Andrew b Kelleher	1	— not out		5
R. Ralph c Andrew b Kelleher	5	— not out		0
K. C. Preston c Manning b Kelleher	9			
I. M. King not out	4			
L-b 7, w 1	8	B 18, w 1		19

1/25 2/35 3/73 4/123 5/237 6/241   298   1/15 2/16 3/33   (7 wkts.) 152
7/242 8/252 9/286 (3.27 an over)   4/68 5/80 6/108 7/152

Northamptonshire

D. Brookes b Bailey	12	— c Taylor b Bailey	5
B. L. Reynolds c Ralph b Preston	11	— b Ralph	169
K. V. Andrew c King b Bailey	0	— c Bailey b Ralph	7
L. Livingston c King b Bailey	0	— c Taylor b Ralph	77
D. W. Barrick c Insole b Bailey	25	— c Ralph b Insole	8
G. E. Tribe c Barker b Ralph	3	— lbw b Bailey	38
J. P. Fellows-Smith lbw b Preston	40	— c Bear b Preston	59
J. S. Manning b Ralph	0	— c Bailey b Ralph	4
F. H. Tyson c Taylor b Ralph	18	— not out	27
M. H. J. Allen c King b Ralph	7	— c Savill b Preston	13
H. R. A. Kelleher not out	2	— not out	9
L-b 2	2	B 3, l-b 2	5

1/18 2/18 3/18 4/32 5/52 6/52 7/52   120   1/6 2/148   (9 wkts., dec.) 421
8/108 9/118 (2.85 an over)   3/175 4/259 5/351 6/363
7/368 8/391 9/409

Northamptonshire Bowling

	O.	M.	R.	W.	O.	M.	R.	W.
Tyson	29	8	88	5	15	7	34	5
Kelleher	25.1	2	101	5	12	6	45	1
Fellows-Smith	11	0	36	0	2	0	12	0
Manning	11	5	18	0	9	2	33	0
Tribe	10	1	38	0	7	5	9	0
Allen	5	1	9	0	2	2	0	1

Essex Bowling

	O.	M.	R.	W.	O.	M.	R.	W.
Bailey	18	6	39	4	28	6	86	2
Preston	12.2	1	42	2	37	8	124	2
Ralph	12	4	37	4	31	4	128	4
Greensmith					3	0	21	0
King					7	0	32	0
Insole					8	3	25	1

Umpires: C. S. Elliott and J. S. Buller.

ESSEX v. OXFORD UNIVERSITY

At Westcliff, June 29, July 1, 2. Essex won by three wickets. Eagar, by
stylish all-round strokes in a stay of two hours twenty minutes, hit nineteen 4's,
and saved Oxford from collapse on a very green pitch on the first day, when
Preston bowled with marked skill. Only Dodds and Ralph achieved much for
Essex against the pace of Bowman, and Oxford gained a lead of 43. Bowman

followed his best bowling performance with his highest innings after the University lost seven wickets for 72 and he and Bailey added 64 for the last wicket. Essex required 226 to win and Dodds and Taylor put them on the way to victory with a second wicket partnership of 108, though Oxford fought to the end.

Oxford University

J. A. D. Hobbs c Greensmith b Preston .	1	— c Preston b Ralph	0
I. Gibson b Preston	0	— lbw b Ralph	11
M. A. Eagar c Taylor b King	99	— c Ralph b Preston	16
C. D. Melville c Taylor b Greensmith	23	— c Bear b Greensmith	17
J. M. Kumleben c Ralph b Preston	6	— c Taylor b Preston	0
R. L. Jowett run out	6	— c Taylor b Preston	7
R. G. Woodcock c Bear b Preston	20	— c King b Preston	12
M. D. Scott c Savill b Preston	3	— c Barker b Greensmith	9
R. Bowman b Greensmith	0	— c Preston b Ralph	75
R. W. Wilson not out	8	— c Taylor b King	2
J. A. Bailey c Savill b King	2	— not out	23
B 1, l-b 1	2	B 7, l-b 3	10

1/0 2/1 3/33 4/45 5/138 6/140   170   1/2 2/27 3/27 4/32 5/37   182
7/143 8/144 9/147   6/50 7/72 8/85 9/118

Essex

T. C. Dodds b Bowman	30	— c Scott b Bowman	62
G. Barker c Hobbs b Bailey	7	— lbw b Bailey	7
B. Taylor c Bailey b Bowman	16	— c sub b Bailey	68
L. Savill c Wilson b Woodcock	6	— c Wilson b Bailey	19
J. Milner c Jowett b Bowman	16	— c Wilson b Bailey	27
M. Bear c Hobbs b Bailey	0	— run out	3
G. Smith b Bowman	6	— c Woodcock b Bailey	0
W. T. Greensmith c Gibson b Bowman	5	— not out	19
R. Ralph c Gibson b Bowman	27	— not out	13
K. C. Preston c Scott b Bowman	14		
I. M. King not out	0		
		B 3, l-b 3, w 1, n-b 1	8

1/31 2/53 3/53 4/69 5/69 6/80 7/81   127   1/21 2/129   (7 wkts.) 226
8/94 9/126   3/146 4/176 5/186 6/186
                                                        7/193

Essex Bowling

	O.	M.	R.	W.		O.	M.	R.	W.
Preston	19	5	41	5	....	19	9	32	4
Ralph	10	1	40	0	....	16	5	39	3
King	22	8	35	2	....	16	5	43	1
Greensmith	13.5	6	52	2	....	19	5	58	2

Oxford University Bowling

	O.	M.	R.	W.		O.	M.	R.	W.
Bailey	20	7	39	2	....	29	9	71	5
Bowman	19.3	5	60	7	....	17.5	3	80	1
Woodcock	12	3	28	1	....	15	2	38	0
					Wilson	4	0	29	0

Umpires: C. S. Elliott and J. S. Buller.

At Sheffield, July 6, 8, 9. ESSEX lost to YORKSHIRE by six wickets.

At Birmingham, July 10, 11, 12. ESSEX drew with WARWICKSHIRE.

ESSEX v. SOMERSET

At Colchester, July 13, 15. Essex beat Somerset by eight wickets, taking 12 points. Bowling strength was the deciding factor, and Ralph, who controlled his medium-fast deliveries admirably, deservedly earned the splendid match analysis of ten wickets for 86 runs. He and Preston were unchanged in the first innings when Somerset were routed on a green pitch by lunch time. McCool, with his leg-spin, troubled Essex but Barker, by sound batting, helped them to gain a lead of 100 by the close. Somerset showed improved form in their second innings, with Tripp, the only Somerset-born batsman in the side, driving and cutting attractively. Essex were left to make 98 to win and when Barker was caught at the wicket with only five runs on the board Somerset hopes rose, but Dodds and Taylor, by free stroke-play which brought 89 runs in an hour, put their side on the road to victory.

Somerset

W. E. Alley c Taylor b Preston	7	— c Ralph b Greensmith 39
J. G. Lomax c Insole b Ralph	22	— c Insole b Preston 2
G. M. Tripp b Preston	6	— lbw b Ralph 62
C. L. McCool c Insole b Ralph	5	— b Ralph 9
G. G. Atkinson lbw b Preston	4	— b Greensmith 37
M. F. Tremlett c and b Ralph	7	— c Preston b Greensmith ... 1
H. W. Stephenson c Dodds b Preston	9	— lbw b Preston 17
K. H. Palmer not out	11	— c Taylor b Preston 1
B. Langford c King b Ralph	2	— lbw b Ralph 4
B. Lobb b Ralph	2	— not out 5
J. W. McMahon c Insole b Ralph	1	— c Taylor b Ralph 17
N-b 1	1	B 1, l-b 1, w 1 3
	77	197

1/8 2/16 3/33 4/40 5/50 6/56 7/60
8/66 9/70 (2.26 an over)

1/3 2/55 3/63 4/79 5/141
6/143 7/187 8/187 9/191

Essex

T. C. Dodds lbw b Alley	8	— not out 47
G. Barker c Tremlett b Lobb	48	— c Stephenson b Lobb 0
B. Taylor c Lomax b Palmer	30	— c Langford b McMahon ... 48
D. J. Insole c Atkinson b Alley	4	— not out 0
T. E. Bailey c and b McMahon	29	
L. Savill c and b McCool	8	
M. Bear b McCool	3	
W. T. Greensmith lbw b McCool	23	
R. Ralph not out	12	
K. C. Preston c Langford b McMahon	1	
I. M. King lbw b McCool	1	
B 5, l-b 5	10	L-b 3 3
	177	(2 wkts.) 98

1/15 2/76 3/81 4/90 5/105 6/111
7/158 8/172 9/173 (2.18 an over)

1/5 2/94

Essex Bowling

	O.	M.	R.	W.	O.	M.	R.	W.
Preston	17	3	43	4	21	7	45	3
Ralph	16.5	6	33	6	28	7	53	4
Greensmith					23	3	65	3
Bailey					2	1	2	0
King					13	3	27	0
Insole					1	0	2	0

Somerset Bowling

	O.	M.	R.	W.		O.	M.	R.	W.
Lobb	14	0	48	1	....	6	0	14	1
Alley..........	25	9	23	2	....	4	1	10	0
Lomax	4	1	10	0	....				
Palmer	10	2	43	1	....	2.5	0	16	0
Langford	2	1	5	0	....	3	0	18	0
McMahon	9	8	1	2	....	7	2	27	1
McCool	17	5	37	4	....	2	0	10	0

Umpires: T. J. Bartley and E. Davies.

ESSEX v. SUSSEX

At Colchester, July 17, 18, 19. Essex won by 184 runs, taking 12 points, after being sent in to bat on a damp pitch. Batting failures were many, Sussex showing in a specially poor light. When set 241 to get to win, they lost their last seven wickets for six runs. T. Bailey, who bore a big part in bringing about this collapse, shared with Barker in the one real stand of the Essex first innings which realised 137 for the third wicket. Barker's first century of the season occupied four hours forty minutes and included sixteen 4's. With Ralph taking three wickets in four balls, Essex led by 91, but fared badly in the second innings till Bear and Greensmith added 62.

Essex

T. C. Dodds b Bates	13	— b James..................	37
G. Barker c Cogger b Bates	107	— c Foreman b Thomson	9
B. Taylor c Suttle b Bates	0	— c Mantell b Bates	0
T. E. Bailey c Mantell b Foreman	61	— c Bates b James	4
L. Savill b James	17	— c Foreman b Bates	8
M. Bear st Mantell b Thomson	25	— b Suttle	42
W. T. Greensmith c Lenham b Thomson	2	— not out	38
R. Ralph run out	8	— c Mantell b Suttle	0
K. C. Preston c Cogger b Bates	0	— not out	11
I. M. King not out	0		
J. A. Bailey lbw b Thomson	0		
L-b 3, n-b 1..................	4		

1/19 2/19 3/156 4/195 5/210 6/221   237   1/29 2/30   (7 wkts., dec.) 149
7/233 8/237 9/237 (2.17 an over)   3/48 4/51 5/71 6/133 7/137

Sussex

A. E. James lbw b King	19	— c Ralph b T. Bailey	10
L. J. Lenham c T. Bailey b J. Bailey....	41	— b Preston	0
K. G. Suttle c Dodds b Ralph..........	18	— c T. Bailey b J. Bailey	15
J. M. Parks lbw b Ralph	27	— b T. Bailey	21
D. J. Foreman st Taylor b Greensmith ..	31	— b J. Bailey	0
G. Potter c Taylor b Greensmith	2	— lbw b T. Bailey	1
R. J. Langridge c Preston b Greensmith ..	0	— not out	2
G. Cogger c Taylor b Ralph	0	— b T. Bailey	0
N. I. Thomson lbw b Ralph	0	— lbw b Greensmith	1
D. N. Mantell b Ralph	0	— b T. Bailey	1
D. L. Bates not out	0	— st Taylor b Greensmith	1
B 4, l-b 3, w 1	8	B 4..................	4

1/40 2/82 3/90 4/128 5/135 6/135   146   1/8 2/10 3/50 4/50 5/51   56
7/144 8/144 9/146 (2.43 an over)   6/51 7/51 8/52 9/53

Sussex Bowling

	O.	M.	R.	W.	O.	M.	R.	W.
Thomson	27.3	7	43	3	16	4	29	1
Bates	26	8	62	4	18	3	51	2
James	35	14	65	1	12	4	30	2
Cogger	4	0	18	0				
Suttle	8	2	32	0	12	2	39	2
Foreman	8	5	13	1				

Essex Bowling

	O.	M.	R.	W.	O.	M.	R.	W.
Preston	15	4	28	0	6	1	13	1
Ralph	15.2	4	29	5	4	1	10	0
King	11	7	20	1				
J. Bailey	12	2	38	1	5	2	11	2
Greensmith	7	0	23	3	7.3	4	4	2
T. Bailey					13	7	14	5

Umpires: E. Davies and T. J. Bartley.

At Ebbw Vale, July 20, 22, 23. ESSEX drew with GLAMORGAN.

At Lord's, July 24, 25, 26. ESSEX lost to MIDDLESEX by 209 runs.

At Manchester, July 27, 29, 30. ESSEX drew with LANCASHIRE.

ESSEX v. MIDDLESEX
(T. C. Dodds's Benefit)

At Leyton, July 31, August 1, 2. Essex won by 74 runs, taking 12 points to four by Middlesex, in their first match at Leyton for 24 years. This was a great achievement considering they were 159 behind on first innings. Essex fared badly on a well-grassed pitch on the opening day and Middlesex, thanks chiefly to Robertson, handicapped by a strain, and Compton, whose 121st century occupied two and a quarter hours and contained one 6 and seventeen 4's, went ahead with seven wickets intact. There followed a remarkable Essex recovery in which Barker, batting five and a quarter hours and hitting eighteen 4's, bore a leading part. Dodds helped him in an opening stand of 70 and Taylor and Insole in partnerships of 113 and 102. When Insole declared, leaving Middlesex 219 to win in two and a half hours, Gale played a gallant innings, but no one else achieved much against the fast-medium bowling of Preston and Bailey. The gate receipts for Dodds's benefit amounted to £1,100 and collections realised £262.

Essex

T. C. Dodds lbw b Bennett	9	— c and b Titmus	48
G. Barker c Murray b Warr	3	— lbw b Hurst	117
B. Taylor b Warr	8	— b Titmus	46
D. J. Insole lbw b Titmus	31	— b Bennett	93
L. Savill b Warr	14	— run out	32
M. Bear run out	31	— run out	1
W. T. Greensmith b Moss	1	— not out	5
R. Ralph c Robertson b Compton	1	— not out	18
K. C. Preston c Baldry b Titmus	4		
J. A. Bailey not out	6		
I. M. King st Murray b Titmus	3		
B 4	4	B 10, l-b 7	17

1/13 2/19 3/24 4/54 5/95 6/100 7/102   115
8/102 9/106 (2.01 an over)

1/70 2/183   (6 wkts., dec.)   377
3/285 4/350 5/352 6/355

Middlesex

	First innings		Second innings	
J. D. Robertson	lbw b Ralph	59	c Dodds b Ralph	11
R. A. Gale	c King b Insole	32	b Greensmith	60
D. O. Baldry	lbw b Greensmith	27	b Bailey	17
R. J. Hurst	c Ralph b Greensmith	0	lbw b Preston	0
D. C. S. Compton	b Ralph	109	b Preston	21
A. C. Walton	lbw b Greensmith	18	c King b Bailey	12
F. J. Titmus	c Insole b Ralph	14	c and b Bailey	10
J. T. Murray	c and b Preston	0	c Insole b Preston	2
D. Bennett	c and b Preston	3	c Ralph b Preston	5
J. J. Warr	not out	2	not out	1
A. E. Moss	lbw b Ralph	0	c and b Preston	1
	B 4, l-b 6	10	L-b 2, n-b 2	4
		274		**144**

1/10 2/111 3/113 4/143 5/186 6/262 7/263 8/267 9/273 (3.04 an over)

1/13 2/72 3/90 4/105 5/123 6/135 7/139 8/140 9/143

Middlesex Bowling

	O.	M.	R.	W.		O.	M.	R.	W.
Moss	12	4	27	1	....	20	3	58	0
Bennett	14	6	21	1	....	6	1	34	1
Warr	15	3	41	3	....	22	5	50	0
Baldry	4	2	7	0	....	5	0	19	0
Titmus	8	5	6	3	....	44	15	104	2
Compton	4	2	9	1	....	5	0	26	0
Hurst						29	12	69	1

Essex Bowling

	O.	M.	R.	W.		O.	M.	R.	W.
Preston	25	7	62	2	....	14	7	42	5
Ralph	21.5	6	62	4	....	6	0	24	1
Bailey	14	4	48	0	....	10	0	42	3
Insole	9	5	14	1	....	1	0	2	0
King	7	1	32	0					
Greensmith	13	2	46	3	....	5	1	30	1

Umpires: H. Elliott and F. S. Lee.

At Canterbury, August 7, 8, 9. ESSEX drew with KENT.

At Wellingborough, August 10, 12, 13. ESSEX lost to NORTHAMPTONSHIRE by eight wickets.

ESSEX v. WORCESTERSHIRE

At Leyton, August 3, 5, 6. Drawn, Essex taking four points. Time had not altered the main characteristic of the Leyton pitch. It remained as favourable to batsmen as in the days when it was the county headquarters. As many as 912 runs were scored in the match and only 23 wickets fell. Essex, normally among the better fielding sides, suffered an unaccountable series of lapses on the first day, and the advantage gained when Kenyon and P. E. Richardson were dismissed for 40 was dissipated. The succeeding batsmen, particularly Horton, built up a strong position. Horton's 93 was his highest of the season, and he made his runs quicker than any of the others. Essex began with a stand of 74 in an hour, and after Insole's bright innings, Bailey and Savill punished some indifferent bowling in a stand of 158. Bailey, who took three and a half hours to reach his hundred, hit two 6's and seventeen 4's. Worcestershire batted throughout the last day, when there was never any likelihood of a definite result.

Worcestershire

D. Kenyon b J. Bailey	4	—	c Preston b Greensmith	22
P. E. Richardson c J. Bailey b Ralph	24	—	c Taylor b J. Bailey	49
G. Dews c J. Bailey b Insole	40	—	c Bear b Greensmith	24
D. W. Richardson c Preston b Ralph	52	—	c Taylor b J. Bailey	1
R. G. Broadbent lbw b Preston	76	—	c Preston b J. Bailey	0
M. J. Horton c Taylor b J. Bailey	93	—	b Greensmith	54
R. Booth b J. Bailey	15	—	c Preston b Greensmith	17
R. O. Jenkins b Preston	13	—	not out	22
G. H. Chesterton c Taylor b J. Bailey	0			
R. Berry not out	2	—	not out	2
B 1, l-b 6, n-b 3	10		B 8, n-b 3	11

1/32 2/40 3/96 4/157   (9 wkts., dec.) 329   1/35 2/82 3/98   (7 wkts.) 202
5/234 6/294 7/316 8/324 9/329   4/98 5/117 6/150 7/187
(2.93 an over)

L. N. Coldwell did not bat.

Essex

T. C. Dodds c Kenyon b Berry	40	W. T. Greensmith not out	21
G. Barker c Dews b Berry	38	B 2, l-b 5, w 1	8
B. Taylor c P. Richardson b Berry	11		
D. J. Insole c Dews b Berry	53		
T. E. Bailey c Dews b Coldwell	132	1/74 2/87 3/104 (7 wkts., dec.) 381	
L. Savill st Booth b Berry	78	4/179 5/337 6/337 7/381	
M. Bear c P. Richardson b Berry	0	(3.20 an over)	

R. Ralph, K. C. Preston and J. A. Bailey did not bat.

Essex Bowling

	O.	M.	R.	W.		O.	M.	R.	W.
Preston	26	4	79	2	....	19	5	41	0
Ralph	24	4	63	2	....	15	5	40	0
J. Bailey	28.2	6	60	4	....	17	6	26	3
Insole	14	4	37	1					
Greensmith	20	2	80	0	....	32	3	82	4
Barker						2	0	2	0

Worcestershire Bowling

	O.	M.	R.	W.
Coldwell	30.3	3	104	1
Chesterton	22	3	76	0
Berry	37	10	115	6
Jenkins	7	0	35	0
Horton	22	8	43	0

Umpires: H. Elliott and F. S. Lee.

ESSEX v. NOTTINGHAMSHIRE

At Southend, August 14, 15, 16. Drawn, without a result on first innings. Rain prevented play on the first two days, but the third produced some remarkable cricket. Sent in to bat, Essex lost three wickets in five balls from Jepson without a run scored. Then Barker, driving and pulling powerfully, and Bailey, specially strong on the leg-side, put on 174 in two hours twenty minutes, but it was unfortunate for Nottinghamshire that Jepson had to retire midway through his sixth over with a torn calf muscle. Barker hit his third century of the season in two and a half hours with one 6 and thirteen 4's among his strokes. Insole's declaration left Nottinghamshire to score at 84 an hour to gain the eight points dependent upon first innings lead, a task they did not attempt.

Essex

T. C. Dodds c Martin b Jepson .. 0	A. Durley st Millman b Dooland.. 1
G. Barker b Matthews 100	W. T. Greensmith not out........ 4
B. Taylor lbw b Jepson 0	B 7....................... 7
D. J. Insole b Jepson 0	
T. E. Bailey b Matthews 74	1/0 2/0 3/0 4/174 (6 wkts., dec.) 188
L. Savill not out 2	5/181 6/184 (3.18 an over)

R. Ralph, K. C. Preston and J. A. Bailey did not bat.

Nottinghamshire

J. D. Springall b J. Bailey 40	N. Hill not out 9
E. J. Martin c T. Bailey b Preston 7	M. Hill not out 15
C. J. Poole b Preston 4	
R. Dooland c Greensmith b Preston 0	1/22 2/32 3/32 4/51 (5 wkts.) 80
G. Goonesena b Ralph 5	5/62 (2.28 an over)

G. Millman, A. Jepson, M. Morgan and C. S. Matthews did not bat.

Nottinghamshire Bowling	O.	M.	R.	W.	Essex Bowling	O.	M.	R.	W.
Jepson	6	5	2	3	T. Bailey......	7	2	17	0
Matthews	14	1	53	2	Preston	14	3	34	3
Morgan.......	9	0	51	0	Ralph	6	1	23	1
Dooland	21	5	33	1	J. Bailey	3	2	2	1
Goonesena ...	9	1	42	0	Greensmith ...	5	2	4	0

Umpires: P. Corrall and W. F. Price.

ESSEX v. WARWICKSHIRE

At Southend, August 17, 19, 20. Drawn, Essex taking two points. Most excitement came on the last day. Warwickshire, set to get 231 at 82 an hour, began quietly, but Smith and Townsend hit freely and with ten minutes remaining they stood within 26 of victory with five wickets left. Then, helped by a wonderful running catch by Barker, Bailey and Preston with the new ball caused a collapse and the total went to 215 for nine wickets. Hollies, the last man, foiled Essex by surviving the last three balls. On the first day Dodds stayed nearly two and a half hours, but six Essex wickets were down for 100. Bailey led a recovery, batting carefully for almost four hours, and Preston hit freely in a stand of 65. Warwickshire started well, but broke down against Preston and Ralph, and though Leach, twice missed, rallied them and Spooner helped put on 58, they finished 26 behind. Taylor, hitting eleven 4's, paved the way to a declaration in the Essex second innings.

Essex

T. C. Dodds b Hollies................. 47	— st Spooner b Wheatley 26
G. Barker c Smith b Bannister 3	— c Smith b Bannister 0
B. Taylor b Wheatley 0	— c Leach b Bannister 88
D. J. Insole b Hollies 20	— c Spooner b Wheatley 0
T. E. Bailey b Carter................. 80	— c Spooner b Hollies 21
L. Savill c Townsend b Carter 2	— st Spooner b Hollies 12
A. Durley lbw b Carter............... 2	— b Hollies 4
W. T. Greensmith c Smith b Bannister .. 9	— c Leach b Bannister 7
R. Ralph lbw b Wheatley 5	— not out 28
K. C. Preston c Gardner b Carter 40	— b Wheatley 0
I. M. King not out 0	— not out 6
B 12, l-b 3 15	B 6, l-b 4, w 1, n-b 1 .. 12

1/5 2/8 3/52 4/87 5/90 6/100 7/149   223   1/8 2/30   (9 wkts., dec.) 204
8/158 9/223 (2.16 an over)   3/30 4/114 5/144 6/162
7/162 8/175 9/189

Warwickshire

F. C. Gardner b Bailey	38	— c Bailey b Greensmith 51
N. F. Horner c Ralph b Preston	29	— lbw b Bailey 6
W. J. Stewart lbw b Ralph	10	— b King 29
M. J. K. Smith st Taylor b Preston	1	— c Savill b King 25
A. Townsend c Durley b Preston	0	— b Bailey 38
C. W. Leach c and b Ralph	67	— c Greensmith b Bailey 24
R. T. Spooner lbw b Greensmith	30	— c Barker b Bailey 15
R. G. Carter run out	1	— c Ralph b Preston 9
J. D. Bannister b Ralph	1	— not out 0
O. S. Wheatley not out	3	— c Durley b Preston 0
W. E. Hollies b Ralph	1	— not out 0
B 13, l-b 2, n-b 1	16	B 5, l-b 11, n-b 2...... 18

1/57 2/82 3/85 4/85 5/114 6/172   197   1/15 2/89 3/99   (9 wkts.) 215
7/181 8/193 9/195 (2.59 an over)   4/132 5/180 6/205 7/205
                                     8/215 9/215

Warwickshire Bowling

	O.	M.	R.	W.		O.	M.	R.	W.
Bannister	22	5	38	2	....	33.3	13	49	3
Wheatley	17	4	25	2	....	15	3	63	3
Carter	25	8	56	4	....	5	0	24	0
Townsend	2	0	12	0	....	3	1	6	0
Hollies	32	8	69	2	....	26	10	50	3
Leach	5	0	8	0					

Essex Bowling

	O.	M.	R.	W.		O.	M.	R.	W.
Preston	25	3	78	3	....	9	3	24	2
Bailey	16	2	51	1	....	14	2	35	4
Ralph	16.1	8	17	4	....	7	2	19	0
King	10	6	16	0	....	11	2	42	2
Greensmith	9	2	19	1	....	14	0	77	1

Umpires: P. Corrall and W. F. Price.

At Leicester, August 21, 22, 23. ESSEX drew with LEICESTERSHIRE.

ESSEX v. KENT

At Clacton, August 24, 26, 27. Essex won by 87 runs, taking 14 points. They were the superior side, but Kent stubbornly contested the issue when set 399 to win. Dodds and Barker played a valuable part in the success by splendid batting during opening partnerships of 161 and 79. In the first innings accurate seam bowling by Smith helped in the dismissal of the last five men for 29 runs, and when Kent went in Preston and Ralph, lively off the pitch, proved difficult. Taylor's hard hitting, which yielded him one 6 and fifteen 4's, enabled Insole to declare on the second evening. Kent scored 56 for two before the close and next day excellent stroke-play by Wilson and Dixon prolonged the game for another four and a half hours. Dixon hit fifteen 4's.

Essex

T. C. Dodds lbw b Smith	97	— lbw b Smith	81
G. Barker lbw b Page	62	— c Phebey b Smith	36
B. Taylor c Phebey b Smith	22	— lbw b Halfyard	91
D. J. Insole c Ridgway b Smith	6	— not out	58
L. Savill c Pettiford b Page	9	— not out	11
W. T. Greensmith c Pettiford b Page	6		
G. Smith b Smith	3		
R. Ralph lbw b Page	8		
K. C. Preston b Smith	6		
J. A. Bailey b Smith	1		
I. M. King not out	4		
L-b 7	7	B 7, l-b 6	13

1/161 2/161 3/177 4/198 5/202 6/209   **231**
7/215 8/225 9/227 (3.30 an over)

1/79 2/164   (3 wkts., dec.) **290**
3/256

Kent

A. H. Phebey lbw b Preston	9	— b Preston	11
R. C. Wilson c Insole b Ralph	4	— run out	78
P. E. Jones c Taylor b Preston	5	— lbw b Greensmith	5
J. Pettiford b Insole	12	— b Bailey	11
J. F. Pretlove lbw b Ralph	52	— c Preston b King	30
A. L. Dixon c King b Ralph	13	— c Smith b Preston	73
A. W. Catt c Taylor b Ralph	12	— c Taylor b King	32
G. Smith b Preston	2	— lbw b Preston	3
F. Ridgway b Preston	8	— c Bailey b Greensmith	33
D. J. Halfyard not out	2	— c King b Greensmith	9
J. C. T. Page b Ralph	2	— not out	8
L-b 1, w 1	2	B 8, l-b 9, n-b 1	18

1/6 2/16 3/23 4/54 5/77 6/103   **123**
7/110 8/110 9/118 (1.98 an over)

1/21 2/30 3/131 4/131   **311**
5/171 6/213 7/252 8/263
9/288

Kent Bowling

	O.	M.	R.	W.		O.	M.	R.	W.
Ridgway	4	0	38	0	....	13	3	56	0
Halfyard	9	0	38	0	....	11	1	56	1
Smith	23.3	4	53	6	....	19	6	38	2
Pettiford	9	0	37	0					
Page	24	10	58	4		9	1	44	0
Dixon						16	0	66	0
Jones						4	0	17	0

Essex Bowling

	O.	M.	R.	W.		O.	M.	R.	W.
Preston	20	7	29	4	....	28	8	71	3
Ralph	23.3	6	52	5	....	16	5	45	0
Bailey	6	1	13	0	....	19	3	70	1
Insole	5	0	12	1					
Greensmith	7	1	15	0	....	34.2	6	88	3
King					....	17	9	19	2

Umpires: W. E. Phillipson and W. Place.

ESSEX v. SURREY

At Clacton, August 28, 29, 30. Essex (12 points) beat Surrey (four points) by two wickets. This remarkable victory, gained despite first innings arrears of 133, was thoroughly deserved. First-rate bowling and fielding in the Surrey second innings followed by resolute batting turned the scale. The absence of May, from Surrey, and Trevor Bailey, from Essex, were compensating losses, but the

Champions, well served by the accurate bowling of A. Bedser and Laker and the attractive batting of Barrington, Constable and Stewart, held the whip hand until after tea on the second day. Then Preston, splendidly supported in the field, proved almost unplayable with his lively pace. At one stage he took three wickets without conceding a run and Surrey left off 61 for five. McIntyre's aggressiveness next morning saw Essex left to make 253 in four hours and thanks to the forceful, stylish stroke-play of Insole, who hit sixteen 4's in making 115 in two hours and fifty minutes, and the assistance given him by Savill and Bear, they won with twenty minutes to spare. Lock, after his great success in the Fifth Test match, was hit for 133 runs in the game and took only one wicket.

Surrey

M. J. Stewart c King b Insole	66	— c Taylor b Ralph	8
T. H. Clark c Taylor b Preston	17	— c Taylor b Preston	0
B. Constable c Savill b Preston	105	— lbw b Preston	19
K. F. Barrington not out	129	— c Taylor b Preston	16
D. G. W. Fletcher c Taylor b Preston	13	— c Ralph b Preston	0
E. A. Bedser b Ralph	13	— b Ralph	15
A. J. McIntyre run out	5	— c Preston b Greensmith	41
G. A. R. Lock c sub b Ralph	0	— run out	1
J. C. Laker not out	4	— not out	13
P. J. Loader (did not bat)		— c King b Greensmith	0
A. V. Bedser (did not bat)		— run out	0
B 5, l-b 9, w 1	15	B 1, l-b 5	6

1/29 2/143 3/260 4/304 (7 wkts., dec.) 367   1/0 2/18 3/42 4/44 5/49 119
5/327 6/345 7/346 (2.95 an over)   6/67 7/68 8/113 9/119

Essex

T. C. Dodds run out	21	— c Lock b Loader	8
G. Barker b Laker	66	— c Laker b Loader	2
B. Taylor b A. Bedser	10	— c Barrington b A. Bedser	7
D. J. Insole c Stewart b Laker	21	— b A. Bedser	115
L. Savill c Barrington b Laker	6	— lbw b A. Bedser	32
W. T. Greensmith c Barrington b A. Bedser	43	— c Lock b Laker	18
M. Bear lbw b A. Bedser	1	— c Fletcher b Loader	41
G. Smith c Fletcher b Lock	25	— c McIntyre b A. Bedser	3
R. Ralph c Fletcher b A. Bedser	22	— not out	2
K. C. Preston b A. Bedser	8	— not out	8
I. M. King not out	1		
B 3, l-b 6, n-b 1	10	B 6, l-b 14	20

1/35 2/49 3/103 4/124 5/129 6/132   234   1/9 2/16 3/22 (8 wkts.) 256
7/178 8/224 9/225 (2.57 an over)   4/103 5/149 6/231 7/245
                                                  8/245

Essex Bowling

	O.	M.	R.	W.		O.	M.	R.	W.
Preston	36	5	88	3	....	25.3	6	59	4
Ralph	36	6	122	2	....	18	3	48	2
Insole	18	4	31	1	....	5	3	3	0
King	22	8	52	0					
Greensmith	13	0	59	0	....	3	2	3	2

Surrey Bowling

	O.	M.	R.	W.		O.	M.	R.	W.
Loader	16	2	48	0	....	17.5	3	60	3
A. Bedser	25.3	7	49	5	....	21	2	61	4
Lock	23	5	79	1	....	12	1	54	0
Laker	20	7	38	3	....	14	2	54	1
E. Bedser	6	3	10	0	....	1	0	7	0

Umpires: W. E. Phillipson and W. Place.

GLAMORGAN

President—SIR HERBERT MERRETT

Captain and Secretary—WILFRED WOOLLER, 6, High Street, Cardiff

W. G. A. Parkhouse   County Badge   J. E. McConnon

Glamorgan enjoyed a much more successful season than was anticipated. Their final placing, joint ninth with Sussex, meant that they moved up four positions compared with 1956. In all, Glamorgan gained ten victories, four coming in successive county games at the end of May and the beginning of June. This fell only three short of the Championship winning total of 1948 and the difference could easily have been reduced to only one. The final match was a touch-and-go struggle, ending in success for Yorkshire by four runs. In addition, rain washed out play at Pontypridd with Glamorgan seemingly well placed against Derbyshire.

One of the biggest talking points concerned the state of the Cardiff pitch. Of the six matches played at The Arms Park, only the first, against Lancashire early in May, went into three days. All the others were completed in two, Glamorgan losing to the West Indies (five wickets), Warwickshire (ten wickets), Northamptonshire (ten wickets) and Yorkshire (four runs). Glamorgan's solitary success there was against Worcestershire, by 91 runs.

It was estimated that these two-day matches meant a loss of about £500 to the county exchequer. Worried by this blow to the finances, Glamorgan discussed the position with the local club and an improvement in the pitch can be expected this year.

This apart, Wooller, Glamorgan's long service captain, must have been well pleased with the summer's cricket. Three batsmen, Parkhouse, Watkins and Hedges, topped 1,000 runs in Championship matches and Shepherd and McConnon took nearly 200 wickets between them with off-breaks and cutters. Shepherd, on whose shoulders fell most of the work in 1956, found the burden eased with the return of McConnon after a year in League cricket.

Though Shepherd once again dominated the bowling, claiming 112 wickets, McConnon showed that he has lost none of his skill. He sent back 83 batsmen and also enjoyed a fair amount of success with the bat which he wielded in vigorous fashion.

With two young fast bowlers, H. D. Davies and Walker, making great strides, Wooller and Watkins were able to take matters more easily in the field. This probably accounted for the return to his best batting form by Watkins who, like Hedges and Parkhouse, hit two centuries. A seventh three-figure innings came from Devereux, who again proved himself an excellent all-rounder.

Best of all, Glamorgan's future prospects seem assured with the development of promising youngsters. Outstanding among these were Walker, a useful all-rounder, and William Davies, a right-hand opening batsman.

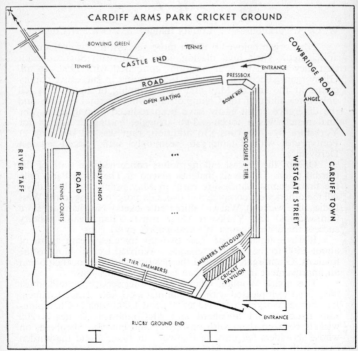

GLAMORGAN RESULTS

All First-Class Matches—Played 30, Won 10, Lost 11, Drawn 9

County Championship Matches—Played 28, Won 10, Lost 9,
Drawn 8, No Decision 1

COUNTY CHAMPIONSHIP AVERAGES
BATTING

	Birthplace	Mtchs.	Inns.	Not Outs	Runs	100's	Highest Inns.	Aver.
W. G. A. Parkhouse	Swansea	25	46	4	1538	2	133	36.61
A. J. Watkins	Usk	24	39	4	1091	2	140	31.17
W. E. Jones......	Carmarthen	17	28	3	703	0	69*	28.12
B. Hedges	Pontypridd	27	51	5	1288	2	139	28.00
L. N. Devereux ..	Exeter	27	49	7	965	1	108*	22.97
P. Walker	Bristol	19	31	1	552	0	60	18.40
J. E. McConnon ..	Newcastle	27	42	3	707	0	52	18.12
D. J. Ward	Tonypandy	9	15	4	174	0	31*	15.81
W. Wooller	Colwyn Bay	20	35	4	432	0	55	13.93
G. Dauncey......	Swansea	2	4	0	54	0	34	13.50
J. Pressdee	Swansea	11	16	2	186	0	32	13.28
W. G. Davies	Barry	12	21	0	269	0	58	12.80
D. J. Shepherd ..	Swansea	24	36	19	214	0	53	12.58
H. G. Davies	Llanelly	26	38	3	372	0	39	10.62
A. Jones..........	Swansea	2	4	0	29	0	12	7.25
H. D. Davies	Pembury	16	18	6	590	0	10	4.91
A. Lewis	Neath	2	4	0	14	0	12	3.50
F. Clark	Cardiff	4	6	2	11	0	8	2.75

Also batted: D. L. Evans (*Ammanford*) 6; P. Gatehouse (*Caerphilly*) played in two matches but did not bat.

BOWLING

	Overs	Maidens	Runs	Wickets	Average
D. J. Shepherd	745.1	230	1829	112	16.33
F. Clark	58.4	13	137	7	19.57
L. N. Devereux	246.2	75	593	29	20.44
J. E. McConnon........	632.5	170	1713	83	20.63
W. E. Jones............	26	4	95	4	23.75
P. Walker	346.3	92	835	33	25.30
H. D. Davies	402.4	72	1397	51	27.39
J. Pressdee	84	19	255	8	31.87
W. G. Davies	36	10	97	3	32.33
W. Wooller	314.4	83	862	25	34.48
A. J. Watkins	396.2	105	899	25	35.96
P. Gatehouse	41	7	153	4	38.25

Also bowled: B. Hedges 0.2—0—4—0.

Amateurs.—W. Wooller, A. Lewis.

GLAMORGAN v. GLOUCESTERSHIRE

At Cardiff, April 29, 30. Glamorgan won by five wickets. Gloucestershire 236 (D. Hawkins 50) and 152; Glamorgan 239 for nine wickets, dec. (W. G. A. Parkhouse 60) and 152 for five (B. D. Wells four for 34).

At Taunton, May 1, 2 (Two Days). GLAMORGAN drew with SOMERSET.

GLAMORGAN v. LANCASHIRE

At Cardiff, May 8, 9, 10. Lancashire won by three wickets, taking 14 points. Spin bowlers were in command after the first few overs on a rain-affected pitch and Lancashire's superiority in this department carried them to victory. None of the Glamorgan batsmen shaped soundly against Hilton and Tattersall who made the most of their opponents' reluctance to use their feet. Washbrook, on the other hand, was not tied to his crease against Shepherd, Glamorgan's most successful bowler, and a forcing innings which included one 6 and ten 4's gave Lancashire an advantage which proved decisive. Though having to bat a second time on drying turf, Lancashire achieved their target of 101 runs in spite of extremely accurate off-spin by Shepherd who took ten wickets for 94 in the match.

Glamorgan

W. G. A. Parkhouse c Wharton b Hilton	21	— c Wilson b Hilton	20
W. G. Davies b Tattersall	4	— b Tattersall	15
B. Hedges c Washbrook b Hilton	8	— c Wharton b Tattersall	5
L. N. Devereux c Collins b Tattersall	21	— c Wharton b Tattersall	23
A. J. Watkins c Grieves b Tattersall	0	— c Collins b Hilton	21
W. Wooller c Collins b Hilton	5	— c Collins b Hilton	22
J. Pressdee c Wharton b Tattersall	12	— c Wilson b Statham	30
D. J. Ward not out	17	— c and b Statham	7
J. E. McConnon c Wharton b Hilton	9	— not out	11
H. G. Davies c Wilson b Hilton	1	— c Edrich b Statham	0
D. J. Shepherd c Washbrook b Hilton	0	— b Statham	6
B 2, l-b 4	6	L-b 7	7

1/21 2/31 3/34 4/34 5/45 6/62 7/78   104   1/0 2/17 3/31 4/63 5/63   167
8/91 9/100 (1.6 an over)   6/107 7/123 8/132 9/155

Lancashire

A. Wharton c Watkins b McConnon	14	— c Hedges b Shepherd	14
J. Dyson c Watkins b McConnon	9	— c Wooller b Shepherd	0
G. A. Edrich b Shepherd	7	— c Devereux b Shepherd	10
C. Washbrook c Ward b Devereux	66	— c Watkins b McConnon	13
K. Grieves c Pressdee b Shepherd	1	— not out	37
J. T. Ikin c and b Devereux	23	— b Devereux	8
R. Collins c W. Davies b Watkins	37	— c Ward b Shepherd	0
M. J. Hilton b Shepherd	0	— lbw b Shepherd	10
J. B. Statham c Wooller b Shepherd	11	— not out	4
A. Wilson b Shepherd	3		
R. Tattersall not out	0		
		B 4, n-b 1	5

1/19 2/30 3/30 4/47 5/114 6/133   171   1/10 2/20 3/35   (7 wkts.) 101
7/133 8/167 9/171 (3.1 an over)   4/35 5/41 6/55 7/97

Lancashire Bowling

	O.	M.	R.	W.	O.	M.	R.	W.
Statham	7	2	8	0	22.1	4	38	4
Wharton	5	1	10	0	2	0	7	0
Hilton	26.2	12	40	6	27	13	51	3
Tattersall	27	11	40	4	37	16	50	3
Collins					6	3	14	0

Glamorgan Bowling

	O.	M.	R.	W.	O.	M.	R.	W.
Wooller	6	1	13	0	9	5	10	0
Watkins	5	1	15	1	4	2	13	0
McConnon	15	3	55	2	10	4	24	1
Shepherd	22	9	51	5	23.5	10	43	5
Devereux	7	2	37	2	4	2	6	1

Umpires: P. Corrall and Harry Elliott.

At The Oval, May 11, 13. GLAMORGAN lost to SURREY by an innings and 166 runs.

At Ilford, May 15, 16, 17. GLAMORGAN drew with ESSEX.

At Gravesend, May 18, 20, 21 GLAMORGAN beat KENT by five wickets.

GLAMORGAN v. SUSSEX

At Swansea, May 25, 27, 28. Drawn, Sussex taking four points. Watkins' first century of the summer was the only bright patch as far as Glamorgan were concerned and took over five hours. Unenterprising methods adopted by the majority of their batsmen not only meant the loss of first innings lead and bonus points but also robbed them of a chance of victory. Fielding, too, did not reach the high standard expected and Smith, who hit 171 for once out, was dropped three times. Sussex, scoring 86 runs an hour, set Glamorgan to get 196 at a similar rate, but apart from Jones (one 6, six 4's) the batsmen made little effort to go for the runs. Hedges stayed eighty minutes for 16.

Sussex

D. V. Smith b Watkins	117	— not out 54
L. J. Lenham lbw b Devereux	30	— st H. G. Davies b Shepherd 5
K. G. Suttle lbw b Shepherd	16	— c and b Wooller 36
J. M. Parks lbw b Shepherd	70	— c Parkhouse b McConnon.. 18
G. Potter c and b McConnon	14	— not out 19
D. J. Foreman c and b Shepherd	34	— c Pressdee b Wooller 26
N. I. Thomson b Shepherd	1	
R. V. Bell run out	0	
R. T. Webb not out	19	— b Wooller 18
A. E. James lbw b Devereux	14	
R. G. Marlar lbw b Devereux	0	
B 6, l-b 1	7	B 3, l-b 1 4

1/98 2/140 3/208 4/246 5/266 6/273   322   1/18 2/38   (5 wkts., dec.) 180
7/283 8/285 9/322 (3.25 an over)   3/77 4/80 5/129

Glamorgan

W. G. A. Parkhouse lbw b Suttle	38	— b Marlar 17
W. G. Davies lbw b James	1	— c Thomson b Smith 13
B. Hedges b Thomson	22	— not out 16
W. E. Jones c Parks b Marlar	56	— not out 43
A. J. Watkins not out	115	
L. N. Devereux b Suttle	4	
J. Pressdee c Foreman b Marlar	25	
W. Wooller lbw b Smith	5	
J. E. McConnon c Bell b Smith	6	
H. G. Davies c Bell b Smith	10	
D. J. Shepherd c Parks b Marlar	13	
B 4, l-b 8	12	B 4, l-b 2 6

1/18 2/58 3/76 4/151 5/163 6/250   307   1/32 2/36   (2 wkts.) 95
7/255 8/261 9/281 (2.13 an over)

Glamorgan Bowling

	O.	M.	R.	W.		O.	M.	R.	W.
Wooller	10	1	36	0	....	18	3	66	3
Watkins	12	2	29	1					
McConnon	22	1	102	1	....	6	1	19	1
Shepherd	33	11	79	4	....	22	5	72	1
Devereux	11.4	1	29	3	....	11	3	19	0
Pressdee	10	2	40	0					

Sussex Bowling

	O.	M.	R.	W.		O.	M.	R.	W.
Thomson	23	9	28	1	....	8	2	21	0
James	15	7	20	1	....	3	1	3	0
Marlar	52.4	18	126	3	....	16	5	39	1
Bell	12	1	41	0	....	3	1	9	0
Suttle	19	9	36	2	....	4	1	3	0
Smith	22	11	44	3	....	8	4	14	1

Umpires: W. Place and C. A. Coleman.

At Manchester, May 29, 30, 31. GLAMORGAN beat LANCASHIRE by 128 runs.

At Sheffield, June 1, 3, 4. GLAMORGAN beat YORKSHIRE by seven wickets.

At Coalville, June 5, 6. GLAMORGAN beat LEICESTERSHIRE by innings and 52 runs.

At Cardiff, June 8, 10. GLAMORGAN lost to WEST INDIES by five wickets. (See WEST INDIES section.)

GLAMORGAN v. SOMERSET

At Swansea, June 12, 13. Glamorgan won by nine wickets, taking 12 points. On a pitch which took spin from the start Glamorgan hurried to their fourth successive Championship victory, thus equalling a feat they had achieved previously only in 1948, their Championship year. Glamorgan were indebted to magnificent off-spin bowling by Shepherd, who received admirable support from McConnon, and Somerset followed-on 170 behind. In spite of a third wicket partnership of 90 between the Australians, Alley and McCool, Glamorgan were left to get only 52 to win and these were obtained before the close on the second day for the loss of Wooller.

Glamorgan

W. G. Davies lbw b Lomax	10	
B. Hedges c Palmer b Langford	34	— not out 37
L. N. Devereux c Alley b Hilton	38	— not out 8
W. E. Jones st Stephenson b Langford	1	
A. J. Watkins b McMahon	45	
P. Walker c Stephenson b Alley	38	
W. Wooller c McCool b Alley	33	— b Lobb 8
J. E. McConnon c Palmer b McMahon	26	
H. D. Davies b Lobb	7	
H. G. Davies c Lobb b McMahon	15	
D. J. Shepherd not out	6	
B 8, w 1	9	L-b 1 1

1/25 2/53 3/59 4/112 5/154 6/204   **262**   1/10   (1 wkt.) **54**
7/227 8/244 9/255 (2.13 an over)

Somerset

W. E. Alley c Walker b Shepherd	17	— c Watkins b Devereux 69
K. E. Palmer b H. D. Davies	1	— lbw b Shepherd 4
P. B. Wight c Devereux b McConnon	32	— c and b McConnon 0
C. L. McCool c H. G. Davies b Shepherd	2	— b Shepherd 48
M. F. Tremlett c Wooller b Shepherd	18	— c and b McConnon 17
J. G. Lomax c and b McConnon	2	— run out 36
H. W. Stephenson c Devereux b Shepherd	2	— c Hedges b Shepherd 24
J. Hilton lbw b McConnon	1	— c Watkins b Devereux 2
B. Langford c Devereux b Shepherd	1	— c Wooller b Shepherd 3
B. Lobb c W. G. Davies b Shepherd	11	— not out 12
J. W. McMahon not out	0	— b Devereux.............. 3
B 5	5	B 1, l-b 1, n-b 1 3

1/7 2/36 3/38 4/66 5/76 6/76 7/79   **92**   1/16 2/19 3/109 4/130   **221**
8/80 9/88 (2.48 an over)   5/145 6/172 7/191 8/200
9/204

Somerset Bowling

	O.	M.	R.	W.		O.	M.	R.	W.
Lobb	22	5	63	1	....	3	0	10	1
Alley..........	20	6	36	2	....	3	0	13	0
Lomax	4	0	15	1					
Langford	30	11	59	2	....	4	1	16	0
McMahon	28	17	39	3	....	3.4	1	14	0
Hilton	19	6	41	1					

Glamorgan Bowling

	O.	M.	R.	W.		O.	M.	R.	W.
H. D. Davies...	8	2	25	1	....	5	1	7	0
Watkins	3	1	3	0	....	4	1	8	0
McConnon	12	2	35	3	....	25	8	76	2
Devereux	2	1	4	0	....	14.4	2	42	3
Shepherd	11.5	5	20	6	....	33	14	71	4
					Wooller..	5	0	14	0

Umpires: J. F. Crapp and John Langridge.

GLAMORGAN v. WARWICKSHIRE

At Cardiff, June 15, 17. Warwickshire won by ten wickets, taking 14 points. An inspired spell of leg-break bowling by Hollies immediately after lunch on the first day led to the ending of Glamorgan's sequence of success. Glamorgan shaped soundly enough in the early play before Hollies, in a spell of eight overs, captured four wickets for 19 runs and the innings closed for 176. Warwickshire went ahead during a fine fifth wicket partnership by Townsend and Spooner who put on 149 in two hours. Glamorgan, needing 181 to make Warwickshire bat again, struggled vainly to loosen the grip of Carter and Hollies. Though Warwickshire had to go in a second time two deliveries sufficed to finish a one-sided match.

Glamorgan

W. G. A. Parkhouse b Singh	57	— c Spooner b Carter	0
W. G. Davies c Spooner b Ibadulla	4	— b Ibadulla	8
B. Hedges c Ibadulla b Leach	52	— b Hollies	37
W. E. Jones c Spooner b Ibadulla	6	— c Townsend b Hollies.....	8
A. J. Watkins c Cartwright b Hollies ..	11	— c and b Carter	32
L. N. Devereux c Spooner b Ibadulla ...	9	— not out	45
P. Walker b Hollies	15	— c Townsend b Hollies.....	8
W. Wooller c Townsend b Hollies	2	— b Carter	7
J. E. McConnon c Spooner b Hollies....	6	— b Carter	6
H. G. Davies b Ibadulla	0	— lbw b Carter	17
D. J. Shepherd not out	2	— c and b Carter	8
B 9, l-b 3	12	B 1, l-b 4	5

1/42 2/87 3/113 4/132 5/138 6/158　176
7/164 8/170 9/170 (2.41 an over)

1/0 2/36 3/52 4/53 5/108　181
6/126 7/147 8/155 9/173

Warwickshire

F. C. Gardner b Shepherd	9		
N. F. Horner c Walker b McConnon ...	15	— not out	4
M. J. K. Smith run out	34		
A. Townsend c and b McConnon	89		
T. W. Cartwright lbw b Shepherd......	8	— not out	0
R. T. Spooner st H. G. Davies b Shepherd	118		
K. Ibadulla c Wooller b Walker	52		
S. Singh c Wooller b Shepherd	0		
C. W. Leach lbw b Shepherd	0		
R. G. Carter c and b Shepherd	5		
W. E. Hollies not out	0		
B 15, l-b 11	26		

1/11 2/31 3/82 4/102 5/251 6/336　356　　　(No wkt.)　4
7/336 8/350 9/356 (3.12 an over)

Warwickshire Bowling

	O.	M.	R.	W.		O.	M.	R.	W.
Carter	16	5	44	0	....	23.3	5	68	6
Townsend	3	0	5	0	....	3	1	2	0
Ibadulla	21.1	8	45	4	....	25	12	45	1
Hollies	25	5	64	4	....	25	11	49	3
Singh	6	3	6	1	....	5	1	12	0
Leach	2	2	0	1	....	2	2	0	0

Glamorgan Bowling

	O.	M.	R.	W.
Wooller	11	0	19	0
Watkins	7	1	17	0
Shepherd	33	8	87	6
McConnon	22	4	97	2
Devereux	21	8	43	0
Walker	10.1	2	67	1
Hedges	0.2	0	4	0

Umpires: J. Wood and John Langridge.

At Chesterfield, June 19, 20, 21. GLAMORGAN drew with DERBYSHIRE.

At Worcester, June 22, 24, 25. GLAMORGAN drew with WORCESTERSHIRE.

At Nottingham, June 26, 27, 28. GLAMORGAN beat NOTTINGHAMSHIRE by 27 runs.

GLAMORGAN v. GLOUCESTERSHIRE
(W. G. A. Parkhouse's Benefit)

At Swansea, June 29, July 1, 2. Gloucestershire won by an innings and 57 runs, taking 14 points. An aggressive opening partnership of 170 between Young and Emmett put Gloucestershire in command and they never relaxed their grip on the game. Emmett, who hit his first century of the summer, jumped down the pitch to the bowling at every opportunity and his delightful innings contained four 6's and twenty 4's. Emmett batted only three and a half hours for his excellent 170. Lack of confidence among the middle batsmen was chiefly responsible for Glamorgan following on 284 behind. The Welsh county offered better resistance in their second innings but Gloucestershire pressed home their advantage in relentless fashion despite a glorious innings from Shepherd. Shepherd hit four 6's and four 4's, one of his sixes going over the roof of the Rugby stand into the Mumbles Road.

Gloucestershire

D. M. Young c Walker b Devereux	71
G. M. Emmett b Shepherd	170
R. B. Nicholls lbw b Walker	23
T. W. Graveney c Parkhouse b H. D. Davies	47
C. A. Milton not out	59
D. Hawkins b Jones	6
J. Mortimore c Parkhouse b Jones	1
A. S. Brown c Dauncey b Walker	6
D. R. Smith c Devereux b Walker	15
R. Etheridge not out	19
L-b 5	5

C. Cook did not bat.

1/170 2/257 (8 wkts., dec.) 422
3/273 4/327 5/344 6/346 7/361
8/384 (3.57 an over)

Glamorgan

W. G. A. Parkhouse lbw b Smith	17	—	lbw b Smith		31
G. Dauncey c Graveney b Cook	34	—	b Mortimore		7
B. Hedges c Graveney b Smith	1	—	c Brown b Smith		9
W. E. Jones b Mortimore	1	—	c Hawkins b Cook		20
L. N. Devereux c and b Mortimore	4	—	b Brown		45
P. Walker b Smith	7	—	c Etheridge b Brown		16
J. E. McConnon c Etheridge b Mortimore	43	—	b Smith		21
W. Wooller st Etheridge b Mortimore	21	—	c Graveney b Mortimore		19
H. G. Davies b Mortimore	0	—	c Cook b Smith		4
H. D. Davies c Mortimore b Cook	4	—	not out		2
D. J. Shepherd not out	0	—	b Cook		53
B 2, l-b 4	6				

1/30 2/44 3/51 4/57 5/57 6/79 7/131   138
8/131 9/138 (2.00 an over)

1/22 2/41 3/52 4/97   227
5/124 6/147 7/149 8/157
9/181

Glamorgan Bowling

	O.	M.	R.	W.	O.	M.	R.	W.
H. D. Davies	19	2	100	1				
Wooller	11	1	30	0				
Shepherd	16	1	83	1				
Walker	37	7	96	3				
McConnon	13	2	37	0				
Devereux	8	2	28	1				
Jones	14	3	43	2				

Gloucestershire Bowling

	O.	M.	R.	W.	O.	M.	R.	W.
Smith	18	4	30	3	33	10	61	4
Brown	8	1	22	0	18	7	46	2
Mortimore	23	9	43	5	32	16	71	2
Cook	13.3	6	15	2	24.4	10	45	2
Graveney	3	1	4	0				
Hawkins	3	0	18	0				
Nicholls					1	0	4	0

Umpires: L. H. Gray and A. R. Coleman.

GLAMORGAN v. KENT

At Neath, July 3, 4, 5. Glamorgan won by 46 runs, taking 12 points to four by Kent. When Glamorgan collapsed in two hours to the pace of Halfyard their chances of success seemed slight but they fought back magnificently and turned the tables on Kent. Halfyard, practically unplayable on a drying pitch, took nine wickets for 39 runs, the best performance of his career. Kent, who passed their opponents' score with only three wickets down, led by 146, but Glamorgan faced up to their task dourly. With Parkhouse leading the resistance they batted so surely that Kent were left to get 207 to win—a task beyond them against inspired off-spin bowling by McConnon. Parkhouse showed his class in a faultless display which lasted five hours twenty minutes. He hit one 6 and eighteen 4's.

Glamorgan

W. G. A. Parkhouse c Ufton b Halfyard.	9	— c Wilson b Wright	133
G. Dauncey c Pretlove b Halfyard	6	— c Ufton b Halfyard	7
B. Hedges c Page b Halfyard	15	— c Page b Wright	37
W. E. Jones c Pettiford b Halfyard	0	— c Fagg b Dixon	41
L. N. Devereux c Wilson b Halfyard	5	— run out	18
P. Walker lbw b Halfyard	0	— c Wilson b Wright	0
D. J. Ward c Dixon b Halfyard	1	— c Wilson b Wright	15
J. E. McConnon c Page b Halfyard	36	— lbw b Halfyard	43
H. G. Davies c Dixon b Halfyard	0	— c Phebey b Dixon	21
D. J. Shepherd c Wilson b Dixon	12	— c Page b Dixon	3
H. D. Davies not out	3	— not out	3
B 1, l-b 1	2	B 24, l-b 7	31

1/10 2/23 3/25 4/32 5/32 6/37 7/48   **89**
8/48 9/77 (2.61 an over)

1/31 2/110 3/207 4/246   **352**
5/250 6/266 7/324 8/346
9/346

Kent

A. H. Phebey c Jones b H. D. Davies	1	— lbw b Walker	4
R. C. Wilson c H. G. Davies b H. D. Davies	0	— b H. D. Davies	35
J. F. Pretlove b McConnon	59	— c H. G. Davies b H. D. Davies	27
J. Pettiford c Parkhouse b H. D. Davies	43	— run out	15
S. E. Leary b Shepherd	40	— c Devereux b McConnon	23
A. L. Dixon c H. D. Davies b Walker	6	— c H. G. Davies b H. D. Davies	27
D. G. Ufton b McConnon	15	— c Walker b McConnon	0
A. E. Fagg, c Devereux b Shepherd	14	— c Shepherd b McConnon	0
D. J. Halfyard c Parkhouse b McConnon	5	— c Shepherd b McConnon	14
D. V. P. Wright not out	28	— not out	7
J. C. T. Page, b H. D. Davies	23	— c Parkhouse b H. D. Davies	2
L-b 1	1	B 1, l-b 4, n-b 1	6

1/1 2/14 3/80 4/115 5/124 6/147   **235**
7/170 8/183 9/187 (2.70 an over)

1/10 2/63 3/74 4/88 5/120   **160**
6/123 7/123 8/144 9/159

Kent Bowling

	O.	M.	R.	W.		O.	M.	R.	W.
Halfyard	17.2	7	39	9	....	38	13	89	2
Dixon	12	3	35	1	....	40.3	13	91	3
Page	5	0	13	0	....	22	7	57	0
Wright						31	14	70	4
Pretlove						1	1	0	0
Pettiford						4	0	14	0

Glamorgan Bowling

	O.	M.	R.	W.		O.	M.	R.	W.
H. D. Davies...	25.3	4	88	4	....	23.4	6	66	4
Walker	20	7	34	1	....	6	2	21	1
Shepherd	21	2	64	2	....	6	0	17	0
McConnon	20	5	48	3	....	12	3	26	4
Devereux						13	4	24	0

Umpires: L. H. Gray and A. R. Coleman.

GLAMORGAN v. NOTTINGHAMSHIRE

At Llanelly, July 6, 8. Glamorgan won by an innings and 120 runs, taking 14 points. They dominated the game from the start. First their batsmen, particularly Hedges, who, hitting nineteen 4's, made the best score of his career, thrashed the Nottinghamshire attack and then McConnon and Gatehouse caused their opponents to follow-on with effective bowling on a rain-affected pitch. Twenty wickets fell on the second day for 234 runs. Gatehouse, a tall, left-arm pace bowler making his Championship debut, took three wickets for six runs in one spell of five overs, and when Nottinghamshire batted a second time Walker claimed three victims without cost in four overs. McConnon gained a match analysis of nine for 86.

Glamorgan

W. G. A. Parkhouse b Dooland ..	64	H. G. Davies b Jepson..........	10
B. Hedges c Smales b Walker.....	139	H. D. Davies not out	1
L. N. Devereux b Jepson.........	0	B 8, l-b 2, w 1	11
W. E. Jones run out	38		
A. J. Watkins lbw b Smales	2		
P. Walker b Jepson ,.. ,.....	52	1/156 2/163 3/238 (8 wkts., dec.) 387	
J. E. McConnon b Smales.......	45	4/248 5/248 6/338 7/370 8/386	
W. Wooller not out	25	(3.36 an over)	

P. Gatehouse did not bat.

Nottinghamshire

J. D. Clay b Gatehouse	16	— c H. D. Davies b Walker....	13
G. Millman c H. G. Davies b Gatehouse.	15	— lbw b Watkins	14
F. W. Stocks c Wooller b McConnon ...	45	— lbw b Walker	0
R. G. Giles b Gatehouse	3	— b Walker	13
R. T. Simpson c Watkins b McConnon..	0	— c and b H. D. Davies	1
M. Hill c and b McConnon	2	— c Wooller b McConnon ...	6
C. J. Poole b Walker	18	— b Jones	18
B. Dooland c Devereux b McConnon ...	20	— c Wooller b McConnon ...	16
A. K. Walker hit wkt b Devereux.......	14	— b McConnon	7
A. Jepson c Wooller b McConnon	12	— c Jones b McConnon	0
K. Smales not out	0	— not out	6
B 16, l-b 3, n-b 2	21	B 1, l-b 4, n-b 2........	7

1/39 2/40 3/49 4/62 5/75 6/115 7/121   166
8/142 9/166 (2.07 an over)

1/7 2/21 3/21 4/30 5/54   101
6/58 7/67 8/88 9/92

Nottinghamshire Bowling

	O.	M.	R.	W.	O.	M.	R.	W.
Walker	25	7	76	1				
Jepson	26	10	58	3				
Dooland	34	9	117	1				
Stocks	5	0	32	0				
Smales	25	8	93	2				

Glamorgan Bowling

	O.	M.	R.	W.	O.	M.	R.	W.
Gatehouse	15	4	27	3	3	2	6	0
H. D. Davies...	11	4	28	0	4	2	5	1
Wooller	5	2	6	0				
McConnon	21.1	10	38	5	28.5	14	48	4
Devereux	13	7	14	1	5	3	3	0
Walker	15	5	32	1	10	6	6	3
Jones					4	1	14	1
Watkins					8	3	12	1

Umpires: J. F. Crapp and A. E. Pothecary.

At Portsmouth, July 10, 11, 12. GLAMORGAN drew with HAMPSHIRE.

GLAMORGAN v. NORTHAMPTONSHIRE

At Cardiff, July 13, 15.   Northamptonshire won by ten wickets, taking 14 points. Glamorgan's decision to bat on a rain- and sun-affected pitch proved disastrous. None of the batsmen could cope with the left-arm spin of Manning and Allen. By steady batting Northamptonshire doubled their opponents' score, an advantage which proved decisive. Facing Tyson in top form, Glamorgan crumpled in their second innings and Northamptonshire needed only five runs to win. Tyson, in one spell of four overs on the second day, took four wickets for five runs.

Glamorgan

W. G. A. Parkhouse c Tyson b Allen ...	16	— c Andrew b Tyson	4
B. Hedges c Tribe b Allen	19	— c Andrew b Tyson	5
L. N. Devereux b Manning	6	— b Tyson	13
W. E. Jones b Manning	0	— b Tyson	18
A. J. Watkins b Manning	2	— b Tyson	0
P. Walker run out	15	— b Tyson	2
J. E. McConnon c Fellows-Smith b Allen	10	— c Brookes b Tribe	17
D. J. Ward lbw b Tribe	5	— lbw b Tribe	23
H. G. Davies not out	21	— c Andrew b Allen	12
D. J. Shepherd b Tribe	0	— not out	10
H. D. Davies b Allen	3	— b Tyson	0
B 4, l-b 2	6	L-b 1, n-b 2	3

1/26 2/41 3/41 4/41 5/49 6/67 7/69   103   1/4 2/13 3/30 4/31 5/44   107
8/82 9/82 (1.83 an over)   6/45 7/74 8/90 9/106

Northamptonshire

D. Brookes lbw b McConnon	38		
P. Arnold lbw b Shepherd	24		
B. Reynolds b Shepherd	14		
D. W. Barrick run out	30		
R. Subba Row run out	43		
G. E. Tribe c H. G. Davies b McConnon	6		
J. P. Fellows-Smith lbw b Shepherd....	30		
J. S. Manning b Watkins	0		
K. V. Andrew not out.................	2	— not out	
F. H. Tyson c H. G. Davies b Watkins..	0		
M. H. J. Allen b Shepherd	5	— not out	4
B 10, l-b 4	14		

1/44 2/78 3/113 4/122 5/135 6/186   206   (No wkts.) 5
7/193 8/199 9/199 (1.96 an over)

Northamptonshire Bowling

	O.	M.	R.	W.		O.	M.	R.	W.
Tyson	4	0	10	0	....	14.5	4	25	7
Fellows-Smith..	4	1	8	0	....	2	1	3	0
Manning	20	9	32	3	....	10	3	34	0
Allen	23.4	10	43	4	....	8	2	19	1
Tribe	4	2	4	2	....	6	1	23	2

Glamorgan Bowling

	O.	M.	R.	W.		O.	M.	R.	W.
H. D. Davies...	4	0	22	0					
Watkins	27	9	46	2	....	0.4	0	5	0
Shepherd	43.2	19	68	4					
McConnon	27	5	49	2					
Walker	4	1	7	0					

Umpires: P. A. Gibb and P. Corrall.

GLAMORGAN v. HAMPSHIRE

At Swansea, July 17, 18, 19. Match abandoned without a ball bowled.

Glamorgan

W. G. A. Parkhouse, B. Hedges, L. N. Devereux, A. Jones, P. Walker, J. Pressdee, J. E. McConnon, W. Wooller, H. G. Davies, D. J. Shepherd and H. D. Davies.

Hampshire

J. R. Gray, R. E. Marshall, H. Horton, A. W. H. Rayment, H. M. Barnard. A. C. D. Ingleby-Mackenzie, P. J. Sainsbury, L. Harrison, D. Shackleton, M. Heath and M. D. Burden.

Umpires: P. A. Gibb and P. Corrall.

GLAMORGAN v. ESSEX

At Ebbw Vale, July 20, 22, 23. Drawn, Glamorgan taking four points. Rain ruined any chance of a definite result. Play was restricted to the last two days and Glamorgan had to be content with first innings lead and bonus points, which they obtained just on time. Bailey and Insole helped Essex to recover after the loss of three wickets for 52, Insole's batting providing the main sparkle in a somewhat drab display. Watkins and Devereux served Glamorgan well in a fourth wicket stand of 118 runs at one a minute. Three interruptions through rain after lunch unsettled Watkins who narrowly failed to reach his century, but vigorous hitting by Haydn Davies and McConnon ensured the lead.

Essex

T. C. Dodds c Pressdee b Watkins 7	R. Ralph c Hedges b Shepherd... 2
G. Barker c Wooller b Watkins... 29	K. C. Preston b Shepherd 31
B. Taylor c Pressdee b Wooller... 6	I. King not out 4
D. J. Insole c Watkins b Pressdee. 47	B 5, l-b 3, w 4 12
T. E. Bailey c Shepherd b Watkins 61	
L. Savill run out 36	
M. Bear c H. G. Davies b H. D. Davies 4	1/31 2/42 3/52 4/113 5/178 239
W. T. Greensmith c H. G. Davies b Shepherd 0	6/189 7/192 8/196 9/235
	(2.62 an over)

Glamorgan

W. G. A. Parkhouse c Bailey b Preston 5	W. Wooller c Taylor b Preston... 0
B. Hedges c Bailey b Preston..... 16	H. G. Davies c Taylor b Ralph... 15
L. N. Devereux c Dodds b Ralph 74	D. J. Shepherd not out 1
J. Pressdee b Preston 3	B 1, l-b 3 4
A. J. Watkins c Bailey b Preston. 96	
P. Walker b Ralph 10	1/5 2/42 3/46 4/164 (8 wkts.) 241
J. E. McConnon not out 17	5/194 6/212 7/212 8/233
	(3.01 an over)

H. D. Davies did not bat.

Glamorgan Bowling

	O.	M.	R.	W.
H. D. Davies .	15	1	71	1
Watkins	18.2	9	21	3
Wooller.......	13	3	46	1
Walker	2	1	6	0
McConnon ...	13	4	21	0
Pressdee	7	3	15	1
Shepherd	23	7	47	3

Essex Bowling

	O.	M.	R.	W.
Bailey	17	1	53	0
Preston	22.5	6	75	5
Ralph	20	2	54	3
King	14	3	30	0
Greensmith ...	5	0	18	0
Insole	1	0	7	0

Umpires: H. Baldwin and R. S. Lay.

At Hastings, July 24, 25, 26. GLAMORGAN drew with SUSSEX.

At Northampton, July 27, 29, 30. GLAMORGAN beat NORTHAMPTONSHIRE by 23 runs.

At Bristol, July 31, August 1, 2. GLAMORGAN lost to GLOUCESTERSHIRE by 266 runs.

At Swansea, August 3, 5, 6. GLAMORGAN lost to WEST INDIES by six wickets. (See WEST INDIES section.)

GLAMORGAN v. DERBYSHIRE

At Pontypridd, August 7, 8, 9. Drawn, Glamorgan taking four points. Rain, which prevented play on the last day, caused the match to be abandoned in an interesting position with Derbyshire, who had one wicket down, requiring 205 more runs to win on a pitch giving help to both pace and spin bowlers. A sound opening partnership between Parkhouse and Hedges provided the foundation of a useful Glamorgan score and then Derbyshire collapsed against McConnon, who took advantage of turf already responsive to spin. Glamorgan, batting a second time with an advantage of 73, faced the Derbyshire attack with determination. Again Parkhouse mastered the bowlers and, aided by Devereux, put on 107 runs for the second wicket. When wickets fell quickly, Wooller declared only to be thwarted by the weather.

Glamorgan

W. G. A. Parkhouse c Dawkes b Revill..	48	— c Morgan b Gladwin 89
B. Hedges b Morgan	40	— lbw b Gladwin............ 12
L. N. Devereux c Lee b Gladwin	5	— c Jackson b Gladwin 38
W. E. Jones c Revill b Carr	26	— c Dawkes b Jackson 1
D. Ward c Revill b Morgan............	9	— not out 5
P. Walker c and b Gladwin	30	— b Jackson 2
J. E. McConnon c Dawkes b Jackson ...	29	— c Morgan b Jackson 0
W. Wooller c Gibson b Gladwin	7	— lbw b Jackson 0
D. L. Evans c Dawkes b Gladwin	6	
D. J. Shepherd not out	1	— not out 19
F. Clarke c Revill b Gladwin...........	0	
L-b 1, n-b 1..................	2	

1/77 2/93 3/98 4/119 5/147 6/176   **203**

7/188 8/200 9/203 (2.25 an over)

1/28 2/135   (7 wkts., dec.) **166**

3/136 4/136 5/140 6/140

7/146

Derbyshire

A. Hamer c Walker b McConnon	39	— b Shepherd 12
C. Lee b McConnon	9	— not out 21
J. M. Kelly c Wooller b Shepherd	6	— not out 0
D. B. Carr c Walker b McConnon	24	
I. M. Gibson lbw b Shepherd	7	
K. Mohan c Parkhouse b McConnon ...	9	
A. C. Revill c Wooller b McConnon ...	13	
D. C. Morgan c and b McConnon	3	
G. O. Dawkes c Jones b McConnon ...	5	
C. Gladwin not out	5	
L. Jackson c Wooller b Shepherd	0	
B 9, w 1	10	B 2.................. 2

1/37 2/52 3/70 4/89 5/95 6/117   **130**

7/119 8/123 9/126 (2.09 an over)

1/35   (1 wkt.) **35**

Derbyshire Bowling

	O.	M.	R.	W.	O.	M.	R.	W.
Jackson	23	9	44	1	21	8	29	4
Gladwin	24	7	45	5	19	5	49	3
Morgan	27	6	65	2	14	4	35	0
Revill	10	6	28	1	7	1	21	0
Carr	6	2	19	1	3	0	13	0
			Gibson		2	0	19	0

Glamorgan Bowling

	O.	M.	R.	W.	O.	M.	R.	W.
Clarke	7	1	22	0				
Walker	5	1	12	0				
McConnon	26	10	37	7	8	2	12	0
Shepherd	24.1	6	49	3	7	2	21	1

Umpires: D. J. Wood and A. E. Pothecary.

At Weston-super-Mare, August 10, 12, 13. GLAMORGAN lost to SOMERSET by ten wickets.

GLAMORGAN v. WORCESTERSHIRE

At Cardiff, August 17, 19. Glamorgan won by 91 runs, taking 12 points. Again the Cardiff pitch proved ideal for off-spinners. Between them Shepherd and McConnon took twelve wickets for Glamorgan and Horton claimed the same number for Worcestershire, but a magnificent innings by Watkins on the awkward pitch put Glamorgan on top in a low-scoring match. Four wickets were down for 42 when Watkins went to the crease and, combining sound defence with powerful stroke-play, he revived Glamorgan's fortunes. Requiring 196 to win, Worcestershire never looked capable of getting the runs.

Glamorgan

W. G. A. Parkhouse c and b Horton	43	— c Coldwell b Horton 1
B. Hedges c Booth b Berry	5	— c Booth b Berry 21
W. G. Davies c Booth b Berry	6	— c Booth b Berry 5
A. Lewis lbw b Horton	2	— lbw b Horton 12
A. J. Watkins lbw b Horton	13	— b Horton 81
L. N. Devereux c D. Richardson b Horton	4	— b Berry 7
P. Walker c Coldwell b Horton.........	48	— c Dews b Berry 11
J. E. McConnon c Dews b Horton......	18	— lbw b Flavell 31
W. Wooller c Dews b Horton	0	— c Dews b Flavell 4
H. G. Davies c D. Richardson b Horton..	0	— c Kenyon b Horton 0
D. J. Shepherd not out	16	— not out 3
		B 2, l-b 5 7

1/29 2/39 3/46 4/62 5/66 6/85 7/121   155   1/3 2/25 3/34 4/42 5/59   183
8/133 9/133 (1.93 an over)   6/101 7/149 8/159 9/176

Worcestershire

D. Kenyon b Walker..................	6	— b McConnon 20
P. E. Richardson c Wooller b Shepherd......	37	— c Walker b Watkins 0
G. Dews c Parkhouse b Watkins........	3	— hit wkt b McConnon 8
D. W. Richardson b McConnon	10	— lbw b Shepherd 18
R. G. Broadbent lbw b Devereux	26	— c Wooller b Shepherd 38
L. Outschoorn c Wooller b Shepherd....	4	— c Wooller b Devereux 1
M. J. Horton c Watkins b Devereux ...	34	— b Devereux................. 0
R. Booth not out	3	— c Watkins b Devereux 4
R. Berry c Watkins b Shepherd........	0	— c Wooller b Shepherd 0
J. Flavell c Lewis b Shepherd	11	— b Shepherd 2
L. N. Coldwell b Shepherd	0	— not out 6
B 4, l-b 4, n-b 1	9	B 4, l-b 3 7

1/8 2/19 3/53 4/61 5/69 6/116 7/127   143   1/2 2/32 3/39 4/88 5/91   104
8/128 9/142 (2.42 an over)   6/92 7/93 8/96 9/96

Worcestershire Bowling

	O.	M.	R.	W.		O.	M.	R.	W.
Flavell	10	3	26	0	...	10	2	12	2
Coldwell	4	1	5	0	...	1	1	0	0
Berry	30	17	37	2	...	29	12	63	4
Horton	36	11	87	8	...	37.1	13	101	4

Glamorgan Bowling

	O.	M.	R.	W.		O.	M.	R.	W.
Walker	5	1	14	1	...	4	2	2	0
Watkins	13	2	29	1	...	5	2	15	1
Shepherd	20	8	37	5	...	16.4	6	26	4
McConnon	14	1	51	1	...	8	1	39	2
Devereux	7	5	3	2	...	8	2	15	3

Umpires: J. S. Buller and T. W. Spencer.

GLAMORGAN v. MIDDLESEX

At Swansea, August 24, 26. Middlesex won by seven wickets, taking 14 points. A dusty pitch, which aided the bowlers of both teams, brought about a finish in two days. Apart from Edrich and Wooller, none of the batsmen shaped confidently. Edrich, after occupying two hours for 35 runs, took 22 off an over from Shepherd with four strokes—6, 6, 6 and 4. Apart from this over Shepherd commanded respect and obtained eight wickets for 84. Batting a second time 111 in arrear, Glamorgan avoided the possibility of an innings defeat through the efforts of Wooller and Haydn Davies whose eighth wicket partnership yielded 77 runs. Wooller, who made his highest score of the summer, hit one 6 and eight 4's. Middlesex needed only 50 to win but lost three wickets to McConnon before accomplishing their task.

Glamorgan

W. G. A. Parkhouse b Moss	10	— c Robertson b Moss 2
B. Hedges c Edrich b Warr	7	— c Murray b Moss 0
L. N. Devereux b Moss	28	— c Hurst b Titmus 9
A. Jones c Edrich b Moss	6	— b Hurst 11
A. J. Watkins run out	5	— c Hurst b Titmus 8
P. Walker c Edrich b Titmus	1	— st Murray b Hurst 20
J. E. McConnon lbw b Hurst	3	— c Delisle b Hurst 0
W. Wooller lbw b Titmus	3	— lbw b Warr 55
H. G. Davies c Hurst b Bennett	28	— b Titmus 39
D. J. Shepherd not out	3	— b Warr 4
F. Clarke b Bennett	8	— not out 1
L-b 4	4	B 11 11

1/15 2/17 3/31 4/38 5/45 6/48 7/55   **106**   1/2 2/7 3/17 4/26 5/48   **160**
8/83 9/95 (3.02 an over)   6/48 7/78 8/155 9/157

Middlesex

J. D. Robertson b Shepherd	22	— st Davies b McConnon 17
R. A. Gale c Hedges b Shepherd	4	— c Clarke b McConnon ... 11
A. C. Walton c Watkins b Devereux	23	— lbw b McConnon 1
G. P. S. Delisle c Wooller b Shepherd	2	— not out 4
W. J. Edrich b Shepherd	77	— not out 10
F. J. Titmus c Walker b Shepherd	23	
J. T. Murray lbw b Shepherd	1	
D. Bennett c and b Shepherd	47	
J. J. Warr b Shepherd	0	
R. J. Hurst not out	7	
B 7, l-b 3, n-b 1	11	B 6, l-b 1, n-b 1 8

1/16 2/51 3/53 4/53   (9 wkts., dec.) **217**   1/3 2/35 3/37   (3 wkts.) **51**
5/83 6/85 7/162 8/166 9/217
(3.50 an over)
A. E. Moss did not bat.

Middlesex Bowling

	O.	M.	R.	W.		O.	M.	R.	W.
Warr..........	6	1	17	1	....	12.2	4	17	2
Moss	13	2	29	3	....	14	5	42	2
Titmus	10	3	34	2	....	11	2	30	3
Hurst	4	0	19	1	....	9	1	37	3
Bennett	2	1	3	2	....	8	4	6	0
			Edrich	....		3	0	17	0

Glamorgan Bowling

	O.	M.	R.	W.		O.	M.	R.	W.
Clarke	9	2	24	0	....	1	0	5	0
Walker	6	0	25	0					
Shepherd	28.4	10	84	8	....	10.3	2	14	0
McConnon	2	0	8	0	....	10	1	24	3
Devereux	16	0	65	1					

Umpires: N. Oldfield and R. S. Lay.

GLAMORGAN v. YORKSHIRE

At Cardiff, August 28, 29. Yorkshire won by four runs, taking 14 points, after a tense finish. This was the fifth match at The Arms Park to be completed in two days; the pitch started to crumble after the opening overs. With spin bowlers again taking command, Yorkshire seemed to have a decisive advantage when they left their opponents to get 173 runs. Glamorgan hit back with a forceful opening partnership between Parkhouse and Hedges who put on 95 runs in sixty-five minutes and they had half their wickets left with 17 runs needed but a second collapse sealed their fate. The end came when Pickles was given the ball for the first time in the match and he hit Haydn Davies' off stump with his third delivery.

Yorkshire

W. B. Stott b Clarke	4	— b Devereux....................	26
W. Watson b Shepherd	10	— c Walker b Shepherd	12
W. H. H. Sutcliffe b Shepherd..........	33	— c McConnon b Shepherd...	16
D. B. Close c Walker b Shepherd	4	— c Parkhouse b Devereux ...	14
J. V. Wilson c Devereux b Shepherd ...	15	— c Watkins b Shepherd	23
D. E. V. Padgett b Shepherd	9	— c Davies b Shepherd.......	1
R. Illingworth b Shepherd	8	— lbw b Shepherd	22
F. S. Trueman st Davies b McConnon ..	0	— run out	26
R. Appleyard c sub b Shepherd	14	— run out	0
J. G. Binks c and b Watkins	0	— not out	2
D. Pickles not out	0	— lbw b McConnon	0
L-b 1, n-b 1.....................	2	B 2, l-b 2	4

	99

1/11 2/24 3/30 4/61 5/76 6/79 7/80
8/96 9/97 (2.02 an over)

1/20 2/55 3/63 4/73 5/77   146
6/111 7/116 8/136 9/146

Glamorgan

W. G. A. Parkhouse c Trueman b Appleyard	12	—	c Wilson b Appleyard		43
B. Hedges b Illingworth	25	—	c and b Appleyard		55
L. N. Devereux c Trueman b Appleyard	6	—	c and b Illingworth		27
A. Lewis c Trueman b Illingworth	0	—	c Close b Appleyard		0
A. J. Watkins c Binks b Illingworth	10	—	c Binks b Illingworth		20
P. Walker b Appleyard	3	—	lbw b Appleyard		2
J. E. McConnon c Illingworth b Appleyard	6	—	lbw b Trueman		4
W. Wooller not out	4	—	b Illingworth		5
H. G. Davies c Close b Illingworth	0	—	b Pickles		1
D. J. Shepherd c Stott b Appleyard	0	—	c Pickles b Illingworth		0
F. Clarke b Illingworth	2	—	not out		0
L-b 5	5		B 8, l-b 3		11

1/35 2/43 3/43 4/49 5/57 6/67 7/67   73   1/95 2/130 3/130 4/130   168
8/69 9/69 (1.97 an over)   5/156 6/159 7/163 8/166
    9/168

Glamorgan Bowling

	O.	M.	R.	W.		O.	M.	R.	W.
Clarke	5	0	12	1					
Walker	6	3	10	0	....	2	0	6	0
Shepherd	19.4	9	30	7	....	18	4	46	5
McConnon	17	6	44	1	....	14.1	3	52	1
Watkins	1	0	1	1	....	3	0	6	0
Devereux					....	7	1	32	2

Yorkshire Bowling

	O.	M.	R.	W.		O.	M.	R.	W.
Trueman	7	1	19	0	....	1	1	0	1
Illingworth	17.3	5	31	5	....	20	5	63	4
Appleyard	12	5	18	5	....	18	1	66	4
Close						5	1	28	0
Pickles						0.3	0	0	1

Umpires: N. Oldfield and A. Skelding.

GLOUCESTERSHIRE

President—THE DUKE OF BEAUFORT
Secretary—C. H. G. THOMAS, County Ground, Bristol, 7
Captain—G. M. EMMETT

R. B. Nicholls   County Badge   D. R. Smith

Gloucestershire, third in the Championship in 1956, flattered only to deceive last summer. They badly fell from grace after a successful period halfway through the season and finished twelfth.

Yet, for all the disappointments, there were compensations. Young players, given their chances, showed much promise and Graveney's reinstatement as a regular England Test batsman brought reflected honour to the county. With the continued inability of McHugh, the fast bowler from Yorkshire, to appear, the retirement of Crapp to become an umpire, and an early injury to Milton which prevented this fine all-rounder from playing in a county game until July, the season was one of experiment. Milton's long absence was a big blow, not only to the batting strength but to the fielding.

Graveney, who hit six centuries in Championship matches—one in each innings against Warwickshire at Birmingham—Young and Emmett bore heavy responsibility. Emmett, the captain, found things very difficult for a long time, but with a remarkable innings of 91 in sixty-seven minutes against the West Indies he showed that, at 44 years of age, his ability to produce masterly strokes was unimpaired. His 170 against Glamorgan at Swansea was Gloucestershire's highest individual score of the season, though Graveney made 258 in the Third Test match against the West Indies. Nicholls, a stylish batsman capable of forceful stroke-play, scored over 1,000 runs for the first time, and in contrast to the previous season the tail-enders often provided lively resistance.

Smith and Brown, two young Bristol-born players who first

helped the county in 1956, came into this batting category, but medium-fast bowling was their prime asset. Smith, a soccer forward with the Bristol City club, took over one hundred wickets in all matches, and in the second half of the season Brown formed an effective opening attack with him. The spin bowlers were not as consistent as in the summer before, Wells, in particular, falling away in marked degree. Cook, in his benefit season, enjoyed fair success but failed to take his usual hundred wickets. Mortimore, given more opportunities with his off-spin bowling, often demonstrated his usefulness.

Etheridge and Meyer shared the wicket-keeping with Rochford who, at the end of the summer, was not re-engaged. Lambert, who had rendered the county valuable service as an all-rounder since 1937, retired when the season finished. Knightley-Smith also left to take up a post at Highgate School, where he was a pupil.

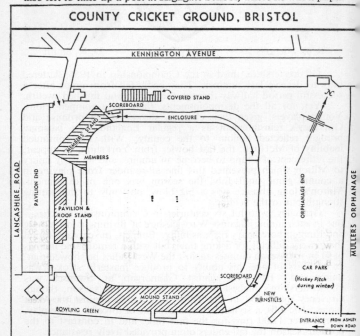

COUNTY CRICKET GROUND, BRISTOL

GLOUCESTERSHIRE RESULTS

All First-Class Matches—Played 31, Won 8, Lost 15, Drawn 8

County Championship Matches—Played 28, Won 8, Lost 13, Drawn 6, No Decision 1

COUNTY CHAMPIONSHIP AVERAGES

BATTING

	Birthplace	Mtchs.	Inns.	Not Outs	Runs	100's	Highest Inns.	Aver.
T. W. Graveney	*Riding Mill*	19	31	3	1393	6	134	49.75
C. A. Milton .	*Bristol*	17	27	9	758	0	89	42.11
D. M. Young .	*Coalville*	28	49	1	1476	1	114	30.75
R. B. Nicholls.	*Shapness*	28	48	1	1303	0	84	27.72
G. M. Emmett.	*Agra, India*	27	47	0	1181	1	170	25.12
D. Hawkins..	*Alveston*	16	28	3	458	1	106	18.32
M. A. Eagar ..	*London*	4	6	0	109	0	35	18.16
A. S. Brown ..	*Bristol*	19	31	8	392	0	45	17.04
W. Knightley-Smith	*London*	7	13	0	207	0	55	15.92
R. Etheridge..	*Gloucester*	12	16	4	155	0	38	12.91
D. R. Smith...	*Bristol*	28	42	9	421	0	63*	12.75
D. Carpenter..	*Stroud*	9	17	0	210	0	48	12.35
J. Mortimore..	*Bristol*	21	29	0	357	0	47	12.31
B. J. Meyer...	*Bournemouth*	6	11	3	94	0	30*	11.75
D. A. Allen...	*Bristol*	7	8	0	72	0	23	9.00
C. Cook	*Tetbury*	27	35	15	173	0	35*	8.65
G. E. Lambert.	*London*	8	14	0	111	0	48	7.92
G. G. M. Wiltshire	*Chipping Sodbury*	3	6	0	46	0	18	7.66
B. D. Wells...	*Gloucester*	15	22	3	141	0	18	7.42
P. Rochford...	*Halifax*	7	9	2	14	0	4*	2.00

* Signifies not out.

BOWLING

	Overs	Maidens	Runs	Wickets	Average
G. M. Emmett	8.3	2	28	2	14.00
J. Mortimore	633.2	234	1381	73	18.91
D. R. Smith	800.3	192	1941	94	20.64
C. Cook	989.3	380	2017	92	21.92
A. S. Brown	381.3	101	988	38	26.00
D. Hawkins	77.2	23	269	10	26.90
D. A. Allen	70.4	27	199	7	28.42
B. D. Wells	656.4	196	1568	55	28.50
G. E. Lambert	210	39	620	21	29.52
T. W. Graveney	28	3	84	2	42.00
G. G. M. Wiltshire......	33	3	133	3	44.33
R. B. Nicholls........	11.1	5	59	1	59.00

Also bowled: C. A. Milton 3—2—1—0; D. M. Young 5—2—14—0.

Amateurs.—M. A. Eagar, W. Knightley-Smith.

At Cardiff, April 29, 30. GLOUCESTERSHIRE lost to GLAMORGAN by five wickets. (Two-day friendly match.)

At Oxford, May 4, 6, 7. GLOUCESTERSHIRE drew with OXFORD UNIVERSITY.

At Hove, May 8, 9, 10. GLOUCESTERSHIRE lost to SUSSEX by seven wickets.

At Lord's, May 11, 13, 14. GLOUCESTERSHIRE lost to MIDDLESEX by 135 runs.

GLOUCESTERSHIRE v. LEICESTERSHIRE

At Gloucester, May 18, 20, 21. Gloucestershire won by 11 runs, taking 14 points. On a rain-affected pitch batsmen were at a disadvantage. Savage judiciously allied flight with off-spin in causing Gloucestershire's first innings breakdown after they were 73 for no wicket, but Smith turned the tables on the last day. Leicestershire, thanks to sound stroke-play by Palmer, had reached 113 for five and required only 29 more to win. The visitors were out for another 17, for Smith was so effective at his fast-medium pace that he took four wickets in seven overs for five runs.

Gloucestershire

D. M. Young b Munden	49	— b Savage	12
D. Carpenter b Savage	21	— b Spencer	4
R. B. Nicholls c and b Savage	25	— lbw b Palmer	32
G. M. Emmett c Munden b Savage	13	— c and b van Geloven	0
D. Hawkins c Firth b Savage	11	— c Hickman b Palmer	17
J. Mortimore c Munden b Savage	1	— b van Geloven	6
G. E. Lambert c van Geloven b Savage	6	— b van Geloven	0
D. R. Smith b Savage	0	— b Spencer	13
P. Rochford c Spencer b Savage	1	— b Spencer	0
C. Cook not out	8	— not out	13
B. D. Wells c Spencer b Palmer	2	— b Palmer	12
B 4, l-b 1, n-b 2	7	B 8, l-b 5, n-b 2	15

1/73 2/83 3/98 4/116 5/126 6/132   144
7/132 8/133 9/140 (2.48 an over)

1/7 2/28 3/33 4/71 5/79   124
6/80 7/87 8/95 9/98

Leicestershire

G. Lester lbw b Wells	8	— c Rochford b Lambert	1
M. R. Hallam b Smith	6	— b Smith	4
L. R. Gardner b Lambert	5	— b Lambert	4
C. H. Palmer c Lambert b Mortimore	23	— c Carpenter b Smith	65
J. van Geloven c Rochford b Wells	4	— b Lambert	17
V. S. Munden c Rochford b Mortimore	8	— b Smith	16
M. Hickman c Mortimore b Lambert	38	— lbw b Smith	0
J. Firth c Smith b Mortimore	5	— lbw b Lambert	1
J. Savage b Wells	14	— run out	0
R. L. Pratt c Emmett b Lambert	8	— c Rochford b Smith	3
C. T. Spencer not out	2	— not out	1
B 3, l-b 2, n-b 1	6	B 6, l-b 12	18

1/8 2/16 3/33 4/45 5/55 6/55 7/69   127
8/100 9/124 (1.56 an over)

1/4 2/14 3/74 4/78 5/98   130
6/113 7/113 8/113 9/129

Leicestershire Bowling

	O.	M.	R.	W.		O.	M.	R.	W.
Spencer	4	0	21	0	....	9	2	28	3
Pratt	5	0	19	0	....	4	0	11	0
Palmer	13.5	11	8	1	....	10.4	9	10	3
van Geloven	9	2	16	0	....	25	12	33	3
Savage	19	5	50	8	....	10	3	27	1
Munden	7	2	23	1					

Gloucestershire Bowling

	O.	M.	R.	W.		O.	M.	R.	W.
Lambert	7.5	3	12	3	....	31	12	37	4
Smith	5	0	9	1	....	25.4	11	43	5
Cook	18	11	20	0	....	8	3	15	0
Wells	27	12	39	3	....	14	7	17	0
Mortimore	23	6	41	3					

Umpires: W. F. Price and W. E. Phillipson.

GLOUCESTERSHIRE v. WORCESTERSHIRE

At Bristol, May 22, 23, 24. Worcestershire won by five wickets, taking 12 points. Batsmen were masters in this game which produced an exciting struggle for the first innings lead and again for the result. Young scored soundly against his former county and Smith drove firmly, but their efforts were surpassed by Kenyon and D. W. Richardson, whose attractive strokes brought them deserved centuries. Worcestershire required 41 for the lead when Aldridge, their last man, went in, but Richardson, farming the bowling, took runs as he liked and reached his hundred with a six which put his side in front. Altogether he hit two 6's and fourteen 4's. Graveney, batting with grace and power, replied with a century in just over three hours for Gloucestershire and Emmett set Worcestershire to make 218 in two hours and forty minutes. This time the senior Richardson excelled. He scored readily with a wide variety of strokes off pace and spin bowling in a splendid innings which occupied him just under two hours, and his team, 173 for three when the extra half-hour was claimed, won with three minutes to spare. Late hours—1.30 to 8.15—were played on the first two days.

Gloucestershire

D. M. Young, c D. Richardson b Berry .	70	— b Flavell	13
D. Carpenter lbw b Horton	31	— c Booth b Flavell	6
T. W. Graveney lbw b Flavell	29	— not out	111
R. B. Nicholls b Aldridge	24	— c Booth b Flavell	59
G. M. Emmett c Outschoorn b Flavell	43	— c Dews b Aldridge	25
D. J. Hawkins b Berry	24	— not out	0
G. E. Lambert c Horton b Aldridge	0		
D. R. Smith not out	63	— b Aldridge	0
C. Cook b Aldridge	15		
P. Rochford not out	4		
B 1, l-b 2, n-b 1	4	B 2, l-b 7	9

1/55 2/119 3/141 4/186 　(8 wkts., dec.) 307　　1/18 2/25 　(5 wkts., dec.) 223
5/212 6/213 7/259 8/287 (2.84 an over)　　3/169 4/210 5/218
B. D. Wells did not bat.

Worcestershire

P. E. Richardson b Cook	25	— st Rochford b Cook	108
D. Kenyon c Hawkins b Cook	115	— c Young b Lambert	8
G. Dews c Lambert b Hawkins	33	— run out	33
D. W. Richardson not out	101	— st Rochford b Cook	4
L. Outschoorn b Cook	4	— not out	2
R. G. Broadbent c Cook b Hawkins	2	— not out	40
M. J. Horton c Rochford b Hawkins	0	— b Cook	14
R. Booth c Carpenter b Smith	11		
R. Berry b Smith	4		
J. Flavell b Smith	0		
J. Aldridge not out	3		
B 13, l-b 1, w 1	15	B 4, l-b 5	9

1/70 2/177 3/189 　　(9 wkts., dec.) 313　　1/8 2/123 3/132 　(5 wkts.) 218
4/193 5/196 6/201 7/214 8/267 9/267　　4/181 5/211
(2.79 an over)

Worcestershire Bowling

	O.	M.	R.	W.		O.	M.	R.	W.
Aldridge	31	6	92	3	....	16	5	58	2
Flavell	25	7	48	2	....	22	5	84	3
Berry	38	15	96	2	....	17	3	48	0
Horton	13	3	58	1	....	6	1	24	0
D. Richardson .	1	0	9	0					

Gloucestershire Bowling

	O.	M.	R.	W.	O.	M.	R.	W.
Lambert	22	4	81	0	8	0	43	1
Smith	26	3	83	3	11	1	42	0
Cook	35	12	80	3	16	2	74	3
Wells	18	5	38	0	7.3	0	50	0
Hawkins	11	6	16	3				

Umpires: W. F. Price and E. Davies.

At Northampton, May 25, 27. GLOUCESTERSHIRE lost to NORTHAMPTONSHIRE by seven wickets.

At Romford, May 29, 30, 31. GLOUCESTERSHIRE lost to ESSEX by six wickets.

GLOUCESTERSHIRE v. WARWICKSHIRE

At Bristol, June 1, 3, 4. Warwickshire won by 95 runs, taking 14 points. Gloucestershire, thanks to Graveney, who drove stylishly in a chanceless century, put up a fairly good fight in the first innings, but sadly disappointed in the second. They needed 213 to win with just over a day left, but failed against Carter, bowling accurate off-spinners at lively pace, and the match ended before lunch on the third morning. Ibadulla, with three wickets for nine runs in four overs, gave him fine help. Gardner's sound batting proved a valuable asset to Warwickshire. He batted pluckily in the first innings, although needing a runner for a long time after pulling a thigh muscle. Wells, using off-spin judiciously, was Gloucestershire's most successful bowler. Hawkins, of similar type, bowled well in the second innings.

Warwickshire

F. C. Gardner b Smith	83	—	not out	54
N. F. Horner c Nicholls b Hawkins	51	—	c Graveney b Hawkins	0
M. J. K. Smith c Emmett b Wells	14	—	b Lambert	0
A. Townsend c Meyer b Cook	6	—	c Hawkins b Cook	34
A. V. Wolton c Graveney b Wells	1	—	b Cook	0
R. T. Spooner lbw b Wells	1	—	b Hawkins	24
K. Ibadulla lbw b Wells	27	—	lbw b Wells	10
S. Singh lbw b Smith	33	—	lbw b Wells	5
R. G. Carter b Wells	21	—	c Wells b Cook	27
J. D. Bannister b Wells	0	—	c Lambert b Hawkins	0
W. E. Hollies not out	0	—	c Wells b Hawkins	2
B 9, l-b 5	14		B 9, l-b 6	15

1/81 2/127 3/129 4/129 5/131 6/181   251   1/3 2/66 3/73 4/73 5/84   171
7/229 8/251 9/251 (2.56 an over)   6/102 7/146 8/146 9/158

Gloucestershire

G. M. Emmett lbw b Bannister	2	—	c Townsend b Carter	5
D. M. Young c sub b Carter	32	—	c sub b Carter	4
W. Knightley-Smith c Horner b Carter	3	—	b Carter	0
T. W. Graveney c sub b Ibadulla	122	—	b Carter	2
R. B. Nicholls run out	7	—	lbw b Carter	25
D. Hawkins b Ibadulla	5	—	c Smith b Ibadulla	12
B. J. Meyer c Bannister b Ibadulla	0	—	c Ibadulla b Carter	0
G. E. Lambert lbw b Ibadulla	0	—	b Ibadulla	48
D. Smith c Spooner b Hollies	12	—	not out	18
C. Cook not out	1	—	b Ibadulla	0
B. D. Wells b Hollies	18	—	c Bannister b Carter	1
B 4, l-b 3, n-b 1	8		L-b 2	2

1/10 2/21 3/81 4/128 5/136 6/142   210   1/9 2/16 3/18 4/20 5/78   117
7/146 8/185 9/191 (2.14 an over)   6/95 7/95 8/106 9/106

Gloucestershire Bowling

	O.	M.	R.	W.		O.	M.	R.	W.
Lambert	12	2	34	0	....	5	1	9	1
Smith	11.1	4	23	2	....	3	0	13	0
Wells	37	11	89	6	....	27	10	54	2
Cook	29	13	46	1	....	26	12	52	3
Hawkins	8	1	41	1	....	15	7	28	4
Nicholls	1	0	4	0					

Warwickshire Bowling

	O.	M.	R.	W.		O.	M.	R.	W.
Banrister	6	3	6	1	....	2	1	6	0
Carter	21	6	55	2	....	20.2	6	57	7
Hollies	37	13	57	2	....	18	3	33	0
Singh	7	2	21	0	....	3	0	10	0
Ibadulla	26	7	62	4	....	4	2	9	3
Townsend	1	0	1	0					

Umpires: R. S. Lay and H. G. Baldwin.

At Bristol, June 5, 6, 7. GLOUCESTERSHIRE lost to WEST INDIES by 154 runs. (See WEST INDIES section.)

At Taunton, June 8, 10, 11. GLOUCESTERSHIRE drew with SOMERSET.

At Birmingham, June 12, 13, 14. GLOUCESTERSHIRE lost to WARWICKSHIRE by six wickets.

At The Oval, June 19, 20. GLOUCESTERSHIRE lost to SURREY by an innings and 149 runs.

GLOUCESTERSHIRE v. ESSEX

At Stroud, June 22, 24, 25. Essex, taking 14 points, won by an innings and 21 runs, Gloucestershire giving an uninspiring display. Missed catches helped Essex to their good first innings score to which the free-driving Dodds, who hit fifteen 4's, and Savill made chief contributions. The home batsmen showed little resolution against fast and slow bowling. Greensmith, with cleverly-flighted leg-breaks, took three wickets in four balls. Gloucestershire followed on and lost four wickets for 73 before the close of the second day. Next morning, despite attractive, forcing stroke-play by Brown, the game was soon over. An unusual incident occurred in the Gloucestershire first innings, Mortimore being run out when standing outside his crease after an unsuccessful leg-before appeal.

Essex

T. C. Dodds lbw b Allen	85
G. Barker c Nicholls b Smith	10
B. Taylor lbw b Allen	25
L. Savill run out	89
M. Bear c Nicholls b Allen	4
G. Smith b Cook	1
W. T. Greensmith b Brown	48
R. Ralph lbw b Smith	8
K. C. Preston b Smith	2
I. M. King c Nicholls b Smith	1
E. Palmer not out	0
B 10, l-b 4, w 1	15

1/43 2/104 3/137 4/157 5/168   288
6/260 7/284 8/287 9/287
(2.90 an over)

Gloucestershire

D. M. Young c Ralph b Palmer	17	—	c Greensmith b Palmer	25
W. Knightley-Smith c and b Preston	35	—	c Taylor b Palmer	5
R. B. Nicholls c Palmer b Ralph	13	—	b Preston	20
G. M. Emmett lbw b Preston	5	—	c Taylor b Preston	13
A. S. Brown c Taylor b Greensmith	3	—	not out	41
J. Mortimore run out	21	—	lbw b Preston	13
D. A. Allen c Preston b Greensmith	0	—	b Greensmith	5
D. Smith c Preston b Greensmith	0	—	b Greensmith	2
B. J. Meyer c Bear b Greensmith	17	—	c Preston b Greensmith	1
G. G. M. Wiltshire b King	1	—	run out	11
C. Cook not out	4	—	lbw b Preston	0
B 4, l-b 2, n-b 2	8		B 4, l-b 2, n-b 1	7

1/25 2/58 3/69 4/76 5/83 6/83 7/83   124   1/20 2/41 3/49 4/60 5/91   143
8/103 9/104 (2.33 an over)   6/92 7/108 8/123 9/139

Gloucestershire Bowling

	O.	M.	R.	W.		O.	M.	R.	W.
Smith	20.2	4	67	4					
Wiltshire	5	2	20	0					
Cook	27	13	57	1					
Mortimore	12	3	33	0					
Allen	23	8	61	3					
Brown	12	2	35	1					

Essex Bowling

	O.	M.	R.	W.		O.	M.	R.	W.
Preston	16	4	28	2		25.2	8	60	4
Ralph	10	1	31	1		1	1	0	0
Palmer	10	3	26	1		16	4	39	2
Greensmith	10.4	3	19	4		13	5	32	3
King	6	3	12	1		5	3	5	0

Umpires: H. G. Baldwin and T. J. Bartley.

GLOUCESTERSHIRE v. CAMBRIDGE UNIVERSITY

At Bristol, June 26, 27. Cambridge won by an innings and 33 runs. James, who scored 168, and Goonesena, who hit 60 and took twelve wickets for 100 runs in the match, were the outstanding figures. Only Milton, who batted excellently in his first game of the season after fracturing a wrist-bone, and Emmett could do much in the first innings against the guileful leg-break and top-spin bowling of the Cambridge captain. In contrast, James dominated the cricket, on-driving and pulling powerfully during a fine display lasting four hours and including six 6's and seventeen 4's. Goonesena helped him in a stand of 141, and when Gloucestershire batted again 173 behind, he once more puzzled his rivals. Cambridge finished the match after ten minutes of the extra half-hour.

Gloucestershire

G. M. Emmett lbw b James	45	—	b Smith	20
D. Carpenter run out	15	—	c and b Goonesena	22
W. Knightley-Smith b James	4	—	b Wheatley	5
T. W. Graveney c and b Goonesena	11	—	c Swift b Goonesena	32
A. S. Brown lbw b Goonesena	5	—	b Goonesena	0
C. A. Milton st Swift b Goonesena	51	—	b Pieris	28
J. Mortimore c Dexter b Goonesena	15	—	c sub b Goonesena	1
J. V. C. Griffiths c Dexter b Goonesena	9	—	lbw b Goonesena	13
D. A. Allen b Wheatley	7	—	lbw b James	6
D. Smith b Goonesena	0	—	st Swift b Goonesena	6
R. J. Etheridge not out	0	—	not out	0
B 12, l-b 3, w 1	16		B 6, l-b 1	7

1/57 2/62 3/74 4/84 5/95 6/128   178   1/22 2/27 3/66 4/66 5/95   140
7/152 8/167 9/175   6/109 7/109 8/109 9/128

Cambridge University

R. W. Barber c Graveney b Griffiths	22
C. S. Smith b Smith	8
D. J. Green st Etheridge b Mortimore	9
E. R. Dexter c Graveney b Smith..	43
R. M. James c Griffiths b Allen...168	
G. Goonesena c Etheridge b Griffiths	60
P. D. Croft lbw b Mortimore	15
G. W. Cook b Mortimore	0
P. I. Pieris b Allen	15
B. T. Swift not out	2
O. S. Wheatley c Allen b Graveney	1
B 5, l-b 2, w 1	8
	351

1/25 2/36 3/48 4/96 5/237
6/262 7/262 8/340 9/345

Cambridge University Bowling

	O.	M.	R.	W.		O.	M.	R.	W.
Smith	7	1	17	0	....	5	1	15	1
Wheatley	12	2	37	1	....	3	0	24	1
Pieris	6	1	11	0	....	16	4	35	1
James	17	10	25	2	....	0.2	0	0	1
Goonesena	24.2	5	60	6	....	20	9	40	6
Cook	10	5	16	0					
Barber					....	5	2	19	0

Gloucestershire Bowling

	O.	M.	R.	W.
Smith	27	6	56	2
Brown	8	2	23	0
Mortimore	37	12	87	3
Griffiths	26	4	105	2
Allen	13	4	33	2
Graveney	9	2	21	1
Milton	6	0	18	0

Umpires: E. Davies and D. Davies.

At Swansea, June 29, July 1, 2. GLOUCESTERSHIRE beat GLAMORGAN by an innings and 57 runs.

GLOUCESTERSHIRE v. DERBYSHIRE

At Gloucester, July 6, 8, 9. Derbyshire won by two wickets, taking 14 points. Gloucestershire, 214 behind on the first innings, fought back so well that their rivals only just scraped home. Kelly and Revill, partners in a third-wicket stand of 138, batted soundly in giving Derbyshire their good start, but Gloucestershire, with the exception of the stubborn Nicholls, fared disastrously against the lively swing bowling of Jackson who took seven for 27 runs. Following on, Gloucestershire batted in much improved style. Young, after defying his opponents for four hours, fell in sight of a century and Derbyshire found themselves left to score 63 to win. On a worn pitch this proved a most difficult task against the fast bowling of Smith and the off-spin of Mortimore. The issue became so close that when Gladwin joined Morgan at the fall of the eighth wicket eight runs were still required and they took half an hour to score them.

Derbyshire

A. Hamer b Smith	0	— b Smith	9
C. Lee run out	24	— lbw b Smith	5
J. Kelly c Emmett b Cook	113	— c Emmett b Mortimore	5
A. C. Revill c Milton b Mortimore	59	— c Etheridge b Smith	19
D. B. Carr c Etheridge b Brown	10	— c Brown b Mortimore	5
H. L. Johnson c Milton b Smith	2	— lbw b Smith	0
D. C. Morgan c Emmett b Mortimore	29	— not out	11
G. O. Dawkes c Etheridge b Mortimore..	30	— b Smith	6
E. Smith c Milton b Brown	15	— run out	1
C. Gladwin lbw b Brown	17	— not out	1
L. Jackson not out	3		
B 5, l-b 3, w 5	13	W 1	1
	315	(8 wkts.)	63

1/0 2/50 3/188 4/206 5/217 6/229
7/273 8/289 9/302 (2.54 an over)

1/11 2/20 3/20
4/36 5/49 6/49 7/54 8/55

Gloucestershire

G. M. Emmett c Dawkes b Jackson	0	— c Carr b Morgan.........	35
D. M. Young lbw b Jackson	11	— c Morgan b Gladwin	99
W. Knightley-Smith c Johnson b Jackson	2	— b Morgan	0
R. B. Nicholls lbw b Jackson	44	— c Lee b Gladwin	20
C. A. Milton c Dawkes b Jackson	5	— lbw b Jackson	4
D. Hawkins b Morgan	5	— c Dawkes b Jackson	29
J. Mortimore b Morgan	0	— c Gladwin b Smith	31
A. S. Brown c Johnson b Gladwin	8	— c and b Gladwin	7
D. Smith c Dawkes b Jackson	11	— lbw b Smith	1
R. Etheridge not out	11	— b Gladwin	29
C. Cook b Jackson	0	— not out	5
B 2, n-b 2	4	B 11, l-b 3, n-b 2......	16
	101		**276**

1/0 2/6 3/15 4/31 5/47 6/53 7/68
8/79 9/101 (1.74 an over)

1/52 2/54 3/119 4/132
5/185 6/217 7/229 8/254
9/267

Gloucestershire Bowling

	O.	M.	R.	W.	O.	M.	R.	W.
Smith	27	6	51	2	19	5	31	5
Brown	23.3	2	81	3	2	0	8	0
Mortimore.....	38	12	93	3	17.5	6	23	2
Cook	29	9	48	1				
Hawkins	6	2	29	0				

Derbyshire Bowling

	O.	M.	R.	W.	O.	M.	R.	W.
Jackson	17.5	11	27	7	28	4	83	2
Gladwin	19	9	29	1	29	11	61	4
Morgan	15	6	26	2	28	14	31	2
Smith	6	2	15	0	20.3	7	38	2
Carr					11	2	36	0
Revill					2	0	11	0

Umpires: A. R. Coleman and P. A. Gibb.

GLOUCESTERSHIRE v. MIDDLESEX

At Gloucester, July 10, 11, 12. Drawn, Gloucestershire taking four points. Rain badly upset cricket, curtailing play on the first two days and preventing a prompt resumption on the last. Nicholls, a strong driver, played a splendid innings for Gloucestershire, and Young, after needing four stitches in a chin cut by a ball from Warr, returned and batted soundly. Etheridge, who hit Moss, with the new ball, for two 6's, helped Smith in a lively ninth wicket stand. Then Smith showed his prowess as a fast-medium bowler by sending back three men for 11 runs while five left for 28 in fifty minutes. Baldry, driving and cutting stylishly, hit eleven 4's in 53, but apart from Bennett he could not find anyone to stay with him. Mortimore, bowling his off-breaks cleverly on damp turf, gave his faster colleagues excellent support.

Gloucestershire

G. M. Emmett c Delisle b Warr	1			
D. M. Young b Baldry	47	— not out		23
R. B. Nicholls c Edrich b Baldry	84			
T. W. Graveney c and b Hurst	32			
C. A. Milton c Edrich b Hurst	2			
D. G. Hawkins lbw b Hurst	3			
R. J. Etheridge b Moss	38	— hit wkt b Robertson		7
A. S. Brown lbw b Titmus	1	— not out		13
J. Mortimore c Bennett b Hurst	0			
D. R. Smith not out	46			
C. Cook run out	5			
L-b 7, n-b 2	9			

1/1 2/78 3/160 4/167 5/171 6/180　　268　　1/25　　　(1 wkt.) 43
7/185 8/188 9/252 (2.79 an over)

Middlesex

J. D. Robertson b Smith	6	J. J. Warr b Mortimore		2
R. A. Gale c Smith b Brown	8	R. J. Hurst not out		5
D. O. Baldry c Brown b Mortimore	53	A. E. Moss c Hawkins b Mortimore		12
G. P. S. Delisle b Brown	0			
F. J. Titmus c Etheridge b Smith	3	B 7, l-b 1, w 2		10
J. T. Murray b Smith	0			
D. Bennett c Graveney b Cook	31	1/8 2/17 3/17 4/28 5/28 6/102		132
W. J. Edrich b Mortimore	2	7/106 8/110 9/119 (1.88 an over)		

Middlesex Bowling

	O.	M.	R.	W.	O.	M.	R.	W.
Moss	21	1	89	1	2	0	4	0
Warr	17.5	3	56	1				
Bennett	4	1	8	0	1	0	1	0
Titmus	18	4	44	1				
Hurst	27	12	47	4				
Baldry	8	2	15	2				
Edrich					7	2	21	0
Robertson					6	0	17	1

Gloucestershire Bowling

	O.	M.	R.	W.
Smith	23	7	45	3
Brown	9	1	18	2
Mortimore	21.2	6	45	4
Cook	17	3	14	1

Umpires: P. A. Gibb and H. Elliott.

At Maidstone, July 13, 15, 16. GLOUCESTERSHIRE lost to KENT by eight wickets.

At Scarborough, July 17, 18, 19. GLOUCESTERSHIRE drew with YORKSHIRE.

At Worcester, July 20, 22, 23. GLOUCESTERSHIRE drew with WORCESTERSHIRE.

At Nottingham, July 24, 25, 26. GLOUCESTERSHIRE beat NOTTINGHAMSHIRE by five wickets.

GLOUCESTERSHIRE v. SURREY

At Bristol, July 27, 29, 30. Gloucestershire won by 38 runs, taking 12 points. Despite the fine performance of Gibson, their new medium-fast bowler who took ten wickets in his first Championship match, Surrey, without May, Loader, Laker and Lock, suffered their second defeat of the season. Gloucestershire, who lacked Graveney, gave a meritorious display. Milton, sound and stylish, helped them to a fair total on the first day when Gibson, lively and very accurate in direction, shared the wickets with A. Bedser. Constable and Fletcher, partners in a fourth-wicket stand of 120, drove and cut attractively for Surrey who lost nine men for 219 to a varied attack before Cox and A. Bedser put Surrey in front. The turning-point came when Emmett and Young, masters of pace and spin, scored 91 without being separated before the close of the second day. Nicholls, a forceful driver, consolidated the advantage next morning and a declaration left Surrey to make 230 in two and three-quarter hours. Clark and Constable were out for 13, and although Stewart and Barrington added 112 in seventy minutes Surrey still needed 49 with only two wickets standing when the extra half-hour was claimed. The task proved too heavy, more good fielding and clever spin bowling finishing the game in Gloucestershire's favour with fifteen minutes to spare.

Gloucestershire

G. M. Emmett c McIntyre b Gibson	42	—	c Stewart b Gibson	60
D. M. Young b Gibson	36	—	c McIntyre b A. Bedser	67
R. B. Nicholls lbw b A. Bedser	39	—	c McIntyre b E. Bedser	58
M. A. Eagar lbw b A. Bedser	28	—	b Cox	1
C. A. Milton b Gibson	61	—	not out	19
A. S. Brown c Stewart b A. Bedser	0	—	b A. Bedser	20
J. Mortimore b Gibson	16	—	lbw b Gibson	11
E. J. Etheridge c Pratt b Gibson	0	—	c Stewart b Gibson	1
D. R. Smith c Stewart b A. Bedser	13	—	b Gibson	0
C. Cook b Gibson	3			
B. D. Wells not out	0			
B 5, l-b 6	11		B 1, l-b 5	6

1/68 2/87 3/139 4/162 5/164 6/206   249   1/103 2/149 (8 wkts., dec.) 243
7/210 8/239 9/246 (2.67 an over)   3/171 4/199 5/228 6/241
7/243 8/243

Surrey

T. H. Clark c Young b Smith	0	—	lbw b Smith	1
M. J. Stewart c Mortimore b Smith	12	—	c Milton b Wells	60
B. Constable c Smith b Wells	80	—	b Brown	5
K. F. Barrington c Mortimore b Smith	1	—	c Milton b Cook	56
D. G. W. Fletcher b Wells	59	—	c Eagar b Mortimore	23
R. C. E. Pratt lbw b Brown	9	—	b Wells	8
E. A. Bedser b Smith	7	—	c Eagar b Mortimore	19
A. J. McIntyre b Brown	24	—	run out	1
D. F. Cox not out	29	—	st Etheridge b Mortimore	6
D. Gibson c and b Wells	11	—	c Etheridge b Cook	3
A. V. Bedser not out	17	—	not out	5
B 6, l-b 6, w 2	14		L-b 4	4

1/0 2/35 3/41 4/161   (9 wkts., dec.) 263   1/8 2/13 3/125 4/125   191
5/162 6/179 7/181 8/205 9/219   5/134 6/168 7/170 8/177
(2.17 an over)   9/183

Surrey Bowling

	O.	M.	R.	W.		O.	M.	R.	W.
A. Bedser	30	8	79	4	....	28	8	68	2
Cox	14	1	51	0	....	7	0	32	1
Gibson	27	6	53	6	....	21	3	73	4
E. Bedser	22	4	55	0	....	24	6	64	1

Gloucestershire Bowling

	O.	M.	R.	W.	O.	M.	R.	W.
Smith	38	11	76	4	9	1	34	1
Brown	29	6	58	2	6	0	38	1
Wells	22	8	45	3	12	0	57	2
Cook	26	10	52	0	20.2	6	47	2
Mortimore	6	3	18	0	6	0	11	3

Umpires: John Langridge and E. A. Roberts.

GLOUCESTERSHIRE v. GLAMORGAN

At Bristol, July 31, August 1, 2. Gloucestershire won by 266 runs, taking 14 points. Their batting strength and the guile of Cook, whose left-arm slow bowling brought him eleven wickets for 84 runs, were the decisive factors. At one stage in the last innings when Glamorgan faced the task of scoring 350 to win in five and a half hours, Cook took five wickets for 15 runs, 12 of them hit in one over by Haydn Davies. Wooller, one of Cook's victims, was twice out first ball. Young and Graveney narrowly missed hundreds for Gloucestershire and Nicholls and Emmett also batted attractively. Walker, Glamorgan's young left-arm medium-paced bowler, accomplished the exceptional feat of bowling for five hours in the first innings with breaks only for lunch and tea. He sent down fifty overs and his skill and accuracy yielded him seven wickets for 116 runs.

Gloucestershire

G. M. Emmett b Walker	57	—	lbw b Wooller	0
D. M. Young lbw b Watkins	97	—	b Walker	8
R. B. Nicholls c Watkins b Walker	17	—	c Davies b Devereux	73
T. W. Graveney b Walker	41	—	b Shepherd	99
C. A. Milton lbw b Wooller	25	—	lbw b Devereux	17
A. S. Brown c Davies b Walker	4	—	not out	9
J. Mortimore b Walker	42			
D. A. Allen lbw b Walker	13			
D. R. Smith c sub b Walker	13			
R. J. Etheridge run out	0			
C. Cook not out	1			
B 1, l-b 6, n-b 1	8		B 1, l-b 2	3

1/103 2/151 3/211 4/217 5/222 6/269   318   1/0 2/38   (5 wkts., dec.) 209
7/299 8/306 9/306 (2.83 an over)   3/135 4/191 5/209

Glamorgan

W. G. A. Parkhouse c Cook b Brown	29	—	c Graveney b Allen	31
B. Hedges lbw b Cook	20	—	c Brown b Mortimore	8
A. Jones b Brown	0	—	c Etheridge b Cook	12
L. N. Devereux lbw b Smith	0	—	c Graveney b Cook	2
A. J. Watkins b Cook	55	—	not out	12
P. Walker c Allen b Cook	7	—	c Graveney b Cook	2
J. E. McConnon st Etheridge b Cook	51	—	c Young b Cook	0
W. Wooller b Mortimore	0	—	c Milton b Cook	0
H. G. Davies c Graveney b Brown	3	—	c Smith b Cook	13
J. Pressdee c Graveney b Mortimore	1	—	absent hurt	0
D. J. Shepherd not out	12	—	lbw b Allen	0
			B 2, l-b 1	3

1/36 2/36 3/37 4/61 5/79 6/140   178   1/25 2/54 3/54 4/58 5/64   83
7/141 8/150 9/154 (2.37 an over)   6/68 7/69 8/83 9/83

Glamorgan Bowling

	O.	M.	R.	W.		O.	M.	R.	W.
Wooller	17	3	64	1	....	7	1	38	1
Watkins	21	3	70	1					
Walker	50.3	10	116	7	....	10	1	30	1
McConnon	16	2	52	0	....	8	2	24	0
Shepherd	7	3	8	0	....	20.3	4	57	1
Devereux					....	15	2	57	2

Gloucestershire Bowling

	O.	M.	R.	W.		O.	M.	R.	W.
Smith	20	4	60	1	....	4	2	6	0
Brown	11	5	25	2	....	3	1	14	0
Cook	23.5	13	42	5	....	18	7	42	6
Mortimore	15	7	26	2	....	13	7	13	1
Allen	5	2	25	0	....	8.1	6	5	2

Umpires: W. F. Price and H. G. Baldwin.

GLOUCESTERSHIRE v. SOMERSET

At Bristol, August 3, 5. Gloucestershire won by an innings and five runs, taking 14 points. Stronger in all departments they finished the game with an hour and a half of the second day to spare. Watched by a crowd of 10,000, Somerset lost eighteen wickets for 293 runs on Bank Holiday Monday and despite the bold hitting of Tremlett, whose 46 included two 6's and seven 4's, they failed to make their rivals bat a second time. The speed and accuracy of Smith and craft of Mortimore, the off-spinner, upset Somerset in their first innings. In the second the spin-bowling combination of Mortimore and Cook decided the issue. Gloucestershire profited by the splendid first-day batting of Graveney, Nicholls and Young. Graveney. sound rather than adventurous, spent three and a quarter hours over his 134; his stylish strokes—the majority powerful drives—brought him one 6 and fourteen 4's.

Gloucestershire

G. M. Emmett c Langford b Biddulph	27
D. M. Young b Langford	50
R. B. Nicholls st Stephenson b McCool	61
T. W. Graveney b Langford	134
C. A. Milton lbw b McCool	4
A. S. Brown c Pickles b McCool	37
J. Mortimore c Langford b McMahon	9
D. A. Allen b Langford	9
D. Smith c McCool b Langford	0
R. J. Etheridge st Stephenson b McCool	12
C. Cook not out	0
B 3, l-b 6	9

1/36 2/110 3/184 4/188 5/276   352
6/305 7/337 8/337 9/342
(3.20 an over)

Somerset

L. Pickles b Smith	5	— c Allen b Mortimore	27
W. E. Alley b Mortimore	35	— c Graveney b Cook	35
D. R. W. Silk not out	48	— c Etheridge b Mortimore	12
P. B. Wight b Smith	0	— b Cook	40
C. L. McCool b Smith	5	— c Milton b Allen	14
M. F. Tremlett c and b Smith	0	— c Mortimore b Cook	46
K. H. Palmer c Brown b Smith	0	— c Brown b Cook	5
H. W. Stephenson b Mortimore	26	— not out	25
B. Langford b Mortimore	0	— lbw b Cook	6
J. W. McMahon c and b Mortimore	0	— b Mortimore	0
K. D. Biddulph b Mortimore	2	— b Mortimore	0
B 1, l-b 3	4	B 4, l-b 8	12

1/24 2/50 3/55 4/73 5/73 6/75   125
7/115 8/119 9/119 (2.19 an over)

1/67 2/73 3/86 4/125   222
5/182 6/189 7/195 8/209
9/222

Somerset Bowling

	O.	M.	R.	W.	O.	M	R.	W.
Biddulph	11	0	53	1				
Alley	9	1	31	0				
McMahon	24	3	76	1				
Langford	32	10	80	4				
McCool	31.5	4	102	4				
Wight	2	1	1	0				

Gloucestershire Bowling

	O.	M.	R.	W.	O.	M	R.	W.
Smith	17	6	25	5	12	1	42	0
Brown	7	2	31	0	3	0	10	0
Cook	15	6	31	0	21	8	34	5
Mortimore	11	6	16	5	28.5	10	93	1
Allen	7	2	18	0	4	0	31	1

Umpires: D. Davies and W. E. Phillipson.

At Leicester, August 7, 8, 9. GLOUCESTERSHIRE drew with LEICESTERSHIRE.

GLOUCESTERSHIRE v. SUSSEX

At Cheltenham, August 10, 12, 13. Drawn. Rain prevented even a first innings decision. Cricket could not start until after lunch on the first two days and there was no play on the third. Nevertheless, the limited cricket proved exciting. Brown, very lively off a damp pitch, took all six Sussex wickets which fell on the opening afternoon for 41 out of 78. His last four victims were dismissed in ten deliveries without cost. Sheppard, who alone played him confidently, went on to hit eleven 4's in a splendid 72 made in two and three-quarter hours. Gloucestershire, in their turn, failed against fast bowling. They lost four men for nine runs and scored only 19 in forty-five minutes before bad light finished play for the day, and, as it happened, for the match, just before half-past five.

Sussex

D. V. Smith b Brown	22
D. S. Sheppard c Nicholls b Mortimore	72
K. G. Suttle c Graveney b Brown	7
J. M. Parks lbw b Brown	8
G. H. G. Doggart b Brown	0
L. J. Lenham c Smith b Brown	0
A. E. James b Brown	0
R. T. Webb not out	31
N. I. Thomson b Mortimore	26
R. G. Marlar b Smith	0
R. V. Bell run out	0
B 1, l-b 2	3

1/45 2/65 3/77 4/77 5/77 6/77   169
7/124 8/162 9/167 (2.28 an over)

Gloucestershire

G. M. Emmett lbw b Thomson	0
D. M. Young b James	6
R. B. Nicholls c Suttle b James	1
T. W. Graveney lbw b Thomson	0
C. A. Milton not out	1
A. S. Brown not out	10
L-b 1	1

1/0 2/6 3/7 4/9   (4 wkts.) 19
(1.58 an over)

J. Mortimore, D. A. Allen, D. R. Smith, P. Rochford and C. Cook did not bat.

Gloucestershire Bowling

	O.	M.	R.	W.
Smith	19	3	53	1
Brown	24	8	55	6
Cook	20	8	32	0
Mortimore	11	4	26	2

Sussex Bowling

	O.	M.	R.	W.
Thomson	6	1	7	2
James	5.3	2	11	2

Umpires: E. Davies and A. E. Pothecary.

GLOUCESTERSHIRE v. HAMPSHIRE

At Cheltenham, August 14, 15. Gloucestershire won by seven wickets, taking 14 points. On a drying pitch bowlers held the upper hand to such an extent that Emmett, the Gloucestershire captain, was top scorer of the match, with 41. Cricket did not commence until half-past two; then Mortimore. pitching his off-spinners accurately and well supported in the field, ran through Hampshire. Gloucestershire were indebted to Emmett for his attractive yet powerful strokes which helped them to reach 70 for three by the close, and next day Cook and Allen earned the bonus points by making 27 in five overs for the last wicket. Hampshire, in the second innings, lost their opening pair without a run on the board and there was no recovery—pluckily though Horton batted for an hour and a half—against the spin of Cook and Mortimore. Sainsbury, who distinguished himself with brilliant catching at short-leg in the first innings off Burden's clever bowling surprised the early Gloucestershire batsmen in the second when only 15 runs were needed for victory.

Hampshire

R. E. Marshall c Emmett b Brown	17 — c Graveney b Brown	0
J. R. Gray lbw b Smith	2 — c Brown b Smith	0
H. Horton run out...................	7 — c Nicholls b Mortimore ...	30
A. W. H. Rayment c Rochford b Mortimore	37 — c Brown b Smith	1
R. W. C. Pitman c Milton b Mortimore .	13 — c Milton b Cook	10
A. C. D. Ingleby-Mackenzie b Mortimore	7 — c Milton b Cook	20
P. J. Sainsbury lbw b Mortimore	13 — b Cook	0
E. D. R. Eagar c Milton b Mortimore...	8 — b Mortimore	1
D. Shackleton c Smith b Mortimore.....	9 — not out	2
M. Heath c Brown b Mortimore........	5 — c Allen b Cook	0
M. D. Burden not out.................	0 — b Mortimore	1
B 4, l-b 2, w 1..................	7 L-b 1	1

1/7 2/27 3/32 4/54 5/62 6/103 7/106   125   1/0 2/0 3/5 4/19 5/57   66
8/113 9/120 (2.27 an over)   6/61 7/63 8/63 9/64

Gloucestershire

G. M. Emmett c Pitman b Sainsbury ...	41 — c Pitman b Sainsbury	0
D. M. Young c Sainsbury b Burden.....	15 — c Horton b Sainsbury......	3
R. B. Nicholls c Gray b Sainsbury	0 — not out	11
T. W. Graveney c Sainsbury b Burden ..	33 — b Sainsbury	0
C. A. Milton c Sainsbury b Burden	14 — not out	0
A. S. Brown c Sainsbury b Burden	14	
J. Mortimore b Burden	14	
D. A. Allen run out..................	23	
D. Smith b Sainsbury................	3	
P. Rochford lbw b Burden............	3	
C. Cook not out.....................	16	
W 1	1 L-b 1	1

1/56 2/56 3/56 4/91 5/106 6/125   177   1/0 2/3 3/3   (3 wkts.) 15
7/134 8/139 9/150 (2.52 an over)

Gloucestershire Bowling

	O.	M.	R.	W.		O.	M.	R.	W.
Smith	12	5	16	1	....	6	3	6	2
Brown	12	1	34	1	....	4	1	6	1
Mortimore.....	17.2	6	37	7	....	16	4	41	3
Cook	14	3	31	0	....	14	10	12	4

Hampshire Bowling

	O.	M.	R.	W.	O.	M.	R.	W.
Shackleton.....	3	1	14	0				
Heath	4	2	5	0				
Sainsbury......	32.1	14	47	3	 4	3	1	3
Burden	31	8	110	6	.... 3.5	2	13	0

Umpires: E. Davies and John Langridge.

GLOUCESTERSHIRE v. YORKSHIRE

(C. Cook's Benefit)

At Cheltenham, August 17, 19. Gloucestershire won by two wickets, taking 14 points. They were fortunate that Yorkshire chose to bat in a match which brought a most exciting conclusion. Smith and Brown, the Gloucestershire seam bowlers, extracted life from the damp turf in breaking the back of their rivals' batting and Illingworth, in confident form, alone stood firm for long. Emmett progressed readily as the pitch became easier and Gloucestershire, at drawing of stumps, led by 27 with five wickets in hand. Next day the drying pitch gave spin bowlers considerable help and Wardle and Illingworth proved so troublesome that Gloucestershire were hard-pressed to hit off 69 for victory. A six by Etheridge off Wardle when six wickets were down for 46 swayed the issue, but eight men were out for 56. After a boundary, from byes, the players, thinking the runs had been obtained, left the field, but they were recalled when the scorers stated that one more was wanted. Eventually, a leg-bye ended the game.

Yorkshire

W. B. Stott b Smith......................	0	— lbw b Cook	22
W. Watson c Milton b Smith	3	— c Etheridge b Cook	14
D. E. F. Padgett c Etheridge b Brown...	18	— b Cook	6
D. B. Close c Mortimore b Brown	7	— c Milton b Wells	10
J. V. Wilson c Milton b Smith	8	— st Etheridge b Wells	45
R. Illingworth c Emmett b Cook	70	— b Wells	4
W. H. H. Sutcliffe c Smith b Wells	18	— c Milton b Wells	3
J. H. Wardle c Graveney b Cook	5	— c Brown b Wells	12
F. S. Trueman b Wells	0	— c Brown b Wells	0
J. G. Binks c Smith b Cook	2	— st Etheridge b Cook	0
D. Pickles not out	2	— not out	0
		L-b 2	2

1/1 2/4 3/15 4/28 5/38 6/115 7/120   133   1/28 2/36 3/60 4/62 5/71   118
8/129 9/129 (2.33 an over)   6/95 7/115 8/115 9/116

Gloucestershire

G. M. Emmett c Pickles b Close	62	— c Wilson b Illingworth ...	6
D. M. Young c Trueman b Wardle	13	— c Stott b Wardle	9
R. B. Nicholls c Wilson b Illingworth....	1	— c Binks b Wardle	7
T. W. Graveney run out	22	— c Wilson b Wardle	5
C. A. Milton c Binks b Wardle	18	— c Trueman b Wardle	8
A. S. Brown b Illingworth	19	— c Close b Wardle	0
J. Mortimore c Binks b Wardle	4	— c and b Illingworth	2
R. J. Etheridge b Illingworth	4	— not out	12
D. R. Smith c Wilson b Illingworth	0	— not out	4
C. Cook b Wardle	1		
B. D. Wells not out	8	— lbw b Wardle	0
B 20, l-b 11	31	B 10, l-b 6	16

1/41 2/52 3/113 4/116 5/160 6/166   183   1/18 2/26 3/30   (8 wkts.)   69
7/168 8/168 9/173 (2.57 an over)   4/35 5/39 6/46 7/56 8/56

Gloucestershire Bowling

	O.	M.	R.	W.		O.	M.	R.	W.
Smith	14	4	27	3	....	6	3	10	0
Brown	14	7	24	2	....	4	1	8	0
Cook	14.4	3	36	3	....	17	8	28	4
Mortimore	4	0	11	0	....	15	6	27	0
Wells	10	2	35	2	....	21.5	8	43	6

Yorkshire Bowling

	O.	M.	R.	W.		O.	M.	R.	W.
Trueman	7	1	23	0	....	2	0	12	0
Pickles	7	3	13	0					
Illingworth	23	5	65	4	....	15	6	16	2
Wardle	24.3	11	29	4	....	16.2	8	25	6
Close	9	2	22	1					

Umpires: John Langridge and D. Davies.

GLOUCESTERSHIRE v. LANCASHIRE

At Bristol, August 24, 26, 27. Drawn. Lancashire took two points for first innings lead, but Gloucestershire, thanks to Young and Milton, proved the faster scorers. Young hit his only hundred of the season. Wharton, in great form, gained his third hundred in 1957, helping Lancashire to a useful advantage. They looked to be well placed when six Gloucestershire second innings wickets were down for 84. Hawkins, however, foiled his opponents and when Lancashire were left to score 150 in an hour and a half the task proved beyond them. They made only 49 in an hour.

Gloucestershire

G. M. Emmett c Wilson b Bowman	7	— c Wilson b Statham 5
D. M. Young c and b Bowman	114	— b Tattersall 17
D. Carpenter run out	14	— run out 12
R. B. Nicholls c Wharton b Tattersall	0	— lbw b Statham 7
C. A. Milton b Ikin	59	— b Tattersall 14
D. G. Hawkins b Statham	7	— not out 68
A. S. Brown lbw b Statham	21	— lbw b Greenhough 13
J. Mortimore lbw b Statham	7	— lbw b Barber 24
D. R. Smith not out	12	— c Bond b Bowman 17
C. Cook c Statham b Tattersall	3	— not out 3
B. D. Wells b Statham	1	
B 4, n-b 2	6	B 5, l-b 4, n-b 3 12

1/7 2/48 3/48 4/186 5/204 6/208   251
7/227 8/236 9/249 (2.61 an over)

1/14 2/26   (8 wkts., dec.) 192
3/43 4/43 5/65 6/84 7/134
8/179

Lancashire

R. W. Barber lbw b Wells	16	— not out 14
A. Wharton c Milton b Brown	103	— lbw b Brown 4
G. Pullar c Nicholls b Smith	28	— b Smith 1
C. Washbrook lbw b Smith	32	— c Young b Brown 9
J. T. Ikin c Hawkins b Mortimore	24	— not out 18
J. D. Bond b Cook	34	
R. Bowman b Wells	21	
J. B. Statham b Wells	0	
T. Greenhough not out	26	
A. Wilson b Smith	0	
R. Tattersall c and b Wells	0	
B 8, l-b 2	10	B 1, l-b 1, w 1 3

1/45 2/107 3/187 4/187 5/219 6/258   294
7/258 8/268 9/289 (2.04 an over)

1/5 2/14 3/15   (3 wkts.) 49

Lancashire Bowling

	O.	M.	R.	W.		O.	M.	R.	W.
Statham	25.1	10	41	4	....	23	10	37	2
Bowman	17	2	47	2	....	14	2	44	1
Tattersall	30	5	84	2	....	15	7	29	2
Greenhough	8	1	34	0	....	23	7	53	1
Wharton	10	2	26	0					
Ikin	6	3	13	1	....	7	3	9	0
Barber					....	4	1	8	1

Gloucestershire Bowling

	O.	M.	R.	W.		O.	M.	R.	W.
Smith	32	4	73	3	....	6	1	22	1
Brown	11	2	23	1	....	4	2	5	2
Cook	35	16	64	1	....	3	2	1	0
Wells	41	18	73	4	....	3	1	2	0
Mortimore	25	11	51	1	....	5	3	8	0
Emmett					....	1	0	8	0
Young					....	1	1	0	0

Umpires: P. A. Gibb and W. F. Price.

GLOUCESTERSHIRE v. NOTTINGHAMSHIRE

At Bristol, August 28, 29, 30. Nottinghamshire won by three wickets, taking 12 points. Dooland, playing his last match for Nottinghamshire, bore a notable part in the success with his firm hitting in both innings. He was at his best on the last day when his side, set to make 220 in two hours and fifty minutes, won with eight minutes to spare. Splendidly supported by Poole in a fourth wicket partnership of 109, Dooland, driving forcefully, hit 70 in an hour and a half and the crowd gave him an ovation. Stylish batting by Emmett and Milton brought no reward for Gloucestershire whose indifferent bowling and fielding in the second innings gave Nottinghamshire their match-winning opportunity.

Gloucestershire

G. M. Emmett c N. Hill b Goonesena	83	— lbw b Dooland	28
D. M. Young c N. Hill b Goonesena	9	— c Dooland b Jepson	3
R. B. Nicholls b Goonesena	0	— lbw b Dooland	36
T. W. Graveney c Dooland b Goonesena	8	— c Martin b Walker	33
C. A. Milton b Dooland	89	— not out	64
D. G. Hawkins c Martin b Walker	14	— st Millman b Goonesena	12
A. S. Brown b Jepson	45	— c Goonesena b Jepson	17
J. Mortimore b Jepson	47	— b Dooland	0
D. R. Smith c Walker b Jepson	0	— not out	13
C. Cook run out	0		
B. D. Wells not out	7		
B 9	9	B 9, l-b 7	16

1/44 2/60 3/100 4/101 5/134 6/213   **311**   1/6 2/51   (7 wkts., dec.) **222**
7/304 8/304 9/304 (3.20 an over)   3/88 4/129 5/168 6/197
                                            7/198

Nottinghamshire

J. D. Springall b Brown	2	— b Smith	8
E. J. Martin b Brown	31	— c Nicholls b Smith	15
N. Hill c Graveney b Wells	56	— run out	9
M. Hill c Graveney b Cook	19	— b Smith	1
C. J. Poole not out	95	— c Milton b Brown	70
B. Dooland c Graveney b Cook	58	— b Brown	70
G. Goonesena not out	26	— c Young b Smith	12
A. K. Walker (did not bat)	—	— not out	7
A. Jepson (did not bat)	—	— not out	7
B 21, l-b 5, n-b 1	27	B 16, l-b 2, w 3	21

1/11 2/60 3/107 4/119   (5 wkts., dec.) 314   1/28 2/40 3/63   (7 wkts) 220
5/231 (2.19 an over)   4/172 5/180 6/190 7/208.
G. Millman and M. Morgan did not bat.

Nottinghamshire Bowling

	O.	M.	R.	W.		O.	M.	R.	W.
Walker	24	7	68	1	....	19	5	56	1
Jepson	16	3	59	3	....	20	5	56	2
Morgan	14	1	61	0					
Goonesena	23	9	58	4	....	13	3	38	1
Dooland	20.1	5	56	1	....	18	3	56	3

Gloucestershire Bowling

	O.	M.	R.	W.		O.	M.	R.	W.
Smith	23	7	46	0	....	19	4	56	4
Brown	21	9	41	2	....	13	1	45	2
Wells	43	13	93	1	....	10	1	29	0
Cook	40.3	21	54	2	....	9	1	49	0
Mortimore	15	2	53	0	....	4	0	20	0

Umpires: D. Davies and J. S. Buller.

At Bournemouth, August 31, September 2. GLOUCESTERSHIRE lost to HAMPSHIRE by an innings and 28 runs.

HAMPSHIRE

President—H. S. ALTHAM

Captain and Secretary—E. D. R. EAGAR, County Ground,
Southampton

R. E. Marshall   County Badge   P. J. Sainsbury

Hampshire's playing fortunes, so high the previous two
summers, declined sharply and the county slumped from sixth to
thirteenth position. They lost twelve games compared with six the
previous season.

Even in 1955 when they finished third, Hampshire did not claim
to be an ideally balanced team and in the season under review
frailties both in batting and bowling were sometimes too easily
exposed. The progress of the younger members continued to be
slow. All too often the onus rested on the hard core of experienced
players and when they failed, as they were bound to do from time
to time, there was little to fall back on. Until the various respon-
sibilities can be more evenly apportioned Hampshire must be
prepared for modest results.

If evidence were needed of the side's dependence on certain
individuals none better could be given than the remarkable record
of Shackleton. Far from having his style of in-swing attack cramped
by the restriction placed on leg-side fieldsmen he bowled more
overs than anyone in the Championship.

Cannings missed nine matches because of injury and did not
touch his true form until the last game of the season at Bournemouth when he routed Gloucestershire. Heath, bowling off a
shorter run, strove to fill the gap and received his county cap. He
has much natural ability and provided he is properly guided, should
develop into a capable seam bowler.

Where Hampshire's attack failed was in the lack of effective
spin bowlers. Neither Sainsbury, left arm, nor Burden, off-breaks,
possessed sufficient "bite" or guile to trouble the better class
batsmen and Marshall scarcely seemed to rate his own potentialities

as a change bowler seriously enough. As for batting, Marshall again stood out as a dashing stroke-maker. Not only did he hit the season's fastest hundred, at Southampton in sixty-six minutes off Kent, but at Portsmouth he hit a century before lunch against Glamorgan and played two glorious attacking innings against the champions, Surrey.

For Eagar the season was his last as captain. Throughout the post-war period, much of it with slender playing resources at his disposal, he inspired those he led by personal example. The left-hander Ingleby-Mackenzie who replaces him completed 1,000 runs for the first time, an encouraging omen for the future. Sainsbury established a county record by holding fifty-six catches, most of them near the bat on the leg side. Harrison took a well-deserved benefit and kept wicket in his customary reliable style.

HAMPSHIRE COUNTY CRICKET GROUND
SOUTHAMPTON

HAMPSHIRE RESULTS

All First-Class Matches—Played 31, *Won* 8, *Lost* 12, *Drawn* 11

County Championship Matches—Played 28, *Won* 7, *Lost* 12,
Drawn 8, *No Decision* 1

COUNTY CHAMPIONSHIP AVERAGES
BATTING

	Birthplace	Mtchs.	Inns.	Not Outs	Runs	100's	Highest Inns.	Aver.
R. E. Marshall.	*West Indies*	27	49	0	1609	4	163	32.83
J. R. Gray	*Southampton*	27	50	4	1316	2	115	28.60
H. Horton	*Hereford*	27	50	4	1296	3	114*	28.17
A. C. D. Ingleby-Mackenzie	*Devon*	26	46	5	974	0	88	23.75
H. M. Barnard.	*Portsmouth*	18	31	2	585	0	71*	20.17
A. W. H. Rayment	*Finchley*	16	28	0	520	0	80	18.57
P. J. Sainsbury.	*Southampton*	27	43	7	639	0	94	17.75
D. Shackleton..	*Todmorden*	27	39	7	478	0	64	14.93
L. Harrison ...	*Mudeford*	26	40	8	435	0	79	13.59
V. H. D. Cannings	*Bighton*	18	24	11	168	0	33*	12.92
R. W. C. Pitman	*Southampton*	7	12	1	142	0	28	12.90
E. D. R. Eagar.	*Cheltenham*	15	23	2	217	0	29	10.33
M. D. Burden..	*Southampton*	17	23	10	81	0	23*	6.23
M. Heath......	*Bournemouth*	19	28	5	75	0	17*	3.26

* *Signifies not out.*

BOWLING

	Overs	Maidens	Runs	Wickets	Average
D. Shackleton	1142.4	418	2260	144	15.69
V. H. D. Cannings......	598.4	203	1295	58	22.32
P. J. Sainsbury	678.3	264	1367	57	23.98
M. D. Burden	474.4	151	1186	45	26.35
M. Heath..............	631	150	1767	67	26.37
A. W. H. Rayment......	64	14	233	6	38.83
J. R. Gray	247	71	613	15	40.86
R. E. Marshall	52	16	132	2	66.00

Also bowled: H. M. Barnard 16—0—92—1; E. D. R. Eagar 5—0—10—2;
L. Harrison 7—1—30—0; H. Horton 16—2—40—0.

Amateurs.—E. D. R. Eagar, A. C. D. Ingleby-Mackenzie.

HAMPSHIRE v. SOMERSET

At Southampton, April 29, 30. Drawn. Somerset 279 (C. L. McCool 116,
P. J. Sainsbury four for 51) and 116 for five wickets, dec.; Hampshire 260 for nine,
dec. and 120 for six. (Friendly.)

At Hove, May 2, 3. HAMPSHIRE drew with SUSSEX. (Friendly.)

HAMPSHIRE v. ROYAL NAVY

At Southampton. Twelve-a-side. May 6, 7. Drawn. Royal Navy 134
(M. D. Burden five for 30) and seven for one wicket; Hampshire 240 for eight
wickets, dec. (H. Horton 127 not out).

N

HAMPSHIRE v. ESSEX

At Southampton, May 8, 9, 10. Essex won by 152 runs, taking 12 points. They always held the initiative against opponents who never looked at ease against the fast-medium attack of Bailey, Preston and Ralph. A fourth wicket partnership of 63 between Savill and Bailey, followed by some bold hitting from Ralph, helped Essex to improve on a poor start. Hampshire made a dismal reply and when Essex batted again Insole put his side in a commanding position with a powerful display of driving. Bear shared a stand of 93 and Hampshire, facing an objective of 307 runs, were always fighting a losing battle after Marshall had gone.

Essex

G. Barker c Horton b Shackleton	4	—	c Gray b Burden	31
L. Savill c Harrison b Cannings	33	—	c Ingleby-Mackenzie b Cannings	4
B. Taylor c Sainsbury b Cannings	2	—	c Barnard b Cannings	0
D. J. Insole c Harrison b Shackleton	2	—	lbw b Shackleton	84
T. E. Bailey c Sainsbury b Burden	30	—	c Sainsbury b Burden	0
M. Bear not out	18	—	c Sainsbury b Burden	35
G. Smith c Eagar b Cannings	0	—	c Marshall b Burden	19
W. T. Greensmith c Harrison b Burden	4	—	not out	4
R. Ralph c Eagar b Shackleton	45	—	lbw b Shackleton	20
K. C. Preston c Shackleton b Gray	6	—	c Gray b Shackleton	39
I. King c Harrison b Cannings	0	—	c Sainsbury b Shackleton	1
B 2	2		B 2, l-b 3	5

1/4 2/6 3/8 4/71 5/71 6/71 7/82 8/129   146
9/146 (1.65 an over)

1/14 2/14 3/50 4/50   242
5/143 6/178 7/178 8/237
9/237

Hampshire

R. E. Marshall c Bear b Preston	17	—	c and b Bailey	53
J. R. Gray c Preston b Bailey	8	—	c King b Ralph	8
H. Horton b Smith b Bailey	5	—	c Preston b Ralph	21
L. Harrison b Bailey	6	—	c Insole b Preston	9
H. M. Barnard lbw b Preston	8	—	c Savill b Ralph	7
A. C. D. Ingleby-Mackenzie c King b Preston	0	—	c Barker b Ralph	27
P. J. Sainsbury lbw b Ralph	7	—	c Insole b Preston	8
E. D. R. Eagar c Ralph b Bailey	13	—	not out	11
D. Shackleton c Insole b Ralph	11	—	c Bear b Bailey	0
V. H. D. Cannings c Preston b Bailey	1	—	c King b Preston	4
M. D. Burden not out	5	—	st Taylor b Preston	0
L-b 1	1		B 5, n-b 1	6

1/12 2/23 3/37 4/41 5/42 6/49 7/55   82
8/74 9/75 (2.15 an over—no Bonus pts.)

1/57 2/64 3/84 4/104   154
5/104 6/127 7/142 8/143
9/154

Hampshire Bowling

	O.	M.	R.	W.		O.	M.	R.	W.
Shackleton	26	12	47	3		21.3	8	62	4
Cannings	25.3	17	19	4		25	9	61	2
Gray	11	7	9	1		10	2	23	0
Sainsbury	6	1	22	0		19	6	36	0
Burden	19	6	47	2		15	5	50	4
Marshall						4	2	5	0

Essex Bowling

	O.	M.	R.	W.	O.	M.	R.	W.
Bailey	13.5	5	35	5	 16	2	47	2
Preston........	15	2	35	3	 20	5	59	4
Ralph	9	2	11	2	 15	3	40	4
King					4	2	2	0

Umpires: R. S. Lay and J. F. Crapp.

At Northampton, May 11, 13, 14. HAMPSHIRE drew with NORTHAMPTONSHIRE.

At Leicester, May 15, 16, 17. HAMPSHIRE beat LEICESTERSHIRE by nine wickets.

HAMPSHIRE v. MIDDLESEX

At Portsmouth, May 18, 20, 21. Hampshire won by three runs in a tense finish, taking 12 points. The bowling of Shackleton, who took eleven wickets for 72, was the deciding factor. Hampshire's first innings performance, apart from Horton and Barnard, was depressing, but Middlesex fared even worse against an accurate seam attack on a difficult but not vicious pitch. Marshall brought more colour to the second innings, with 62 out of 86 in a little over an hour. Horton again batted well, and Harrison showed glimpses of his best form. Middlesex, needing 244 to win, were given a good start by Robertson and Edrich, but after Compton was fifth out Delisle took on the task of sheltering the tail. He received sound assistance from Hurst, but his gallant effort failed when he was l.b.w. trying a sweep to decide the issue.

Hampshire

R. E. Marshall c Delisle b Bennett	8	— c Hurst b Angus	62
J. R. Gray c Edrich b Bennett	5	— c Melluish b Warr	9
H. Horton b Titmus	46	— lbw b Compton	48
A. C. D. Ingleby-Mackenzie c Delisle b Bennett	5	— lbw b Angus	2
P. J. Sainsbury b Bennett	2	— c Titmus b Warr	9
H. M. Barnard b Hurst	35	— c Robertson b Titmus	1
L. Harrison c Robertson b Titmus	7	— c Melluish b Compton	34
E. D. R. Eagar lbw b Titmus	0	— not out	23
D. Shackleton c and b Hurst	9	— c Hurst b Compton	1
M. D. Heath c and b Titmus	4	— run out	0
V. H. D. Cannings not out	0	— c Melluish b Bennett	7
B 7, l-b 5	12	B 10, l-b 12	22

1/5 2/14 3/30 4/36 5/112 6/112　　　　133　　　　1/34 2/86 3/90 4/108　　　　218
7/112 8/129 9/129 (2.14 an over)　　　　5/109 6/181 7/188 8/192
　　　　　　　　　　　　　　　　9/196

Middlesex

J. D. Robertson c Harrison b Shackleton.	6	— c Barnard b Gray	49
R. A. Gale b Shackleton	0	— c Harrison b Shackleton ...	7
W. J. Edrich c Gray b Heath	33	— c Barnard b Shackleton ...	50
G. P. S. Delisle c Barnard b Cannings...	8	— lbw b Shackleton	50
D. C. S. Compton b Heath	11	— b Shackleton	52
F. J. Titmus c Barnard b Heath	33	— b Shackleton	0
D. Bennett b Cannings	7	— c Harrison b Heath	13
M. E. L. Melluish b Shackleton	1	— b Heath	3
J. J. Warr b Shackleton	2	— c Sainsbury b Shackleton...	0
R. J. Hurst not out	2	— c Sainsbury b Heath	0
T. Angus lbw b Shackleton	2	— not out	4
B 3, l-b 2	5	B 4, l-b 8	12

1/3 2/8 3/23 4/44 5/87 6/95 7/100　　　　108　　　　1/13 2/100 3/125 4/125　　　　240
8/103 9/103 (2.20 an over)　　　　5/184 6/207 7/211 8/212
　　　　　　　　　　　　　　　　9/232

Middlesex Bowling

	O.	M.	R.	W.		O.	M.	R.	W.
Warr	11	3	19	0	...	21	6	47	2
Bennett	11	4	17	4	...	14.4	2	37	1
Titmus	20.2	5	53	4	...	16	4	40	1
Angus	5	2	6	0	...	15	4	32	2
Hurst	15	7	26	2	...	13	5	25	0
Compton					...	11	4	15	3

Hampshire Bowling

	O.	M.	R.	W.		O.	M.	R.	W.
Shackleton	12.3	2	31	5	...	32	16	41	6
Cannings	19	9	33	2	...	24	3	56	0
Heath	12	1	35	3	...	30	5	70	3
Sainsbury	5	4	4	0	...	3	2	1	0
Marshall					...	4	0	9	0
Gray					...	16	4	51	1

Umpires: P. A. Gibb and J. Wood.

At Nottingham, May 22, 23, 24. HAMPSHIRE drew with NOTTINGHAMSHIRE.

At Romford, May 25, 27, 28. HAMPSHIRE lost to ESSEX by 46 runs.

HAMPSHIRE v. WARWICKSHIRE

At Southampton, May 29, 30, 31. Drawn. Hampshire taking four points. They found the task of scoring 203 to win at 93 an hour beyond them after a match of batting contrasts. A stylish innings by Smith helped Warwickshire out of trouble against a well-directed attack. Hampshire, in turn, were saved from collapse by the painstaking defence of Gray whose 100 out of 196 took four and a half hours. Lively hitting by Shackleton saw his side into the lead and this gay mood was also reflected in the stroke-play of Horner and Smith who enabled Warwickshire to set Hampshire their sizeable fourth innings target. Burden bowled his off-breaks skilfully.

Warwickshire

F. C. Gardner b Sainsbury	22	— b Sainsbury	22
M. F. Horner c Eagar b Sainsbury	20	— c and b Burden	87
M. J. K. Smith c Harrison b Cannings	84	— b Burden	52
A. Townsend run out	12	— st Harrison b Burden	15
A. V. Wolton b Cannings	19	— run out	23
R. T. Spooner b Cannings	8	— b Sainsbury	5
K. Ibadulla lbw b Sainsbury	29	— not out	15
S. Singh lbw b Shackleton	59	— c Sainsbury b Burden	16
R. G. Carter b Burden	1	— run out	0
J. D. Bannister c Shackleton b Burden	12	— c Sainsbury b Burden	0
W. E. Hollies not out	0	— not out	5
B 5, l-b 2	7	B 7, l-b 4	11

1/41 2/46 3/66 4/149 5/165 6/176   273   1/80 2/130 (9 wkts., dec.) 251
7/225 8/226 9/264 (2.16 an over)   3/173 4/198 5/203 6/220
                                           7/228 8/233 9/237

Hampshire

R. E. Marshall b Carter	1	— b Singh	35
J. R. Gray c Horner b Singh	115	— lbw b Carter	16
L. Harrison c Singh b Bannister	18		
H. Horton c Townsend b Singh	10	— b Ibadulla	6
P. J. Sainsbury run out	35		
H. M. Barnard c and b Hollies	7	— not out	24
A. C. D. Ingleby-Mackenzie c Singh b Carter	9	— b Hollies	16
E. D. R. Eagar c Spooner b Hollies	8		
D. Shackleton b Bannister	53	— not out	39
V. H. D. Cannings not out	33		
M. D. Burden not out	23		
B 4, l-b 5, w 1	10	L-b 3	3

1/16 2/51 3/69 4/125   (9 wks., dec.) 322   1/35 2/61 3/71   (4 wkts.) 139
5/139 6/170 7/193 8/231 9/280   4/91
(2.57 an over)

Hampshire Bowling

	O.	M.	R.	W.		O.	M.	R.	W.
Shackleton	28.3	6	67	1	....	15	2	37	0
Gray	14	3	24	0					
Cannings	26	10	47	3	....	9	1	37	0
Burden	17	7	38	2	....	26	4	83	5
Sainsbury	34	11	83	3	....	31	9	83	2
Marshall	5	3	7	0					

Warwickshire Bowling

	O.	M.	R.	W.		O.	M.	R.	W.
Bannister	29	5	87	2	....	6	0	30	0
Carter	16	4	37	2	....	5	0	13	1
Townsend	4	1	8	0					
Singh	31	7	84	2	....	5	1	17	1
Hollies	45	14	96	2	....	15	4	47	1
			Ibadulla			9	1	29	1

Umpires: John Langridge and D. Davies.

At Oxford, June 1, 3, 4. HAMPSHIRE drew with OXFORD UNIVERSITY

HAMPSHIRE v. KENT

At Southampton, June 8, 10, 11. Drawn, Kent taking two points. A century in sixty-six minutes by Marshall, the fastest for Hampshire since 1927, was the highlight of a match during which Ingleby-Mackenzie and Leary received their county caps. Barnard and Ingleby-Mackenzie shared a fifth wicket stand of 104 in just over an hour for Hampshire. Leary hit an excellent hundred when Kent replied, Cowdrey helping in a fourth wicket partnership of 101. Marshall's dashing innings followed, though by then there was little hope of a definite result, rain having prevented play on the second day until after lunch.

Hampshire

R. E. Marshall b Ridgway	2	— c Smith b Wright	103
J. R. Gray b Smith	54	— not out	56
H. Horton b Smith	41	— not out	18
E. D. R. Eagar c Cowdrey b Leary	29		
H. M. Barnard c and b Ridgway	67		
A. C. D. Ingleby-Mackenzie c Pretlove b Halfyard	88		
P. J. Sainsbury not out	37		
L. Harrison not out	15		
B 4, l-b 6	10	B 1, w 1, n-b 1	3

1/3 2/87 3/108 4/147   (6 wkts., dec.) 343   1/120   (1 wkt., dec.) 180
5/251 6/311 (3.20 an over)

D. Shackleton, V. H. D. Cannings and M. D. Burden did not bat.

Kent

A. H. Phebey c Burden b Cannings	50		
R. C. Wilson b Cannings	9		
J. F. Pretlove c Eagar b Cannings	56		
M. C. Cowdrey c Ingleby-Mackenzie b Sainsbury	46	— not out	2
S. E. Leary c and b Sainsbury	108	— not out	13
A. L. Dixon lbw b Burden	16	— c Burden b Eagar	1
T. G. Evans c Sainsbury b Shackleton	39	— c Shackleton b Cannings	16
G. Smith not out	5	— c Marshall b Shackleton	25
D. J. Halfyard b Sainsbury	5	— c and b Eagar	0
F. Ridgway not out	0		
L-b 7, w 1, n-b 2	10	L-b 4	4

1/24 2/113 3/133 4/234   (8 wkts., dec.) 344   1/32 2/47 3/54   (4 wkts.) 61
5/286 6/333 7/334 8/343 (2.52 an over)   4/58

D. V. P. Wright did not bat.

Kent Bowling

	O.	M.	R.	W.		O.	M.	R.	W.
Ridgway	20	7	40	2	....	3	1	14	0
Smith	35	8	118	2	....	5	2	13	0
Halfyard	15.5	3	54	1					
Wright	23	3	72	0	....	11	3	53	1
Cowdrey	1	0	1	0					
Leary	10	0	37	1	....	7	1	53	0
Pretlove	2	0	11	0	....	3	0	18	0
Evans						4	0	26	0
Dixon						1	1	0	0

Hampshire Bowling

	O.	M.	R.	W.		O.	M.	R.	W.
Shackleton	44.3	22	101	1	....	5	1	20	1
Cannings	30	12	60	3	....	4	0	23	1
Burden	22	6	72	1					
Gray	16	5	46	0					
Sainsbury	18	7	41	3	....	5	4	4	0
Marshall	5	2	14	0					
Eagar						5	0	10	2

Umpires: J. Wood and W. F. Price.

At Lord's, June 12, 13, 14. HAMPSHIRE lost to MIDDLESEX by 116 runs.

At Bath, June, 15, 17. HAMPSHIRE beat SOMERSET by an innings and 43 runs.

HAMPSHIRE v. SUSSEX

At Portsmouth, June 19, 20, 21. Drawn, Hampshire taking four points. Most of the excitement was crowded into the final morning after the first day's play had been washed out by rain. Hampshire then wanted only 50 for the lead with eight wickets remaining, but accurate fast-medium bowling by Bates and Thomson caused such a transformation that seven were still required when the last pair came together. The runs came after five tense overs. Four hours twenty minutes remained and Sussex batted out time.

Sussex

A. E. James c Marshall b Shackleton....	27	— lbw b Rayment	17
L. J. Lenham lbw b Shackleton.........	13	— lbw b Barnard	30
K. G. Suttle c Barnard b Sainsbury	53	— c and b Sainsbury	59
J. M. Parks b Cannings	32	— not out	93
D. J. Foreman c Sainsbury b Cannings .	8	— c Gray b Rayment	29
G. Potter not out	32	— not out	18
D. A. Stripp not out	32		
L-b 4	4	B 6, l-b 1	7

1/30 2/53 3/123 4/131   (5 wkts., dec.) 201   1/35 2/79   (4 wkts.) 253
5/135 (2.42 an over)   3/123 4/192

N. I. Thomson, D. N. Mantell, R. G. Marlar and D. L. Bates did not bat.

Hampshire

R. E. Marshall c Mantell b Stripp.	56	D. Shackleton lbw b Thomson....	1
J. R. Gray lbw b Bates	12	L. Harrison not out	8
H. Horton c Stripp b Bates.......	36	V. H. D. Cannings c Foreman b	
A. C. D. Ingleby-Mackenzie c		Bates	4
Potter b Thomson	54	M. Heath not out	2
A. W. H. Rayment c Foreman b		L-b 6, n-b 1	7
Bates	16		
H. M. Barnard run out	9	1/33 2/83 3/156 (9 wkts., dec.) 205	
P. J. Sainsbury c Foreman b		4/166 5/189 6/189 7/189 8/190	
Thomson	0	9/195 (3.47 an over)	

Hampshire Bowling

	O.	M.	R.	W.		O.	M.	R.	W.
Shackleton.....	25	8	53	2	....	4	2	3	0
Cannings	21	6	44	2	....	5	2	7	0
Heath	17	2	49	0	....	4	2	4	0
Gray	6	3	12	0					
Sainsbury......	14	3	39	1	....	26	11	47	1
Rayment					.....	22	3	92	2
Horton					....	12	2	26	0
Barnard					......	6	0	37	1
Harrison					.....	7	1	30	0

Sussex Bowling

	O.	M.	R.	W.
Bates	18	3	58	4
Thomson	23.3	9	53	3
James	6	2	24	0
Stripp	7	0	43	1
Marlar	4	0	20	0

Umpires: J. F. Crapp and T. W. Spencer.

HAMPSHIRE v. NOTTINGHAMSHIRE

At Cowes, June 22, 24, 25. Hampshire won by 80 runs, taking 14 points. Another brilliant display of batting by Marshall put them on top from the start. Marshall, who hit one 6 and eighteen 4's in two hours, shared a stand of 123 with Horton, who batted nearly twice as long. Despite a second wicket partnership of 122 by Giles and Clay, Nottinghamshire faltered against the pace of Shackleton and Hampshire, leading by 27, were enabled by brisk batting on the part of Rayment (twelve 4's) to declare a second time. Left to get 195, Nottinghamshire again found Shackleton too good for them and the end came with ten minutes to spare.

Hampshire

R. E. Marshall c Smales b Matthews	...107	— c and b Dooland	....	19
J. R. Gray c Stocks b Jepson	 13	— lbw b Walker	....	9
H. Horton not out	114	— c Millman b Walker	......	0
A. W. H. Rayment c Smales b Dooland	. 21	— b Dooland	....	80
H. M. Barnard run out	 12	— b Smales	....	24
A. C. D. Ingleby-Mackenzie c Millman b Walker	 14	— not out	....	31
P. J. Sainsbury not out	 3	— not out	....	0
L-b 2	 2	B 2, l-b 1, n-b 1	......	4

1/25 2/148 3/217 4/236　(5 wkts., dec.) 286　　　1/11 2/11　(5 wkts., dec.) 167
5/273 (3.66 an over)　　　　　　　　　　　　　3/48 4/109 5/167

L. Harrison, D. Shackleton, M. D. Burden and M. Heath did not bat.

Nottinghamshire

R. T. Simpson c Burden b Shackleton	.. 3	— lbw b Shackleton	....	0
J. D. Clay c Barnard b Shackleton	 59	— c Harrison b Shackleton	.....	13
R. J. Giles lbw b Heath	101	— lbw b Shackleton	......	6
F. W. Stocks c Sainsbury b Shackleton	.. 0	— c Sainsbury b Heath	.....	31
C. J. Poole b Shackleton	 19	— b Shackleton	....	1
B. Dooland c Barnard b Shackleton	 1	— c Rayment b Shackleton	.....	0
A. K. Walker b Heath	 6	— c Sainsbury b Gray	.....	28
G. Millman not out	 35	— not out	....	5
A. E. Jepson c Harrison b Heath	 11	— c and b Shackleton	.....	14
K. Smales b Shackleton	 6	— c Sainsbury b Heath	.....	6
C. S. Matthews c Marshall b Shackleton	12	— c Shackleton b Gray	......	8
B 5, l-b 1	 6	L-b 2	....	2

1/14 2/136 3/139 4/180 5/181 6/191　259　　　1/0 2/19 3/28 4/38 5/46　114
7/196 8/212 9/227 (2.87 an over)　　　　　　　6/60 7/77 8/100 9/104

Nottinghamshire Bowling

	O.	M.	R.	W.		O.	M.	R.	W.
Walker	21	4	71	1	....	6	2	12	2
Jepson	23	2	102	1	....	7	1	18	0
Matthews	15	0	53	1					
Dooland	18	2	56	1	....	9	1	23	2
Smales	1	0	2	0	....	15	2	72	1
Stocks					....	7	0	38	0

Hampshire Bowling

	O.	M.	R.	W.		O.	M.	R.	W.
Shackleton	32.1	7	81	7	....	19	7	54	6
Heath	28	10	92	3	....	12.5	1	49	2
Gray	9	2	22	0	....	6	2	9	2
Sainsbury	13	4	31	0					
Burden	8	1	27	0					

Umpires: T. W. Spencer and J. F. Crapp.

At Guildford, June 26, 27. HAMPSHIRE lost to SURREY by an innings and 73 runs.

HAMPSHIRE v. CAMBRIDGE UNIVERSITY

At Bournemouth, June 29, July 1, 2. Hampshire won by 99 runs. After two wickets fell for seven runs, Gray (twenty-one 4's) and Rayment put on 171 and Ingleby-Mackenzie (two 6's, twelve 4's) added 139 without being parted. Barber, with a maiden century scored in just over two hours and including fifteen 4's, was mainly responsible for Cambridge gaining a lead of 28, but Rayment and Barnard joined in a stand of 148 and Ingleby-Mackenzie again drove freely, so that Hampshire declared and set their opponents 295 to get. Though the county attack, already much weakened, lost White with a pulled muscle, the University batsmen never looked like making a fight.

Hampshire

H. Horton c Swift b Wheatley	2	—	b Smith	27
J. R. Gray c Swift b Wheatley	124	—	c Swift b Smith	33
R. W. C. Pitman c Swift b Wheatley	0	—	b Barber	12
A. W. H. Rayment c Swift b Cook	77	—	c Newman b Cook	62
H. M. Barnard not out	41	—	b Barber	86
A. C. D. Ingleby-Mackenzie not out	109	—	b Smith	61
E. D. R. Eagar (did not bat)		—	b Smith	14
D. T. Tulk (did not bat)		—	not out	8
D. W. White (did not bat)		—	c Cook b Dexter	2
B 4, l-b 2	6		B 3, l-b 14	17

1/3 2/7 3/178 4/220   (4 wkts., dec.) 359

1/61 2/68   (8 wkts., dec.) 322
3/82 4/230 5/230 6/260
7/319 8/322

M. D. Burden and A. Wassell did not bat.

Cambridge University

R. W. Barber c Horton b Burden	106	—	c Rayment b Gray	9
I. M. McLachlan c Gray b White	36	—	c Ingleby-Mackenzie b Barnard	12
D. J. Green b White	1	—	b Burden	32
E. R. Dexter c Gray b Barnard	40	—	hit wkt b Rayment	26
R. M. James b Gray	49	—	b Rayment	5
C. S. Smith c Barnard b White	13	—	c Gray b Wassell	19
R. G. Newman c Barnard b Wassell	44	—	c Tulk b Burden	43
G. W. Cook c and b Burden	26	—	c Eagar b Wassell	14
P. I. Pieris c Eagar b Wassell	46	—	c Barnard b Rayment	18
B. T. Swift c White b Burden	17	—	c Gray b Rayment	2
O. S. Wheatley not out	0	—	not out	0
B 4, l-b 1, w 4	9		B 8, l-b 6, w 1	15

1/78 2/80 3/156 4/192 5/251 6/255   387
7/300 8/358 9/386

1/27 2/31 3/79 4/95 5/97   195
6/154 7/158 8/183 9/195

Cambridge University Bowling

	O.	M.	R.	W.	O.	M.	R.	W.
Smith	17	1	69	0	22	5	57	4
Wheatley	19	4	87	3	20	3	87	0
Pieris	10	1	31	0	4	2	9	0
Dexter	9	2	25	0	2.2	0	21	1
Barber	11	0	57	0	17	4	70	2
James	8	2	36	0	6	1	23	0
Cook	13	3	48	1	14	4	38	1

Hampshire Bowling

	O.	M.	R.	W.		O.	M.	R.	W.
White	21	2	78	3	....	2	0	5	0
Tulk	3	0	22	0					
Gray	16	3	49	1	....	6	1	6	1
Burden	20	1	127	3	....	12	1	52	2
Barnard	7	2	31	1	....	7	2	20	1
Wassell........	15.2	6	41	2	....	9	5	15	2
Rayment	5	1	30	0	....	21	2	75	4
			Eagar			3	0	7	0

Umpires: D. Davies and H. G. Baldwin.

HAMPSHIRE v. LEICESTERSHIRE

At Bournemouth, July 3, 4. Hampshire won by four wickets, taking 12 points to two by Leicestershire. Bowlers were in command almost throughout in a game which remained an open issue although lasting only two days. Sent in to bat on a drying pitch, the Leicestershire batsmen generally were in difficulties, though Gardner defended commendably for an hour and three-quarters. Hampshire's reply was no better against the fast-medium attack of Boshier and Spencer, Boshier having a spell of four wickets for seven runs. A stand of 50 in eighty-five minutes between Lester and Palmer saved Leicestershire from utter rout and Hampshire were left to get 109. They experienced many uncertain moments before vigorous batting by Rayment and Barnard steered them to safe waters.

Leicestershire

G. Lester b Shackleton	7	— c Horton b Burden	31
M. R. Hallam b Sainsbury	24	— c Sainsbury b Shackleton ..	2
P. Smith c and b Sainsbury	0	— lbw b Shackleton	2
C. H. Palmer b Shackleton	17	— run out	25
L. R. Gardner hit wkt b Heath	30	— c Horton b Burden	7
R. A. Diment c Rayment b Heath	20	— c Gray b Shackleton	9
J. Firth lbw b Shackleton	5	— not out	4
J. Savage c Burden b Sainsbury	5	— c Sainsbury b Shackleton ..	0
R. C. Smith c Marshall b Gray	19	— b Burden	0
C. T. Spencer not out	15	— c Marshall b Shackleton ..	4
B. Boshier run out	2	— c and b Burden	0
L-b	6	L-b 2	2

1/20 2/30 3/31 4/66 5/97 6/102   150   1/3 2/5 3/55 4/67 5/73   86
7/111 8/124 9/140 (1.64 an over)   6/77 7/77 8/80 9/85

Hampshire

R. E. Marshall c Boshier b Spencer	15	— c Diment b Boshier	26
J. R. Gray b Boshier	7	— c Firth b Spencer	0
H. Horton c Spencer b Boshier	25	— c Firth b Spencer	3
A. W. H. Rayment c Hallam b Spencer..	12	— b Savage	47
H. M. Barnard c Hallam b Spencer	0	— b Palmer	26
A. C. D. Ingleby-Mackenzie c Spencer b			
Boshier..............................	44	— c Gardner b Savage	0
P. J. Sainsbury c Firth b Spencer	3	— not out	2
L. Harrison c Spencer b Boshier	2	— not out	2
D. Shackleton c Spencer b Boshier	3		
M. Heath not out	3		
M. D. Burden c Firth b Spencer	4		
B 4, l-b 4, n-b 2	10	L-b 3	3

1/18 2/24 3/48 4/48 5/108 6/116   128   1/13 2/21 3/47   (6 wkts.) 109
7/118 8/118 9/121 (3.20 an over)   4/105 5/105 6/105

Hampshire Bowling

	O.	M.	R.	W.	O.	M.	R.	W.
Shackleton	24.4	11	27	3	18	11	16	5
Heath	17	4	49	2	12	4	30	0
Burden	29	11	49	0	21.1	7	32	4
Sainsbury	18	11	14	3	6	3	6	0
Gray	2	1	5	1				

Leicestershire Bowling

	O.	M.	R.	W.	O.	M.	R.	W.
Spencer	15.2	1	53	5	10	0	37	2
Boshier	15	4	28	5	11	2	25	1
R. Smith	5	2	7	0	1	0	12	0
Savage	3	1	16	0	8.5	2	20	2
Palmer	2	0	14	0	6	3	12	1

Umpires: D. Davies and H. G. Baldwin.

At Hove, July 6, 8, 9. HAMPSHIRE lost to SUSSEX by six wickets.

HAMPSHIRE v. GLAMORGAN

At Portsmouth, July 10, 11, 12. Drawn, Hampshire taking four points. A high-scoring game including centuries by Watkins and Marshall and six other innings of over fifty. Glamorgan made a splendid recovery after Shackleton took the first three wickets at a personal cost of five runs on a pitch still moist from overnight rain. Watkins, who shared three-figure partnerships with Parkhouse and Walker, showed splendid judgment, especially early in his innings while the ball was lifting awkwardly. Marshall, in his most dashing vein, led Hampshire's free-scoring reply, hitting one 6 and eighteen 4's. Rain curtailed the second day's play but Ingleby-Mackenzie (two 6's and nine 4's) ensured Hampshire of the lead. The remaining play carried little point, rain ending the game twenty minutes early.

Glamorgan

W. G. A. Parkhouse c Rayment b Gray	77	— not out	53
B. Hedges c Harrison b Shackleton	0	— c and b Rayment	42
L. N. Devereux b Shackleton	0	— not out	15
W. E. Jones c Sainsbury b Shackleton	0		
A. J. Watkins c Harrison b Shackleton	140		
P. Walker b Shackleton	60		
J. E. McConnon b Heath	29		
D. J. Ward not out	31		
H. G. Davies not out	12		
B 1, l-b 4	5	L-b 1	1

1/1 2/4 3/12 4/137   (7 wkts., dec.) 354   1/78   (1 wkt.) 111
5/281 6/288 7/321 (3.02 an over)

H. D. Davies and P. Gatehouse did not bat.

Hampshire

J. R. Gray c Parkhouse b Gatehouse	57	L. Harrison c Watkins b Walker	6
R. E. Marshall c H. G. Davies b Walker	163	D. Shackleton not out	2
		M. Heath c McConnon b Walker	1
H. Horton c Parkhouse b Walker	46	V. H. D. Cannings not out	0
A. W. H. Rayment c Walker b H. D. Davies	23	B 5	5
H. M. Barnard c McConnon	19		
A. C. D. Ingleby-Mackenzie c H. G. Davies b Watkins	77	1/163 2/254 (9 wkts., dec.) 406	
P. J. Sainsbury c Parkhouse b H. D. Davies	7	3/271 4/309 5/309 6/356 7/393 8/405 9/406 (3.94 an over)	

Hampshire Bowling

	O.	M.	R.	W.		O.	M.	R.	W.
Shackleton	38	12	94	5	....	5	2	10	0
Cannings	21	7	44	0					
Heath	30	5	105	1	....	10	2	27	0
Sainsbury	3	0	11	0	....	15	3	35	0
Gray	15	0	40	1					
Barnard	10	0	55	0					
Rayment						8	3	24	1
Horton						4	0	14	0

Glamorgan Bowling

	O.	M.	R.	W.
Gatehouse	23	1	120	1
H. D. Davies	32	6	115	2
Walker	16	2	56	4
McConnon	12	4	34	1
Watkins	16	1	65	1
Devereux	4	0	11	0

Umpires: R. S. Lay and J. S. Buller.

At Southampton, July 13, 15, 16. HAMPSHIRE drew with WEST INDIES. (See WEST INDIES section.)

HAMPSHIRE v. SOMERSET

At Bournemouth, July 20, 22. Somerset won by eight wickets, taking 12 points. They owed much to Alley who took ten wickets for 61 runs, and Hampshire, twice having the worst of the pitch, were beaten with a day to spare. Sent in to bat, they were always struggling. Gray did his best to rally the side but the last six wickets fell in half an hour for 16 to the seam bowling of Lobb and Alley. Somerset went ahead with the eighth pair together, McCool batting with fine judgment when Shackleton and Heath threatened to run through the side. Batting again, Hampshire once more found themselves on drying turf and were unable to cope with Alley whose right-arm in-swingers made haste off the pitch.

Hampshire

R. E. Marshall b Alley	11	—	b McMahon	16
J. R. Gray lbw b Lobb	56	—	c Palmer b McMahon	4
H. Horton c McCool b McMahon	4	—	b Lobb	29
A. W. H. Rayment c Wight b Langford	0	—	c McCool b McMahon	0
H. M. Barnard b Langford	22	—	c Palmer b Alley	3
A. C. D. Ingleby-Mackenzie b Lobb	32	—	c and b Alley	6
P. J. Sainsbury c McMahon b Alley	0	—	lbw b Alley	0
L. Harrison c Wight b Alley	0	—	lbw b Alley	6
D. Shackleton st Stephenson b Alley	10	—	lbw b Alley	0
M. Heath c and b Lobb	2	—	b Alley	0
M. D. Burden not out	3	—	not out	0
B 6, l-b 8	14		L-b 2, n-b 1	3

1/21 2/39 3/40 4/87 5/138 6/139   154   1/18 2/23 3/23 4/26 5/44   67
7/139 8/139 9/150 (3.01 an over)   6/44 7/59 8/59 9/61

Somerset

L. Pickles c Barnard b Heath	7	— b Shackleton 11
W. E. Alley b Sainsbury	31	— run out 14
P. B. Wight c Sainsbury b Shackleton ...	37	— not out 4
M. F. Tremlett b Heath	9	— not out 19
C. L. McCool c Horton b Heath	50	
G. G. Atkinson c Marshall b Heath.....	0	
K. E. Palmer c Sainsbury b Shackleton..	3	
H. W. Stephenson b Shackleton	0	
B. Langford not out	23	
B. Lobb b Shackleton	6	
J. W. McMahon c Sainsbury b Shackleton	0	
B 4, l-b 3	7	B 1, l-b 1 2

1/29 2/42 3/73 4/99 5/108 6/127   173   1/26 2/27   (2 wkts.) 50
7/127 8/155 9/171 (2.79 an over)

Somerset Bowling

	O.	M.	R.	W.		O.	M.	R.	W.
Lobb	12.1	2	27	3	....	7.5	1	24	1
Alley..........	13	3	39	4	....	18	12	22	6
Langford	11	1	33	2					
McMahon	13	3	31	1	....	11	5	18	3
Palmer	2	0	10	0					

Hampshire Bowling

	O.	M.	R.	W.		O.	M.	R.	W.
Shackleton.....	31	11	75	5	....	10.5	3	23	1
Heath	25	6	75	4	....	4	0	15	0
Sainsbury......	6	1	16	1	....	6	2	10	0

Umpires: F. S. Lee and L. H. Gray.

HAMPSHIRE v. YORKSHIRE

At Bournemouth, July 24, 25, 26. Yorkshire won by five wickets, taking 14 points. They were much the better all-round team. Hampshire were soon in difficulties against keen bowling and fielding, Wilson and Illingworth making spectacular diving catches. Yorkshire did not find progress easy and were indebted to a resolute innings by Illingworth for their lead. Marshall, driving and pulling in an exhilarating display of attacking strokes, gave Hampshire a much better start to their second innings but his colleagues failed to implement this performance. Illingworth hurried through the rest of the batting and Yorkshire, left to get 142, made light of their task.

Hampshire

R. E. Marshall b Pickles................	2	— c Binks b Close 71
J. R. Gray b Pickles	2	— b Illingworth 19
H. Horton c Wilson b Close	33	— c Binks b Wardle 19
A. W. H. Rayment run out	35	— b Illingworth 21
H. M. Barnard b Wardle	8	— c Wilson b Illingworth 17
A. C. D. Ingleby-Mackenzie c Watson b Close	3	— b Illingworth 11
P. J. Sainsbury b Close	0	— not out 38
L. Harrison c Illingworth b Close	4	— c Watson b Illingworth 3
D. Shackleton st Binks b Wardle	2	— c Watson b Illingworth 0
M. Heath c Wilson b Wardle	16	— c Binks b Cowan........ 4
M. D. Burden not out..................	0	— c Watson b Pickles 1
B 1, l-b 4	5	B 2, l-b 11, n-b 1 14

1/2 2/5 3/67 4/82 5/86 6/86 7/87   110   1/39 2/104 3/124 4/155   218
8/94 9/110 (1.92 an over)   5/156 6/179 7/195 8/195
9/213

Yorkshire

W. B. Stott b Heath	35	—	c Gray b Sainsbury	50
K. Taylor lbw b Heath	1	—	b Burden	34
J. V. Wilson c Gray b Shackleton	24	—	b Sainsbury	8
D. B. Close lbw b Shackleton	4	—	b Sainsbury	37
W. Watson b Burden	17	—	c Barnard b Sainsbury	3
R. Illingworth c Sainsbury b Gray	48	—	not out	5
W. H. H. Sutcliffe c Barnard b Shackleton	6	—	not out	0
J. H. Wardle b Heath	10		
J. G. Binks b Shackleton	22		
D. Pickles b Gray	0		
M. J. Cowan not out	0		
B 9, l-b 7, n-b 4	20		L-b 5	5

1/14 2/54 3/64 4/87 5/99 6/113　　　187　　1/76 2/95 3/95　(5 wkts.) 142
7/136 8/183 9/183 (2.01 an over)　　　　　　　　4/123 5/138

Yorkshire Bowling

	O.	M.	R.	W.		O.	M.	R.	W.
Pickles	8	2	16	2	....	10	1	28	1
Cowan	6	1	15	0	....	7	2	20	1
Wardle	21	6	48	3	....	36	18	65	1
Illingworth	11	6	13	0	....	30	12	62	6
Close	11.2	5	13	4	....	8	1	29	1

Hampshire Bowling

	O.	M.	R.	W.		O.	M.	R.	W.
Shackleton	37.3	18	55	4	....	9	3	24	0
Heath	30	11	64	3	....	5	1	20	0
Gray	5	1	14	2					
Burden	20	9	34	1	....	18.1	4	41	1
Sainsbury						15	4	52	4

Umpires: F. S. Lee and L. H. Gray.

HAMPSHIRE v. THE ARMY

At Southampton, July 27, 29, 30. Hampshire won by seven wickets. The Army 212 (M. D. Burden five for 60) and 160 for four, declared (Cpl. J. A. Pitt 69 not out); Hampshire 187 for six, declared (A. W. H. Rayment 58) and 188 for three (C. Harrison 66, B. R. Harrison 60 not out). Not first-class.

At Coventry, July 31, August 1, 2. HAMPSHIRE beat WARWICKSHIRE by nine wickets.

At Canterbury, August 3, 5, 6. HAMPSHIRE lost to KENT by 74 runs.

HAMPSHIRE v. SURREY

At Portsmouth, August 7, 8. Surrey won by an innings and 35 runs, taking 14 points. They treated the large crowd to a fine display of batting on the opening day. Stewart, with eleven 4's, was very strong in his on-side play, but May overshadowed his colleagues with an immaculate exhibition of driving, scoring his 97 (thirteen 4's) in two and a quarter hours. Though Hampshire were dismissed twice on the second day, Surrey needing only eight minutes of the extra half-hour to finish the match, Marshall mastered the champions' bowling with two spectacular innings of 56 and 111. Always attacking the bowling, he was caught in the deep in his first venture. When Hampshire followed on he needed only one hour and fifty minutes to make 111 out of 153 with seventeen 4's as his chief strokes. He treated all four Surrey bowlers with scant respect, but apart from Horton and Ingleby-Mackenzie, the remaining Hampshire batsmen proved very disappointing. As usual Surrey fielded superbly, giving fine support to Lock who took eleven wickets for 97 runs.

Surrey

T. H. Clark lbw b Gray	45	D. G. W. Fletcher c and b Sainsbury	5
M. J. Stewart c Ingleby-Mackenzie b Sainsbury	92	A. J. McIntyre not out	28
B. Constable c Marshall b Sainsbury	23	G. A. R. Lock not out	43
		N-b 1	1
P. B. H. May c Ingleby-Mackenzie b Sainsbury	97		
K. F. Barrington b Sainsbury	52	1/90 2/140 3/189 (6 wkts., dec.)	386

1/90 2/140 3/189 (6 wkts., dec.) 386
4/296 5/310 6/315 (3.41 an over)

J. C. Laker, P. J. Loader and A. V. Bedser did not bat.

Hampshire

R. E. Marshall c Bedser b Lock	56	— b Laker	111
J. R. Gray c and b Loader	5	— b Lock	16
H. Horton b Bedser	10	— c Stewart b Laker	39
A. W. H. Rayment lbw b Bedser	4	— c Barrington b Lock	1
E. D. R. Eagar c Stewart b Lock	4	— b Laker	0
A. C. D. Ingleby-Mackenzie c Lock b Bedser	0	— b Laker	35
P. J. Sainsbury c Barrington b Lock	0	— c Stewart b Lock	0
L. Harrison not out	16	— c Stewart b Lock	9
D. Shackleton st McIntyre b Laker	18	— not out	4
V. H. D. Cannings b Lock	1	— st McIntyre b Lock	2
M. Heath c Barrington b Lock	0	— b Lock	4
B 4, n-b 2	6	B 8, l-b 2	10

1/17 2/69 3/75 4/77 5/81 6/81 7/86   120
8/119 9/120 (2.61 an over)

1/34 2/153 3/164 4/165   231
5/196 6/199 7/221 8/221
9/227

Hampshire Bowling

	O.	M.	R.	W.	O.	M.	R.	W.
Shackleton	30	4	97	0				
Cannings	20	1	77	0				
Heath	23	4	84	0				
Sainsbury	31	6	98	5				
Gray	9	1	29	1				

Surrey Bowling

	O.	M.	R.	W.	O.	M.	R.	W.
Loader	8	4	16	1	9	2	22	0
Bedser	13	6	23	3	12	0	49	0
Laker	14	4	51	1	22	3	77	4
Lock	11	5	24	5	19.5	4	73	6

Umpires: P. Corrall and W. Place.

HAMPSHIRE v. DERBYSHIRE

At Portsmouth, August 10, 12, 13. Drawn, Hampshire taking four points. Sporting declarations on the last day led to a tense finish. In a bold attempt to produce a definite result after rain limited the opening day's play to two and a half hours, Carr, the Derbyshire captain, conceded first innings lead and bonus points. Hampshire acknowledged this generous gesture by going all out for runs and Gray failed by only seven to complete a century before lunch. Immediately he reached three figures Hampshire declared, leaving Derbyshire to obtain 222 runs at 78 an hour. After a poor start Derbyshire looked well placed to win until Shackleton and Cannings swung the game Hampshire's way again; but the ninth pair, Gibson and Gladwin, held out despite a cluster of fieldsmen round the bat.

Hampshire

J. R. Gray c Morgan b Jackson	0	— not out	103
R. E. Marshall c Jackson b Gladwin	70	— c Carr b Jackson	23
H. Horton c Gibson b Gladwin	35	— c Morgan b Jackson	12
A. W. H. Rayment c Jackson b Gladwin	8	— c Gibson b Carr	20
R. W. C. Pitman c Gibson b Revill	23	— c Dawkes b Jackson	15
A. C. D. Ingleby-Mackenzie c Dawkes b Revill	28	— not out	17
P. J. Sainsbury lbw b Jackson	20		
L. Harrison c Revill b Morgan	5		
D. Shackleton not out	24		
V. H. D. Cannings not out	17		
N-b 1	1	L-b 2	2

1/4 2/97 3/107 4/118　　(8 wkts., dec.) 231　　　1/33 2/53　　(4 wkts., dec.) 192
5/164 6/165 7/185 8/204 (2.78 an over)　　　　　3/108 4/162
M. Heath did not bat.

Derbyshire

A. Hamer c and b Heath	37	— b Shackleton	4
C. Lee c and b Sainsbury	47	— b Shackleton	9
J. M. Kelly c Pitman b Sainsbury	25	— c and b Rayment	30
D. B. Carr c Ingleby-Mackenzie b Sainsbury	22	— st Harrison b Shackleton	4
A. C. Revill c Cannings b Heath	22	— c Cannings b Rayment	33
I. M. Gibson not out	34	— not out	18
K. F. Mohan c Horton b Shackleton	2	— b Rayment	0
D. C. Morgan c Horton b Shackleton	2	— b Cannings	51
G. O. Dawkes c Rayment b Cannings	3	— c and b Sainsbury	23
C. Gladwin not out	6	— not out	1
L-b 2	2	B 1, l-b 2, n-b 1	4

1/53 2/105 3/112 4/142　　(8 wkts., dec.) 202　　1/12 2/13 3/64　　(8 wkts.) 177
5/162 6/182 7/187 8/194 (2.11 an over)　　　　　4/103 5/151 6/157 7/159
　　　　　　　　　　　　　　　　　　　　　　　8/160

L. Jackson did not bat.

Derbyshire Bowling

	O.	M.	R.	W.		O.	M.	R.	W.
Jackson	27	11	49	2	....	13	0	50	3
Gladwin	25	7	76	3	....	13	1	43	0
Morgan	16	5	38	1	....	11	2	37	0
Carr	6	1	24	0	....	13	1	43	1
Revill	9	1	43	2	....	5	0	17	0

Hampshire Bowling

	O.	M.	R.	W.		O.	M.	R.	W.
Shackleton	24	10	43	2	....	15	6	23	3
Cannings	17	5	42	1	....	9	2	22	1
Heath	23	11	40	2	....	7	2	19	0
Marshall	6	1	15	0					
Sainsbury	22	7	60	3	....	14	1	57	1
Rayment						17	5	52	3

Umpires: P. Corrall and W. Place.

At Cheltenham, August 14, 15. HAMPSHIRE lost to GLOUCESTERSHIRE by seven wickets.

At Old Trafford, August 17, 19, 20. HAMPSHIRE lost to LANCASHIRE by 95 runs.

At Worcester, August 21, 22, 23. HAMPSHIRE drew with WORCESTERSHIRE.

HAMPSHIRE v. NORTHAMPTONSHIRE
(L. Harrison's Benefit)

At Bournemouth, August 28, 29, 30. Northamptonshire won by seven wickets, taking 12 points. The left-arm spin trio of Tribe, Manning and Allen took 15 of the 17 wickets which fell to Northamptonshire bowlers. Sent in to bat on a drying pitch Hampshire did well to score 160 after losing half the side for 64. Northamptonshire did not gain the lead until the ninth pair were together, Tribe steering his side through a critical period when Burden's off-breaks threatened a complete breakdown. Without Marshall, ill with influenza, Hampshire looked like faring even worse than in their first innings until Harrison, the beneficiary, and Shackleton halted the spinners' successful progress. They added 92 in a grand seventh wicket partnership but Northamptonshire easily obtained the 187 runs necessary for victory. Tribe fittingly marked an excellent all-round performance by completing the "double" of 100 wickets and 1,000 runs for the sixth consecutive season.

Hampshire

R. E. Marshall b Kelleher	3	— absent ill	0
J. R. Gray c Subba Row b Manning	41	— lbw b Allen	18
H. Horton b Manning	14	— lbw b Tribe	9
E. D. R. Eagar b Manning	3	— b Tyson	26
R. W. C. Pitman lbw b Tribe	0	— run out	0
A. C. D. Ingleby-Mackenzie lbw b Allen	31	— c Andrew b Tribe	4
P. J. Sainsbury c and b Allen	19	— run out	22
L. Harrison b Tribe	32	— c Kelleher b Tribe	28
D. Shackleton b Manning	3	— c Arnold b Tribe	64
V. H. D. Cannings not out	7	— not out	1
M. D. Burden lbw b Tribe	0	— c Arnold b Tribe	9
B 4, l-b 3	7	B 4, l-b 11, n-b 1	16

1/10 2/52 3/63 4/64 5/64 6/111   160
7/120 8/127 9/160 (2.35 an over)

1/25 2/27 3/28 4/36 5/87   197
6/92 7/184 8/187

Northamptonshire

D. Brookes c Harrison b Sainsbury	25	— lbw b Shackleton	22
P. Arnold run out	33	— b Sainsbury	68
R. Subba Row b Burden	35	— not out	49
D. W. Barrick c Sainsbury b Shackleton	13	— c Gray b Shackleton	11
B. L. Reynolds c Eagar b Burden	11		
G. E. Tribe c sub b Burden	22	— not out	33
J. S. Manning lbw b Shackleton	0		
K. V. Andrew c Sainsbury b Burden	10		
F. H. Tyson not out	5		
M. H. J. Allen c sub b Burden	10		
H. R. A. Kelleher b Burden	0		
B 4, l-b 2, w 1	7	B 2, l-b 3, w 2	7

1/58 2/65 3/98 4/120 5/127 6/130   171
7/145 8/160 9/171 (1.85 an over)

1/58 2/109   (3 wkts.) 190
3/130

Northamptonshire Bowling

	O.	M.	R.	W.		O.	M.	R.	W.
Tyson	3	1	6	0	....	21	9	36	1
Kelleher	4	0	9	1	....	15	7	35	0
Allen	18	6	28	2	....	22	14	24	1
Manning	26	6	67	4	....	26	17	36	0
Tribe	16.5	4	43	3	....	24.3	7	50	5
Subba Row						1	1	0	0

Hampshire Bowling

	O.	M.	R.	W.	O.	M.	R.	W.
Shackleton	31	18	43	2	19	5	34	2
Cannings	5	2	9	0	9	3	21	0
Burden	37	16	87	6	28	6	84	0
Sainsbury	15	10	14	1	20.2	10	44	1
Marshall	4	1	11	0				

Umpires: C. S. Elliott and E. Davies.

HAMPSHIRE v. GLOUCESTERSHIRE

At Bournemouth, August 31, September 2. Hampshire won by an innings and 28 runs, taking 14 points. Gloucestershire collapsed in extraordinary fashion to the seam bowling of Shackleton and Cannings, the match ending abruptly on the second evening. Facing arrears of 67 they were routed in eighty-five minutes, five wickets falling at 35. Cannings took six of the first seven wickets in twelve overs on a pitch which never recovered from a soaking the previous day. That Hampshire established a first innings lead was due mainly to a cheerful partnership between Ingleby-Mackenzie (two 6's and eight 4's) and Sainsbury. They put on 65 in less than forty minutes.

Gloucestershire

G. M. Emmett c Gray b Cannings	11	—	b Cannings	11
D. M. Young c Harrison b Sainsbury	41	—	b Shackleton	5
R. B. Nicholls c Harrison b Cannings	0	—	c Harrison b Cannings	2
T. W. Graveney c Sainsbury b Burden	10	—	b Cannings	4
C. A. Milton c Sainsbury b Shackleton	27	—	c Sainsbury b Cannings	8
D. G. Hawkins c Sainsbury b Burden	1	—	lbw b Shackleton	0
A. S. Brown not out	13	—	b Cannings	0
J. Mortimore lbw b Shackleton	15	—	lbw b Cannings	0
D. R. Smith c Harrison b Shackleton	0	—	not out	0
C. Cook lbw b Shackleton	0	—	b Shackleton	0
B. D. Wells c Marshall b Shackleton	0	—	b Shackleton	4
L-b 2, n-b 1	3		L-b 5	5

1/21 2/21 3/40 4/92 5/93 6/93   121   1/19 2/21 3/27 4/27 5/35   39
7/121 8/121 9/121 (1.80 an over)   6/35 7/35 8/35 9/35

Hampshire

R. E. Marshall c Brown b Cook	12	L. Harrison b Cook	2
J. R. Gray c and b Mortimore	35	D. Shackleton c Milton b Cook	3
H. Horton c Brown b Mortimore	14	V. H. D. Cannings b Smith	0
E. D. R. Eagar b Mortimore	10	M. D. Burden not out	6
R. W. C. Pitman lbw b Wells	11	B 11, l-b 2 w 1	14
A. C. D. Ingleby-Mackenzie c Hawkins b Cook	59	1/23 2/63 3/78 4/89 5/91 6/156	188
P. J. Sainsbury lbw b Wells	22	7/179 8/179 9/180 (2.35 an over)	

Hampshire Bowling

	O.	M.	R.	W.	O.	M.	R.	W.
Shackleton	21	9	36	5	12.4	8	15	4
Cannings	12	7	16	2	12	4	19	6
Burden	19	6	53	2				
Sainsbury	15	10	13	1				

Gloucestershire Bowling

	O.	M.	R.	W.
Smith	15	2	33	1
Brown	7	6	5	0
Cook	13.3	6	31	4
Wells	26	10	61	2
Mortimore	18	4	44	3

Umpires: P. A. Gibb and E. Davies.

KENT

President—Sir Edward Hardy

Secretary—Nevill Christopherson, St. Lawrence Ground, Canterbury

Captain—M. C. Cowdrey

R. C. Wilson

County Badge

D. J. Halfyard

Even the astute captaincy of Cowdrey, who led them for the first time, failed to inspire Kent and they finished thirteenth, a rise of only three places compared with 1956. In some respects there were hopeful signs for the future. The decision to appoint L. E. G. Ames general manager showed that Kent were alive to their deficiencies and determined to improve.

Two bright prospects emerged in Halfyard and Brown. Both showed much ability when bowling with the new ball and Halfyard, formerly of Surrey, not only took over one hundred wickets in Championship matches, but achieved two singular performances when he finished with nine wickets for 39 runs against Glamorgan at Neath and did the hat-trick against Worcestershire at Folkestone. Another promising young player was Pretlove, the Cambridge Blue, who was one of five men who scored 1,000 runs in all matches. Halfyard and Pretlove were awarded their county caps.

In many ways Kent followed their form of the previous summer. Again they began the season in a blaze of glory with an innings victory over Middlesex at Lord's—a win which confounded even their sternest critics. Alas, as in 1956, two months then passed before another Championship success came their way. A second revival early in August brought three wins in five matches but the last four engagements, including that against West Indies, all brought defeat and much disappointment to their supporters.

Inconsistency in both batting and bowling was responsible for Kent's poor record. They often received an excellent start from their opening batsmen, Phebey and the left-handed Wilson. Both, however, were inclined to allow the opposing bowlers to settle down to a steady length, but on twelve occasions they shared partnerships of 50 or more. Kent badly needed a batsman or two of the Ames class to push the score along at a brisk pace.

Perhaps the biggest disappointment in this respect was the captain himself. Cowdrey, although remarkably consistent for England with scores of 4, 154, 152, 55, 68 and 2, he played only one big innings for Kent—165 against Nottinghamshire at Trent Bridge. Nevertheless, the calls of representative cricket kept Cowdrey and Evans out of ten or more Championship matches and although Ufton and Catt proved adequate deputies behind the stumps for Evans, Kent had no one to replace Cowdrey.

Whereas Ridgway and Smith helped Halfyard to maintain an adequate seam attack, Kent were weak in spin. Page, concentrating mainly on off-breaks, was never a dominant bowler, and Wright, who deservedly received a second benefit in the twilight of his career, made only occasional appearances before deciding to retire.

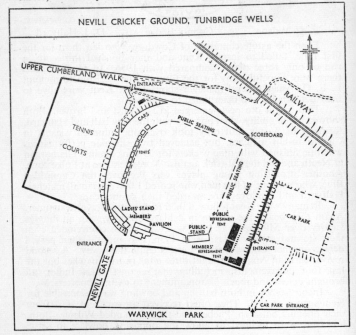

NEVILL CRICKET GROUND, TUNBRIDGE WELLS

KENT RESULTS

All First-Class Matches—Played 30, *Won* 7, *Lost* 14, *Drawn* 9
County Championship Matches—Played 28, *Won* 6, *Lost* 13, *Drawn* 9

COUNTY CHAMPIONSHIP AVERAGES
BATTING

	Birthplace	Mtchs.	Inns.	Not Outs	Runs	100's	Highest Inns.	Aver.
M. C. Cowdrey	*Bangalore, India*	16	27	5	979	1	165	44.50
R. C. Wilson..	*Bapchild*	27	49	1	1760	3	157	36.66
S. E. Leary....	*Cape Town*	23	42	9	1102	2	108	33.39
A. H. Phebey..	*Catford*	28	51	0	1368	1	111	26.82
J. F. Pretlove..	*Camberwell*	27	47	3	1085	1	101	24.65
G. W. Cook ...	*Beckenham*	4	5	1	89	0	51*	22.25
T. G. Evans ...	*Finchley*	14	25	1	527	0	84*	21.95
J. Pettiford ...	*Sydney*	20	34	6	555	0	57	19.82
A. E. Fagg....	*Chartham*	10	20	2	290	0	45*	16.11
D. G. Ufton ...	*Crayford*	11	19	1	281	0	55	15.61
A. L. Dixon...	*Dartford*	16	30	1	448	0	73	15.44
A. W. Catt....	*Edenbridge*	3	5	0	54	0	32	10.80
G. Smith.....	*Huddersfield*	10	17	4	137	0	32	10.53
B. Disbury....	*Bedford*	2	3	0	29	0	19	9.66
J. C. T. Page..	*Mereworth*	22	29	15	119	0	23	8.50
D. J. Halfyard..	*Middlesex*	25	40	5	281	0	32	8.02
D. V. P. Wright	*Sidcup*	12	14	6	62	0	28*	7.75
P. H. Jones...	*Woolwich*	4	8	0	58	0	15	7.25
F. Ridgway...	*Stockport*	18	25	4	144	0	33	6.85
R. S. Thresher.	*Tonbridge*	2	3	0	20	0	19	6.66
J. M. Allan...	*Leeds*	6	10	1	31	0	8*	3.44
A. Brown....	*Nottingham*	7	10	2	27	0	9*	3.37

Also batted: A. R. B. Neame (*Faversham*) 20 and 2.

* *Signifies not out.*

BOWLING

	Overs	Maidens	Runs	Wickets	Average
M. C. Cowdrey	8.1	1	28	2	14.00
G. Smith	389.1	109	923	57	16.19
J. Pettiford	77	23	210	11	19.09
J. F. Pretlove	45	18	98	5	19.60
D. J. Halfyard	843.4	225	2271	112	20.27
D. V. P. Wright	286.3	93	871	38	22.92
A. Brown	177.3	34	536	23	23.30
F. Ridgway	467.1	94	1407	60	23.45
J. C. T. Page	621.2	203	1565	64	24.45
J. M. Allan	93	29	272	8	34.00
S. E. Leary	72.1	11	308	9	34.22
R. S. Thresher	60	8	232	6	38.66
A. L. Dixon	270.3	69	820	17	48.23

Also bowled: G. W. Cook 11—3—36—0; B. Disbury 1—0—7—0; T. G. Evans 6—1—28—0; P. H. Jones 4—0—17—0; A. H. Phebey 1.2—1—4—0.

Amateurs.—J. M. Allan, G. W. Cook, M. C. Cowdrey, A. R. B. Neame, J. F. Pretlove, R. S. Thresher.

At Lord's, May 8, 9, 10. KENT beat MIDDLESEX by an innings and 59 runs.

At Manchester, May 11, 13, 14. KENT lost to LANCASHIRE by 60 runs.

KENT v. GLAMORGAN

At Gravesend, May 18, 20, 21. Glamorgan won by five wickets, taking 12 points. Both teams batted poorly on a good pitch until the last day, when Watkins led Glamorgan to their first victory of the season. Wilson gave Kent a reasonable start but after passing 100 with only two men out they collapsed against the spin of McConnon and pace of Hugh Davies. Glamorgan looked equally uncertain against Wright, though W. G. Davies presented a solid front for three hours ten minutes in scoring his maiden 50. The coolness of Pressdee enabled them to win a tense struggle for the lead and then Kent broke down again. Wooller took advantage of much rash stroke-play, but Leary received fine help from Halfyard (two 6's) and Page in his effort to restore Kent's position. Despite an attractive innings by Parkhouse, it seemed that Glamorgan might find their task too much against Wright until the left-handed Watkins forced the leg-spinner out of the attack with some powerful hooking and driving.

Kent

R. C. Wilson lbw b McConnon	63	— c H. G. Davies b H. D. Davies	0
A. H. Phebey lbw b Wooller	5	— c McConnon b Wooller	17
J. F. Pretlove c H. G. Davies b Watkins	6	— c W. G. Davies b Devereux	26
A. E. Fagg c H. D. Davies b McConnon	34	— c H. G. Davies b McConnon	10
S. E. Leary lbw b McConnon	4	— not out	55
J. Pettiford lbw b H. D. Davies	14	— run out	4
T. G. Evans c Wooller b H. D. Davies	27	— st H. G. Davies b McConnon	3
D. J. Halfyard c Watkins b H. D. Davies	0	— b Wooller	32
F. Ridgway c H. G. Davies b H. D. Davies	2	— c Watkins b Wooller	0
D. V. P. Wright c Ward b McConnon	3	— c H. G. Davies b H. D. Davies	1
J. C. T. Page not out	0	— b Wooller	19
B 4, l-b 3	7	B 4	4

1/20 2/35 3/102 4/112 5/121 6/152   **165**
7/156 8/158 9/163 (2.57 an over)

1/0 2/19 3/51 4/59 5/71   **171**
6/77 7/129 8/127 9/138

Glamorgan

W. G. A. Parkhouse c Evans b Halfyard	11	— lbw b Wright	51
W. G. Davies c Leary b Wright	58	— c Evans b Ridgway	1
B. Hedges lbw b Ridgway	1	— b Wright	11
L. N. Devereux c Leary b Halfyard	4	— not out	31
W. Wooller b Page	8	— not out	11
A. J. Watkins c Leary b Page	45	— b Pettiford	56
J. Pressdee not out	17	— b Pretlove	10
D. J. Ward lbw b Wright	1		
J. E. McConnon c Fagg b Wright	13		
H. G. Davies b Wright	0		
H. D. Davies b Halfyard	1		
B 2, l-b 2, n-b 3	7	L-b 1, n-b 1	2

1/13 2/14 3/24 4/51 5/133 6/133   **166**
7/134 8/152 9/152 (2.12 an over)

1/5 2/64 3/65   (5 wkts.) **173**
4/137 5/150

Glamorgan Bowling

	O.	M.	R.	W.	O.	M.	R.	W.
H. D. Davies	8	0	39	4	17	3	47	2
Watkins	12	2	25	1	11	4	20	0
Wooller	13	1	46	1	18.4	7	38	4
Devereux	14	7	30	0	8	3	19	1
McConnon	16.3	7	18	4	10	0	43	2

Kent Bowling

	O.	M.	R.	W.		O.	M.	R.	W.
Ridgway	14	4	32	1	....	14	1	43	1
Halfyard	16	5	37	3	....	16.2	4	35	0
Wright	18	8	40	4	....	17	6	47	2
Page	30	16	50	2	....	10	4	24	0
Pettiford						7	2	16	1
Pretlove						2	0	6	1

Umpires: H. G. Baldwin and R. S. Lay

KENT v. LEICESTERSHIRE

At Gravesend, May 22, 23, 24. Drawn, Kent taking four points. With Wilson, Pretlove and Cowdrey in excellent batting form Kent outplayed Leicestershire and looked set for victory but rain prevented any cricket on the last day. Pretlove showed Kent the way in a stylish, enterprising innings which brought him his first century for the county. Hitting seventeen 4's he made 101 out of 160 put on with Wilson in two hours forty minutes. Very slow at first, Wilson stayed five hours for his 157 which contained one 6 and twenty-five 4's. He and Cowdrey added 126 in seventy minutes and at the end of the first day Kent dismissed Hallam and van Geloven. Leicestershire were in severe trouble when four wickets were down for 31, but a stand of 103 by Palmer and Gardner, who like Hickman hit strongly, prevented a complete rout. As Wright had bowled for three hours and forty minutes without relief—a grand performance—Cowdrey did not enforce the follow-on; instead he proceeded to give another entertaining display of powerful driving.

Kent

A. H. Phebey c Firth b Munden 27	— lbw b Spencer 15
R. C. Wilson hit wkt b Palmer 157	— c Palmer b Boshier 9
J. F. Pretlove b Lester................. 101	
M. C. Cowdrey c and b Palmer 86	— not out 63
S. E. Leary st Firth b Palmer 5	
T. G. Evans b Spencer 0	— c Savage b Boshier 22
D. J. Halfyard not out 6	— b Spencer 3
B. E. Disbury did not bat............. —	— c and b Spencer........... 19
B 8, l-b 2 10	L-b 3 3

1/61 2/221 3/347 (6 wkts., dec.) 392   1/16 2/29 (5 wkts., dec.) 134
4/375 5/376 6/392 (3.69 an over)   3/86 4/129 5/134

F. Ridgway, D. V. P. Wright and J. C. T. Page did not bat.

Leicestershire

G. Lester c Leary b Wright....... 19	J. Savage not out 6
M. R. Hallam c Leary b Halfyard... 0	C. T. Spencer c and b Cowdrey .. 0
J. van Geloven b Ridgway 3	B. Boshier c Wilson b Cowdrey.... 0
J. Firth c Wilson b Wright 5	B 1, l-b 5, n-b 3............. 9
C. H. Palmer c Cowdrey b Wright. 57	
L. R. Gardner c and b Halfyard... 47	1/0 2/3 3/20 4/31 5/134 6/134 199
M. J. Hickman b Wright 38	7/182 8/192 9/199 (2.51 an over)
V. S. Munden b Ridgway 15	

Leicestershire Bowling

	O.	M.	R.	W.		O.	M.	R.	W.
Spencer	14	0	57	1	....	16.5	4	66	3
Boshier	13	1	62	0	....	16	2	65	2
van Geloven	9	0	38	0					
Palmer	16.2	3	72	3					
Munden	27	10	83	1					
Savage	21	9	48	0					
Lester	6	1	22	1					

Kent Bowling

	O.	M.	R.	W.
Ridgway	14	7	19	2
Halfyard	14	5	31	2
Wright	35	12	105	4
Page	14	6	33	0
Cowdrey	2	0	2	2

Umpires: H. G. Baldwin and R. S. Lay.

At Cambridge, May 25, 27, 28. KENT beat CAMBRIDGE UNIVERSITY by 117 runs.

KENT v. SOMERSET

At Gillingham, June 1, 3, 4. Somerset won by five wickets, taking 14 points. They deserved their success for superior and more attractive cricket. They made full use of winning the toss by scoring at an exceptional rate on the first day. Alley set the mood and Tremlett hit Page for three 6's. Kent lost three wickets cheaply before the close and, despite a brisk innings by Leary, followed-on 183 behind. They had reached 134 for one when a thunderstorm ended the second day before tea and on the last morning the pitch aided spin considerably. Kent's nine remaining wickets added only 112 against Langford and McMahon, and Wright bowled his leg-breaks so well that Somerset might have found another 50 runs beyond them.

Somerset

W. E. Alley c Wilson b Page	86	—	c Phebey b Page	27
K. E. Palmer run out	2	—	b Wright	7
P. B. Wight c Pretlove b Halfyard	27	—	not out	21
C. L. McCool c Wright b Page	44	—	c Ufton b Wright	3
M. F. Tremlett c Wilson b Halfyard	42	—	b Wright	4
H. W. Stephenson b Halfyard	32	—	not out	0
J. Hilton not out	51	—	c Phebey b Wright	0
J. Harris c Ufton b Ridgway	15			
B. Langford c Phebey b Leary	17			
B. Lobb c Disbury b Leary	0			
J. W. McMahon b Wright	0			
B 1, l-b 3	4		B 1, l-b 1	2
	320		(5 wkts.)	64

1/18 2/72 3/143 4/197 5/201 6/240
7/263 8/316 9/316 (3.85 an over)

1/29 2/41 3/54 (5 wkts.)
4/62 5/62

Kent

A. H. Phebey c Stephenson b Langford..	22	— c Tremlett b Langford	86
R. C. Wilson c and b Hilton	17	— b Langford	27
J. F. Pretlove lbw b Langford	2	— run out	46
B. E. Disbury st Stephenson b Hilton....	10	— lbw b Langford	0
S. E. Leary run out	58	— b McMahon..............	30
A. E. Fagg c Lobb b Hilton	0	— c Hilton b McMahon	1
D. G. Ufton st Stephenson b Langford...	4	— lbw b McMahon	8
D. J. Halfyard c Stephenson b Lobb	12	— c Harris b Langford	19
F. Ridgway b Lobb	6	— not out	10
D. V. P. Wright c McMahon b Langford	1	— lbw b Langford	3
J. C. T. Page not out	0	— b McMahon..............	1
B 1, l-b 4	5	B 6, l-b 9	15

1/34 2/41 3/42 4/99 5/114 6/118   **137**   1/47 2/146 3/159 4/204   **246**
7/118 8/134 9/137 (2.49 an over)   5/204 6/211 7/230 8/232
9/237

Kent Bowling

	O.	M.	R.	W.		O.	M.	R.	W.
Ridgway	14	1	52	1					
Halfyard	20	2	82	3	....	5	2	6	0
Page	22	6	93	2	....	13	3	44	1
Wright	21.3	7	72	1	....	8.2	3	12	4
Leary	4	1	10	2					
Disbury	1	0	7	0					

Somerset Bowling

	O.	M.	R.	W.		O.	M.	R.	W.
Lobb	3.3	0	13	2	...	3	2	9	0
Alley..........	2	0	13	0	...	4	0	9	0
Langford	25	7	57	4	...	42	14	87	5
Hilton	17	5	39	3	...	18	2	45	0
McMahon	7	2	10	0	...	28	6	81	4

Umpires: J. Wood and P. A. Gibb.

At Southampton, June 8, 10, 11. KENT drew with HAMPSHIRE.

At Leicester, June 12, 13, 14. KENT drew with LEICESTERSHIRE.

At Rushden, June 15, 17, 18. KENT drew with NORTHAMPTONSHIRE.

KENT v. WARWICKSHIRE

At Dartford, June 19, 20, 21. Warwickshire won by 19 runs, taking 12 points. Kent made a creditable attempt to deprive Warwickshire of their fifth successive Championship victory, but in the end failed narrowly against the sustained pace-and-spin attack of Bannister and Hollies. Ufton, deputising for Evans behind the wicket, distinguished himself on the first day by holding four excellent catches while Warwickshire concentrated on building a sound score. Leary produced the best and brightest batting of the match when Kent replied but received so little support that Warwickshire gained a comfortable lead. This stood them in good stead for they broke down in their second innings against the hostile fast-medium bowling of Smith, who achieved his best performance to date. Left to score 210 in four hours forty minutes, Kent made the mistake of waiting for runs to come. Despite a good innings by Wilson his colleagues proved disappointing.

Warwickshire

F. C. Gardner c Ufton b Smith	16	—	c Leary b Dixon	15
N. F. Horner c Wilson b Ridgway	10	—	c Fagg b Halfyard	0
M. J. K. Smith c Ufton b Dixon	27	—	c Ufton b Dixon	29
A. Townsend c Ufton b Halfyard	92	—	c Wilson b Smith	45
T. W. Cartwright c Ufton b Dixon	23	—	lbw b Smith	0
R. T. Spooner lbw b Smith	47	—	c Ufton b Smith	4
K. Ibadulla b Halfyard	7	—	b Smith	14
S. Singh c sub b Halfyard	27	—	c Dixon b Smith	5
R. G. Carter not out	2	—	b Dixon	0
J. D. Bannister (did not bat)		—	not out	6
W. E. Hollis (did not bat)		—	b Smith	0
B 5, l-b 5, n-b 2	12		B 14, l-b 6	20

1/23 2/49 3/53 4/119 (8 wkts., dec.) 263
5/220 6/228 7/261 8/263 (2.77 an over)

1/1 2/38 3/79 4/84 5/96 138
6/112 7/126 8/126 9/132

Kent

A. H. Phebey c Ibadulla b Townsend	20	—	b Bannister	24
R. C. Wilson b Carter	8	—	c Horner b Bannister	69
J. F. Pretlove c Cartwright b Townsend	24	—	c Townsend b Hollies	22
A. E. Fagg c Cartwright b Townsend	10	—	c Smith b Bannister	3
S. E. Leary not out	74	—	b Hollies	8
A. L. Dixon c Horner b Bannister	6	—	b Hollies	0
D. G. Ufton b Hollies	21	—	b Bannister	13
J. M. Allan c Spooner b Hollies	1	—	c Townsend b Bannister	8
G. Smith b Bannister	11	—	c Spooner b Bannister	7
D. J. Halfyard c Bannister b Ibadulla	16	—	not out	16
F. Ridgway c Spooner b Ibadulla	0	—	c Singh b Bannister	2
L-b 1	1		B 15, l-b 2, n-b 1	18

1/18 2/43 3/62 4/62 5/89 6/137 192
7/139 8/158 9/190 (2.86 an over)

1/46 2/91 3/99 4/112 190
5/112 6/141 7/156 8/160
9/183

Kent Bowling

	O.	M.	R.	W.		O.	M.	R.	W.
Ridgway	11	1	27	1					
Halfyard	23.4	5	65	3		8	4	11	1
Smith	33	9	68	2		29.3	13	60	6
Dixon	21	2	71	2		22	10	47	3
Allan	7	3	20	0					

Warwickshire Bowling

	O.	M.	R.	W.		O.	M.	R.	W.
Bannister	20	5	57	2		36.1	10	95	7
Carter	17	1	53	1		4	1	7	0
Townsend	11	0	51	3		4	0	7	0
Hollies	15	6	29	2		31	13	55	3
Ibadulla	3.4	3	1	2		3	1	8	0

Umpires: A. E. Pothecary and W. F. Price.

KENT v. SUSSEX

At Tunbridge Wells, June 22, 24, 25. Sussex won by nine wickets, taking 14 points. They were the better of two poor batting sides on a pitch that throughout encouraged seam-bowlers. Kent gave an inept display against Thomson, who until punished by Halfyard and Smith had taken six for 16 in the first innings. Their only other stand of note was between Wilson and Pretlove in the second innings. Smith bowled just as well for Kent but did not enjoy the same fielding support. Nevertheless he improved his best analysis in first-class cricket for the second time in a week. James, in his new role as opening batsman, batted solidly.

Kent

A. H. Phebey c Suttle b Bates	1	— c Suttle b Thomson	1
R. C. Wilson c Potter b Thomson	6	— c and b Thomson	77
J. F. Pretlove c Parks b Thomson	0	— c Foreman b Thomson	45
D. G. Ufton c Parks b James	18	— c Suttle b Thomson	1
S. E. Leary lbw b Thomson	0	— c James b Bates	12
A. L. Dixon c Bates b Thomson	20	— b Bates	16
J. M. Allan c Foreman b Thomson	0	— lbw b Bates	0
A. E. Fagg c Stripp b Thomson	4	— c James b Thomson	28
D. J. Halfyard b Stripp	20	— c Stripp b Thomson	4
G. Smith b Stripp	32	— c Potter b Thomson	0
D. V. P. Wright not out	5	— not out	0
		B 12, l-b 3	15

1/7 2/7 3/7 4/7 5/31 6/31 7/41　106　　1/2 2/83 3/93 4/131 5/156　199
8/51 9/97 (2.71 an over)　　6/162 7/172 8/182 9/194

Sussex

L. J. Lenham c Ufton b Smith	4	— not out	16
A. E. James c and b Smith	52	— c sub b Halfyard	10
K. G. Suttle b Smith	5	— not out	28
J. M. Parks c Phebey b Smith	74		
D. J. Foreman c Fagg b Wright	10		
G. Potter c Smith b Halfyard	47		
D. A. Stripp c Halfyard b Smith	12		
N. I. Thomson c Phebey b Smith	0		
D. N. Mantell c Ufton b Smith	34		
R. G. Marlar c Wilson b Smith	8		
D. L. Bates not out	0		
B 4, l-b 3, w 1	8		

1/10 2/30 3/121 4/145 5/151 6/181　254　　1/11　　(1 wkt.) 54
7/185 8/235 9/250 (2.76 an over)

Sussex Bowling

	O.	M.	R.	W.		O.	M.	R.	W.
Thomson	20	8	45	6	....	32.2	6	57	7
Bates	12	3	32	1		21	4	45	3
James	5	2	17	1		5	3	6	0
Stripp	2.1	0	12	2		5	1	19	0
Marlar						18	5	41	0
Suttle						7	2	16	0

Kent Bowling

	O.	M.	R.	W.		O.	M.	R.	W.
Smith	38	4	110	8	....	9	2	24	0
Halfyard	21	4	59	1		9.5	1	30	1
Dixon	12	3	27	0					
Wright	15	8	32	1					
Allan	4	2	13	0					
Leary	2	0	5	0					
Pretlove						1	1	0	0

Umpires: John Langridge and A. Skelding.

KENT v. YORKSHIRE

At Tunbridge Wells, June 26, 27. Yorkshire won by ten wickets, taking 12 points. Kent lost again, chiefly through disappointing batting. Yorkshire, who won the toss, began badly on a lively pitch and seven wickets should have been down for 120. Instead Wardle, missed when two, hit hard for an hour. Another dropped catch proved costly as Cowan, who escaped when ten, helped Appleyard to add 77 for the last wicket. Appleyard made the highest score of his career. Although Kent collapsed badly they deprived Yorkshire of bonus points. Following-on 197 behind they just saved the innings defeat. Phebey stayed nearly two and a half hours and Evans, who hit eleven 4's, took only fifty-one minutes over 61. His 50 came in twenty-eight minutes.

Yorkshire

D. B. Close c Pretlove b Halfyard	8	
W. B. Stott c Jones b Thresher	39	
J. V. Wilson c Pretlove b Dixon	13 — not out	4
D. E. V. Padgett c Evans b Dixon	17	
R. Illingworth c Dixon b Thresher	2	
K. Taylor c Evans b Halfyard	23	
W. H. H. Sutcliffe c Cowdrey b Leary	38	
J. H. Wardle c Jones b Allan	46	
J. G. Binks c Evans b Thresher	11	
R. Appleyard run out	63	
M. J. Cowan not out	19 — not out	2
B 8, n-b 5	13	

1/10 2/43 3/83 4/83 5/86 6/116   292   (No wkt.) 6
7/183 8/196 9/215 (2.83 an over)

Kent

A. H. Phebey b Appleyard	7 — c Wilson b Illingworth	61
J. M. Allan c Wardle b Cowan	0 — c Wilson b Wardle	5
J. F. Pretlove b Cowan	7 — c Appleyard b Illingworth	15
M. C. Cowdrey c Sutcliffe b Cowan	10 — b Illingworth	0
D. J. Halfyard b Cowan	0 — b Illingworth	1
S. E. Leary not out	29 — c Binks b Wardle	17
T. G. Evans c Sutcliffe b Appleyard	0 — c and b Wardle	61
P. H. Jones b Cowan	5 — st Binks b Wardle	12
J. Pettiford c Binks b Appleyard	3 — not out	26
A. L. Dixon c Wilson b Illingworth	8 — lbw b Wardle	0
R. S. Thresher b Wardle	19 — b Illingworth	0
B 8, l-b 1	9	

1/7 2/9 3/21 4/21 5/33 6/36 7/49   97   1/34 2/69 3/69 4/102   198
8/56 9/74 (3.03 an over)   5/156 6/177 7/177 8/197
                                 9/198

Kent Bowling

	O.	M.	R.	W.	O.	M.	R.	W.
Halfyard	33	11	101	2				
Thresher	25	6	70	3				
Dixon	28	14	51	2				
Allan	11	5	30	1				
Leary	5.3	0	27	1				
Evans					2	1	2	0
Phebey					1.2	1	4	0

Yorkshire Bowling

	O.	M.	R.	W.	O.	M.	R.	W.
Cowan	12	1	32	5	10	5	12	0
Appleyard	12	5	23	3	7	1	23	0
Wardle	4.3	0	17	1	26	8	75	5
Illingworth	3	0	16	1	26	12	61	5
Close					6	3	27	0

Umpires: John Langridge and A. Skelding.

At Birmingham, June 29, July 1, 2. KENT drew with WARWICKSHIRE.

At Neath, July 3, 4, 5. KENT lost to GLAMORGAN by 46 runs.

At The Oval, July 6, 8. KENT lost to SURREY by ten wickets.

KENT v. WORCESTERSHIRE

At Folkestone, July 10, 11, 12. Kent won by 128 runs, taking 12 points. For their first victory since the opening match of the season. Kent were heavily indebted to three players. Phebey and Wilson gave the batting an excellent start in each innings and Halfyard again bowled excellently in gaining the best match-figures of his career. Having returned the best analysis of the season with nine for 39 against Glamorgan the previous week, Halfyard recorded the first hat-trick by dismissing Booth, Horton and Jenkins with successive balls in Worcestershire's first innings. Flavell also found the pitch responsive to his lively seam attack in causing Kent's first innings breakdown. Phebey provided the backbone of the innings by staying nearly four and a half hours. Despite a splendid fighting display by Kenyon, Worcestershire had little chance of avoiding defeat on the last day when the ball kicked viciously off rain-damaged turf. Halfyard again bowled unchanged and finished with thirteen wickets for 94 runs.

Kent

A. H. Phebey c Horton b Flavell 111	— c P. Richardson b Horton..	38
R. C. Wilson lbw b Horton 43	— c D. Richardson b Horton .	45
J. F. Pretlove b Jenkins 7	— lbw b Horton............	1
M. C. Cowdrey c Dews b Jenkins....... 4	— not out	47
S. E. Leary c Horton b Flavell 5	— c Kenyon b Flavell	19
J. Pettiford c Horton b Flavell 0	— not out	14
D. G. Ufton not out 25		
A. L. Dixon c Booth b Flavell 0		
D. J. Halfyard b Flavell 0		
D. V. P. Wright c Booth b Flavell 3		
J. C. T. Page b Flavell 12		
L-b 3 3	B 4, w 1	5

1/107 2/126 3/132 4/147 5/149   213   1/84 2/86   (4 wkts., dec.) 169
6/187 7/187 8/187 9/191 (2.42 an over)   3/93 4/139

Worcestershire

D. Kenyon b Halfyard 4	— b Halfyard	79
P. E. Richardson c Ufton b Halfyard ... 47	— c Cowdrey b Halfyard	6
G. Dews not out 47	— c Wilson b Page	12
D. W. Richardson c Leary b Halfyard.. 0	— c Page b Halfyard	7
R. G. Broadbent c Pretlove b Wright ... 6	— c Wilson b Halfyard	7
M. J. Horton c Ufton b Halfyard 0	— c Phebey b Halfyard	5
R. Booth c Cowdrey b Halfyard 0	— c Ufton b Halfyard........	2
R. O. Jenkins c Leary b Halfyard 0	— c Wilson b Page	4
R. Berry c Cowdrey b Halfyard 4	— c Pretlove b Page	2
J. Flavell run out 5	— c Leary b Page	0
L. Coldwell c Leary b Wright 0	— not out	4
B 2, l-b 9, w 1, n-b 1 13	L-b 4, w 1	5

1/4 2/64 3/64 4/88 5/98 6/98 7/102   126   1/20 2/53 3/64 4/84 5/89   128
8/106 9/119 (3.23 an over)   6/104 7/109 8/124 9/124

Worcestershire Bowling

	O.	M.	R.	W.		O.	M.	R.	W.
Flavell	21.3	6	46	7	....	11	1	50	1
Coldwell	17	3	45	0	....	4	0	15	0
Horton	16	6	46	1	....	25	9	62	3
Berry	12	4	22	0	....	23	10	37	0
Jenkins	21	8	51	2					

Kent Bowling

	O.	M.	R.	W.		O.	M.	R.	W.
Halfyard	20	5	45	7	....	26.1	12	49	6
Dixon	7	1	30	0	....	4	0	23	0
Wright	12.1	3	38	2					
					Page	22	7	51	4

Umpires: T. J. Bartley and T. W. Spencer.

KENT v. GLOUCESTERSHIRE

At Maidstone, July 13, 15, 16. Kent won by eight wickets, taking 12 points. Kent went a long way towards gaining their second successive victory on the first day when, after putting Gloucestershire in on a pitch helping spin, they finished 13 behind with one wicket down. Brown began Gloucestershire's troubles with two splendid catches and only a workmanlike innings by Nicholls prevented complete collapse against Wright and Page. The turf was saturated by week-end rain and Kent made heavy weather of building a useful lead, Wilson spending over an hour in the 90's. Although Kent dropped several catches some good ones were held, particularly that by Dixon which removed Graveney cheaply for the second time, and not even stout hitting by Brown, Mortimore and Smith could set Kent more than a token task. Phebey and Wilson ensured victory with their fifth successive partnership of over 50.

Gloucestershire

G. M. Emmett c and b Brown	9	— c Evans b Halfyard	3
D. M. Young c Evans b Page	28	— c Cowdrey b Page	24
R. B. Nicholls c Pretlove b Wright	70	— c Leary b Halfyard	13
T. W. Graveney c Brown b Page	4	— c sub b Page	0
C. A. Milton lbw b Wright	6	— lbw b Brown	7
D. G. Hawkins b Page	16	— c Evans b Halfyard	2
A. S. Brown c Evans b Wright	4	— c Evans b Halfyard	39
J. Mortimore c Brown b Page	1	— lbw b Page	41
R. Etheridge not out	18	— b Halfyard	0
D. Smith b Wright	18	— b Page	41
C. Cook b Brown	0	— not out	6
B 9, n-b 1	10	B 9, l-b 1, n-b 1	11

1/21 2/40 3/44 4/65 5/94 6/113   184   1/8 2/39 3/42 4/47 5/47   187
7/134 8/144 9/179 (3.40 an over)   6/125 7/132 8/139 9/140

Kent

A. H. Phebey b Mortimore	36	— c Graveney b Emmett	29
R. C. Wilson c Graveney b Cook	102	— not out	42
J. F. Pretlove run out	73	— lbw b Emmett	0
M. C. Cowdrey c Hawkins b Mortimore	14		
S. E. Leary b Mortimore	25	— not out	4
J. Pettiford not out	24		
T. G. Evans c Brown b Mortimore	3		
D. J. Halfyard c Brown b Cook	9		
D. V. P. Wright c Milton b Mortimore	1		
J. C. T. Page b Cook	0		
A. Brown c Hawkins b Mortimore	0		
B 4, l-b 5	9	L-b 1	1

1/60 2/210 3/227 4/246 5/262 6/274   296   1/58 2/58   (2 wkts.) 76
7/286 8/289 9/289 (2.14 an over)

Kent Bowling

	O.	M.	R.	W.		O.	M.	R.	W.
Halfyard	8	2	26	0	....	32	11	72	5
Brown	9.4	1	35	2	....	7	1	18	1
Page	18	1	74	4	....	29	11	58	4
Wright	18	8	39	4	....	8	3	28	0

Gloucestershire Bowling

	O.	M.	R.	W.		O.	M.	R.	W.
Smith	17	3	49	0	....	5	1	13	0
Brown	11	2	39	0	....	3	1	6	0
Cook	49	25	62	3	....	3	0	18	0
Mortimore	61	20	137	6	....	4	1	10	0
Graveney						6	0	24	0
Emmett						5.1	2	4	2

Umpires: J. S. Buller and F. S. Lee.

KENT v. LANCASHIRE

At Maidstone, July 17, 18, 19. Drawn, Lancashire taking four points. Bad weather robbed them of almost certain victory by restricting play to half an hour on the last day, Kent finishing only 77 ahead with three wickets left. Kent fared well on the first day, reaching 105 for two by lunch but two unnecessary run-outs began a breakdown which Wharton completed with the new ball. Lancashire, in turn, began badly against Halfyard but in the absence of Wright, Kent could not prevent Ikin and Bond regaining the initiative. Kent's shortage of slow-bowling was reflected in the success of Dyson, Hilton, Tattersall and Greenhough, whose spin caused their subsequent collapse.

Kent

A. H. Phebey b Hilton	30	— c Grieves b Hilton	34
R. C. Wilson c Grieves b Greenhough	16	— st Wilson b Wharton	0
J. F. Pretlove b Hilton	44	— c Wilson b Dyson	5
A. E. Fagg not out	45	— c and b Dyson	8
S. E. Leary run out	1	— lbw b Dyson	2
J. Pettiford c Wharton b Hilton	3	— not out	40
D. G. Ufton run out	10	— b Tattersall	4
A. L. Dixon b Wharton	29	— c Wilson b Greenhough	5
G. Smith c Grieves b Wharton	0	— not out	11
D. J. Halfyard b Wharton	0		
J. C. T. Page b Wharton	0		
B 9, l-b 3, n-b 2	14	B 11	11

1/36 2/90 3/111 4/117 5/120 6/133   192   1/5 2/24 3/42   (7 wkts.) 120
7/178 8/178 9/192 (2.31 an over)   4/44 5/83 6/91 7/106

Lancashire

A. Wharton c Page b Halfyard	35	A. Wilson b Halfyard	5
J. Dyson c Pretlove b Smith	11	R. Tattersall not out	1
J. T. Ikin c Ufton b Page	68	B 1, l-b 3	4
C. Washbrook lbw b Halfyard	18		
K. Grieves b Page	5		
G. Pullar c Ufton b Smith	4		
J. D. Bond c Ufton b Halfyard	51		
M. J. Hilton c Fagg b Smith	4	1/34 2/64 3/104 4/117 5/124 235
T. W. Greenhough c Leary b Halfyard	29	6/169 7/186 8/200 9/226
		(2.52 an over)

Lancashire Bowling

	O.	M.	R.	W.		O.	M.	R.	W.
Wharton	12.4	4	20	4	....	6	2	9	1
Tattersall	15	4	41	0	....	17	7	39	1
Greenhough	23	5	61	1	....	8	1	11	1
Hilton	28	15	53	3	....	16	7	26	1
Dyson	4	2	3	0	....	18	9	24	3

Kent Bowling

	O.	M.	R.	W.
Halfyard	30.5	5	89	5
Smith	27	10	46	3
Page	31	8	83	2
Dixon	4	1	13	0

Umpires: J. S. Buller and F. S. Lee.

KENT v. SURREY

At Blackheath, July 20, 22, 23. Surrey won by 73 runs, taking 12 points, but Kent came nearer to victory than the score suggests. The pitch on the third day was easier than at any time in the match and, had Cowdrey not fallen to an exceptional ball from Loader that broke in at an acute angle and flattened the leg-stump, Kent might well have scored the 229 runs needed to win. The pitch was never vicious but quicker bowlers found it helpfully two-paced after rain delayed the start until four o'clock on the first day. Surrey lost five wickets for 118 by the close and then twenty-three wickets went down on a remarkable second day. Halfyard and Brown quickly wound up the Surrey innings but Loader struck back so swiftly that within forty minutes Kent's score read 10 for five. Bold hitting by Evans and Dixon partly restored the innings and then Surrey broke down in turn against Brown and Halfyard, losing their first three men for eight runs. Kent's shortage of change bowling helped May and E. Bedser to halt the slide, and Halfyard, after bowling May, retired with back trouble following his seventeenth consecutive over. Surrey snatched Phebey's wicket before the close but Kent appeared to be making good progress until Cowdrey's remarkable dismissal on the last morning. Dixon again batted admirably, especially in a last-wicket stand with Brown.

Surrey

T. H. Clark c Wilson b Halfyard	0	— lbw b Brown	2
M. J. Stewart c Wilson b Halfyard	30	— b Halfyard	0
B. Constable c Wilson b Page	39	— c Evans b Brown	1
P. B. H. May c Pettiford b Brown	19	— b Halfyard	51
K. F. Barrington c Pretlove b Brown	18	— b Brown	4
E. A. Bedser c Page b Halfyard	20	— c Wilson b Page	46
A. J. McIntyre c Dixon b Brown	10	— not out	21
G. A. R. Lock c Phebey b Halfyard	0	— c Evans b Dixon	4
J. C. Laker not out	14	— not out	4
P. J. Loader b Brown	0		
A. V. Bedser c Pettiford b Halfyard	12		
B	1	B 5, l-b 3	8

1/0 2/50 3/84 4/91 5/110 6/132 7/136   163   1/2 2/2 3/8 (7 wkts., dec.) 141
8/144 9/144 (2.26 an over)   4/28 5/90 6/132 7/137

Kent

A. H. Phebey lbw b Loader	0	— lbw b Loader	4
R. C. Wilson b Lock	16	— c May b Lock	39
J. F. Pretlove b A. Bedser	1	— b Lock	10
M. C. Cowdrey b Loader	0	— b Loader	8
S. E. Leary c Stewart b Loader	0	— lbw b Lock	0
J. Pettiford lbw b Loader	1	— lbw b Loader	30
T. G. Evans c Constable b Loader	23	— c and b Lock	4
A. L. Dixon b A. Bedser	31	— b Laker	31
D. J. Halfyard c Barrington b Loader	1	— b Lock	2
J. C. T. Page b Loader	0	— c Barrington b Lock	10
A. Brown not out	0	— not out	9
B 1, l-b 1, n-b 1	3	B 5, l-b 3	8

1/2 2/3 3/6 4/8 5/10 6/42 7/48   76   1/8 2/35 3/46 4/47 5/89   155
8/69 9/76 (2.37 an over)   6/101 7/106 8/117 9/127

Kent Bowling

	O.	M.	R.	W.	O.	M.	R.	W.
Halfyard	25	8	51	5	17	7	44	2
Brown	27	7	65	4	16	3	60	3
Page	20	4	46	1	11	3	24	1
Dixon					1	0	5	1

Surrey Bowling

	O.	M.	R.	W.	O.	M.	R.	W.
Loader	16.2	5	30	7	21	7	45	3
A. Bedser	10	3	17	2	12	1	29	0
Lock	6	1	26	1	24	4	64	6
Laker					11.1	7	9	1

Umpires: J. F. Crapp and Harry Elliott.

At Taunton, July 24, 25, 26. KENT lost to SOMERSET by ten wickets.

At Hastings, July 27, 29, 30. KENT drew with SUSSEX.

At Nottingham, July 31, August 1, 2. KENT beat NOTTINGHAMSHIRE by eight
wickets.

KENT v. HAMPSHIRE

(D. V. P. Wright's Second Benefit)

At Canterbury, August 3, 5, 6. Kent won by 74 runs with eight minutes to
spare, taking 12 points. Although back trouble prevented Wright playing, he won
the toss, but Hampshire caused surprise when Shackleton captured the first three
wickets for 19 runs. Stubborn batting by Leary who stayed for three hours,
hitting twelve 4's, brought about a recovery before Evans (one 6, eleven 4's),
enjoying some luck, hit freely for his not out 84. Hampshire lost their first seven
wickets for 95, a collapse partly due to Marshall hooking a ball from Ridgway
into his face. The injury required several stitches and when he returned he found
a valuable partner in Sainsbury, who defied the Kent bowlers for two hours and
twenty minutes. A fine display by Cowdrey quickly augmented Kent's lead of 71
and in the end they left Hampshire to score 269 to win in three and three-quarter
hours. Thanks to Marshall and Gray the visitors began their task promisingly,
but after Gray was fifth out at 144 Kent's keen bowling and fielding turned the
scale.

O

Kent

A. H. Phebey c Rayment b Shackleton ..	5	— c Ingleby-Mackenzie b Shackleton	4
R. C. Wilson c Harrison b Shackleton...	9	— c Gray b Shackleton......	15
J. Pettiford c Horton b Heath	28	— b Shackleton	32
M. C. Cowdrey c Marshall b Shackleton.	4	— c Harrison b Cannings ...	63
S. E. Leary b Heath	75	— b Sainsbury	33
J. F. Pretlove b Sainsbury	24	— c Harrison b Heath	8
T. G. Evans not out	84	— b Cannings	4
G. Smith c Harrison b Heath	4	— lbw b Shackleton	2
D. J. Halfyard c Sainsbury b Heath ...	14	— c Eagar b Heath	2
F. Ridgway c Horton b Heath	3	— not out	17
J. C. T. Page c Horton b Heath	1	— not out	2
B 4, l-b 2	6	B 10, l-b 2, n-b 3	15

1/14 2/15 3/19 4/84 5/141 6/153   257   1/8 2/25   (9 wkts., dec.) 197
7/157 8/213 9/249 (2.40 an over)   3/125 4/125 5/133 6/140
                                                   7/174 8/177 9/178

Hampshire

J. R. Gray c Cowdrey b Ridgway	11	— c Ridgway b Smith	73
R. E. Marshall c Page b Smith	52	— c Halfyard b Ridgway ...	32
H. Horton c Cowdrey b Smith	9	— b Pettiford	10
A. W. H. Rayment c Smith b Halfyard .	12	— c Leary b Smith	7
E. D. R. Eagar b Smith	0	— c Cowdrey b Smith	9
A. C. D. Ingleby-Mackenzie b Halfyard.	0	— b Halfyard	28
P. J. Sainsbury c Cowdrey b Smith	47	— not out	4
L. Harrison b Ridgway	8	— c Wilson b Ridgway	28
D. Shackleton c Pretlove b Smith	8	— b Halfyard	0
V. H. D. Cannings not out	29	— c Leary b Pettiford	0
M. Heath b Halfyard	2	— c Leary b Page	1
B 1, l-b 4, w 1, n-b 2	8	B 1, l-b 1	2

1/38 2/56 3/62 4/62 5/63 6/78 7/95   186   1/49 2/67 3/116 4/120   194
8/127 9/171 (2.86 an over)   5/144 6/152 7/188 8/189
                                                 9/189

Hampshire Bowling

	O.	M.	R.	W.		O.	M.	R.	W.
Shackleton....	25	9	41	3	....	26	9	56	4
Cannings	27	7	65	0	....	21	7	61	2
Gray	14	6	23	0	....	9	2	23	0
Heath	25.5	4	88	6	....	11	4	36	2
Sainsbury......	15	6	34	1	....	6	1	6	1

Kent Bowling

	O.	M.	R.	W.		O.	M.	R.	W.
Ridgway	18	2	50	2	....	9		39	2
Halfyard	26.5	8	75	3	....	19	3	66	2
Smith	20	6	53	5	....	14	1	55	3
Pettiford			13	8		20	2		
Leary			8	5		12	0		
Page			1.2	1		0	1		

Umpires: C. S. Elliott and R. S. Lay.

KENT v. ESSEX

At Canterbury, August 7, 8, 9. Drawn, Kent taking two points. A painstaking opening stand of 171 by Phebey and Wilson which came only eight runs behind their previous best—against Middlesex at Lord's earlier in the season—put Kent on top and Cowdrey declared first thing Thursday morning. Essex found themselves trapped on a rain-affected pitch and were put out for 144, Smith, the local amateur seam bowler, dismissing Taylor, Trevor Bailey and Savill in four balls. Following on 157 behind, Essex soon lost Dodds, but Barker and Taylor made a defiant stand and the total stood at 98 for three at the end of the second day. Next morning Insole and Bailey shaped most confidently, Insole clearing the arrears with a 6, but when Essex were 25 ahead and still had six wickets left, rain ruined the prospect of an interesting finish. During the Essex first innings, the band of the Buffs stopped playing after lunch on the second day at the request of Taylor and Insole, who complained that the music disturbed them.

Kent

A. H. Phebey c Insole b T. Bailey	95	D. G. Ufton b Preston	19
R. C. Wilson c Ralph b Preston ..	82	G. Smith not out	6
M. C. Cowdrey c Barker b Preston	2	B 16, l-b 4, w 1	21
S. E. Leary c T. Bailey b Preston..	3		
J. Pettiford c T. Bailey b J. Bailey	26	1/171 2/175 3/187 (6 wkts., dec.) 301	
J. F. Pretlove not out	47	4/207 5/236 6/271 (2.86 an over)	

D. J. Halfyard, F. Ridgway and J. C. T. Page did not bat.

Essex

T. C. Dodds b Ridgway	27	— b Ridgway	11
G. Barker c Wilson b Halfyard	0	— b Pettiford	36
B. Taylor c and b Smith	39	— c Ufton b Pettiford	36
D. J. Insole b Halfyard	26	— not out	68
T. E. Bailey c Cowdrey b Smith	0	— not out	22
L. Savill c Ufton b Smith	0		
M. Bear c Ufton b Ridgway	1		
W. T. Greensmith c Cowdrey b Smith	12		
R. Ralph not out	24	— c Leary b Halfyard	5
K. C. Preston b Ridgway	10		
J. A. Bailey c Ufton b Smith	1		
B 4	4	B 2, l-b 2	4

1/2 2/52 3/90 4/90 5/90 6/93 7/109	144	1/13 2/71 3/90 (4 wkts.) 182	
8/120 9/141 (3.42 an over)		4/105	

Essex Bowling

	O.	M.	R.	W.	O.	M.	R.	W.
T. Bailey	23	7	59	1				
Preston	28	4	81	4				
Ralph	27	2	61	0				
J. Bailey	18	4	45	1				
Greensmith	9	0	34	0				

Kent Bowling

	O.	M.	R.	W.	O.	M.	R.	W.
Ridgway	19	3	63	3	9.4	2	32	1
Halfyard	10	0	39	2	17	4	51	1
Smith	12.4	2	38	5	22	8	30	0
Page					13	2	39	0
Pettiford					7	0	26	2

Umpires: C. S. Elliott and R. S. Lay.

At Leeds, August 10, 12, 13. KENT drew with YORKSHIRE.

At Derby, August 14, 15, 16. KENT beat DERBYSHIRE by an innings and 50 runs.

KENT v. NORTHAMPTONSHIRE

At Dover, August 17, 19, 20. Northamptonshire won by six wickets. taking 12 points to four by Kent, and with their thirteenth victory of the season, set up a record for the county. Kent batted slowly in the first innings. Wilson and Phebey began with a stand of 81, but, despite brisk work by Evans, the pace bowling of Tyson and Kelleher caused the fall of the last nine wickets for 133. Although Subba Row stayed three hours forty minutes, Northamptonshire also broke down, the last six wickets realising only 55 runs. Kent, 29 ahead, were saved in the second innings by Cowdrey, and Northamptonshire required 189 to win. A second wicket partnership of 99 by Brookes and Livingston virtually settled the issue.

Kent

A. H. Phebey lbw b Allen	38	— lbw b Tyson	0
R. C. Wilson c Tyson b Tribe	67	— b Tyson	24
J. Pettiford c Tribe b Kelleher	17	— b Tyson	5
M. C. Cowdrey c Livingston b Kelleher .	2	— b Manning	70
J. F. Pretlove b Kelleher	0	— lbw b Tribe	2
G. W. Cook c Andrew b Kelleher	16	— c Andrew b Manning	5
T. G. Evans c Andrew b Tyson	43	— c Subba Row b Tribe	26
G. Smith b Tyson	2	— b Tribe	12
F. Ridgway c Andrew b Tyson	0	— c Manning b Tribe	5
D. J. Halfyard run out	16	— c Subba Row b Allen	0
J. C. T. Page not out	0	— not out	0
B 6, l-b 4, n-b 3	13	B 3, l-b 6, n-b 1	10

1/81 2/129 3/129 4/129 5/136 6/173   214   1/0 2/10 3/51 4/96 5/107   159
7/182 8/182 9/212 (2.37 an over)   6/112 7/139 8/158 9/159

Northamptonshire

D. Brookes lbw b Halfyard	17	— c Ridgway b Page	47
P. Arnold lbw b Ridgway	0	— run out	29
L. Livingston c Pretlove b Halfyard	20	— b Halfyard	49
R. Subba Row c Wilson b Smith	70	— c Pettiford b Page	1
B. L. Reynolds c Ridgway b Halfyard	20	— not out	37
G. E. Tribe c Cowdrey b Page	7	— not out	12
J. S. Manning b Smith	8		
K. V. Andrew b Ridgway	18		
F. H. Tyson b Smith	12		
M. H. J. Allen not out	1		
H. R. A. Kelleher c Ridgway b Smith	1		
B 1, l-b 7, w 1, n-b 2	11	L-b 13, n-b 1	14

1/17 2/21 3/75 4/130 5/145 6/145   185   1/35 2/134   (4 wkts.)   189
7/159 8/182 9/184 (1.81 an over)   3/135 4/144

Northamptonshire Bowling

	O.	M.	R.	W.		O.	M.	R.	W.
Tyson	19	3	60	3	....	9	1	29	3
Kelleher	23.5	6	60	4	....	11	4	28	0
Manning	12	4	20	0	....	19	5	57	2
Allen	18	7	27	1	....	1	1	0	1
Tribe	17	6	34	1	....	12.3	2	35	4

Kent Bowling

	O.	M.	R.	W.		O.	M.	R.	W.
Ridgway	22	4	61	2	....	10	1	41	0
Halfyard	19	9	43	3	....	21	3	66	1
Page	29	14	28	1	....	11	4	37	2
Smith	30	15	35	4	....	11	4	27	0
Pettiford	2	0	7	0					
					Cowdrey	0.1	0	4	0

Umpires: A. E. Pothecary and L. H. Gray.

KENT v. MIDDLESEX

At Dover, August 21, 22. Middlesex won by 231 runs, taking 14 points. They were superior at all points, though they began badly, losing five wickets to the pace bowlers for 70 runs. Titmus and Murray restored the position by adding 82. Moss, fast, and Titmus, off-breaks. soon disposed of Kent, for whom the left-handed Pretlove alone stayed long. Leading by 95, Middlesex lost six wickets for 86, but Titmus (two 6's, nine 4's) again stemmed the tide, and Kent required 275 to win. This time their breakdown was complete, the innings being all over in seventy-five minutes. Moss, bowling at a fine pace, took seven wickets for 24 runs, the best analysis of his career, bringing his match record to twelve for 59.

Middlesex

J. D. Robertson b Halfyard	7	— c Phebey b Ridgway	31
R. A. Gale c Pettiford b Ridgway	18	— c Pretlove b Ridgway	5
W. J. Edrich lbw b Ridgway	10	— b Page	30
D. C. S. Compton b Ridgway	5	— b Page	4
G. P. S. Delisle lbw b Brown..........	10	— b Page	5
F. J. Titmus c Pretlove b Halfyard	62	— b Page	70
J. T. Murray c Ridgway b Halfyard	46	— b Ridgway	0
J. J. Warr b Brown	9	— c Ridgway b Page	5
R. J. Hurst c Catt b Brown	1	— c Pretlove b Pettiford	6
A. E. Moss b Ridgway	12	— not out	4
T. Angus not out	18	— b Page	10
L-b 5	5	B 1, l-b 8	9

1/11 2/36 3/44 4/45 5/70 6/152   203   1/19 2/44 3/44 4/53 5/77   179
7/165 8/173 9/173 (2.90 an over)   6/86 7/120 8/157 9/167

Kent

A. H. Phebey b Moss	12	— lbw b Moss	0
R. C. Wilson c Robertson b Titmus	11	— c Titmus b Warr	7
J. Pettiford c Murray b Moss	0	— c Gale b Warr	2
P. E. Jones b Titmus	6	— c Murray b Moss	10
J. F. Pretlove st Murray b Titmus	50	— lbw b Moss	0
A. L. Dixon c Robertson b Titmus	4	— b Moss	0
A. W. Catt lbw b Moss	6	— b Moss	4
F. Ridgway c Gale b Moss	14	— c Angus b Edrich	4
D. J. Halfyard c Murray b Moss	0	— c Murray b Moss	6
A. Brown run out	3	— b Moss	5
J. C. T. Page not out...............	0	— not out	1
L-b 1, n-b 1..................	2	L-b 4	4

1/18 2/18 3/29 4/30 5/44 6/55 7/87   108   1/0 2/3 3/6 4/18 5/20   43
8/87 9/108 (1.74 an over)   6/26 7/31 8/35 9/42

Kent Bowling

	O.	M.	R.	W.		O.	M.	R.	W.
Ridgway	19.1	1	52	4	....	13	3	36	3
Halfyard	28	4	84	3	....	10	1	32	0
Brown	16	6	40	3	....	7	1	28	0
Page	7	1	22	0	....	25.3	6	61	6
Pettiford						6	2	13	1

Middlesex Bowling

	O.	M.	R.	W.		O.	M.	R.	W.
Moss	17	8	35	5	....	9.3	2	24	7
Angus	3	0	7	0					
Titmus	27.3	13	49	4					
Compton	11	3	14	0					
Warr	3	2	1	0	....	5	1	7	2
Edrich						4	2	8	1

Umpires: A. E. Pothecary and L. H. Gray.

At Clacton, August 24, 26, 27. KENT lost to ESSEX by 87 runs.

At Canterbury, August 28, 29, 30. KENT lost to WEST INDIES by seven wickets.
(See WEST INDIES section.)

LANCASHIRE

Patron—HER MAJESTY THE QUEEN

President—THE EARL OF DERBY

Secretary—C. G. HOWARD, County Cricket Ground, Old Trafford, Manchester, 16

Captain—CYRIL WASHBROOK

| J. B. Statham | County Badge | C. Washbrook |

After the manner in which they harried Surrey in 1956, finishing second only twenty points behind the Champions, hopes were high that Lancashire would do even better in the centenary year of cricket at Old Trafford, celebrated with a match against M.C.C. in June. Optimism rose rapidly when Lancashire made such a splendid beginning and took such full advantage of the new bonus points rule that the maximum 70 points were gained from the first five Championship games.

Pessimism set in just as quickly when the team failed to gain a point from their next five games, and this note of depression persisted for the rest of the season. Only 86 points were gained from the last 23 Championship matches, and Lancashire fell to sixth place in the table.

The beginning of Lancashire's decline coincided with the departure of Washbrook, their captain, and Statham, the spearhead of the attack, on Test Match duties. Washbrook himself fell off in his run-getting; Grieves made a good start to the season, but could do little right later when the pitches became predominantly wet. Little was seen of Edrich in first-class cricket because his skill and experience were used to develop the second team as captain and coach.

In bowling, too, there were disappointments. Again the burden of the opening attack fell heavily on the willing shoulders of Statham, but he lacked adequate support until late in the season

when Smith, after good work at Cambridge, bowled well. Similarly
with the spin bowling, Tattersall, returning to his best form with
his off-breaks after a mixed season in 1956, seldom found a worthy
partner. Malcolm Hilton lacked accuracy and penetration with
his left-arm slows, and Greenhough's leg-breaks did not fully
maintain the promise of the previous summer, so that each had
spells out of the side. A further blow was that Jordan, who kept
wicket so well in 1956, missed well over half the games through
injury, Wilson deputising.

The batting depended largely on three left-handers, Wharton,
a reliable opener, Ikin, who enjoyed a good last season with the
county, and Pullar, a graceful, hard-hitting young player, whose
advance was one of the brightest features of the year. Bond came
into the side with success; he played several enterprising innings,
fielded excellently, and looked a prospect for the future.

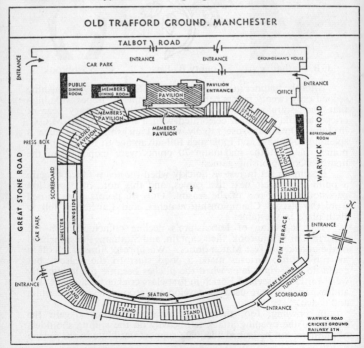

LANCASHIRE RESULTS

All First-Class Matches—Played 36, *Won* 11, *Lost* 10, *Drawn* 15

County Championship Matches—Played 28, *Won* 10, *Lost* 8, *Drawn* 8, *No Decision* 2

COUNTY CHAMPIONSHIP AVERAGES
BATTING

	Birthplace	Mtchs.	Inns.	Not Outs	Runs	100's	Highest Inns.	Aver.
R. W. Barber...	*Manchester*	4	7	3	198	0	50	49.50
A. Wharton....	*Heywood*	25	42	1	1421	3	114	34.65
G. Pullar	*Swinton*	19	33	3	814	2	138	27.13
J. T. Ikin	*Stoke*	28	46	3	1074	1	141*	24.97
C. Washbrook ..	*Barrow*	22	34	2	793	0	94	24.78
K. Grieves	*Sydney*	24	40	6	750	0	68	22.05
G. A. Edrich ...	*Lingwood*	7	14	0	295	0	72	21.07
J. Dyson	*Oldham*	18	29	1	576	0	88	20.57
J. D. Bond	*Kearsley*	19	26	1	446	0	72	17.84
R. Collins	*Manchester*	11	19	1	313	0	54	17.38
P. Whiteley	*Rochdale*	3	4	0	64	0	32	16.00
C. S. Smith	*Didsbury*	8	13	0	193	0	42	14.84
J. B. Statham...	*Manchester*	21	27	4	255	0	53	11.08
M. J. Hilton ...	*Chadderton*	15	22	1	227	0	43	10.80
R. Bowman ...	*Cleveleys*	3	3	0	32	0	21	10.66
T. Greenhough.	*Rochdale*	19	27	6	176	0	29	8.38
C. Hilton	*Atherton*	2	4	1	24	0	17	8.00
J. M. Jordan...	*Clough Fold*	11	17	1	128	0	31	8.00
R. Tattersall...	*Bolton*	28	38	20	143	0	20*	7.94
E. A. Kelly.....	*Liverpool*	2	4	1	22	0	11*	7.33
W. Heys.......	*Oswaldtwistle*	3	4	0	19	0	10	4.75
A. Wilson	*Newton-le-Willows*	14	16	4	54	0	11	4.50

Also batted: J. Roberts (*Bolton*) 0 and 0*; A. Bolton (*Darwen*) 6.

* *Signifies not out.*

BOWLING

	Overs	Maidens	Runs	Wickets	Average
J. B. Statham	647.3	190	1257	100	12.57
C. S. Smith	184.2	38	414	29	14.27
R. Tattersall...........	1000	354	2079	122	17.04
T. Greenhough	423	118	1084	56	19.35
M. J. Hilton	458.3	187	974	46	21.17
J. T. Ikin	82.4	30	173	8	21.62
J. Dyson	155	64	311	12	25.91
R. Bowman	68	10	189	7	27.00
A. Wharton	270.4	66	718	24	29.91
R. Collins	67	16	194	6	32.33
P. Whiteley	36	12	82	2	41.00
E. A. Kelly	44	10	158	3	52.66
C. Hilton	36	5	122	2	61.00

Also bowled: R. W. Barber 13—5—24—2; J. Roberts 21—6—72—0.

Amateurs.—R. W. Barber, R. Bowman, C. S. Smith.

At Oxford, May 1, 2. LANCASHIRE beat OXFORD UNIVERSITY by ten wickets.

At Taunton, May 4, 6, 7. LANCASHIRE beat SOMERSET by seven wickets.

At Cardiff, May 8, 9, 10. LANCASHIRE beat GLAMORGAN by three wickets.

LANCASHIRE v. KENT

At Manchester, May 11, 13, 14. Lancashire won by 60 runs, taking 14 points. Lancashire played enterprising cricket and deserved victory in a game frequently interrupted by rain. On a green pitch, admirable pace bowling by Halfyard and Ridgway, well supported by the off-breaks of Page, gave Lancashire an uncomfortable time. Kent, however, fared even worse against an aggressive opening spell of pace by Statham and the subsequent spin attack of Tattersall and Hilton. Between the showers, Wharton, Grieves and Collins batted briskly in Lancashire's second innings, and Washbrook made a bold declaration, allowing Kent well over four hours to make 220. Tattersall (skilful off-breaks), Statham and Hilton justified their captain's confidence.

Lancashire

A. Wharton b Ridgway	6	—	c Phebey b Page	42
J. Dyson c Phebey b Page	23	—	c Cowdrey b Wright	19
G. A. Edrich c Leary b Ridgway	12	—	b Wright	7
C. Washbrook c Evans b Halfyard	3	—	c Phebey b Wright	21
K. Grieves run out	12	—	not out	47
J. T. Ikin b Halfyard	25	—	c Cowdrey b Page	5
R. Collins c and b Halfyard	14	—	not out	38
M. J. Hilton c Cowdrey b Halfyard	1	—	c Pretlove b Ridgway	1
J. Jordan c Wilson b Page	0			
J. B. Statham c Halfyard b Page	4			
R. Tattersall not out	2		B 4	4
L-b 4	4			

1/6 2/16 3/28 4/40 5/63 6/96 7/99 — 106
8/100 9/100 (1.85 an over)

1/61 2/61 (6 wkts., dec.) 184
3/89 4/91 5/103 6/113

Kent

A. H. Phebey lbw b Statham	4	—	b Statham	35
R. C. Wilson c Wharton b Tattersall	12	—	c Jordan b Tattersall	19
J. M. Allan c Jordan b Statham	2	—	c Edrich b Hilton	0
J. F. Pretlove c Statham b Tattersall	9	—	c Statham b Hilton	46
D. V. P. Wright b Statham	0	—	not out	3
M. C. Cowdrey c Wharton b Hilton	26	—	c Jordan b Statham	2
S. E. Leary c Grieves b Hilton	10	—	st Jordan b Tattersall	22
T. G. Evans c Edrich b Hilton	0	—	c Ikin b Tattersall	24
F. Ridgway c Wharton b Tattersall	0	—	c Jordan b Tattersall	4
D. J. Halfyard c Dyson b Tattersall	6	—	c Collins b Tattersall	0
J. C. T. Page not out	0	—	c Washbrook b Tattersall	0
B 2	2		B 2, l-b 2	4

1/12 2/18 3/18 4/18 5/51 6/51 7/57 — 71
8/58 9/68 (1.42 an over)

1/31 2/101 3/103 4/109 — 159
5/151 6/152 7/152 8/152
9/156

Kent Bowling

	O.	M.	R.	W.		O.	M.	R.	W.
Ridgway	20	5	51	2	....	13	2	33	1
Halfyard	28	13	36	4	....	9	3	33	0
Page	8.4	3	15	3	....	17	2	84	2
Wright						9	3	18	3
Allan						2	0	12	0

Lancashire Bowling

	O.	M.	R.	W.		O.	M.	R.	W.
Statham	16	10	18	3	....	12	2	27	2
Wharton	4	0	10	0					
Tattersall	20	9	30	4	....	21.5	4	83	6
Hilton	9.3	5	11	3	....	21	5	43	2
Collins						3	2	2	0

Umpires: J. S. Buller and D. Davies.

LANCASHIRE v. SCOTLAND

At Manchester, May 15, 16. 17. Drawn. Lancashire lost their first four wickets for 53, but recovered splendidly, mainly because of a stylish innings by Pullar, the left-hander. Making his first appearance of the season, Pullar hit his highest score to date. He batted three and a quarter hours and hit one 6 and twelve 4's. Rain prevented play on the second day, and on resuming Scotland found the spin of Tattersall, Hilton and Greenhough too much for them.

Lancashire

A. Wharton c Chisholm b Wilson	13	— not out 23
J. Dyson b Wilson	12	— not out 5
G. A. Edrich c Cosh b Livingstone	8	
J. D. Bond b Drummond	1	
K. Grieves c Dudman b Allan	44	
G. Pullar c Courtenay b Drummond	121	
M. J. Hilton b Allan	11	
J. Jordan c Cosh b Barr	20	
R. Tattersall not out	14	
T. Greenhough b Livingstone	3	
E. A. Kelly b Livingstone	0	
B 6, l-b 1	7	B 4 4

1/28 2/29 3/30 4/53 5/112 6/152   254   (No wkt.) 32
7/192 8/249 9/254

Scotland

R. H. E. Chisholm c Tattersall b Greenhough 13	J. Brown c Jordan b Hilton 8
L. Dudman b Greenhough 15	D. W. Drummond c Jordan b Hilton 4
Rev. J. Aitchison c and b Hilton .. 22	D. Livingstone lbw b Tattersall.... 2
J. M. Allan c Grieves b Hilton.... 11	J. S. Wilson st Jordan b Hilton.... 1
G. W. L. Courtenay c Hilton b Tattersall 4	B 5 5
D. Barr not out 29	1/22 2/38 3/66 4/70 5/70 114
S. H. Cosh c Grieves b Hilton 0	6/70 7/78 8/80 9/95

Scotland Bowling

	O.	M.	R.	W.	O.	M.	R.	W.
Wilson	24	3	66	2	4	2	8	0
Drummond	22	3	71	2	4	1	8	0
Livingstone	24	11	35	3	5	1	9	0
Barr	9	3	24	1				
Allan	16	2	51	2	6	5	3	0

Lancashire Bowling

	O.	M.	R.	W.
Kelly	7	1	17	0
Tattersall	22	14	29	2
Hilton	22.3	10	38	6
Greenhough	11	2	25	2

Umpires: W. Place and D Davies.

At Coventry, May 18, 20. LANCASHIRE beat WARWICKSHIRE by an innings and 105 runs.

At Cambridge, May 22, 23, 24. LANCASHIRE drew with CAMBRIDGE UNIVERSITY

At WORCESTER, May 25, 27. LANCASHIRE beat WORCESTERSHIRE by an innings and 22 runs.

LANCASHIRE v. GLAMORGAN

At Manchester, May 29, 30, 31. Glamorgan won by 128 runs, taking 14 points. After gaining maximum points from each of their first five championship games, Lancashire sadly disappointed against a hard-fighting Glamorgan side. After Parkhouse, W. Davies and Jones had given the Welsh county a sound start, Devereux made his first century in county cricket. Despite determined resistance for four and a half hours by Dyson, and a fiercely hit innings from Collins, Lancashire managed to avert the follow-on only with the last pair together. Then they declared, but Glamorgan again rose to the occasion. After a third declaration they bowled too well for Lancashire, McConnon and Shepherd, with their off-breaks, ensuring a comfortable victory for the Welsh county.

Glamorgan

W. G. A. Parkhouse c Ikin b Kelly	86	— c Dyson b Tattersall 30
W. G. Davies b Greenhough	35	— c Ikin b Wharton 3
B. Hedges c Ikin b Tattersall	3	— c Pullar b Hilton 40
W. E. Jones c Heys b Collins	42	— st Heys b Greenhough 41
A. J. Watkins c Ikin b Kelly	16	— c Dyson b Hilton 1
L. N. Devereux not out	108	— c Hilton b Tattersall 0
J. Pressdee c and b Kelly	32	— c Tattersall b Greenhough.. 7
J. E. McConnon st Heys b Wharton	37	— not out 9
H. G. Davies not out	2	
B 3, l-b 6	9	L-b 1 1

1/65 2/70 3/153 4/179 (7 wkts., dec.) 370
5/212 6/294 7/351 (2.56 an over)
H. D. Davies and D. J. Shepherd did not bat.

1/20 2/50 (7 wkts., dec.) 132
3/90 4/91 5/92 6/117 7/132

Lancashire

A. Wharton c W. G. Davies b Shepherd..	33	— c and b Shepherd 58
J. Dyson c Shepherd b H. D. Davies	71	— c Hedges b H. D. Davies... 6
J. T. Ikin lbw b Shepherd	10	— b McConnon 15
G. Pullar c H. G. Davies b Shepherd....	5	— c Jones b McConnon 6
K. Grieves b McConnon	8	— c Pressdee b McConnon 7
R. Collins c Pressdee b Shepherd	54	— c W.G. Davies b H.D. Davies 18
M. J. Hilton c Devereux b Pressdee	5	— st H. G. Davies b McConnon 30
R. Tattersall c H. G. Davies b Shepherd..	8	— c H. G. Davies b Shepherd.. 4
W. Heys c Parkhouse b H. D. Davies	10	— b Shepherd 0
E. A. Kelly not out	11	— b McConnon 4
T. Greenhough not out	3	— not out 1
L-b 1, n-b 3	4	B 2, l-b 1 3

1/52 2/74 3/80 4/89 (9 wkts., dec.) 222
5/156 6/168 7/184 8/201 9/209
(2.38 an over)

1/22 2/50 3/73 4/85 152
5/103 6/114 7/130 8/130
9/137

Lancashire Bowling

	O.	M.	R.	W.		O.	M.	R.	W.
Kelly	27	8	77	3	....	5	1	22	0
Wharton	16	3	63	1	....	8	3	10	1
Hilton	33	10	70	0	....	14	4	32	2
Tattersall	33	16	40	1	....	20	5	48	2
Greenhough	28	6	84	1	....	2.3	0	11	2
Collins	7	2	27	1	....	1	0	8	0

Glamorgan Bowling

	O.	M.	R.	W.		O.	M.	R.	W.
H. D. Davies	19	4	46	2	....	9	2	26	2
Watkins	17	3	29	0	....	7	0	20	0
Shepherd	30	10	69	5	....	16	4	47	3
McConnon	13	4	45	1	....	13.4	3	56	5
Pressdee	14	4	29	1					

Umpires: L. H. Gray and A. Skelding.

LANCASHIRE v. DERBYSHIRE

At Liverpool, June 1, 3. Derbyshire won by an innings and 66 runs, taking 14 points. Playing with great confidence for their fifth successive championship win, Derbyshire outclassed Lancashire who were without Washbrook and Statham. On the first day Hamer, Lee, Kelly, Johnson and Morgan so belaboured the depleted attack that four 6's and fifty-six 4's were struck before Carr declared in time to give Lancashire forty minutes' batting. Apart from aggressive hitting by Collins, Lancashire could do little in their first innings against the lively attack of Jackson, Gladwin and Morgan. They followed-on and despite a sound display by Ikin, fared even worse against Morgan, who was well supported by the off-breaks of Smith.

Derbyshire

A. Hamer c Jordan b Hilton	.....	104
C. Lee c Grieves b Tattersall	.....	73
J. Kelly c and b Wharton	.....	68
A. C. Revill c Jordan b Collins	....	10
D. B. Carr c Jordan b Tattersall	...	24
G. O. Dawkes b Wharton	....	0
H. L. Johnson not out	....	88
D. C. Morgan st Jordan b Tattersall		41
E. Smith c Collins b Tattersall	....	0
B 4, l-b 5	....	9

C. Gladwin and L. Jackson did not bat.

1/158 2/201 (8 wkts., dec.) 417
3/226 4/275 5/277 6/306 7/411
8/417 (3.62 an over)

Lancashire

A. Wharton c Carr b Gladwin	....	7	— c and b Gladwin	 8
J. Dyson c Revill b Jackson	....	12	— c Carr b Morgan	 29
J. T. Ikin c Kelly b Gladwin	....	9	— b Morgan	 49
G. Pullar c Dawkes b Jackson	....	9	— b Smith	 26
K. Grieves lbw b Jackson	....	32	— c Lee b Morgan	 7
R. Collins c Smith b Morgan	....	54	— b Smith	 0
M. J. Hilton b Jackson	....	23	— b Morgan	 7
J. Jordan lbw b Morgan	....	14	— c Revill b Morgan	 0
R. Tattersall c Lee b Jackson	....	18	— not out	 20
T. Greenhough not out	....	2	— b Morgan	 0
E. A. Kelly b Jackson	....	2	— c Carr b Smith	 5
B 4, l-b 4, w 1, n-b 1		10	B 4, l-b 3, w 1	8

1/14 2/26 3/34 4/39 5/117 6/147   192
7/161 8/171 9/188 (3.20 an over)

1/9 2/81 3/108 4/126   159
5/127 6/128 7/129 8/136
9/140

Lancashire Bowling

	O.	M.	R.	W.	O.	M.	R.	W.
Kelly	12	1	59	0				
Wharton	22	5	79	2				
Tattersall	30.2	6	89	4				
Hilton	27	6	90	1				
Greenhough ...	16	7	56	0				
Collins	8	1	35	1				

Derbyshire Bowling

	O.	M.	R.	W.	O.	M.	R.	W.
Jackson	20	1	63	5	11	3	21	0
Gladwin	18	12	31	2	9	5	18	1
Morgan	17	5	63	3	23	9	65	6
Smith	5	0	25	0	23	9	39	3
Carr					5	3	8	0

Umpires: T. W. Spencer and L. H. Gray.

LANCASHIRE v. M.C.C.
(Old Trafford Centenary)

At Manchester, June 5, 6, 7. Drawn. As part of the festivities to mark the completion of 100 years of cricket at Old Trafford, Lancashire played this match against a team raised by the Marylebone Club. Coming just before Whitsun and in bitterly cold weather, the match was watched by only a few spectators, but those who attended enjoyed a superb display by Sir Leonard Hutton, who appeared in first-class cricket for the first time in two years. Flawless in defence, he drove in his most stylish manner, hitting ten 4's. Three Sussex players, Smith, Parks and Dexter also batted well. Parks (two 6's and nineteen 4's) spent only two and a half hours over his not out 132. For Lancashire, Wharton seized the opportunity to make his highest score. He hit two 6's and twenty-one 4's and, with Ikin, Washbrook and Grieves equally comfortable on a perfect pitch, the County declared. Rain ruined the last day when play was reduced to eighty minutes.

M.C.C.

Sir L. Hutton c Pullar b Hilton	76	—	c Dyson b Tattersall	25
D. V. Smith c Jordan b Statham	49	—	c Wharton b Collins	55
W. Watson c Jordan b Statham	0	—	b Statham	7
J. M. Parks not out	132	—	c Ikin b Wharton	1
E. R. Dexter b Ikin	22	—	c Ikin b Hilton	61
G. Goonesena c and b Ikin	2	—	not out	23
F. R. Brown b Statham	13	—	not out	11
T. G. Evans c Collins b Hilton	25			
D. Shackleton c Jordan b Tattersall	14			
F. S. Trueman not out	0			
B 4, l-b 3	7		B 4, l-b 1	5

1/99 2/101 3/155 4/188 (8 wkts., dec.) 340
5/194 6/216 7/287 8/327

1/9 2/16 3/121 (5 wkts.) 188
4/125 5/163

R. G. Marlar did not bat.

Lancashire

A. Wharton c Smith b Goonesena	164		G. Pullar lbw b Goonesena	7
J. Dyson c Brown b Dexter	15		R. Collins not out	0
J. T. Ikin lbw b Marlar	42		B 5, l-b 5, w 1	11
C. Washbrook c Trueman b Shackleton	50			—
K. Grieves c Marlar b Smith	76		1/39 2/160 3/253 (6 wkts., dec.) 365
			4/312 5/349 6/365	

M. J. Hilton, J. Jordan, J. B. Statham and R. Tattersall did not bat.

Lancashire Bowling

	O.	M.	R.	W.	O.	M.	R.	W.
Statham	19	5	69	3	4	1	4	1
Wharton	16	4	55	0	10	1	53	1
Tattersall	21	5	84	1	11	1	30	1
Hilton	17	2	86	2	14	1	65	1
Collins	11	4	23	0	8	2	23	1
Ikin	10	3	16	2	2	0	8	0

M.C.C. Bowling

	O.	M.	R.	W.
Trueman	17	0	72	0
Shackleton	19	8	35	1
Dexter	10	0	51	1
Goonesena	19	1	97	2
Marlar	20	6	62	1
Brown	9	2	22	0
Smith	4.2	1	15	1

Umpires: T. W. Spencer and W. E. Phillipson.

LANCASHIRE v. YORKSHIRE

At Manchester, June 8, 10, 11. Drawn, Yorkshire taking four points. After an exciting match of varying fortunes, Lancashire saved the game with their last pair together during the extra half-hour. Rain curtailed the first day, but allowed time for the Yorkshire first innings, the backbone of which was a stand of 72 between two left-handers, Wilson and Stott. After they were parted, the last five wickets fell rapidly in face of the left-arm slows of Hilton. On Whit-Monday came an even more pronounced collapse by Lancashire after the fifth wicket pair, Pullar and Washbrook, added 64. The remaining wickets added only four runs, Wardle proving most effective. Tattersall's off-breaks were troublesome when Yorkshire batted again, but Illingworth batted soundly and Trueman hit strongly. Apart from Edrich, Grieves and Washbrook, the Lancashire batsmen struggled in the second innings, but Statham and Tattersall held out

Yorkshire

F. A. Lowson lbw b Wharton	2	—	c Edrich b Tattersall	10
D. B. Close c Pullar b Wharton	14	—	b Statham	0
J. V. Wilson c Pullar b Hilton	54	—	b Tattersall	15
K. Taylor b Statham	15	—	b Tattersall	0
R. Illingworth c Jordan b Tattersall	16	—	b Tattersall	53
W. B. Stott c Pullar b Tattersall	44	—	b Tattersall	29
W. H. H. Sutcliffe c Jordan b Hilton	0	—	b Wharton	11
J. H. Wardle st Jordan b Hilton	0	—	b Statham	11
F. S. Trueman st Jordan b Hilton	0	—	not out	40
J. G. Binks not out	6	—	run out	10
M. Ryan b Tattersall	2	—	b Statham	1
			L-b 3	3

1/15 2/24 3/41 4/68 5/140 6/140   153
7/140 8/142 9/145 (2.25 an over)

1/4 2/12 3/12 4/63 5/98   183
6/117 7/128 8/134 9/179

Lancashire

A. Wharton c Wilson b Ryan	8	—	c Close b Trueman	16
G. A. Edrich c Binks b Trueman	4	—	c Lowson b Illingworth	31
J. T. Ikin b Illingworth	7	—	b Trueman	3
K. Grieves b Close	16	—	c Illingworth b Wardle	50
G. Pullar c Binks b Ryan	30	—	b Illingworth	0
C. Washbrook b Wardle	43	—	c Close b Wardle	41
R. Collins c Binks b Wardle	1	—	c and b Illingworth	8
M. J. Hilton lbw b Ryan	2	—	lbw b Illingworth	6
J. Jordan c Stott b Wardle	0	—	lbw b Trueman	0
J. B. Statham c Trueman b Wardle	1	—	not out	6
R. Tattersall not out	0	—	not out	0
W 1	1		B 3, l-b 10, n-b 1	14

1/9 2/17 3/22 4/46 5/109 6/109   113
7/110 8/110 9/113 (1.71 an over)

1/24 2/28 3/91   (9 wkts.) 175
4/136 5/148 6/159 7/162
8/162 9/168

Lancashire Bowling

	O.	M.	R.	W.		O.	M.	R.	W.
Statham	21	7	55	1	....	30.5	11	54	3
Wharton	10	5	19	2	....	8	1	32	1
Tattersall	23.3	8	49	3	....	39	23	51	5
Collins	8	1	24	0	....	2	0	6	0
Hilton	5	2	6	4	....	14	6	37	0
Ikin					....	1	1	0	0

Yorkshire Bowling

	O.	M.	R.	W.		O.	M.	R.	W.
Trueman	13	5	28	1	....	14	5	34	3
Ryan	13	4	13	3	....	7	1	35	0
Illingworth	8	4	17	1	....	12	5	31	4
Wardle	20.3	6	43	4	....	24	8	61	2
Close	11	5	11	1					

Umpires: T. J. Bartley and P. Corrall.

At Brentwood, June 12, 13, 14. LANCASHIRE lost to ESSEX by seven wickets.

LANCASHIRE v. SURREY

At Manchester, June 15, 17, 18. Surrey won by an innings and 51 runs, taking 14 points. On top throughout, they needed only ninety minutes of the third day to complete the victory. In glorious weather on the first day Surrey batted consistently against a well-sustained attack. May hit his century in two and three-quarter hours, including fourteen 4's. Lancashire began well, Wharton and Edrich making 97 for the first wicket. Then the left-arm slows of Lock caused a complete collapse. Lancashire followed on 217 behind and though the Surrey catching fell from its normal high standard, seven chances being wasted, Lock again proved too much for the batsmen.

Surrey

T. H. Clark c Bond b Tattersall....	30	E. A. Bedser not out	34
M. J. Stewart c Bond b Tattersall..	55	B 2, l-b 1	3
B. Constable c Edrich b Tattersall.	32		—
P. B. H. May c Bond b Tattersall..100			
D. G. W. Fletcher b Wharton	47	1/74 2/101 3/140 (5 wkts., dec.) 352	
K. F. Barrington not out.........	51	4/259 5/277 (2.90 an over)	

A. J. McIntyre, G. A. R. Lock, P. J. Loader and A. V. Bedser did not bat.

Lancashire

A. Wharton c Stewart b Lock	56	— lbw b Loader	47
G. A. Edrich lbw b Loader	39	— b A. Bedser	11
J. T. Ikin lbw b Lock	2	— b Lock	23
K. Grieves c McIntyre b A. Bedser ...	19	— b E. Bedser	2
G. Pullar lbw b Lock	4	— c May b Lock	37
J. D. Bond c E. Bedser b A. Bedser ...	12	— c and b Lock	9
R. Collins b E. Bedser	0	— c Barrington b Lock	5
J. Jordan b E. Bedser	0	— run out	26
J. B. Statham not out	0	— b Lock	0
R. Tattersall c Stewart b Lock	0	— c Constable b E. Bedser....	2
J. Roberts c and b Lock	0	— not out	0
L-b 3, n-b 1	4	B 1, l-b 3	4
	—		—
1/97 2/101 3/105 4/108 5/130 6/135	135	1/24 2/77 3/80 4/91 5/146	166
7/135 8/135 9/135 (1.87 an over)		6/151 7/163 8/163 9/166	

Lancashire Bowling

	O.	M.	R.	W.
Statham	30	5	61	0
Roberts	21	6	72	0
Wharton	16	2	58	1
Tattersall	44	7	135	4
Ikin...........	6	0	20	0
Collins	2	1	3	0

Surrey Bowling

	O.	M.	R.	W.	O.	M.	R.	W.
Loader	19	6	42	1	9	2	24	1
A. Bedser	17	6	27	2	18	7	33	1
Lock	22.4	8	37	5	26.1	11	78	5
E. Bedser	13	5	25	2	18	9	25	2
Clark					4	2	2	0

Umpires: E. Davies and H. Elliott.

LANCASHIRE v. CAMBRIDGE UNIVERSITY

At Liverpool, June 19, 20. Cambridge won by an innings and 31 runs. Despite good batting by McLachlan, the University lost eight men for 209 to a weakened Lancashire side, for whom Dyson bowled off-breaks well. Then Cook and Smith, who is qualified for Lancashire, added 200 in a splendid ninth wicket stand of two and a half hours. On a dusty pitch on the second day Lancashire failed twice against the University spin bowlers. The only consolation for the county was that Barber, who bowled leg-breaks skilfully, was also a Lancashire-qualified player, and Bond, a young player being tried in the senior eleven, exceeded 50 in each innings.

Cambridge University

R. W. Barber b Booth	19
I. M. McLachlan c and b Dyson	89
D. J. Green c Bond b Wharton	43
E. R. Dexter b Dyson	37
R. M. James b Hilton	2
P. D. Croft lbw b Dyson	4
S. A. U. Fakir b Dyson	6
P. I. Pieris c and b Dyson	0
G. W. Cook c Pullar b Hilton	111
C. S. Smith c Pullar b Dyson	87
B. T. Swift not out	2
B 13, l-b 2, n-b 1	16
	416

1/59 2/148 3/166 4/168 5/185
6/208 7/208 8/209 9/409

Lancashire

A. Wharton c and b Smith	4	— lbw b Dexter	16
J. Dyson c Green b Dexter	2	— c Dexter b Cook	16
J. D. Bond c Swift b Barber	53	— c Smith b Cook	59
A. Bolton b Smith	6	— not out	14
K. Grieves b Pieris	2	— b Pieris	3
G. Pullar c James b Cook	76	— c Fakir b Cook	17
B. Booth c Cook b Barber	0	— c Cook b Barber	4
G. A. Edrich b Pieris	26	— lbw b Pieris	24
J. Jordan c Smith b Barber	27	— b Barber	2
C. Hilton b Barber	0	— st Swift b Barber	0
J. Roberts not out	0	— b Smith	5
B 15, l-b 11	26	B 1, l-b 2	3
	222		163

1/4 2/6 3/25 4/28 5/150 6/154 7/168
8/222 9/222

1/29 2/56 3/101 4/127
5/137 6/142 7/142 8/146
9/146

Lancashire Bowling

	O.	M.	R.	W.
Roberts	5	2	18	0
C. Hilton	22	4	67	2
Wharton	23	7	42	1
Booth	36	7	133	1
Dyson	40.5	12	106	6
Bolton	3	0	17	0
Edrich	3	0	17	0

Cambridge University Bowling

	O.	M.	R.	W.		O.	M.	R.	W.
Smith	18	8	37	2	....	8.5	3	21	1
Dexter	6	5	2	1	....	6	1	20	1
Pieris	16	5	35	2	....	11	6	27	2
Cook	30	11	66	1	....	14	4	46	3
James	6	2	15	0					
Barber	17.2	7	41	4	....	11	1	46	3

Umpires: E. Davies and Harry Elliott.

At Leicester, June 22, 24, 25. LANCASHIRE lost to LEICESTERSHIRE by five wickets.

LANCASHIRE v. SOMERSET

At Manchester, June 26, 27. Lancashire won by an innings and 173 runs, taking 14 points. Re-discovering their early season form, Lancashire were always on top, apart from a break-down of the middle batting after Wharton and Dyson gave them a splendid start. Bond and Tattersall, in a ninth wicket stand, ensured an adequate total. Splendid fast bowling by Statham caused a Somerset first innings collapse, and when they followed on 247 behind the leg-breaks of Ikin, seldom employed at this stage of his career, quickly finished the match with a day to spare.

Lancashire

A. Wharton lbw b McMahon.....	83
J. Dyson c Stephenson b Alley....	88
J. T. Ikin c Tripp b Lobb........	29
C. Washbrook c Alley b McMahon	11
K. Grieves c Alley b Lobb........	0
G. Pullar c and b Hilton........	7
J. D. Bond c Tremlett b McMahon	72
M. J. Hilton b Lobb	4

J. B. Statham c McCool b Hilton..	3
R. Tattersall c McMahon b Hilton	10
A. Wilson not out	8
B 8, l-b 12, w 2	22

1/128 2/214 3/216 4/216 5/223 ... 337
6/238 7/252 8/259 9/328
(2.78 an over)

Somerset

J. G. Lomax c Grieves b Wharton	0	— b Wharton	5
W. E. Alley c Grieves b Statham	1	— c and b Ikin	8
P. B. Wight c Grieves b Statham	34	— c Grieves b Statham	16
G. M. Tripp c Wilson b Statham	0	— b Ikin	11
M. F. Tremlett b Tattersall	17	— b Statham..............	0
C. L. McCool b Tattersall	12	— c Wharton b Hilton	0
K. E. Palmer c Ikin b Statham	7	— c Hilton b Ikin	3
H. W. Stephenson lbw b Statham	0	— c Dyson b Hilton	20
J. Hilton c Wilson b Statham	0	— c Ikin b Statham	11
B. Lobb not out	17	— c Grieves b Ikin	0
J. W. McMahon b Tattersall	0	— not out	0
L-b 2	2		

1/1 2/2 3/34 4/65 5/65 6/67 7/68 ... 90
8/70 9/83 (1.80 an over)

1/10 2/28 3/29 4/33 5/37 ... 74
6/46 7/49 8/62 9/62

Somerset Bowling

	O.	M.	R.	W.	O.	M.	R.	W.
Lobb	26	5	46	3				
Alley	23	10	40	1				
Hilton	31.1	7	88	3				
Lomax	3	0	18	0				
McMahon	27	5	91	3				
McCool	11	2	32	0				

Lancashire Bowling

	O.	M.	R.	W.	O.	M.	R.	W.
Statham	18	9	19	6	10	4	12	3
Wharton	8	3	10	1	5	1	8	1
Tattersall	13.3	3	33	3	3	2	2	0
Hilton	5	3	8	0	18.5	10	34	2
Dyson	3	1	7	0				
Ikin	2	0	11	0	11	3	18	4

Umpires: N. Oldfield and R. S. Lay.

At Lord's, June 29, July 1, 2. LANCASHIRE beat MIDDLESEX by 72 runs.

At Northampton, July 6, 8. LANCASHIRE lost to NORTHAMPTONSHIRE by 59 runs.

LANCASHIRE v. SUSSEX

At Manchester, July 10, 11, 12. Drawn, the match being the first of the season in the county championship abandoned without a first innings decision. Despite the wet pitch, Lancashire batted consistently, but Sussex looked likely to make a close fight. Suttle, the left-hander, batted with admirable enterprise. More rain, however, prevented a resumption of the match after tea on the second day.

Lancashire

A. Wharton c Foreman b Marlar .. 33
J. Dyson b Suttle 28
J. T. Ikin c Parks b Foreman 35
C. Washbrook lbw b Suttle 12
K. Grieves b Foreman 24
J. D. Bond c Foreman b Suttle ... 17
M. J. Hilton st Mantell b Thomson 42
J. B. Statham b Thomson 22
A. Wilson c Lenham b Dexter 11

T. W. Greenhough c James b Marlar 16
R. Tattersall not out 11
B 15, l-b 4 19

1/64 2/86 3/106 4/147 5/148   270
6/178 7/227 8/236 9/254
(2.38 an over)

Sussex

L. J. Lenham c Wharton b Tattersall 9
D. V. Smith c Grieves b Tattersall 15
K. G. Suttle not out 58
J. M. Parks c Statham b Hilton... 26

E. R. Dexter not out 2

1/21 2/24 3/102   (3 wkts.) 110
(2.38 an over)

D. J. Foreman, G. Cogger, N. I. Thomson, A. E. James, R. G. Marlar and D. N. Mantell did not bat.

Sussex Bowling

	O.	M.	R.	W.
Thomson	12	2	43	2
Dexter	15	5	38	1
Cogger	3	1	8	0
James	8	2	12	0
Marlar	36.3	16	60	2
Suttle	28	7	67	3
Foreman	10	2	23	2

Lancashire Bowling

	O.	M.	R.	W.
Statham	9	1	28	0
Wharton	4	1	8	0
Tattersall	14	7	32	2
Hilton	13	7	25	1
Greenhough	4	0	17	0
Dyson	2	2	0	0

Umpires: J. Wood and N. Oldfield.

LANCASHIRE v. MIDDLESEX

At Manchester, July 13, 15, 16. Drawn, no decision. Compensation for the loss of the first two days through rain came with a brilliant hundred from Denis Compton, in his farewell season. After Middlesex lost three wickets for 25, Edrich and Compton added 127 in splendid style, and Compton hit three 6's and eleven 4's. With a chance of eight points, Lancashire disappointed their supporters by failing to accept the challenge to score 188 in a hundred and twenty-five minutes. After Wharton and Ikin fell at the same score, they played out time.

Middlesex

J. D. Robertson c Washbrook b Statham	5	F. J. Titmus not out 14
R. A. Gale c and b Statham	8	J. T. Murray not out 2
D. O. Baldry c Dyson b Tattersall	3	B 8, l-b 3 11
D. C. S. Compton run out 104		
W. J. Edrich c Hilton b Tattersall	40	1/6 2/23 3/25 (5 wkts., dec.) 187
		4/152 5/176 (2.79 an over)

D. Bennett, H. W. Tilly, R. J. Hurst and A. E. Moss did not bat.

Lancashire

A. Wharton b Hurst	30	B 1 1
J. Dyson not out	34	
J. T. Ikin b Hurst	0	
G. Pullar b Hurst	4	1/42 2/42 3/52 (3 wkts.) 78
K. Grieves not out	9	(2.23 an over)

C. Washbrook, J. D. Bond, M. J. Hilton, J. B. Statham, A. Wilson and R. Tattersall did not bat.

Lancashire Bowling

	O.	M.	R.	W.
Statham	20	2	61	2
Wharton	4	2	3	0
Tattersall	26	7	73	2
Hilton	11	5	25	0
Dyson	6	3	14	0

Middlesex Bowling

	O.	M.	R.	W.
Moss	4	2	5	0
Bennett	2	0	11	0
Titmus	9	3	14	0
Hurst	14	6	20	3
Compton	6	0	27	0

Umpires: J. Wood and C. A. Coleman.

At Maidstone, July 17, 18, 19. LANCASHIRE drew with KENT.

At Derby, July 20, 22, 23. LANCASHIRE drew with DERBYSHIRE.

LANCASHIRE v. LANCASHIRE LEAGUE XI

(Not First-class)

At Manchester, July 24, 25, 26. Drawn. Rain ruined this match, preventing any cricket after tea on the first day. With the League including four Test players—Reid (New Zealand), Fuller (South Africa), Fazal Mahmood (Pakistan) and Gupte (India)—a keen contest was anticipated. Reid and Entwistle gave the League a promising start with a stand of 50, but on a drying pitch the spin of Tattersall, Hilton and Dyson proved too much for the remainder who seemed uncertain whether to play their normal Saturday afternoon hitting game or adopt more cautious methods. When the County batted, Dyson took half an hour to open his score. M.C.C. decided in December, 1957, that this was not a first-class match.

Lancashire League

J. J. Reid c Bond b Hilton 28	S. P. Gupte b Dyson 0
S. Entwistle lbw b Tattersall 22	W. Horsfield b Tattersall 0
H. Dawson b Tattersall 5	D. Payne not out 0
V. E. Jackson c Bond b Tattersall.. 21	B 2 2
D. Hardman c Bond b Dyson..... 3	
D. Riley st Wilson b Hilton...... 14	
E. R. H. Fuller c Pullar b Tattersall 18	1/50 2/56 3/64 4/81 5/81 6/100 126
Fazal Mahmood lbw b Dyson 13	7/118 8/122 9/126

Lancashire

A. Wharton lbw b Mahmood 21	N-b 1 1
J. Dyson not out 8	
J. T. Ikin not out 2	1/26 (1 wkt.) 32

K. Grieves, G. Pullar, C. S. Smith, J. D. Bond, R. Tattersall, M. J. Hilton, A. Wilson and J. Roberts did not bat.

Lancashire Bowling

	O.	M.	R.	W.
Smith	8	1	22	0
Roberts	4	1	16	0
Tattersall	26.3	11	49	5
Hilton	22	10	23	2
Dyson	8	4	14	3

League Bowling

	O.	M.	R.	W.
Fazal Mahmood	8	1	20	1
Horsfield......	3	2	4	0
Fuller	4	1	7	0

LANCASHIRE v. ESSEX

At Manchester, July 27, 29, 30. Drawn, Essex taking four points. This was the fourth successive Lancashire home match spoiled by rain in July. No play was possible on Saturday and when Insole won the toss on Monday the three Essex seam bowlers, Bailey, Preston and Ralph, supported by splendid catching, needed only two and a half hours to dismiss Lancashire for 73. It was their lowest total in all matches against Essex and their lowest in county cricket for two years. The pitch eased with another rolling and with Dodds (eight 4's) hitting attractively and Bailey and Savill shaping confidently, Essex enjoyed a lead of 128 with half their wickets still standing at the close. A strained shoulder reduced Bailey to half speed on the last day when Wharton, Ikin, Washbrook and Grieves steered Lancashire into a safe position.

Lancashire

A. Wharton c Insole b Bailey	0	— c Barker b Bailey	30
J. Dyson c Ralph b Preston	3	— b Ralph	9
J. T. Ikin c Preston b Bailey	0	— c Taylor b Insole	51
C. Washbrook c Greensmith b Ralph ...	10	— not out	76
K. Grieves c Ralph b Preston	19	— not out	36
J. D. Bond lbw b Preston	4		
C. S. Smith b Preston	3		
M. J. Hilton c Greensmith b Preston ...	9		
J. Jordan b Ralph	0		
J. B. Statham c Insole b Ralph	14		
R. Tattersall not out	8		
B 2, l-b 1	3	B 2, l-b 1	3

1/0 2/0 3/6 4/27 5/36 6/37 7/46   73   1/32 2/46 3/150   (3 wkts.) 205
8/47 9/58 (1.69 an over)

Essex

T. C. Dodds c Wharton b Dyson..	58	W. T. Greensmith b Smith	2
G. Barker c Hilton b Dyson......	14	R. Ralph not out	0
B. Taylor st Jordan b Dyson.....	0	B 8, l-b 1	9
D. J. Insole b Hilton	22		
T. E. Bailey c Statham b Dyson..	41		
L. Savill b Statham.............	40	1/48 2/48 3/83 (9 wkts., dec.) 210
K. C. Preston b Smith	22	4/113 5/175 6/202 7/204 8/210
M. Bear c Jordan b Smith........	2	9/210 (2.61 an over)

I. King did not bat.

Essex Bowling

	O.	M.	R.	W.	O.	M.	R.	W.
Bailey	15	5	25	2	....	10	6	13	1
Preston........	16	5	34	5	....	11	1	34	0
Ralph	11.1	6	11	3	....	19	6	34	1
Greensmith ...						19	3	57	0
King						18	7	35	0
Insole						10	2	29	1

Lancashire Bowling

	O.	M.	R.	W.
Statham	17	2	41	1
Smith	11.2	2	33	3
Tattersall	12	5	23	0
Hilton	19	9	29	1
Dyson	20	5	75	4

Umpires: C. S. Elliott and A. Skelding.

LANCASHIRE v. NORTHAMPTONSHIRE

At Blackpool, July 31, August 1, 2. Northamptonshire won by 212 runs, taking 12 points. Superior all-round cricket, and astute captaincy by Brookes, who timed two declarations well, enabled Northamptonshire to complete the first "double" in their history over Lancashire. Brookes, batting four hours, laid sound foundations on the first day and shared a third wicket stand of 129 with Barrick. The varied left-arm spin of Allen, Tribe and Broderick proved too much for the Lancashire batsmen except the enterprising Wharton and Bond in their first innings. After more sound batting by Brookes, Tribe and Broderick, Lancashire collapsed against some more clever bowling by Tribe.

Northamptonshire

D. Brookes lbw b Greenough 103	— c Greenough b Smith	49
P. Arnold c Ikin b Greenough	26	— c Wharton b Smith	0
L. Livingston lbw b Greenough	12	— c Bond b Smith	9
D. W. Barrick c Jordan b Dyson	97	— c Bond b Greenough	9
B. L. Reynolds c Jordan b Greenough..	0	— c Grieves b Tattersall	0
G. E. Tribe c Wharton b Smith	9	— not out	59
V. Broderick b Tattersall	16	— lbw b Tattersall	34
K. V. Andrew not out.................	16	— not out	1
F. H. Tyson not out	1		
B 2, l-b 3, n-b 2	7	B 11, l-b 8	19

1/53 2/70 3/199 4/199 (7 wkts., dec.) 287	1/6 2/26 (6 wkts., dec.) 180
5/222 6/269 7/269 (2.51 an over)	3/43 4/46 5/92 6/168

M. H. J. Allen and M. Dilley did not bat.

Lancashire

A. Wharton c and b Allen	51	— c Andrew b Tyson	19
C. S. Smith lbw b Tyson	4	— c Allen b Tyson	0
J. T. Ikin b Tribe	16	— c Arnold b Tribe	27
C. Washbrook b Tribe	0	— c Livingston b Tribe	1
K. Grieves c Andrew b Allen	0	— c Allen b Tribe	0
J. D. Bond c Reynolds b Broderick	51	— lbw b Allen	11
J. Dyson run out	13	— run out	18
J. Jordan st Andrew b Allen	0	— absent hurt	0
J. B. Statham b Broderick	17	— c and b Tribe	6
T. Greenhough c Andrew b Broderick	0	— st Andrew b Tribe	0
R. Tattersall not out	0	— not out	4
B 6, l-b 4, n-b 1	11	B 2, l-h 4	6
	163		92

1/24 2/75 3/79 4/79 5/81 6/116 7/120
8/162 9/162 (2.62 an over)

1/1 2/28 3/41 4/41 5/51
6/65 7/79 8/88 9/92

Lancashire Bowling

	O.	M.	R.	W.		O.	M.	R.	W.
Statham	19	4	44	0	....	13.4	4	31	0
Smith	18	4	31	1	....	9	2	29	3
Wharton	4	0	9	0					
Tattersall	28	7	58	0	....	18	7	39	2
Greenhough	25	7	85	4	....	18	11	25	1
Ikin	3	0	18	0					
Dyson	17	6	35	1	....	7	1	37	0

Northamptonshire Bowling

	O.	M.	R.	W.		O.	M.	R.	W.
Tyson	13	4	33	0	....	10	0	31	2
Dilley	7	2	25	0	....	4	2	8	0
Allen	18	7	44	3	....	10	5	12	1
Tribe	23	8	48	2	....	13.5	5	30	5
Broderick	1.2	0	2	3	....	1	0	5	0

Umpires: N. Oldfield and A. Skelding.

At Sheffield, August 3, 5, 6. LANCASHIRE drew with YORKSHIRE.

LANCASHIRE v. NOTTINGHAMSHIRE

At Manchester, August 7, 8, 9. Drawn, Lancashire taking four points. Pullar, the left-hander, who batted four hours and hit twenty-one 4's by means of splendid driving and pulling, gave Lancashire a splendid start. He received good support from Grieves. After an early breakdown, Nottinghamshire easily saved the follow-on, despite a rain-soaked pitch on the second day. Then, following a declaration by each side, Nottinghamshire were set to make 192 in two and a half hours, a task which became out of the question when rain caused a further delay.

Lancashire

C. S. Smith st Millman b Morgan	35	— c Goonesena b Matthews .. 1
J. T. Ikin run out	15	— lbw b Jepson 22
G. Pullar st Millman b Vowles	137	— c Vowles b Jepson 22
C. Washbrook st Millman b Goonesena ..	0	— c Poole b Jepson 23
K. Grieves c Morgan b Vowles	59	— not out 17
J. D. Bond c Morgan b Vowles	5	— not out 15
P. Whitley c Morgan b Dooland	18	
T. Greenhough c Matthews b Dooland ..	5	
J. B. Statham c Millman b Goonesena ..	4	
A. Wilson run out	5	
R. Tattersall not out	1	
B 1, l-b 9	10	L-b 2 2

1/25 2/112 3/121 4/243 5/256 6/269   294   1/8 2/32   (4 wkts., dec.) 102
7/283 8/288 9/288 (2.42 an over)   3/61 4/71

Nottinghamshire

J. D. Springall c Grieves b Smith	24	— not out 10
G. Millman b Statham	6	— c Wilson b Smith 9
N. Hill c Greenhough b Whiteley	54	— not out 21
M. Hill b Smith	4	
C. J. Poole c Ikin b Statham	27	
B. Dooland b Statham	56	
G. Goonesena c Wilson b Smith	21	
R. C. Vowles not out	2	
A. Jepson c Statham b Smith	5	
M. Morgan not out	0	
L-b 3, n-b 3	6	N-b 1 1

1/21 2/32 3/36 4/86   (8 wkts., dec.) 205   1/16   (1 wkt.) 41
5/163 6/197 7/197 8/204 (2.32 an over)

C. S. Matthews did not bat.

Nottinghamshire Bowling

	O.	M.	R.	W.		O.	M.	R.	W.
Jepson	19	13	24	0	....	13	1	38	3
Matthews	16	4	35	0	....	7	0	19	1
Goonesena	26.1	6	63	2	....	2	1	7	0
Dooland	34	12	59	2	....	7	1	36	0
Morgan	19	4	64	1					
Vowles	7	0	39	3					

Lancashire Bowling

	O.	M.	R.	W.		O.	M.	R.	W.
Statham	17	6	34	3	....	2	1	2	0
Smith	22.2	6	61	4	....	3	1	12	1
Tattersall	25	10	47	0	....	8	2	15	0
Greenhough	12	5	21	0	....	1	1	0	0
Whiteley	12	3	36	1	....	8	5	11	0

Umpires: J. F. Crapp and H. G. Baldwin.

At Manchester, August 10, 12, 13. LANCASHIRE lost to WEST INDIES by nine wickets. (See WEST INDIES section.)

At Worthing, August 14, 15, 16. LANCASHIRE lost to SUSSEX by four wickets.

LANCASHIRE v. HAMPSHIRE

At Manchester, August 17, 19, 20. Lancashire won by 95 runs, taking 12 points; Hampshire took two points. Shackleton, Lancashire-born, bowled splendidly at fast-medium pace for Hampshire in both innings, but in vain. In the first innings Pullar alone showed real resistance, and the young left-hander followed with a splendid hundred, hitting one 6 and thirteen 4's. Although Hampshire succeeded in building a substantial lead, they could not score fast enough against keen bowling to gain bonus points, and they collapsed in their second innings when set to make 177 in two and a quarter hours.

Lancashire

J. T. Ikin b Heath	15	— b Shackleton	1
C. S. Smith b Shackleton	6	— b Shackleton	5
G. Pullar c Rayment b Heath	39	— run out	138
C. Washbrook lbw b Shackleton	13	— c Sainsbury b Shackleton	0
K. Grieves b Heath	1	— c Shackleton b Heath	1
J. D. Bond b Shackleton	4	— c Gray b Shackleton	52
P. Whiteley b Shackleton	0	— c Gray b Shackleton	32
J. B. Statham b Shackleton	1	— b Heath	4
A. Wilson not out	7	— not out	4
T. Greenhough b Shackleton	3	— c Harrison b Shackleton	7
R. Tattersall c Horton b Shackleton	0	— lbw b Shackleton	4
		B 4, l-b 1, w 1	6

1/21 2/21 3/45 4/46 5/53 6/55 7/69   89   1/6 2/13 3/15 4/16 5/131   250
8/85 9/89 (2.40 an over)   6/232 7/239 8/239 9/239

Hampshire

R. E. Marshall c Wilson b Statham	30	— c Wilson b Smith	10
J. R. Gray b Statham	0	— c Whiteley b Smith	2
H. Horton c Bond b Tattersall	27	— c Tattersall b Whiteley	7
A. W. H. Rayment b Greenhough	30	— run out	1
R. W. C. Pitman lbw b Greenhough	8	— b Greenhough	11
A. C. D. Ingleby-Mackenzie b Greenhough	9	— lbw b Greenhough	8
P. J. Sainsbury not out	25	— b Greenhough	0
L. Harrison b Tattersall	8	— b Greenhough	8
D. Shackleton c Wilson b Greenhough	10	— c Bond b Smith	12
M. Heath lbw b Statham	4	— not out	0
M. D. Burden b Statham	0	— b Statham	0
B 3, l-b 2, n-b 7	12	B 10, l-b 8, n-b 4	22

1/1 2/55 3/77 4/101 5/102 6/111   163   1/12 2/13 3/20 4/24 5/33   81
7/137 8/153 9/163 (2.11 an over)   6/33 7/47 8/70 9/72

Hampshire Bowling

	O.	M.	R.	W.	O.	M.	R.	W.
Shackleton	18.5	5	51	7	34.5	7	60	7
Heath	18	6	38	3	24	7	71	2
Gray					12	2	43	0
Burden					17	6	48	0
Sainsbury					13	4	22	0

Lancashire Bowling

	O.	M.	R.	W.	O.	M.	R.	W.
Statham	17.3	3	34	4	6.3	4	4	1
Smith	12	2	26	0	6	2	20	3
Tattersall	26	10	39	2	10	3	10	0
Greenhough	16	4	42	4	15	7	20	4
Whiteley	5	0	10	0	7	3	5	1

Umpires: Harry Elliott and T. J. Bartley.

At Nottingham, August 21, 22, 23. LANCASHIRE drew with NOTTINGHAMSHIRE.

At Bristol, August 24, 26, 27. LANCASHIRE drew with GLOUCESTERSHIRE.

LANCASHIRE v. WARWICKSHIRE

At Manchester, August 28, 29, 30. Lancashire won by six wickets, taking 12 points. They owed much to the splendid fast bowling of Statham, although generally rain-affected turf was more suitable to spin. That Lancashire gained first innings lead was due to a hard-hit innings of 91 by Wharton, but other batsmen were so subdued by the leg-spin of Hollies that no bonus points were obtained. Sustained hostility by Statham caused Warwickshire to be dismissed cheaply a second time before sound batting by Wharton and Ikin took Lancashire to a comfortable victory.

Warwickshire

F. C. Gardner c Wharton b Statham ...	17	— lbw b Statham 3
N. F. Horner lbw b Greenhough	20	— c Wilson b Statham 0
W. J. Stewart b Statham..............	4	— c Statham b Ikin 48
M. J. K. Smith b Statham.............	4	— b Statham........... 30
A. Townsend c Wharton b Collins	18	— c Bond b Collins 6
C. W. Leach c Bond b Tattersall	21	— b Statham........... 0
S. Singh c Collins b Tattersall	43	— b Statham........... 0
R. T. Spooner b Collins	21	— c Wilson b Statham 23
O. S. Wheatley not out	6	— c Barber b Tattersall 5
R. G. Thompson run out	0	— not out 5
W. E. Hollies c Ikin b Collins	10	— c Washbrook b Tattersall .. 0
B 12, l-b 3, n-b 1	16	L-b 1 1

1/37 2/41 3/46 4/49 5/67 6/138   180   1/1 2/18 3/65 4/88 5/88   121
7/139 8/168 9/168 (2.64 an over)   6/88 7/97 8/108 9/116

Lancashire

A. Wharton st Spooner b Hollies	91	— b Hollies 31
R. W. Barber b Hollies	34	— not out 20
G. Pullar c Stewart b Singh	2	— c Horner b Singh 12
J. T. Ikin b Hollies	0	— not out 34
C. Washbrook b Leach	6	— lbw b Wheatley 4
J. D. Bond b Wheatley	20	
R. Collins lbw b Wheatley	9	— c Spooner b Wheatley 8
T. Greenhough st Spooner b Hollies ...	11	
A. Wilson not out	3	
J. B. Statham b Wheatley	7	
R. Tattersall st Spooner b Hollies.......	4	
B 5, n-b 1	6	B 1................. 1

1/92 2/95 3/96 4/127 5/149 6/162   193   1/21 2/31   (4 wkts.) 110
7/177 8/181 9/188 (1.77 an over)   3/47 4/73

Lancashire Bowling

	O.	M.	R.	W.	O.	M.	R.	W.
Statham	24	5	46	3	16	6	22	6
Wharton	6	1	15	0	2	0	16	0
Tattersall	20	6	40	2	9.4	0	37	2
Greenhough ...	8	1	23	1	3	0	12	0
Collins	10	0	40	3	11	4	21	1
Ikin					6	3	12	1

Warwickshire Bowling

	O.	M.	R.	W.	O.	M.	R.	W.
Wheatley	20	7	42	3	14	0	50	2
Thompson	4	2	11	0				
Singh	35	20	69	1	6	3	9	1
Hollies	40.3	14	53	5	20	6	46	1
Leach	5	2	6	1				
Townsend	4	1	6	0				
Smith					0.2	0	4	0

Umpires: H. Elliott and C. A. Coleman.

LANCASHIRE v. WORCESTERSHIRE

At Blackpool, August 31, September 2. Lancashire won by an innings and 56 runs, taking 14 points. A lively pitch proved to the liking of Statham who, bowling with pace and life, troubled the Worcestershire batsmen in both innings. He received good support from Smith. Wharton and Barber, with a hard-hitting opening stand, put Lancashire in a strong position. Wharton batted nearly four hours and hit one 6 and fourteen 4's; Barber hit ten boundaries in his sparkling 50.

Worcestershire

D. Kenyon b Wharton	25	— c Wilson b Statham	2
P. E. Richardson c Wilson b Statham	0	— c Wilson b Statham	3
G. Dews c Wilson b Statham	6	— hit wkt b Tattersall	16
D. W. Richardson b Smith	2	— b Statham	2
L. Outschoorn lbw b Statham	1	— b Barber	26
M. J. Horton c Wilson b Statham	30	— b Smith	9
R. Booth b Ikin	11	— lbw b Smith	0
R. O. Jenkins lbw b Smith	15	— not out	20
R. Berry not out	8	— c Wilson b Statham	3
G. H. Chesterton b Smith	0	— run out	0
J. Flavell b Smith	0	— c Bond b Statham	13
B 4, l-b 5, n-b 2	11	L-b 4, n-b 1	5

1/7 2/18 3/27 4/34 5/44 6/84 7/90   **109**   1/2 2/7 3/9 4/37 5/50   **99**
8/109 9/109 (1.84 an over)   6/50 7/71 8/76 9/84

Lancashire

R. W. Barber st Booth b Horton	50	C. S. Smith b Chesterton	9
A. Wharton c D. Richardson b Horton	114	J. B. Statham not out	22
R. Collins b Flavell	20	R. Tattersall c Berry b Flavell	10
A. Wilson b Flavell	0	L-b 1	1
G. Pullar run out	19		
C. Washbrook lbw b Chesterton	14	1/102 2/140 3/140 4/186 5/205 **264**
J. T. Ikin b Horton	0	6/205 7/219 8/223 9/239
J. D. Bond c Booth b Flavell	5	(2.23 an over)

Lancashire Bowling

	O.	M.	R.	W.	O.	M	R.	W.
Statham	23	5	39	4	18.4	6	21	5
Smith	13.4	2	29	4	16	3	35	2
Wharton	9	3	15	1	2	0	6	0
Ikin	11	3	12	1	10	6	8	0
Tattersall	2	0	3	0	6	3	3	1
Collins					4	1	5	0
Barber					9	4	16	1

Worcestershire Bowling

	O.	M.	R.	W.
Flavell	24.3	5	79	4
Chesterton	21	5	52	2
Horton	35	17	69	3
Jenkins	2	0	12	0
Berry	35	17	51	0

Umpires: P. Corrall and T. W. Spencer.

At Blackpool, September 4, 5, 6. LANCASHIRE drew with WEST INDIES. (See WEST INDIES section.)

LEICESTERSHIRE

President—S. H. B. LIVINGSTON

Captain and Secretary—C. H. PALMER, Spencer Chambers.

4, Market Place, Leicester

M. R. Hallam   County Badge   J. van Geloven

Leicestershire were anxious for better fortune to mark the last season of Palmer as captain and secretary. Yet there was little foundation for optimism, as with the departure of Jackson to League cricket and the death of Tompkin, the talent at the disposal of the county was very limited. Furthermore, no young players of great promise, with the possible exception of Savage and Gardner, came to light.

The record over the season made dismal reading. Victory in only two matches left Leicestershire at the bottom of the Championship table again and only once, in the drawn match with Kent, did they earn bonus points. Bad luck could not be put forward as an excuse. Palmer won the toss in all the last fourteen games and the side actually batted first in each of the final 15 matches played, nine of which they lost. During that period the county led four times on first innings without ever scoring the faster. In all matches they were dismissed for under 100 on twelve occasions, including twice by the West Indies and once by the R.A.F., who won by an innings margin.

The batting was anything but dependable. Hallam in all matches scored over 2,000 runs for the first time in his career and hit four centuries but otherwise only Palmer exceeded 1,000 in Championship games. Lester had only three scores of over fifty in 56 innings and Firth, the wicket-keeper, could do little right. During one period of eight innings he failed to get off the mark six times. Van Geloven gave some stubborn displays after an indifferent start and Gardner, a neat, stylish right-handed batsman, impressed at times.

Rarely did the bowlers have any runs to play with. Spencer

and Boshier generally played their parts well in opening the attack. Boshier giving a fine performance in taking eight Essex first innings wickets for 45 runs at Brentwood. Savage, off-spin, who also took eight wickets against Gloucestershire, finished at the top of the county averages but the rest of the slow bowlers, including V. Munden, who was not re-engaged, accomplished little of note.

Palmer frequently resorted to "donkey-drops." These strange, high-tossed deliveries often surprised the opposition, and in the West Indies match accounted for Kanhai, Asgarali and Worrell. Palmer followed that game by hitting a splendid century against Essex on his last appearance at Leicester as captain, which was a fitting finale from one who had served the county well for eight years. To offset the loss of Palmer, Leicestershire engaged Watson from Yorkshire and Revill from Derbyshire for 1958.

GRACE ROAD   CRICKET GROUND   LEICESTER
by courtesy of City of Leicester Education Committee

LEICESTERSHIRE RESULTS

All First-Class Matches—Played 30, Won 3, Lost 17, Drawn 10

County Championship Matches—Played 28, Won 2, Lost 16,
Drawn 9, No Decision 1

COUNTY CHAMPIONSHIP AVERAGES
BATTING

	Birthplace	Mtchs.	Inns.	Not Outs	Runs	100's	Highest Inns.	Aver.
M. R. Hallam..	*Leicester*	27	52	1	1617	4	176	31.70
C. H. Palmer...	*Old Hill*	27	50	4	1208	3	117	26.26
J. van Geloven.	*Leeds*	23	44	3	849	0	63	20.70
R. A. Diment..	*Tortworth*	16	29	0	531	0	67	18.31
G. Lester......	*Long Whatton*	27	52	1	920	0	73	18.03
L. R. Gardner..	*Ledbury*	27	50	5	798	0	69*	17.73
P. Munden	*Leicester*	2	3	0	42	0	38	14.00
M. Hickman...	*Market Harborough*	8	14	0	152	0	38	10.85
V. Munden	*Leicester*	11	19	3	166	0	26*	10.37
J. Firth........	*Cottingley*	27	47	5	425	0	51	10.11
R. C. Smith....	*Stanford*	20	34	6	211	0	22	7.53
J. Goodwin....	*Audley*	7	12	8	29	0	10	7.25
C. T. Spencer..	*Leicester*	27	48	5	308	0	46	7.16
B. Boshier.....	*Leicester*	17	29	12	118	0	30	6.94
J. Savage......	*Ramsbottom*	24	41	3	258	0	33	6.78
P. Smith.......	*Leicester*	3	6	0	20	0	9	3.33
R. L. Pratt.....	*Stoney Stanton*	3	6	0	15	0	8	2.50

Also batted: E. F. Phillips (*Bridgnorth*) 1 and 27*.

* *Signifies not out.*

BOWLING

	Overs	Maidens	Runs	Wickets	Average
J. Savage	517.4	155	1436	75	19.14
B. Boshier	388.4	71	1081	51	21.19
C. H. Palmer	403.3	164	842	36	23.38
R. C. Smith............	373.3	140	829	35	23.68
C. T. Spencer	684.5	110	2049	75	27.32
J. van Geloven	172	41	461	16	28.81
V. Munden	205	80	497	17	29.23
J. Goodwin	182.5	28	576	19	30.31
R. L. Pratt	45	3	144	4	36.00
G. Lester	50	14	163	4	40.75

Amateurs.—R. A. Diment, C. H. Palmer.

LEICESTERSHIRE v. WORCESTERSHIRE

At Leicester, April 25, 26. Drawn. Leicestershire 194 (G. Lester 69, L. R. Gardner 54); Worcestershire 339 for seven wickets (P. E. Richardson 62, D. Kenyon 54). (Friendly match.)

LEICESTERSHIRE v. YORKSHIRE

At Leicestershire (Grace Road), May 8, 9, 10. Drawn, Leicester taking two points. Palmer, the Leicestershire captain, played a major part in a match otherwise spoiled by rain. On the first day he batted just over three and a half hours, hitting twenty 4's, and, after rain reduced the cricket on Thursday to twenty minutes, his bowling did much to deny Yorkshire the lead. Even so, Leicestershire could not contain the Yorkshire batsmen sufficiently to bring the extra reward for faster scoring. Sutcliffe hit two 6's and eleven 4's in a fine innings.

Leicestershire

G. Lester c Lowson b Platt	5	J. S. Savage b Platt	33
M. R. Hallam c Wilson b Wardle	50	C. T. Spencer b Platt	1
L. R. Gardner b Wardle	5	T. J. Goodwin not out	2
C. H. Palmer c Wilson b Wardle	117	B 3, l-b 12, n-b 1	16
M. Hickman b Wardle	0		
V. S. Munden b Wardle	15		—
J. van Geloven c Illingworth b Close	41	1/30 2/47 3/74 4/84 5/140 6/234	336
J. Firth lbw b Platt	51	7/254 8/317 9/319 (2.68 an over)	

Yorkshire

F. A. Lowson b Spencer	14	J. G. Binks b Palmer	9
D. B. Close c Firth b Palmer	62	R. K. Platt not out	2
J. V. Wilson c van Geloven b Palmer	22	B 7, l-b 2, n-b 4	13
D. E. V. Padgett c Hallam b Munden	26		
W. Watson c Palmer b Savage	24		
W. H. H. Sutcliffe b Munden	75		—
R. Illingworth c Goodwin b Munden	8	1/29 2/93 3/110 4/127 5/149	278
J. H. Wardle c and b Spencer	18	6/186 7/208 8/215 9/270	
F. S. Trueman c Hickman b Goodwin	5	(3.05 an over)	

Yorkshire Bowling	O.	M.	R.	W.
Trueman	25	6	63	0
Platt	23.1	10	48	4
Wardle	43	14	124	5
Close	21	7	47	1
Illingworth	13	1	38	0

Leicestershire Bowling	O.	M.	R.	W.
Spencer	17	2	57	2
Goodwin	14	1	71	1
Palmer	23.4	10	28	3
Savage	16	3	56	1
Munden	20	7	53	3

Umpires: T. W. Spencer and N. Oldfield.

LEICESTERSHIRE v. DERBYSHIRE

At Leicester (Aylestone Road), May 11, 13. Derbyshire won by an innings and 132 runs, taking 14 points. They were given a splendid start by Hamer and Lee, the Yorkshire-born opening pair, who put on 112, and the total assumed greater proportions when Gladwin, Jackson and Morgan each took a wicket in the final forty minutes of the first day. During that time Leicestershire scored only two runs, one for a wide, in eleven overs. Rain on Sunday ruined Leicestershire's chances of fighting back. On a drying pitch they had no answer to the off-spin of Smith, who took the last three wickets of the first innings in one over and six for 19 during the final seventy minutes' play after tea.

Derbyshire

A. Hamer c Goodwin b Spencer ..	31	
C. Lee c Spencer b Goodwin	83	
J. Kelly c Lester b Spencer	4	
A. C. Revill c Firth b Savage	25	
D. B. Carr c Hallam b Munden...	19	
G. O. Dawkes c Palmer b Goodwin	28	
H. L. Johnson c Hickman b Spencer	30	
D. C. Morgan c Lester b Goodwin .	14	

E. Smith not out	3
C. Gladwin c Firth b Spencer.....	0
L. Jackson run out	2
B 2, l-b 3	5

1/112 2/120 3/126 4/166 5/166   244
6/206 7/235 8/241 9/242
(2.80 an over)

Leicestershire

G. Lester b Jackson..................	6	— b Morgan	....	15
M. R. Hallam b Gladwin	0	— b Jackson	....	5
L. R. Gardner b Jackson	0	— lbw b Smith	....	10
C. H. Palmer b Morgan	0	— lbw b Morgan	....	1
M. Hickman b Gladwin	10	— b Smith	....	0
V. S. Munden c Gladwin b Morgan	1	— c Dawkes b Smith....		1
J. van Geloven not out	11	— c Carr b Smith	....	1
J. Firth c Carr b Jackson	12	— c Lee b Smith	....	9
J. S. Savage lbw b Smith	13	— b Smith	....	4
C. T. Spencer c Johnson b Smith	0	— c Jackson b Morgan	..	1
T. J. Goodwin c Dawkes b Smith	0	— not out	....	0
B 1, l-b 2, w 1.................	4	B 3, l-b 4, n-b 1.......		8

1/0 2/1 3/2 4/11 5/18 6/18 7/36   57
8/57 9/57 (0.86 an over)

1/10 2/33 3/34 4/37 5/37   55
6/39 7/42 8/54 9/55

Leicestershire Bowling

	O.	M.	R.	W.	O.	M.	R.	W.
Spencer	22.4	3	69	4				
Goodwin	23	3	69	3				
Palmer	4	0	8	0				
Munden	17	6	41	1				
Savage	20	7	52	1				

Derbyshire Bowling

	O.	M.	R.	W.	O.	M.	R.	W.
Jackson	18	13	8	3	8	7	1	1
Gladwin	19	13	9	2	6	2	7	0
Morgan	20	11	19	2	14.2	10	10	3
Smith	9	4	17	3	16	5	19	6
Carr..........					3	0	10	0

Umpires: T. W. Spencer and E. Davies.

LEICESTERSHIRE v. HAMPSHIRE

At Leicester (Aylestone Road), May 15, 16, 17. Hampshire won by nine wickets, taking 14 points. They owed much to Shackleton for their first victory of the season. He wrecked Leicestershire's chances of saving the game in a late spell of five wickets for 12 runs. Throughout, the bowlers, and mainly those of pace, held the upper hand on a pitch changing in character. Consequently, praise was due to Palmer, who, despite the handicap of lumbago, helped to rescue Leicestershire from a bad start. Marshall replied in his own inimitable style, hitting seven powerful 4's, and Sainsbury and Barnard added 52 in a spirited sixth wicket stand.

Leicestershire

G. Lester c Sainsbury b Cannings	6	— c Shackleton b Burden 31
M. R. Hallam b Shackleton	12	— b Shackleton 4
L. R. Gardner b Burden	37	— b Shackleton 0
C. H. Palmer c Sainsbury b Burden	49	— c Ingleby-Mackenzie b Burden 14
M. Hickman run out	0	— c Horton b Shackleton..... 11
V. S. Munden b Shackleton	7	— not out 26
J. van Geloven b Cannings	45	— c Eagar b Cannings 3
J. Firth lbw b Sainsbury	20	— lbw b Shackleton 0
J. S. Savage b Cannings	5	— c Harrison b Shackleton .. 2
R. L. Pratt lbw b Cannings	0	— b Shackleton 0
C. T. Spencer not out	2	— b Shackleton 16
B 1, l-b 4, n-b 1	6	

1/13 2/19 3/102 4/105 5/107 6/127   **189**
7/158 8/172 9/182 (1.53 an over)

1/5 2/5 3/12 4/43 5/63   **107**
6/63 7/63 8/69 9/71

Hampshire

R. E. Marshall c Hallam b Munden	58	— c Gardner b Spencer 13
J. R. Gray b Spencer	1	— not out 38
H. Horton b Spencer	0	— not out 28
E. D. R. Eagar c Palmer b Spencer	8	
A. C. D. Ingleby-Mackenzie b Spencer	0	
P. J. Sainsbury b Pratt	43	
H. M. Barnard lbw b Pratt	24	
L. Harrison c Spencer b Savage	24	
D. Shackleton c Gardner b Munden	32	
V. H. D. Cannings b Savage	0	
M. D. Burden not out	9	
B 6, l-b 10, n-b 2	18	L-b 1 1

1/17 2/17 3/47 4/53 5/88 6/140   **217**
7/147 8/197 9/198 (2.30 an over)

1/28   (1 wkt.)   **80**

Hampshire Bowling

	O.	M.	R.	W.		O.	M.	R.	W.
Shackleton	30	14	35	2	....	30	19	20	7
Cannings	26.4	10	41	4	....	19	9	22	1
Sainsbury	29	8	49	1					
Gray	10	5	10	0	....	3	1	12	0
Burden	25	9	39	2	....	27	11	53	2
Marshall	2	0	9	0					

Leicestershire Bowling

	O.	M.	R.	W.		O.	M.	R.	W.
Spencer	25	7	58	4	....	8	3	16	1
Pratt	20	3	62	2	....	8	0	24	0
Munden	26	11	46	2	....	4.1	0	8	0
Savage	20.5	9	27	2	....	10	4	15	0
Palmer	2	1	6	0					
van Geloven						5	1	6	0
Lester						2	0	10	0

Umpires: E. Davies and J. F. Crapp.

At Gloucester, May 18, 20, 21. LEICESTERSHIRE lost to GLOUCESTERSHIRE by 11 runs.

At Gravesend, May 22, 23, 24. LEICESTERSHIRE drew with KENT.

P

LEICESTERSHIRE v. SURREY

At Leicester (Grace Road), May 25, 27. Surrey won by 222 runs, taking 14 points and gaining victory inside two days for the third time in their last four matches. Leicestershire's satisfaction in dismissing their opponents fairly cheaply did not last long. Although Lock and Laker, opening the attack on a dusty surface, achieved little success at first, the batsmen were constantly in trouble as soon as A. Bedser and Loader came into the attack. Bedser took four wickets for 13 runs in an excellent spell of sixteen overs. A good third wicket stand of 121 between Clark (sixteen 4's) and May against bowlers unable to exploit a crumbling pitch enabled Surrey to declare midway through the afternoon of the second day. Then Lock, supplementing his five wickets with three good catches, and Laker further tormented Leicestershire with spin.

Surrey

T. H. Clark b Spencer	18	— c Hallam b Lester		93
M. J. Stewart b Munden	43	— c Hickman b Savage		24
K. Barrington c Spencer b Savage	26	— c Palmer b Munden		6
P. B. H. May b Munden	8	— c van Geloven b Savage		58
M. D. Willett c Gardner b Savage	0	— c Lester b Savage		0
E. A. Bedser c Savage b Palmer	18	— not out		25
A. J. McIntyre b Savage	0	— not out		37
G. A. R. Lock c and b Spencer	41			
J. C. Laker b Spencer	0			
P. J. Loader not out	24			
A. V. Bedser b Palmer	8			
B 5, l-b 5	10	B 4, l-b 1		5

1/39 2/79 3/99 4/99 5/106 6/106   196   1/37 2/56   (5 wkts., dec.) 248
7/162 8/162 9/162 (3.76 an over)   3/177 4/185 5/185

Leicestershire

G. Lester lbw b Loader	25	— c Stewart b Loader		4
M. R. Mallam b A. V. Bedser	11	— lbw b Lock		40
J. van Geloven c Stewart b Lock	6	— c Lock b Laker		9
C. H. Palmer c Lock b A. V. Bedser	28	— lbw b Lock		26
L. R. Gardner hit wkt b Loader	22	— c Lock b Laker		2
V. S. Munden lbw b A. V. Bedser	0	— c E. A. Bedser b Laker		0
M. Hickman c Willett b Lock	1	— c Lock b Laker		0
J. Firth c McIntyre b A. V. Bedser	1	— c Barrington b Lock		12
J. S. Savage b E. A. Bedser	13	— c Barrington b Lock		3
C. T. Spencer b E. A. Bedser	0	— c McIntyre b Lock		1
B. S. Boshier not out	5	— not out		1
B 6, l-b 1, n-b 3	10	L-b 1, w 1		2

1/22 2/30 3/53 4/85 5/85 6/90 7/95   122   1/7 2/41 3/55 4/76 5/82   100
8/114 9/115 (1.74 an over)   6/83 7/83 8/97 9/99

Leicestershire Bowling

	O.	M.	R.	W.		O.	M.	R.	W.
Spencer	14	3	50	3	....	7	0	28	0
Boshier	5	0	20	0	....	2	0	10	0
van Geloven	6	2	16	0					
Savage	12	1	64	3	....	24	5	79	3
Palmer	5.3	2	10	2	....	10	4	23	0
Munden	9	3	26	2	....	22	9	52	1
					Lester	10	2	51	1

Surrey Bowling

	O.	M.	R.	W.	O.	M.	R.	W.
Lock	21	8	48	2	14	3	33	5
Laker	20	9	21	0	13	5	32	4
A. V. Bedser	16	9	13	4	4	0	7	0
Loader	11	4	22	2	5	1	26	1
E. A. Bedser	2.2	2	8	2				

Umpires: W. E. Phillipson and P. A. Gibb.

LEICESTERSHIRE v. R.A.F.

At Melton Mowbray, May 29, 30. R.A.F. won by an innings and 17 runs. Leicestershire 143 (G. Lester 53, R. Subba Row four for 33) and 99 (Subba Row four for 22); Royal Air Force 259 (Subba Row 106, B. R. Knight 87, C. T. Spencer four for 88).

At Hove, June 1, 3, 4. LEICESTERSHIRE beat SUSSEX by 99 runs.

LEICESTERSHIRE v. GLAMORGAN

At Coalville, June 5, 6. Glamorgan won by an innings and 52 runs, taking 14 points. Hedges, mastering pace and spin, gave them an excellent start, hitting seventeen 4's during an innings of four and a quarter hours. Wooller and McConnon added 78 for the seventh wicket. Leicestershire were always struggling against bowlers able to make the occasional ball lift and well supported in the field. They lost all twenty wickets on the second day. Shepherd proved the most successful bowler for Glamorgan.

Glamorgan

W. G. A. Parkhouse lbw b Palmer .	16	H. G. Davies c Firth b Palmer .	4
B. Hedges c Firth b Goodwin .	128	H. D. Davies not out .	9
W. E. Jones b van Geloven .	47	D. J. Shepherd c and b van Geloven	5
L. N. Devereux c van Geloven b Spencer	36	B 9, l-b 11, w 1 .	21
A. J. Watkins c Firth b Spencer	10		—
J. Pressdee b Spencer	8	1/35 2/169 3/225 4/244 5/259	369
W. Wooller c Firth b van Geloven	34	6/266 7/344 8/349 9/355	
J. F. McConnon b van Geloven .	51	(3.41 an over)	

Leicestershire

G. Lester c Devereux b H. D. Davies .	15	— c Hedges b McConnon .	40
M. R. Hallam b Wooller .	23	— c and b H. D. Davies .	9
J. van Geloven c Devereux b H. D. Davies	0	— c Hedges b Shepherd .	27
C. H. Palmer b Shepherd .	17	— c H. G. Davies b Shepherd .	0
L. R. Gardner run out .	0	— c McConnon b Devereux .	40
R. A. Diment c H. G. Davies b H. D. Davies	54	— lbw b McConnon .	10
J. Firth c Wooller b Shepherd .	34	— c Wooller b Shepherd .	10
R. C. Smith c H. G. Davies b Devereux .	6	— c H. G. Davies b Shepherd .	4
C. T. Spencer c Pressdee b Devereux .	8	— c and b Devereux .	5
J. Goodwin not out .	0	— b Shepherd .	5
J. S. Savage c Watkins b Devereux .	0	— not out .	0
L-b 3, n-b 3 .	6	L-b 3, n-b 1 .	4

1/20 2/20 3/56 4/56 5/56 6/125 7/142   163
8/163 9/163 (2.54 an over)

1/10 2/60 3/64 4/83 5/113   154
6/134 7/144 8/144 9/154

Leicestershire Bowling

	O.	M.	R.	W.	O.	M.	R.	W.
Spencer	28	2	98	3				
Goodwin	28	5	83	1				
Palmer	15	3	44	2				
Savage	5	2	26	0				
Smith	11	2	43	0				
van Geloven	21	6	54	4				

Glamorgan Bowling

	O.	M.	R.	W.		O.	M.	R.	W.
H. D. Davies	11	2	55	3	....	8	1	39	1
Wooller	9	4	14	1	....	2	0	11	0
Shepherd	22	9	41	2	....	14	8	22	5
McConnon	8	4	15	0	....	10	5	21	2
Pressdee	3	2	4	0	....	10	2	28	0
Watkins	6	3	8	0	....	6	3	3	0
Devereux	4.4	0	20	3	....	18.2	7	26	2

Umpires: N. Oldfield and T. J. Bartley.

At Northampton, June 8, 10, 11. LEICESTERSHIRE lost to NORTHAMPTONSHIRE by an innings and 29 runs.

LEICESTERSHIRE v. KENT

At Leicester, June 12, 13, 14. Drawn, Leicestershire taking four points. With Hallam, last out, hitting one 6 and thirty-one 4's in five hours' batting for his highest score, Leicestershire were in a good position, but although Spencer followed with spirited fast bowling the effort was not sustained. Cowdrey, dropped off an easy chance when 28, and Dixon added 71 for the seventh wicket and Kent restricted their arrears to 52. Spencer also proved capable with the bat when promoted in the order on the second day, but by then Leicestershire had surrendered much of the advantage. On the last day Allan, of Kent, was no-balled once and Palmer, of Leicestershire, twice for having more than five fieldsmen on the leg-side. They were the first to be "called" for this offence since the new rule came into force at the start of the season.

Leicestershire

G. Lester lbw b Ridgway	14	— lbw b Wright	45
M. R. Hallam c Evans b Wright	176	— b Page	6
L. R. Gardner b Ridgway	0	— st Evans b Allan	6
C. H. Palmer b Page	11	— run out	1
J. van Geloven b Wright	5	— b Ridgway	6
R. A. Diment c Evans b Pretlove	34	— b Wright	17
M. Hickman b Pretlove	12	— lbw b Allan	0
J. Firth lbw b Wright	10	— not out	24
R. C. Smith c and b Wright	0	— b Allan	9
C. T. Spencer b Wright	3	— c Wilson b Allan	46
T. J. Goodwin not out	4	— b Page	10
B 17, l-b 6, n-b 2	25	B 9, l-b 4, n-b 1	14

1/22 2/22 3/81 4/104 5/183 6/235   294   1/14 2/27 3/28 4/60 5/119   184
7/251 8/251 9/266 (3.06 an over)   6/122 7/138 8/149 9/159

Kent

A. H. Phebey lbw b Spencer	27	— b Palmer	22
R. C. Wilson c Diment b Palmer	23	— c van Geloven b Palmer	50
J. M. Allan b Spencer	7		
J. F. Pretlove c Hallam b Lester	3	— not out	1
M. C. Cowdrey c Firth b Goodwin	73	— b Palmer	33
S. Leary lbw b Goodwin	32	— st Firth b van Geloven	12
T. G. Evans c Diment b Palmer	3	— c Spencer b van Geloven	12
A. L. Dixon b Spencer	52	— b van Geloven	1
F. Ridgway lbw b Palmer	6	— not out	0
D. V. P. Wright not out	7		
J. C. T. Page b Spencer	3		
B 4, l-b 1, n-b 1	6	B 16, l-b 11, n-b 2	29

1/35 2/52 3/59 4/77 5/139 6/145 242 1/60 2/73 3/134 (6 wkts.) 160
7/216 8/223 9/238 (2.30 an over) 4/147 5/153 6/153

Kent Bowling

	O.	M.	R.	W.		O.	M.	R.	W.
Ridgway	9	5	20	2	....	21	9	28	1
Page	27	9	90	1	....	16	8	35	2
Wright	25.3	7	87	5	....	18	5	64	2
Dixon	7	3	27	0					
Pretlove	13	8	22	2					
Allan	14	6	23	0	....	14	2	43	4

Leicestershire Bowling

	O.	M.	R.	W.		O.	M.	R.	W.
Spencer	30.1	9	56	4	....	14	3	29	0
Goodwin	17	3	52	2					
Palmer	30	12	64	3	....	21	8	54	3
Lester	9	5	21	1	....	4	3	1	0
Smith	15	5	35	0	....	3	3	0	0
van Geloven	4	2	8	0	....	17	5	47	3

Umpires: C. S. Elliott and W. E. Phillipson.

At Brentwood, June 15, 17, 18. LEICESTERSHIRE lost to ESSEX by 181 runs.

At Oxford, June 19, 20, 21. LEICESTERSHIRE beat OXFORD UNIVERSITY by ten wickets.

LEICESTERSHIRE v. LANCASHIRE

At Leicester, June 22, 24, 25. Leicestershire won by five wickets, taking 12 points to Lancashire's four. They looked badly placed in a low-scoring game when needing 71 for victory with only five wickets left, but Palmer and Gardner hit off the runs without being parted. Lancashire, after losing four men for 45. were saved from complete failure by a stand of 70 between Grieves and Pullar, Leicestershire in turn broke down against spin bowling. Then Boshier, the six-feet-five-inches-tall fast bowler, started another Lancashire collapse by taking five of the first six wickets at a personal cost of 16 runs. Left to score 141, Leicestershire owed much to the skill of their captain. With wristy late cuts and good off-drives, Palmer did most of the scoring while Gardner played defensively.

Lancashire

A. Wharton lbw b Boshier	29	— c Hallam b Palmer	33
J. Dyson c Diment b Boshier	9	— c P. Smith b Boshier	3
J. T. Ikin c Firth b Boshier	6	— c Spencer b Boshier	0
J. D. Bond b Spencer	1	— b Boshier	8
K. Grieves lbw b Palmer	47	— c and b Boshier	12
G. Pullar c Munden b Palmer	21	— c Palmer b Spencer	27
G. A. Edrich b R. Smith	7	— b Boshier	0
J. Jordan not out	10	— run out	31
R. Tattersall b R. Smith	2	— c Gardner b Palmer	3
T. Greenhough b Palmer	0	— c Hallam b R. Smith	6
C. Hilton c Hallam b R. Smith	0	— not out	0
B 1, l-b 2, n-b 1	4	B 6, l-b 5	11

1/29 2/40 3/45 4/45 5/115 6/120   136
7/126 8/128 9/129 (1.86 an over)

1/10 2/10 3/30 4/60 5/61   134
6/62 7/103 8/118 9/134

Leicestershire

G. Lester c Wharton b Hilton	3	— c Grieves b Tattersall	6
M. R. Hallam b Tattersall	12	— b Dyson	21
P. Smith b Greenhough	9	— b Tattersall	2
C. H. Palmer run out	18	— not out	47
L. R. Gardner b Greenhough	9	— not out	27
R. A. Diment c Edrich b Tattersall	10	— c Greenhough b Dyson	23
V. S. Munden b Tattersall	26		
J. Firth c Jordan b Dyson	8		
R. T. Smith run out	0		
C. T. Spencer c Ikin b Tattersall	13	— c Hilton b Tattersall	10
B. Boshier not out	1		
B 15, l-b 4, n-b 2	21	B 2, l-b 2, w 1	5

1/6 2/18 3/44 4/56 5/57 6/72 7/103   130
8/106 9/125 (1.54 an over)

1/12 2/38 3/61   (5 wkts.) 141
4/66 5/70

Leicestershire Bowling

	O.	M.	R.	W.		O.	M.	R.	W.
Spencer	13	2	30	1	....	17	4	54	1
Boshier	20	7	47	3	....	15	3	42	5
Palmer	16	8	20	3	....	13	7	18	2
Munden	4	4	0	0					
R. Smith	20.2	12	35	3	....	3.3	0	9	1

Lancashire Bowling

	O.	M.	R.	W.		O.	M.	R.	W.
Hilton	10	4	18	1	....	5	0	28	0
Wharton	1	0	3	0					
Tattersall	40	18	39	4	....	24.1	5	56	3
Greenhough	9	2	24	2	....	1	0	4	0
Dyson	24	13	25	1	....	20	6	40	2
			Ikin			3	1	8	0

Umpires: R. S. Lay and P. Corrall.

LEICESTERSHIRE v. SOMERSET

At Leicester, June 29, July 1. Somerset won by 58 runs, taking 12 points. Two poor batting sides had no answer to the turning ball on a dusty pitch and on the second day 23 wickets fell for 153 runs. Leicestershire, needing 100 to win, were dismissed for 41 in one hour twenty-five minutes by Langford, off-breaks, and McMahon, left-arm slow. They bowled throughout the innings, Langford taking five wickets for 15 runs (nine for 60 in the match) and McMahon five wickets for 24 runs. Earlier on the last day Leicestershire had been warned of the difficulties ahead by the success of their own off-spinner, Savage, whose analysis of six wickets for 28 runs gave him match figures of eleven for 81.

Somerset

J. G. Lomax c Diment b R. Smith	....	36	— b Spencer	....	5
J. Hilton b R. Smith	....	4	— c Firth b Boshier	....	3
P. B. Wight b Savage	....	30	— b Savage	....	18
G. M. Tripp c Firth b R. Smith	....	18	— c Spencer b Boshier	......	0
C. L. McCool b Savage	....	0	— c Spencer b Savage	....	30
G. Atkinson b Savage	....	29	— c Lester b Savage	....	6
M. F. Tremlett c Firth b Savage	....	24	— b Savage	....	22
H. W. Stephenson b R. Smith	....	5	— c and b Savage	....	1
B. Langford b R. Smith	....	1	— st Firth b Savage	....	2
B. Lobb b Savage	....	0	— c Firth b R. Smith	......	2
J. W. McMahon not out	....	0	— not out	....	0
B 1, l-b 2		3	B 6		6

1/36 2/61 3/81 4/85 5/109 6/139   150   1/6 2/12 3/13 4/35 5/66   95
7/144 8/150 9/150 (2.112 an over)   6/77 7/81 8/92 9/95

Leicestershire

G. Lester lbw b McMahon	....	5	— lbw b McMahon	....	10
M. R. Hallam b Hilton	....	27	— lbw b McMahon	....	1
P. Smith lbw b Langford	....	1	— lbw b Langford	....	6
C. H. Palmer c McCool b McMahon	..	19	— b McMahon	....	5
L. R. Gardner c Atkinson b Langford	..	12	— lbw b McMahon	......	1
R. A. Diment b McMahon	....	22	— c Atkinson b Langford	.....	0
J. Firth c Tripp b Langford	....	10	— not out	....	2
J. Savage c Tripp b Hilton	....	18	— b McMahon	....	4
R. Smith c Wight b Langford	....	21	— c Wight b Langford	......	0
C. T. Spencer c Stephenson b Lobb	..	3	— c McCool b Langford	.....	3
B. Boshier not out	....	0	— c Hilton b Langford	......	7
B 4, l-b 4		8	B 2		2

1/26 2/37 3/41 4/67 5/79 6/91 7/118   146   1/10 2/11 3/16 4/16 5/23   41
8/133 9/146 (2.115 an over)   6/27 7/28 8/32 9/33

Leicestershire Bowling

	O.	M.	R.	W.		O.	M.	R.	W.
Spencer	9	5	10	0	....	7	1	21	1
Boshier.......	9	0	31	0	....	7	1	10	2
Palmer	6	2	9	0					
R. Smith	28.1	15	44	5	....	15.4	4	30	1
Savage	19	3	53	5	....	16	5	28	6

Somerset Bowling

	O.	M.	R.	W.		O.	M.	R.	W.
Lobb	6	1	6	1					
Langford	30.1	16	45	4	....	13.3	6	15	5
McMahon	26	5	63	3	....	13	6	24	5
Hilton	7	2	24	2					

Umpires: J. Wood and W. Place.

At Bournemouth, July 3, 4, 5. LEICESTERSHIRE lost to HAMPSHIRE by four wickets.

At Birmingham, July 6, 8, 9. LEICESTERSHIRE lost to WARWICKSHIRE by four wickets.

At Hull, July 10, 11, 12. LEICESTERSHIRE lost to YORKSHIRE by an innings and 12 runs.

LEICESTERSHIRE v. SUSSEX

At Ashby-de-la-Zouch, July 13, 15, 16. Drawn, Leicestershire taking two points. A rain-affected match was notable for a fine duel between Smith, the Sussex opening batsman, and the Leicestershire bowlers. Facing a total of 150, the product of careful batting on a pitch of varying pace, Sussex lost Sheppard, who was playing in his first Championship match of the season, at 19 and only the skill of Smith saved them from complete disaster. He stayed just over two hours, hitting two 6's off Palmer and six 4's in scoring 61 out of a total of 91. Boshier, bowling throughout an innings of two hours ten minutes, caused trouble with his hostile pace, and Savage, off-breaks, took the last three wickets, including that of Smith, in five balls. Hallam supported his bowlers with fine batting before the rain intervened. No play was possible on the last day.

Leicestershire

G. Lester lbw b Suttle	14	— c Sheppard b Bates	13
M. R. Hallam c Suttle b Marlar	28	— not out	71
R. A. Diment c Sheppard b Thomson	23		
C. H. Palmer b Suttle	0		
L. R. Gardner c Parks b Dexter	49		
J. van Geloven b Suttle	3	— not out	27
J. Firth lbw b Bates	11		
J. Savage c Smith b Thomson	3		
R. Smith lbw b Dexter	2		
C. T. Spencer run out	10		
B. Boshier not out	3		
B 2, l-b 1, n-b 1	4	B 4, l-b 1	5
	150	(1 wkt.)	116

1/39 2/43 3/47 4/76 5/104 6/107   1/27
7/133 8/136 9/144 (1.57 an over)

Sussex

D. V. Smith b Savage	61	N. I. Thomson run out	5
Rev. D. S. Sheppard c Firth b Boshier	6	R. G. Marlar not out	3
K. G. Suttle lbw b Palmer	4	D. N. Mantell b Savage	0
J. M. Parks c Firth b Boshier	6	D. L. Bates c van Geloven b Savage	0
E. R. Dexter b Palmer	1	B 1, l-b 1, n-b 1	3
D. J. Foreman c Spencer b Boshier	0		
G. Cogger b Boshier	2		91

1/19 2/27 3/46 4/53 5/58 6/68
7/75 8/91 9/91 (2.60 an over)

Sussex Bowling

	O.	M.	R.	W.	O.	M.	R.	W.
Thomson	23	12	22	2	15	5	29	0
Bates	16	6	33	1	10	3	25	1
Suttle	20	11	21	3	5	2	9	0
Marlar	17	7	33	1	9	1	33	0
Foreman	10	3	15	0				
Dexter	9	2	22	2	2	0	4	0
Smith					5	1	11	0

Leicestershire Bowling

Spencer	5	0	26	0
Boshier	17	5	31	4
Palmer	12	5	31	2
Savage	0.5	0	0	3

Umpires: W. F. Price and D. Davies.

At The Oval, July 17, 18, 19. Leicestershire lost to Surrey by ten wickets.

LEICESTERSHIRE v. WARWICKSHIRE

At Hinckley, July 20, 22, 23. Drawn, Warwickshire taking four points. Leicestershire, who lost their last six first innings wickets for 25 runs, struggled against the accuracy of Hollies. On a slow surface, this leg-break bowler did not concede a run during one spell of 78 balls and Ibadulla supported him well. Lester alone faced this pair successfully, staying four hours ten minutes. On Monday, Warwickshire had to fight hard for the lead on a drying pitch and the last batsmen were together when Griffiths put them ahead by sweeping Savage for 6. Van Geloven batted well in Leicestershire's second innings and Warwickshire needed 164 to win, but with the game in an interesting position rain intervened.

Leicestershire

G. Lester c Gardner b Ibadulla	73	— b Carter	11
M. R. Hallam b Griffiths	12	— b Hollies	36
J. van Geloven c and b Ibadulla	28	— lbw b Ibadulla	62
C. H. Palmer b Hollies	7	— c Smith b Ibadulla	0
L. R. Gardner lbw b Hollies	34	— b Ibadulla	10
V. S. Munden not out	10	— c Cartwright b Ibadulla	0
J. Firth c Carter b Ibadulla	1	— c Cartwright b Hollies	8
J. Savage lbw b Ibadulla	4	— b Hollies	0
R. Smith b Hollies	3	— not out	15
C. T. Spencer st Lewis b Hollies	4	— st Lewis b Hollies	10
B. Boshier b Hollies	0	— c Lewis b Ibadulla	4
B 5, l-b 1, w 1	7	B 4, l-b 3, n-b 1	8

1/26 2/71 3/85 4/158 5/161 6/162   183
7/166 8/169 9/183 (1.67 an over)

1/28 2/76 3/77 4/101   164
5/101 6/120 7/120 8/140
9/157

Warwickshire

F. C. Gardner c van Geloven b Savage	26	— b Spencer	8
N. F. Horner c Firth b Spencer	4	— lbw b Savage	33
W. J. Stewart c Boshier b Savage	23	— c Gardner b Savage	19
M. J. K. Smith b Savage	43	— c Spencer b Savage	1
A. Townsend c Gardner b Smith	6	— not out	22
T. W. Cartwright c Spencer b Palmer	22	— lbw b Savage	12
K. Ibadulla not out	23	— not out	2
R. G. Carter b Munden	8		
E. B. Lewis b Munden	1		
W. E. Hollies c and b Savage	1		
S. S. Griffiths b Savage	14		
B 10, l-b 3	13	B 3, l-b 5, n-b 1	9

1/6 2/42 3/53 4/60 5/119 6/141 7/154   184
8/161 9/162 (1.93 an over)

1/32 2/50 3/68   (5 wkts.) 106
4/69 5/90

Warwickshire Bowling

	O.	M.	R.	W.		O.	M.	R.	W.
Carter	21	4	55	0		9	2	39	1
Griffiths	12	1	33	1		4	1	8	0
Ibadulla	34	12	52	4		30.5	13	49	5
Hollies	36.3	22	30	5		38	17	60	4
Townsend	5	2	6	0					

Leicestershire Bowling

	O.	M.	R.	W.		O.	M.	R.	W.
Spencer	9	4	16	1		8	0	22	1
Boshier	15	8	21	0		7	3	21	0
Palmer	11	6	16	1		3.3	1	8	0
Savage	29.4	9	71	5		10	3	34	4
Smith	12	7	30	1					
Munden	18	12	17	2		6	3	12	0

Umpires: T. J. Bartley and D. J. Wood.

At Stourbridge, July 24, 25, 26. LEICESTERSHIRE lost to WORCESTERSHIRE by an innings and 73 runs.

At Taunton, July 27, 29, 30. LEICESTERSHIRE drew with SOMERSET.

At Chesterfield, July 31, August 1. LEICESTERSHIRE lost to DERBYSHIRE by an innings and 123 runs.

LEICESTERSHIRE v. NORTHAMPTONSHIRE

At Leicester, August 3, 5, 6. Northamptonshire won by eight wickets, taking 14 points and reaching a total of 150 points in the County Championship for the first time. Victory would have been even more emphatic but for Palmer, who was top scorer for Leicestershire in both innings. Skill and concentration brought him a sorely needed 50 on the first day when his colleagues groped on a pitch sometimes producing lift for the seamers and occasionally helping the spin bowlers. Allen, left-arm slow, caused the final collapse with five wickets for four runs in 35 deliveries. Northamptonshire, helped by good scores from the later batsmen, led by 73 runs. Leicestershire started the last day only 23 ahead with half the side out but the bespectacled Palmer, although worried by misty rain, attacked scientifically, hitting 35 of the 36 runs added in half an hour. During this period Tribe, also left-arm slow, took three wickets with his first four balls.

Leicestershire

G. Lester c Andrew b Kelleher	7	— c and b Allen		13
M. R. Hallam b Tyson	23	— c Andrew b Tyson		5
J. van Geloven b Tribe	39	— c Tyson b Kelleher		8
C. H. Palmer c Kelleher b Tribe	50	— not out		79
L. R. Gardner lbw b Allen	20	— lbw b Broderick		25
R. A. Diment lbw b Allen	7	— b Tyson		0
J. Firth b Tyson	0	— b Tribe		0
J. Savage b Allen	9	— b Tribe		0
R. Smith lbw b Allen	0	— b Tribe		0
C. T. Spencer b Allen	4	— b Tyson		0
B. Boshier not out	1	— run out		1
B 1, l-b 5, n-b 1	7	W 1		1

1/13 2/44 3/110 4/131 5/145 6/146   167   1/9 2/18 3/37 4/86 5/87   132
7/155 8/155 9/166 (2.25 an over)   6/96 7/96 8/96 9/101

Northamptonshire

D. Brookes c Diment b Boshier	2	— c Diment b Spencer		17
P. Arnold c Hallam b Savage	55	— not out		23
L. Livingston lbw b Spencer	19	— b Spencer		11
D. W. Barrick b Boshier	0	— not out		9
B. L. Reynolds c van Geloven b Spencer	34			
G. E. Tribe b Smith	24			
V. Broderick b Smith	1			
K. V. Andrew b Savage	23			
F. H. Tyson b Boshier	40			
M. H. J. Allen lbw b Savage	26			
H. R. A. Kelleher not out	3			
B 7, l-b 4, n-b 2	13			

1/3 2/26 3/27 4/101 5/132 6/140   240   1/26 2/46   (2 wkts.) 60
7/149 8/198 9/232 (2.44 an over)

Northamptonshire Bowling

	O.	M.	R.	W.		O.	M.	R.	W.
Tyson	17	3	43	2	....	15	0	61	3
Kelleher	19	6	44	1	....	10	4	13	1
Tribe	21	5	55	2	....	12	4	35	3
Broderick	8	6	9	0	....	9	2	15	1
Allen	8.5	6	9	5	....	11	6	7	1

Leicestershire Bowling

	O.	M.	R.	W.		O.	M.	R.	W.
Spencer	15	5	32	2	....	7	0	36	2
Boshier	24	4	64	3	....	6.5	0	24	0
Palmer	16	6	36	0					
Savage	23.1	4	61	3					
Smith	20	8	34	2					

Umpires: J. S. Buller and John Langridge.

LEICESTERSHIRE v. GLOUCESTERSHIRE

At Leicester, August 7, 8, 9. Drawn, Gloucestershire taking four points. Despite spirited resistance for over three hours by van Geloven (twelve 4's) Leicestershire were poorly placed at the end of the first day. Gloucestershire led by 44 runs with seven first innings wickets left, Nicholls and Graveney having put on 143 in one hundred minutes for the third wicket. Graveney, in a flawless innings which included one 6 and fourteen 4's, finished within five of a century. He added only two runs to his score on a rainy second day when the Leicestershire attack made good use of changing conditions. Even so, Gloucestershire were still in a favourable position when rain washed out the final day.

Leicestershire

G. Lester c Etheridge b Smith	2	— not out 35
M. R. Hallam c Brown b Smith	9	— c Etheridge b Brown 17
J. van Geloven st Etheridge b Mortimore	63	— not out 20
C. H. Palmer c Graveney b Mortimore	11	
L. R. Gardner c Milton b Allen	0	
R. A. Diment c Nicholls b Cook	10	
C. T. Spencer c Nicholls b Cook	0	
J. Firth b Mortimore	0	
J. Savage c Young b Mortimore	0	
R. Smith not out	13	
B. Boshier c Milton b Brown	30	
B 1, l-b 1	2	B 2, l-b 1 3

1/10 2/11 3/49 4/50 5/77 6/77 7/77   140   1/20   (1 wkt.) 75
8/77 9/102 (1.75 an over)

Gloucestershire

G. M. Emmett c Gardner b Spencer	0	D. Smith c Smith b Boshier 9
D. M. Young c Firth b Boshier	16	R. Etheridge c Savage b Spencer.. 4
R. B. Nicholls b Smith	62	C. Cook not out 1
T. W. Graveney b Savage	97	L-b 5, w 1, n-b 1 7
C. A. Milton c Firth b Smith	28	
A. Brown c Hallam b Smith	0	1/0 2/32 3/175 4/189 5/190 241
J. Mortimore c Firth b Smith	0	6/190 7/211 8/236 9/236
D. A. Allen c Diment b Boshier	17	(3.39 an over)

Gloucestershire Bowling

	O.	M.	R.	W.		O.	M.	R.	W.
Smith	18	6	35	2	....	8	2	15	0
Brown	10	4	19	1	....	6	1	20	1
Cook	18	9	30	2	....	11	6	22	0
Mortimore	25	16	38	4	....	6	4	6	0
Allen	9	4	16	1	....	7.3	4	9	0

Leicestershire Bowling

	O.	M.	R.	W.
Spencer	16	1	58	2
Boshier	20	4	62	3
Smith	23	2	77	4
Savage	10	3	26	1
Palmer	2	0	11	0

Umpires: F. S. Lee and T. J. Bartley.

LEICESTERSHIRE v. WORCESTERSHIRE

At Loughborough, August 10, 12, 13. Drawn, Leicestershire taking two points. Neither side was able to score at an entertaining rate on a pitch noted for its help to seam bowlers. Sixteen Leicestershire wickets fell to Flavell and Chesterton and only van Geloven and Palmer in a third wicket stand of 72 in the second innings mastered the attack for any period. Worcestershire were equally unconvincing. When set to score 176 runs in two and three-quarter hours to win, they were glad of a sound innings by D. Richardson, who met spin and pace with certainty during the last two hours. A fine catch by Spencer provided one of the few highlights. Fielding at forward short leg, he dived sideways at incredible speed to hold a ball inches from the turf when Dews made a fierce hit at a "donkey-drop" from Palmer.

Leicestershire

G. Lester c D. Richardson b Chesterton	46	— c Booth b Horton	14
M. R. Hallam b Horton	6	— b Chesterton	0
J. van Geloven st Booth b Berry	23	— b Flavell	58
C. H. Palmer c Horton b Berry	0	— c P. Richardson b Chesterton	58
L. R. Gardner lbw b Flavell	6	— c Booth b Chesterton	5
R. A. Diment c P. Richardson b Chesterton	39	— c Broadbent b Flavell	3
J. Firth lbw b Flavell	0	— b Flavell	1
J. Savage c Booth b Flavell	6	— b Flavell	4
R. Smith b Chesterton	0	— not out	0
C. T. Spencer c Outschoorn b Chesterton	7	— c P. Richardson b Chesterton	10
B. Boshier not out	0	— c Kenyon b Chesterton	4
B 6, l-b 3	9	B 5	5

1/23 2/73 3/73 4/84 5/89 6/91 7/135   142
8/135 9/142 (1.42 an over)

1/2 2/37 3/109 4/130   162
5/137 6/139 7/144 8/157
9/162

Worcestershire

D. Kenyon b Spencer	7	— b Spencer	16
P. E. Richardson b Boshier	13	— c Firth b Spencer	5
G. Dews b Spencer	15	— c Spencer b Palmer	7
D. W. Richardson b Boshier	6	— not out	47
R. G. Broadbent b Savage	48	— c van Geloven b Spencer	11
L. Outschoorn c Spencer b Palmer	17	— st Firth b Smith	6
M. J. Horton c Palmer b Savage	12	— lbw b Smith	0
R. Booth c van Geloven b Smith	8	— not out	5
J. Flavell b Savage	0		
G. H. Chesterton lbw b Savage	0		
R. Berry not out	0		
B 1, n-b 2	3	B 4, l-b 4, w 1, n-b 1 ..	10

1/10 2/22 3/43 4/45 5/89 6/120 7/121   129   1/13 2/25 3/33   (6 wkts.) 107
8/121 9/123 (1.63 an over)   4/60 5/90 6/94

Worcestershire Bowling

	O.	M.	R.	W.		O.	M.	R.	W.
Flavell	13	6	37	3	....	20	4	38	4
Chesterton	17.5	7	26	4	....	25.5	14	58	5
Horton	38	24	35	1	....	19	6	37	1
Berry	30	16	27	2	....	11	2	24	0
P. Richardson	1	0	8	0					

Leicestershire Bowling

	O.	M.	R.	W.		O.	M.	R.	W.
Spencer	14	2	30	2	....	12	5	19	3
Boshier	17	6	34	2	....	7	2	21	0
Savage	16	8	27	4	....	11	8	10	0
Smith	18.4	6	25	1	....	11	2	27	2
Palmer	13	9	10	1	....	8	2	20	1

Umpires: L. H. Gray and R. S. Lay.

At Lord's, August 14, 15, 16. MIDDLESEX v. LEICESTERSHIRE. No play because of rain.

At Leicester, August 17, 19, 20. LEICESTERSHIRE lost to WEST INDIES by an innings and 212 runs. (See WEST INDIES section.)

LEICESTERSHIRE v. ESSEX

At Leicester, August 21, 22, 23. Drawn, Leicestershire taking two points. The match will be remembered for the efforts of Palmer. On his last appearance at Leicester before retiring from county cricket he gave his side a good send-off by winning the toss for the thirteenth successive time and then playing one of his best innings of the summer. Concentrating for just over four and a half hours against tight bowling, Palmer hit twelve 4's in a fine century. Savage, the off-spinner, backed up his captain with excellent bowling which included one spell of four wickets for seven runs in two overs and it seemed that Palmer might mark his farewell with victory. Rain, however, thwarted him after he had set Essex to score 247 runs in three hours ten minutes. Phillips, a young batsman from Shropshire, showed great promise in Leicestershire's second innings.

Leicestershire

G. Lester c and b Greensmith	26	— run out	19
M. R. Hallam c Bailey b Greensmith	42	— c Preston b King	74
R. A. Diment st Taylor b Greensmith	40	— b King	20
C. H. Palmer c Preston b Bailey	103	— c Dodds b King	7
L. R. Gardner b Insole	4	— b Preston	19
E. F. Phillips lbw b Bailey	1	— not out	27
J. Firth b Bailey	10	— not out	14
J. Savage b Ralph	4		
C. T. Spencer b Bailey	10	— c Savill b Preston	1
R. L. Pratt c Durley b Bailey	4	— c Bailey b Preston	0
R. Smith not out	0		
B 10, l-b 4	14	B 2, l-b 4, w 1	7

1/68 2/80 3/139 4/171 5/179 6/211   258   1/26 2/66 (7 wkts., dec.) 188
7/236 8/248 9/252 (2.11 an over)   3/82 4/127 5/139 6/146
                                                         7/147

Essex

T. C. Dodds c Spencer b Pratt	11	K. C. Preston lbw b Savage	6
G. Barker c Hallam b Savage	44	J. A. Bailey c and b Smith	15
B. Taylor c Spencer b Pratt	0	I. M. King not out	1
D. J. Insole b Smith	8	B 8, l-b 4, n-b 2	14
L. Savill c Hallam b Savage	40		
W. T. Greensmith c Spencer b Savage	61		
A. Durley b Savage	0	1/23 2/23 3/69 4/75 5/166	200
R. Ralph b Savage	0	6/166 7/173 8/174 9/189	
		(2.40 an over)	

Essex Bowling

	O.	M.	R.	W.		O.	M.	R.	W.
Preston	21	5	45	0	....	16	1	55	3
Ralph	21	3	70	1	....	5	0	15	0
Bailey	32	8	68	5	....	7	2	12	0
Greensmith	26	13	36	3	....	16	2	49	0
King	19	12	24	0	....	26	10	50	3
Insole	3	2	1	1					

Leicestershire Bowling

	O.	M.	R.	W.
Spencer	18	5	35	0
Pratt	8	0	28	2
Smith	20	9	43	2
Savage	28	11	69	6
Palmer	9	5	11	0

Umpires: J. F. Crapp and H. G. Baldwin.

At Nottingham, August 24, 26, 27. LEICESTERSHIRE lost to NOTTINGHAMSHIRE by one wicket.

MIDDLESEX

President—R. H. TWINING
Hon. Secretary—F. G. MANN, Lord's Cricket Ground,
St. John's Wood Road, London, N.W.8
Captain—W. J. EDRICH

J. D. Robertson   County Badge   J. T. Murray

Season 1957 saw the end of an important chapter in the history of Middlesex. The previous year several established players dropped out, but last summer brought the finish of regular cricket for Denis Compton as a professional and the retirement from the captaincy of W. J. Edrich, who had led the side for the past five years. He also shared the position with Compton in 1951 and 1952.

Once more Middlesex lacked consistency. They lost twelve Championship matches, even more than Worcestershire, who finished one from bottom, but against that they won ten games and only three of the matches were drawn. In addition three games ended without a result on first innings because of the weather. An astonishing sequence of results at the start of the season showed the unreliability of the side. The first eleven Championship matches resulted as follows: Won, Lost, Won, Lost, Won, Lost, Lost, Won, Won, Lost, Lost. The first draw did not come until the end of June. Whatever the deficiencies of the side, it could not be said that they lacked the essential will to win. Always in the upper half of the table, Middlesex were never far away from their final position of seventh, a decline of two places compared with 1956.

Pitches at Lord's helped bowlers throughout the season and this caused the high number of finished matches. Middlesex were concerned in only two games which failed to bring a result there— that against West Indies and the fixture with Leicestershire in August when not a ball could be bowled. Fast-medium bowlers gained most benefit and for a long time the spinners received few opportunities. Titmus took only 38 wickets in the first two months of the season, but later more use was found for his off-breaks and for the third year running he completed the "double." Hurst, the slow left-hander, bowled with economical effectiveness.

Batting often let down the side, but no fault could be found with Robertson who, at the age of 40, returned to his best form and enjoyed his most successful season since 1952. For the ninth time he scored over 2,000 runs in all first-class games in a season. His opening partner, the left-handed Gale, also played many fine and attractive innings, but his big scores were interspersed with periods when he did little of note. Many of the displays of Compton were not far short of his best which made his decision to give up regular cricket because of his knee even more regrettable.

The season brought special distinction to Murray, the wicket-keeper, who became only the second player in history to score 1,000 runs and claim 100 victims.

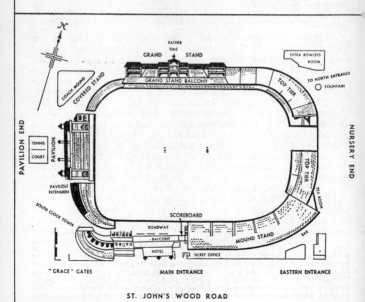

LORD'S CRICKET GROUND

MIDDLESEX RESULTS

All First-Class Matches—Played 31, Won 11, Lost 13, Drawn 7

County Championship Matches—Played 28, Won 10, Lost 12,
Drawn 3, No Decision 3

COUNTY CHAMPIONSHIP AVERAGES
BATTING

	Birthplace	Mtchs.	Inns.	Not Outs	Runs	100's	Highest Inns.	Aver.
D. C. S. Compton	Hendon	20	37	0	1404	3	143	37.94
J. D. Robertson	Chiswick	27	50	1	1852	3	201*	37.79
W. J. Edrich...	Lingwood	26	46	2	1016	0	77	23.09
A. C. Walton..	British Guiana	8	15	0	341	0	59	22.73
J. T. Murray...	Kensington	26	46	3	908	1	120	21.11
R. Gale	Old Warden	26	48	0	997	1	126	20.77
F. J. Titmus...	Kentish Town	27	49	3	952	0	70	20.69
T. Angus	Gateshead	2	4	2	34	0	18*	17.00
G. P. S. Delisle.	St. Kitts	14	27	4	388	0	76*	16.86
D. Bennett.....	Wakefield	26	42	8	564	0	51*	16.58
D. O. Baldry...	Acton	11	19	0	313	0	61	16.47
J. J. Warr.....	Ealing	24	36	12	277	0	40*	11.54
R. J. Hurst.....	Hampton Hill	27	37	16	155	0	16	7.38
H. W. Tilly...	Edmonton	3	4	0	28	0	21	7.00
A. E. Moss....	Tottenham	25	33	8	139	0	24	5.56
D. A. Bick.....	Hampstead	2	4	0	13	0	10	3.25

Also batted: R. W. Hooker (*Shoreditch*) 7 and 0; M. E. L. Melhuish (*Westcliff*) 1 and 3; W. E. Russell (*Glasgow*) 6 and 8.

* *Signifies not out.*

BOWLING

	Overs	Maidens	Runs	Wickets	Average
A. E. Moss	600.5	137	1628	94	17.31
R. J. Hurst	556.4	204	1404	72	19.50
F. J. Titmus	705.4	206	1758	88	19.97
J. J. Warr	606.3	148	1465	68	21.54
T. Angus	23	6	45	2	22.50
D. C. S. Compton	268.2	55	838	35	23.94
D. O. Baldry	44	12	104	4	26.00
D. Bennett.............	385.4	69	1092	41	26.63
R. Gale	13	1	64	2	32.00
W. J. Edrich	76.2	21	173	5	34.60

Also bowled: J. D. Robertson 6—0—17—1; H. W. Tilly 19—5—61—4.

Amateurs.—G. P. S. Delisle, W. J. Edrich, M. E. L. Melhuish, A. C. Walton, J. J. Warr.

MIDDLESEX v. NOTTINGHAMSHIRE

At Lord's, May 4, 6, 7. Middlesex won by 115 runs, taking 14 points. They began their first game by losing three wickets for 24 runs, but eventually won comfortably. Nottinghamshire, without Simpson and Stocks, were unfortunate to lose Walker, who returned home suffering from mumps, after he had caused Middlesex trouble by taking seven wickets for 56 runs, the best performance of his career. Murray and Bennett rescued Middlesex, who turned the tables by bringing about a Nottinghamshire collapse on a pitch which always helped fast bowlers. Dooland resisted for two hours, but Middlesex led by 53 and consolidated the position with consistent batting against a weakened attack. Needing 324, Nottinghamshire made Middlesex work hard for victory but they were always fighting a losing battle.

Middlesex

J. D. Robertson c Millman b Walker....	15	— b Dooland	80
R. A. Gale b Walker	0	— c and b Smales	21
W. J. Edrich c Millman b Walker	8	— c Harvey b Smales	26
F. J. Titmus lbw b Walker	26	— c C. Poole b Dooland	45
J. T. Murray c C. Poole b Walker	65	— lbw b Dooland	6
G. P. S. Delisle c K. Poole b Walker....	0	— c Harvey b Jepson	43
R. W. Hooker c Millman b Walker	7	— lbw b Smales	0
D. Bennett c Millman b Smales	46	— c Smales b Jepson	46
J. J. Warr b Jepson	15	— b K. Poole	1
R. J. Hurst b Smales	12	— not out	0
A. E. Moss not out	0		
B 2, l-b 2	4	L-b 2	2

1/1 2/23 3/24 4/95 5/99 6/116   **198**   1/48 2/84 (9 wkts., dec.) **270**
7/125 8/153 9/189 (2.78 an over)   3/144 4/158 5/189 6/191
7/256 8/270 9/270

Nottinghamshire

R. J. Giles c Titmus b Moss	6	— b Moss	9
J. D. Clay lbw b Moss	1	— c Edrich b Titmus	32
H. M. Winfield c Titmus b Warr	27	— b Moss	26
C. J. Poole c Edrich b Moss	18	— c Edrich b Titmus	11
P. F. Harvey b Moss	21	— c Moss b Titmus	34
B. Dooland b Moss	50	— lbw b Hurst	14
K. J. Poole b Bennett	18	— c Hooker b Hurst	19
G. Millman c Murray b Warr	1	— not out	15
A. E. Jepson not out	0	— c Delisle b Warr	4
K. Smales lbw b Warr	0	— b Moss	15
A. K. Walker absent ill	—	— absent ill	—
B 3	3	B 13, l-b 13, n-b 3	29

1/6 2/9 3/33 4/65 5/91 6/119   **145**   1/26 2/69 3/86 4/91   **208**
7/139 8/145 9/145 (2.07 an over)   5/144 6/152 7/174 8/203
9/203

Nottinghamshire Bowling

	O.	M.	R.	W.		O.	M.	R.	W.
Walker	21	3	56	7					
Jepson	18	5	45	1	....	24.1	4	65	2
K. Poole	9	1	26	0	....	25	2	117	1
Dooland	21	5	56	0	....	14	2	42	3
Smales	1.4	0	11	2	....	13	4	44	3

Middlesex Bowling

	O.	M.	R.	W.		O.	M.	R.	W.
Moss	19.3	5	51	5		17	5	40	3
Bennett	18	3	43	1	....	9	1	29	0
Warr	22	7	31	3	....	11.5	4	19	1
Titmus	10	3	17	0	....	27	11	47	3
				Hurst		13	4	44	2

Umpires: J. Langridge and J. Wood.

MIDDLESEX v. KENT

At Lord's, May 8, 9, 10. Kent won by an innings and 59 runs, taking 12 points. Middlesex were outplayed and their only satisfaction was that by scoring faster in the first innings they deprived Kent of two points. Kent were given a great start by Phebey and Wilson who scored 179, and good innings by Leary, Pretlove and Evans enabled them to declare and capture two wickets cheaply before the close. Trapped on a difficult pitch on the second day Middlesex attempted to hit their way out of trouble. Compton and Edrich were the only batsmen to reach double figures and Middlesex followed on 238 behind. Compton made his second fifty of the match, but Kent won comfortably before lunch on the last day. The ball often rose nastily and Kent used a slow bowler, Wright, for only six overs in the match.

Kent

A. H. Phebey c Murray b Moss ..	86	J. Pettiford not out 1
R. C. Wilson c Edrich b Titmus...	92	G. Smith not out 0
J. F. Pretlove c Robertson b Hurst	41	B 13, l-b 8, w 1, n-b 2 24
M. C. Cowdrey c Warr b Moss ...	0	
S. E. Leary c Murray b Titmus ...	60	
T. G. Evans c Delisle b Titmus ...	37	1/179 2/205 (8 wkts., dec.) 346
F. Ridgway b Titmus	3	3/208 4/290 5/336 6/345 7/345
D. J. Halfyard c Murray b Moss..	0	8/345 (3.32 an over)

D. V. P. Wright did not bat.

Middlesex

J. D. Robertson lbw b Halfyard	4	— c Halfyard b Ridgway ..	22
R. A. Gale b Ridgway	1	— b Halfyard	21
R. J. Hurst c Evans b Halfyard	0	— c Halfyard b Smith	0
A. E. Moss c Leary b Ridgway	4	— c Evans b Smith	2
W. J. Edrich c Smith b Halfyard	36	— c Evans b Ridgway	0
D. C. S. Compton b Halfyard	50	— st Evans b Smith	53
F. J. Titmus c Wilson b Smith	2	— c Evans b Halfyard	19
J. T. Murray c Ridgway b Smith	5	— c Leary b Smith	22
G. P. S. Delisle c Phebey b Smith.......	0	— c Wright b Halfyard	23
D. Bennett c and b Halfyard	2	— b Halfyard	3
J. J. Warr not out	0	— not out	12
B 4	4	B 1, n-b 1	2

1/5 2/5 3/5 4/11 5/69 6/78 7/95   108   1/28 2/28 3/63 4/66   179
8/95 9/108 (3.6 an over)   5/123 6/134 7/159 8/165
                                   9/166

Middlesex Bowling

	O.	M.	R.	W.	O.	M.	R	W.
Moss	22	3	84	3				
Warr.........	20	3	64	0				
Bennett	5	1	24	0				
Titmus	32	5	95	4				
Hurst	19	7	40	1				
Compton	6	0	15	0				

Kent Bowling

	O.	M.	R.	W.		O.	M.	R	W.
Ridgway	6	2	28	2	....	12	3	39	2
Halfyard	14.4	2	46	5	....	21	7	61	4
Smith	9	2	30	3	....	13.3	2	47	4
					Wright ...	6	0	30	0

Umpires: P. A. Gibb and H. G. Baldwin.

MIDDLESEX v. GLOUCESTERSHIRE

At Lord's, May 11, 13, 14. Middlesex won by 135 runs, taking 14 points. They made the most of their fortune in batting first on a good pitch which later proved ideal for spin bowlers. Gale hit well when helping Edrich add 123 in one hundred minutes for the second wicket and Compton completed his third fifty in successive innings. Graveney gave a masterly display in saving Gloucestershire from complete collapse. He took out his bat for 101 (seventeen 4's) scored in three and a half hours. Hawkins alone gave him much support in a fifth wicket stand of 80. Leading by 116, Middlesex also struggled, but Gloucestershire, set to get 250, again broke down. Hurst took eleven wickets for 80. As in the corresponding game in 1956, Graveney scored a century and 0.

Middlesex

J. D. Robertson c Carpenter b Lambert .	1	—	c Lambert b Cook		37
R. A. Gale c Hawkins b Wells	82	—	c Nicholls b Wells		17
W. J. Edrich c Carpenter b Smith	76	—	c Young b Cook		0
D. C. S. Compton c Hawkins b Wells	50	—	c Carpenter b Cook		26
F. J. Titmus c Rochford b Smith	26	—	c Emmett b Cook		16
J. T. Murray b Smith	43	—	b Wells		19
G. P. S. Delisle b Smith	23	—	not out		2
D. Bennett b Smith	6	—	c Graveney b Cook		8
J. J. Warr b Lambert	11				
R. J. Hurst b Lambert	0				
A. E. Moss not out	0				
B 6, l-b 4	10		B 7, l-b 1		8

1/2 2/125 3/214 4/215 5/282 6/289   **329**   1/31 2/31   (7 wkts., dec.) **133**
7/316 8/323 9/324 (3.16 an over)   3/73 4/93 5/110 6/118 7/133

Gloucestershire

D. M. Young c Bennett b Warr	8	—	c Titmus b Hurst		35
D. Carpenter b Moss	6	—	lbw b Warr		0
T. W. Graveney not out	101	—	c Murray b Warr		0
G. M. Emmett c Delisle b Warr	2	—	b Titmus		0
R. B. Nicholls lbw b Warr	19	—	lbw b Hurst		26
D. Hawkins b Hurst	40	—	st Murray b Hurst		4
G. E. Lambert c Gale b Hurst	0	—	c Titmus b Hurst		4
D. R. Smith lbw b Titmus	8	—	c Compton b Hurst		14
P. Rochford c Murray b Hurst	2	—	c Murray b Titmus		4
C. Cook c Murray b Hurst	10	—	not out		7
B. D. Wells c Murray b Hurst	8	—	st Murray b Hurst		4
B 4, l-b 5	9		B 14, l-b 2		16

1/11 2/25 3/35 4/75 5/145 6/145   **213**   1/12 2/12 3/70 4/71 5/71   **114**
7/156 8/159 9/189 (2.76 an over)   6/75 7/82 8/99 9/109

Gloucestershire Bowling

	O.	M.	R.	W.		O.	M.	R.	W.
Lambert	19.1	3	67	3	....	4	0	12	0
Smith	29	8	73	5	....	5	2	9	0
Wells	30	7	87	2	....	20	2	58	2
Cook	23	4	85	0	....	18.5	5	46	5
Hawkins	3	1	7	0					

Middlesex Bowling

	O.	M.	R.	W.		O.	M.	R.	W.
Moss	13	3	34	1	....	4	0	20	0
Warr	25	9	55	3	....	6	3	7	2
Bennett	5	0	22	0					
Hurst	13.1	3	47	5	....	20.3	9	33	6
Titmus	21	1	46	1	....	23	10	38	2

Umpires: A. E. Pothecary and A. Skelding.

At Portsmouth, May 18, 20, 21. MIDDLESEX lost to HAMPSHIRE by three runs.

At Oxford, May 22, 23, 24. MIDDLESEX lost to OXFORD UNIVERSITY by four wickets.

MIDDLESEX v. SOMERSET

At Lord's, May 25, 27, 28. Middlesex won by nine runs, taking twelve points to four gained by Somerset. Seam bowlers dominated the match. Lobb and Alley (Somerset) and Moss and Warr (Middlesex) made the most of a pitch which remained helpful throughout, and they were further aided on the first day by a high wind from the Nursery end. Only Titmus distinguished himself with the bat in both innings, and largely through his efforts and example Middlesex were able to leave a target of 230. McCool and Palmer, who added 78 for the fourth wicket at a run a minute, and Stephenson and Tremlett, the sixth pair, put Somerset within striking distance, but the new ball in the hands of Warr (three for 16) swung the game to Middlesex, in spite of stubborn resistance from the last pair, Hilton and McMahon.

Middlesex

J. D. Robertson c McCool b Lobb	1	— c and b McMahon	53
R. A. Gale b Alley	17	— c McCool b Lobb	14
W. J. Edrich b Lobb	17	— c Stephenson b Lobb	56
D. C. S. Compton c Lomax b Alley	0	— c Stephenson b Lobb	14
F. J. Titmus b Lobb	51	— c Stephenson b Lobb	65
W. E. Russell hit wkt b Lomax	6	— st Stephenson b Lomax	8
J. T. Murray b Alley	11	— c Palmer b McCool	4
D. Bennett c Harris b McMahon	8	— b McCool	9
J. J. Warr st Stephenson b McMahon	15	— b Harris	10
R. J. Hurst not out	14	— not out	0
A. E. Moss lbw b McCool	0	— lbw b Lobb	0
B 2, l-b 5	7	B 2, l-b 7	9

1/2 2/35 3/35 4/35 5/55 6/81 7/96   147   1/30 2/113 3/129 4/140   242
8/116 9/146 (2.07 an over)   5/173 6/179 7/202 8/232
                                        9/242

Somerset

W. E. Alley b Moss	16	— c Murray b Moss	37
J. G. Lomax b Moss	2	— b Moss	0
P. B. Wight b Moss	46	— b Moss	22
C. L. McCool b Warr	35	— b Titmus	49
K. E. Palmer b Warr	8	— c Murray b Compton	23
H. W. Stephenson lbw b Bennett	15	— c Murray b Warr	33
M. F. Tremlett c Warr b Moss	18	— b Bennett	21
J. Harris run out	8	— b Moss	3
J. Hilton c Murray b Moss	1	— not out	5
B. Lobb b Bennett	10	— c Bennett b Warr	4
J. W. McMahon not out	0	— c Murray b Warr	8
N-b 1	1	B 10, l-b 5	15

1/16 2/23 3/84 4/104 5/121 6/123   160   1/9 2/41 3/60 4/138 5/148   220
7/149 8/149 9/160 (3.33 an over)   6/186 7/200 8/200 9/208

Somerset Bowling

	O.	M.	R.	W.		O.	M.	R.	W.
Lobb	21	5	53	3	....	23.4	2	69	5
Alley	15	7	21	3	....	7	1	16	0
Harris	12	2	21	0	....	7	2	19	1
Lomax	6	0	20	1	....	5	0	20	1
McMahon	13	2	22	2	....	10	3	26	1
McCool	3.5	1	3	1	....	11	3	35	2
Palmer						4	0	23	0
Hilton						11	3	25	0

Middlesex Bowling

	O.	M.	R.	W.		O.	M.	R.	W.
Moss	18.2	2	62	5	....	23	6	41	4
Warr	11	0	45	2	....	22.3	9	44	3
Bennett	12	3	31	2	....	15	2	46	1
Titmus	6	2	20	0	....	15	5	46	1
Compton	1	0	1	0	....	3	0	11	1
					Hurst	7	1	17	0

Umpires: C. S. Elliott and F. S. Lee.

MIDDLESEX v. NORTHAMPTONSHIRE

At Lord's, June 1, 3, 4. Northamptonshire won by 47 runs, taking 12 points to four gained by Middlesex. They recovered splendidly after being 67 behind on first innings. Winning the toss, Northamptonshire lost eight men by lunch for 87 to excellent fast bowling by Warr and Moss, but Manning, one of five left-handers, aided by Andrew, improved the position with a partnership of 75. Middlesex owed their lead largely to sensible batting by Murray but a dashing stand of 174 in as many minutes between Livingston and Reynolds swung the game in Northamptonshire's favour. After an hour and forty minutes was lost on the last morning Middlesex were left to score 176 in two hours forty minutes but, with the pitch helping the spin bowlers, they were unequal to the task. Compton, batting with a runner because of a recurrence of knee trouble, resisted pluckily for forty minutes.

Northamptonshire

D. Brookes lbw b Warr	11	—	lbw b Warr	0
B. L. Reynolds b Moss	29	—	c Murray b Warr	93
L. Livingston b Warr	0	—	c Delisle b Hurst	93
D. W. Barrick c Compton b Warr	2	—	c Murray b Moss	3
R. Subba Row lbw b Warr	12	—	b Moss	4
G. E. Tribe b Moss	6	—	b Moss	16
J. S. Manning c Delisle b Compton	55	—	lbw b Moss	10
F. H. Tyson b Moss	0	—	c Moss b Warr	6
M. H. J. Allan c Titmus b Moss	5	—	c Murray b Warr	3
K. V. Andrew c Murray b Compton	36	—	not out	11
H. R. A. Kelleher not out	1	—	b Warr	2
L-b 4, n-b 2	6		L-b 1	1

1/11 2/12 3/14 4/28 5/66 6/67 7/67   163   1/0 2/174 3/187 4/193   242
8/87 9/162 (2.58 an over)   5/194 6/204 7/217 8/221
                                                           9/239

Middlesex

J. D. Robertson c Tyson b Manning	34	—	c Livingston b Tyson	18
D. A. Bick b Kelleher	10	—	b Kelleher	0
W. J. Edrich c Andrew b Manning	33	—	c Brookes b Kelleher	0
D. C. S. Compton b Tribe	29	—	c Subba Row b Tribe	29
F. J. Titmus b Tribe	16	—	c Subba Row b Manning	31
G. P. S. Delisle lbw b Tribe	10	—	c Livingston b Tyson	16
J. T. Murray b Manning	49	—	lbw b Allen	22
D. Bennett c Andrew b Kelleher	16	—	c Allen b Manning	3
J. J. Warr not out	20	—	lbw b Tribe	3
R. J. Hurst c Livingston b Tyson	6	—	c Allen b Manning	3
A. E. Moss c Andrew by Tyson	1	—	not out	0
L-b 4, n-b 2	6		N-b 1, w 2	3

1/16 2/73 3/98 4/110 5/120 6/143   230   1/18 2/18 3/18 4/44 5/76   128
7/203 8/203 9/226 (3.10 an over)   6/92 7/92 8/117 9/128

Middlesex Bowling

	O.	M.	R.	W.		O.	M.	R.	W.
Moss	16	1	39	4	....	21	3	72	4
Warr	16	3	38	4	....	22.3	3	72	5
Bennett	10	5	24	0	....	7	0	44	0
Compton	4	0	14	2					
Titmus	9	1	30	0	....	12	3	35	0
Hurst	8	4	12	0	....	6	2	18	1

Northamptonshire Bowling

	O.	M.	R.	W.		O.	M.	R.	W.
Tyson	18.5	2	68	2	....	8	2	46	2
Kelleher	18	6	44	2	....	7	2	22	2
Manning	17	2	54	3	....	12	3	37	3
Tribe	17	5	45	3	....	3.4	2	5	2
Subba Row	3	0	13	0					
					Allen	8	4	15	1

Umpires: N. Oldfield and F. S. Lee.

MIDDLESEX v. DERBYSHIRE

At Lord's, June 5, 6, 7. Derbyshire won by 163 runs, taking 14 points. They gave a useful all-round display whereas Middlesex failed twice with the bat on a pitch always helpful to the faster bowlers. Derbyshire began shakily, but good innings by Carr, Johnson and Morgan helped them recover. Middlesex found the fast-medium attack of Jackson too much for them, particularly on the second morning when five of his six wickets were obtained for 23 runs. Leading by 96, Derbyshire again made a disappointing start, but once more Carr rescued them. He and Dawkes added 109 in eighty-five minutes. Middlesex never looked like scoring the 339 they needed to win.

Derbyshire

A. Hamer c Edrich b Moss	18	— b Moss	7
C. Lee b Moss	0	— c Moss b Warr	9
J. Kelly b Warr	21	— lbw b Bennett	20
A. C. Revill c Bennett b Edrich	14	— b Moss	4
D. B. Carr b Warr	45	— c Murray b Titmus	68
G. O. Dawkes c Murray b Bennett....	8	— c Gale b Warr	56
H. L. Johnson lbw b Hurst	45	— lbw b Moss	17
D. C. Morgan not out	34	— c Gale b Bennett	32
E. Smith b Bennett	3	— hit wkt b Moss	4
C. Gladwin lbw b Moss	19	— run out	9
L. Jackson c Robertson b Warr	2	— not out	2
B 4, 1-b 10	14	B 12, 1-b 2	14

1/8 2/27 3/47 4/68 5/89 6/124 7/169   223   1/11 2/21 3/30 4/56 5/165   242
8/174 9/218 (2.82 an over)   6/185 7/201 8/213 9/239

Middlesex

J. D. Robertson c Dawkes b Jackson....	0	— c Gladwin b Jackson	27
D. A. Bick c Revill b Gladwin	1	— c Morgan b Gladwin	2
W. J. Edrich b Jackson	18	— c Lee b Gladwin	12
R. A. Gale c Lee b Carr	25	— c Hamer b Smith	8
F. J. Titmus c Revill b Jackson	9	— c Dawkes b Gladwin	27
G. P. S. Delisle b Gladwin	15	— c Lee b Morgan	16
J. T. Murray c and b Morgan	22	— b Gladwin	7
D. Bennett c Dawkes b Jackson	10	— c Dawkes b Morgan	46
J. J. Warr b Jackson	12	— b Revill	10
R. J. Hurst not out	4	— c Hamer b Smith	14
A. E. Moss lbw b Jackson	0	— not out	6
B 4, l-b 7	11		

1/0 2/6 3/43 4/57 5/58 6/88 7/98   127   1/2 2/22 3/47 4/54 5/80   175
8/120 9/127 (2.18 an over)   6/98 7/112 8/138 9/159

Middlesex Bowling

	O.	M.	R.	W.	O.	M.	R.	W.
Warr..........	21.3	7	67	3	20	1	62	2
Moss	21	4	46	3	16	2	51	4
Bennett	15	0	49	2	11.3	0	52	2
Edrich	4	0	10	1				
Hurst	11	5	24	1	9	2	38	0
Titmus	6	1	13	0	12	2	25	1

Derbyshire Bowling

	O.	M.	R.	W.	O.	M.	R.	W.
Jackson	22.3	13	37	6	18	4	44	1
Gladwin	21	7	38	2	15	2	41	4
Morgan	12	3	37	1	21	12	34	2
Carr	2	1	4	1	4	1	7	0
Smith					18.3	8	37	2
Revill					2	0	12	1

Umpires: J. Wood and D. Davies.

MIDDLESEX v. SUSSEX

At Lord's, June 8, 10, 11. Middlesex won by 54 runs, taking 14 points. They looked like having to be satisfied with a draw until Sussex collapsed badly at the end. Robertson and Gale gave Middlesex a great start by making 209 for the first wicket. On an easy pitch Robertson scored 101 in two hours before lunch, but added only 18 in the next hour. He hit twenty-one 4's in 119. Gale, missed in the slips when one, scored his maiden century and his 126 included twenty-three 4's. Smith and Lenham made a good reply for Sussex with a first wicket stand of 98. Smith scored 149 in four and a half hours. Sussex declared 76 behind and Robertson played another bright innings. Needing 238 in three hours, Sussex had seven wickets left forty-five minutes from the close and required another 80 runs. Then Hurst and Moss finished the match in under half an hour.

Middlesex

J. D. Robertson c Bates b James	119	— c Smith b Suttle 65
R. A. Gale b Smith	126	— b Bates 4
W. J. Edrich b Smith	16	— c Thomson b Marlar 37
D. C. S. Compton run out	7	— c Lenham b James 27
F. J. Titmus c Marlar b Bates	11	— b Suttle 1
G. P. S. Delisle not out	29	— b Suttle 0
J. T. Murray b James	62	— lbw b Marlar 4
D. Bennett (did not bat)		— not out 17
J. J. Warr (did not bat)		— not out 1
B 4, l-b 1	5	L-b 5 5

1/209 2/265 3/266 4/282 (6 wkts., dec.) 375
5/284 6/375 (3.82 an over)

1/24 2/107 (7 wkts., dec.) 161
3/107 4/108 5/108 6/113
7/151

R. J. Hurst and A. E. Moss did not bat.

Sussex

D. V. Smith c Moss b Titmus	149	— c Compton b Bennett 68
L. J. Lenham lbw b Hurst	44	— c Hurst b Titmus 26
K. G. Suttle c Warr b Titmus	59	— b Titmus 10
J. M. Parks b Bennett	7	— c Murray b Moss 37
D. J. Foreman b Bennett	0	— c Bennett b Hurst 22
R. H. Willson run out	3	— c Compton b Hurst 0
N. I. Thomson lbw b Titmus	1	— c Compton b Moss 11
R. T. Webb b Moss	19	— not out 3
A. E. James not out	7	— c Titmus b Moss 0
R. G. Marlar lbw b Titmus	0	— c and b Hurst 0
D. L. Bates not out	7	— st Murray b Hurst 0
B 2, l-b 1	3	B 1, l-b 5 6

1/98 2/129 3/183 4/196 (9 wkts., dec.) 299
5/207 6/228 7/260 8/289 9/289
(3.21 an over)

1/77 2/92 3/114 4/161 183
5/168 6/179 7/180 8/182
9/182

Sussex Bowling

	O.	M.	R.	W.		O.	M.	R.	W.
Thomson	21	3	100	0	....	13	4	27	0
Bates	25	7	67	1	....	6	0	32	1
James	25	7	85	2	....	8	3	24	1
Smith	21	5	88	2					
Marlar	6	0	30	0	....	10	1	29	2
Suttle					....	16	4	44	3

Middlesex Bowling

	O.	M.	R.	W.		O.	M.	R.	W.
Moss	28	4	94	1	....	8	3	32	3
Warr	22	3	61	0	....	12	0	42	0
Bennett	23	4	59	2	....	9	0	40	1
Compton	4	1	23	0					
Hurst	3	2	4	1	....	5.5	1	28	4
Titmus	13	1	55	4	....	14	5	35	2

Umpires: R. S. Lay and A. Skelding.

MIDDLESEX v. HAMPSHIRE

At Lord's, June 12, 13, 14. Middlesex won by 116 runs, taking 14 points. Bowlers did well for Hampshire but the batsmen let them down. Robertson played another good innings for Middlesex and once more Gale gave him useful support, but the others were worried by the fast-medium attack of Cannings, Heath and Shackleton. Gray saved Hampshire from complete collapse and the tail-end batsmen gave useful support, but Middlesex led by 35. Compton gave a dashing display in the second innings and Edrich and Titmus were also in form, Hampshire needed 263 in just under five hours, but were always struggling and apart from Horton and Eagar offered weak resistance. Middlesex won with an hour and a quarter left.

Middlesex

J. D. Robertson c Marshall b Cannings..	71	—	c Harrison b Heath	20
R. A. Gale c Harrison b Heath	35	—	b Gray	9
W. J. Edrich c Barnard b Cannings	16	—	c Horton b Marshall	45
D. C. S. Compton c Eagar b Cannings	25	—	st Harrison b Sainsbury	61
F. J. Titmus run out	17	—	lbw b Heath	43
G. P. S. Delisle hit wkt b Heath	10	—	c Harrison b Heath	11
J. T. Murray b Shackleton	19	—	c and b Sainsbury	10
D. Bennett b Heath	0	—	b Heath	7
J. J. Warr c Gray b Heath	0	—	c Harrison b Shackleton	1
R. J. Hurst not out	0	—	not out	0
A. E. Moss lbw b Shackleton	0	—	b Shackleton	9
B 7, l-b 2	9		B 9, l-b 2	11

1/69 2/121 3/150 4/155 5/182 6/182   **202**
7/186 8/190 9/202 (2.52 an over)

1/12 2/46 3/124 4/125   **227**
5/159 6/209 7/210 8/218
9/218

Hampshire

J. R. Gray b Hurst	76	—	st Murray b Compton	10
R. E. Marshall c Bennett b Warr	5	—	lbw b Warr	0
H. Horton lbw b Moss	3	—	c Murray b Compton	49
E. D. R. Eagar c Murray b Warr	1	—	b Titmus	29
H. M. Barnard c and b Compton	4	—	lbw b Hurst	14
A. C. D. Ingleby-Mackenzie c Murray b Warr	14	—	c Edrich b Hurst	1
P. J. Sainsbury c Murray b Compton	4	—	c Edrich b Compton	6
L. Harrison b Moss	19	—	not out	14
D. Shackleton b Bennett	9	—	b Bennett	13
V. H. D. Cannings not out	26	—	b Bennett	2
M. Heath b Moss	3	—	b Bennett	0
B 1, l-b 2	3		L-b 6, n-b 2	8

1/14 2/23 3/28 4/35 5/56 6/78 7/112   **167**
8/121 9/147 (2.06 an over)

1/0 2/21 3/67 4/100 5/102   **146**
6/113 7/116 8/134 9/134

Hampshire Bowling

	O.	M.	R.	W.		O.	M.	R.	W.
Shackleton	26.5	9	54	2		23.3	11	42	2
Cannings	20.3	4	67	3					
Heath	21	8	49	4		30	6	93	4
Gray	8	1	19	0		6	2	17	1
Sainsbury	3	2	4	0		14	3	43	2
					Marshall	6	1	21	1

Middlesex Bowling

	O.	M.	R.	W.		O.	M.	R.	W.
Moss	13	1	54	3		12	2	23	0
Warr	18	8	22	3		6	2	9	1
Compton	17	4	38	2		11	2	46	3
Bennett	15	5	19	1		14.2	5	20	3
Titmus	5	1	13	0		13	6	26	1
Hurst	13	6	18	1		16	10	14	2

Umpires: A. Skelding and H. G. Baldwin.

MIDDLESEX v. YORKSHIRE

At Lord's, June 15, 17, 18. Yorkshire won by ten wickets, taking 12 points. They were far too strong all round for Middlesex. A crowd of 20,000 saw Yorkshire bat steadily on Saturday. Lowson hit his first century of the season, batting stylishly for four and three-quarter hours. His 116 included sixteen 4's. He received best support from Wilson and Watson. Towards the end of a scorching day Wardle hit 33 in half an hour. On Monday, Middlesex lost 16 wickets. They failed in the first innings on a lively pitch against the pace of Trueman, Cowan and Appleyard and followed on 179 behind. Mainly through the enterprise of Robertson, who made 49 out of 54 in an hour, Middlesex deprived Yorkshire of bonus points. Appleyard again bowled cleverly in the second innings and Yorkshire needed only 45 to win.

Yorkshire

D. B. Close hit wkt b Moss	4	— not out	24
F. A. Lowson c Edrich b Bennett	116	— not out	18
J. V. Wilson c Edrich b Hurst	32		
W. B. Stott c Hurst b Titmus	10		
W. Watson lbw b Bennett	53		
W. H. H. Sutcliffe not out	19		
J. H. Wardle c Compton b Titmus	33		
F. S. Trueman not out	22		
B 10, l-b 10, w 1	21	L-b 2, n-b 1	3

1/5 2/96 3/131 4/221   (6 wkts., dec.) 310   (No wkt.) 45
5/238 6/275 (2.69 an over)
J. G. Binks, R. Appleyard and M. J. Cowan did not bat.

Middlesex

J. D. Robertson c Close b Appleyard	49	— c Wilson b Cowan	37
R. A. Gale c Sutcliffe b Trueman	0	— c Trueman b Appleyard	10
W. J. Edrich c Appleyard b Trueman	14	— lbw b Trueman	8
F. J. Titmus lbw b Cowan	4	— c Lowson b Appleyard	6
D. C. S. Compton c Close b Trueman	19	— c Binks b Appleyard	36
G. P. S. Delisle c Binks b Appleyard	9	— b Trueman	20
J. T. Murray b Trueman	18	— c Wilson b Cowan	6
D. Bennett b Appleyard	10	— c Binks b Appleyard	22
J. J. Warr b Cowan	4	— not out	40
R. J. Hurst not out	3	— c Binks b Appleyard	7
A. E. Moss b Cowan	0	— b Appleyard	17
L-b 1, n-b 4	5	L-b 5, n-b 9	14

1/13 2/54 3/55 4/83 5/87 6/109 7/119   131   1/49 2/55 3/62 4/90 5/103   223
8/126 9/128 (2.91 an over)   6/114 7/148 8/171 9/185

Middlesex Bowling

	O.	M.	R.	W.		O.	M.	R.	W.
Warr	18	8	31	0	....	2	0	4	0
Moss	15	3	31	1	....	3	0	10	0
Bennett	23	2	54	2	....	4	0	13	0
Compton	4	0	24	0	....	1	0	14	0
Titmus	29	10	59	2					
Hurst	26	8	90	1					
Edrich						0.2	0	1	0

Yorkshire Bowling

	O.	M.	R.	W.		O.	M.	R.	W.
Trueman	14	1	49	4	....	15	1	67	2
Cowan	13.4	3	38	3	....	17	3	42	2
Appleyard	17	3	39	3	....	25	7	60	6
Wardle						10	0	36	0
Close						1	0	4	0

Umpires: D. Davies and N. Oldfield.

At Nottingham, June 19, 20, 21. MIDDLESEX lost to NOTTINGHAMSHIRE by two wickets.

At Leeds, June 22, 24, 25. MIDDLESEX drew with YORKSHIRE.

MIDDLESEX v. LANCASHIRE

At Lord's, June 29, July 1, 2. Lancashire won by 72 runs, taking 12 points. The Lord's pitch belied its reputation by being at least as helpful to spin bowlers as to those using the seam, and Lancashire owed much to excellent off-break bowling by Tattersall. Statham bowled with persistence, pace and accuracy in each innings. Wharton, Dyson and Ikin gave Lancashire a good start, but Hurst began a collapse that was retrieved by the last wicket pair, Pullar and Hilton who added 72. A dour display by Edrich was the backbone of the Middlesex first innings. They conceded the lead, but deprived Lancashire of bonus points by slightly faster scoring. Again the Lancashire middle batting broke down, Titmus taking four wickets in eleven balls, but, despite fine stroke-play by Robertson, Middlesex found their task of scoring 236 too much.

Lancashire

A. Wharton b Baldry	38	—	c Gale b Compton	33
J. Dyson c Moss b Warr	63	—	c Compton b Warr	5
J. T. Ikin c Murray b Bennett	47	—	c Warr b Titmus	48
C. Washbrook b Hurst	9	—	lbw b Hurst	6
K. Grieves b Hurst	5	—	b Hurst	29
G. Pullar not out	69	—	c and b Titmus	0
J. D. Bond lbw b Hurst	1	—	b Titmus	0
J. Jordan b Compton	1	—	b Titmus	0
J. B. Statham c Hurst b Compton	6	—	c Edrich b Moss	26
R. Tattersall run out	0	—	not out	6
C. Hilton run out	17	—	b Moss	7
B 1, l-b 5, n-b 2	8		B 16, l-b 2, n-b 1	19

1/84 2/141 3/154 4/162 5/174 6/175   264
7/184 8/190 9/192 (2.69 an over)

1/18 2/26 3/77 4/128   179
5/128 6/128 7/128 8/154
9/171

Middlesex

J. D. Robertson c Ikin b Hilton	9	—	c Hilton b Statham	70
R. A. Gale b Statham	4	—	c Wharton b Tattersall	11
W. J. Edrich b Tattersall	69	—	c sub b Tattersall	0
F. J. Titmus c Jordan b Wharton	23	—	c Ikin b Statham	25
D. O. Baldry lbw b Wharton	3	—	st Jordan b Tattersall	8
D. C. S. Compton b Statham	25	—	lbw b Statham	0
J. T. Murray c Jordan b Wharton	30	—	c Bond b Tattersall	28
D. Bennett c Grieves b Tattersall	13	—	b Tattersall	1
J. J. Warr b Wharton	19	—	not out	2
R. J. Hurst not out	4	—	b Tattersall	0
A. E. Moss b Statham	3	—	c Wharton b Tattersall	0
B 1, l-b 5	6		B 16, l-b 2	18

1/10 2/22 3/69 4/77 5/106 6/161   208
7/169 8/188 9/202 (2.77 an over)

1/32 2/32 3/35 4/109   163
5/120 6/140 7/161 8/163
9/163

Middlesex Bowling

	O.	M.	R.	W.	O.	M.	R.	W.
Moss	11	3	35	0	.... 15.3	4	34	2
Warr..........	20	4	50	1	 10	4	10	1
Bennett	17	3	45	1	 4	0	8	0
Baldry	11	2	29	1				
Compton	16	8	37	2	 9	0	29	1
Hurst	20.3	6	58	3	 19	10	24	2
Titmus	2	1	2	0	 26	7	55	4

Lancashire Bowling

	O.	M.	R.	W.	O.	M.	R.	W.
Statham	22.2	5	51	3	 19	7	35	3
Hilton	13	1	38	1	 8	0	38	0
Tattersall	21	4	53	2	.... 25.3	9	39	7
Wharton	16	2	59	4	 5	1	17	0
Ikin...........	3	2	1	0				
					Dyson 2	0	16	0

Umpires: John Langridge and A. E. Pothecary.

At Kidderminster, July 6, 8. MIDDLESEX beat WORCESTERSHIRE by 134 runs.

At Gloucester, July 10, 11, 12. MIDDLESEX drew with GLOUCESTERSHIRE.

At Manchester, July 13, 15, 16. MIDDLESEX drew with LANCASHIRE.

At Chesterfield, July 17, 18, 19. MIDDLESEX lost to DERBYSHIRE by an innings and 22 runs.

At Lord's, July 20, 22, 23. MIDDLESEX drew with WEST INDIES. (See WEST INDIES section.)

MIDDLESEX v. ESSEX

At Lord's, July 24, 25, 26. Middlesex won by 209 runs, taking 14 points. A great innings by Robertson on the first day put them on top from the start. He dominated the play for almost five and a half hours and his 201 included twenty-eight 4's. Useful support came from Baldry, Edrich, Titmus and Murray, but the next best score was only 38. Essex were saved from complete disaster by Insole but despite his defiant innings they were 151 behind on first innings. The pace of Moss and Bennett worried them most. Middlesex did not enforce the follow-on and with Gale batting soundly they built up a lead of 292. Overnight rain made the pitch difficult and after a declaration first thing, Essex were dismissed in two and a half hours before lunch. Titmus made the ball turn sharply when the pitch took spin after the first hour.

Middlesex

J. D. Robertson not out 201	—	c and b Preston	25
R. A. Gale lbw b Ralph	13	—	c and b Preston	66
A. C. Walton c Insole b Ralph	0	—	c Greensmith b King	17
D. O. Baldry st Taylor b Greensmith...	30	—	b Bailey	5
W. J. Edrich c Bear b Insole	38	—	b Preston	2
F. J. Titmus st Taylor b Ralph	28	—	b Bailey	0
J. T. Murray lbw b Bailey	20	—	not out	21
D. Bennett not out	0	—	not out	1
L-b 6, n-b 1	7		L-b 4	4

1/26 2/50 3/118 4/191   (6 wkts., dec.) 337   1/36 2/76   (6 wkts., dec.) 141
5/275 6/333 (3.27 an over)   3/91 4/91 5/129 6/137

J. J. Warr, R. J. Hurst and A. E. Moss did not bat.

Essex

T. C. Dodds c Murray b Moss	22	— c Edrich b Warr	11
G. Barker c Murray b Warr	0	— c Murray b Moss	0
R. Ralph c Edrich b Moss	5	— b Titmus	1
B. Taylor c Titmus b Moss	7	— c Gale b Moss	19
D. J. Insole c Walton b Bennett	90	— c Moss b Titmus	22
L. Savill b Moss	24	— c Titmus b Moss	0
M. Bear c Edrich b Bennett	18	— c Robertson b Titmus	4
W. T. Greensmith c Murray b Bennett	3	— lbw b Titmus	12
K. C. Preston b Bennett	0	— c Hurst b Titmus	0
J. A. Bailey c Murray b Bennett	5	— c Robertson b Hurst	1
I. King not out	0	— not out	1
B 7, l-b 5	12	B 9, l-b 3	12

1/1 2/10 3/34 4/35 5/125 6/157 7/169   **186**   1/6 2/32 3/32 4/42 5/54   **83**
8/169 9/179 (2.86 an over)   6/73 7/76 8/76 9/81

Essex Bowling

	O.	M.	R.	W.		O.	M.	R.	W.
Preston	33	3	88	0	....	14	3	39	3
Ralph	28	8	82	3	....	7	1	21	0
Bailey	7	0	49	1	....	13	2	51	2
King	13	3	32	0	....	7	1	26	1
Greensmith	15	1	42	1					
Insole	7.1	0	37	1					

Middlesex Bowling

	O.	M.	R.	W.		O.	M.	R.	W.
Warr	8	2	26	1	....	7	2	17	1
Moss	15	4	42	4	....	8	2	29	3
Baldry	8	4	22	0					
Bennett	11.1	1	36	5					
Titmus	6	1	15	0	....	11	5	15	5
Hurst	15	8	30	0	....	7	4	7	1
Gale	2	0	3	0					
Edrich						4	2	3	0

Umpires: J. F. Crapp and W. Place.

At Birmingham, July 27, 29, 30. MIDDLESEX beat WARWICKSHIRE by 47 runs.

At Leyton, July 31, August 1, 2. MIDDLESEX lost to ESSEX by 74 runs.

At Hove, August 3, 5, 6. MIDDLESEX lost to SUSSEX by 99 runs.

At Northampton, August 7, 8. 9. MIDDLESEX drew with NORTHAMPTONSHIRE.

At The Oval, August 10, 12, 13. MIDDLESEX drew with SURREY.

MIDDLESEX v. LEICESTERSHIRE

At Lord's, August 14, 15, 16. Match abandoned without a ball bowled.

Middlesex: J. D. Robertson, R. A. Gale, A. C. Walton, D. C. S. Compton, W. J. Edrich, F. J. Titmus, J. T. Murray, D. Bennett, J. J. Warr, R. J. Hurst, A. E. Moss.

Leicestershire: G. Lester, M. R. Hallam, J. van Geloven, C. H. Palmer, L. R. Gardner, J. Firth, R. A. Diment, J. Savage, R. C. Smith, C. T. Spencer, B. Boshier.

Umpires: C. S. Elliott and W. Place.

MIDDLESEX v. SURREY

At Lord's, August 17, 19, 20. Surrey won by 102 runs, taking 14 points. Bowlers always held the advantage in this match which took place after rain had prevented any cricket at the M.C.C.'s headquarters since the previous Saturday. Surrey were in trouble until Lock, hitting cleanly, led a recovery. Then Laker and Lock put out Middlesex for 100 so that Surrey finished the first day 81 ahead with all their second innings wickets intact. The pitch was firmer on Monday when Clark and Eric Bedser batted in enterprising fashion. Middlesex wanted 286 to win, but Lock caught Robertson superbly with the left hand following a full-blooded hook and Alec Bedser dismissed Gale, Compton and Edrich in the course of four deliveries, putting Surrey completely on top. Walton (one 6 and eight 4's) and Titmus (two 6's and five 4's) countered splendidly, but the leeway was too big and Surrey needed only an hour on the last day to capture the last four wickets.

Surrey

M. J. Stewart c Titmus b Warr	....	16	—	b Hurst	11
T. H. Clark c Gale b Moss	....	9	—	hit wkt b Compton	 48
B. Constable b Titmus	....	23	—	c Gale b Warr	 31
P. B. H. May c Bennett b Titmus	....	16	—	c Murray b Warr	 0
K. F. Barrington b Hurst	....	0	—	b Warr	 6
E. A. Bedser c Walton b Titmus	....	26	—	st Murray b Hurst	 65
A. J. McIntyre b Titmus	....	13	—	lbw b Moss	 19
G. A. R. Lock c Warr b Titmus	....	46	—	c Murray b Titmus	 2
J. C. Laker b Titmus	....	3	—	c Titmus b Hurst	 2
P. J. Loader c Edrich b Hurst	....	6	—	b Titmus	 0
A. V. Bedser not out	....	15	—	not out	 6
B 5		5		B 6, l-b 11	17
		178			**207**

1/20 2/34 3/55 4/61 5/77 6/104
7/104 8/114 9/137 (3.56 an over)

1/20 2/90 3/93 4/99
5/122 6/162 7/179 8/198
9/199

Middlesex

J. D. Robertson c Barrington b A. Bedser		27	—	c Lock b Loader	 7
R. A. Gale c Stewart b Lock	....	3	—	lbw b A. Bedser	 7
A. C. Walton lbw b Laker	....	5	—	c Barrington b Lock	 59
W. J. Edrich c Stewart b Lock	....	16	—	b A. Bedser	 0
D. C. S. Compton c May b Laker	....	5	—	lbw b A. Bedser	 0
F. J. Titmus c Stewart b Laker	....	0	—	c E. Bedser b Lock	 54
D. Bennett not out	....	28	—	lbw b Lock	 1
J. T. Murray b Laker	....	1	—	c May b Lock	 33
J. J. Warr c Lock b Laker	....	1	—	b Laker	 10
R. J. Hurst c Stewart b Laker	....	0	—	not out	 10
A. E. Moss lbw b Lock	....	2	—	b Laker	 0
B 11, l-b 1		12		B 1, l-b 1	 2
		100			**183**

1/8 2/34 3/51 4/60 5/62 6/68 7/77
8/83 9/87 (1.72 an over)

1/8 2/14 3/14 4/14 5/97
6/103 7/148 8/163 9/183

Middlesex Bowling

	O.	M.	R.	W.	O.	M.	R.	W.
Warr	10	1	28	1	 16	1	52	3
Moss	9	3	17	1	 11	4	35	1
Titmus	18.5	2	86	6	 19	2	42	2
Hurst	12	3	42	2	.... 14.3	6	22	3
Compton					 10	3	39	1

Surrey Bowling

	O.	M.	R.	W.	O.	M.	R.	W.
A. Bedser	15	7	15	1	 13	3	30	3
Lock	19.4	5	42	3	 23	8	70	4
Laker	23	8	31	6	.... 13.5	4	42	2
Loader					19	6	39	1

Umpires: E. Davies and W. Place.

At Dover, August 21, 22. MIDDLESEX beat KENT by 231 runs.

At Swansea, August 24, 26. MIDDLESEX beat GLAMORGAN by seven wickets.

MIDDLESEX v. WORCESTERSHIRE

At Lord's, August 28, 29, 30. Worcestershire won by two wickets, taking 12 points. After a thrilling finish the deciding run came off the fifth ball of the final over. Denis Compton, on his last appearance as a professional for Middlesex, stole the limelight. He scored 191 runs in the match including a sparkling 143 in the first innings. He and Robertson shared a third wicket stand of 225 when Middlesex batted first on an easy pitch. Compton batted three hours and hit one 6 and seventeen 4's. Worcestershire began shakily, but Derek Richardson led a recovery with a century in just over three hours. Broadbent, who helped him add 144, and Horton gave good support. Worcestershire declared four runs ahead. Middlesex were unable to force the pace, but Worcestershire were set to get 200 to win in two hours twenty-five minutes. A fine struggle developed with Worcestershire, who needed 28 in the last ten minutes, just succeeding.

Middlesex

J. D. Robertson c Kenyon b Coldwell	..104	— b Coldwell	5
R. A. Gale c Broadbent b Flavell	17	— st Booth b Chesterton	25
A. C. Walton c Booth b Coldwell	37	— c and b Chesterton	42
D. C. S. Compton b Flavell	143	— c Outschoorn b Horton	48
W. J. Edrich b Flavell	9	— c Kenyon b Horton	22
J. T. Murray st Booth b Chesterton	27	— b Flavell	30
F. J. Titmus not out	8	— c Broadbent b Horton	18
D. Bennett (did not bat)		— not out	1
J. J. Warr (did not bat)		— not out	1
B 1, l-b 4	5	B 8, l-b 2, n-b 1	11

1/24 2/76 3/301 4/305　　(6 wkts., dec.) 350
5/330 6/350 (3.72 an over)

1/9 2/61　　(7 wkts., dec.) 203
3/90 4/131 5/157 6/201
7/201

R. J. Hurst and A. E. Moss did not bat.

Worcestershire

D. Kenyon c Compton b Hurst	51	— hit wkt b Bennett	32
P. E. Richardson c Edrich b Warr	6	— run out	27
G. Dews c Walton b Hurst	28	— b Bennett	27
D. W. Richardson st Murray b Compton	113	— c Walton b Hurst	9
R. G. Broadbent c Edrich b Warr	56	— st Murray b Titmus	42
L. Outschoorn c Gale b Hurst	16	— lbw b Titmus	1
M. J. Horton not out	51	— c Moss b Hurst	13
R. Booth st Murray b Compton	1	— not out	22
G. H. Chesterton b Hurst	1	— not out	6
J. Flavell run out	2	— c Edrich b Titmus	8
L. N. Coldwell not out	11		
B 12, l-b 5, n-b 1	18	B 9, l-b 4	13

1/14 2/89 3/90 4/234　　(9 wkts., dec.) 354
5/276 6/286 7/292 8/293 9/296
(2.76 an over)

1/57 2/85 3/96　　(8 wkts.) 200
4/108 5/138 6/149 7/162
8/172

Worcestershire Bowling

	O.	M.	R.	W.		O.	M.	R.	W.
Flavell	18	0	83	3	....	20	1	58	1
Coldwell	28	4	121	2	....	8	1	30	1
Chesterton	27.4	5	91	1	....	14	3	42	2
Horton	20	5	50	0	....	19	3	62	3

Middlesex Bowling

	O.	M.	R.	W.		O.	M.	R.	W.
Moss	21	7	59	0	....	6	0	15	0
Warr	20	4	56	2	....	6	0	17	0
Compton	26.1	5	66	2	....	7	1	38	0
Bennett	13	2	33	0	....	4	1	11	0
Hurst	31	12	70	4	....	15.5	2	69	2
Gale	4	1	12	0	....	2	0	13	0
Titmus	11	3	37	0	....	7	1	24	3
Edrich	2	0	3	0					

Umpires: F. S. Lee and R. S. Lay.

I ZINGARI MATCHES

Matches 28, Won 12, Lost 6, Drawn 6, Abandoned 4

May 4	v. Trinity College, Cambridge	Trinity won by 48 runs
May 11	v. Charterhouse School	I Zingari won by three wickets
May 11	v. Hon. Artillery Company	I Zingari won by 76 runs
May 18	v. Magdalene College	Drawn
May 18	v. Magdalen College	Drawn
May 19	v. Duke of Norfolk's XI	Duke of Norfolk's XI won by three wickets
May 25	v. Green Jackets	Green Jackets won by 163 runs
May 25	v. Christ Church, Oxford	I Zingari won by eight wickets
June 1	v. Royal Engineers	R.E.'s won by 36 runs
June 1	v. Royal Navy	I Zingari won by two wickets
June 5	v. Household Brigade	Drawn
June 8, 9	v. Royal Artillery	Drawn
June 15	v. Westminster School	I Zingari won by nine wickets
June 19	v. Middlesex Regt.	I Zingari won by nine wickets
June 22	v. Harrow School	I Zingari won by two runs
June 25	v. Winchester College	Winchester won by 69 runs
June 29	v. Royal Naval College, Greenwich	I Zingari won by seven wickets
June 29	v. E.R.A. de Rothschild's XI	I Zingari won by 89 runs
July 6	v. Eton College 1st XI	I Zingari won by four wickets
July 6	v. Eton College 2nd XI	I Zingari won by four wickets
July 13	v. Aldershot Services	Drawn
July 20	v. Wellington College	Abandoned
July 20	v. Royal Fusiliers	I Zingari won by four wickets
July 20	v. Sir William Worsley's XI	Abandoned
July 21	v. Ampleforth College	Abandoned
July 27	v. R.M. Academy, Sandhurst	R.M.A. won by 54 runs
July 27	v. Staff College, Camberley	Drawn
August 10	v. Lord Porchester's XI	Abandoned

NORTHAMPTONSHIRE

President—G. A. T. VIALS

Secretary—LIEUT.-COL. A. ST. G. COLDWELL, County Cricket
Ground, Wantage Road, Northampton

Captain—DENNIS BROOKES

G. E. Tribe

County Badge

K. V. Andrew

Northamptonshire's astute team building and steady improvement over the three previous years were amply rewarded in 1957.
They enjoyed the most successful season in their history, finishing
second in the county Championship, and although 94 points
behind Surrey, were the only side who offered any challenge to
the leaders in the last month. Northamptonshire were also runners-
up to Yorkshire in 1912, with ten victories in eighteen games, but
the achievements of that season were easily surpassed by a team
which contained only one regular player born in the county. The
fifteen Championship victories in 1957 constituted a new record
for the county, and they suffered only two defeats—fewer than any
other contestant.

It was fitting that Brookes should lead the side to this exalted
position in the twentieth season since winning his county cap.
No player has served the county more loyally; as a batsman he
remained a model of correctness and steadiness, even though
greater responsibility was thrust upon him by the inconsistency of
others. Early in the season he completed 25,000 runs for the
county, and his innings of 100 against Surrey at The Oval earned
him the distinction of having scored a century against every side
in the Championship.

The biggest disappointment was the form of Livingston, who
scored little more than half as many runs as in 1956, being troubled
throughout the season by an injury to his left knee. This induced
him to play most of his strokes off the back foot, and it was not

until the last few matches that he revealed glimpses of his usual aggressive form. In the absence of Subba Row, still in the R.A.F., the all-rounder, Tribe, often looked the soundest batsman apart from the captain, and he performed the "double" for the sixth successive season. To the bowlers must be given the main credit for their county's success. Tyson, for the first time in his career, exceeded 100 wickets, and his splendid performance in taking thirteen wickets for 112 runs was the deciding factor in the win at The Oval, Northamptonshire's fourth successive defeat of Surrey.

In these days, when so many sides rely mainly upon the off-spinner, it was really remarkable that between them the three left-arm slow bowlers, Tribe, Manning and Allen, captured 305 wickets in Championship matches alone. The fielding did not approach Surrey's magnificent standard, although Andrew kept wicket excellently.

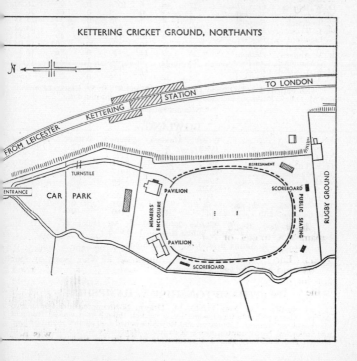

NORTHAMPTONSHIRE RESULTS

All First-Class Matches—Played 29, *Won* 15, *Lost* 3, *Drawn* 11

County Championship Matches—Played 28, *Won* 15, *Lost* 2,
Drawn 10, *No Decision* 1

COUNTY CHAMPIONSHIP AVERAGES
BATTING

	Birthplace	Mtchs.	Inns.	Not Outs	Runs	100's	Highest Inns.	Aver.
D. Brookes ...	*Kippax*	28	49	3	1428	4	148*	31.04
L. Livingston..	*Sydney*	20	33	1	988	0	95	30.87
R. Subba Row	*Croydon*	5	8	1	214	0	70	30.57
B. L. Reynolds	*Kettering*	28	45	5	1157	2	169	28.92
J. P. Fellows-Smith	*Durban*	12	20	1	546	1	109	28.73
P. Arnold	*Wellington, N.Z.*	18	32	3	808	0	86	27.86
D. W. Barrick.	*Fitzwilliam*	27	46	6	1076	0	97	26.90
M. Norman...	*Northampton*	2	3	0	79	0	64	26.33
V. Broderick .	*Bacup*	4	4	1	76	0	34	25.33
G. E. Tribe...	*Melbourne*	27	43	6	911	0	92	24.62
A. Lightfoot ..	*Woore, Crewe*	7	9	0	192	0	49	21.33
F. H. Tyson...	*Bolton*	24	31	10	379	0	70*	18.04
K. V. Andrew.	*Oldham*	28	39	11	429	0	76	15.32
J. S. Manning.	*Adelaide*	25	35	3	460	1	132	14.37
H. R. A. Kelleher	*Bermondsey*	22	23	11	145	0	25	12.08
M. J. H. Allen.	*Bedford*	28	32	7	174	0	29	6.96

Also batted: L. McGibbon (*Newcastle*) 0* and 0*; R. W. Clarke (*Finedon*)
and M. Dilley (*Rushden*) each played in one match but did not bat.

* *Signifies not out.*

BOWLING

	Overs	Maidens	Runs	Wickets	Average
V. Broderick	105.3	47	156	12	13.00
M. J. H. Allen	603	241	1225	77	15.90
G. E. Tribe	792.2	222	2071	124	16.70
J. S. Manning	881.5	330	1917	104	18.43
F. H. Tyson	598.5	136	1586	86	18.44
H. R. A. Kelleher	452.2	131	1127	42	26.83
A. Lightfoot	11	3	32	1	32.00
D. W. Barrick	7	1	25	0	——
J. P. Fellows-Smith	61	13	180	0	——

Also bowled: R. W. Clarke 29—2—93—0: M. Dilley 11—4—33—0;
L. McGibbon 5—2—14—0; R. Subba Row 4—1—13—0.

Amateurs.—R. Subba Row, J. P. Fellows-Smith.

At Northampton, May 4, 6, 7. NORTHAMPTON lost to WEST INDIES by four
wickets. (See WEST INDIES section.)

NORTHAMPTONSHIRE v. HAMPSHIRE

At Northampton, May 11, 13, 14. Drawn, Northamptonshire taking two
points. The match produced some lively cricket, though rain caused frequent
interruptions. Brookes, Livingston and Reynolds batted well against tight bowling,
and following Northamptonshire's declaration Hampshire were struggling until
Horton and Sainsbury shared a partnership of 73 for the sixth wicket. After

quick scoring, Northamptonshire set Hampshire to score 224 in a little under three hours, a task which was never seriously attempted after Marshall was dismissed.

Northamptonshire

D. Brookes c Sainsbury b Burden	77 — b Shackleton	0
M. Norman lbw b Sainsbury	11 — b Cannings	4
L. Livingston b Shackleton	39 — lbw b Cannings	16
D. W. Barrick c Burden b Sainsbury	24 — lbw b Shackleton	52
B. Reynolds c Harrison b Sainsbury	43 — b Sainsbury	54
G. E. Tribe b Cannings	13 — not out	23
J. S. Manning not out	7 — not out	6
F. H. Tyson c Marshall b Shackleton	4	
B 1, l-b 5, w 1	7	B 6, l-b 6 12

1/48 2/109 3/132 4/183   (7 wkts., dec.) 225   1/0 2/20   (5 wkts., dec.) 167
5/206 6/214 7/225 (2.14 an over)   3/23 4/113 5/153

M. H. J. Allen, K. V. Andrew and H. R. A. Kelleher did not bat.

Hampshire

R. E. Marshall b Kelleher	24 — lbw b Tribe	52
J. R. Gray b Kelleher	0 — st Andrew b Allen	44
H. Horton b Tribe	64 — b Tribe	0
L. Harrison b Manning	0 — not out	1
H. M. Barnard b Tyson	0 — b Tribe	3
A. C. D. Ingleby-Mackenzie lbw b Manning	5 — not out	48
P. J. Sainsbury lbw b Manning	42	
E. D. R. Eagar c Livingston b Manning	13	
D. Shackleton not out	11	
V. H. D. Cannings c and b Manning	0	
M. D. Burden b Tribe	4	
B 4, l-b 2	6	B 1, l-b 7 8

1/9 2/32 3/43 4/48 5/59 6/132 7/150   169   1/85 2/87 3/111   (4 wkts.) 156
8/156 9/164 (2.25 an over)   4/128

Hampshire Bowling

	O.	M.	R.	W.		O.	M.	R.	W.
Shackleton	34.5	15	59	2	....	25	5	44	2
Cannings	23	7	55	1	....	14	4	36	2
Sainsbury	21	10	46	3	....	25	10	49	1
Burden	19	7	41	1	....	9	2	26	0
Marshall	7	2	17	0					

Northamptonshire Bowling

	O.	M.	R.	W.		O.	M.	R.	W.
Tyson	9	3	17	1	....	5	0	14	0
Kelleher	8	3	21	2	....	4	1	17	0
Manning	30	17	46	5	....	16	4	33	0
Tribe	18.3	5	56	2	....	23	5	56	3
Allen	9	2	23	0	....	7	0	28	1

Umpires: W. E. Phillipson and C. S. Elliott.

At Worcester, May 15, 16. NORTHAMPTONSHIRE beat WORCESTERSHIRE by five wickets. (Two-day friendly.)

At Nottingham, May 18, 20, 21. NORTHAMPTONSHIRE drew with NOTTINGHAM-SHIRE.

NORTHAMPTONSHIRE v. GLOUCESTERSHIRE

At Northampton, May 25, 27. Northamptonshire won by seven wickets, taking 12 points. Brilliant batting by Reynolds and fine bowling by Allen and Tribe were the decisive factors. Allen caused a remarkable Gloucestershire collapse. After a fourth stand of 99 by Emmett and Graveney, the remaining six wickets fell for 28. Northamptonshire, too, found difficulty against accurate spin bowling. They owed everything to Reynolds, who stayed four hours for the highest score of his career. While he was at the crease his seven partners between them scored only 42. The most successful of these was Kelleher, with whom he added 84 for the last wicket. Tribe was the destroyer in Gloucestershire's second innings, and Northamptonshire easily hit off the 62 runs needed to win.

Gloucestershire

D. M. Young c Reynolds b Kelleher	1	— lbw b Tribe	44
D. Carpenter st Andrew b Tribe	12	— b Tribe	12
T. W. Graveney lbw b Manning	57	— c Andrew b Tribe	23
R. B. Nicholls b Allen	32	— b Manning	6
G. M. Emmett c Brookes b Allen	72	— c Kelleher b Allen	31
D. Hawkins not out	19	— run out	10
G. E. Lambert b Allen	0	— c Tyson b Tribe.........	14
D. R. Smith b Allen	0	— b Tribe	4
C. Cook c Livingston b Tribe	0	— b Tribe	0
P. Rochford lbw b Tribe	0	— not out	0
B. D. Wells b Allen	2	— b Tribe	4
B 8, l-b 3, n-b 1	12	L-b 3, n-b 1	4

1/1 2/72 3/80 4/179 5/190 6/190   207   1/34 2/68 3/87 4/89 5/115   152
7/190 8/195 9/204 (3.13 an over)   6/133 7/146 8/146 9/147

Northamptonshire

D. Brookes b Lambert	10	— c Graveney b Wells	1
P. Arnold c Lambert b Wells..........	31	— b Cook	0
L. Livingston lbw b Cook	18	— st Rochford b Wells	13
D. W. Barrick c Graveney b Wells ...	29	— not out	23
B. Reynolds not out	157	— not out	25
G. E. Tribe c Lambert b Cook	3		
J. Manning b Wells	0		
F. H. Tyson c Young b Cook	0		
M. H. J. Allen c Lambert b Cook	3		
K. V. Andrew c Smith b Cook	5		
H. R. A. Kelleher lbw b Hawkins	21		
B 11, l-b 10	21		

1/26 2/63 3/64 4/116 5/135 6/136   298   1/1 2/1 3/18   (3 wkts.)   62
7/153 8/167 9/214 (2.54 an over)

Northamptonshire Bowling

	O.	M.	R.	W.		O.	M.	R.	W.
Tyson	12	2	32	0	....	6	1	18	0
Kelleher	6	1	22	1	....	4	1	8	0
Manning	19	4	56	1	....	18	6	43	1
Tribe	19	4	57	3	....	22.2	5	68	7
Allen	9.5	2	28	5	....	6	1	11	1

Gloucestershire Bowling

	O.	M.	R.	W.	O.	M.	R.	W.
Lambert	13	3	34	1				
Smith	8	2	23	0				
Cook	46	16	98	5	 9	1	29	1
Wells	42	11	104	3	 7	2	21	2
Hawkins	6.2	1	16	1				
Nicholls	2	0	2	0				
Graveney					2	0	7	0
Emmett					0.4	0	5	0

Umpires: Harry Elliott and J. Wood.

At The Oval, May 29, 30, 31. NORTHAMPTONSHIRE beat SURREY by 72 runs.

At Lord's, June 1, 3, 4. NORTHAMPTONSHIRE beat MIDDLESEX by 47 runs.

NORTHAMPTONSHIRE v. SURREY

At Northampton, June 5, 6, 7. Surrey won by ten wickets, taking 14 points. The match was made memorable by Stewart holding seven catches during the Northamptonshire second innings. No fielder in first-class cricket other than a wicket-keeper had previously taken so many during a single innings, and only twice had even a wicket-keeper held seven. On rain-affected turf, Stewart fielded very close to the accurate bowling of Alec Bedser, Lock and Laker. He took six catches at backward short-leg and one in the gully. None was really difficult. Apart from aggressive driving by Barrick, Northamptonshire struggled against keen bowling on a good pitch during their first innings. Surrey, too, had to earn runs, but they batted consistently, with May in particularly good form. Their lead of 98 proved most valuable when rain livened the pitch and made conditions possible for Stewart's catching feat.

Northamptonshire

D. Brookes c Lock b A. Bedser	7	—	c Lock b A. Bedser........	6
B. L. Reynolds b Loader	2	—	c Stewart b A. Bedser....	26
L. Livingston b A. Bedser	0	—	c Stewart b A. Bedser....	0
D. W. Barrick c McIntyre b Lock	86	—	c Barrington b A. Bedser...	33
A. Lightfoot lbw b Laker	29	—	c Stewart b Lock..........	5
G. E. Tribe b E. Bedser	22	—	c Stewart b Lock..........	11
J. S. Manning b E. Bedser	0	—	c Stewart b Laker..........	10
K. V. Andrew run out	6	—	not out	12
F. H. Tyson not out	34	—	c Stewart b Laker..........	4
M. H. J. Allen b A. Bedser	5	—	c McIntyre b Lock..........	0
H. R. A. Kelleher b Laker	13	—	c Stewart b Lock..........	0
B 2, l-b 6, n-b 1	9		B 4......	4

1/9 2/9 3/9 4/86 5/145 6/145 7/147   213   1/11 2/11 3/52 4/59 5/71   111
8/161 9/184 (2.02 an over)   6/87 7/95 8/98 9/101

Surrey

D. G. W. Fletcher c Manning b Tribe ..	37	— not out	8
M. J. Stewart c Andrew b Manning	24	— not out	6
B. Constable b Allen	42		
P. B. H. May c Kelleher b Tyson	96		
K. F. Barrington b Kelleher	10		
E. A. Bedser c Livingston b Tyson	46		
A. J. McIntyre b Tribe	27		
G. A. R. Lock st Andrew b Tribe	0		
J. C. Laker c Manning b Tribe	11		
P. J. Loader c Brookes b Tribe	4		
A. V. Bedser not out	0		
B 7, l-b 7	14		

1/58 2/78 3/157 4/212 5/224 6/269   311   (No wkt.) 14
7/281 8/299 9/310 (2.59 an over)

Surrey Bowling

	O.	M.	R.	W.		O.	M.	R.	W.
Loader	26	9	54	1	....	9	2	26	0
A. Bedser......	26	6	58	3	....	16	5	43	4
Laker	13.3	10	14	2	....	12	6	14	2
Lock	23	10	45	1	....	9.2	1	20	4
E. Bedser	16	2	33	2	....	1	0	4	0

Northamptonshire Bowling

	O.	M.	R.	W.					
Tyson	25.4	8	47	2					
Kelleher	22	7	39	1					
Manning	26	10	81	1	....	1.5	1	8	0
Tribe	26	3	73	5					
Allen	20	8	57	1	....	1	0	6	0

Umpires: F. S. Lee and A. Skelding.

NORTHAMPTONSHIRE v. LEICESTERSHIRE

At Northampton, June 8, 10, 11. Northamptonshire won by an innings and 29 runs, taking 14 points. Brookes completed 25,000 runs for the county in the course of a chanceless innings, and his stand of 139 with Livingston was followed by another enterprising partnership with the aggressive Barrick. Brookes batted patiently for five hours and a half and hit thirteen 4's. Northamptonshire's left-arm spin attack, even without Tribe, soon had Leicestershire in difficulties. Broderick, playing his first county match of the season, enjoyed a personal triumph in the first innings and when Leicestershire followed on 162 behind, Manning marked his 33rd birthday by taking five wickets, including three for one run in three overs.

Northamptonshire

D. Brookes not out 135	B 5, l-b 5, n-b 1.............	11
B. L. Reynolds b Spencer 5		
L. Livingston c Firth b Spencer... 76	1/21 2/160 (2 wkts., dec.)	277
D. W. Barrick not out 50	(2.88 an over)	

A. Lightfoot, V. Broderick, J. S. Manning, K. V. Andrew, F. H. Tyson, M. H. J. Allen and H. R. A. Kelleher did not bat.

Leicestershire

G. Lester lbw b Broderick	16	— c Manning b Allen	11
M. R. Hallam c Andrew b Tyson	15	— c Manning b Allen	13
J. van Geloven c Kelleher b Broderick	3	— lbw b Manning	10
C. H. Palmer c Brookes b Manning	3	— b Allen	0
L. R. Gardner c Andrew b Manning	28	— c Kelleher b Manning	13
R. A. Diment lbw b Allen	14	— lbw b Manning	2
M. Hickman c Allen b Broderick	18	— c and b Manning	24
J. Firth lbw b Broderick	0	— b Broderick	15
R. Smith c Allen b Broderick	2	— run out	10
C. T. Spencer c and b Manning	4	— c Barrick b Manning	14
J. Goodwin not out	0	— not out	6
B 11, n-b 1	12	B 1, l-b 12, n-b 2	15

1/27 2/38 3/43 4/43 5/73 6/105 7/105   115   1/29 2/34 3/34 4/58 5/61   133
8/109 9/113 (1.88 an over)   6/62 7/94 8/110 9/113

Leicestershire Bowling

	O.	M.	R.	W.	O.	M.	R.	W.
Spencer	25	4	72	2				
Goodwin	27	2	98	0				
van Geloven	14	1	41	0				
Palmer	14	5	29	0				
Smith	16	4	26	0				

Northamptonshire Bowling

	O.	M.	R.	W.		O.	M.	R.	W.
Tyson	11	4	15	1	....	2	1	1	0
Kelleher	7	3	19	0	....	2	1	1	0
Broderick	19.3	11	29	5	....	32	13	40	1
Manning	20	11	34	3	....	35.4	18	48	5
Allen	3	1	6	1	....	27	19	24	3
Barrick						2	1	4	0

Umpires: P. A. Gibb and Harry Elliott.

At Hove, June 12, 13, 14. NORTHAMPTONSHIRE beat SUSSEX by 142 runs.

NORTHAMPTONSHIRE v. KENT

At Rushden, June 15, 17, 18. Drawn, Northamptonshire taking four points. They were generally the superior side, but Halfyard bowled splendidly for Kent, taking five wickets in each innings. When Northamptonshire lost six men for 157 their ultimate total seemed unlikely, but Fellows-Smith, who had only made his county debut in the previous match when he scored 109 and 65 not out, continued in the same vein, hitting one 6 and seventeen 4's in his brilliant 90 which came in two and a quarter hours. Tyson was equally aggressive. Although Cowdrey and Leary shaped well for Kent and Evans made 41 by means of twelve scoring strokes, Tribe upset the tail and Northamptonshire led by 126. Although they experienced difficulty in strengthening their position against more keen bowling they left Kent to make 324 in four hours forty minutes. Phebey and Wilson replied by making 162 for the first wicket, but the stand lasted nearly three hours and although Cowdrey was twice missed Kent gave up the fight.

Northamptonshire

D. Brookes c Evans b Halfyard	9	— c Halfyard b Ridgway	31
B. L. Reynolds c Phebey b Allan	44	— c Evans b Halfyard	44
A. Lightfoot lbw b Halfyard	49	— c Leary b Halfyard	13
D. W. Barrick b Halfyard	18	— c and b Halfyard	1
G. E. Tribe c Leary b Wright	12	— b Ridgway	42
J. P. Fellows-Smith lbw b Dixon	90	— c and b Allan	32
J. S. Manning c Cowdrey b Halfyard	5	— b Halfyard	17
K. V. Andrew c Pretlove b Halfyard	11	— lbw b Ridgway	8
F. H. Tyson not out	70	— b Halfyard	1
M. H. J. Allen b Allan	10	— not out	1
H. R. A. Kelleher not out	15		
B 4, l-b 10, n-b 1	15	B 1, l-b 5, n-b 1	7

1/9 2/82 3/117 4/122   (9 wkts., dec.) 348
5/152 6/157 7/214 8/291 9/310
(3.73 an over)

1/51 2/104   (9 wkts., dec.) 197
3/114 4/114 5/142 6/182
7/186 8/187 9/197

Kent

A. H. Phebey b Kelleher	12	— lbw b Tribe	90
R. C. Wilson b Kelleher	0	— c Andrew b Manning	77
J. F. Pretlove c Andrew b Tyson	24		
M. C. Cowdrey lbw b Tyson	68	— not out	31
S. E. Leary c Brookes b Manning	45	— b Manning	7
T. G. Evans c Andrew b Manning	41	— c Lightfoot b Tribe	14
A. L. Dixon c Allen b Tribe	14	— not out	13
J. M. Allan not out	8		
F. Ridgway c Reynolds b Tribe	2		
D. V. P. Wright lbw b Tribe	0		
D. J. Halfyard b Tribe	0		
B 8	8	B 9, l-b 3	12

1/4 2/19 3/60 4/143 5/195 6/206   222
7/218 8/220 9/222 (3.41 an over)

1/162 2/184   (4 wkts.) 244
3/197 4/215

Kent Bowling

	O.	M.	R.	W.		O.	M.	R.	W.
Ridgway	17	1	84	0	....	28.4	6	79	3
Halfyard	29	8	81	5	....	25	6	60	5
Allan	30	9	80	2	....	11	2	51	1
Wright	10	0	64	1					
Dixon	7	2	24	1					

Northamptonshire Bowling

	O.	M.	R.	W.		O.	M.	R.	W.
Tyson	18	2	71	2	....	15	2	59	0
Kelleher	13	4	32	2	....	15	6	26	0
Fellows-Smith	5	0	16	0					
Tribe	12.3	2	49	4	....	18	2	62	2
Manning	10	6	21	2	....	23	8	66	2
Allen	6	1	25	0	....	6	0	19	0

Umpires: W. E. Phillipson and A. E. Pothecary.

At Harrogate, June 19, 20, 21. NORTHAMPTONSHIRE drew with YORKSHIRE.

NORTHAMPTONSHIRE v. ROYAL AIR FORCE

At Northampton, June 22, 24, 25. Drawn. Northamptonshire 229 (V. Broderick 63, G. Hill five for 57) and 167 for eight, dec.; Royal Air Force 213 for six, dec. (S. A. Leadbetter 57) and 130 for seven wickets (R. Subba Row 58). Not first-class.

At Westcliff, June 26, 27, 28. NORTHAMPTONSHIRE drew with ESSEX.

NORTHAMPTONSHIRE v. NOTTINGHAMSHIRE

At Kettering, June 29, July 1, 2. Northamptonshire won by five wickets, taking 14 points. Bowlers held the whip hand throughout, and a praiseworthy innings by Tribe tipped the balance in favour of the home side. Nottinghamshire reached three figures with only three men out, but the later batsmen failed against spin. Northamptonshire fared even worse for a time, but furious hitting by Tribe, whose 92 included four 6's and eleven 4's and occupied only two hours, put Northamptonshire ahead. Pace bowlers did the damage when Nottinghamshire batted again and though Northamptonshire were set only 73 to win they lost five men before the winning hit came.

Nottinghamshire

R. T. Simpson c Livingston b Allen	11	— lbw b Tyson	1
J. D. Clay run out	33	— lbw b Tyson	12
R. J. Giles lbw b Allen	2	— lbw b Kelleher	7
F. W. Stocks lbw b Tyson	30	— b Kelleher	5
C. J. Poole c Tribe b Manning	33	— b Tyson	10
M. Hill c Livingston b Tribe	9	— b Tyson	15
B. Dooland c Tyson b Manning	7	— b Tyson	13
A. K. Walker b Tribe	14	— c Andrew b Kelleher	13
G. Millman c Andrew b Tribe	4	— c Barrick b Manning	0
A. Jepson c Fellows-Smith b Manning	0	— c Fellows-Smith b Kelleher	24
K. Smales not out	0	— not out	1
B 12, l-b 4	16	N-b 3	3

1/31 2/34 3/73 4/110 5/128 6/138   159   1/14 2/15 3/25 4/27 5/44   104
7/143 8/154 9/159 (2.30 an over)   6/59 7/75 8/78 9/82

Northamptonshire

D. Brookes b Jepson	29	— c and b Dooland	18
B. L. Reynolds b Jepson	13	— c Millman b Jepson	16
L. Livingston c Dooland b Smales	17		
D. W. Barrick c Millman b Jepson	8	— b Jepson	9
G. E. Tribe b Walker	92	— not out	12
J. P. Fellows-Smith c Millman b Dooland	4	— c Clay b Dooland	0
J. S. Manning c and b Dooland	10	— c Hill b Dooland	1
K. V. Andrew b Jepson	0	— not out	6
F. H. Tyson b Dooland	4		
M. H. J. Allen lbw b Jepson	5		
H. R. A. Kelleher not out	0		
B 9	9	B 3, l-b 8	11

1/34 2/59 3/59 4/70 5/85 6/117   191   1/25 2/47 3/47   (5 wkts.) 73
7/121 8/140 9/169 (2.69 an over)   4/49 5/65

Northamptonshire Bowling

	O.	M.	R.	W.		O.	M.	R.	W.
Tyson	11	1	23	1	....	18	5	37	5
Kelleher	4	1	11	0	....	16.2	6	41	4
Allen	12	3	14	2					
Manning	26.2	9	47	3	....	9	4	23	1
Tribe	16	1	48	3					

Nottinghamshire Bowling

	O.	M.	R.	W.		O.	M.	R.	W.
Walker	8	1	28	1		7	4	12	0
Jepson	34	14	46	5	....	15	3	38	2
Dooland	18	3	75	3	....	7.5	3	12	3
Smales	11	4	33	1					

Umpires: W. F. Price and P. A. Gibb.

NORTHAMPTONSHIRE v. SOMERSET

At Northampton, July 3, 4, 5. Northamptonshire won by 124 runs, taking 14 points. Spin bowlers were dominant, only six wickets falling to pace in the match. Northamptonshire's first innings struggle was relieved only by Fellows-Smith, who drove with great assurance, but Somerset fared no better, though their last pair added 35 before an unfortunate run out ended their chances of the lead. Barrick batted steadily in Northamptonshire's second innings, but McMahon, who took his match analysis to ten wickets for 87 runs, was more than a match for the rest. Overnight rain provided a suitable pitch for Tribe and Manning on the last day, and they dismissed Somerset for 82, sharing the wickets equally.

Northamptonshire

D. Brookes lbw b Hilton	29	— b Hilton	20
P. Arnold c Tripp b Alley	7	— c Langford b McMahon	22
B. Reynolds c and b Langford	17	— c Tripp b McMahon	9
D. W. Barrick c Tripp b Langford	0	— b McMahon	50
G. E. Tribe b Lobb	14	— lbw b Langford	8
J. P. Fellows-Smith c Stephenson b McMahon	48	— c and b McMahon	10
J. S. Manning c Tripp b Hilton	7	— c Hilton b Langford	8
K. V. Andrew c McCool b McMahon	3	— c Stephenson b McMahon	29
M. H. J. Allen c Lomax b McMahon	10	— st Stephenson b McMahon	3
H. R. A. Kelleher run out	3	— c Lomax b Lobb	25
L. McGibbon not out	0	— not out	0
B 9, l-b 2	11	B 11, n-b 1	12

1/16 2/47 3/49 4/63 5/90 6/100 7/117   **149**
8/140 9/143 (2.61 an over)

1/38 2/44 3/62 4/82 5/99   **196**
6/108 7/155 8/161 9/192

Somerset

W. E. Alley b Allen	23	— c Andrew b Manning	19
J. G. Lomax c Tribe b Manning	6	— c Fellows-Smith b Manning	8
P. B. Wight c Allen b Kelleher	32	— b Manning	1
G. M. Tripp lbw b Allen	2	— c and b Manning	9
C. L. McCool lbw b Manning	0	— c Kelleher b Tribe	16
M. F. Tremlett c Kelleher b Tribe	4	— c Allen b Manning	0
H. W. Stephenson c and b Manning	29	— c Fellows-Smith b Tribe	1
J. Hilton c Tribe b Kelleher	1	— c Andrew b Tribe	2
B. Lobb b Kelleher	2	— c and b Tribe	0
B. Langford not out	27	— c Fellows-Smith b Tribe	16
J. McMahon run out	9	— not out	1
L-b 4	4	B 6, l-b 3	9

1/27 2/33 3/37 4/48 5/61 6/88 7/90   **139**
8/96 9/104 (2.04 an over)

1/31 2/35 3/36 4/45 5/45   **82**
6/46 7/52 8/73 9/77

Somerset Bowling

	O.	M.	R.	W.	O.	M.	R.	W.
Lobb	17	4	41	1	11.4	1	26	1
Alley	4	0	12	1	7	4	11	0
Hilton	22.2	9	57	2	16	7	35	1
Langford	7	1	15	2	19	5	38	2
McMahon	7	1	13	3	29	10	74	6

Northamptonshire Bowling

	O.	M.	R.	W.	O.	M.	R.	W.
Kelleher	12	3	32	3	3	2	5	0
McGibbon	3	1	10	0	2	1	4	0
Allen	18	9	25	2	3	2	4	0
Manning	27	14	52	3	25	8	44	5
Tribe	8	2	16	1	21.5	15	16	5

Umpires: C. S. Elliott and R. S. Lay.

NORTHAMPTONSHIRE v. LANCASHIRE

At Northampton, July 6, 8. Northamptonshire won by 59 runs, taking 12 points. This match served to illustrate the changing character of the Northampton pitch. From the start of the season spin bowlers had been gaining a greater measure of success. Now they reaped a rich harvest, only one wicket in a low-scoring match falling to pace bowling. The most remarkable performance was that of Allen, who came on at a time when Lancashire looked to be heading for the lead, and in eight overs took his five wickets for seven runs. Thanks to Arnold, who batted soundly, and Tribe, who hit lustily, Northamptonshire passed 100 with only three wickets down in their second innings, but when they were parted the rest went cheaply. Lancashire, needing 165 to win, collapsed after a stand of 53 by Washbrook and Wharton, Northamptonshire gaining their first home victory over the northern county for 43 years.

Northamptonshire

D. Brookes c Grieves b Tattersall	3	— lbw b Tattersall	17
P. Arnold c Pullar b Hilton	19	— b Hilton	58
B. L. Reynolds c Hilton b Tattersall	1	— lbw b Greenhough	10
D. W. Barrick c Grieves b Tattersall	20	— c Bond b Hilton	4
G. E. Tribe c Washbrook b Greenhough	27	— lbw b Hilton	30
J. P. Fellows-Smith lbw b Greenhough	11	— c Ikin b Greenhough	0
J. S. Manning c Hilton b Tattersall	1	— c Hilton b Tattersall	4
K. V. Andrew lbw b Greenhough	2	— c Ikin b Hilton	7
F. H. Tyson lbw b Greenhough	25	— b Greenhough	0
M. H. J. Allen c Hilton b Greenhough	10	— not out	1
H. R. A. Kelleher not out	7	— b Greenhough	0
L-b 3	3	B 11, l-b 1	12
	129		**143**

1/7 2/23 3/34 4/45 5/68 6/69 7/80   129
8/95 9/120 (1.92 an over)

1/44 2/71 3/86 4/110   143
5/127 6/127 7/131 8/140
9/142

Lancashire

A. Wharton b Manning	7	— b Manning	26
J. Dyson b Tribe	16	— b Tyson	0
J. T. Ikin b Allen	22	— c Andrew b Tribe	7
C. Washbrook b Tribe	13	— c Tribe b Manning	26
K. Grieves c Arnold b Allen	28	— c Reynolds b Manning	1
G. Pullar c Manning b Allen	0	— lbw b Tribe	4
J. D. Bond lbw b Manning	2	— c Tyson b Manning	8
M. J. Hilton b Manning	4	— c Reynolds b Manning	8
A. Wilson hit wkt b Allen	7	— b Tribe	0
R. Tattersall c Manning b Allen	0	— not out	1
T. Greenhough not out	0	— b Tribe	12
B 4, l-b 5	9	B 8, l-b 4	12
	108		**105**

1/19 2/29 3/49 4/81 5/81 6/92 7/99   108
8/108 9/108 (2.25 an over)

1/1 2/13 3/66 4/66 5/71   105
6/73 7/84 8/84 9/88

Lancashire Bowling

	O.	M.	R.	W.	O.	M.	R.	W.
Wharton	5	2	9	0				
Tattersall	25	10	38	4	23	12	36	2
Hilton	21	10	52	1	27	14	51	4
Greenhough	15.5	5	27	5	21.3	2	44	4
Dyson					2	2	0	0

Northamptonshire Bowling

	O.	M.	R.	W.		O.	M.	R.	W.
Tyson	6	1	18	0	....	4	1	6	1
Kelleher	3	2	4	0	....	2	1	1	0
Manning	17	5	38	3	....	20	5	44	5
Tribe	14	7	32	2	....	18.2	8	42	4
Allen	7.5	3	7	5					

Umpires: P. Corrall and A. Skelding.

At Yeovil, July 10, 11, 12. NORTHAMPTONSHIRE drew with SOMERSET.

At Cardiff, July 13, 15. NORTHAMPTONSHIRE beat GLAMORGAN by ten wickets.

NORTHAMPTONSHIRE v. WARWICKSHIRE

At Northampton, July 17, 18, 19. Northamptonshire drew with Warwickshire, taking four points. Again spin bowlers held the whip hand throughout a rain-affected match. Smith batted extremely well on a drying pitch while the rest of the Warwickshire batsmen were falling easy victims to Tribe and Manning. Tribe followed his excellent bowling with a sound innings that carried his side to a lead of 25. Ibadulla's figures were the best of his career. Warwickshire batted better in the second innings, but their declaration left Northamptonshire little over an hour and a quarter to score the 143 needed for victory, and, in failing light, the home side were content to play out time.

Warwickshire

T. W. Cartwright c Arnold b Allen	39	— c Kelleher b Allen	18
N. F. Horner c Fellows-Smith b Manning	0	— b Tribe	14
W. J. Stewart c Barrick b Manning	4	— c Kelleher b Allen	37
M. J. K. Smith c Kelleher b Manning	61	— run out	31
A. Townsend c Barrick b Tribe	6	— c and b Manning	28
A. V. Wolton b Tribe	4	— b Allen	12
K. Ibadulla b Tribe	4	— not out	13
C. Hawkins lbw b Tribe	2	— not out	11
E. Leadbeater b Tribe	12		
R. G. Carter c Kelleher b Manning	0	— b Tribe	2
S. S. Griffiths not out	0		
B 1, l-b 5	6	N-b 1	1

1/11 2/17 3/74 4/87 5/92 6/100 7/106   138   1/18 2/68   (7 wkts., dec.) 167
8/138 9/138 (1.79 an over)   3/69 4/111 5/135 6/143
                                            7/148

Northamptonshire

D. Brookes c Cartwright b Ibadulla	16	— lbw b Leadbeater	12
P. Arnold c Smith b Griffiths	15	— c Hawkins b Carter	0
L. Livingston c and b Carter	23	— not out	16
D. W. Barrick c Smith b Ibadulla	4	— not out	0
B. L. Reynolds c Townsend b Ibadulla	11		
G. E. Tribe b Ibadulla	52		
J. P. Fellows-Smith c Wolton b Ibadulla	4		
J. S. Manning b Ibadulla	4		
K. V. Andrew c and b Ibadulla	19		
M. H. J. Allen not out	5		
H. R. A. Kelleher run out	1		
B 6, w 2, n-b 1	9	B 2, l-b 2	4

1/26 2/50 3/58 4/62 5/94 6/109 7/118   163   1/1 2/32   (2 wkts.) 32
8/154 9/161 (1.87 an over)

Northamptonshire Bowling

	O.	M.	R.	W.		O.	M.	R.	W.
Kelleher	8	3	11	0	....	3	1	3	0
Fellows-Smith..	5	2	8	0					
Manning	30	10	55	4	....	22	10	36	1
Allen	16	8	25	1	....	21	8	63	3
Tribe	18.1	8	33	5	....	30	10	64	2

Warwickshire Bowling

	O.	M.	R.	W.			M.	R.	W.
Carter.........	22	12	35	1	....	3	0	10	1
Griffiths	25	6	52	1	....	3	1	7	0
Ibadulla	40.1	17	67	7	....	5	2	7	0
Leadbeater ...						5	2	4	1

Umpires: D. Davies and T. W. Spencer.

NORTHAMPTONSHIRE v. SUSSEX

At Peterborough, July 20, 22, 23. Drawn, Sussex taking four points. Northamptonshire fought back splendidly after a calamitous first innings, in which they had no effective counter to splendid medium-pace bowling by Thomson and Dexter on a rain-affected pitch. The Sussex batting, by comparison, was carefree. Parks gave an exhilarating display, hitting 72 in less than an hour and a half. Dexter, Suttle and Smith were equally aggressive, but in attempting to keep up the pace the later batsmen fell cheaply to Allen. Arnold inspired Northamptonshire's recovery, and though his partners scored more quickly, it was not until arrears of 183 had been wiped out that he fell. Arnold batted four and a quarter hours, hitting one 6 and twelve 4's. Despite a spell of three wickets for six runs in seven overs by Thomson early on the third day, Northamptonshire set Sussex to score 145 in two and a half hours, but rain frustrated hopes of an interesting finish.

Northamptonshire

D. Brookes c Sheppard b Thomson	3	— c Marlar b Thomson	17
P. Arnold c Foreman b Dexter	21	— c Bates b Smith	86
L. Livingston c Dexter b Thomson......	0	— b Dexter	34
D. W. Barrick c Mantell b Thomson ...	13	— b Suttle	34
B. L. Reynolds c Lenham b Thomson ..	3	— c Mantell b Thomson......	42
G. E. Tribe c Bates b Thomson	4	— lbw b Thomson	22
J. P. Fellows-Smith c Sheppard b Thomson	0	— b Thomson................	14
J. S. Manning c Mantell b Thomson	0	— c Mantell b Bates	34
K. V. Andrew not out.................	4	— b Suttle	8
F. H. Tyson b Dexter	1	— not out	11
M. H. J. Allen c Marlar b Dexter.......	0	— b Bates	0
B 2, l-b 4, n-b 2	8	B 16, l-b 3, w 1, n-b 5 .	25

1/5 2/5 3/35 4/45 5/46 6/46 7/46   57   1/38 2/92 3/173 4/205   327
8/53 9/56 (1.46 an over)   5/259 6/260 7/291 8/310
                                                        9/327

Sussex

D. V. Smith c Tribe b Allen	39	— not out	7
Rev. D. S. Sheppard c Livingston b Manning	10	— not out	3
K. G. Suttle st Andrew b Allen	25		
J. M. Parks c and b Allen	72		
E. R. Dexter st Andrew b Tribe	63		
D. J. Foreman b Allen	8		
L. J. Lenham b Tribe	7		
N. I. Thomson c Tyson b Allen	1		
R. G. Marlar c sub b Allen	8		
D. N. Mantell b Allen	0		
D. L. Bates not out	0		
B 4, 1-b 2, w 1	7		

1/20 2/59 3/118 4/185 5/203 6/230   240   (No wkt.) 10
7/231 8/233 9/240 (3.63 an over)

Sussex Bowling

	O.	M.	R.	W.	O.	M.	R.	W.
Bates	6	3	14	0	18.1	4	44	2
Thomson	19	13	12	7	45	21	82	4
Dexter	14	5	23	3	16	6	31	1
Marlar					27	11	56	0
Suttle					24	9	41	2
Smith					25	13	48	1

Northamptonshire Bowling

	O.	M.	R.	W.	O.	M.	R.	W.
Tyson	17	6	43	0	2	1	6	0
Fellows-Smith	2	0	8	0	1	0	4	0
Manning	10	1	43	1				
Tribe	16	1	57	2				
Allen	20.5	3	82	7				

Umpires: T. W. Spencer and N. Oldfield.

NORTHAMPTONSHIRE v. GLAMORGAN

At Northampton, July 27, 29, 30. Glamorgan won by 23 runs, taking 14 points. Rain interfered on the first day, and the match seemed to be heading for a lifeless draw until Brookes declared Northamptonshire's first innings 90 behind. Tyson justified this venture by sending back the first five Glamorgan batsmen for 25, but an unfinished sixth-wicket stand of 100 by Jones and Walker paved the way to a declaration leaving Northamptonshire 216 to get in two hours forty minutes. Until a vigorous sixth-wicket stand by Tribe and Fellows-Smith was broken, Northamptonshire progressed satisfactorily, but a collapse followed.

Glamorgan

W. G. A. Parkhouse lbw b Allen	36	— b Tyson	12
B. Hedges c Allen b Manning	61	— c Andrew b Tyson	0
L. N. Devereux b Manning	8	— b Tyson	2
D. J. Ward b Manning	8	— c Brookes b Tyson	9
W. E. Jones st Andrew b Tribe	55	— not out	59
A. J. Watkins c Livingston b Allen	31	— b Tyson	0
P. Walker b Allen	2	— not out	38
J. E. McConnon b Tribe	13		
J. Pressdee not out	20		
H. G. Davies lbw b Tribe	16		
D. J. Shepherd b Tribe	0		
B 5, 1-b 1, n-b 1	7	L-b 5	5

1/75 2/108 3/119 4/120 5/169 6/177   257   1/1 2/13   (5 wkts., dec.) 125
7/212 8/229 9/257 (2.42 an over)   3/14 4/25 5/25

Northamptonshire

D. Brookes run out	32	—	lbw b Watkins	13
P. Arnold c Davies b Watkins	9	—	c Parkhouse b McConnon	36
L. Livingston c Davies b McConnon	42	—	c Walker b McConnon	42
D. W. Barrick not out	43	—	lbw b Shepherd	0
B. L. Reynolds c Watkins b Shepherd	15	—	c Ward b McConnon	20
G. E. Tribe c Watkins b Shepherd	0	—	c Pressdee b Shepherd	40
J. P. Fellows-Smith run out	0	—	run out	22
K. V. Andrew not out	18	—	b Shepherd	6
F. H. Tyson (did not bat)		—	c Watkins b Shepherd	0
M. H. J. Allen (did not bat)		—	c Shepherd b Watkins	1
J. S. Manning (did not bat)		—	not out	0
B 2, l-b 5, n-b 1	8		B 5, l-b 7	12

1/25 2/70 3/94 4/121   (6 wkts., dec.) 167   1/34 2/83 3/88 4/98 5/132 192
5/121 6/121 (1.91 an over)   6/175 7/177 8/185 9/192

Northamptonshire Bowling

	O.	M.	R.	W.		O.	M.	R.	W.
Tyson	27	4	64	0	....	10	4	13	5
Fellows-Smith	5	0	18	0	....	5	1	19	0
Manning	29	5	62	3					
Tribe	23	6	51	4	....	16	3	53	0
Allen	22	6	55	3	....	12	4	30	0
Barrick					....	1	0	5	0

Glamorgan Bowling

	O.	M.	R.	W.		O.	M.	R.	W.
Watkins	27	10	53	1	....	13.2	:	58	2
Walker	10	2	21	0	....	6	1	14	0
Shepherd	28	11	42	2	....	6	4	48	4
McConnon	22	8	43	1	....	9	0	60	3

Umpires: W. Place and A. R. Coleman.

At Blackpool, July 31, August 1, 2. NORTHAMPTONSHIRE beat LANCASHIRE by
212 runs.

At Leicester, August 3, 5, 6. NORTHAMPTONSHIRE beat LEICESTERSHIRE by eight
wickets.

NORTHAMPTONSHIRE v. MIDDLESEX

At Northampton, August 7, 8, 9. Drawn, Northamptonshire taking four
points. Rain ruined prospects of an interesting finish. Robertson dominated the
Middlesex batting in both innings. In the first he was complete master of the
spin attack, but until Titmus shared a sixth wicket stand of 40, could find no one
to stay with him. He fell to Tyson with the new ball after three hours forty
minutes of determined resistance. Livingston, who reached 50 in an hour, was
equally outstanding for Northamptonshire, but after his departure they had to
struggle for their narrow lead. Middlesex lost three wickets cheaply at the start
of their second innings before Robertson and Edrich steadied them, and the later
batsmen made useful scores by judicious hitting. Only three overs were possible
on the last day when Middlesex, declaring at their overnight total, set Northamptonshire to score 174 for victory.

Middlesex

J. D. Robertson c and b Allen	94	—	b Allen		41
R. A. Gale c Arnold b Tribe	9	—	c Livingston b Tyson		8
A. C. Walton c Tribe b Allen	10	—	c Allen b Tyson		0
D. O. Baldry lbw b Tribe	0	—	c Andrew b Allen		9
W. J. Edrich b Tribe	12	—	c Allen b Broderick		28
D. Bennett st Andrew b Allen	12	—	c Tribe b Allen		9
F. J. Titmus b Tyson	20	—	c Tyson b Allen		14
J. J. Warr c Allen b Tyson	0	—	not out		10
J. T. Murray c Andrew b Tyson	0	—	st Andrew b Tribe		30
R. J. Hurst b Tribe	12	—	c Allen b Broderick		16
A. E. Moss not out	20				
B 1, l-b 2	3		B 12, l-b 1, n-b 1		14

1/32 2/50 3/53 4/77 5/119 6/159   192   1/29 2/29   (9 wkts., dec.) 179
7/159 8/159 9/166 (2.28 an over)   3/52 4/85 5/105 6/107
                                          7/126 8/152 9/179

Northamptonshire

D. Brookes b Moss	6	—	not out	4
P. Arnold c Murray b Hurst	39	—	not out	5
L. Livingston b Moss	61			
D. W. Barrick b Hurst	4			
B. L. Reynolds c and b Titmus	24			
A. Lightfoot c Robertson b Edrich	4			
G. E. Tribe c Murray b Titmus	9			
V. Broderick not out	25			
K. V. Andrew c Edrich b Titmus	2			
F. H. Tyson b Titmus	5			
M. H. J. Allen b Titmus	0			
B 15, l-b 4	19			

1/18 2/96 3/100 4/126 5/147 6/161   198   (No wkt.) 9
7/161 8/186 9/198 (2.44 an over)

Northamptonshire Bowling

	O.	M.	R.	W.	O.	M.	R.	W.
Tyson	18	5	32	3	14	5	28	2
Lightfoot	4	1	10	0	3	0	13	0
Tribe	26.1	7	77	4	16	5	35	1
Allen	23	10	48	3	30	12	55	4
Broderick	13	6	22	0	21.4	9	34	2

Middlesex Bowling

	O.	M.	R.	W.	O.	M.	R.	W.
Moss	12	3	17	2	2	0	5	0
Warr	4	0	14	0	1	0	4	0
Titmus	28	14	46	5				
Bennett	2	0	7	0				
Gale	4	0	35	0				
Hurst	17	3	44	2				
Edrich	14	5	16	1				

Umpires: J. S. Buller and John Lang·idge.

NORTHAMPTONSHIRE v. ESSEX

At Wellingborough, August 10, 12, 13. Northamptonshire won by eight wickets, taking 14 points. This was their twelfth win of the season, equalling their previous highest total in 1912. The bowling of Manning was the deciding factor. Only Bailey, who stayed over two and a half hours, could cope with Manning's sharp spin, though Barker hit brightly against the pace bowlers. By contrast the Essex spin attack held no terrors, and Northamptonshire were able to build up a lead of 157 before declaring. Unusually restrained, Livingston batted over four and a half hours, hitting one 6 and twelve 4's in his highest score of the season. Essex again started badly, losing three wickets for 32. Then Taylor and Bailey shared an exhilarating stand of 144 in an hour and a half, Taylor reaching his century in under two hours, with one 6 and sixteen 4's. After his dismissal Essex collapsed completely and Northamptonshire were left to score only 48 to win.

Essex

T. C. Dodds lbw b Kelleher	9	— run out 16
G. Barker c Andrew b Manning	38	— c Allen b Kelleher 2
B. Taylor b Manning	16	— lbw b Tyson 105
D. J. Insole c Andrew b Manning	8	— b Kelleher 1
T. E. Bailey not out	36	— c Andrew b Manning 51
L. Savill c Allen b Manning	3	— c sub b Manning 1
M. Bear b Manning	0	— lbw b Tribe 1
W. T. Greensmith st Andrew b Allen	13	— c Kelleher b Manning 4
R. Ralph b Manning	0	— not out 10
K. C. Preston b Tribe	13	— b Tribe 0
I. M. King c Allen b Tribe	1	— run out 0
B 1, l-b 2, n-b 1	4	B 8, l-b 5 13

1/17 2/57 3/68 4/71 5/80 6/80   141

7/103 8/104 9/129 (1.80 an over)

1/10 2/25 3/32 4/176   204
5/185 6/190 7/194 8/194
9/194

Northamptonshire

D. Brookes c Taylor b King	31	— hit wkt b King 14
P. Arnold c Insole b King	75	— not out 23
L. Livingston c Preston b Bailey	95	
D. W. Barrick c Taylor b Bailey	22	— c King b Greensmith 5
B. L. Reynolds not out	47	— not out 2
G. E. Tribe b Preston	3	
J. S. Manning b Preston	9	
K. V. Andrew run out	2	
F. H. Tyson not out	3	
B 10, l-b 1	11	B 4 4

1/81 2/153 3/212 4/259   (7 wkts., dec.) 298   1/29 2/36   (2 wkts.) 48
5/262 6/286 7/288 (2.50 an over)

M. H. J. Allen and H. R. A. Kelleher did not bat.

Northamptonshire Bowling

	O.	M.	R.	W.	O.	M.	R.	W.
Tyson	10	1	37	0	11	2	35	1
Kelleher	8	4	19	1	8	3	22	2
Manning	29	19	37	6	18	4	59	3
Allen	27	14	38	1	6	1	38	0
Tribe	3.5	1	6	2	11	2	37	2

Essex Bowling

	O.	M.	R.	W.	O.	M.	R.	W.
Bailey	30	4	91	2				
Preston	37	3	105	2	5	1	13	0
Ralph	9	1	28	0	4	1	11	0
King	33	16	44	2	3.1	1	6	1
Greensmith	10	3	19	0	3	1	14	1

Umpires: R. Coleman and H. Elliott.

At Worcester, August 14, 15, 16. NORTHAMPTONSHIRE drew with WORCESTERSHIRE.

At Dover, August 17, 19, 20. NORTHAMPTONSHIRE beat KENT by six wickets.

NORTHAMPTONSHIRE v. DERBYSHIRE

At Northampton, August 21, 22, 23. Northamptonshire won by 135 runs, taking 12 points; Derbyshire four points. Spin bowlers dominated the match, and Northamptonshire's trio were much more effective than Derbyshire's pair, Smith and Carr. Livingston, Barrick and Lightfoot were the only batsmen to survive long in the Northamptonshire first innings, but Derbyshire in their turn were soon struggling after Brookes had given his spin bowlers the new ball. Kelly and Short, playing in his first county match, put Derbyshire on the way to the lead, and a seventh partnership between Johnson and Dawkes took them ahead. The best batting of the match came later from Tribe. With Lightfoot, he shared a stand of 64 after five wickets had fallen cheaply. Manning and Kelleher, who hit his 23 in eight scoring strokes, helped to boost the Northamptonshire total and Derbyshire were set to score 187 to win. They collapsed for 51, Manning finishing with eleven wickets for 87 and Tribe seven for 53.

Northamptonshire

D. Brookes c Morgan b Jackson........	5	— c Carr b Jackson 1
P. Arnold c Morgan b Jackson	14	— c Lee b Smith 17
L. Livingston lbw b Carr	27	— c Carr b Jackson 3
D. W. Barrick c Jackson b Smith	22	— b Smith 11
B. L. Reynolds c Lee b Carr	0	— c and b Smith 28
A. Lightfoot lbw b Carr	26	— run out 28
G. E. Tribe c Short b Carr...........	9	— c Morgan b Smith 63
J. S. Manning b Carr	6	— b Smith 17
K. V. Andrew c Carr b Smith	3	— c Dawkes b Morgan 1
M. H. J. Allen b Smith	0	— not out 8
H. R. A. Kelleher not out	0	— c and b Morgan 23
L-b 4, n-b 1.............	5	B 12, l-b 3 15

1/19 2/26 3/73 4/73 5/73 6/86   117   1/8 2/14 3/30 4/41 5/71   215
7/106 8/117 9/117 (1.74 an over)   6/135 7/167 8/172 9/192

Derbyshire

A. Hamer c Andrew b Manning	0	— lbw b Manning 2
C. Lee b Allen	6	— b Tribe 13
J. Kelly c Livingston b Manning......	30	— b Manning 5
D. B. Carr c Kelleher b Allen	0	— c Tribe b Manning 10
M. Morgan b Manning	2	— c Brookes b Tribe 0
J. D. Short b Tribe	22	— b Tribe 0
H. L. Johnson not out	49	— lbw b Tribe 3
G. O. Dawkes c Livingston b Manning ..	28	— not out 11
H. J. Rhodes b Manning	0	— b Tribe 4
E. Smith c Allen b Manning	1	— b Tribe 0
L. Jackson lbw b Manning............	3	— c and b Manning 1
L-b 5	5	B 2.......... 2

1/0 2/6 3/6 4/13 5/60 6/82 7/133   146   1/4 2/20 3/22 4/30 5/30   51
8/134 9/138 (2.65 an over)   6/30 7/44 8/50 9/50

Derbyshire Bowling

	O.	M.	R.	W.		O.	M.	R.	W.
Jackson	17	7	24	2	....	19	7	21	2
Rhodes........	4	1	10	0	....	8	1	23	0
Smith	21.3	8	39	3	....	34	17	77	5
Morgan	5	2	8	0	....	30.1	13	43	2
Carr	19	11	31	5	....	11	6	25	0
				Johnson		3	0	11	0

Northamptonshire Bowling

	O.	M.	R.	W.		O.	M.	R.	W.
Manning	27.5	8	65	7	....	17.5	10	22	4
Allen	15	5	39	2	....	7	2	11	0
Tribe	12	3	37	1	....	10	3	16	0

Umpires: A. R. Coleman and W. E. Phillipson.

At Buxton, August 24, 26, 27. NORTHAMPTONSHIRE drew with DERBYSHIRE (no decision).

At Bournemouth, August 28, 29, 30. NORTHAMPTONSHIRE beat HAMPSHIRE by seven wickets.

THE ASHES

The Ashes were originated in 1882 when, on August 29, Australia defeated the full strength of England on English soil for the first time. The Australians won by the narrow margin of seven runs, and the following day the *Sporting Times* printed a mock obituary notice, written by Shirley Brooks, son of an editor of *Punch*, which read:

"In affectionate remembrance of English Cricket which died at The Oval, 29th August, 1882. Deeply lamented by a large circle of sorrowing friends and acquaintances. R.I.P. N.B. The body will be cremated and the Ashes taken to Australia."

The following winter the Hon. Ivo Bligh, afterwards Lord Darnley, set out to Australia to recover these mythical Ashes. Australia won the first match by nine wickets, but England won the next two, and the real ashes came into being when some Melbourne women burnt a stump used in the third game and presented the ashes in an urn to Ivo Bligh.

When Lord Darnley died in 1927, the urn, by a bequest in his will, was given to M.C.C., and it held a place of honour in the Long Room at Lord's until early 1953 when, with other cricket treasures, it was moved to the newly built Imperial Cricket Memorial near the pavilion. There it stands permanently, together with the velvet bag in which the urn was originally given to Lord Darnley and the score card of the 1882 match.

NOTTINGHAMSHIRE

President—MAJOR J. K. LANE

Secretary—H. A. BROWN, County Cricket Ground,
Nottingham

Captain—R. T. Simpson

G. Millman   County Badge   C. J. Poole

Beset by illness and injury from the opening day of the 1957
season, Nottinghamshire experienced a depressing summer and
finished third from the bottom of the Championship. Only five
victories were recorded and two of these came in the last week of
the campaign. Stocks, the experienced left-hand batsman, was
unavailable during May as he sustained a broken finger at the nets
two days before the first match. This was against Middlesex, at
Lord's, where Walker, the Australian left-arm fast bowler, after
taking seven wickets for 56 runs in the first innings, went down
with mumps, and he, too, was absent for the rest of May.

Worst of all was the back trouble which laid low Simpson, the
captain, whose appearances were confined to ten matches in the
middle of the season when he rarely looked like his true self.
Jepson, who captained the side for most of the summer, had also
to shoulder the bulk of the seam bowling. This was a big task for
a player of 42. He did well to take 68 wickets.

The Australian leg-spin bowler, Dooland, finished top of the
bowling, but it was not until late in the season that he found his
best form. In fact, he completed his 1,000 runs before he claimed
his 100th wicket. He did this on August 13th, and that same day
announced that after completing five years' service with the county
he would be returning home. His departure immediately following
his benefit left a gap that will be hard to fill. Fortunately it is
anticipated that the 1957 Cambridge University captain, Goonesena,
will be available next summer. Like Dooland he completed the
double, for although he did not appear in Championship matches

until after the University match, he took 49 wickets and scored 343 runs for the county.

So disappointing were the results by mid-summer that the Nottinghamshire Committee decided to introduce several young ground staff players. This meant the disappearance from the eleven of such well-tried batsmen as Clay, Stocks, Giles and off-spinner Smales. The new policy produced some satisfaction. Maurice and Norman Hill (unrelated) established first-team places. The former, a stylish right-hand batsman, completed 1,000 runs and N. Hill, a tenacious left-hander, was also a brilliant close-to-the-wicket fielder. Springall, formerly on the M.C.C. staff, proved a useful successor to Clay. Morgan, a Welshman signed on special registration, showed promise as an off-spin bowler. One cap was awarded in 1957, to Millman, who was regarded as one of the best young wicket-keepers in the country.

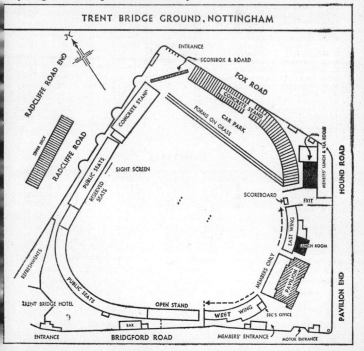

TRENT BRIDGE GROUND, NOTTINGHAM

NOTTINGHAMSHIRE RESULTS

All First-Class Matches—Played 30, *Won* 5, *Lost* 13, *Drawn* 12

County Championship Matches—Played 28, *Won* 5, *Lost* 13,
Drawn 9, *No Decision* 1

COUNTY CHAMPIONSHIP AVERAGES

BATTING

	Birthplace	Mtchs.	Inns.	Not Outs	Runs	100's	Highest Inns.	Aver.
C. J. Poole.....	*Forest Town*	23	44	5	1425	1	110*	36.53
B. Dooland ...	*Adelaide*	28	53	3	1374	1	115*	27.48
F. W. Stocks ..	*Hucknall*	11	22	1	544	2	103*	25.90
T. Atkinson....	*Millom*	3	6	4	51	0	21*	25.50
J. D. Springall..	*Rotherhithe*	13	25	1	609	0	83	25.37
N. Hill	*Holbeck*	16	29	2	659	1	119	24.40
J. D. Clay	*W. Bridgford*	20	39	0	917	0	86	23.51
M. Winfield...	*Gainsborough*	9	17	0	398	0	74	23.41
M. Hill........	*Scunthorpe*	24	45	1	1030	0	95	23.40
G. Goonesena..	*Colombo*	11	19	3	343	0	51	21.43
R. J. Giles.....	*Chilwell*	11	21	0	413	1	101	19.66
P. F. Harvey...	*Linby*	3	6	1	94	0	34	18.80
A. K. Walker..	*Manly, N.S.W.*	14	24	2	400	0	73	18.18
E. Martin	*Lambley*	8	15	1	242	0	38	17.28
R. T. Simpson..	*Sherwood*	9	18	0	306	1	113	17.00
G. Millman ...	*Bedford*	23	40	7	538	0	58	16.30
K. J. Poole ...	*Thurgarton*	7	12	1	161	0	32	14.63
R. C. Vowles ..	*Grimsby*	4	7	2	72	0	54	14.40
A. Jepson	*Selsdon*	26	45	7	525	0	61	13.81
K. Smales	*Horsforth*	17	29	10	202	0	48	10.63
C. S. Matthews	*Worksop*	13	15	5	53	0	12	5.30
M. Morgan ...	*Ynyshir*	10	11	5	19	0	8*	3.16
E. J. Rowe.....	*Netherfield*	5	7	7	10	0	5*	—

* *Signifies not out.*

BOWLING

	Overs	Maidens	Runs	Wickets	Average
B. Dooland	1204.2	380	2867	129	22.22
G. Goonesena..........	387.3	93	1104	49	22.53
R. C. Vowles	34	4	145	6	24.16
A. Jepson	713	176	1853	66	28.07
C. S. Matthews	306.5	64	879	28	31.39
A. K. Walker	355.4	78	1030	29	35.51
K. Smales	513.5	169	1349	36	37.47
M. Morgan	231.4	66	631	12	52.58
K. J. Poole	121	13	447	5	89.40
T. Atkinson...........	59	11	184	2	92.00
F. W. Stocks	26	2	136	1	136.00

Also bowled: R. J. Giles 2—1—3—0; M. Hill 1—0—2—0; R. T. Simpson 0.2—0—4—0.

Amateurs.—G. Goonesena, R. T. Simpson.

At Lord's, May 4, 6, 7. NOTTINGHAMSHIRE lost to MIDDLESEX by 115 runs.

At Frome, May 11, 13, 14. NOTTINGHAMSHIRE lost to SOMERSET by 92 runs.

At Birmingham, May 15, 16, 17. NOTTINGHAMSHIRE drew with WARWICKSHIRE.

NOTTINGHAMSHIRE v. NORTHAMPTONSHIRE

At Nottingham, May 18, 20, 21. Drawn, Northamptonshire taking four points. Conditions were so much in favour of the bat that once Northamptonshire gained first innings lead early on the final day only formal interest remained. The disappointing form of several experienced players led Nottinghamshire to try two 21-year-old batsmen, Maurice Hill, a right-hander, and Norman Hill, a left-hander. M. Hill seized his chance with an elegant innings, full of attractive forward strokes. Winfield and Dooland also batted well and Jepson declared first thing on Monday. Another young batsman, Norman, then distinguished himself for Northamptonshire by sharing an opening partnership of 155 with Brookes that placed his side well on the road to the first innings lead and bonus points.

Nottinghamshire

R. Giles lbw b Kelleher	0	— c and b Tribe	84
J. D. Clay lbw b Manning	38	— run out	24
H. M. Winfield run out	74	— c Clarke b Tribe	63
N. Hill lbw b Manning	3	— b Manning	12
M. Hill c Brookes b Manning	85	— c Norman b Allen	29
B. Dooland c Reynolds b Manning	56	— not out	34
K. J. Poole lbw b Kelleher	0	— not out	4
G. Millman not out	24		
A. Jepson b Kelleher	17		
K. Smales not out	1		
B 4, l-b 5, n-b 1	10	B 5, l-b 2, w 1, n-b 3	11

1/0 2/83 3/89 4/188   (8 wkts., dec.) 308
5/242 6/248 7/273 8/306 (2.67 an over)
C. S. Matthews did not bat.

1/45 2/166 3/185 (5 wkts.) 261
4/193 5/256

Northamptonshire

D. Brookes lbw b Jepson	95	G. E. Tribe not out	11
M. Norman c K. Poole b Dooland	64	B 1, l-b 3	4
L. Livingston b Matthews	75		
D. W. Barrick not out	59	1/155 2/176 3/280 (4 wkts., dec.) 312
B. Reynolds lbw b Jepson	4	4/295 (2.73 an over)

J. S. Manning, M. H. J. Allen, K. V. Andrew, R. W. Clarke and H. R. A. Kelleher did not bat.

Northamptonshire Bowling

	O.	M.	R.	W.	O.	M.	R.	W.
Kelleher	35	6	65	3	18	5	36	0
Clarke	21	1	70	0	8	1	23	0
Tribe	19	5	48	0	28	10	79	2
Manning	31	8	92	4	25	7	50	1
Allen	8	3	20	0	20	5	49	1
Barrick	1	0	3	0	3	0	13	0

Nottinghamshire Bowling

	O.	M.	R.	W.
Jepson	15	1	40	2
Matthews	19.5	1	74	1
Dooland	35	13	73	1
Smales	28	6	55	0
K. Poole	16	0	66	0

Umpires: T. W. Spencer and T. J. Bartley.

NOTTINGHAMSHIRE v. HAMPSHIRE

At Nottingham, May 22, 23, 24. Drawn, Nottinghamshire taking two points. When Marshall and Gray began Hampshire's second innings with a breezy partnership of 137 in ninety minutes it looked as though an interesting finish was in prospect. After Marshall's dismissal at 150, however, the scoring became progressively slower and Eagar delayed his declaration until Nottinghamshire were left to make 268 in two hours. Then rain intervened and the game was abandoned. A painstaking century by Horton, who batted nearly four hours, and sustained bowling by Dooland were the features of the opening day. Dooland bowled for four hours and twenty minutes of the five and a half hours Hampshire batted. Nottinghamshire scored even more laboriously against accurate defensive bowling by Sainsbury and Shackleton until M. Hill and Dooland put on 109 in eighty-five minutes.

Hampshire

R. E. Marshall c Rowe b Smales	43	— st Rowe b Dooland	87
J. R. Gray lbw b Dooland	54	— c Clay b Dooland	51
H. Horton c Matthews b Dooland	106	— b Jepson	1
P. J. Sainsbury b Dooland	0	— c Dooland b Poole	42
H. M. Barnard b Dooland	8	— not out	71
A. C. D. Ingleby-Mackenzie c Jepson b Smales	6	— c M. Hill b Poole	2
L. Harrison c Rowe b Dooland	2	— not out	6
E. D. R. Eagar b Matthews	17		
D. Shackleton c Jepson b Dooland	30		
V. H. D. Cannings not out	6		
M. D. Burden st Rowe b Dooland	2		
B 2, l-b 2, w 1	5	L-b 12, n-b 1	13

1/78 2/109 3/115 4/127 5/156 6/166   **279**
7/193 8/270 9/275 (2.21 an over)

1/137 2/138   (5 wkts., dec.)   **273**
3/150 4/247 5/255

Nottinghamshire

R. J. Giles c Eagar b Sainsbury	22	A. Jepson b Cannings	8
J. D. Clay b Sainsbury	40	C. S. Matthews not out	5
H. M. Winfield b Sainsbury	17		
N. Hill b Burden	31	B 1, l-b 6	7
M. Hill run out	63		
B. Dooland b Cannings	83	1/57 2/66 3/109 (9 wkts., dec.) **285**
K. J. Poole run out	5	4/125 5/234 6/247 7/271 8/271
K. Smales c Eagar b Shackleton	4	9/285 (2.08 an over)

E. J. Rowe did not bat.

Nottinghamshire Bowling

	O.	M.	R.	W.	O.	M.	R.	W.
Jepson	11	3	20	0	10	1	41	1
Matthews	18	3	62	1	11	3	33	0
Dooland	52.2	23	94	7	29	9	77	2
Poole	8	2	20	0	12	0	46	2
Smales	37	12	78	2	18	3	60	0
Giles					2	1	3	0

Hampshire Bowling

	O.	M.	R.	W.
Shackleton	31	14	55	1
Cannings	24.2	5	62	2
Sainsbury	49	25	79	3
Burden	27	11	62	1
Gray	6	1	20	0

Umpires: L. H. Gray and J. S. Buller.

At Nottingham, May 25, 27, 28. NOTTINGHAMSHIRE drew with WEST INDIES. (See WEST INDIES section.)

NOTTINGHAMSHIRE v. WORCESTERSHIRE

At Nottingham, June 1, 3, 4. Nottinghamshire won by six wickets, taking 12 points to two by Worcestershire. They fought back splendidly after once looking in danger of following-on. Walker, playing his first game after a long absence through mumps, led such a spirited rally that Worcestershire only just gained first innings lead. Despite more hard hitting by Dews, Worcestershire broke down in the second innings against Smales. As in the first innings, the two Hills checked a second bad start by Nottinghamshire and in two hours Maurice was within sight of his maiden century. Then he jumped out to drive and was smartly stumped. He hit two 6's and thirteen 4's.

Worcestershire

D. Kenyon b Dooland	34	— c Rowe b Jepson	40
L. Outschoorn lbw b Jepson	6	— c Rowe b Jepson	2
G. Dews c N. Hill b Dooland	73	— c N. Hill b Dooland	83
D. W. Richardson c Rowe b Jepson	35	— b Smales	2
R. G. Broadbent c Dooland b K. Poole	21	— c Dooland b Smales	0
M. J. Horton c Rowe b Dooland	73	— c N. Hill b Smales	4
R. Booth c K. Poole b Dooland	37	— c Rowe b Dooland	13
R. O. Jenkins b Jepson	22	— c Rowe b Smales	2
R. Berry c Dooland b Smales	1	— lbw b Smales	0
J. Flavell c N. Hill b Smales	4	— not out	13
J. Aldridge not out	0	— c and b Smales	6
B 4, l-b 1	5	B 5, l-b 1	6

1/8 2/64 3/141 4/157 5/185 6/280   311
7/284 8/291 9/297 (2.61 an over)

1/2 2/88 3/91 4/91 5/125   171
6/141 7/147 8/147 9/159

Nottinghamshire

J. D. Clay c Broadbent b Aldridge	5	— lbw b Horton	10
H. M. Winfield c and b Aldridge	1	— c Dews b Berry	9
M. Hill c Booth b Berry	43	— st Booth b Jenkins	95
N. Hill c Booth b Aldridge	50	— c Aldridge b Jenkins	27
C. J. Poole c and b Berry	0	— not out	28
B. Dooland lbw b Berry	12	— not out	4
K. J. Poole c Horton b Berry	32		
A. K. Walker b Flavell	61		
K. Smales c Broadbent b Flavell	48		
A. Jepson c Booth b Flavell	40		
E. J. Rowe not out	5		
B 4, l-b 5, n-b 1	10	B 1, l-b 1, w 1	3

1/6 2/9 3/72 4/72 5/90 6/140 7/150   307
8/232 9/274 (3.33 an over)

1/18 2/26 3/110   (4 wkts.) 176
4/168

Nottinghamshire Bowling

	O.	M.	R.	W.		O.	M.	R.	W.
Walker	16	2	35	0	....	7	1	16	0
Jepson	17.2	3	39	3	....	11	3	25	2
Dooland	43	12	108	4	....	20	8	52	2
Smales	33	12	84	2	....	17.1	4	55	6
K. Poole	10	2	40	1	....	4	1	17	0

Worcestershire Bowling

	O.	M.	R.	W.		O.	M.	R.	W.
Flavell	16.4	1	43	3	....	4	0	6	0
Aldridge	18	3	64	3	....	4	1	8	0
Berry	36	10	94	4	....	19	6	66	1
Horton	17	4	80	0	....	20.1	5	53	1
Jenkins	4	1	16	0	....	8	1	40	2

Umpires: J. F. Crapp and W. E. Phillipson.

NOTTINGHAMSHIRE v. SOMERSET

At Nottingham, June 5, 6, 7. Drawn, Nottinghamshire taking four points. Only eighty-five minutes' play was possible on the last day because of rain; otherwise Nottinghamshire would almost certainly have gained full reward for superior cricket. Simpson and Stocks, both making their first appearance of the season, celebrated with excellent innings and Dooland bowled cleverly in bringing about Somerset's first innings collapse. Two more Australians, Alley and McCool, took chief honours for Somerset.

Nottinghamshire

R. T. Simpson c Wight b McMahon	....	78	— b Lobb	0
J. D. Clay c and b McMahon		54	— b Hilton	19
M. Hill c Atkinson b McMahon		20	— c sub b McMahon	5
N. Hill c Stephenson b McMahon		0	— b Hilton	3
F. W. Stocks c Palmer b Alley		46	— c McMahon b Lobb	101
H. M. Winfield lbw b Alley		22	— st McCool b McMahon	42
B. Dooland c Stephenson b Alley		8	— c Alley b McMahon	16
A. K. Walker c Hilton b Alley		7	— run out	16
K. Smales b Alley		4	— c and b Lobb	20
A. Jepson c McCool b McMahon		2	— b Alley	3
E. J. Rowe not out		0	— not out	1
B 8, w 1		9	B 5, l-b 4, w 3, n-b 1	13

1/120 2/149 3/155 4/158 5/233 6/233   250   1/0 2/62 3/62 4/71 5/71   239
7/239 8/249 9/250 (2.80 an over)   6/122 7/166 8/220 9/233

Somerset

W. E. Alley c Clay b Dooland		37	— lbw b Jepson	12
K. E. Palmer c Rowe b Dooland		16	— not out	36
P. B. Wight b Dooland		7	— not out	17
C. L. McCool b Dooland		65		
G. G. Atkinson lbw b Dooland		3		
M. F. Tremlett b Dooland		13		
H. W. Stephenson lbw b Jepson		0		
J. Hilton c Walker b Dooland		6		
B. Langford b Smales		0		
J. W. McMahon run out		0		
B. Lobb not out		1		
B 2, l-b 4		6		

1/52 2/57 3/64 4/70 5/118 6/119   154   1/19   (1 wkt.) 65
7/144 8/146 9/150 (2.10 an over)

Somerset Bowling

	O.	M.	R.	W.		O.	M.	R.	W.
Lobb	16	7	29	0	....	13.3	2	54	3
Alley	12.1	3	31	5	....	13	3	34	1
McCool	15	2	63	0					
McMahon	29	15	69	5	....	28	11	63	3
Langford	9	2	27	0	....	2	0	7	0
Hilton	8	3	22	0	....	16	4	62	2
Atkinson					....	2	0	6	0

Nottinghamshire Bowling

	O.	M.	R.	W.		O.	M.	R.	W.
Jepson	22	3	46	1	....	12	4	28	1
Walker	5	2	16	0	....	10	0	20	0
Dooland	30.1	10	50	7	....	4	0	15	0
Smales	16	7	36	1	....	2	1	2	0

Umpires: Harry Elliott and L. H. Gray.

NOTTINGHAMSHIRE v. SURREY

At Nottingham, June 8, 10, 11. Surrey won by an innings and 119 runs, taking 14 points. Although helped by the after-effects of a fierce storm which ended play on the opening day after they had reached 147 for two, Surrey were always masters. Stewart fell early on the second morning, but May shared a partnership of 103 in an hour with Fletcher before declaring. Lock's biting left-hand spin upset Nottinghamshire in their first innings and when they followed-on 178 behind they found Laker virtually unplayable on the third day.

Surrey

T. H. Clark c Rowe b Stocks 40	K. F. Barrington not out......... 10
M. J. Stewart b Smales 80	B 4, l-b 2 6
B. Constable c and b Walker..... 31	
P. B. H. May b Jepson 83	1/74 2/135 3/172 (4 wkts., dec.) 303
D. G. W. Fletcher not out 53	4/275 (3.56 an over)

E. A. Bedser, A. J. McIntyre, G. A. R. Lock, J. C. Laker and A. V. Bedser did not bat.

Nottinghamshire

R. T. Simpson c Fletcher b A. Bedser ...	5	— b A. Bedser	5
J. D. Clay c and b Lock	26	— c Barrington b Lock	1
H. M. Winfield c Lock b A. Bedser	3	— c Lock b Laker	0
M. Hill c Stewart b Lock	14	— b Laker	19
N. Hill c E. Bedser b Lock	7	— b Laker	16
F. W. Stocks c May b Lock	15	— c Lock b Laker	1
B. Dooland c Constable b Lock	22	— lbw b Laker	7
A. K. Walker c Laker b Lock	1	— c Fletcher b Lock	4
K. Smales b Laker	15	— c McIntyre b Laker	0
A. Jepson b Lock....................	10	— c May b Laker	2
E. J. Rowe not out	0	— not out	0
B 4, l-b 2, n-b 1	7	B 4...................	4

1/9 2/12 3/49 4/54 5/63 6/93 7/98   125   1/6 2/6 3/10 4/39 5/46   59
8/102 9/125 (1.73 an over)   6/47 7/52 8/58 9/59

Nottinghamshire Bowling

	O.	M.	R.	W.		O.	M.	R.	W.
Walker	14	1	49	1					
Jepson	22	3	62	1					
Dooland	28	4	100	0					
Smales	18	1	70	1					
Stocks	3	0	16	1					

Surrey Bowling

	O.	M.	R.	W.		O.	M.	R.	W.
A. Bedser......	18	8	41	2	....	4	2	4	1
Lock	32.2	13	49	7	....	19	4	35	2
Laker	19	9	26	1	....	15.5	10	16	7
E. Bedser	3	2	2	0					

Umpires: E. Davies and C. S. Elliott.

At Bradford, June 12, 13. NOTTINGHAMSHIRE lost to YORKSHIRE by eight wickets.

NOTTINGHAMSHIRE v. CAMBRIDGE UNIVERSITY

At Nottingham, June 15, 17, 18. Drawn. The match was specially memorable for Dooland. When within three runs of his first century in England, he sacrificed his wicket after being called for a sharp run. His leg-spin and googlies proved too much for most of the Cambridge batsmen in the first innings, but when his bowling would almost certainly have brought victory, stomach trouble kept him away on the last day. In his absence Walker turned to spin-bowling with reasonable success but, though they claimed the extra half-hour, Nottinghamshire left themselves insufficient time to win.

Nottinghamshire

R. T. Simpson b Wheatley	0	— hit wkt b Smith	12
J. D. Clay b Wheatley.................	44	— b Goonesena	16
R. J. Giles c Swift b Cook	77	— c Smith b Goonesena	28
M. Hill b Wheatley	1	— c Swift b Wheatley	0
C. J. Poole b Cook	46	— not out	64
J. P. Springall c Barber b Goonesena....	40	— b Pieris	18
B. Dooland run out	97		
G. Millman c Swift b Goonesena	0	— c McLachlan b Goonesena .	11
A. K. Walker c Smith b Goonesena	5	— not out	20
A. Jepson not out	36		
M. Morgan st Swift b Goonesena......	0		
B 14, l-b 4	18	B 9, l-b 2	11

1/11 2/89 3/91 4/172 5/179 6/256   364   1/30 2/36   (6 wkts., dec.) 180
7/256 8/292 9/331   3/67 4/71 5/75 6/127

Cambridge University

R. W. Barber c Hill b Dooland........	25	— b Walker	9
I. McLachlan c Millman b Dooland	38	— run out	5
D. J. Green c Jepson b Walker	23	— c Springall b Walker	24
G. Goonesena c and b Dooland	0	— c Simpson b Morgan	8
R. M. James run out	63	— c Giles b Morgan	34
S. A. U. Fakir b Morgan	1	— c and b Walker	18
C. S. Smith c Millman b Dooland	35	— not out	0
G. W. Cook b Morgan	8	— not out	9
P. I. Pieris c Clay b Dooland	13	— b Morgan	31
B. T. Swift c Morgan b Dooland	25		
O. S. Wheatley not out	17		
B 10, w 1	11		

1/53 2/76 3/76 4/90 5/105 6/162   259   1/14 2/16 3/72   (7 wkts.) 138
7/175 8/211 9/214   4/72 5/98 6/106 7/134

Cambridge University Bowling

	O.	M.	R.	W.		O.	M.	R.	W.
Smith	23	5	66	0	....	14	5	26	1
Wheatley	23	6	52	3	....	11	2	33	1
Pieris	22	4	75	0	....	9	2	24	1
Goonesena	25.1	5	84	4	....	19	6	51	3
Cook	24	10	63	2	....	8	1	35	0
Fakir	1	0	2	0					
James	1	0	4	0	....	1	1	0	0

Nottinghamshire Bowling

	O.	M.	R.	W.		O.	M.	R.	W.
Walker	24	11	26	1	....	28	12	57	3
Jepson	17	2	41	0	....	6	2	7	0
Morgan	33	3	102	2	....	22	8	74	3
Dooland	35	17	70	6					
M. Hill	3	0	9	0					

Umpires: J. S. Buller and F. S. Lee.

NOTTINGHAMSHIRE v. MIDDLESEX

At Nottingham, June 19, 20, 21. Nottinghamshire won by two wickets, taking 14 points. A sparkling innings by C. J. Poole enabled them to score at the necessary rate of 100 runs an hour, the winning hit being made with seven minutes left. The pitch always favoured batsmen, the best of several good innings on the first day being Murray's maiden century. Murray batted altogether two and a half hours and hit twenty-two 4's. Nottinghamshire responded with an even more consistent display led by Simpson, and they claimed bonus points by 0.007 runs an over—the slenderest margin recorded since the award was introduced. A characteristic exhibition of forcing strokes by Compton distinguished the Middlesex second innings.

Middlesex

J. D. Robertson c Poole b Dooland	 41	— c Millman b Walker 28
R. A. Gale b Walker	 20	— c Walker b Smales 64
W. J. Edrich c and b Dooland	 49	
D. C. S. Compton b Jepson	 14	— b Jepson 77
F. J. Titmus b Dooland	 8	— c Millman b Walker 6
D. O. Baldry b Dooland	 15	— lbw b Jepson 2
G. P. S. Delisle lbw b Dooland	 0	— not out 76
J. T. Murray st Millman b Walker	120	— not out 11
D. Bennett not out	 51	
J. J. Warr not out	 24	
B 2, l-b 4	6	B 5, l-b 8 13

1/45 2/79 3/106 4/125   (8 wkts., dec.) 348   1/46 2/70   (5 wkts., dec.) 277
5/138 6/138 7/179 8/310 (3.00 an over)   3/124 4/251 5/260
R. J. Hurst did not bat.

Nottinghamshire

R. T. Simpson c and b Edrich	113	— c Edrich b Bennett	2
J. D. Clay b Titmus	50	— c Gale b Compton	37
R. J. Giles lbw b Edrich	7	— st Murray b Titmus	37
F. W. Stocks c Murray b Bennett	46	— c Murray b Titmus	0
M. Hill c Murray b Warr	32	— run out	24
C. J. Poole not out	65	— c Hurst b Compton	65
B. Dooland c Edrich b Warr	16	— c Gale b Titmus	18
A. K. Walker c Baldry b Titmus	19	— c Delisle b Warr	0
A. E. Jepson c Baldry b Titmus	18	— not out	31
G. Millman b Titmus	5		
K. Smales (did not bat)		— not out	9
B 16, l-b 5, w 2	23	B 10	10

1/148 2/162 3/180 4/266 (9 wkts., dec.) 394
5/268 6/295 7/338 8/365 9/394
(3.007 an over)

1/3 2/75 3/75   (8 wkts.) 233
4/86 5/101 6/143 7/145
8/217

Nottinghamshire Bowling

	O.	M.	R.	W.		O.	M.	R.	W.
Walker	21	4	66	2	....	24	5	93	2
Jepson	27	8	67	1	....	18	2	71	2
Smales	24	6	70	0	....	20	3	85	1
Dooland	42	12	112	5	....	2	0	15	0
Stocks	2	0	27	0					

Middlesex Bowling

	O.	M.	R.	W.		O.	M.	R.	W.
Warr	21	5	37	2	....	6	0	31	1
Bennett	17	3	56	1	....	8	2	29	1
Compton	16	1	55	0	....	12	0	68	2
Hurst	14	2	60	0	....	5	0	33	0
Titmus	29	14	79	4	....	14	1	62	3
Edrich	34	10	84	2					

Umpires: J. S. Buller and P. Corrall.

At Cowes, June 22, 24, 25.   NOTTINGHAMSHIRE lost to HAMPSHIRE by 80 runs.

NOTTINGHAMSHIRE v. GLAMORGAN

At Nottingham, June 26, 27, 28. Glamorgan won by 27 runs, taking 12 points to four by Nottinghamshire. Glamorgan made a splendid recovery after following-on 193 behind. They lost six wickets in clearing the arrears, but a determined stand by Jones and the more aggressive McConnon helped them build a lead of 102. Although the pitch was never vicious, Wooller and H. D. Davies bowled with such admirable spirit that seven Nottinghamshire wickets fell for 39. Then Shepherd completed one of the most dramatic victories of the season by taking the last three wickets. Wooller, at the age of 43, bowled throughout the two hours in intense heat. Everything went in favour of the home side for the first two days when, after consistent batting, their spin bowlers shattered Glamorgan's first innings.

Nottinghamshire

R. T. Simpson c Shepherd b Wooller....	31	—	c Parkhouse b H. D. Davies	5
J. D. Clay c H. G. Davies b H. D. Davies	20	—	c H. G. Davies b H. D. Davies	4
R. J. Giles c Walker b McConnon	39	—	b Wooller	3
F. W. Stocks c Hedges b Walker	15	—	c and b Wooller	2
C. J. Poole b McConnon	58	—	c Shepherd b Wooller	16
M. Hill c Wooller b H. D. Davies	46	—	c McConnon b H. D. Davies	6
B. Dooland b Walker	28	—	c H. G. Davies b H. D. Davies	0
A. K. Walker c H. G. Davies b H. D. Davies	73	—	b Shepherd	26
G. Millman c Jones b Wooller	42	—	not out	11
A. Jepson c Shepherd b Wooller	1	—	c H. G. Davies b Shepherd	0
K. Smales not out	0	—	b Shepherd	1
L-b 1	1	—	N-b 1	1

1/43 2/56 3/81 4/148 5/173 6/222   354   1/7 2/10 3/13 4/17 5/33   75
7/256 8/348 9/349 (3.30 an over)   6/37 7/39 8/71 9/73

Glamorgan

W. G. A. Parkhouse c Poole b Jepson ..	6	—	c Simpson b Jepson	9
B. Hedges c Millman b Dooland	30	—	b Dooland	24
L. N. Devereux c Stocks b Walker	16	—	lbw b Walker	59
W. E. Jones c and b Smales	17	—	lbw b Dooland	63
A. J. Watkins c Stocks b Smales	2	—	lbw b Dooland	13
P. M. Walker c Poole b Dooland	40	—	c Millman b Dooland	23
W. Wooller c Poole b Dooland	20	—	c Stocks b Smales	9
J. E. McConnon c Hill b Dooland	5	—	lbw b Jepson	52
H. G. Davies st Millman b Dooland	15	—	b Dooland	19
H. D. Davies not out	3	—	b Dooland	3
D. J. Shepherd c Walker b Smales	2	—	not out	5
B 1, l-b 3, n-b 1	5	—	B 12, l-b 4	16

1/7 2/28 3/65 4/71 5/77 6/128   161   1/9 2/75 3/104 4/141   295
7/134 8/156 9/158 (2.23 an over)   5/152 6/177 7/260 8/270
9/288

Glamorgan Bowling

	O.	M.	R.	W.		O.	M.	R.	W.
H. D. Davies...	18.5	3	74	3	....	13	2	30	4
Wooller	24	8	80	3		18	4	35	3
Walker	25	9	56	2					
McConnon	20	5	68	2					
Shepherd	16	4	59	0	....	4.2	2	9	3
Devereux	3	0	16	0					

Nottinghamshire Bowling

	O.	M.	R.	W.		O.	M.	R.	W.
Walker	11	4	20	1	....	21	8	60	1
Jepson	11	3	18	1	....	23	7	43	2
Smales	27	13	41	3	....	32	16	74	1
Dooland	23	7	77	5	....	37.4	11	91	6
				Stocks		3	0	11	0

Umpires: T. W. Spencer and F. S. Lee.

At Kettering, June 29, July 1, 2. NOTTINGHAMSHIRE lost to NORTHAMPTONSHIRE by five wickets.

R

At Worcester, July 3, 4, 5. NOTTINGHAMSHIRE drew with WORCESTERSHIRE.

At Nottingham, June 4, 5, 6, 8, 9. ENGLAND drew with WEST INDIES (Third Test).
(See WEST INDIES section.)

At Llanelly, July 6, 8. NOTTINGHAMSHIRE lost to GLAMORGAN by an innings and
120 runs.

NOTTINGHAMSHIRE v. DERBYSHIRE

At Nottingham, July 13, 15, 16. Match drawn, Nottinghamshire taking two
points. In an exciting climax, Nottinghamshire's last-wicket pair, Walker and
Smales, held out for the final quarter of an hour with all hope of victory gone.
Nottinghamshire began their task of scoring 203 at 82 an hour promisingly. They
reached 100 in eighty-three minutes and Poole and Goonesena hit 50 in half
an hour for the fifth wicket. When they were parted, however, the initiative
passed to Derbyshire. Goonesena, fresh from his double century in the University
match, completed an excellent week. In his first Championship match of the
season he produced his best bowling performance for the county on the first day,
receiving great help from Clay, whose six catches at slip established a Nottinghamshire record. After Hill and Poole retrieved a bad start by Nottinghamshire with
a spirited stand of 146, Goonesena repaired the damage done by Gladwin and
Jackson with the new ball and piloted his side to a lead of 43. Derbyshire cleared
this without loss but were in a precarious situation until Morgan helped Carr to
add 76 in fifty minutes.

Derbyshire

A. Hamer b Dooland	56	— run out	44
C. Lee st Millman b Goonesena	13	— st Millman b Goonesena	32
J. Kelly c Clay b Goonesena	1	— b Jepson	43
A. C. Revill c Clay b Goonesena	17	— lbw b Dooland	14
D. B. Carr c Hill b Goonesena	5	— not out	50
D. J. Green c Clay b Goonesena	50	— b Jepson	0
G. O. Dawkes c Clay b Goonesena	17	— b Goonesena	3
D. C. Morgan not out	28	— not out	46
E. Smith c Clay b Goonesena	0	— lbw b Jepson	6
C. Gladwin c Clay b Dooland	4		
L. Jackson run out	4		
L-b 8, w 1	9	B 2, l-b 4, w 1	7

1/54 2/56 3/84 4/98 5/107 6/143   204   1/74 2/78   (7 wkts., dec.) 245
7/182 8/182 9/196 (2.91 an over)   3/103 4/158 5/158 6/161
                                           7/169

Nottinghamshire

J. D. Clay lbw b Jackson	2	— c Jackson b Gladwin	32
J. D. Springall b Morgan	31	— lbw b Gladwin	21
F. W. Stocks c Green b Gladwin	2	— c Jackson b Gladwin	3
M. Hill b Gladwin	66	— c Lee b Morgan	17
C. J. Poole c Carr b Jackson	79	— c Morgan b Smith	31
G. Goonesena not out	29	— c Lee b Smith	25
B. Dooland b Gladwin	11	— lbw b Jackson	22
A. K. Walker c Carr b Gladwin	0	— not out	3
G. Millman b Jackson	6	— c and b Morgan	0
K. Smales b Jackson	3	— not out	0
A. Jepson run out	13	— c Carr b Morgan	12
B 4, l-b 1	5	B 4, l-b 2, n-b 1	7

1/6 2/33 3/35 4/181 5/181 6/192   247   1/36 2/40 3/69   (9 wkts.) 173
7/192 8/209 9/221 (2.24 an over)   4/73 5/123 6/134 7/170
                                           8/170 9/173

Nottinghamshire Bowling

	O.	M.	R.	W.		O.	M.	R.	W.
Walker	7	3	14	0	....	13	2	59	0
Jepson	7	0	24	0	....	19	7	55	3
Dooland	25	8	76	2	....	25	10	42	1
Goonesena	28	8	75	7	....	22.2	7	64	2
Smales	3	1	6	0	....	6	2	18	0

Derbyshire Bowling

	O.	M.	R.	W.		O.	M.	R.	W.
Jackson	30	8	63	4	....	12	5	27	1
Gladwin	29	16	40	4	....	12	1	52	3
Morgan	24	9	56	1	....	16	2	58	3
Smith	19	7	47	0	....	4	0	29	2
Carr	5	1	23	0					
Revill	3	1	13	0					

Umpires: W. E. Phillipson and W. Place.

NOTTINGHAMSHIRE v. YORKSHIRE
(B. Dooland's Benefit)

At Nottingham, July 20, 22, 23. Yorkshire won by 205 runs, taking 12 points. Although Dooland celebrated his benefit match with a fine all-round display, the match was specially memorable for the batting of Yorkshire's new young opening pair, Stott and Taylor. In the first innings they shared the county's first century opening stand of the season; in the second they left this far behind by putting on 230, the best partnership for any Yorkshire wicket for five years. The left-handed Stott scored his third century of the month out of 186, hitting sixteen 4's, and Taylor's first hundred of the season contained twenty boundaries. Apart from these two, Yorkshire's batting was undistinguished against Dooland but Nottinghamshire fared worse, losing their first three wickets to Trueman and Pickles for no runs. Hard hitting by Dooland deprived Yorkshire of bonus points. Set the immense task of scoring 349 to win, Nottinghamshire again suffered early shocks from Pickles and never recovered. The combination of cheerless weather and a bus strike seriously affected Dooland's receipts from the game.

Yorkshire

W. B. Stott c K. Poole b Smales	50	— c Millman b Jepson 114
K. Taylor lbw b Dooland.............	79	— not out 140
J. V. Wilson c Millman b Dooland	6	— not out 37
D. B. Close b Dooland	14	
R. Illingworth c Smales b Dooland	7	
W. H. H. Sutcliffe c K. Poole b Dooland	7	
J. H. Wardle b Dooland	30	
F. S. Trueman b Dooland	0	
J. G. Binks st Millman b Smales........	6	
D. Pickles b Smales ....:.	0	
M. J. Cowan not out.................	0	
B 7, l-b 5, w 1.................	13	

1/122 2/133 3/148 4/157 5/167 6/177   212   1/230   (1 wkt., dec.) 291
7/177 8/206 9/206 (2.30 an over)

Nottinghamshire

J. D. Clay lbw b Trueman	0	— c Sutcliffe b Pickles	9
J. D. Springall c Close b Pickles	0	— c Cowan b Pickles	3
F. W. Stocks lbw b Trueman	0	— c Trueman b Wardle	26
M. Hill run out	10	— c Close b Wardle	0
C. J. Poole c Wilson b Trueman	23	— b Cowan	42
G. Goonesena c Trueman b Illingworth	17	— c Trueman b Illingworth	24
B. Dooland b Wardle	69	— c Illingworth b Trueman	8
K. J. Poole b Wardle	13	— c Illingworth b Wardle	21
G. Millman b Wardle	10	— b Close	2
K. Smales b Wardle	0	— c Wilson b Close	1
A. Jepson not out	5	— not out	0
B 5, l-b 1, w 1, n-b 1	8	L-b 5, n-b 2	7

1/0 2/0 3/0 4/30 5/44 6/60 7/95   155   1/8 2/13 3/65 4/101   143
8/148 9/150 (2.31 an over)   5/111 6/127 7/129 8/134
                                  9/143

Nottinghamshire Bowling

	O.	M.	R.	W.		O.	M.	R.	W.
Jepson	12	4	17	0	....	19	3	81	1
K. Poole	6	1	16	0	....	16	2	56	0
Dooland	33.1	16	55	7	....	19	4	72	0
Goonesena	11	2	53	0	....	11	1	46	0
Smales	30	15	58	3	....	15	3	36	0

Yorkshire Bowling

	O.	M.	R.	W.		O.	M.	R.	W.
Trueman	15	5	29	3	....	14	6	27	1
Pickles	14	3	24	1	....	10	4	29	2
Illingworth	13	3	29	1	....	7	5	4	1
Cowan	12	2	35	0	....	12	3	32	1
Wardle	13	4	30	4	....	17	8	40	3
Close						6	5	4	2

Umpires: D. Davies and A. Skelding.

NOTTINGHAMSHIRE v. GLOUCESTERSHIRE

At Nottingham, July 24, 25, 26. Gloucestershire won by five wickets, taking 12 points and Nottinghamshire two. They made a remarkable recovery in the face of Nottinghamshire's formidable first innings score. This was based on fine attacking innings by Springall, with his highest score for the county, and Poole, who so dominated the scene that his first century of the season came out of 145. Thanks to Nicholls and Milton, Gloucestershire looked as though they would challenge strongly for the lead but a spell of four wickets for 11 by Goonesena wrecked their hopes. Batting again with a lead of 96, the home side broke down completely against the fast-medium bowling of Smith, who achieved the best performance of his career. Gloucestershire were left ample time to make the 208 needed to win but when three men were out for 96 victory looked doubtful. Then Nicholls and Milton took command for the second time in the match. Nottinghamshire's last chance went when Nicholls was dropped at mid-off with the total 138.

Nottinghamshire

J. D. Clay b Smith	34	— lbw b Smith	11
J. D. Springall b Smith	83	— b Brown	5
F. W. Stocks b Wells	35	— c Nicholls b Smith	9
M. Hill c Carpenter b Mortimore	27	— b Smith	5
C. J. Poole not out	110	— c and b Brown	16
G. Goonesena c Nicholls b Smith	6	— b Smith	2
B. Dooland c Carpenter b Wells	26	— c Milton b Smith	41
G. Millman lbw b Wells	1	— run out	1
K. Smales lbw b Brown	0	— run out	16
A. Jepson c Wells b Mortimore	11	— b Smith	4
C. S. Matthews c Nicholls b Wells	5	— not out	0
B 6, l-b 5, w 1	12	L-b 2	2

1/119 2/124 3/183 4/191 5/227 6/292   350
7/299 8/306 9/340 (2.71 an over)

1/14 2/18 3/29 4/34   112
5/38 6/58 7/86 8/98 9/108

Gloucestershire

G. M. Emmett b Goonesena	41	— c Millman b Mathews	21
D. M. Young c and b Mathews	0	— b Jepson	17
R. B. Nicholls b Mathews	75	— b Dooland	69
M. A. Eagar lbw b Dooland	35	— b Goonesena	27
C. A. Milton not out	59	— not out	58
D. Carpenter c Clay b Goonesena	5	— lbw b Jepson	0
A. S. Brown c and b Goonesena	1	— not out	13
J. Mortimore c Stocks b Goonesena	10		
R. J. Etheridge c Stocks b Goonesena	0		
D. R. Smith run out	4		
B. D. Wells b Dooland	11		
B 7, l-b 6	13	B 3, l-b 3	6

1/22 2/58 3/127 4/175 5/186 6/188   254
7/210 8/210 9/222 (3.52 an over)

1/39 2/39 3/96   (5 wkts.) 211
4/185 5/186

Gloucestershire Bowling

	O.	M.	R.	W.		O.	M.	R.	W.
Smith	26	5	76	3	....	18.1	5	45	6
Brown	30	6	86	1	....	16	3	50	2
Wells	50.2	19	90	4	....	11	6	10	0
Mortimore	23	2	86	2	....	11	7	5	0

Nottinghamshire Bowling

	O.	M.	R.	W.		O.	M.	R.	W.
Jepson	6	2	30	0	....	18	4	45	2
Matthews	14	4	35	2	....	14	1	38	1
Goonesena	22	4	87	5	....	18	8	51	1
Dooland	22.1	3	58	2	....	28.4	13	60	1
Smales	8	2	31	0	....	7	2	11	0

Umpires: N. Oldfield and C. A. Coleman.

At Ilkeston, July 27, 29, 30. NOTTINGHAMSHIRE drew with DERBYSHIRE.

NOTTINGHAMSHIRE v. KENT

At Nottingham, July 31, August 1, 2. Kent won by eight wickets, taking 12 points. Superb batting by Cowdrey, who scored 216 runs in the match for once out, was the deciding factor. Nottinghamshire appeared to have gained a satisfactory position on the opening day when they made 265 and took the first three Kent wickets for 32, but on Thursday, Cowdrey, driving magnificently, hit his first century of the season for his county, scoring 165 out of 213 in four hours, 104 of his runs coming from boundary strokes. In contrast, Wilson spent three and a quarter hours for 41 and Leary also batted patiently, but their stubborn work was invaluable, for though Kent failed to gain the bonus points they obtained a lead of 72. Two Australian leg-spinners, Dooland and Pettiford, also accomplished much effective work, the latter bringing about a Nottinghamshire collapse so that Kent needed only 113 to win, a task they accomplished rather easily after Dooland disposed of their opening pair. Altogether Dooland sent down seventy overs and took seven wickets for no more than 97 runs. He waged a rare duel with Cowdrey.

Nottinghamshire

J. D. Clay c Cowdrey b Ridgway	6	—	lbw b Ridgway	5
J. D. Springall c Cook b Ridgway	6	—	lbw b Pettiford	60
N. Hill c Phebey b Halfyard	30	—	b Ridgway	0
M. Hill b Page	55	—	c Pettiford b Halfyard	48
C. J. Poole c Leary b Ridgway	24	—	c Ufton b Leary	29
B. Dooland c Leary b Page	50	—	c Halfyard b Pettiford	0
R. Vowles run out	2	—	c Leary b Pettiford	10
G. Millman not out	54	—	b Page	19
A. Jepson c Halfyard b Leary	34	—	c and b Pettiford	0
C. S. Matthews b Page	1	—	not out	0
M. Morgan run out	1	—	b Page	0
L-b 1, n-b 1	2		B 11, l-b 1, n-b 1	13

1/7 2/12 3/98 4/98 5/130 6/148   265   1/8 2/10 3/89 4/140 5/142   184
7/177 8/248 9/255 (2.78 an over)   6/159 7/184 8/184 9/184

Kent

A. H. Phebey run out	18	—	c N. Hill b Dooland	33
R. C. Wilson c Vowles b Morgan	41	—	c N. Hill b Dooland	1
J. C. T. Page b Jepson	2			
J. F. Pretlove c Millman b Matthews	2	—	not out	25
M. C. Cowdrey b Dooland	165	—	not out	51
S. E. Leary not out	60			
G. W. Cook b Dooland	8			
J. Pettiford c Clay b Dooland	6			
D. G. Ufton c Springall b Morgan	0			
D. J. Halfyard st Millman b Dooland	4			
F. Ridgway c Millman b Dooland	20			
B 5, l-b 6	11		B 4	4

1/24 2/27 3/32 4/175 5/245 6/255   337   1/23 2/40   (2 wkts.) 114
7/271 8/276 9/285 (2.55 an over)

Kent Bowling

	O.	M.	R.	W.		O.	M.	R.	W.
Ridgway	21	5	69	3	....	10	2	34	2
Halfyard	27	5	98	1	....	19	3	44	1
Cook	11	3	36	0					
Page	32	18	43	3	....	22.5	14	30	2
Leary	4	1	17	1	....	5	1	19	1
Pettiford						15	8	23	4
Cowdrey						5	1	21	0

Nottinghamshire Bowling

	O.	M.	R.	W.		O.	M.	R.	W.
Jepson	15	3	49	1		2	1	9	0
Matthews	27	3	85	1		7	0	36	0
Vowles	11	2	42	0					
Dooland	43.1	21	69	5		27	8	28	2
Morgan	36	13	81	2		12	2	37	0

Umpires: L. H. Gray and W. Place.

At The Oval, August 3, 5, 6. NOTTINGHAMSHIRE lost to SURREY by six wickets.

At Manchester, August 7, 8, 9. NOTTINGHAMSHIRE drew with LANCASHIRE.

NOTTINGHAMSHIRE v. WARWICKSHIRE

At Nottingham, August 10, 12, 13. Nottinghamshire won by 175 runs, taking 14 points. A maiden century by Norman Hill and fine all-round work by Dooland, who on the last day became the first player to complete the double in 1957, carried Nottinghamshire to a meritorious victory after three declarations. No play was possible before lunch on the opening day when Nottinghamshire, having won the toss, spent four hours making 173 for five wickets. N. Hill, 54 not out, went on to reach 119, hitting four 6's and seven 4's, and he and Dooland put on 123 for the sixth wicket. Subsequently, Gardner, by rigid defence, alone withstood the wiles of Dooland and Goonesena. When Warwickshire finished the second day with a first innings total of 120 for four wickets a definite result seemed unlikely, but M. J. K. Smith declared 148 behind. Nottinghamshire accepted the challenge, Poole showing commendable enterprise in getting 50 in forty minutes. Altogether Nottinghamshire batted only eighty minutes, leaving the visitors to score 249 in three hours twenty minutes. Again Dooland and Goonesena, admirably supported behind the stumps by Millman who had just been awarded his county cap, carried all before them and Nottinghamshire won with nearly two hours to spare.

Nottinghamshire

J. D. Springall b Griffiths	51	—	c and b Leach	27
G. Millman b Hollies	16	—	lbw b Hollies	6
E. J. Martin c Cartwright b Leach	17	—	not out	0
M. Hill c Singh b Hollies	18	—	c Stewart b Leach	4
N. Hill b Leach	119			
C. J. Poole c Spooner b Cartwright	15	—	not out	50
B. Dooland b Hollies	59	—	c Cartwright b Hollies	1
G. Goonesena not out	3			
A. Jepson c Hollies b Leach	0	—	b Leach	12
L-b 5, w 1, n-b 2	8			

1/42 2/84 3/88 4/116   (8 wkts., dec.) 306
5/157 6/280 7/306 8/306 (2.48 an over)

1/21 2/51   (5 wkts., dec.) 100
3/65 4/90 5/99

M. Morgan and C. S. Matthews did not bat.

Warwickshire

F. C. Gardner c Millman b Dooland	72	—	c Millman b Dooland	1
D. P. Ratcliffe c N. Hill b Dooland	11	—	c Millman b Goonesena	1
W. J. Stewart c Jepson b Morgan	16	—	c Millman b Jepson	10
M. J. K. Smith c Dooland b Goonesena	14	—	c Morgan b Dooland	11
T. W. Cartwright c Millman b Dooland	9	—	c Millman b Goonesena	13
C. W. Leach lbw b Dooland	10	—	lbw b Dooland	1
R. T. Spooner c N. Hill b Dooland	4	—	c N. Hill b Matthews	9
S. Singh not out	16	—	not out	25
J. D. Bannister not out	0	—	c Springall b Goonesena	0
S. S. Griffiths (did not bat)		—	st Millman b Goonesena	0
W. E. Hollies (did not bat)		—	b Dooland	1
B 1, l-b 4, w 1	6		L-b 1	1

1/25 2/61 3/84 4/105   (7 wkts., dec.) 158
5/121 6/133 7/146 (1.75 an over)

1/13 2/21 3/38 4/45 5/45   73
6/47 7/47 8/60 9/62

Warwickshire Bowling

	O.	M.	R.	W.		O.	M.	R.	W.
Bannister	22	9	46	0	....	3	1	8	0
Griffiths	13	2	27	1	....	4	1	7	0
Hollies	43	18	85	3	....	9	2	24	2
Singh	21	5	66	0					
Leach	9.5	2	37	3	....	5	0	50	3
Cartwright	14	1	37	1	....	4	1	11	0

Nottinghamshire Bowling

	O.	M.	R.	W.		O.	M.	R.	W.
Jepson	4	2	7	0	....	7	1	13	1
Matthews	6	3	6	0	....	5	0	24	1
Dooland	39	11	68	5	....	7.1	3	5	4
Goonesena	32	7	49	1	....	6	2	30	4
Morgan	9	3	22	1					

Umpires: T. J. Bartley and P. A. Gibb.

At Southend, August 14, 15, 16. NOTTINGHAMSHIRE drew with ESSEX.

At Worthing, August 17, 19, 20. NOTTINGHAMSHIRE lost to SUSSEX by 23 runs.

NOTTINGHAMSHIRE v. LANCASHIRE

At Nottingham, August 21, 22, 23. Drawn, Nottinghamshire taking four points. Except when eased on the last day by rain which prematurely ended the game, the pitch helped spin bowlers. Apart from Poole, the left-hander, who stayed two and a half hours, few of the Nottinghamshire batsmen could do much with the off-breaks of Tattersall on the opening day. With 104 runs on the board and two men out, Lancashire seemed admirably situated, but Dooland caused such a breakdown that they finished the innings 28 behind. Dooland achieved his best analysis of the season. Nottinghamshire batted more solidly at the second attempt and Lancashire, needing 279 to win, did well till the weather intervened.

Nottinghamshire

J. D. Springall c Ikin b Statham	6	— c Bolton b Bowman	2
E. J. Martin c Ikin b Statham	16	— b Tattersall	33
N. Hill c Bowman b Tattersall	24	— b Tattersall	22
M. Hill c Barber b Bowman	7	— lbw b Tattersall	3
C. J. Poole c Statham b Tattersall	75	— c and b Greenhough	39
B. Dooland c Wharton b Tattersall	3	— b Statham	32
G. Goonesena c Wharton b Tattersall	2	— c Ikin b Greenhough	48
A. K. Walker c Wharton b Tattersall	23	— c Bond b Tattersall	29
G. Millman b Statham	6	— run out	38
T. Atkinson not out	3	— c Bowman b Ikin	0
M. Morgan b Tattersall	0	— not out	0
L-b 3	3	B 1, l-b 3	4

1/21 2/28 3/46 4/64 5/67 6/69 7/125   168   1/8 2/38 3/44 4/82 5/127   250
8/152 9/168 (2.40 an over)   6/135 7/186 8/234 9/241

Lancashire

A. Wharton c Atkinson b Dooland	37	— retired hurt............... 12
R. W. Barber b Dooland	29	— not out 35
G. Pullar c N. Hill b Dooland	9	— not out 42
J. T. Ikin c N. Hill b Goonesena	35	
J. D. Bond c Atkinson b Dooland	3	
A. Bolton c N. Hill b Dooland	6	
R. Bowman lbw b Dooland	3	
T. Greenhough st Millman b Goonesena	4	
J. B. Statham c Springall b Dooland	9	
A. Wilson c and b Dooland	1	
R. Tattersall not out	1	
L-b 3	3	B 4, n-b 1 5

1/53 2/63 3/104 4/114 5/121 6/124   140   (No wkt.) 94
7/129 8/129 9/139 (2.33 an over)

Lancashire Bowling

	O.	M.	R.	W.		O.	M.	R.	W.
Statham	18	4	38	3	....	16	6	27	1
Bowman	12	3	27	1	....	12	1	30	1
Wharton	9	2	22	0	....	7	3	20	0
Tattersall	21	5	53	6	....	29	6	73	4
Greenhough ...	10	2	25	0	....	22	3	57	2
				Ikin	....	10.4	3	39	1

Nottinghamshire Bowling

	O.	M.	R.	W.		O.	M.	R.	W.
Walker	6	2	22	0	....	4	0	16	0
Atkinson	5	0	29	0	....	2	0	7	0
Dooland	24.5	12	42	8	....	10	2	21	0
Goonesena ...	13	1	34	2	....	9	1	29	0
Morgan	11	7	10	0	....	6	2	16	0

Umpires: C. S. Elliott and T. J. Bartley.

NOTTINGHAMSHIRE v. LEICESTERSHIRE

At Nottingham, August 24, 26, 27. Nottinghamshire won by one wicket, taking 14 points. An exciting struggle took place for first innings lead, which Nottinghamshire gained by two runs, and when, set 197 to win, they lost nine men for 190, they again had to battle for success. Hallam took practically all the batting honours on the first day. He gave three chances in a stay of five hours ten minutes, but displayed splendid defence and ability to punish the loose ball, hitting twenty-four 4's. Of seven wickets which fell for 96, Goonesena took the last four for three runs. Nottinghamshire lost six wickets for 116 and though Dooland and Goonesena came to the rescue with a bold stand of 92, did not go ahead till their last batsmen were together. As in the first innings, a breakdown against the leg-break bowlers followed a good start when Leicestershire batted again, but capital left-arm bowling by Smith kept the result in doubt to the very end.

Leicestershire

G. Lester b Dooland	28	— b Dooland	34
M. R. Hallam b Goonesena	152	— c Goonesena b Dooland	39
J. van Geloven st Millman b Morgan	32	— c Dooland b Goonesena	27
C. H. Palmer b Dooland	4	— b Jepson	44
L. R. Gardner lbw b Dooland	0	— c Poole b Goonesena	0
R. A. Diment c Millman b Jepson	4	— st Millman b Goonesena	10
J. Firth b Atkinson	3	— lbw b Dooland	1
J. Savage c Morgan b Goonesena	10	— b Goonesena	4
R. C. Smith not out	9	— lbw b Dooland	7
C. T. Spencer st Millman b Goonesena	0	— c Jepson b Goonesena	10
J. Goodwin b Goonesena	2	— not out	0
B 2, l-b 3, w 1	6	B 9, l-b 12	21

1/59 2/135 3/154 4/154 5/185 6/198   250   1/73 2/80 3/81 4/108   197
7/234 8/240 9/240 (2.31 an over)   5/121 6/122 7/141 8/160
                                              9/183

Nottinghamshire

J. D. Springall c Firth b Goodwin	20	— c sub b Smith	23
E. J. Martin b Spencer	3	— b Goodwin	9
G. Millman c Firth b Spencer	17	— c Hallam b Smith	1
N. Hill c Goodwin b Spencer	2	— b Smith	19
M. Hill c Hallam b Smith	38	— c Hallam b Savage	41
C. J. Poole b Savage	19	— lbw b Smith	8
B. Dooland b Spencer	72	— c sub b Smith	51
G. Goonesena b Savage	51	— c sub b Smith	8
A. Jepson b Goodwin	1	— c Lester b Smith	17
T. Atkinson c and b Goodwin	19	— not out	8
M. Morgan not out	0	— not out	5
B 2, l-b 3, n-b 5	10	B 1, l-b 6, n-b 1	8

1/13 2/40 3/43 4/44 5/76 6/116 7/208   252   1/18 2/52 3/61   (9 wkts.) 198
8/209 9/242 (3.45 an over)   4/99 5/105 6/128 7/148
                                              8/173 9/190

Nottinghamshire Bowling

	O.	M.	R.	W.	O.	M.	R.	W.
Jepson	14	3	28	1	9.2	3	18	1
Atkinson	16	3	42	1	4	0	17	0
Dooland	34	12	72	3	32	9	78	4
Goonesena	31	8	77	4	35	13	58	5
Morgan	13	5	25	1	6	4	5	0

Leicestershire Bowling

	O.	M.	R.	W.	O.	M.	R.	W.
Spencer	22	1	93	4	14	1	36	0
Goodwin	22.5	4	61	3	6	0	19	1
Smith	11	5	26	1	30	13	54	7
Savage	16	1	58	2	20	7	74	1
Palmer	1	0	4	0	3	1	7	0

Umpires: T. J. Bartley and Harry Elliott.

At Bristol, August 28, 29, 30. NOTTINGHAMSHIRE beat GLOUCESTERSHIRE by three
    wickets.

SOMERSET

President: THE BISHOP OF BATH AND WELLS

Secretary—R. ROBINSON, County Cricket Ground, St. James's Street, Taunton

Captain—M. F. TREMLETT

W. E. Alley   County Badge   M. F. Tremlett

Somerset, who in 1956 took their first steps along the road to recovery, improved still further in 1957. They finished in the middle of the Championship table, and though at times the cricket lapsed into its former slipshod character, there were encouraging pointers for the future, notably in the performances of several of the younger players. In the main the nine victories were achieved against weak opposition, but they constituted the best performance since 1946. Having established a winning position, the side did not let the advantage slip so readily as had often been the case. Perhaps they gave their best performance in defeat, when they lost to Surrey at Weston-super-Mare by only three wickets with eight minutes remaining.

The inclusion of another Australian in the left-handed Alley gave the batting a more solid appearance. In the early part of the season he was the backbone of the innings, despite a technique not really suited to opening. Later he had a short spell lower in the order. Alley was awarded one of the quickest county caps in Somerset history, after only four matches, a compliment his all-round performances over the season fully justified. After a slow start McCool was again the leading scorer, though his aggregate and average were both reduced.

Tremlett, too, was slow to find his touch, but finished the season in great style. His captaincy at times invoked criticism, though, like his batting, it throve on success in the later matches. Silk once again proved a great asset when available.

Lobb, a much improved player, was the outstanding bowler. He became the first Somerset pace bowler since the war to exceed a hundred wickets in a season, a distinction he thoroughly deserved. Wellard took over a hundred in 1946, but was by then bowling off-spinners. Alley, right-arm medium-fast, proved a capable ally to Lobb, and Dickinson's presence in August helped to balance the attack. McMahon enjoyed a successful season, but was not re-engaged, a decision which proved highly controversial. Langford gained in control as the season progressed, and by the end was bowling extremely well. McCool was sparingly used, and Hilton, who subsequently resigned, could not win a regular place. Stephenson kept wicket with unfailing excellence, but his batting was disappointing, though he hit a fine century in his benefit year against Kent.

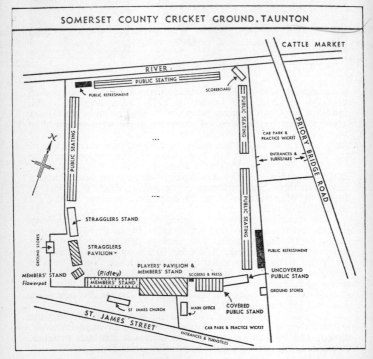

SOMERSET COUNTY CRICKET GROUND, TAUNTON

SOMERSET RESULTS

All First-Class Matches—Played 32, Won 9, Lost 15, Drawn 8

County Championship Matches—Played 28, Won 9, Lost 14, Drawn 5

COUNTY CHAMPIONSHIP AVERAGES
BATTING

	Birthplace	Mtchs.	Inns.	Not Outs	Runs	100's	Highest Inns.	Aver.
D. R. W. Silk...	*California*	7	12	3	409	0	73	45.44
C. L. McCool...	*Sydney*	28	49	3	1382	1	100*	30.04
P. B. Wight	*Georgetown*	25	44	3	1164	0	88	28.39
M. F. Tremlett..	*Stockport*	28	49	3	1285	2	144	27.93
W. E. Alley	*Sydney*	27	51	2	1310	1	108	26.73
G. G. Atkinson .	*Lofthouse*	8	13	1	247	0	52	20.58
H. W. Stephenson	*Stockton-on-Tees*	28	47	5	843	1	104*	20.07
K. E. Palmer....	*Winchester*	20	34	6	532	0	56*	19.00
L. Pickles.......	*Wakefield*	12	23	2	386	0	70	18.38
J. Harris	*Taunton*	4	5	0	71	0	41	14.20
J. G. Lomax....	*Rochdale*	14	27	0	314	0	36	11.62
J. Hilton	*Chadderton*	17	28	6	202	0	51*	9.18
K. Biddulph ...	*Chingford*	2	4	1	26	0	22	8.66
G. M. Tripp	*Clevedon*	8	15	0	121	0	62	8.06
B. Langford.....	*Birmingham*	22	34	3	244	0	31*	7.87
B. Lobb	*Birmingham*	26	38	8	176	0	30*	5.86
T. E. Dickinson..	*Paramatta*	4	6	3	11	0	7*	3.66
J. W. McMahon.	*S. Australia*	24	36	14	78	0	17	3.54

Also batted: B. Roe (*Cleethorpes*) 47 and 0*; C. Greetham (*Wargrave*) 31 and 15; R. Virgin (*Taunton*) 5 and 14*.

* *Signfies not out.*

BOWLING

	Overs	Maidens	Runs	Wickets	Average
P. B. Wight	40	14	101	10	10.10
B. Langford	548.2	190	1201	63	19.06
T. E. Dickinson	115.4	20	309	16	19.31
W. E. Alley	532.1	133	1288	64	20.12
J. W. McMahon........	709.1	228	1737	81	21.44
B. Lobb	716.5	152	1910	88	21.70
M. F. Tremlett	20.2	3	70	3	23.33
J. G. Lomax	110.3	13	359	13	27.61
C. L. McCool	299.2	61	938	33	28.42
J. Hilton	300.5	80	743	24	30.95
K. Biddulph	40	6	138	4	34.50
K. E. Palmer..........	103.5	15	359	10	35.90
J. Harris	56	9	147	3	49.00

Also bowled: G. G. Atkinson 8—1—22—0; L. Pickles 2—0—10—0; B. Roe 2—0—3—0; H. W. Stephenson 2—1—11—0.

Amateurs.—D. R. W. Silk, T. E. Dickinson.

At Southampton, April 29, 30. SOMERSET drew with HAMPSHIRE. (Two-day friendly.)

SOMERSET v. GLAMORGAN

At Taunton, May 1, 2. Drawn. Glamorgan 253 (A. J. Watkins 62) and 125 for six wickets, dec. (J. Hilton four for 13); Somerset 257 for nine wickets, dec. (G. M. Tripp 74, M. F. Tremlett 55) and 86 for five wickets.

SOMERSET v. LANCASHIRE

At Taunton, May 4, 6, 7. Lancashire won by seven wickets, taking 14 points. Somerset were outplayed from first to last. Only Lobb of the bowlers looked menacing and three easy chances off his bowling were dropped early on. He gained solace from a final spell of four wickets for seven runs in 27 balls, but by then Lancashire were in a commanding position, thanks to stands of 117 by Washbrook and Edrich and 94 by Grieves and Ikin. Statham and Tattersall upset the Somerset batting until Stephenson dominated a ninth wicket stand of 43, but were not effective after the follow-on. Pickles and McCool counter-attacked intelligently, and when an innings defeat had been avoided Lobb hit out cheerfully. Next, Lobb and Alley claimed the first three Lancashire wickets for 16, but Washbrook and Grieves saw their side home.

Lancashire

A. Wharton c Stephenson b Alley	50	— b Alley	12
J. Dyson lbw b Alley	17	— c McCool b Lobb	2
G. A. Edrich c Tremlett b McMahon	64	— c Lomax b Lobb	0
C. Washbrook c Tripp b McMahon	64	— not out	22
K. Grieves c Stephenson b McCool	51	— not out	8
J. T. Ikin c Tremlett b Lobb	51		
M. J. Hilton b Lomax	4		
J. Jordan b Lobb	0		
J. B. Statham c Hilton b Lobb	12		
T. Greenhough b Lobb	0		
R. Tattersall not out	4		
B 9, l-b 3	12	L-b 1	1

1/45 2/80 3/197 4/208 5/302 6/312   329   1/10 2/14 3/16   (3 wkts.)   45
7/312 8/316 9/316 (2.91 an over)

Somerset

L. Pickles b Statham	10	— b Statham	46
J. G. Lomax b Statham	11	— c Edrich b Hilton	14
J. Hilton c Grieves b Tattersall	27	— b Wharton	15
W. E. Alley, c Jordan b Hilton	27	— b Tattersall	16
C. L. McCool b Statham	10	— b Hilton	54
P. B. Wight b Tattersall	0	— b Statham	0
M. F. Tremlett b Greenhough	16	— b Statham	20
G. Tripp b Statham	0	— c Grieves b Hilton	0
H. W. Stephenson not out	41	— b Tattersall	9
J. W. McMahon b Tattersall	3	— c Greenhough b Hilton	0
B. Lobb b Statham	0	— not out	30
B 6, l-b 2	8	B 13, l-b 3	16

1/14 2/21 3/81 4/81 5/81 6/105   153   1/32 2/81 3/103 4/103   220
7/106 8/107 9/150 (2.18 an over)   5/124 6/125 7/158 8/180
9/182

Somerset Bowling

	O.	M.	R.	W.		O.	M.	R.	W.
Lomax	13	1	55	1					
Lobb	24.3	5	64	4	....	6	2	16	2
Alley	21	7	50	2	....	6	1	28	1
Hilton	17	2	44	0					
McCool	18	3	52	1					
McMahon	19	7	52	2					

Lancashire Bowling

	O.	M.	R.	W.		O.	M.	R.	W.
Statham	21	9	31	5	....	20	8	46	3
Wharton	9	2	34	0	....	10.3	3	33	1
Tattersall	16	9	26	3	....	22	9	53	2
Hilton	14	9	27	1	....	26	10	61	4
Greenhough	10	1	27	1	....	4	1	11	0

Umpires: D. Davies and J. S. Buller.

At Cambridge, May 8, 9, 10. SOMERSET drew with CAMBRIDGE UNIVERSITY.

SOMERSET v. NOTTINGHAMSHIRE

At Frome, May 11, 13, 14. Somerset won by 92 runs, taking 14 points, thanks to slightly stronger batting on a rain-affected pitch. The Nottinghamshire spin bowlers posed perplexing problems for the earlier batsmen, and the pace attack made short work of the tail, but Nottinghamshire fared even worse. Lobb dismissed the first four batsmen early on the second day, the remainder showed lack of resolution against spin. Again the Nottinghamshire bowlers gained the ascendancy over all the batsmen except Tremlett, and Matthews took the last four wickets in the course of four maiden overs. Somerset called on seven bowlers in the Nottinghamshire second innings and they achieved their first championship points of the season before lunch on the third day.

Somerset

L. Pickles c Matthews b Jepson	10	— run out	5
W. E. Alley lbw b Smales	26	— lbw b Smales	36
P. B. Wight b Dooland	33	— st Millman b Dooland	10
C. L. McCool b Dooland	0	— hit wkt b Dooland	1
M. F. Tremlett c Jepson b Smales	22	— c Giles b Matthews	57
J. G. Lomax run out	6	— b Smales	6
H. W. Stephenson b Jepson	30	— b Smales	22
B. Langford lbw b Jepson	16	— not out	7
J. Hilton b Matthews	0	— b Matthews	0
B. Lobb c Jepson b Matthews	6	— st Millman b Matthews	1
J. W. McMahon not out	1	— b Matthews	0
B 5, l-b 7	12	B 1	1

1/18 2/63 3/64 4/81 5/95 6/106   162   1/32 2/42 3/43 4/62 5/89   146
7/143 8/148 9/158 (1.95 an over)   6/138 7/138 8/138 9/146

Nottinghamshire

R. J. Giles b Lobb	9	— lbw b Langford	14
J. D. Clay hit wkt b Lobb	15	— c and b McMahon	13
M. Winfield c Lomax b Hilton	13	— lbw b Hilton	6
E. J. Martin c Stephenson b Lobb	0	— b Hilton	6
C. J. Poole b Lobb	6	— c Lobb b McMahon	19
P. F. Harvey not out	11	— c Stephenson b Lobb	1
B. Dooland c Pickles b McMahon	0	— c Stephenson b McMahon	27
G. Millman lbw b McMahon	0	— b Langford	1
K. Smales b Hilton	1	— not out	22
A. Jepson b McMahon	9	— c Pickles b Alley	19
C. S. Matthews run out	0	— b Lomax	1
B 10, l-b 5	15	B 5, l-b 2 w 1	8
	—		—
	79		137

1/29 2/38 3/42 4/48 5/66 6/66
7/66 8/69 9/78 (1.54 an over)

1/22 2/33 3/33 4/52 5/53
6/74 7/80 8/94 9/122

Nottinghamshire Bowling

	O.	M.	R.	W.		O.	M.	R.	W.
Jepson	10.4	2	30	3	....	10	3	18	0
Matthews	9	2	21	2	....	7	5	3	4
Dooland	32	11	56	2	....	20	7	51	2
Smales	31	12	43	2	....	26	9	73	3

Somerset Bowling

	O.	M.	R.	W.		O.	M.	R.	W.
Lobb	15	7	19	4	....	17	4	33	1
Lomax	4	1	3	0	....	4.3	1	10	1
Hilton	12.2	5	16	2	....	10	1	24	2
McMahon	17	7	22	3	....	17	7	32	3
Langford	3	2	4	0	....	13	6	9	2
McCool						6	4	8	0
Alley						3	0	13	1

Umpires: P. Corrall and Harry Elliott.

At Leeds, May 18, 20. SOMERSET lost to YORKSHIRE by an innings and 48 runs.

At Birmingham, May 22, 23, 24. SOMERSET lost to WARWICKSHIRE by six wickets.

At Lord's, May 25, 27, 28. SOMERSET lost to MIDDLESEX by nine runs.

SOMERSET v. WORCESTERSHIRE

At Taunton, May 29, 30, 31. Drawn, Somerset taking two points. The batting of D. W. Richardson, Wight and Tremlett were the features of a match which ended tamely. Richardson dominated both Worcestershire innings. In the first he hit an invigorating century in less than two and a half hours and only a declaration robbed him of the chance of scoring a hundred in each innings. Somerset started their first innings badly, but a stand of 127 in two hours between Wight and Tremlett brought about a recovery and they gained a narrow lead. Set to score 199 in a little under two hours to win, Somerset contented themselves with playing out time.

Worcestershire

L. Outschoorn lbw b Alley	30	— c Wight b Lobb	9
D. Kenyon c Alley b Harris	27	— b Alley	13
G. Dews c Palmer b McMahon	38	— b Alley	23
D. W. Richardson c McCool b Palmer	110	— not out	93
R. G. Broadbent c Palmer b Harris	31	— b Lobb	1
M. J. Horton lbw b McCool	12	— c McCool b Hilton	54
R. Booth c Hilton b Alley	44	— not out	3
R. O. Jenkins not out	17		
J. Flavell b Lobb	0		
B 7, l-b 1, w 1	9	L-b 5	5

1/41 2/73 3/149 4/244 (8 wkts., dec.) 318
5/252 6/265 7/318 8/318 (3.08 an over)
R. Berry and J. Aldridge did not bat.

1/17 2/28 (5 wkts., dec.) 201
3/41 4/30 5/188

Somerset

W. E. Alley b Aldridge	13	— c Dews b Berry	17
K. E. Palmer c Booth b Flavell	8	— st Booth b Jenkins	33
P. B. Wight c Booth b Berry	87		
C. L. McCool c Flavell b Berry	23	— not out	11
H. W. Stephenson c Booth b Jenkins	0		
R. Virgin lbw b Berry	5	— not out	14
M. F. Tremlett c Berry b Aldridge	92		
J. Harris c Dews b Horton	41		
J. Hilton not out	30		
B. Lobb c Flavell b Berry	7		
J. W. McMahon not out	7		
L-b 6, w 2	8	L-b 3	3

1/11 2/33 3/79 4/80 (9 wkts., dec.) 321
5/92 6/219 7/243 8/302 9/313
(2.60 an over)

1/44 2/56 (2 wkts.) 78

Somerset Bowling

	O.	M.	R.	W.	O.	M.	R.	W.
Alley	19	7	42	2	7	0	22	2
Lobb	26.1	2	88	1	12	1	50	2
Harris	18	2	59	2				
McCool	20	2	69	1	7	1	22	0
Hilton	5	2	6	0	16	1	44	1
McMahon	12	3	32	1	27.3	10	58	0
Palmer	3	0	13	1				

Worcestershire Bowling

	O.	M.	R.	W.	O.	M.	R.	W.
Flavell	25	5	80	1	6	0	29	0
Outschoorn	1	0	4	0	2	1	6	0
Aldridge	19	4	69	2	6	0	12	0
Berry	40	20	61	4	5	3	4	1
Jenkins	11	2	36	1	4	0	16	1
Horton	27	10	63	1	3	1	8	0

Umpires: R. S. Lay and H. G. Baldwin.

At Gillingham, June 1, 3, 4. SOMERSET beat KENT by five wickets.

At Nottingham, June 5, 6, 7. SOMERSET drew with NOTTINGHAMSHIRE.

SOMERSET v. GLOUCESTERSHIRE

At Taunton, June 8, 10, 11. Drawn, rain intervening on the first and second days. Splendid batting by Wight on an awkward pitch was the feature of Somerset's first innings and Atkinson showed defiance while wickets were falling cheaply to Smith. The last six went for 54. Gloucestershire lost their last six wickets for exactly the same amount, but Graveney, with a flawless exhibition of stroke-play, Nicholls and Knightley-Smith, put them well ahead. There was never any likelihood of a result, but McCool batted splendidly in scoring Somerset's first century of the season in two and a half hours. He hit fourteen 4's.

Somerset

W. E. Alley b Lambert	5	— c Young b Smith	8
P. B. Wight b Smith	67	— lbw b Smith	26
C. Greetham lbw b Cook	31	— c Wells b Cook	15
C. L. McCool c and b Smith	33	— not out	100
G. G. Atkinson c Hawkins b Lambert	52	— c Young b Hawkins	31
H. W. Stephenson c Graveney b Smith	0	— lbw b Smith	22
M. F. Tremlett b Wells	11	— not out	22
J. Harris b Smith	4		
J. Hilton b Smith	2		
B. Lobb b Smith	0		
J. W. McMahon not out	0		
B 1, l-b 1	2	B 5, l-b 1	6

1/18 2/91 3/111 4/153 5/153 6/175   207   1/15 2/44   (5 wkts., dec.) 230
7/193 8/203 9/203 (2.32 an over)   3/64 4/124 5/161

Gloucestershire

D. M. Young lbw b Alley	45	D. Smith c Alley b McCool	2
G. M. Emmett c Harris b Alley	5	C. Cook not out	12
W. Knightley-Smith b McMahon	55	B. D. Wells b Lobb	14
T. W. Graveney c McCool b Lobb	99	B 13, l-b 9, w 2	24
R. B. Nicholls st Stephenson b McCool	65		
D. Hawkins run out	0	1/5 2/102 3/132 4/273 5/273	327
B. J. Meyer c Stephenson b Lobb	0	6/289 7/295 8/299 9/299	
G. E. Lambert c Alley b McCool	6	(3.02 an over)	

Gloucestershire Bowling

	O.	M.	R.	W.		O.	M.	R.	W.
Lambert	21	4	57	2	....	6	2	12	0
Smith	24	6	58	6	....	16	5	45	3
Wells	24	8	50	1	....	15	1	62	0
Cook	18	7	35	1	....	16	3	35	1
Graveney	2	0	5	0	....	7	1	17	0
Hawkins						13	4	44	1
Nicholls						1	0	9	0

Somerset Bowling

	O.	M.	R.	W.
Lobb	27	8	79	3
Alley	23	5	47	2
Harris	19	3	48	0
Hilton	13	2	43	0
McMahon	15	2	46	1
McCool	11	2	40	3

Umpires: John Langridge and A. E. Pothecary.

At Swansea, June 12, 13. SOMERSET lost to GLAMORGAN by nine wickets.

SOMERSET v. HAMPSHIRE

At Bath, June 15, 17. Hampshire won by an innings and 43 runs, taking 14 points. Somerset collapsed twice against the splendid pace bowling of Shackleton (eight for 110 in the match) and Heath (eleven for 106). A consistent, if colourless, batting display put Hampshire in a strong position, and having gained the advantage they never relaxed their grip. Their innings was notable for one curious incident. Following a run out, Horton returned to the pavilion, but was recalled when the new batsman, Rayment, was already at the wicket. Following a consultation, it was decided Gray was the man run out, and Horton resumed. Later Horton was run out, this time conclusively.

Hampshire

R. E. Marshall b Lobb	48		D. Shackleton c Atkinson b Lomax	9	
J. R. Gray run out	43		M. Heath not out	17	
H. Horton run out	39		M. D. Burden b Lobb	11	
A. W. H. Rayment b Lomax	4		B 4, l-b 1, w 5	10	
H. M. Barnard lbw b McMahon	34				
A. C. D. Ingleby-Mackenzie lbw b Hilton	47		1/82 2/104 3/112 4/172 5/195	275	
P. J. Sainsbury c Lomax b Lobb	12		6/231 7/238 8/241 9/251		
L. Harrison c Tremlett b Lobb	1		(3.12 an over)		

Somerset

W. E. Alley c Sainsbury b Shackleton	8	— c Harrison b Heath	19
J. G. Lomax c Barnard b Shackleton	24	— c Harrison b Heath	25
P. B. Wight c Harrison b Heath	13	— b Shackleton	3
C. L. McCool lbw b Shackleton	3	— b Sainsbury	8
G. G. Atkinson not out	15	— c Harrison b Heath	19
M. F. Tremlett b Heath	2	— c Ingleby-Mackenzie b Heath	22
H. W. Stephenson c Shackleton b Heath	10	— c Barnard b Heath	0
J. Hilton c Harrison b Heath	1	— b Heath	8
B. Langford b Shackleton	7	— c Marshall b Heath	15
B. Lobb b Shackleton	10	— c Harrison b Shackleton	13
J. W. McMahon c Barnard b Shackleton	0	— not out	5
B 1	1	B 1	1

1/12 2/25 3/47 4/48 5/53 6/65 7/67	94	1/35 2/44 3/54 4/62 5/83	138
8/84 9/94 (2.68 an over)		6/83 7/98 8/117 9/130	

Somerset Bowling

	O.	M.	R.	W.	O.	M.	R.	W.
Lobb	27	2	98	4				
Alley	14	3	48	0				
Langford	9	4	20	0				
Lomax	18	2	55	2				
Tremlett	3	0	14	0				
McMahon	13	5	30	1				
Hilton	4	4	0	1				

Hampshire Bowling

	O.	M.	R.	W.	O.	M.	R.	W.
Shackleton	17.3	8	42	6	18	4	68	2
Heath	17	5	51	4	22.2	5	55	7
Marshall					2	1	8	0
Gray					2	2	0	0
Sainsbury					5	3	6	1

Umpires: P. A. Gibb and H. G. Baldwin.

SOMERSET v. ESSEX

At Bath, June 19, 20, 21. Somerset won by seven wickets, taking 14 points. Essex, weakened by the absence of Insole and Bailey, never looked like saving the game. For once all Somerset's middle batsmen succeeded, particularly Tremlett, who hit Greensmith for two 6's off successive deliveries in the course of a bold innings. Still, Greensmith was easily the most successful member of a modest attack. Essex broke down against the varied Somerset bowling but recovered well after following-on 176 behind. Smith and Bear led the way, and a stand of 95 by the seventh pair, Greensmith and Ralph, ensured that Somerset would have to bat again. Ralph's 66 was his highest for Essex.

Somerset

W. E. Alley lbw b Preston	0	— lbw b Ralph	16
J. G. Lomax b Preston	28	— c Preston b Palmer	22
P. B. Wight b Greensmith	47	— c Taylor b Ralph	0
C. L. McCool c Barker b Greensmith	53	— not out	26
M. F. Tremlett st Taylor b Greensmith	63	— not out	24
K. E. Palmer c and b Preston	51		
H. W. Stephenson c Preston b Greensmith	2		
B. Langford c Ralph b King	1		
J. Hilton c Taylor b Greensmith	0		
B. Lobb st Taylor b Greensmith	0		
J. W. McMahon not out	5		
B 1, l-b 8, n-b 1	10	L-b 1	1

1/0 2/52 3/84 4/159 5/224 6/226   **260**   1/21 2/25 3/54   (3 wkts.) **89**
7/227 8/248 9/248 (2.70 an over)

Essex

T. C. Dodds c Langford b Lobb	4	— c Langford b Lobb	4
G. Barker c Stephenson b Lobb	0	— st Stephenson b Lomax	29
B. Taylor lbw b Langford	9	— c Langford b Alley	1
L. Savill c Lomax b Hilton	11	— c Wight b McMahon	6
M. Bear b McMahon	24	— b Lomax	42
G. Smith c Wight b Lomax	8	— c McCool b Lomax	53
W. T. Greensmith lbw b McMahon	1	— c and b McMahon	38
R. Ralph c McCool b Lomax	0	— c Stephenson b McCool	66
K. C. Preston b Lobb	4	— b Lobb	9
I. M. King c Hilton b Alley	2	— c McMahon b Lobb	1
E. Palmer not out	9	— not out	0
B 4, l-b 8	12	B 9, l-b 6	15

1/3 2/4 3/26 4/33 5/56 6/57 7/58   **84**   1/8 2/21 3/38 4/55 5/135   **264**
8/64 9/74 (1.58 an over)   6/152 7/247 8/260 9/262

Essex Bowling

	O.	M.	R.	W.		O.	M.	R.	W.
Preston	22.1	8	55	3	....	6	1	27	0
Palmer	15	4	56	0	....	2	0	15	1
Ralph	12	4	29	0	....	8	1	24	2
Greensmith	33	11	76	6	....	3	0	15	0
King	14	6	34	1					
Bear						5	0	7	0

Somerset Bowling

	O.	M.	R.	W.		O.	M.	R.	W.
Lobb	17	5	34	3	....	20	5	64	3
Alley	7	2	11	1	....	9	0	25	1
Langford	6	5	1	1	....	5	1	14	0
McMahon	14.2	8	18	2	....	24.4	9	54	2
Hilton	6	5	1	1					
Lomax	3	0	7	2	....	15	1	42	3
Palmer						6	1	11	0
McCool						11	3	34	1
Wight						1	0	5	0

Umpires: H. G. Baldwin and G. Coleman.

SOMERSET v. DERBYSHIRE

At Bath, June 22, 24, 25. Derbyshire won by nine wickets, taking 14 points. For the second time in the course of the Bath Festival, Somerset collapsed almost completely against high-class seam bowling. Derbyshire fared little better and Kelly's 87 was sufficient to put them on the way to victory. Somerset were trapped on the rain-affected pitch, and Gladwin and Jackson ran through them. Lobb and Alley looked equally menacing, and Derbyshire owed their lead of 96 solely to Kelly and Morgan. They came together with six wickets down for 56 and put on 100 in just over an hour. For Somerset, Wight, in a polished and assured display, scored 81 out of 108. Then Gladwin started another collapse and his final analysis was thirteen wickets for 86. Derbyshire needed only 35 to win.

Somerset

W. E. Alley b Jackson	4	— c Gladwin b Smith	0
J. G. Lomax c Kelly b Jackson	12	— c Carr b Gladwin	1
P. B. Wight c Dawkes b Gladwin	11	— lbw b Gladwin............	81
C. L. McCool c Johnson b Jackson	7	— c Lee b Gladwin	20
M. F. Tremlett b Gladwin	2	— b Gladwin	6
K. E. Palmer b Morgan	6	— c Morgan b Gladwin	0
H. W. Stephenson run out	18	— c Johnson b Gladwin	17
B. Langford b Gladwin	0	— c Carr b Gladwin	0
J. Hilton c Morgan b Gladwin	1	— c Johnson b Jackson	0
B. Lobb st Dawkes b Gladwin	0	— not out	0
J. W. McMahon not out	0	— b Gladwin	4
N-b 1	1	N-b 1	1

1/4 2/27 3/27 4/35 5/42 6/56	62	1/1 2/30 3/90 4/90 5/108 130
7/56 8/58 9/58 (1.87 an over)		6/108 7/113 8/117 9/126

Derbyshire

A. Hamer c Wight b Lobb	9	— c Langford b Alley	8
C. Lee lbw b Alley..................	1	— not out	14
J. M. Kelly c Palmer b Tremlett	87	— not out	13
A. C. Revill b Alley.................	0		
D. B. Carr c Stephenson b Lobb	7		
G. O. Dawkes c Hilton b Alley	1		
H. L. Johnson lbw b Lobb...........	10		
D. C. Morgan b Tremlett	35		
E. Smith c Lomax b Lobb	0		
C. Gladwin not out	0		
L. Jackson c Stephenson b Lobb	0		
B 5, l-b 3	8		

1/10 2/10 3/10 4/25 5/30 6/56 7/156	158	1/9 (1 wkt.) 35
8/158 9/158 (3.67 an over)		

Derbyshire Bowling

	O.	M.	R.	W.		O.	M.	R.	W.
Jackson	11	4	22	3	....	20	10	41	1
Gladwin	16	7	29	5	....	24.3	10	57	8
Morgan	6	3	10	1	....	10	2	19	0
Smith						6	1	12	1

Somerset Bowling

	O.	M.	R.	W.		O.	M.	R.	W.
Lobb	15.3	3	36	5	....	4.4	1	15	0
Alley	7	0	18	3	....	2	0	8	1
Lomax	3	0	15	0					
McMahon	5	1	22	0					
Langford	4	0	20	0					
Hilton	2	0	10	0					
Tremlett	6	1	29	2	....	2	0	12	0

Umpires: L. H. Gray and A. R. Coleman.

At Manchester, June 26, 27. SOMERSET lost to LANCASHIRE by nine wickets.

At Leicester, June 29, July 1. SOMERSET beat LEICESTERSHIRE by 58 runs.

At Northampton, July 3, 4, 5. SOMERSET lost to NORTHAMPTONSHIRE by 124 runs.

SOMERSET v. R.A.F.

At Glastonbury, July 6, 8, 9. R.A.F. won by 94 runs. R.A.F. 220 (G. G. Atkinson 76, B. Langford four for 57) and 227 (R. Subba Row 81, Langford five for 81); Somerset 160 (W. E. Alley 53, D. B. Pearson five for 33) and 193 (G. Hill six for 69). Not first-class.

SOMERSET v. NORTHAMPTONSHIRE

At Yeovil, July 10, 11, 12. Drawn, Northamptonshire taking two points. Rain reduced the match to a keen struggle for first innings lead which Northamptonshire gained on the stroke of time with their last pair together. Alley and McCool batted soundly, but Tyson swept through the rest on a slow pitch that offered him no assistance. Only seven overs were possible on the second day. Brookes and Barrick shared a brisk stand of 101; then Manning hit 17 in an over from Langford, but with the new ball Alley took four for 21 in the course of 13 overs. Andrew resisted stubbornly and made the hit which decided the destination of the two points. Northamptonshire were 0.005 runs per over behind on the scoring rate.

Somerset

W. E. Alley b Kelleher	71
J. G. Lomax st Andrew b Manning	22
P. B. Wight b Tyson	5
C. L. McCool b Tyson	77
M. F. Tremlett b Tyson	15
G. M. Tripp b Tribe	3
H. W. Stephenson c Barrick b Tribe	0
B. Langford lbw b Tyson	17
J. Hilton not out	18
B. Lobb b Tyson	6
J. W. McMahon c Andrew b Tyson	0
B 9, l-b 5	14

248

1/60 2/85 3/135 4/172 5/178
6/178 7/211 8/226 9/238
(2.455 an over)

Northamptonshire

D. Brookes c McCool b Lobb	84
P. Arnold c Tripp b Langford	16
D. Reynolds b Langford	0
D. W. Barrick b Lobb	63
G. E. Tribe lbw b Langford	5
J. P. Fellows-Smith lbw b Alley	5
J. S. Manning b Alley	34
K. V. Andrew not out	30
F. H. Tyson b Alley	0
M. H. J. Allen b Alley	4
H. R. A. Kelleher not out	3
B 5, l-b 1	6

1/46 2/48 3/149 4/160 (9 wkts.) 250
5/170 6/195 7/219 8/219 9/237
(2.450 an over)

Northamptonshire Bowling

	O.	M.	R.	W.
Tyson	24.3	6	53	6
Kelleher	20	5	44	1
Allen	11	5	17	0
Manning	24	7	49	1
Tribe	21	4	71	2

Somerset Bowling

	O.	M.	R.	W.
Lobb	28	6	65	2
Hilton	10	1	26	0
Alley	19.1	4	41	4
Langford	21	5	61	3
McMahon	21	6	46	0
Lomax	3	0	5	0

Umpires: A. E. Pothecary and J. F. Crapp.

At Colchester, July 13, 15. SOMERSET lost to ESSEX by eight wickets.

At Taunton, June 17, 18, 19. SOMERSET drew with WEST INDIES. (See WEST INDIES section.)

At Bournemouth, July 20, 22. SOMERSET beat HAMPSHIRE by eight wickets.

SOMERSET v. KENT

At Taunton, July 24, 25, 26. Somerset won by ten wickets, taking 14 points. Kent fielded a weak bowling side, but that did not detract from the merit of Somerset's achievement. To concede over 300 runs in the first innings and still win was a notable feat under any circumstances—particularly since, having won the toss, Tremlett invited Kent to bat first. Wilson and Pretlove foiled that gamble with a stand of 110, and though McCool captured three wickets in rapid succession, Wilson found another useful partner in Ufton. Wilson spent nearly five hours over his 146, hitting one 6 and sixteen 4's. Somerset tackled a formidable task with heartening enthusiasm. All the batsmen, with the exception of Alley, found their form. The best innings was played by Stephenson, whose first century of the season occupied only two hours. The 18-year-old Roe showed distinct promise in his first championship game. Another stand by Pretlove and Wilson held up Somerset in their drive for victory, and Ufton hit powerfully, but Somerset needed only 53 to complete the double over Kent.

Kent

A. H. Phebcy c Pickles b McMahon ...	15	— c Stephenson b Lobb	10
R. Wilson c Pickles b Langford	146	— b McMahon	61
J. F. Pretlove lbw b McCool	56	— b McCool	24
A. L. Dixon c Lobb b McCool	14	— lbw b McMahon	1
S. E. Leary c McMahon b McCool	5	— c Stephenson b Lobb	16
J. Pettiford lbw b Lobb	6	— lbw b Lobb	13
D. G. Ufton st Stephenson b McCool ...	38	— b Lobb	55
A. E. Fagg b Lobb	13	— c Tremlett b McMahon	21
A. Brown b Lobb	1	— st Stephenson b McMahon .	0
J. C. T. Page not out................	1	— not out	0
R. S. Thresher (did not bat)...........		— b Alley	1
B 2, l-b 5, w 3..............	10	B 8, l-b 2, w 2	12

1/38 2/148 3/168 4/184 (9 wkts., dec.) 305
5/215 6/273 7/297 8/298 9/305
(2.58 an over)

1/27 2/92 3/101 4/108 214
5/127 6/132 7/175 8/191
9/211

Somerset

L. Pickles b Thresher	70	— not out	24
W. E. Alley c Page b Brown	4	— not out	31
P. B. Wight c Ufton b Page	55		
M. F. Tremlett c Fagg b Leary	64		
C. L. McCool c Dixon b Page	92		
B. Roe c Pretlove b Thresher	47		
H. W. Stephenson not out	104		
K. E. Palmer run out	6		
B. Langford lbw b Thresher	4		
B. Lobb b Brown	6		
J. W. McMahon not out	1		
B 1, l-b 10, w 1, n-b 2	14		

1/13 2/89 3/192 4/205   (9 wkts., dec.) 467   (No wkt.) 55
5/310 6/404 7/422 8/446 9/453
(3.51 an over)

Somerset Bowling

	O.	M.	R.	W.		O.	M.	R.	W.
Lobb	15.3	2	39	3	....	15	3	44	4
Alley	21	3	53	0	....	3.3	1	15	1
Langford	32	12	74	1	....	1	1	0	0
McMahon	21	6	51	1	....	20	3	68	4
Palmer	7	1	25	0	....	5	0	17	0
McCool	21	7	53	4	....	21	6	58	1

Kent Bowling

	O.	M.	R.	W.		O.	M.	R.	W.
Brown	31	9	119	2	....	4	0	15	0
Thresher	33	2	145	3	....	2	0	17	0
Dixon	24	5	78	0					
Page	36	12	87	2					
Pretlove	2	0	6	0	....	3	1	5	0
Leary	7	0	18	1	....	1.4	0	18	0

Umpires: E. Davies and W. F. Price.

SOMERSET v. LEICESTERSHIRE

At Taunton, July 27, 29, 30. Drawn, Somerset taking four points. A splendid innings by Hallam saved Leicestershire when defeat by an innings seemed likely. The Somerset bowlers had the assistance of a rain-affected pitch in the Leicestershire first innings, and only van Geloven, who batted nearly three hours, and Munden. in his first county match, offered serious resistance. For the second game in succession Somerset's batsmen excelled. Tremlett, whose century was his first of the season, batted four hours and hit sixteen 4's. His stand of 187 with Wight contained the brightest batting of the match. Leicestershire were left with all the third day to try to avoid defeat, and on turf which offered no help to bowlers, gave one of their soundest batting displays for some time. Hallam, staying nearly four and a half hours, hit twenty-one 4's.

Leicestershire

G. Lester lbw b Alley	1	— c Palmer b Langford	13
M. R. Hallam st Stephenson b McCool	30	— c Stephenson b Tremlett	151
J. van Geloven c Stephenson b Lobb	57	— c Wight b McMahon	32
L. R. Gardner c Pickles b McMahon	9	— not out	19
C. H. Palmer c Stephenson b McMahon	26	— not out	62
P. Munden b Lobb	38		
J. Firth lbw b Alley	5		
J. Savage c Palmer b Lobb	2		
R. C. Smith run out	4		
C. T. Spencer c Wight b Alley	0		
B. Boshier not out	0		
B 5, l-b 6, w 5	16	B 7, l-b 5, w 5, n-b 1	18

1/1 2/34 3/67 4/121 5/137 6/160   188   1/56 2/137   (3 wkts.) 295
7/183 8/188 9/188 (2.29 an over)   3/252

Somerset

L. Pickles b Spencer	3	B. Langford c Firth b Boshier	23
W. E. Alley c Spencer b Boshier	7	B. Roe not out	0
P. B. Wight run out	88	B 1, l-b 2, n-b 2	5
M. F. Tremlett c Gardner b Spencer	144		
C. L. McCool c Firth b Spencer	3		
H. W. Stephenson c Hallam b van		1/10 2/10 3/197 (7 wkts., dec.) 368	
Geloven	39	4/223 5/270 6/303 7/363	
K. E. Palmer not out	56	(3.71 an over)	

J. W. McMahon and B. Lobb did not bat.

Somerset Bowling

	O.	M.	R.	W.	O.	M.	R.	W.
Lobb	28	13	49	3	13	2	39	0
Alley	24.3	3	61	3	9	2	32	0
Palmer	3	1	4	0	8	2	30	0
McCool	12	2	42	1	11	1	37	0
McMahon	12	7	12	2	35	11	76	1
Langford	2	1	4	0	18	7	29	1
Pickles					2	0	10	0
Wight					4	3	1	0
Tremlett					4	0	9	1
Roe					2	0	3	0
Stephenson					2	1	11	0

Leicestershire Bowling

	O.	M.	R.	W.
Spencer	24	2	65	3
Boshier	20	1	96	2
Palmer	18	5	63	0
Savage	3	0	12	0
Smith	10	2	40	0
van Geloven	18	2	63	1
Lester	6	1	24	0

Umpires: E. Davies and W. F. Price.

At Worcester, July 31, August 1, 2. SOMERSET beat WORCESTERSHIRE by 57 runs.

At Bristol, August 3, 4. SOMERSET lost to GLOUCESTERSHIRE by an innings and five runs.

SOMERSET v. SUSSEX

At Weston-super-Mare, August 7, 8, 9. Sussex won by an innings and 44 runs, taking 14 points. They gave an attractive batting display, backed up by excellent seam bowling. Suttle and Parks exposed the limitations of the Somerset attack during a brisk stand of 165, Smith having retired hurt at 16. Both fell attempting big hits. Smith returned and hit powerfully, Webb helping him add 63 in three-quarters of an hour. Somerset started badly, recovered partially while Tremlett and McCool were adding 79 in a little over an hour, then lost the last six wickets for 41. Three second innings wickets were down for 19, but again Tremlett came to the rescue. Though only Pickles stayed with him for any length of time, the Somerset captain made a splendid 106 in three and a half hours, hitting fifteen 4's, but it was not enough to save his side from an innings defeat.

Sussex

D. V. Smith lbw b Alley	78	R. T. Webb not out	25
Rev. D. S. Sheppard c Stephenson		R. G. Marlar c and b Alley	0
b Palmer	17	N. I. Thomson not out	6
K. G. Suttle c McMahon b McCool	94	B 5, l-b 9, w 1, n-b 1	16
J. M. Parks c Pickles b Lobb	92		
G. H. G. Doggart lbw b Langford	48	1/38 2/203 3/241 (8 wkts., dec.) 384
L. J. Lenham c Silk b McCool	8	4/268 5/302 6/303 7/366 8/366
A. E. James c Stephenson b McCool	0	(3.45 an over)

R. V. Bell did not bat.

Somerset

L. Pickles c and b Thomson	6	— c Parks b James	25
W. E. Alley c Lenham b Thomson	4	— c Suttle b James	0
P. B. Wight c Sheppard b Thomson	0	— c Webb b Thomson	12
M. F. Tremlett b Bell	51	— c and b Bell	106
C. L. McCool c Webb b Thomson	38	— c Suttle b James	20
D. R. W. Silk not out	20	— b James	0
H. W. Stephenson c and b Bell	15	— c Webb b Suttle	0
K. E. Palmer c Webb b James	3	— not out	18
B. Langford c Parks b James	0	— c Sheppard b Marlar	4
B. Lobb run out	1	— st Webb b Marlar	4
J. W. McMahon b James	1	— c Sheppard b Marlar	1
N-b 2	2	B 6, l-b 2, n-b 1	9

1/5 2/6 3/21 4/100 5/100 6/121   141   1/4 2/4 3/19 4/97 5/136   199
7/132 8/136 9/137 (2.47 an over)   6/139 7/180 8/187 9/191

Somerset Bowling

	O.	M.	R.	W.	O.	M.	R.	W.
Lobb	24	4	85	1				
Alley	24	2	65	2				
Palmer	15	1	57	1				
Langford	15	5	32	1				
McCool	19	4	62	3				
McMahon	14	1	67	0				

Sussex Bowling

	O.	M.	R.	W.	O.	M.	R.	W.
Thomson	18	8	46	4	19	9	38	1
James	19.3	10	32	3	31	11	72	4
Marlar	4	0	22	0	15.1	4	46	3
Bell	15	5	39	1	11	6	15	1
Suttle					15	7	19	1

Umpires: D. Davies and W. F. Price.

SOMERSET v. GLAMORGAN

At Weston-super-Mare, August 10, 12, 13. Somerset won by ten wickets, taking 14 points. Glamorgan never recovered from the blows dealt them in their first innings by the seam bowlers, Lobb and Dickinson, a former Lancashire player, who was making his debut for Somerset. They shared the ten wickets, and only two batsmen, Parkhouse and Walker, reached double figures against them. All but one of the wickets fell to catches behind the bat. Parkhouse defended well for two and a half hours, and Walker helped in a stand of 57. Somerset also started badly, but a fourth stand of 160 by McCool and Wight put them on the road to victory. At one stage they put on 100 in an hour. Then the pitch, which had been damp, became tricky under the effects of sun and wind and after the fourth wicket fell Shepherd and McConnon routed the remainder for the addition of 50 runs. Langford found conditions ideal for his off-spin, and bowled Somerset to their eighth victory of the season, a performance which earned him his county cap.

Glamorgan

W. G. A. Parkhouse c McCool b Lobb .	58 —	lbw b Dickinson 20
B. Hedges c McCool b Dickinson	1 —	c Wight b Langford 21
W. G. Davies c Stephenson b Lobb	0 —	b Langford 10
W. E. Jones c Stephenson b Lobb	5 —	b Dickinson 0
A. J. Watkins c Palmer b Lobb........	3 —	c Silk b Langford 28
L. N. Devereux c Stephenson b Dickinson	5 —	c Silk b Wight 16
P. Walker c McCool b Dickinson	35 —	b Wight 0
J. E. McConnon c Stephenson b Dickinson	9 —	b Langford 9
W. Wooller c Stephenson b Lobb	0 —	b Langford 31
H. G. Davies b Dickinson	9 —	c Stephenson b Langford... 1
D. J. Shepherd not out	6 —	not out 2
		L-b 3 3

1/4 2/5 3/25 4/29 5/43 6/100 7/108   131   1/21 2/52 3/53 4/53 5/92   141
8/108 9/118 (2.62 an over)   6/92 7/104 8/113 9/116

Somerset

L. Pickles b Walker	1 —	not out 6
W. E. Alley c Jones b Walker	8 —	not out 10
P. B. Wight c Watkins b Shepherd	79	
M. F. Tremlett c Watkins b Walker	21	
C. L. McCool run out.................	95	
H. W. Stephenson lbw b Shepherd	12	
D. R. W. Silk c Walker b Shepherd	0	
K. E. Palmer not out	22	
B. Langford c Walker b Shepherd	1	
T. E. Dickinson c Watkins b McConnon	0	
B. Lobb c Jones b McConnon...........	15	
L-b 3	3	

1/8 2/15 3/47 4/207 5/207 6/207   257   (No wkt.) 16
7/220 8/222 9/235 (3.17 an over)

Somerset Bowling

	O.	M.	R.	W.		O.	M.	R.	W.
Lobb	23	7	63	5	....	17	10	24	0
Dickinson	17.4	4	36	5	....	12	4	24	2
Alley..........	9	1	32	0	....	3	2	1	0
Langford						25.1	9	61	6
Wight						6	0	20	2
McCool						2	1	8	0

Glamorgan Bowling

	O.	M.	R.	W.		O.	M.	R.	W.
Wooller	16	4	68	0					
Walker	20	7	33	3					
Watkins	9	2	20	0					
Shepherd	22	2	92	4	....	3	1	5	0
McConnon	13.1	3	34	2	....	2.2	1	11	0
Devereux	1	0	7	0					

Umpires: A. Skelding and D. J. Wood.

SOMERSET v. SURREY

(H. W. Stephenson's Benefit)

At Weston-super-Mare, August 14, 15, 16. Surrey won by three wickets, taking 14 points, and thus assuring themselves of the County Championship for the sixth consecutive year. To their credit, Somerset ran them close, for only eight minutes of extra time remained when Laker made the winning hit. Despite a patient innings by Wight, six Somerset wickets were down for 150 before Stephenson and Palmer gained complete mastery in a stand of 92. When it was broken the remaining wickets fell cheaply. May and Clark batted splendidly for Surrey, but Stewart was never at ease and it was left to McIntyre and Lock to take Surrey into the lead. Somerset lost two wickets wiping out the arrears and then Tremlett played a magnificent attacking innings of 83 in just over an hour. Wight completed his fourth score of over 50 in his last four innings against Surrey, but Laker, with a spell of five for 19 in eight overs, regained the initiative for his side. Surrey needed 153 to win and found themselves struggling against both the clock and a determined attack. May played another fine innings and Barrington hit briskly to see Surrey home and provide a thrilling climax to Stephenson's successful benefit.

Somerset

L. Pickles lbw b Loader	0	—	b Loader	1	
D. R. W. Silk c Lock b A. Bedser	33	—	b Laker	16	
P. B. Wight b Lock	65	—	lbw b Laker	58	
M. F. Tremlett b A. Bedser	2	—	c Constable b A. Bedser	83	
C. L. McCool c Stewart b Lock	21	—	c and b Lock	9	
W. E. Alley c Loader b Laker	18	—	c McIntyre b Laker	1	
H. W. Stephenson b A. Bedser	47	—	c Lock b Laker	4	
K. E. Palmer b E. Bedser	49	—	c Stewart b Laker	10	
B. Langford b Loader	0	—	lbw b Loader	5	
T. E. Dickinson not out	0	—	c McIntyre b Laker	0	
B. Lobb b A. Bedser	4	—	not out	0	
B 6, l-b 3, n-b 2	11		N-b 1	1	

1/0 2/89 3/92 4/116 5/148 6/150   **250**
7/242 8/242 9/246 (2.23 an over)

1/8 2/29 3/140 4/152   **188**
5/153 6/157 7/175 8/188
9/188

Surrey

T. H. Clark b Langford	55	—	lbw b Lobb	21	
M. J. Stewart st Stephenson b Wight	48	—	lbw b Langford	29	
B. Constable c Palmer b Langford	1	—	c Pickles b Langford	9	
P. B. H. May b Dickinson	62	—	c Alley b Lobb	38	
K. F. Barrington c Stephenson b Langford	6	—	c and b McCool	32	
E. A. Bedser c Dickinson b McCool	4	—	not out	10	
A. J. McIntyre b Dickinson	53	—	lbw b Dickinson	2	
G. A. R. Lock b Palmer	30	—	c Pickles b McCool	5	
P. J. Loader c Tremlett b Dickinson	2				
J. C. Laker not out	3	—	not out	1	
A. V. Bedser b Dickinson	8				
B 6, l-b 8	14		B 4, l-b 2	6	

1/85 2/89 3/145 4/164 5/169 6/209   **286**
7/268 8/274 9/274 (3.07 an over)

1/44 2/54 3/71   (7 wkts.) **153**
4/78 5/111 6/146 7/152

Surrey Bowling

	O.	M.	R.	W.		O.	M.	R.	W.
Loader	23	7	40	2	....	11.2	1	25	2
A. Bedser.....	26	6	47	4	....	12	3	38	1
Lock	28	9	67	2	....	16	1	47	1
Laker	29	8	72	1	....	20	. 3	66	6
E. Bedser......	6	1	13	1	....	1	0	11	0

Somerset Bowling

	O.	M.	R.	W.		O.	M.	R.	W.
Lobb	15	1	50	0	....	9	1	29	2
Dickinson	23,4	3	80	4	....	14	1	58	1
Alley..........	9	0	30	0	....	3	1	5	0
Langford	28	10	60	3	....	17.1	6	49	2
McCool	5	0	24	1	....	2	1	6	2
Wight	6	1	16	1					
Palmer	6	3	12	1					

Umpires: T. W. Spencer and A. Skelding.

At Chesterfield, August 17, 19, 20. Somerset beat Derbyshire by an innings and 21 runs.

SOMERSET v. SUSSEX
(Friendly)

At Imperial Athletic Ground, Bristol, August 21, 22, 23. Somerset's first visit to Bristol for many years for a home fixture produced entertaining cricket in this friendly match, but no play was possible on the third day. For the second time in three weeks Tremlett scored two fifties in a match against the Sussex attack, and most of the other batsmen found the rest from competitive cricket conducive to attractive stroke play.

Somerset

D. R. W. Silk c Suttle b Bell............	79	— c Webb b Bates	11
W. E. Alley b Bell	58	— lbw b Cogger	18
P. B. Wight run out....................	10	— b Bates	10
C. L. McCool c Bell b Bates............	85	— not out	7
K. E. Palmer lbw b Bates	25	— b Bates	11
H. W. Stephenson c Webb b Bates	18	— b Bates	0
M. F. Tremlett c Semmence b Bates ...	52	— c Bates b Bell............	51
B. Langford lbw b Suttle	13	— not out	1
B. Lobb b Bates	2		
T. E. Dickinson b Suttle	0		
A. Whitehead not out	0		
B 6, n-b 3	9	B 8.................	8

1/114 2/135 3/179 4/258 5/261   351   1/26 2/37 3/41   (6 wkts.) 117
6/309 7/339 8/349 9/349   4/48 5/79 6/116

Sussex

L. J. Lenham c and b McCool ...	62	G. Cogger c Stephenson b McCool	1
R. H. Willson b Dickinson	0	R. V. Bell c Stephenson b White-	
R. T. Webb lbw b McCool	35	head	6
K. G. Suttle lbw b McCool	18	D. L. Bates not out	1
G. Potter lbw b McCool	78	B 2, l-b 4	6
Nawab of Pataudi lbw b Langford	19		
D. V. Smith c Whitehead b Wight..	10	1/6 2/72 3/116 4/121 5/176	241
D. J. Semmence b Whitehead	5	6/197 7/217 8/222 9/229	

Sussex Bowling

	O.	M.	R.	W.		O.	M.	R.	W.
Bates	28	5	74	5	....	12	1	41	4
Cogger	22	1	74	0	....	5	0	25	1
Smith	9	3	34	0	....	11	4	28	0
Bell	28 .	4	107	2	....	5	3	15	1
Suttle	18.3	3	53	2					

Somerset Bowling

	O.	M.	R.	W.
Dickinson	7	4	12	1
Lobb	5	1	18	0
McCool	42	8	107	5
Whitehead	25	8	46	2
Langford	14	4	35	1
Wight	4	2	17	1

Umpires: C. Buttle and A. H. Mills.

SOMERSET v. YORKSHIRE

At Taunton, August 24, 26, 27. Yorkshire won by seven wickets, taking 12 points to Somerset's four. They were greatly indebted to their young fast bowler, Pickles, who achieved easily his best performance in taking twelve wickets for 133 runs. Somerset flattered to deceive when Silk and Alley gave them an excellent start in a stand of 89 and Silk stayed to put on 101 with McCool for the fourth wicket. The turning-point came when Pickles took the new ball and in the course of twenty-nine deliveries obtained five wickets for only six runs. Yorkshire themselves struggled for runs and, despite a commendable effort by Illingworth, failed by three runs to get the lead. Next, the combination of Pickles and Appleyard put Yorkshire completely on top and though Langford and Biddulph staged a late rally they needed only 159 to win. Finally, Sutcliffe, the Yorkshire captain, played an enterprising innings, bringing the match to an exciting climax by hitting the last two balls each for 6. He received splendid support from Watson on a pitch which offered some help to bowlers.

Somerset

D. R. W. Silk c Close b Cowan	61	— c Wilson b Pickles	17
W. E. Alley b Illingworth	64	— b Cowan	11
P. B. Wight c Binks b Pickles	1	— b Pickles	7
M. F. Tremlett c Close b Pickles	4	— b Pickles	1
C. L. McCool c and b Illingworth	77	— b Appleyard	35
G. G. Atkinson lbw b Pickles	11	— lbw b Pickles	16
K. E. Palmer b Pickles	0	— b Appleyard	0
H. W. Stephenson c Wilson b Pickles ...	11	— c Binks b Appleyard	7
B. Langford b Pickles	0	— c Binks b Pickles	31
K. D. Biddulph not out	2	— c and b Appleyard	22
T. E. Dickinson c Binks b Pickles.......	0	— not out	7
B 1	1	L-b 2	2

1/89 2/90 3/100 4/201 5/208 6/209   232   1/21 2/30 3/32 4/39 5/80   156
7/225 8/225 9/232 (3.36 an over)   6/80 7/88 8/98 9/135

Yorkshire

W. B. Stott b Dickinson	43	— c Palmer b Alley	18
W. Watson b Biddulph	3	— c Langford b Dickinson....	48
W. H. H. Sutcliffe c Stephenson b Biddulph	13	— not out	70
D. B. Close c Dickinson b Langford	40	— st Stephenson b Langford..	20
J. V. Wilson b Alley	41	— not out	1
D. E. V. Padgett st Stephenson b McCool	14		
R. Illingworth not out	47		
J. G. Binks b Alley	4		
R. Appleyard c Biddulph b Wight	13		
D. Pickles b Biddulph	4		
M. J. Cowan lbw b Dickinson	0		
L-b 7, n-b 1	8	B 1, l-b 5	6

1/3 2/23 3/81 4/115 5/153 6/171 7/177   230   1/34 2/92 3/140   (3 wkts.) 163
8/198 9/211 (3.02 an over)

Yorkshire Bowling

	O.	M.	R.	W.		O.	M.	R.	W.
Pickles	20	4	61	7	....	24	6	72	5
Cowan	17	0	74	1	....	23	5	42	1
Appleyard	8	1	21	0	....	11.4	1	28	4
Illingworth	21	6	56	2	....	12	4	12	0
Close	3	0	19	0					

Somerset Bowling

	O.	M.	R.	W.		O.	M.	R.	W.
Dickinson	21.2	2	59	2	....	8	2	22	1
Biddulph	19	5	53	3	....	10	1	32	0
Langford	16	4	41	1	....	20.2	8	54	1
Alley	11	3	34	2	....	10	4	20	1
Palmer	2	0	10	0					
Wight	4	0	9	1	....	6	2	20	0
McCool	3	0	16	1					
Atkinson						2	0	9	0

Umpires: John Langridge and J. Wood.

At Hove, August 28, 29, 30. SOMERSET lost to SUSSEX by 232 runs. (Friendly match.)

SURREY

Patron—HER MAJESTY THE QUEEN
President—Marshal of the Royal Air Force Lord Tedder
Secretary—B. K. Castor, Kennington Oval, London, S.E.11
Captain—P. B. H. May

E. A. Bedser

County Badge

K. F. Barrington

For the sixth successive year incomparable Surrey carried all before them. Their high skill, ruthless efficiency, matchless team spirit and appetite for quick runs left no reasonable doubt that their record run of Championship victories would be extended. Once they had taken the lead theirs was a lonely supremacy, and in the final table they were separated from Northamptonshire, the runners-up, by the wide margin of 94 points. On August 16 they clinched the title, a date which equalled Warwickshire's post-war record, set in 1951, of winning by the earliest date.

Surrey's policy of persistent aggression from the first ball to the last never wavered, even in the rare threat of defeat. As many as nine of their 21 Championship victories were gained inside two days. Nor was it a coincidence that they scored faster than any other side—an example of their dynamic approach to the game.

Throughout the season Surrey were the dominant side, attracting large crowds wherever they appeared. They played, acted, thought and looked like the magnificent champions they are. Surrey's achievements undoubtedly entitle them to be considered the greatest county combination of all time.

Though it was yet another glorious record of uninterrupted success the season marked a new chapter in Surrey cricket. After five triumphant years Stuart Surridge retired and the captaincy passed to P. B. H. May, England's captain since 1955. As May was an automatic choice to lead the national side again, there were fears that his dual responsibility, and his absence in many county fixtures—he missed nine—would react unfavourably against Surrey. May's services to England virtually meant his sharing the Surrey captaincy with his newly-appointed deputy, senior professional, Alec Bedser.

Bedser was May's own recommendation to the Surrey Committee, and it proved from every conceivable angle a wise and happy choice. Bedser was a brilliant deputy. His wide experience, deep technical knowledge, shrewdness and willingness to encourage the new members earned him a new stature in English cricket. When they played together May made no secret of his reliance on Bedser's advice. At the end of the season May paid the warmest of tributes to the qualities of his vice-captain. "Alec has been splendid in every direction," he said. "So much has depended on him. He and I run the show including team selection."

For the first time since he suffered from shingles when touring with Hutton's team in Australia in 1954–55, Bedser was also once again a great medium-pace bowler, sharing with Lock and Loader the distinction of taking over 100 wickets for his club.

Captain and vice-captain shared the credit for the maintenance of Surridge's legacy of a great team spirit. It was a spirit born of success, and thrived because, by habit and practice, Surrey played as a side and not as a collection of brilliant individualists.

Once again Surrey's international-standard attack was superb; so was the supporting fielding and catching, especially close to the wicket. The sight of their alert fieldsmen crouched near the bat is a familiar and thrilling feature of English cricket. The side's striking power was reflected in the first-class bowling averages. Lock, at the top, took 200 wickets for the second time in three years, including 153 in the Championship at the remarkably low cost of 11.58 apiece. Laker, Loader and the Bedser twins were also in the first ten bowlers to take 70 or more wickets. Whatever the type of pitch Surrey had the bowlers to use it. Loader and Alec Bedser rarely failed to strike with the new ball, and there was Laker and Lock, the world's most dangerous spinning partnership, to follow, with Eric Bedser's off-breaks as good measure.

Under Surridge, who believed catches were to be had off defensive shots if fieldsmen were prepared to stand close enough, Surrey developed a standard of fielding comparable with the greatest. May and Bedser saw to it that their side did not deviate from Surridge's level. Lock again made many breathless catches and Stewart, as the shortest of short-legs, or in any position near the bat, was one of the most daring and brilliant catchers in the country. He took 77 catches, only one short of W. R. Hammond's record established in 1928. Stewart, however, had the rich compensation of creating a new world record for a fielder other than a wicket-keeper by making seven catches at Northampton in June.

To stand at Stewart's "pocket picking" distance at short-leg needs more than a safe pair of hands, quick reflexes and a stout heart; it demands complete faith in his bowlers to maintain an accurate length. They never failed him. Barrington, in his first season as a slip, shared with Stewart and Lock the outstanding performance of exceeding 60 catches. Surrey, by having their youngest players in the positions nearest the wicket, further prove this modern theory is the soundest.

Barrington also made a welcome return to form with the bat. He enjoyed his best season since his premature selection for England in 1955 led to his falling off. Stewart and Clark, who was on the fringe of Test honours, also topped the 1,500 mark in all matches, and Constable fell just short of that target. None could match the consistently high performance of May, who scored in his 19 Championship games 1,391 of his first-class aggregate of 2,347 runs.

Generally Surrey could hope for runs down to number nine. Their batsmen cheerfully took risks in the interests of their side; their true worth lay in their determination to give the team's bowlers time and runs in which to dismiss the opposition twice. Surrey's batting has often been unjustly criticised; almost always under-rated. For long periods five Surrey batsmen and five Surrey bowlers were in the averages. The mammoth totals of pre-war Oval days are happily no longer reached. The wicket has undergone a radical change; the lush, beautifully maintained outfield is no longer fast. Runs are harder to come by, and Surrey strive, not necessarily for large, dreary draw-producing totals, but winning ones.

McIntyre lost none of his wicket-keeping ability. Throughout the Test series he stood by as reserve to Evans and there can be little doubt that he is England's second best 'keeper. Keeping to Surrey's varied attack, especially on a pitch helpful to the bowlers, calls for the highest skill and McIntyre was seldom wanting.

A last but not inconsiderable reason for Surrey's triumph was their fund of adequate reserves to fill the gaps left by England's heavy calls. Without their loyal and excellent service Surrey would be hard pressed to maintain their position.

At the end of the year Surrey parted company with B. K. Castor who retired after being secretary since 1946. He had been a county official since 1930 when he joined Essex, and to mark his long and efficient period of office all the first-class County secretaries presented him with a radiogram and records at their annual meeting at Lord's in December. Commander B. O. Babb, the asistant-secretary, has succeeded Mr. Castor at The Oval.— A. B.

(Owing to the exigencies of space, the diagram of The Oval ground has been omitted for this edition.)

SURREY RESULTS

All First-Class Matches—Played 35, Won 25, Lost 4, Drawn 6

County Championship Matches—Played 28, Won 21, Lost 3, Drawn 3, No Decision 1

COUNTY CHAMPIONSHIP AVERAGES
BATTING

	Birthplace	Mtchs	Inns.	Not Outs	Runs	100's	Highest Inns.	Aver.
P. B. H. May ...	*Reading*	19	27	2	1391	3	125	33.04
D. F. Cox	*Bermondsey*	6	7	3	142	0	54	35.50
K. F. Barrington.	*Reading*	28	41	9	1129	3	129*	35.28
D. G. W. Fletcher	*Sutton*	16	24	5	659	1	101	34.68
M. J. Stewart ...	*Herne Hill*	27	40	2	1290	2	140	33.94
T. H. Clark	*Luton*	23	35	3	995	0	95	31.09
B. Constable ..	*Molesey*	25	35	2	929	2	107	28.15
A. J. McIntyre..	*Kennington*	28	31	5	606	0	96	23.30
R. C. E. Pratt...	*Balham*	9	12	5	163	0	40	23.28
E. A. Bedser ...	*Reading*	26	31	4	587	0	65	21.74
G. A. R. Lock..	*Limpsfield*	22	22	4	331	0	46	18.38
M. D. Willett ...	*Norwood*	5	8	1	99	0	26	14.14
A. V. Bedser ...	*Reading*	27	20	10	103	0	17*	10.30
P. J. Loader	*Wallington*	25	19	4	152	0	38	10.13
J. C. Laker	*Bradford*	18	18	8	86	0	14*	8.60
D. Gibson	*Mitcham*	2	3	0	14	0	11	4.66

Also batted: D. A. D. Sydenham (*Surbiton*) 0; R. Swetman (*Reading*) played in one match but did not bat.

BOWLING

	Overs	Maidens	Runs	Wickets	Average
G. A. R. Lock	810.3	296	1773	153	11.58
J. C. Laker	563	229	1055	85	12.41
E. A. Bedser	395.4	130	804	60	13.40
D. Gibson	73	11	198	14	14.14
P. J. Loader	632.4	155	1488	101	14.73
A. V. Bedser	823.1	217	1698	109	15.57
K. F. Barrington	23	4	70	3	23.33
D. F. Cox	69.1	6	218	5	43.60

Also bowled: T. H. Clark 4—2—2—0; R. C. E. Pratt 1—0—3—0; D. A. D. Sydenham 13—2—56—1.

Amateur.—P. B. H. May.

At Cambridge, April 27, 29, 30. SURREY beat CAMBRIDGE UNIVERSITY by ten wickets.

At Lord's, May 1, 2, 3. SURREY beat M.C.C. by 238 runs.

SURREY v. COMBINED SERVICES

At The Oval, May 4, 6, 7. Drawn. Rain after tea on the final day spoiled hopes of a definite result, for Surrey were looking to Lock to exploit a pitch beginning to take spin. Even so the match provided extremely useful practice for Surrey and also showed that the Services, with considerable talent to draw upon, compared favourably with many county sides. Though Stewart (sixteen 4's) and Barrington (eleven 4's) hit centuries in sharing an unbroken second wicket partnership of 235 in three hours forty minutes, Surrey did not have matters all their own way. Two young pace bowlers, Pearson (Worcestershire) and Hodgson (Yorkshire) worried the county batsmen in the first innings, and Parsons, himself a Surrey amateur, and his captain, Shirreff, batted soundly for the Services.

Surrey

T. H. Clark c Fenner b Standring	52	— c Fenner b Standring 15
M. J. Stewart c Fenner b Pearson	9	— not out 114
B. Constable c Shirreff b Hodgson	84	
K. F. Barrington c Atkinson b Pearson..	7	— not out 110
D. G. W. Fletcher lbw b Pearson	0	
R. C. E. Pratt c Pearson b Standring	1	
E. A. Bedser c Parsons b Hodgson	24	
A. J. McIntyre not out	17	
G. A. R. Lock c Shirreff b Hodgson	0	
P. J. Loader c Parsons b Semmence	17	
A. V. Bedser b Pearson	10	
B 3, l-b 3, w 1, n-b 6	13	B 10, l-b 4, n-b 3 17

1/23 2/104 3/123 4/123 5/128 6/187   234   1/21   (1 wkt., dec.) 256
7/190 8/190 9/221

Combined Services

L/A/C S. A. Leadbetter c Lock b A. Bedser	4	— c Loader b Barrington 46
L/Cpl. P. J. Sharpe c sub b A. Bedser ...	44	— c McIntyre b Loader 11
Gnr. A. B. D. Parsons b Loader	52	— c Fletcher b E. Bedser ... 18
A/C G. A. Atkinson c Lock b Loader ..	4	— not out 36
Dvr. J. Edrich b E. Bedser	7	— run out 0
A/C D. J. Semmence b Loader	0	— not out 5
Sqdn/Ldr. A. C. Shirreff c Barrington b Lock	69	
Spr. K. E. Standring b Lock	22	
F/Lt. M. D. Fenner c Stewart b A. Bedser	3	
A/C D. B. Pearson c Lock b A. Bedser ..	4	
L/A/C P. Hodgson not out	1	
B 3, l-b 6, n-b 3	12	B 4, l-b 5, w 2, n-b 1 12

1/17 2/106 3/106 4/112 5/112 6/127   222   1/20 2/67   (4 wkts.) 128
7/209 8/214 9/219   3/116 4/116

Combined Services Bowling

	O.	M.	R.	W.		O.	M.	R.	W.
Pearson	20	2	65	4	....	14	2	58	0
Hodgson	21	1	66	3	....	10	1	43	0
Standring	21	4	47	2	....	22	3	69	1
Semmence	7	0	43	1					
Shirreff						26	7	61	0
Leadbetter						2	0	8	0

Surrey Bowling

	O.	M.	R.	W.	O.	M.	R.	W.
Loader	31	5	76	3	11	4	19	1
A. Bedser......	32.5	7	58	4				
Lock	33	13	53	2	15	10	21	0
E. Bedser	12	5	23	1	12	1	45	1
Clark					11	4	14	0
Pratt					1	0	5	0
Barrington					3	1	12	1

Umpires: H. G. Baldwin and L. H. Gray.

SURREY v. GLAMORGAN

At The Oval, May 11, 13. Surrey won by an innings and 166 runs, taking 14 points. This was their first Championship match since the retirement of Surridge, and fortunate to bat first before week-end rain made the conditions ideal for Laker and Lock, they dismissed Glamorgan twice on the second day in the space of three and a half hours. The pitch was damp enough to help the Glamorgan bowlers on the opening day, but after tea McIntyre used the cut and cover drive with devastating effect. Beside hitting twelve 4's he drove Wooller for 6, scoring his 96 in just over two hours. Glamorgan were unfortunate when Parkhouse split his chin hooking Loader, for after this mishap only Devereux and Watkins withstood the Surrey spin bowlers. Lock finished with twelve wickets for only 34 runs. As usual, Surrey fielded brilliantly close to the wicket and they dismissed Glamorgan the second time in sixty-five minutes. May's run-out caused much controversy. The Surrey captain thought Hedges had held the ball when he dived towards the stumps from mid-on, but the ball was under Hedges as he lay on the ground. Hedges signalled no catch, but May had arrived at the pavilion end where Barrington had not moved. Wooller, the Glamorgan captain, broke the stumps at the vacant end.

Surrey

T. H. Clark c Pressdee b W. G. Davies	12	
M. J. Stewart b H. D. Davies.....	1	
B. Constable c H. G. Davies b Wooller	16	
P. B. H. May run out	10	
K. F. Barrington c Watkins b McConnon	52	
E. A. Bedser c Pressdee b Shepherd	22	
A. J. McIntyre c Watkins b H. D. Davies	96	

G. A. R. Lock c Watkins b Pressdee 29
J. C. Laker c Pressdee b Wooller.. 5
D. F. Cox not out 9
P. J. Loader run out............ 1
    B 2, l-b 4 6

1/1 2/28 3/46 4/48 5/102 6/127   259
7/167 8/205 9/256 (2.84 an over)

Glamorgan

W. G. A. Parkhouse retired hurt	20	— absent hurt	0
W. G. Davies b Lock	1	— lbw b Lock	4
B. Hedges c Barrington b Lock	4	— c Lock b Laker	1
L. N. Devereux c Stewart b Lock	22	— c Barrington b Laker	8
A. J. Watkins c Stewart b Laker	7	— not out	11
W. Wooller c Loader b Lock........	2	— c Cox b Lock.............	1
J. Pressdee lbw b Lock	0	— c Stewart b Lock.........	0
J. McConnon c Clark b Lock	0	— lbw b Lock...............	0
H. G. Davies c Barrington b Laker	0	— c Stewart b Lock.........	0
H. D. Davies c Stewart b Laker	0	— c Constable b Lock	0
D. J. Shepherd not out	4	— b Laker	0
L-b 1, n-b 1	2	B 4, l-b 2	6

1/16 2/25 3/56 4/56 5/58 6/58 7/58   62   1/5 2/6 3/10 4/22 5/25   31
8/58 9/62 (1.31 an over)   6/25 7/25 8/29 9/31

Glamorgan Bowling

	O.	M.	R.	W.	O.	M.	R.	W.
H. D. Davies ..	18.4	3	51	2				
Watkins	13	1	32	0				
W. G. Davies ..	7	1	18	1				
Wooller	24	5	60	2				
Shepherd	20	6	53	1				
McConnon	5	1	13	1				
Pressdee	3	0	26	1				

Surrey Bowling

	O.	M.	R.	W.	O.	M.	R.	W.
Loader	13	5	22	0				
Cox...........	2	0	8	0				
Laker	12.2	7	10	3	11.3	7	11	3
Lock	20	13	20	6	11	6	14	6

Umpires: W. F. Price and D. J. Wood.

SURREY v. WORCESTERSHIRE

At The Oval, May 18, 20. Surrey won by eight wickets, taking 12 points. They were far better equipped in attack for a pitch which helped bowlers considerably, and again Lock and Laker, splendidly supported in the field, made the most of their opportunities. Worcestershire, who chose to bat first after rain, were always worried by the quick spin and hostility of the left-arm bowler who gained a match analysis of eleven wickets for 61. Lock also shone as a batsman and he scored the last 15 runs Surrey needed for first innings lead. Surrey, left to make only 90 for victory, lost their opening pair for two before May, driving superbly through the covers, and Barrington showed that bold stroke-play could bring runs in adverse conditions.

Worcestershire

D. Kenyon c May b A. Bedser	3	— c Stewart b Lock	13
P. E. Richardson c Barrington b Lock...	23	— c Barrington b Laker	17
G. Dews c McIntyre b Laker..........	5	— b Lock	7
D. W. Richardson c Pratt b Lock.......	5	— b Laker	2
L. Outschoorn c Fletcher b A. Bedser ...	45	— c and b Lock	7
R. G. Broadbent c Barrington b A. Bedser	1	— c Stewart b Laker	9
M. J. Horton c Stewart b Lock	1	— c Stewart b Lock...........	2
R. Booth c McIntyre b Lock	0	— c Barrington b Lock	18
R. Berry b A. Bedser...............	10	— c Stewart b Laker	3
J. Flavell c Fletcher b Lock	7	— b Lock	2
J. Aldridge not out	0	— not out	0
B 6, l-b 1, n-b 1	8	B 5, l-b 5	10

1/3 2/15 3/22 4/69 5/70 6/75 7/77   108
8/98 9/107 (2.29 an over)

1/36 2/36 3/46 4/46 5/65   90
6/65 7/73 8/88 9/90

Surrey

D. G. W. Fletcher b Flavell	5	— lbw b Flavell	0
M. J. Stewart c and b Berry..........	16	— b Flavell	1
K. F. Barrington c Kenyon b Berry	36	— not out	30
P. B. H. May c P. Richardson b Berry ..	7	— not out	51
R. C. E. Pratt c Dews b Berry.........	1		
E. A. Bedser c Dews b Horton	0		
A. J. McIntyre b Aldridge	8		
G. A. R. Lock not out	32		
J. C. Laker c Dews b Aldridge	0		
P. J. Loader c Dews b Flavell	4		
A. V. Bedser c D. Richardson b Aldridge	0		
		B 3, l-b 5	8

1/11 2/46 3/62 4/65 5/65 6/65 7/83   109
8/83 9/94 (2.22 an over)

1/2 2/2   (2 wkts.) 90

Surrey Bowling

	O.	M.	R.	W.	O.	M.	R.	W.
Loader	4	2	5	0	7	2	10	0
A. Bedser	14	2	21	4	8	1	18	0
Laker	12	2	34	1	19.1	8	31	4
Lock	17.2	6	40	5	19	12	21	6

Worcestershire Bowling

	O.	M.	R.	W.	O.	M.	R.	W.
Flavell	11	1	41	2	7	2	14	2
Aldridge	10.2	2	16	3	7	3	15	0
Horton	14	5	34	1	6	2	17	0
Berry	14	8	18	4	9.1	2	36	0

Umpires: A. R. Coleman and F. S. Lee.

SURREY v. SUSSEX

At The Oval, May 22, 23, 24. Drawn, Surrey taking four points. Rain limited cricket on the last day to two hours twenty minutes. On the opening day Clark drove and hooked splendidly, hitting two 6's and twelve 4's. He shared in stands of 92 with Stewart and 75 with May. Missed when 18, May, who drove beautifully, overshadowed Willett in a partnership of 101, his share being 82, and he hit sixteen 4's. Sussex began moderately well, but after lunch on the second day Lock and Loader bowled so successfully against irresolute batsmen that the last six wickets fell for 55. The pitch remaining good, May, despite a lead of 176, did not enforce the follow-on, and he (one 6, ten 4's) and Stewart again batted well before a second declaration left Sussex to get 313. When four men were out for 73, Surrey looked to possess a chance of victory, but Parks hooked and cut courageously till rain caused an abandonment.

Surrey

T. H. Clark c Bates b Marlar	95	— c Lenham b Bates	9
M. J. Stewart b Smith	51	— c Webb b Bates	56
K. F. Barrington c Lenham b Marlar	11	— b Thomson	5
P. B. H. May c Lenham b Thomson	117	— c Webb b Thomson	64
M. D. Willett c and b Thomson	23	— not out	2
E. A. Bedser c Webb b Thomson	9	— c Bell b Bates	0
A. J. McIntyre not out	9		
G. A. R. Lock c Parks b Thomson	0		
J. C. Laker not out	3		
L-b 1, n-b 1	2		

1/92 2/119 3/194   (7 wkts., dec.) 320   1/18 2/24   (5 wkts., dec.) 136
4/295 5/300 6/309 7/309 (3.10 an over)   3/118 4/123 5/136
P. J. Loader and A. V. Bedser did not bat.

Sussex

D. V. Smith c McIntyre b Laker	19	— c A. Bedser b Lock	29
L. J. Lenham c McIntyre b Laker	29	— b Laker	22
K. G. Suttle lbw b Lock	38	— c Laker b Lock	8
J. M. Parks c Lock b Laker	0	— not out	66
G. Potter c Willett b Lock	2	— c Willett b Lock	5
D. J. Foreman c McIntyre b Lock	6	— not out	11
N. I. Thomson c E. Bedser b Lock	27		
R. V. Bell c Lock b Loader	5		
R. T. Webb b Loader	4		
R. G. Marlar b Loader	5		
D. L. Bates not out	0		
L-b 8, n-b 1	9		

1/45 2/63 3/77 4/89 5/102 6/107   144   1/44 2/59 3/59   (4 wkts.) 141
7/120 8/134 9/140 (2.28 an over)   4/73

Sussex Bowling

	O.	M.	R.	W.		O.	M.	R.	W.
Thomson	20	3	74	4	....	14	2	37	2
Bates	20	3	67	0	....	11.5	2	26	3
Smith	15	4	40	1	....	9	2	36	0
Bell	15	3	43	0					
Marlar	22	4	76	2	....	1	0	5	0
Suttle	11	4	18	0	....	5	1	32	0

Surrey Bowling

	O.	M.	R.	W.		O.	M.	R.	W.
Loader	19.4	0	53	3	....	13	3	51	0
A. Bedser......	7	1	12	0	....	11	2	48	0
Laker	17	10	15	3	....	14	3	23	1
Lock	12	4	43	4	....	16	10	19	3
E. Bedser	7	3	12	0					

Umpires: P. A. Gibb and F. S. Lee.

At Leicester, May 25, 27. SURREY beat LEICESTERSHIRE by an innings and 222 runs.

SURREY v. NORTHAMPTONSHIRE

At The Oval, May 29, 30, 31. Northamptonshire won by 72 runs, taking 12 points to Surrey's four. The match was dominated by three England pace bowlers—A. V. Bedser, Loader and Tyson. Bedser and Loader routed Northamptonshire on a helpful pitch, but Tyson, thirteen wickets for 112 runs, recapturing the form which made him the toast of English cricket during the M.C.C. Australian tour of 1954–55, was an even more difficult proposition. His first innings figures were the best of his career; nearly half the runs scored off him came from the edge. Brookes and Barrick put Northamptonshire on top with a lively stand of 92 in seventy minutes. Brookes took four hours over his hundred, and hit only six 4's. Then Loader and Bedser, with the new ball, rent the innings asunder, the last five wickets falling while 40 runs were added. Cox, who opened the Surrey second innings because Clark received a blow on the hand in the first, stayed nearly three hours, despite being struck on the head by a Tyson bouncer; the rest had little defence to offer against the sheer pace of Tyson and the guile of Tribe.

Northamptonshire

D. Brookes c Stewart b A. Bedser	9	— c Fletcher b Loader	100
P. Arnold lbw b Loader	8	— c Willett b Loader	26
L. Livingston lbw b Loader	22	— c Stewart b A. Bedser...	12
D. W. Barrick c Cox b Loader	4	— c A. Bedser b Barrington...	57
B. L. Reynolds c Barrington b A. Bedser.	7	— c and b Barrington	0
G. E. Tribe c Constable b Cox	38	— c McIntyre b A. Bedser ...	2
J. S. Manning c Barrington b A. Bedser..	1	— c sub b A. Bedser	11
F. H. Tyson c Barrington b A. Bedser ..	2	— b A. Bedser	2
M. H. J. Allen b A. Bedser	1	— c Cox b Loader	1
K. V. Andrew b E. Bedser	16	— c Barrington b A. Bedser...	5
H. R. A. Kelleher not out	0	— not out	0
L-b 3, n-b 2....................	5	B 8, l-b 4, n-b 4........	16

1/11 2/24 3/38 4/48 5/66 6/67 7/73   113   1/64 2/94 3/186 4/186   232
8/75 9/111 (1.73 an over)   5/191 6/219 7/224 8/225
                                               9/228

Surrey

T. H. Clark c Andrew b Tyson	3	— lbw b Tribe 10
M. J. Stewart b Manning	24	— c Allen b Tyson............. 0
B. Constable c Allen b Tyson	11	— b Manning 29
K. F. Barrington b Tyson	4	— c Arnold b Tribe 5
D. G. W. Fletcher c and b Tyson	29	— c Kelleher b Tyson 12
M. D. Willett b Tyson	4	— c Reynolds b Manning ... 26
D. F. Cox c Tribe b Tyson	5	— b Tribe 54
E. A. Bedser b Kelleher	17	— c Andrew b Tyson 1
A. J. McIntyre c Andrew b Tyson	7	— b Tyson 0
P. J. Loader c and b Tyson	7	— b Tyson 4
A. V. Bedser not out	3	— not out 12
N-b 2	2	B 4................... 4

1/20 2/32 3/56 4/63 5/71 6/92 7/102   116   1/0 2/54 3/77 4/102 5/102   157
8/106 9/107 (2.27 an over)   6/103 7/103 8/130 9/135

Surrey Bowling

	O.	M.	R.	W.	O.	M.	R.	W.
Loader	26	5	51	3	22	2	68	3
A. Bedser......	24	7	28	5	25.5	6	51	5
Cox...........	12.1	2	27	1	11	1	38	0
E. Bedser	3	1	2	1	11	3	25	0
Barrington					11	1	34	2

Northamptonshire Bowling

	O.	M.	R.	W.	O.	M.	R.	W.
Tyson	20.5	2	60	8	22	7	52	5
Kelleher	23	6	46	1	8	3	19	0
Manning	7	2	8	1	12.3	9	12	2
Tribe					25	6	64	3
Allen					2	1	6	0

Umpires: W. E. Phillipson and J. Wood.

SURREY v. ESSEX

At The Oval, June 1, 3. Surrey won by an innings and 87 runs, gaining 14 points. A capital century by Fletcher placed them in a much better position on the opening day than at first appeared likely. Fletcher, driving and hitting to leg skilfully, obtained two 6's and eleven 4's before being unluckily run out. Although Surrey never missed some of their best men, Essex sadly felt the absence of Insole and Bailey on the Monday, when they were twice dismissed. They broke down against the pace of Loader and followed-on 223 behind. At the second attempt they failed in face of the off-breaks of E. Bedser, supported by smart fielding, the match ending in the fourth over of extra time.

Surrey

R. C. E. Pratt c Taylor b Palmer..	27	D. F. Cox not out 30
M. J. Stewart b Preston	14	P. J. Loader c Dodds b Preston... 38
B. Constable c Taylor b Ralph....	43	L-b 1, w 1, n-b 3 5
K. F. Barrington c Preston b King	44	
D. G. W. Fletcher run out	101	1/29 2/43 3/125 (9 wkts., dec.) 346
M. D. Willett c Taylor b Preston..	20	4/131 5/195 6/242 7/252 8/297
E. A. Bedser c King b Preston....	15	9/346 (2.93 an over)
A. J. McIntyre b Preston.........	9	

A. V. Bedser did not bat.

Essex

T. C. Dodds b Loader	24	—	c Fletcher b A. Bedser	....	3
G. Barker lbw b A. Bedser	7	—	c Stewart b Loader	......	8
B. Taylor b Loader	0	—	lbw b Loader	......	20
G. W. Horrex c Pratt b Cox	1	—	c Fletcher b Barrington	....	17
M. Bear not out	37	—	c Stewart b E. Bedser	......	10
G. Smith b Loader	26	—	c Willett b E. Bedser	......	21
W. T. Greensmith c Cox b Loader	7	—	c and b E. Bedser	....	18
R. Ralph c Fletcher b Loader	0	—	c Fletcher b E. Bedser	....	3
K. C. Preston b E. Bedser	2	—	b E. Bedser	....	2
I. King c Stewart b Loader	1	—	b Loader	....	17
E. J. Palmer c Loader b A. Bedser	10	—	not out	....	11
B 2, l-b 6	8		L-b 6	....	6

1/18 2/23 3/34 4/43 5/75 6/95 7/95   123

8/98 9/99 (2.24 an over)

1/11 2/13 3/46 4/58 5/70   136

6/93 7/101 8/104 9/111

Essex Bowling

	O.	M.	R.	W.	O.	M.	R.	W.
Preston	32.5	10	76	5				
Ralph	23	6	70	1				
Palmer	11	3	41	1				
Greensmith	20	1	60	0				
King	31	7	94	1				

Surrey Bowling

	O.	M.	R.	W.	O.	M.	R.	W.
Loader	19	3	48	6	16.5	3	52	3
A. Bedser	10.3	4	17	2	12	3	23	1
Cox	7	0	23	1	2	0	5	0
E. Bedser	18	8	27	1	21	9	32	5
Barrington					8	2	18	1

Umpires: D. Davies and John Langridge.

At Northampton, June 5, 6, 7. SURREY beat NORTHAMPTONSHIRE by ten wickets.

At Nottingham, June 8, 10, 11. SURREY beat NOTTINGHAMSHIRE by an innings and 119 runs.

At The Oval, June 12, 13, 14. SURREY drew with WEST INDIES. (See WEST INDIES section.)

At Manchester, June 15, 17, 18. SURREY beat LANCASHIRE by an innings and 51 runs.

SURREY v. GLOUCESTERSHIRE

At The Oval, June 19, 20. Surrey won by an innings and 149 runs, taking 14 points. The largely inexperienced Gloucestershire side were outplayed so completely that the match was all over half an hour before tea-time on the second day. After risking first innings on a "green" pitch, Emmett alone faced Surrey's formidable attack with assurance, scoring 33 out of 42. Gloucestershire were all out twenty minutes after lunch and Surrey's batting was in such dominant contrast that by tea they led by 22 with nine wickets standing. Constable spent three hours over his first century of the season and Barrington played a most attractive innings, full of excellent drives and pulls which brought him four 6's and twelve 4's. Going in again on a pitch showing signs of wear, Gloucestershire had no hope of withstanding A. Bedser in the conditions, though Mortimore played admirably for over an hour.

Gloucestershire

G. M. Emmett lbw b Loader	33	— b A. Bedser	2
D. M. Young c McIntyre b Loader	4	— c Stewart b Lock	7
W. Knightley-Smith lbw b Loader	1	— b A. Bedser	13
R. B. Nicholls c Lock b A. Bedser	0	— lbw b A. Bedser	9
A. S. Brown c Cox b Lock	5	— b A. Bedser	1
J. Mortimore c McIntyre b A. Bedser	13	— st McIntyre b Lock	22
D. A. Allen c McIntyre b Lock	1	— c and b A. Bedser	4
B. J. Meyer not out	7	— lbw b Loader	0
G. G. M. Wiltshire b Loader	0	— c Stewart b Lock	2
D. Smith lbw b Lock	0	— not out	26
C. Cook b Lock	2	— c Stewart b A. Bedser	7
L-b 2	2	B 4, l-b 4, n-b 3	11

1/17 2/29 3/30 4/42 5/57 6/58 7/59   68   1/2 2/2 3/30 4/39 5/39   104
8/61 9/62 (1.74 an over)   6/46 7/58 8/67 9/81

Surrey

T. H. Clark c Young b Wiltshire	21	B 4, l-b 2	6
M. J. Stewart b Cook	59		
B. Constable b Cook	107		
K. F. Barrington not out	124	1/39 2/125 3/293 (3 wkts., dec.)	321
R. C. E. Pratt not out	4	(3.60 an over)	

E. A. Bedser, A. J. McIntyre, G. A. R. Lock, D. F. Cox, P. J. Loader and A. V. Bedser did not bat.

Surrey Bowling

	O.	M.	R.	W.	O.	M.	R.	W.
Loader	16	5	30	4	5	2	11	1
A. Bedser	14	4	29	2	22	8	49	6
Lock	8.5	4	7	4	19	8	33	3

Gloucestershire Bowling

	O.	M.	R.	W.
Smith	18	2	75	0
Wiltshire	15	0	63	1
Mortimore	13	1	50	0
Cook	25	7	59	2
Allen	7	1	34	0
Brown	11	0	34	0

Umpires: L. H. Gray and H. P. Sharp.

SURREY v. OXFORD UNIVERSITY

At Guildford, June 22, 24, 25. Surrey won by 138 runs. Rain and a late rally by the University almost denied them the victory they deserved, for only ten minutes of the extra half-hour remained when the last wicket fell. Any other result would have been an injustice as Surrey were immensely superior throughout. All their leading batsmen scored almost at will, though Clark got himself out in both innings when he had a century within his grasp. Constable (thirteen 4's) hit his second hundred in successive innings. Oxford also began well and with a fine partnership by Walton and Melville yielding 104 they reached 158 at the fall of their third wicket, but thereupon they experienced great difficulty against the varied styles of the two Bedsers. The follow-on was averted by only three runs and before Surrey declared a second time runs again came easily to the county. Oxford broke down in their second innings but a late stand by Melville and Scott nearly saved them. Stewart gave Eric Bedser grand support in the final innings when he held four excellent catches at short leg.

Surrey

T. H. Clark lbw b Bowman	82	—	lbw b Bowman	94
M. J. Stewart c Scott b Bowman	5	—	b Bowman	24
B. Constable c Matthews b Wilson	100	—	not out	37
K. F. Barrington b Jowett	76			
R. C. E. Pratt not out	76			
E. A. Bedser not out	18			
D. F. Cox (did not bat)		—	not out	5
B 4, l-b 2, w 3, n-b 2	11		L-b 2	2

1/11 2/143 3/221 4/297 (4 wkts., dec.) 368   1/97 2/146 (2 wkts., dec.) 162

D. E. Pratt, R. Swetman, D. Gibson and A. V. Bedser did not bat.

Oxford University

J. A. D. Hobbs b Gibson	25	—	c Swetman b Cox	6
M. A. Eagar c Swetman b Gibson	26	—	b Gibson	20
A. C. Walton lbw b Cox	70	—	c Cox b A. Bedser	15
C. D. Melville c Swetman b E. Bedser	65	—	c Stewart b E. Bedser	36
J. M. Kumleben c R. Pratt b E. Bedser	0	—	c Stewart b E. Bedser	23
R. L. Jowett c Stewart b A. Bedser	3	—	c Stewart b E. Bedser	6
M. J. Matthews c R. Pratt b A. Bedser	0	—	lbw b E. Bedser	2
R. G. Woodcock c A. Bedser b E. Bedser	5	—	c Stewart b E. Bedser	0
M. D. Scott not out	13	—	c Barrington b A. Bedser	52
R. W. Wilson b A. Bedser	1	—	not out	1
R. Bowman b A. Bedser	2	—	c R. Pratt b A. Bedser	1
B 6, l-b 2, n-b 3	11		B 5, l-b 2, w 2	9

1/52 2/54 3/158 4/158 5/163 6/163   221   1/13 2/39 3/88 4/89 5/95   171
7/182 8/216 9/217   6/106 7/106 8/162 9/169

Oxford University Bowling

	O.	M.	R.	W.		O.	M.	R.	W.
Bowman	21	4	95	2	....	18	2	71	2
Melville	11	1	43	0	....	5	1	22	0
Wilson	26	4	62	1	....	15	2	46	0
Woodcock	25	5	84	0					
Jowett	18	1	58	1	....	3	0	21	0
Matthews	3	0	15	0					

Surrey Bowling

	O.	M.	R.	W.		O.	M.	R.	W.
A. Bedser	22.2	5	67	4	....	8.2	4	8	3
Cox	13	3	33	1	....	14	2	40	1
Gibson	16	4	43	2	....	13	3	24	1
E. Bedser	23	8	57	3	....	23	9	48	5
D. Pratt	3	1	10	0	....	12	3	28	0
Barrington						3	0	14	0

Umpires: A. E. Pothecary and W. F. Price.

SURREY v. HAMPSHIRE

At Guildford, June 26, 27. Surrey won by an innings and 73 runs, taking
14 points. Hampshire never recovered from being dismissed in less than one hour
forty minutes and the match was over by three o'clock on the second afternoon.
Loader and A. Bedser, swinging the ball considerably and gaining pace off the
pitch, caused the trouble after Hampshire had won the toss. By the end of the
first day Surrey had established a lead of 181, thanks largely to excellent batting
by Clark, May and Barrington. When Hampshire were sent in again the following
morning Laker, with three wickets in his first eleven balls, broke the back of the

innings which was polished off after lunch by Loader. Afterwards the teams staged an exhibition game, the last half-hour of which was watched by the Queen and the Duke of Edinburgh. They were visiting Guildford as part of the town's celebrations of the 700th anniversary of the granting of its first known charter by King Henry III. During a break in play the teams and officials were presented to the Royal visitors.

Hampshire

J. R. Gray lbw b Loader	0	— c Stewart b Laker	14
R. E. Marshall c Pratt b Loader	6	— b Laker	10
H. Horton b Loader	8	— c Pratt b E. Bedser	13
A. W. H. Rayment c McIntyre b Loader	12	— b Laker	0
H. M. Barnard c and b Loader	13	— c E. Bedser b Laker	15
A. C. D. Ingleby-Mackenzie b A. Bedser	9	— b Loader	35
P. J. Sainsbury lbw b Loader	0	— c Barrington b Laker	9
L. Harrison c Constable b A. Bedser	4	— c and b Loader	2
D. Shackleton c and b Loader	8	— c and b Loader	4
M. Heath c Stewart b A. Bedser	0	— not out	0
M. D. Burden not out	2	— b Loader	0
B 4	4	B 6	6

1/0 2/9 3/22 4/29 5/42 6/43 7/52   66
8/52 9/64 (2.64 an over)

1/30 2/31 3/31 4/57 5/58   108
6/102 7/104 8/106 9/108

Surrey

M. J. Stewart c Sainsbury b Gray	28	R. C. E. Pratt not out	7
T. H. Clark b Sainsbury	82	B 4, l-b 4	8
B. Constable c sub b Burden	26		
P. B. H. May c Barnard b Heath	56	1/66 2/143 3/145 (4 wkts., dec.) 247
K. F. Barrington not out	40	4/230 (2.90 an over)

E. A. Bedser, A. J. McIntyre, J. C. Laker, P. J. Loader and A. V. Bedser did not bat.

Surrey Bowling

	O.	M.	R.	W.	O.	M.	R.	W.
Loader	13	2	36	7	17.3	6	34	4
A. Bedser	12.1	4	26	3	10	4	11	0
Laker					20	6	46	5
E. Bedser					5	2	11	1

Hampshire Bowling

	O.	M.	R.	W.
Shackleton	25	6	60	0
Heath	22	4	68	1
Gray	8	1	30	1
Sainsbury	17	6	43	1
Burden	13	0	38	1

Umpires: A. E. Pothecary and W. F. Price.

SURREY v. YORKSHIRE

At The Oval, June 29, July 1, 2. Surrey won by an innings and 19 runs, taking 14 points. Again they were in a most enterprising mood. Clark set the pace, hitting two 6's and eight 4's, and although Trueman bowled splendidly in a temperature of 90 deg., May, driving at his best and hitting freely to leg, scored 125 in three hours twenty-five minutes, including fifteen 4's. Barrington had a shaky beginning against Trueman but helped May to add 130. Apart from Watson in both innings and Wilson in the second the Yorkshire batting was most disappointing. When they followed-on needing 193 to avert the innings defeat,

Yorkshire began with four left-handers, Watson, Stott, Wilson and Close. A fine partnership of 123 by Watson and Wilson occupied two and a half hours, but as soon as this was broken, Eric Bedser and Lock carried all before them. The remaining eight Yorkshire wickets went down in less than an hour for only 29 more runs, Surrey gaining their seventh consecutive Championship victory before lunch on Tuesday. Altogether Watson batted for six and a half hours in the match. As usual Surrey fielded excellently, Stewart making two more remarkable catches at short square-leg. Rain had moistened the pitch when Yorkshire started batting on Monday but at no time were the conditions really difficult.

Surrey

T. H. Clark c Close b Trueman....	75
M. J. Stewart b Appleyard	16
B. Constable c Wilson b Trueman	23
P. B. H. May c Appleyard b Illingworth	125
K. F. Barrington c Binks b Trueman	53
E. A. Bedser c Sutcliffe b Trueman	0
A. J. McIntyre b Wardle	38

G. A. R. Lock c Wilson b Wardle..	8
J. C. Laker b Trueman	6
P. J. Loader not out	14
A. V. Bedser c Stott b Wardle....	0
B 2, l-b 5	7
	365

1/38 2/97 3/128 4/258 5/258
6/336 7/337 8/347 9/355
(3.65 an over)

Yorkshire

D. B. Close c Laker b Lock	13	— b Lock 0
W. Watson c Stewart b Lock...........	53	— c McIntyre b E. Bedser 72
J. V. Wilson c Lock b A. Bedser......	5	— c McIntyre b E. Bedser 64
D. E. V. Padgett c McIntyre b Loader...	13	— c May b Lock 0
R. Illingworth b Lock	5	— c Stewart b Lock.......... 10
W. B. Stott b Laker	4	— b Loader................ 13
W. H. H. Sutcliffe c May b A. Bedser ..	38	— c McIntyre b E. Bedser 0
J. H. Wardle lbw b Laker	20	— b Loader................ 5
F. S. Trueman b Loader	3	— b E. Bedser 0
J. G. Binks b A. Bedser	6	— c Lock b E. Bedser 0
R. Appleyard not out	0	— not out 0
B 5, l-b 6, n-b 1	12	B 8, l-b 2 10
	172	174

1/20 2/65 3/84 4/93 5/99 6/99 7/143
8/156 9/167 (1.86 an over)

1/22 2/145 3/146 4/146
5/160 6/163 7/170 8/170
9/174

Yorkshire Bowling

	O.	M.	R.	W.	O.	M.	R.	W.
Trueman	22	4	67	5				
Appleyard	18	0	85	1				
Illingworth	24	3	77	1				
Wardle	30.5	8	100	3				
Close	5	0	29	0				

Surrey Bowling

	O.	M.	R.	W.		O.	M.	R.	W.
Loader	21	3	33	2	....	10	3	23	2
A. Bedser......	16.3	5	24	3	....	14	4	31	0
Laker	26	9	44	2	....	14	8	19	0
Lock	27	9	58	3	....	19	3	64	3
E. Bedser......	1	0	1	0	....	15.5	6	27	5

Umpires: F. S. Lee and A. Skelding.

SURREY v. KENT

At The Oval, July 6, 8. Surrey won by ten wickets, taking 14 points. They gained a tight grip on the game on the first morning when Kent, after choosing to bat first on a rain-affected pitch, were routed by the varied spin of Lock and E. Bedser. Surrey also found the conditions difficult, but Kent had no bowlers capable of making full use of the pitch, although Brown, 21 year old right-arm medium-fast, marked his championship debut by disposing of Clark and Constable in eight balls. More rain over the week-end left the turf lifeless and a patient innings by Phebey enabled Kent to make a reasonable recovery in their second innings. With eight wickets standing they needed only 14 to make Surrey bat again, but A. Bedser and Loader dismissed Phebey, Pettiford, Dixon and Leary in eight balls while the score remained unchanged. Despite colourful hitting by Ufton and Halfyard, Surrey's final task caused Clark and Fletcher little trouble.

Kent

A. H. Phebey c Willett b Lock	8	— c Barrington b A. Bedser	58
R. C. Wilson b Loader	1	— c Barrington b A. Bedser	20
J. F. Pretlove c Lock b E. Bedser	12	— c Lock b A. Bedser	1
J. Pettiford b E. Bedser	3	— b Loader	15
S. E. Leary c Willett b Lock	0	— st McIntyre b A. Bedser	0
A. L. Dixon c Loader b Lock	2	— lbw b Loader	0
D. G. Ufton c Constable b E. Bedser	20	— c Pratt b Loader	28
A. E. Fagg b E. Bedser	6	— c Pratt b Lock	16
D. J. Halfyard c Barrington b Lock	3	— b Lock	20
J. C. T. Page not out	2	— not out	12
A. Brown c Barrington b Lock	0	— b Loader	0
		B 14, l-b 3, w 1, n-b 2	20

1/3 2/21 3/21 4/24 5/26 6/26 7/52   57
8/53 9/57 (1.67 an over)

1/55 2/61 3/110 4/110   190
5/110 6/110 7/131 8/155
9/190

Surrey

T. H. Clark c Page b Brown	4	— not out	37
D. G. W. Fletcher lbw b Dixon	30	— not out	25
B. Constable c Pretlove b Brown	10		
K. Barrington c Wilson b Pretlove	43		
R. C. E. Pratt lbw b Dixon	9		
M. D. Willett c Fagg b Page	24		
E. A. Bedser c Leary b Dixon	25		
A. J. McIntyre b Page	18		
G. A. R. Lock c Ufton b Page	2		
A. V. Bedser not out	0		
P. J. Loader c Brown b Page	6		
B 8, l-b 2	10	B 1, l-b 4	5

1/5 2/15 3/89 4/89 5/103 6/151 7/162   181
8/170 9/175 (2.74 an over)

(No wkt.) 67

Surrey Bowling

	O.	M.	R.	W.		O.	M.	R.	W.
Loader	7	2	9	1	....	25.4	8	50	4
A. Bedser	5	1	11	0	....	29	10	48	4
Lock	11.3	4	19	5	....	19	5	55	2
E. Bedser	10	5	18	4	....	9	4	17	0

Kent Bowling

	O.	M.	R.	W.		O.	M.	R.	W.
Halfyard	4	1	9	0	....	7	3	10	0
Brown	10	0	29	2	....	9.5	0	31	0
Page	12.4	0	36	4					
Dixon	21	5	69	3	....	4	0	21	0
Pretlove	12	5	17	1					
Leary	6	1	11	0					

Umpires: T. J. Bartley and John Langridge.

SURREY v. DERBYSHIRE

At The Oval, July 10, 11, 12. Drawn, Surrey taking four points. Rain, which interfered with the game on all three days and cut the playing time by half, dramatically deprived Surrey of victory. In semi-darkness they went in soon after lunch on the last day needing 24 to win, lost Barrington to the first ball, and with only two runs made and four balls sent down, heavy rain and hail ended the match. Using a "green" pitch admirably, Alec Bedser and Loader dismissed Derbyshire in their first innings in just over two hours. After Clark had retired with a head wound when struck by a rising ball, Stewart and Constable took Surrey ahead without the loss of a wicket. Then Stewart and May handled the fast-medium attack so roughly that 105 were added in fifty minutes. May made 68 in that time, hitting two 6's and eight 4's in a fine display. Stewart, strong to the on, hit thirteen 4's. Hamer batted admirably in Derbyshire's second innings. Although the ball often turned and lifted abruptly, he gave no chances, hit ten 4's by strong pulling and cutting, and deservedly carried his bat.

Derbyshire

A. Hamer c Barrington b A. Bedser	28	— not out	112
C. Lee lbw b A. Bedser	15	— c Barrington b A. Bedser	10
J. Kelly c Barrington b Loader	2	— c McIntyre b Lock	9
A. C. Revill c May b A. Bedser	3	— c May b E. Bedser	20
D. B. Carr c Barrington b Loader	3	— b E. Bedser	0
D. J. Green c Stewart b Lock	1	— c Barrington b Lock	21
G. O. Dawkes c Fletcher b A. Bedser	22	— c McIntyre b Lock	4
D. C. Morgan run out	0	— lbw b A. Bedser	9
E. Smith b Loader	5	— b A. Bedser	2
C. Gladwin b Loader	0	— hit wkt b Lock	14
L. Jackson not out	0	— st McIntyre b A. Bedser	2
		B 2, l-b 1, n-b 2	5

1/26 2/29 3/32 4/47 5/51 6/53   79   1/29 2/58 3/86 4/86 5/144   208
7/53 8/67 9/67 (2.25 an over)   6/155 7/170 8/176 9/203

Surrey

T. H. Clark retired hurt	7		
M. J. Stewart c Carr b Morgan	87		
B. Constable c Lee b Gladwin	23	— not out	1
P. B. H. May c Kelly b Morgan	68		
K. F. Barrington b Morgan	4	— c Dawkes b Jackson	0
D. G. W. Fletcher b Jackson	26		
E. A. Bedser b Morgan	13		
A. J. McIntyre b Jackson	21	— not out	1
P. J. Loader c Kelly b Gladwin	8		
G. A. R. Lock c Morgan b Gladwin	0		
A. V. Bedser not out	2		
B 4, l-b 1	5		

1/85 2/190 3/191 4/194 5/214 6/251   264   1/0   (1 wkt.)   2
7/254 8/262 (4.55 an over)

Surrey Bowling

	O.	M.	R.	W.		O.	M.	R.	W.
Loader	12	2	52	4	....	6	1	14	0
A. Bedser	17.2	6	24	4	....	34.1	6	65	4
Lock	6	4	3	1	....	40	14	78	4
E. Bedser						23	7	46	2

Derbyshire Bowling

	O.	M.	R.	W.		O.	M.	R.	W.
Jackson	16	2	54	2	....	0.4	0	2	1
Gladwin	20.3	5	98	3					
Morgan	14	3	71	4					
Smith	7	0	36	0					

Umpires: E. Davies and H. G. Baldwin.

At Bradford, July 13, 15, 16. SURREY drew with YORKSHIRE.

SURREY v. LEICESTERSHIRE

At The Oval, July 17, 18, 19. Surrey won by ten wickets, taking 14 points. They gained the release of Lock from the Players' side at Lord's where May, Clark and Laker were appearing, and taking eleven wickets in the match for 58 runs, Lock carried his county to their thirteenth championship victory. Palmer must have regretted his decision to bat first because from the start the damp pitch was helpful to bowlers. Gardner, who stayed two and a quarter hours, alone offered real resistance. Rain greatly interfered with the cricket, but by enterprising batting Surrey declared with only three wickets down and Leicestershire in the last forty minutes on Thursday lost Lester and Hallam for 15. The next morning Lock and Eric Bedser wrought such havoc that the eight remaining wickets fell in seventy-five minutes for 63 more runs, so that Surrey were comfortable winners before lunch.

Leicestershire

G. Lester c Stewart b A. Bedser	1	— c and b Lock		7
M. R. Hallam c Swetman b Lock	9	— c McIntyre b Lock		1
J. van Geloven b Loader	8	— c Stewart b E. Bedser		7
C. H. Palmer c Barrington b Lock	4	— c Fletcher b Lock		1
L. R. Gardner not out	38	— lbw b Lock		5
V. S. Munden c Barrington b E. Bedser	10	— c Barrington b E. Bedser		0
J. Firth c Stewart b E. Bedser	0	— b E. Bedser		9
J. Savage lbw b Lock	0	— b E. Bedser		1
R. Smith c Pratt b Lock	15	— c Barrington b Lock		11
C. T. Spencer b Lock	0	— c and b Lock		18
B. Boshier b Loader	0	— not out		16
B 1, n-b 1	2	B 2		2

1/5 2/18 3/22 4/22 5/37 6/39 7/40   **87**
8/80 9/80 (1.52 an over)

1/2 2/11 3/16 4/21 5/22   **78**
6/22 7/27 8/32 9/52

Surrey

R. C. E. Pratt c Lester b Munden	28	— not out		3
M. J. Stewart c Firth b Savage	31	— not out		8
B. Constable b Palmer	32			
K. F. Barrington not out	59			
D. G. W. Fletcher not out	1			
B 3, l-b 2, n-b 1	6	L-b 1		1

1/53 2/70 3/152   (3 wkts., dec.) **157**   (No wkt.) **12**
(3.34 an over)

R. Swetman, E. A. Bedser, A. J. McIntyre, G. A. R. Lock, P. J. Loader and A. V. Bedser did not bat.

Surrey Bowling

	O.	M.	R.	W.		O.	M.	R.	W.
Loader	14.3	5	23	2					
A. Bedser	7	2	8	1	....	5	0	13	0
Lock	21	10	33	5	....	20.2	14	25	6
E. Bedser......	14	7	21	2	....	17	9	38	4

Leicestershire Bowling

	O.	M.	R.	W.		O.	M.	R.	W.
Spencer	13	3	37	0	....	2	1	3	0
Boshier........	10	0	25	0					
Savage	8	2	38	1					
Smith	4	0	17	0					
Palmer	5	2	11	1					
Munden	7	0	23	1	....	1.5	1	8	0

Umpires: L. H. Gray and J. F. Crapp.

At Blackheath, July 20, 22, 23. SURREY beat KENT by 73 runs.

At Bristol, July 27, 29, 30. SURREY lost to Gloucestershire by 38 runs.

At The Oval, July 31, August 1, 2. SURREY lost to WEST INDIES by seven wickets. (See WEST INDIES section.)

SURREY v. NOTTINGHAMSHIRE

At The Oval, August 3, 5, 6. Surrey beat Nottinghamshire by six wickets, taking 14 points. Despite some fine-leg spin bowling by Goonesena and Dooland, Nottinghamshire could not extend Surrey. Millman, opening the innings for the first time, defied the Surrey attack for three and a half hours, but when the second new ball became available Loader and Bedser took the last five wickets for the addition of 61 runs. Consistent rather than brilliant batting marked Surrey's first innings. Fletcher justified his return to the side by playing well for 99 and Eric Bedser (one 6 and seven 4's) hit strongly. When Nottinghamshire batted again Springall shaped promisingly, but the combined efforts of Loader, Alec Bedser, Laker and Lock, plus the customary excellent fielding, left Surrey to get 107 in just over two and a half hours. This time some masterly cover-driving by May enabled the champions to complete their task with three-quarters of an hour to spare. Dooland again bowled splendidly and received fine assistance from Millman behind the stumps.

Nottinghamshire

J. D. Springall b Loader	15	—	c McIntyre b Lock	45
G. Millman b E. Bedser	58	—	c Lock b Laker	16
N. Hill st McIntyre b Laker	25	—	b Laker	29
M. Hill lbw b Loader	6	—	c Stewart b Lock	14
C. J. Poole c McIntyre b E. Bedser	36	—	c McIntyre b Laker	5
B. Dooland b A. Bedser	39	—	lbw b A. Bedser	27
G. Goonesena c Lock b Loader	9	—	b Loader	15
R. Vowles c McIntyre b Loader	1	—	lbw b Loader	2
A. Jepson c Laker b A. Bedser	26	—	not out	8
M. Morgan c McIntyre b Loader	0	—	c Barrington b Loader	0
C. S. Matthews not out	1	—	c May b Loader	0
B 5, l-b 3, w 1, n-b 1	10		B 2, l-b 8, n-b 2	12

1/30 2/91 3/108 4/135 5/166 6/197   226   1/30 2/84 3/94 4/102   173
7/197 8/208 9/208 (2.32 an over)   5/115 6/147 7/161 8/161
                                           9/169

Surrey

D. G. W. Fletcher c N. Hill b Goonesena	99	—	c Millman b Dooland	16
M. J. Stewart c Matthews b Goonesena..	21	—	st Millman b Dooland	17
B. Constable c Dooland b Goonesena...	16	—	c Millman b Dooland	9
P. B. H. May lbw b Goonesena	29	—	not out	51
K. F. Barrington c Jepson b Goonesena	19	—	st Millman b Morgan	8
E. A. Bedser c Vowles b Dooland	52	—	not out	2
A. J. McIntyre b Goonesena	12			
G. A. R. Lock c Millman b Jepson	19			
J. C. Laker c Millman b Jepson	0			
P. J. Loader not out	12			
A. V. Bedser c N. Hill b Dooland	6			
B 2, l-b 6	8		B 2, l-b 2	4

1/40 2/66 3/139 4/180 5/188 6/204   293   1/33 2/38 3/57   (4 wkts.) 107
7/252 8/252 9/280 (2.61 an over)   4/96

Surrey Bowling

	O.	M.	R.	W.		O.	M.	R.	W.
Loader	22	5	55	5	....	16	3	50	4
A. Bedser	16.4	2	51	2	....	6	1	11	1
Lock	25	9	49	0	....	28	11	42	2
Laker	21	13	20	1	....	32	13	58	3
E. Bedser	13	1	41	2					

Nottinghamshire Bowling

	O.	M.	R.	W.		O.	M.	R.	W.
Jepson	18	2	46	2	....	4	2	5	0
Matthews	17	5	40	0	....	3	1	3	0
Goonesena	30	3	107	6	....	9	0	32	0
Dooland	32.5	17	64	2	....	14	3	32	3
Morgan	14	2	28	0	....	5.4	0	29	1
					M. Hill	1	0	2	0

Umpires: P. A. Gibb and A. R. Coleman.

At Portsmouth, August 7, 8. SURREY beat HAMPSHIRE by an innings and 35 runs.

SURREY v. MIDDLESEX

(D. G. W. Fletcher's Benefit)

At The Oval, August 10, 12, 13. Drawn, no decision. Rain washed out the third day, and restricted play on the other two to a total of just over six hours. The best feature of the match was the batting of Walton and Clark on the treacherous pitch. Walton, though frequently beaten, made his strokes with the utmost confidence, but after his partnership of 61 with Compton, the Middlesex innings disintegrated before the controlled swing of A. V. Bedser and the spin of Lock. Clark dominated the Surrey batting before falling to Moss, who took three wickets at a personal cost of four runs on the second day before rain ended the match.

Middlesex

J. D. Robertson b Loader	0	J. T. Murray c Stewart b A. Bedser	8
R. A. Gale c May b Lock	16	J. J. Warr b Lock	7
A. C. Walton c Barrington b A.		R. J. Hurst not out	3
Bedser	50	A. E. Moss c Constable b A. Bedser	2
D. C. S. Compton c Loader b Lock	24	L-b 1, w 1, n-b 1	3
W. J. Edrich c Clark b Lock	0		
D. Bennett c May b A. Bedser	0	1/1 2/31 3/92 4/92 5/92 6/92	114
F. J. Titmus c May b Lock	1	7/99 8/101 9/111 (2.07 an over)	

Surrey

T. H. Clark c Murray b Moss	50	G. A. R. Lock not out..........	10
M. J. Stewart b Warr	0	J. C. Laker not out.............	1
B. Constable lbw b Titmus	6	L-b 1, w 1	2
P. B. H. May lbw b Warr	20		
K. F. Barrington b Warr	1		—
D. G. W. Fletcher b Moss	8	1/4 2/30 3/54 4/60　(7 wkts.)	100
A. J. McIntyre c Walton b Moss..	2	5/86 6/87 7/90 (2.43 an over)	

P. J. Loader and A. V. Bedser did not bat.

Surrey Bowling

	O.	M.	R.	W.
Loader	8	4	8	1
A. Bedser	14.3	3	38	4
Laker	13	5	33	0
Lock	19	10	32	5

Middlesex Bowling

	O.	M.	R.	W.
Moss	12	5	22	3
Warr	16	6	31	3
Hurst........	7	1	32	0
Titmus	6	2	13	1

Umpires: J. S. Buller and C. S. Elliott.

At Weston-super-Mare, August 14, 15, 16. SURREY beat SOMERSET by three wickets.

At Lord's, August 17, 19, 20. SURREY beat MIDDLESEX by 102 runs.

At The Oval, August 22, 23, 24. ENGLAND beat WEST INDIES in the Fifth Test by an innings and 237 runs. (See WEST INDIES section.)

At Birmingham, August 24, 26, 27. SURREY beat WARWICKSHIRE by ten wickets.

At Clacton, August 28, 29, 30. SURREY lost to ESSEX by two wickets

SURREY v. WARWICKSHIRE

At The Oval, August 31, September 2. Surrey won by an innings and 70 runs, taking 14 points, the match being completed before three o'clock on the second afternoon. Stewart set the key-note to another enterprising exhibition by the champions. Excelling with the drive and hook, he hit eleven 4's while making a splendid century against a keen attack in which Carter did well in dismissing Clark, May and Barrington cheaply. After Loader had disposed of Horner, Alec Bedser took three wickets for three runs, being helped by two amazing short-leg catches by Lock. Warwickshire had lost seven for 69 by Saturday evening and on Monday more wonderful all-round work by Lock, who finished with ten wickets for 60 runs, took Surrey to another easy win. For Warwickshire, the match brought distinction to M. J. K. Smith who completed 2,000 runs in his first season as captain and Hollies ended a notable championship career with 100 wickets for the fourteenth time. The crowd and the Surrey players applauded Hollies when he returned to the pavilion for the last time.

Surrey

T. H. Clark c Spooner b Carter..	9	G. A. R. Lock lbw b Hollies	27
M. J. Stewart c Wheatley b Townsend	103	J. C. Laker c Spooner b Townsend	12
B. Constable b Wheatley	19	P. J. Loader b Townsend	13
P. B. H. May c Horner b Carter..	29	A. V. Bedser not out	0
K. F. Barrington lbw b Carter...	0	L-b 4	4
E. A. Bedser c Smith b Wheatley.	5		
A. J. McIntyre c Townsend b Hollies	30	1/17 2/56 3/98 4/98 5/116 6/165	251
		7/223 8/231 9/240 (3.34 an over)	

Warwickshire

F. C. Gardner lbw b A. Bedser	15	— c Lock b Laker		9
N. F. Horner b Loader	4	— c May b Lock		24
W. J. Stewart c Lock b A. Bedser	2	— b A. Bedser		0
M. J. K. Smith b Loader	14	— c and b Lock		2
A. Townsend c Lock b A. Bedser	0	— c and b Lock		0
C. W. Leach b Lock	16	— c Stewart b Lock		13
S. Singh c A. Bedser b Lock	30	— c E. Bedser b Lock		14
R. T. Spooner c and b Lock	1	— b Laker		17
R. G. Carter b Loader	2	— b Laker		3
O. S. Wheatley not out	1	— c and b Lock		2
W. E. Hollies c and b Lock	1	not out		0
B 3, l-b 6	9	B 2		2

1/13 2/20 3/33 4/33 5/55 6/59 7/69   95   1/30 2/30 3/35 4/35 5/38   86
8/90 9/90 (2.26 an over)   6/56 7/70 8/79 9/80

Warwickshire Bowling

	O.	M.	R.	W.	O.	M.	R.	W.
Wheatley	17	5	55	2				
Carter	16	2	76	3				
Townsend	14	3	40	3				
Singh	13	5	41	0				
Hollies	15	2	35	2				

Surrey Bowling

	O.	M.	R.	W.	O.	M.	R.	W.
Loader	14	2	44	3	4	2	9	0
A. Bedser	14	6	14	3	8	1	12	1
Laker	7	3	14	0	9.4	2	17	3
Lock	6.3	3	14	4	15	6	46	6

Umpires: R. S. Lay and J. S. Buller.

At Hove, September **4, 5, 6**. SURREY beat SUSSEX by seven wickets

At Scarborough, September 11, 12, 13. SURREY (Champion County) beat THE REST by six wickets. (See OTHER MATCHES.)

SUSSEX

President—THE DUKE OF NORFOLK

Secretary—LIEUT.-COL. G. D. GRIMSTON, County Ground,
Eaton Road, Hove 3, Sussex

Captain—R. G. MARLAR

| J. M. Parks | County Badge | N. I. Thomson |

So far as the final records were concerned, the season for Sussex very much resembled that of 1956, with the difference that the county this time started moderately and finished well. They beat Gloucestershire in their opening Championship engagement, but experienced so lean a spell that it was not until near the end of June that they registered another win. During August, when Sheppard, Doggart and Cox provided much-needed bolstering to the batting, they registered four of their eight victories.

With so much depending upon the success or failure of a few players, Sussex were at no time a well-balanced side, and only too often the batting "tail" was deplorably long. Smith, helped by three centuries, headed the batting figures, and he found a place in the England team in three Test matches. Parks, showing no sign of the indisposition which compelled his early return from the M.C.C. tour of South Africa, was again the chief run-getter, and Suttle and Lenham also each scored over 1,000 runs; but though Foreman was responsible for an occasional good innings and James, when called upon to open the innings when Smith responded to representative calls, acquitted himself creditably, the remainder of the batting was far from reliable. Lenham, in his first season as a professional, created a highly favourable impression as an opening batsman of pleasing style and sound defence, and he hit his maiden century against Derbyshire at Hove. Another encouraging feature was the promising form displayed in three games by the young Nawab of Pataudi, of Winchester College, son of the former Worcestershire batsman. The loss of Oakman for almost the entire season with back trouble, which began while he was with M.C.C. in South Africa, was severely felt.

Thomson once more formed the spearhead of the attack, again taking over 100 wickets, including seven for 12 runs against Northamptonshire at Peterborough; Bates, though at times a little costly, supported him well as opening bowler. Both suffered from the failure to unearth a slip fieldsman of the calibre of John Langridge. Except that he dismissed eight batsmen for 75 in the Warwickshire first innings at Eastbourne, Marlar, with his off-breaks, for a long time met with little success, but he developed greater effectiveness towards the close of the summer as pitches became more responsive to spin. Not so often called upon as in the previous year, the left-handed Smith took correspondingly fewer wickets at higher cost.

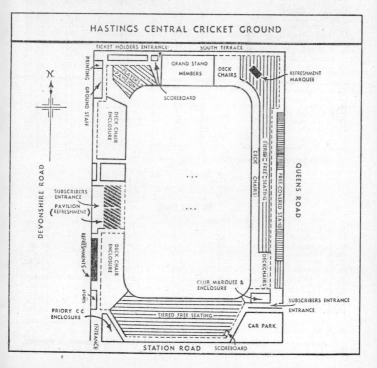

SUSSEX RESULTS

All First-Class Matches—Played 32, *Won* 9, *Lost* 10, *Drawn* 13

County Championship Matches—Played 28, *Won* 8, *Lost* 9, *Drawn* 9, *No Decision* 2

COUNTY CHAMPIONSHIP AVERAGES

BATTING

	Birthplace	Mtchs.	Inns.	Not Outs	Runs	100's	Highest Inns.	Aver.
D. V. Smith ...	*Broadwater*	21	38	2	1580	3	166	43.88
J. M. Parks ...	*Haywards Hth.*	27	48	5	1861	2	101	43.27
E. R. Dexter ..	*Milan*	3	3	1	66	0	63	33.00
K. G. Suttle...	*Kensington*	28	51	2	1500	2	165	30.61
L. Lenham ...	*Lancing*	26	48	3	1224	1	130	27.20
Rev. D. S. Sheppard	*Reigate*	8	13	2	290	1	117	26.36
D. J. Foreman..	*Cape Town*	18	31	3	651	0	61	23.25
G. H. G. Doggart	*Earls Court*	9	16	0	332	0	84	20.75
A. S. M. Oakman	*Hastings*	2	4	0	78	0	52	19.50
R. T. Webb ...	*Harrow*	13	21	6	276	0	31*	18.40
G. Potter	*Dormansland*	11	19	4	240	0	47	16.00
D. A. Stripp ...	*Crawley*	5	8	2	87	0	32*	14.50
A. E. James ...	*Bletchley*	23	39	4	498	0	52	14.22
N. I. Thomson .	*Walsall*	27	40	4	509	0	59	14.13
R. G. Marlar ..	*Eastbourne*	27	39	9	324	0	37	10.80
G. Cox	*Horsham*	2	4	0	37	0	33	9.25
R. V. Bell	*Chelsea*	9	12	5	52	0	14	7.42
R. J. Langridge	*Brighton*	3	5	1	25	0	12	6.25
D. N. Mantell..	*Acton*	15	20	2	98	0	34	5.44
D. L. Bates ...	*Hove*	22	31	11	94	0	21	4.70
G. L. Cogger...	*Uckfield*	6	7	1	11	0	5	1.83
R. H. Willson..	*Seaford*	2	4	0	6	0	3	1.50

Also batted: Nawab of Pataudi (*Bhopal*) 0 and 23.

* *Signifies not out.*

BOWLING

	Overs	Maidens	Runs	Wickets	Average
E. R. Dexter	56	18	118	7	16.85
D. Foreman	28	10	51	3	17.00
G. L. Cogger	41	10	91	5	18.20
N. I. Thomson	936	292	2143	105	20.40
A. E. James...........	593	209	1380	53	26.03
R. G. Marlar	781	205	2161	83	26.03
K. G. Suttle	438.1	153	943	35	26.94
D. L. Bates	611.2	127	1787	61	29.29
R. V. Bell	158	49	460	14	32.85
D. V. Smith	321	100	895	25	35.80
D. A. Stripp	25.1	2	127	3	42.33

Also bowled: G. H. G. Doggart 2.5—1—5—1; L. Lenham 2—0—11—0; A. S. M. Oakman 10—3—27—0; J. M. Parks 4—1—10—0.

Amateurs.—E. R. Dexter, G. H. G. Doggart, R. G. Marlar, Nawab of Pataudi, Rev. D. S. Sheppard.

SUSSEX v. HAMPSHIRE

At Hove, May 2, 3. Drawn (12-a-side). Hampshire 271 for ten wickets, dec. (H. M. Barnard 78, R. E. Marshall 53, L. Harrison 52) and 204 for four wickets, dec. (H. Horton 77, R. W. C. Pitman 62); Sussex 233 (L. Lenham 83) and 89 for two wickets.

SUSSEX v. GLOUCESTERSHIRE

At Hove, May 8, 9, 10. Sussex won by seven wickets, taking 12 points to Gloucestershire's four. Set to get 267 in three and a quarter hours, Sussex triumphed with ten minutes to spare, thanks to a magnificent display of forceful batting by the left-handed D. V. Smith. Smith was the dominating partner in an opening stand of 163 in one and three-quarter hours with Lenham and he hit nine 6's and eleven 4's while obtaining 166 out of 253 in a little under three hours. The feature of the Gloucestershire first innings was a maiden century by Hawkins which earned him his county cap. Becoming free after a slow start, he reached three figures in two and a half hours and he hit one 5 and nineteen 4's. For Sussex, who found run-getting difficult against the slows of Cook, Lenham was unfortunate not to emulate the feat of Hawkins, for he was out in playing a ball on to his boot, from whence it rebounded into the hands of short leg.

Gloucestershire

D. M. Young c Webb b Bates	12	— b Marlar		30
D. Carpenter st Webb b Marlar	36	— c sub b Smith		48
T. W. Graveney c Potter b Marlar	37	— c Bates b Smith		35
R. B. Nicholls lbw b Smith	26	— st Webb b James		54
G. M. Emmett c Smith b Suttle	39	— c Potter b Marlar		12
D. G. Hawkins c Smith b Suttle	106	— b James		13
G. E. Lambert b Suttle	8	— c Lenham b James		4
D. R. Smith c Lenham b Thomson	4	— not out		4
P. Rochford lbw b Thomson	0			
C. Cook not out	35			
B. D. Wells c Webb b Thomson	4			
B 10, l-b 1, n-b 4	15	B 19, l-b 3, n-b 1		23

1/27 2/77 3/97 4/135 5/173 6/193   322   1/72 2/131   (7 wkts., dec.) 223
7/215 8/215 9/305 (3.06 an over)   3/132 4/148 5/205 6/215
                                           7/223

Sussex

D. V. Smith c and b Wells	40	— lbw b Lambert		166
L. J. Lenham c Lambert b Wells	95	— st Rochford b Cook		34
K. G. Suttle b Cook	48	— run out		12
J. M. Parks c Hawkins b Cook	40	— not out		27
G. Potter b Wells	0			
N. I. Thomson c Carpenter b Cook	16			
D. J. Foreman c Graveney b Cook	0	— not out		10
R. T. Webb not out	20			
A. E. James c Smith b Wells	1			
D. L. Bates c Rochford b Cook	7			
R. G. Marlar c Lambert b Cook	2			
B 5, l-b 4, n-b 1	10	B 6, l-b 13		19

1/72 2/161 3/209 4/209 5/237 6/237   279   1/163 2/185   (3 wkts.) 268
7/254 8/262 9/277 (2.7 an over)   3/253

Sussex Bowling

	O.	M.	R.	W.	O.	M.	R.	W.
Bates	25	5	74	1	 10	2	30	0
Thomson	20.1	6	70	3	 6	3	11	0
James	8	2	27	0	.... 5.2	1	21	3
Marlar	10	3	32	2	 31	13	72	2
Suttle	20	6	43	3	 14	2	40	0
Smith	19	5	52	1	 15	4	26	2
Parks	3	1	9	0				

Gloucestershire Bowling

	O.	M.	R.	W.	O.	M.	R.	W.
Lambert	9	0	37	0	 17	1	65	1
D. Smith	7	0	18	0	.... 13.4	1	39	0
Wells	38	10	101	4	 11	2	51	0
Cook	41.5	18	84	6	 19	1	61	1
Hawkins	7	0	29	0	 2	0	33	0

Umpires: F. S. Lee and L. H. Gray.

At Cambridge, May 18, 20, 21. SUSSEX beat CAMBRIDGE UNIVERSITY by an innings and 148 runs.

At The Oval, May 22, 23, 24. SUSSEX drew with SURREY.

At Swansea, May 25, 27, 28. SUSSEX drew with GLAMORGAN.

At Derby, May 29, 30, 31. SUSSEX lost to DERBYSHIRE by 197 runs.

SUSSEX v. LEICESTERSHIRE

At Hove, June 1, 3, 4. Leicestershire won by 99 runs, taking 12 points to four by Sussex. Credit for Leicestershire's first victory of the season went largely to Hallam, Diment and Goodwin. Diment saved the side from failure on the opening day. He drove specially well, hitting eleven 4's, and he and Gardner added 90. Sussex batted solidly, but capital left-arm fast-medium bowling by Goodwin restricted their lead to 63. Hallam followed with the highest innings of his career, hitting twenty-two 4's in nearly four and a half hours. He and Lester shared in a stand of 114. Sussex, left 216 to get in two hours twenty minutes, at first went for the runs, but good work by Firth behind the wicket helped in a batting breakdown.

Leicestershire

G. Lester c Suttle b Thomson	5	— lbw b James	52
M. R. Hallam b Bates.................	24	— c Webb b Bates	146
J. van Geloven c Webb b Bates........	2	— c Parks b Thomson	33
C. H. Palmer b Bates	7	— c Marlar b Thomson	33
L. R. Gardner c Bates b Marlar	33	— not out	10
R. A. Diment c Webb b James...............	67		
J. Firth c Webb b James...............	11		
J. Savage c Webb b James	5		
R. C. Smith c Lenham b James........	4		
C. T. Spencer b Bates	9		
J. Goodwin not out	0		
B 7, l-b 4, w 1	12	B 2, l-b 2	4

1/20 2/23 3/44 4/45 5/135 6/157   179   1/114 2/223 (4 wkts., dec.) 278
7/162 8/166 9/171 (2.29 an over)   3/248 4/278

Sussex

D. V. Smith b Goodwin	23	—	c Firth b Spencer	17
L. J. Lenham c Firth b Goodwin	25	—	c Savage b Goodwin	12
K. G. Suttle b Goodwin	1	—	c Hallam b Savage	25
J. M. Parks c van Geloven b Goodwin	20	—	c Firth b Spencer	0
G. Potter c Hallam b Goodwin	23	—	c Firth b Spencer	7
R. T. Webb c Spencer b Savage	28	—	lbw b Lester	7
D. J. Foreman lbw b Spencer	43	—	c Spencer b Goodwin	3
N. I. Thomson c and b Goodwin	15	—	b Savage	8
R. G. Marlar b van Geloven	33	—	not out	0
A. E. James not out	20	—	c Hallam b Smith	5
D. L. Bates c Goodwin b Spencer	0	—	c and b Smith	21
B 1, l-b 7, n-b 3	11		B 7 l-b 4	11

1/40 2/50 3/62 4/78 5/119 6/127   242   1/19 2/40 3/42 4/47 5/66   116
7/165 8/208 9/242 (2.71 an over)   6/68 7/81 8/81 9/111

Sussex Bowling

	O.	M.	R.	W.		O.	M.	R.	W.
Bates	18.3	5	56	4	....	14	1	86	1
Thomson	16	7	25	1	....	18.5	2	63	2
Smith	9	3	21	0	....	5	1	14	0
James	20	10	32	4	....	25	13	32	1
Marlar	8	2	25	1	....	16	3	54	0
Suttle	6	4	8	0	....	11	5	25	0

Leicestershire Bowling

	O.	M.	R.	W.		O.	M.	R.	W.
Spencer	29.5	6	78	2	....	13	4	35	3
Goodwin	35	8	90	6	....	10	2	33	2
Palmer	16	8	30	0					
Savage	7	2	17	1	....	11	5	30	2
van Geloven	1	0	16	1					
Lester						6	2	7	1
Smith						2.1	2	0	2

Umpires: W. F. Price and A. E. Pothecary.

SUSSEX v. ROYAL NAVY

At Hove, June 6, 7. Sussex won by 69 runs. Sussex 276 (L. J. Lenham 85, D. A. Stripp 50, O/A. R. D. Healey six for 114) and 101 for one wicket, dec. (K. G. Suttle 57 not out); Royal Navy 177 for nine wickets, dec. (Sub.-Lt. A. J. T. Brown 55, R. V. Bell four for 51) and 131 (Suttle five for 23).

At Lord's, June 8, 10, 11. SUSSEX lost to MIDDLESEX by 54 runs.

SUSSEX v. NORTHAMPTONSHIRE

At Hove, June 12, 13, 14. Northamptonshire won by 142 runs, taking 12 points. They recovered well from a bad start. After playing awkwardly at first, the pitch turned easy. Fellows-Smith, making his Championship debut, led Northamptonshire's recovery, hitting six 6's and ten 4's in a stay of just under three hours. Tyson and Allen followed with a ninth wicket stand of 83. Smith and Lenham gave Sussex a good start, but of the others only Foreman did much. Lenham retired with a damaged thumb when 58 and returned at the fall of the fourth wicket. Marlar, scoring 20 in twelve minutes, prevented Northamptonshire taking bonus points by a narrow margin. Fellows-Smith played another bright innings, this time with two 6's and nine 4's, and Sussex were set to get 268 in three and a quarter hours. Never up with the clock, they lost with forty minutes remaining.

Northamptonshire

D. Brookes c Mantell b Thomson	14	— c Mantell b Smith	3
B. Reynolds b James	2	— c Parks b Marlar	42
L. Livingston c Lenham b Thomson	15		
D. W. Barrick b James	4	— c Foreman b Marlar	46
G. E. Tribe lbw b James	28	— b Marlar	39
J. P. Fellows-Smith c Foreman b James	109	— not out	65
J. S. Manning c Parks b Marlar	19	— b James	29
K. V. Andrew b Suttle	8	— not out	9
F. H. Tyson not out	61	— c Parks b James	9
M. H. J. Allen c Marlar b Bell	29		
B 5, l-b 1	6	L-b 2, n-b 1	3

1/10 2/18 3/35 4/37   (9 wkts., dec.) 295
5/84 6/137 7/190 8/212 9/295
(2.92 an over)

1/31 2/49   (6 wkts., dec.) 245
3/120 4/137 5/202 6/216

H. R. A. Kelleher did not bat.

Sussex

L. J. Lenham c Brookes b Manning	93	— b Tribe	30
D. V. Smith c Manning b Tribe	48	— lbw b Kelleher	3
K. G. Suttle b Tribe	11	— c Allen b Tribe	14
J. M. Parks c Andrew b Tribe	3	— lbw b Allen	31
D. J. Foreman b Tyson	55	— st Andrew b Manning	2
N. I. Thomson c Manning b Tyson	22	— st Andrew b Manning	15
R. H. Willson c Tribe b Kelleher	3	— c Andrew b Manning	0
D. N. Mantell c sub b Tyson	5	— b Allen	3
A. E. James b Tyson	8	— b Tribe	2
R. V. Bell b Kelleher	0	— not out	11
R. G. Marlar not out	20	— c and b Tribe	4
B 3, n-b 2	5	B 2, l-b 7, n-b 1	10

1/94 2/115 3/128 4/133 5/188 6/238   273
7/239 8/244 9/249 (2.96 an over)

1/5 2/34 3/57 4/68 5/68   125
6/105 7/105 8/106 9/117

Sussex Bowling

	O.	M.	R.	W.	O.	M.	R.	W.
Thomson	32	8	91	2				
James	35	15	73	4	17	2	66	2
Smith	12	3	39	0	7	1	22	1
Marlar	8	1	38	1	30	7	73	3
Suttle	9	4	21	1	22	9	52	0
Bell	5	2	27	1	4	0	29	0

Northamptonshire Bowling

	O.	M.	R.	W.	O.	M.	R.	W.
Tyson	23.5	8	40	4	5	0	21	0
Kelleher	23	5	86	2	5	0	13	1
Manning	13	6	37	1	21	8	42	3
Tribe	21	4	70	3	15.4	6	36	4
Fellows-Smith	7	2	23	0				
Allen	4	1	12	0	6	4	3	2

Umpires: L. H. Gray and W. F. Price.

At Hove, June 15, 17, 18. SUSSEX lost to WEST INDIES by 235 runs. (See WEST INDIES section.)

At Portsmouth, June 19, 20, 21. SUSSEX drew with HAMPSHIRE.

At Tunbridge Wells, June 22, 24, 25. SUSSEX beat KENT by nine wickets.

SUSSEX v. WARWICKSHIRE

At Eastbourne, June 26, 27, 28. Warwickshire won by two wickets in the last over of extra time, gaining 14 points. Only Parks (eleven 4's), Smith and Foreman achieved much in the Sussex first innings. Gardner showed great patience for nearly five and a quarter hours, and he and Smith took Warwickshire ahead in the course of a fourth wicket partnership of 128. Sussex lost three men before clearing their first innings arrears of 139, but a stubborn innings by Suttle left Warwickshire 140 runs to get with ninety-five minutes remaining.

Sussex

D. V. Smith b Carter	48	— b Hollies	34
L. J. Lenham b Carter	7	— lbw b Carter	9
A. E. James b Townsend	2	— b Hollies	14
J. M. Parks c and b Ibadulla	74	— lbw b Townsend	37
K. G. Suttle st Spooner b Ibadulla	1	— b Hollies	93
D. J. Foreman b Bannister	39	— c Cartwright b Hollies	34
G. Potter c Smith b Hollies	8	— not out	23
N. I. Thomson b Bannister	6	— lbw b Ibadulla	5
D. N. Mantell b Carter	3	— lbw b Hollies	4
R. G. Marlar b Bannister	1	— b Hollies	6
D. L. Bates not out	9	— b Hollies	4
B 4, l-b 7, w 1, n-b 2	14	B 8, l-b 7	15

1/17 2/39 3/106 4/137 5/144 6/173   212
7/195 8/200 9/202 (2.55 an over)

1/15 2/60 3/61 4/151   278
5/213 6/238 7/243 8/254
9/268

Warwickshire

F. C. Gardner b Marlar	126	— not out	26
N. F. Horner c Bates b James	41	— c Suttle b Thomson	6
W. J. Stewart b Marlar	14	— b Thomson	5
R. G. Carter b Marlar	0	— not out	2
M. J. K. Smith c Mantell b Smith	69	— lbw b Thomson	15
A. Townsend b Marlar	29	— c Smith b Marlar	40
T. W. Cartwright lbw b Marlar	0	— b Bates	30
R. T. Spooner b Marlar	15	lbw b Bates	3
K. Ibadulla not out	6	— b Thomson	10
J. D. Bannister c Suttle b Marlar	21	— c Suttle b Thomson	1
W. E. Hollies c Potter b Marlar	16		
B 4, l-b 10	14	L-b 3, w 1	4

1/66 2/97 3/97 4/225 5/259 6/259   351
7/297 8/310 9/334 (2.78 an over)

1/13 2/18 3/27   (8 wkts.) 142
4/47 5/67 6/71 7/89 8/131

Warwickshire Bowling

	O.	M.	R.	W.		O.	M.	R.	W.
Bannister	17	5	30	3	....	14	4	32	0
Carter	14.1	4	48	3	....	15	4	48	1
Hollies	26	4	60	1	....	43.2	10	95	7
Townsend	6	1	25	1	....	20	5	50	1
Ibadulla	20	9	35	2	....	27	10	38	1

Sussex Bowling

	O.	M.	R.	W.		O.	M.	R.	W.
Thomson	22	5	49	0	....	15	0	72	5
Bates	19	1	56	0	....	9.2	0	31	2
Smith	24	7	65	1					
James	23	9	56	1					
Marlar	27	7	75	8	....	5	0	35	1
Suttle	11	1	36	0					

Umpires: J. F. Crapp and W. E. Phillipson.

SUSSEX v. WORCESTERSHIRE

At Eastbourne, June 29, July 1, 2. Drawn with the scores level. Sussex took four points and Worcestershire six points. This was the first instance of a side gaining six points in this way since the system of scoring in the Championship was amended in 1953. Previously the side leading on the first innings took eight points and their opponents four points. Worcestershire wanted 209 in two hours ten minutes and when Thomson came to bowl the final ball of extra time they needed a single to equal the scores and two for victory. This meant that Worcestershire were in the position of getting 0, 6 or 12 points from this very last ball. Sussex spread their field deep and Broadbent pulled to mid-wicket. Both Broadbent and Horton went flat out for two runs. Suttle, dashing in, made a wild return across the pitch but as Broadbent raced for the second run, Parks picked up and threw the ball behind Broadbent and between his legs, hitting the stumps with Broadbent only inches the wrong side of the crease.

Sussex

D. V. Smith c Booth b Flavell	66	— c Broadbent b Horton	34
A. E. James b Berry	42	— c P. Richardson b Berry	48
K. G. Suttle b Berry	40	— b Flavell	15
J. M. Parks lbw b Flavell	76	— not out	61
D. J. Foreman c Dews b Flavell	15	— c Broadbent b Berry	26
G. Potter c Jenkins b Flavell	8		
D. A. Stripp b Coldwell	5	— b Flavell	2
N. I. Thomson not out	50	— b Flavell	6
D. N. Mantell c Booth b Flavell	2		
R. G. Marlar c P. Richardson b Coldwell	15		
D. L. Bates st Booth b Berry	9		
L-b 4	4	B 1, l-b 6	7

1/94 2/121 3/150 4/214 5/232 6/249   332   1/65 2/97   (6 wkts., dec.) 199
7/263 8/277 9/298 (2.91 an over)   3/101 4/168 5/182 6/199

Worcestershire

D. Kenyon c and b Marlar	123	— b Thomson	35
P. E. Richardson b Thomson	10	— b Bates	24
G. Dews b Bates	19	— c and b Bates	31
D. W. Richardson b James	18	— c Marlar b James	23
R. G. Broadbent run out	0	— run out	43
M. J. Horton run out	29	— not out	45
R. Booth c Thomson b James	42		
R. O. Jenkins c Parks b Marlar	31		
R. Berry b Thomson	12		
J. Flavell c Bates b Marlar	18		
L. N. Coldwell not out	0		
B 10, l-b 11	21	B 2, l-b 5	7

1/16 2/41 3/87 4/103 5/188 6/217   323   1/42 2/62 3/110   (5 wkts.) 208
7/290 8/290 9/323 (2.76 an over)   4/128 5/208

Worcestershire Bowling

	O.	M.	R.	W.		O.	M.	R.	W.
Flavell	27	6	81	5	....	21.2	3	67	3
Coldwell	30	5	103	2	....	9	1	24	0
Berry	29.3	13	53	3	....	24	8	83	2
Horton	21	3	68	0	....	7	2	18	1
P. Richardson	2	1	1	0					
Jenkins	4	0	22	0					

Sussex Bowling

	O.	M.	R.	W.	O.	M.	R.	W.
Bates	17	2	56	1	 14	0	80	2
Thomson	26.2	4	72	2	 8	1	40	1
James	25	9	58	2	 12	1	51	1
Smith	12	5	39	0				
Marlar	32	9	60	3				
Stripp	5	1	17	0	 5	0	30	0

Umpires: J. F. Crapp and W. E. Phillipson.

At Birmingham, July 3, 4, 5. SUSSEX lost to WARWICKSHIRE by 93 runs.

SUSSEX v. HAMPSHIRE

At Hove, July 6, 8, 9. Sussex won by six wickets, taking 14 points, after sending in their opponents to bat. This move did not bring quite the results anticipated, for the pitch soon lost its helpfulness to bowlers and good batting by the careful Horton and the more enterprising Barnard, who added 69, assured Hampshire of a useful total. Parks and Foreman, sharing in a stand of 76, placed Sussex in a strong position. Then the last six wickets fell for 72 and the lead amounted to only 19. Gray batted solidly in the Hampshire second innings, but another collapse left Sussex to get no more than 137. Again Parks gave a masterly display.

Hampshire

R. E. Marshall c Foreman b Bates	1	— b Cogger.................... 14
J. R. Gray c Suttle b Thomson	13	— c and b Marlar 53
H. Horton c Mantell b Thomson	71	— c Mantell b James....... 15
A. W. H. Rayment lbw b Marlar	5	— b Thomson............... 20
H. M. Barnard b James	52	— c Cogger b Suttle 17
A. C. D. Ingleby-Mackenzie lbw b Marlar	10	— b James................. 10
P. J. Sainsbury c Cogger b Thomson ...	12	— c Mantell b Cogger...... 12
L. Harrison lbw b Thomson	0	— not out 6
D. Shackleton b Thomson	20	— c Stripp b Thomson 4
M. Heath c Suttle b Thomson	0	— b Thomson............... 2
M. D. Burden not out................	1	— b Cogger................ 0
B 5, l-b 3, n-b 1	9	B 1, l-b 1 2

1/5 2/17 3/33 4/102 5/127 6/158   **194**
7/158 8/193 9/193 (2.10 an over)

1/30 2/73 3/93 4/93   **155**
5/116 6/142 7/142 8/148
9/150

Sussex

A. E. James c Harrison b Shackleton....	5	— c Harrison b Heath 0
L. J. Lenham c Horton b Shackleton ...	11	— lbw b Heath 29
K. G. Suttle c Ingleby-Mackenzie b Heath	39	— c Sainsbury b Burden.... 36
J. M. Parks lbw b Sainsbury	52	— c Barnard b Burden...... 53
D. J. Foreman c Sainsbury b Shackleton	61	— not out 18
D. A. Stripp c Barnard b Burden	4	— not out 0
G. Cogger c Heath b Burden	5	
N. I. Thomson c Harrison b Shackleton..	5	
D. N. Mantell b Heath	2	
R. G. Marlar not out	11	
D. L. Bates run out	1	
B 15, l-b 2	17	L-b 1 1

1/11 2/36 3/65 4/141 5/152 6/170   **213**
7/193 8/200 9/206 (2.50 an over)

1/1 2/70 3/107   (4 wkts.) **137**
4/124

Sussex Bowling

	O.	M.	R.	W.		O.	M.	R.	W.
Thomson	21	9	35	6	....	21	8	37	3
Bates	17	4	46	1	....	13	3	28	0
Marlar	20	4	55	2	....	20	7	35	1
Stripp	1	0	6	0					
James	18	10	20	1	....	15	3	30	2
Suttle	15	3	23	0	....	9	6	3	1
Cogger						13	5	20	3

Hampshire Bowling

	O.	M.	R.	W.		O.	M.	R.	W.
Shackleton.....	20	6	33	4	....	16	7	27	0
Heath	27	6	61	2	....	16	1	61	2
Gray	21	6	57	0	....	4	2	7	0
Burden	13	4	34	2	....	10.3	3	25	2
Sainsbury......	4	1	11	1	....	12	6	16	0

Umpires: R. S. Lay and W. F. Price.

At Manchester, July 10, 11, 12. SUSSEX drew with LANCASHIRE.

At Ashby-de-la-Zouch, July 13, 15, 16. SUSSEX drew with LEICESTERSHIRE.

At Colchester, July 17, 18, 19. SUSSEX lost to ESSEX by 184 runs.

At Peterborough, July 20, 22, 23. SUSSEX drew with NORTHAMPTONSHIRE.

SUSSEX v. GLAMORGAN

At Hastings, July 24, 25, 26. Drawn, Sussex taking four points. A game almost as dreary as the corresponding fixture at Hove the previous year. Despite the easy character of the pitch the batting until the last afternoon was almost entirely of a defensive nature. At the end of the second day the Glamorgan captain, Wooller, dissatisfied at the slow scoring rate, bowled five under-arm deliveries to his rival captain, Marlar. Sussex, sent in to bat, passed 100 with only three wickets down but though Parks played a pleasing innings, his colleagues failed against a persistent attack. Glamorgan fared even worse against Thomson who took the last four wickets in 14 balls for two runs. Sussex, by cautious methods, increased their lead of 90 to 196 but by then rain, which delayed play on the final day until late afternoon, ruled out the chance of a definite result. Ironically, Glamorgan's opening pair, Parkhouse and Wooller, then played the most adventurous cricket of the match. They hit Marlar for 53 runs in ten overs and completed a century partnership.

Sussex

L. J. Lenham c Hedges b McConnon ...	31	— c Parkhouse b Watkins	0
A. E. James c Watkins b McConnon ...	39	— c Davies b Watkins	11
K. G. Suttle c Walker b McConnon ...	14	— lbw b Watkins	4
J. M. Parks b Watkins	60	— c Davies b Shepherd.......	41
D. J. Foreman c Wooller b Shepherd...	4	— c Wooller b Clark	18
R. J. Langridge c Davies b Shepherd ...	0	— b Watkins	11
G. Cogger c Parkhouse b McConnon ...	4	— not out	0
N. I. Thomson b Clark	24	— c McConnon b Clark	5
R. G. Marlar not out	0	— c Shepherd b Clark	13
D. N. Mantell b Clark	0	— not out	0
D. L. Bates lbw b Clark	0		
B 3, n-b 2	5	B 2, n-b 1	3

1/69 2/77 3/95 4/110 5/110 6/121   181   1/3 2/16   (8 wkts., dec.) 106
7/181 8/181 9/181 (2.08 an over)   3/21 4/58 5/84 6/101 7/106
                 8/106

Glamorgan

W. G. A. Parkhouse c Langridge b Cogger	25	— not out	51
B. Hedges c Mantell b Thomson	12	— b Suttle	0
L. N. Devereux c Cogger b Bates	13	— not out	1
D. J. Ward b Thomson	16		
A. J. Watkins c Foreman b Marlar	8		
P. Walker b Marlar	6		
J. E. McConnon lbw b Thomson	0		
W. Wooller not out	0	— c Foreman b Suttle	50
H. G. Davies b Thomson	2		
D. J. Shepherd c Parks b Thomson	0		
F. Clark c Foreman b Thomson	0		
B 5, l-b 3, w 1	9	L-b 1	1

1/24 2/41 3/62 4/69 5/83 6/84 7/84   91   1/100 2/102   (2 wkts.) 103
8/87 9/87 (1.71 an over)

Glamorgan Bowling

	O.	M.	R.	W.		O.	M.	R.	W.
Clark	16	4	26	3	....	20.4	6	48	3
Watkins	11	6	14	1	....	22	11	27	4
Wooller	9	3	16	0	....	12	7	12	0
Shepherd	20	6	43	2	....	10	2	16	1
Walker	8	2	24	0					
McConnon	23	5	53	4					

Sussex Bowling

	O.	M.	R.	W.		O.	M.	R.	W.
Thomson	23	11	25	6	....	10	6	8	0
Bates	12	4	35	1	....	3	0	11	0
James	9	4	9	0	....	6	3	5	0
Suttle	1	0	7	0	....	10	2	25	2
Cogger	4	1	6	1					
Marlar	4	4	0	2	....	10	2	53	0

Umpires: H. Elliott and A. E. Pothecary.

SUSSEX v. KENT

At Hastings, July 27, 29, 30. Drawn, Sussex taking four points after being sent in on a well-grassed pitch. Thanks to effective fast-medium bowling by Ridgway, returning after an absence of six weeks through injury, Kent got down three wickets for 40 runs, but the left-handed Suttle came to the rescue with his highest innings in first-class cricket. In five hours and a quarter Suttle, by drives and leg-side strokes, hit 165 out of 248, giving only one chance. Kent also began badly, but Leary, strong in defence for nearly four and a half hours, checked the collapse. On the last day Kent declared 62 behind and big hitting by Lenham enabled Sussex to close their innings and leave their opponents 186 to get in just over two hours twenty minutes. Two Kent wickets fell for four runs, but Wilson and Fagg, by adding 66, virtually made the game safe.

T

Sussex

A. S. M. Oakman c Leary b Ridgway ...	6	—	c Pettiford b Halfyard	18
L. J. Lenham c Ufton b Ridgway	2	—	not out	61
K. G. Suttle c Leary b Ridgway	165	—	c Halfyard b Smith	4
J. M. Parks lbw b Ridgway	9	—	c Halfyard b Smith	5
A. E. James c Page b Ridgway	17			
R. J. Langridge c Leary b Smith	12			
R. G. Marlar c Leary b Smith..........	1	—	c Pretlove b Halfyard	9
N. I. Thomson c Phebey b Halfyard	23	—	c Wilson b Leary	21
G. Cogger b Halfyard	0			
D. N. Mantell c Ufton b Halfyard	5			
D. L. Bates not out	0			
B 9, l-b 8, n-b 2	19		L-b 5	5

1/7 2/8 3/40 4/102 5/142 6/152   259   1/25 2/29   (5 wkts., dec.) 123
7/223 8/243 9/255 (2.64 an over)   3/43 4/96 5/123

Kent

A. H. Phebey c Mantell b Cogger ...	25	—	c Marlar b Bates	1
R. C. Wilson c Mantell b Bates	4	—	b Suttle	35
J. F. Pretlove c Lenham b Bates	9	—	c Oakman b Thomson	0
D. G. Ufton c Parks b Bates	0	—	c Suttle b Thomson	2
S. E. Leary not out	100	—	not out	17
J. Pettiford run out	15	—	not out	10
A. E. Fagg lbw b Marlar	11	—	b Thomson	38
G. Smith b Suttle	15			
D. J. Halfyard c Mantell b Bates	3			
F. Ridgway lbw b Thomson	0			
B 8, l-b 6, n-b 1	15		W 2	2

1/8 2/22 3/36 4/58   (9 wkts., dec.) 197   1/3 2/4 3/70   (5 wkts.) 105
5/117 6/149 7/180 8/196 9/197   4/76 5/79
(1.95 an over)

J. C. T. Page did not bat.

Kent Bowling

	O.	M.	R.	W.		O.	M.	R.	W.
Ridgway	27	5	89	5	....	6	0	23	0
Halfyard	24.3	7	57	3	....	10.5	4	22	2
Smith	27	8	52	2	....	11	3	26	2
Page	19	4	42	0					
Leary.........						6	0	47	1

Sussex Bowling

	O.	M.	R.	W.		O.	M.	R.	W.
Thomson	26	12	31	1	....	15	2	47	3
Bates	27	7	63	4	....	11	4	34	1
Cogger	17	3	39	1					
James	8	4	7	0	....	4	1	12	0
Suttle	10	6	12	1	....	5	3	8	1
Oakman	5	1	10	0					
Marlar	8	0	20	1	....	4	3	2	0

Umpires: H. Elliott and A. E. Pothecary.

SUSSEX v. YORKSHIRE

At Hove, July 31, August 1, 2. Yorkshire won by nine wickets, taking 14 points. The batting of Sussex was very patchy. They lost three wickets for 33 before Sheppard, making his first appearance of the season at Hove, and Smith added 103. Sheppard, last out, directed his strokes perfectly, hitting sixteen 4's in a faultless century. When Sussex batted a second time, only Oakman and

Doggart did much against a competent attack and even they were fortunate. For Yorkshire, Close showed excellent form in hitting 103 out of 167 in two and three-quarter hours and Stott was a model of accuracy. Taylor, less sure, severely punished loose deliveries. Watson, leading the side, spent an hour over his first 12 runs and while he and Close were together the Sussex captain and off-spin bowler, Marlar, ended a long spell by sending down one ball—a wide—left-arm. Marlar declined a new ball when Yorkshire went in to score 34 to win.

Sussex

L. J. Lenham lbw b Trueman	0	c Appleyard b Trueman	10
D. V. Smith c Appleyard b Illingworth	69	c Wilson b Trueman	0
A. S. M. Oakman c Taylor b Trueman	2	c Wardle b Close	52
K. G. Suttle st Binks b Wardle	16	c Binks b Illingworth	6
Rev. D. S. Sheppard c Taylor b Pickles	117	b Wardle	1
G. H. G. Doggart c Wilson b Illingworth	9	c Close b Wardle	50
A. E. James b Appleyard	11	lbw b Appleyard	4
N. I. Thomson b Wardle	1	c Wilson b Appleyard	0
R. G. Marlar b Trueman	8	c Binks b Appleyard	0
D. N. Mantell c Wilson b Pickles	4	not out	9
D. L. Bates not out	0	c Binks b Wardle	17
L-b 1, n-b 5	6	B 4, l-b 10, n-b 1	15

1/4 2/8 3/33 4/136 5/157 6/205 7/210   243
8/223 9/238 (2.73 an over)

1/4 2/23 3/42 4/43 5/108   164
6/136 7/136 8/136 9/136

Yorkshire

W. B. Stott c Sheppard b Marlar	48	— not out	15
K. Taylor lbw b Marlar	90	lbw b Doggart	14
J. V. Wilson c and b Marlar	0	— not out	5
D. B. Close c Suttle b Bates	103		
W. Watson c Bates b Smith	68		
R. Illingworth b Smith	9		
J. H. Wardle c Mantell b Smith	3		
F. S. Trueman not out	29		
J. G. Binks b Smith	4		
R. Appleyard c Smith b Marlar	4		
D. Pickles b Marlar	0		
B 6, l-b 4, w 3, n-b 3	16		

1/115 2/115 3/165 4/282 5/332 6/335   374   1/19   (1 wkt.) 34
7/338 8/356 9/374 (2.87 an over)

Yorkshire Bowling

	O.	M.	R.	W.	O.	M.	R.	W.
Trueman	12	3	34	3	11	6	14	2
Pickles	17.1	4	48	2	5	4	2	0
Wardle	25	6	60	2	30.5	13	50	3
Appleyard	13	3	39	1	14	4	35	3
Illingworth	22	9	56	2	12	3	32	1
Close					7	2	16	1

Sussex Bowling

	O.	M.	R.	W.	O.	M.	R.	W.
Thomson	27	9	54	0	3	1	7	0
Bates	14	1	56	1				
Suttle	20	4	46	0				
Oakman	5	2	17	0				
James	24	6	63	0				
Smith	16	1	68	4				
Marlar	23.4	7	54	5	5	0	22	0
Doggart					2.5	1	5	1

Umpires: T. J. Bartley and P. Corrall.

SUSSEX v. MIDDLESEX

At Hove, August 3, 5, 6. Sussex won by 99 runs, taking 14 points, despite a fine all-round effort by Compton. On the first day Parks scored attractively and James (nine 4's) joined in a stand of 73 with Thomson, checking a collapse brought about by Compton with left-arm slows. Robertson and Gale began with a partnership of 55 for Middlesex, who looked comfortably placed till Marlar, with off-breaks, caused a breakdown in which the last six wickets fell for 37. Leading by 65, Sussex gained a strong position when the left-handers, Smith and Suttle, added 94, but again Compton hurried the innings to a close. Needing 266 to win, the Middlesex batsmen, apart from Compton, showed little enterprise, and Suttle this time helped in their downfall.

Sussex

D. V. Smith c Murray b Warr	26	—	c and b Compton	59
L. J. Lenham lbw b Warr	0	—	c and b Compton	6
K. G. Suttle c Murray b Bennett	26	—	c Murray b Hurst	66
J. M. Parks lbw b Compton	60	—	c Murray b Gale	37
Rev. D. S. Sheppard c Edrich b Compton	7	—	c Compton b Moss	1
G. H. G. Doggart lbw b Compton	0	—	st Murray b Compton	11
A. E. James c and b Moss	52	—	c Titmus b Gale	5
N. I. Thomson c Robertson b Warr	45	—	not out	7
R. G. Marlar not out	19	—	b Compton	4
D. N. Mantell lbw b Compton	6	—	run out	0
D. L. Bates lbw b Compton	0	—	c and b Compton	0
L-b 2	2		L-b 2, n-b 2	4

1/16 2/29 3/71 4/91 5/101 6/134 243
7/207 8/225 9/243 (2.79 an over)

1/3 2/97 3/130 4/145 200
5/162 6/188 7/189 8/194
9/198

Middlesex

J. D. Robertson c Doggart b James	50	—	c Mantell b James	32
R. A. Gale c Sheppard b Marlar	31	—	c Bates b James	1
R. J. Hurst b Thomson	10	—	c Mantell b Suttle	1
A. C. Walton b James	25	—	run out	42
D. C. S. Compton c Parks b James	16	—	c Bates b Thomson	44
W. J. Edrich c Suttle b Marlar	2	—	b Marlar	8
F. J. Titmus c Doggart b Marlar	6	—	c James b Marlar	15
J. T. Murray c Doggart b Marlar	0	—	c Doggart b Suttle	9
D. Bennett c Lenham b Marlar	3	—	lbw b Suttle	7
J. J. Warr not out	19	—	b Marlar	1
A. E. Moss c Suttle b Marlar	4	—	not out	2
B 1, l-b 9, n-b 2	12		B 4	4

1/55 2/78 3/113 4/141 5/144 6/151 178
7/152 8/152 9/169 (2.31 an over)

1/28 2/37 3/101 4/120 166
5/143 6/154 7/155 8/162
9/164

Middlesex Bowling

	O.	M.	R.	W.		O.	M.	R.	W.
Moss	15	1	45	1	....	9	3	18	1
Warr	20	6	50	3	....	3	0	17	0
Bennett	12	1	34	1					
Titmus	12	1	41	0	....	16	6	55	0
Compton	17.4	6	40	5	....	24.3	5	71	5
Hurst	10	1	31	0	....	18	9	34	1
Gale					....	1	0	1	2

Sussex Bowling

	O.	M.	R.	W.	O.	M.	R.	W.
Thomson	15	5	42	1	 16	8	24	1
Bates	17	5	35	0	 6	2	13	0
Marlar	23.3	5	50	6	 38	9	86	3
James	20	8	37	3	 18	8	37	2
Suttle	1	0	2	0	.... 8.1	6	2	3

Umpires: T. J. Bartley and P. Corrall.

At Weston-super-Mare, August 7, 8, 9. Sussex beat Somerset by an innings and 44 runs.

At Cheltenham, August 10, 12, 13. Sussex drew with Gloucestershire.

SUSSEX v. LANCASHIRE

At Worthing, August 14, 15, 16. Sussex won by four wickets, taking 12 points. Lancashire, put in after the loss of the first day through rain, gained four points, but their attack failed at a crucial period. Ikin showed much patience in the first innings. Tattersall, pitching accurately, puzzled the Sussex batsmen. At one stage he dismissed four men in ten balls for four runs. Aggressive batting by Pullar showed Lancashire to more advantage in the second innings and a sporting declaration by Washbrook assured a good finish. Set to score 161 in two hours and ten minutes, Sussex were hard pressed until Doggart and Sheppard, who played splendidly despite an injured finger, stood firm. When Sussex claimed the extra half-hour, they still needed 38, but Sheppard saw them through to victory with seven minutes to spare.

Lancashire

C. S. Smith c Webb b Bates............	7	— run out	30
J. T. Ikin c Parks b Smith............	76	— c Suttle b Thomson	0
G. Pullar c and b Bell	16	— not out	70
C. Washbrook c Smith b Thomson	28		
K. Grieves c Suttle b Bates	5		
J. B. Bond b Thomson	14		
P. Whiteley c Smith b Thomson	14		
R. Bowman c Parks b Smith	8		
W. Heys c Webb b Bell	1		
T. Greenhough c Marlar b Thomson ...	13		
R. Tattersall not out	0		
B 6, l-b 7, n-b 1	14	B 2, l-b 1, n-b 2.......	5

1/10 2/56 3/96 4/103 5/132 6/163   196   1/0 2/105   (2 wkts., dec.) 105
7/175 8/178 9/192 (2.54 an over)

Sussex

D. V. Smith lbw b Greenhough	42	— c Heys b Bowman	7
L. J. Lenham lbw b Greenhough	18	— b Greenhough	20
K. G. Suttle b Greenhough	0	— b Tattersall...............	4
J. M. Parks c Bond b Tattersall	0	— b Bowman	39
G. H. G. Doggart c Bowman b Tattersall	49	— c Grieves b Tattersall	39
D. S. Sheppard lbw b Greenhough	4	— not out	34
R. T. Webb c Grieves b Tattersall	1		
N. I. Thomson c Whiteley b Tattersall ..	0	— c Washbrook b Smith	1
R. G. Marlar c Bowman b Tattersall ...	10	— not out	9
R. V. Bell not out	0		
D. L. Bates b Tattersall	0		
B 4, l-b 10, n-b 3	17	B 7, l-b 1	8

1/63 2/63 3/66 4/66 5/72 6/83 7/83   141   1/12 2/26 3/94   (6 wkts.) 161
8/137 9/141 (2.51 an over)   4/110 5/123 6/126

Sussex Bowling

	O.	M.	R.	W.		O.	M.	R.	W.
Thomson	24.5	11	51	4	....	12	5	35	1
Bates	20	4	47	2	....	6.1	1	23	0
Bell	12	0	46	2					
Marlar	11	3	20	0	....	5	1	12	0
Smith	9	4	18	2	....	5	2	30	0

Lancashire Bowling

	O.	M.	R.	W.		O.	M.	R.	W.
Smith	8	1	18	0	....	12	1	36	1
Bowman	4	1	13	0	....	9	1	28	2
Tattersall	23.5	10	42	6	....	10	0	68	2
Whiteley	4	1	20	0					
Greenhough ...	16	4	31	4	....	4	0	21	1

Umpires: F. S. Lee and A. R. Coleman.

SUSSEX v. NOTTINGHAMSHIRE

At Worthing, August 17, 19, 20. Sussex won by 23 runs, taking 12 points. Nottinghamshire gained four points for first innings lead and faster scoring, but their rivals turned the tables in a close finish. Left to make 230 to win, Nottinghamshire started well, but lost three wickets at 73. Poole and Goonesena made plucky efforts and the last wicket proved stubborn, but Sussex won with fifteen minutes of the extra half-hour to spare. Dooland gained honour in his side's defeat by a memorable match performance. He hit his first Championship hundred and, by clever leg-spin bowling, took ten wickets for 102 runs. Smith, Lenham and Parks played excellent innings for the winners.

Sussex

D. V. Smith c Dooland b Morgan	71	— b Matthews	44
L. J. Lenham c Springall b Morgan	25	— b Dooland	89
K. G. Suttle c Morgan b Goonesena	39	— b Dooland	35
J. M. Parks c Matthews b Dooland	93	— c and b Goonesena	3
Rev. D. S. Sheppard c Millman b Dooland	14	— b Dooland	4
G. H. G. Doggart c Dooland b Goonesena	0	— b Dooland	19
R. T. Webb b Matthews	6	— c Poole b Goonesena	9
A. E. James b Atkinson	3	— b Goonesena	0
N. I. Thomson c Poole b Dooland	15	— not out	4
R. G. Marlar lbw b Dooland	23	— st Millman b Dooland	2
R. V. Bell not out	2	— b Dooland	4
B 1, l-b 2, n-b 1	4	B 10, l-b 4, n-b 3....	17

1/77 2/114 3/150 4/201 5/202 6/216   295   1/102 2/166 3/175 4/180   230
7/239 8/264 9/269 (2.80 an over)   5/195 6/208 7/219 8/219
9/221

Nottinghamshire

J. D. Springall c Parks b Smith	27	— b Marlar	37
E. J. Martin c Suttle b Smith..........	38	— c Doggart b Suttle	31
N. Hill lbw b Thomson	5	— b Suttle	23
M. Hill c Doggart b Smith............	0	— c Doggart b Marlar	0
C. J. Poole c James b Thomson	88	— c Doggart b Marlar	24
B. Dooland not out	115	— c Smith b Suttle	11
G. Goonesena b James	12	— c Doggart b Marlar	28
G. Millman b James	5	— b Suttle	5
T. Atkinson not out	0	— not out	21
C. S. Matthews (did not bat)		— c Thomson b Marlar	9
M. Morgan (did not bat)		— lbw b James	5
B 6	6	B 9, l-b 3	12

1/58 2/71 3/71 4/73   (7 wkts., dec.) 296   1/73 2/73 3/73 4/123   206
5/236 6/258 7/284 (2.87 an over)   5/127 6/135 7/152 8/166
9/180

Nottinghamshire Bowling

	O.	M.	R.	W.	O.	M.	R.	W.
Matthews	19	4	46	1	15	2	47	1
Atkinson	20	4	58	1	12	4	31	0
Morgan	25	6	74	2	21	10	42	0
Dooland	21.1	6	54	4	17	1	48	6
Goonesena	20	2	59	2	17	6	45	3

Sussex Bowling

	O.	M.	R.	W.	O.	M.	R.	W.
Thomson	27	5	76	2	4	1	9	0
James	27.1	9	69	2	4.3	3	2	1
Marlar	14	6	29	0	26	6	109	5
Suttle	6	1	15	0	20	7	49	4
Smith	25	7	73	3	7	2	25	0
Bell	4	0	28	0				

Umpires: F. S. Lee and A. R. Coleman.

At Bristol (friendly), August 21, 22, 23. SUSSEX drew with SOMERSET.

At Worcester, August 24, 26, 27. SUSSEX drew with WORCESTERSHIRE.

SUSSEX v. SOMERSET
(Friendly)

At Hove, August 28, 29, 30. Sussex won by 232 runs. Cox, making his first appearance for Sussex since his appointment as cricket coach at Winchester College in 1956, took the honours with fine innings of 74 and 100 not out. At 46 years of age he exhibited the firm attacking strokes of his younger days. Willson, in splendid driving form, helped him in an unfinished fourth wicket stand of 149 in the second innings. Bell, turning the ball awkwardly, played a big part in disposing cheaply of Somerset when they were left to make 348 to win in four hours. The young Nawab of Pataudi showed promise in a short but useful innings for Sussex on the first day.

Sussex

A. E. James b Lobb	16	— c McMahon b Langford	8
L. J. Lenham lbw b McMahon	17	— c Wight b Langford	26
R. H. Willson c Stephenson b Lobb	0	— not out	113
G. H. G. Doggart b Lobb	42	— c Wight b Langford	34
Nawab of Pataudi c Stephenson b Whitehead	27		
G. Cox run out	74	— not out	100
D. J. Semmence c Alley b Tremlett	33		
R. T. Webb b Lobb	4		
R. G. Marlar b Lobb	2		
R. V. Bell not out	23		
D. L. Bates c Lobb b McMahon	14		
B 10, l-b 6, n-b 1	17	B 14, l-b 2	16

1/23 2/23 3/49 4/88 5/127 6/197   269   1/14 2/64   (3 wkts., dec.) 297
7/214 8/222 9/238   3/148

Somerset

L. Pickles b James	3	— c Pataudi b Bell	22
W. E. Alley b James	20	— c Cox b Bell	13
P. B. Wight c Doggart b Bell	47	— c Cox b Bell	13
D. R. W. Silk c Webb b Bell	24	— c Doggart b Bell	3
B. Langford c Doggart b Marlar	24	— lbw b Marlar	0
H. W. Stephenson c Willson b Marlar	7	— c Doggart b Bell	26
M. F. Tremlett b Marlar	53	— c Lenham b Bell	30
K. G. Biddulph st Webb b Bell	6	— c Bates b Marlar	5
B. Lobb c Nawab of Pataudi b Bell	21	— b Bell	2
J. W. McMahon not out	12	— c Bell b Marlar	0
A. Whitehead b Marlar	0	— not out	1
W 1, n-b 1	2		
	219		**115**

1/22 2/25 3/89 4/100 5/107 6/167
7/186 8/186 9/217

1/18 2/22 3/27 4/28 5/49
6/54 7/90 8/113 9/114

Somerset Bowling

	O.	M.	R.	W.		O.	M.	R.	W.
Biddulph	16	4	40	0	....	7	1	16	0
Silk	2	1	1	0	....	3	1	22	0
Lobb	21	1	61	5	....	5	0	10	0
Langford	13	3	27	0	....	32	6	106	3
McMahon	21	5	72	2	....	19	3	53	0
Whitehead	17	4	37	1	....	13	2	36	0
Wight	7	1	12	0	....	7	2	15	0
Tremlett	2	0	2	1	....	4	0	23	0

Sussex Bowling

	O.	M.	R.	W.		O.	M.	R.	W.
Bates	14	4	41	0	....	5	1	10	0
James	16	5	38	2	....	2	1	8	0
Bell	33	14	55	4	....	17	6	36	7
Marlar	28.4	5	76	4	....	15	1	61	3
Doggart	3	0	6	0					
Lenham	1	0	1	0					

Umpires: John Langridge and A. E. Pothecary.

SUSSEX v. DERBYSHIRE

At Hove, August 31, September 2, 3. Sussex won by four runs, taking 12 points. Derbyshire, who gained four points, were set to score 235 for victory in three hours and ten minutes. Although Carr batted well, they lost five men for 109, and nine wickets were down for 225. Dawkes, limping badly, held fast, but Jackson fell with five runs wanted. Marlar's clever off-spin bowling was the match-winning factor—his figures were eleven wickets for 144—but a second innings stand by Lenham and Doggart of 174 proved important in helping Sussex to recover after being 90 behind on the first innings. Lenham hit his first century for the county.

Sussex

D. V. Smith b Rhodes	39	—	lbw b Smith		35
L. J. Lenham lbw b Jackson	39	—	c Morgan b Rhodes		130
K. G. Suttle run out	3	—	c and b Smith		4
J. M. Parks lbw b Jackson	0	—	c Carr b Smith		13
G. H. G. Doggart c Revill b Smith	0	—	run out		84
G. Cox c Carr b Smith	1	—	b Smith		33
R. T. Webb b Morgan	24	—	c Smith b Rhodes		0
A. E. James c Smith b Jackson	0	—	c Jackson b Smith		6
R. V. Bell b Rhodes	14	—	not out		8
R. G. Marlar not out	17	—	c Dawkes b Jackson		4
D. L. Bates b Morgan	2	—	not out		1
			B 5, l-b 1		6

1/53 2/69 3/69 4/70 5/76 6/86 7/86   **139**   1/52 2/76   (9 wkts., dec.) **324**
8/109 9/132 (1.95 an over)   3/98 4/272 5/273 6/274
                                    7/301 8/312 9/319

Derbyshire

A. Hamer b Bell	51	—	c Doggart b Bell		37
C. Lee c Cox b Bell	36	—	c Webb b Bates		4
J. M. Kelly c James b Marlar	20	—	c Parks b James		1
A. C. Revill c Webb b Bell	11	—	b Marlar		30
D. B. Carr c Suttle b Marlar	30	—	c Bell b Marlar		51
D. C. Morgan b Marlar	9	—	c Suttle b Marlar		13
H. L. Johnson b Marlar	27	—	c sub b Marlar		26
G. O. Dawkes c Smith b Bell	13	—	not out		32
H. J. Rhodes c Doggart b Marlar	6	—	c sub b Marlar		12
E. Smith not out	7	—	b Bates		9
L. Jackson b Marlar	7	—	b James		1
B 6, l-b 6	12		B 9, l-b 5		14

1/82 2/97 3/121 4/123 5/161 6/162   **229**   1/13 2/14 3/64 4/81 5/109 **230**
7/183 8/204 9/215 (2.10 an over)   6/167 7/169 8/195 9/225

Derbyshire Bowling

	O.	M.	R.	W.		O.	M.	R.	W.
Jackson	20	5	45	3	....	29	13	49	1
Rhodes	13	4	32	2	....	22	3	82	2
Morgan	14.3	7	23	2	....	12	2	49	0
Smith	23	9	39	4	....	36	9	97	5
Carr					....	7	0	28	0
Revill					....	10	5	13	0

Sussex Bowling

	O.	M.	R.	W.		O.	M.	R.	W.
Bates	13	5	28	0	....	10	0	34	2
James	5	1	13	0	....	10.1	3	30	2
Smith	13	2	35	0					
Marlar	25.5	4	65	6	....	21	3	79	5
Bell	46	22	73	4	....	13	0	51	1
Suttle	6	4	3	0	....	9	1	22	0

Umpires: C. S. Elliott and D. J. Wood.

SUSSEX v. SURREY

At Hove, September 4, 5, 6. Surrey won by seven wickets, taking 14 points from a match of low scoring. Lenham, batting without serious fault for nearly four hours, carried his bat through the Sussex first innings, but he alone achieved much. Surrey in turn fared badly, particularly against the off-breaks of Marlar. They lost six wickets for 100, but May hit a 6 and six 4's and McIntyre (seven 4's) employed forceful methods, and the Champions gained a lead of 47. Fine fast bowling by Loader caused a remarkable Sussex collapse in the second innings when six wickets went down for 20 runs, all to Loader at a cost of 10 runs. Then Thomson attacked the bowling fiercely, hitting 59, including three 6's and six 4's, out of 79 in three-quarters of an hour before being caught on the boundary. So Surrey needed 89 to win and though they lost two men cheaply the result was in no doubt.

Sussex

Batsman	1st		2nd	
D. V. Smith c Stewart b Lock	17	— c Lock b Loader	0	
L. J. Lenham not out	66	— lbw b Loader	10	
K. G. Suttle c Constable b Laker	27	— b Loader	4	
J. M. Parks c Barrington b Lock	7	— lbw b Loader	0	
G. H. G. Doggart lbw b Laker	3	— b Loader	2	
G. Cox b Laker	3	— c Stewart b Loader	0	
R. T. Webb c and b A. Bedser	13	— c Laker b Loader	14	
N. I. Thomson c May b E. Bedser	1	— c Loader b Laker	59	
R. V. Bell c May b E. Bedser	2	— not out	6	
R. G. Marlar c and b E. Bedser	4	— lbw b Laker	9	
D. L. Bates c Lock b Laker	0	— b Laker	2	
L-b 4	4	B 4, l-b 5	9	
	147		115	

1/30 2/76 3/84 4/88 5/102 6/126
7/131 8/135 9/142 (1.68 an over)

1/0 2/12 3/18 4/18 5/20
6/20 7/53 8/99 9/111

Surrey

Batsman	1st		2nd	
T. H. Clark lbw b Thomson	2	— c Webb b Thomson	9	
M. J. Stewart c Parks b Thomson	0	— b Marlar	5	
B. Constable c Doggart b Marlar	18	— not out	19	
P. B. H. May c Doggart b Marlar	48	— c Suttle b Bell	25	
K. F. Barrington c Smith b Bell	10	— not out	27	
E. A. Bedser b Bell	14			
A. J. McIntyre c Suttle b Marlar	46			
G. A. R. Lock st Webb b Marlar	17			
J. C. Laker c Smith b Marlar	4			
P. J. Loader not out	8			
A. V. Bedser b Marlar	0			
B 6, l-b 1	7	B 3, n-b 1	4	
	174	(3 wkts.)	89	

1/1 2/4 3/45 4/76 5/84 6/100 7/146
8/164 9/169 (3.16 an over)

1/10 2/18 3/55

Surrey Bowling

	O.	M.	R.	W.		O.	M.	R.	W.
Loader	4	1	12	0	....	19	7	33	7
A. Bedser	16	4	29	1	....	6	0	28	0
Laker	25.1	11	48	4	....	5.4	2	11	3
Lock	33	15	46	2	....	8	4	34	0
E. Bedser	9	5	8	3					

Sussex Bowling

	O.	M.	R.	W.		O.	M.	R.	W.
Thomson	18	6	29	2	....	9	1	23	1
Bates	9	1	24	0	....	1	0	8	0
Bell	14	7	41	2	....	4	2	18	1
Marlar	14.2	1	73	6	....	12	2	36	1
Suttle						1	1	0	0

Umpires: C. S. Elliott and L. H. Gray.

WARWICKSHIRE

President—LORD BENNETT OF EDGBASTON
Secretary—L. T. DEAKINS, County Ground, Birmingham, 3
Captain—M. J. K. SMITH

| M. J. K. Smith | County Badge | K. Ibadulla |

Warwickshire's cricket in 1957 was the subject of sharp contrasts. Early in July, having won six consecutive Championship fixtures for the first time in the club's history, the county stood second to Surrey. Those who followed the day-to-day happenings recognised that Warwickshire were not really as powerful as that position indicated. Even so they were unprepared for the extra-ordinary decline which followed. Not one of the last eleven games which included matches against West Indies and Combined Services, was won and, as a result, Warwickshire dropped to eleventh in the final placings.

At times during this unhappy period it was difficult to accept the fact that Warwickshire were being represented by the players who had previously achieved so much. Flaws suddenly appeared in the batting and collapses in the middle of the order could not always be ascribed to the quality of opposing bowling. Sometimes there was a lack of resolution, almost as if defeat was inevitable. Viewing the season in its entirety it was clear Warwickshire remained an ill-balanced side, over-burdened with opening bowlers and lacking spinners to support the seemingly ageless Hollies.

Still, the summer was not without its compensations. M. J. K. Smith brought a young man's spirit of enthusiasm and enterprise to his newly appointed role of county captain. No one could have started the season on a more unnerving note. He failed to score in each of his first three innings, two of them played for M.C.C. against Yorkshire at Lord's. Yet such were his gifts of determination and technique that he went on to make over 2,000 runs, many of them when those around him failed.

Just as Smith stood supreme among Warwickshire's batsmen so, too, did Hollies among the bowlers. At 45, and in his farewell season, the leg-spinner not only took a hundred wickets for the fourteenth time but sent down more overs than any other bowler in the Championship. What an example he has set to young cricketers; Warwickshire's team will not seem the same without this genial player.

Horner, whose aggregate of runs was his highest for the county, Gardner, and Townsend, all passed 1,000 runs. Ibadulla, from Pakistan, and Singh, who returned to India at the end of the season, proved useful all-rounders. Bannister, Carter, who could turn effectively to off-spin, Wheatley, the Cambridge Blue, and Griffiths all enjoyed periods of success with the new ball. Spooner kept wicket efficiently and was unlucky to miss his benefit match because of injury.

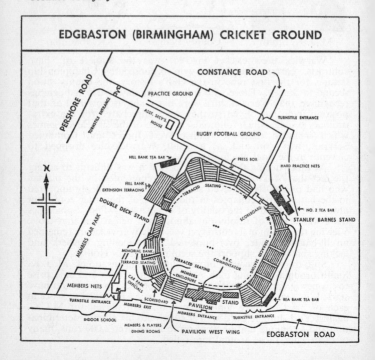

EDGBASTON (BIRMINGHAM) CRICKET GROUND

WARWICKSHIRE RESULTS

All First-Class Matches—Played 33, *Won* 11, *Lost* 7, *Drawn* 15
County Championship Matches—Played 28, *Won* 9, *Lost* 7,
Drawn 11, *No Decision* 1

COUNTY CHAMPIONSHIP AVERAGES
BATTING

	Birthplace	Mtchs.	Inns.	Not Outs	Runs	100's	Highest Inns.	Aver.
M. J. K. Smith.	Leicester	28	51	5	1761	3	127	38.28
F. C. Gardner..	Coventry	27	51	8	1464	2	163	34.04
N. F. Horner...	Queensbury	27	52	3	1440	1	152	29.38
K. Ibadulla	Pakistan	19	29	11	508	0	53	28.22
A. Townsend...	Stockton-on-Tees	27	47	3	1201	1	154	27.29
W. J. Stewart...	Carmarthenshire	14	25	0	631	1	104	25.24
R. T. Spooner..	Stockton-on-Tees	22	36	3	755	1	118	22.87
S. Singh	India	20	31	6	571	0	59	22.84
C. W. Leach...	India	10	17	0	318	0	67	18.70
A. V. Wolton..	Maidenhead	8	14	0	209	0	48	14.92
T. W. Cartwright	Coventry	13	24	2	328	0	43	14.90
R. G. Carter...	Birmingham	21	31	5	196	0	27	7.53
J. D. Bannister.	Wolverhampton	19	27	6	150	0	34	7.14
S. S. Griffiths..	West Indies	9	10	3	38	0	17*	5.42
E. B. Lewis....	Shirley	5	8	0	43	0	17	5.37
R. G. Thompson	Coventry	3	3	2	5	0	5*	5.00
E. Leadbeater..	Huddersfield	3	3	0	13	0	12	4.33
O. S. Wheatley.	Co. Durham	5	9	3	22	0	6*	3.66
W. E. Hollies..	Old Hill (Staffs)	25	30	12	59	0	16	3.27

Also batted: C. Hawkins (*Slough*) 2 and 11*; D. L. Ratcliffe (*Birmingham*) 11 and 1; R. T. Weekes (*Camborne*) 14*.

* *Signifies not out.*

BOWLING

	Overs	Maidens	Runs	Wickets	Average
K. Ibadulla	519.5	202	912	53	17.20
C. W. Leach	52.2	15	159	9	17.66
W. E. Hollies	1174.4	397	2381	123	19.35
E. Leadbeater	59	21	123	6	20.50
J. D. Bannister	610.1	165	1546	64	24.15
O. S. Wheatley	127	27	342	14	24.42
A. Townsend	307.1	65	761	28	27.17
R. G. Carter	618.5	141	1829	67	27.29
S. S. Griffiths	222.1	42	537	19	28.26
R. G. Thompson	29	11	61	2	30.50
S. Singh	412.5	148	905	28	32.32
T. E. Cartwright.......	35	4	92	1	92.00

Also bowled: F. C. Gardner 1.2—0—11—0; M. J. K. Smith 1.2—0—5—0; R. T. Weekes 22—10—69—1.

Amateurs.—E. B. Lewis, S. Singh, M. J. K. Smith, O. S. Wheatley.

At Dudley, May 4, 6, 7. WARWICKSHIRE drew with WORCESTERSHIRE.

At Middlesbrough, May 11, 13, 14. WARWICKSHIRE drew with YORKSHIRE.

WARWICKSHIRE v. NOTTINGHAMSHIRE

At Birmingham, May 15, 16, 17. Drawn, Warwickshire taking two points. Two ninth wicket partnerships were features of a match in which bowlers were generally on top. Jepson and Smales added 81 after Nottinghamshire lost eight wickets for 90 on a pitch affected by rain. The Warwickshire wicket-keeper, Spooner, distinguished himself by holding six catches. Warwickshire, in turn, found scoring far from easy but spirited batting by Ibadulla, a young Pakistani, and Bannister advanced the total from 109 for eight to 180 in an hour and a quarter, whereupon Smith declared. The earlier batsmen did better when Nottinghamshire batted again, though Hollies flighted his leg breaks so intelligently that the last six wickets fell after lunch for 37. Despite a dashing start by Horner and Spooner, Warwickshire found the task of scoring 228 to win in two hours and a quarter beyond them.

Nottinghamshire

R. J. Giles c Spooner b Townsend	2	— lbw b Hollies	25
J. D. Clay c Spooner b Carter	0	— st Spooner b Hollies	57
H. M. Winfield c Spooner b Carter	1	— lbw b Hollies	39
E. J. Martin c Spooner b Carter	9	— run out	27
C. J. Poole c Spooner b Bannister	3	— c Horner b Ibadulla	24
B. Dooland b Carter	21	— c Wolton b Hollies	16
K. J. Poole b Singh	31	— c Ibadulla b Hollies	4
G. Millman b Carter	12	— not out	10
K. Smales c Spooner b Singh	21	— c Ibadulla b Hollies	1
A. Jepson b Singh	61	— c Horner b Ibadulla	11
C. S. Matthews not out	1	— c Gardner b Ibadulla	6
B 15, n-b 2	17	B 4, l-b 4	8

1/2 2/2 3/9 4/16 5/22 6/40 7/84   179
8/90 9/171 (2.35 an over)

1/46 2/103 3/138 4/173   228
5/196 6/205 7/208 8/212
9/212

Warwickshire

F. C. Gardner b Matthews	6	— not out	1
N. F. Horner c C. Poole b Jepson	1	— c Jepson b Dooland	49
M. J. K. Smith b Matthews	1	— lbw b Jepson	1
A. Townsend run out	42	— c Smales b Dooland	14
A. V. Wolton c C. Poole b K. Poole	32	— c K. Poole b Jepson	13
R. T. Spooner c Clay b Dooland	10	— b Smales	44
S. Singh run out	3	— c Winfield b Dooland	15
K. Ibadulla not out	41	— c Millman b Dooland	38
R. G. Carter b Smales	0	— not out	0
J. D. Bannister b Matthews	34		
L-b 9, w 1	10	B 6, l-b 4	10

1/10 2/10 3/19 4/73   (9 wkts., dec.) 180
5/96 6/100 7/103 8/109 9/180
(2.11 an over)

1/75 2/80 3/114 (7 wkts.) 185
4/122 5/138 6/151 7/185

W. E. Hollies did not bat.

Warwickshire Bowling

	O.	M.	R.	W.	O.	M.	R.	W.
Bannister	20	8	54	1	11	4	24	0
Carter	24	7	56	5	4	1	9	0
Townsend	10	2	20	1	5	2	7	0
Ibadulla	4	2	3	0	18	3	58	3
Hollies	8	2	18	0	37	9	78	6
Singh	9.3	5	11	3	17	3	44	0

Nottinghamshire Bowling

	O.	M.	R.	W.		O.	M.	R.	W.
Jepson	12	3	33	1	....	14	0	50	2
Matthews......	19	10	42	3	....	7	0	23	0
K. Poole	11	2	20	1	....	4	0	23	0
Dooland	20	5	45	1	....	12	1	45	4
Smales	23	13	30	1	....	12	3	34	1

Umpires: W. E. Phillipson and A. Skelding.

WARWICKSHIRE v. LANCASHIRE

At Coventry, May 18, 20. Lancashire won by innings and 105 runs, taking 14 points. A notable bowling performance by their England fast bowler, Statham, earned Lancashire victory in two days. Controlling his length and making splendid use of his faster ball, Statham took 15 wickets in the match for 89, and was never mastered. Warwickshire were dismissed in their first innings in less than two and a half hours, and though Lancashire lost several wickets cheaply, Washbrook kept the innings together with a display of considerable technical ability. Jordan gave him useful support in a seventh wicket stand of 60 when Bannister threatened to run through the side. On Warwickshire facing arrears of 195, Statham swung the ball in the damp atmosphere and took the first seven wickets in ten overs for 22. Spooner tried to counter his accuracy by some powerful driving but Greenhough's leg-breaks hastened the end.

Warwickshire

F. C. Gardner c Collins b Statham......	11	— b Statham.................	2
N. F. Horner c Jordan b Wharton	6	— lbw b Statham	4
M. J. K. Smith c Jordan b Statham	5	— c Jordan b Statham	2
A. Townsend lbw b Statham	0	— c Greenhough b Statham...	10
A. V. Wolton b Statham	4	— c Greenhough b Statham...	2
R. T. Spooner c Greenhough b Wharton..	1	— c Grieves b Greenhough ...	44
S. Singh c Dyson b Statham	6	— c Washbrook b Statham ...	2
K. Ibadulla not out	19	— c Jordan b Statham	2
R. G. Carter b Statham	17	— b Greenhough	16
J. D. Bannister b Statham	1	— not out	0
W. E. Hollies c Grieves b Statham	0	— st Jordan b Greenhough ...	2
L-b 1	1	L-b 3, n-b 1	4

1/9 2/18 3/18 4/22 5/23 6/32 7/35   71   1/6 2/7 3/12 4/14 5/31   90
8/69 9/71 (1.77 an over)   6/33 7/37 8/87 9/88

Lancashire

A. Wharton b Bannister	16	J. B. Statham b Bannister	53
J. Dyson b Bannister	37	R. Tattersall not out	1
J. T. Ikin c Spooner b Bannister ..	11	T. Greenhough lbw b Hollies	2
C. Washbrook st Spooner b Hollies	94	B 10, l-b 8	18
K. Grieves lbw b Bannister	0		
G. Pullar lbw b Bannister	0		
R. Collins b Carter	16	1/24 2/50 3/73 4/73 5/79 6/106 266
J. Jordan b Hollies	18	7/166 8/263 9/263 (2.95 an over)	

Lancashire Bowling

	O.	M.	R.	W.	O.	M.	R.	W.
Statham	18.4	6	34	8	17	2	55	7
Wharton	12	4	23	2	10	2	14	0
Tattersall	8	3	11	0				
Greenhough	1	0	2	0	7	2	17	3

Warwickshire Bowling

	O.	M.	R.	W.
Bannister	38	8	107	6
Carter	28	5	87	1
Townsend	14	2	36	0
Singh	3	2	1	0
Hollies	6.5	1	17	3

Umpires: A. E. Pothecary and E. Davies.

WARWICKSHIRE v. SOMERSET

At Birmingham, May 22, 23, 24. Warwickshire won by six wickets, taking 12 points to four gained by Somerset. Warwickshire recovered splendidly after being 131 runs behind on first innings. A forcing innings by the left-handed Alley laid the foundations of a big Somerset total. Stephenson and Palmer shared a seventh wicket partnership of 140. Lobb jolted his former county by dismissing three of the first four Warwickshire batsmen at a personal cost of 13, but Ibadulla, showing sound judgment, stayed over two hours and was largely responsible for the follow-on being averted. Somerset's inability to press home their advantage when batting again was due to excellent fast bowling by Bannister who took six wickets for 37 runs. Only Alley, who batted lower in the order in the second innings, succeeded in defying him. Warwickshire began the last day needing 232 and though Horner gave them a fine start, not until Smith and Spooner came together did they look likely to get the runs. Smith, blossoming out after a shaky start, was the dominant partner in an unbroken fifth stand of 117 in an hour and a half.

Somerset

L. Pickles b Bannister	3	c and b Hollies	27
W. E. Alley b Singh	80	c Townsend b Hollies	51
J. G. Lomax hit wkt b Hollies	18	b Bannister	0
C. L. McCool b Hollies	38	c Singh b Bannister	10
G. M. Tripp c Spooner b Bannister	8	b Carter	0
M. F. Tremlett b Bannister	30	c Spooner b Bannister	0
H. W. Stephenson not out	81	lbw b Bannister	0
K. E. Palmer b Townsend	56	b Bannister	8
J. Hilton (did not bat)	—	st Spooner b Singh	0
J. W. McMahon (did not bat)	—	lbw b Bannister	4
B. Lobb (did not bat)	—	not out	0
B 4, l-b 10, n-b 7	21		

1/38 2/94 3/121 4/147 (7 wkts., dec.) 335
5/172 6/195 7/335 (2.63 an over)

1/0 2/8 3/8 4/31 5/39   100
6/41 7/75 8/90 9/96

Warwickshire

F. C. Gardner lbw b Lobb		17	— b Alley		15
N. F. Horner c Tripp b Alley		30	— c McCool b McMahon		61
M. J. K. Smith lbw b Lobb		5	— not out		97
A. Townsend c Stephenson b Lobb		0	— c Hilton b McMahon		11
A. V. Wolton b Alley		40	— c Tripp b Lobb		4
R. T. Spooner b Alley		3	— not out		38
S. Singh c Pickles b Lomax		15			
K. Ibadulla not out		49			
R. G. Carter b McMahon		16			
J. D. Bannister c Tripp b Alley		18			
W. E. Hollies b Alley		1			
B 8, l-b 2		10	B 5, l-b 1		6

1/42 2/47 3/47 4/74 5/92 6/119   204   1/56 2/83 3/105   (4 wkts.) 232
7/121 8/150 9/202 (2.48 an over)   4/115

Warwickshire Bowling

	O.	M.	R.	W.		O.	M.	R.	W.
Bannister	25	9	37	3	....	13	5	37	6
Carter	17	2	61	0	....	13	4	27	1
Townsend	8.5	1	22	1	....	5	1	15	0
Singh	34	10	82	1	....	4	3	3	1
Hollies	38	8	90	2	....	8.3	4	18	2
Ibadulla	4	0	22	0					

Somerset Bowling

	O.	M.	R.	W.		O.	M.	R.	W.
Lobb	23	4	66	3	....	14	1	55	1
Alley	23.5	5	52	5	....	21	5	59	1
Palmer	3	0	15	0					
Lomax	14	3	37	1	....	5	1	19	0
McCool	7	3	12	0	....	7	2	18	0
McMahon	8	4	11	1	....	24	7	61	2
Hilton	3	2	1	0	....	4	0	14	0
Tremlett						1.2	1	0	0

Umpires: A. E. Pothecary and D. Davies.

At Oxford, May 25, 27, 28. WARWICKSHIRE beat OXFORD UNIVERSITY by three wickets.

At Southampton, May 29, 30, 31. WARWICKSHIRE drew with HAMPSHIRE.

At Birmingham, May 30, 31, June 1, 3, 4. ENGLAND and WEST INDIES drew the First Test Match. (See WEST INDIES section.)

At Bristol, June 1, 3, 4. WARWICKSHIRE beat GLOUCESTERSHIRE by 95 runs.

WARWICKSHIRE v. DERBYSHIRE

At Birmingham, June 8, 10, 11. Warwickshire won by nine wickets, taking 12 points. Derbyshire could make little of the leg-breaks of Hollies, a ninth wicket stand of 52 between Smith and Gladwin being the only worthwhile resistance. Warwickshire's batting was also a patchwork affair but Ibadulla's first fifty in Championship cricket—a pleasing mixture of solid defence and atrractive stroke-play—won them the lead. With the pitch still helping spin bowlers, Hollies broke the back of Derbyshire's second innings, taking four wickets for seven runs in his first nine overs. Carter again gave him useful support and Warwickshire hit off the runs without trouble.

Derbyshire

A. Hamer lbw b Hollies	36	— run out		42
C. Lee c Spooner b Carter	1	— lbw b Hollies		10
J. M. Kelly c Singh b Carter	11	— b Hollies		33
A. C. Revill c Spooner b Hollies	25	— b Singh		1
D. B. Carr b Ibadulla	3	— lbw b Hollies		27
G. O. Dawkes c Horner b Hollies	16	— c Gardner b Hollies		6
H. L. Johnson lbw b Ibadulla	31	— b Carter		2
D. C. Morgan c and b Hollies	10	— lbw b Hollies		1
E. Smith not out	31	— b Carter		18
C. Gladwin run out	20	— not out		17
L. Jackson c Cartwright b Hollies	0	— b Carter		4
L-b 5, w 1	6	B 10, l-b 1		11

1/3 2/42 3/51 4/78 5/78 6/116   **190**   1/34 2/60 3/65 4/111   **172**
7/134 8/138 9/190 (2.18 an over)   5/118 6/125 7/126 8/129
9/168

Warwickshire

F. C. Gardner c Morgan b Smith	10	— not out		55
N. F. Horner c Carr b Gladwin	10	— c and b Morgan		41
M. J. K. Smith c Dawkes b Carr	22	— not out		31
A. Townsend run out	37			
R. G. Carter c Dawkes b Jackson	10			
T. W. Cartwright c Lee b Carr	43			
R. T. Spooner c and b Carr	33			
K. Ibadulla b Morgan	53			
S. Singh b Jackson	9			
J. D. Bannister not out	7			
W. E. Hollies b Jackson	0			
L-b 1, w 1	2	B 3		3

1/14 2/35 3/48 4/58 5/133 6/133   **236**   1/62   (1 wkt.) **130**
7/202 8/221 9/235 (2.01 an over)

Warwickshire Bowling

	O.	M.	R.	W.	O.	M.	R.	W.
Bannister	12	4	33	0	5	0	14	0
Carter	15	4	42	2	23	6	60	3
Hollies	31.4	12	52	5	38	18	47	5
Ibadulla	24	8	49	2	14	6	24	0
Townsend	3	0	8	0				
Singh	1	1	0	0	10	5	16	1

Derbyshire Bowling

	O.	M.	R.	W.	O.	M.	R.	W.
Jackson	17.4	6	39	3	4	1	10	0
Gladwin	16	10	30	1	12	4	17	0
Morgan	14	5	31	1	15	10	21	1
Smith	36	16	54	1	14	3	48	0
Carr	32	14	72	3	7	2	22	0
Revill	1	0	8	0				
Johnson					1.1	0	9	0
Lee					1	1	0	0

Umpires: F. S. Lee and J. S. Buller.

WARWICKSHIRE v. GLOUCESTERSHIRE

At Birmingham, June 12, 13, 14. Warwickshire won by six wickets, taking 12 points. Two separate hundreds by Graveney, who also became the first to complete 1,000 runs for the season, failed to save Gloucestershire. On the opening day Graveney made 106 out of 130 in just under two hours, a display rich in graceful strokes. Hollies, bowling with great steadiness, took six wickets. The Warwickshire innings was dominated by the monumental patience of Gardner who stayed five and three-quarter hours, hitting a 6 and twenty-three 4's. Graveney's second century was even more impressive than his first. He showed exceptional skill against the turning ball skilfully delivered by Hollies and timed his strokes so well that 80 of his runs came in boundaries. When Warwickshire went in again wanting 119, Gloucestershire opened with their spinners, but though they gained early successes another admirable innings by Gardner saw Warwickshire through to victory.

Gloucestershire

G. M. Emmett b Hollies	52	— c Spooner b Ibadulla	25
D. M. Young c Smith b Hollies	29	— lbw b Hollies	18
W. Knightley-Smith c Spooner b Hollies	4	— c Singh b Ibadulla	16
T. W. Graveney c Townsend b Carter	106	— not out	101
R. B. Nicholls c Cartwright b Hollies	14	— lbw b Ibadulla	8
J. Mortimore c Townsend b Ibadulla	2	— c Townsend b Ibadulla	4
B. J. Meyer c Spooner b Carter	13	— lbw b Bannister	8
G. G. M. Wiltshire b Bannister	18	— c Townsend b Singh	14
D. R. Smith c Smith b Hollies	15	— c Smith b Singh	14
C. Cook not out	2	— lbw b Hollies	0
B. D. Wells hit wkt b Hollies	13	— lbw b Hollies	6
L-b 2	2	B 4, l-b 2, n-b 1	7

1/81 2/85 3/86 4/160 5/185 6/215   270   1/45 2/51 3/89 4/99 5/103   221
7/222 8/240 9/257 (2.90 an over)   6/138 7/175 8/193 9/200

Warwickshire

F. C. Gardner c Knightley-Smith b Cook	163	— not out	73
N. F. Horner c Graveney b Cook	29	— run out	4
M. J. K. Smith c Smith b Graveney	59	— c Young b Wells	0
A. Townsend b Graveney	0	— c and b Mortimore	12
T. W. Cartwright c Graveney b Wiltshire	22	— b Mortimore	2
R. T. Spooner c Meyer b Wiltshire	10	— not out	27
K. Ibadulla c Meyer b Wells	20		
S. Singh lbw b Cook	37		
R. G. Carter c Smith b Cook	8		
J. D. Bannister c Wiltshire b Cook	1		
W. E. Hollies not out	0		
B 17, l-b 7	24	L-b 1	1

1/38 2/170 3/170 4/229 5/239 6/286   373   1/18 2/21 3/63   (4 wkts.)   119
7/357 8/367 9/373 (2.82 an over)   4/69

Warwickshire Bowling

	O.	M.	R.	W.		O.	M.	R.	W.
Bannister	15	3	67	1	....	12	2	29	1
Carter	13	1	53	2	....	11	4	30	0
Townsend	8	3	15	0					
Ibadulla	19	7	33	1	....	29	11	48	4
Hollies	25.5	4	62	6	....	43	18	66	3
Singh	12	1	38	0	....	20	6	41	2

Gloucestershire Bowling

	O.	M.	R.	W.	O.	M.	R.	W.
Smith	20	3	62	0				
Wiltshire	13	1	50	2				
Cook	41	13	86	5	 13	3	30	0
Wells	37	8	89	1	 14	1	48	1
Mortimore.....	13	3	35	0	 11	0	28	2
Graveney	8	1	27	2				
Emmett					1	0	8	0
Nicholls					0.1	0	4	0

Umpires: T. J. Bartley and W. Place.

At Cardiff, June 15, 17, 18. WARWICKSHIRE beat GLAMORGAN by ten wickets.

At Dartford, June 19, 20, 21. WARWICKSHIRE beat KENT by 19 runs.

WARWICKSHIRE v. CAMBRIDGE UNIVERSITY

At Birmingham, June 22, 24, 25. Drawn. A feature of this rain-affected match was a century by C. S. Smith, the first of his career. Normally a number eight batsman, Smith was promoted to open the University innings and took part in two big stands, 138 with Barber and 95 with Dexter. Driving strongly, particularly against the spin bowlers, he hit one 6 and twelve 4's. Smith also distinguished himself by taking five wickets with his fast-medium bowling. His namesake, the Warwickshire captain, playing a forcing innings, enabled the county to set the University to get 158 in two hours, but though Dexter hit briskly Cambridge found the task beyond them.

Warwickshire

W. J. Stewart c Green b Goonesena.....	83	— b James.................	38
T. W. Cartwright c Swift b Wheatley ,..	26	— lbw b Goonesena	21
M. J. K. Smith c Swift b Goonesena	5	— b James.................	52
A. V. Wolton c and b Smith	26	— c Wheatley b James	2
K. Ibadulla b Smith	54	— c sub b James	0
S. Singh b Wheatley	12	— lbw b Wheatley	6
C. W. Leach run out	12	— not out	19
G. G. Hawkins c McLachlan b Smith ...	2	— not out	1
E. Leadbeater c Dexter b Smith	3		
R. G. Carter b Smith	5		
R. G. Thompson not out	4		
B 10, l-b 2	12	B 4, l-b 3	7

1/86 2/103 3/122 4/164 5/180 6/210 244   1/54 2/64   (6 wkts., dec.) 146
7/218 8/234 9/237   3/66 4/66 5/87 6/139

Cambridge University

R. W. Barber c Hawkins b Leadbeater ..	63	— not out	4
C. S. Smith not out	103	— c Cartwright b Leadbeater..	14
E. R. Dexter c Thompson b Carter	58	— run out	36
R. M. James (did not bat)		— c Wolton b Ibadulla	2
G. Goonesena (did not bat)		— c Smith b Leadbeater	3
D. J. Green (did not bat)		— not out	21
P. D. Croft (did not bat)		— c Smith b Leach	22
B 4, l-b 4, w 1	9	L-b 1	1

1/138 2/233   (2 wkts., dec.) 233   1/43 2/52 3/52   (5 wkts.) 103
                                               4/55 5/96

I. M. McLachlan, G. W. Cook, B. T. Swift and O. S. Wheatley did not bat.

Cambridge Bowling

	O.	M.	R.	W.		O.	M.	R.	W.
Smith	24	5	40	5	....	6	0	29	0
Wheatley	20	6	52	2	....	11	3	33	1
Dexter	3	0	24	0					
James	8	3	18	0	....	9	5	5	4
Goonesena	22	6	63	2	....	15	3	50	1
Cook	17	7	27	0	....	7	1	22	0
Barber	3	1	8	0					

Warwickshire Bowling

	O.	M.	R.	W.		O.	M.	R.	W.
Carter	16.5	5	52	1	....	4	0	19	0
Thompson	15	3	44	0	....	3	0	25	0
Ibadulla	20	8	46	0	....	5	1	8	1
Cartwright	4	1	14	0					
Singh	7	3	13	0					
Leach	9	7	6	0	....	4	3	4	1
Leadbeater	12	2	49	1	....	13	3	39	2
Wolton						3	1	7	0

Umpires: H. Elliott and N. Oldfield.

At Eastbourne, June 26, 27, 28. WARWICKSHIRE beat SUSSEX by two wickets.

WARWICKSHIRE v. KENT

At Birmingham, June 29, July 1, 2. Drawn, Warwickshire taking four points. A definite result rarely appeared possible on a pitch which afforded bowlers little help. Phebey, Pettiford, Leary and Wilson, though barracked by a section of the crowd, took batting honours in the Kent first innings. For Warwickshire, Gardner shared stands of 77 with Horner and 114 with Stewart, and with Smith and Townsend adding 139 the lead amounted to 155. Throughout the last day most of the Kent batsmen remained on the defensive, but Dixon (ten 4's) punished any loose delivery.

Kent

A. H. Phebey c Smith b Carter	69	— lbw b Hollies 29
R. C. Wilson b Hollies	45	— c Townsend b Hollies 23
P. H. Jones b Hollies	0	— b Hollies 15
J. Pettiford c Townsend b Bannister	57	— b Bannister............ 36
S. E. Leary not out	57	— b Ibadulla............ 16
A. L. Dixon st Spooner b Hollies	4	— c Townsend Ibadulla 61
A. R. B. Neame c Bannister b Townsend	20	— c Townsend b Hollies...... 2
T. G. Evans c Spooner b Townsend	5	— c Spooner b Hollies 15
A. E. Fagg c Spooner b Townsend	0	— not out 28
D. J. Halfyard c Spooner b Hollies	8	— not out 8
J. C. T. Page not out	10	
B 6, l-b 6, n-b 1	13	B 4, l-b 1 5

1/89 2/93 3/129 4/205   (9 wkts., dec.) 288   1/39 2/54 3/78   (8 wkts.) 238
5/215 6/249 7/255 8/255 9/268   4/110 5/115 6/140 7/210
(2.34 an over)   8/225

Warwickshire

F. C. Gardner c Jones b Leary	85	R. G. Carter b Page 19
N. F. Horner c Wilson b Page	41	J. D. Bannister b Page 5
W. J. Stewart c Halfyard b Page	62	W. E. Hollies c Fagg b Page...... 8
M. J. K. Smith c Neame b Page	66	B 12, l-b 5, n-b 1 18
A. Townsend b Page	68	
T. W. Cartwright b Page	16	1/77 2/191 3/196 4/335 5/335 443
R. T. Spooner b Dixon	19	6/368 7/378 8/411 9/425
K. Ibadulla not out	36	(3.81 an over)

Warwickshire Bowling

	O.	M.	R.	W.		O.	M.	R.	W.
Bannister	28	3	67	1	....	22	4	58	1
Carter	18	5	44	1	....	19	8	52	0
Townsend	22	6	40	3	....	4	1	4	0
Cartwright	4	0	10	0					
Ibadulla	20	7	39	0	....	28	12	52	2
Hollies	31	9	75	4	....	45	20	67	5

Kent Bowling

	O.	M.	R.	W.
Halfyard	25	3	85	0
Dixon	39	6	142	1
Page	39.2	8	117	8
Pettiford	7	0	47	0
Leary	6	1	34	1

Umpires: E. Davies and T. J. Bartley.

WARWICKSHIRE v. SUSSEX

At Birmingham, July 3, 4, 5. Warwickshire won by 93 runs, taking 12 points to four points gained by Sussex. Apart from a stand of 62 in forty minutes between Horner and Stewart, Warwickshire were generally struggling against an attack in which Suttle took three wickets in four balls. Warwickshire should have gained first innings lead, but slipshod fielding enabled Bates and Marlar to give Sussex the points with a partnership of 62 for the ninth wicket. Still, splendid stroke play by Horner and Smith quickly put Warwickshire on top and when Sussex went in again needing 251 they found the spin of Hollies and Ibadulla too much.

Warwickshire

F. C. Gardner c Stripp b Marlar	13	— b Bates	8
N. F. Horner b Bates	52	— c Foreman b Thomson	67
W. J. Stewart c Mantell b Bates	30	— b Marlar	37
M. J. K. Smith lbw b Marlar	21	— c Parks b James	95
A. Townsend c Foreman b Suttle	44	— not out	41
T. W. Cartwright c Mantell b Marlar	15	— not out	3
R. T. Spooner c Parks b Bates	44		
K. Ibadulla lbw b Suttle	0		
R. G. Carter c and b Suttle	0		
J. D. Bannister b Bates	3		
W. E. Hollies not out	4		
B 15, l-b 5, n-b 1	21	B 6, l-b 3	9

1/43 2/105 3/110 4/142 5/182 6/214   **247**   1/17 2/76   (4 wkts., dec.) **260**
7/214 8/214 9/242 (2.54 an over)   3/138 4/252

Sussex

A. E. James c and b Carter	6	— c Cartwright b Hollies	9
L. J. Lenham c Spooner b Carter	5	— c Spooner b Ibadulla	15
K. G. Suttle b Bannister	16	— c Spooner b Hollies	38
J. M. Parks c Townsend b Ibadulla	53	— lbw b Hollies	40
D. J. Foreman c Spooner b Townsend	41	— lbw b Ibadulla	19
G. Potter st Spooner b Hollies	4	— b Ibadulla	5
D. A. Stripp b Carter	32	— c Townsend b Hollies	4
N. I. Thomson c Spooner b Hollies	36	— c Cartwright b Hollies	4
D. N. Mantell c Cartwright b Carter	16	— b Ibadulla	4
R. G. Marlar run out	37	— not out	15
D. L. Bates not out	0	— c Cartwright b Hollies	0
B 7, n-b 4	11	B 8	8

1/10 2/19 3/28 4/111 5/131 6/131   **257**   1/11 2/59 3/71 4/124   **157**
7/173 8/191 9/253 (2.73 an over)   5/124 6/124 7/133 8/135
     9/146

Sussex Bowling

	O.	M.	R.	W.		O.	M.	R.	W.
Thomson	17	6	24	0		19	3	69	1
Bates	16.2	6	23	4		7	1	13	1
James	5	0	17	0		18	4	46	1
Marlar	39	5	135	3		20	4	62	1
Suttle	20	10	27	3		16	4	61	0

Warwickshire Bowling

	O.	M.	R.	W.		O.	M.	R.	W.
Bannister	18	4	53	1		2	1	1	0
Carter	21	4	64	4		11	2	42	0
Hollies	25.1	9	71	2		32	13	60	6
Ibadulla	17	7	21	1		23	8	41	4
Townsend	13	0	37	1		1	0	5	0

Umpires: P. A. Gibb and H. Elliott.

WARWICKSHIRE v. LEICESTERSHIRE

At Birmingham, July 6, 8, 9. Warwickshire won by four wickets, taking 14 points. Leadbeater, a former Yorkshire leg-spin bowler, and Griffiths, a fast bowler from Barbados, making their Championship debuts, proved capable deputies for Hollies and Bannister. With Carter they were chiefly responsible for Leicestershire's poor first innings total. A maiden championship century by Stewart was a feature of Warwickshire's reply. His innings of two and three-quarter hours was an admirable blend of restraint and judicious hitting which brought him fifteen 4's. Leicestershire, batting again, owed most to the stubborn batting of L. R. Gardner, and Warwickshire did not win without anxious moments, especially from Savage, on a pitch helping both fast and spin bowlers.

Leicestershire

G. Lester c Townsend b Singh	38	— lbw b Griffiths	6
M. R. Hallam c Townsend b Carter	17	— c Spooner b Griffiths	2
R. A. Diment lbw b Carter	10	— c Townsend b Ibadulla	56
C. H. Palmer c Townsend b Leadbeater	27	— lbw b Carter	6
L. R. Gardner b Leadbeater	9	— not out	69
J. van Geloven c Carter b Leadbeater	42	— lbw b Griffiths	12
J. Firth not out	42	— lbw b Griffiths	12
J. Savage b Griffiths	1	— b Leadbeater	5
R. C. Smith c Leadbeater b Carter	12	— b Carter	4
C. T. Spencer b Griffiths	6	— b Townsend	15
B. Boshier c Spooner b Carter	8	— c Spooner b Townsend	0
B 1, l-b 1, n-b 5	7	B 13, l-b 2, w 4	19

1/26 2/42 3/85 4/105 5/106 6/107   177   1/8 2/9 3/28 4/97 5/103   194
7/119 8/142 9/155 (2.01 an over)   6/133 7/161 8/172 9/194

Warwickshire

F. C. Gardner b Spencer	10	— c van Geloven b Savage	45
N. F. Horner c Firth b Boshier	40	— c Firth b Spencer	10
W. J. Stewart c Diment b Spencer	104	— c van Geloven b Savage	22
M. J. K. Smith c Diment b Savage	16	— c Firth b Savage	13
A. Townsend b Palmer	2	— b Savage	7
R. T. Spooner lbw b Palmer	6	— c Diment b van Geloven	34
K. Ibadulla b Boshier	7	— not out	11
S. Singh not out	15	— not out	0
E. Leadbeater c Hallam b Boshier	0		
R. G. Carter b Boshier	0		
S. S. Griffiths b Boshier	0		
B 6, l-b 9, w 1	16	B 5, l-b 9, w 1, n-b 1	16

1/18 2/87 3/136 4/157 5/188 6/192   216   1/22 2/59 3/93 (6 wkts.) 158
7/208 8/216 9/216 (2.95 an over)   4/104 5/128 6/154

Warwickshire Bowling

	O.	M.	R.	W.		O.	M.	R.	W.
Carter.........	18.2	4	65	4	....	19	3	63	2
Griffiths	24	4	45	2	....	19	4	45	3
Townsend	7	2	14	0	....	5.2	2	5	2
Ibadulla	11	6	8	0	....	15	11	12	1
Singh	7	4	4	1	....	6	3	9	0
Leadbeater	21	10	34	3	....	20	7	41	2

Leicestershire Bowling

	O.	M.	R.	W.		O.	M.	R.	W.
Spencer	25	5	68	2	....	16	2	37	1
Boshier........	18.3	1	46	5	....	7	0	12	0
Palmer	13	6	18	2	....	9	3	14	0
Smith	7	3	32	0					
Savage	9	2	36	1	....	19.2	4	59	4
Lester						1	0	1	0
van Geloven...						9	2	19	1

Umpires: L. H. Gray and C. S. Elliott.

WARWICKSHIRE v. ESSEX

At Birmingham, July 10, 11, 12. Drawn, Warwickshire taking four points. Despite rain which interrupted play each day there was an exciting finish. Essex, wanting 82 to win in just under an hour and a half, struck out eagerly but, losing fifteen minutes because of showers, could not force the pace sufficiently against the accurate attack of Griffiths and Carter who handled a wet ball skilfully. Smith, playing many fine attacking strokes, dominated Warwickshire's batting on the first day. Insole and Savill shared a partnership of 85 for Essex, whose bowlers Ralph and Preston gave their side a winning opportunity by dismissing Warwickshire a second time in an hour and twenty-five minutes. Both made excellent use of a cross wind and a pitch freshened by rain.

Warwickshire

F. C. Gardner b Insole	68	— c and b Ralph	8
N. F. Horner c Dodds b Preston	44	— run out	6
W. J. Stewart b Insole.................	30	— c Preston b Ralph	18
M. J. K. Smith not out.................	85	— c Preston b Ralph	2
A. Townsend lbw b Preston	31	— lbw b Preston	5
R. T. Spooner not out	22	— b Ralph	4
K. Ibadulla (did not bat)		— b Ralph	0
S. Singh (did not bat)		— c King b Preston	7
E. Leadbeater (did not bat)		— lbw b Preston	1
R. G. Carter (did not bat)		— not out	2
S. S. Griffiths (did not bat)		— lbw b Preston	1
B 7, l-b 1, n-b 1	9	N-b 1	1

1/77 2/137 3/158 4/215   (4 wkts., dec.) 289   1/10 2/20 3/26 4/35 5/41   53
(2.97 an over)   6/41 7/43 8/50 9/53

Essex

T. C. Dodds c Ibadulla b Carter	0	— run out	8
G. Barker b Griffiths	3	— c Spooner b Griffiths	8
R. Ralph c Spooner b Griffiths	9	— not out	2
B. Taylor lbw b Townsend	23	— run out	0
D. J. Insole b Singh	80	— b Carter	16
L. Savill b Griffiths	78	— not out	1
M. Bear b Singh	12		
G. Smith lbw b Carter	22	— lbw b Griffiths	9
W. T. Greensmith lbw b Carter	1	— run out	1
K. C. Preston c and b Ibadulla	9	— b Griffiths	15
I. M. King not out	6		
B 1, l-b 15, n-b 2	18	B 5, l-b 1	6

1/2 2/16 3/30 4/60 5/145 6/169   261   1/20 2/20 3/20   (7 wkts.) 66
7/226 8/228 9/243 (2.30 an over)   4/44 5/62 6/62 7/64

Essex Bowling

	O.	M.	R.	W.		O.	M.	R.	W.
Preston	29	3	72	2	....	12.5	4	30	4
Ralph	23	4	72	0	....	12	2	22	5
King	13	6	33	0					
Insole	19	4	49	2					
Greensmith	10	3	35	0					
Smith	3	0	19	0					

Warwickshire Bowling

	O.	M.	R.	W.		O.	M.	R.	W.
Carter	25	6	55	3	....	8	0	36	1
Griffiths	19.1	3	53	3	....	7	0	24	3
Townsend	12	1	30	1					
Leadbeater	13	2	44	0					
Ibadulla	27	7	36	1					
Singh	17	6	25	2					

Umpires: D. Davies and A. R. Coleman.

WARWICKSHIRE v. WORCESTERSHIRE

At Birmingham, July 13, 15, 16. Rain again intervened, preventing play on the last day. It also caused two delays on the first day when Smith and Townsend, appreciating the easier batting conditions after tea, helped to place Warwickshire in a sound position. Griffiths, bowling Kenyon and P. E. Richardson in his opening over, started a disastrous Worcestershire collapse which was halted only by the resoluteness of Booth, ably supported first by Horton and then by Jenkins, with whom 66 were added before the weather had the final word.

Warwickshire

F. C. Gardner c Broadbent b Coldwell	3	S. Singh c Broadbent b Coldwell	15
N. F. Horner c Booth b Flavell	30	R. G. Carter not out	0
W. J. Stewart c Flavell b Berry	11	L-b 6	6
M. J. K. Smith c Flavell b Horton	74		
A. Townsend c Booth b Flavell	36	1/9 2/44 3/44 (8 wkts., dec.) 216
R. T. Spooner c Coldwell b Berry	34	4/152 5/171 6/199 7/211 8/216
K. Ibadulla c Dews b Coldwell	7	(2.45 an over)

W. E. Hollies and S. S. Griffiths did not bat.

Worcestershire

D. Kenyon b Griffiths	1
P. E. Richardson b Griffiths	0
G. Dews c Spooner b Carter	1
D. W. Richardson b Hollies	15
R. G. Broadbent c Gardner b Townsend	10
M. J. Horton c Gardner b Griffiths	21

R. Booth not out	68
R. O. Jenkins not out	19
B 6, l-b 4	10
	—
1/1 2/2 3/2 4/31 5/31 (6 wkts.)	145
6/79 (2.04 an over)	

R. Berry, J. Flavell and L. N. Coldwell did not bat.

Worcestershire Bowling

	O.	M.	R.	W.
Flavell	28	7	70	2
Coldwell	21.4	7	47	3
Horton	8	0	29	1
Berry	20	10	29	2
Jenkins	8	1	27	0
P. E. Richardson	2	0	8	0

Warwickshire Bowling

	O.	M.	R.	W.
Carter	22	4	47	1
Griffiths	17	3	38	3
Ibadulla	2	0	2	0
Hollies	19	10	32	1
Townsend	2	1	2	1
Singh	9	1	14	0

Umpires: T. W. Spencer and A. Skelding.

At Northampton, July 17, 18, 19. WARWICKSHIRE drew with NORTHAMPTONSHIRE.

At Hinckley, July 20, 22, 23. WARWICKSHIRE drew with LEICESTERSHIRE.

WARWICKSHIRE v. SCOTLAND

At Birmingham, July 24, 25, 26. Warwickshire won by an innings and 75 runs. Although fielding few of their regular Championship team Warwickshire outplayed Scotland, the game ending on the third morning. The county built up a sound total before declaring and Scotland at once were in trouble against the lively fast bowling of Bannister. They were all out in just under three hours and, batting again, they failed against the left-arm spin of Youll and the swing of Thompson.

Warwickshire

T. W. Cartwright c Livingstone b Wilson	84
D. P. Ratcliffe c Barr b Wilson	17
W. J. Stewart c Kemsley b Barr	3
M. J. K. Smith c Wilson b Livingstone	36
S. Singh not out	68

B. E. Fletcher b Barr	23
C. W. Leach not out	51
B 1, l-b 3, n-b 1	5
	—
1/30 2/33 3/126 (5 wkts., dec.)	287
4/147 5/192	

C. G. Hawkins, M. Youll, J. D. Bannister and R. G. Thompson did not bat.

Scotland

R. H. E. Chisholm c Ratcliffe b Thompson	0	— b Thompson	4
L. Dudman lbw b Bannister	0	— c Hawkins b Bannister	0
J. Aitchison b Bannister	6	— run out	23
J. N. Kemsley c Cartwright b Bannister	12	— c Hawkins b Bannister	0
D. Barr b Cartwright	11	— c sub b Thompson	43
S. H. Cosh b Bannister	9	— c Leach b Thompson	38
J. Brown c Cartwright b Leach	1	— c Cartwright b Youll	5
J. B. Roberts c Hawkins b Bannister	11	— c Leach b Youll	15
D. Livingstone lbw b Youll	5	— b Youll	3
J. S. Wilson not out	0	— c and b Thompson	12
D. R. Lawrence b Bannister	1	— not out	1
B 2, l-b 5	7	L-b 5	5

1/0 2/2 3/15 4/22 5/38 6/38 7/41	63	1/4 2/6 3/7 4/55 5/110	149
8/58 9/63		6/117 7/119 8/133 9/143	

Scotland Bowling

	O.	M.	R.	W.	O.	M.	R.	W.
Wilson	23	3	80	2				
Lawrence	20	4	55	0				
Barr	15	5	43	2				
Roberts	22	6	54	0				
Livingstone	22	6	50	1				

Warwickshire Bowling

	O.	M.	R.	W.	O.	M.	R.	W.
Thompson	10	7	4	1	18.5	6	50	4
Bannister	17.2	6	28	6	5	0	13	2
Cartwright	6	2	9	1	3	0	20	0
Leach	11	8	4	1	3	2	1	0
Youll	2	0	7	1	14	0	60	3
Singh	11	8	4	0				

Umpires: C. S. Elliott and R. S. Lay.

WARWICKSHIRE v. MIDDLESEX

(R. T. Spooner's Benefit)

At Birmingham, July 27, 29, 30. Middlesex won by 47 runs, taking 12 points. They always held the initiative after rain restricted the first day's play to eighty minutes. Carefree batting by Compton and Edrich, who pulled a leg muscle, helped Middlesex to make up for the time lost, and when Warwickshire replied Titmus caused trouble on a drying pitch with his off spin. In five overs he took four wickets for seven runs. Smith declared 148 behind and Middlesex, equally anxious to force an outright decision, followed suit by making the third declaration of the match. While Smith was batting Warwickshire always had a chance of getting the 292 runs wanted for victory. He completed his first hundred for the county and shared a fifth-wicket stand of 108 with Gardner in an hour and a half. When Smith left, however, the fast bowling of Moss and Warr proved too much for the tail batsmen.

Middlesex

J. D. Robertson b Hollies	42	— st Lewis b Bannister	39
R. A. Gale c Hollies b Bannister	42	— c sub b Hollies	35
D. O. Baldry c Lewis b Griffiths	14	— run out	24
D. C. S. Compton c Leach b Bannister	60	— b Bannister	4
W. J. Edrich retired hurt	49		
F. J. Titmus c Leach b Bannister	5	— not out	31
J. T. Murray b Hollies	14		
D. Bennett not out	2		
A. E. Moss (did not bat)		— b Leach	7
B 13. l-b 2	15	B 1, l-b 2	3

1/82 2/94 3/116 4/194 (6 wkts., dec.) 243
5/216 6/243 (2.61 an over)

1/74 2/78 (5 wkts., dec.) 143
3/80 4/123 5/143

J. J. Warr and R. J. Hurst did not bat.

Warwickshire

F. C. Gardner c Baldry b Titmus	17	—	c Murray b Moss	38
N. F. Horner c Compton b Warr	11	—	lbw b Compton	37
T. W. Cartwright c Hurst b Titmus	31	—	b Warr	2
M. J. K. Smith c Murray b Titmus	12	—	c Titmus b Warr	110
A. Townsend b Titmus	0	—	lbw b Hurst	19
C. W. Leach lbw b Compton	2	—	run out	4
K. Ibadulla not out	10	—	b Moss	2
J. D. Bannister b Titmus	1	—	b Warr	3
E. B. Lewis b Compton	7	—	c Murray b Moss	11
S. S. Griffiths not out	1	—	c Titmus b Moss	4
W. E. Hollies (did not bat)		—	not out	0
L-b 3	3		B 4, l-b 10	14

1/12 2/48 3/61 4/61   (8 wkts., dec.) 95   1/6 2/59 3/95 4/104 5/212   244
5/74 6/76 7/77 8/90 (2.63 an over)   6/220 7/225 8/229 9/239

Warwickshire Bowling

	O.	M.	R.	W.		O.	M.	R.	W.
Griffiths	20	6	40	1	....	3	1	9	0
Bannister	23	5	75	3	....	17	4	56	2
Townsend	14	2	40	0					
Ibadulla	6	4	5	0					
Hollies	28.2	8	66	2	....	14	2	71	1
Leach	2	0	2	0	....	0.3	0	4	1

Middlesex Bowling

	O.	M.	R.	W.		O.	M.	R.	W.
Moss	8	2	17	0	....	13.2	3	41	4
Warr	5	1	12	1	....	8	2	17	3
Titmus	13	4	23	5	....	22	3	68	0
Bennett	4	0	20	0	....	6	0	21	0
Hurst	2	1	11	0	....	13	5	31	1
Compton	4	1	9	2	....	13	1	52	1

Umpires: J. F. Crapp and W. E. Phillipson.

WARWICKSHIRE v. HAMPSHIRE

At Coventry, July 31, August 1, 2. Hampshire won by nine wickets, taking 14 points. A notable spell against his former county by Cannings, one of four seam bowlers included in the team, played a big part in Hampshire's success. Cannings, recalled after an absence of nine matches, prevented Warwickshire from establishing a commanding position by taking the last five second innings wickets in twenty-eight balls for 15 runs. Hampshire, left to get 151, made light of their task, Gray hitting twelve 4's in his not out 82. Chief feature of the earlier play was a restrained hundred by Horton which held Hampshire's first innings together. He stayed four and three-quarter hours and hit one 6 and seventeen 4's.

Warwickshire

F. C. Gardner run out	17	— lbw b Gray		36
N. F. Horner b Cannings	6	— lbw b Shackleton		19
T. W. Cartwright lbw b Cannings	0	— c Sainsbury b Shackleton		6
M. J. K. Smith b Gray	38	— c Harrison b Gray		29
A. Townsend b Gray	13	— c Harrison b Heath		9
C. W. Leach st Harrison b Sainsbury	57	— c and b Cannings		8
S. Singh c Horton b Cannings	45	— not out		58
R. G. Carter c Sainsbury b Shackleton	25	— b Cannings		1
J. D. Bannister c Eagar b Shackleton	1	— b Cannings		1
E. B. Lewis c Harrison b Shackleton	17	— c Sainsbury b Cannings		3
W. E. Hollies not out	0	— lbw b Cannings		0
B 4, l-b 1, n-b 1	6	B 2, l-b 5, n-b 1		8

1/12 2/12 3/35 4/52 5/119 6/168 7/190 225
8/191 9/220 (2.52 an over)

1/33 2/39 3/84 4/96 178
5/100 6/146 7/160 8/174
9/178

Hampshire

R. E. Marshall c Lewis b Bannister	4	— lbw b Hollies	30
J. R. Gray c Lewis b Carter	14	— not out	82
H. Horton st Lewis b Hollies	106	— not out	36
A. W. H. Rayment c Townsend b Bannister	14		
E. D. R. Eagar b Hollies	1		
R. W. Pitman b Carter	28		
P. J. Sainsbury c Townsend b Hollies	32		
L. Harrison run out	0		
D. J. Shackleton c Leach b Bannister	26		
V. H. D. Cannings not out	19		
M. Heath c Hollies b Singh	4		
L-b 2, n-b 3	5	B 1, l-b 1, w 1	3

1/5 2/23 3/38 4/40 5/90 6/150 7/152 253   1/70   (1 wkt.) 151
8/193 9/236 (2.72 an over)

Hampshire Bowling

	O.	M.	R.	W.	O.	M.	R.	W.
Shackleton	24.3	8	61	3	31	12	46	2
Cannings	21	6	52	3	22.4	8	60	5
Heath	18	5	52	0	20	4	39	1
Gray	11	3	37	2	8	2	25	2
Sainsbury	14	6	17	1				

Warwickshire Bowling

	O.	M.	R.	W.	O.	M.	R.	W.
Bannister	24	7	71	3	5	1	16	0
Carter	20	4	77	2	6.3	1	27	0
Hollies	25	9	54	3	16	3	44	1
Singh	13	6	27	1	16	7	39	0
Townsend	9	3	19	0	4	0	21	0
Leach	2	2	8	0				
Smith					1	0	1	0

Umpires: E. Davies and P. A. Gibb.

At Derby, August 3, 5, 6. WARWICKSHIRE drew with DERBYSHIRE.

At Birmingham, August 7, 8, 9. WARWICKSHIRE drew with WEST INDIES. (See
WEST INDIES section.)

At Nottingham, August 10, 12, 13. WARWICKSHIRE lost to NOTTINGHAMSHIRE
by 175 runs.

WARWICKSHIRE v. COMBINED SERVICES

At Birmingham, August 14, 15, 16. Drawn. Rain which limited play on the first two days spoilt the chances of a definite result. The county included several young players among whom Wheatley, the fast-medium Cambridge bowler, and Leach, left-arm spinner, showed promise. Stewart, sharing profitable partnerships with Cartwright and Smith, enabled Warwickshire to gain a comfortable lead but less than three hours remained when the Services batted again. Sharpe was soon out and Leadbetter retired after being struck in the stomach but Parsons and Atkinson steered their side to safety.

Combined Services

P. J. Sharpe b Leach	40 — b Thomson	21
A. B. D. Parsons lbw b Wheatley	0 — st Hawkins b Youll	15
A. C. Shirreff c Hawkins b Wheatley	35 — not out	13
G. G. Atkinson b Leach	4 — c Cartwright b Wolton	53
S. A. Leadbetter c Thompson b Leach	36 — retired hurt	9
E. J. Hewitt c Hawkins b Thompson	14	
K. B. Standring not out	27	
M. D. Fenner c Ratcliffe b Wheatley	8	
A. Pitt st Hawkins b Youll	10 — not out	26
C. Hill c Leach b Leadbeater	0	
P. Hodgson not out	0	
N-b 1	1	B 4, l-b 2, w 2	8

1/0 2/68 3/80 4/80   (9 wkts., dec.) 175   1/26 2/75 3/117   (3 wkts.) 145
5/108 6/150 7/161 8/171 9/175

Warwickshire

T. W. Cartwright c Fenner b Hill	27	E. Leadbeater c Pitt b Shirreff	4
D. P. Ratcliffe c Hewitt b Shirreff	11	O. S. Wheatley c Fenner b Hodgson	0
W. J. Stewart c Hill b Shirreff	91	R. G. Thompson not out	0
M. J. K. Smith c Fenner b Standring	66	L-b 5, n-b 3	8
A. V. Wolton lbw b Hodgson	26		
C. W. Leach c Sharpe b Hodgson	28		
C. G. Hawkins c Sharpe b Hodgson	0	1/21 2/62 3/181 4/206 5/235	270
M. Youll b Shirreff	9	6/242 7/263 8/268 9/270	

Warwickshire Bowling

	O.	M.	R.	W.		O.	M.	R.	W.
Thompson	12	4	28	1	....	7	4	20	1
Wheatley	20	6	41	3	....	8	5	13	0
Cartwright	5	0	30	0					
Leach	20	8	19	3	....	7	2	14	0
Leadbeater	14	4	36	1	....	16	6	42	0
Youll	6	0	20	1	....	12	1	32	1
Wolton	1	1	0	0	....	12	4	16	1

Combined Services Bowling

	O.	M.	R.	W.
Hill	16	7	39	1
Standring	27	4	84	1
Shirreff	20.2	7	69	4
Hodgson	24	6	66	4
Pitt	3	1	4	0

Umpires: J. F. Crapp and H. G. Baldwin.

At Southend, August 17, 19, 20. WARWICKSHIRE drew with ESSEX.

WARWICKSHIRE v. YORKSHIRE

At Birmingham, August 21, 22, 23. Drawn, Yorkshire taking four points Rain denied Yorkshire the chance of forcing victory, limiting the final day's play to twenty minutes. Two left-handers, Watson and Stott, laid the foundation of Yorkshire's big total with an opening stand of 117. Warwickshire's attack was handicapped by the retirement of Bannister suffering from back strain. Smith, playing with skill and patience, did his best to help his side recover from a poor start but Warwickshire followed on 172 behind. The first wicket pair, Gardner and Horner, did better this time before the weather brought the game to its disappointing conclusion.

Yorkshire

W. B. Stott c Horner b Wheatley	60
W. Watson c Gardner b Wheatley	116
W. H. H. Sutcliffe c Townsend b Carter	10
D. B. Close b Carter	2
J. V. Wilson b Hollies	76

R. Illingworth not out	61
J. H. Wardle not out	41
B 21, l-b 9, n-b 2	32

1/117 2/141 3/151 (5 wkts., dec.) 401
4/245 5/311 (3.10 an over)

J. G. Binks, R. Appleyard, D. Pickles and M. J. Cowan did not bat.

Warwickshire

F. C. Gardner lbw b Appleyard	9	— not out	19
N. F. Horner c Watson b Cowan	6	— not out	39
W. J. Stewart c Close b Appleyard	46		
M. J. K. Smith c Binks b Pickles	127		
A. Townsend c Close b Cowan	11		
C. W. Leach st Binks b Appleyard	2		
R. T. Spooner c Sutcliffe b Appleyard	9		
R. G. Carter c Binks b Illingworth	0		
J. D. Bannister not out	6		
O. S. Wheatley c Close b Pickles	0		
W. E. Hollies c Binks b Pickles	0		
B 6, l-b 4, w 2, n-b 1	13	B 4, w 1	5

1/12 2/32 3/103 4/120 5/128 6/152   229   (No wkt.) 63
7/167 8/229 9/229 (2.57 an over)

Warwickshire Bowling

	O.	M.	R.	W.	O.	M.	R.	W.
Bannister	7	1	18	0				
Wheatley	31	6	69	2				
Townsend	22	7	56	0				
Carter	30	2	107	2				
Hollies	37	9	113	1				
Leach	2	0	6	0				

Yorkshire Bowling

	O.	M.	R.	W.	O.	M.	R.	W.
Pickles	19	5	31	3	9	1	36	0
Cowan	19	3	70	2	5	1	9	0
Appleyard	23	4	67	4	6	2	10	0
Wardle	8	1	17	0				
Illingworth	14	8	14	1	2	0	3	0
Close	6	2	17	0				

Umpires: D. Davies and J. S. Buller.

WARWICKSHIRE v. SURREY

At Birmingham, August 24, 26, 27. Surrey won by ten wickets, taking 14 points. Even without May, Laker, Lock and Loader, Surrey outplayed Warwickshire. Smith, completing 2,000 runs in his first full season for the county, batted skilfully against Surrey's varied attack in which the Bedser brothers commanded most respect. Two fine centuries by M. J. Stewart and Barrington, who shared a third wicket partnership of 184, helped Surrey to a commanding position and from that point Warwickshire were always struggling to save the game. Horner, who pulled E. Bedser for two 6's in one over, stayed two hours but once his stand with W. J. Stewart ended, the Surrey bowlers took control. When last man Hollies went in to play his final innings at Edgbaston for Warwickshire on the third morning, the players formed a guard of honour in appreciation of the 45-year-old leg-break bowler who first appeared for the county twenty-five years ago.

Warwickshire

F. C. Gardner b A. Bedser	0	—	c and b Gibson	8
N. F. Horner c McIntyre b A. Bedser	39	—	b E. Bedser	99
W. J. Stewart lbw b Sydenham	20	—	c Stewart b E. Bedser	30
M. J. K. Smith c Barrington b Gibson	77	—	c McIntyre b A. Bedser	8
A. Townsend c McIntyre b Gibson	12	—	c Gibson b E. Bedser	16
C. W. Leach c McIntyre b A. Bedser	20	—	c Barrington b Gibson	6
S. Singh c McIntyre b E. Bedser	7	—	b E. Bedser	1
E. B. Lewis c Stewart b E. Bedser	4	—	lbw b E. Bedser	0
S. S. Griffiths b E. Bedser	0	—	not out	17
O. S. Wheatley lbw b E. Bedser	0	—	b E. Bedser	5
W. E. Hollies not out	0	—	c Constable b E. Bedser	7
B 6, n-b 1	7		B 13, l-b 8	21

1/0 2/55 3/61 4/88 5/128 6/143   186
7/155 8/172 9/186 (2.69 an over)

1/11 2/136 3/151 4/169   218
5/169 6/174 7/174 8/183
9/196

Surrey

T. H. Clark c Townsend b Hollies	48 — not out 6
M. J. Stewart b Townsend	140
B. Constable b Hollies	0
K. F. Barrington b Townsend	101
D. G. W. Fletcher b Townsend	0
R. C. E. Pratt b Singh	40 — not out 7
E. A. Bedser c and b Singh	37
A. J. McIntyre c Smith b Singh	0
A. V. Bedser c Hollies b Singh	9
D. Gibson c Townsend b Singh	0
D. Sydenham not out	0
B 14, l-b 3	17

1/93 2/93 3/277 4/281 5/322 6/372   392
7/372 8/391 9/391 (2.90 an over)

(No wkt.) 13

Surrey Bowling

	O.	M.	R.	W.	O.	M.	R.	W.
A. Bedser	22	4	53	3	30	7	66	1
Gibson	15	1	46	2	10	1	26	2
Sydenham	9	2	22	1	4	0	34	0
E. Bedser	23.1	5	58	4	26.2	10	53	7
Barrington					4	1	18	0

Warwickshire Bowling

	O.	M.	R.	W.	O.	M.	R.	W.
Wheatley	13	2	38	0				
Griffiths	15	1	43	0				
Singh	43.2	8	132	5				
Hollies	33	9	82	2	2	1	2	0
Leach	17	5	46	0				
Townsend	14	1	34	3				
Gardner					1.2	0	11	0

Umpires: C. S. Elliott and J. S. Buller.

At Manchester, August 20, 29, 30. WARWICKSHIRE lost to LANCASHIRE by six wickets.

At The Oval, August 31, September 2. WARWICKSHIRE lost to SURREY by an innings and 70 runs.

U

WORCESTERSHIRE

President—Sir Geoffrey Tomkinson

Joint Secretaries—J. Lister and P. E. Richardson, County Ground, Worcester

Captain—P. E. Richardson

D. W. Richardson   County Badge   J. Flavell

Considering that Worcestershire possessed Peter Richardson, the regular England opening batsman, and that his brother, Derek, played well enough to make his debut in Test cricket, their final place, second from the bottom in the Championship table, came as a great disappointment.

They had not been so low since 1934. Four wins, one each month and all away from Worcester, in 28 county matches of which 14 were left drawn, seemed a poor reward for such a talented batting side. The fact that three of these successes came after opponents had declared twice and that the other was over Leicestershire, last in the table, reduced even the merit of these victories.

Lack of success could be traced mainly to the ineffectiveness of the spin attack. Frequently the pace bowlers dismissed the opposing early batsmen at reasonable cost and then progress came to a halt. Jenkins bridged the gap in 1956 with over 100 wickets, but at 38 years of age he could no longer indulge in long spells and his number of victims fell appreciably. Consequently the main responsibility fell on Berry (left-arm) and Horton (off-breaks), neither of whom reproduced his form of previous years. This was particularly so of Horton, who, though he took twelve wickets rather expensively against Glamorgan on the suspect Cardiff pitch, managed to gain only seventy-five wickets in all matches at an average of just over 30.00.

Flavell, the most successful bowler, took 101 wickets and only four of those were outside the Championship. He received splendid support in opening the attack from Aldridge, Coldwell and Chesterton but too often their efforts were dissipated. Coldwell performed the first hat-trick of his career against Leicestershire at Stourbridge.

Inability to dismiss opponents twice within reasonable time meant that runs, of which there were plenty, lost their value. Worcestershire totalled 300 or more eleven times in county matches, and when set targets against the clock the batsmen were always willing to face up to the task. Kenyon, who twelve months earlier fell only six runs short of completing 2,000 for the seventh successive season, hit 2,231 runs in all matches, including his fifth double hundred and fiftieth century of his career. Five other batsmen, the brothers Richardson, Dews, Broadbent and Horton, exceeded 1,000 and only Outschoorn fell below normal standard. D. Richardson enjoyed his best season with 1,830 runs, but undoubtedly frequent calls on P. E. Richardson for representative matches were a great handicap. Besides the loss of his batting, changes of leadership did not help the side to settle down into an effective combination.

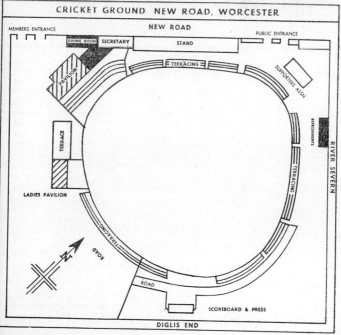

WORCESTERSHIRE RESULTS
All First-Class Matches—Played 32, *Won* 6, *Lost* 10, *Drawn* 16
County Championship Matches—Played 28, *Won* 4, *Lost* 9, *Drawn* 14, *No Decision* 1

COUNTY CHAMPIONSHIP AVERAGES
BATTING

	Birthplace	Mtchs.	Inns.	Not Outs	Runs	100's	Highest Inns.	Aver.
D. Kenyon	*Wordsley*	28	50	2	1847	5	200*	38.47
R. G. Broadbent	*Beckenham*	26	46	6	1301	0	77*	32.52
D. W. Richardson	*Hereford*	25	46	5	1310	5	169	31.95
P. E. Richardson	*Hereford*	19	34	0	1034	2	116	30.41
G. Dews	*Ossett*	28	50	1	1324	1	115	27.02
M. J. Horton...	*Worcester*	27	45	4	1032	0	93	25.17
R. O. Jenkins..	*Worcester*	19	29	10	405	0	60	21.31
L. Outschoorn..	*Ceylon*	19	32	1	566	1	115	18.25
R. Booth......	*Marsden*	28	44	6	586	0	68*	15.42
R. Berry......	*Manchester*	26	31	10	184	0	32	8.76
J. Aldridge.....	*Evesham*	9	11	7	34	0	18*	8.50
L. Coldwell	*Newton Abbot*	20	20	9	71	0	19	6.45
J. Lister	*Thirsk*	3	4	0	22	0	9	5.50
J. Flavell	*Wall Heath*	26	33	4	148	0	18	5.10
G. H. Chesterton	*Chisbury*	5	7	2	9	0	6*	1.80

* Signifies not out.

BOWLING

	Overs	Maidens	Runs	Wickets	Average
J. Aldridge	265.2	52	790	33	23.93
G. H. Chesterton	162.2	41	454	18	25.22
J. Flavell	795	128	2474	97	25.50
R. Berry	965	369	2195	76	28.88
R. O. Jenkins	259.4	45	860	29	29.65
L. Coldwell	591	123	1746	55	31.74
M. J. Horton	800.4	279	1926	60	32.10
D. W. Richardson	17	1	79	1	79.00
L. Outschoorn	8	2	25	0	——
P. E. Richardson	11	2	36	0	——

Amateurs.—G. H. Chesterton, J. Lister, P. E. Richardson.

At Leicester, April 25, 26. WORCESTERSHIRE drew with LEICESTERSHIRE. (Friendly match.)

At Worcester, May 1, 2. WORCESTERSHIRE lost to WEST INDIES by an innings and 77 runs. (See WEST INDIES section.)

WORCESTERSHIRE v. WARWICKSHIRE

At Dudley, May 4, 6, 7. Drawn, Warwickshire taking four points. After Smith, the Warwickshire captain, had been dismissed without scoring for the third successive time, Townsend laid the foundations for a big total. Passing 100 for the first time in a Championship match since the game at Worcester in 1953, he hit 154, including one 6 and twenty 4's, in just under five hours. For Worcestershire, Broadbent occupied nearly three hours over 40. Good batting by Booth limited the Warwickshire lead to 102 but Smith, making amends for his earlier failure during a brilliant innings of an hour and a half, set Worcestershire to score 290 in three hours twenty minutes to win. Kenyon (seventeen 4's) set a lively pace but with half the side out for 172 the end became an anti-climax. Horton hit a boundary in the final over for the only scoring stroke during the last hour, when 24 successive maidens were sent down.

Warwickshire

F. C. Gardner c Booth b Aldridge	11	— not out	57
N. F. Horner c P. Richardson b Berry...	47	— c Booth b Flavell	39
M. J. K. Smith lbw b Flavell	0	— not out	77
A. Townsend c Flavell b Berry 154			
A. V. Wolton c Booth b Aldridge.........	48		
R. T. Spooner b Aldridge...............	10		
S. Singh not out	42		
J. D. Bannister c and b Jenkins.........	2		
R. T. Weeks not out	14		
L-b 1	1	B 4, l-b 10	14

1/19 2/20 3/104 4/235 (7 wkts., dec.) 329   1/69   (1 wkt., dec.) 187
5/251 6/296 7/299 (2.86 an over)
W. E. Hollies and R. G. Thompson did not bat.

Worcestershire

D. Kenyon lbw b Bannister	18	— b Hollies	88
P. E. Richardson c Bannister b Thompson	15	— c Horner b Hollies	17
R. G. Broadbent lbw b Hollies	40	— c Spooner b Hollies	9
D. W. Richardson b Bannister	10	— run out	54
G. Dews st Spooner b Hollies	1	— c Gardner b Singh	3
M. J. Horton c Gardner b Hollies	46	— not out	5
R. O. Jenkins c Spooner b Thompson ..	7	— not out	0
R. Booth c Spooner b Bannister	65	— c Wolton b Hollies	0
J. Flavell c Gardner b Hollies	13		
R. Berry c Spooner b Weeks	8		
J. Aldridge not out	3		
L-b 1	1		

1/26 2/34 3/48 4/49 5/117 6/136   227   1/49 2/79 3/146 (6 wkts.) 176
7/145 8/173 9/202 (1.78 an over)   4/159 5/172 6/172

Worcestershire Bowling

	O.	M.	R.	W.		O.	M.	R.	W.
Flavell	23	4	78	1	....	22	4	65	1
Aldridge.......	23	2	66	3	....	14	2	64	0
Berry	42	15	105	2	....	2	0	16	0
Jenkins	13	1	44	1					
Horton	14	3	35	0	....	4	2	10	0
D. Richardson.					....	4	0	18	0

Warwickshire Bowling

	O.	M.	R.	W.		O.	M.	R.	W.
Bannister	32.2	6	81	3	....	7	4	15	0
Thompson	14	7	21	2	....	5	0	18	0
Hollies	41	16	59	4	....	28	13	54	4
Singh	22	11	23	0	....	13	7	13	1
Weeks	15	8	31	1	....	7	2	38	0
Townsend	3	0	11	0	....	10	4	38	0

Umpires: W. Place and C. Elliott.

At Cambridge, May 11, 13, 14. Worcestershire drew with Cambridge University.

WORCESTERSHIRE v. NORTHAMPTONSHIRE

At Worcester, May 15, 16. Northamptonshire won by five wickets. Worcestershire 115 for three wickets, declared, and 143 for four wickets, declared; Northamptonshire 109 for six wickets, declared, and 150 for five wickets (D. Brookes 53). (Friendly match.)

At The Oval, May 18, 20. WORCESTERSHIRE lost to SURREY by eight wickets.

At Bristol, May 22, 23, 24. WORCESTERSHIRE beat GLOUCESTERSHIRE by five wickets.

WORCESTERSHIRE v. LANCASHIRE

At Worcester, May 25, 27. Lancashire won by an innings and 22 runs, taking 14 points and maintaining their hundred per cent record from five matches. A commendable concerted bowling effort followed a fine innings by Ikin. He went to the wicket when Wharton was caught off the first ball and remained undefeated five hours twenty minutes later, having hit eighteen 4's. There were no signs of the coming debacle when Kenyon and P. Richardson put on 37 before the close of the first day but, with Tattersall and Greenhough making the ball turn and lift on a wearing pitch on Monday, Worcestershire followed on 159 runs behind ten minutes before lunch. Statham began another collapse by dismissing Kenyon at two and, after another good spell of leg-breaks from Greenhough, he supplied the finishing effort with three wickets for four runs.

Lancashire

A. Wharton c Dews b Flavell	0
J. Dyson lbw b Flavell	5
J. T. Ikin not out 141	
C. Washbrook c Flavell b Berry ..	12
K. Grieves b Aldridge	35
R. Collins c D. Richardson b Horton	13
M. J. Hilton b Aldridge..........	1
W. Heys b Horton	8
J. B. Statham b Jenkins	10
R. Tattersall c D. Richardson b Jenkins	17
T. Greenhough st Booth b Horton.	0
B 10, l-b 8	18

1/0 2/15 3/31 4/89 5/110 6/111 7/145 8/164 9/259 (2.52 an over) **260**

Worcestershire

D. Kenyon c Heys b Statham	17	— lbw b Statham	2
P. E. Richardson c Grieves b Tattersall..	20	— c Heys b Hilton...........	27
G. Dews c Washbrook b Hilton	26	— lbw b Greenhough	42
D. W. Richardson b Tattersall	9	— c Wharton b Greenhough ...	17
R. G. Broadbent c and b Tattersall	3	— b Greenhough	0
M. J. Horton c Wharton b Greenhough .	5	— c Grieves b Tattersall	8
R. Booth c Grieves b Greenhough	4	— b Statham...............	22
R. O. Jenkins st Heys b Hilton	1	— b Statham...............	0
R. Berry lbw b Tattersall	6	— not out	6
J. Flavell c Greenhough b Tattersall	2	— b Statham...............	0
J. Aldridge not out	0	— c Hilton b Greenhough	2
B 4, l-b 3, n-b 1	8	B 4, l-b 7	11

1/37 2/39 3/62 4/72 5/88 6/92 7/92 8/94 9/101 (2.02 an over) **101**

1/2 2/46 3/79 4/83 5/100 6/100 7/111 8/124 9/124 **137**

Worcestershire Bowling

	O.	M.	R.	W.
Flavell	19	5	48	2
Aldridge.......	24	7	36	2
Berry	21	9	61	1
Jenkins	13	1	41	2
Horton	25.4	6	56	3

Lancashire Bowling

	O	M.	R.	W.		O	M.	R.	W.
Statham	12	2	28	1	....	8	2	15	4
Wharton	2	0	7	0	....	3	1	6	0
Tattersall	17	9	22	5	....	13	6	37	1
Greenhough ...	8	5	11	2	....	14.1	5	34	4
Hilton	11	4	25	2	....	14	5	25	1
			Collins			5	1	9	0

Umpires: A. E. Pothecary and W. F. Price.

At Taunton, May 29, 30, 31. WORCESTERSHIRE drew with SOMERSET.

At Nottingham, June 1, 3, 4. WORCESTERSHIRE lost to NOTTINGHAMSHIRE by six wickets.

At Oxford, June 5, 6, 7. WORCESTERSHIRE beat OXFORD UNIVERSITY by 178 runs.

WORCESTERSHIRE v. ESSEX

At Worcester, June 8, 10, 11. Drawn, Worcestershire taking four points. Insole, the Essex captain, deprived them of full reward. Going in with his side 12 for two and needing another 120 to save an innings defeat, he remained till the end, having batted just over five hours. Bailey, in a typical innings of one hour forty minutes for 19, and Bear helped their captain. Essex, put in after rain, gave a patchy display in their first innings and Worcestershire went ahead for the loss of three wickets. P. Richardson and Kenyon began with a confident stand of 84, and a stylish century followed from D. Richardson. He batted two hours forty minutes and hit seventeen 4's.

Essex

T. C. Dodds b Aldridge	48	— b Flavell	0
G. Barker b Horton	14	— c D. Richardson b Aldridge	17
B. Taylor b Aldridge	19	— c Outschoorn b Coldwell ..	4
D. J. Insole lbw b Horton	5	— not out 150	
T. E. Bailey c Booth b Coldwell	25	— c D. Richardson b Aldridge	19
M. Bear b Horton	31	— c Booth b Flavell	34
G. Smith c P. Richardson b Berry	27	— b Coldwell	8
W. T. Greensmith lbw b Aldridge	8	— c D. Richardson b Coldwell	0
R. Ralph c Booth b Aldridge	8	— c Booth b Flavell	14
K. C. Preston not out	5	— not out	0
I. M. King b Horton	1		
L-b 8	8	L-b 4	4

1/62 2/62 3/72 4/100 5/116 6/169 **199**   1/1 2/12 3/30 (8 wkts.) **250**
7/177 8/189 9/198 (1.97 an over)   4/95 5/202 6/213 7/213
                                        8/238

Worcestershire

D. Kenyon lbw b King	46	R. Berry b Ralph	1
P. E. Richardson c Greensmith b King	60	J. Flavell not out	8
		L. Coldwell b Bailey	2
G. Dews c Bear b Greensmith....	20	J. Aldridge b Bailey	2
D. W. Richardson b Bailey ...115		B 15, l-b 2, n-b 1............	18
L. Outschoorn c King b Greensmith	15		
M. J. Horton b Bailey	34	1/84 2/113 3/168 4/204 5/291 **331**	
R. Booth lbw b Bailey	10	6/306 7/311 8/319 9/323	
		(3.06 an over)	

Worcestershire Bowling

	O.	M.	R.	W.		O.	M.	R.	W.
Flavell	11	0	52	0	....	23	2	69	3
Coldwell	15	5	23	1	....	33	4	82	3
Aldridge	22	6	44	4	....	13	3	45	2
Horton	36.3	20	44	4	....	1	0	3	0
Berry	16	10	28	1	....	21	10	32	0
			Outschoorn	...		5	1	15	0

Essex Bowling

	O.	M.	R.	W.
Bailey	29.4	7	85	5
Preston	15	5	54	0
Ralph	23	4	63	1
King	19	4	56	2
Greensmith	21	6	55	2

Umpires: C. A. Coleman and W. Place.

WORCESTERSHIRE v. ROYAL AIR FORCE

At Worcester, June 12, 13, 14. Royal Air Force beat Worcestershire by eight wickets. Worcestershire 159 (P/O R. Subba Row five for 47) and 259 (R. G. Broadbent 111, P/O R. Subba Row four for 85); Royal Air Force 286 (A/C P. H. Parfitt 75, A/C G. Atkinson 50, L. Coldwell four for 48) and 126 for two wickets (L/A/C S. A. Leadbetter 58 not out). (Not first class.)

At Derby, June 15, 17, 18. WORCESTERSHIRE drew with DERBYSHIRE.

WORCESTERSHIRE v. COMBINED SERVICES

At Worcester, June 19, 20. Worcestershire won by nine wickets. The Combined Services batsmen succumbed to temptation in face of cunning leg-breaks from Jenkins. Stepping out to drive inviting deliveries tossed high, seven of them were dismissed by balls moving considerably in the cross-wind. Even so, Services led by eight runs on the first innings but they collapsed when the fast-medium bowler, Coldwell, joined Jenkins in making good use of the conditions. Swinging the ball in to the bat, Coldwell took five of the first seven wickets for nine runs. Jenkins, who previously had taken only eight wickets in six games, finished with a match analysis of eleven for 129. Kenyon hit his second fifty in helping the county to score 97 to win.

Combined Services

P. J. Sharpe b Jenkins	49	— lbw b Coldwell	6
P. H. Parfitt b Jenkins	33	— c Booth b Coldwell	1
A. B. D. Parsons c and b Jenkins	45	— not out	36
R. Subba Row b Jenkins	4	— b Jenkins	6
G. A. Atkinson c Booth b Horton	33	— c and b Jenkins	0
D. J. Semmence b Jenkins	0	— c Outschoorn b Coldwell	1
A. C. Shirreff b Jenkins	0	— c Booth b Coldwell	9
B. Knight c Kenyon b Horton	16	— b Jenkins	5
K. B. Standring not out	18	— c Booth b Coldwell	4
C. Clayton c Horton b Jenkins	0	— lbw b Jenkins	12
D. B. Pearson c Kenyon b Flavell	15	— c Kenyon b Flavell	3
B 4, l-b 6, w 1	11	L-b 4, w 1	5

1/67 2/95 3/105 4/168 5/171 6/171   224   1/3 2/8 3/31 4/31 5/32   88
7/176 8/203 9/203   6/42 7/46 8/57 9/79

Worcestershire

D. Kenyon lbw b Pearson	61	— not out	54
L. Outschoorn b Pearson	2	— lbw b Knight	11
D. W. Richardson b Knight	50	— not out	30
R. G. Broadbent c Parfitt b Knight	0		
M. J. Horton b Pearson	10		
J. Lister b Pearson	21		
R. Booth c Parfitt b Knight	43		
R. Jenkins b Standring	12		
B. Hall c Subba Row b Knight	0		
J. Flavell run out	1		
L. Coldwell not out	4		
B 4, l-b 3, w 1, n-b 4	12	L-b 1, w 1	2

1/11 2/99 3/103 4/131 5/132 6/164   216   1/59   (1 wkt.) 97
7/204 8/204 9/205

Worcestershire Bowling

	O.	M.	R.	W.		O.	M.	R.	W.
Flavell	8	2	18	1	....	13.5	5	24	1
Coldwell	9	3	16	0	....	15	6	20	5
Hall	6	2	14	0	....	1	0	8	0
Horton	28	6	67	2					
Jenkins	28	4	98	7	....	16	5	31	4

Combined Services Bowling

	O.	M.	R.	W.		O.	M.	R.	W.
Pearson	17	3	50	4	....	6	0	20	0
Standring	16	5	35	1	....	4	1	8	0
Knight	15.1	1	55	4	....	11	2	31	1
Shirreff	17	3	43	0	....	10	1	36	0
Subba Row	6	2	21	0					

Umpires: P. A. Gibb and J. Wood.

WORCESTERSHIRE v. GLAMORGAN

At Worcester, June 22, 24, 25. Drawn, Worcestershire taking two points
A thunderstorm which reduced cricket on the second day to the pre-lunch period
influenced the game. Before that Glamorgan, replying to a total of 148, struggled
against the pace and swing of Coldwell and Flavell and lost their last eight first
innings wickets for the addition of 65 runs. Coldwell took seven wickets for the
first time in his career. Worcestershire, for whom Broadbent hit his first fifty of
the summer, led by 34 runs, but as the pitch dried so they, too, found batting
difficult. McConnon, bowling off-breaks unchanged for thirty-two overs, turned
the ball sharply and took eight for 56. Kenyon batted well before the collapse,
becoming the first Worcestershire batsman to complete 1,000 runs.

Worcestershire

D. Kenyon b Walker	17	— c Walker b Devereux	53
L. Outschoorn lbw b Wooller	15	— lbw b McConnon	39
G. Dews lbw b Wooller	0	— c and b McConnon	10
D. W. Richardson c Parkhouse b Wooller	12	— c Wooller b McConnon	1
R. G. Broadbent c Watkins b Shepherd	62	— c Shepherd b McConnon	1
M. J. Horton lbw b Wooller	14	— lbw b McConnon	17
R. Booth b H. D. Davies	1	— b McConnon	0
R. O. Jenkins lbw b Walker	19	— b McConnon	11
R. Berry c H. G. Davies b Walker	7	— not out	12
J. Flavell c and b Walker	0	— b McConnon	0
L. Coldwell not out	0	— run out	4
L-b 1	1	B 5, l-b 6	11

1/28 2/28 3/36 4/44 5/93 6/98 7/133   148   1/66 2/92 3/104 4/110   159
8/143 9/143 (1.85 an over)   5/112 6/113 7/136 8/139
9/139

Glamorgan

W. G. A. Parkhouse lbw b Coldwell	21	— not out 31
B. Hedges lbw b Coldwell	2	— not out 25
L. N. Devereux lbw b Coldwell	13	
W. E. Jones b Coldwell	29	
A. J. Watkins c Booth b Coldwell	0	
P. Walker b Flavell	11	
W. Wooller b Flavell	0	
J. E. McConnon b Coldwell	16	
H. G. Davies c Richardson b Flavell ..	16	
H. D. Davies b Coldwell	4	
D. J. Shepherd not out	0	
L-b 1, n-b 1	2	L-b 3 3

1/12 2/27 3/50 4/50 5/61 6/61 7/80   114   (No wkt.) 59
8/103 9/111 (2.42 an over)

Glamorgan Bowling

	O.	M.	R.	W.		O.	M.	R.	W.
H. D. Davies...	17	6	47	1	....	7	2	17	0
Wooller	28	12	49	4	....	6	2	11	0
Walker	23.2	12	32	4	....	7.3	2	18	0
Shepherd	12	6	19	1	....	6	0	23	0
McConnon ...						32	16	56	8
Devereux						20	11	23	1

Worcestershire Bowling

	O.	M.	R.	W.		O.	M.	R.	W.
Flavell	20	5	52	3	....	7	2	19	0
Coldwell	23.2	4	52	7	....	6	0	22	0
Berry	3	1	5	0	....	5	2	4	0
Jenkins	1	0	3	0					
Horton						6	1	11	0

Umpires: P. A. Gibb and J. Wood.

WORCESTERSHIRE v. DERBYSHIRE

At Dudley, June 26, 27, 28. Worcestershire won by two wickets, taking 14 points. The match produced 1,208 runs for the loss of twenty-one wickets, an average of over 57 runs per wicket, three declarations and an exciting finish. Kenyon and P. Richardson did much towards Worcestershire's success when for the first hour of the second day they defied Jackson and Gladwin on a rain-affected pitch. Twice Richardson was struck painful blows by balls lifting off a good length. The stubborn defence of these two made matters comparatively easy for D. Richardson when he batted under better conditions. He hit twenty-five 4's in 169, his highest score and his fourth century of the season, and with Broadbent put on 151 in one and three-quarter hours. Broadbent scored only 20 of those runs. An enterprising century by Hamer, who hit two 6's and twenty-one 4's, enabled Derbyshire to set Worcestershire to score 243 in two hours forty minutes, which they did with three balls and two wickets to spare.

Derbyshire

A. Hamer c D. Richardson b Flavell ...	7	— c Dews b Horton	134
C. Lee c and b Jenkins	38	— c Horton b Flavell	0
J. M. Kelly c Booth b Flavell	97	— c Flavell b Horton	71
A. C. Revill c Flavell b Jenkins	29	— not out	26
D. B. Carr st Booth b Jenkins	15		
G. O. Dawkes c Dews b Flavell	27		
H. L. Johnson not out	79	— not out	10
D. C. Morgan not out	64		
L-b 1, w 1	2	L-b 3	3

1/20 2/64 3/114 4/135 　(6 wkts., dec.) 358
5/205 6/224 (3.08 an over)

1/4 2/158 　(3 wkts., dec.) 244
3/217

E. Smith, C. Gladwin and L. Jackson did not bat.

Worcestershire

D. Kenyon c Dawkes b Jackson	70	— c Lee b Gladwin	15
P. E. Richardson c Dawkes b Jackson ..	32	— c Hamer b Gladwin	20
G. Dews c Dawkes b Carr	65	— c Kelly b Morgan	68
D. W. Richardson c Carr b Revill	169	— c Morgan b Smith	21
R. G. Broadbent not out	20	— b Carr	55
M. J. Horton (did not bat)		— c and b Smith	21
J. Flavell (did not bat)		— run out	1
R. Booth (did not bat)		— not out	15
R. O. Jenkins (did not bat)		— c and b Jackson	19
L. Coldwell (did not bat)		— not out	0
L-b 4	4	L-b 10, n-b 1	11

1/42 2/121 3/209 4/360 　(4 wkts., dec.) 360
(3.36 an over)

1/34 2/47 3/117 　(8 wkts.) 246
4/143 5/186 6/188 7/213
8/241

R. Berry did not bat.

Worcestershire Bowling

	O.	M.	R.	W.		O.	M.	R.	W.
Flavell	23	2	87	3	....	21	1	78	1
Coldwell	23	2	74	0	....	14.3	8	50	0
P. Richardson..	1	1	0	0	....	1	0	9	0
Jenkins	31	6	108	3	....	4	0	13	0
Berry	32	12	69	0	....	5	1	26	0
Horton	6	2	18	0	....	17	6	65	2

Derbyshire Bowling

Jackson	22	6	60	2	....	8.3	1	30	1
Gladwin	24	10	50	0	....	10	2	42	2
Morgan	14	1	49	0	....	11	1	51	1
Smith	33	6	123	0	....	14	3	77	2
Carr	11	0	60	1	....	6	0	35	1
Revill	2.4	0	14	1					

Umpires: W. Place and T. J. Bartley.

At Eastbourne, June 29, July 1, 2, WORCESTERSHIRE drew with SUSSEX.

WORCESTERSHIRE v. NOTTINGHAMSHIRE

At Worcester, July 3, 4, 5. Drawn, Worcestershire taking two points. There were several notable batting performances on a pitch which gave the seam bowlers assistance at first and helped the spinners later. Clay, who hit thirteen 4's, helped Nottinghamshire through a bad period when Flavell and Coldwell moved the ball in the air and off the seam, and Kenyon hit the fifth double century and the 50th hundred of his career. Mindful that the Worcestershire batting was below strength because of Test match calls, Kenyon started carefully but, when taking out his bat after an innings of six and a quarter hours, he had hit thirty-one 4's. Jenkins declared 27 runs ahead but without bonus points. As Nottinghamshire declined to set them a task, he might have gained by batting a little longer.

Nottinghamshire

R. T. Simpson c Broadbent b Coldwell	1	— c Berry b Horton 30
J. D. Clay c Dews b Berry	86	— b Berry 22
R. J. Giles b Coldwell	14	— c Outschoorn b Horton ... 10
G. Millman b Flavell	27	— c Flavell b Horton 11
F. W. Stocks lbw b Horton	29	— not out 103
M. Hill b Flavell	44	— c Horton b Jenkins 6
C. J. Poole c Broadbent b Flavell	9	— b Flavell 14
B. Dooland c Broadbent b Coldwell	31	— c Kenyon b Coldwell 1
A. K. Walker c Broadbent b Coldwell	11	— c and b Berry 29
A. Jepson c Outschoorn b Flavell	1	— not out 3
K. Smales not out	1	
B 10, l-b 1	11	B 11, l-b 1, w 1 13

1/5 2/41 3/113 4/141 5/177 6/224   265   1/28 2/36   (8 wkts., dec.) 242
7/241 8/258 9/264 (2.88 an over)   3/48 4/69 5/142 6/163
                                                  7/164 8/229

Worcestershire

D. Kenyon not out	200	J. Lister c Dooland b Jepson..... 9
L. Outschoorn b Walker	3	R. O. Jenkins not out 20
G. Dews lbw b Walker	0	B 1, l-b 4, n-b 1........... 6
R. G. Broadbent c Dooland b Jepson	50	
M. J. Horton b Walker	4	1/15 2/15 3/182 (6 wkts., dec.) 292
R. Booth c Millman b Walker	0	4/215 5/215 6/234 (2.60 an over)

R. Berry, J. Flavell and L. Coldwell did not bat.

Worcestershire Bowling

	O.	M.	R.	W.	O.	M.	R.	W.
Flavell	21.1	3	57	4	15	2	37	1
Coldwell	29	9	68	4	10	4	21	1
Berry	26	10	65	1	25	11	47	2
Horton	16	2	64	1	49	19	75	3
Jenkins					19	4	49	1

Nottinghamshire Bowling

	O.	M.	R.	W.
Walker	33.4	6	88	4
Jepson	26	9	70	2
Dooland	32	9	72	0
Smales	14	5	44	0
Stocks	6	2	12	0

Umpires: E. Davies and N. Oldfield.

WORCESTERSHIRE v. MIDDLESEX

At Kidderminster, July 6, 8. Middlesex won by 134 runs, taking 14 points. They owed much to Compton, who, in his typical style, hit a whirlwind 48 in thirteen scoring strokes in the first innings and became top scorer of the match when batting a second time. On both occasions he was dismissed by Berry but not before that bowler had received some punishment. Compton hit him for three 6's and five 4's in his first innings, his other scoring strokes being one 4, one 3 and three singles. On Monday, when 24 wickets fell for 309 runs, Compton alone was capable of forcing runs off Berry and Horton, both of whom turned the ball appreciably on a crumbling pitch. Berry took eleven wickets for 142 runs. Worcestershire's second innings lasted under two hours in face of the spin of Titmus (off-breaks) and Hurst (left-arm).

Middlesex

J. D. Robertson c Dews b Coldwell	28	— c Coldwell b Berry 40
R. A. Gale c Jenkins b Flavell	18	— c Jenkins b Horton 16
D. O. Baldry c Coldwell b Berry	61	— c Coldwell b Berry 8
D. C. S. Compton c and b Berry	48	— st Booth b Berry 82
W. J. Edrich c Dews b Berry	1	— b Horton 1
F. J. Titmus b Jenkins	12	— c Broadbent b Berry 10
J. T. Murray b Jenkins	7	— b Horton 0
D. Bennett c Horton b Berry	6	— c Booth b Berry 7
H. W. Tilly b Berry	7	— c Broadbent b Berry 21
R. J. Hurst not out	1	— not out 4
A. E. Moss c Coldwell b Jenkins	24	— c Flavell b Horton 1
L-b 1	1	

1/39 2/59 3/121 4/131 5/168 6/168   214   1/47 2/63 3/66 4/67 5/106   190
7/176 8/186 9/189 (3.24 an over)   6/107 7/136 8/184 9/185

Worcestershire

D. Kenyon c Murray b Moss	3	— c Titmus b Hurst 28
L. Outschoorn b Moss	8	— lbw b Titmus 14
G. Dews c Murray b Bennett	16	— c Gale b Titmus 14
R. G. Broadbent c Tilly b Compton	14	— c Tilly b Titmus 4
M. J. Horton c Murray b Titmus	55	— b Hurst 0
R. Booth c Moss b Bennett	24	— c Baldry b Hurst 9
J. Lister c Tilly b Compton	2	— c Baldry b Titmus 4
R. O. Jenkins b Hurst	31	— c Tilly b Titmus 2
R. Berry not out	2	— b Hurst 2
J. Flavell c Hurst b Titmus	1	— not out 11
L. Coldwell c Murray b Hurst	0	— c Tilly b Hurst 19
N-b 4	4	B 3 3

1/4 2/31 3/31 4/92 5/100 6/103   160   1/20 2/56 3/57 4/60 5/60   110
7/153 8/157 9/160 (2.50 an over)   6/72 7/76 8/78 9/80

Worcestershire Bowling

	O.	M.	R.	W.		O.	M.	R.	W.
Flavell	10	3	40	1	....	3	0	15	0
Coldwell	10	1	37	1	....	3	0	24	0
Berry	23	9	66	5	....	26	5	76	6
Horton	14	7	29	0	....	26.3	5	75	4
Jenkins	9	0	41	3					

Middlesex Bowling

	O.	M.	R.	W.	O.	M.	R.	W.
Moss	12	3	21	2	 3	0	5	0
Bennett	8	1	27	2	 2	0	15	0
Tilly	6	1	16	0				
Compton	16	4	40	2				
Titmus	15	5	39	2	 16	6	34	5
Hurst	7.2	3	13	2	.... 15.5	6	53	5

Umpires: H. Elliott and N. Oldfield.

At Folkestone, July 10, 11, 12. WORCESTERSHIRE lost to KENT by 128 runs.

At Birmingham, July 13, 15. WORCESTERSHIRE drew with WARWICKSHIRE.

WORCESTERSHIRE v. GLOUCESTERSHIRE

(D. Kenyon's Benefit)

At Worcester, July 20, 22, 23. Drawn, Gloucestershire taking four points. Rain reduced cricket on the first day to less than an hour and destroyed the likelihood of a definite result. Worcestershire, put in to bat, lost three wickets for 45 runs to the young Gloucestershire pace bowler, Smith, but Broadbent and D. W. Richardson, playing through eleven maiden overs at the start of their partnership, stopped the collapse. Broadbent again batted well for nearly two hours after Gloucestershire gained the lead and the bonus points.

Worcestershire

D. Kenyon lbw b Smith	24	— b Smith	14
P. E. Richardson c Nicholls b Smith	12	— b Smith	20
G. Dews c Brown b Smith	4	— b Mortimore	24
D. W. Richardson c Etheridge b Mortimore	60	— c Mortimore b Cook	3
R. G. Broadbent c Eagar b Mortimore	42	— not out	60
R. Booth run out	1	— c Graveney b Cook	14
M. J. Horton b Smith	20	— c and b Nicholls	0
R. O. Jenkins not out	20	— not out	12
B 6	6	L-b 4	4

1/35 2/36 3/45 4/140   (7 wkts., dec.) 189   1/22 2/45   (6 wkts., dec.) 151
5/145 6/145 7/189 (1.98 an over)   3/53 4/71 5/112 6/113

R. Berry, J. Flavell and L. Coldwell did not bat.

Gloucestershire

G. M. Emmett c Booth b Coldwell	45	M. A. Eagar c D.Richardson b Berry 18
D. M. Young c Booth b Flavell	56	A. S. Brown not out 23
R. B. Nicholls lbw b Berry	22	B 4, l-b 5 9
T. W. Graveney b Berry	1	
R. J. Etheridge c Dews b Berry	0	1/62 2/121 3/133 (6 wkts., dec.) 192
C. A. Milton not out	18	4/133 5/133 6/155 (2.37 an over)

J. Mortimore, D. R. Smith and C. Cook did not bat.

Gloucestershire Bowling

	O.	M.	R.	W.		O.	M.	R.	W.
Smith	23.3	8	40	4	....	15	4	41	2
Brown	21	6	47	0	....	6	3	17	0
Cook	26	14	41	0	....	14	8	23	2
Mortimore	23	7	47	2	....	18	10	23	1
Nicholls	1	0	8	0	....	5	0	28	1
Young					....	4	1	14	0
Milton					....	3	2	1	0

Worcestershire Bowling

	O.	M.	R.	W.
Flavell	22	4	63	1
Coldwell	23	8	56	1
Berry	32	16	57	4
Jenkins	4	0	7	0

Umpires: C. S. Elliott and P. Corrall.

WORCESTERSHIRE v. LEICESTERSHIRE

At Stourbridge, July 24, 25 26. Worcestershire won by an innings and 73 runs, taking 14 points. They established a commanding position almost from the start. Flavell took a wicket at four and when Horton came on to allow the fast bowler to change ends, his off-breaks proved so effective that the next four wickets fell to him in 17 balls at a cost of five runs. Then, after a shower, Coldwell, fast-medium, performed the first hat-trick of his career, and although Gardner batted resolutely Leicestershire could not recover. They collapsed again after Dews, who hit seventeen 4's in his first century of the summer, and Broadbent and Horton helped Worcestershire to a lead of 210. On a drying pitch, Horton conceded only 37 runs in 42.4 overs, 24 of them maidens, and took five wickets. He finished with match figures of nine wickets for 48 runs.

Leicestershire

G. Lester lbw b Flavell	4	—	b Jenkins	46
M. R. Hallam b Horton	6	—	st Booth b Jenkins	41
J. van Geloven st Booth b Horton	6	—	c Outschoorn b Horton	2
C. H. Palmer c Outschoorn b Horton	0	—	b Flavell	6
L. R. Gardner c Flavell b Coldwell	50	—	st Booth b Jenkins	3
V. S. Munden c Dews b Horton	2	—	not out	21
J. Firth lbw b Coldwell	13	—	c Lester b Jenkins	0
J. Savage c Booth b Coldwell	0	—	b Horton	0
R. Smith c Booth b Coldwell	0	—	c Outschoorn b Horton	13
C. T. Spencer b Coldwell	6	—	c Coldwell b Horton	0
B. Boshier not out	0	—	b Horton	0
B 1, l-b 2	3		B 1, w 4	5

1/4 2/12 3/12 4/21 5/29 6/55 7/55   90   1/76 2/81 3/92 4/97 5/110 137
8/55 9/89 (2.30 an over)   6/110 7/110 8/129 9/129

Worcestershire

D. Kenyon b Savage	15	J. Lister c Munden b van Geloven	7
L. Outschoorn b Spencer	5	J. Flavell not out	5
G. Dews c Palmer b Savage	115	B 1, l-b 2	3
R. G. Broadbent c Firth b Spencer	66		
M. J. Horton not out	70	1/7 2/27 3/173 (6 wkts., dec.) 300
R. Booth c Firth b Munden	14	4/234 5/265 6/288 (2.54 an over)

R. Berry, R. O. Jenkins and L. Coldwell did not bat.

Worcestershire Bowling

	O.	M.	R.	W.		O.	M.	R.	W.
Flavell	14	1	58	1	....	10	2	19	1
Coldwell	11.5	5	18	5	....	4	1	7	0
Horton	12	8	11	4	....	42.4	24	37	5
Berry	1	1	0	0	....	4	2	7	0
					Jenkins	35	11	62	4

Leicestershire Bowling

	O.	M.	R.	W.
Spencer	21	0	64	2
Boshier	17	4	41	0
Savage	30	9	75	2
Smith	29	14	59	0
Palmer	7	1	22	0
Munden	10	5	20	1
van Geloven	4	0	16	1

Umpires: John Langridge and H. G. Baldwin.

WORCESTERSHIRE v. YORKSHIRE

At Worcester, July 27, 29, 30. Yorkshire won by seven wickets, taking 14 points. When the last day commenced with Yorkshire only 56 ahead on first innings with three wickets left, there seemed little to suggest the victory ahead. Success was made possible by the accurate off-spin of Illingworth, who utilised a spot on otherwise placid turf. He took nine wickets for 42 runs, his best performance, and Yorkshire, left to score 67 in an hour, won with seven minutes to spare. The previous day Illingworth showed excellent batting form. Watson, much less enterprising, took more than three and a half hours over 80.

Worcestershire

D. Kenyon b Illingworth	47	—	b Illingworth		28
L. Outschoorn b Illingworth	32	—	lbw b Illingworth		60
G. Dews c Taylor b Appleyard	21	—	lbw b Illingworth		6
D. W. Richardson st Binks b Wardle	20	—	st Binks b Wardle		13
R. G. Broadbent b Pickles	14	—	c Stott b Illingworth		16
M. J. Horton c Binks b Wardle	38	—	c Close b Illingworth		12
R. Booth st Binks b Appleyard	2	—	b Illingworth		11
R. O. Jenkins b Appleyard	26	—	not out		7
R. Berry b Illingworth	12	—	c Wilson b Illingworth		8
J. Flavell c and b Pickles	3	—	st Binks b Illingworth		0
L. Coldwell not out	0	—	c Stott b Illingworth		1
B 9, l-b 6, n-b 7	22		B 9, l-b 1		10

1/72 2/85 3/128 4/128 5/172 6/179   237
7/189 8/206 9/217 (2.52 an over)

1/57 2/71 3/107 4/127   172
5/132 6/147 7/154 8/168
9/168

Yorkshire

W. B. Stott c Jenkins b Flavell	21	—	b Berry		5
K. Taylor c Richardson b Berry	27	—	lbw b Berry		8
J. V. Wilson c Booth b Horton	38	—	c Jenkins b Coldwell		1
D. B. Close b Jenkins	38	—	not out		41
W. Watson c and b Jenkins	80	—	not out		9
R. Illingworth c Broadbent b Richardson	58				
W. H. H. Sutcliffe lbw b Berry	27				
J. H. Wardle b Coldwell	1				
J. G. Binks st Booth b Jenkins	19				
R. Appleyard c Berry b Jenkins	23				
D. Pickles not out	0				
B 2, l-b 4, w 4 n-b 1	11		L-b 3, n-b 1		4

1/25 2/79 3/91 4/133 5/223 6/291   343
7/292 8/317 9/330 (3.14 an over)

1/13 2/14 3/18   (3 wkts.) 68

Yorkshire Bowling

	O.	M.	R.	W.		O.	M.	R.	W.
Pickles	14	2	35	2	...	4	0	25	0
Appleyard	23	5	63	3	...	3	0	18	0
Illingworth	23	10	49	3	...	32	15	42	9
Close	10	1	34	0	...	6	2	26	0
Wardle	24	14	34	2	...	31	16	51	1

Worcestershire Bowling

	O.	M.	R.	W.		O.	M.	R.	W.
Flavell	11	3	31	1					
Coldwell	27	7	73	1	...	8	1	21	1
Berry	23	3	73	2	...	7.5	0	43	2
Horton	23	12	57	1					
Jenkins	16.4	3	68	4					
Richardson	8	1	30	1					

Umpires: P. A. Gibb and T. J. Bartley.

WORCESTERSHIRE v. SOMERSET

At Worcester, July 31, August 1, 2. Somerset won by 57 runs, taking 14 points. McMahon, the Australian left-arm spin bowler, struck the final blow by dismissing the last man with only six minutes left for play. His fellow-countrymen, Alley and McCool, took the honours at the start, when Somerset exceeded 350 runs in an innings for the third match running. Alley, a left-hander, hit twenty-one 4's in his maiden century in county cricket. Silk, the former Cambridge University captain, playing in his first county match of the season, helped McCool add 99 runs for the fifth wicket. Jenkins and Berry, watching the turning ball carefully, rescued Worcestershire after seven wickets fell for 125 runs and Somerset's lead was kept down to 112. Following another good innings by Silk, Somerset set Worcestershire to score 274 runs in three hours twenty minutes, a task which proved beyond them. McMahon, though turning the ball only slowly, flighted it well and was a constant threat to batsmen trying to keep up with the clock.

Somerset

L. Pickles c D. Richardson b Jenkins	51	— b Coldwell	2
W. E. Alley c Booth b Aldridge	108	— c Dews b Coldwell	0
P. B. Wight b Coldwell	20	— b Coldwell	9
M. F. Tremlett b Aldridge	10	— c P. Richardson b Horton	25
C. L. McCool c Dews b Aldridge	81	— c Booth b Coldwell	1
D. R. W. Silk b Coldwell	58	— not out	71
H. W. Stephenson c P. Richardson b Aldridge	14	— c Booth b Coldwell	9
K. H. Palmer not out	17	— st Booth b Berry	38
B. Langford (did not bat)		— c Booth b Coldwell	0
B. Lobb (did not bat)		— b Aldridge	1
J. W. McMahon (did not bat)		— not out	2
L-b 5	5	L-b 3	3

1/145 2/174 3/182 (7 wkts., dec.) 364
4/196 5/295 6/321 7/364 (2.95 an over)

1/1 2/2 (9 wkts., dec.) 161
3/11 4/22 5/40 6/130 7/153
8/153 9/156

Worcestershire

D. Kenyon lbw b Palmer	5	—	c Stephenson b McMahon	16
P. E. Richardson c Tremlett b Langford	39	—	c Palmer b Alley	10
G. Dews c McCool b Langford	32	—	hit wkt b McMahon	40
D. W. Richardson c McCool b Langford	10	—	c Palmer b Langford	14
R. G. Broadbent c Silk b Langford	18	—	run out	76
M. J. Horton c Stephenson b McMahon	15	—	c McCool b McMahon	9
R. Booth c Tremlett b Lobb	2	—	c Langford b McMahon	41
R. O. Jenkins c McCool b Langford	60	—	not out	2
R. Berry c Alley b Langford	32	—	c Silk b McMahon	4
L. Coldwell b McMahon	14	—	b Lobb	0
J. Aldridge not out	18	—	lbw b McMahon	0
B 3, l-b 2, w 1, n-b 1	7		B 4	4

1/27 2/50 3/68 4/104 5/107 6/112   252

7/125 8/215 9/224 (2.59 an over)

1/10 2/65 3/66 4/86   216

5/130 6/205 7/210 8/211

9/216

Worcestershire Bowling

	O.	M.	R.	W.	O.	M.	R.	W.
Coldwell	21.5	3	60	2	22	6	58	6
Aldridge	17	2	69	4	10	1	27	1
Horton	35	12	87	0	14	3	43	1
Berry	35	13	81	0	11	7	19	1
Jenkins	11	2	43	1	2	0	11	0
D. W. Richardson	3	0	19	0				

Somerset Bowling

	O.	M.	R.	W.	O.	M.	R.	W.
Lobb	24	6	39	1	10	2	27	1
Alley	5	0	27	0	6	1	26	1
Palmer	2	0	6	1				
McMahon	21.4	2	82	2	26.2	7	93	6
Langford	28	11	44	6	20	8	52	1
McCool	12	2	41	0	2	0	14	0
Tremlett	4	1	6	0				

Umpires: J. F. Crapp and W. E. Phillipson.

At Leyton, August 3, 5, 6. WORCESTERSHIRE drew with ESSEX.

At Scarborough, August 7, 8, 9. WORCESTERSHIRE drew with YORKSHIRE.

At Loughborough, August 10, 12, 13. WORCESTERSHIRE drew with LEICESTERSHIRE.

WORCESTERSHIRE v. NORTHAMPTONSHIRE

At Worcester, August 14, 15, 16. Drawn, Northamptonshire taking four points. Floodwater from the Severn overflowed inside the boundary and prevented cricket on the first day. The pitch was still damp when P. Richardson sent Northamptonshire in to bat but his bowlers received little assistance. Brookes stayed throughout the second day—bad light reduced play after tea— and he batted just over five and a quarter hours, hitting sixteen 4's, before declaring. With four and three-quarter hours left, Worcestershire began well, P. Richardson and Dews putting on 133 at a run a minute for the second wicket, but the two left-arm slow bowlers, Allen and Tribe, became increasingly difficult to face on the drying turf. They took the last eight wickets for 88 runs and Northamptonshire gained four points with ten minutes to spare.

Northamptonshire

D. Brookes not out	148	K. V. Andrew b Coldwell	1
P. Arnold b Berry	23	F. H. Tyson not out	18
L. Livingston c Kenyon b Horton	52	L-b 7, w 2	9
D. W. Barrick c Dews b Berry	27		
B. L. Reynolds b Flavell	9	1/43 2/158 3/204 (7 wkts., dec.)	290
G. E. Tribe lbw b Flavell	0	4/230 5/236 6/247 7/248	
J. S. Manning b Flavell	3	(2.98 an over)	

M. H. J. Allen and H. R. A. Kelleher did not bat.

Worcestershire

D. Kenyon c Andrew b Tyson	21	R. Berry b Tribe	5
P. E. Richardson c Tyson b Tribe	70	J. Flavell b Allen	5
G. Dews lbw b Allen	71	L. Coldwell not out	0
D. W. Richardson b Allen	3	B 1, l-b 4, n-b 1	6
R. G. Broadbent b Allen	38		
L. Outschoorn c Reynolds b Allen	21	1/27 2/160 3/164 4/175 5/216	248
M. J. Horton st Andrew b Allen	5	6/230 7/237 8/237 9/246	
R. Booth lbw b Tribe	3	(2.66 an over)	

Worcestershire Bowling

	O.	M.	R.	W.
Flavell	23	1	83	3
Coldwell	21	4	76	1
Berry	34	10	75	2
Horton	19	3	47	1

Northamptonshire Bowling

	O.	M.	R.	W.
Tyson	11	0	45	1
Kelleher	6	1	8	0
Manning	24	8	64	6
Allen	29	9	67	0
Tribe	22.4	6	58	3

Umpires: D. J. Wood and D. Davies.

At Cardiff, August 17, 19. WORCESTERSHIRE lost to GLAMORGAN by 91 runs.

WORCESTERSHIRE v. HAMPSHIRE

At Worcester, August 21, 22, 23. Drawn, Hampshire taking four points. The match entered extra time with Worcestershire, set to score 171 runs in two and a quarter hours, having made 106 for four and needing another 65 runs to win. Then Shackleton and Cannings took five wickets while 41 runs were added and the game ended with the last pair struggling to save defeat. They played safely through the final sixteen deliveries with nine fieldsmen clustered round the bat. This exciting finish was made possible by two declarations. Jenkins called in the Worcestershire players 101 runs behind after Outschoorn had batted six and a half hours for 115, his only century of the season, and Ingleby-Mackenzie replied by declaring Hampshire's second innings at 69 for four.

Hampshire

J. R. Gray lbw b Flavell	18	— c Outschoorn b Flavell	7
R. E. Marshall b Coldwell	8	— c Dews b Coldwell	13
H. Horton b Flavell	8	— b Coldwell	14
A. W. H. Rayment b Berry	66	— c Berry b Coldwell	23
R. W. C. Pitman c Booth b Berry	16	— not out	7
A. C. D. Ingleby-Mackenzie b Horton	57	— not out	5
P. J. Sainsbury c Berry b Coldwell	94		
L. Harrison st Booth b Berry	79		
D. Shackleton b Flavell	12		
V. H. D. Cannings not out	0		
M. Heath c Dews b Berry	1		
L-b 11	11		

1/20 2/32 3/45 4/77 5/166 6/184	370	1/20 2/20 (4 wkts., dec.) 69
7/338 8/363 9/367 (3.24 an over)		3/50 4/57

Worcestershire

D. Kenyon b Marshall	33	—	c Gray b Shackleton	29
L. Outschoorn c Sainsbury b Heath	115	—	c Harrison b Shackleton	39
G. Dews lbw b Sainsbury	0	—	c Pitman b Cannings	22
D. W. Richardson c and b Sainsbury	27	—	c Gray b Cannings	6
R. G. Broadbent not out	77	—	c Pitman b Cannings	34
M. J. Horton (did not bat)		—	c Sainsbury b Cannings	3
R. Booth (did not bat)		—	c Sainsbury b Shackleton	4
R. O. Jenkins (did not bat)		—	run out	1
J. Flavell (did not bat)		—	b Shackleton	1
L. Coldwell (did not bat)		—	not out	0
R. Berry (did not bat)		—	not out	0
B 9, l-b 7, n-b 1	17		L-b 8	8

1/64 2/65 3/119 4/269   (4 wkts., dec.) 269   1/55 2/86 3/97   (9 wkts.) 147
(2.06 an over)   4/97 5/107 6/135 7/140
                                                      8/143 9/147

Worcestershire Bowling

	O.	M.	R.	W.		O.	M.	R.	W.
Flavell	27	4	101	3	....	9	0	48	1
Coldwell	28	1	85	2	....	8.2	3	21	3
Berry	39.2	11	105	4					
Horton	20	4	68	1					

Hampshire Bowling

	O.	M.	R.	W.		O.	M.	R.	W.
Shackleton	28	8	42	0	....	20	5	54	4
Cannings	29	9	46	0	....	14	3	46	4
Heath	16	2	49	1	....	6	0	39	0
Sainsbury	27	13	28	2					
Marshall	7	3	16	1					
Rayment	17	3	65	0					
Gray	6	4	6	0					

Umpires: T. W. Spencer and A. Skelding.

WORCESTERSHIRE v. SUSSEX

At Worcester, August 24, 26, 27. Drawn, Sussex taking four points. Parks, released from his duties as twelfth man in the Test, hit a century in each innings for the first time. His second hundred, which took only two and a half hours, came at an opportune time, for Sussex were 76 for five and only 78 runs on. Parks hit fourteen 4's in his first innings, during which he retired hurt after being struck on the knee. Suttle, who helped to add 110 runs in ninety minutes for the seventh wicket, also reached three figures. So did Kenyon, of Worcestershire, who completed 2,000 runs for the seventh time in ten years. He spent two and a half hours over his first 50, reached 100 in another forty-five minutes and then occupied over an hour in adding 19. Despite a last wicket stand of 42, Worcestershire failed to gain the lead by three runs. Flavell, their fast bowler, took eleven wickets for 155 runs in the match.

Sussex

D. V. Smith c Booth b Flavell	12	— c Booth b Flavell	6
L. J. Lenham b Jenkins	51	— lbw b Flavell	6
K. G. Suttle c and b Flavell	103	— c Booth b Flavell	25
J. M. Parks lbw b Flavell	101	— not out	100
G. H. G. Doggart b Jenkins	9	— c Booth b Coldwell	9
Nawab of Pataudi b Flavell	0	— c Kenyon b Flavell	23
R. T. Webb b Jenkins	0	— not out	14
N. I. Thomson b Flavell	7		
A. E. James b Flavell	0	— b Flavell	4
R. G. Marlar c Flavell b Jenkins	20		
D. L. Bates not out	2		
B 1, l-b 5, w 1	7	B 1, l-b 2	3

1/42 2/82 3/114 4/115 5/116 6/133   312   1/7 2/20   (6 wkts., dec.) 190
7/243 8/243 9/309 (3.31 an over)   3/32 4/49 5/76 6/143

Worcestershire

D. Kenyon c Doggart b Thomson	119	— not out	29
L. Outschoorn c Nawab of Pataudi b Bates	0	— b Bates	0
G. Dews c Doggart b Bates	30	— c and b Bates	24
D. W. Richardson st Webb b Smith	22	— not out	6
R. G. Broadbent st Webb b Marlar	27		
M. J. Horton c Doggart b Bates	43		
R. Booth b Bates	6		
R. O. Jenkins c Webb b Bates	2		
R. Berry not out	26		
J. Flavell b Bates	9		
L. Coldwell run out	10		
B 4, l-b 11, n-b 1	16	L-b 4	4

1/2 2/52 3/103 4/185 5/218 6/243   310   1/3 2/47   (2 wkts.) 63
7/249 8/256 9/268 (2.64 an over)

Worcestershire Bowling

	O.	M.	R.	W.		O.	M.	R.	W.
Flavell	28	5	68	6	....	24	2	87	5
Coldwell	15	2	70	0	....	24	5	63	1
Jenkins	30	4	103	4	....	2	0	12	0
Berry	15	5	40	0	....	4.2	0	25	0
Horton	6	1	24	0					

Sussex Bowling

	O.	M.	R.	W.		O.	M.	R.	W.
Thomson	24	6	49	1	....	6	0	27	0
Bates	30	8	99	6	....	9	1	18	2
Smith	14	6	26	1					
Marlar	29.2	12	72	1	....	1	0	3	0
Suttle	12	2	32	0					
Parks	1	0	1	0					
James	7	5	15	0					
			Lenham		....	2	0	11	0

Umpires: A. Skelding and D. Davies.

At Lord's, August 28, 29, 30. WORCESTERSHIRE beat MIDDLESEX by two wickets.

At Blackpool, August 31, September 2. WORCESTERSHIRE lost to LANCASHIRE by an innings and 56 runs.

YORKSHIRE

President—T. L. TAYLOR

Secretary—J. H. NASH, Old Bank Chambers, Park Row, Leeds, 1

Captain—W. H. H. Sutcliffe

R. Illingworth   County Badge   W. B. Stott

Considering the many problems which beset them, Yorkshire did well to finish third, four places higher than in 1956. During the season W. H. H. Sutcliffe announced that he would not be available to captain the side in 1958; Watson, one of the stalwarts for many years, accepted an appointment with Leicestershire; Lowson, the opening batsman, developed leg trouble and could not play again after mid-June and some of the established players lost form. Against that a number of the younger members showed considerable advancement and although there were certain to be teething troubles while the side was being reorganised, the future looked promising.

The most important difficulty the county had to overcome was to find a successor to Sutcliffe, for no obvious replacement was available. During the two years Sutcliffe held the position he tried his utmost to infuse new life into the team, but it must be said that he did not always receive the support his efforts deserved.

Yorkshire began shakily last year, but improvement came and they steadily climbed the table. Early in August they took over third place and held the position for the rest of the season. After looking a very ordinary side and losing badly to Surrey at The Oval, Yorkshire met with only one reverse in the next seventeen first-class games.

The selection of the side did not always meet with approval. In a number of instances the balance of the bowling was upset in the effort to give stability to the suspect batting. Occasionally only one fast bowler was included, with Appleyard sharing the new ball. The development of a new opening pair in Stott and Taylor did much to improve the side. The left-handed Stott joined the team against Scotland at the end of May and made rapid progress. He scored 181 and 139 in successive matches against Essex and Leicestershire and made another century against Nottinghamshire. His sound defence and strong driving attracted much attention. Taylor also gave several fine displays and against Nottinghamshire at Trent Bridge they began with a hundred in each innings. In the second innings their stand of 230 was the best for any Yorkshire wicket for five years.

Illingworth's good all-round work enabled him to achieve the "double" in all matches for the first time in his career, but even more successful as bowlers were Trueman and Wardle. Late in the season Pickles, a young fast-medium bowler, accomplished a number of splendid performances and looked like developing into a valuable member of the side.

Sheffield United Cricket & Football Club Ltd. Bramall Lane Ground

YORKSHIRE RESULTS

All First-Class Matches—Played 35, *Won* 16, *Lost* 5, *Drawn* 14
County Championship Matches—Played 28, *Won* 13, *Lost* 4,
Drawn 11

COUNTY CHAMPIONSHIP AVERAGES
BATTING

	Birthplace	Mtchs.	Inns.	Not Outs	Runs	100's	Highest Inns.	Aver.
W. Watson	*Bolton-on-Dearne*	20	29	1	1177	3	162	42.03
F. A. Lowson..	*Bradford*	9	14	2	442	2	116	36.83
R. Illingworth..	*Pudsey*	27	40	8	1066	0	97	33.31
W. B. Stott	*Yeadon*	23	39	1	1248	3	181	32.84
K. Taylor	*Huddersfield*	13	23	2	643	1	140*	30.61
D. B. Close ...	*Rawdon*	24	39	2	1068	3	120	28.86
J. V. Wilson...	*Scampston*	28	48	7	1009	0	76	24.60
M. J. Cowan...	*Leeds*	12	7	6	23	0	19*	23.00
W. H. H. Sutcliffe	*Armley*	26	39	8	631	0	75	20.35
J. H. Wardle...	*Ardsley*	24	31	5	422	0	46	16.23
R. K. Platt.....	*Holmfirth*	5	5	3	32	0	17	16.00
R. Appleyard ..	*Bradford*	19	19	7	166	0	63	13.83
F. S. Trueman..	*Stainton*	18	24	5	255	0	63	13.42
D. E. V. Padgett	*Bradford*	14	23	1	264	0	48	12.00
J. G. Binks	*Hull*	28	33	4	210	0	22	7.24
M. Ryan	*Huddersfield*	3	4	1	17	0	7*	5.66
D. Pickles	*Halifax*	12	13	5	17	0	6	2.15

Also batted: J. B. Bolus (*Leeds*) 13; D. Wilson (*Settle*) 0.

* Signifies not out.

BOWLING

	Overs	Maidens	Runs	Wickets	Average
F. S. Trueman	438.2	104	1177	76	15.48
R. Illingworth	682.2	248	1502	86	17.46
J. H. Wardle	819.5	330	1707	92	18.55
D. Pickles	217.4	49	591	31	19.06
R. Appleyard	506.5	122	1302	60	21.70
R. K. Platt	110.1	33	298	11	27.09
D. B. Close	197.2	60	544	20	27.20
M. Ryan	94	19	293	10	29.30
M. J. Cowan	310	59	898	29	30.96
K. Taylor	22	88	39	1	39.00

Also bowled: D. Wilson 24—6—74—1.

Amateur.—W. H. H. Sutcliffe.

At Lord's, April 27, 29, 30. YORKSHIRE lost to M.C.C. by two runs.

At Cambridge, May 1, 2, 3. YORKSHIRE beat CAMBRIDGE UNIVERSITY by 212 runs.

YORKSHIRE v. DERBYSHIRE

At Bradford, May 4, 6. Yorkshire won by nine wickets, taking 14 points. The bowling of Trueman and the batting of Close and Illingworth gave Yorkshire a fine start to their home programme. In the first innings Derbyshire were upset by the pace and fire of Trueman. Yorkshire were also in difficulties against the faster bowlers, but Close played a grand innings, scoring 108 out of 173 (twenty-one 4's) in two and three-quarter hours. On the second day, Illingworth consolidated the position with a fine display. Derbyshire, 116 behind, began disastrously and only a courageous effort by Lee, the former Yorkshire player, saved them from complete rout. Trueman, in the match, took ten wickets for 90 runs.

Derbyshire

A. Hamer c and b Close	38	— b Trueman	1
C. Lee b Trueman	0	— b Trueman	81
J. Kelly b Trueman	14	— b Platt	9
A. C. Revill c Wardle b Trueman	34	— c Wilson b Wardle	1
D. B. Carr c Wilson b Wardle	21	— c Trueman b Wardle	8
G. O. Dawkes lbw b Trueman	2	— absent hurt	—
H. L. Johnson c Wilson b Close	5	— c and b Illingworth	6
D. C. Morgan lbw b Trueman	13	— b Trueman	11
E. Smith b Close	2	— b Trueman	0
C. Gladwin not out	13	— not out	5
L. Jackson run out	0	— b Trueman	2
B 5, l-b 2	7	B 8, l-b 6	14

1/1 2/31 3/70 4/113 5/115 6/119   149
7/121 8/123 9/148 (2.57 an over)

1/10 2/26 3/37 4/63 5/83   138
6/119 7/119 8/132 9/138

Yorkshire

F. A. Lowson c Johnson b Gladwin	15	— not out	9
D. B. Close c Kelly b Smith	108	— c Gladwin b Morgan	7
J. V. Wilson b Gladwin	4	— not out	2
K. Taylor b Gladwin	0		
W. Watson b Jackson	23		
W. H. H. Sutcliffe b Morgan	0		
R. Illingworth c sub b Gladwin	80		
J. H. Wardle b Carr	6		
F. S. Trueman c Morgan b Carr	2		
J. G. Binks b Morgan	10		
R. K. Platt not out	12		
B 1, l-b 4	5	L-b 4, n-b 1	5

1/32 2/36 3/40 4/111 5/112 6/173   265
7/182 8/186 9/212 (3.04 an over)

1/9   (1 wkt.)   23

Yorkshire Bowling

	O.	M.	R.	W.		O.	M.	R.	W.
Trueman	19	2	66	5	....	14.3	5	24	5
Platt	8	3	18	0	....	8	3	26	1
Wardle	18.3	11	24	1	....	14	5	34	2
Close	10	3	26	3	....	8	3	22	0
Illingworth	2	0	8	0	....	4	1	18	1

Derbyshire Bowling

	O.	M.	R.	W.		O.	M.	R.	W.
Jackson	21	4	61	1					
Gladwin	20.5	6	47	4	....	3	1	8	0
Morgan	15	2	50	2	....	2.4	0	10	1
Smith	16	6	60	1					
Carr	12	4	33	2					
Revill	2	0	9	0					

Umpires: A. Skelding and W. E. Phillipson.

At Leicester, May 8, 9, 10. YORKSHIRE drew with LEICESTERSHIRE.

YORKSHIRE v. WARWICKSHIRE

At Middlesbrough, May 11, 13, 14. Drawn, Yorkshire taking two points. Rain seriously interfered with the match and the only interest was the exciting struggle for first innings' lead. Trueman bowled superbly on Saturday, his pace being too much for most of the Warwickshire batsmen. Despite a useful innings by Wilson, Yorkshire were so troubled by the medium paced bowling of Townsend and Singh that when their eighth wicket fell 32 were needed for the lead. Illingworth saw Yorkshire ahead with a fine display of sound defence and judicious hitting. Binks helped him add 58. Four hours were lost on the second day and not a ball could be bowled on Tuesday.

Warwickshire

F. C. Gardner lbw b Trueman	6	— not out	4
N. F. Horner lbw b Trueman	37	— not out	7
M. J. K. Smith b Trueman	4		
A. Townsend c and b Platt	34		
A. V. Wolton c Binks b Trueman	7		
R. T. Spooner lbw b Platt	18		
S. Singh c Padgett b Trueman	21		
K. Ibadulla lbw b Platt	1		
J. D. Bannister run out	0		
R. G. Thompson not out	0		
W. E. Hollies b Trueman	0		
B 8, l-b 4, n-b 2	14		

1/16 2/20 3/93 4/93 5/112 6/132   142   (No wkt.)   11
7/136 8/136 9/142 (2.68 an over)

Yorkshire

F. A. Lowson b Townsend	19		F. S. Trueman c Hollies b Singh	2
D. B. Close c Spooner b Bannister	2		J. G. Binks c Singh b Townsend	12
J. V. Wilson c Townsend b Singh	40		R. K. Platt c Townsend b Singh	0
D. E. V. Padgett b Townsend	0		B 4, l-b 4, n-b 1	9
W. Watson c Townsend b Singh	28			
W. H. H. Sutcliffe b Townsend	4			
R. Illingworth not out	54		1/2 2/36 3/40 4/89 5/94 6/106	170
J. H. Wardle b Townsend	0		7/106 8/111 9/169 (2.12 an over)	

Yorkshire Bowling

	O.	M.	R.	W.	O.	M.	R.	W.
Trueman	18.5	2	46	6	4	3	1	0
Platt	19	4	50	3	3	0	7	0
Illingworth	7	1	22	0	2	0	3	0
Wardle	7	5	6	0	2	2	0	0
Close	1	0	4	0				

Warwickshire Bowling

	O.	M.	R.	W.
Bannister	15	6	38	1
Thompson	6	2	11	0
Townsend	23	7	42	5
Ibadulla	10	6	12	0
Singh	21	10	44	4
Hollies	5	2	14	0

Umpires: C. A. R. Coleman and N. Oldfield.

At Oxford, May 15, 16. YORKSHIRE beat OXFORD UNIVERSITY by an innings and 41 runs.

YORKSHIRE v. SOMERSET

At Leeds, May 18, 20. Yorkshire won by an innings and 48 runs, taking 14 points. They had much the better of the conditions and overplayed Somerset. Put in to bat on a pitch affected by heavy overnight rain, Somerset began with a stand of 64 but collapsed before Wardle and were out for the addition of 80. Yorkshire, thanks mainly to a stylish innings by Taylor, went ahead with three men out. Illingworth batted carefully for three and three-quarter hours and Trueman, hitting at nearly everything, scored 63 of an eighth wicket stand of 116 in seventy minutes. Somerset, 152 behind, again failed against spin on a pitch further damaged by afternoon rain.

Somerset

L. Pickles c Wilson b Wardle	33	— c Taylor b Wardle	13
W. E. Alley c Trueman b Wardle	47	— run out	39
G. M. Tripp c Trueman b Wardle	0	— b Trueman	2
C. L. McCool b Illingworth	1	— c Wilson b Illingworth	18
M. F. Tremlett c Cowan b Wardle	2	— c Trueman b Wardle	5
J. G. Lomax c Wilson b Wardle	1	— c Wilson b Appleyard	0
H. W. Stephenson c Watson b Trueman	29	— c Watson b Wardle	19
B. Langford c Wilson b Wardle	10	— c Wilson b Illingworth	0
J. Hilton not out	12	— not out	1
B. Lobb b Trueman	0	— c Sutcliffe b Illingworth	0
J. W. McMahon c Binks b Wardle	5	— b Wardle	0
B 2, l-b 1, n-b 1	4	L-b 3, n-b 4	7
	144		**104**

1/64 2/64 3/65 4/68 5/78 6/95 7/109 8/127 9/127 (2.44 an over)

1/46 2/49 3/58 4/75 5/76 6/102 7/102 8/103 9/103

Yorkshire

F. A. Lowson c Lomax b Hilton	25	J. H. Wardle b Lobb	3
K. Taylor c Tremlett b Alley	68	F. S. Trueman b Lobb	63
J. V. Wilson lbw b Hilton	0	R. Appleyard not out	0
R. Illingworth lbw b McMahon	97	B 4, l-b 7	11
W. Watson b Alley	26		
W. H. H. Sutcliffe c Stephenson b Hilton	0	(9 wkts., dec.)	296
J. G. Binks b Lobb	3		

M. J. Cowan did not bat

1/49 2/51 3/112 4/159 5/160 6/174 7/180 8/296 9/296 (2.50 an over)

Yorkshire Bowling

	O.	M.	R.	W.		O.	M.	R.	W.
Trueman	12	4	31	2		11	2	32	1
Cowan	4	1	16	0		6	2	14	0
Appleyard	8	4	27	0		8	4	8	1
Wardle	25.2	11	34	7		17.2	8	36	4
Illingworth	10	3	32	1		6	4	7	3

Somerset Bowling

	O.	M.	R.	W.
Lobb	27.1	6	72	3
Lomax	6	2	28	0
McMahon	29	10	62	1
Hilton	33	7	76	3
Langford	2	0	10	0
Alley	21	7	37	2

Umpires: P. Corrall and J. S. Buller.

At Sheffield, May 22, 23, 24. YORKSHIRE drew with WEST INDIES. (See WEST INDIES section.)

At Chesterfield, May 25, 27, 28. YORKSHIRE lost to DERBYSHIRE by 84 runs.

At Paisley, May 29, 30, 31. YORKSHIRE drew with SCOTLAND.

YORKSHIRE v. GLAMORGAN

At Sheffield, June 1, 2, 4. Glamorgan won by seven wickets, taking 12 points. They completed a splendid week, having defeated Lancashire in their previous match. The early Yorkshire batsmen, apart from Lowson, struggled on a good pitch but the tail improved the position. Lowson, sixth out, batted stylishly for four hours. Glamorgan owed most to Devereux for their lead of 11. When the eighth wicket fell at 191, Yorkshire looked to be on top but H. D. Davies kept up his end for an hour and scored ten of a ninth wicket stand of 69. Devereux, lucky at times, nevertheless batted extremely well for three and a half hours. When Yorkshire declared, Glamorgan needed 181 in two hours ten minutes. They made the runs with eight minutes to spare, Hedges and Watkins finishing the match with an unbroken stand of 108 in an hour.

Yorkshire

F. A. Lowson c Pressdee b McConnon	100	— c Watkins b H. D. Davies .. 3
W. B. Stott run out	1	— c Parkhouse b H. D. Davies 40
J. V. Wilson c Hedges b W. G. Davies ..	31	— c Jones b H. D. Davies 53
R. Illingworth b W. G. Davies	0	— c H. G. Davies b H. D. Davies 3
K. Taylor c Shepherd b Watkins	4	— c Parkhouse b H. D. Davies 42
D. E. V. Padgett lbw b Pressdee	32	— run out 4
W. H. H. Sutcliffe b Watkins	25	— c Parkhouse b Pressdee 24
J. H. Wardle b Watkins	8	— not out 0
J. G. Binks st H. G. Davies b Pressdee	20	— b H. D. Davies 8
R. Appleyard c McConnon b Pressdee	18	— not out 0
M. Ryan not out	7	
B 1, l-b 10, n-b 1	12	B 9, l-b 5 14

1/4 2/66 3/66 4/99 5/174 6/176 7/189 258   1/8 2/98 (8 wkts., dec.) 191
8/222 9/249 (2.55 an over)   3/105 4/106 5/112 6/182
                                                    7/183 8/191

Glamorgan

W. G. A. Parkhouse lbw b Wardle	32	— c Taylor b Ryan 20
J. E. McConnon c Wilson b Appleyard ..	6	— c Taylor b Ryan 2
B. Hedges c Wilson b Appleyard	20	— not out 92
W. G. Davies b Wardle	22	
W. E. Jones c Lowson b Wardle	3	
A. J. Watkins b Ryan	58	— not out 54
L. N. Devereux c Lowson b Appleyard ..	83	— c and b Appleyard 10
J. Pressdee c Stott b Wardle	9	
H. G. Davies c Appleyard b Ryan	11	
H. D. Davies c Padgett b Appleyard	10	
D. J. Shepherd not out	9	
B 4, l-b 1, n-b 1	6	L-b 5 5

1/8 2/58 3/62 4/68 5/117 6/151 269   1/40 2/47 3/75 (3 wkts.) 183
7/179 8/191 9/260 (2.03 an over)

Glamorgan Bowling

	O.	M.	R.	W.		O.	M.	R.	W.
H. D. Davies...	23	6	63	0	....	22	1	85	6
Watkins	29	6	71	3	....	16	3	50	0
W. G. Davies..	14	6	29	2	....	3	1	7	0
Shepherd	5	0	23	0	....	3	2	1	0
McConnon	12	3	26	1	....	5	4	5	0
Pressdee	17.4	4	34	3	....	7	2	29	1

Yorkshire Bowling

	O.	M.	R.	W.	O.	M.	R.	W.
Ryan	31	9	72	2	 12	1	49	2
Appleyard	40	15	87	4	.... 13.3	1	62	1
Wardle	49	22	85	4	 10	0	67	0
Illingworth	11	5	18	0				
Taylor	1	0	1	0				

Umpires: W. Place and Harry Elliott.

At Jesmond, June 5, 6. YORKSHIRE beat NORTHUMBERLAND by an innings and 158 runs.

At Manchester, June 8, 10, 11. YORKSHIRE drew with LANCASHIRE.

YORKSHIRE v. NOTTINGHAMSHIRE

At Bradford, June 12, 13. Yorkshire won by eight wickets, taking 14 points. They gained a comfortable victory although at one stage on the second day Nottinghamshire looked to be getting on top. Apart from Winfield, who defended doggedly for two and a quarter hours, the Nottinghamshire batsmen were mostly baffled by the varied spin of Wardle and were out in under three and a quarter hours. Yorkshire also struggled, but Lowson and Stott stood firm and they took the lead with half their wickets in hand. Nottinghamshire, 39 behind, cleared their arrears and played themselves into a useful position during a second wicket stand of 66 between Clay and Winfield. Then the last eight wickets fell for 61 and Yorkshire needed only 97 to win.

Nottinghamshire

R. T. Simpson b Wardle..............	18	— c Sutcliffe b Trueman	2
J. D. Clay b Illingworth	15	— c Trueman b Illingworth	45
H. M. Winfield run out	32	— lbw b Wardle	23
M. Hill c Lowson b Wardle	22	— b Trueman	6
N. Hill c Trueman b Wardle	5	— b Close	6
B. Dooland c Wilson b Wardle	0	— lbw b Trueman	0
P. F. Harvey b Trueman	12	— b Close	15
K. J. Poole c Wilson b Wardle	0	— lbw b Trueman	14
A. K. Walker c Trueman b Wardle ...	0	— c Binks b Trueman	9
A. Jepson b Trueman	5	— c and b Close...........	3
E. J. Rowe not out	1	— not out	3
L-b 1, n-b 2..............	3	B 1, l-b 7, w 1	9

1/27 2/43 3/78 4/92 5/92 6/104   113   1/8 2/74 3/78 4/90 5/90   135
7/106 8/106 9/112 (1.85 an over)   6/105 7/108 8/118 9/121

Yorkshire

F. A. Lowson b Jepson..............	34	— run out	30
D. B. Close c Rowe b Jepson	16	— c Simpson b Walker	27
J. V. Wilson b Walker	3	— not out	13
K. Taylor lbw b Walker	0	— not out	23
R. Illingworth b Dooland.............	12		
W. B. Stott run out	36		
W. H. H. Sutcliffe c Rowe b Walker....	14		
J. H. Wardle c Rowe b Dooland	24		
F. S. Trueman not out	1		
J. G. Binks b Jepson..............	0		
R. K. Platt absent hurt	0		
B 4, l-b 8	12	L-b 3, w 1	4

1/26 2/39 3/39 4/58 5/82 6/118   152   1/54 2/59   (2 wkts.) 97
7/150 8/151 9/152 (2.14 an over)

Yorkshire Bowling

	O.	M.	R.	W.		O.	M.	R.	W.
Trueman	17.3	4	46	2	....	15.3	1	30	5
Platt	3	1	7	0					
Wardle	27	15	36	6	....	27	15	43	1
Illingworth	13	8	21	1	....	23	10	29	1
Close						11	4	17	3
Taylor						2	1	7	0

Nottinghamshire Bowling

	O.	M.	R.	W.		O.	M.	R.	W.
Walker	21	5	43	3	....	11	3	34	1
Jepson	21.3	3	58	3	....	8	1	31	0
Dooland	28	17	39	2	....	6	1	24	0
Simpson						0.2	0	4	0

Umpires: E. Davies and P. Corrall.

At Lord's, June 15, 17, 18. YORKSHIRE beat MIDDLESEX by ten wickets.

YORKSHIRE v. NORTHAMPTONSHIRE

At Harrogate, June 19, 20, 21. Drawn, Northamptonshire taking two points. The pitch was so easy paced that batsmen were in control almost throughout. Lowson and Watson gave Yorkshire their first three-figure start of the season and Watson batted five and a half hours for 162 which included twenty-four 4's. Lively batting from Illingworth followed before Sutcliffe declared. Northamptonshire were in danger of following on when their fifth wicket fell at 105, but Tribe and Manning started a recovery which Manning and Andrew completed. Their stand of 191 was the highest made for the seventh wicket against Yorkshire and each hit the best score of his career. Northamptonshire led by 27 and although Yorkshire lost three wickets cheaply they were never in danger.

Yorkshire

F. A. Lowson c Kelleher b Tribe	47			
W. Watson c Andrew b Tribe	162			
J. V. Wilson b Kelleher	23	— c Allen b Manning	18
D. E. V. Padgett c Kelleher b Manning..	2	— c Andrew b Tyson	5
W. B. Stott c Allen b Tyson	29	— b Manning	20
R. Illingworth not out	64	— not out	34
W. H. H. Sutcliffe st Andrew b Tribe ...	13	— not out	30
J. G. Binks b Manning	16		
L-b 5	5	B 4, l-b 6	10

1/105 2/150 3/187   (7 wkts., dec.) 361   1/10 2/42 3/43   (3 wkts.) 117
4/258 5/286 6/326 7/361 (3.10 an over)

R. Appleyard, D. Wilson and M. J. Cowan did not bat.

Northamptonshire

D. Brookes c Lowson b Appleyard	26	K. V. Andrew run out	76
B. L. Reynolds c Binks b Illing-worth	17	F. H. Tyson c Cowan b Appleyard	16
A. Lightfoot b Cowan	19	M. H. J. Allen not out	3
D. W. Barrick c Sutcliffe b Apple-yard	24	H. R. A. Kelleher c Cowan b Illingworth	16
G. E. Tribe b D. Wilson	28	B 17, l-b 10, n-b 1...........	28
J. Fellows-Smith st Binks b Illing-worth	3		
J. S. Manning b Appleyard	132		

1/39 2/43 3/79 4/102 5/105   388
6/157 7/348 8/349 9/369
(2.62 an over)

Northamptonshire Bowling

	O.	M.	R.	W.		O.	M.	R.	W.
Tyson	25	3	80	1	....	9	3	24	1
Kelleher	16	2	62	1	....	5	2	13	0
Fellows-Smith..	5	1	16	0	....	7	5	9	0
Manning	26.5	7	72	2	....	12	5	23	2
Tribe	34	8	103	3	....	13	5	34	0
Allen	7	1	23	0	....	9	8	4	0

Yorkshire Bowling

	O.	M.	R.	W.
Cowan	39	10	105	1
Appleyard	50	14	98	4
Illingworth	40	19	99	3
D. Wilson	19	4	58	1

Umpires: F. S. Lee and W. Place.

YORKSHIRE v. MIDDLESEX

At Leeds, June 22, 24, 25. Drawn, Middlesex taking four points. After gaining a big lead Middlesex could not force victory, partly because of rain and also because Yorkshire defended solidly in their second innings. Sutcliffe probably regretted his decision to bat for on a lively pitch the Middlesex pace bowlers were menacing. Yorkshire were dismissed cheaply, the last six wickets falling in an hour for 26. Robertson made 65 of an opening stand of 95 and with bright displays coming from Compton and Murray, Middlesex led by 283. Rain held up play shortly after Yorkshire started their second innings and also caused an interruption of seventy minutes on the last afternoon. Watson played another good innings and Wilson and Illingworth batted cautiously.

Yorkshire

W. Watson lbw b Baldry	41	— c Murray b Hurst 50
W. B. Stott b Moss	10	— c Murray b Titmus 13
J. V. Wilson c Murray b Bennett	12	— not out 36
D. E. V. Padgett c Compton b Bennett ..	6	— b Moss 16
R. Illingworth b Moss	19	— not out 30
W. H. H. Sutcliffe c Murray b Moss ...	1	
J. G. Binks b Warr	0	
R. Appleyard b Warr	0	
M. Ryan b Moss	7	
D Wilson b Moss	0	
M. J. Cowan not out.................	2	B 12, l-b 5, n-b 1...... 18

1/19 2/43 3/69 4/72 5/82 6/83 7/83   98   1/53 2/81 3/108   (3 wkts.) 163
8/95 9/95 (1.92 an over)

Middlesex

J. D. Robertson c Illingworth b Cowan 65	D. Bennett st Binks b Appleyard.. 30
R. A. Gale b Cowan 36	J. J. Warr c Padgett b Ryan 7
W. J. Edrich c Binks b Ryan ... 30	R. J. Hurst not out 10
D. C. S. Compton c J. V. Wilson b Ryan 82	A. E. Moss b Illingworth 3
F. J. Titmus lbw b Cowan 6	L-b 10 10
D. O. Baldry b Cowan........... 29	1/95 2/110 3/160 4/175 5/252 381
J. T. Murray c and b Illingworth.. 73	6/253 7/312 8/333 9/373
	(3.28 an over)

Middlesex Bowling

	O.	M.	R.	W.		O.	M.	R.	W.
Moss	16.4	5	43	5	....	14	9	19	1
Warr	18	7	24	2	....	18	5	44	0
Bennett	9	1	26	2	....	8	4	13	0
Baldry	7	2	5	1	....	1	0	7	0
Titmus						13	7	15	1
Hurst						10	5	20	1
Edrich						4	0	10	0
Compton						9	4	17	0

Yorkshire Bowling

	O.	M.	R.	W.
Cowan	32	5	104	4
Ryan	31	4	124	3
Appleyard	39	4	96	1
Illingworth	8.5	1	31	2
D. Wilson	5	2	16	0

Umpires: F. S. Lee and W. Place.

At Tunbridge Wells, June 26, 27. YORKSHIRE beat KENT by ten wickets.

At The Oval, June 29, July 1, 2. YORKSHIRE lost to SURREY by an innings and 19 runs.

At Harrogate, July 3, 4, 5. Yorkshire 146 (R. Illingworth 66, G. Hill four for 20); R.A.F. 124 (R. Subba Row 67, M. J. Cowan four for 31). Drawn. No play first two days.

YORKSHIRE v. ESSEX

At Sheffield, July 6, 8, 9. Yorkshire won by six wickets, taking 14 points. Sutcliffe chose wisely in giving Essex first innings, although his policy did not seem to be successful when Dodds and Barker scored 75 for the first wicket. In a remarkable forty minutes to lunch the Essex total changed to 92 for seven, Wardle taking four for one and Illingworth three for 15 in this period. Greensmith and Ralph added 73 for the eighth wicket and Yorkshire took two hours to capture the last three wickets. Stott dominated the Yorkshire innings, scoring 181, his maiden century, in six and a quarter hours. Drives and hooks brought him most of his two 6's and nineteen 4's. Yorkshire led by 158 and although Insole and Savill made a good effort to check them, they needed only 24 to win. They lost four wickets in scoring them.

Essex

T. C. Dodds c Wilson b Illingworth	34	— c Close b Cowan	11
G. Barker b Wardle....................	48	— b Cowan	24
B. Taylor b Illingworth	4	— st Binks b Wardle	3
D. J. Insole lbw b Illingworth	0	— b Illingworth	47
L. Savill b Wardle	0	— b Cowan	51
M. Bear st Binks b Wardle	0	— c Close b Illingworth	3
G. W. Horrex c Sutcliffe b Wardle	0	— lbw b Wardle	1
W. T. Greensmith not out	55	— c and b Close............	13
R. Ralph c Binks b Close	31	— lbw b Wardle	11
K. C. Preston b Cowan	27	— c Binks b Cowan..........	1
I. King b Cowan	6	— not out	6
B 5, l-b 6	11	B 4, l-b 6	10

1/75 2/89 3/89 4/89 5/89 6/91 7/92   216
8/165 9/212 (2.66 an over)

1/22 2/37 3/43 4/110   181
5/122 6/123 7/139 8/165
9/173

Yorkshire

D. B. Close c Insole b Ralph	7	— b Ralph		4
W. B. Stott c Savill b King	181	— b Ralph		6
J. V. Wilson lbw b Greensmith	20	— lbw b Preston		7
R. Illingworth b Preston	28	— lbw b Ralph		3
W. H. H. Sutcliffe lbw b Ralph	9	— not out		5
D. E. V. Padgett b Greensmith	48	— not out		0
J. B. Bolus st Taylor b King	13			
J. H. Wardle c King b Ralph	20			
J. G. Binks c Barker b Ralph	12			
R. Appleyard not out	6			
B 21, l-b 7, n-b 2	30			

1/7 2/63 3/132 4/164   (9 wkts., dec.) 374   1/10 2/17 3/17   (4 wkts.) 25
5/253 6/325 7/328 8/361 9/374   4/23
(2.75 an over)
M. J. Cowan did not bat.

Yorkshire Bowling

	O.	M.	R.	W.		O.	M.	R.	W.
Cowan	17.5	1	72	2	....	27	2	79	4
Appleyard	12	4	36	0	....	17	5	45	0
Illingworth	22	10	30	3	....	20	12	16	2
Wardle	22	8	55	4	....	24.2	14	26	3
Close	7	2	12	1	....	5	4	5	1

Essex Bowling

	O.	M.	R.	W.		O.	M.	R.	W.
Preston	34	8	83	1	....	4.4	1	9	1
Ralph	31.2	6	98	4	....	4	0	16	3
King	28	11	77	2					
Greensmith	33	13	60	2					
Insole	10	1	26	0					

Umpires: J. Wood and W. Place.

YORKSHIRE v. LEICESTERSHIRE

At Hull, July 10, 11, 12. Yorkshire won by an innings and 12 runs, taking 14 points. They were vastly superior all round. On a lively pitch Leicestershire found the bowling of Appleyard troublesome, but led by van Geloven they rallied and the last four wickets added 103. Yorkshire were placed in a commanding position by their first four batsmen, all left-handers. Stott hit his second century in successive matches, driving and hooking well for five and a quarter hours. Yorkshire took the lead with one wicket down and declared 182 ahead. Trueman began Leicestershire's second breakdown and Illingworth upset the remaining batsmen. Only Hallam and Gardner, in a stand of 67, checked Yorkshire for long.

Leicestershire

G. Lester b Appleyard	6	— b Trueman		0
M. R. Hallam b Appleyard	12	— c Wilson b Illingworth		60
R. A. Diment c Close b Trueman	23	— lbw b Trueman		0
C. H. Palmer b Appleyard	4	— c Binks b Trueman		11
L. R. Gardner lbw b Appleyard	0	— c Trueman b Illingworth		39
J. van Geloven lbw b Appleyard	59	— c Trueman b Close		0
J. Firth b Trueman	9	— c Trueman b Illingworth		5
J. Savage lbw b Appleyard	24	— b Cowan		29
R. C. Smith c Binks b Cowan	22	— lbw b Illingworth		2
C .T. Spencer not out	19	— b Illingworth		0
B. Boshier b Trueman	5	— not out		12
B 4, l-b 3	7	B 2, l-b 10		12

1/17 2/26 3/44 4/44 5/48 6/87 7/138   190   1/0 2/0 3/28 4/95 5/96   170
8/161 9/171 (2.28 an over)   6/115 7/134 8/142 9/144

X

Yorkshire

W. Watson c van Geloven b Savage	49
W. B. Stott c Savage b Boshier	139
J. V. Wilson b Boshier	49
D. B. Close c Gardner b Spencer	60
R. Illingworth c Boshier b Smith	24
W. H. H. Sutcliffe c Spencer b Boshier	18
J. H. Wardle not out	6

M. J. Cowan did not bat.

F. S. Trueman c Hallam b Spencer	3
J. G. Binks b Boshier	0
R. Appleyard not out	2
B 7, l-b 13, w 2	22

1/109 2/237 3/268 (8 wkts., dec.) 372
4/333 5/351 6/360 7/366 8/367
(3.07 an over)

Yorkshire Bowling

	O.	M.	R.	W.		O.	M.	R.	W.
Trueman	16.5	6	38	3	....	12	3	38	3
Cowan	16	5	46	1	....	6.3	3	16	1
Appleyard	22	10	35	6	....	5	3	5	0
Illingworth	9	4	17	0	....	27	11	52	5
Wardle	11	6	21	0	....	19	9	32	0
Close	8	1	26	0	....	12	4	15	1

Leicestershire Bowling

	O.	M.	R.	W.
Spencer	30	3	103	2
Boshier	22	3	54	4
Palmer	18	6	48	0
Smith	24	11	52	1
Savage	12	6	32	1
van Geloven	14	1	51	0
Lester	1	0	10	0

Umpires: W. Place and W. E. Phillipson.

YORKSHIRE v. SURREY

(J. H. Wardle's Benefit)

At Bradford, July 15, 16. Drawn, Surrey taking four points. Although rain prevented play until three o'clock on the second day Surrey made a splendid attempt to win. Put in to bat, they made light of difficult conditions and, led by May, who scored 63 in an hour and three-quarters, they reached 196 for seven by the close. May declared first thing on the last morning and the Surrey bowlers once more rose to the occasion. Yorkshire collapsed completely against Laker and Lock and followed on 105 behind under two-day rules. When the seventh wicket fell in their second innings Yorkshire still needed two runs to clear the arrears and forty-five minutes remained. Wardle and Trueman held out in bad light against good bowling and May gave up the attempt to win with eighteen minutes of extra time remaining.

Surrey

T. H. Clark c Binks b Illingworth	34
M. J. Stewart b Trueman	4
B. Constable run out	26
P. B. H. May b Trueman	63
K. F. Barrington c Trueman b Illingworth	2
E. A. Bedser lbw b Wardle	23

A. J. McIntyre c Binks b Appleyard	22
G. A. R. Lock not out	15
B 1, l-b 6	7

1/8 2/65 3/66 (7 wkts., dec.) 196
4/88 5/156 6/156 7/196
(2.80 an over)

J. C. Laker, P. J. Loader and A. V. Bedser did not bat.

Yorkshire

W. Watson c E. Bedser b Lock	14	— b Lock 11
W. B. Stott b Lock	8	— lbw b E. Bedser 10
J. V. Wilson c May b Laker	9	— lbw b Laker 28
D. B. Close b Lock	30	— c Lock b Laker 20
R. Illingworth b Laker	3	— lbw b Lock............. 16
D. E. V. Padgett lbw b Laker	0	— c May b Lock 3
W. H. H. Sutcliffe c Barrington b Lock..	5	— c Stewart b Lock......... 0
J. H. Wardle b Laker	1	— not out 16
F. S. Trueman b Laker	6	— not out 3
R. Appleyard c Barrington b Laker	7	
J. G. Binks not out	0	
B 4, l-b 4	8	B 4, l-b 10 14

1/22 2/27 3/37 4/48 5/48 6/67   91   1/22 2/30 3/69   (7 wkts.) 121
7/74 8/78 9/84 (2.67 an over)   4/91 5/91 6/94 7/103

Yorkshire Bowling

	O.	M.	R.	W.	O.	M.	R.	W.
Trueman	18	5	46	2				
Appleyard	11.4	1	27	1				
Wardle	22	10	44	1				
Illingworth	16	3	53	2				
Close	2	0	19	0				

Surrey Bowling

	O.	M.	R.	W.	O.	M.	R.	W.
A. Bedser......	3	0	6	0	 4	2	14	0
Loader	4	0	11	0				
Laker	14.1	7	23	6	 29	18	35	2
Lock	13	1	43	4	 26	10	44	4
				E. Bedser	9	5	14	1

Umpires: C. S. Elliott and Jim Langridge.

YORKSHIRE v. GLOUCESTERSHIRE

    At Scarborough, July 17, 18, 19. Drawn, Gloucestershire taking four points. Yorkshire's batting again disappointed and Gloucestershire gave a much more impressive display. Milton, the acting captain, put Yorkshire in on a difficult pitch and only Close and Stott offered serious resistance. The last five wickets fell for 17. Gloucestershire went ahead during a fourth-wicket stand of 125 between Young and Milton who each batted well against a varied attack. Yorkshire, 90 behind when Milton declared, stood only three ahead when their fifth wicket fell with almost an hour left. Wardle again showed his ability to defend in a crisis and with Sutcliffe helped to save the game. Mortimore, the Gloucestershire off-break bowler, caused most concern to Yorkshire during the match and was never mastered.

Yorkshire

W. B. Stott c Etheridge b Brown	20	— c Brown b Mortimore	35
K. Taylor b Brown	0	— c Milton b Smith	15
J. V. Wilson b Brown	2	— c Eagar b Mortimore	17
D. B. Close run out	57	— lbw b Mortimore	18
R. Illingworth b Cook	8	— c Eagar b Cook	0
W. H. H. Sutcliffe c Young b Mortimore	12	— not out	11
J. H. Wardle c Carpenter b Mortimore	4	— not out	16
R. Appleyard c Smith b Cook	6		
J. G. Binks c Etheridge b Cook	0		
D. Pickles st Etheridge b Mortimore	6		
M. J. Cowan not out	0		
B 4, l-b 2, n-b 1	7	L-b 5	5

1/0 2/14 3/44 4/68 5/105 6/107 7/115   **122**   1/17 2/68 3/76   (5 wkts.) **117**
8/116 9/122 (1.93 an over)   4/87 5/93

Gloucestershire

T. W. Carpenter b Pickles	0	D. Hawkins b Pickles	5
D. M. Young c Close b Pickles	84	A. S. Brown not out	5
R. B. Nicholls c Wilson b Illing-		B 4, l-b 3	7
worth	27		
M. A. Eagar lbw b Illingworth	0	1/6 2/63 3/63 (5 wkts., dec.) 212	
C. A. Milton not out	84	4/188 5/198 (2.52 an over)	

J. Mortimore, R. J. Etheridge, D. R. Smith and C. Cook did not bat.

Gloucestershire Bowling

	O.	M.	R.	W.		O.	M.	R.	W.
Smith	9	2	19	0	....	7	5	12	1
Brown	12	7	14	3	....	10	3	24	0
Cook	17.4	5	38	3	....	21	10	40	1
Mortimore	24	14	44	3	....	24	18	28	3
					Hawkins	3	1	8	0

Yorkshire Bowling

	O.	M.	R.	W.
Cowan	8	1	25	0
Pickles	13	1	39	3
Wardle	24	9	47	0
Illingworth	19	5	43	2
Close	6	1	21	0
Appleyard	14	3	30	0

Umpires: C. S. Elliott and John Langridge.

At Nottingham, July 20, 22, 23. YORKSHIRE beat NOTTINGHAMSHIRE by 205 runs.

At Bournemouth, July 24, 25, 26. YORKSHIRE beat HAMPSHIRE by five wickets.

At Leeds, July 25, 26, 27. ENGLAND beat WEST INDIES in the Fourth Test by an innings and five runs. (See WEST INDIES section.)

At Worcester, July 27, 29, 30. YORKSHIRE beat WORCESTERSHIRE by seven wickets.

At Hove, July 31, August 1, 2. YORKSHIRE beat SUSSEX by nine wickets.

YORKSHIRE v. LANCASHIRE

At Sheffield, August 3, 5, 6. Drawn, Lancashire taking four points. After four successive victories Yorkshire were overplayed by their traditional rivals and were fortunate to escape a heavy defeat. Wharton, who hit the first hundred for Lancashire against Yorkshire since 1949, batted three and a quarter hours and hit sixteen 4's in 102, but he was missed before scoring and escaped again when 42 and 90. Smith shared an opening stand of 136 and good innings also came from Grieves and Washbrook. Yorkshire lost Taylor in the opening over and, despite a defiant innings by Wilson, never really recovered. Following on 200 behind, they again fared badly, but thunderstorms restricted play to an hour and three-quarters on the last day, and although Washbrook claimed the extra half-hour Lancashire could not force a win.

Lancashire

A. Wharton b Wardle	102	A. Wilson b Trueman	0
C. S. Smith c Binks b Appleyard	42	R. Tattersall not out	3
J. T. Ikin c Appleyard b Trueman	16	B 4, l-b 4, w 2, n-b 1	11
C. Washbrook lbw b Pickles	49		
K. Grieves c Illingworth b Pickles	68		
J. D. Bond b Trueman	0		
J. Dyson lbw b Illingworth	29		
J. B. Statham b Trueman	6	1/136 2/148 3/196 4/218 5/223	351
T. Greenhough c Appleyard b Trueman	25	6/282 7/299 8/329 9/331 (2.56 an over)	

Yorkshire

W. B. Stott b Smith	20	— c Bond b Statham	0
K. Taylor lbw b Statham	3	— c Bond b Greenhough	32
J. V. Wilson run out	45	— b Tattersall	6
D. B. Close c Bond b Smith	5	— b Tattersall	2
R. Illingworth c Grieves b Greenhough	14	— not out	32
W. H. H. Sutcliffe c Bond b Greenhough	14	— not out	6
J. H. Wardle b Statham	6		
F. S. Trueman c Statham b Tattersall	31		
J. G. Binks c Bond b Tattersall	0	— c Wilson b Smith	4
R. Appleyard c Smith b Tattersall	4		
D. Pickles not out	0		
B 2, l-b 4, n-b 3	9	L-b 2, n-b 2	4

1/5 2/33 3/39 4/70 5/101 6/109 7/113   151   1/0 2/19 3/25   (5 wkts.) 86
8/134 9/138 (2.35 an over)   4/44 5/60

Yorkshire Bowling

	O.	M.	R.	W.	O.	M.	R.	W.
Trueman	31	9	75	5				
Pickles	23	6	70	2				
Appleyard	22	5	50	1				
Wardle	31	11	75	1				
Illingworth	27	9	55	1				
Close	3	0	15	0				

Lancashire Bowling

	O.	M.	R.	W.	O.	M.	R.	W.
Statham	13	2	30	2	12	6	23	1
Smith	15	5	30	2	11	1	15	1
Tattersall	9.5	2	24	3	13	9	7	2
Greenhough	17	7	50	2	15	3	37	1
Dyson	9	3	8	0	5	5	0	0

Umpires: T. W. Spencer and L. H. Gray.

YORKSHIRE v. WORCESTERSHIRE

At Scarborough, August 7, 8, 9. Drawn, Yorkshire taking four points. Although rain ruined the match, an exciting struggle took place for the lead. Yorkshire owed nearly everything to Watson and Close who, on an easy pitch, scored all but 96 of the total. Close, in dashing form, hit fifteen 4's in a chanceless 93 made in two and a quarter hours. Watson, more subdued, batted three hours forty minutes for his century. A careful innings by Peter Richardson helped Worcestershire to make a reasonable start but rain ended play shortly after half-past three on the second day and a resumption was not possible until three o'clock the next afternoon. Only ninety minutes were left and Worcestershire needed 93 for the lead with five wickets left. Appleyard, with three wickets in five balls, put Yorkshire on top and the last wicket fell to the fifth ball of the final over of extra time.

Yorkshire

W. B. Stott b Chesterton	29	
W. Watson b Flavell	102	
J. V. Wilson c Dews b Coldwell	1	
D. B. Close c Flavell b Coldwell	93	
R. Illingworth b Flavell	20	
W. H. H. Sutcliffe b Flavell	10	
J. H. Wardle c Outschoorn b Chesterton	16	
F. S. Trueman st Booth b Chesterton	3	
J. G. Binks not out	3	
R. Appleyard c Broadbent b Chesterton	5	
D. Pickles b Flavell	5	
L-b 3, w 1	4	
	—	
	291	

1/47 2/50 3/216 4/229 5/247 6/270 7/276 8/278 9/284
(3.34 an over)

Worcestershire

D. Kenyon b Trueman	34	
P. E. Richardson c Watson b Illingworth	72	
G. Dews c Trueman b Wardle	30	
D. W. Richardson b Wardle	0	
R. G. Broadbent c Pickles b Appleyard	63	
L. Outschoorn c Wilson b Illingworth	0	
M. J. Horton c Wilson b Wardle	52	
R. Booth c Close b Appleyard	1	
J. Flavell c Trueman b Appleyard	0	
G. H. Chesterton not out	2	
L. Coldwell b Wardle	0	
B 5, l-b 7	12	
	—	
	266	

1/86 2/125 3/127 4/197 5/198 6/257 7/258 8/258 9/266
(2.63 an over)

Worcestershire Bowling

	O.	M.	R.	W.
Flavell	27.5	0	80	4
Coldwell	20	6	72	2
Chesterton	34	4	109	4
Horton	4	0	23	0
D. Richardson	1	0	3	0

Yorkshire Bowling

	O.	M.	R.	W.
Trueman	20	6	41	1
Pickles	17	3	55	0
Appleyard	20	3	65	3
Wardle	25.5	6	48	4
Illingworth	18	7	45	2

Umpires: T. W. Spencer and L. H. Gray.

YORKSHIRE v. KENT

At Leeds, August 10, 12, 13. Drawn, Yorkshire taking two points. They owed most to a devastating spell by Trueman just when Kent looked to be getting the upper hand in the fight for first innings lead. Three hours were lost while the pitch dried on the first day and the second day was a complete blank, so there was never a chance of a definite finish. Yorkshire were in a subdued mood but they batted consistently although not very effectively. Kent were 107 for three when Trueman swung the game by dismissing Pretlove and Catt with successive balls. Cowdrey hit a brisk 58 which robbed Yorkshire of bonus points but Trueman sent him and Ridgway back in three balls. Altogether, Trueman took five for 10 in six overs and the last wicket fell with three minutes of extra time left.

Yorkshire

W. B. Stott b Brown	1
W. Watson c Cowdrey b Page	36
J. V. Wilson c Ridgway b Brown	6
D. B. Close c Cowdrey b Page	22
D. E. V. Padgett c Catt b Pretlove	27
R. Illingworth c Catt b Brown	29
J. H. Wardle c Cowdrey b Brown	39
F. S. Trueman b Ridgway	14
J. G. Binks b Ridgway	10
R. Appleyard not out	1
D. Pickles b Ridgway	0
N-b 3	3

1/2 2/24 3/57 4/72 5/111 6/163   188
7/167 8/187 9/188 (2.37 an over)

Kent

A. H. Phebey c Illingworth b Appleyard	16
R. C. Wilson lbw b Wardle	13
J. Pettiford c Appleyard b Illingworth	32
M. C. Cowdrey b Trueman	58
J. F. Pretlove lbw b Trueman	3
A. L. Dixon c Wilson b Trueman	0
A. W. Catt c Binks b Trueman	0
G. W. Cook st Binks b Wardle	9
F. Ridgway c Close b Trueman	0
J. C. T. Page not out	8
A. S. Brown lbw b Wardle	9
L-b 2, w 1	3

1/28 2/34 3/96 4/107 5/107   151
6/108 7/127 8/127 9/135
(2.74 an over)

Kent Bowling

	O.	M.	R.	W.
Ridgway	22.4	3	65	3
Brown	28	5	61	4
Page	22	9	46	2
Pretlove	6	2	13	1

Yorkshire Bowling

	O.	M.	R.	W.
Trueman	11	4	26	5
Pickles	3	0	7	0
Wardle	12	4	32	3
Appleyard	14	4	36	1
Illingworth	15	3	47	1

Umpires: N. Oldfield and W. E. Phillipson.

At Bradford, August 14, 15, 16. YORKSHIRE v. WEST INDIES abandoned without a ball bowled.

At Cheltenham, August 17 19. YORKSHIRE lost to GLOUCESTERSHIRE by two wickets.

At Birmingham, August 21, 22, 23. YORKSHIRE drew with WARWICKSHIRE.

At Taunton, August 24, 26, 27. YORKSHIRE beat SOMERSET by seven wickets.

At Cardiff, August 28, 29. YORKSHIRE beat GLAMORGAN by four runs.

YORKSHIRE v. M.C.C.

At Scarborough, August 31, September 2, 3. Yorkshire won by eight wickets. They were always on top of the useful-looking side opposed to them and gained a comfortable victory. Rain restricted play to four hours on the first day when M.C.C. fared badly against a keen attack. Yorkshire, with Stott playing a fine innings, went ahead with only two wickets down and looked like building a big lead until Tyson and Warr caused a breakdown. The last six wickets fell for 42. M.C.C. collapsed completely when facing arrears of 94 and lost their first seven wickets for 75. Pickles, in one spell of lively fast bowling, took three wickets in six balls. Taylor and Tyson stopped the rot with a stand of 55. Tyson's 63 took only forty-five minutes and then Yorkshire hit off the 77 runs they required in under an hour.

M.C.C.

R. A. Gale lbw b Appleyard	34	— b Trueman		9
W. J. Edrich b Pickles	13	— b Appleyard		6
A. C. Walton c Close b Pickles	27	— b Pickles		4
D. J. Insole c Wardle b Pickles	8	— b Pickles		0
E. R. Dexter c Binks b Wardle	33	— b Pickles		0
B. Taylor b Appleyard	0	— c Close b Trueman		61
T. E. Bailey b Appleyard	4	— lbw b Appleyard		7
G. Goonesena c Binks b Wardle	2	— b Appleyard		5
F. H. Tyson not out	24	— c Wardle b Trueman		63
J. J. Warr b Trueman	6	— not out		6
D. J. Shepherd c Padgett b Trueman	8	— c Wilson b Illingworth		4
B 5, l-b 8, n-b 1	14	B 5		5

1/48 2/50 3/68 4/117 5/129 6/129   173
7/135 8/135 9/159

1/12 2/19 3/19 4/19 5/35   170
6/59 7/75 8/130 9/163

Yorkshire

W. B. Stott b Goonesena	91	— b Tyson		2
D. E. V. Padgett b Bailey	43			
W. H. H. Sutcliffe b Goonesena	29	— lbw b Tyson		1
D. B. Close b Warr	37	— not out		34
J. V. Wilson c and b Tyson	26			
R. Illingworth lbw b Tyson	23	— not out		35
J. H. Wardle b Tyson	0			
F. S. Trueman c Walton b Warr	1			
R. Appleyard b Warr	2			
J. G. Binks not out	0			
D. Pickles b Warr	1			
B 4, l-b 2, w 6, n-b 2	14	B 4, l-b 1, n-b 1		6

1/85 2/143 3/180 4/225 5/259 6/259   267
7/260 8/266 9/266

1/3 2/11   (2 wkts.) 78

Yorkshire Bowling

	O.	M.	R.	W.		O.	M.	R.	W.
Trueman	14.4	3	35	2	....	13	5	20	3
Pickles	12	3	31	3	....	9	1	29	3
Appleyard	22	3	64	3	....	7	0	40	3
Wardle	7	2	18	2	....	1	1	0	0
Illingworth	3	1	11	0	....	7	1	76	1

M.C.C. Bowling

	O.	M.	R.	W.		O.	M.	R.	W.
Tyson	19	2	61	3	....	6	1	33	2
Warr	16.2	2	52	4	....	4	0	12	0
Bailey	12	1	27	1					
Dexter	8	2	26	0					
Goonesena	17	3	58	2	....	3	0	15	0
Shepherd	11	3	29	0					
Gale						2	0	12	0

Umpires: H. G. Baldwin and A. R. Coleman.

THE UNIVERSITIES IN 1957

CAMBRIDGE

Captain—G. GOONESENA (Royal College, Colombo and Queens')
Hon. Secretary—E. R. DEXTER (Radley and Jesus)
Captain for 1958—E. R. DEXTER
Hon. Secretary—D. J. GREEN (Burton-on-Trent G. S. and Christ's)

Following a most disappointing home season at Fenner's where of the twelve chief fixtures seven were lost and five drawn, Cambridge showed considerable improvement on tour. After drawing with Nottinghamshire at Trent Bridge they gained a capital win at Liverpool over Lancashire who, dismissed twice on the second day, were beaten by an innings and 31 runs. Later, at Bristol, similar success over Gloucestershire put the side in good heart, so that when they encountered Oxford at Lord's they took command of the game from the outset.

Although the Dark Blues won the toss and elected to bat they received a shock when Wheatley delivered a decisive blow by taking five wickets for 15 runs. Oxford never really recovered, the match ending with a win for the Light Blues by an innings and 186 runs, the heaviest defeat ever recorded against the Dark Blues in the history of University matches.

For this achievement Cambridge owed a very great deal to their captain, Gamini Goonesena, who, with a great innings of 211, the highest ever played by a Cambridge man against Oxford, also bowled his leg spinners with success, and concluded his career at Cambridge by capturing the last wicket in the match.

Two record partnerships were established after Cambridge left Fenner's. In the University match Goonesena, in conjunction with Cook, who made 111, set up fresh figures for the seventh wicket of 289, previously held by F. R. Brown and J. T. Morgan with 257 in 1930. Another record, this time for the ninth wicket, in which Cook also made 111, in association with Smith, created new figures of 200 against Lancashire.

Despite these performances, the batting honours of the season easily went to Dexter, a stylist without parallel at either University. His innings of 185 against Lancashire at Fenner's was the forerunner of other achievements, and when on the same day he was in the running for being the first batsman in the country to reach a thousand runs with P. B. H. May and T. W. Graveney, the latter gained the distinction with 102 before luncheon. In July, Dexter was invited to replace T. E. Bailey in the England twelve chosen for Headingley, but an injury compelled him to decline.

James, after a disappointing series of batting at Fenner's, re-established himself with a sparkling display of driving in a score of 168 at Bristol. Besides Cook and Dexter, three other batsmen made their initial centuries in first-class cricket: Barber 106 against Hampshire, Smith 103 not out against Warwickshire, and McLachlan 101 against Essex.

Before the team left Fenner's a blow fell when Goonesena was seized with sinus trouble. Fortunately he recovered in time to give his supreme performance against Oxford.

Goonesena and Smith headed the bowling averages with 53 and 54 wickets respectively; they received effective support from Wheatley whose fast-medium action earned 41 wickets. Cook showed his all-round qualities with several good spells of off-spin bowling; Pieris also kept a steady length and occasionally caused some disturbance by some spirited tail-end batting.

Cambridge found a new wicket-keeper in Swift, a Freshman from St. Peter's, Adelaide, who had about the best record of anyone in this position for quite a number of years. With 38 caught and ten stumped he was certainly outstanding.

Goonesena, Dexter and Smith were chosen to play for the Gentlemen against the Players at Lord's.   P. PIGGOTT.

CAMBRIDGE UNIVERSITY RESULTS
First-Class Matches—Played 19, *Won* 3, *Drawn* 8, *Lost* 8

AVERAGES
First-Class Matches
BATTING

	Matches	Inns.	Not Outs	Runs	100's	Highest Innings	Average
R. G. Newman	2	3	0	123	0	44	41.00
E. R. Dexter	18	32	1	1209	2	185	39.00
G. Goonesena	13	23	0	753	1	211	32.73
G. W. Cook	18	30	5	742	2	111*	29.68
I. M. McLachlan	14	24	1	613	1	101	26.65
C. S. Smith	16	28	7	536	1	103*	25.52
R. W. Barber	10	17	1	405	1	106	25.31
R. M. James	17	29	1	652	1	168	23.28
D. J. Green	17	30	2	650	0	75	23.21
R. Bairamian	2	3	1	45	0	24	22.50
P. I. Pieris	12	19	3	359	0	55*	22.43
M. Kasippillai	6	11	2	201	0	62*	22.33
P. D. Croft	4	5	0	98	0	43	19.60
G. Edge	2	4	0	55	0	33	13.75
B. T. Swift	17	23	7	160	0	25	10.00
J. T. Davies	4	8	0	66	0	29	8.25
S. A. V. Fakir	5	9	0	61	0	18	6.77
O. S. Wheatley	17	21	10	60	0	17*	5.45
J. R. Rutherford	8	15	2	63	0	10	4.84
J. Norman	2	3	0	12	0	9	4.00
J. M. Watson	2	3	0	4	0	3	1.33

Also batted: J. A. Bokhari 1 and 7; M. S. Meeson 21 and 4; D. J. Smith 0 and 6.

* Signifies not out.

BOWLING

	Overs	Maidens	Runs	Wickets	Average
G. Goonesena..........	407.5	95	1135	53	21.41
C. S. Smith	472.5	96	1213	54	22.46
R. M. James	158.1	41	446	16	27.87
O. S. Wheatley	433	103	1240	41	30.24
E. R. Dexter	107.2	24	333	11	30.27
R. W. Barber	78.2	16	295	9	32.77
G. W. Cook...........	415.1	113	1192	30	39.73
S. A. V. Fakir........	11	0	44	1	44.00
P. I. Pieris	319	81	910	20	45.50
J. R. Rutherford	123.1	21	383	8	47.87
M. Kasippillai	34	6	124	2	62.00

Also bowled: R. Bairamian 1.1—0—6—1; J. A. Bokhari 1.2—0—7—0; G. Edge 2—1—2—0; D. J. Green 2.5—1—4—0; I. M. McLachlan 1—0—3—0; D. J. Smith 12.4—1—37—2; J. M. Watson 1—1—0—0.

CAMBRIDGE UNIVERSITY v. SURREY

At Cambridge, April 27, 29. Surrey won by ten wickets. The Champions were too strong for the University at this early stage of the season. The Fenner's pitch proved more helpful than usual to bowlers and Alec Bedser and Loader dealt deadly blows before resistance came from Goonesena, Cook and Swift. Cook gave a very sound display. Surrey were inclined to sacrifice wickets seeking runs after receiving a sound start from Clark and Stewart, but with Eric Bedser and Laker hitting well on Monday morning the county led by 100. Then Laker and Lock made the most of the responsive turf, although Cook and Green batted soundly.

Cambridge University

R. W. Barber c Stewart b A. Bedser	8	— c Lock b A. Bedser........	4
I. A. Bokhari c McIntyre b Loader	1	— c Lock b Laker...........	7
D. J. Green c Lock b A. Bedser	0	— b Laker................	23
E. R. Dexter c Fletcher b A. Bedser....	11	— b Lock	7
R. M. James hit wkt b Loader	7	— c Stewart b Lock........	11
G. Goonesena c Constable b Lock	20	— c A. Bedser b Lock.......	2
C. S. Smith c McIntyre b Laker	4	— b Laker	2
G. W. Cook not out	64	— c Barrington b Lock	24
B. T. Swift c Stewart b Lock	17	— b Laker	14
D. J. Smith c Laker b Lock	0	— c Barrington b Lock	6
O. S. Wheatley c Barrington b Lock	7	— not out	1
B 1	1	B 1	1

1/9 2/9 3/9 4/23 5/29 6/48 7/58   140
8/114 9/126

1/5 2/17 3/40 4/43 5/57   104
6/63 7/71 8/89 9/103

Surrey

T. H. Clark c Cook b Goonesena	42	— not out	7
M. J. Stewart b Cook	40	— not out	0
B. Constable c Green b C. Smith	18		
K. Barrington b C. Smith.............	16		
G. A. R. Lock c Swift b Goonesena	12		
D. G. W. Fletcher c Cook b Goonesena..	6		
E. A. Bedser b C. Smith	52		
A. J. McIntyre c C. Smith b Wheatley..	2		
J. C. Laker c Wheatley b D. Smith	44		
P. J. Loader c James b D. Smith	1		
A. V. Bedser not out	0		
B 5, l-b 2	7		

1/80 2/90 3/119 4/126 5/136 6/155   240
7/162 8/217 9/234

(No wkt.)   7

Surrey Bowling

	O.	M.	R.	W.		O.	M.	R.	W.
Loader	16	2	43	2	....	7	2	8	0
A. Bedser......	10	5	10	3	....	11	6	17	1
Laker	16	4	46	1	....	24	7	38	4
Lock	21.4	8	40	4	....	19.5	7	40	5

Cambridge Bowling

	O.	M.	R.	W.
C. Smith	22	4	47	3
Wheatley	9	1	39	1
Dexter	4	1	15	0
D. Smith	12.4	1	37	2
Goonesena	22	3	59	3
Cook	10	1	36	1
Bokhari.......	1.2	0	7	0
Green	1	1	0	0

Umpires: F. S. Lee and H. Palmer.

CAMBRIDGE UNIVERSITY v. YORKSHIRE

At Cambridge, May 1, 2, 3. Yorkshire won by 212 runs, thanks mainly to the splendid fast bowling of Trueman. A patient performance by Lowson, who batted four hours and hit a 6 and thirteen 4's, and a more enterprising knock by Watson, put Yorkshire in a strong position. Cambridge owed much to the Freshman, Green, who defied Yorkshire for three hours. Yorkshire did not enforce the follow-on, and when Cambridge wanted 347 to win, Trueman was again in form, making his match analysis eleven wickets for 75 runs. Close took the last four wickets in the course of six overs. Cook, who carried his bat through the innings, gave another highly promising batting performance for the University.

Yorkshire

F. A. Lowson st Swift b Goonesena.....154			
D. B. Close c Green b Smith 0	— c Goonesena b James	46	
K. Taylor c Barber b Goonesena 36	— lbw b Cook	44	
D. E. V. Padgett c Swift b Wheatley ... 36	— b Rutherford	21	
W. Watson c Green b Cook 73	— not out	0	
W. H. H. Sutcliffe c Smith b Goonesena.. 8	— b Cook	11	
R. Illingworth b Goonesena............ 2	— c Swift b Smith	15	
J. H. Wardle c Cook b Goonesena 9	— not out	7	
F. S. Trueman b Cook 13			
J. G. Binks not out 11			
B 2, l-b 4 6	B 4, l-b 8, w 1	13	

1/1 2/62 3/169 4/256   (9 wkts., dec.) 348   1/41 2/83 (5 wkts., dec.) 157
5/288 6/298 7/312 8/325 9/348   3/111 4/145 5/156
R. K. Platt did not bat.

Cambridge University

R. W. Barber c Watson b Trueman	....	1	— c Binks b Trueman	....	8
G. W. Cook c Taylor b Trueman	......	0	— not out	....	61
C. S. Smith b Trueman		1	— lbw b Close	....	0
D. J. Green b Trueman	....	75	— c Binks b Trueman	......	0
I. M. McLachlan b Trueman	....	0	— b Platt	....	15
E. R. Dexter b Close	....	24	— c Lowson b Close	....	31
R. M. James c Trueman b Close	....	0	— c and b Trueman	....	8
G. Goonesena b Trueman	......	42	— c Taylor b Close	....	3
J. R. Rutherford b Close	....	1	— b Trueman	....	3
B. T. Swift b Trueman	....	5	— b Close	....	0
O. S. Wheatley not out	....	0	— c Platt b Close	....	1
B 7, l-b 2, n-b 1		10	L-b 2, n-b 2	....	4

1/1 2/4 3/17 4/17 5/89 6/89   159
7/135 8/154 9/154

1/8 2/16 3/16 4/42 5/99   134
6/122 7/132 8/132 9/132

Cambridge Bowling

	O.	M.	R.	W.		O.	M.	R.	W.
Smith	21	5	50	1	....	8	1	29	1
Wheatley	24	6	85	1	....	5	1	24	0
Rutherford	6	0	26	0	....	11	2	24	1
Goonesena	36	5	109	5	....	3	0	20	0
Cook	22.5	4	66	2	....	4	0	7	2
Dexter	3	1	3	0	....	4	0	14	0
McLachlan	1	0	3	0					
James						12	2	26	1

Yorkshire Bowling

	O.	M.	R.	W.		O.	M.	R.	W.
Trueman	19	7	37	7	....	10	1	38	4
Platt	12	5	29	0	....	10	1	24	1
Wardle	12	7	29	0	....	24	14	34	0
Taylor	3	1	5	0					
Illingworth	8	0	19	0	....	5	3	5	0
Close	15	6	30	3	....	16.4	9	29	5

Umpires: W. F. Price and H. Palmer.

CAMBRIDGE UNIVERSITY v. ESSEX

At Cambridge, May 4, 5, 6. Drawn. Unimaginative batting by the University and Essex ruined the chances of a definite result, despite three declarations. From a Cambridge viewpoint, the only satisfactory performances produced in the match were the centuries by McLachlan and Dexter. They alone treated the bowling on its merit and refused to be hurried into making mistakes. The other University batsmen, showing signs of immaturity, were rarely comfortable against an attack which lacked fire, and often accuracy.

Cambridge University

R. W. Barber c Ralph b King	25	— b Preston	17
G. W. Cook b Preston	0	— lbw b Bailey	2
D. J. Green b Preston	44	— c Smith b Preston	5
I. M. McLachlan st Taylor b King	101	— lbw b Ralph	33
E. R. Dexter b Preston	24	— not out	100
G. Goonesena b Preston	29	— c Insole b King	3
R. M. James lbw b Bailey	3	— not out	5
C. S. Smith b King	24		
J. R. Rutherford run out	10	— lbw b Preston	6
B. T. Swift not out	6		
B 5, l-b 4, n-b 1	10	L-b 3	3

1/4 2/63 3/96 4/129   (9 wkts., dec.) 276
5/190 6/205 7/251 8/270 9/276
O. S. Wheatley did not bat.

1/9 2/23   (6 wkts., dec.) 174
3/24 4/37 5/128 6/136

Essex

G. Barker c Swift b Goonesena	29	— b Cook	57
L. A. Savill b Goonesena	21	— st Swift b Goonesena	14
B. Taylor lbw b Smith	15	— not out	23
D. J. Insole c Swift b Cook	8		
T. E. Bailey c Goonesena b Wheatley	66		
M. Bear lbw b Goonesena	5	— not out	22
G. Smith c James b Wheatley	64		
W. T. Greensmith lbw b James	14		
R. Ralph b Wheatley	4		
K. C. Preston not out	5		
B 1, l-b 6	7	L-b 5	5

1/42 2/57 3/72 4/79   (9 wkts., dec.) 238
5/86 6/197 7/214 8/219 9/238
I. King did not bat.

1/58 2/78   (2 wkts.) 121

Essex Bowling

	O.	M.	R.	W.	O.	M.	R.	W.
Bailey	22.1	5	57	1	16	3	31	1
Preston	24	6	55	4	14	4	38	3
Ralph	13	3	26	0	14	2	39	1
Greensmith	19	2	47	0	3	2	25	0
King	27	8	67	3	9	1	38	1
Insole	7	0	14	0				

Cambridge Bowling

	O.	M.	R.	W.	O.	M.	R.	W.
Smith	28	6	64	1	4	0	10	0
Wheatley	20	5	48	3	3	0	13	0
Goonesena	26	5	66	3	8	0	32	1
Rutherford	7	1	21	0	7	3	16	0
Cook	12	2	26	1	10	5	10	1
James	2.5	0	6	1				
Barber					10	1	35	0

Umpires: F. S. Lee and H. Palmer.

CAMBRIDGE UNIVERSITY v. SOMERSET

At Cambridge, May 8, 9, 10. Drawn. That the University were able to draw this match was almost entirely due to the first innings performance of their captain, Goonesena. He fell four short of a century after hitting thirteen 4's, and added 126 in a sixth wicket stand with Dexter. Heavy rain seriously affected the pitch, but this was not entirely responsible for the University's pathetic batting in the second innings. Somerset needed 176 to win in less than two hours, and though Lomax, Alley and Stephenson made gallant efforts to force the pace, they were still 34 behind with three wickets standing at the end.

Cambridge University

J. T. Davies c Tremlett b Lobb	1	— b Hilton	11
G. W. Cook b Lobb	24	— c Tremlett b Hilton	22
D. J. Green b Lobb	3	— c Stephenson b Lobb	2
I. M. McLachlan b Lobb	0	— c McMahon b Lobb	2
E. R. Dexter lbw b McMahon	64	— b Hilton	5
M. Kasippillai c Alley b Lobb	0	— c Lomax b Hilton	3
G. Goonesena b Lobb	96	— c McMahon b Lobb	4
C. S. Smith c Tremlett b McCool	30	— not out	0
J. R. Rutherford b Lobb	4	— c Lomax b Lobb	0
B. T. Swift b McMahon	19	— c Tremlett b Hilton	0
O. S. Wheatley not out	15	— run out	0
B 15, l-b 8	23	B 4, l-b 1	5

1/4 2/14 3/14 4/33 5/37 6/163   279   1/37 2/37 3/40 4/43 5/49   54
7/211 8/215 9/243   6/49 7/53 8/53 9/54

Somerset

J. G. Lomax b Wheatley	12	— c and b Cook	25
J. Hilton c Dexter b Smith	9	— c Dexter b Goonesena	8
P. B. Wight c Goonesena b Wheatley	49	— c Swift b Dexter	0
C. L. McCool lbw b Goonesena	45	— c Swift b Goonesena	18
J. W. McMahon c Kasippillai b Goonesena	0		
W. E. Alley c Swift b Smith	0	— lbw b Cook	43
L. Pickles c McLachlan b Goonesena	26	— not out	7
M. F. Tremlett c Swift b Wheatley	2	— b Cook	7
H. W. Stephenson c Swift b Smith	9	— c Green b Cook	23
G. Tripp c Swift b Smith	5	— not out	4
B. Lobb not out	0		
N-b 1	1	B 6, l-b 1	7

1/21 2/21 3/113 4/113 5/114 6/128   158   1/53 2/58 3/90   (7 wkts.) 142
7/134 8/148 9/154   4/90 5/106 6/131 7/131

Somerset Bowling

	O.	M.	R.	W.		O.	M.	R.	W.
Lobb	28	5	63	7	....	10.2	3	23	4
Lomax	16	5	32	0	....	2	0	6	0
Alley	12	4	34	0					
McCool	10.3	0	37	1					
McMahon	29	10	78	2	....	2	0	6	0
Hilton	4	1	12	0	....	5	2	8	5
Tremlett					....	2	1	6	0

Cambridge Bowling

	O.	M.	R.	W.		O.	M.	R.	W.
Smith	13	0	46	4	....	7	0	35	0
Wheatley	12	4	30	3	....	3	0	13	0
Goonesena	13.5	4	44	3	....	12	4	21	2
Rutherford	5	0	24	0	....	1	0	5	0
Cook	7	1	13	0	....	17	5	45	4
Dexter					....	3	0	16	1

Umpires: W. F. Price and H. Palmer.

CAMBRIDGE UNIVERSITY v. WORCESTERSHIRE

At Cambridge, May 11, 13, 14. Drawn. Cautious batting on a good pitch, but against steady bowling, made the game dull for onlookers. D. Richardson, Dews and Booth infused some excitement into the match with fine stroke-play for the county, but only Dexter and, to a certain extent, Green, followed the example when Cambridge went in. A resolute partnership of 114 by Dews and D. Richardson enabled Worcestershire to set Cambridge to make 256 in three hours. The start was disastrous, three men falling for four runs, but Green and Dexter checked the breakdown in a stand of 75. Nevertheless, Cambridge had only three wickets left at the finish.

Worcestershire

P. E. Richardson c Davies b Wheatley ..	20	— lbw b Smith 6
D. Kenyon b Wheatley	4	— lbw b Smith 6
G. Dews b Cook	8	— c Swift b Rutherford 89
D. W. Richardson c Dexter b Cook	86	— b Wheatley 65
R. G. Broadbent lbw b Wheatley	7	— not out 23
M. J. Horton c Wheatley b Rutherford ..	49	— c Goonesena b Rutherford . 2
R. Booth c Cook b Rutherford	56	
R. O. Jenkins c and b Rutherford	14	
R. Berry b Goonesena	1	
L. Coldwell lbw b Smith..............	9	
J. Aldridge not out	2	
B 2, l-b 4, n-b 1	7	L-b 3 3

1/7 2/21 3/79 4/101 5/176 6/181   263   1/8 2/13   (5 wkts., dec.) 194
7/205 8/206 9/261   3/127 4/192 5/194

Cambridge University

J. T. Davies c Kenyon b Horton........	29	— b Aldridge 0
G. W. Cook c Dews b Aldridge	19	— b Aldridge 0
D. J. Green c Kenyon b Horton	15	— b Berry 48
I. M. McLachlan c P. Richardson b Horton	11	— run out 1
E. R. Dexter b Aldridge	70	— c Kenyon b Berry 32
G. Goonesena lbw b Horton	0	— c P. Richardson b Horton . 5
M. Kasippillai c Berry b Horton	6	— b Jenkins 30
C. S. Smith not out	33	— not out 5
J. R. Rutherford b Horton..............	10	— not out 1
B. T. Swift b Aldridge................	0	
O. S. Wheatley b Aldridge	0	
B 4, l-b 4, n-b 1	9	L-b 1, w 1 2

1/21 2/64 3/65 4/96 5/96 6/122   202   1/0 2/3 3/4   (7 wkts) 124
7/161 8/185 9/186   4/79 5/92 6/114 7/119

Cambridge Bowling

	O.	M.	R.	W.		O.	M.	R.	W.
Smith	12	2	27	1	....	19	5	43	2
Wheatley	15	3	31	3	....	23	9	33	1
Cook	19	8	57	2	....	15	4	53	0
Goonesena	22	6	72	1	....	15	2	42	0
Rutherford	15.5	2	53	3	....	14.2	3	20	2
Kasippillai	4	0	16	0					

Worcestershire Bowling

	O.	M.	R.	W.		O.	M.	R.	W.
Aldridge	12.5	5	31	4	....	7	0	20	2
Coldwell	10	3	24	0	....	5	2	8	0
Horton	40	19	76	6	....	19	8	38	1
Jenkins	8	2	21	0	....	21	11	47	1
Berry	24	12	41	0	....	10	7	9	2

Umpires: F. S. Lee and H. Palmer.

At Cambridge, May 15, 16, 17. CAMBRIDGE UNIVERSITY drew with WEST INDIES. (See WEST INDIES section.)

CAMBRIDGE UNIVERSITY v. SUSSEX

At Cambridge, May 18, 20, 21. Sussex won by an innings and 148 runs. In the absence of Goonesena, the captain, and C. S. Smith, Cambridge were no match for Sussex. Weak, hesitant batting caused them to be dismissed in two and three-quarter hours by a moderate attack on a good pitch, and then Sussex proceeded to flay the weakened University attack. Suttle hit fourteen 4's in a masterly exhibition and Parks, who helped him to put on 151, turned from defence to attack, finishing with one 6 and thirteen 4's in his 124. Cambridge made another poor start, losing half their wickets for 55, and although James and Pieris held up the Sussex bowlers for a time the pace and swing of Thomson and Bates brought the county a comfortable victory with ample time to spare.

Cambridge University

J. T. Davies c Webb b Bates	0	— b Thomson	1
G. W. Cook b Bates	3	— lbw b Bates	27
D. J. Green b Smith	15	— b Bates	0
G. Edge c Suttle b Thomson	7	— b Thomson	10
E. R. Dexter b Bates	18	— b Bates	8
R. M. James c Foreman b Thomson	4	— lbw b Bell	26
P. I. Pieris c Smith b Bell	13	— c and b Marlar	37
M. Kasippillai b Smith	11	— c Webb b Thomson	7
J. R. Rutherford b Smith	7	— not out	5
B. T. Swift not out	18	— b Bates	0
O. S. Wheatley c Smith b Bates	2	— b Thomson	0
L-b 1, n-b 1	2	B 11, l-b 4, n-b 5	20

1/3 2/9 3/20 4/45 5/45 6/54 7/73   **100**   1/11 2/28 3/46 4/46 5/55   **141**
8/77 9/81   6/111 7/136 8/136 9/138

Sussex

D. V. Smith retired hurt	27	R. V. Bell not out 14
L. J. Lenham c Davies b Wheatley	16	
K. G. Suttle c Kasippillai b Cook	91	
J. M. Parks b Swift b Pieris	124	
G. Potter c Pieris b Rutherford	63	B 5, l-b 8, n-b 3 16
D. J. Foreman c Swift b Kasippillai	17	
N. I. Thomson c Rutherford b Kasippillai	21	1/49 2/200 3/293 (6 wkts., dec.) **389** 4/324 5/366 6/389

R. T. Webb, R. G. Marlar and D. L. Bates did not bat.

Sussex Bowling

	O.	M.	R.	W.	O.	M.	R.	W.
Thomson	15	7	27	2	19	8	27	4
Bates	14	5	35	4	20.4	6	48	4
Smith	10	4	20	3				
Bell	3	0	16	1	10	4	21	1
Marlar					6	1	25	1

Cambridge Bowling

	O.	M.	R.	W.
Rutherford	14	1	50	1
Wheatley	36	9	78	1
Pieris	38	8	142	1
Cook	13	3	45	1
Dexter	4	0	20	0
Kasippillai	9	1	36	2
James	1	0	2	0

Umpires: K. McCanlis and H. Palmer.

CAMBRIDGE UNIVERSITY v. LANCASHIRE

At Cambridge, May 22, 23, 24. Drawn. Two brilliant individual efforts marked this match. First, Dexter, driving magnificently, made 185 for Cambridge of which 105 came before lunch on the first day. In all, he batted four hours, hitting three 6's and twenty-seven 4's. It was considered the finest innings for the University since David Sheppard made 239 at Worcester in 1952. Lancashire, however, lacked the help of Statham and Tattersall. The next day Grieves hit the first double century of his career, staying five and a half hours for his 224 which included thirty-six 4's.

Cambridge University

I. M. McLachlan lbw b Wharton	8	— not out		62
S. A. V. Fakir b Wharton	7	— c Collins b Greenhough		6
D. J. Green b Kelly	10	— not out		17
E. R. Dexter b Collins	185			
R. M. James st Jordan b Hilton	39			
R. G. Newman b Wharton	36			
P. I. Pieris b Wharton	0			
M. Kasippillai c Wharton b Greenhough	17			
J. R. Rutherford c Jordan b Greenhough	0			
B. T. Swift not out	14			
O. S. Wheatley st Jordan b Greenhough	3			
B 5, l-b 9, w 1	15	L-b 1		1

1/14 2/15 3/27 4/148 5/239   334   1/37   (1 wkt.) 86
6/239 7/295 8/295 9/327

Lancashire

A. Wharton c Fakir b Pieris	21	T. Greenhough b James	2
J. Dyson c Swift b Wheatley	7	E. A. Kelly not out	16
J. T. Ikin b Pieris	5	J. Jordan absent hurt	0
G. Pullar c sub b Pieris	15	B 2, l-b 6, w 1	9
K. Grieves c Dexter b James	224		
M. J. Hilton b Pieris	13		
C. Washbrook lbw b James	43	1/13 2/30 3/33 4/71 5/99 6/226	400
R. Collins b Wheatley	45	7/324 8/331 9/400	

Lancashire Bowling

	O.	M.	R.	W.		O.	M.	R.	W.
Kelly	17	5	61	1	....	5	3	12	0
Wharton	12	3	43	4	....	4	1	8	0
Greenhough ...	24.5	4	86	3	....	11	3	18	1
Collins	10	2	47	1	....	6	0	24	0
Dyson	12	0	48	0					
Hilton	14	4	34	1					
Ikin						5	0	23	0

Cambridge Bowling

	O.	M.	R.	W.
Wheatley	28	4	107	2
Rutherford	19	4	59	0
Pieris	32	7	117	4
Kasippillai	16	3	59	0
James	14.1	1	46	3
Dexter	3	0	3	0

Umpires: John Langridge and H. Palmer.

CAMBRIDGE UNIVERSITY v. KENT

At Cambridge, May 25, 27, 28. Kent won by 117 runs. A great all-round performance by Leary gave them success in an exciting finish. After sharing an unbroken stand of 187 with Phebey in two hours twenty minutes, of which he scored 102, Leary proceeded to spin his side to victory. Set to make 273 to win in two and three-quarter hours, the University batsmen played lightheartedly, which proved costly against Leary, who took five wickets for 34 runs. Pieris and Kasippillai endeavoured to retrieve the situation, but their efforts came too late.

Kent

A. H. Phebey b Smith	59	— not out 100
J. M. Allen c Smith b Dexter	35	— c Dexter b Wheatley....... 8
S. E. Leary run out	27	— not out 102
D. E. Disbury b Pieris	11	
A. R. B. Neame c and b Cook	9	
D. G. Ufton c Norman b Pieris	9	
J. F. Pretlove c Dexter b Wheatley	54	
M. C. Cowdrey c Watson b Cook	54	
D. J. Halfyard c Pieris b Cook	20	
J. C. T. Page c Kasippillai b Cook	3	
A. Brown not out	10	
B 10, l-b 6, n-b 2	18	B 6, l-b 3, w 2, n-b 2 .. 13

1/81 2/126 3/135 4/145 5/153   309   1/36   (1 wkt., dec.) 223
6/163 7/269 8/292 9/292

Cambridge University

S. A. V. Fakir run out	6	—	lbw b Halfyard	15	
C. S. Smith c Leary b Page	51	—	c Pretlove b Leary	22	
G. W. Cook c Leary b Brown	46	—	st Pretlove b Leary	0	
E. R. Dexter hit wkt b Pretlove	31	—	b Halfyard	8	
R. M. James c Leary b Halfyard	31	—	b Brown	10	
M. S. Meeson c Page b Pretlove	21	—	c Neame b Page	4	
P. I. Pieris not out	55	—	st Pretlove b Leary	34	
M. Kasippillai not out	9	—	c Page b Leary	48	
J. M. Watson (did not bat)		—	c Disbury b Leary	0	
J. Norman (did not bat)		—	b Page	3	
O. S. Wheatley (did not bat)		—	not out	0	
B 6, l-b 4	10		B 8, l-b 3	11	

1/13 2/106 3/112	(6 wkts., dec.) 260	
4/155 5/171 6/235		

1/28 2/42 3/66 4/88 5/121   155
6/121 7/151 8/152 9/152

Cambridge Bowling

	O.	M.	R.	W.		O.	M.	R.	W.
Smith	22	2	71	1	....	12	1	27	0
Wheatley	18	2	51	1	....	11	3	29	1
Dexter	12	3	36	1					
Cook	26.2	8	74	4	....	17	3	45	0
Pieris	21	4	59	2	....	9	1	38	0
Fakir						7	0	32	0
James						15.1	3	39	0

Kent Bowling

	O.	M.	R.	W.		O.	M.	R.	W.
Halfyard	24	7	42	1	....	8	1	36	2
Brown	31	7	53	1	....	8	0	48	1
Page	32	13	74	1	....	3.2	0	4	2
Allan	17	7	41	0	....	3	0	22	0
Leary	2	0	6	0	....	10	2	34	5
Pretlove	8	0	34	2					

Umpires: L. H. Gray and H. Palmer.

CAMBRIDGE UNIVERSITY v. MIDDLESEX

At Cambridge, May 29, 30, 31. Middlesex won by nine wickets, outplaying a side considerably weakened by examinations. Cambridge were put out in three hours on a good pitch, only a stand of 59 for the fourth wicket by Dexter and James checking the Middlesex attack. In command from the start, Middlesex took the lead during a fourth wicket partnership of 197 in two and a quarter hours by Delisle and Robertson who each hit centuries. Delisle's 130 took only two and three-quarter hours and included one 6 and twenty 4's. Cambridge did a little better in the second innings but Middlesex needed only six to win.

Cambridge University

J. M. Watson c Bennett b Warr	1	— c Hurst b Warr	3
G. W. Cook lbw b Hurst	30	— b Hurst	44
G. Edge lbw b Baldry	5	— b Robins	33
E. R. Dexter b Bennett	46	— lbw b Robins	0
R. M. James lbw b Robins	25	— st Murray b Hurst	24
P. I. Pieris c Murray b Warr	11	— c Murray b Hurst	5
M. Kasippillai b Hurst	8	— not out	62
R. Bairamian b Hurst	20	— c Murray b Warr	24
O. S. Wheatley not out	5	— b Warr	2
J. R. Rutherford b Bennett	1	— c Murray b Bennett	6
J. Norman run out	0	— run out	9
B 11, w 2	13	B 13, w 5	18

1/10 2/20 3/52 4/111 5/123 6/131   165   1/19 2/76 3/77 4/112   230
7/151 8/160 9/165   5/117 6/128 7/193 8/203
9/216

Middlesex

R. A. Gale c Norman b Cook	23
D. A. Bick c Bairamian b Cook	67
D. O. Baldry c Kasippillai b Dexter	53
G. P. S. Delisle run out	130
J. D. Robertson not out	105
W. E. Russell not out	8 — not out	6
R. V. C. Robins (did not bat)	— c Norman b Bairamian .. 0
J. T. Murray (did not bat)	— not out	0
L-b 3, n-b 1	4

1/46 2/130 3/156 4/353   (4 wkts., dec.) 390   1/0   (1 wkt.) 6

D. Bennett, J. J. Warr and R. J. Hurst did not bat.

Middlesex Bowling

	O.	M.	R.	W.	O.	M.	R.	W.
Bennett	15	3	36	2	15	2	49	1
Warr	12	7	13	2	17.4	6	34	3
Baldry	5	1	9	1				
Robins	14	0	46	1	33	5	92	2
Hurst	18.5	8	40	3	24	6	37	3
Russell	1	0	8	0				

Cambridge Bowling

	O.	M.	R.	W.
Wheatley	18	4	78	0
Rutherford	14	2	54	0
Pieris	16	6	31	0
Dexter	7	1	22	1
Cook	36	11	114	2
Kasippillai	5	2	13	0
James	18	3	72	0
Edge	2	1	2	0
Bairamian	1.1	0	6	1
Watson	1	1	0	0

Umpires: F. S. Lee and H. Palmer.

CAMBRIDGE UNIVERSITY v. FREE FORESTERS

At Cambridge, June 8, 10, 11. Free Foresters won by 15 runs. The match was notable, not only for the good finish but for the re-appearance of Ian Craig, Australian's newly appointed captain, in first-class cricket in England. He was in the country taking a pharmaceutical course. Craig did not disappoint, giving two splendid displays. In the first innings he batted carefully while getting his eye in but his century took only three hours, the second 50 coming in an hour. His 127 included seventeen 4's. Buckingham helped him add 115 for the second wicket. Rain limited play to fifty-five minutes on the second day. Cambridge declared 75 behind after good innings by McLachlan, Goonesena and Dexter. Foresters followed suit and Cambridge were set to get 202 in two and a quarter hours. They looked to be winning comfortably until the last four wickets fell for four runs.

Free Foresters

A. D. Buckingham c Smith b Goonesena	61	— c McLachlan b Smith	4
D. E. Blake c Dexter b Smith	8	— b Cook	50
I. D. Craig b Smith	127	— c Wheatley b Cook	44
A. R. B. Neame c Cook b Dexter	19	— st Swift b Goonesena	12
F. R. Brown b Dexter	8		
F. G. Mann b Smith	41	— not out	4
J. P. Fellows-Smith b Pieris	3	— st Swift b Goonesena	10
B. A. Barnett b Smith	22		
R. V. C. Robins not out	10		
T. A. Hall b Smith	0		
B 1, l-b 1, n-b 5	7	L-b 1, n-b 1	2

1/18 2/133 3/222 4/226   (9 wkts. dec.) 306
5/232 6/255 7/293 8/298 9/306

1/16 2/93   (5 wkts., dec.) 126
3/106 4/121 5/126

C. J. M. Kenny did not bat.

Cambridge University

C. S. Smith b Brown	11	— st Barnett b Kenny	13
I. M. McLachlan c and b Hall	82	— b Hall	0
D. J. Green lbw b Brown	2	— c Fellows-Smith b Kenny	61
E. R. Dexter b Kenny	46	— b Kenny	37
G. Goonesena lbw b Kenny	50	— b Kenny	51
R. M. James b Hall	3	— b Hall	0
P. I. Pieris not out	14	— b Kenny	1
B. T. Swift c Mann b Kenny	3	— b Kenny	0
G. W. Cook not out	4	— run out	12
R. Bairamian (did not bat)		— not out	1
O. S. Wheatley (did not bat)		— lbw b Kenny	1
B 10, l-b 1, w 2, n-b 3	16	B 5, l-b 2, w 1, n-b 1	9

1/30 2/36 3/130 4/195   (7 wkts., dec.) 231
5/203 6/212 7/216

1/0 2/33 3/110 4/121   186
5/122 6/182 7/184 8/184
9/186

Cambridge Bowling

	O.	M.	R.	W.		O.	M.	R.	W.
Smith	19	3	44	5	....	7	0	28	1
Wheatley	8	1	22	0	....	4	0	10	0
Dexter	21	4	60	2					
Goonesena	25	2	91	1	....	1.1	0	3	2
Pieris	18	5	43	1	....	7	0	34	0
Cook	16	4	39	0	....	11	1	49	2

Free Foresters Bowling

	O.	M.	R.	W.		O.	M.	R.	W.
Hall	15	4	32	2	....	8	2	29	2
Kenny	22	7	51	3	....	14.5	0	45	7
Fellows-Smith	5	1	19	0	....	11	0	53	0
Brown	22	2	78	2	....	6	0	34	0
Robins	5	2	13	0	....	1	0	16	0
Neame	9	2	22	0					

Umpires: L. H. Gray and H. Palmer.

CAMBRIDGE UNIVERSITY v. DERBYSHIRE

At Cambridge, June 12, 13, 14. Derbyshire won by six wickets and the University finished their home programme without a victory. Cambridge failed to make the most of an easy-paced pitch and, despite a useful innings by Dexter, seven wickets were down for 134 before Croft and Pieris brought some improvement by adding 53. Derbyshire began slowly but on the second day Carr gave a fine display for three hours. Even so, Cambridge were only 13 behind on first innings. Again they disappointed and Derbyshire, needing 154 to win, did so easily although the first two wickets fell for 13.

Cambridge University

I. M. McLachlan b Smith	26	— b Morgan	34
S. A. V. Fakir c Dawkes b Jackson	0	— lbw b Jackson	2
D. J. Green b Smith	19	— b Jackson	8
E. R. Dexter b Morgan	47	— run out	22
G. Goonesena st Dawkes b Revill	6	— c Carr b Morgan	13
R. M. James b Morgan	16	— lbw b Hall	49
P. D. Croft b Hall	43	— lbw b Johnson	14
G. W. Cook b Hall	7	— b Hall	8
P. I. Pieris b Hall	25	— c Dawkes b Hall	0
C. S. Smith not out	15	— b Hall	10
B. T. Swift b Smith	1	— not out	1
B 4, n-b 1	5	B 4, l-b 1	5

1/8 2/37 3/54 4/79 5/113 6/115   **210**   1/6 2/18 3/51 4/78 5/81   **166**
7/134 8/187 9/190   6/103 7/139 8/164 9/165

Derbyshire

C. Lee b Pieris	41	— b Smith	1
M. Bentley c and b Smith	2	— b Smith	10
J. Kelly b Smith	0	— st Swift b Goonesena	28
A. C. Revill c Cook b Goonesena	18	— c Green b Fakir	83
D. B. Carr c Swift b Smith	88	— not out	26
G. O. Dawkes b Goonesena	12	— not out	0
H. L. Johnson not out	33		
D. C. Morgan c Green b Smith	12		
E. Smith c Green b Smith	0		
L. Jackson c Swift b Pieris	9		
D. Hall lbw b Smith	0		
B 2, l-b 6	8	B 5, l-b 1	6

1/9 2/9 3/44 4/112 5/133 6/177   **223**   1/2 2/13 3/92   (4 wkts.) **154**
7/201 8/201 9/216   4/152

Derbyshire Bowling

	O.	M.	R.	W.		O.	M.	R.	W.
Jackson	18	9	26	1	....	15	8	19	2
Morgan	21	8	42	2	....	18	13	15	2
Hall	19	5	57	3	....	19.3	5	64	4
Smith	25.4	10	47	3	....	19	11	40	0
Revill	7	1	33	1	....	1	0	7	0
Johnson						5	0	16	1

Cambridge Bowling

	O.	M.	R.	W.		O.	M.	R.	W.
Smith	28	5	66	6	....	11	0	38	2
Dexter	7	3	9	0	....	5	1	14	0
Goonesena	29	10	68	2	....	13	5	28	1
Pieris	26	7	60	2	....	5	0	19	0
Cook	5	2	12	0	....	4	0	26	0
James						2	0	9	0
Fakir						3	0	10	1
Green						1.5	0	4	0

Umpires: K. McCanlis and H. Palmer.

At Nottingham, June 15, 17, 18. CAMBRIDGE UNIVERSITY drew with NOTTINGHAM-SHIRE.

At Liverpool, June 19, 20. CAMBRIDGE UNIVERSITY beat LANCASHIRE by an innings and 31 runs.

At Birmingham, June 22, 24, 25. CAMBRIDGE UNIVERSITY drew with WARWICK-SHIRE.

At Bristol, June 26, 27. CAMBRIDGE UNIVERSITY beat GLOUCESTERSHIRE by an innings and 33 runs.

At Bournemouth, June 29, July 1, 2. CAMBRIDGE UNIVERSITY lost to HAMPSHIRE by 99 runs.

At Lord's, July 3, 4, 5. CAMBRIDGE UNIVERSITY drew with M.C.C.

At Lord's, July 6, 8, 9. CAMBRIDGE beat OXFORD in the University Match by an innings and 186 runs. (See OTHER MATCHES AT LORD'S.)

OXFORD

Captain—A. C. WALTON (Radley and Lincoln)

Hon. Secretary—J. A. BAILEY (Christ's Hospital and University)

Captain for 1958—J. A. BAILEY

Hon. Secretary—M. A. Eagar (Rugby and Worcester)

Most unusually, Oxford University won three games in the Parks, beating Middlesex, Free Foresters and the Army, but on the whole they were an uninspired and uninspiring side. The crowning though not unexpected disappointment was their inept performance at Lord's. Cambridge were clearly the superior side, but Oxford should have made a better fight.

It is understandable that a captain is loath to give invitations to play against Cambridge until he is convinced that the men are worthy. It soon became clear that there were two or three obvious choices and, no doubt, prolonged uncertainty had an adverse effect on individual performances because players did not show their best form while in a state of suspense. That Oxford never developed into a really sound team was the more surprising because, with the University season finished, Walton, Bailey, Gibson and Bowman all played notable parts in first-class county cricket.

As captain, Walton had his problems, not least among them being the search for an opening pair of batsmen. Hobbs always batted well and confidently, making several useful scores, including a fine 151 against the Army. With Gibson rarely available because of examinations, however, no one else showed pretentions to forming a satisfactory partner for Hobbs.

Judged on their previous records, the strength of the batting clearly rested upon Walton and Eagar, but, though playing well on occasion, neither showed the consistency required or expected if the side were to score adequately. It was extraordinary how often the combined efforts of the lower batsmen—Melville, Woodcock and Scott—repaired earlier omissions and extricated the side from dire trouble.

A University team should be able to make up for other shortcomings by keen fielding, and Oxford in this way certainly saved many runs. Walton and Eagar always set a good example and Scott proved an excellent wicket-keeper.

The choice of bowlers against Cambridge must have presented another big difficulty. In Bailey, Phillips and Clube, Walton had at his disposal three old blues, though Phillips and Clube, never able to spare much time for cricket were, in the end, not chosen for Lord's. Bailey, a certainty as one of the pace bowlers, would have gained a better average with a little more luck.

The other opener, Bowman, gained confidence as the season progressed and often bowled extremely well. Adequate spinners to succeed J. M. Allan were hard to find, but Woodcock and Wilson filled the bill quite well, though generally having to bowl on unhelpful pitches.

C. VENABLES.

OXFORD UNIVERSITY RESULTS

First-Class Matches—Played 15, *Won* 3, *Drawn* 2, *Lost* 10

AVERAGES
First-Class Matches

BATTING

	Matches	Inns.	Not Outs	Runs	100's	Highest Innings	Average
C. D. Melville	11	21	2	715	2	142	37.63
R. Jowett	10	19	2	489	0	122	28.76
M. A. Eagar	14	27	1	647	0	99	24.88
I. M. Gibson	8	16	1	358	1	100*	23.86
A. C. Walton	12	23	0	514	0	95	22.34
J. D. Currie	4	8	0	164	0	38	20.50
J. A. D. Hobbs	15	30	1	581	0	95	20.03
J. M. Kumleben	8	16	1	294	1	100	19.60
R. G. Woodcock	14	27	5	390	0	57	17.72
M. D. Scott	14	26	4	380	0	52	17.27
R. Bowman	9	16	5	172	0	75	15.63
R. A. Bowles	3	6	0	92	0	43	15.33
A. Wolfe-Murray	3	5	2	43	0	25	14.33
G. S. Seaton	3	6	0	73	0	26	12.16
L. D. Watts	3	5	0	50	0	26	10.00
J. A. Bailey	10	16	4	97	0	23*	8.08
R. W. Wilson	11	20	5	100	0	17*	6.66
S. V. M. Clube	4	5	1	25	0	9*	6.25
J. B. Phillips	3	5	2	9	0	5	3.00
M. J. A. Matthews	2	4	0	9	0	5	2.25

Also batted: D. A. C. Marshall 54* and 14*; J. G. Raybould 2 and 1.
A. L. Hichens and G. B. Gauntlett each played in one match but did not bat.

BOWLING

	Overs	Maidens	Runs	Wickets	Average
M. J. A. Matthews	28	8	77	6	12.83
I. M. Gibson	52.4	11	186	8	23.25
J. A. Bailey	363.5	112	910	37	24.59
S. V. M. Clube	102	15	299	12	24.91
R. Bowman	313.5	61	995	34	29.26
R. G. Woodcock	415	108	1139	35	32.54
R. W. Wilson	395	91	1078	31	34.77
R. Jowett	142	25	432	12	36.00
A. Wolfe-Murray	42	2	155	3	51.66
C. D. Melville	109	22	368	6	61.33
J. B. Phillips	74	16	255	4	63.75

Also bowled: A. L. Hichens 13—3—25—0; J. G. Raybould 10—1—30—0; A. C. Walton 1.3—0—8—0.

OXFORD UNIVERSITY v. LANCASHIRE

At Oxford, May 1, 2, 3. Lancashire won by ten wickets. A missed catch offered by Wharton off the third ball of the match cost the University dearly. The left-hander went on to score the first century of the season. With the exception of Grieves, the remainder of the county batsmen were kept subdued by the pace of Bailey and the spin of Woodcock. Oxford fared badly against the spin bowlers, and, losing their last eight wickets for 34 runs, followed on 161 behind. Five men were out for 68, but a fine innings by Eagar, cousin of the Hampshire captain, avoided an innings beating.

Lancashire

A. Wharton c Walton b Woodcock	106		
J. Dyson b Bailey	16		
G. A. Edrich c Scott b Woodcock	21		
C. Washbrook st Scott b Woodcock	16		
K. Grieves b Bailey	75		
J. T. Ikin c and b Clube	10		
M. J. Hilton st Scott b Woodcock	0		
J. Jordan c Hobbs b Bailey	15	— not out	6
T. Greenhough c Scott b Bailey	4	— not out	0
J. B. Statham b Phillips	0		
R. Tattersall not out	0		
L-b 2	2		

1/19 2/112 3/150 4/175 5/190 6/193   265   (No wkt.) 6
7/244 8/256 9/265

Oxford University

I. Gibson lbw b Hilton	25	— c Ikin b Tattersall	15
J. A. D. Hobbs b Statham	33	— b Wharton	1
M. D. Scott st Jordan b Hilton	12	— st Jordan b Hilton	10
A. C. Walton lbw b Tattersall	5	— b Statham	8
L. D. Watts b Statham	1	— lbw b Greenhough	12
M. A. Eagar lbw b Greenhough	20	— c Edrich b Hilton	73
C. D. Melville c Edrich b Tattersall	2	— st Jordan b Greenhough	2
R. G. Woodcock c Hilton b Tattersall	0	— c Jordan b Greenhough	9
J. A. Bailey c Statham b Greenhough	1	— c Wharton b Hilton	17
S. V. M. Clube c Greenhough b Tattersall	4	— c Washbrook b Statham	4
J. B. Phillips not out	0	— not out	3
N-b 1	1	B 7, l-b 4	11

1/45 2/70 3/72 4/74 5/81 6/99 7/99   104   1/10 2/23 3/30 4/62 5/68   165
8/100 9/104   6/81 7/114 8/155 9/158

Oxford Bowling

	O.	M.	R.	W.	O.	M.	R.	W.
Bailey	18.1	4	60	4				
Phillips	21	7	58	1				
Gibson	5	0	37	0				
Woodcock	28	9	72	4				
Clube	14	2	36	1				
Walton					0.4	0	6	0

Lancashire Bowling

	O.	M.	R.	W.	O.	M.	R.	W.
Statham	14	6	18	2	14	4	21	2
Wharton	4	0	17	0	7	3	6	1
Hilton	16	9	25	2	22	7	41	3
Greenhough	10	4	28	2	18	3	62	3
Tattersall	8.5	3	15	4	14	6	24	1

Umpires: D. Hendren and H. Baldwin.

OXFORD UNIVERSITY v. GLOUCESTERSHIRE

At Oxford, May 4, 6, 7. Drawn. Gloucestershire batted consistently, with a third wicket stand of 148 between Graveney and Emmett the feature. The Oxford batting showed improvement. In the first innings Walton drove magnificently through the covers, hitting fifteen 4's, and Eagar played fine attacking strokes. When the University needed 270 to win, Gibson, who hit a maiden century, and Hobbs experienced little difficulty with the county attack, but they could not maintain the necessary scoring rate of 77 an hour and rain eventually ended the proceedings.

Gloucestershire

D. M. Young b Phillips	50	— c Hobbs b Bailey	64
D. Carpenter c Scott b Woodcock	24	— c Melville b Bailey	2
T. W. Graveney c Hobbs b Phillips	85	— c Eagar b Phillips	17
G. M. Emmett c Walton b Woodcock	68	— b Melville	55
R. B. Nicholls st Scott b Woodcock	26	— not out	23
D. Hawkins c Clube b Woodcock	55	— not out	14
G. E. Lambert c Melville b Bailey	20		
D. R. Smith c Scott b Melville	10		
P. Rochford c Melville b Bailey	0		
C. Cook not out	7		
B. D. Wells not out	28		
B 4, l-b 9	13	B 4	4

1/48 2/86 3/234 4/241 (9 wkts., dec.) 386
5/293 6/334 7/347 8/351 9/351

1/23 2/116 (4 wkts., dec.) 179
3/126 4/155

Oxford University

I. Gibson c Emmett b Smith	4	— not out	100
J. A. D. Hobbs b Lambert	22	— not out	51
A. C. Walton lbw b Wells	88		
L. D. Watts b Cook	26		
M. A. Eagar c Rochford b Lambert	60		
C. D. Melville c Nicholls b Wells	43		
M. D. Scott c Emmett b Lambert	2		
R. G. Woodcock not out	21		
J. A. Bailey b Wells	0		
S. V. M. Clube b Wells	8		
J. B. Phillips b Wells	1		
B 11, l-b 7, n-b 3	21	L-b 1	1

1/19 2/43 3/117 4/168 5/246 296
6/248 7/277 8/278 9/292

(No wkt.) 152

Oxford Bowling

	O.	M.	R.	W.		O.	M.	R.	W.
Bailey	29	10	75	2	....	20	4	44	2
Phillips	20	4	79	2	....	15	1	67	1
Clube	22	2	85	0					
Woodcock	39	6	99	4	....	3	0	32	0
Gibson	2	0	14	0					
Melville	6	3	21	1	....	9	1	32	1

Gloucestershire Bowling

	O.	M.	R.	W.		O.	M.	R.	W.
Lambert	25	5	70	3	....	10	3	35	0
Smith	16	1	54	1	....	12	2	37	0
Cook	28	10	64	1	....	4	0	12	0
Wells	38.1	15	67	5	....	4	0	14	0
Hawkins	9	5	20	0	....	7	1	26	0
Emmett						4	0	27	0

Umpires: D. Hendren and E. Davies.

At Oxford, May 8, 9, 10. OXFORD UNIVERSITY lost to the WEST INDIES by an innings and 90 runs. (See WEST INDIES section.)

OXFORD UNIVERSITY v. YORKSHIRE

At Oxford, May 15, 16. Yorkshire won by an innings and 41 runs. They batted unevenly against a weakened attack, but a partnership of 111 between the left-handed Wilson (one 6, seventeen 4's) and Lowson ensured a good total. The University failed badly in face of the pace of Cowan and the off-breaks of Appleyard and followed on 237 behind. This time they broke down against the left-arm slows of Wardle, nine men being out for 120. Then Melville, going in last because of an injured thumb, added 76 in fifty minutes with a fellow South African, Kumleben, who, in his first match of the season for the University, completed a maiden century.

Yorkshire

D. B. Close c Melville b Woodcock 37	J. H. Wardle c Wilson b Woodcock 8
K. Taylor b Wilson 19	J. G. Binks not out.............. 34
J. V. Wilson c Walton b Woodcock132	R. Appleyard not out............ 9
D. E. V. Padgett b Wilson 1	B 10, l-b 2, w 1 13
F. A. Lowson c Woodcock b Wilson 46	
W. Watson lbw b Bowman 2	
W. H. H. Sutcliffe c Melville b	1/39 2/59 3/60 (8 wkts., dec.) 332
Wilson 31	4/171 5/204 6/259 7/270 8/293

M. J. Cowan did not bat.

Oxford University

J. A. D. Hobbs b Appleyard	10	— c Wardle b Cowan	16
A. C. Walton c Close b Bowman	0	— c Binks b Cowan.........	2
M. D. Scott c Wilson b Appleyard	5	— b Wardle	7
J. M. Kumleben c Appleyard b Cowan ...	0	— run out	100
M. A. Eagar b Appleyard	4	— lbw b Wardle	0
C. D. Melville c Binks b Cowan	3	— not out	26
J. D. Currie b Wardle	38	— c Padgett b Close	18
J. G. Raybould b Cowan	2	— b Wardle	1
R. G. Woodcock c Appleyard b Wardle .	18	— c Wilson b Wardle	0
R. W. Wilson not out	4	— b Cowan	9
R. Bowman b Cowan	4	— b Wardle	0
B 1, l-b 4, n-b 1, w 1	7	B 2, l-b 9, n-b 6.......	17

1/1 2/10 3/15 4/15 5/22 6/22 7/35   95
8/71 9/86

1/10 2/20 3/45 4/58   196
5/72 6/72 7/86 8/115 9/120

Oxford Bowling

	O.	M.	R.	W.	O.	M.	R.	W.
Bowman	28	8	69	1				
Melville	18	6	50	0				
Wilson	22	4	79	4				
Woodcock	38	8	91	3				
Raybould......	10	1	30	0				

Yorkshire Bowling

	O.	M.	R.	W.		O.	M.	R.	W.
Cowan	16.5	4	33	5	....	19	3	64	3
Appleyard	13	6	26	3	....	22	8	45	0
Wardle	9	4	13	2	....	23	7	65	5
Close	6	1	16	0	....	5	3	5	1

Umpires: D. Hendren and H. G. Baldwin.

OXFORD UNIVERSITY v. MIDDLESEX

At Oxford, May 22, 23, 24. Oxford won by four wickets in a dramatic finish, registering just on time their first victory against a county since May, 1950. The University owed much to Bailey, Brown and Woodcock, who between them accounted for all but three of their opponents' wickets. Their performances were achieved without help from the pitch and they always had the Middlesex batsmen struggling. Hobbs failed by five to reach his first century, and with Eagar dealt decisively with the Middlesex attack. Bick, Gale and Baldry gave sound batting displays for Middlesex, but received inadequate support.

Middlesex

D. A. Bick b Bowman	53	—	c and b Wilson	50
R. A. Gale c Woodcock b Bailey	0	—	c and b Woodcock	80
W. J. Edrich c Eagar b Bailey	0	—	st Scott b Woodcock	17
W. E. Russell b Bowman	0	—	hit wkt b Woodcock	0
D. O. Baldry c Seaton b Bowman	52	—	run out	17
G. P. S. Delisle c Scott b Bowman	0	—	c Scott b Bailey	25
J. T. Murray c Eagar b Bowman	8	—	c Seaton b Woodcock	1
F. J. Titmus c Scott b Bailey	15	—	lbw b Bowman	37
R. V. C. Robins b Wilson	7	—	c Kumleben b Bailey	8
J. J. Warr b Bailey	14	—	b Bowman	4
T. Angus not out	0	—	not out	0
B 6	6		B 3, l-b 4, n-b 1	8
	155			247

1/1 2/1 3/4 4/87 5/91 6/107 7/120 8/132 9/140

1/95 2/143 3/143 4/150 5/189 6/192 7/192 8/210 9/231

Oxford University

J. A. D. Hobbs b Titmus	95	—	c Murray b Warr	8
G. S. Seaton b Titmus	26	—	c Murray b Angus	6
A. C. Walton c and b Angus	35	—	c Murray b Angus	2
J. M. Kumleben b Angus	0	—	not out	21
J. D. Currie b Warr	23	—	run out	11
M. A. Eagar c Murray b Baldry	73	—	run out	1
R. G. Woodcock lbw b Titmus	35	—	run out	0
M. D. Scott c Edrich b Angus	22	—	not out	6
R. W. Wilson b Titmus	1			
R. Bowman not out	13			
J. A. Bailey c Murray b Angus	0			
B 10, l-b 14, n-b 1	25			
	348		(6 wkts.)	55

1/55 2/125 3/127 4/171 5/212 6/303 7/305 8/318 9/344

1/14 2/14 3/20 4/45 5/47 6/48

Oxford Bowling

	O.	M.	R.	W.		O.	M.	R.	W.
Bailey	24.4	7	49	4	....	30	11	60	2
Bowman	18	1	44	5	....	24.5	6	66	2
Wilson	19	4	36	1	....	19	2	59	1
Woodcock	13	7	20	0	....	30	12	54	4

Middlesex Bowling

	O.	M.	R.	W.		O.	M.	R.	W.
Warr	23	5	31	1	....	10	1	25	1
Angus	29.1	4	81	4	....	9.4	1	30	2
Titmus	34	7	83	4					
Robins	16	3	77	0					
Russell	5	2	15	0					
Baldry	13	4	36	1					

Umpires: D. Hendren and P. Corrall.

OXFORD UNIVERSITY v. WARWICKSHIRE

At Oxford, May 25, 27, 28. Warwickshire won by three wickets in an exciting finish. The county were left to score 209 in two hours and twenty-five minutes, and Gardner, whose first innings century took him as long as five hours, decided the issue by hitting the last ball of the match for 6. Unenterprising play by the early Oxford batsmen marked the first innings. Though the county bowling possessed no special sting, five wickets fell for 76 before the Freshman, Jowett, making his debut for the University, and Woodcock added 77.

Oxford University

J. A. D. Hobbs c Gardner b Leach	23	—	b Carter		28
G. S. Seaton c Carter b Griffiths	0	—	c and b Leach		24
A. C. Walton run out	13	—	c Gardner b Singh		17
J. D. Currie hit wkt b Youll	20	—	lbw b Singh		37
M. A. Eagar b Carter	5	—	c Lewis b Leach		0
R. G. Woodcock c Ibadulla b Leach	55	—	c Ibadulla b Leach		31
R. Jowett not out	81	—	lbw b Singh		7
M. D. Scott c Smith b Griffiths	30	—	not out		43
R. W. Wilson c Lewis b Griffiths	2	—	c Lewis b Griffiths		2
R. Bowman b Griffiths	0	—	c Lewis b Griffiths		3
J. A. Bailey c Lewis b Griffiths	4	—	not out		2
B 11, l-b 1, n-b 2, w 5	19		B 8, l-b 7, n-b 5, w 13		33

	252	227

1/0 2/25 3/44 4/57 5/76 6/153   1/50 2/66   (9 wkts., dec.) 227
7/228 8/230 9/230   3/80 4/80 5/146 6/166
                             7/166 8/182 9/206

Warwickshire

F. C. Gardner b Bowman	110	—	not out		47
T. W. Cartwright c Bowman b Wilson	36	—	lbw b Bailey		57
M. J. K. Smith c Hobbs b Wilson	72	—	lbw b Bailey		3
K. Ibadulla b Bowman	36	—	lbw b Bailey		15
B. Fletcher not out	16	—	b Bowman		36
C. W. Leach (did not bat)		—	lbw b Bailey		0
S. Singh (did not bat)		—	c Currie b Woodcock		33
R. G. Carter (did not bat)		—	b Bowman		9
E. B. Lewis (did not bat)		—	not out		4
L-b 1	1		B 4, l-b 5		9

(4 wkts., dec.)	271	(7 wkts.) 213

1/49 2/152 3/224 4/271   (4 wkts., dec.) 271   1/0 2/72 3/122   (7 wkts.) 213
                                     4/130 5/132 6/168 7/191

M. Youll and S. S. Griffiths did not bat.

Warwickshire Bowling

	O.	M.	R.	W.	O.	M.	R.	W.
Carter	24	4	80	1	18	4	61	1
Griffiths	24.5	9	39	5	17	6	29	2
Cartwright	5	1	15	0				
Leach	26	9	49	2	23	4	49	3
Singh	9	3	17	0	18	8	30	3
Youll	9	1	33	1	8	1	25	0
Ibadulla					2	2	0	0

Oxford Bowling

	O.	M.	R.	W.	O.	M.	R.	W.
Bailey	25	9	65	0	14	2	66	4
Bowman	26.5	3	75	2	12	2	38	2
Wilson	28	9	72	2	9	0	43	0
Woodcock	19	7	41	0	8	1	57	1
Jowett	7	1	17	0				

Umpires: D. Hendren and H. Baldwin.

OXFORD UNIVERSITY v. HAMPSHIRE

At Oxford, June 1, 3, 4. Drawn. After a moderate start, Oxford enjoyed the best of the game. Melville overshadowed everybody in their first innings, strong driving enabling him to reach three figures in two and three-quarter hours. Marshall and Horton began well for the county, but following a fifth wicket partnership of 82 by the hard-hitting Barnard and Ingleby-Mackenzie, the new ball caused a collapse. Rain prevented cricket before lunch on the last day when Eagar, twice missed at slip, and Kumleben, by putting on 94, did most to enable Oxford to declare and set Hampshire 240 to get in two and three-quarter hours, a task they did not attempt.

Oxford University

G. S. Seaton c Ingleby-Mackenzie b Burden	11	— c Gray b Heath	6
J. A. D. Hobbs b Burden	24	— b Burden	20
M. A. Eagar b Heath	8	— not out	90
J. M. Kumleben c and b Burden	35	— run out	20
C. D. Melville not out	140	— run out	6
R. G. Woodcock c Cannings b Gray	0	— not out	3
R. Jowett c Roper b Heath	48		
M. D. Scott lbw b Gray	12		
R. W. Wilson b Burden	4		
R. Bowman not out	13		
B 10, l-b 12	22	B 1, l-b 5	6

1/30 2/49 3/49 4/137 (8 wkts., dec.) 317
5/144 6/231 7/260 8/295

1/13 2/39 (4 wkts., dec.) 151
3/133 4/141

J. A. Bailey did not bat.

Hampshire

R. E. Marshall c Bailey b Woodcock	27	— c Wilson b Bailey	43
H. Horton c Hobbs b Wilson	20	— c Scott b Woodcock	51
J. R. Gray c and b Woodcock	0	— c Seaton b Bailey	3
B. R. S. Harrison c Eagar b Woodcock	16	— not out	3
H. M. Barnard c and b Wilson	70	— not out	18
A. C. D. Ingleby-Mackenzie b Bailey	62	— c Bailey b Wilson	8
C. Roper c Hobbs b Bailey	7		
M. Heath lbw b Bowman	0		
E. D. R. Eagar not out	11	— b Bailey	7
V. H. D. Cannings b Bowman	4		
M. D. Burden b Bowman	4		
B 4, l-b 4	8	L-b 4	4

1/51 2/51 3/51 4/101 5/183 6/207 229
7/210 8/211 9/215

1/21 2/86 3/108 (5 wkts.) 137
4/110 5/124

Hampshire Bowling

	O.	M.	R.	W.		O.	M.	R.	W.
Heath	22	5	62	2	....	16	3	56	1
Cannings	14	3	50	0	....	14	4	32	0
Gray	19	8	28	2	....	10	7	8	0
Barnard	7	2	21	0					
Burden	30	9	81	4	....	13	1	49	1
Eagar	2	0	6	0					
Marshall	8	2	21	0					
Horton	4	0	26	0					

Oxford Bowling

	O.	M.	R.	W.	O.	M.	R.	W.
Bailey	20	8	33	2	19	10	46	3
Bowman	13.5	4	34	3	6	1	20	0
Woodcock	21	4	72	3	10	3	32	1
Wilson	32	11	62	2	3	1	10	1
Jowett	9	1	20	0				
Melville					6	1	25	0

Umpires: D. Hendren and J. S. Buller.

OXFORD UNIVERSITY v. WORCESTERSHIRE

At Oxford, June 5, 6, 7. Worcestershire won by 178 runs over a University team much below full strength. P. Richardson led the way in solid county batting in the first innings, and after Hobbs and Gibson began for the University with a stand of 99, Coldwell performed so effectively with the new ball that in one spell he dismissed six men for as many runs. So Worcestershire led by 100 and brisk hitting by Kenyon and D. Richardson, who added 125 together, paved the way to a second declaration. With Coldwell again in fine bowling form, and Horton supporting him ably, Oxford never looked like obtaining the 308 needed for victory.

Worcestershire

D. Kenyon c Hobbs b Wilson	43	— st Scott b Jowett	119
P. E. Richardson lbw b Woodcock	76	— c Watts b Wolfe-Murray	11
L. Outschoorn c Jowett b Woodcock	31	— not out	0
M. J. Horton c Gibson b Wilson	8	— c Jowett b Woodcock	1
A. Spencer c Gibson b Wolfe-Murray	16		
D. W. Richardson c Eagar b Bailey	35	— st Scott b Jowett	58
G. Dews not out	29	— lbw b Wilson	13
R. Booth c Wolfe-Murray b Wilson	41		
B. C. Hall not out	1		
B 6, n-b 2	8	B 4, l-b 1	5

1/83 2/137 3/158 4/158 (7 wkts., dec.) 288
5/211 6/219 7/285

1/28 2/64 (5 wkts., dec.) 207
3/189 4/206 5/207

R. Berry and L. J. Coldwell did not bat.

Oxford University

J. A. D. Hobbs c P. Richardson b Berry	57	— c Booth b Coldwell	25
I. Gibson c Booth b Outschoorn	53	— c Outschoorn b Coldwell	10
R. A. Bowles lbw b Coldwell	18	— c Dews b Horton	43
M. A. Eagar b Berry	8	— c Booth b Coldwell	0
L. D. Watts lbw b Berry	7	— b Coldwell	4
R. G. Woodcock c Dews b Coldwell	18	— c and b Horton	16
R. L. Jowett c Booth b Coldwell	0	— lbw b Horton	0
M. D. Scott c P. Richardson b Coldwell	6	— b Coldwell	13
R. W. Wilson b Coldwell	1	— not out	13
J. A. Bailey b Coldwell	6	— c Dews b Horton	0
A. Wolfe-Murray not out	1	— b Horton	0
B 4, l-b 8, w 1	13	B 4, l-b 1	5

1/99 2/119 3/134 4/148 5/156 6/156 188
7/174 8/181 9/187

1/37 2/40 3/40 4/44 5/74 129
6/80 7/103 8/121 9/121

Y

Oxford Bowling

	O.	M.	R.	W.		O.	M.	R.	W.
Bailey	25	9	41	1	....	1	0	8	0
Wolfe-Murray..	16	1	69	1	....	8	0	33	1
Wilson	34	8	94	3	....	19	2	54	1
Woodcock	23	8	61	2	....	22.1	4	76	1
Jowett	5	2	10	0	....	5	0	31	2
Gibson	4	2	5	0					

Worcestershire Bowling

	O.	M.	R.	W.		O.	M.	R.	W.
Coldwell	16	6	30	6	....	19	11	18	5
Hall	11	2	33	0	....	9	2	24	0
Horton	31	11	63	0	....	23.5	11	37	5
Berry	25	13	40	3	....	15	5	32	0
Spencer	4	2	4	0					
D. Richardson	1	0	1	0					
Outschoorn	1	0	4	1	....	3	0	13	0
P. Richardson..	1	1	0	0					

Umpires: D. Hendren and E. Davies.

OXFORD UNIVERSITY v. THE ARMY

At Oxford, June 12, 13, 14. Oxford won by an innings and 27 runs. Oxford University 456 for seven wickets, dec. (J. A. D. Hobbs 151, M. A. Eagar 86, R. A. Bowles 59, M. J. Matthews 52); The Army 132 (L/Cpl. P. J. Sharp 54) and 297 (Major K. C. Came 67, Spr. K. B. Standring 63, R. W. Wilson six for 106). (Not first-class.)

OXFORD UNIVERSITY v. FREE FORESTERS

At Oxford, June 15, 17, 18. Oxford won by 187 runs. They were always the masters. Walton hit one 6 and fourteen 4's in a stay of two hours ten minutes and he and Eagar put on 105. Then Jowett, very free for two and a half hours, shared with Marshall in a stand of 127. The Free Foresters batsmen, with the exception of Buckingham and Whitcombe, failed against the spin of Clube and Jowett, but though leading by 201 Oxford did not enforce the follow-on. Eagar again scored readily and in the end the Foresters required 368 to win. After a fair start the last seven wickets fell for 68 to the bowling of Matthews and Jowett, the match ending soon after lunch on the third day.

Oxford University

J. A. D. Hobbs b Dickinson	21	— c Buckingham b Wilson	26
R. A. Bowles c Wilson b Dickinson	14	— lbw b Whitcombe	5
M. A. Eagar lbw b Wilson	37	— c Buckingham b Glerum	53
A. C. Walton lbw b Glerum	95	— c Came b Dickinson	19
R. L. Jowett c Tyrwhitt-Drake b Woodhouse	105	— not out	30
M. J. A. Matthews c Powell b Glerum	2	— b Dickinson	5
D. A. C. Marshall not out	54	— not out	14
A. Wolfe-Murray not out	0		
B 11, l-b 8, n-b 1	19	B 9, l-b 5	14

1/25 2/41 3/146 4/196 (6 wkts., dec.) 347
5/198 6/325

1/34 2/58 (5 wkts., dec.) 166
3/108 4/118 5/130

S. V. M. Clube, A. L. Hichens and G. B. Gauntlett did not bat.

Free Foresters

A. D. Buckingham c Gauntlett b Jowett..	34	— c Jowett b Clube	....	16
T. W. Tyrwhitt-Drake b Wolfe-Murray..	11	— c Marshall b Clube	....	38
A. R. B. Neame b Clube	13	— lbw b Matthews	....	38
A. J. P. Woodhouse b Jowett	12	— b Jowett	....	17
H. W. Glerum c Gauntlett b Clube	0	— b Matthews	....	1
R. E. S. Wyatt c Eagar b Clube	1	— c Eagar b Jowett	....	6
P. A. Whitcombe c Gauntlett b Matthews	39	— c Clube b Jowett	....	1
H. G. Powell c and b Clube	8	— b Matthews	....	5
K. C. Came c Hobbs b Jowett	6	— lbw b Matthews	....	6
R. W. Wilson b Clube	7	— b Matthews	....	17
D. C. Dickinson not out	2	— not out	....	21
B 5, l-b 6, n-b 2	13	B 6, l-b 4, n-b 3, w 1 ..		14

1/16 2/53 3/73 4/74 5/73 6/82 7/108   146
8/123 9/142

1/48 2/73 3/112 4/113   180
5/122 6/128 7/131 8/136
9/143

Free Foresters Bowling

	O.	M.	R.	W.		O.	M.	R.	W.
Came	12	3	34	0	....	3	1	12	0
Whitcombe	23	10	55	0	....	7	1	18	1
Dickinson	19	2	53	2	....	19	7	37	2
Wilson	26	8	77	1	....	12	2	48	1
Neame	12	3	37	0	....	4	0	21	0
Wyatt	10	4	28	0					
Glerum	4	0	16	2	....	7	3	16	1
Buckingham ...	2	0	8	0					
Woodhouse ...	3	0	20	1					

Oxford Bowling

	O.	M.	R.	W.		O.	M.	R.	W.
Hichens	7	0	10	0	....	6	3	15	0
Wolfe-Murray..	8	1	20	1	....	2	0	9	0
Clube	22	5	49	5	....	17	3	50	2
Jowett	16	3	50	3	....	20	6	34	3
Matthews......	4	2	4	1	....	21	6	58	5

Umpires: D. Hendren and A. D. Smith.

OXFORD UNIVERSITY v. LEICESTERSHIRE

At Oxford, June 19, 20, 21. Leicestershire won by ten wickets. The University made a wretched start against the pace bowling of Spencer and Boshier, but after the fall of five wickets for 42 Melville and Woodcock led a recovery with a stand of 73. Hallam batted splendidly for Leicestershire and, sharing in stands of 103 with Lester and 107 with Gardner, took the county ahead for the loss of one wicket. In the end Oxford faced arrears of 187 and, though Melville drove admirably, hitting nineteen 4's, Leicestershire needed no more than 76 to win.

Oxford University

J. A. D. Hobbs c Firth b Spencer	8	— c P. Munden b Spencer 0
R. A. Bowles b Boshier	8	— c Spencer b Lester 4
A. C. Walton c Boshier b Spencer	0	— c Firth b Boshier 9
C. D. Melville c Firth b Spencer	55	— b Spencer 142
J. Kumleben c Firth b Boshier	9	— c Spencer b Savage 22
R. L. Jowett b Boshier	4	— b V. Munden 8
R. G. Woodcock c P. Munden b Savage..	57	— lbw b V. Munden 0
M. A. Scott b Savage	16	— b Boshier 29
R. W. Wilson c Firth b Savage	11	— b Spencer 5
J. Wolfe-Murray c P. Munden b Savage..	17	— c Gardner b Spencer 25
R. Bowman not out	8	— not out 7
B 2, l-b 3, n-b 2	7	B 1, l-b 8, w 2 11

1/12 2/12 3/16 4/38 5/42 6/115   196   1/0 2/11 3/64 4/107 5/136 262
7/142 8/167 9/176   6/136 7/198 8/217 9/246

Leicestershire

G. Lester c Hobbs b Jowett	42	— not out 21
M. R. Hallam c Walton b Woodcock	118	— not out 55
L. R. Gardner b Wilson	82	
R. A. Diment lbw b Jewett	0	
J. van Geloven lbw b Wilson	24	
P. Munden st Scott b Woodcock	33	
V. S. Munden c Wolfe-Murray b Bowman	14	
J. Firth c Hobbs b Melville	0	
C. T. Spencer c Scott b Wilson	26	
J. Savage not out	12	
B. Boshier c Wolfe-Murray b Wilson	2	
B 11, l-b 15, n-b 4	30	

1/103 2/210 3/222 4/270 5/295 6/327   383   (No wkt.) 76
7/330 8/351 9/379

Leicestershire Bowling

	O.	M.	R.	W.		O.	M.	R.	W.
Spencer	23	7	59	3	....	23.4	6	70	4
Boshier.........	15	3	52	3	....	20	7	55	2
V. Munden	5	2	23	0	....	14	8	13	2
Savage	9.2	1	44	4	....	15	3	48	1
van Geloven ..	3	1	11	0					
Lester						24	6	65	1

Oxford Bowling

	O.	M.	R.	W.		O.	M.	R.	W.
Bowman	23	5	81	1	....	5	1	20	0
Wolfe-Murray..	5	0	10	0	....	3	0	14	0
Wilson	44.5	12	99	4	....	6	1	20	0
Woodcock	35	18	53	2	....	4	1	7	0
Jowett	37	11	81	2					
Melville	9	1	29	1	....	1	0	13	0
Walton						0.5	0	2	0

Umpires: D. Hendren and K. McCanlis.

At Guildford, June 22, 24, 25. OXFORD UNIVERSITY lost to SURREY by 138 runs.

At Lord's, June 26, 27, 28. OXFORD UNIVERSITY lost to M.C.C. by 129 runs.

At Westcliff, June 29, July 1, 2. OXFORD UNIVERSITY lost to ESSEX by three wickets.

At Eastbourne, July 3, 4, 5. OXFORD UNIVERSITY beat D. R. JARDINE'S XI by 55 runs.

At Lord's, July 6, 8, 9. OXFORD lost to CAMBRIDGE by an innings and 186 runs. (See OTHER MATCHES AT LORD'S section.)

LIST OF BLUES

From 1880–1957

To save space, Blues prior to 1880 are omitted, except some of special interest for personal or family reasons.

OXFORD

Abell, G. E. B. (Marlborough), 1924, 1926–27
Allan, J. M. (Edinburgh Academy), 1953–56
Altham, H. S. (Repton), 1911–12
Arenhold, J. A. (Diocesan Coll., S.A.), 1954
Arkwright, H. A. (Eton), 1895
Arnall-Thompson, H. T. (Rugby), 1886
Asher, A. G. G. (Loretto), 1883
Awdry, R. W. (Winchester), 1904

Bailey, J. A. (Christ's Hospital), 1956–57
Ballance, T. G. L. (Uppingham), 1935, 1937
Bannon, B. D. (Tonbridge), 1898
Barber, A. T. (Shrewsbury) (Capt. in 1929), 1927–29
Bardsley, R. V. (Shrewsbury), 1911–13
Bardswell, G. R. (Uppingham) (Capt. in 1897), 1894, 1896–97
Barlow, E. A. (Shrewsbury), 1932–34
Barnard, F. H. (Charterhouse), 1922, 1924
Barnes, R. G. (Harrow), 1906–07
Bartlett, J. N. (Chichester), 1946, 1951
Barton, M. R. (Winchester), 1936–37
Bassett, H. (Bedford House, Oxford), 1889–91
Bastard, E. W. (Sherborne), 1883–85
Bathurst, F. (Winchester), 1848
Bathurst, L. C. V. (Radley), 1893–94
Bathurst, R. A. (Winchester), 1838–39
Bathurst, S. E. (Winchester), 1836
Bell, G. F. (Repton), 1919
Belle, B. H. (Forest School), 1936
Benn, A. (Harrow), 1935
Benson, E. T. (Blundell's), 1928–29
Berkeley, G. F. H. (Wellington), 1890–93
Bettington, R. H. B. (The King's School, Parramatta) (Capt. in 1923), 1920–23
Bickmore, A. F. (Clifton), 1920–21
Bird, W. S. (Malvern) (Capt. in 1906), 1904–06
Birrell, H. B. (St. Andrews, South Africa), 1953–54
Blagg, P. H. (Shrewsbury), 1939

Blaikie, K. G. (Maritzburg), 1924
Blake, P. D. S. (Eton) (Capt. in 1952), 1950–52
Bloy, N. C. F. (Dover), 1946–47
Boger, A. J. (Winchester), 1891
Bolitho, W. E. T. (Harrow), 1883, 1885
Bonham-Carter, M. (Winchester), 1902
Boobbyer, B. (Uppingham), 1949–52
Bosanquet, B. J. T. (Eton), 1898–1900
Boswell, W. G. K. (Eton), 1913–14
Bowman, R. (Fettes), 1957
Bowring, T. (Rugby), 1907–08
Bradby, H. C. (Rugby), 1890
Braddell, R. L. (Charterhouse), 1910–11
Bradshaw, W. H. (Malvern), 1930–31
Brain, J. H. (Clifton) (Capt. in 1887), 1884–87
Brain, W. H. (Clifton), 1891–93
Brandt, D. R. (Harrow), 1907
Branston, G. T. (Charterhouse), 1904–06
Brett, P. J. (Winchester), 1929
Bristowe, O. C. (Eton), 1914
Bromley-Martin, G. E. (Eton), 1897–98
Brooke, R. H. J. (St. Edward's, Oxford), 1932
Brougham, H. (Wellington), 1911
Brownlee, L. D. (Clifton), 1904
Bruce, C. N. (now Lord Aberdare) (Winchester), 1907–08
Buckland, E. H. (Marlborough), 1884–87
Burn, R. C. W. (Winchester), 1902–05
Bush, J. E. (Magdalen Coll. Sch.), 1952
Butterworth, R. E. C. (Harrow), 1927
Buxton, R. V. (Eton), 1906

Campbell, I. P. (Canford), 1949–50
Campbell, I. P. F. (Repton) (Capt. in 1913), 1911–13
Carlisle, K. M. (Harrow) (Capt. in 1905), 1903–05
Carr, D. B. (Repton) (Capt. in 1950), 1949–51
*Case, T. B. (Winchester), 1891–92
Cazalet, P. V. F. (Eton), 1927
Chalk, F. G. H. (Uppingham) (Capt. in 1934), 1931–34

* Case came into the game of 1891, by permission of the Cambridge captain, through the Hon. F. J. N. Thesiger being injured soon after play began.

Champain, F. H. B. (Cheltenham) (Capt. in 1899), 1897–1900
Chesterton, G. H. (Malvern), 1949
Clube, S. V. M. (St. John's, Leatherhead), 1956
Cobb, A. R. (Winchester), 1886
Cochrane, A. H. J. (Repton), 1885–86, 1888
Colebrooke, E. L. (Charterhouse), 1880
Collins, L. P. (Marlborough), 1899
Colman, G. R. R. (Eton), 1913–14
Coutts, I. D. F. (Dulwich), 1952
Cowdrey, M. C. (Tonbridge) (Capt. in 1954), 1952–54
Coxon, A. J. (Harrow C.S.), 1952
Crawford, J. W. F. (Merchant Taylors), 1900–01
Crawley, A. M. (Harrow), 1927–30
Croome, A. C. M. (Wellington), 1888–89
Crutchley, G. E. V. (Harrow), 1912
Cunliffe, F. H. E. (Eton)(Capt. in 1898), 1895–98
Curwen, W. J. H. (Charterhouse), 1906

Darwall-Smith, R. F. H. (Charterhouse), 1935–38
Dauglish, M. J. (Harrow), 1889–90
Davidson, W. W. (Brighton), 1947–48
Davies, P. H. (Brighton), 1913–14
Delisle, G. P. S. (Stoneyhurst), 1955–56
De Montmorency, R. H. (Cheltenham and St. Paul's), 1899
de Saram, F. C. (Royal College, Colombo), 1934–35
Dillon, E. W. (Rugby), 1901–02
Divecha, R. V. (Bombay University), 1950–51
Dixon, E. J. H. (St. Edward's, Oxford) (Capt. in 1939), 1937–39
Donnelly, M. P. (Canterbury University, New Zealand) (Capt. in 1947), 1946–47
Dowding, A. L. (St. Peter's, Adelaide) (Capt. in 1953), 1952–53
Dyson, J. H. (Charterhouse), 1936

Eagar, E. D. R. (Cheltenham). 1939
Eagar, M. A. (Rugby), 1956–57
Eccles, A. (Repton), 1897–99
Eggar, J. D. (Winchester), 1938
Evans, A. H. (Rossall and Clifton) (Capt. in 1881), 1878–81
Evans, A. J. (Winchester) (Capt. in 1911), 1909–12
Evans, E. N. (Haileybury), 1932
Evans, G. (St. Asaph), 1939
Evans, W. H. B. (Malvern) (Capt. in 1904), 1902–05
Evelyn, F. L. (Rugby), 1880

Fane, F. L. (Charterhouse), 1897–98

Fasken, D. K. (Wellington), 1953–55
Fellows-Smith, J. P. (Durban High School, South Africa), 1953–55
Findlay, W. (Eton) (Capt. in 1903), 1901–03
Fisher, C. D. (Westminster), 1900
Forbes, D. H. (Eton), 1894
Ford, G. J. (King's College, London), 1839–40
Ford, N. M. (Harrow), 1928–30
Forster, H. W. (Eton), 1887–89
Foster, G. N. (Malvern), 1905–08
Foster, H. K. (Malvern), 1894–96
Foster, R. E. (Malvern) (Capt. in 1900), 1897–1900
Fowler, G. (Clifton), 1888
Fox, R. W. (Wellington), 1897–98
Franklin, H. W. F. (Christ's Hospital), 1924
Fraser, J. N. (Church of England Grammar School, Melbourne, and Melbourne University), 1912–13
Frazer, J. E. (Winchester), 1924
Fry, C. B. (Repton) (Capt. in 1894), 1892–95

Garland-Wells, H. M. (St. Paul's), 1928–30
Garthwaite, P. F. (Wellington), 1929
Gibson, I. M. (Manchester G.S.), 1955–57
Gilbert, H. (Charterhouse), 1907–09
Gilliat, I. A. W. (Charterhouse), 1925
Gilligan, F. W. (Dulwich) (Capt. in 1920), 1919–20
Gordon, J. H. (Winchester), 1906–07
Greenstock, J. W. (Malvern), 1925–27
Greeson, F. H. (Winchester), 1887–89
Grover, J. N. (Winchester) (Capt. in 1938), 1936–38
Guise, J. L. (Winchester) (Capt. in 1925), 1924–25

Halliday, J. G. (City of Oxford High School), 1935
Hamilton, W. D. (Haileybury), 1882
Harris (Lord), G. R. C. (Eton), 1871–72, 1874
Harrison, G. C. (Malvern and Clifton), 1880–81
Hart, T. M. (Strathallan), 1931–32
Hartley, J. C. (Marlborough and Tonbridge), 1896–97
Hatfeild, C. E. (Eton), 1908
Hedges, L. P. (Tonbridge), 1920–22
Henderson, D. (St. Edwards, Oxford), 1950
Henley, D. F. (Harrow), 1947
Henley, F. A. H. (Forest School), 1905
Hewetson, E. P. (Shrewsbury), 1923–25
Hewett, H. T. (Harrow), 1886
Hildyard, L. D'Arcy (Private), 1884–86
Hill, V. T. (Winchester), 1892

Hill-Wood, C. K. (Eton), 1928–30
Hill-Wood, D. J. (Eton), 1928
Hine-Haycock, T. R. (Wellington), 1883–84
Hirst, E. T. (Rugby), 1878–80
Hobbs, J. A. D. (Liverpool Coll.), 1957
Hofmeyr, M. B. (Pretoria, South Africa) (Capt. in 1951), 1949–51
Holdsworth, R. L. (Repton), 1919–22
Hollins, A. M. (Eton), 1899
Hollins, F. H. (Eton), 1901
Holmes, E. R. T. (Malvern) (Capt. in 1927), 1925–27
Hone, B. W. (Adelaide University) (Capt. in 1933), 1931–33
Hooman, C. V. L. (Charterhouse), 1909–10
Hopkins, H. O. (St. Peter's College, Adelaide), 1923
Howell, M. (Repton) (Capt. in 1919), 1914, 1919
Hurst, C. S. (Uppingham) (Capt. in 1909), 1907–09

Jackson, K. L. T. (Rugby), 1934
Jardine, D. R. (Winchester), 1920–21, 1923
Jardine, M. R. (Fettes) (Capt. in 1891), 1889–92
Jenkins, V. G. J. (Llandovery), 1933
Jones, R. T. (Eton), 1892
Jose, A. D. (Adelaide University), 1950–51
Jowett, D. C. P. R. (Sherborne), 1952–55
Jowett, R. L. (Bradford G.S.), 1957

Kamm, A. (Charterhouse), 1954
Kardar, A. H. (Punjab University), 1947–49
Keighley, W. G. (Eton), 1947–48
Kelly, G. W. F. (Stonyhurst), 1901–02
Kemp, M. C. (Harrow) (Capt. in 1883–84), 1881–84
Kentish, E. S. M. (Cornwall College, Jamaica), 1956
Key, K. J. (Clifton), 1884–87
Kimpton, R. C. M. (Melbourne University), 1935, 1937–38
Kingsley, P. G. T. (Winchester) (Capt. in 1930), 1928–30
Knight, D. J. (Malvern), 1914, 1919
Knight, N. S. (Uppingham), 1934
Knott, C. H. (Tonbridge) (Capt. in 1924), 1922–24
Knott, F. H. (Tonbridge) (Capt. in 1914), 1912–14
Knox, F. P. (Dulwich) (Capt. in 1901), 1899–1901

Lagden, R. O. (Marlborough), 1909–12
Le Couteur, P. R. (Warrnambool Academy and Melbourne University), 1909–11

Lee, E. C. (Winchester), 1898
Legard, A. R. (Winchester), 1932,.1935
Legge, G. B. (Malvern) (Capt. in 1926), 1925–26
Leslie, C. F. H. (Rugby), 1881–83
Leveson Gower, H. D. G. (Winchester) (Capt. in 1896), 1893–96
Lewis, D. J. (Cape Town University), 1951
Lewis, R. P. (Winchester), 1894–96
Lindsay, W. O'B. (Harrow), 1931
Llewelyn, W. D. (Eton), 1890–91
Lomas, J. M. (Charterhouse), 1938–39
Lowe, J. C. M. (Uppingham), 1907–09
Lowndes, W. G. L. F. (Eton), 1921
Lyon, B. H. (Rugby), 1922–23
Lyon, G. W. F. (Brighton), 1925

McBride, W. N. (Westminster), 1926
McCanlis, M. A. (Cranleigh) (Capt. in 1928), 1926–28
Macindoe, D. H. (Eton) (Capt. in 1946), 1937–39, 1946
McIntosh, R. I. F. (Uppingham), 1927–28
M'Iver, C. D. (Forest School), 1903–04
McKinna, G. H. (Manchester Grammar School), 1953
M'Lachlan, N. (Loretto) (Capt. in 1882), 1879–82
Mallett, A. W. H. (Dulwich), 1947–48
Marshall, J. C. (Rugby), 1953
Marsham, A. J. B. (Eton), 1939
Marsham, C. D. B. (Private) (Capt. in 1857–58), 1854–58
Marsham, C. H. B. (Eton) (Capt. in 1902), 1900–02
Marsham, C. J. B. (Private), 1851
Marsham, R. H. B. (Private), 1856
Marsland, G. P. (Rossall), 1954
Martin, E. G. (Eton), 1903–06
Martyn, H. (Exeter Grammar School), 1899–1900
Matthews, M. H. (Westminster), 1936–37
Maudsley, R. H. (Malvern), 1946–47
Mayhew, J. F. N. (Eton), 1930
Medlicott, W. S. (Harrow) 1902
Melle, B. G. von B. (South African College School and South African College, Cape Town), 1913–14
Melville, A. (Michaelhouse, South Africa) (Capt. in 1931–32), 1930–33
Melville, C. D. (Michaelhouse S.A.), 1957
Metcalfe, S. G. (Leeds Grammar School), 1956
Mitchell, R. A. H. (Eton) (Capt. in 1863–65), 1862–65
Mitchell, W. M. (Dulwich), 1951–52
Mitchell-Innes, N. S. (Sedbergh) (Capt. in 1936), 1934–37
Monro, R. W. (Harrow), 1860

Moore, D. N. (Shrewsbury) (Capt. in 1931, when he did not play v. Cambridge, owing to illness), 1930

Mordaunt, G. J. (Wellington) (Capt. in 1895), 1893–96

More, R. E. (Westminster), 1900–01

Moss, R. H. (Radley), 1889

Munn, J. S. (Forest School), 1901

Murray-Wood, W. (Mill Hill), 1936

Naumann, F. C. G. (Malvern), 1914, 1919

Nepean, E. A. (Sherborne), 1887–88

Neser, V. H. (South African College, Cape Town), 1921

Newman, G. C. (Eton), 1926–27

Newton, A. E. (Eton), 1885

Newton-Thompson, J. O. (Diocesan College, Rondebosch, South Africa), 1946

Nicholls, B. E. (Winchester), 1884

Nunn, J. A. (Sherborne), 1926–27

O'Brien, T. C. (St. Charles' College, Notting Hill), 1884–85

Oldfield, P. C. (Repton), 1932–33

Ottaway, C. J. (Eton) (Capt. in 1873), 1870–73

Owen-Smith, H. G. (Diocesan College, South Africa), 1931–33

Page, H. V. (Cheltenham) (Capt. in 1885–86), 1883–86

Palairet, L. C. H. (Repton) (Capt. in 1892–93), 1890–93

Palairet, R. C. N. (Repton), 1893–94

Pataudi, Nawab of (Chief's College, Lahore), 1929–31

Patten, M. (Winchester), 1922–23

Patterson, J. I. (Chatham House, Ramsgate), 1882

Patterson, W. H. (Chatham House, Ramsgate, and Harrow), 1880–81

Pawson, A. C. (Winchester), 1903

Pawson, A. G. (Winchester) (Capt. in 1910), 1908–11

Pawson, H. A. (Winchester) (Capt. in 1948), 1947–48

Payne, A. (Private) (Capt. in 1856), 1852, 1854–56

Payne, A. F. (Private), 1855

Payne, C. A. L. (Charterhouse), 1906–07

Peake, E. (Marlborough), 1881–83

Pearse, G. V. (Maritzburg College, Natal), 1919

Peat, C. U. (Sedbergh), 1913

Peebles, I. A. R. (Glasgow Academy), 1930

Pershke, W. J. (Uppingham), 1938

Pether, S. (Magdalen College School), 1939

Philipson, H. (Eton) (Capt. in 1889), 1887–89

Phillips, F. A. (Rossall), 1892, 1894–95

Phillips, J. B.(King's, Canterbury), 1955

Pilkington, C. C. (Eton), 1896

Pilkington, H. C. (Eton), 1899–1900

Pilkington, W. (Midhurst), 1827

Potts, H. J. (Stand G. S.), 1950

Price, V. R. (Bishop's Stortford) (Capt. in 1921), 1919–22

Proud, R. B. (Winchester), 1939

Pycroft, J. (Bath), 1836

Raikes, D. C. G. (Shrewsbury), 1931

Raikes, G. B. (Shrewsbury), 1894–95

Raikes, T. B. (Winchester), 1922–24

Randolph, B. M. (Charterhouse), 1855–56

Randolph, C. (Eton), 1844–45

Randolph, J. (Westminster), 1843

Randolph, L. C. (Westminster), 1845

Raphael, J. E. (Merchant Taylors), 1903–05

Rashleigh, W. (Tonbridge) (Capt. in 1888), 1886–89

Rice, R. W. (Cardiff), 1893

Richardson, J. V. (Uppingham), 1925

Ricketts, G. W. (Winchester), 1887

Ridding A. (Winchester), 1846–50

Ridding, C. H. (Winchester), 1845–49

Ridding, W. (Winchester) (Capt. in 1849 and 1851, also in 1851 but did not play v. Cambridge, owing to illness), 1849–50, 1852–53

Robertson-Glasgow, R. C. (Charterhouse), 1920–23

Robinson, G. E. (Burton), 1881–83

Robinson, H. B. (North Shore College, Vancouver), 1947–48

Robinson, R. L. (St. Peter's College, Adelaide, and Adelaide University), 1908–09

Royle, Vernon (Rossall), 1875–76

Rucker, C. E. S. (Charterhouse), 1914

Rucker, P. W. (Charterhouse), 1919

Rudd, C. R. D. (Eton), 1949

Ruggles-Brise, H. G. (Winchester), 1883

Rumbold, J. S. (St. Andrew's College New Zealand), 1946

Sale, R. (Repton), 1910

Sale, R. (*junior*) (Repton), 1939, 1946

Salter, M. G. (Cheltenham), 1909–10

Samson, O. M. (Cheltenham), 1903

Schwann, H. S. (Clifton), 1890

Scott, Lord Geo. (Eton), 1887–89

Scott, M. D. (Winchester), 1957

Scott, K. B. (Winchester), 1937

Scott, R. S. G. (Winchester), 1931

Seamer, J. W. (Marlborough), 1934–36

Seitz, J. A. (Scotch College and Melbourne University), 1909

---

* Thesiger began to play in the game of 1891, but retired injured soon after the start. The Cambridge captain allowed his place to be taken by T. B. Case.

CAMBRIDGE

Aird, R. (Eton), 1923
Alexander, F. C. M. (Wolmer's Coll., Jamaica), 1952–53
Allen, A. W. (Eton), 1933–34
Allen, B. O. (Clifton), 1933
Allen, G. O. (Eton), 1922–23
Allom, M. J. C. (Wellington), 1927–28
Arnold, A. C. P. (Malvern), 1914
Ashton, C. T. (Winchester) (Capt. in 1923), 1921–23
Ashton, G. (Winchester) (Capt. in 1921), 1919–21
Ashton, H. (Winchester) (Capt. in 1922), 1920–22
Austin, H. M. (Melbourne), 1924

Baggallay, M. E. C. (Eton), 1911
Bagnall, H. F. (Harrow), 1923
Bailey, T. E. (Dulwich), 1947–48
Baily, E. P. (Harrow), 1872, 1874
Baily, R. E. H. (Harrow), 1908
Bainbridge, H. W. (Eton) (Capt. in 1886), 1884–86
Barber, R. W. (Ruthin), 1956–57
Baker, E. C. (Brighton), 1912, 1914
Bartlett, H. T. (Dulwich) (Capt. in 1936), 1934–36
Bennett, C. T. (Harrow) (Capt. in 1925, 1923, 1925)
Blake, J. P. (Aldenham), 1939
Blaker, R. N. (Elizabeth College, Guernsey), 1842–43
Blaker, R. N. R. (Westminster), 1900–02
Bligh, Ivo F. W. (Lord Darnley) (Eton) (Capt. in 1881), 1878–81
Block, S. A. (Marlborough), 1929
Blundell, E. D. (Waitaki, New Zealand), 1928–29
Bodkin, P. E. (Bradfield) (Capt. in 1946), 1946
Bray, E. (Westminster), 1871–72
Bray, E. H. (Charterhouse), 1896–97
Bridgeman, W. C. (Eton), 1887
Brocklebank, J. M. (Eton), 1936
Brodhurst, A. H. (Malvern), 1939
Bromley-Davenport, H. R. (Eton), 1892–93
Brooke-Taylor, G. P. (Cheltenham), 1919–20
Brown, F. R. (Leys), 1930–31
Browne, F. B. R. (Aldro School and Eastbourne College), 1922
Brunton, J. du V. (Lancaster Grammar School), 1894
Bryan, J. L. (Rugby), 1921
Buchanan, J. N. (Charterhouse) (Capt. in 1909), 1906–09
Buckston, G. M. (Eton), 1903
Burnett, A. C. (Lancing), 1949
Burnup, C. J. (Malvern), 1896–98

Burrough, J. (King's School, Bruton, and Shrewsbury), 1895
Bushby, M. H. (Dulwich) (Capt. in 1954), 1952–54
Butler, E. M. (Harrow), 1888–89
Butterworth, H. R. W. (Rydal Mount), 1929
Buxton, C. D. (Harrow) (Capt. in 1888), 1885–88

Calthorpe, F. S. G. (Repton), 1912–14, 1919
Cameron, J. H. (Taunton), 1935–37
Cangley, B. G. (Felsted), 1947
Carris, B. D. (Harrow), 1938–39
Carris, H. E. (Mill Hill), 1930
Cawston, E. (Lancing), 1932
Chapman, A. P. F. (Oakham and Uppingham), 1920–22
Christopherson, J. C. (Uppingham), 1931
Cobbold, P. W. (Eton), 1896
Cobbold, R. H. (Eton), 1927
Cobden, F. C. (Harrow), 1870–72
Cockett, J. A. (Aldenham), 1951
Colbeck, L. G. (Marlborough), 1905–06
Collins, D. C. (Wellington College, Wellington, N.Z.), 1910–11
Comber, J. T. H. (Marlborough), 1931–33
Conradi, E. R. (Oundle), 1946
Coode, A. T. (Fauconberge School, Beccles), 1898
Cook, G. W. (Dulwich), 1957
Cowie, A. G. (Charterhouse), 1910
Crawley, E. (Harrow), 1887–89
Crawley, L. G. (Harrow), 1923–25
Croft, P. D. (Gresham's, Holt), 1955
Crookes, D. V. (Michaelhouse, South Africa), 1953
Cumberlege, B. S. (Durham), 1913

Daniell, J. (Clifton), 1899–1901
Datta, P. B. (Asutosh College, Calcutta), 1947
Davies, G. B. (Rossall), 1913–14
Davies, J. G. W. (Tonbridge), 1933–34
Dawson, E. W. (Eton) (Capt. in 1927), 1924–27
Day, S. H. (Malvern) (Capt. in 1901), 1899–1902
De Little, E. R. (Geelong Grammar School), 1889
De Paravicini, P. J. (Eton), 1882–85
De Zoete, H. W. (Eton), 1897–98
Dewes, J. G. (Aldenham), 1948–50
Dexter, E. R. (Radley), 1956–57
Dickinson, D. C. (Clifton), 1953
Dickinson, P. J. (K.C.S., Wimbledon), 1939

Doggart, A. G. (Bishop's Stortford), 1921–22
Doggart, G. H. G. (Winchester) (Capt. in 1950), 1948–50
Dorman, A. W. (Dulwich), 1886
Douglas, J. (Dulwich), 1892–94
Douglas, R. N. (Dulwich), 1890–92
Downes, K. D. (Rydal), 1939
Dowson, E. M. (Harrow) (Capt. in 1903), 1900–03
Driffield, L. T. (Leatherhead), 1902
Druce, N. F. (Marlborough) (Capt. in 1897), 1894–97
Druce, W. G. (Marlborough) (Capt. in 1895), 1894–95
Duleepsinhji, K. S. (Cheltenham), 1925–26, 1928

Ebden, C. H. M. (Eton), 1902–03
Elgood, B. C. (Bradfield), 1948
Enthoven, H. J. (Harrow) (Capt. in 1926), 1923–26
Estcourt, N. S. D. (Plumtree, Southern Rhodesia), 1954
Evans, R. G. (King Edward, Bury St. Edmunds), 1921
Eyre, C. H. (Harrow) (Capt. in 1906), 1904–06

Fabian, A. H. (Highgate), 1929–31
Fairbairn, G. A. (Church of England Grammar School, Geelong), 1913–14, 1919
Falcon, M. (Harrow) (Capt. in 1910), 1908–11
Fargus, A. H. C. (Clifton and Haileybury), 1900–01
Farnes, K. (Royal Liberty School, Romford), 1931–33
Fernie, A. E. (Wellingborough), 1897, 1900
Fiddian-Green, C. A. (Leys), 1921–22
Field, E. (Clifton), 1894
Foley, C. P. (Eton), 1889–91
Foley, E. (Eton), 1880
Ford, A. F. J. (Repton), 1878–81
Ford, F. G. J. (Repton) (Capt. in 1889) 1887–90
Ford, W. J. (Repton), 1873
Francis, T. E. S. (Tonbridge), 1925
Franklin, W. B. (Repton), 1912
Fraser, T. W. (Jeppe, S. Africa), 1937
Freeman-Thomas F. (Lord Willingdon) (Eton), 1886–89
Frere, J. (Eton), 1827
Fry, K. R. B. (Cheltenham), 1904

Gaddum, F. D. (Uppingham and Rugby), 1882
Gay, L. H. (Marlborough and Brighton), 1892–93
Gibb, P. A. (St. Edward's, Oxford), 1935–38

Gibson, C. H. (Eton), 1920–21
Gillespie, D. W. (Uppingham), 1939
Gilligan, A. E. R. (Dulwich), 1919–20
Gilman, J. (St. Paul's), 1902
Godsell, R. T. (Clifton), 1903
Goodwin, H J. (Marlborough), 1907–08
Goonesena, G. (Royal Coll., Colombo), (Capt. in 1957), 1954–57
Gosling, R. C. (Eton), 1888–90
Grace, W. G., junr. (Clifton), 1895–96
Grant, G. C. (Trinidad), 1929–30
Grant, R. S. (Trinidad), 1933
Gray, H. (Perse), 1894–95
Green, C. E. (Uppingham) (Capt. in 1868), 1865–68
Green, D. J. (Burton G.S.), 1957
Grierson, H. (Bedford Grammar), 1911
Griffith, S. C. (Dulwich), 1935
Griffiths, W. H. (Charterhouse), 1946–48
Grimshaw, J. W. T. (King William's College, Isle of Man), 1934–35

Hadingham, A. W. G. (St. Paul's), 1932
Hale, H. (Hutchins School, Hobart), 1887, 1889–90
Hall, P. J. (Geelong), 1949
Harbinson, W. K. (Marlborough), 1929
Harper, L. V. (Rossall), 1901–03
Harrison, W. P. (Rugby), 1907
Hawke, M. B. (Lord) (Eton) (Capt. in 1885), 1882–83, 1885
Hawkins, H. H. B. (Whitgift), 1898–99
Hayward, W. I. D. (St. Peter's College, Adelaide), 1950–51, 1953
Hazlerigg, A. G. (Eton) (Capt. in 1932), 1930–32
Hemingway, W. McG. (Uppingham), 1895–96
Henery, P. J. T. (Harrow), 1882–83
Hewan, G. E. (Marlborough), 1938
Hill, A. J. L. (Marlborough), 1890–93
Hill-Wood, W. W. (Eton), 1922
Hind, A. E. (Uppingham), 1898–1901
Hobson, B. S. (Taunton), 1946
Holloway, N. J. (Leys), 1910–12
Hone, N. T. (Rugby), 1881
Hopley, F. J. V. (Harrow), 1904
Hopley, G. W. (Harrow), 1912
Hotchkin, N. S. (Eton), 1935
Howard-Smith, G. (Eton), 1903
Hughes, O. (Malvern), 1910
Hunt, R. G. (Aldenham), 1937
Human, J. H. (Repton) (Capt. in 1934), 1932–34
Human, R. H. C. (Repton), 1930–31

Imlay, A. D. (Clifton), 1907
Insole, D. J. (Monoux, Walthamstow) (Capt. in 1949), 1947–49
Ireland, J. F. (Marlborough) (Capt. in 1911), 1908–11
Irvine, L. G. (Taunton), 1926–27

Napier, G. G. (Marlborough), 1904–07
Nason, J. W. W. (University School, Hastings), 1909–10
Naumann, J. H. (Malvern), 1913, 1919
Nelson, R. P. (St. George's, Harpenden), 1936
Norman, C. L. (Eton), 1852–53
Norman, F. H. (Eton) (Capt. in 1860), 1858–60

O'Brien, R. (Wellington), 1955–56
Olivier, E. (Repton), 1908–09
Orford, L. A. (Uppingham), 1886–87

Page, C. C. (Malvern), 1905–06
Palmer, C. (Uppingham), 1907
Parker, G. W. (Crypt Gloucester) (Capt. in 1935), 1934–35
Parry, D. M. (Merchant Taylors), 1931
Parsons, A. B. D. (Brighton), 1954–55
Partridge, N. E. (Malvern), 1920
Patterson, W. S. (Uppingham) (Capt. in 1877), 1875–77
Pawle, J. H. (Harrow), 1936–37
Payne, A. U. (St. Edmund's, Canterbury), 1925
Payne, M. W. (Wellington) (Capt. in 1907), 1904–07
Payton, W. E. G. (Nottingham High School), 1937
Pelham, A. G. (Eton), 1934
Pelham, F. G. (Eton) (Capt. in 1866–67), 1864–67
Penn, E. F. (Eton), 1899, 1902
Pepper, J. (The Leys), 1946–48
Perkins, H. (Bury St. Edmunds), 1854
Perkins, T. T. N. (Leatherhead), 1893–94
Phillips, E. S. (Marlborough), 1904
Pickering, E. H. (Eton) (Capt. in 1829), 1827, 1829
Pickering, W. P. (Eton), 1840, 1842
Pieris, P. I. (St. Thomas, Colombo), 1957
Ponsonby, F. G. B. (Lord Bessborough) (Harrow), 1836
Pope, C. G. (Harrow), 1894
Popplewell, O. B. (Charterhouse), 1949–51
Powell, A. G. (Charterhouse), 1934
Prest, E. B. (Eton), 1850
Prest, H. E. W. (Malvern), 1909, 1911
Pretlove, J. F. (Alleyn's), 1954–56
Pryer, B. J. K. (City of London), 1948

Ramsay, R. C. (Harrow), 1882
Ranjitsinhji, K. S. (Rajkumar College, India), 1893
Ratcliffe, A. (Rydal School), 1930–32
Rees-Davies, W. R. (Eton), 1938
Riddell, V. H. (Clifton), 1926
Riley, W. N. (Worcester Grammar School), 1912

Rimell, A. G. J. (Charterhouse), 1949–50
Roberts, F. B. (Rossall), 1903
Robertson, W. P. (Harrow), 1901
Robins, R. W. V. (Highgate), 1926–28
Robinson, J. J. (Appleby), 1894
Rock, C. W. (Launceston Grammar School, Tasmania), 1884–86
Roe, W. N. (Clergy Orphan School, Canterbury), 1883
Rotherham G. A. (Rugby), 1919
Rought-Rought, D. C. (Private), 1937
Rought-Rought, R. C. (Private), 1930, 1932
Rowe, F. C. C. (Harrow), 1881
Rowell, W. I. (Marlborough), 1891

Savile, A. (Eton), 1840
Savile, G. (Eton and Rossall), 1868
Saville, S. H. (Marlborough) (Capt. in 1914), 1911–14
Seabrook, F. J. (Haileybury) (Capt. in 1928), 1926–28
Seddon, R. (Bridgnorth Grammar School), 1846–47
Shelmerdine, G. O. (Cheltenham), 1922
Sheppard, D. S. (Sherborne) (Capt. in 1952), 1950–52
Sherwell, N. B. (Tonbridge), 1923–25
Shine, E. B. (King Edward VI School, Saffron Walden), 1896–97
Shirley, W. R. (Eton), 1924
Shirreff, A. C. (Dulwich), 1939
Shuttleworth, G. M. (Queen Elizabeth Grammar School), 1946–48
Silk, D. R. W. (Christ's Hospital), (Capt. in 1955), 1953–55
Singh, S. (Khalsa and Punjab U.), 1955–56
Slack, J. K. E. (U.C.S.), 1954
Smith, C. A. (Charterhouse), 1882–85
Smith, C. S. (William Hulme's G.S.), 1954–57
Smith, D. J. (Stockport G.S.), 1955–56
Spencer, R. (Harrow), 1881
Spiro, D. G. (Harrow), 1884
Stanning, J. (Rugby), 1900
Steel, A. G. (Marlborough) (Capt. in 1880), 1878–81
Steel, D. Q. (Uppingham), 1876–79
Stevenson, M. H. (Rydal), 1949–52
Stogdon, J. H. (Harrow), 1897–99
Streatfeild, E. C. (Charterhouse), 1890–93
Studd, C. T. (Eton) (Capt. in 1883), 1880–83
Studd, G. B. (Eton) (Capt. in 1882), 1879–82
Studd, J. E. K. (Eton) (Capt. in 1884), 1881–84
Studd, P. M. (Harrow) (Capt. in 1939), 1937–39
Studd, R. A. (Eton), 1895

Subba Row, R. (Whitgift), 1951–53

Sutthery, A. M. (Uppingham and Oundle), 1887

Swift, B. T. (St. Peter's, Adelaide), 1957

Taylor, T. L. (Uppingham) (Capt. in 1900), 1898–1900

Thompson, J. R. (Tonbridge), 1938–39

Thornton, C. I. (Eton) (Capt. in 1872), 1869–72

Tindall, M. (Harrow) (Capt. in 1937), 1935–37

Tomlinson, W. J. V. (Felsted), 1923

Topham, H. G. (Repton), 1883–84

Toppin, C. (Sedbergh), 1885–87

Tordoff, G. G. (Normanton G.S.), 1952

Trapnell, B. M. W. (U.C.S.), 1946

Tufnell, N. C. (Eton), 1909–10

Turnbull, M. J. (Downside) Capt. in 1929), 1926, 1928–29

Turner, J. A. (Uppingham), 1883–86

Urquhart, J. R. (King Edward VI School, Chelmsford), 1948

Valentine, B. H. (Repton), 1929

Vincent, H. G. (Haileybury), 1914

Wait, O. J. (Dulwich), 1949, 1951

Ward, E. E., Rev. (Bury St. Edmunds), 1870–71

Warr, J. J. (Ealing County Grammar School) (Capt. in 1951), 1949–52

Watts, H. E. (Downside), 1947

Webster, J. (Bradford G.S.), 1939

Webster, W. H. (Highgate), 1932

Weigall, G. J. V. (Wellington), 1891–92

Wells, C. M. (Dulwich), 1891–93

Wells, T. U. (King's College, Auckland, N.Z.), 1950

Wheatley, O. S. (King Edward's, Birmingham), 1957

White, A. F. T. (Uppingham), 1936

White, A. H. (Geelong), 1924

Whitfeld, H. (Eton), 1878–81

Wilcox, D. R. (Dulwich) (Capt. in 1933), 1931–33

Wild, J. V. (Taunton), 1938

Wilenkin, B. C. G. (Harrow), 1956

Willatt, G. L. (Repton) (Capt. in 1947), 1946–47

Wilson, C. E. M. (Uppingham) (Capt. in 1898), 1895–98

Wilson, C. P. (Uppingham and Marlborough), 1880–81

Wilson, E. R. (Rugby) (Capt. in 1902), 1899–02

Wilson, F. B. (Harrow) (Capt. in 1904), 1902–04

Wilson, G. (Harrow), 1919

Winlaw, R. de W. K. (Winchester), 1932–34

Winter, A. H. (Westminster), 1865–67

Winter, C. E. (Uppingham), 1902

Winter, G. E. (Winchester), 1898–99

Wood, G. E. C. (Cheltenham) (Capt. in 1920), 1914, 1919–20

Woodroffe, K. H. C. (Marlborough), 1913–14

Woods, S. M. J. (Brighton) (Capt. in 1890), 1888–91

Wooller, W. (Rydal), 1935–36

Wright, C. C. G. (Tonbridge), 1907–08

Wright, C. W. (Charterhouse), 1882–85

Wright, P. A. (Wellingborough), 1922–24

Wykes, N. G. (Oundle), 1928

Yardley, N. W. D. (St. Peter's, York) (Capt. in 1938), 1935–38

Yardley, W. (Rugby) (Capt. in 1871), 1869–72

Young, R. A. (Repton) (Capt. in 1908), 1905–08

OTHER MATCHES IN 1957

SCOTLAND v. YORKSHIRE

At Paisley, May 29, 30, 31. Drawn. Lack of enterprise by the Scottish batsmen on a pitch which remained true throughout the three days prevented a definite result. Missed before scoring, Aitchison spent three hours over 53, but Brown, the wicket-keeper, hit freely. D. Wilson bowled his left-arm slows accurately on his first appearance for Yorkshire who had to thank Watson and Lowson for seeing them into a strong position by making 190 for the opening stand. Watson drove splendidly while getting his first century of the season. On the last day, when Yorkshire were handicapped through injuries to Binks and Platt, steady defence by Chisholm saved Scotland.

Scotland

R. H. E. Chisholm c Binks b Cowan	...	32	— not out	61
L. Dudman b Appleyard	....	21	— c Watson b Cowan	3
Rev. J. Aitchison lbw b D. Wilson		53	— c Cowan b Appleyard	23
J. N. Kemsley c Lowson b Cowan	......	2	— c and b Stott	27
D. Barr c J. Wilson b Appleyard	....	6	— not out	13
S. H. Cosh c and b Platt	....	15		
J. Brown b D. Wilson	....	90		
W. D. F. Dow b D. Wilson	....	15		
D. Livingstone b Appleyard	....	0		
M. Kerrigan lbw b Appleyard	....	6		
J. S. Wilson not out	....	9		
B 5, l-b 4, n-b 3	....	12	B 4, l-b 4, n-b 2	10
		—		—
		261	(3 wkts.)	137

1/41 2/70 3/86 4/100 5/121 6/153 7/216 8/217 9/225

1/19 2/51 3/113

Yorkshire

F. A. Lowson c Cosh b Kerrigan	.	90	D. Wilson not out	4
W. Watson hit wkt b Dow	....	134	M. J. Cowan c Barr b Kerrigan	0
J. V. Wilson b Wilson	....	19	J. G. Binks absent hurt	0
W. H. H. Sutcliffe c Barr b Kerrigan		67	L-b 1, n-b 4	5
K. Taylor c Brown b Wilson	.....	25		—
W. B. Stott run out	...	21		374
R. K. Platt run out	....	7		
R. Appleyard c Dudman b Chisholm		2		

1/190 2/247 3/247 4/296 5/356 6/366 7/369 8/372 9/374

Yorkshire Bowling

	O.	M.	R.	W.	O.	M.	R.	W.
Platt	24	5	70	1	4	3	1	0
Cowan	32	9	89	2	13	4	27	1
D. Wilson	26.4	12	28	3	14	7	22	0
Appleyard	27	8	48	4	16	5	43	1
Taylor	5	1	6	0				
Stott	2	0	8	0	6	3	10	1
Watson					3	1	9	0
J. Wilson					3	1	8	0
Sutcliffe.......					1	0	7	0

Scotland Bowling

	O.	M.	R.	W.
Dow	22	1	82	1
Wilson	24	3	66	2
Kerrigan	36.3	11	92	3
Livingstone	29	4	80	0
Chisholm	4	0	13	1
Barr	12	3	36	0

Umpires: C. B. Hirst and C. C. Black.

NORTHUMBERLAND v. YORKSHIRE

At Jesmond, June 5, 6. Yorkshire won by an innings and 158 runs. Northumberland 194 (P. Shaw 74, J. H. Wardle four for 63) and 117 (J. H. Wardle five for 61); Yorkshire 469 for six wickets, declared (D. E. V. Padgett 102 not out, R. Illingworth 79, W. H. H. Sutcliffe 63, F. A. Lowson 56, D. B. Close 51).

D. R. JARDINE'S XI v. OXFORD UNIVERSITY

At Eastbourne, July 3, 4, 5. Oxford University won by 55 runs. A splendid century by Jowett turned the scales in a match where bowlers, helped by a rain-soaked pitch, acquitted themselves satisfactorily, Wait, Bailey and Gibson each took five wickets and Thresher (twice) and Allan claimed four. An early morning storm prevented play before lunch on the opening day when Oxford collapsed, but Jardine's side also fared badly until the tail came to the rescue. When Oxford lost seven second innings wickets for 75 they seemed hopelessly placed, but Scott stayed while Jowett drove and pulled to such purpose that he hit seventeen 4's. Finally, some admirable leg-spin bowling by Gibson saw Oxford home, despite a stubborn effort by Parsons who stayed nearly two hours.

Oxford University

I. Gibson b Thresher	27	—	c Melluish b Thresher	8
J. A. D. Hobbs c and b Wait	0	—	c Robins b Thresher	19
A. C. Walton lbw b Thresher	1	—	lbw b Wait	2
C. D. Melville run out	7	—	c Parsons b Thresher	12
M. A. Eagar c Melluish b Allan	10	—	lbw b Wait	3
R. L. Jowett b Thresher	0	—	b Thresher	122
J. M. Kumleben c and b Allan	1	—	c Allan b Wait	5
R. G. Woodcock b Thresher	9	—	b Wait	0
M. D. Scott not out	18	—	c and b Allan	31
R. W. Wilson c Melluish b Allan	1	—	b Wait	8
J. A. Bailey c Thoy b Allan	12	—	not out	1
			B 6, l-b 1, n-b 1	8

1/2 2/3 3/31 4/35 5/35 6/36 7/53   86   1/12 2/24 3/41 4/48   219
8/63 9/64   5/48 6/50 7/75 8/156 9/197

D. R. Jardine's XI

J. M. Allan b Bailey	1	—	b Gibson	9
M. E. Melluish c Bailey b Melville	5	—	b Bailey	0
A. D. B. Parsons b Wilson	15	—	c Melville b Woodcock	42
C. E. Winn b Bailey	0	—	c Wilson b Woodcock	13
L. Church b Bailey	1	—	lbw b Gibson	0
R. E. Thoy c Hobbs b Bailey	13	—	b Wilson	5
R. V. C. Robins c Bailey b Wilson	26	—	b Wilson	7
K. Pestell c Jowett b Wilson	16	—	b Gibson	21
J. G. Walker c Wilson b Bailey	26	—	b Gibson	15
O. J. Wait c Kumleben b Wilson	19	—	b Gibson	7
R. S. Thresher not out	2	—	not out	0
B 1, l-b 1	2		B 2, l-b 3	5

1/2 2/10 3/11 4/13 5/35 6/35 7/70   126   1/1 2/21 3/30 4/42 5/67   124
8/83 9/120   6/82 7/112 8/112 9/121

D. R. Jardine's XI Bowling

	O.	M.	R.	W.	O.	M.	R.	W.
Wait	11	5	22	1	27	5	85	5
Thresher	21	12	29	4	22.2	7	42	4
Allan	14	6	35	4	12	2	50	1
Church					4	0	16	0
Pestell					5	2	17	0
Robins					1	0	1	0

Oxford Bowling

	O.	M.	R.	W.	O.	M.	R.	W.
Bailey	30	11	58	5	7	2	8	1
Melville	9	4	19	1	5	2	7	0
Wilson	22.4	4	42	4	23	7	54	2
Jowett	2	0	5	0				
Gibson					14.4	4	29	5
Woodcock					7	0	21	2

Umpires: T. Medhurst and J. R. Funnell.

SCOTLAND v. M.C.C.

At Aberdeen, July 3, 4, 5. Drawn. M.C.C., under the inspiring captaincy of F. R. Brown, made a great recovery after being 149 behind on the first innings. Set to make 275 in two hours fifty minutes they came within 18 of their target. Despite steady and prolonged bowling by Brown who took six wickets in 46 overs, Scotland built up a substantial total with Kemsley scoring a century in as many minutes. Paterson, the former Essex secretary, batted splendidly for M.C.C. in both innings, but in pulling the match round they also owed much to Knott, the former Hampshire off-spinner who took eight wickets for only 38 runs. Neame, the former Harrow captain, and Taylor gave Paterson good support when M.C.C. hit so freely on the last afternoon that only two maiden overs were delivered by the Scottish bowlers.

Scotland

R. H. E. Chisholm c Taylor b Wilson ...	35	— lbw b Knott	40
L. C. Dudman lbw b Muncer	48	— c Taylor b Knott	46
Rev. J. Aitchison c Muncer b Brown	52	— lbw b Knott	0
J. N. Kemsley c and b Brown	103	— c Taylor b Knott........	2
D. Barr c Sharp b Brown	40	— b Muncer	18
S. H. Cosh c Taylor b Brown	35	— c Neame b Knott	0
J. Brown run out	11		
J. B. Roberts st Taylor b Brown	21	— not out	9
M. Kerrigan lbw b Brown	13	— c Neame b Knott	3
D. Livingstone lbw b Wilson	0	— b Knott...............	3
D. R. Lawrence not out	6	— c Swallow b Knott	3
B 11, l-b 3, w 3, n-b 1	18	B 4...................	4

1/85 2/106 3/166 4/252 5/312 6/339   384   1/77 2/77   (9 wkts., dec.) 125
7/347 8/363 9/365   3/101 4/101 5/110 6/110
                                         7/116 8/121 9/125

M.C.C.

R. F. T. Paterson c Aitchison b Roberts.	52	— c Barr b Kerrigan	88
R. Swallow c Brown b Livingstone	21	— b Barr	6
B. Taylor c and b Roberts	27	— c sub b Livingstone	42
A. R. B. Neame b Lawrence	0	— c Cosh b Barr	69
J. S. Mendl c Livingstone b Lawrence ...	17	— not out	12
H. P. Sharp b Lawrence	4	— not out	2
F. R. Brown lbw b Lawrence	48	— b Lawrence	29
B. L. Muncer run out	37		
R. L. Whitby c Aitchison b Livingstone .	11		
C. J. Knott not out	2		
G. C. Wilson not out	7		
B 2, l-b 5, n-b 2	9	B 6, l-b 2, n-b 1.......	9

1/56 2/104 3/105 4/105   (9 wkts., dec.) 235   1/27 2/106   (5 wkts.) 257
5/110 6/170 7/187 8/219 9/226   3/190 4/234 5/254

M.C.C. Bowling

	O.	M.	R.	W.	O.	M.	R.	W.
Brown	46.5	10	147	6	 9	2	33	0
Wilson	34	9	85	2	 7	0	24	0
Muncer	18	6	37	1	 8	1	14	1
Whitby	18	4	50	0	 5	1	12	0
Knott	20	8	38	0	.... 15.2	4	38	8
Neame	3	0	9	0				

Scotland Bowling

	O.	M.	R.	W.	O.	M.	R.	W.
Lawrence	29	5	56	4	 13	0	58	1
Barr	15	3	31	0	 11	0	52	2
Livingstone	26	10	52	2	 9	0	45	1
Kerrigan	20	3	40	0	 9	1	36	1
Roberts	22	8	36	2	 9	1	39	0
Chisholm	3	0	11	0	 3	0	18	0

Umpires: C. B. Hirst and J. Boyd.

COL. L. C. STEVEN'S XI v. ROYAL AIR FORCE

At Eastbourne, July 24, 25. Drawn. Royal Air Force 226 (G. G. Atkinson 63, R. Subba Row 57) and 145 for eight wickets, declared (M. D. Fenner 47, D. Goodson four for 76); Col. L. C. Steven's XI 94 and 241 for eight wickets (G. Potter 105, S. Leadbetter 66).

IRELAND v. SCOTLAND

At Dublin, July 27, 29. Ireland won by 38 runs with a day to spare. Exceptional spin bowling and wicket-keeping marked this match in which the highest individual score was 30. Frank Fee, the 23-year-old off-spinner, achieved an Irish record in taking nine wickets for 26 runs. He finished with twelve for 60 and Livingstone, specialising in leg-breaks, took eleven wickets for 51 for Scotland. He owed much to the competency of Brown who equalled the world's wicket-keeping record with seven victims in one innings.

Ireland

S. F. Bergin b Barr	13	— c Brown b Lawrence	17
K. Quinn st Brown b Livingstone	25	— c Brown b Wilson	2
A. Finlay b Lawrence	24	— st Brown b Livingstone	9
L. A. Warke c Dudman b Livingstone...	1	— c Brown b Wilson	4
J. S. Pollock c Dudman b Barr	21	— b Livingstone	17
W. I. Lewis c Barr b Wilson	10	— c Brown b Livingstone	4
A. P. Hollick b Livingstone	0	— b Roberts	0
G. W. Fawcett c Wilson b Livingstone..	9	— st Brown b Livingstone	3
I. B. J. Wilson st Brown b Livingstone..	7	— c Aitchison b Livingstone ..	4
F. Fee c Cosh b Livingstone	7	— not out	9
E. H. Bodell not out	9	— st Brown b Roberts	0
B 1, l-b 3, w 1, n-b 8	13	B 1, l-b 1, n-b 2.........	4

1/27 2/54 3/59 4/72 5/92 6/99   139   1/17 2/23 3/28 4/38 5/42   73
7/106 8/113 9/123   6/47 7/52 8/63 9/72

Scotland

R. H. E. Chisholm b Fee	12	—	lbw b Bodell		3
L. C. Dudman b Fee	7	—	c Hollick b Fee		17
Rev. J. Aitchison c Bergin b Fee	3	—	b Fee		30
J. N. Kemsley c Warke b Fee	3	—	b Bodell		0
D. Barr c Warke b Fee	12	—	b Bodell		2
S. H. Cosh b Fee	0	—	b Bodell		2
J. Brown not out	25	—	c Fee b Wilson		7
J. B. Roberts c Warke b Fee	0	—	c Fee b Wilson		6
D. Livingstone b Fee	6	—	not out		16
J. S. Wilson c Fawcett b Fee	0	—	b Wilson		1
D. R. Lawrence b Warke	10	—	b Fee		0
B 2, l-b 1, n-b 1	4		B 3, l-b 5		8

1/13 2/22 3/27 4/34 5/34 6/41 7/41   82   1/6 2/46 3/46 4/50 5/56   92
8/49 9/49   6/56 7/72 8/75 9/89

Scotland Bowling

	O.	M.	R.	W.		O.	M.	R.	W.
Wilson	14	5	23	1	....	9	5	22	2
Lawrence	14	4	24	1	....	6	1	19	1
Barr	13	2	27	2	....	4	2	5	0
Roberts	11	4	19	0	....	8	5	5	2
Livingstone	23.5	6	33	6	....	14	5	18	5

Ireland Bowling

	O.	M.	R.	W.		O.	M.	R.	W.
Bodell	23	6	45	0	....	14	6	24	4
Warke	3.4	1	7	1	....	3	0	16	0
Fee	22	12	26	9	....	21	7	34	3
Wilson	2	2	0	0	....	10	6	10	3

Umpires: J. Connerton and K. Orme.

ROYAL NAVY v. ROYAL AIR FORCE

At Portsmouth, July 31, August 1. Drawn. Royal Navy 212 (C. D. White 46, K. Serpanchy 46, A. C. Shirreff six for 61) and 160 (B. Knight four for 45, R. Subba Row four for 24); Royal Air Force 190 for five wickets, declared (R. Subba Row 50 not out) and 170 for eight wickets (G. Atkinson 46).

SCARBOROUGH FESTIVAL

At Scarborough, August 31, September 2, 3. YORKSHIRE beat M.C.C. by eight wickets. (See YORKSHIRE section.)

GENTLEMEN v. PLAYERS

At Scarborough, September 4, 5, 6. Players won by six wickets. Enterprising batting by both sides amply compensated spectators for much time lost through rain on the first day. The Players did well to win, for on the second day when Bailey, accurate with his medium-fast bowling, took four of their first five wickets for 18 runs out of 35, they were in sore straits. Aggressive stroke-play by Reynolds and his Northamptonshire colleague Tyson, who shared in a stand of 114, turned the tide and Gentlemen eventually led on the first innings by eight runs. The exciting cricket continued on the last day. Dexter driving powerfully, and Smith helped the Gentlemen score 226 in two and a half hours before a declaration, and the Players were set to make 235 in just under two and three-quarter hours. When Close and Gale began with a partnership of 133, victory for the professionals seemed assured, but Warr, fast and lively, caused them anxious moments before D. W. Richardson, hitting forcefully, decided the issue. Even so, the Players had only eight minutes to spare at the finish.

Gentlemen

P. E. Richardson c Gale b Shepherd	 54	— lbw b Trueman	 2
W. H. H. Sutcliffe b Tyson	 1	— not out	 8
M. J. K. Smith b Tyson	 1	— c Close b Wardle	 50
W. J. Edrich c Reynolds b Shepherd	 29	— b Graveney	 34
A. C. Walton c Graveney b Wardle	 28	— c Shepherd b Graveney	 30
E. R. Dexter c Evans b Close	 6	— c Taylor b Trueman	 88
D. J. Insole b Wardle	 35		
T. E. Bailey not out	 31		
G. Goonesena not out	 22		
L-b 3, n-b 4	 7	B 4, l-b 5, n-b 5	 14

1/9 2/20 3/74 4/106   (7 wkts., dec.) 214   1/2 2/93   (5 wkts., dec.) 226
5/121 6/127 7/173   3/163 4/209 5/226
J. J. Warr and M. E. L. Melluish did not bat.

Players

D. B. Close b Warr	 4	— run out	 79
R. A. Gale lbw b Bailey	 4	— st Melluish b Goonesena	.. 83
T. W. Graveney b Bailey	 13	— b Warr	 6
D. W. Richardson b Bailey	 0	— not out	 54
B. Taylor lbw b Bailey	 6	— c Insole b Warr	 2
B. Reynolds c Edrich b Insole	 75		
T. G. Evans lbw b Dexter	 13	— not out	 4
F. H. Tyson c Edrich b Insole	 63		
J. H. Wardle c Bailey b Goonesena	 1		
F. S. Trueman run out	 7		
D. J. Shepherd not out	 10		
B 4, w 5, n-b 1	 10	B 4, l-b 3	 7

1/4 2/8 3/8 4/24 5/35 6/59 7/173   206   1/133 2/200   (4 wkts.) 235
8/174 9/188   3/219 4/226

Players Bowling

	O.	M.	R.	W.		O.	M.	R.	W.
Trueman	14	1	44	0	....	8	1	23	2
Tyson	13	4	22	2	....	7	1	26	0
Close	11	7	18	1	....	2	0	21	0
Shepherd	24	7	70	2	....	12	0	47	0
Wardle	23	5	53	2	....	10	1	60	1
Graveney						6.2	0	35	2

Gentlemen Bowling

	O.	M.	R.	W.		O.	M.	R.	W.
Warr	17	1	52	1	....	12.4	2	72	2
Bailey	20	6	38	4	....	17	2	62	0
Dexter	8	0	32	1	....	4	0	24	0
Goonesena	11	0	58	1	....	5	0	31	1
Insole	4.1	0	16	2	....	4	0	39	0

Umpires: H. G. Baldwin and A. R. Coleman.

At Scarborough, September 7, 9, 10. T. N. PEARCE'S XI drew with WEST INDIES.
(See WEST INDIES section.)

CHAMPION COUNTY (SURREY) v. THE REST

At Scarborough, September 11, 12, 13. Surrey won by six wickets. The
Champions lived up to their reputation by almost outplaying the Rest who, compelled to follow on 159 behind, never looked like saving the match. Superb
driving by May (sixteen 4's) and Barrington (three 6's and twenty-one 4's), whose
partnership realised 152, gave Surrey the initiative on the opening day and they

never looked back. For The Rest, Marshall made 55 out of a first wicket stand of 85 punishing Lock for 24 in one over, and then the Surrey attack took complete command. Graveney, Compton, Bailey and Tribe all offered stubborn resistance in The Rest's second innings. When Surrey needed 81 to win, Trueman put in a great effort but with Constable shaping confidently the Champions were not extended. Owing to a strained leg muscle May took no part in the cricket on the last two days when Alec Bedser had the honour of leading the team in their final triumph of a memorable season.

Surrey

T. H. Clark c Tyson b Bailey	18	— b Trueman	13
M. J. Stewart c Bailey b Trueman	19	— c Evans b Trueman	7
B. Constable b Tyson	20	— not out	41
P. B. H. May b Wardle	97		
K. F. Barrington c Tribe b Bailey	136	— b Trueman	4
E. A. Bedser c Evans b Bailey	14	— c Evans b Bailey	0
A. J. McIntyre c Marshall b Tribe	4	— not out	15
G. A. R. Lock not out	28		
J. C. Laker not out	17		
B 4, l-b 11, w 1	16	L-b 2	2

1/25 2/46 3/81 4/233 (7 wkts., dec.) 369   1/14 2/27 (4 wkts.) 82
5/273 6/310 7/324   3/45 4/54
P. J. Loader and A. V. Bedser did not bat.

The Rest

P. E. Richardson c Loader b Laker	32	— c E. Bedser b Lock	8
R. E. Marshall c McIntyre b A. Bedser	55	— run out	0
T. W. Graveney b A. Bedser	10	— b Laker	53
D. W. Richardson c Stewart b Lock	23	— c Constable b Lock	23
D. C. S. Compton c Barrington b Lock	20	— c sub b Lock	41
T. E. Bailey b Loader	0	— b E. Bedser	35
G. E. Tribe c Stewart b Laker	7	— b Lock	44
T. G. Evans not out	22	— b A. Bedser	6
F. H. Tyson c E. Bedser b Laker	11	— lbw b Loader	10
J. H. Wardle c E. Bedser b Lock	9	— c McIntyre b Loader	0
F. S. Trueman lbw b Lock	9	— not out	4
B 7, l-b 5	12	B 6, l-b 9	15

1/85 2/101 3/110 4/141 5/142 6/156   210   1/0 2/23 3/95 4/123   239
7/158 8/178 9/187   5/132 6/185 7/195 8/222
9/224

The Rest Bowling

	O.	M.	R.	W.	O.	M.	R.	W.
Trueman	19	3	66	1	12	2	35	3
Tyson	19	2	74	1	6	1	19	0
Bailey	17	2	72	3	3.1	0	18	5
Wardle	9	1	33	1	1	0	4	0
Tribe	12	0	91	1	2	0	4	0
Compton	1	0	17	0				

Surrey Bowling

	O.	M.	R.	W.	O.	M.	R.	W.
Loader	14	2	37	1	16	3	37	2
A. Bedser	11	4	22	2	19	3	65	1
Lock	21.4	3	98	4	24.5	6	59	4
Laker	11	3	32	3	19	5	36	1
E. Bedser	4	1	9	0	17	5	27	1

Umpires: A. Skelding and D. Davies.

HASTINGS FESTIVAL

At Hastings, August 31, September 2, 3. WEST INDIES beat L. E. G. AMES'S XI by four wickets. (See WEST INDIES section.)

AN ENGLAND XI v. A COMMONWEALTH XI

At Hastings, September 4, 5, 6. England XI won by three wickets with seven minutes remaining. Sent in to bat on a green pitch, the Commonwealth, none too strongly represented, were saved in the first innings by Pettiford, who hit his highest score of the season. Bright play by Milton and Cowdrey, who put on 120, led to the England XI going ahead with seven wickets in hand and Carr declared with a lead of 86. On the last day, when the regular England XI bowlers took little part in the attack, the Commonwealth scored 307 runs in two and a half hours for the loss of their last nine wickets, leaving their opponents 281 to get in two and three-quarter hours. Cowdrey hit thirteen 4's while making his fifth century of the season in ninety minutes and Barrick and Carr helped in the ready run-getting.

A Commonwealth XI

L. Outschoorn b Jackson	18	—	b Bennett	9
P. Arnold b Moss	1	—	c Moss b Cowdrey	77
J. Pettiford c Jackson b Moss	59	—	b Jackson	42
D. G. Phadkar c Milton b Cowdrey	31	—	c Barrick b Carr	17
C. G. Pepper run out	17	—	st Murray b Cowdrey	35
G. E. Tribe c Milton b Jackson	10	—	c Carr b Barrick	46
B. Dooland c Hamer b Moss	4	—	c Dewes b Cowdrey	28
J. S. Manning c Milton b Moss	1	—	st Murray b Hamer	30
R. Bartels c Carr b Cowdrey	18	—	b Cowdrey	27
B. A. Barnett c Milton b Moss	27	—	not out	14
S. P. Gupte not out	2	—	c Barrick b Hamer	31
B 1, l-b 1, w 1	3		B 6, l-b 4	10

1/8 2/32 3/104 4/126 5/139 6/143   191
7/144 8/149 9/187

1/17 2/104 3/137 4/180   366
5/195 6/247 7/271 8/310
9/328

An England XI

A. Hamer b Manning	27	—	st Barnett b Pettiford	35
J. R. Gray lbw b Dooland	30	—	c and b Bartels	20
C. A. Milton c Barnett b Tribe	74	—	c Dooland b Gupte	32
M. C. Cowdrey b Manning	62	—	c Outschoorn b Tribe	100
J. G. Dewes c Dooland b Gupte	47	—	st Barnett b Dooland	1
D. W. Barrick not out	27	—	b Tribe	26
D. B. Carr (did not bat)		—	c Arnold b Gupte	44
D. Bennett (did not bat)		—	not out	16
J. T. Murray (did not bat)		—	not out	3
B 5, l-b 5	10		L-b 2, w 2	4

1/39 2/71 3/191 4/199   (5 wkts., dec.) 277
5/277

1/32 2/68 3/115   (7 wkts.) 281
4/124 5/178 6/239 7/273

A. E. Moss and L. Jackson did not bat.

An England XI Bowling

	O.	M.	R.	W.	O.	M.	R.	W.
Moss	21	2	62	5	 5	0	25	0
Jackson	19	4	50	2	 12	0	32	1
Bennett	12	4	29	0	 5	0	20	1
Gray	4	1	14	0	 2	1	4	0
Carr	1	0	5	0	 9	2	49	1
Cowdrey	6.3	1	28	1	 17	0	109	4
Hamer					3.1	0	28	2
Barrick					13	0	89	1

A Commonwealth XI Bowling

	O.	M.	R.	W.	O.	M.	R.	W.
Phadkar	7	1	20	0	 3	0	19	0
Bartels	5	0	13	0	 8	0	31	1
Manning	13	0	64	2	 5	0	32	0
Dooland	16	0	69	1	.... 7.5	0	51	1
Gupte	14.2	4	45	1	 15	2	46	2
Pepper	6	0	30	0				
Tribe	6	0	26	1	 8	0	56	2
Pettiford					8	0	42	1

Umpires: F. S. Lee and A. E. Pothecary.

TORQUAY FESTIVAL

If not quite so shabbily served by the weather as in 1956, when play was possible on only one of the six days and caused a financial loss of nearly £2,000 to the organisers, the Torquay Festival was spoiled by a cold wind and heavy showers of rain. Nevertheless, Mr. David Haines, the enterprising secretary, stated that the promoters intended to carry on because they felt that given good weather there was a big public in the south-west corner of England keen to support first-class cricket.

AN ENGLAND XI v. A COMMONWEALTH XI

At Torquay, September 4, 5, 6. Drawn. A sparkling century by Emmett, who hit his second 50 in eighteen minutes, provided a fine start for the Festival. Driving and pulling with tremendous power he hit five 6's and fourteen 4's, completing three figures in ninety-two minutes. Khan Mohammad, the Pakistan fast bowler, achieved a fine performance in taking seven wickets. On the second day the conditions were ideal for spin bowlers and Titmus, Ramchand and McCool proved effective. Commonwealth found themselves wanting 393 to win in five and a half hours on the last day. Unfortunately two hours were lost through rain, yet only a fighting innings by Jackson, the Commonwealth captain, saved his side from defeat. Favoured by the helpful pitch, Titmus and Illingworth each seized the opportunity to take the necessary wickets he required to complete the double.

An England XI

D. Brookes b Khan Mohammad	2	— b McCool	68
J. D. Robertson c Stephenson b Ramchand	24	— c McCool b Jackson	30
D. Kenyon b Khan Mohammad	13	— hit wkt b Ramchand	42
G. M. Emmett c Desai b Jackson	114	— b Ramchand	14
C. H. Palmer c Marshall b Khan Mohammad	59	— lbw b McCool	15
A. J. Watkins c Stephenson b Khan Mohammad	25	— c Livingston b Ramchand	36
R. Illingworth b Khan Mohammad	1	— b McCool	6
F. J. Titmus c Wight b Khan Mohammad	24	— st Stephenson b McCool	2
K. V. Andrew c Stephenson b Khan Mohammad	2	— c Wight b Ramchand	8
C. Gladwin c Jackson b Desai	6	— not out	12
M. J. Cowan not out	1	— b Ramchand	5
B 7, l-b 6	13	B 3, l-b 5	8
	284		**246**

1/11 2/43 3/45 4/204 5/230 6/242
7/250 8/266 9/277

1/60 2/136 3/157 4/164
5/188 6/198 7/202 8/225
9/234

A Commonwealth XI

R. E. Marshall c Palmer b Gladwin	26	— c Robertson b Illingworth	47
W. E. Alley c Palmer b Gladwin	1	— c Andrew b Illingworth	41
L. Livingston c Andrew b Illingworth	40	— c Brookes b Illingworth	6
P. B. Wight c Illingworth b Titmus	34	— b Titmus	1
C. L. McCool b Titmus	1	— b Illingworth	22
G. Ramchand b Illingworth	1	— b Illingworth	7
V. E. Jackson b Titmus	11	— not out	52
A. Desai b Titmus	4	— c Robertson b Illingworth	7
H. W. Stephenson b Titmus	15	— b Titmus	7
A. K. Walker b Titmus	3	— not out	9
Khan Mohammad not out	1		
N-b 1	1	B 6, l-b 3, n-b 1	10
	138	(8 wkts.)	**209**

1/2 2/55 3/80 4/81 5/82 6/101
7/105 8/125 9/137

1/29 2/94 3/95
4/96 5/105 6/139 7/175
8/182

A Commonwealth XI Bowling

	O.	M.	R.	W.	O.	M.	R.	W.
Khan Mohammad	23	3	56	7	5	1	16	0
Walker	19	2	67	0	5	1	43	0
Ramchand	12	4	18	1	23	3	58	5
Desai	8.1	0	48	1				
Wight	10	1	56	0	9	3	36	0
Jackson	5	0	26	1	8	2	18	1
McCool					22	3	67	4

An England XI Bowling

	O.	M.	R.	W.	O.	M.	R.	W.
Cowan	9	1	32	0	8	2	33	0
Gladwin	10	1	47	2	7	1	20	0
Illingworth	12	7	14	2	28	7	61	6
Titmus	11	0	44	6	26	7	73	2
Watkins					3	0	12	0

Umpires: W. F. Price and J. S. Buller.

NORTH v. SOUTH

At Torquay, September 7, 9, 10. South won by one wicket with fifty minutes to spare. Throughout this match the pitch proved so encouraging to bowlers that batsmen only succeeded by taking chances. The presence of Lock, who took ten wickets—completing his 200 for the season—gave the South a tremendous advantage, but on the opening day Livingston and Palmer both hit splendidly for the North and Emmett and McCool replied for South in similar vein. A deluge prevented any cricket on Monday, but although his side were 76 in arrear Emmett declared first thing Tuesday. South proceeded to dismiss the opposition in two hours before lunch, leaving themselves to make 220 in three and a half hours. Although Marshall hit fearlessly South seemed doomed to defeat when six men were out for 99, but again Emmett and McCool rose to the occasion. Nevertheless 33 were still needed when Stephenson, the last man, joined Watkins. Then, mainly by steady methods, the runs were obtained amidst great excitement.

North

D. Kenyon b Watkins	9	— c Stephenson b Loader	7
D. Brookes b Lock	23	— c McCool b Lock	18
L. Livingston c Tremlett b Titmus	53	— b Lock	16
C. H. Palmer c Loader b Lock	56	— b Lock	15
A. Wharton st Stephenson b Titmus	2	— c Titmus b Lock	6
R. Illingworth b Titmus	2	— c Lock b Titmus	11
J. S. Manning c Titmus b McCool	27	— b Lock	3
K. V. Andrew c Watkins b Lock	11	— b Lock	24
C. Gladwin c and b Titmus	1	— not out	21
J. B. Statham c Tremlett b Lock	16	— c Titmus b Alley	3
M. J. Cowan not out	15	— b Alley	8
B 9, l-b 1	10	B 6, l-b 3, w 1, n-b 1	11

1/15 2/51 3/89 4/96 5/110 6/153   225
7/179 8/186 9/192

1/13 2/44 3/45 4/52 5/74   143
6/77 7/84 8/113 9/119

South

J. D. Robertson b Statham	8	— c Illingworth b Gladwin	13
R. E. Marshall c and b Gladwin	9	— c Brookes b Illingworth	43
W. E. Alley b Gladwin	4	— c Livingston b Manning	21
G. M. Emmett c Statham b Illingworth	47	— b Palmer	49
C. L. McCool b Palmer	71	— c Livingston b Illingworth	47
M. F. Tremlett not out	6	— c Cowan b Illingworth	2
A. J. Watkins not out	0	— not out	15
G. A. R. Lock (did not bat)		— b Gladwin	4
P. J. Loader (did not bat)		— b Illingworth	1
F. J. Titmus (did not bat)		— st Andrew b Illingworth	1
H. W. Stephenson (did not bat)		— not out	16
L-b 3, n-b 1	4	B 5, l-b 3	8

1/18 2/18 3/25 4/111   (5 wkts., dec.) 149
5/148

1/15 2/59 3/60   (9 wkts.) 220
4/67 5/69 6/99 7/167
8/183 9/187

South Bowling

	O.	M.	R.	W.	O.	M.	R.	W.
Loader	7	1	14	0	5	0	13	1
Watkins	9	2	16	1	4	0	18	0
Titmus	17	3	68	4	10	1	45	1
Lock	23	3	90	4	14	5	35	6
McCool	8	0	27	1				
Alley					4.3	0	21	2

North Bowling

	O.	M.	R.	W.		O.	M.	R.	W.
Statham	5	1	20	1	....	5	1	11	0
Gladwin	6	2	4	2	....	7	0	40	2
Cowan	7	1	23	0	....	4	1	5	0
Manning	8	2	43	0	....	10	0	49	1
Illingworth	7	1	39	1	....	18	3	84	5
Palmer	4	1	16	1	....	2.2	0	23	1

Umpires: W. F. Price and J. S. Buller.

IRELAND v. M.C.C. (1956)

At Dublin, September 1, 3, 4, 1956. M.C.C. won by 22 runs. By an unfortunate oversight the report and full scores of this match were omitted from last year's *Wisden*. Two memorable bowling performances provided the main feature. Fee, the North of Ireland schoolmaster and off-spinner, took fourteen wickets, equalling the Irish record of S. S. Huey, for exactly 100 runs. In the M.C.C. first innings Pollock held five excellent leg-side catches off the bowling of Fee. Chesterton, the M.C.C. captain and Malvern schoolmaster, took ten wickets for 52 runs in the match with his medium-pace bowling.

M.C.C.

W. Knightley-Smith c Pollock b Huey	27	— c Lewis b Fee	17
R. E. Bird c Neville b Warke	1	— c Neville b Fee	19
G. P. S. Delisle c Warke b Fee	14	— run out	23
J. M. A. Marshall c Pollock b Fee	12	— b Wilson	10
W. Murray-Wood b Fee	6	— c Martin b Fee	0
J. P. Fellows-Smith c Pollock b Fee	27	— c Martin b Fee	28
M. H. Stevenson c Fawcett b Huey	12	— c Wilson b Fee	10
P. A. Whitcombe c Martin b Fee	14	— not out	4
C. B. R. Featherstonhaugh c Pollock b Fee	6	— c Pollock b Fee	1
P. I. Bedford not out	6	— b Fee	20
G. H. Chesterton c Pollock b Fee	3	— c Fawcett b Wilson	2
B 3, l-b 2, w 2	7	B 1, n-b 2	3

1/9 2/33 3/54 4/65 5/74 6/95 7/118   **135**   1/25 2/54 3/58 4/85 5/92   **137**
8/124 9/124   6/107 7/126 8/132 9/134

Ireland

H. Martin c Bird b Chesterton	6	— c Stevenson b Whitcombe	33
S. F. Bergin c Bird b Chesterton	10	— b Whitcombe	28
L. A. Warke c Bird b Chesterton	2	— c Bird b Chesterton	46
J. S. Pollock c Bird b Chesterton	0	— c Knightley-Smith b Whitcombe	5
P. A. Neville c Fellows-Smith b Chesterton	0	— c Bedford b Chesterton	17
W. I. Lewis run out	0	— c Bird b Chesterton	2
G. W. Fawcett c Marshall b Fellows-Smith	1	— c Bird b Fellows-Smith	7
S. S. Huey c Chesterton b Fellows-Smith	4	— b Fellows-Smith	10
I. B. J. Wilson b Bedford b Chesterton	12	— c Stevenson b Whitcombe	18
F. Fee c Stevenson b Chesterton	1	— b Fellows-Smith	7
S. W. Ferris not out	3	— not out	4
B 6, l-b 4, n-b 3	13	B 14, l-b 8, w 1, n-b 2	25

1/15 2/23 3/23 4/23 5/26 6/27   **48**   1/61 2/72 3/80 4/118   **202**
7/30 8/30 9/32   5/122 6/147 7/147 8/176
      9/187

Ireland Bowling

	O.	M.	R.	W.		O.	M.	R.	W.
Ferris	6	2	8	0	....	4	1	15	0
Warke	4	1	11	1	....	3	1	5	0
Fee	24	8	56	7	....	28	11	44	7
Wilson	6	1	12	0	....	13	1	40	2
Huey	16	4	41	2	....	14	3	30	0

M.C.C. Bowling

	O.	M.	R.	W.		O.	M.	R.	W.
Whitcombe	6	3	9	0	....	24	17	24	4
Chesterton	15.4	9	14	7	....	33	19	38	3
Fellows-Smith	10	6	12	2	....	22.4	7	43	3
Bedford						15	1	49	0
Marshall						11	4	23	0

Umpires: C. Fox and J. Connerton.

THE MINOR COUNTIES IN 1957

Yorkshire Second Eleven won the Minor Counties Championship for the second time. In 1947 they carried off the title by beating Surrey, then leaders, in the Challenge match. This time Yorkshire's superiority in the competition was more convincing. Not only did they head the table but they showed themselves to be the better all-round side in the drawn Challenge match with Warwickshire at Scarborough.

Undoubtedly one of the main reasons for Yorkshire's success was the captaincy of J. R. Burnet, who had led the second eleven for five years. Though a firm disciplinarian, Burnet gave the younger members of the side the utmost encouragement and impressed on them the need for a progressive outlook to the game. Not surprisingly, therefore, he was asked to lead the county eleven in 1958.

In all, Yorkshire called upon 31 players. Of these the most successful were G. W. Moore, J. B. Bolus, E. I. Lester, D. E. V. Padgett and P. J. Sharpe of the batsmen, and R. Appleyard, J. Birkenshaw, D. Wilson, R. K. Platt, D. Pickles, M. Ryan and M. Cowan, bowlers. In addition E. Legard kept wicket capably.

Warwickshire, too, were indebted to their captain, H. E. Dollery, for an extremely satisfactory season. Under his experienced and shrewd leadership the team quickly settled down and six of the first seven matches ended in victory. The other was abandoned. Though Warwickshire could not maintain this splendid record the side were unbeaten until the last match when Northamptonshire won by four wickets in a low-scoring encounter. M. Youll, an 18-year-old left-arm bowler of unorthodox style, claimed 62 victims and E. Leadbeater, the former Yorkshire leg-spin bowler, took 42 wickets. R. G. Thompson was the main seam bowler. The batsmen earned praise for their high rate of scoring, with W. J. Stewart and D. P. Ratcliffe impressing most.

Berkshire, the leading Minor County, at one time headed the Championship but they fell away towards the end of August. Even so, had they scored only three runs more in their last match with Dorset they would have established the right to challenge Yorkshire. As usual the captain, G. R. Langdale, was a tower of strength in both batting and bowling.

Hertfordshire, who rose from fifteenth to seventh position, obtained 34 points from the first five matches but were unable to maintain this satisfactory start. Under the enterprising leadership of C. V. L. Marques, every match was played to win regardless of the risk of defeat.

Early in the season G. A. Edrich was appointed captain of **Lancashire Second Eleven**. His main task was to bring on the younger players under conditions as close as possible to those experienced in first-class cricket. This policy brought excellent results and a higher position than seemed likely in an experimental year. Edrich set a splendid example in batting and fielding and took a very real interest in the development of the young professionals. He will continue to lead the team during the next three seasons and also "double" as assistant-coach to T. S. Worthington. Of the batsmen, J. D. Bond, G. Pullar and A. Bolton showed most promise, with J. Roberts and R. Booth (fast-medium) and P. Whiteley (left-arm slow) the pick of the bowlers.

Cambridgeshire experienced a satisfactory season, thanks to the bowling of I. Craig and the all-round ability of W. B. Morris. Craig, whose well-controlled run-up at times camouflaged devastating speed, took almost twice as many wickets as any other bowler in the side. Of the batsmen, two newcomers, C. Morris and D. Gubbins, achieved the distinction of scoring centuries.

The experience of J. E. Walsh as captain was most beneficial to **Leicestershire Second Eleven,** not only from the point of view of his leadership but also from his ability to dismiss obstinate batsmen. Altogether the county had a most encouraging season with all the young players contributing towards the success of the side.

Injuries and other causes seriously weakened **Durham** after an excellent start; the departure of M. E. Scott and J. G. Williamson to Northamptonshire were particularly heavy blows.

Staffordshire, too, have lost one of their most promising youngsters to a senior county, for K. Higgs, a fast bowler, topped the averages in his first season and then joined Lancashire. D. M. Haynes, who led the side since 1954, resigned for business reasons.

Cornwall won only one match. Their lack of success was due in no small measure to poor fielding. The captain, W. N. Dorning, scored most runs and the bowling honours went to R. Pellew who took 24 wickets before his departure, early in August, to the Far East.

Lack of confidence among the batsmen was the chief reason for **Lincolnshire** experiencing their worst season for 24 years. H. M. A. Cherry-Downes bowled magnificently and A. W. Lea and J. D. Walton provided admirable support.

Though **Norfolk** failed to achieve victory for the second successive year, E. G. Witherden scored 801 runs—the highest aggregate for the county since 1911—and also took 26 wickets. Witherden, formerly with Kent, hit four centuries.

Bedfordshire, weakened by the departure in recent years of R. A. Gale, P. Watts, B. Disbury and G. Millman to senior counties, again suffered a disappointing season. M. Ashenden, a young Sussex-born fast bowler on National Service with the R.A.F., headed the averages.

Derbyshire Second Eleven, who finished bottom, were badly hit by injuries to the bowlers, D. Hall and H. J. Rhodes. F. C. Brailsford showed considerable improvement as an opening batsman and scored 70 and 66 against Northamptonshire and Lancashire.

Derbyshire, Middlesex, Surrey and Kent have decided to leave the Minor Counties Competition at the end of 1958. The following second elevens will remain: Lancashire, Yorkshire, Warwickshire, Nottinghamshire, Northamptonshire, Somerset, Gloucestershire, Essex and Leicestershire. So in 1959 there will be 26 competing counties—the same number as in 1953.

MINOR COUNTIES' CHAMPIONSHIP

FINAL RESULTS, 1957

	Played	Won	Lost	Won 1st Inns.	Lost 1st Inns.	No Result	Points	Average
Yorkshire 2nd XI....	18	11	*3	2	0	2	123	6.83
Warwickshire 2nd XI.	20	11	*1	4	3	1	130	6.50
Somerset 2nd XI.....	16	8	1	4	3	0	95	5.93
Berkshire	10	5	*3	0	1	1	56	5.60
Suffolk	8	4	*3	1	0	0	44	5.50
Middlesex 2nd XI ...	12	5	*1	2	4	0	63	5.25
Hertfordshire	10	4	*2	2	1	1	52	5.20
Lancashire 2nd XI ..	22	8	*3	4	2	5	107	4.86
Cambridgeshire	8	3	1	1	2	1	37	4.62
Leicestershire 2nd XI.	12	4	†3	2	3	0	55	4.58
Notts 2nd XI	18	4	1	7	4	2	69	3.83
Northants 2nd XI....	14	4	*4	0	3	3	52	3.71
Dorset	12	3	*3	2	3	1	44	3.66
Gloucestershire 2nd XI	10	2	1	4	2	1	36	3.60
Durham	12	3	3	2	2	2	42	3.50
Oxfordshire	10	2	*4	3	0	1	34	3.40
Devon	10	2	*3	2	2	1	33	3.30
Staffordshire	12	2	*2	3	3	2	39	3.25
Buckinghamshire	10	2	3	2	2	1	30	3.00
Wiltshire	10	2	4	1	1	2	28	2.80
Northumberland	12	2	4	1	3	2	30	2.50
Essex 2nd XI	12	1	4	5	1	1	28	2.33
Kent 2nd XI	14	1	*3	4	5	1	32	2.28
Surrey 2nd XI......	14	1	3	4	4	2	30	2.14
Cornwall	10	1	3	0	3	3	19	1.90
Lincolnshire	10	1	*6	1	1	1	19	1.90
Cheshire...........	10	1	*5	0	3	1	18	1.80
Norfolk	12	0	*4	5	3	0	21	1.75
Bedfordshire	8	0	2	1	2	3	11	1.37
Shropshire	8	0	*3	0	3	2	10	1.25
Cumberland	8	0	*5	1	0	2	10	1.25
Derbyshire 2nd XI ..	12	0	6	3	2	1	13	1.08

* 3 points for 1st Innings' lead in one match lost.
† 3 points for 1st Innings' lead in two matches lost.

System of Scoring:—

Ten points for a win in completed Two-Day match, and for a lead on the first innings in a One-Day match, provided the match cannot be played out.

Three points to the winner and one to the loser in a Two-Day match decided on the first innings.

Two points to each County in a match in which there is no result on the first innings.

When the match is a tie, the ten points shall be equally divided.

For a tie on first innings in an unfinished match, two points to each side.

First innings qualifying points (3) gained shall be retained irrespective of the final result of a match provided that a County shall receive not more than ten points in such match.

The challenge match between Yorkshire Second XI and Warwickshire Second XI was drawn, and Yorkshire accordingly became Champion County by virtue of Rule 16.

CHALLENGE MATCH

YORKSHIRE II v. WARWICKSHIRE II

At Scarborough, September 18, 19, 20. Drawn. Warwickshire, who needed an outright win to overthrow the leaders, were foiled by stubborn Yorkshire batting and the weather. Because of rain, which limited play on the first day to under two hours, and to a natural reluctance of the Yorkshire batsmen to endanger their position, the Champions' first innings lasted half of the game. Warwickshire failed against the pace of Pickles and Ryan, and though Cartwright wrought havoc with his off-spin when Yorkshire batted again, the Challengers were left the almost impossible task of scoring 210 in just over two hours against an accurate attack.

Yorkshire II

W. E. Bolus c Leadbeater b Griffiths	0	— b Cartwright 39
P. J. Sharpe b Griffiths	17	— c Carter b Cartwright...... 14
D. E. V. Padgett b Griffiths	18	— c Leadbeater b Cartwright.. 2
G. W. Moore b Carter	72	— c Leadbeater b Cartwright.. 8
E. Legard c Dollery b Wolton	13	— c Hawkins b Griffiths 1
J. Birkenshaw c Ratcliffe b Leach	17	— c Youll b Cartwright 5
E. J. Lester b Griffiths	1	— c and b Cartwright 0
J. R. Burnet c Ratcliffe c Cartwright	48	— run out 5
M. Ryan b Cartwright.............	3	— c Hawkins b Cartwright ... 5
D. Wilson not out	2	— b Carter 0
D. Pickles c Griffiths b Leach	1	— not out 0
B 18, l-b 4, w 1, n-b 2	25	B 22, l-b 1, n-b 2 25

1/0 2/28 3/47 4/93 5/140 6/143   217   1/15 2/19 3/37 4/70 5/70   104
7/194 8/215 9/215   6/81 7/81 8/100 9/104

Warwickshire II

T. W. Cartwright c and b Ryan	38		
D. P. Ratcliffe b Pickles	4	— not out	2
C. W. Leach b Ryan	9	— c Lester b Padgett	1
A. V. Wolton c Wilson b Ryan	0	— b Ryan	7
D. Livingstone c Wilson b Birkenshaw	12	— not out	55
H. E. Dollery b Pickles	32	— lbw b Wilson	11
M. Youll b Pickles	4		
C. G. Hawkins c Moore b Pickles	10		
E. Leadbeater b Pickles	0		
R. G. Carter b Ryan	3		
S. S. Griffiths not out	0		
		B 1, l-b 1	2

1/5 2/16 3/16 4/52 5/93 6/99 7/99   112   1/5 2/13 3/55   (3 wkts.) 78
8/109 9/112

Warwickshire II Bowling

	O.	M.	R.	W.		O.	M.	R.	W.
Griffiths	28	7	52	4	....	15	5	31	1
Carter	35	13	53	1	....	13.4	6	29	1
Leach	16.4	5	37	2					
Wolton	5	2	4	1					
Leadbeater	9	2	32	0					
Cartwright	5	1	8	2	....	26	17	19	7
Youll	2	0	6	0					

Yorkshire II Bowling

	O.	M.	R.	W.		O.	M.	R.	W.
Pickles	19	5	44	5	....	8	3	9	0
Ryan	17.2	4	34	4	....	8	0	36	1
Birkenshaw	7	2	22	1	....	5	1	15	0
Wilson	1	0	12	0	....	5	3	8	1
Padgett						1	0	2	1
Bolus						1	0	1	0
Lester						1	0	4	0
Burnet						1	0	1	0

Umpires: L. K. W. Martin and W. E. Brown.

BEDFORDSHIRE

Secretary—F. CROMPTON, Shire Hall, Bedford

*Matches 8—Lost 2, Won on first innings 1, Lost on first innings 2,
No result 3*

		1st Innings	2nd Innings	Result	
June 10, 11	Bedfordshire	185	—	No result	
Woodhall Spa	Lincolnshire	77 for 2	—		
June 18, 19	Cambridgeshire	318* for 4	63 for 5	Won on	first
Ely	Bedfordshire	389* for 5	—	innings	
July 3, 4	Hertfordshire	261	80 for 4	Lost by	six
Hitchin	Bedfordshire	139	207	wickets	
July 24, 25	Bedfordshire	155	146* for 6	Lost on	first
Luton	Staffordshire	181* for 5	98 for 5	innings	
August 5, 6	Cambridgeshire	378* for 8	—	Lost on	first
Bedford School	Bedfordshire	234	145 for 8	innings	

		1st Innings	2nd Innings	Result
August 7, 8	Bedfordshire	44	169	Lost by eight wickets
Bedford School	Lincolnshire	147	68 for 2	
August 9, 10	Hertfordshire	152* for 8	—	No result
Bedford School	Bedfordshire	114 for 7		
August 14, 15	Staffordshire	177* for 9	—	No result
Uttoxeter	Bedfordshire	12 for 2		

Innings declared closed.

Batting Averages

	Innings	Not Outs	Runs	Highest Innings	Average
J. A. R. Oliver†	10	3	399	114	57.00
M. Jordan	11	1	257	127*	25.70
N. S. Gunn	10	1	196	47	21.77
B. Robinson	7	2	87	26*	17.40
G. L. B. August	8	0	130	37	16.25
F. Whittingham	9	0	125	45	13.88
R. W. Street	5	0	68	33	13.60
I. Davison	8	2	78	24*	13.00
R. D. Lowings	5	0	55	24	11.00
M. Ashenden	8	3	33	9	6.60
T. R. McIntyre	5	0	24	21	4.80

Also batted: J. G. Owen 36, 67, 26; F. Breeze 2, 22, 7, 4; F. J. Comerford 6, 13, 4, 3; S. T. Morris 24, 4, 10, 6; D. G. Jenkins 0, 0*, 2*; G. Dawson 12, 29*; A. Greene 1, 24; M. A. Crouch 15, 7*, 0*; J. Legate 1, 12; D. C. Eldridge 4.

* Signifies not out. † Captain.

Bowling Averages

	Overs	Maidens	Runs	Wickets	Average
M. Ashenden	121.1	24	404	20	20.20
D. G. Jenkins	40	4	128	6	21.33
J. A. R. Oliver	113	24	295	13	22.69
I. Davison	174	35	463	19	24.36

Also bowled: J. G. Owen 37.5—4—118—4; D. C. Eldridge 4—0—10—0; N. S. Gunn 27—3—95—3; M. Jordan 1—0—4—0; F. Breeze 49—9—156—1; R. A. King 3—1—9—0; R. W. Street 13—0—63—0; J. Legate 38—10—75—4; S. T. Morris 0.4—0—4—0.

Professionals.—None.

BERKSHIRE

Secretary—H. L. Lewis, c/o Huntley & Palmers Ltd., Reading

Matches 10—Won 5, Lost 3, Lost on first innings 1, No result 1

		1st Innings	2nd Innings	Result
July 31, August 1	Cornwall	234* for 7	102 for 3	Lost by seven wickets
Falmouth	Berkshire	127	208	
August 2, 3	Berkshire	145	279* for 7	Won by 121 runs
Torquay	Devon	165	138	
August 5, 6	Buckinghamshire	231	201	Won by 87 runs
Reading	Berkshire	272* for 7	170	
August 7, 8	Oxfordshire	129	107	Won by 93 runs
Reading	Berkshire	151	176	
August 9, 10	Berkshire	198* for 9	—	†Won by 144 runs
Slough	Buckinghamshire	54	—	
August 12, 13	Berkshire	185* for 7	—	No result

		1st Innings	2nd Innings	Result
Newbury	Cornwall	111 for 4	—	
August 16, 17	Berkshire	222* for 5	143* for 5	Won by 173 runs
Reading	Devon	142	50	
August 21, 22	Dorset	274* for 5	195	Lost by 52 runs
Reading	Berkshire	278* for 4	139	
August 23, 24	Oxfordshire	228* for 4	—	Lost on first innings
Oxford	Berkshire	128	212 for 7	
August 26, 27	Dorset	228* for 6	67	Lost by two runs
Poole	Berkshire	205	88	

* Innings declared closed.
† Reduced to one day because of rain.

Batting Averages

	Innings	Not Outs	Runs	Highest Innings	Average
R. M. James	10	1	406	173*	45.11
A. A. Hillary	13	0	532	164	40.92
M. A. Salmon..............	5	0	198	81	39.60
J. A. Mence	9	0	277	88	30.77
G. R. Langdale†	16	3	368	50	28.30
C. E. W. Brooks	13	3	241	69	24.10
J. G. C. Surridge	8	0	155	36	19.37
A. T. Davis	15	1	247	37*	17.64
C. M. S. Crombie	10	0	167	56	16.70
J. E. Scott	5	0	72	52	14.40
K. C. Came	8	1	93	44	13.28
F. C. Pickett	11	0	128	30	11.63
J. Carless	6	1	49	29	9.80
J. M. Pavey	6	0	52	26	8.66
K. M. Hooper	6	1	15	9	3.00
T. Ingram	6	2	4	3	1.00

* *Signifies not out.* † *Captain.*

Bowling Averages

	Overs	Maidens	Runs	Wickets	Average
M. N. Morgan	39	16	50	8	6.25
D. E. Young	77.3	24	176	13	13.53
G. R. Langdale	314.1	107	592	43	13.76
R. M. James	147	30	339	21	16.14
K. M. Hooper	50.5	11	143	8	17.87
F. C. Pickett	146.2	36	363	17	21.35
C. E. W. Brooks	139.3	26	451	13	34.69

Professionals.—None.

BUCKINGHAMSHIRE

Secretary—C. ANTHONY PRINCE, 10, Ashbourne Road, London, W.5

Matches 10—Won 2, Lost 3, Won on first innings 2, Lost on first innings 2, No result 1

		1st Innings	2nd Innings	Result
July 29, 30	Oxfordshire	189	124	Won by one wicket
High Wycombe	Buckinghamshire	98	216 for 9	
July 31, August 1	Buckinghamshire	201	205 for 0	Lost on first innings
Norwich	Norfolk	343* for 2	—	

		1st Innings	2nd Innings	Result
August 2, 3	Oxfordshire	276* for 9	126* for 5	Lost on first
Cowley (Morris Motors)	Buckinghamshire	138	163 for 8	innings
August 5, 6	Buckinghamshire	231	201	Lost by 87 runs
Reading	Berkshire	272* for 7	170	
August 7, 8	Buckinghamshire	272* for 8	189* for 2	Won on first
High Wycombe	Hertfordshire	254	111 for 8	innings
August 9, 10	Berkshire	198* for 9	—	†Lost by 144
Slough	Buckinghamshire	54	—	runs
August 12, 13	Buckinghamshire	41 for 3	—	No result
Chesham	Kent II	—	—	
August 16, 17	Kent II	227	179	Won by six
Canterbury	Buckinghamshire	290* for 9	118 for 4	wickets
August 19, 20	Hertfordshire	174	77	Lost by 19 runs
Watford	Buckinghamshire	139	93	
August 23, 24	Buckinghamshire	142* for 4	108* for 7	Won on first
Ascott Park, Wing	Norfolk	96	145 for 9	innings

* Innings declared closed.
† Reduced to one day because of rain.

Batting Averages

	Innings	Not Outs	Runs	Highest Innings	Average
D. F. Johns†	12	0	459	122	38.25
B. A. Barnett	13	3	338	61	33.80
G. Reynolds	5	1	132	63	33.00
N. V. Butler	11	1	300	132*	30.00
D. Mackinnon	9	1	215	66*	26.87
L. Hitchings	10	0	227	66	22.70
G. Atkins	10	1	154	40	17.11
D. M. A. Steele	9	0	150	62	16.66
R. G. L. Janaway	15	2	207	73*	15.92
J. A. Cockett	8	0	89	46	11.12
K. W. A. Butler	5	1	42	20	10.50
R. Avery	7	2	41	14	8 60
C. W. Smith	10	3	37	17*	5.28
D. R. Peppiatt	5	0	24	24	4.80
A. J. Hughes	9	5	14	9*	4.66

Also batted: P. L. B. Stoddart 193 runs; M. Tilbury 31; A. Harvey 14; R. Nickless 22; F. Harris 7; B. Janes 27; R. P. Farr 6; G. Irving 8; R. Plested 2.

* *Signifies not out.* † *Captain.*

Bowling Averages

	Overs	Maidens	Runs	Wickets	Average
A. J. Hughes	288.1	69	678	47	14.42
K. W. A. Butler	157.3	57	290	19	15.26
D. F. Johns	132.2	33	335	21	15.95
R. Avery	97	28	261	11	23.73
C. W. Smith	230.1	59	617	14	44.07

Also bowled: R. G. L. Janaway 5—2—15—2; B. Janes 20—5—54—3; F. Harris 23—8—39—2; N. V. Butler 40—7—107—5; G. Reynolds 12—5—44—1: G. Irving 73—15—207—3; R. Plested 34—5—98—1; G. Atkins 6—0—35—0: D. R. Peppiatt 13—2—42—0.

Professionals.—None.

CAMBRIDGESHIRE

Secretary—F. W. WILKINSON, "Charnwood," 43, Cambridge Road, Ely

Matches 8—Won 3, Lost 1, Won on first innings 1, Lost on first innings 2, No result 1.

		1st Innings	2nd Innings	Result
June 18, 19	Cambridgeshire	318* for 4	63 for 5	Lost on first
Ely	Bedfordshire	389* for 5	—	innings
June 25, 26	Cambridgeshire	129	241	Lost on first
Wisbech	Essex II	173	139 for 6	innings
July 10, 11	Lincolnshire	146* for 3	201* for 5	Won by seven
Cambridge	Cambridgeshire	157* for 5	193 for 3	wickets
July 24, 25	Lincolnshire	85	65	Won by one
Bourne	Cambridgeshire	47	104 for 9	wicket
July 31, August 1	Hertfordshire	207	145* for 9	Lost by three
Sawston	Cambridgeshire	162* for 5	187	runs
August 5, 6	Cambridgeshire	378	—	Won on first
Bedford	Bedfordshire	234	145 for 8	innings
August 12, 13	Essex II	—	—	No result
Chingford	Cambridgeshire	—	—	
August 21, 22	Hertfordshire	92* for 8	99	Won by seven
Letchworth	Cambridgeshire	100* for 9	93 for 3	wickets

* Innings declared closed.

Batting Averages

	Innings	Not Outs	Runs	Highest Innings	Average
W. B. Morris	11	4	307	83	43.85
D. Gubbins	6	2	155	101*	38.75
J. Cornwell	9	2	248	76	35.42
M. A. Crouch†	12	0	319	108	26.58
D. Howarth	4	1	75	47	25.00
R. A. Gautrey	11	2	225	70	25.00
R. Hawes	11	0	234	80	21.27
H. A. Godfrey	6	1	100	49	20.00
B. Gadsby	7	3	24	17*	6.00
J. Hoyles	6	0	19	12	3.14

Also batted: J. Palmby 0, 0, 1; R. A. Taylor 9*, 25, 4; A. B. Thomas 49, 0; R. Nunn 0, 0, 11, 7; P. A. Shippey 4, 1; D. Johnson 0*, 17; C. A. Morris 104*, 1, 4; W. Ashton 9; C. Reed 2, 38; D. Wickham 5; D. Fairey 3*.

* *Signifies not out.*   † *Captain.*

Bowling Averages

	Overs	Maidens	Runs	Wickets	Average
I. T. Craig	221	84	358	31	11.54
R. A. Taylor	50.1	12	112	9	12.44
D. Johnson	22	2	85	5	17.00
W. B. Morris	140	47	334	18	18.55
B. Gadsby	186.3	31	349	16	21.81
J. Hoyles	81	17	179	8	22.37
C. A. Morris	50	4	158	6	26.33

Also bowled: H. Wale 33—4—115—0; H. Spragg 22—4—58—1; J. Palmby 24—2—79—1; H. A. Godfrey 31—4—102—1; E. Parish 5—0—19—1; D. Fairey 3—1—3—0.

Professional.—W. B. Morris.

CHESHIRE

Secretary—L. WILSON, San Remo, Ruff Lane, Ormskirk, Lancs.

Matches 10—Won 1, Lost 5, Lost on first innings 3, No result 1

		1st Innings	2nd Innings	Result
May 27, 28	Yorkshire II	240	—	Lost by innings
Salts, Saltaire	Cheshire	41	110	and 89 runs
May 29, 30	Cheshire	180	179	Lost by nine
Newcastle	Northumberland	173	187 for 1	wickets
June 5, 6	Cheshire	97	227	Lost by six
Neston	Lancashire II	208* for 6	119 for 4	wickets
June 12, 13	Lancashire II	164	153* for 9	Lost by 53 runs
Old Trafford	Cheshire	115	149	
June 19, 20	Yorkshire II	386	47 for 1	Lost by nine
Oxton	Cheshire	232	200	wickets
July 3, 4	Cheshire	122	193 for 8	Lost on first
Macclesfield	Warwickshire II	177	108 for 8	innings
July 10, 11	Cheshire	94	101 for 5	Lost on first
Norton	Staffordshire	118		innings
July 22, 23	Warwickshire II	175* for 9	124* for 9	Lost on first
Edgbaston	Cheshire	154	115 for 7	innings
August 7, 8	Cheshire	134	169	Won by two
Middlewich	Staffordshire	135* for 7	166	runs
August 14, 15	Northumberland	264	—	No result
Hoylake	Cheshire	100 for 0	—	

* Innings declared closed.

Batting Averages

	Innings	Not Outs	Runs	Highest Innings	Average
F. W. Millett	19	1	492	58	27.30
R. Fox	11	1	261	69	26.10
A. Vickery	8	0	203	50	25.37
B. M. Lowe†	14	1	249	59	19.15
B. S. Jones	10	1	132	38	14.66
K. F. Holding.............	17	3	188	46	13.42
M. J. B. Riley	16	0	215	45	13.43
R. J. Digman	11	5	44	13*	7.33
B. E. Jones	10	0	60	36	6.00
M. J. James...............	8	3	27	15	5.40

* *Signifies not out.*   † Captain.

Bowling Averages

	Overs	Maidens	Runs	Wickets	Average
K. E. Young	53	9	177	12	14.75
M. J. B. Riley	133	28	383	25	15.32
D. J. Smith	85	27	216	14	15.42
R. J. Digman	235	59	646	26	24.84
A. Vickery	130	32	317	12	26.41

Professionals.—None.

CORNWALL

Secretary—A. LUGG, Wendron, 18, Trevean Road, Truro

Matches 10—Won 1, Lost 3, Lost on first innings 3, No result 3

		1st Innings	2nd Innings	Result
June 21, 22	Cornwall	217* for 9	158	Lost on first
Penzance	Somerset II	219* for 9	57 for 0	innings
July 5, 6	Cornwall	172	169	Lost on first
Falmouth	Gloucestershire II	217* for 9	51 for 5	innings
July 19, 20	Devon	112	—	No result
Liskeard	Cornwall	31 for 0	—	
July 31, August 1	Cornwall	234* for 7	102 for 3	Won by seven
Falmouth	Berkshire	127	208	wickets
August 2, 3	Dorset	275* for 7	146* for 3	Lost by 126
Camborne	Cornwall	167	128	runs
August 7, 8	Cornwall	36	294	Lost by seven
Bath	Somerset II	201* for 7	132 for 3	wickets
August 9, 10	Dorset	86	—	No result
Blandford	Cornwall	7 for 1	—	
August 12, 13	Berkshire	185* for 7	—	No result
Newbury	Cornwall	111 for 4		
August 14, 15	Gloucestershire II	219* for 8	117* for 3	Lost by 45 runs
Bristol	Cornwall	131* for 7	160	
August 26, 27	Devon	309* for 9	15 for 0	Lost on first
Exeter	Cornwall	256		innings

* Innings declared closed.

Batting Averages

	Innings	Not Outs	Runs	Highest Innings	Average
W. N. Dorning†	14	5	426	61	47.33
A. W. Smith	6	0	208	96	34.66
R. D. I. Charlesworth	7	1	184	50	30.66
R. F. Hosking	15	1	419	56	29.92
J. W. Murphy	15	2	378	79	29.07
O. Trenwith	4	2	45	24	22.50
J. Vincent	6	1	65	27	13.00
D. I. Roberts	4	0	51	29	12.75
T. W. Cory	5	0	46	19	9.20
R. Harris	13	1	108	32	9.00
T. B. Bax	4	1	22	12	7.33
R. Pellew	7	2	36	16	7.20
A. Rodda	4	0	28	15	7.00
H. Watts	8	0	54	15	6.75
M. C. Weeks	5	1	22	13*	5.50
A. Opie	5	0	23	13	4.60
M. J. Tobin	6	1	21	11	4.20
B. Read	6	1	18	8	3.60
I. J. Skinner	4	0	13	7	3.25

Also batted: G. B. Carter 9; R. Sharp 4; W. M. Buzza 28*.

* *Signifies not out.*   † Captain.

Bowling Averages

	Overs	Maidens	Runs	Wickets	Average
A. W. Smith	104	34	190	11	17.27
R. Pellew	177.3	47	426	24	17.75
O. Trenwith	82	14	240	12	20.00
H. Watts	144.4	30	448	16	28.00
B. Read	94	15	323	10	32.30
J. W. Murphy	91	21	237	4	59.25

Also bowled: R. F. Hosking 43—3—178—8; M. C. Weeks 51—11—154—6; A. Opie 60.3—14—174—6; I. J. Skinner 63—16—115—2; R. Harris 2—1—7—0 T. W. Cory 7—0—25—0.

Professionals.—None.

CUMBERLAND

Secretary—N. WISE, 18, Banklands, Workington

Matches 8—Lost 5, Won on first innings 1, No result 2

		1st Innings	2nd Innings	Result
May 15, 16	Northumberland	90	34 for 1	Won on first
Workington	Cumberland	95	—	innings
May 29, 30	Durham	330	—	Lost by innings
Carlisle	Cumberland	168	144	and 18 runs
July 1, 2	Cumberland	149	94	Lost by innings
York	Yorkshire II	338* for 4	—	and 95 runs
July 8, 9	Cumberland	151	98	Lost by five
Kendal	Yorkshire II	92	158 for 5	wickets
July 15, 16	Cumberland	157 for 7	—	No result
Gosforth	Northumberland	—	—	
July 17, 18	Cumberland	135	92	Lost by ten
Bishop Auckland	Durham	194	34 for 0	wickets
July 22, 23	Lancashire II	255* for 7	—	Lost by innings
Southport	Cumberland	97	46	and 112 runs
August 14, 15	Cumberland	—	—	No result
Keswick	Lancashire II	—	—	

* Innings declared closed.

Batting Averages

	Innings	Not Outs	Runs	Highest Innings	Average
H. Halliday	10	0	260	45	26.00
D. J. Hair	4	0	79	40	19.75
I. Park	5	1	64	28	16.00
R. Shepherd	6	0	93	32	15.50
J. M. S. Burrow	12	1	164	82*	14.90
J. H. Millican	12	0	170	44	14.16
R. Stewart	4	0	38	26	9.50
J. Rudd	4	2	16	12*	8.00
R. Faville	10	0	71	26	7.10
M. Beaty	12	5	45	11*	6.42
P. Sarjeant	6	1	25	10	5.00
T. McKegg	5	0	20	12	4.00
T. Thompson	6	0	22	20	3.66
W. D. F. Dow	4	1	7	4	2.33
R. S. Ellwood†	6	0	13	6	2.16

Also batted: J. B. Parker 31, 20*, 6; J. Cowan 24, 2; R. Bowman 48, 2; N. Emery 9, 8; W. Dennis 13, 1; J. Dennis 16, 2; P. Hartley 10, 0; A. Metcalfe 5, 0, 0.

* *Signifies not out.*   † Captain.

Bowling Averages

	Overs	Maidens	Runs	Wickets	Average
H. Halliday	56	14	130	8	16.25
J. B. Parker	22	2	67	4	16.75
P. Sarjeant................	24	4	69	4	17.25
W. D. F. Dow	47.3	9	166	8	20.75
J. H. Millican	71.5	15	222	10	22.20
J. Dennis	50.4	13	135	6	22.50
R. S. Ellwood	22	4	59	2	29.50
T. Thompson	42.2	12	93	3	31.00
A. Metcalfe	29	6	99	3	33.00
J. Cowan	9	0	41	1	41.00
J. Rudd	38	7	89	2	44.50
R. Stewart	26	9	59	1	59.00
W. Dennis	30	3	112	1	112.00

Professionals.—H. Halliday, J. Dennis, W Dennis.

DERBYSHIRE SECOND ELEVEN

Secretary—W. T. TAYLOR, County Cricket Ground,
Nottingham Road, Derby

*Matches 12—Lost 6, Won on first innings 3, Lost on first innings 2,
No result 1*

		1st Innings	2nd Innings	Result
May 22, 23	Derbyshire II	165	195	Lost by three
Coalville	Leicestershire II	169* for 5	192 for 7	wickets
May 27, 28	Derbyshire II	96	258	Lost by ten
Old Trafford	Lancashire II	230* for 8	125* for 0	wickets
June 5, 6	Shropshire	244	100 for 7	Won on first
Derby	Derbyshire II	246* for 9	—	innings
June 10, 11	Derbyshire II	149	140	Lost by ten
Derby	Warwickshire II	284* for 9	6 for 0	wickets
June 26, 27	Derbyshire II	113	201	Lost by innings
Northampton	Northants II	350* for 4	—	and 36 runs
July 10, 11	Derbyshire II	103	77	Lost on first
Newark	Notts II	155* for 6	—	innings
July 17, 18	Shropshire	206		No result
St. Georges	Derbyshire II	5 for 0	—	
July 24, 25	Notts II	185	212* for 4	Won on first
Chesterfield	Derbyshire II	261* for 8		innings
August 5, 6	Derbyshire II	158	126	Lost by innings
Edgbaston	Warwickshire II	307* for 6	—	and 23 runs
August 12, 13	Derbyshire II	149	138* for 3	Lost on first
Derby	Leicestershire II	152* for 5	53 for 4	innings
August 21, 22	Derbyshire II	300* for 8	—	Won on first
Derby	Northants II	165	246 for 7	innings
August 28, 29	Lancashire II	311 for 5	112* for 8	Lost by 27 runs
Derby	Derbyshire II	249* for 8	147	

* Innings declared closed.

Batting Averages

	Innings	Not Outs	Runs	Highest Innings	Average
A. Revill	6	1	188	85	37.60
J. A. Holmes	14	1	366	85	28.15
J. D. Short	15	0	323	58	21.53
G. Wyatt	19	2	360	59	21.17
F. C. Brailsford	17	0	335	70	19.70
K. F. Mohan	10	0	197	50	19.70
G. A. Beet	16	0	304	67	19.00
D. J. Green	7	0	110	56	15.71
J. B. Furniss	12	4	117	25	14.62
H. L. Johnson	5	1	56	28*	14.00
N. West	10	0	105	25	10.50
L. S. Marples†	18	5	133	29	10.23
D. Hall	7	5	16	8*	8.00
H. Rhodes	8	0	54	17	6.75
W. Bedford	5	0	33	12	6.60

Also batted: C. Lee 55; J. Kelly 9, 58; J. Lomas 21, 6, 36, 0*; J. Whiteley 18*, 2, 14, 5*; I. Gibson 12, 5, 15, 19; R. Dawes 20, 4; N. Else 12; I. Buxton 5, 9, 12, 11; D. Millner 13, 7; A. Eato 11, 6, 0, 13; P. Eyre 3; F. C. Cresswell 0.

Signifies not out.   † *Captain.*

Bowling Averages

	Overs	Maidens	Runs	Wickets	Average
D. Hall	163.5	38	441	26	16.96
H. Rhodes	160.2	37	410	18	22.77
I. Gibson	63.5	13	163	6	27.16
J. A. Holmes	52.5	6	176	6	29.33
J. B. Furniss	194.1	46	712	24	29.66
W. Bedford	61	17	179	6	29.83
J. Whiteley	52	10	188	5	37.60
A. Eato	65.4	14	195	5	39.00
G. A. Beet	151	40	525	12	43.75
A. Revill	89	22	264	6	44.00

Also bowled: J. D. Short 2—0—2—1; K. F. Mohan 30—11—77—3; R. Dawes 18—1—66—1; N. West 0.2—0—2—0; P. Eyre 4—0—18—0; N. Else 12—5—19—0; F. C. Cresswell 11—1—38—0; D. Millner 7—1—46—0; L. Johnson 29—5—94—1; J. Kelly 1—0—5—0.

Amateurs.—J. A. Holmes, J. D. Short, D. J. Green, L. S. Marples, W. Bedford, I. Gibson, I. Buxton, F. C. Cresswell.

DEVON

Secretary—T. H. KIRKHAM, "Ewelme," 17, Shiphay Lane, Torquay

Matches 10—Won 2, Lost 3, Won on first innings 2, Lost on first innings 2, No result 1

		1st Innings	2nd Innings	Result
July 19, 20	Devon	112	—	No result
Liskeard	Cornwall	31 for 0		
August 2, 3	Berkshire	145	279* for 7	Lost by 121
Torquay	Devon	165	138	runs
August 5, 6	Dorset	234	99	Lost on first
Seaton	Devon	190	81 for 4	innings

		1st Innings	2nd Innings	Result	
August 12, 13	Devon	176	71* for 2	Won on	first
Dorchester	Dorset	97	84 for 5	innings	
August 14, 15	Oxfordshire	109	—	†Won by	six
Oxford	Devon	110 for 4	—	wickets	
August 16, 17	Berkshire	222* for 5	143* for 5	Lost by	173
Reading	Devon	142	50	runs	
August 19, 20	Devon	91	55	Lost by	nine
Newton Abbot	Somerset II	134	13 for 1	wickets	
August 26, 27	Devon	309* for 9	15 for 0	Won on	first
Exeter	Cornwall	256	—	innings	
August 28, 29	Oxfordshire	202	81	Won by	five
Paignton	Devon	202	82 for 5	wickets	
August 30, 31	Somerset II	284* for 9	—	Lost on	first
Chard	Devon	70	173 for 5	innings	

* Innings declared closed.
† Reduced to one day because of rain.

Batting Averages

	Innings	Not Outs	Runs	Highest Innings	Average
D. H. Cole	16	2	534	90	38.14
D. Stilwell	5	1	96	44	24.00
R. Smith	12	2	226	57	22.60
H. D. Fairclough†	17	1	321	58	20.06
W. T. Selley	12	2	177	38*	17.70
N. F. Borrett	9	0	129	48	14.33
N. C. F. Bloy	12	0	169	45	14.08
J. T. Stevens	8	1	60	35	8.57
B. H. Lock	14	1	107	25*	8.23
P. Atkinson	14	1	105	20	8.07
N. Thomas	10	0	80	35	8.00
R. Healey	5	0	23	19	4.60
C. E. Wensley	4	1	10	4*	3.33
J. E. Bonner	8	4	3	2	0.75

Also batted: P. W. Stearns 3 innings 58 runs; M. P. Arscott 2—3; G. R. Thompson 3—24; H. Uren 2—3; H. Crichand 2—5; A. Hitchman 3—8; S. Cray 2—25; S. Mountford 3—59; J. Wacker 17; J. R. P. Ousley 4; D. Rippon 2; R. Seatherton 3; J. Rodgers 4; D. Medway 6; A. E. Smith 4; R. Horswell 8; P. Gaunt 6.

* Signifies not out. † Captain.

Bowling Averages

	Overs	Maidens	Runs	Wickets	Average
A. E. Smith	22	3	45	5	9.00
A. S. Crichand	25	5	61	5	12.20
R. Smith	201	60	331	25	13.24
N. F. Borrett	37	5	114	8	14.25
H. D. Fairclough	115	39	257	16	16.06
P. Gaunt	21	2	58	3	19.33
D. H. Cole	222	57	472	22	21.45
A. Hitchman	76	9	183	7	26.14
P. Atkinson	186	41	496	17	29.18
N. C. F. Bloy	34	4	127	4	31.75
R. Healey	57	11	177	5	35.40

Also bowled: G. R. Thompson 31—8—38—1; P. W. Stearns 22—3—57—1; R. Seatherton 5—1—11—0; D. Rippon 11—4—16—0.

Professionals.—None.

DORSET

Secretary—S. Hey, "Greenroyd," Horsecastles Lane,
Sherborne

*Matches 12—Won 3, Lost 3, Won on first innings 2, Lost on first
innings 3, No result 1*

		1st Innings	2nd Innings	Result
August 2, 3	Dorset	275* for 7	146* for 3	Won by 126
Camborne	Cornwall	167	128	runs
August 5, 6	Dorset	234	99	Won on first
Seaton	Devon	190	81 for 4	innings
August 7, 8	Wiltshire	188	190* for 7	Won on first
Sherborne	Dorset	192* for 9	137 for 6	innings
August 9, 10	Dorset	86	—	No result
Blandford	Cornwall	7 for 1		
August 12, 13	Devon	176	71* for 2	Lost on first
Dorchester	Dorset	97	84 for 5	innings
August 16, 17	Wiltshire	172	135	Lost by 60 runs
Marlborough	Dorset	146	101	
August 19, 20	Dorset	277	142* for 6	Lost by six
Banbury	Oxfordshire	205	215 for 4	wickets
August 21, 22	Dorset	274* for 5	195	Won by 52 runs
Reading	Berkshire	278* for 4	139	
August 23, 24	Dorset	100	158	Lost on first
Sherborne	Somerset II	107* for 9	122 for 6	innings
August 26, 27	Dorset	228* for 6	67	Won by two
Poole	Berkshire	205	88	runs
August 28, 29	Dorset	160	108	Lost by five
Yeovil	Somerset II	167* for 5	102 for 5	wickets
August 30, 31	Oxfordshire	135	133* for 7	Lost on first
Wimborne	Dorset	78	64 for 2	innings

* Innings declared closed.

Batting Averages

	Innings	Not Outs	Runs	Highest Innings	Average
M. M. Walford	22		728	131*	34.66
D. C. P. R. Jowett	8	1	213	65	30.42
G. W. L. Courtenay	16	1	389	88	25.93
G. G. L. Hebden	17	1	410	82	25.62
M. Hardwicke	22	1	347	64	16.52
D. A. Bulfield	19	1	276	53	15.33
G. E. S. Woodhouse	13	2	135	26*	12.27
M. E. Doggrell	19	4	172	44	11.46
D. J. W. Bridge†	20	1	202	48	10.63
H. G. Hunt	9	1	77	43	9.62
R. R. Dovey	14	1	73	18	5.61
P. A. Deane	7		36	27	5.14

Also batted: J. Aiken 5, 1*, 3, 0*, 0*; H. L. Baker 5, 1; A. P. F. Alexander
0*, 3*, 0*, 0, 2, 4*, 15, 4; M. B. Bovill 12, 89*, 19, 3; D. Hardman 19*, 12;
D. Hardwicke 2, 5, 4; W. H. Ives 0*; D. Nickell 4*, 0; C. A. H. White 7*;
I. Wilson 0, 15.

     * *Signifies not out.*   † Captain.

Bowling Averages

	Overs	Maidens	Runs	Wickets	Average
R. R. Dovey	464.4	199	757	61	12.41
D. J. W. Bridge	331	112	772	48	16.08
P. A. Deane	94	25	247	12	20.58
M. E. Doggrell	248.5	49	745	24	31.04
A. P. F. Alexander	123	18	408	11	37.09

Also bowled: D. A. Bulfield 22.5—2—117—5; D. Hardman 23.4—3—89—7; G. G. L. Hebden 12—2—36—2; W. H. Ives 1—0—1—0; D. C. P. R. Jowett 8—4—19—0.

Professionals.—None.

DURHAM

Secretary—J. ILEY, "Farndale," Fieldhouse Lane, Durham City

Matches 12—*Won* 3, *Lost* 3, *Won on first innings* 2, *Lost on first innings* 2, *No result* 2

		1st Innings	2nd Innings	Result
May 13, 14	Durham	112	133	Lost by eight
Edgbaston	Warwickshire II	177* for 9	—	wickets
May 29, 30	Durham	330	—	Won by innings
Carlisle	Cumberland	168	144	and 18 runs
June 10, 11	Durham	242	19 for 0	Won by ten
Jesmond	Northumberland	112	148	wickets
June 26, 27	Durham	262	—	Won on first
South Shields	Staffordshire	127	117 for 2	innings
July 17 18	Cumberland	135	92	Won by ten
Bishop Auckland	Durham	194	34 for 0	wickets
July 24, 25	Durham	128 for 8	—	No result
Stockton-on-Tees	Lancashire II	—	—	
July 31, August 1	Durham	243	135 for 5	Lost on first
Darlington	Warwickshire II	244* for 4	—	innings
August 5, 6	Durham	218	145 for 6	Lost on first
Sunderland	Northumberland	279* for 9	—	innings
August 7, 8	Durham	154	109	Lost by innings
Blackhill	Yorkshire II	300* for 7	—	and 36 runs
August 19, 20	Durham	90	79	Lost by innings
Middlesbrough	Yorkshire II	193* for 9	—	and 24 runs
August 26, 27	Lancashire II	—	—	No result
Old Trafford	Durham	—	—	
August 28, 29	Durham	289	—	Won on first
Leek	Staffordshire	184	73 for 4	innings

* Innings declared closed.

Batting Averages

	Innings	Not Outs	Runs	Highest Innings	Average
H. D. Bell	15	2	393	90	30.23
J. G. Fox	13	6	196	41	28.00
M. P. Weston	10	1	235	74	26.11
G. C. Lamb	14	0	358	52	25.57
K. H. Thompson	16	0	388	60	24.25
J. M. Watson	16	1	301	47	20.06
D. W. Hardy†	15	0	287	51	19.13
D. Kirby	5	0	77	55	15.40
S. H. Young	6	3	44	17	14.66
R. Aspinall	13	1	154	37	12.83
G. M. Crawford	7	1	70	33	11.66
N. H. Pigg	8	3	42	22	8.40

Also batted: G. L. Lake 0, 14*; W. G. Moffitt 34, 15, 2, 3; J. G. Keeler 21, 4; M. J. Tate 15, 0; K. Longstaff 20, 0, 8*, 0, 0; K. Williamson 7; R. Inglis 0, 8; W. Wake 2, 6; S. G. C. Stoker 8, 0; V. A. Reed 6, 11; G. Molloy 3, 0*; J. N. Watson 0, 3; F. Forster 0*, 0*.

        * *Signifies not out.*   † Captain.

Bowling Averages

	Overs	Maidens	Runs	Wickets	Average
S. H. Young	136.4	41	266	21	12.66
D. W. Hardy	135	36	311	21	14.80
J. M. Watson	204.5	66	478	29	16.48
R. Aspinall	224.1	67	513	26	19.73
N. H. Pigg	116.1	28	328	15	21.86

Also bowled: J. N. Watson 10—3—17—3; W. Wake 10—2—18—1; D. Kirby 12.2—6—27—1; F. Forster 27—11—49—1; M. J. Tate 32—3—121—2; K. Williamson 16—3—62—1; S. G. C. Stoker 34—10—67—1; M. P. Weston 21.1—1—75—1; H. D. Bell 1—0—3—0; G. Molloy 6—0—30—0.

Professionals.—R. Aspinall, F. Forster, J. G. Keeler, J. M. Watson.

ESSEX SECOND ELEVEN

Secretary—T. E. BAILEY, 60, London Road, Chelmsford

Matches 12—Won 1, Lost 4, Won on first innings 5, Lost on first innings 1, No result 1

		1st Innings	2nd Innings	Result
May 23, 24	Essex II	159	167	Won on first
Taunton	Somerset II	134	152 for 8	innings
June 4, 5	Surrey II	54* for 0	282* for 5	Won on first
Frinton-on-Sea	Essex II	55* for 0	212 for 5	innings
June 12, 13	Essex II	129	278* for 9	Lost by seven
Sittingbourne	Kent II	246* for 6	162 for 3	wickets
June 19, 20	Essex II	197	196* for 9	Lost on first
Purfleet	Kent II	200* for 7	83 for 1	innings
June 25, 26	Cambridgeshire	129	241	Won on first
Wisbech	Essex II	173	139 for 6	innings
July 3, 4	Middlesex II	237* for 7	148* for 2	Lost by 25 runs
Winchmore Hill	Essex II	139* for 3	221	
July 5, 6	Suffolk	176	89	Lost by 13 runs
Mistley	Essex II	80	172	
July 23, 24	Essex II	160	103	Lost by eight
Harlow	Somerset II	165* for 5	100 for 2	wickets
July 27, 29	Surrey II	82	44 for 1	Won on first
The Oval	Essex II	238* for 8	—	innings
August 5, 6	Essex II	278* for 6	78 for 3	Won by seven
Felixstowe	Suffolk	91	264	wickets
August 7, 8	Essex II	279	120* for 4	Won on first
Chelmsford	Middlesex II	199* for 5	79 for 7	innings
August 12, 13	Essex II	—	—	No result
Chingford	Cambridgeshire	—	—	

        * Innings declared closed.

Batting Averages

	Innings	Not Outs	Runs	Highest Innings	Average
G. Horrex	3	0	275	116	91.66
L. Savill	6	2	199	102*	49.75
J. Milner	6	1	180	63	36.00
A. Durley	26	2	757	101	31.54
D. Moore	4	1	82	35	27.33
J. Taylor	6	1	123	50	24.60
A. B. Quick†	20	2	440	94	24.44
V. Paul	4	0	92	48	23.00
J. Wright	14	1	295	86	22.69
G. Smith	15	1	304	64	21.71
K. Wallace	12	1	233	89	21.18
P. Spicer	22	3	352	61*	18.52
G. Nolan	16	4	200	37	16.66
B. Knight	3	1	33	21	16.50
D. Bryant	4	2	33	28*	16.50
P. Palmer	5	0	73	46	14.60
D. Daniels	12	7	68	33*	13.60
E. Palmer	10	2	103	41*	12.87
A. Tillim	5	1	48	18	12.00
F. Rumsey	4	0	39	13	9.75
T. Lester	8	0	65	31	8.12
D. Watt	5	3	16	10*	8.00
J. Cadman	5	0	22	8	4.40
P. Phelan	12	2	41	9	4.10
C. Wheatley	5	2	4	2*	1.33

Also batted: P. Shott 2 innings 47 runs; F. Rist 2—51; M. Eastman 2—40; M. Kolham 2—3; M. Davey 1—22; P. Clark 1—6; C. Earthy 1—0; A. Hurd 1—0.

* Signifies not out.   † *Captain.*

Bowling Averages

	Overs	Maidens	Runs	Wickets	Average
D. Watt	68	16	207	14	14.78
B. Knight	57	12	200	13	15.38
P. Phelan	201.2	41	528	33	16.00
E. Palmer	188	50	498	26	19.15
J. Cadman	21	5	89	4	22.25
P. Spicer	255.3	55	747	33	22.63
G. Smith	39	6	128	5	25.60
A. Tillim	58.1	10	191	7	27.28
A. Hurd	47	9	191	7	27.28
J. Wright	27.4	2	112	4	28.00
F. Rumsey	50	7	164	5	32.80
C. Wheatley	55	12	165	5	33.00
D. Daniels	214.3	25	791	16	49.43

Also bowled: P. Shott 19.5—3—66—5; C. Earthy 14—2—46—1; D. Bryant 3—2—9—0; M. Eastman 3—0—20—0; M. Kolham 3—0—15—0; A. B. Quick 18.4—0—92—0; M. Davey 3—1—5—0; B. Francis 11—1—65—1.

Amateurs.—A. B. Quick, G. Horrex, J. Taylor, V. Paul, K. Wallace, D. Bryant, E. Palmer, T. Lester, P. Phelan, M. Eastman, C. Earthy, D. Moore, J. Wright, G. Nolan, P. Palmer, F. Rumsey, J. Cadman, P. Shott, M. Davey.

GLOUCESTERSHIRE SECOND ELEVEN

Secretary—C. H. G. Thomas, County Ground, Bristol, 7

Matches 10—Won 2, Lost 1, Won on first innings 4, Lost on first innings 2, No result 1

		1st Innings	2nd Innings	Result
May 15, 16	Lancashire II	210	—	No result
Bristol	Gloucestershire II	—	—	
May 27, 28	Gloucestershire II	209	133* for 3	Won on first
Bristol	Somerset II	139	180 for 7	innings
June 12, 13	Gloucestershire II	190	95	Lost by six
Bristol	Warwickshire II	191* for 9	97 for 4	wickets
June 17, 18	Gloucestershire II	249	149	Won by 69 runs
Bristol	Surrey II	194	135	
June 20, 21	Warwickshire II	348* for 1	155 for 2	Won on first
Edgbaston	Gloucestershire II	350* for 7	—	innings
June 24, 25	Gloucestershire II	178* for 8	137 for 6	Lost on first
Old Trafford	Lancashire II	227		innings
July 3, 4	Gloucestershire II	291* for 5	112* for 4	Won on first
Glastonbury	Somerset II	194* for 9	67 for 2	innings
July 5, 6	Cornwall	172	169	Won on first
Falmouth	Gloucestershire II	217* for 9	51 for 5	innings
August 14, 15	Gloucestershire II	219* for 8	117* for 3	Won by 46 runs
Bristol	Cornwall	131* for 7	160	
August 29, 30	Gloucestershire II	178	232* for 8	Lost on first
The Oval	Surrey II	200* for 1	151 for 7	innings

* Innings declared closed.

Batting Averages

	Innings	Not Outs	Runs	Highest Innings	Average
R. K. Whiley	4	1	151	69	50.33
A. V. Avery†	8	5	129	41*	43.00
D. Carpenter	15	0	626	193	41.73
D. A. Allen	9	1	310	72*	38.75
G. E. Lambert	5	2	116	41	38.66
J. Mortimore	4	0	140	62	35.00
D. Hawkins	10	0	285	86	28.50
J. V. C. Griffiths	15	0	322	43	21.18
D. G. A'Court	8	3	104	48*	20.80
G. Wiltshire	7	3	78	35	19.50
D. C. Mills	13	2	212	67	19.27
A. S. Brown	8	1	111	41*	15.85
R. J. Etheridge	7	0	84	22	12.00
G. J. Lake	9	5	42	18*	10.50
B. Meyer	7	0	72	22	10.28

Also batted: M. Dash 21, 7, 6, 7*; W. Knightley-Smith 4*, 5, 15, 8; P. Rochford 6, 3*, 0, 9; J. Bernard 9, 24; A. F. Martin 6, 9; L. D. Watts 3, 13; R. Newman 7, 0; H. Jarman 9; A. Milton 2.

* *Signifies not out.*   † *Captain.*

Bowling Averages

	Overs	Maidens	Runs	Wickets	Average
G. Wiltshire	104.1	29	191	13	14.68
J. Mortimore	88.3	27	221	13	17.00
G. J. Lake	152.1	47	323	17	19.00
D. A. Allen	194.1	56	522	25	20.88
D. Hawkins	67.4	19	188	9	20.88

	Overs	Maidens	Runs	Wickets	Average
A. S. Brown	38	8	101	4	25.25
J. V. C. Griffiths	236	68	625	24	26.04
G. E. Lambert	69	13	231	7	33.00
B. D. Wells	38.5	8	146	4	36.50
D. G. A'Court	63	16	192	4	48.00

Also bowled: D. Carpenter 1 wicket for 40 runs; D. C. Mills 0—22; C. A. Milton 1—4; B. Meyer 0—9; J. Bernard 1—91; P. Rochford 0—22; R. Nicholls 1—2.

Amateurs.—R. K. Whiley, D. G. A'Court, D. C. Mills, M. Dash, W. Knightley-Smith, J. Bernard, A. F. Martin, L. D. Watts, R. Newman, H. Jarman.

HERTFORDSHIRE

Secretary—Major H. G. Lay, High Croft, Springfields, Broxbourne

Matches 10—Won 4, Lost 2, Won on first innings 2, Lost on first innings 1, No result 1

		1st Innings	2nd Innings	Result
July 3, 4	Hertfordshire	261	86 for 4	Won by six
Hitchin	Bedfordshire	139	207	wickets
July 17, 18	Norfolk	156* for 8	—	Won on first
Hertford	Hertfordshire	157 for 8		innings
July 31, August 1	Hertfordshire	207	145* for 9	Won by three
Sawston	Cambridgeshire	162* for 5	187	runs
August 5, 6	Norfolk	153* for 1	136	Won by four
Lakenham	Hertfordshire	127	164 for 6	wickets
August 7, 8	Buckinghamshire	272* for 8	189* for 2	Lost on first
High Wycombe	Hertfordshire	254	111 for 8	innings
August 9, 10	Hertfordshire	152* for 8	—	No result
Bedford	Bedfordshire	114 for 7		
August 12, 13	Suffolk	246* for 4	181* for 6	Won on first
Felixstowe	Hertfordshire	250* for 3	54 for 2	innings
August 19, 20	Hertfordshire	174	77	Won by 19 runs
Watford	Buckinghamshire	139	93	
August 21, 22	Hertfordshire	92* for 8	99	Lost by seven
Letchworth	Cambridgeshire	100* for 9	93 for 3	wickets
August 23, 24	Hertfordshire	159* for 8	80* for 9	Lost by five
St. Albans	Suffolk	106	134 for 5	wickets

* Innings declared closed.

Batting Averages

	Innings	Not Outs	Runs	Highest Innings	Average
B. S. Darvell	11	6	139	54*	27.80
L. Bateman	9	2	185	60*	26.42
A. O'Neill	16	0	413	88	25.81
G. A. Smithson	13	1	298	63	24.83
T. L. Clough	17	2	339	64*	22.60
A. N. Bradbeer...........	5	0	99	54	19.80
R. G. Simons	12	0	203	71	16.91
R. W. Smith	16	1	229	46	15.26
D. V. Cooper	8	0	122	57	15.25
T. G. Morley	14	5	105	26*	11.66
J. A. Standen	5	0	56	28	11.20
C. V. L. Marquest..........	15	2	131	25*	10.00
R. C. Hughes	5	1	28	17	7.00
G. Meadowcroft...........	6	1	32	15*	6.40

Also batted: R. B. Marriott 18, 4; B. Hatley 18, 8, 0; R. Vine 0*, 3*, 0*, 0; C. Clapham 5, 0; D. Pratt 0*, 0, 2*, 0*; T. A. Bell 1, 1; G. Cole 1.

* Signifies not out.   † Captain.

Bowling Averages

	Overs	Maidens	Runs	Wickets	Average
G. Meadowcroft	116.2	32	261	22	11.86
D. Pratt	99.5	24	261	17	15.35
T. G. Morley	204.1	43	532	27	19.70
C. V. L. Marques	225.1	50	647	25	25.88
B. S. Darvell	117	27	384	12	32.00
R. Vine	99	35	193	5	38.60
R. C. Hughes	62	13	195	5	39.00

Also bowled: G. Cole 26.4—10—60—3; J. A. Standon 22—6—58—3; A. N. Bradbeer 2—0—12—0; G. A. Smithson 5—0—46—1; L. Bateman 3—0—15—0; A. O'Neill 2—0—15—0.

Professionals.—G. A. Smithson, T. G. Morley, J. A. Standen.

KENT SECOND ELEVEN

Secretary—N. CHRISTOPHERSON, St. Lawrence Ground, Canterbury

Matches 14—Won 1, Lost 3, Won on first innings 4, Lost on first innings 5, No result 1

		1st Innings	2nd Innings	Result
May 15, 16	Middlesex II	138	187 for 8	Won on first innings
Lord's	Kent II	239* for 8		
June 8, 10	Surrey II	205* for 5	104 for 5	Won on first innings
The Oval	Kent II	220* for 3		
June 12, 13	Essex II	129	278* for 9	Won by seven wickets
Sittingbourne	Kent II	246* for 6	162 for 3	
June 19, 20	Essex II	197	196* for 9	Won on first innings
Purfleet	Kent II	200* for 7	83 for 1	
July 1, 2	Somerset II	249* for 8	90* for 9	Lost on first innings
Taunton	Kent II	150* for 8	110 for 3	
July 4, 5	Surrey II	182	17 for 1	Lost on first innings
Beckenham	Kent II	159		
July 8, 9	Norfolk	348* for 5	94* for 4	Lost on first innings
Ditton	Kent II	250* for 8	44 for 0	
July 23, 24	Norfolk	197	180* for 8	Lost on first innings
Hunstanton	Kent II	176	111 for 6	
July 25, 26	Somerset II	149* for 9	50	Lost by seven wickets
Broadstairs	Kent II	145	47 for 3	
July 31, August 1	Middlesex II	162	161	Won on first innings
Folkestone	Kent II	187	135 for 9	
August 12, 13	Buckinghamshire	41 for 3	—	No result
Chesham	Kent II	—	—	
August 16, 17	Kent II	227	179	Lost by six wickets
Canterbury	Buckinghamshire	290* for 9	118 for 4	
August 19, 20	Kent II	247	114* for 3	Lost by one wicket
Chippenham	Wiltshire	159* for 8	203 for 9	
August 26, 27	Wilshire	157	214* for 3	Lost on first innings
Tonbridge	Kent II	120	191 for 6	

* Innings declared closed.

Batting Averages

	Innings	Not Outs	Runs	Highest Innings	Average
D. G. Ufton	6	1	247	94	49.50
P. Jones	19	2	564	74	33.17
A. Dixon	7	1	190	73	31.66
B. Disbury	5	1	123	40*	30.75
A. E. Fagg†	7	1	162	100	27.00
A. Brazier	20	2	454	100*	25.22
B. Luckhurst	15	5	230	55	23.00
A. R. B. Neame	6	0	126	40	21.00
J. Prodger	23	1	370	47	16.81
A. Catt	12	2	151	46	15.10
R. Wilkinson	12	1	137	63*	12.45
M. Bristow	12	3	93	17*	10.33
D. V. P. Wright	6	1	33	16*	6.60
A. Brown	6	0	36	10	6.00

Also batted: J. F. Pretlove 56*, 27; M. Millard 47*, 28, 3; C. Lewis† 9, 0*, 8, 2, 0; R. Beard 20, 17; F. Ridgway 0, 9; C. F. Anson 0, 7; R. Thresher 2, 2; J. Dancy 1, 9; G. W. Cook 12, 7; R. M. Prideaux 43, 40; S. Knight 18; I. C. Potter 5; I. Moir 11; M. Checksfield 2; J. Lock 1. J. Pettiford scored 144 runs in three innings and was not out on each occasion.

* *Signifies not out.*　　　　† *Joint Captain.*

Bowling Averages

	Overs	Maidens	Runs	Wickets	Average
R. Thresher	64	15	126	11	11.45
S. Knight	31.3	9	83	7	11.85
J. C. T. Page	88.5	32	193	14	13.78
F. Ridgway	70	27	148	10	14.80
B. Luckhurst	258.5	85	611	33	18.51
P. Jones	151.1	52	356	19	18.73
A. Brown	199.4	43	498	25	19.92
A. Dixon	140	49	389	19	20.47
A. F. Brazier	60	16	167	8	20.87
J. Pettiford	85	27	247	10	24.70
D. V. P. Wright	64	19	186	6	31.00
J. B. Phillips	110	24	279	8	34.87
R. Wilkinson	122.3	37	379	8	47.37

Also bowled: J. Dancy 27—7—46—2; I. C. Potter 21—5—61—2; J. Lock 26—7—51—1; C. Lewis 13—2—44—0; G. W. Cook 9—4—23—0; A. R. B. Neame 15—5—15—1; J. F. Pretlove 3—0—15—0; D. G. Ufton 1—0—3—0; R. Beard 6—1—31—0; M. Millard 2—1—3—0; J. Prodger 6—3—13—1.

Amateurs.—A. R. B. Neame, J. F. Pretlove, M. Millard, R. Beard, C. F. Anson, R. Thresher, J. Dancy, G. W. Cook, R. M. Prideaux, I. C. Potter, I. Moir, M. Checksfield, J. Lock, J. B. Phillips.

LANCASHIRE SECOND ELEVEN

Secretary—C. G. Howard, Old Trafford, Manchester, 16

Matches 22—Won 8, Lost 3, Won on first innings 4, Lost on first innings 2, No result 5

		1st Innings	2nd Innings	Result
May 13, 14	Lancashire II	269* for 9	—	Won on first
Urmston	Northumberland	133	13 for 1	innings
May 15, 16	Lancashire II	210	—	No result
Bristol	Gloucestershire II	4 for 0	—	
May 20, 21	Surrey II	169	—	†Won by six
Old Trafford	Lancashire II	174 for 4	—	wickets

		1st Innings	2nd Innings	Result
May 22, 23	Lancashire II	143	207	Lost by six
Old Trafford	Warwickshire II	194	160 for 4	wickets
May 27, 28	Derbyshire II	96	258	Won by ten
Old Trafford	Lancashire II	230* for 8	125 for 0	wickets
May 29, 30	Notts II	210	114	Won by six
Wollaton	Lancashire II	242	86 for 4	wickets
June 5, 6	Cheshire	97	227	Won by six
Neston	Lancashire II	208* for 6	119 for 4	wickets
June 10, 11	Lancashire II	136	—	Lost on first
Harrogate	Yorkshire II	138 for 4	—	innings
June 12, 13	Lancashire II	164	153* for 9	Won by 53 runs
Old Trafford	Cheshire	115	149	
June 24, 25	Gloucestershire II	178* for 8	137 for 6	Won on first
Old Trafford	Lancashire II	227	—	innings
June 26, 27	Lancashire II	161	183	Lost by seven
Birmingham	Warwickshire II	303* for 6	42 for 3	wickets
July 1, 2	Northants II	249	123	Won by nine
Old Trafford	Lancashire II	312	63 for 1	wickets
July 8, 9	Lancashire II	274	71 for 7	Lost on first
Mitcham	Surrey II	343	—	innings
July 10, 11	Northants II	240	—	No result
Northampton	Lancashire II	207 for 4	—	
July 22, 23	Lancashire II	255* for 7	—	Won by innings
Southport	Cumberland	97	46	and 112 runs
July 24, 25	Durham	128 for 8	—	No result
Stockton-on-Tees	Lancashire II	—	—	
August 5, 6	Yorkshire II	210	208* for 9	Lost by 70 runs
Old Trafford	Lancashire II	212* for 3	136	
August 7, 8	Northumberland	343* for 9	—	Won on first
Jesmond	Lancashire II	345 for 9	—	innings
August 16, 17	Lancashire II	—	—	No result
Keswick	Cumberland	—	—	
August 21, 22	Notts II	219	247 for 6	Won on first
Old Trafford	Lancashire II	380* for 7	—	innings
August 26, 27	Lancashire II	—	—	No result
Old Trafford	Durham	—	—	
August 28, 29	Lancashire II	311* for 5	112* for 8	Won by 27 runs
Derby	Derbyshire II	249* for 8	147	

* Innings declared closed.

† Reduced to one day because of rain.

Batting Averages

	Innings	Not Outs	Runs	Highest Innings	Average
G. A. Edrich†	22	7	873	130*	58.20
G. Pullar	6	1	242	89	48.40
J. D. Bond	12	0	551	181	45.91
R. Collins	14	1	513	145	39.46
P. Marner	18	2	562	109	35.12
B. Booth	27	0	767	134	28.40
A. Bolton	21	3	486	54*	27.00
M. J. Hilton	5	0	110	42	22.00
A. Wilson	7	0	129	37	18.42
N. H. Cooke	24	0	435	83	18.12
B. Ogden	6	1	89	37*	17.80
P. Whiteley	9	2	119	64*	17.00
F. Moore	15	7	131	22*	16.37
C. Gradwell	5	1	64	21	16.00
W. Heys	16	3	127	26*	9.76
J. Roberts	7	4	19	6*	6.33
G. Coombe	10	1	50	14	5.55

Also batted: P. Dobing 4, 0, 0, 5; T. Greenhough 2, 0; K. B. Standring 19, 29, 10; G. Clayton 0, 0, 4*; A. Sutton 0; B. Quinton 0, 5, 6; B. Bulcock 4*; S. Anderson 7*; C. Hilton 1; P. N. Hutson 55; E. A. Kelly 2; G. Ashfield 0*, 1, 4*, 0*; G. Taylor 0; J. Hindle 8*, 9*, 14; R. Bowman 9; C. S. Smith 13*, 26*; C. Burton 6.

* *Signifies not out.* † Captain.

Bowling Averages

	Overs	Maidens	Runs	Wickets	Average
T. Greenhough	63.5	17	143	18	7.94
J. Roberts	267.1	82	681	50	13.62
P. Whiteley	141.1	47	288	17	16.94
E. A. Kelly	71	19	178	10	17.80
B. Booth	292	71	925	49	18.87
R. Collins	155.2	47	358	17	21.05
M. J. Hilton	164.5	60	437	19	23.00
F. W. Moore	321.2	77	872	33	26.42

Also bowled: N. H. Cooke 88—26—196—8; A. Bolton 41.4—4—167—3; A. Sutton 2—0—2—0; K. B. Standring 36—11—64—4; C. Burton 43—17—80—4; B. Bulcock 48—16—142—3; P. Dobing 25—7—82—3; C. Hilton 12—1—50—1; S. Anderson 3—0—26—0; B. Quinton 19—6—67—1; G. O. Ashfield 44—6—149—5; D. Bailey 25.4—4—69—7; P. Marner 42—8—137—5; C. S. Smith 24—5—77—1; G. Taylor 7—0—27—0; G. A. Edrich 2.4—0—19—0; R. Bowman 28—6—33—3.

Amateurs.—C. Gradwell, P. Dobing, K. B. Standring, A. Sutton, B. Quinton, B. Bulcock, S. Anderson, P. N. Hutson, G. Ashfield, G. Taylor, J. Hindle, R. Bowman, C. S. Smith, C. Burton, D. Bailey.

LEICESTERSHIRE SECOND ELEVEN

Secretary—R. A. DIMENT, Spencer Chambers, 4, Market Place, Leicester

Matches 12—*Won* 4, *Lost* 3, *Won on first innings* 2, *Lost on first innings* 3

		1st Innings	2nd Innings	Result
May 16, 17	Leicestershire II	44	143	Lost by innings
Birmingham	Warwickshire II	189* for 9	—	and 2 runs
May 22, 23	Derbyshire II	165	195	Won by three
Coalville	Leicestershire II	169* for 5	192 for 7	wickets
May 29, 30	Lincolnshire	182	83	Won by five
Grantham	Leicestershire II	184* for 7	82 for 5	wickets
June 3, 4	Leicestershire II	177	139	Won by 47 runs
Leicester	Somerset II	138	131	
June 19, 20	Leicestershire II	233* for 8	163 for 6	Won on first
Leicester	Northants II	164	112 for 4	innings
July 2, 3	Notts II	308* for 9	—	Lost on first
Melton	Leicestershire II	201	80 for 6	innings
July 8, 9	Warwickshire II	266	106* for 2	Lost on first
Loughborough	Leicestershire II	205	41 for 2	innings
July 29, 30	Notts II	143	149	Lost by 11 runs
Worksop	Leicestershire II	148* for 6	133	
August 5, 6	Leicestershire II	149	124	Won by 106
Rothwell	Northants II	101	66	runs
August 12, 13	Derbyshire II	149	138 for 3	Won on first
Derby	Leicestershire II	152* for 5	53 for 4	innings
August 21, 22	Leicestershire II	187	201* for 8	Lost on first
Leicester	Lincolnshire	203	117 for 6	innings
August 26, 27	Leicestershire II	121	86	Lost by seven
Keynsham	Somerset II	141	94 for 3	wickets

* Innings declared closed.

Batting Averages

	Innings	Not Outs	Runs	Highest Innings	Average
V. S. Munden	14	1	352	132	27.08
E. F. Phillips	16	0	370	67	23.12
P. A. Munden	16	1	345	85	23.00
J. E. Walsh†	21	4	365	60*	21.47
R. C. Smith	5	1	82	36	20.50
R. A. Diment	4	0	77	53	19.25
G. Burch	23	4	365	53	19.21
P. T. Smith	22	1	393	62	18.71
R. Julian	13	3	146	29*	14.60
M. Hickman	10	0	144	40	14.50
G. A. Hickinbottom	8	4	54	20*	13.50
F. M. Turner	18	8	120	18*	12.00
R. L. Pratt	9	0	87	17	9.66
B. S. Boshier	4	1	27	10	9.00
J. Smith	17	0	96	44	5.64
T. J. Goodwin	7	1	30	14	5.00

Also batted: M. Goodson 28, 1; P. Marrion 30, 34; J. van Geloven 49; D. Goodson 13, 2; P. Colville 3, 1; J. M. Josephs 14*, 0*; J. Pywell 0, 1; I. Foster 3, 0.

* Signifies not out.   † *Captain.*

Bowling Averages

	Overs	Maidens	Runs	Wickets	Average
R. C. Smith	91.4	42	183	16	11.43
F. M. Turner	161	40	432	30	14.40
T. J. Goodwin	248.5	50	617	42	14.69
R. L. Pratt	229	52	663	42	15.78
J. E. Walsh	181	56	471	29	16.24
B. S. Boshier	82	17	199	10	19.90
V. S. Munden	134	47	264	8	33.00

Also bowled: D. Goodson 34—5—105—4; J. Smith 9—1—18—0; J. van Geloven 6—2—14—0.

Amateurs.—R. A. Diment, M. Goodson, P. Marrion, D. Goodson, P. Colville, J. M. Josephs, J. Pywell, I. Foster.

LINCOLNSHIRE

Secretary—R. J. CHARLTON, Glen Cottage, Little Bytham, near Grantham

Matches 10—*Won* 1, *Lost* 6, *Won on first innings* 2, *No result* 1

		1st Innings	2nd Innings	Result
May 29, 30	Lincolnshire	182	83	Lost by five
Grantham	Leicestershire II	184* for 7	82 for 5	wickets
June 10, 11	Bedfordshire	185	—	No result
Woodhall Spa	Lincolnshire	77 for 2	—	
June 17, 18	Lincolnshire	191	160	Lost by two
Mirfield	Yorkshire II	213	139 for 8	wickets
June 26, 27	Lincolnshire	129	134	Lost by nine
Grimsby	Notts II	245	19 for 1	wickets
July 10, 11	Lincolnshire	146* for 3	201* for 5	Lost by seven
Cambridge	Cambridgeshire	157* for 5	193 for 3	wickets
July 24, 25	Lincolnshire	85	65	Lost by one
Bourne	Cambridgeshire	47	104 for 9	wicket
August 5, 6	Notts II	308* for 9	113 for 9	Lost first on
Trent Bridge	Lincolnshire	185	—	innings
August 7, 8	Bedfordshire	44	169	Won by eight
Bedford School	Lincolnshire	147	68 for 2	wickets

		1st Innings	2nd Innings	Result
August 12, 13	Yorkshire II	245* for 6	—	Lost by innings
Scunthorpe	Lincolnshire	35	71	and 139 runs
August 21, 22	Leicestershire II	187	201* for 8	Won on first
Leicester	Lincolnshire	203	117 for 6	innings

* Innings declared closed.

Batting Averages

	Innings	Not Outs	Runs	Highest Innings	Average
J. H. Taylor	17	0	530	78	31.17
E. M. Senior	8	2	176	70*	29.33
D. W. Taylor	15	0	270	48	18.00
R. C. Inman	8	2	108	40	18.00
R. P. Lascelles	8	1	123	69	17.57
B. C. Ehrenfried†	18	1	269	69	15.82
G. A. Marlow	4	0	63	35	15.75
J. D. Walton	13	3	127	28	12.70
G. R. Mawer	6	0	73	18	12.16
J. R. C. Todd	12	0	137	36	11.41
M. J. Keyworth	8	1	76	25	10.85
K. M. Cook	13	0	125	48	9.61
R. J. Chambers	6	0	57	34	9.50
N. Chatterton	4	1	26	20	8.66
A. W. Lea	11	2	76	28	8.44
G. Flower	7	1	49	14*	8.16
R. Kelsey	13	1	96	24	8.00
H. M. A. Cherry-Downes....	13	8	37	15*	7.40
J. Clark	4	0	16	13	4.00

Also batted: J. L. Thompson 14, 0; S. Beckett 7, 0; R. Beeson 8, 0, 0; K. Watson 2, 0*, 0; D. Merryweather 0, 0.

* *Signifies not out.* † Captain.

Bowling Averages

	Overs	Maidens	Runs	Wickets	Average
H. M. A. Cherry-Downes..	341.1	89	938	65	14.43
J. D. Walton	182.5	44	469	25	18.76
K. Watson	30	5	114	5	22.80
A. W. Lea	213.5	39	668	28	23.85
G. Flower	46	10	115	4	28.75

Also bowled: John Watson 15—4—41—2; E. M. Renier 31.5—4—121—2; J. Clark 10.3—2—33—1; N. Chatterton 23.3—8—48—1; K. M. Cook 45—7—175—1; G. A. Marlow 31—7—90—1; B. C. Ehrenfried 5—0—15—0; D. Merryweather 1—0—5—0.

Professionals.—None.

MIDDLESEX SECOND ELEVEN

Secretary—F. G. MANN, Lord's Cricket Ground, London, N.W.8

Matches 12—Won 5, Lost 1, Won on first innings 2, Lost on first innings 4

		1st Innings	2nd Innings	Result
May 15, 16	Middlesex II	138	187 for 8	Lost on first
Lord's	Kent II	239* for 8	—	innings
June 5, 6	Middlesex II	182	219* for 8	Won by 17 runs
Enfield	Northants II	185* for 4	199	
June 24, 25	Middlesex II	168* for 6	132* for 8	Lost on first
The Oval	Surrey II	176* for 7	8 for 0	innings

		1st Innings	2nd Innings	Result
July 3, 4	Middlesex II	237* for 7	148* for 2	Won by 25 runs
Winchmore Hill	Essex II	139* for 3	221	
July 10, 11	Middlesex II	243* for 6	202* for 3	Won on first innings
Ealing	Norfolk	241	157 for 6	
July 24, 25	Northants II	141	193	Lost by six runs
Corby	Middlesex II	186* for 4	142	
July 29, 30	Norfolk	132	131	Won by eight wickets
Norwich	Middlesex II	247* for 4	20 for 2	
July 31, August 1	Middlesex II	162	161	Lost on first innings
Folkestone	Kent II	187	135 for 9	
August 7, 8	Essex II	279	120* for 4	Lost on first innings
Chelmsford	Middlesex II	199* for 5	79 for 7	
August 9, 10	Middlesex II	222	—	Won by innings and 84 runs
Lowestoft	Suffolk	77	61	
August 21, 22	Middlesex II	215* for 4	201* for 3	Won by 107 runs
Southgate	Suffolk	217* for 4	92	
August 24, 26	Middlesex II	285* for 7	—	Won on first innings
Lord's	Surrey II	148	257 for 7	

* Innings declared closed.

Batting Averages

	Innings	Not Outs	Runs	Highest Innings	Average
R. A. White	20	3	660	105	38.82
R. W. Hooker	21	3	654	95	36.33
D. A. Bick	16	1	424	69	28.26
R. V. C. Robins	11	2	239	39*	26.55
D. J. Rayment	9	3	159	44	26.50
D. O. Baldry	6	0	134	118	25.66
D. Widows	9	3	141	60*	23.50
D. L. Newman†	10	1	194	47	21.55
W. E. Russell	16	0	298	57	18.62
A. Biggs	9	0	152	38	16.88
H. W. Tilly	10	4	91	20	15.16
A. J. Card	12	5	80	20*	11.42
K. B. Day	6	2	8	5	2.00
T. Angus	5	4	2	2*	2.00
S. J. Iisley	3	1	1	1*	0.50

Also batted: C. D. Drybrough 3 inns., 2 n.os 159 runs; P. H. Parfitt 3—1—156; M. E. L. Melluish 3—0—12; A. R. Day 2—1—48; H. J. Felton 2—0—92; J. L. Swann 2—0—21; C. C. Holton 1—0—25; D. Bennett 1—0—3.

* Signifies not out.   † Captain.

Bowling Averages

	Overs	Maidens	Runs	Wickets	Average
R. W. Hooker	80	25	207	15	13.80
H. W. Tilly	328.5	104	697	40	17.42
T. Angus	214.5	53	595	34	17.50
D. O. Baldry	54	18	143	8	17.87
W. E. Russell	102.2	30	274	15	18.26
R. V. C. Robins	154.1	34	480	24	20.00
S. J. Ilsley	78.3	29	160	7	22.85
R. A. White	36	9	117	5	23.40
D. A. Bick	76.5	16	232	8	29.00
A. J. Card	81.1	19	263	8	32.87
A. Biggs	27	3	96	1	96.00

Also bowled: D. L. Newman 9—2—24—1; D. Bennett 29.1—9—61—3; C. C. Holton 4—1—9—1; J. L. Swann 8—3—20—1; P. H. Parfitt 13—4—45—1; C. D. Drybrough 2—0—16—0; D. J. Rayment 3—1—16—0; D. Widows 2—0—17—0.

Amateurs.—D. L. Newman, R. V. C. Robins, C. D. Drybrough, M. E. L. Melluish, A. R. Day, H. J. Felton, J. L. Swann, C. C. Holton.

NORFOLK

Secretary—G. A. STEVENS, 37, St. Peter's Street, Norwich

Matches 12—Lost 4, Won on first innings 5, Lost on first innings 3

		1st Innings	2nd Innings	Result
July 8, 9	Norfolk	348* for 5	94* for 4	Won on first
Ditton	Kent II	250* for 8	44 for 0	innings
July 10, 11	Middlesex II	243* for 6	202* for 3	Lost on first
Ealing	Norfolk	241	157 for 6	innings
July 17, 18	Norfolk	156* for 8	—	Lost on first
Hertford	Hertfordshire	157 for 8	—	innings
July 23, 24	Norfolk	197	180* for 8	Won on first
Hunstanton	Kent II	176	111 for 6	innings
July 29, 30	Norfolk	132	131	Lost by eight
Norwich	Middlesex II	247* for 4	20 for 2	wickets
July 31, August 1	Buckinghamshire	201	205 for 0	Won on first
Norwich	Norfolk	343* for 2	—	innings
August 5, 6	Norfolk	153* for 1	136	Lost by four
Norwich	Hertfordshire	127	164 for 6	wickets
August 7, 8	Suffolk	256* for 6	183* for 4	Lost by 142
Norwich	Norfolk	183	114	runs
August 9, 10	Norfolk	175	4 for 1	Won on first
Norwich	Notts II	163	—	innings
August 16, 17	Suffolk	280* for 5	—	Lost by innings
Felixstowe	Norfolk	103	134	and 43 runs
August 23, 24	Buckinghamshire	142* for 4	108* for 7	Lost on first
Ascott Park, Wing	Norfolk	96	145 for 9	innings
August 28, 29	Norfolk	298* for 6	130* for 4	Won on first
Trent Bridge	Notts II	207* for 9	199 for 7	innings

* Innings declared closed.

Batting Averages

	Innings	Not Outs	Runs	Highest Innings	Average
N. H. Moore	5	2	263	163*	87.66
J. C. Bate	4	0	251	139	62.75
E. G. Witherden	19	3	801	120*	50.06
R. Reynolds	20	1	398	74*	20.94
G. G. Fidler	13	3	204	36*	20.40
W. O. Thomas	8	0	163	78	20.37
P. G. Powell†	22	2	405	45	20.25
M. E. Thorne	11	2	165	45	18.33
A. G. Coomb	10	1	159	48	17.66
T. L. Brayne	10	1	150	49	16.66
P. W. Wesley	6	0	83	34	13.83
H. C. Blofeld	7	0	93	34	13.28
E. J. Greatrex	9	3	57	17	9.50
R. J. Farrer	6	1	46	18*	9.20
P. G. Walmsley	8	4	34	24*	8.50
T. D. Bowett	8	3	36	15*	7.20
R. Schofield	8	1	38	15	5.42
B. G. W. Stevens	5	0	18	8	3.60
N. J. Tilney	5	0	3	1	0.60

Also batted: J. C. C. Blofeld 10, 36; D. Phipps 0; W. D. Hancock 13, 1; T. A. Hall 0, 4; J. J. W. Tomlinson 0*, 0*, 11*, 6*; E. A. Kent played in two matches but did not bat.

* *Signifies not out.*   † Captain.

Bowling Averages

	Overs	Maidens	Runs	Wickets	Average
J. J. W. Tomlinson	26	2	101	5	20.20
A. G. Coomb	232	58	623	27	23.07
R. Schofield	143.1	21	452	19	23.78
N. H. Moore	40.5	11	99	4	24.75
E. G. Witherden	280.5	87	664	26	25.53
T. A. Hall	36	5	104	4	26.00
P. G. Walmsley	197.3	49	535	18	29.72
N. J. Tilney	50	14	152	5	30.40
E. A. Kent	25	3	81	2	40.50
G. G. Fiddler	77	13	251	5	50.20
R. J. Farrer	85.1	26	243	2	121.50

Also bowled: W. D. Hancock 16—2—51—2; M. E. Thorne 6—1—23—0;
T. L. Braync 6—0—24—0; W. O. Thomas 6—0—35—0; R. Reynolds 8—1—40—0;
P. W. Wesley 5—0—22—0; P. G. Powell 5—1—19—0; D. Phipps 2—0—13—0.

Professional.—E. G. Witherden.

NORTHAMPTONSHIRE SECOND ELEVEN

Secretary—Lt.-Col. A. St. G. Coldwell, County Cricket
Ground, Northampton

Matches 14—*Won* 4, *Lost* 4, *Lost on first innings* 3, *No result* 3

		1st Innings	2nd Innings	Result
May 1, 2	Warwickshire II	237	201	Lost by 20 runs
Northampton	Northants II	111	127	
May 20, 21	Northants II	237* for 6	25* for 3	Lost on first
Retford	Notts II	287	—	innings
May 22, 23	Yorkshire II	137	119	Won by three
Northampton	Northants II	110	147 for 7	wickets
June 5, 6	Middlesex II	182	219* for 8	Lost by 17 runs
Enfield	Northants II	185* for 6	199	
June 19, 20	Leicestershire II	233* for 8	163* for 6	Lost on first
Leicester	Northants II	164	112 for 4	innings
June 26, 27	Derbyshire II	113	201	Won by innings
Northampton	Northants II	350* for 4	—	and 36 runs
July 1, 2	Northants II	249	123	Lost by nine
Old Trafford	Lancashire II	312	63 for 1	wickets
July 3, 4	Yorkshire II	—	—	No result
Doncaster	Northants II	—	—	
July 10, 11	Northants II	240	—	No result
Northampton	Lancashire II	207 for 4	—	
July 24, 25	Northants II	141	193	Won by six
Corby	Middlesex II	186* for 4	142	runs
August 5, 6	Leicestershire II	149	124	Lost by 106
Rothwell	Northants II	101	66	runs
August 14, 15	Northants II	231* for 6	—	No result
Northampton	Notts II	103 for 2	—	
August 21, 22	Derbyshire II	300* for 8	—	Lost on first
Derby	Northants II	165	246 for 7	innings
August 28, 29	Warwickshire II	142	57	Won by four
Coventry	Northants II	141	61 for 6	wickets

* Innings declared closed.

Batting Averages

	Innings	Not Outs	Runs	Highest Innings	Average
P. Arnold	7	0	353	113	50.42
J. P. Fellows-Smith	15	3	470	100*	39.16
M. Norman	18	0	474	113	26.33
A. Lightfoot	14	0	355	77	25.35
V. Broderick†	20	2	376	64	20.88
S. Leadbetter	7	0	115	51	16.42
J. Smith	12	1	174	45	15.81
L. Rowe	21	2	271	42	14.26
R. Peacock	6	0	82	25	13.66
J. Edmonds	11	5	70	30	11.66
J. Wild	8	2	69	16*	11.50
P. Watts	19	2	182	83	10.70
M. Dilley	14	2	65	24*	5.41
L. McGibbon	10	2	17	8	2.12

Also batted: B. Reynolds 79, 11; R. Clarke 1, 2; E. Davis 101*, 2, 11, 20; P. Davis 2*, 4*; E. J. Belton 6, 35; M. McMillan 4, 2, 5; R. Rowe 5; H. Kelleher 1, 2*; A. L. Wells 1, 0; A. Liddell 38; E. Lane Fox 20; R. Mayes 55; J. Minney 13, 44, 0, 6, 8; D. Coulson 22, 0, 6, 0*.

* *Signifies not out.* † *Captain.*

Bowling Averages

	Overs	Maidens	Runs	Wickets	Average
V. Broderick	319.1	125	709	58	12.22
L. McGibbon	158.3	53	378	25	15.12
J. Wild	119	25	341	18	18.94
M. Dilley	202	40	602	22	27.36
J. Edmonds	133.4	22	408	14	29.14
P. Watts	159	38	519	17	30.52
J. P. Fellows-Smith	70.4	14	279	7	39.85

Also bowled: R. Clarke 12—1—42—1; M. Allen 42.4—20—72—9; A. Lightfoot 41.5—13—82—5; R. Rowe 7—1—36—1; H. Kelleher 9—0—34—1.

Amateurs.—J. P. Fellows-Smith, J. Smith, R. Peacock, E. Davis, E. J. Belton, M. McMillan, R. Rowe, A. L. Wells, A. Liddell, E. Lane Fox, R. Mayes, J. Minney, D. Coulson.

NORTHUMBERLAND

Secretary—G. H. MALLEN, 94, St. George's Terrace, Newcastle upon Tyne, 2

Matches 12—Won 2, Lost 4, Won on first innings 1, Lost on first innings 3, No result 2

		1st Innings	2nd Innings	Result
May 13, 14	Lancashire II	269* for 9	—	Lost on first
Urmston	Northumberland	133	13 for 1	innings
May 15, 16	Northumberland	90	34 for 1	Lost on first
Workington	Cumberland	95	—	innings
May 29, 30	Cheshire	180	179	Won by nine
Newcastle	Northumberland	173	187 for 1	wickets
June 10, 11	Durham	242	19 for 0	Lost by ten
Newcastle	Northumberland	112	148	wickets
June 24, 25	Staffordshire	429* for 5	—	Lost by innings
Newcastle	Northumberland	223	187	and 19 runs

		1st Innings	2nd Innings	Result
June 26, 27	Northumberland	238	131	Won by 110
Newcastle	Yorkshire II	164	95	runs
July 15, 16	Cumberland	157 for 7	—	No result
Gosforth	Northumberland	—		
July 22, 23	Yorkshire II	255* for 9	93* for 1	Lost by 117
Redcar	Northumberland	165	66	runs
August 5, 6	Durham	218	145 for 6	Won on first
Sunderland	Northumberland	279* for 9	—	innings
August 7, 8	Northumberland	343* for 9	—	Lost on first
Newcastle	Lancashire II	345 for 9	—	innings
August 12, 13	Northumberland	120	—	†Lost by six
Porthill	Staffordshire	121 for 4	—	wickets
August 14, 15	Northumberland	264	—	No result
Hoylake	Cheshire	100 for 0	—	

* Innings declared closed.
† Reduced to one day because of rain.

Batting Averages

	Innings	Not Outs	Runs	Highest Innings	Average
C. R. M. Atkinson	6	0	247	105	41.16
R. W. Smithson	8	0	264	106	33.00
K. D. Smith	10	2	223	92	27.87
P. Shaw	11	0	293	106	26.63
C. Pearson	5	0	130	37	26.00
G. Walton	9	1	206	100*	25.75
R. G. Clough	17	3	334	74*	23.85
J. Oakes	16	0	351	83	21.93
L. E. Liddell†	9	0	169	46	18.77
K. Savage	4	2	32	17	16.00
R. Jowsey	4	0	63	34	15.75
G. K. Knox	7	0	105	38	15.00
H. B. Henderson	15	2	184	35	14.15
F. Clayforth	14	5	65	19*	7.22
K. Norton	11	4	42	12	6.00
D. Hall	4	1	9	4	3.00
E. Sisterson	6	1	10	4	2.00
M. Glaister	3	0	1	1	0.33

Also batted: D. Carr 4, 0*; A. Bartle 5, 2; J. B. Rowell 5, 1; L. F. Gordon 4, 0; A. C. Evans 4, 0; J. Wake 0, 0; K. Earl 4.

* *Signifies not out.*   † *Captain.*

Bowling Averages

	Overs	Maidens	Runs	Wickets	Average
E. Sisterson	90	24	265	16	16.56
K. Norton	194.4	71	412	22	18.72
J. Oakes	212.4	65	501	24	20.87
D. Hall	62	13	165	7	23.57
R. G. Clough	45.1	8	159	6	26.50
F. Clayforth	327.4	88	863	32	26.96

Also bowled: C. R. M. Atkinson 23—4—58—3; K. J. Earl 34.1—7—68—3; J. Wake 40—13—78—2; M. Glaister 35—7—95—2; J. B. Rowell 21—5—49—1; K. D. Smith 18—2—74—1; C. Pearson 13—4—43—0; D. R. Carr 15—3—62—0; A. C. Evans 25—6—80—0; R. W. Smithson 2—0—4—0; P. Shaw 2—2—0—0; H. B. Henderson 1—1—0—0; L. E. Liddell 1—1—0—0.

Professionals.—No full-time.

NOTTINGHAMSHIRE SECOND ELEVEN

Secretary—H. A. Brown, County Ground, Trent Bridge,
Nottingham

Matches 18—*Won* 4, *Lost* 1, *Won on first innings* 7, *Lost on
first innings* 4, *No result* 2

		1st Innings	2nd Innings	Result
May 20, 21 Retford	Northants II Notts II	237* for 6 287	25 for 3 —	Won on first innings
May 29, 30 Wollaton	Notts II Lancashire II	210 242* for 8	114* for 7 86 for 4	Lost by six wickets
June 17, 18 Leamington	Notts II Warwickshire II	308* for 7 296* for 9	91 for 2 —	Won on first innings
June 24, 25 Trent Bridge	Shropshire Notts II	161 292* for 7	232 for 7 —	Won on first innings
June 26, 27 Grimsby	Lincolnshire Notts II	129 245	134 19 for 1	Won by nine wickets
July 2, 3 Melton Mowbray	Notts II Leicestershire II	308* for 9 201* for 9	— 80* for 6	Won on first innings
July 4, 5 Shrewsbury	Shropshire Notts II	139* for 7 93* for 1	156* for 9 203 for 3	Won by seven wickets
July 10, 11 Newark	Derbyshire II Notts II	103 155* for 6	77 —	Won on first innings
July 17, 18 Nottingham	Notts II Warwickshire II	204* for 2 105* for 5	142* for 7 108 for 7	Won on first innings
July 24, 25 Chesterfield	Notts II Derbyshire II	185 261* for 8	212 for 4 —	Lost on first innings
July 29, 30 Worksop	Notts II Leicestershire II	143 148* for 6	149 133	Won by 11 runs
July 31, August 1 Bridlington	Yorkshire II Notts II	185 206	107 89 for 1	Won by nine wickets
August 5, 6 Trent Bridge	Notts II Lincolnshire	308* for 9 185	— 113 for 9	Won on first innings
August 9, 10 Lakenham	Norfolk Notts II	175 163	4 for 1 —	Lost on first innings
August 14, 15 Northampton	Northants II Notts II	231* for 6 103 for 2	— —	No result
August 21, 22 Old Trafford	Notts II Lancashire II	219 380* for 7	247 for 6 —	Lost on first innings
August 26, 27 Worksop	Yorkshire II Notts II	255* for 9 68 for 1	— —	No result
August 28, 29 Trent Bridge	Norfolk Notts II	298* for 6 207* for 9	130* for 4 199 for 7	Lost on first innings

* Innings declared closed.

Batting Averages

	Innings	Not Outs	Runs	Highest Innings	Average
N. Hill	10	3	421	135	60.14
M. Winfield	23	7	728	137	45.50
J. D. Springall	9	2	298	63	42.57
C. J. Poole	2	0	82	76	41.00
E. Martin	20	1	710	133	37.36
J. D. Clay	7	1	209	81	34.83
J. H. Parks	3	1	68	35	34.00
R. C. Vowles	13	6	231	67	33.00
K. Smales	7	0	208	63	29.71
F. W. Stocks	6	1	146	51	29.20
R. Giles	13	0	359	52	27.61

	Innings	Not Outs	Runs	Highest Innings	Average
M. Hall	13	0	315	73	24.23
J. B. Riley	7	1	138	64*	23.00
J. Kelly	14	2	274	38	22.83
P. F. Harvey†	18	2	302	47*	18.87
A. K. Walker	7	1	108	48	18.00
P. Taylor	6	3	45	26*	15.00
K. J. Poole	12	3	113	38	12.55
E. J. Rowe	9	3	55	34*	9.16
C. S. Matthews	3	1	12	6	6.00
T. Atkinson	7	0	35	16	5.00
M. Morgan	6	2	17	8*	4.25
J. Cotton	7	0	21	18	3.00

* *Signifies not out.* † Captain.

Bowling Averages

	Overs	Maidens	Runs	Wickets	Average
M. Morgan	163.5	65	290	21	13.80
R. C. Vowles	135.3	35	349	22	15.86
J. Cotton	110	15	385	24	16.04
A. Walker	132.3	31	334	20	16.70
K. Smales	190	79	423	24	17.62
P. F. Harvey	384	151	911	51	17.86
T. Atkinson	182.1	43	427	20	21.35
C. S. Matthews	144.4	39	347	12	28.91
K. J. Poole	173.1	31	592	18	32.88
F. W. Stocks	29	8	106	3	35.33
J. Kelly	139.2	57	244	6	40.66
P. Taylor	98.2	18	285	6	47.50

Also bowled: J. Walters 4—1—12—1; E. Martin 1—1—0—0; J. H. Parks 1—0—1—0.

Amateur.—J. B. Riley.

OXFORDSHIRE

Secretary—L. B. Frewer, "Tal-y-Fan," 58, Sunderland Avenue, Oxford

Matches 10—Won 2, Lost 4, Won on first innings 3, No result 1

		1st Innings	2nd Innings	Result
July 29, 30 High Wycombe	Oxfordshire Buckinghamshire	189 98	124 216 for 9	Lost by one wicket
August 2, 3 Cowley (Morris Motors)	Oxfordshire Buckinghamshire	276* for 9 138	126* for 5 163 for 8	Won on first innings
August 7, 8 Reading (Earley)	Berkshire Oxfordshire	151 129	176 107	Lost by 91 runs
August 9, 10 Trowbridge	Oxfordshire Wiltshire	157 137	— —	†Won by 20 runs
August 12, 13 Oxford Sports Club	Oxfordshire Wiltshire	— —	— —	No result
August 14, 15 Oxford Sports Club	Oxfordshire Devon	109 110 for 4	— —	†Lost by six wickets
August 19, 20 Banbury (NAC)	Dorset Oxfordshire	277 205	142* for 6 215 for 4	Won by six wickets

		1st Innings	2nd Innings	Result	
August 23, 24	Oxfordshire	228* for 4	—	Won on	first
Oxford (Christ Church)	Berkshire	128	212 for 7	innings	
August 28, 29	Oxfordshire	202	81	Lost by	five
Paignton	Devon	202	82 for 5	wickets	
August 30, 31	Oxfordshire	135	133* for 7	Won on	first
Wimborne	Dorset	78	64 for 2	innings	

* Innings declared closed.
† Reduced to one day because of rain.

Batting Averages

	Innings	Not Outs	Runs	Highest Innings	Average
G. D. Roynon	4	2	200	133*	100.00
K. Talboys	7	0	255	90	36.42
J. E. Bush†	15	0	485	122	32.33
D. E. Martin	9	2	171	50*	24.44
P. J. Taylor	3	0	67	40	22.33
R. Wheeler	7	0	140	85	20.00
T. A. Gibson	6	3	58	41*	19.33
D. Banton	13	0	197	63	15.15
J. W. Carter	12	0	173	34	14.41
C. Carr	12	0	155	36	12.91
H. J. Locke	6	1	63	25	12.60
D. J. Laitt	12	3	110	15	12.22
R. A. Winstone	12	3	109	14*	12.11
A. H. P. Beater	3	0	28	21	9.33
A. L. Hichens	10	5	28	10*	5.60
A. D. Pickering	7	0	31	14	4.42
R. D. J. Surman	4	0	10	5	2.50

Also batted: P. Capel Smith 3, 18; A. F. R. Green 2; B. C. Page 1; D. Cross 1, 9.

* *Signifies not out.* † *Captain.*

Bowling Averages

	Overs	Maidens	Runs	Wickets	Average
D. Banton	182.4	51	437	33	13.24
R. D. J. Surman	85	21	207	13	15.92
D. J. Laitt	254	54	623	38	16.39
A. L. Hichens	219.1	48	662	35	18.91

Also bowled: J. E. Bush 1—0—4—1; G. D. Roynon 4—1—12—1; A. D. Pickering 3—0—16—1; A. H. P. Beater 6—1—17—1; H. J. Locke 24—5—54—3; T. A. Gibson 39—11—89—2; B. C. Page 15—6—31—0; A. F. R. Green 13—3—48—0; R. A. Winstone 5—0—15—0.

Professionals.—None.

SHROPSHIRE

Secretary—S. L. ROBINSON, 98, Copthorne Road, Shrewsbury

Matches 8—Lost 3, Lost on first innings 3, No result 2

		1st Innings	2nd Innings	Result	
May 16, 17	Shropshire	102	—	No result	
Wolverhampton	Staffordshire	—	—		
May 29, 30	Shropshire	174	204* for 9	Lost on	first
Market Drayton	Staffordshire	188	136 for 2	innings	
June 5, 6	Shropshire	244	100 for 7	Lost on	first
Derby	Derbyshire II	246* for 9		innings	

		1st Innings	2nd Innings	Result
June 24, 25	Shropshire	161	232 for 7	Lost on first
Trent Bridge	Notts II	292* for 7	—	innings
July 4, 5	Shropshire	139* for 7	156* for 9	Lost by seven
Shrewsbury	Notts II	93* for 1	203 for 3	wickets
Jully 11, 12	Shropshire	54	110	Lost by ten
Newport	Warwickshire II	164* for 6	1 for 0	wickets
July 17, 18	Shropshire	206	—	No result
St. Georges	Derbyshire II	5 for 0	—	
August 19, 20	Warwickshire II	206	4 for 0	Lost by ten
Edgbaston	Shropshire	71	135	wickets

* Innings declared closed.

Batting Averages

	Innings	Not Outs	Runs	Highest Innings	Average
K. W. Powell	14	5	242	78	26.88
G. Laking	10	5	123	30*	24.60
J. H. Apperley	8	0	192	48	24.00
D. Jones	14	0	307	57	21.92
D. S. Parry	14	0	275	94	19.64
G. V. Othen	6	1	74	32	14.80
F. B. Everall	13	1	162	45	13.50
W. E. Rooker	3	0	34	24	11.33
A. J. Huntbach	5	3	22	21*	11.00
F. H. Apperley†	14	0	150	36	10.71
K. Arch	11	1	106	27	10.60
J. T. Davies	2	0	21	14	10.50
P. Bradley	11	2	90	33	10.00
J. Home	11	0	97	26	8.81
T. Savage	5	0	39	14	7.80
B. C. France	4	0	27	10	6.75
J. A. Harvey	2	0	2	2	1.00

* Signifies not out.   *† Captain.*

Bowling Averages

	Overs	Maidens	Runs	Wickets	Average
J. H. Apperley	31	7	117	6	19.50
A. J. Huntbach	25	4	81	4	20.25
P. Bradley	125.1	22	470	22	21.36
G. V. Othen	32	6	109	3	36.33
K. Arch	79.2	11	307	6	51.16
D. S. Parry	41	3	174	3	58.00
G. Laking	36.3	3	131	2	65.50

Also bowled: F. B. Everall 4—0—23—0; B. C. France 6—0—25—0; W. E. Rooker 8—0—23—0; J. A. Harvey 5—0—28—0.

Professionals.—None.

SOMERSET SECOND ELEVEN

Secretary—R. ROBINSON, County Cricket Ground, Taunton

Matches 16—Won 8, Lost 1, Won on first innings 4, Lost on first innings 3

		1st Innings	2nd Innings	Result
May 23, 24	Essex II	159	167	Lost on first
Taunton	Somerset II	134	152 for 8	innings
May 27, 28	Gloucestershire II	209* for 8	133* for 3	Lost on first
Bristol	Somerset II	139	180 for 7	innings

		1st Innings	2nd Innings	Result
June 3, 4	Leicestershire II	177	139	Lost by 47 runs
Leicester	Somerset II	138	131	
June 21, 22	Cornwall	217* for 9	158	Won on first
Penzance	Somerset II	219* for 9	57 for 0	innings
July 1, 2	Somerset II	249* for 8	90* for 9	Won on first
Taunton	Kent II	150* for 8	110 for 3	innings
July 3, 4	Gloucestershire II	291* for 5	112* for 4	Lost on first
Glastonbury	Somerset II	194* for 9	67 for 2	innings
July 23, 24	Essex II	160	103	Won by eight
Harlow	Somerset II	165* for 5	100 for 2	wickets
July 25, 26	Kent II	145	50	Won by seven
Broadstairs	Somerset II	149* for 9	47 for 3	wickets
August 2, 3	Wiltshire	238* for 7	130	Won by one
Trowbridge	Somerset II	239* for 6	131 for 9	wicket
August 7, 8	Cornwall	36	294	Won by seven
Bath	Somerset II	201* for 7	132 for 3	wickets
August 19, 20	Devon	91	55	Won by nine
Newton Abbot	Somerset II	134	13 for 1	wickets
August 21, 22	Wiltshire	44	171	Won by innings
Midsomer Norton	Somerset II	222* for 6	—	and seven runs
August 23, 24	Dorset	100	158	Won on first
Sherborne	Somerset II	107* for 9	122 for 6	innings
August 26, 27	Leicestershire II	121	86	Won by seven
Keynsham	Somerset II	114	94 for 3	wickets
August 28, 29	Dorset	160	108	Won by five
Yeovil	Somerset II	167* for 5	102 for 5	wickets
August 30, 31	Somerset II	284* for 9	—	Won on first
Chard	Devon	70	173 for 5	innings

* Innings declared closed.

Batting Averages

	Innings	Not Outs	Runs	Highest Innings	Average
G. Tripp	19	5	455	71	32.50
J. G. Lomax	19	3	443	64	27.68
B. Roe	22	5	452	83	26.58
R. Virgin	22	7	397	64	26.46
C. Greetham	29	2	645	64	23.88
J. Harris	18	5	244	31	18.76
P. Eele	21	1	364	113	18.20
J. M. Woolley	17	2	264	68	17.60
J. Hilton	10	3	97	35*	13.85
K. Biddulph	12	3	83	43	9.22
A. Whitehead	12	7	25	7*	5.00

Also batted: A. J. Davies 35*, 1; K. Palmer 21, 0, 30, 6*, 86; J. Baker 10, 0, 7, 26; F. J. Herting 17, 12, 48, 8, 0, 7, 13; W. H. R. Andrews† 4*, 0, 25, 18, 2*, 0*; G. L. Keith 16, 11, 18, 6, 0, 0; M. Kitchen 0, 5*, 11, 1; R. Taylor 0, 0*; B. Langford 4, 0; E. Bryant 0, 0*, 1, 8, 2, 8*; G. Atkinson 46; T. E. Dickinson 4*, 1*; J. McMahon 11, 3.

* *Signifies not out.* † Captain.

Bowling Averages

	Overs	Maidens	Runs	Wickets	Average
J. G. Lomax	259	74	543	49	11.08
T. E. Dickinson	58.3	13	180	16	11.25
J. Hilton	229.3	68	582	47	12.38
K. Biddulph	276.5	67	711	55	12.92
A. Whitehead	170.4	56	411	22	18.68
J. Harris	186.2	41	502	25	20.08

Also bowled: W. H. R. Andrews 55—16—123—13; C. Greetham 70—20—227—11; F. J. Herting 85.5—24—225—9; J. McMahon 48.2—11—134—8; P. Eele 25—5—63—6; R. Taylor 39—9—161—5; J Baker 31—2—109—4; K. Palmer 40—10—81—3; E. Bryant 48—21—94—3; B. Langford 22—5—67—1; R. Virgin 2—0—10—0; G. Keith 1—0—9—0.

Amateurs.—J. M. Woolley, A. J. Davies, J. Baker, F. J. Herting, R. Taylor, T. E. Dickinson.

STAFFORDSHIRE

Secretary—L. W. Hancock, 4, Kingsland Avenue, Oakhill, Stoke-on-Trent

Matches 12—*Won* 2, *Lost* 2, *Won on first innings* 3, *Lost on first innings* 3, *No result* 2

		1st Innings	2nd Innings	Result
May 15, 16	Shropshire	102	—	No result
Wolverhampton (Goodyear Gnd.)	Staffordshire	—	—	
May 29, 30	Shropshire	174	204* for 9	Won on first innings
Market Drayton	Staffordshire	188	136 for 2	
June 12, 13	Yorkshire II	339* for 4	—	Lost by innings and 55 runs
Longton	Staffordshire	142	142	
June 24, 25	Staffordshire	429* for 5	—	Won by innings and 19 runs
Newcastle	Northumberland	223	187	
June 26, 27	Durham	262	—	Lost on first innings
South Shields	Staffordshire	127	117 for 2	
July 10, 11	Cheshire	94	101 for 5	Won on first innings
Norton	Staffordshire	118	—	
July 24, 25	Bedfordshire	155	146* for 6	Won on first innings
Luton	Staffordshire	181* for 5	98 for 5	
August 7, 8	Cheshire	134	169	Lost by two runs
Middlewich	Staffordshire	135* for 7	166	
August 12, 13	Northumberland	120	—	†Won by six wickets
Porthill	Staffordshire	121 for 4	—	
August 14, 15	Staffordshire	177* for 9	—	No result
Uttoxeter	Bedfordshire	12 for 2	—	
August 21, 22	Staffordshire	126	164* for 8	Lost on first innings
Scarborough	Yorkshire II	127* for 7	101 for 7	
August 28, 29	Durham	289* for 8	—	Lost on first innings
Leek	Staffordshire	184	73 for 4	

* Innings declared closed.
† Reduced to one day because of rain.

Batting Averages

	Innings	Not Outs	Runs	Highest Innings	Average
F. R. Bailey	10	1	320	120	35.55
D Bean	18	1	473	99	27.82
S. Crump	10	2	217	71	27.12
F. Butler	7	0	177	48	25.28
D. M. Haynes†	14	2	267	61	22.25
H. Boon	16	2	307	108*	21.92
B. Crump	15	0	300	50	20.00
H. G. Searle	3	0	56	43	18.66
T. Whittaker	6	1	88	44	17.60
S. B. Boon	10	2	128	39*	16.00
D. S. G. Swift	5	2	38	19	12.66

AA

	Innings	Not Outs	Runs	Highest Innings	Average
B. Shardlow	10	1	84	28	9.33
K. Higgs	5	2	17	13*	5.66
A. D. Giles	4	2	8	4*	4.00
W. Smith	3	0	12	6	4.00
B. Hayward................	5	0	9	5	1.80

Also batted: F. H. V. Davis 8, 1; J. Bailey 13, 0; P. W. Calderbank 16, 16; J. C. Norcup 0, 1; J. M. Ellsmore 2*, 18*; N. G. W. Banks 11; H. H. Wood 12; R. Joynes 6; E. Lowell 20.

* Signifies not out.   *† Captain.*

Bowling Averages

	Overs	Maidens	Runs	Wickets	Average
K. Higgs	258.4	76	604	46	13.13
B. Shardlow	256.2	78	571	37	15.43
S. Crump	119.1	37	252	13	19.38
J. M. Ellsmore	23	7	67	3	22.33
B. Hayward..............	149.3	50	358	14	25.57
R. Joynes	22	7	52	2	26.00
J. C. Norcup	73	26	163	6	27.16
S. B. Boon..............	73	26	152	5	30.40
B. Crump	159	41	408	13	31.38
H. G. Searle	17	4	34	1	34.00
T. Whittaker	24	7	93	1	93.00

Also bowled: E. Lowell 6—1—12—1; H. Boon 4—1—15—0; F. Butler 3—1—11—0.

Professionals.—None.

SUFFOLK

Secretary—G. T. Barnard, 24 and 26, Museum Street, Ipswich

Matches 8—Won 4, Lost 3, Lost on first innings 1

			1st Innings	2nd Innings	Result
July 5, 6	Suffolk		176	89	Won by 13 runs
Mistley	Essex II		80	172	
August 5, 6	Essex II		278* for 6	78 for 3	Lost by seven wickets
Felixstowe	Suffolk		91	264	
August 7, 8	Suffolk		256* for 6	183* for 4	Won by 142 runs
Lakenham	Norfolk		183	114	
August 9, 10	Middlesex II		222	—	Lost by innings and 84 runs
Lowestoft	Suffolk		77	61	
August 12, 13	Suffolk		246* for 4	181* for 6	Lost on first innings
Felixstowe	Hertfordshire		250* for 3	54 for 2	
August 16, 17	Suffolk		280* for 5	—	Won by innings and 43 runs
Felixstowe	Norfolk		103	134	
August 21, 22	Middlesex II		215* for 4	201* for 3	Lost by 107 runs
Southgate	Suffolk		217* for 4	92	
August 23, 24	Hertfordshire		159* for 8	80* for 9	Won by five wickets
St. Albans	Suffolk		106	134 for 5	

* Innings declared closed.

Batting Averages

	Innings	Not Outs	Runs	Highest Innings	Average
C. B. T. Gibbons	13	5	344	71*	43.00
W. A. D. Whitfield	6	3	126	40	42.00
D. F. Henley-Welch	4	0	131	71	32.75

	Innings	Not Outs	Runs	Highest Innings	Average
R. F. Clark	4	0	115	70	28.75
K. C. Girkin	15	1	351	93	25.07
B. A. Wilson	12	1	267	107*	24.27
B. H. Belle	13	0	308	102	23.69
R. Mayes	15	0	306	104	20.40
I. D. Prior	4	0	53	33	13.25
G. C. Perkins	9	2	72	23	10.28
A. G. Cutter	9	2	63	25	9.00
M. D. Corke†	12	1	69	16	6.27
R. C. Upson	6	2	21	7*	5.25
J. V. Bailey	3	0	7	4	2.33

Also batted: R. A. Hewitt 8, 2; B. E. Workman 4, 3; W. Aldous 0* 0*; I. F. Hammond 10*, 27; P. B. Hudson 0*, 29. J. G. Crisp played in two matches and C. A. Studd in one match but did not bat.

* Signifies not out.   † *Captain.*

Bowling Averages

	Overs	Maidens	Runs	Wickets	Average
G. C. Perkins	290.2	129	433	33	13.12
J. G. Crisp	54	11	132	10	13.20
K. C. Girkin	70.3	16	211	12	17.58
B. A. Wilson	99.5	26	308	14	22.00
P. B. Hudson	51	12	156	7	22.28
A. G. Cutter	155.5	39	479	18	26.61
D. F. Henley-Welch	34	9	87	3	29.00
R. C. Upson	46	11	153	4	38.25

Also bowled: R. Mayes 4—0—14—0; M. D. Corke 5—2—20—0; B. H. Belle 2—0—16—0; W. A. D. Whitfield 29—6—107—1; J. V. Bailey 18—5—55—1; I. F. Hammond 7—2—28—0.

Professionals.—G. C. Perkins, R. Mayes, B. A. Wilson.

SURREY SECOND ELEVEN

Secretary—COMMANDER B. BABB, Kennington Oval, S.E.11

Matches 14—Won 1, Lost 3, Won on first innings 4, Lost on first innings 4, No result 2

		1st Innings	2nd Innings	Result
May 8, 9	Warwickshire II	254	—	No result
Edgbaston	Surrey II	105 for 6	—	
May 20, 21	Surrey II	169	—	†Lost by seven
Old Trafford	Lancashire II	174 for 3	—	wickets
June 4, 5	Surrey II	54* for 0	282* for 5	Lost on first
Frinton-on-Sea	Essex II	55* for 0	212 for 5	innings
June 8, 10	Surrey II	205* for 5	104 for 5	Lost on first
The Oval	Kent II	220* for 3	—	innings
June 17, 18	Gloucestershire II	249	149	Lost by 69 runs
Bristol	Surrey II	194	135	
June 24, 25	Middlesex II	168* for 6	132* for 8	Won on first
The Oval	Surrey II	176* for 7	8 for 0	innings
July 4, 5	Surrey II	182	17 for 1	Won on first
Beckenham	Kent II	159* for 9	—	innings

		1st Innings	2nd Innings	Result
July 8, 9	Lancashire II	274	71 for 7	Won on first
Mitcham	Surrey II	343		innings
July 15, 16	Warwickshire II	213	87* for 8	Lost by 79 runs
Beddington	Surrey II	127	94	
July 27, 29	Surrey II	82	44 for 1	Lost on first
The Oval	Essex II	238* for 8	—	innings
August 5, 6	Surrey II	296* for 9	—	Won by innings
Swindon	Wiltshire	151	139	and six runs
August 14, 15	Surrey II	—	—	No result
The Oval	Wiltshire	—	—	
August 24, 26	Middlesex II	285* for 7	—	Lost on first
Lord's	Surrey II	148	257 for 7	innings
August 29, 30	Gloucestershire II	178	232* for 8	Won on first
The Oval	Surrey II	200* for 1	156 for 7	innings

* Innings declared closed.

† Reduced to one day because of rain.

Batting Averages

	Innings	Not Outs	Runs	Highest Innings	Average
R. Swetman	16	4	527	195	43.91
D. F. Cox	11	3	343	106	42.87
A. B. D. Parsons	12	2	342	105	34.20
D. Gibson	11	3	236	37	29.50
J. H. Edrich	12	2	289	116*	28.90
D. E. Pratt	14	2	308	68	25.66
R. C. E. Pratt	6	0	149	50	24.83
A. H. Brown	9	1	139	64	17.37
M. W. Ricketts	5	0	85	48	17.00
M. D. Willett	19	4	246	103*	16.40
V. J. Ransom†	12	2	127	24	12.70
P. G. McKelvey	12	6	75	28*	12.50
D. Sydenham	10	3	82	30	11.71
L. A. Johnson	8	1	55	14	7.85
R. A. E. Tindall	13	2	59	16	5.36

Also batted: G. J. Chidgey 0, 9; T. H. Clark 106; J. K. Hall 4, 14; C. Harding 0; W. A. Smith 0; M. F. Woodhouse 1.

* *Signifies not out.*   † Captain.

Bowling Averages

	Overs	Maidens	Runs	Wickets	Average
D. Sydenham	210	55	537	31	17.32
M. D. Willett	186.1	58	453	25	18.12
D. Gibson	168.2	34	517	22	23.50
P. G. McKelvey	164.5	41	430	18	23.88
D. F. Cox	88.4	21	255	10	25.50
V. J. Ransom	59	18	133	5	26.60
D. Pratt	132	31	392	14	28.01
R. A. E. Tindall	41.3	8	157	6	26.16
J. K. Hall	84	13	254	7	36.28

Also bowled: H. K. Christian 17—1—75—0; T. H. Clark 3—1—9—0; C. Harding 22—5—80—3; A. B. D. Parsons 1—0—14—0; J. Pegley 1—0—5—0; R. C. E. Pratt 17.4—3—38—0; W. A. Smith 28—0—111—1.

Amateurs.—V. J. Ransom, A. B. D. Parsons, A. H. Brown, M. W. Ricketts, G. J. Chidgey, J. K. Hall, M. F. Woodhouse, H. K. Christian, J. Pegley.

WARWICKSHIRE SECOND ELEVEN

Secretary—L. T. DEAKINS, County Ground, Edgbaston,
Birmingham, 5

*Matches 21—Won 11, Lost 1, Won on first innings 4, Lost on
first innings 4, No result 1*

		1st Innings	2nd Innings	Result
May 1, 2	Warwickshire II	237	111	Won by 20 runs
Northampton	Northants II	201	127	
May 8, 9	Warwickshire II	254	—	No result
Edgbaston	Surrey II	105 for 6	—	
May 13, 14	Durham	112	133	Won by eight
Edgbaston	Warwickshire II	117* for 9	70 for 2	wickets
May 16, 17	Leicestershire II	44	143	Won by innings
M. & B. Ground	Warwickshire II	189* for 9		and two runs
Birmingham				
May 22, 23	Lancashire II	143	207	Won by six
Old Trafford	Warwickshire II	194	160 for 4	wickets
June 10, 11	Derbyshire II	149	140	Won by ten
Derby	Warwickshire II	284* for 9	2 for 0	wickets
June 12, 13	Gloucestershire II	190	95	Won by six
Bristol	Warwickshire II	191* for 9	97 for 4	wickets
June 17, 18	Notts II	308* for 7	91 for 2	Lost on first
Leamington	Warwickshire II	296	—	innings
June 20, 21	Warwickshire II	348* for 1	155 for 2	Lost on first
Edgbaston	Gloucestershire II	350* for 7		innings
June 26, 27	Lancashire II	161	183	Won by seven
M. & B. Ground,	Warwickshire II	303* for 6	42 for 3	wickets
Birmingham				
July 3, 4	Cheshire	122	193 for 8	Won on first
Macclesfield	Warwickshire II	177	108 for 8	innings
July 8, 9	Warwickshire II	266	106* for 2	Won on first
Loughborough	Leicestershire II	205	41 for 2	innings
July 11, 12	Shropshire	54	110	Won by ten
Newport	Warwickshire II	164* for 0	1 for 0	wickets
July 15, 16	Warwickshire II	213	87* for 8	Won by 79 runs
Beddington	Surrey II	127	94	
July 17, 18	Notts II	204* for 2	142* for 7	Lost on first
Nottingham	Warwickshire II	105* for 5	108 for 7	innings
July 22, 23	Warwickshire II	175* for 9	124* for 9	Won on first
Edgbaston	Cheshire	154	115 for 7	innings
July 31, August 1	Durham	243	135 for 5	Won on first
Darlington	Warwickshire II	244* for 4	—	innings
August 5, 6	Derbyshire II	158	126	Won by innings
Edgbaston	Warwickshire II	307* for 6	—	and 23 runs
August 19, 20	Warwickshire II	206	4 for 0	Won by ten
Edgbaston	Shropshire	71	135	wickets
August 28, 29	Warwickshire II	142	57	Lost by four
Coventry	Northants II	141	61 for 6	wickets
		Challenge Match		
Sept. 18, 19, 20	Yorkshire II	217	104	Lost on first
Scarborough	Warwickshire II	112	78 for 3	innings

* Innings declared closed.

Batting Averages

	Innings	Not Outs	Runs	Highest Innings	Average
W. J. Stewart	15	1	623	184*	44.50
A. V. Wolton	21	2	669	198*	35.21
R. T. Weeks	7	3	129	34	32.25
T. W. Cartwright	16	0	514	100	32.12

	Innings	Not Outs	Runs	Highest Innings	Average
H. E. Dollery†	16	5	344	50	31.27
D. P. Ratcliffe	26	5	617	109	29.38
D. A. Livingstone	29	6	533	79*	23.17
B. E. Fletcher	24	5	405	51	21.31
C. W. Leach	22	2	426	59	21.30
H. J. Latham	7	1	116	62	19.33
C. G. Hawkins	26	6	369	46	18.45
M. Youll	25	12	238	42	18.30
E. Leadbeater	20	2	214	47*	11.88
B. T. Glynn	4	0	34	16	8.50
S. S. Griffiths	6	3	24	16	8.00
R. G. Thompson	8	3	34	13	6.80
R. G. Carter	7	0	37	23	5.40

Also batted: R. Sewell 76, 9; R. E. Hitchcock 26, 1, 0; J. L. Wilkins 14, 11; G. H. Hill 16, 5, 3, 0; K. R. Dollery 14, 6*; K. Ibadulla 10; T. A. Pargetter 8; M. S. Cook 3, 0; R. J. Devereux 0.

Bowling Averages

	Overs	Maidens	Runs	Wickets	Average
T. W. Cartwright	146	62	221	25	8.84
J. D. Bannister	101	28	277	21	13.19
A. V. Wolton	74	28	119	9	13.22
C. W. Leach	288.5	141	448	31	14.45
O. S. Wheatley	55.3	16	118	8	14.75
S. S. Griffiths	161	39	354	23	15.39
H. J. Latham	121.4	33	283	18	15.72
R. G. Carter	157.3	43	335	21	15.95
M. Youll	313.4	63	1018	62	16.41
R. G. Thompson	358.1	114	723	44	16.43
G. H. Hill	70	27	134	8	16.75
E. Leadbeater	391.3	122	926	42	22.04
R. T. Weeks	119.1	40	305	11	27.72

Also bowled: K. Ibadulla 12—5—9—2; T. A. Pargetter 25—7—56—2; B. E. Fletcher 6—2—14—1; J. Billingham 12—3—31—1; R. W. Wilson 20—6—46—1; J. L. Wilkins 1—1—0—0; W. J. Stewart 4—2—13—0; K. R. Dollery 13—5—14—0; D. A. Livingstone 25.1—7—72—0.

Amateurs.—H. J. Latham, R. Sewell, R. E. Hitchcock, J. L. Wilkins, G. H. Hill, K. R. Dollery, T. A. Pargetter, M. S. Cook, R. J. Devereux, O. S. Wheatley, J. Billingham, R. W. Wilson.

WILTSHIRE

Secretary—R. A. C. FORRESTER, 11–12, High Street, Chippenham

Matches 10—Won 2, Lost 4, Won on first innings 1, Lost on first innings 1, No result 2

		1st Innings	2nd Innings	Result
August 2, 3	Wiltshire	238* for 7	130	Lost by one
Trowbridge	Somerset II	239* for 6	131 for 9	wicket
August 5, 6	Wiltshire	151	139	Lost by innings
Swindon	Surrey II	296* for 9	—	and six runs
(B.R. Ground)				
August 7, 8	Wiltshire	188	190* for 7	Lost on first
Sherborne	Dorset	192* for 9	137 for 6	innings

		1st Innings	2nd Innings	Result
August 9, 10	Oxfordshire	157	—	†Lost by 20 runs
Trowbridge	Wiltshire	137	—	
August 12, 13	Wiltshire	—	—	No result
Oxford	Oxfordshire	—	—	
August 14, 15	Wiltshire	—	—	No result
The Oval	Surrey II	—	—	
August 16, 17	Wiltshire	172	135	Won by 60 runs
Marlborough Col.	Dorset	146	101	
August 19, 20	Kent II	247	114* for 3	Won by one
Chippenham	Wiltshire	159* for 8	203 for 9	wicket
August 21, 22	Wiltshire	44	171	Lost by innings
Midsomer Norton	Somerset II	222* for 6		and seven runs
August 26, 27	Wiltshire	157	214* for 3	Won on first
Tonbridge .	Kent II	120	191 for 6	innings

* Innings declared closed.
† Reduced to one day because of rain.

Batting Averages

	Innings	Not Outs	Runs	Highest Innings	Average
A. B. Chivers	4	2	106	47	53.00
A. M. Smith	11	2	320	113*	35.55
J. R. Thompson	15	0	483	133	32.20
R. J. Knight	9	0	198	80	22.00
I. R. Lomax	9	1	143	67	17.87
A. H. Mills	6	0	95	41	15.83
M. H. Lloyd	13	0	189	50	14.53
M. H. Martin	9	4	68	17	13.60
P. C. Dunn	13	1	162	54	13.50
J. Hurn†	14	0	186	44	13.28
A. G. Marshall	11	2	107	24	11.88
M. Hanna	6	0	39	17	6.50
J. H. Merryweather	14	0	79	19	5.64
G. A. Thurgood	7	2	27	9	5.40

Also batted: V. T. Baddeley 1, 6.
* *Signifies not out.*   † *Captain.*

Bowling Averages

	Overs	Maidens	Runs	Wickets	Average
V. T. Baddeley	33.1	6	100	7	14.28
J. H. Merryweather	335.2	72	684	45	15.20
A. G. Marshall	160.4	37	472	21	22.47
M. H. Martin	115	23	386	13	29.69
K. P. Jones	69.4	16	225	5	45.00
P. C. Dunn	23	4	143	3	47.66

Also bowled: I. R. Lomax 1 wicket for 99 runs; J. R. Thompson 0—5; A. Smith 0—43; A. B. Chivers 0—10.

Professional.—A. G. Marshall.

YORKSHIRE SECOND ELEVEN

Secretary—J. H. NASH, Old Bank Chambers, Leeds, 1

Matches 19—Won 11, Lost 3, Won on first innings 3, Lost on first innings 2, No result 2

		1st Innings	2nd Innings	Result
May 22, 23	Yorkshire II	137	119	Lost by three
Northampton	Northants II	110	147 for 7	wickets
May 27, 28	Yorkshire II	240	—	Won by innings
Salts' Saltaire	Cheshire	41	110	and 89 runs

		1st Innings	2nd Innings	Result
June 10, 11	Lancashire II	136	—	Won on first
Harrogate	Yorkshire II	138 for 4	—	innings
June 12, 13	Yorkshire II	339* for 4	—	Won by innings
Longton	Staffordshire	142	142	and 55 runs
June 17, 18	Lincolnshire	191	160	Won by two
Mirfield	Yorkshire II	213	139 for 8	wickets
June 19, 20	Yorkshire II	386	47 for 1	Won by nine
Oxton	Cheshire	232	200	wickets
June 26, 27	Northumberland	238	131	Lost by 110
Jesmond	Yorkshire II	164	95	runs
July 1, 2	Cumberland	149	94	Won by innings
York	Yorkshire II	338* for 4	—	and 95 runs
July 3, 4	Yorkshire II	—	—	No result
Doncaster	Northants II	—		
July 8, 9	Cumberland	151	98	Won by five
Kendal	Yorkshire II	92	158 for 5	wickets
July 22, 23	Yorkshire II	255* for 9	93* for 1	Won by 117
Redcar	Northumberland	165	66	runs
July 31, August 1	Yorkshire II	185	107	Lost by nine
Bridlington	Notts II	206	89 for 1	wickets
August 5, 6	Yorkshire II	210	208* for 9	Won by 70 runs
Old Trafford	Lancashire II	212* for 3	136	
August 7, 8	Durham	154	109	Won by innings
Black Hill	Yorkshire II	300* for 7	—	and 37 runs
August 12, 13	Yorkshire II	245* for 6	—	Won by innings
Scunthorpe	Lincolnshire	35	71	and 139 runs
August 19, 20	Durham	90	79	Won by innings
Middlesbrough	Yorkshire II	193* for 9	—	and 24 runs
August 21, 22	Staffordshire	126	164* for 8	Won on first
Scarborough	Yorkshire II	127* for 7	101 for 7	innings
August 26, 27	Yorkshire II	255* for 9	—	No result
Shireoaks	Notts II	68 for 1	—	
		Challenge Match		
Sept. 18, 19, 20	Yorkshire II	217	104	Won on first
Scarborough	Warwickshire II	112	78 for 3	innings

* Innings declared closed.

Batting Averages

	Innings	Not Outs	Runs	Highest Innings	Average
K. Taylor	4	1	126	58	42.00
D. E. V. Padgett	11	1	409	134	40.90
G. W. Moore	23	3	713	93	35.65
P. J. Sharpe	11	1	327	67	32.70
J. B. Bolus	24	1	747	127	32.47
J. R. Burnett†	22	2	417	64	20.85
M. Naylor	15	1	283	55	20.21
E. I. Lester	27	3	467	79	19.45
D. Wilson	14	7	133	43*	19.00
W. F. Oates	8	1	129	39*	18.42
R. L. Jowett	8	1	120	39	17.14
J. Birkenshaw	10	1	153	39	17.00
B. Handley	5	0	84	63	16.80
H. D. Bird	5	0	68	45	13.60
E. Legard	20	6	170	27*	12.14
M. Ryan	13	2	128	29	11.63
R. K. Platt	5	3	18	7*	9.00
D. Pickles	8	1	34	14	4.85
M. J. Cowan	5	2	10	4*	3.33

Also batted: R. Appleyard 8, 2, 1; A. B. Bainbridge 33; P. N. Broughton 6*, 0*, 0; F. W. Goddard 7, 5*; P. J. Kippax 7, 5; J. Pitt 18*; E. Slingsby 14, 3; W. B. Stott 19, 2, 78; W. P. Tiler 3*, 4, 0, 0; W. Watson 35, 107; R. Wood 13.

      * *Signifies not out.*   † Captain.

Bowling Averages

	Overs	Maidens	Runs	Wickets	Average
R. Appleyard	131	51	240	31	7.74
J. Birkenshaw	151.3	50	307	32	9.59
D. Wilson	303	114	667	48	13.89
R. K. Platt	169.3	62	312	22	14.18
D. Pickles	173.3	45	385	27	14.25
M. Ryan	269.4	60	633	44	14.38
M. J. Cowan	116.2	25	308	20	15.40
W. P. Tiler	80.1	17	231	14	16.50
B. Handley	77.3	23	229	13	17.61
M. Naylor	116.3	21	463	20	23.15
P. N. Broughton	42	9	121	5	24.20

Also bowled: A. B. Bainbridge 18.3—4—30—4; J. B. Bolus 15.3—6—51—3; J. R. Burnet1—0—1—0; F. W.Goddard 4—1—10—0; R. L. Jowett 14—5—27—0; P. J. Kippax 20—9—45—2; E. I. Lester 1—0—4—0; D. E. V. Padgett 1—0—2—1; J. A. Pitt 22—11—31 3; K. Taylor 1—0—1—0; C. Wood 6—4—5—1; R. Wood 24—6—75—2.

Amateurs.—J. R. Burnet, G. W. Moore, P. J. Sharpe, R. L. Jowett, P. J. Kippax.

MINOR COUNTIES' AVERAGES, 1957
BATTING
(Qualification: 8 innings, average 25.00)

	County	Innings	Not Outs	Runs	Highest Innings	Average
N. Hill	*Notts II*	10	3	421	135	60.14
G. A. Edrich	*Lancashire II*	22	7	873	130*	58.20
J. A. R. Oliver	*Bedfordshire*	10	3	399	114	57.00
E. G. Witherden	*Norfolk*	19	3	801	120*	50.06
D. E. V. Padgett	*Yorkshire II*	9	1	389	134	48.62
W. H. Dorning	*Cornwall*	14	5	426	61	47.33
J. D. Bond	*Lancashire II*	12	0	551	181	45.91
M. Winfield	*Notts II*	23	7	728	137	45.50
R. M. James	*Berkshire*	10	1	406	173*	45.11
W. J. Stewart	*Warwickshire II*	15	1	623	184*	44.50
R. Swetman	*Surrey II*	16	4	527	195	43.91
W. B. Morris	*Cambridgeshire*	11	4	307	83	43.85
C. B. T. Gibbon	*Suffolk*	13	5	344	71*	43.00
A. V. Avery	*Gloucestershire II*	8	5	129	41*	43.00
D. F. Cox	*Surrey II*	11	3	343	106	42.87
J. D. Springall	*Notts II*	9	2	298	63	42.57
D. Carpenter	*Gloucestershire II*	15	0	626	193	41.74
A. A. Hillary	*Berkshire*	13	0	532	164	40.92
R. Collins	*Lancashire II*	14	1	513	145	39.46
J. P. Fellows-Smith	*Northants II*	15	3	470	100*	39.16
A. V. Wolton	*Warwickshire II*	19	2	662	198*	38.94
E. A. White	*Middlesex II*	20	3	660	105*	38.82
D. Allen	*Gloucestershire II*	9	1	310	72*	38.75
D. F. Johns	*Buckinghamshire*	12	0	459	122	38.25

      * *Signifies not out.*

	County	Innings	Not Outs	Runs	Highest Innings	Average
D. H. Cole	Devon	16	2	534	90	38.14
E. Martin	Notts II	20	1	710	133	37.36
P. J. Sharpe.......	Yorkshire II	9	1	296	67	37.00
R. W. Hocker	Middlesex II	21	3	654	95	36.33
A. M. Smith	Wiltshire	11	2	320	113*	35.55
J. Cornwell	Cambridgeshire	9	2	248	76	35.42
G. W. Moore	Yorkshire II	21	3	633	93	35.16
P. Marner	Lancashire II	18	2	562	109	35.12
M. M. Walford ..	Dorset	22	1	728	131*	34.66
A. B. D. Parsons ..	Surrey II	12	2	342	105	34.20
B. A. Barnett	Buckinghamshire	13	3	338	61	33.80
J. B. Bolus	Yorkshire II	22	1	708	127	33.71
F. R. Bailey	Staffordshire	10	1	320	120	33.55
H. E. Dollery	Warwickshire II	14	5	301	50	33.44
P. Jones	Kent II	19	2	564	74	33.17
R. C. Vowles	Notts II	13	6	231	67	33.00
R. W. Smithson ..	Northumberland	8	0	264	106	33.00
G. Tripp	Somerset II	19	5	455	71	32.50
J. E. Bush	Oxfordshire	15	0	485	122	32.33
J. R. Thompson ..	Wiltshire	15	0	483	133	32.20
T. W. Cartwright .	Warwickshire II	15	0	476	100	31.73
A. Durley	Essex II	26	2	757	101	31.54
J. H. Taylor	Lincolnshire	17	0	530	78	31.17
J. A. Mence	Berkshire	9	0	277	88	30.77
D. P. Ratcliffe ...	Warwickshire II	24	4	611	109	30.55
D. C. P. R. Jowett	Dorset	8	1	213	65	30.42
H. D. Bell	Durham	15	2	393	90	30.23
N. V. Butler	Buckinghamshire	11	1	300	132*	30.00
R. F. Hosking	Cornwall	15	1	419	56	29.92
D. Gibson	Surrey II	11	3	236	37	29.50
E. M. Senior	Lancashire II	8	2	176	70*	29.33
J. W. Murphy	Cornwall	15	2	378	79	29.07
J. Edrich	Surrey II	12	2	289	116*	28.90
D. Hawkins.......	Gloucestershire II	10	0	285	86	28.50
B. Booth	Lancashire II	27	0	767	134	28.40
G. R. Langdale ...	Berkshire	16	3	368	50	28.30
D. A. Bick	Middlesex II	16	1	424	69	28.26
J. A. Holmes......	Derbyshire II	14	1	366	85	28.15
J. G. Fox	Durham	13	6	196	41	28.00
K. D. Smith	Northumberland	10	2	223	92	27.87
D. Bean	Staffordshire	18	1	473	99	27.82
B. S. Darvell	Hertfordshire	11	6	139	54*	27.80
J. G. Lomax	Somerset II	19	3	443	64	27.68
R. Giles	Notts II	13	0	359	52*	27.61
F. W. Millett	Cheshire	19	1	492	58	27.33
S. Crump	Staffordshire	10	2	217	71	27.12
V. S. Munden	Leicestershire II	14	1	352	132	27.07
A. Bolton	Lancashire II	21	3	486	54*	27.00
K. W. Powell	Shropshire	14	5	242	78	26.88
D. Mackinnon	Buckinghamshire	9	1	215	66*	26.87
P. Shaw	Northumberland	11	0	293	106	26.63
B. Roe	Somerset II	22	5	452	83	26.58
M. A. Crouch	Cambridgeshire	12	0	319	108	26.58
R. Virgin	Somerset II	22	7	397	64	26.46
L. Bateman	Hertfordshire	9	2	185	60*	26.42
M. Norman	Northants II	18	0	474	113	26.33
M. P. Weston	Durham	10	1	235	74	26.11
R. Fox	Cheshire	11	1	261	69	26.10
G. W. L. Courteney	Dorset	16	1	389	88	25.93
A. O'Neill	Hertfordshire	16	0	413	88	25.81

* *Signifies not out.*

	County	Innings	Not Outs	Runs	Highest Innings	Average
G. Walton	Northumberland	9	1	206	100*	25.75
M. Jordan	Bedfordshire	11	1	257	127*	25.70
D. E. Pratt	Surrey II	14	2	308	68	25.66
G. G. L. Hebden..	Dorset	17	1	410	82	25.62
G. C. Lamb	Durham	14	0	358	52	25.57
A. Vickery	Cheshire	8	0	203	50	25.37
A. F. Brazier......	Kent II	20	2	454	100*	25.22
K. C. Girkin	Suffolk	15	1	351	93	25.07
R. A. Gautrey	Cambridgeshire	11	2	225	70	25.00

Signifies not out.

BOWLING

(Qualification: 20 wickets, average 24.00)

	County	Overs	Maidens	Runs	Wickets	Average
R. Appleyard ...	Yorkshire II	131	51	240	31	7.74
J. Birkenshaw ..	Yorkshire II	139.3	47	270	31	8.70
J. G. Lomax	Somerset II	259	74	543	49	11.08
I. T. Craig	Cambridgeshire	221	84	353	31	11.38
G. Meadowcroft..	Hertfordshire	116.2	32	261	22	11.86
V. Broderick ...	Northants II	319.1	125	709	58	12.22
J. Hilton	Somerset II	229.3	68	582	47	12.38
R. R. Dovey	Dorset	464.4	199	757	61	12.40
S. H. Young	Durham	136.4	41	266	21	12.66
K. Biddulph	Somerset II	276.5	67	711	55	12.92
M. J. B. Riley..	Cheshire	133	27	326	25	13.04
G. C. Perkins ...	Suffolk	290.2	129	433	33	13.12
K. Higgs	Staffordshire	258.4	76	604	46	13.13
J. D. Bannister..	Warwickshire II	101	28	277	21	13.19
D. Banton	Oxfordshire	182.4	51	437	33	13.24
J. Roberts	Lancashire II	267.1	82	681	50	13.62
D. Wilson	Yorkshire II	297	111	647	47	13.76
G. R. Langdale..	Berkshire	314.1	107	592	43	13.76
M. Morgan	Notts II	163.5	65	290	21	13.80
R. Smith	Devon	161.4	53	292	21	13.90
C. W. Leach ...	Warwickshire II	272.1	136	411	29	14.17
R. K. Platt	Yorkshire II	169.3	62	312	22	14.18
F. M. Turner ...	Leicestershire II	161	40	432	30	14.40
A. J. Hughes ...	Buckinghamshire	288.1	69	678	47	14.42
H. M. A. Cherry-Downes ...	Lincolnshire	341.1	89	938	65	14.43
M. Ryan	Yorkshire II	244.2	56	563	39	14.43
T. J. Goodwin ..	Leicestershire II	248.5	50	617	42	14.69
D. W. Hardy ...	Durham	135	36	311	21	14.80
D. Pickles	Yorkshire II	146.3	37	332	22	15.09
L. McGibbon ...	Northants II	158.3	53	378	25	15.12
M. H. Merry-weather	Wiltshire	335.2	72	684	45	15.20
M. J. Cowan ...	Yorkshire II	116.2	25	308	20	15.40
B. Shardlow ...	Staffordshire	256.2	78	571	37	15.43
R. L. Pratt	Leicestershire II	229	52	663	42	15.78
R. C. Vowles ...	Notts II	135.3	35	349	22	15.86
D. F. Johns ...	Buckinghamshire	132.2	33	335	21	15.95
P. Phelan	Essex II	201.2	41	528	33	16.00
J. Cotton	Notts II	110	15	385	24	16.04
D. J. W. Bridge..	Dorset	331	112	772	48	16.08
R. M. James ...	Berkshire	147	30	339	21	16.14
J. E. Walsh	Leicestershire II	181	56	471	29	16.24

	County	Overs	Maidens	Runs	Wickets	Average
M. Youll	Warwickshire II	311.4	63	1012	62	16.32
D. J. Laitt	Oxfordshire	254	64	623	38	16.39
R. G. Thompson	Warwickshire II	358.1	114	723	44	16.43
J. M. Watson ...	Durham	204.5	66	478	29	16.48
A. Walker	Notts II	132.3	31	334	20	16.70
D. Hall	Derbyshire II	163.5	38	441	26	16.96
D. Sydenham ...	Surrey II	210	55	537	31	17.32
H. W. Tilly	Middlesex II	328.5	104	697	40	17.42
T. Angus.......	Middlesex II	214.5	53	595	34	17.50
K. Smales	Notts II	190	79	423	24	17.62
R. Pellew	Cornwall	177.3	47	426	24	17.75
P. F. Harvey ...	Notts II	384	151	911	51	17.86
M. D. Willett ...	Surrey II	186.1	58	453	25	18.12
B. Luckhurst ...	Kent II	258.5	85	611	33	18.51
A. Whitehead ...	Somerset II	170.4	56	411	22	18.68
K. Norton	Northumberland	194.1	71	412	22	18.72
J. D. Walton ...	Lincolnshire	182.5	44	469	25	18.76
B. Booth	Lancashire II	292	71	925	49	18.87
A. L. Hichens ..	Oxfordshire	219.1	48	662	35	18.91
E. Palmer	Essex II	188	50	498	26	19.15
T. G. Morley ...	Hertfordshire	204.1	43	532	27	19.70
R. Aspinall	Durham	224.1	67	513	26	19.73
A. Brown.......	Kent II	199.4	43	498	25	19.92
R. V. C. Robins.	Middlesex II	154.1	34	480	24	20.00
J. Harris	Somerset II	186.2	41	502	25	20.08
M. Ashenden ...	Bedfordshire	121.1	24	404	20	20.20
J. Oakes	Northumberland	212.4	65	501	24	20.87
D. Allen........	Gloucestershire II	194	56	522	25	20.88
E. Leadbeater ..	Warwickshire II	382.3	120	894	42	21.28
T. Atkinson.....	Notts II	182.1	43	427	20	21.35
P. Bradley	Shropshire	125.1	22	470	22	21.36
D. H. Cole	Devon	211.3	59	472	22	21.45
A. G. Marshall..	Wiltshire	160.4	37	472	21	22.47
P. Spicer	Essex II	255.3	55	747	33	22.63
A. G. Coomb ...	Norfolk	232	58	623	27	23.07
M. Naylor	Yorkshire II	116.3	21	463	20	23.15
D. Gibson	Surrey II	168.2	34	517	22	23.50
A. W. Lea	Lincolnshire	213.5	39	668	28	23.85

THE PUBLIC SCHOOLS IN 1957

By E. M. Wellings

After years of complaint about the unworthy standard of Public Schools fielding the 1957 season at last gave us solid reason to applaud the boys in that vital branch of the game. Not only were there outstanding individuals in the representative matches at Lord's, but the general level was appreciably higher than in previous seasons. Moreover the reports which arrived from cricket masters about their individual school teams were more than usually concerned with fielding.

The improvement was general; ground fielding, catching and throwing which in many recent representative games has been wild enough to exhaust the good temper of the most placid wicket-keeper. For six years Surrey have been winning the County Championship primarily by deadly fielding in support of their magnificent attack. With a certain time lag Public Schools cricket follows the trends in county cricket. And now, when surely the fielding standard in the county game is higher than ever, the boys have profited from the men's example.

The first boy mentioned this year, then, shall be G. Atkins of Dr. Challoner's Grammar School, for on the four days of the representative games he never failed to impress on all his skill as a fielder. Atkins arrived at Lord's well recommended by the runs he had scored for the Club Cricket Conference against M.C.C. He was anything but a disappointment as a left-handed batsman, but he made a much more lasting impression by his brilliant fielding at cover. If Atkins set the standard the others followed him ably, and not all the fielding skill was concentrated among the eleven who were chosen against Combined Services. P. J. Kippax (Bedford Modern) was a reserve who fielded particularly well in the first of the two matches. If he had extended either of his two highly promising innings as an opening batsman by a few runs, he must have won selection for the second game.

Not only in fielding but in bowling also, recent trends in county cricket left their mark on schoolboy cricket. It is not so long ago that the emphasis in English first-class cricket was placed on pace bowling, following the successes against England of Lindwall, Miller and Johnston. The result has been the fast bowling era of Trueman, Statham, Tyson, Loader, Moss and others. Allowing for the time-lag it was, then, not surprising that the leading school bowlers of 1957 were almost exclusively those of some pace who used the new ball.

There was little spin bowling of class in the sides for the Lord's games. But reports from the schools frequently mentioned promising spinners of ages qualifying them still for the Under 16

Colts teams. The influence of Lock, Laker and Wardle has reached the younger boys and we may expect a change of bowling emphasis among the selected boys at Lord's in the next year or two.

In the absence of spin it was not surprising that, for once, the batting was clearly superior to the bowling. It was a good year for school batting despite the road accident early in June that put H. C. Blofeld (Eton) out of the game for the rest of the term. Until that event Blofeld was most people's bet as the best schoolboy batsman of the year, and his loss was a grave misfortune not only to Eton.

Happily there were worthy players to offer themselves as candidates for top position in his stead. The two most prominent were C. D. Drybrough, a games player and athlete of wide interests and ability from Highgate, and D. Kirby of St. Peter's, York. Drybrough did most of his good things in the first of the two games at Lord's. His 128, starting when the Southern Schools were 15 for three, was a magnificent piece of sensibly aggressive cricket. By the time he had driven the bowlers of The Rest straight and hard while advancing to 50 in no more than sixty-five minutes the game was turned. If he was stronger on the front foot than the back, Drybrough looked a most excellent school batsman. He had the same aggressive attitude towards batting as did E. R. Dexter while a schoolboy, and he may well develop in the same successful way.

Kirby was a consistently good scorer during the four days. His most attractive stroke was the cover drive, and generally he played in a manner to make comparison between him and Drybrough invidious. Together they may have been the leaders, but they did not leave their fellows far behind. At the youthful age of 16 the Nawab of Pataudi, having spent the term scoring freely for Winchester, made an immediate mark at Lord's, where there was just time at the end of the second day for him to play himself into the representative XI. He had failed in the first innings, and if his second had started half an hour later he might not have been given the chance to play his splendid innings of 71 against Combined Services.

At one time only County Championship matches were arranged so that stumps could be drawn on the last day at 6 p.m., the final half-hour until 6.30 being used only if necessary to obtain a result. Of late years the practice has spread to all manner of matches, in which the players are not similarly pressed for time in the catching of trains to their next playing engagement. It is with some indignation, having probably been deprived of some good cricket, that I ask why the practice has been extended quite unnecessarily to a School trial game at Lord's, in which the result has no significance. That the game started on the second day at 11 a.m. is no argument in favour of stopping half an hour early on a perfect summer's evening, when spectators and batsman alike were enjoying Pataudi's innings. He himself at 27 not out looked appealingly at his team's balcony in the vain hope that someone would decide that the final half-hour was necessary.

A two-day game is all too short to sift the material before choosing the representative side. To sacrifice half an hour needlessly may be unfair to the boys. Two members of the side whose fielding on this occasion was thus cut short have particular cause for complaint. A. W. M. Bain (Fettes) accordingly bowled only nine overs in the match and M. K. S. Shatrushalyasinhji only eight. As the latter, a nephew of K. S. Duleepsinhji, came to Lord's as an all-rounder and had no reasonable time for batting in either innings he must have felt that the trial game was much too short.

Having played in two Oxford sides with his father, I was asked how the present holder of the title compared with the first cricketing Nawab of Pataudi. Except that they both were endowed with natural talent and ball sense they are not comparable. The father was physically frail and was essentially a batsman of finesse rather than force, though he was also a fast scorer. His son is built more strongly, and if he shows the delicate touch of his father in the cut strokes, which he plays with obvious relish, he is clearly a more robust batsman. As yet his bat is not so straight as his father's and he takes more chances. In August he played three times for Sussex promisingly, and reports from Hove of his good fielding were particularly pleasing.

Although J. R. Bernard (Clifton) failed in the trial game after an earlier triumph at Lord's against Tonbridge, there were three strong batting candidates for the two opening positions, R. A. C. Luckin (Felsted), Kippax and G. J. Sharman (Lancing). Kippax was perhaps the one who appeared to promise most, and he was the most vigorous batsman of the three. He was also the one who had to be omitted, for the other two scored more heavily. The soundness of Luckin and the undaunted patience of Sharman gained the positions.

At the time I recall muttering unkind things whilst Sharman was taking nearly an hour to reach double figures. But Sharman had his place and his role among the more eager stroke-making batsmen. He himself was a reluctant stroke-maker and largely concealed his ability in that direction, but he was wonderfully patient and watchful. With Atkins the Schools had already six batsmen, and all-rounders considerably extended their batting.

Their stumper, H. S. Cook (Warwick), won his place from I. P. Morton, a neat wicket-keeper from Christ's Hospital, mainly on his superior batting. He was the second player of the same name from Warwick in recent years to represent the Public Schools. Like the earlier one, who was largely a bowler, H. S. Cook batted left-handed. He had the left-hander's typical strokes past cover and to leg, where he was particularly strong, and he scored heavily in both the games at Lord's. Bowlers A. T. C. Allom (Charterhouse) and D. M. Green (Manchester Grammar School) were also batsmen of considerable merit and value.

Of the batsmen who did not win selection against the Services Kippax, who has been already mentioned, and A. R. Day of Aldenham looked the best. Day was miserably unlucky in being run out in his first innings through no fault of his own. In the second innings he was among the first four southerners who fell for 47 on a fast and fiery pitch to some equally fiery bowling.

That pitch was not unlike the one on which the Second Test match two months earlier had come to a distressingly early finish. It knocked up badly on the second day to give the pace bowlers a tremendous advantage. If M.C.C. wish to encourage boy cricketers to bowl spinners, they will not do so by giving them pitches of that sort.

The Rest had just the bowlers for those conditions, and the Southern batsmen were fiercely assailed. C. D. R. Barker (The King's School, Macclesfield) brought the ball round their ribs, and H. G. Owen-Hughes (Shrewsbury) mowed them down at the other end. Owen-Hughes was one of those unusual players who bowl off the wrong foot and whose peculiar action inevitably produces leg cut. On that very responsive pitch he was bowling fast leg-breaks, and until he and Barker began to tire the Southern batsmen were in sore trouble.

In the event Barker was not in the final XI, though he was in the dozen from whom that side was chosen on the morning of the match. I would have been reluctant to leave him out, but in addition to Owen-Hughes both Allom and I. C. Potter (King's School, Canterbury) staked strong claims to inclusion. Potter was the steadiest of the four as well as being the smallest. The others were all tall. Allom was only two inches short of seven feet. He bowled at medium pace, a lively medium, and from his vast height made the ball bounce awkwardly. He may be said to have overcome the disadvantage of excessive height by keeping his pace down. Like Pataudi, Allom is the son of a distinguished father. M. J. C. Allom was one of the best medium-fast bowlers between the wars and bowled for England in Test cricket.

Barker also made good use of his height, and if he was mainly an inswing bowler he showed himself to be a decidedly good one of his type. Taken together the pace bowlers were more than adequate and toiled hard to cover the shortage of good spin. Potentially the best spinner was Drybrough, for he was a left-hander with considerable ability to impart spin, but as yet his bowling lacked variety. The attack was completed in its main ingredients by Green, who had established himself as the pick of the off-spinners.

In a year when the spin was so moderate it was perhaps surprising that A. W. Allen, who had a highly successful season as a slow left-hander at Repton, was not tried at Lord's. But selection of these sides is an uncommonly difficult task and must depend largely on recommendations from the schools. The great need is a preliminary trial, from which, say, the dozen most obvious selections for the Southern Schools *v.* The Rest match would be excluded. This could be done by cutting out some of the inter-schools matches at Lord's. Though writing as an old boy of a school which would lose its match at Lord's, I must confess to seeing no good reason for any inter-schools match being played there except Eton *v.* Harrow. I believe that Public Schools cricket would benefit from having more representative and less inter-schools cricket on show.

Two of the best sides of the year were among those who played at Lord's, Clifton with success but Haileybury arriving only to suffer a surprise defeat by Cheltenham. After a depressing start to the season Clifton rallied to become one of the schools' best teams—and a fine fielding one—and played their last ten matches without defeat. For Cheltenham, playing above themselves, the win at Lord's was compensation for disappointing displays in other inter-schools matches. For Haileybury it was anti-climax at the end of a season which had marked them as being among the leaders of Public School cricket. Yet, even in defeat they shaped in the manner of cricketers entitled to success and continually looked worth more than they actually achieved at Lord's.

Of all the year's team performances the best was perhaps that of Winchester. Although they began the season with only two old Colours and habitually meet stronger opposition than the majority, they were unbeaten for the second year running. The Nawab of Pataudi's 851 runs at an average of 65.47 was among the best two or three batting performances on paper at any of the bigger schools. It stood with Drybrough's 706 at 78.44 for Highgate. The next best average at Highgate was only 17.4 and the second aggregate merely 273. As Drybrough's 32 wickets were also the school's highest total his tremendous influence on his team's cricket was obvious.

In the West, Downside, who suffered their only defeat and that by a very narrow margin in the final match, rivalled Clifton. With three bowlers aged 15 taking 103 out of 123 wickets they could contemplate the future with more relish than most. The leading side in the north would seem to have been St. Peter's, York. They, too, with Kirby heading the batsmen, lost only once and won seven of the other 13 games. If Winchester are given first position among the powerful group of Southern Schools, they had obvious rivals in Charterhouse and Haileybury. King's, Canterbury, were another strong and successful side. Eton's season was disrupted by Blofeld's misfortune, and Harrow were no more than an ordinary side worried by slender bowling resources.

Douai went through 1957 unbeaten, and there were others beaten only once, but several of them drew an excessive number of their games even making allowance for ill luck with the weather. Repton were among the single losers. They drew 11 out of 18 games. Radley drew 9 of 15, Rossall 7 of 11, and Malvern also lost only once but drew often.

In East Anglia, Leys began, like Winchester, with only two old Colours and yet developed their players so well that they won six inter-schools matches. They must be counted among the team successes of the summer, and it is clear that there were a number of good sides. It was clear, too, that attention paid to fielding played a notable part in their development.

Every school season produces remarkable individual performances when set against the modest deeds of others in the same sides. The year 1957 was no exception. A. H. Jinnah dominated Epsom cricket in the manner of Drybrough at Highgate with 590 runs for an average of 65.56 and 38 wickets at 10.57 runs each. At Aldenham, Day's average of 49.4 against a next best of 20.87 is support for the impression that he was a player good enough to make a big impression at Lord's with reasonable luck. Kippax had similar success at Bedford Modern, where his 49.5 average was nearly twice as good as that of his nearest rival. Bedford Modern's season was also notable for J. S. Orpin taking 25 wickets at 11.8, for he was only 14 and one of a considerable number of very young left-arm spinners who did well during the summer.

R. M. Prideaux (Tonbridge) was another who dominated his side's batting with an average twice as large as the next one. Even more so did G. Neil-Dwyer prop up the Ruthin batting. His 593 runs gave him an average of 53.9, while none of the others was able to reach 20 an innings.

The heavy scoring of the first four Lancing batsmen, whose total was 2,449, recalls similar scoring at Radley when E. R. Dexter and A. C. Walton were their leading batsmen. No round-up of the season would be complete without mention of a tremendous partnership at Bloxham. Playing against the XL Club, D. N. Adey and C. C. W. Rodgers put on 287 together. And finally there was M. G. Waller's 59 wickets at under 11 runs each for Uppingham. As that is the greatest number ever taken for the School it is a good item on which to end discussion of a decidedly encouraging season.

Following are the destinations of some of the members of last year's XIs:—

	OXFORD	CAMBRIDGE
Blundells	R. A. W. Sharpe	
Bradford G.S.	J. P. Bayley	
	J. M. Hewitt	
Bristol G.S.	R. J. Short	
	R. C. Tanner	
Bryanston	M. F. J. Checksfield	J. R. Brock
		J. E. Goldsmith
		D. M. Ladd
Cheltenham		A. F. Benke
Christ's Hospital	I. P. Morton	
	N. P. Thompson	
City of London		G. B. Green
Dean Close		R. I. Ireland
		R. L. Johns
Downside		P. A. Kavanagh
Eton	J. D. Ayer	H. C. Blofeld
		E. J. Lane-Fox
Felstead		A. T. P. Higgins
		R. A. G. Luckin
Fettes		R. J. B. Hoare
Highgate	C. D. Drybrough	C. J. S. Garner
	M. H. Wadsworth	
Kingswood		R. G. J. Hopkins
Lancing	G. J. Sharman	
Leeds G.S.		J. D. Brooke
Leys		D. S. Bousfield
Marlborough	B. A. C. Marr	C. A. Morris
Merchiston		J. M. Boyle
Millfield		T. L. de Z. Adihetty
Monkton Combe	I. H. Glasgow	C. P. C. Hunt
		N. B. Matthewson
Oundle	N. M. Stephens	J. H. Minney
		P. B. Reddaway
Radley	T. W. Morkill	
	P. J. Mackeown	
Repton		P. H. Vaughan
Rossall	G. M. Attenborough	M. J. Reece
Rugby		P. R. Colville
		T. B. L. Coghlan
Ruthin		G. Neil-Dwyer
St. Paul's	A. N. Sperryn	
St. Peter's		D. Kirby
Sedbergh	C. G. Midgley	M. R. Grundy
		J. R. Miller
Shrewsbury	H. G. Owen-Hughes	
Stamford		J. B. Bayley
Stonyhurst	C. P. Cheetham	
Tonbridge		R. M. Prideaux
Trinity College	J. L. MacDonald	D. H. MacPherson
Trinity School		S. E. Reid
Victoria	P. J. B. le Brocq	
Wellingborough		N. Iqbal
Whitgift		D. Mills
Winchester	Nawab of Pataudi	
Worcester R.G.S.	C. G. Clarke	
	A. P. Mobbs	
Wrekin	N. H. Grenfell	

THE SCHOOLS

* Signifies not out. † *Indicates captain.*

ALDENHAM SCHOOL

Although an inexperienced side, Aldenham had a successful season against other schools. They had wins against Highgate, Beaumont and Mill Hill to set against defeats by Felsted and Merchant Taylor's. Their captain, A. R. Day, enjoyed a particularly good season and repeatedly carried his side.

Played 12, *Won* 5, *Lost* 3, *Drawn* 4

Batting

	Innings	Not outs	Runs	Highest inns.	Average
†A. R. Day	12	2	494	94*	49.40
A. Dey	11	3	167	42	20.87
J. D. Hughes	12	1	213	50	19.36
D. R. Barker	11	2	154	40*	17.11
B. C. Wharton	8	1	119	81	17.00
R. E. Harris	12	0	196	61	16.33

Bowling

	Overs	Maidens	Runs	Wickets	Average
J. J. Irwin	123.5	25	319	21	15.19
Z. H. Hidayatallah	96.3	4	355	19	18.68
D. R. Barker	144.5	29	386	20	19.30
A. R. Day	121.5	33	333	11	30.27

ALLEYN'S SCHOOL

Played 16, *Won* 5, *Lost* 3, *Drawn* 8

Batting

	Innings	Not outs	Runs	Highest inns.	Average
†M. J. Edwards	14	4	339	95	33.90
R. F. Dorey	14	2	268	48*	22.33
I. N. Trafford	12	0	277	70	23.08

Bowling

	Overs	Maidens	Runs	Wickets	Average
R. Devo	52.5	21	105	16	6.56
R. J. Coulson	123	38	266	23	11.56
R. F. Dorey	110.4	36	278	24	11.58

ALLHALLOWS SCHOOL

The season at Allhallows was interrupted by a period of quarantine at a time when the team was developing promisingly. The batting generally was thin and the bowling more steady than dangerous. Palmer, the captain, and Rowe were splendid all-rounders.

Played 10, *Won* 5, *Lost* 4, *Drawn* 1

Batting

	Innings	Not outs	Runs	Highest inns.	Average
P. G. Rowe	10	0	292	88	29.20
†D. W. M. Palmer	10	1	203	83*	22.55
M. Damji	10	0	222	63	22.20
N. P. Jenney	9	1	113	21	14.12

Bowling

	Overs	Maidens	Runs	Wickets	Average
N. P. Jenney	91	20	249	25	9.96
P. N. G. Murdoch	103	29	307	22	13.95
P. G. Rowe	73	15	202	14	14.42
D. W. M. Palmer	51	7	236	13	18.15

AMPLEFORTH COLLEGE

At their best Ampleforth were a strong side. The bowling was always good, particularly the left-arm spinners of R. Lorimer, but the batsmen, with the exception of Morris, were unreliable. The side started badly as fielders but reached a high standard before the end of the term, and W. Sparling was outstandingly good.

Played 14, Won 5, Lost 4, Drawn 5

Batting

	Innings		Not outs		Runs		Highest inns.		Average
†B. J. Morris	14	..	2	..	388	..	60	..	32.33
P. Chambers	13	..	2	..	269	..	71*	..	24.45
M. A. King	14	..	2	..	279	..	50	..	23.25
R. Lorimer	11	..	4	..	161	..	44*	..	23.00
A. King	14	..	0	..	194	..	32	..	13.85

Bowling

	Overs		Maidens		Runs		Wickets		Average
H. Lorimer	41.4	..	16	..	81	..	11	..	7.36
R. Lorimer	178.3	..	43	..	509	..	44	..	11.56
Master of Lovat	147.2	..	43	..	388	..	22	..	17.63
D. H. Glynn	140.4	..	43	..	335	..	15	..	22.33
A. R. Iveson	134	..	35	..	381	..	16	..	23.81

ARDINGLY COLLEGE

Played 13, Won 7, Lost 4, Drawn 2

Batting

	Innings		Not outs		Runs		Highest inns.		Average
R. W. Joyce	13	..	3	..	327	..	86	..	32.70
J. D. Gurney...........	12	..	6	..	186	..	79	..	31.00
J. R. Rivers	13	..	0	..	337	..	109	..	25.92
R. A. Perrin	13	..	1	..	268	..	63	..	22.33
M. J. Lambert	13	..	0	..	252	..	49	..	19.37

Bowling

	Overs		Maidens		Runs		Wickets		Average
P. J. Lane	128.2	..	26	..	334	..	28	..	11.92
†S. C. Mounsey	140.5	..	23	..	417	..	31	..	13.45

BANCROFT'S SCHOOL

During a particularly successful season Bancroft's lost only one inter-schools match, against St. Dunstan's.

Played 15, Won 7, Lost 2, Drawn 6

Batting

	Innings		Not outs		Runs		Highest inns.		Average
†A. G. Meredith	15	..	0	..	413	..	74	..	27.53
G. L. Rice	15	..	1	..	312	..	61	..	22.28
C. F. Barrow	14	..	5	..	191	..	39*	..	21.22
A. R. Thompson	15	..	3	..	218	..	66*	..	18.16
R. S. Furniss...........	9	..	2	..	106	..	39	..	15.14
E. J. Smith	15	..	0	..	218	..	53	..	14.53
J. D. Hoskin	9	..	1	..	104	..	53*	..	13.00
M. Robinson	13	..	2	..	143	..	30	..	13.00

Bowling

	Overs		Maidens		Runs		Wickets		Average
G. L. Rice	143.3	..	33	..	327	..	33	..	9.90
D. H. C. Thompson	144.1	..	34	..	357	..	34	..	10.50
A. J. Fairservice	191.4	..	39	..	460	..	27	..	17.03
D. P. Munroe	85.4	..	15	..	265	..	15	..	17.66

BEAUMONT COLLEGE

After a disappointing start, when the experienced batsmen were failing, Beaumont improved steadily and became a well-balanced side. The bowlers, headed by Baker and Stevens, were always good and the fielding excellent.

Played 14, *Won* 5, *Lost* 4, *Drawn* 1, *Tie* 1, *Abandoned* 3

Batting

	Innings	Not outs	Runs	Highest inns.	Average
B. L. Baker	14	1	311	79	23.92
C. R. Johnson	15	1	322	55	23.00
M. Bulfield	14	3	239	54*	21.72
T. Wood	12	3	151	39*	16.77
†I. F. Sinclair	14	3	184	66*	16.72
H. C. Stevens	12	1	179	43	16.27
A. O'Connor	11	3	126	34	15.75
M. Barr	13	0	150	36	11.53

Bowling

	Overs	Maidens	Runs	Wickets	Average
B. L. Baker	163.1	44	433	34	12.73
I. F. Sinclair	122.2	19	394	22	17.90
H. C. Stevens	137.3	27	406	21	19.33
R. Vickers	109	22	295	12	24.58

BEDFORD MODERN SCHOOL

Their results were a pleasant surprise to Bedford Modern, for the side was young and generally inexperienced. They played attractive cricket and developed well under an exceptionally good captain in Brannan. While Kippax stood out among the batsmen the leading bowler was Orpin, a left-arm spinner who was only 14.

Played 11, *Won* 5, *Lost* 4, *Drawn* 2

Batting

	Innings	Not outs	Runs	Highest inns.	Average
P. J. Kippax	12	1	545	106	49.54
M. R. Theobald	12	1	283	101	25.71
R. J. Slaughter	6	0	110	62	18.33
J. S. Watson	10	1	135	70	15.00
B. N. Antell	10	1	131	50*	14.55
†A. M. Brannan	12	1	153	41	13.90

Bowling

	Overs	Maidens	Runs	Wickets	Average
J. S. Orpin	93	20	295	25	11.80
D. G. Jones	110	28	270	20	13.50
P. J. Kippax	110.1	14	352	19	18.52
A. W. J. Norcott	118	21	307	13	23.61

BEDFORD SCHOOL

An inexperienced team were well led by Eldridge who headed the batting and bowling and captained the Rest against Southern Schools at Lord's. The bowling depended mainly on the accurate off-spinners of Eldridge and the excellent leg-break bowling of Cooper, being splendidly supported by lively and dependable fielding.

Played 11, *Won* 2, *Lost* 4, *Drawn* 5

Batting

	Innings	Not outs	Runs	Highest inns.	Average
†D. C. Eldridge	13	1	327	102*	27.25
S. G. Cook	13	1	283	74	23.58
K. Rischmiller	12	0	232	75	19.33
M. G. Hearth	13	0	226	56	17.38
I. M. W. Pettigrew	11	0	176	69	16.00
P. A. Pettigrew	11	1	153	48	15.30

Bowling

	Overs	Maidens	Runs	Wickets	Average
D. C. Eldridge	248.4	.. 53	.. 752	.. 45	.. 16.71
A. D. Cooper	129.3	.. 1	.. 575	.. 28	.. 20.53

BERKHAMSTED SCHOOL

Berkhamsted brought a lean spell lasting several years to an end in 1957. In a much stronger side than of late Mackrill, their captain, batted with splendid consistency and only twice during the season were the whole team dismissed.

Played 14, Won 5, Lost 2, Drawn 7

Batting

	Innings	Not outs	Runs	Highest inns.	Average
†A. J. Mackrill	13	.. 3	.. 445	.. 69	.. 44.50
C. W. Grace	12	.. 1	.. 295	.. 59	.. 26.81
D. J. Bucknell..........	14	.. 1	.. 246	.. 53*	.. 18.92
T. B. Stanier	11	.. 5	.. 113	.. 23*	.. 18.83
C. J. S. Webb	11	.. 4	.. 131	.. 41*	.. 18.71
R. M. Stanier	14	.. 1	.. 237	.. 63*	.. 18.23
S. A. U. Fakir	10	.. 3	.. 114	.. 35	.. 16.28
R. M. Mitchell	11	.. 1	.. 129	.. 32*	.. 12.90

Bowling

	Overs	Maidens	Runs	Wickets	Average
A. V. B. MacLaine	87.4	.. 19	.. 299	.. 21	.. 14.23
J. B. Rush	148.1	.. 26	.. 407	.. 27	.. 15.07
C. W. Grace	157.3	.. 31	.. 439	.. 24	.. 18.29
A. D. Dunningham	135	.. 22	.. 403	.. 15	.. 26.86

BISHOP'S STORTFORD COLLEGE

A young side, ably led by Thorogood and often inspired by their opening batsmen, Davies and Hickling, enjoyed a more successful season than in 1956. Hickling is developing into the best left-handed batsman the school has had since the war.

Played 10, Won 3, Lost 2, Drawn 5

Batting

	Innings	Not outs	Runs	Highest inns.	Average
T. L. Hickling..........	9	.. 2	.. 398	.. 90	.. 56.85
C. V. P. McDonald	7	.. 1	.. 184	.. 45	.. 30.66
W. J. Davies	8	.. 2	.. 165	.. 42	.. 27.50
J. S. Thorogood	7	.. 0	.. 151	.. 70	.. 21.57
J. H. M. Duke	7	.. 2	.. 103	.. 31	.. 20.60

Bowling

	Overs	Maidens	Runs	Wickets	Average
C. V. P. McDonald	137.5	.. 30	.. 322	.. 20	.. 16.10
J. S. Thorogood	127.1	.. 29	.. 389	.. 23	.. 16.91
J. H. M. Duke	75.2	.. 12	.. 242	.. 11	.. 22.00

BLOXHAM SCHOOL

Two of the Bloxham defeats followed declarations. The batting was good, especially that of two young players, Adey and Rodgers, who had a record partnership of 287 against the XL Club. The bowling, apart from Carter and Rodgers, was moderate and the catching at times deplorable.

Played 12, Won 1, Lost 6, Drawn 5

Batting

	Innings	Not outs	Runs	Highest inns.	Average
D. N. Adey	14	.. 1	.. 420	.. 183*	.. 32.30
C. C. W. Rodgers	13	.. 3	.. 282	.. 101*	.. 28.20
J. S. Carter	13	.. 3	.. 142	.. 45	.. 14.20
A. J. Lindsay	10	.. 0	.. 131	.. 46	.. 13.10

Bowling

	Overs		Maidens		Runs		Wickets		Average
J. S. Carter	119	..	23	..	401	..	23	..	17.43
C. C. W. Rodgers	91.1	..	12	..	265	..	15	..	17.66

BLUNDELL'S SCHOOL

A powerful batting side at Blundell's lost only to St. Luke's College. With Clarke and Tarrant scoring heavily there were four partnerships of over 100 during the season. In the later matches Harvey won his place in the side at the age of 15 and formed a splendid opening partnership with Tarrant. Though Taylor was effective with his leg-breaks the strength of the bowling did not match that of the batting.

Played 13, Won 5, Lost 1, Drawn 7

Batting

	Innings		Not outs		Runs		Highest inns.		Average
C. J. A. Clarke	13	..	2	..	511	..	135*	..	46.45
G. R. Harvey	7	..	1	..	275	..	78	..	45.83
P. D. Tarrant	14	..	1	..	593	..	185	..	45.61
R. A. W. Sharp	11	..	4	..	198	..	70*	..	28.28
A. R. Tinniswood	14	..	1	..	348	..	110	..	26.76
C. Mumford	11	..	2	..	197	..	41	..	21.88
F. J. Davis	10	..	3	..	113	..	32*	..	16.14

Bowling

	Overs		Maidens		Runs		Wickets		Average
D. V. Taylor	176.2	..	35	..	603	..	38	..	15.86
C. J. A. Clarke	175.4	..	40	..	464	..	26	..	17.84
F. J. Davis	99.1	..	23	..	285	..	15	..	19.00
R. G. Shore	140	..	31	..	401	..	12	..	33.41

BRADFIELD COLLEGE

Played 15, Won 3, Lost 2, Drawn 10

Batting

	Innings		Not outs		Runs		Highest inns.		Average
J. P. Allday	16	..	1	..	503	..	136*	..	33.53
P. J. Workman	16	..	1	..	469	..	140*	..	31.26
P. J. P. Eacersall	16	..	6	..	269	..	62*	..	26.90
H. A. S. Reid	8	..	1	..	187	..	55	..	26.71
J. H. George	11	..	1	..	201	..	59*	..	20.10
J. L. Davison	12	..	1	..	176	..	42	..	16.00
P. J. H. Daubney	13	..	1	..	173	..	33	..	14.44

Bowling

	Overs		Maidens		Runs		Wickets		Average
P. J. Workman	139.2	..	36	..	341	..	20	..	17.05
P. J. P. Eacersall	161.4	..	36	..	437	..	19	..	23.00
E. N. Thomas	286.5	..	71	..	771	..	32	..	24.09
P. J. H. Daubney	147.1	..	37	..	341	..	14	..	24.35

BRADFORD GRAMMAR SCHOOL

But for vital chances being missed by an otherwise fair bowling side the school team would have had a still better record. Gray, the outstanding batsman, and Tiffany gave the side many good starts.

Played 14, Won 7, Lost 3, Drawn 4

Batting

	Innings		Not outs		Runs		Highest inns.		Average
A. J. C. Gray	14	..	4	..	453	..	106*	..	45.30
E. Tiffany	14	..	2	..	217	..	43	..	18.08
†I. M. Hewitt	12	..	1	..	189	..	40	..	17.18
M. S. Throup	9	..	1	..	132	..	65	..	16.50
J. A. Schofield	12	..	3	..	143	..	50*	..	15.88

Bowling

	Overs	Maidens	Runs	Wickets	Average
P. A. Boddy	142	.. 38	.. 305	.. 34	.. 8.91
M. S. Throup	59.4	.. 14	.. 133	.. 13	.. 10.23
J. P. Bailey	147.4	.. 38	.. 338	.. 27	.. 12.51
I. M. Hewitt	121.4	.. 25	.. 241	.. 19	.. 12.68
R. A. Rowe	145	.. 49	.. 267	.. 21	.. 12.71

BRENTWOOD SCHOOL

Consistent and often enterprising batting was the feature of Brentwood's season. The bowling of a side well led by Ryan improved during the season, but the fielding was below the expected standard.

Played 15, Won 5, Lost 3, Drawn 7

Batting

	Innings	Not outs	Runs	Highest inns.	Average
M. A. Ries	7	.. 3	.. 113	.. 43*	.. 28.25
A. R. Wadsworth	9	.. 2	.. 191	.. 59	.. 27.28
B. L. G. Squirrell	13	.. 0	.. 325	.. 67	.. 25.00
J. N. Pawsey	11	.. 2	.. 207	.. 68	.. 23.00
†M. A. J. Ryan	12	.. 2	.. 193	.. 50*	.. 19.30
M. D. Clapham	11	.. 1	.. 165	.. 67*	.. 16.50
M. D. Thurgur	5	.. 0	.. 82	.. 41	.. 16.40
R. H. Parr	11	.. 0	.. 154	.. 42	.. 14.00

Bowling

	Overs	Maidens	Runs	Wickets	Average
A. C. Godfrey	155	.. 54	.. 334	.. 23	.. 14.52
R. W. Webber	110	.. 29	.. 299	.. 20	.. 14.95
M. D. Clapham	141	.. 32	.. 397	.. 25	.. 15.88
J. W. Hodgins	76	.. 10	.. 228	.. 13	.. 17.53
J. N. Pawsey	124	.. 37	.. 305	.. 15	.. 20.33
M. A. J. Ryan	65	.. 11	.. 260	.. 11	.. 23.63

BRIGHTON COLLEGE

The team failed to emulate the unbeaten eleven of 1956 by losing surprisingly to Hurstpierpoint and the Old Brightonians. The most remarkable game was with Christ's Hospital since 556 runs were scored in the day. Lewis, an aggressive left-hander, was again the leading batsman, and Pickering's off-spinners showed great promise.

Played 13, Won 7, Lost 2, Drawn 4

Batting

	Innings	Not outs	Runs	Highest inns.	Average
†R. W. Lewis	13	.. 3	.. 612	.. 114	.. 61.20
P. M. Lush	6	.. 1	.. 225	.. 71	.. 45.00
J. M. Morgan	13	.. 1	.. 372	.. 107*	.. 31.00
D. J. Pickering	13	.. 2	.. 297	.. 56*	.. 27.00
J. H. Smith	13	.. 2	.. 252	.. 64	.. 22.90
S. F. Grose	12	.. 2	.. 101	.. 22	.. 10.10

Bowling

	Overs	Maidens	Runs	Wickets	Average
D. J. Pickering	219.2	.. 39	.. 634	.. 45	.. 14.11
R. W. Lewis	139.3	.. 30	.. 381	.. 23	.. 16.56
D. J. Marshall	130.1	.. 28	.. 378	.. 19	.. 19.89

BRISTOL GRAMMAR SCHOOL

Their solid batting, particularly by Redwood and Sleigh, and the often devastating bowling of Brees brought the school notable successes.

Played 15, Won 8, Lost 3, Drawn 4

Batting

	Innings		Not outs		Runs		Highest inns.		Average
B. W. Redwood	12	..	3	..	244	..	63*	..	27.11
B. S. Sleigh	14	..	2	..	325	..	79	..	27.08
R. J. Burgin	10	..	4	..	120	..	31*	..	20.00
R. H. Brees	10	..	2	..	108	..	43	..	13.50
R. C. Tanner	12	..	0	..	161	..	43	..	13.41
N. J. Ellis	14	..	2	..	146	..	38	..	12.16

Bowling

	Overs		Maidens		Runs		Wickets		Average
R. H. Brees	187	..	55	..	409	..	53	..	7.70
B. W. Redwood	152	..	34	..	411	..	32	..	12.84
B. W. Padfield	132.1	..	38	..	342	..	22	..	15.54
R. J. Short	67	..	12	..	237	..	13	..	18.23

BRYANSTON SCHOOL

It was not until the middle of the term that Bryanston settled down. Although the batting was never reliable the bowling and fielding afterwards developed well and the team were well handled by Checksfield.

Played 15, Won 5, Lost 3, Drawn 7

Batting

	Innings		Not outs		Runs		Highest inns.		Average
†M. F. J. Checksfield	13	..	1	..	275	..	61	..	22.91
D. M. Ladd	14	..	2	..	257	..	45*	..	21.41
J. E. Goldsmith	13	..	1	..	227	..	65	..	18.91
C. J. Packard	13	..	5	..	134	..	39*	..	16.75
R. A. R. Burton	11	..	4	..	133	..	37*	..	16.14
J. R. Brock	11	..	3	..	117	..	38	..	14.62

Bowling

	Overs		Maidens		Runs		Wickets		Average
M. R. D. North	39.2	..	13	..	89	..	16	..	5.56
D. M. Ladd	136.2	..	34	..	355	..	27	..	13.14
J. R. Brock	223.1	..	54	..	542	..	36	..	15.05
D. C. Evans	158	..	44	..	386	..	24	..	16.08

CANFORD SCHOOL

Canford's season proved that batting alone cannot win matches when the bowling is weak. Outstanding in a strong batting side were Palin and Bown, a powerful striker who hit fourteen 6's for the side.

Played 12, Won 1, Lost 4, Drawn 7

Batting

	Innings		Not outs		Runs		Highest inns.		Average
†R. H. Palin	13	..	1	..	564	..	112	..	47.00
N. N. Bown	13	..	1	..	450	..	116	..	37.50
G. D. Lunn	13	..	0	..	305	..	72	..	23.46
A. T. Scrivener	13	..	2	..	229	..	71*	..	20.81
D. M. Hopkins	10	..	3	..	138	..	52	..	15.33
N. R. Aker	10	..	0	..	138	..	51	..	13.80

Bowling

	Overs		Maidens		Runs		Wickets		Average
N. N. Bown	193	..	49	..	487	..	22	..	22.13
W. R. Foster-Mitchell	86.2	..	19	..	228	..	10	..	22.80
R. H. Palin	103	..	21	..	296	..	11	..	26.90

CATERHAM SCHOOL

Among the ingredients which went into the making of a successful season were the captaincy and batting of Harper and excellent fielding.

Played 13, Won 5, Lost 2, Drawn 6

Batting

	Innings		Not outs		Runs		Highest inns.		Average
†N. J. Harper	13	..	5	..	489	..	77*	..	61.12
G. M. Bayly	13	..	2	..	367	..	75*	..	33.36
D. Boston	12	..	5	..	159	..	60*	..	22.71
B. C. Matthews	10	..	5	..	100	..	53*	..	20.00
C. R. Thompson	12	..	0	..	170	..	32	..	14.16

Bowling

	Overs		Maidens		Runs		Wickets		Average
A. C. Gliddon	111.5	..	28	..	309	..	34	..	9.08
J. M. Kelly	112.5	..	26	..	353	..	33	..	10.69
R. Bull	119.5	..	34	..	319	..	27	..	11.82

CHARTERHOUSE SCHOOL

The main strength during a successful season lay in the all-round form of Allom, who bowled accurately at medium pace, was a powerful stroke-player and a fine slip-field. Comer and Sutton were also successful batsmen, and 15-year-old Craig showed much promise. The fielding was good and Levy was a wicket-keeper of great possibilities.

Played 14, Won 6, Lost 2, Drawn 6

Batting

	Innings		Not outs		Runs		Highest inns.		Average
E. J. Craig	7	..	1	..	213	..	63*	..	35.50
A. T. C. Allom	15	..	3	..	420	..	87	..	35.00
†G. E. F. Gross	8	..	6	..	64	..	27	..	32.00
D. D. S. Comer	16	..	1	..	474	..	92	..	31.60
R. J. Sutton	16	..	2	..	415	..	92	..	29.64
A. A. H. White	14	..	3	..	260	..	54*	..	23.63
M. E. I. A. Wells	12	..	2	..	215	..	50	..	21.50
R. H. Sclater	13	..	1	..	222	..	52	..	18.50
J. C. W. Murray	12	..	5	..	105	..	28*	..	15.00

Bowling

	Overs		Maidens		Runs		Wickets		Average
J. C. W. Murray	160	..	28	..	456	..	31	..	14.70
A. T. C. Allom	216.3	..	48	..	589	..	34	..	17.32
G. E. F. Gross	153.1	..	38	..	465	..	27	..	17.22
J. J. Ullman	98.4	..	23	..	304	..	16	..	19.00

CHELTENHAM COLLEGE

Against club sides the form of the Cheltenham team was consistently good, but the record was marred by disappointing displays in three away school matches. Stutchbury, the leading scorer, was a fine stroke-player, and Prain a particularly promising young batsman. Benke, the captain, who took 48 wickets with off-breaks, was prominent in a good fielding side whose throwing was excellent.

Played 13, Won 4, Lost 6. Drawn 3

Batting

	Innings		Not outs		Runs		Highest inns.		Average
T. G. Lynch-Staunton ..	10	..	6	..	214	..	58*	..	53.50
P. W. F. Stutchbury.....	16	..	0	..	521	..	89	..	32.56
R. C. H. Terdre........	16	..	2	..	443	..	65	..	31.64
G. L. Prain	16	..	2	..	352	..	59	..	25.14
C. M. Brain	16	..	0	..	250	..	41	..	15.62
C. R. Purvis	16	..	2	..	213	..	36*	..	15.21
R. K. O. Carey.........	15	..	1	..	206	..	39*	..	14.71
C. G. Hoole	12	..	2	..	101	..	22	..	10.10

Bowling

	Overs		Maidens		Runs		Wickets		Average
T. G. Lynch-Staunton ..	114.3	..	27	..	267	..	20	..	13.35
†A. F. Benke...........	247	..	50	..	720	..	48	..	15.00
B. Lowe	186.5	..	31	..	545	..	28	..	19.46
C. G. Hoole	150	..	23	..	479	..	18	..	26.61

CHIGWELL SCHOOL

Fielding was the best feature of the Chigwell season. Well as their captain, Joslin, played as an all-rounder, the batting often failed to take advantage of favourable conditions, and the bowling was seldom dangerous.

Played 14, Won 5, Lost 6, Drawn 3

Batting

	Innings		Not outs		Runs		Highest inns.		Average
†C. P. Joslin	14	..	5	..	283	..	62	..	31.44
T. J. Norris	14	..	2	..	247	..	60	..	25.83
E. P. R. Hutton	14	..	0	..	269	..	43	..	19.21
B. D. Wood	13	..	6	..	128	..	22	..	18.28
S. A. Brewer	14	..	0	..	225	..	52	..	16.07

Bowling

	Overs		Maidens		Runs		Wickets		Average
C. P. Joslin	74	..	15	..	239	..	20	..	11.95
D. P. Sweet	43.5	..	6	..	133	..	10	..	13.30
J. S. Collecott	58.4	..	17	..	148	..	11	..	13.45
K. W. Burnell	209.3	..	53	..	504	..	26	..	19.38
A. M. Smith	161	..	27	..	448	..	17	..	26.35

CHRIST'S HOSPITAL

The captaincy of Thompson and splendid fielding were the main factors in the team's successful season.

Played 13, Won 8, Lost 4, Drawn 1

Batting

	Innings		Not outs		Runs		Highest inns.		Average
D. A. G. Simon	13	..	2	..	355	..	142*	..	32.27
†N. P. Thompson	12	..	1	..	348	..	57*	..	31.63
J. C. Haylock	13	..	1	..	285	..	65	..	23.75
M. P. Berry	10	..	1	..	196	..	51*	..	21.77
T. C. Phillips	13	..	0	..	256	..	68	..	19.69
I. P. Morton	12	..	2	..	172	..	46	..	17.20

Bowling

	Overs		Maidens		Runs		Wickets		Average
J. C. Haylock	142.5	..	69	..	446	..	43	..	10.37
D. Farrar.............	85	..	18	..	253	..	18	..	14.05
G. C. Emmans	108	..	26	..	330	..	22	..	15.00
N. P. Thompson	144.4	..	45	..	418	..	21	..	19.90

CITY OF LONDON SCHOOL

Good fielding, steady bowling and inconsistent batting added up to an average season. Most encouraging was the batting of Brearley, who scored over 400 runs at the age of 15.

Played 16, Won 6, Lost 6, Drawn 4

Batting

	Innings	Not outs	Runs	Highest inns.	Average
J. M. Brearley..........	16	.. 3	.. 412	.. 73*	.. 31.69
A. J. Bowtell	9	.. 2	.. 134	.. 43*	.. 19.14
T. S. Lacamp	11	.. 5	.. 113	.. 31	.. 18.82
D. J. Lidgate	11	.. 2	.. 164	.. 45*	.. 18.22
J. W. B. Peer	13	.. 2	.. 172	.. 45*	.. 15.63
†G. B. Green	16	.. 0	.. 239	.. 44	.. 14.93
A. D. Simpson	13	.. 2	.. 156	.. 56*	.. 14.18

Bowling

	Overs	Maidens	Runs	Wickets	Average
J. Leech	162.3	.. 36	.. 437	.. 33	.. 13.24
J. W. B. Peer	133.1	.. 28	.. 490	.. 26	.. 18.84
T. S. Lacamp	174.2	.. 34	.. 444	.. 21	.. 21.14

CLIFTON COLLEGE

After losing their first five matches, four of them narrowly, Clifton settled down to become probably their best side for several years, with wins against Marlborough, Cheltenham and Tonbridge. Their strength lay in fielding, which greatly helped an accurate slow bowling attack, of which Mathias was the most successful with leg-breaks. Bernard, who captained the side well, was outstanding with the bat and received good support.

Played 15, Won 5, Lost 5, Drawn 5

Batting

	Innings	Not outs	Runs	Highest inns.	Average
†J. R. Bernard	16	.. 0	.. 641	.. 104	.. 40.06
M. F. King	13	.. 1	.. 343	.. 72	.. 28.58
J. M. Cleese	10	.. 6	.. 91	.. 18*	.. 22.75
G. I. Arthurs	14	.. 4	.. 224	.. 57	.. 22.40
C. H. Pickwoad	16	.. 1	.. 308	.. 51	.. 20.53
R. W. Mathias	16	.. 5	.. 176	.. 47	.. 16.00
D. J. Carter	16	.. 0	.. 209	.. 34	.. 13.06
J. Cottrell	13	.. 2	.. 129	.. 23	.. 11.72
C. J. U. Coates	16	.. 1	.. 175	.. 19	.. 11.66

Bowling

	Overs	Maidens	Runs	Wickets	Average
R. W. Mathias	175	.. 46	.. 398	.. 34	.. 11.70
G. I. Arthurs	114	.. 36	.. 256	.. 21	.. 12.19
J. M. Cleese	65	.. 17	.. 171	.. 13	.. 13.15
M. H. Filer	99	.. 29	.. 253	.. 19	.. 13.31
J. R. Bernard	157	.. 46	.. 343	.. 19	.. 18.05
J. Cottrell	173	.. 34	.. 495	.. 26	.. 19.03

CRANBROOK SCHOOL

Cranbrook's team was better than the results, several of which were close, would suggest. If the batting was unreliable with the exception of Fagg, the bowlers allowed no opponents a total of 200 and Barham, a young leg-spinner, did particularly well.

Played 14, Won 2, Lost 5, Drawn 7

Batting

	Innings		Not outs		Runs		Highest inns.		Average
M. T. Fagg	15	..	3	..	472	..	68	..	39.33
K. G. D. Batchelor	15	..	1	..	284	..	80	..	20.28
M. C. Porter	14	..	1	..	190	..	29	..	14.61
J. G. Barham	15	..	0	..	217	..	43	..	14.46
†J. Piper	14	..	1	..	167	..	51	..	12.84
R. V. Harding	15	..	0	..	180	..	42	..	12.00

Bowling

	Overs		Maidens		Runs		Wickets		Average
J. G. Barham	218.5	..	75	..	511	..	39	..	13.10
R. L. S. Clark	76	..	22	..	179	..	13	..	13.76
J. F. Gunn	144.1	..	52	..	280	..	18	..	15.55
M. C. Porter	204.3	..	67	..	383	..	23	..	16.65
J. Piper	124.1	..	24	..	356	..	14	..	25.42

CRANLEIGH SCHOOL

Considering Cranleigh had six old Colours the season proved disappointing with only one win. Overall, the batting lacked determination and the opening bowlers, Hutchins and Hunter, well as they performed, were overworked in an attack lacking a spinner. Missed catches proved costly.

Played 13, Won 1, Lost 5, Drawn 7

Batting

	Innings		Not outs		Runs		Highest inns.		Average
†J. W. McDermott	14	..	1	..	554	..	114*	..	42.61
B. D. Hickman	14	..	1	..	416	..	98*	..	32.00
J. Hutchins	14	..	1	..	271	..	43	..	20.84
R. G. S. Sykes	14	..	0	..	222	..	45	..	15.85
I. C. Haydon	9	..	0	..	106	..	30	..	11.77
K. H. Richmond	9	..	0	..	106	..	23	..	11.77
V. G. Ward	12	..	2	..	114	..	34	..	11.40

Bowling

	Overs		Maidens		Runs		Wickets		Average
J. Hutchins	225	..	45	..	715	..	38	..	18.81
J. W. McDermott	131	..	15	..	482	..	22	..	21.90
N. J. F. Hunter	201	..	36	..	606	..	26	..	23.30

CULFORD SCHOOL

Played 16, Won 5, Lost 6, Drawn 5

Batting

	Innings		Not outs		Runs		Highest inns.		Average
†J. M. Fisher	16	..	3	..	406	..	57	..	31.23
D. E. Goodchild	13	..	3	..	200	..	35	..	20.00
B. O. Adesigbin	13	..	4	..	168	..	27	..	18.66

Bowling

	Overs		Maidens		Runs		Wickets		Average
G. H. Hazell	139.1	..	23	..	346	..	27	..	12.80
C. M. Pettet	231.1	..	67	..	592	..	42	..	14.09

DEAN CLOSE SCHOOL

Inconsistent batting accounted for a moderate record at Dean Close. The side had three good bowlers, and Knight, who headed the averages in his fourth season, should go far as an off-spinner.

Played 12, Won 3, Lost 4, Drawn 5

Batting

	Innings		Not outs		Runs		Highest inns.		Average
R. L. Johns	12	..	1	..	290	..	104*	..	26.36
R. M. McMahon	10	..	3	..	168	..	52*	..	24.00
R. I. Ireland	12	..	0	..	272	..	95	..	22.66
J. P. Sedgwick	12	..	2	..	180	..	29	..	18.00
†P. H. Knight	10	..	1	..	148	..	79	..	16.44
A. S. Elliott	12	..	2	..	143	..	39	..	14.30

Bowling

	Overs		Maidens		Runs		Wickets		Average
P. H. Knight	165	..	47	..	460	..	37	..	12.43
C. E. N. Blake	153	..	41	..	407	..	22	..	18.50
V. J. Walters	77	..	22	..	276	..	12	..	23.00

DENSTONE COLLEGE

A young inexperienced side contained some promising batsmen but the bowling was weak. Barnes kept wicket well.

Played 11, Won 2, Lost 2, Drawn 7

Batting

	Innings		Not outs		Runs		Highest inns.		Average
R. H. Lees	11	..	5	..	238	..	71*	..	39.66
H. C. Illingworth	10	..	1	..	247	..	58	..	27.44
†T. H. Peake	11	..	0	..	235	..	86	..	21.36
P. J. Hoddell	10	..	1	..	176	..	70	..	19.55
J. L. Foster	10	..	0	..	182	..	45	..	18.20
T. M. Melrose	10	..	1	..	125	..	37	..	13.88

Bowling

	Overs		Maidens		Runs		Wickets		Average
J. C. Standerwick	138	..	33	..	372	..	22	..	16.90

DOUAI SCHOOL

Douai went through their season unbeaten. They had an outstanding batsman in their captain, Segal, and he was also the leading bowler, being well supported by his fellow-opener Horgan and John, a slow left-hander.

Played 12, Won 6, Lost 0, Drawn 6

Batting

	Innings		Not outs		Runs		Highest inns.		Average
†C. R. Segal	12	..	1	..	323	..	76	..	29.36
M. J. Horgan	11	..	0	..	164	..	42	..	14.90
P. D. Filmer	11	..	0	..	161	..	45	..	14.63
C. Allanson	12	..	1	..	151	..	33	..	13.72

Bowling

	Overs		Maidens		Runs		Wickets		Average
C. A. John	80.5	..	9	..	209	..	26	..	8.03
C. R. Segal	164.5	..	50	..	389	..	45	..	8.64
M. J. Horgan	127	..	33	..	383	..	24	..	15.95

DOVER COLLEGE

Played 15, Won 6, Lost 3, Drawn 6

Batting

	Innings		Not outs		Runs		Highest inns.		Average
J. R. A. Widgery	15	..	1	..	302	..	48	..	21.57
G. T. Rouse	13	..	5	..	137	..	31	..	17.12
R. P. King	15	..	0	..	255	..	85	..	17.00
A. J. Kilbee	15	..	0	..	215	..	71	..	14.33
M. J. Otway	15	..	0	..	208	..	65	..	13.86

Bowling

	Overs	Maidens	Runs	Wickets	Average
D. J. Smith	242.1	61	655	54	12.12
C. J. Clare	46.3	12	156	12	13.00
J. R. A. Widgery	304.5	90	677	46	14.71
M. J. Otway	112	28	321	18	17.83

DOWNSIDE SCHOOL

In one of their most successful years Downside's only defeat was by one wicket in the last over of the game. The leading batsman, Kavanagh, passed 50 five times and twice went on beyond 100, while the attacking batting of their captain, Chignell, set the side a splendid example. The three leading bowlers, Pearson who is fast, and spinners Sadler and Fletcher, were all aged 15. The fielding was good.

Played 12, Won 8, Lost 1, Drawn 3

Batting

	Innings	Not outs	Runs	Highest inns.	Average
P. A. Kavanagh	13	1	581	119	48.41
T. Redman	15	3	310	72*	25.83
†A. H. Chignell	15	1	345	68	24.64
W. J. C. Roberts	13	1	288	53	24.00
J. B. Bourke	10	4	137	70*	22.83
A. J. MacKenzie	12	3	155	44*	17.22

Bowling

	Overs	Maidens	Runs	Wickets	Average
A. J. G. Pearson	186.5	59	409	38	10.76
R. J. Sadler	158.2	26	517	38	13.60
C. A. Fletcher	141.4	23	418	27	15.48
A. H. Chignell	57.5	14	210	11	19.09

DULWICH COLLEGE

In spite of having a strong batting side, nine of their innings being ended by declarations, lack of pace bowling kept Dulwich from success. Mayatt led his side well, Soldan batted attractively and Shirley played confidently in his first full season.

Played 15, Won 3, Lost 3, Drawn 9

Batting

	Innings	Not outs	Runs	Highest inns.	Average
J. R. Soldan	15	3	515	88*	42.91
D. A. Shirley	15	1	589	127*	42.07
P. Simmonds	14	1	376	69	28.92
†P. H. Mayatt	15	0	406	90	27.06
R. M. Trembath	10	4	110	35	18.33

Bowling

	Overs	Maidens	Runs	Wickets	Average
B. G. Rogers	269.1	63	668	43	15.53
M. Kirkman	163.5	19	517	28	18.46

EASTBOURNE COLLEGE

Played 13, Won 3, Lost 4, Drawn 6

Batting

	Innings	Not outs	Runs	Highest inns.	Average
T. D. Wainwright	14	2	460	95	39.33
C. B. G. Masefield	14	1	414	108	31.84
P. G. Parsons	13	0	308	53	23.69
R. Gedney	14	1	303	78	23.30
M. S. C. Hill	12	4	152	40*	19.00
G. E. W. Bowyer	13	0	197	48	15.15
T. T. Laycock	14	0	141	37	10.07

Bowling:

	Overs		Maidens		Runs		Wickets		Average
P. J. Colbourne	247	..	60	..	587	..	32	..	18.34
M. Walter	204.3	..	53	..	470	..	25	..	18.80
J. M. E. Wilmot	166.5	..	71	..	421	..	22	..	19.13
†A. J .G. Glossop	168	..	33	..	461	..	23	..	20.04

THE EDINBURGH ACADEMY

The Edinburgh Academy had a successful season. Most of the side could make runs, six bowlers shared the wickets, and the fielding was safe. Wins were recorded over Fettes, Loretto, Strathallan and Watson's, and each of the defeats was by a narrow margin—seven runs by Glenalmond and two wickets, following a declaration, by a club side. The centenary match with Merchiston was unfortunately ruined by rain. This, the oldest inter-school match in Scotland, has been a regular fixture since 1857. For some years it was played twice each season and the number of matches which have taken place is 122. Of these the Academy have won 50, Merchiston 41, and 31 have been drawn.

Played 13, Won 7, Lost 2, Drawn 4

Batting

	Innings		Not outs		Runs		Highest inns.		Average
P. J. Burnet	15	..	2	..	489	..	85	..	37.61
M. H. Bond	14	..	2	..	357	..	66*	..	29.75
†D. M. Henderson......	12	..	1	..	282	..	74*	..	25.63
R. Mathieson	14	..	1	..	310	..	56	..	23.84

Bowling

	Overs		Maidens		Runs		Wickets		Average
D. B. Gillan	90	..	27	..	168	..	16	..	10.50
D. J. L. Proudlock......	133	..	30	..	337	..	23	..	14.65
D. M. Henderson.......	162	..	44	..	355	..	23	..	15.43
K. L. G. Sinclair	131	..	18	..	421	..	26	..	16.19
J. E. N. Harris	117	..	20	..	332	..	19	..	17.47

ELTHAM COLLEGE

Played 14, Won 3, Lost 5, Drawn 6

Batting

	Innings		Not outs		Runs		Highest inns.		Average
†I. R. Gillham	13	..	3	..	433	..	72*	..	43.30
J. H. Bradnock	12	..	1	..	305	..	103*	..	27.72
D. W. Hart	9	..	0	..	138	..	46	..	15.33
K. Green	11	..	0	..	112	..	30	..	10.18

Bowling

	Overs		Maidens		Runs		Wickets		Average
E. G. Moore	130	..	45	..	239	..	26	..	9.19
A. J. H. Ruffle	49.2	..	20	..	122	..	11	..	11.09
N. J. Martin	138.1	..	31	..	338	..	28	..	12.07
D. J. Norris	131	..	38	..	277	..	20	..	13.85

EPSOM COLLEGE

Epsom depended greatly on the all-round form of Jinnah, who was outstanding both as batsman and bowler. Though the left-handed Jaques supported him well the batting generally was not good enough.

Played 11, Won 4, Lost 4, Drawn 3

Batting

	Innings		Not outs		Runs		Highest inns.		Average
A. H. Jinnah	12	..	3	..	590	..	147*	..	65.56
C. T. C. Jaques	12	..	3	..	388	..	76*	..	43.11
M. C. Ribeiro	13	..	1	..	243	..	49	..	20.25
N. B. Merlin	11	..	4	..	127	..	50*	..	18.14

Bowling

	Overs		Maidens		Runs		Wickets		Average
A. H. Jinnah	173	..	51	..	402	..	38	..	10.57
C. T. C. Jaques	92	..	18	..	274	..	15	..	18.26
N. B. Merlin	192	..	60	..	445	..	24	..	18.54
M. R. B. Clarke	165	..	35	..	429	..	22	..	19.50

ETON COLLEGE

An accident on June 7 deprived Eton of their captain and outstanding cricketer, H. C. Blofeld. E. J. Lane-Fox took over the captaincy and J. Baskervyle-Glegg kept wicket respectably well. But Blofeld's loss affected the team's morale in June. The batting was strong, and Clegg made a notable advance as an opener to support Lane-Fox, while Burrows, Leonard and Baring all played usefully. The bowling depended too much on the fast-medium out-swingers of Scott, and the off-spin of the 15-year-old Fellowes. The fielding was good, Dunning, Burrows, Ayer and Goodier being outstanding.

Played 15, Won 3, Lost 6, Drawn 6

Batting

	Innings		Not outs		Runs		Highest inns.		Average
†E. J. Lane-Fox	17	..	1	..	594	..	102	..	37.12
W. G. A. Clegg	16	..	0	..	502	..	86	..	31.37
A. R. Burrows	15	..	4	..	344	..	68*	..	31.27
J. W. Leonard	15	..	2	..	326	..	45*	..	25.07
E. J. R. Scott	9	..	3	..	108	..	26	..	18.00
R. Fellowes	13	..	5	..	142	..	28	..	17.75
M. L. Dunning	13	..	4	..	148	..	24*	..	16.44
J. Baskervyle-Glegg	14	..	1	..	192	..	40	..	14.70

Bowling

	Overs		Maidens		Runs		Wickets		Average
E. J. R. Scott	219	..	43	..	618	..	32	..	19.31
A. R. B. Burrows	88	..	22	..	203	..	10	..	20.30
R. Fellowes	232	..	59	..	766	..	33	..	23.21
E. J. Lane-Fox	155	..	38	..	426	..	15	..	28.40

EXETER SCHOOL

Played 13, Won 6, Lost 4, Drawn 3

Batting

	Innings		Not outs		Runs		Highest inns.		Average
†R. R. Cockroft	13	..	3	..	408	..	87*	..	40.80
M. J. C. Tozer	13	..	0	..	255	..	51	..	19.61
D. I. Yeabsley	12	..	4	..	143	..	56*	..	17.87
J. S. Veryard	13	..	1	..	168	..	65	..	14.00

Bowling

	Overs		Maidens		Runs		Wickets		Average
D. I. Yeabsley	187.5	..	42	..	451	..	52	..	8.67
M. J. Tozer	83	..	16	..	269	..	23	..	11.69
D. Westcott	45	..	10	..	159	..	11	..	14.45
R. J. P. Gray	133.3	..	33	..	289	..	19	..	15.21

FELSTED SCHOOL

Although beaten three times the school side was again good. There was plenty of batting, even though Luckin did not quite maintain his great form of 1956, and the team had two admirably persistent bowlers, the opener Ball and Higgins with his left-arm spinners.

Played 13, Won 5, Lost 3, Drawn 5

Batting

	Innings		Not outs		Runs		Highest inns.		Average
S. R. Walters	14	..	1	..	607	..	134*	..	46.69
R. A. G. Luckin........	14	..	1	..	547	..	87	..	42.07
R. L. Tyrrell	12	..	3	..	354	..	102*	..	39.33
S. D. Culling	14	..	0	..	454	..	72	..	32.42
A. Pickard	11	..	3	..	161	..	56	..	20.12
†A. T. P. Higgins	13	..	0	..	226	..	53	..	17.38

Bowling

	Overs		Maidens		Runs		Wickets		Average
D. W. Ball	206.1	..	62	..	546	..	38	..	14.36
A. T. P. Higgins	215.1	..	52	..	627	..	37	..	16.94
S. C. S. Beresford	59.1	..	15	..	196	..	10	..	19.60
R. A. G. Luckin........	64.4	..	7	..	272	..	11	..	24.72
S. D. Culling...........	178.3	..	48	..	542	..	17	..	31.88

FETTES COLLEGE

The school side achieved much more than had been expected, and for that much of the credit belonged to the captain, Hoare, both as leader and player, while Bain proved an outstandingly successful new-ball bowler.

Played 16, *Won* 6, *Lost* 3, *Drawn* 7

Batting

	Innings		Not outs		Runs		Highest inns.		Average
†R. J. B. Hoare	18	..	2	..	483	..	64	..	30.18
I. M. S. Graham	17	..	3	..	363	..	54	..	25.92
C. G. Hamilton	18	..	1	..	314	..	104	..	18.47
S. Dakers.............	14	..	3	..	200	..	41*	..	18.18
J. A. P. Shackleton	14	..	0	..	254	..	73	..	18.14
B. O. Lloyd	16	..	4	..	201	..	51*	..	16.75
J. A. B. Armit	13	..	3	..	101	..	34	..	10.10

Bowling

	Overs		Maidens		Runs		Wickets		Average
A. W. M. Bain	284.2	..	82	..	564	..	50	..	11.28
R. J. B. Hoare	37.5	..	2	..	160	..	10	..	16.00
R. C. Roy	174.3	..	36	..	537	..	32	..	16.78
J. A. B. Armit	196.4	..	57	..	386	..	23	..	16.78
J. A. P. Shackleton	62	..	13	..	178	..	10	..	17.80

FOREST SCHOOL

Batting and bowling honours were equally shared, and the fielding was good without being outstanding. The average runs (26 per wicket) was better than the average of opponents, which was a fair reflection of the team's standard. Saady completed three good seasons of captaincy.

Played 13, *Won* 5, *Lost* 4, *Drawn* 4

Batting

	Innings		Not outs		Runs		Highest inns.		Average
M. H. W. Rogers	12	..	2	..	334	..	66*	..	33.40
G. Leleu	14	..	1	..	344	..	52	..	26.46
†D. J. Saady	11	..	3	..	200	..	63	..	25.00
D. Wilson	13	..	0	..	319	..	76	..	24.53
C. J. Foster	12	..	1	..	264	..	83	..	24.00
D. R. Peacock	10	..	2	..	112	..	45*	..	14.00

Bowling

	Overs		Maidens		Runs		Wickets		Average
M. H. W. Rogers	138	..	44	..	310	..	26	..	11.92
A. D. Chandler	124.3	..	31	..	250	..	18	..	13.89
D. Wilson	122.5	..	35	..	301	..	21	..	14.33
R. W. G. Banks	116.4	..	35	..	297	..	20	..	14.85

FRAMLINGHAM COLLEGE

Too much was thrust on bowlers Larter and Turnbull. Larter bowled fast and well and made the most of his 6 ft. 4 ins. They deserved better support from the batsmen.

Played 14, Won 6, Lost 6, Drawn 2

Batting

	Innings	Not outs	Runs	Highest inns.	Average
A. W. Hancock	14	.. 1	.. 339	.. 71	.. 26.07
N. H. Porter	13	.. 3	.. 194	.. 48	.. 19.40
†J. Iliffe	15	.. 1	.. 227	.. 44	.. 16.21
A. G. Wright	15	.. 0	.. 229	.. 47	.. 15.26
M. A. G. Spencer	14	.. 0	.. 182	.. 46	.. 13.00

Bowling

	Overs	Maidens	Runs	Wickets	Average
J. D. F. Larter	242.4	.. 75	.. 495	.. 52	.. 9.51
D. L. Turnbull	211.4	.. 51	.. 533	.. 41	.. 13.00

GEORGE HERIOT'S SCHOOL

Played 15, Won 7, Lost 1, Drawn 7

Batting

	Innings	Not outs	Runs	Highest inns.	Average
E. H. Tainsh	15	.. 0	.. 495	.. 70	.. 33.00
H. K. More	15	.. 2	.. 349	.. 75*	.. 26.84
†G. F. Goddard	15	.. 2	.. 283	.. 77	.. 21.76
C. W. Ford	12	.. 2	.. 136	.. 28	.. 13.60
J. A. G. Fiddes	11	.. 2	.. 108	.. 34	.. 12.00
W. L. McClure	9	.. 2	.. 81	.. 24*	.. 11.57

Bowling

	Overs	Maidens	Runs	Wickets	Average
G. F. Goddard	226.4	.. 84	.. 339	.. 54	.. 6.27
J. R. O'Malley	59.7	.. 18	.. 98	.. 15	.. 6.53
R. R. Sanders	124	.. 28	.. 252	.. 19	.. 13.26
H. K. More	75.4	.. 10	.. 149	.. 11	.. 13.54

GEORGE WATSON'S COLLEGE

Played 15, Won 3, Lost 9, Drawn 3

Batting

	Innings	Not outs	Runs	Highest inns.	Average
P. McLaren	11	.. 2	.. 215	.. 74	.. 23.88
S. R. Murray	14	.. 1	.. 267	.. 42	.. 20.53
†I. S. Sangster	13	.. 0	.. 224	.. 47	.. 17.23
R. M. Bain	12	.. 1	.. 115	.. 28	.. 10.45

Bowling

	Innings	Not outs	Runs	Highest inns.	Average
M. T. R. Smith	37	.. 12	.. 115	.. 15	.. 7.66
S. R. Murray	145	.. 46	.. 279	.. 24	.. 11.62
W. I. Laing	194.3	.. 58	.. 492	.. 28	.. 17.57

GLASGOW ACADEMY

Played 13, Won 6, Lost 4, Drawn 3

Batting

	Innings	Not outs	Runs	Highest inns.	Average
†J. C. Henderson	12	.. 0	.. 284	.. 62	.. 23.66
D. Naismith	8	.. 1	.. 164	.. 35	.. 23.42
H. M. Jackson	9	.. 6	.. 124	.. 25	.. 41.33

Bowling

	Overs		Maidens		Runs		Wickets		Average
H. M. Jackson	138.5	..	42	..	347	..	28	..	12.39
J. D. Mackinlay	109.4	..	20	..	352	..	28	..	12.57
J. C. Henderson	74.6	..	9	..	335	..	20	..	16.75
M. Graham	142.5	..	31	..	349	..	20	..	17.45

GORDONSTOUN SCHOOL

In spite of batting failures the consistent medium-paced bowling of Innes and good fielding produced a good record at Gordonstoun.

Played 10, Won 7, Lost 2, Drawn 1

Batting

	Innings		Not outs		Runs		Highest inns.		Average
†J. A. F. Vallance	10	..	0	..	222	..	65	..	22.20
N. T. Otty	10	..	4	..	131	..	38*	..	21.83
S. MacDonald	10	..	0	..	188	..	47	..	18.80

Bowling

	Overs		Maidens		Runs		Wickets		Average
J. A. Innes	100.4	..	40	..	188	..	28	..	6.71
J. A. F. Vallance	66.3	..	9	..	201	..	22	..	9.13
J. J. F. Mungall	47	..	13	..	112	..	11	..	10.18

GRESHAM'S SCHOOL, HOLT

Played 13, Won 2, Lost 3, Drawn 8

Batting

	Innings		Not outs		Runs		Highest inns.		Average
P. C. Jones	13	..	0	..	437	..	75	..	33.61
M. P. M. Prentice	11	..	3	..	202	..	40	..	25.25
R. J. Barry	13	..	1	..	282	..	69	..	23.50
P. R. Bodington	10	..	3	..	164	..	59	..	23.42
A. C. K. Day	9	..	3	..	123	..	38*	..	20.50
H. J. Stevenson	8	..	1	..	143	..	45	..	20.42
G. C. S. Andrews	13	..	3	..	155	..	50*	..	15.50
N. E. Day	10	..	1	..	135	..	30*	..	15.00

Bowling

	Overs		Maidens		Runs		Wickets		Average
P. S. Salinson	79.3	..	9	..	283	..	16	..	17.68
R. J. Barry	118.5	..	7	..	489	..	25	..	19.54
P. C. Jones	160	..	30	..	477	..	19	..	25.10
C. R. Burrell	106	..	11	..	366	..	12	..	30.50

HABERDASHERS' ASKE'S SCHOOL

For the first time in many seasons the school enjoyed reliable batting, but an opening bowling weakness kept the side from genuine success. English was a promising young medium pacer, and late in the season the attack was strengthened when Scofield found his form with leg-breaks and googlies.

Played 14, Won 3, Lost 6, Drawn 5

Batting

	Innings		Not outs		Runs		Highest inns.		Average
N. H. Healey	13	..	3	..	225	..	50*	..	22.50
†I. D. Scofield	14	..	1	..	280	..	53	..	21.53
R. Purvis	11	..	0	..	208	..	44	..	18.90
J. Bustard	13	..	3	..	124	..	24	..	12.40
C. Bradford	14	..	2	..	132	..	32*	..	11.00

Bowling

	Overs	Maidens	Runs	Wickets	Average
D. English	98	30	226	17	13.29
T. R. Treadwell	91	21	204	14	14.57
I. D. Scofield	110	17	445	26	17.11
M. R. Hunt	99	23	263	13	20.23

HAILEYBURY AND I.S.C.

Not until their last game, against Cheltenham at Lord's, was an inter-school match lost. Previously Tonbridge, Bedford and Uppingham had been beaten in the course of a splendid season. The ingredients of success were the enthusiastic leadership of Lofting, the willingness of the batsmen to attack and an admirable fighting spirit. It was a team without any outstanding players whose fielding was always keen and their throwing above average.

Played 12, *Won* 5, *Lost* 2, *Drawn* 5

Batting

	Innings	Not outs	Runs	Highest inns.	Average
†J. G. Lofting	14	0	382	67	27.28
P. J. Parsons	15	1	342	61	24.42
A. G. Roberts	13	4	205	44*	22.77
D. Moeller	14	1	296	52	22.76
M. Higginbottom	6	0	119	51	19.83
I. N. Smith	13	2	198	52	18.00
D. A. Crichton	15	3	211	48*	17.58
C. J. Ledger	9	2	106	37	15.14
I. A. McDonald	12	1	152	51*	13.81

Bowling

	Overs	Maidens	Runs	Wickets	Average
C. J. Ledger	122.5	22	304	27	11.25
D. Moeller	79.4	25	194	14	13.85
I. N. Smith	134.1	40	322	22	14.63
A. G. Roberts	200	55	509	32	15.90

HARROW SCHOOL

For Harrow 1957 was a season of team building, complicated by lack of form of various old "flannels," and the side was a long time settling down. The batting possibilities were never quite fulfilled. Vargas, naturally a fine aggressive player, took a long time to get going after breaking a leg in the football season. Lockett compensated for lack of strokes by becoming sheet anchor in an inexperienced side. Nicholson looked a good player when on the attack on a fast wicket but had limitations of technique. Foster showed considerable promise and verve for the future. The bowling depended greatly upon Champniss's legbreaks and googlies but he never acquired accuracy.

Played 13, *Won* 2, *Lost* 4, *Drawn* 7

Batting

	Innings	Not outs	Runs	Highest inns.	Average
J. D. C. Vargas	15	1	461	101*	32.92
J. B. Lockett	14	3	342	71*	31.09
N. F. Nicholson	12	0	309	74	25.75
D. R. J. Foster	10	0	202	43	20.20
A. J. Anderson	9	0	171	39	19.00
†L. J. Champniss	14	0	252	66	18.00
A. B. Cable	15	2	175	42	13.46

Bowling

	Overs	Maidens	Runs	Wickets	Average
M. J. H. Weedon	224.3	46	593	31	19.12
L. J. Champniss	205.1	29	668	23	29.04
P. E. d'Abo	137	26	386	12	32.16
B. S. Raper	152.5	29	418	11	38.00

HEREFORD CATHEDRAL SCHOOL

Form in the first six matches was disappointing; but, thanks to the fine batting of Brown, and to an effective fast attack, the side gained confidence and won six of their last seven matches.

Played 13, Won 7, Lost 2, Drawn 4

Batting

	Innings		Not outs		Runs		Highest inns.		Average
†R. B. Brown	13	..	2	..	538	..	117	..	48.90
A. Howgate	13	..	1	..	243	..	62	..	20.25
P. R. Shepherd	12	..	0	..	199	..	39	..	16.58
J. S. Daybell	13	..	0	..	212	..	46	..	16.30

Bowling

	Overs		Maidens		Runs		Wickets		Average
A. Howgate	130.3	..	27	..	353	..	38	..	9.28
J. A. S. Duckenfield	102	..	32	..	187	..	18	..	10.38
R. A. Shepherd	111.5	..	20	..	331	..	24	..	13.79

HIGHGATE SCHOOL

After a good start Highgate were disappointing in inter-schools matches, though their defeats were by narrow margins. Drybrough was outstanding as batsman and also the best bowler, while Webster, son of the former Cambridge Blue and Middlesex batsman, was a promising medium-paced bowler. The season was notable for the splendid throwing in the field. Garner made superb catches, and Drybrough, Plummer and Holland were outstandingly good fielders.

Played 16, Won 6, Lost 7, Drawn 3

Batting

	Innings		Not outs		Runs		Highest inns.		Average
†C. D. Drybrough	15	..	6	..	706	..	156*	..	78.44
A. D. Izzard	14	..	0	..	244	..	58	..	17.42
D. W. Plummer	14	..	1	..	225	..	58*	..	17.30
R. P. Juniper	16	..	0	..	273	..	81	..	17.06
M. W. Webster	14	..	1	..	207	..	35	..	15.92
M. H. Wadsworth	14	..	1	..	200	..	57*	..	15.38
N. L. Hancock	11	..	1	..	138	..	46	..	13.80
C. J. S. Garner	13	..	2	..	148	..	22	..	13.45

Bowling

	Overs		Maidens		Runs		Wickets		Average
M. W. Webster	125	..	24	..	292	..	25	..	11.68
C. D. Drybrough	172	..	39	..	418	..	32	..	13.06
D. A. Holland	110.5	..	24	..	370	..	20	..	18.50
M. H. Wadsworth	132	..	33	..	308	..	16	..	19.25
N. L. Hancock	128.1	..	23	..	400	..	17	..	23.52

HURSTPIERPOINT COLLEGE

Hurstpierpoint had an improved season with a young side. The batting was generally more consistent than in recent years, and the opening bowlers, Pollock and Williams, were a very good pair, though the rest of the attack was thin.

Played 15, Won 4, Lost 8, Drawn 3

Batting

	Innings		Not outs		Runs		Highest inns.		Average
B. W. Berks	15	..	0	..	271	..	67	..	18.06
W. G. Pollock	14	..	1	..	230	..	62*	..	17.69
A. J. Bradford	15	..	0	..	233	..	54	..	15.53
A. J. Snow	15	..	1	..	204	..	42	..	14.57

Bowling

	Overs	Maidens	Runs	Wickets	Average
M. B. Williams	186	.. 38	.. 451	.. 41 ..	11.00
W. G. Pollock	220	.. 60	.. 569	.. 40 ..	14.22

IPSWICH SCHOOL

Ipswich owed their successes to all-round efforts rather than individual success, although Whitfield, an aggressive left-hander who played several times for Suffolk, enjoyed an outstanding season with the bat.

Played 13, *Won* 5, *Lost* 2, *Drawn* 6

Batting

	Innings	Not outs	Runs	Highest inns.	Average
†W. A. D. Whitfield	13	.. 4	.. 494	.. 152* ..	54.88
R. H. Hagger	12	.. 2	.. 172	.. 42* ..	17.20
D. R. D. Newell	13	.. 0	.. 215	.. 106 ..	16.53
P. A. Connell	13	.. 0	.. 209	.. 77 ..	16.07
R. P. B. Kemp	13	.. 0	.. 195	.. 48 ..	15.00
J. H. Cook	13	.. 1	.. 147	.. 42 ..	12.25

Bowling

	Overs	Maidens	Runs	Wickets	Average
J. G. Burgess	68.2	.. 13	.. 217	.. 18 ..	12.05
G. M. Pell	70.2	.. 21	.. 249	.. 17 ..	14.64
R. H. Hagger	98.2	.. 15	.. 334	.. 18 ..	18.55
R. P. B. Kemp	160	.. 47	.. 448	.. 24 ..	18.66
W. A. D. Whitfield	123	.. 19	.. 388	.. 17 ..	22.82

KELLY COLLEGE

Played 16, *Won* 6, *Lost* 6, *Drawn* 4

Batting

	Innings	Not outs	Runs	Highest inns.	Average
D. J. Codd	14	.. 2	.. 333	.. 90* ..	27.76
M. T. Whitworth	15	.. 2	.. 244	.. 55 ..	18.76
R. B. Warren	16	.. 1	.. 271	.. 74* ..	18.06
H. T. V. Penberthy	12	.. 2	.. 154	.. 34 ..	15.40

Bowling

	Overs	Maidens	Runs	Wickets	Average
J. S. M. Mitchell	184.3	.. 57	.. 376	.. 30 ..	12.53
E. D. Torrens	179.1	.. 34	.. 542	.. 41 ..	13.21

KING EDWARD'S SCHOOL, BIRMINGHAM

Played 18, *Won* 3, *Lost* 10, *Drawn* 5

Batting

	Innings	Not outs	Runs	Highest inns.	Average
G. E. Phillips	17	.. 0	.. 432	.. 67 ..	25.41
P. B. Rothwell	18	.. 0	.. 322	.. 63 ..	17.88
M. J. Disney	17	.. 0	.. 304	.. 85 ..	17.88
T. P. Lee	12	.. 2	.. 164	.. 50 ..	16.40
A. E. H. Hornig	18	.. 4	.. 188	.. 39 ..	13.42
†R. G. Dauncey	17	.. 3	.. 165	.. 40 ..	11.78
A. B. Clayton	12	.. 1	.. 126	.. 29 ..	11.45

Bowling

	Overs	Maidens	Runs	Wickets	Average
R. C. Spiers	116.4	.. 35	.. 364	.. 22 ..	16.54
A. E. H. Hornig	86.5	.. 14	.. 354	.. 21 ..	16.85
M. J. Disney	126.1	.. 35	.. 332	.. 19 ..	17.47
R. A. Green	71.3	.. 18	.. 204	.. 10 ..	20.40
R. G. Dauncey	136	.. 36	.. 414	.. 20 ..	20.70

KING EDWARD'S SCHOOL, STOURBRIDGE

Fast scoring enabled decisions to be reached in all but one game. A strong batting side, the spin bowling of J. M. Cockin and M. J. Clinton and good fielding contributed to an excellent record.

Played 16, Won 14, Lost 1, Drawn 1

Batting	Innings		Not outs		Runs		Highest inns.		Average
D. Sturman	14	..	4	..	308	..	67	..	30.80
R. E. Lloyd-Jones	16	..	3	..	377	..	79*	..	29.00
†J. M. Cockin..........	13	..	3	..	203	..	51*	..	20.30
A. J. Banbery	14	..	2	..	228	..	52	..	19.00
M. R. Swinnerton	11	..	1	..	150	..	41	..	15.00

Bowling	Overs		Maidens		Runs		Wickets		Average
M. J. Clinton	163.3	..	84	..	207	..	40	..	5.17
J. M. Cockin..........	157.3	..	47	..	314	..	55	..	5.70
M. R. Swinnerton	85	..	32	..	173	..	19	..	9.10
K. R. Adams	99	..	26	..	225	..	21	..	10.71

KING WILLIAM'S COLLEGE, ISLE OF MAN
Played 15, Won 5, Lost 7, Drawn 3

Batting	Innings		Not outs		Runs		Highest inns.		Average
M. Fitzhugh	9	..	0	..	140	..	96	..	15.55
W. Crowe	15	..	3	..	162	..	27	..	13.50
A. Bashforth	16	..	0	..	202	..	28	..	12.62
†H. A. Galbraith	16	..	0	..	186	..	34	..	11.62
T. J. Brennan	13	..	0	..	132	..	28	..	10.15

Bowling	Overs		Maidens		Runs		Wickets		Average
M. Wood..........	106.1	..	39	..	198	..	23	..	8.60
J. A. Wilde	116	..	28	..	276	..	29	..	9.51
A. H. Johnson	149.2	..	48	..	312	..	28	..	11.14
T. Dixon	70	..	12	..	220	..	11	..	20.00

KING'S COLLEGE, TAUNTON
Played 12, Won 3, Lost 6, Drawn 3

Batting	Innings		Not outs		Runs		Highest inns.		Average
†R. Osborn	16	..	5	..	260	..	68*	..	23.63
M. Prew..........	15	..	1	..	316	..	72	..	22.57
J. Carnegie	9	..	3	..	121	..	30	..	20.16
R. Taylor..........	16	..	3	..	242	..	86*	..	18.61
P. Twose	16	..	1	..	241	..	110*	..	16.06
W. Price..........	13	..	0	..	175	..	54	..	13.46
M. Fussell	14	..	2	..	148	..	31	..	12.33

Bowling	Overs		Maidens		Runs		Wickets		Average
R. Stoneman	97.5	..	8	..	371	..	27	..	13.74
D. Walters..........	141.3	..	22	..	448	..	27	..	16.59
P. Twose	182.1	..	33	..	577	..	33	..	17.48

KING'S SCHOOL, BRUTON

The team's strength lay in the bowling, a good opening attack by Tucker and Maffey being well supported by varied spin-bowling, particularly that of Pinco, who was perhaps the most promising off-spin bowler the School has had for years. The main burden of the batting was carried by Gifford and Maffey, a 14-year-old left-handed all-rounder.

Played 10, Won 5, Lost 3, Drawn 1, Abandoned 1

Batting

	Innings	Not outs	Runs	Highest inns.	Average
P. J. Maffey	7	3	139	45*	34.75
†J. A. Gifford	9	3	131	39	21.83
M. G. Read	10	1	184	38*	20.44

Bowling

	Overs	Maidens	Runs	Wickets	Average
D. R. Tucker	49	13	126	11	11.45
P. F. Canning	50	20	124	10	12.40
R. M. Pinco	108	24	335	24	13.95
P. J. Maffey	94	36	202	13	15.53

KINGS' SCHOOL, ELY

Played 15, Won 7, Lost 1, Drawn 7

Batting

	Innings	Not outs	Runs	Highest inns.	Average
†R. W. Clark	13	1	380	105*	31.66
D. J. Brewin	12	3	181	87*	20.11
P. D. Dunbar	9	3	107	36	17.83
R. J. Jessop	13	2	176	56*	16.00
R. Morris	12	2	131	26	13.10

Bowling

	Overs	Maidens	Runs	Wickets	Average
P. D. Dunbar	132	32	327	37	8.83
P. D. McClure	55	22	100	11	9.11
R. W. Clark	330	51	382	39	9.79

THE KING'S SCHOOL, MACCLESFIELD

With only one old Colour available, results were satisfactory, though several matches were lost through inconsistent batting after opponents had been dismissed for moderate totals. Barker had a good season as an all-rounder and afterwards played for Cheshire.

Played 17, Won 7, Lost 7, Drawn 3

Batting

	Innings	Not outs	Runs	Highest inns.	Average
†C. D. R. Barker	17	3	321	40	22.92
J. K. Belfield	17	0	264	58	15.52
M. L. T. Cooper	14	2	153	34	12.75
J. K. Arnold	15	2	159	50	12.23

Bowling

	Overs	Maidens	Runs	Wickets	Average
C. D. R. Barker	149.2	36	330	41	8.04
S. B. Bryning	159	28	486	41	11.85
M. Cole	122	22	368	31	11.87

KING'S SCHOOL, ROCHESTER

King's School, Rochester, were unbeaten by other schools, winning six and drawing two of the eight school matches. The batting of Reader, the captain, and Burren was impressive both by virtue of its power and consistence. Aided by alert, competent fielding, the bowlers, especially Spyer, a fast right-hander, were equal to their task. The wicket-keeping of Webster, the vice-captain, was often outstandingly good. Six old Colours remain as the nucleus of the 1958 side.

Played 12, Won 7, Lost 2, Drawn 3

Batting

	Innings	Not outs	Runs	Highest inns.	Average
†D. C. Reader	12	4	477	102*	59.63
C. Burren	12	1	341	99*	31.00
F. B. Melhuish	10	2	148	36*	18.50
J. P. Hughes	7	0	101	34	14.42
K. J. Webster	12	1	143	38	13.00
N. R. J. Funnell	12	2	121	32*	12.10

Bowling

	Overs	Maidens	Runs	Wickets	Average
R. C. Spyer	170	51	315	36	8.75
D. C. Reader	97	32	213	21	10.14
F. B. Melhuish	116.5	27	352	28	12.57

KINGSWOOD SCHOOL

Played 10, Won 5, Lost 4, Drawn 1

Batting

	Innings	Not outs	Runs	Highest inns.	Average
R. G. J. Hopkins	11	2	208	52	23.11
D. M. Eadie	11	2	152	30	16.88
A. G. P. Lang..........	11	0	153	41	13.90

Bowling

	Overs	Maidens	Runs	Wickets	Average
D. M. Eadie	80	14	237	21	11.28
†A. W. Fearn	151	44	338	22	15.36
A. J. Jarvis	104	38	248	15	16.53
D. J. Fornette	81.2	13	216	12	18.00

LANCING COLLEGE

Lancing's term was a triumph for the leading four batsmen. Together they made 2,429 runs and made them so fast that early declarations were the rule.

Played 15, Won 3, Lost 5, Drawn 7

Batting

	Innings	Not outs	Runs	Highest inns.	Average
G. J. Sharman	16	3	786	123*	60.46
†T. J. Goodwin	16	2	678	129*	47.42
J. W. Bridge	16	2	506	89*	36.14
N. H. S. Evans	15	1	479	99	34.21
C. J. Saunders	12	4	164	57	20.50
G. Davies	10	3	124	63*	17.71
G. C. Herbert	10	1	117	36	13.00

Bowling

	Overs	Maidens	Runs	Wickets	Average
T. J. Goodwin	214	45	587	23	25.52
G. J. Sharman	242	26	821	32	25.62
N. H. S. Evans	174	27	540	20	27.00
C. J. Hale	110	19	367	11	33.36

LEEDS GRAMMAR SCHOOL

Played 11, Won 3, Lost 4, Drawn 4

Batting

	Innings	Not outs	Runs	Highest inns.	Average
†J. D. Brooke	10	0	247	65	24.70
J. A. Windsor	8	2	105	26*	17.50
I. J. Matthews	9	0	141	49	15.66
J. I. Sleightholme	9	2	108	30	15.42
G. A. Chrispin	9	0	113	42	12.55

Bowling

	Overs		Maidens		Runs		Wickets		Average
J. A. Windsor	120.4	..	35	..	319	..	40	..	7.97
G. A. Chrispin	39	..	7	..	141	..	10	..	14.10
K. M. Roberts	87	..	13	..	320	..	22	..	14.54

THE LEYS SCHOOL

A side built round only two old Colours did particularly well in school matches with victories over Bedford, Felsted, St. Paul's, Bishop's Stortford, Gresham's and Wellingborough. Bousfield was the most mature bat, and Fairey, slow left-arm, was the best of the attack.

Played 14, *Won* 7, *Lost* 1, *Drawn* 6

Batting

	Innings		Not outs		Runs		Highest inns.		Average
Y. M. Munjee	5	..	1	..	152	..	82*	..	38.00
D. S. Bousfield	12	..	1	..	332	..	103	..	30.18
S. G. G. Benson	12	..	2	..	301	..	80	..	30.10
J. P. Pashley	14	..	2	..	291	..	51*	..	24.25
D. H. R. Fairey	13	..	1	..	263	..	68	..	21.91
S. B. Turner	10	..	2	..	167	..	49	..	20.87
P. G. R. Rigg	13	..	0	..	265	..	62	..	20.38
S. C. Amey	12	..	5	..	102	..	39	..	14.57
A. J. Leach	12	..	1	..	123	..	31	..	11.18

Bowling

	Overs		Maidens		Runs		Wickets		Average
Y. M. Munjee	48.3	..	7	..	139	..	11	..	12.63
D. H. R. Fairey	225.5	..	72	..	497	..	38	..	13.07
J. P. Pashley	160.3	..	47	..	492	..	30	..	16.40

LIVERPOOL COLLEGE

In spite of starting without a single old Colour, the College lost only one match by other than a narrow margin. McCullagh was a valuable all-rounder, and Turner a reliable batsman in difficult situations.

Played 9, *Won* 2, *Lost* 4, *Drawn* 3

Batting

	Innings		Not outs		Runs		Highest inns.		Average
D. M. Turner	9	..	1	..	176	..	56	..	22.00
R. A. McCullagh	9	..	1	..	160	..	60*	..	20.00
†J. R. Kerr	9	..	0	..	140	..	46	..	15.55

Bowling

	Overs		Maidens		Runs		Wickets		Average
R. A. McCullagh	143.4	..	27	..	387	..	29	..	13.34
D. Searle	144	..	32	..	332	..	23	..	14.43

LLANDOVERY COLLEGE

The team played well together and owed much to the captaincy of Bevan. The bowling was steady and better than results suggested, but the batting was uncertain.

Played 14, *Won* 6, *Lost* 6, *Drawn* 2

Batting

	Innings		Not outs		Runs		Highest inns.		Average
D. I. Gealy	10	..	2	..	261	..	52	..	32.62
C. B. Elliott	14	..	1	..	342	..	76*	..	26.30
D. N. Stimson	12	..	4	..	189	..	39*	..	23.62
R. J. Harris	14	..	0	..	244	..	44	..	17.42
†H. E. D. Bevan	13	..	0	..	199	..	41	..	15.30

Bowling

	Overs	Maidens	Runs	Wickets	Average
P. M. Davies	117.3	35	256	18	14.22
N. Arundel	172.5	36	465	25	18.60
H. E. D. Bevan	84	7	286	13	22.00
C. B. Elliott	154.2	36	412	18	22.88

LORETTO

During a successful inter-schools season the bowling was carried by the openers, Pattullo and Barr, who bowled 406 overs out of 699 and took 80 wickets out of 124. They suffered from missed slip catches.

Played 16, Won 5, Lost 3, Drawn 8

Batting

	Innings	Not outs	Runs	Highest inns.	Average
A. N. G. Barker	18	4	417	113*	29.78
J. A. McOrr	18	0	456	58	25.33
†P. R. Prenter	18	1	336	60	19.76
W. A. Burnet	18	1	324	50	19.05
G. R. G. Graham	11	4	126	44	18.00
D. A. Macaulay	18	3	246	80	16.40
J. C. G. Barr	11	1	105	30	10.50

Bowling

	Overs	Maidens	Runs	Wickets	Average
A. H. Pattullo	192	51	441	36	12.25
J. C. G. Barr	214.3	45	647	44	14.70
P. R. Prenter	61	14	189	10	18.90

MAGDALEN COLLEGE SCHOOL

The school's successes were achieved by team effort under the able captaincy of Jones, who was a stubborn batsman and safe wicket-keeper.

Played 13, Won 8, Lost 3, Drawn 2

Batting

	Innings	Not outs	Runs	Highest inns.	Average
J. S. Baxter	12	2	367	94*	36.70
D. Tinbergen	12	1	249	41	22.63
†D. R. H. Jones	9	2	116	32	16.57
M. J. Harrison	10	0	154	46	15.40
M. E. North	12	2	125	40*	12.50

Bowling

	Overs	Maidens	Runs	Wickets	Average
I. D. K. Weedon	138.4	38	331	35	9.45
A. J. Warnock	107	18	332	22	15.09
A. E. Tidbury	79.1	23	188	11	17.09
R. Dodshon	62.3	10	213	12	17.75

MALVERN COLLEGE

Malvern were at their best when set to score against the clock. Davies led his side well and set an excellent example in the field. The batting feature was the steady improvement of Wilcox, while Shatrushalyasinhji, a nephew of K. S. Duleepsinhji, made good use of his ability to bowl off-breaks at an unusually speedy pace.

Played 14, Won 6, Lost 1, Drawn 7

Batting

	Innings		Not outs		Runs		Highest inns.		Average
J. W. T. Wilcox	16	..	5	..	377	..	60*	..	34.27
†J. M. Davies	17	..	2	..	462	..	100	..	30.80
R. Devereux	16	..	3	..	376	..	111*	..	28.92
I. D. Preston-Jones	17	..	1	..	422	..	85	..	26.37
H. J. Bailey	8	..	1	..	166	..	48	..	23.71
M. K. S. Shatrushalyasinhji	10	..	3	..	166	..	74*	..	23.71
P. G. Jagger	11	..	2	..	198	..	44	..	22.00
M. J. Theobald	8	..	2	..	122	..	41*	..	20.33

Bowling

	Overs		Maidens		Runs		Wickets		Average
M. K. S. Shatrushalyasinhji	205.3	..	42	..	635	..	42	..	15.11
N. C. Naumann	200.5	..	55	..	526	..	31	..	16.96
H. J. Bailey	69	..	23	..	197	..	11	..	17.81
P. G. Jagger	315.4	..	113	..	732	..	33	..	22.18
A. J. S. Henman	119.1	..	21	..	404	..	13	..	31.07

MANCHESTER GRAMMAR SCHOOL

With only three regular members of the 1956 side available, Manchester Grammar School experienced a moderate season. Green was the most accomplished and successful batsman. Humphries and Hanmer, the opening bowlers, worked hard and Green and Hambleton gave most support as change bowlers.

Played 19, Won 8, Lost 6, Drawn 5

Batting

	Innings		Not outs		Runs		Highest inns.		Average
†D. M. Green	16	..	2	..	502	..	120	..	35.85
G. Hambleton	16	..	2	..	317	..	53*	..	22.64
N. J. A. Glassey	17	..	1	..	292	..	63	..	18.25

Bowling

	Overs		Maidens		Runs		Wickets		Average
K. Hanmer	140	..	40	..	243	..	22	..	11.04
A. Humphries	182.5	..	61	..	364	..	29	..	12.55
D. M. Green	122.4	..	32	..	312	..	23	..	13.56
B. Whetton	76	..	14	..	225	..	15	..	15.00
G. Hambleton	140	..	21	..	339	..	20	..	16.95

MARLBOROUGH COLLEGE

Weak bowling, for which good fielding and throwing could not compensate, largely accounted for a disappointing season. If the batting did not come up to expectations Morris and Pyemont shaped well on occasions, and Goodfellow played attractively. Goodfellow, the off-spinner, was the leading bowler, and at the end of the season S. H. Compton, a late arrival in the side who took nine wickets for 157, strengthened the opening attack.

Played 14, Won 2, Lost 4, Drawn 8

Batting

	Innings		Not outs		Runs		Highest inns.		Average
P. Pyemont	10	..	4	..	237	..	63*	..	39.50
C. A. Morris	14	..	2	..	339	..	112*	..	28.25
A. Goodfellow	14	..	0	..	330	..	70	..	23.57
J. J. Hall-Smith	12	..	1	..	224	..	74	..	20.36
†B. A. C. Marr	14	..	1	..	247	..	52*	..	19.00
J. W. Flecker	10	..	0	..	112	..	27	..	11.20

Bowling

	Overs		Maidens		Runs		Wickets		Average
A. Goodfellow	146.1	..	43	..	407	..	25	..	16.28
C. A. Morris	58.4	..	13	..	195	..	10	..	19.50
P. L. Bell	163.2	..	46	..	382	..	16	..	23.87
C. R. Reiss	159.4	..	38	..	431	..	13	..	33.15

MERCERS' SCHOOL

Played 16, Won 2, Lost 10, Drawn 4

Batting

	Innings		Not outs		Runs		Highest inns.		Average
T. Kay	10	..	1	..	207	..	49	..	23.00
M. S. Richards	16	..	1	..	271	..	51	..	18.06
D. G. Eames	14	..	0	..	226	..	41	..	16.14
R. G. Linger	16	..	5	..	172	..	34*	..	15.63

Bowling

	Overs		Maidens		Runs		Wickets		Average
F. A. Robson	146.5	..	30	..	440	..	24	..	18.33
†P. W. J. Tabert	89.5	..	13	..	296	..	15	..	19.73
N. C. H. James	171	..	35	..	517	..	26	..	19.92

MERCHANT TAYLORS' SCHOOL

Played 14, Won 6, Lost 5, Drawn 3

Batting

	Innings		Not outs		Runs		Highest inns.		Average
D. D. Phelps	14	..	3	..	312	..	80*	..	28.36
C. F. Worrell	13	..	1	..	215	..	48	..	17.91
D. E. Sidwell	14	..	1	..	230	..	48	..	17.69
W. F. Urmson	13	..	3	..	166	..	41*	..	16.60
N. W. Griffin	11	..	1	..	139	..	39*	..	13.90
S. C. Smails	14	..	2	..	139	..	34*	..	11.58
†C. G. F. Harding	12	..	0	..	147	..	37	..	12.25

Bowling

	Overs		Maidens		Runs		Wickets		Average
B. J. Northcott	253.1	..	46	..	716	..	51	..	14.03
C. W. S. Matts	210.3	..	35	..	525	..	28	..	18.75
J. D. R. Newhouse	153	..	20	..	453	..	23	..	19.69

MERCHANT TAYLORS' SCHOOL, CROSBY

Played 15, Won 8, Lost 1, Drawn 6

Batting

	Innings		Not outs		Runs		Highest inns.		Average
I. A. Corless	15	..	1	..	396	..	75	..	28.28
J. Dowler	8	..	2	..	165	..	44*	..	27.50
†R. W. T. Myall	15	..	3	..	317	..	50	..	26.41
W. A. Davies	15	..	0	..	328	..	62	..	21.86
A. Veevers	11	..	3	..	137	..	29	..	17.12
B. St. J. Birchall	14	..	2	..	199	..	41*	..	16.58
D. J. Roberts	12	..	0	..	193	..	32	..	16.08

Bowling

	Overs		Maidens		Runs		Wickets		Average
B. St. J. Birchall	195	..	69	..	439	..	50	..	8.78
E. A. Field	109	..	36	..	213	..	22	..	9.68
F. R. H. Birchall	119	..	30	..	307	..	24	..	12.79
A. Veevers	109	..	26	..	333	..	15	..	22.20
T. G. Bennett	91	..	22	..	270	..	11	..	24.54

MERCHISTON CASTLE SCHOOL

Merchiston lost only to Fettes in school matches, Boyle scoring over 600 runs for the second successive year.

Played 15, *Won* 4, *Lost* 2, *Drawn* 9

Batting

	Innings		Not outs		Runs		Highest inns.		Average
†J. M. Boyle	16	..	6	..	628	..	74*	..	62.80
R. D. Morton	15	..	3	..	349	..	53	..	29.08
I. M. McLauchlan	14	..	3	..	282	..	76*	..	25.63
W. A. M. Crow	12	..	2	..	227	..	65	..	22.70
J. A. S. Tuill	13	..	1	..	152	..	23	..	12.66
J. P. Jackson	11	..	2	..	103	..	25	..	11.44

Bowling

	Overs		Maidens		Runs		Wickets		Average
B. R. Donald	76	..	24	..	121	..	12	..	10.08
G. L. Maguire	59	..	19	..	148	..	14	..	10.57
R. D. Morton	215	..	63	..	446	..	39	..	11.43
W. A. Forbes	112	..	31	..	235	..	18	..	13.05
I. M. McLauchlan	211	..	59	..	476	..	23	..	20.69

MILLFIELD SCHOOL

Played 11, *Won* 7, *Lost* 1, *Drawn* 2, *Abandoned* 1

Batting

	Innings		Not outs		Runs		Highest inns.		Average
A. A. Hoodbhoy	9	..	4	..	347	..	62	..	69.40
J. C. Taylor	8	..	3	..	264	..	61*	..	52.80
W. G. M. Craig	11	..	0	..	314	..	71	..	28.54
Th. de Z. Adhihetty	6	..	1	..	130	..	60*	..	26.00
F. J. Herting	9	..	1	..	118	..	35	..	14.75

Bowling

	Overs		Maidens		Runs		Wickets		Average
F. J. Herting	105.2	..	32	..	233	..	28	..	8.32
J. C. Taylor	91.2	..	29	..	217	..	15	..	14.46
C. G. Hutchinson	102	..	23	..	294	..	17	..	17.29
G. S. Little	74.4	..	15	..	225	..	11	..	20.45

MILL HILL SCHOOL

A strong and determined batting side was almost able to off-set unpenetrative though steady bowling.

Played 13, *Won* 2, *Lost* 4, *Drawn* 7

Batting

	Innings		Not outs		Runs		Highest inns.		Average
J. R. Ivens	12	..	3	..	238	..	46*	..	26.44
†K. L. H. Smith	11	..	4	..	185	..	51	..	26.42
K. L. Thomas	13	..	1	..	301	..	73	..	25.08
J. M. Bunyard	13	..	1	..	295	..	52	..	24.58
T. J. Lee	9	..	0	..	211	..	57	..	23.40
P. B. Armitage	12	..	2	..	181	..	43	..	18.10
R. H. Goude	13	..	1	..	202	..	49	..	16.83

Bowling

	Overs		Maidens		Runs		Wickets		Average
R. H. Goude	142.4	..	18	..	467	..	20	..	23.35
A. Scobie	90	..	19	..	259	..	10	..	25.90
F. M. N. Wills	215.2	..	42	..	675	..	23	..	29.34
M. R. Wollerton	111.2	..	16	..	401	..	12	..	33.41

MONKTON COMBE SCHOOL

Monkton Combe's improved record included a victory over Kingswood School for the first time since 1947. The batting was good all the way down the order, the most successful being Walton, a Colt with a wide range of scoring strokes.

Played 12, *Won* 4, *Lost* 2, *Drawn* 4, *Abandoned* 2

Batting

	Innings	Not outs	Runs	Highest inns.	Average
N. Walton	10	2	223	91	27.87
N. B. Matthewson	11	1	199	51	19.90
S. W. Sykes	10	2	147	52*	18.37
C. J. Chester	9	2	124	26*	17.71
C. P. C. Hunt	11	0	178	36	16.18
†I. H. Glasgow	11	2	121	31	13.44

Bowling

	Overs	Maidens	Runs	Wickets	Average
J. F. Woods	155.2	43	414	39	10.61
C. G. Reeves	92	21	271	18	15.05
I. H. Glasgow	114.3	17	389	21	18.52

NEWCASTLE ROYAL GRAMMAR SCHOOL

Played 17, *Won* 5, *Lost* 2, *Drawn* 10

Batting

	Innings	Not outs	Runs	Highest inns.	Average
D. F. Taylor	11	4	182	61*	26.00
D. M. Dallas	13	4	224	87*	24.88
D. Beckham	8	2	126	47	21.00
H. Spall	12	2	200	31	20.00
M. I. Dickinson	15	2	231	60*	17.76
M. M. Oakley	10	1	151	50	16.77
M. Floyd	14	2	185	45	15.41
N. White	15	1	180	45	12.85

Bowling

	Overs	Maidens	Runs	Wickets	Average
J. R. Scott	180	40	479	42	11.40
B. R. Reid	195	30	610	36	16.94

NOTTINGHAM HIGH SCHOOL

Played 15, *Won* 2, *Lost* 3, *Drawn* 10

Batting

	Innings	Not outs	Runs	Highest inns.	Average
R. G. Moore	13	3	371	74	37.10
N. Bishop	14	4	357	74	35.70
J. E. Chambers	15	1	284	43	20.28
D. C. Slater	14	1	227	50	17.46
K. A. Bancroft	12	1	113	41	10.27

Bowling

	Overs	Maidens	Runs	Wickets	Average
A. W. Cavender	208.1	35	557	25	22.28
J. W. Taylor	168.2	24	577	25	23.08
N. Bishop	97	10	421	18	23.38
A. C. Hudson	156	25	525	16	32.81

OAKHAM SCHOOL
Played 14, *Won* 6, *Lost* 3, *Drawn* 5

Batting

	Innings		Not outs		Runs		Highest inns.		Average
L. A. Wilson	13	..	3	..	514	..	96*	..	51.40
†W. N. Houghton	14	..	2	..	510	..	93	..	42.50
J. M. Scorer	13	..	3	..	280	..	42	..	28.00
S. G. Schanschieff	12	..	1	..	301	..	67	..	27.36
J. H. Berry	7	..	2	..	104	..	37*	..	20.80
A. J. M. Betmead	11	..	2	..	130	..	46	..	14.44
C. T. Garton	10	..	0	..	140	..	41	..	14.00

Bowling

	Overs		Maidens		Runs		Wickets		Average
R. G. Marrion	255.3	..	86	..	509	..	46	..	11.06
W. N. Houghton	133	..	27	..	435	..	27	..	16.11
T. J. Case	78	..	13	..	210	..	11	..	19.09
A. J. M. Betmead	185.2	..	29	..	466	..	20	..	23.30

THE ORATORY SCHOOL
Played 15, *Won* 1, *Lost* 6, *Drawn* 8

Batting

	Innings		Not outs		Runs		Highest inns.		Average
L. C. Fynn	16	..	2	..	525	..	94	..	37.50
M. H. Hasslacher	12	..	1	..	268	..	72	..	24.36
N. Simpson	16	..	1	..	271	..	40	..	18.06
†J. H. Hudson	16	..	0	..	228	..	54	..	14.25
M. Creasy	13	..	0	..	158	..	27	..	12.15
J. Townley	13	..	3	..	100	..	31	..	10.00

Bowling

	Overs		Maidens		Runs		Wickets		Average
J. Hawkes	93.4	..	15	..	264	..	19	..	13.89
J. H. Hudson	170	..	30	..	609	..	24	..	25.37
P. Sorapure	130	..	32	..	400	..	15	..	26.66

OUNDLE SCHOOL

Oundle began badly by losing their first three matches on wet pitches. Minney, the best batsman, scored two early centuries and received steady support from Reddaway. Stephens showed promise in his first year. Saul (the captain), medium-paced left-arm, was the spearhead of the attack in which Crabbe was useful with the new ball and Wilson bowled leg-breaks skilfully.

Played 14, *Won* 3, *Lost* 4, *Drawn* 7

Batting

	Innings		Not outs		Runs		Highest inns.		Average
P. B. Reddaway	10	..	4	..	244	..	62	..	40.66
J. H. Minney	16	..	0	..	644	..	105	..	40.25
N. M. Stephens	16	..	4	..	454	..	96*	..	37.83
C. F. Hacking	12	..	1	..	224	..	70	..	20.35
P. D. T. Crabbe	13	..	1	..	151	..	48	..	12.58
S. B. Cartledge	15	..	1	..	173	..	35*	..	12.35

Bowling

	Overs		Maidens		Runs		Wickets		Average
K. Wilson	158	..	28	..	418	..	25	..	16.72
†G. H. Saul	236.2	..	56	..	705	..	38	..	18.55
P. D. T. Crabbe	211.2	..	42	..	585	..	26	..	22.50
N. G. Carling	129	..	28	..	368	..	16	..	23.00

PERSE SCHOOL

With several batsmen of more than average competence and no tail, Perse scored heavily, and lost only two matches out of nineteen, but only four were won, for the catching was unreliable. Islip bowled fast with consistent hostility, and Stone spun his off-breaks sharply.

Played 19, *Won* 4, *Lost* 2, *Drawn* 13

Batting

	Innings		Not outs		Runs		Highest inns.		Average
A. S. Crawford	19	..	3	..	606	..	91	..	37.87
E. L. Kemp	19	..	2	..	632	..	106*	..	37.17
J. W. Huckle	14	..	4	..	334	..	80	..	33.40
D. G. Earl	11	..	4	..	211	..	80	..	30.14
N. P. R. Blyth	16	..	6	..	285	..	53	..	28.50
I. R. F. Gordon	18	..	3	..	266	..	54	..	17.73
K. J. Hardingham	13	..	1	..	147	..	52	..	12.25

Bowling

	Overs		Maidens		Runs		Wickets		Average
I. A. R. Stone	142	..	34	..	403	..	33	..	12.21
†I. A. Islip	240	..	38	..	618	..	42	..	14.71
T. D. Plumridge	93	..	13	..	288	..	15	..	19.20
I. R. F. Gordon	178	..	45	..	484	..	22	..	22.00
N. P. R. Blyth	79	..	7	..	342	..	12	..	28.50

POCKLINGTON SCHOOL

Played 12, *Won* 4, *Lost* 2, *Drawn* 6

Batting

	Innings		Not outs		Runs		Highest inns.		Average
P. D. Briggs	13	..	1	..	285	..	53	..	23.75
A. Atkins	9	..	2	..	108	..	24	..	15.42
C. J. Berry	11	..	0	..	134	..	45	..	12.18
J. A. Davies	10	..	0	..	114	..	45	..	11.40
E. H. Green	13	..	1	..	125	..	35*	..	10.41

Bowling

	Overs		Maidens		Runs		Wickets		Average
P. W. Train	105	..	29	..	204	..	28	..	7.28
J. M. Norris	151.5	..	34	..	458	..	39	..	11.74
P. D. Briggs	74	..	12	..	235	..	14	..	16.78
I. S. Bird	110	..	20	..	331	..	18	..	18.39

QUEEN ELIZABETH GRAMMAR SCHOOL, WAKEFIELD

Played 16, *Won* 7, *Lost* 2, *Drawn* 7

Batting

	Innings		Not outs		Runs		Highest inns.		Average
F. Green	15	..	2	..	573	..	94	..	44.07
†T. Cass	16	..	1	..	290	..	46*	..	19.33
R. A. Dyson	16	..	1	..	270	..	64	..	18.00
A. B. Holdsworth	14	..	8	..	106	..	28*	..	17.66
J. M. Bromley	14	..	1	..	212	..	68	..	16.30
M. J. Scott	16	..	1	..	155	..	22	..	10.33

Bowling

	Overs		Maidens		Runs		Wickets		Average
R. A. Dyson	102.2	..	37	..	210	..	26	..	8.07
K. M. Young	149.5	..	60	..	250	..	30	..	8.33
J. H. Holt	185	..	59	..	373	..	44	..	8.47
D. Pryor	95	..	36	..	177	..	20	..	8.85

RADLEY COLLEGE

Radley lost only to the Authentics. In a strong batting side Mackeown, who hit ten fifties, and Morkill were outstanding. The bowling was not quite penetrative enough on the hard pitches of May and June, but Morkill and Wigley were steady openers. Lane, a useful all-rounder, was brilliant in the field.

Played 15, *Won* 5, *Lost* 1, *Drawn* 9

Batting

	Innings		Not outs		Runs		Highest inns.		Average
P. J. Mackeown	16	..	3	..	816	..	87	..	62.76
†T. W. Morkill	16	..	3	..	463	..	126*	..	35.61
J. R. Russell	15	..	1	..	426	..	75	..	30.42
P. H. Raby	16	..	1	..	400	..	93	..	26.60
I. L. J. Stevens	7	..	1	..	140	..	40	..	23.33
R. D. Freshman	13	..	2	..	249	..	59	..	22.63
R. A. Lane	11	..	5	..	129	..	64	..	21.50

Bowling

	Overs		Maidens		Runs		Wickets		Average
R. A. Lane	107	..	32	..	268	..	17	..	15.76
I. L. J. Stevens	143.1	..	55	..	284	..	18	..	15.77
M. D. Wigley	203.3	..	58	..	494	..	28	..	17.64
T. W. Morkill	237.3	..	93	..	487	..	27	..	18.03
J. F. Fuller-Sessions	128	..	40	..	316	..	14	..	22.57

READING SCHOOL

Played 15, *Won* 7, *Lost* 5, *Drawn* 2, *Tied* 1

Batting

	Innings		Not outs		Runs		Highest inns.		Average
P. A. Merrett	15	..	4	..	404	..	100*	..	36.72
A. P. Sadler	15	..	1	..	347	..	91	..	24.78
R. M. Owen	15	..	1	..	334	..	75*	..	23.85
R. A. Ruskin	12	..	3	..	187	..	66	..	20.77
C. D. C. Councell	8	..	1	..	109	..	47*	..	15.57
A. Cooper	14	..	1	..	172	..	65	..	13.23
D. I. Hill	15	..	0	..	197	..	41	..	13.13

Bowling

	Overs		Maidens		Runs		Wickets		Average
M. Phillips	22.3	..	3	..	63	..	10	..	6.30
P. A. Merrett	170	..	45	..	414	..	41	..	10.09
A. P. Sadler	113.5	..	22	..	281	..	19	..	14.78
R. A. Ruskin	145.3	..	23	..	506	..	34	..	14.87
J. A. Thompsett	120	..	32	..	225	..	14	..	16.07

REPTON SCHOOL

In the 400th year of the school, Repton lost only one match, by three wickets to the Derbyshire Club and Ground. Vaughan led a particularly young side admirably. The batting was somewhat brittle, but Warner's last four innings brought him 300 runs and Vaughan made runs when wanted, though on the whole he had a disappointing year. The bowling, supported by excellent fielding, was invariably accurate. Allen, left-arm slow, was the most successful and has two more years in the side.

Played 18, *Won* 6, *Lost* 1, *Drawn* 11

Batting

	Innings		Not outs		Runs		Highest inns.		Average
C. A. Fry...............	19	..	2	..	697	..	138*	..	41.00
C. S. Warner...........	13	..	1	..	444	..	91	..	37.00
†P. H. Vaughan	18	..	3	..	531	..	75	..	35.40
D. C. M. Vaughan......	12	..	3	..	216	..	52	..	24.00
B. J. Hare	17	..	3	..	304	..	51*	..	21.71
R. F. Gresley	11	..	1	..	133	..	44	..	13.30

Bowling

	Overs		Maidens		Runs		Wickets		Average
A. W. Allen	314.2	..	81	..	853	..	59	..	14.45
G. W. L. Foster	147	..	42	..	325	..	21	..	15.47
C. R. Pilkington	66	..	4	..	218	..	14	..	15.57
J. J. W. Tomlinson	186	..	45	..	502	..	25	..	20.08

ROSSALL SCHOOL

A strong batting side was not dismissed entirely until the last match against Sedbergh, but the bowling depended too much on Reece. In his fifth year in the team Reece bowled his in-swingers untiringly and economically.

Played 11, *Won* 3, *Lost* 1, *Drawn* 7

Batting

	Innings		Not outs		Runs		Highest inns.		Average
J. S. Blower............	9	..	4	..	194	..	52*	..	38.80
P. D. Stokes	9	..	6	..	100	..	39*	..	33.33
R. C. Fairbairn	10	..	3	..	216	..	40	..	30.85
R. Bennett	12	..	1	..	337	..	78	..	30.63
†M. J. Reece	11	..	0	..	335	..	82	..	30.45
G. M. Attenborough ...	12	..	1	..	323	..	65	..	29.36

Bowling

	Overs		Maidens		Runs		Wickets		Average
M. J. Reece	311.5	..	89	..	703	..	48	..	14.64
R. B. Sinker	90.2	..	24	..	254	..	16	..	15.87
R. C. Fairbairn	86.2	..	21	..	237	..	14	..	16.92
G. M. Attenborough ...	108	..	25	..	293	..	13	..	22.53

RUGBY SCHOOL

After a slow start Rugby developed into a good side in July. T. B. L. Coghlan had a disappointing season, and Colville had a lean time between his good start and good finish to the term. Cuthbertson was a highly promising all-rounder at the age of 15.

Played 14, *Won* 3, *Lost* 5, *Drawn* 6

Batting

	Innings		Not outs		Runs		Highest inns.		Average
P. R. Colville	16	..	2	..	440	..	68	..	31.42
A. G. L. Coghlan........	16	..	2	..	317	..	68	..	22.64
M. F. Attenborough	11	..	0	..	214	..	53	..	19.45
J. O. Trumper...........	12	..	5	..	132	..	46*	..	18.85
J. L. Cuthbertson	8	..	2	..	109	..	33	..	15.57
P. D. Snell...........	14	..	0	..	242	..	40	..	17.28
S. J. Y. Robinson	13	..	2	..	147	..	47	..	13.36
T. B. L. Coghlan	11	..	1	..	127	..	42	..	12.70

Bowling

	Overs		Maidens		Runs		Wickets		Average
J. L. Cuthbertson	131.3	..	58	..	258	..	22	..	11.72
A. G. L. Coghlan.......	118.4	..	32	..	313	..	21	..	14.90
S. J. Y. Robinson.......	168.1	..	26	..	451	..	23	..	19.60
J. O. Trumper...........	98	..	14	..	290	..	13	..	22.30

RUTHIN SCHOOL

Ruthin's season was a triumph for their captain, Neil-Dwyer, who carried the batting and whose wicket-keeping was of a particularly high standard.

Played 16, Won 8, Lost 5, Drawn 3

Batting

	Innings		Not outs		Runs		Highest inns.		Average
†G. Neil-Dwyer	16	..	5	..	593	..	111	..	53.90
N. S. Casson	16	..	2	..	263	..	49	..	18.78
P. B. Schofield	16	..	1	..	243	..	74	..	16.20
R. G. L. Williams	13	..	2	..	174	..	35*	..	15.81
R. Carlile	12	..	3	..	134	..	69	..	13.88
D. L. Whiteley	15	..	1	..	160	..	46	..	11.42
A. J. Falconer	14	..	1	..	100	..	30*	..	7.69

Bowling

	Overs		Maidens		Runs		Wickets		Average
A. J. Falconer	99.4	..	31	..	259	..	36	..	7.19
I. S. Thelwell	100	..	30	..	217	..	24	..	9.04
R. E. G. Jones	75	..	21	..	197	..	20	..	9.85
P. B. Schofield	193.5	..	57	..	454	..	44	..	10.31

RYDAL SCHOOL

Rydal ended their season with a great win by ten wickets against the M.C.C. The medium-pace Thomas with seven for 22 had the M.C.C. out for 70, and the captain, C. D. Pighills, and Fish hit off the runs. Throughout the season Dale batted with great resolution and obvious signs of class.

Played 11, Won 4, Lost 3, Drawn 4

Batting

	Innings		Not outs		Runs		Highest inns.		Average
J. H. Dale	10	..	1	..	334	..	81	..	37.11
P. S. Fish	11	..	2	..	251	..	46*	..	27.88
R. M. H. Thomas	9	..	1	..	190	..	63	..	23.75

Bowling

	Overs		Maidens		Runs		Wickets		Average
R. M. H. Thomas	182.5	..	43	..	435	..	31	..	14.03
D. C. Jones	65	..	12	..	203	..	11	..	18.90
J. C. Davies	126.1	..	14	..	448	..	19	..	23.57

ST. BEES SCHOOL

Results tended to flatter St. Bees. There was inadequate batting support for the Hewitson brothers, who scored nearly half the runs, and the spin bowlers, Bell and Boulter, suffered in the same way, while the fielding fell below the standard of previous years.

Played 11, Won 6, Lost 3, Drawn 2

Batting

	Innings		Not outs		Runs		Highest inns.		Average
†W. N. Hewitson	10	..	2	..	251	..	100*	..	31.37
J. R. Hewitson	11	..	2	..	246	..	57*	..	27.33
J. A. Ingham	7	..	0	..	137	..	43	..	19.57
M. Scott	10	..	0	..	108	..	45	..	10.80

Bowling

	Overs		Maidens		Runs		Wickets		Average
M. W. R. Bell	128.3	..	26	..	309	..	26	..	11.88
H. J. Boulter	87	..	12	..	324	..	24	..	13.50

ST. DUNSTAN'S COLLEGE

The team failed on several occasions to exploit a favourable position. Matten scored consistently throughout the season, his 102 not out against Wilson's at The Oval being a particularly fine performance.

Played 15, Won 5, Lost 3, Drawn 6, Abandoned 1

Batting

	Innings		Not outs		Runs		Highest inns.		Average
C. Matten	14	..	2	..	490	..	102*	..	40.83
N. A. Dolder	12	..	1	..	262	..	65	..	23.81
A. J. Asbridge	9	..	4	..	104	..	31	..	20.80
†E. Marsh	14	..	2	..	242	..	59	..	20.18
D. S. Clift	13	..	3	..	183	..	40	..	18.30
R. L. Hobcraft	13	..	2	..	139	..	33	..	12.63
M. A. Wright	14	..	0	..	166	..	34	..	11.98

Bowling

	Overs		Maidens		Runs		Wickets		Average
D. S. Clift	82.4	..	17	..	234	..	19	..	12.31
D. Landon	101.3	..	18	..	342	..	25	..	13.68
N. A. Dolder	131	..	40	..	296	..	20	..	14.80
C. E. Dixon	60	..	11	..	216	..	10	..	21.60
N. T. Bradley	105	..	31	..	347	..	14	..	24.78

ST. EDWARD'S SCHOOL, OXFORD

Some of the most promising cricketers in the side will still be available in 1958, including Trotman, the most likely batsman, Davis, a left-arm slow bowler, Appleby and Tyacke. Dale was not only a good captain but also a fielder in a class on his own.

Played 16, Won 4, Lost 4, Drawn 8

Batting

	Innings		Not outs		Runs		Highest inns.		Average
J. N. Tyacke	10	..	7	..	111	..	27*	..	37.00
J. D. Davis	18	..	2	..	425	..	85	..	26.56
T. W. Brett	18	..	0	..	469	..	101	..	26.05
E. A. Appleby	15	..	7	..	194	..	50*	..	24.25
M. A. Trotman	18	..	0	..	419	..	64	..	23.27
†H. Dale	18	..	0	..	345	..	72	..	19.16
J. H. Fletcher	15	..	0	..	246	..	71	..	16.40
D. G. Davis	16	..	2	..	193	..	37	..	13.78
J. D. G. Hancock	15	..	1	..	156	..	28	..	11.14

Bowling

	Overs		Maidens		Runs		Wickets		Average
A. R. N. Appleby	132.4	..	33	..	347	..	22	..	15.77
D. G. Davis	198.2	..	41	..	553	..	27	..	20.48
C. H. Shirley	117	..	23	..	336	..	15	..	22.40
J. N. Tyacke	200.5	..	37	..	584	..	24	..	24.33
M. A. Trotman	142.3	..	16	..	481	..	18	..	26.72
E. A. Appleby	112.2	..	11	..	391	..	14	..	27.92

ST. LAWRENCE COLLEGE

The two most talented batsmen, de Saram and Prior, in a well-balanced side remain for next season. Both were essentially attacking players though as yet with defensive flaws. Thomas led the side well and made good use of his left-arm googly type bowling. Hodder's defensive batting was of much value to the side.

Played 14, Won 5, Lost 4, Drawn 5

Batting

	Innings	Not outs	Runs	Highest inns.	Average
M. F. Hodder	13	8	263	49*	52.60
G. N. de Saram	14	2	313	123*	26.08
†R. L. Thomas	13	1	282	57*	23.50
A. R. M. Watson	11	4	161	62	23.00
D. C. L. Prior	14	1	294	72*	22.61
R. A. G. Marshall	13	0	228	64	17.53

Bowling

	Overs	Maidens	Runs	Wickets	Average
M. G. Hill	129	27	346	24	14.40
J. S. Irvine	145	32	441	27	16.33
R. L. Thomas	107.2	8	395	21	18.80
M. P. M. Watson	159.3	43	389	20	19.45
G. N. de Saram	97.3	19	337	10	33.70

ST. PAUL'S SCHOOL

Although Neate and Sperryn laid the foundation for numerous good scores, the bowling was not good enough to support their excellent efforts. Francis, who was quick and persevering, was the only class bowler. Both Neate and Francis remain for next season, when there is the prospect of a better record.

Played 13, Won 1, Lost 6, Drawn 6

Batting

	Innings	Not outs	Runs	Highest inns.	Average
F. W. Neate	13	1	619	151*	51.58
†A. N. Sperryn	13	2	372	65	33.81
A. R. Crabtree	10	3	143	29*	20.43
D. O. Hilton	12	0	221	54	18.41
M. M. Flett	13	1	197	33	16.41
C. A. Murray	13	0	194	61	14.92
P. P. McCowen	12	2	145	36*	14.50

Bowling

	Overs	Maidens	Runs	Wickets	Average
D. O. Francis	173.4	38	487	34	14.32
D. Hunkin	105	23	259	12	21.58
A. D. Grimes	105	28	292	13	22.46
A. R. Crabtree	145.1	31	436	18	24.22

ST. PETER'S SCHOOL, YORK

St. Peter's lost only one match against a club side in the final week of term. Much credit for their success must go to the captain, Kirby, for his leadership and fine all-round cricket.

Played 14, Won 7, Lost 1, Drawn 6

Batting

	Innings	Not outs	Runs	Highest inns.	Average
†D. Kirby	13	3	529	132*	52.90
A. McCallum	14	1	413	127	31.76
J. F. Middleton	13	1	280	77*	23.33
D. B. Irvin	12	1	232	44	21.09
J. J. F. Knapton	12	3	182	69*	20.22
J. A. Bygate	11	0	214	56	19.45

Bowling

	Overs	Maidens	Runs	Wickets	Average
†D. Kirby	218	67	446	47	9.48
J. F. Middleton	128.1	36	305	26	11.73
P. B. Burbidge	140	32	345	20	17.25
S. J. S. Wroe	104.2	34	271	12	22.58

SEDBERGH SCHOOL

Bad weather seriously interfered with Sedbergh's season and prevented a useful team from developing its full strength. The batting was good far down the side, and three centuries were scored, while there was ample variety in the bowling.

Played 11, Won 4, Lost 2, Drawn 5

Batting

	Innings	Not outs	Runs	Highest inns.	Average
†C. G. Midgley	10	.. 4	.. 469	.. 103*	.. 78.16
T. P. Goodman	7	.. 3	.. 187	.. 45	.. 46.75
M. R. Grundy	8	.. 1	.. 309	.. 111	.. 44.14
M. W. Broadbent	9	.. 1	.. 197	.. 67*	.. 24.62
R. N. Swarbrick	6	.. 0	.. 131	.. 48	.. 21.83
J. D. Dorman	10	.. 0	.. 137	.. 53	.. 13.70

Bowling

	Overs	Maidens	Runs	Wickets	Average
J. R. Miller	147	.. 39	.. 361	.. 28	.. 12.89
H. M. S. Holme	116	.. 22	.. 371	.. 22	.. 16.86
J. Walker	90	.. 30	.. 253	.. 15	.. 16.86

SHERBORNE SCHOOL

A young, inexperienced side had a poor season. The batting relied too much on Brookes, who had a fine record, and the bowling on the left-arm spin of Curtis and the off-breaks of Yeldham. Pegg kept wicket excellently.

Played 12, Won 1, Lost 4, Drawn 7

Batting

	Innings	Not outs	Runs	Highest inns.	Average
M. C. Brookes	13	.. 1	.. 374	.. 74*	.. 31.16
C. R. J. Pink	9	.. 1	.. 139	.. 51	.. 17.37
D. B. Hill	13	.. 3	.. 169	.. 50	.. 16.90
R. M. Morgan	10	.. 1	.. 152	.. 54	.. 16.88
R. J. A. Hughes	13	.. 0	.. 205	.. 39	.. 15.76
J. A. D. Curtis	11	.. 3	.. 100	.. 29	.. 12.50
S. T. O. Shirley	10	.. 0	.. 122	.. 40	.. 12.20

Bowling

	Overs	Maidens	Runs	Wickets	Average
J. A. D. Curtis	212.3	.. 61	.. 625	.. 34	.. 18.38
C. W. Yeldham	233.5	.. 59	.. 644	.. 24	.. 26.83
C. R. J. Pink	125	.. 38	.. 340	.. 11	.. 30.90

SHREWSBURY SCHOOL

Weak batting inevitably produced a sorry record. It fell away badly after a promising start to the term, and the individual batsmen lost confidence in themselves. Happily the fielding was excellent and the opening bowling of Owen-Hughes was outstanding. His 50 wickets represented a high-class performance. Macaulay and Holden gave him good support.

Played 12, Won 1, Lost 4, Drawn 7

Batting

	Innings	Not outs	Runs	Highest inns.	Average
†A. J. Cordle	14	.. 0	.. 219	.. 64	.. 15.64
D. P. Pearson	15	.. 1	.. 205	.. 63	.. 14.64
J. S. Ker	7	.. 0	.. 100	.. 27	.. 14.28
A. J. Garden	13	.. 2	.. 145	.. 45*	.. 13.18
T. A. J. Nicholson	15	.. 1	.. 182	.. 46	.. 13.00
W. L. Ward	14	.. 1	.. 163	.. 46	.. 12.53
D. L. Wright	13	.. 1	.. 131	.. 29	.. 10.91

Bowling

	Overs	Maidens	Runs	Wickets	Average
H. G. Owen-Hughes	210.5 ..	48 ..	533 ..	50 ..	10.66
A. Holden	117.2 ..	26 ..	336 ..	23 ..	14.61
A. T. Macaulay	160.3 ..	37 ..	433 ..	27 ..	16.03

SOLIHULL SCHOOL

The captain, Stratford, and Lea usually gave Solihull a good start, but the middle batting was unreliable. The bowling was fair and was supported by keen fielding, but the side lacked an opener of real pace.

Played 12, *Won* 3, *Lost* 4, *Drawn* 5

Batting

	Innings	Not outs	Runs	Highest inns.	Average
†D. Stratford	12 ..	0 ..	346 ..	56 ..	28.83
C. J. Lea	12 ..	0 ..	315 ..	62 ..	26.25
R. A. D. Cooper	11 ..	1 ..	204 ..	41 ..	20.40
P. J. W. Taylor	12 ..	0 ..	202 ..	72 ..	16.83
C. J. Thomas	11 ..	3 ..	104 ..	25 ..	13.00
R. N. Stober	11 ..	1 ..	122 ..	42 ..	12.20

Bowling

	Overs	Maidens	Runs	Wickets	Average
C. J. Thomas	109 ..	27 ..	298 ..	24 ..	12.41
A. J. Hames	121.2 ..	21 ..	400 ..	22 ..	18.18

STAMFORD SCHOOL

A young and rather inexperienced eleven did well in club matches but failed to do themselves justice against other schools. The consistent batting of Watson was the season's chief feature.

Played 11, *Won* 4, *Lost* 6, *Drawn* 1

Batting

	Innings	Not outs	Runs	Highest inns.	Average
D. L. Watson	8 ..	0 ..	261 ..	78 ..	32.62
†J. B. Bayley...........	11 ..	0 ..	336 ..	101 ..	30.55
J. A. H. Mitchell	11 ..	2 ..	227 ..	75 ..	25.22
P. D. Stanbury	9 ..	1 ..	122 ..	32 ..	15.25

Bowling

	Overs	Maidens	Runs	Wickets	Average
D. L. Watson	65.3 ..	8 ..	204 ..	10 ..	20.40
G. F. Allen	75 ..	12 ..	290 ..	12 ..	24.16
R. White	121 ..	25 ..	425 ..	15 ..	28.33
J. A. H. Mitchell	146.4 ..	33 ..	432 ..	15 ..	28.80

STONYHURST COLLEGE

The features of a season which began well with three wins in the first six matches before the July rains were the all-round play of Cheetham and Corbett and the excellent wicket-keeping of Moorhouse.

Played 13, *Won* 4, *Lost* 2, *Drawn* 7

Batting

	Innings	Not outs	Runs	Highest inns.	Average
S. Maxwell-Scott	11 ..	3 ..	218 ..	52 ..	27.25
M. T. Corbett	9 ..	0 ..	241 ..	76 ..	26.77
†C. P. Cheetham	8 ..	4 ..	106 ..	33 ..	26.50
P. Moorhouse	8 ..	0 ..	106 ..	30 ..	13.25
J. Shuter	9 ..	1 ..	101 ..	21 ..	12.62

Bowling

	Overs		Maidens		Runs		Wickets		Average
C. P. Cheetham	88.5	..	17	..	293	..	28	..	10.46
M. T. Corbett	175.3	..	31	..	393	..	32	..	12.28
T. Drake-Lee	140.5	..	37	..	368	..	14	..	26.28

STOWE SCHOOL

Stowe had limited success. The bowling was generally adequate, but the batting was most uncertain.

Played 12, Won 3, Lost 5, Drawn 4

Batting

	Innings		Not outs		Runs		Highest inns.		Average
J. H. Harris	12	..	1	..	282	..	50	..	25.63
C. J. G. Atkinson	12	..	0	..	227	..	55	..	18.91
R. Sherjan	12	..	4	..	136	..	42	..	17.00
G. Harwood	12	..	0	..	193	..	33	..	16.08
G. M. Shaw	11	..	1	..	145	..	40	..	14.50

Bowling

	Overs		Maidens		Runs		Wickets		Average
J. H. Harris	129.1	..	39	..	271	..	23	..	11.78
R. Sherjan	111.3	..	38	..	249	..	16	..	15.56
D. G. Garwood-Gowers	137.1	..	22	..	359	..	23	..	15.60
C. J. G. Shillington	98.3	..	24	..	297	..	19	..	15.63

STRATHALLAN SCHOOL

Played 14, Won 3, Lost 5, Drawn 6

Batting

	Innings		Not outs		Runs		Highest inns.		Average
G. T. Hudson	16	..	4	..	360	..	89*	..	30.00
†W. R. Galbraith	15	..	2	..	277	..	51*	..	21.30
A. W. Beattie	16	..	1	..	267	..	46	..	17.80
D. C. Duncan	14	..	1	..	163	..	30*	..	12.53

Bowling

	Overs		Maidens		Runs		Wickets		Average
W. R. Galbraith	39	..	5	..	147	..	16	..	9.18
M. S. Jamieson	172	..	52	..	328	..	41	..	9.46
B. D. C. Watts	110	..	32	..	309	..	22	..	14.04

TAUNTON SCHOOL

Taunton, ably captained by Gray, were particularly strong in batting, scoring over 200 runs on five occasions. The bowling was not so successful, though C. H. Webb was difficult to score off.

Played 15, Won 4, Lost 4, Drawn 7

Batting

	Innings		Not outs		Runs		Highest inns.		Average
G. V. H. Cameron	13	..	2	..	370	..	79	..	33.63
†J. B. Gray	13	..	1	..	399	..	84	..	33.25
D. F. Miller	11	..	2	..	205	..	59*	..	22.77
M. G. Peaker	11	..	2	..	199	..	80	..	22.11
R. P. Lewis	13	..	0	..	275	..	62	..	21.15

Bowling

	Overs		Maidens		Runs		Wickets		Average
R. P. Tarr	80	..	15	..	226	..	13	..	17.38
D. J. Mantell	64	..	4	..	217	..	12	..	18.08
C. H. Webb	191	..	36	..	457	..	24	..	19.04
J. A. Jameson	174	..	26	..	543	..	27	..	20.11

TONBRIDGE SCHOOL

With better batting support for Prideaux, Tonbridge would have had a really good side. Time and again a balanced attack gave the batsmen chances which they did not take. Meredith at medium-pace and Hudson, a leg-spinner, bowled particularly well. Prideaux, a mature player, made runs consistently.

Played 12, *Won* 5, *Lost* 4, *Drawn* 3

Batting

	Innings	Not outs	Runs	Highest inns.	Average
†R. M. Prideaux	13	2	485	106*	44.09
R. H. C. Page	10	2	176	59*	22.00
P. Rylands............	14	2	257	88	21.60
J. H. Foskett...........	13	0	205	36	15.76
R. M. Giles	13	1	160	50*	13.33
M. S. Connell	12	0	138	32	11.50

Bowling

	Overs	Maidens	Runs	Wickets	Average
P. Meredith	238	75	531	44	12.06
A. B. E. Hudson	163	31	497	33	15.06
R. M. Giles	139	19	362	21	17.23
D. J. Evans	90	17	264	15	17.60
R. H. C. Page	118	36	326	17	19.17

TRENT SCHOOL

Trent's record barely did them justice, for they narrowly failed to win four of the drawn games. Norgrove, a stylish and aggressive opener, was particularly noticeable as a newcomer to the side. The batting generally was good, and Blakeley, fast and accurate, was the spearpoint of a useful attack.

Played 13, *Won* 5, *Lost* 1, *Drawn* 7

Batting

	Innings	Not outs	Runs	Highest inns.	Average
R. J. Holden	13	4	255	61	28.34
M. W. Norgrove	13	1	324	57	27.00
G. T. Foster	13	1	275	61	22.91
E. J. Bows	13	0	214	34	16.46
†A. K. Blakeley	10	0	156	52	15.60
J. W. Smalley	12	2	128	21	12.80

Bowling

	Overs	Maidens	Runs	Wickets	Average
A. K. Blakeley	181.2	54	445	40	11.12
R. L. Strickland	109	42	217	14	15.50
R. J. Holden	106.3	33	227	14	16.21
R. A. S. Everett	77	16	184	11	16.72

TRINITY COLLEGE, GLENALMOND

On hard wickets the eleven were unbeaten until June 18, but on the softer pitches later the batting became unsound. The spin bowling was effective, particularly that of Macpherson, the fielding and throwing uniformly good, and the wicket-keeping of C. H. Kennedy excellent. He caught 11 and stumped 11.

Played 18, *Won* 3, *Lost* 5, *Drawn* 10

Batting

	Innings	Not outs	Runs	Highest inns.	Average
J. L. Macdonald........	17	2	359	61	23.93
A. C. Fairbairn	17	2	239	47	15.93
M. K. Fairbairn	12	3	127	32*	14.11
†D. H. Macpherson.....	17	0	225	56	13.23
S. F. Martineau	12	1	131	29	11.90
C. I. Emmerson	13	5	88	15	11.00
K. B. D. Aitken	11	0	119	45	10.81

Bowling

	Overs		Maidens		Runs		Wickets		Average
D. H. Macpherson	180	..	37	..	477	..	49	..	9.73
J. W. Black	133	..	40	..	199	..	19	..	10.47
C. I. Emmerson	70	..	27	..	161	..	13	..	12.38
A. C. Fairbairn	190	..	45	..	452	..	34	..	13.29

TRINITY SCHOOL, CROYDON
Played 15, Won 2, Lost 5, Drawn 8

Batting

	Innings		Not outs		Runs		Highest inns.		Average
†G. R. Symons	14	..	2	..	291	..	49	..	24.25
A. V. L. Williams	7	..	1	..	110	..	34	..	18.33
J. Tait	14	..	3	..	197	..	43*	..	17.90
K. G. Manley	14	..	1	..	225	..	37	..	17.30
S. E. Reid	12	..	2	..	141	..	33*	..	14.10

Bowling

	Overs		Maidens		Runs		Wickets		Average
P. B. Smith	63	..	23	..	136	..	13	..	10.46
S. E. Reid	192.3	..	58	..	435	..	32	..	13.59
M. J. Doyle	74.5	..	13	..	184	..	13	..	14.15
M. R. Mead	144.5	..	39	..	336	..	22	..	15.27
M. J. F. Goldsmith	117.1	..	23	..	362	..	21	..	17.23

UNIVERSITY COLLEGE SCHOOL

On unreliable pitches the batting of the school team inevitably suffered, but Anderson and Jones promised well as batsmen for next season.

Played 13, Won 4, Lost 7, Drawn 2

Batting

	Innings		Not outs		Runs		Highest inns.		Average
C. D. Elston	13	..	2	..	235	..	58*	..	21.36
R. T. Jones	11	..	1	..	148	..	47*	..	14.80
†A. M. E. Wood	12	..	0	..	170	..	60	..	14.16

Bowling

	Overs		Maidens		Runs		Wickets		Average
P. J. Meader	114.2	..	28	..	264	..	25	..	10.56
H. J. Masterton-Smith	138.5	..	27	..	434	..	35	..	12.40
R. T. Jones	105	..	21	..	278	..	13	..	21.88

UPPINGHAM SCHOOL

Uppingham's main strength lay in the bowling, with Waller outstanding. This was supported by excellent fielding and throwing, but although some good scores were made the batting was unreliable and caused the loss of two school matches which ought to have been won.

Played 14, Won 3, Lost 4, Tied 1, Drawn 6

Batting

	Innings		Not outs		Runs		Highest inns.		Average
D. P. Green	16	..	2	..	495	..	100*	..	35.35
H. Raby	16	..	1	..	409	..	75	..	27.26
J. L. Watson	15	..	0	..	320	..	60	..	21.33
E. L. Gothard	15	..	1	..	291	..	67	..	20.78
M. S. Dorman	16	..	3	..	261	..	50*	..	20.07

Bowling

	Overs		Maidens		Runs		Wickets		Average
M. G. Waller	256.1	..	69	..	643	..	59	..	10.89
I. G. Phillips	73	..	24	..	147	..	11	..	13.36
A. C. Usborne	127.1	..	32	..	393	..	26	..	15.11
J. W. Thompson	171	..	19	..	515	..	27	..	19.07

VICTORIA COLLEGE, JERSEY
Played 14, *Won* 3, *Lost* 5, *Drawn* 6

Batting

	Innings		Not outs		Runs		Highest inns.		Average
P. J. B. LeBrocq	14	..	1	..	281	..	52	..	21.61
D. G. Carpenter	12	..	1	..	305	..	78*	..	27.72
F. R. Falle	14	..	2	..	181	..	58	..	15.08
A. O. Brown	11	..	8	..	176	..	41*	..	22.00
J. M. Gallichan	8	..	3	..	121	..	40	..	24.20
J. Tosterin	12	..	0	..	187	..	51	..	15.58
D. Ferguson	14	..	0	..	176	..	37	..	12.57

Bowling

	Overs		Maidens		Runs		Wickets		Average
F. R. Falle	108.4	..	16	..	354	..	27	..	13.11
J. M. Gallichan	93.5	..	13	..	390	..	20	..	18.50
F. P. LeQuesne	92	..	8	..	322	..	25	..	12.88
D. J. Watkins	99.6	..	21	..	338	..	21	..	16.09

WALLASEY GRAMMAR SCHOOL

Wallasey had their best post-war season. Two left-handers, Brown and Watkins, headed the batting. Watkins was also an outstanding cover-point, and at the wicket Brown had more than 20 successes. Atkinson with slow leg-breaks and Whitehead, a young and particularly promising fast bowler, carried the main attack.

Played 15, *Won* 10, *Lost* 4, *Drawn* 1

Batting

	Innings		Not outs		Runs		Highest inns.		Average
G. J. Brown	15	..	2	..	495	..	79	..	38.07
R. D. Watkins	13	..	4	..	323	..	76*	..	35.88
M. J. Walker	12	..	3	..	188	..	48	..	20.88
R. C. Steere	13	..	2	..	212	..	63*	..	19.27
†J. M. Atkinson	14	..	1	..	192	..	53	..	14.76

Bowling

	Overs		Maidens		Runs		Wickets		Average
J. M. Atkinson	169	..	42	..	427	..	51	..	8.37
R. E. Hill	58	..	19	..	117	..	12	..	9.75
C. G. Whitehead	201.2	..	50	..	507	..	48	..	10.56
B. E. D. Sutcliffe	111.3	..	34	..	291	..	13	..	22.38

WELLINGBOROUGH SCHOOL
Played 15, *Won* 3, *Lost* 7, *Drawn* 5

Batting

	Innings		Not outs		Runs		Highest inns.		Average
M. Iqbal	15	..	2	..	344	..	69	..	26.46
J. D. Pember	13	..	1	..	292	..	63	..	24.33
†M. J. R. Barker	14	..	2	..	266	..	51*	..	22.16
I. Ross	15	..	1	..	205	..	24	..	14.64
B. R. Leadsom	13	..	1	..	162	..	42	..	13.50
D. A. Peck	15	..	0	..	198	..	69	..	13.23

Bowling

	Overs		Maidens		Runs		Wickets		Average
J. D. Pember	241.2	..	54	..	607	..	41	..	14.80
R. J. Wesley	86	..	23	..	223	..	13	..	17.15
M. Iqbal	160.1	..	29	..	592	..	30	..	19.73
I. Ross	79	..	12	..	262	..	10	..	26.20

WELLINGTON COLLEGE

A team of all-round ability, in which seven batsmen played innings of more than 60, performed admirably after recovering from the shock of losing the first two matches. The old colours, Yeldham, Robertson, Pavey and Stephenson, all did well, and among the wins was one by 15 runs against Eton.

Played 14, Won 4, Lost 3, Drawn 7

Batting

	Innings		Not outs		Runs		Highest inns.		Average
R. J. B. Yeldham	14	..	3	..	365	..	74*	..	33.18
J. M. Pavey	14	..	2	..	362	..	74*	..	30.16
J. R. G. Stephenson	10	..	3	..	225	..	63	..	30.13
M. F. de Vries	14	..	0	..	378	..	94	..	27.00
M. J. Neale	8	..	0	..	194	..	68	..	24.25
W. D. Robertson	14	..	0	..	328	..	71	..	23.42
T. A. Soutry	13	..	2	..	212	..	67	..	19.27
R. C. G. Fortin	14	..	1	..	181	..	34	..	13.92

Bowling

	Overs		Maidens		Runs		Wickets		Average
W. D. Robertson	202.2	..	64	..	442	..	26	..	17.00
J. R. G. Stephenson	199.5	..	42	..	614	..	34	..	18.05
D. T. Adams	166.3	..	38	..	516	..	25	..	20.64
P. T. Johnson	96	..	18	..	356	..	16	..	22.25

WELLINGTON SCHOOL, SOMERSET

Played 15, Won 7, Lost 3, Drawn 5

Batting

	Innings		Not outs		Runs		Highest inns.		Average
F. Mawji	15	..	2	..	335	..	77	..	25.76
D. Russell	14	..	2	..	207	..	44	..	17.25
D. Bromfield	13	..	1	..	108	..	39	..	16.50
J. B. Byas	14	..	1	..	213	..	42	..	16.38
W. Painter	14	..	2	..	196	..	41	..	16.33

Bowling

	Overs		Maidens		Runs		Wickets		Average
F. Mawji	60	..	12	..	148	..	18	..	8.22
C. Hawkins	208	..	40	..	524	..	50	..	10.48
P. Clarke	95	..	15	..	273	..	22	..	12.40
D. Russell	120	..	21	..	339	..	22	..	15.40

WESTMINSTER SCHOOL

Spry, the captain of whom much was hoped as a left-handed batsman and off-break bowler, had a disappointing season, and his team lacked confidence in themselves. Lewis, next year's captain, alone scored consistently, and except in the case of the fast-medium Wakely the bowling was no more than steady.

Played 14, Won 1, Lost 8, Drawn 5

Batting

	Innings		Not outs		Runs		Highest inns.		Average
G. A. Lewis	13	..	3	..	468	..	107*	..	46.80
F. H. I. Rahimtoola....	11	..	5	..	146	..	40*	..	24.33
C. de Peyor	14	..	1	..	342	..	69	..	26.30
†R. G. M. Spry	14	..	2	..	226	..	70*	..	18.83
A. Naylor-Smith	12	..	1	..	207	..	42	..	18.81
G. R. Poole...........	12	..	0	..	174	..	37	..	14.50
A. G. Cheyne	8	..	0	..	104	..	58	..	13.00

Bowling

	Overs		Maidens		Runs		Wickets		Average
K. G. Wakely	225.2	..	26	..	430	..	27	..	15.92
R. G. M. Spry	79	..	2	..	315	..	15	..	21.00

WHITGIFT SCHOOL

Played 14, Won 2, Lost 5, Drawn 7

Batting

	Innings		Not outs		Runs		Highest inns.		Average
†D. Evans	12	..	2	..	393	..	94	..	39.30
D. Mills	14	..	1	..	324	..	80*	..	24.92
A. M. Osborne	14	..	0	..	324	..	85	..	23.14
P. A. Beattie	9	..	1	..	130	..	44*	..	16.25
J. M. H. Kelly	11	..	2	..	116	..	28*	..	12.88
R. J. Bence	11	..	0	..	129	..	28	..	11.72
B. A. W. Finch	14	..	1	..	147	..	37	..	11.30

Bowling

	Overs		Maidens		Runs		Wickets		Average
D. Evans	42.5	..	3	..	226	..	12	..	18.83
J. M. H. Kelly	171.3	..	45	..	513	..	29	..	17.68
D. R. Steele	142.1	..	29	..	404	..	21	..	19.23
J. B. Bowden	165	..	30	..	528	..	16	..	33.00

WINCHESTER COLLEGE

Though starting with only two members of the 1956 side, Winchester went through a second season unbeaten. The outstanding player was the Nawab of Pataudi with his 851 runs, and Jefferson was the find of the season. At 15 he made 135 in his first inter-school match. The bowling became more and more steady as the season progressed, and Charlton's leg-breaks were particularly successful against other schools. The side was well led by Dunlop. Four out of five inter-school matches were won.

Played 16, Won 6, Lost 0, Drawn 10

Batting

	Innings		Not outs		Runs		Highest inns.		Average
Nawab of Pataudi	18	..	5	..	851	..	127*	..	65.46
J. F. Charlton	9	..	6	..	136	..	52*	..	45.33
†D. W. S. Dunlop	5	..	3	..	59	..	45*	..	29.50
R. I. Jefferson	14	..	1	..	376	..	135	..	28.92
P. J. L. Wright	10	..	4	..	162	..	47*	..	27.00
V. A. L. Powell	12	..	2	..	243	..	50	..	24.30
J. C. D. Townsend	17	..	1	..	354	..	94	..	22.12
J. D. T. Greenall	18	..	1	..	336	..	56*	..	19.76
M. A. P. S. Downham	16	..	1	..	296	..	82	..	19.73
D. R. Woolley	14	..	3	..	208	..	41	..	18.90

Bowling

	Overs		Maidens		Runs		Wickets		Average
R. I. Jefferson	84	..	30	..	158	..	16	..	9.87
D. W. S. Dunlop	187	..	42	..	455	..	24	..	18.95
J. F. Charlton	200.4	..	27	..	685	..	35	..	19.57
J. R. Dinwiddy	161.5	..	31	..	469	..	23	..	20.39
Nawab of Pataudi	87.3	..	21	..	312	..	10	..	31.20

WORCESTER ROYAL GRAMMAR SCHOOL

A young side performed creditably throughout the season. Dinsdale, a newcomer, bowled accurately and well merited his 68 wickets. He was ably supported behind the stumps by Elliott, also in his first season, whose victims numbered 28.

Played 18, Won 9, Lost 5, Drawn 4

Batting

	Innings	Not outs	Runs	Highest inns.	Average
M. H. Sobey	16	1	349	74	23.26
S. D. Fudger	15	1	273	71	19.50
E. J. Pearce	10	1	128	38	14.22
C. G. Clarke	15	1	161	32	11.50
J. W. Elliott	15	2	139	45*	10.69

Bowling

	Overs	Maidens	Runs	Wickets	Average
B. V. Dinsdale	323	108	583	68	8.72
†A. P. Mobbs	141.4	20	413	36	11.47
B. Hodson	71.4	17	191	13	14.69
M. D. Hawkins	204.1	50	462	23	20.08

WORKSOP COLLEGE

The loss of their captain, the all-rounder Sykes, for seven matches and of an opening bowler for 12, unsettled the side. Walter, who made a century against Repton, and Swinney batted well, as did Sykes on his return. Walter shared seven opening partnerships of over 50. Barber, the leading bowler, was well supported.

Played 17, Won 4, Lost 5, Drawn 8

Batting

	Innings	Not outs	Runs	Highest inns.	Average
†W. G. D. Sykes	10	4	275	59*	45.83
G. W. Walter	19	0	542	111	28.52
P. R. Swinney	18	1	355	62	20.88
M. K. Pasha	12	1	216	59	19.63
D. B. Moody	17	0	307	52	18.05
J. M. Farrow	18	1	235	33	13.82
T. M. Turner	18	3	207	30	13.80

Bowling

	Overs	Maidens	Runs	Wickets	Average
W. G. D. Sykes	64	2	212	12	17.66
T. G. W. Barber	187.5	33	560	28	20.00
I. B. A. Grieve	87.5	14	361	17	21.23
D. B. Moody	101	20	308	14	22.00

WREKIN COLLEGE

Wrekin's batting was superior to their bowling, and Grenfell and Edwards each scored a good century.

Played 14, Won 4, Lost 3, Drawn 7

Batting

	Innings	Not outs	Runs	Highest inns.	Average
†N. H. Grenfell	15	4	456	101*	41.45
B. R. Edwards	15	3	423	118*	35.25
J. J. White	13	0	311	61	23.92
C. L. Hartley	12	2	229	51	22.90
D. I. Robertson	14	1	256	70	19.69

Bowling

	Overs	Maidens	Runs	Wickets	Average
J. J. White	135.5	13	388	25	15.52
W. W. Eaves	191	34	565	33	17.12
J. H. E. Baldwin	171.1	31	482	28	17.21
B. R. Edwards	53	5	201	11	18.27

CC

WYCLIFFE COLLEGE

An exceptionally strong attack based on the fast-medium pace of Treadaway, the leg-breaks of Lewis and the left-arm slow bowling of Evans offset some disappointing batting.

Played 13, *Won* 6, *Lost* 4, *Drawn* 3

Batting

	Innings		Not outs		Runs		Highest inns.		Average
W. B. Gauntlett	13	..	3	..	229	..	86*	..	22.90
A. M. Porter	10	..	3	..	139	..	40*	..	19.85
D. W. Lewis	12	..	5	..	105	..	27*	..	15.00
N. J. Treadaway	12	..	1	..	153	..	47	..	13.90
A. M. Vaughan	13	..	0	..	172	..	46	..	13.23
†L. R. Drury	13	..	0	..	160	..	37	..	12.30
A. M. Parker	12	..	0	..	121	..	26	..	10.08

Bowling

	Overs		Maidens		Runs		Wickets		Average
D. W. Lewis	103	..	25	..	299	..	32	..	9.34
N. J. Treadaway.......	149.3	..	40	..	285	..	30	..	9.50
D. A. Evans	114.5	..	33	..	268	..	27	..	9.92
A. M. Porter	81.5	..	19	..	203	..	13	..	15.61

PUBLIC SCHOOL MATCHES IN 1957

For Eton v. *Harrow, Beaumont* v. *Oratory, Clifton* v. *Tonbridge, Rugby* v.
Marlborough, Cheltenham v. *Haileybury, Southern Schools* v. *The Rest and Public
Schools* v. *Combined Services, see Other Matches at Lord's.*

SHREWSBURY v. UPPINGHAM

At Shrewsbury, June 11, 12. Shrewsbury won by 18 runs. Except for a brief
period on the first afternoon, the pitch gave little help to bowlers. Yet so rife
were batting failures that forty wickets fell for an aggregate of 274 runs. Ker
played pluckily in both innings for Shrewsbury, as did Kenyon for Uppingham.

Shrewsbury

T. A. J. Nicholson b Waller	10	— b Thompson	12
D. P. Pearson b Thompson	4	— b Waller	1
D. L. Wright c Green b Thompson	0	— c Kenyon b Waller	0
A. J. Cordle c Gothard b Bulley	0	— b Waller	0
W. L. Ward b Raby b Usborne	12	— c Gothard b Thompson	9
A. J. Garden c Waller b Usborne	1	— b Waller	8
J. S. Ker b Thompson	18	— b Waller	27
A. Holden c Green b Waller	7	— lbw b Thompson	0
A. T. Macaulay b Thompson	2	— run out	2
H. G. Owen-Hughes c Gothard b Waller	3	— c Kenyon b Thompson	4
P. R. Hunt not out	0	— not out	1
Extras	10	Extras	8
	74		**72**

Uppingham

E. L. Gothard c Ward b Macaulay	11	— lbw b Owen-Hughes	3
H. Raby b Owen-Hughes	4	— c Holden b Macaulay	2
D. P. Green c Ker b Macaulay	7	— b Macaulay	5
C. M. Kenyon c Hunt b Holden	12	— c Holden b Owen-Hughes	32
J. L. Watson b Owen-Hughes	5	— b Owen-Hughes	0
M. S. Dorman c Holden b Owen-Hughes	6	— b Owen-Hughes	14
P. C. Watson not out	1	— run out	0
J. W. Thompson c Hunt b Holden	2	— c Hunt b Owen-Hughes	3
R. H. Bulley b Owen-Hughes	1	— not out	3
M. G. Waller c Macaulay b Owen-Hughes	1	— b Macaulay	0
A. C. Usborne b Holden	0	— c Holden b Macaulay	2
Extras	4	Extras	10
	54		**74**

BRADFIELD v. RADLEY

At Bradfield, June 21, 22. Drawn. Missed first ball, Workman played
splendidly when Bradfield followed on 177 behind and they easily saved the game.
Stands of 127 by Morkill and Stevens and of 96 by Lane and Fuller-Sessions
brought about a Radley recovery after the loss of four men for 22.

Radley

P. J. Mackeown b Eacersall	5	R. A. Lane st Emberton b Daubney	64
J. R. Russell b Workman	5	D. J. H. Fisher not out	16
P. H. Raby b Workman	0	J. G. Aspinall c Daubney b Thomas	4
T. W. Morkill b Daubney	89	M. D. Wigley run out	0
R. D. Freshman lbw b Workman	4	Extras	14
I. L. J. Stevens b Workman	38		**277**
J. F. Fuller-Sessions c and b Thomas	38		

Bradfield

P. J. Workman lbw b Wigley	5	— not out	140
J. P. Allday run out	38	— c Fisher b Lane	52
J. L. Davison c Russell b Wigley	3		
P. J. P. Eacersall b Lane	9	— b Raby	18
J. H. George b Lane	5		
P. J. H. Daubney b Lane	2		
T. A. N. Woof lbw b Wigley	12		
H. A. S. Reid lbw b Lane	10	— st Aspinall b Stevens	44
E. N. Thomas not out	6		
P. M. Emberton c Aspinall b Morkill	0		
M. J. Angold b Morkill	0		
Extras	10	Extras	12
	100		**(3 wkts.) 266**

WESTMINSTER v. LANCING

At Vincent Square, June 22. Lancing, superior all round, won by 156 runs.

Lancing

J. W. Bridge lbw b Wareley	14	Extras	6
G. J. Sharman not out	121		
T. J. Goodwin c Cheyne b Harrison	42		
N. H. S. Evans c Cheyne b Spry	99	**(3 wkts., dec.) 282**	

G. C. Herbert, G. Davies, C. J. Saunders, J. C. W. Burrough, A. P. McCutcheon J. T. P. Crowe and C. J. Hale did not bat.

Westminster

C. de Peyer b Hale	1	K. G. Warely c Saunders b Goodwin	2
G. R. Poole b Sharman	13	P. C. Medawar b Sharman	0
G. A. Lewis b Sharman	38	D. V. Harrison not out	0
R. M. G. Spry c Davies b Evans	1	R. H. Bailey b Sharman	0
A. Naylor-Smith lbw b Sharman	37	Extras	10
A. G. Cheyne obstructed the field	23		
F. H. I. Rahimtoola lbw b Goodwin	1		**126**

HARROW v. CHARTERHOUSE

At Harrow, June 28, 29. Drawn. Harrow, needing 229 to win, played defensive cricket till the last hour when Foster scored with some freedom. Comer and Allom batted well for Charterhouse, and in the first Harrow innings Murray took five wickets for 25 runs.

Charterhouse

D. D. S. Comer c Cable b Weedon	65	— b Champniss	30
E. J. Craig c Vargas b Weedon	0	— st Cable b Faith	24
R. J Sutton c Champniss b Weedon	12	— lbw b Champniss	5
R. H. Sclater lbw b Faith	4	— b Weedon	5
A. T. C. Allom lbw b Champniss	19	— not out	79
A. A. H. White c Vargas b Champniss	0	— lbw b Weedon	4
J. J. Ullman c Cable b Champniss	27	— c Cable b Weedon	0
M. E. I. A. Wells c and b Champniss	12	— b Weedon	3
G. E. F. Gross not out	13	— not out	1
J. C. W. Murray run out	8	— lbw b Champniss	19
P. L. Levy lbw b Weedon	1		
Extras	27	Extras	9
	188		**(8 wkts., dec.) 179**

Harrow

H. F. Nicholson c Sclater b Murray.....	23	— b Wells	4
A. J. Anderson b Allom	0	— run out	19
J. B. Locket lbw b Murray............	9	— st Levy b Gross	40
J. D. C. Vargas c Allom b Murray	7	— c Levy b Gross	70
A. B. Cable c Levy b Murray	12	— not out	6
D. R. J. Foster c Craig b Allom	6	— lbw b Allom..............	43
L. J. Champniss c Ullman b Gross.....	12	— c Levy b Allom	4
P. W. Faith lbw b Allom	3	— not out	5
B. S. Raper b Murray	9		
M. J. H. Weedon c Allom b Gross.....	26	— b Gross	0
P. E. d'Abo not out..................	9		
Extras........................	23	Extras	18
	139	(7 wkts.)	209

WINCHESTER v. ETON

At Winchester, June 28, 29. Drawn. Set 156 to get in an hour and a half, Eton did not attempt the task. Winchester began by losing half their wickets for 67. Then Jefferson and Woolley began a recovery by adding 57 and Wright and Charlton hit freely in an eighth wicket stand of 68. Eton batted carefully but consistently, but not till the last pair were together did they establish a lead of 10 runs. Charlton bowled leg-breaks cleverly. Efforts to force the pace cost Winchester wickets in the second innings, but an unbroken partnership of 76 by Woolley and Wright enabled them to declare.

Winchester

J. D. T. Greenall lbw b Ayer	24	— c Baskervyle-Clegg b Burrows	4
J. C. D. Townsend c Baskervyle-Clegg b Burrows	6	— b Fellowes................	12
Nawab of Pataudi c Baskervyle-Clegg b Ayer	0	— c Dunning b Fellowes......	38
R. I. Jefferson lbw b Dunning	50	— c Lane Fox b Fellowes.....	15
V. A. L. Powell b Burrows............	21	— run out	12
M. A. P. S. Downham c Baskervyle-Clegg b Burrows	2	— c Baskervyle-Clegg b Fellowes	0
D. R. Woolley b Ayer................	19	— not out	21
J. F. Charlton c Lane Fox b Burrows ...	34	— c Baskervyle-Clegg b Scott..	0
P. J. L. Wright not out	52	— not out	47
D. W. S. Dunlop b Fellowes	10		
J. R. Dinwiddy b Scott	0		
W 1, n-b 3	4	B 12, l-b 1, w 1, n-b 2 .	16

1/19 2/20 3/39 4/65 5/67 6/124   222   1/7 2/62   (7 wkts., dec.) 165
7/124 8/192 9/221   3/66 4/87 5/87 6/88 7/89

Eton

W. G. A. Clegg c Charlton b Dunlop ...	42	— c Greenall b Pataudi	21
J. Baskervyle-Clegg b Dunlop	17	— not out	22
E. J. Lane Fox c Wright b Dunlop......	0	— b Charlton	4
J. W. Leonard c Wright b Jefferson	45	— not out	10
A. R. B. Burrows b Charlton	30		
P. Baring c Woolley b Charlton	30		
W. F. Goodier c Powell b Charlton	33		
R. Fellowes st Wright b Charlton	0		
E. J. R. Scott c Powell b Charlton	2		
M. L. Dunning lbw b Dinwiddy	13		
J. D. Ayer not out	9		
B 5, l-b 5, n-b 1	11	B 2...................	2

1/62 2/62 3/71 4/134 5/144 6/203   232   1/38 2/45   (2 wkts.) 59
7/203 8/207 9/220

Eton Bowling

	O.	M.	R.	W.		O.	M.	R.	W.
Burrows	16	2	53	4	....	15	6	36	1
Scott	15.4	2	41	1	....	22	5	53	1
Ayer	12	2	56	3	....	3	1	6	0
Fellowes	9	5	17	1	....	19	8	39	4
Lane Fox	11	2	35	0	....	4	1	10	0
Dunning	5	0	16	1	....	1	0	5	0

Winchester Bowling

	O.	M.	R.	W.		O.	M.	R.	W.
Jefferson	19	5	20	1	....	5	2	6	0
Dinwiddy	20	6	39	1	....	6	2	14	0
Dunlop	22	2	65	3	....	2	0	13	1
Charlton	31	8	71	5	....	8	1	13	1
Pataudi	7	1	23	0	....	4	1	11	1
Townsend	2	0	3	0					

Umpires: W. Harrington and R. B. Hunt.

REPTON v. MALVERN

At Repton, July 2, 3. Drawn. Set 210 to get to win, Malvern broke down badly after a fair start and narrowly avoided defeat.

Repton

C. A. Fry c Wilcox b Sat	36 —	c French b Jagger 1
H. Everard lbw b Naumann	11 —	lbw b Devereux 2
C. S. Warner c Wilcox b Sat	29 —	b Jagger 48
P. H. Vaughan c Wilcox b Naumann	23 —	c Bailey b Jagger 48
B. J. Hare b Naumann	0 —	c Wilcox b Jagger 12
R. F. Gresley c Naumann b Bailey	44 —	lbw b Sat 9
D. C. M. Vaughan c Preston-Jones b Henman	12 —	b Sat 0
C. R. Pilkington b Jagger	6 —	not out 6
A. W. Allen run out	24 —	not out 10
G. W. L. Foster not out	0	
J. J. W. Tomlinson st French b Henman..	8	
Extras	34	Extras 11
	227	(7 wkts., dec.) 147

Malvern

J. M. Davies c Fry b Foster	3 —	b Pilkington 16
I. D. Preston-Jones c and b Tomlinson	9 —	c and b Tomlinson 14
R. J. Devereux b Foster	4 —	c Vaughan b Allen 6
J. W. T. Wilcox b Pilkington	17 —	b Foster 34
T. R. G. Carter st Fry b Allen	14 —	c Vaughan b Foster 7
M. K. S. Sat c Vaughan b Allen	5 —	c Fry b Allen 3
P. G. Jagger c Fry b Pilkington	44 —	not out 5
H. J. Bailey c Foster b Allen	37 —	c Vaughan b Foster 2
R. P. French run out	20 —	c Foster b Allen 0
N. C. Naumann not out	5 —	not out 0
A. J. S. Henman run out	0	
Extras	7	Extras 10
	165	(8 wkts.) 97

WORKSOP v. DENSTONE

At Worksop, July 3. Worksop won by four wickets. Sykes took five Denstone wickets for 41 runs.

Denstone

A. C. Illingworth c Little b Barber	2	P. J. Hoddell not out	40
J. L. Foster b Sykes	23	J. C. Standerwick c Walter b Sykes	5
T. A. Peake lbw b Farrow	14	G. E. Sweet c Sykes b Pasha......	0
T. H. Melrose run out	22	R. A. Harrison b Sykes	7
R. H. Lees b Sykes	13	Extras	5
S. H. Barnes lbw b Sykes	5		—
J. A. Norris b Swinney	14		150

Worksop

D. B. Moody c Foster b Harrison	12	I. R. Dugdale not out	8
E. W. Walter c Peake b Standerwick	51	M. K. Pasha not out	17
J. M. Turner c Barnes b Norris...	3	Extras	10
W. G. D. Sykes b Harrison	26		—
P. R. Swinney c and b Standerwick	21	(6 wkts.)	151
J. M. Farrow c Peake b Standerwick	3		

J. B. Scott, T. B. Little and T. G. W. Barber did not bat.

HAILEYBURY v. UPPINGHAM

At Haileybury, July 5, 6. Haileybury won by seven runs. Fine bowling by Waller (nine wickets for 44) and good batting by Raby enabled Uppingham to gain a first innings lead of 87, but Haileybury recovered and gained an exciting victory in the last over of the game.

Haileybury

J. Lofting b Waller	11	— c Green b Waller	6
M. Higginbottom c P. C. Watson b Phillips	25	— run out	30
D. Moeller lbw b Waller	0	— c Gothard b Usborne	12
P. J. Parsons c Gothard b Waller	0	— c Gothard b Phillips	23
D. H. Crichton b Waller	0	— c Kenyon b Phillips	2
I. A. McDonald c Kenyon b Waller...	36	— c Phillips b Usborne	0
I. N. Smith b Waller	3	— c and b Phillips	15
A. G. Roberts lbw b Waller......	0	— c Waller b Thompson......	15
C. J. Ledger b Waller	12	— c Gothard b Usborne	37
J. E. Denison c Kenyon b Waller......	2	— c Waller b Thompson......	41
R. W. Golding not out	2	— not out	1
Extras......................	1	Extras	14
	—		—
	92		196

Uppingham

E. L. Gothard b Roberts	1	— b Parsons	6
H. Raby c Smith b Parsons	72	— c Higginbottom b Parsons..	29
D. P. Green b Roberts	4	— b Roberts	31
C. M. Kenyon b Roberts	2	— lbw b Lofting	7
J. L. Watson c Higginbottom b Lofting..	49	— c McDonald b Smith	2
M. S. Dorman b Parsons	15	— lbw b Parsons	18
P. C. Watson b Roberts	9	— c and b Smith	1
J. W. Thompson not out	12	— c Moeller b Smith	3
I. G. Phillips not out	6	— not out	1
A. C. Usborne (did not bat)		— c Golding b Parsons	0
M. G. Waller (did not bat)		— lbw b Smith	0
Extras......................	9	Extras	4
	—		—
	179		102

M.C.C. TEAM IN SOUTH AFRICA, 1956–57

By Leslie Smith

For the second time in eighteen months South Africa showed their powers of recovery against England. In 1955 they found themselves two down in the series after the first two Tests, then fought back to level matters only to lose the final Test at The Oval. This time, in their own country, they were again two down with three to play, but they drew the Third Test and won the next two, thus sharing the rubber with England for the second time in the history of matches between the two countries. England had won the previous five series.

The tour will be remembered for the remarkably low rate of scoring in the Test matches. Over the five games England averaged 32.69 and South Africa 29.04 runs an hour.

The M.C.C. team originally set sail with the following sixteen players—P. B. H. May (Surrey) (captain), D. J. Insole (Essex) (vice-captain), T. E. Bailey (Essex), P. E. Richardson (Worcestershire), M. C. Cowdrey (Kent), A. S. M. Oakman (Sussex), D. C. S. Compton (Middlesex), J. H. Parks (Sussex), T. G. Evans (Kent), B. Taylor (Essex), J. H. Wardle (Yorkshire), J. B. Statham (Lancashire), F. H. Tyson (Northamptonshire), P. J. Loader (Surrey), G. A. R. Lock (Surrey), J. C. Laker (Surrey), with F. R. Brown, the manager.

Almost as soon as he landed Parks developed eye trouble, and after playing one match he flew home. A short while later he attempted to return to South Africa, but collapsed when about to leave by aeroplane. M.C.C. decided not to send a replacement and the tour continued with fifteen players. Fortunately the team did not suffer much from injuries and the absence of Parks was not too severe a handicap, although as the series developed it became obvious that another batsman, preferably a left-hander to counter the bowling of Goddard and Tayfield, would have been invaluable.

It was expected before the team sailed that the bowling would be one of the most powerful forces ever to undertake a tour. So it proved, and it is remarkable to record that in the twenty-two matches played, all but two first-class, only one three-figure partnership came off the M.C.C. attack and only two South African batsmen obtained centuries. The batting, England's weakness for several years, failed again and almost entirely through this England were unable to win a series which at one point looked like being a walk-over for them.

South Africa also had their batting problems and the

dominance of bowlers over batsmen in practically every innings was largely responsible for the slow scoring in the series. Other factors which contributed were the run-saving fields usually employed by the captains, the accuracy of the two attacks in bowling to their fields and the sluggishness of some of the pitches, but undoubtedly the fact that the majority of batsmen were unwilling to take the slightest chance was the major cause.

The pattern was set in the First Test when Richardson, normally a fairly fast-scoring batsman, took a little over eight hours to reach his hundred, the slowest century ever made in official Test cricket. Richardson's innings helped considerably to win the match and these methods were adopted by the majority of the Test batsmen.

An attempt was made to show that the slow scoring was driving people away from the matches, but this proved to be a fallacy. Record crowds turned up almost everywhere M.C.C. played and the Test matches were often exciting and pleasing to the public. Slow cricket does not necessarily mean dull cricket and four of the Tests developed into closely contested matches; only on the first day of each game, before the state of the match had developed, was the dullness really felt. At the same time, from a personal point of view, I hope never again to watch a series in which so many batsmen were frightened to make forcing strokes and mere occupation of the crease was the prime consideration of nearly everyone.

Outside the Tests M.C.C. often gave attractive displays, but the batsmen could usually afford to take risks then because of the complete superiority of the bowling over the majority of the South African sides.

Biggest disappointment to the English side in the Test Matches came in the form of May, the captain. Acknowledged to be in a class of his own, May had an outstanding tour, doing almost as he pleased in every match except in the five games against South Africa. He began with five centuries, one a double hundred, in his first six first-class matches and his magnificent form caused a wave of depression to sweep over the South African supporters. This changed completely when Heine dismissed him first ball in the Transvaal match, and when the Tests started he just could not get going.

At first May was a little unfortunate to lose his wicket to some remarkable catches, but later it seemed that he was becoming a little anxious over his run of low scores and even in his only innings of any size, 61 in the Fourth Test, he was never a dominating force.

May had proved his big match temperament so many times before that his failures could hardly be put down to that. It appeared that he became a little over-anxious to do well and the strain of captaincy on and off the field became increasingly severe on him. Well before the end he looked rather tired and drawn. A charming person, always polite and ready to please, May, like many before him, found that captaining a team abroad was a vastly different proposition from leading a side at home. He won many friends by his charm at the numerous social functions, but he rarely seemed completely at ease on these occasions.

On the field May made few mistakes, usually adopting a safe policy. Possibly worried about the uncertainty of the batting, he at times appeared unwilling to risk a few runs in the field in the effort to snatch a wicket or two. I remember on one occasion, in particular, when at the start of a match, not a Test, he employed only one slip for Statham and not until the second ball had been edged to the vacant second slip position, and several other snicks went close there, was a normal attacking field set. Apart from leading England in two home series May had had little experience as captain, but having since been appointed to that position with Surrey this should be remedied. Perhaps he will get more appreciation of the right time to make a bold move without erring on the side of recklessness.

As for his batting, May, taking the tour as a whole, again showed himself to be head and shoulders above the rest. He thrilled thousands of South Africans by the quality and grace of his stroke-play and he was one of the few batsmen throughout the tour who regarded a half-volley without suspicion. With batting in most countries at a low ebb, May stands out like a beacon and England are fortunate to possess such a magnificent player.

The highest Test average for either side, 39.00, was achieved by Insole, the vice-captain, who also finished second to May in the full tour record. Somewhat ungainly in style and often suspect outside the off stump, Insole improved tremendously as the tour progressed and proved his splendid temperament and fighting qualities on several vital occasions. A powerful on-side player, he made the most of his fine eye both as a batsman and fieldsman, usually at slip where he held many brilliant catches. His success proved most popular for he was an excellent tourist, being full of humour off the field and extremely keen on it.

Bailey yet again showed his value as England's one top class all-rounder. A highly intelligent player, he often saved his best form for the Test Matches. Forced into the role of opening batsmen when Cowdrey forsook that position, Bailey became more than an adequate stop-gap, but more important was his bowling which helped largely to win one Test and gave him first place in the Test averages.

Cowdrey had a moderate tour for a player of his capabilities. There were days when he looked in the highest class, but on other occasions he found himself tied down completely by slow bowling, particularly that of Tayfield. Because of his splendid anticipation,

Cowdrey developed into a first-class slip field to the slow bowlers. Far better on the big occasion than in the minor matches, Richardson again showed his ideal temperament for Test Matches and his fielding at cover was excellent. For Compton it was not altogether a happy tour. Occasionally he revealed glimpses of past glories, but inability to get down the pitch as much as he used to do because of his knee trouble reduced his effectiveness and he became bogged down by steady bowling. In the field his lack of speed and agility cost many runs, but considering the extent of his handicap he did as well as might have been expected.

The Test batting was virtually settled from the start, for with Parks absent and Oakman and Taylor unable to get going properly there was no challenge to the established players.

In a powerful all-round bowling side, Wardle stood out above the rest and his feat of taking 105 wickets in all matches is unlikely to be surpassed for a long time on a tour of South Africa. Wardle usually bowled left-handed off-breaks and googlies and he often mesmerised batsmen who had seen little of this type of attack. Never afraid of being hit, he often invited punishment, but his control of flight and spin was so good that attempts to attack him were rarely successful. A humorist on the field, he made himself a great favourite throughout Southern Africa.

Lock, the other slow left-hander who took the second highest number of wickets on the tour, was kept out of the Test side by Wardle, playing only in the last Test when injury to the Yorkshire-man gave him his chance. Extremely keen throughout, Lock again showed his brilliance as a short-leg fieldsman and his batting continued to improve. The other slow bowler, Laker, took 50 wickets, but only eleven in the Tests and, compared with the South African off-break bowler Tayfield, he had a disappointing time. Laker found he could not spin the ball to anything like the same extent as in England and he did not look happy under punishment.

Even though Tyson lost much of his speed and accuracy, the fast bowling combination of Statham, Tyson and Loader, with support from Bailey, was always menacing. Statham had days when he looked the best fast bowler in the world, but was sometimes worried by injuries and towards the end lost his snap. On the other hand Loader made a big advance, bowling far better than his figures show. Always experimenting, he revealed excellent control of pace and direction, and judged on the number of times he beat the bat without reward he was by far the unluckiest bowler in the side. Taylor, the second wicket-keeper, tried hard, but came nowhere near challenging Evans, who maintained his astonishingly high standard behind the stumps. Evans showed positive brilliance on a most difficult pitch in the Fifth Test at Port Elizabeth.

The South Africans were expected to be stronger in batting than England, but this was not the case, although in the last two

Tests the length of the batting helped to bring improvement after complete collapses in the first two games. The loss of their captain and leading batsman, McGlew, who developed injuries to a knee and shoulder, proved a severe blow. He was able to play in only one of the Tests.

Goddard, the left-hander, showed himself to be one of the big personalities in world cricket, displaying splendid form with the bat and steadiness with the ball which the England batsmen found difficult to overcome. He usually attacked on or outside the leg stump to two short fine legs and four other fieldsmen on the leg side, and although this method was not pretty to watch it was certainly effective.

McLean played two big Test innings and, at times, looked good, but was inconsistent. Van Ryneveld took over the captaincy from McGlew and his boyish enthusiasm became infectious, the South Africans being keen and lively in the field even when things were going against them.

In fact, the biggest advantage South Africa held throughout the series was their magnificent ground work. Both sides took their catches well, but the South Africans saved many more runs than England largely because of the way they threw themselves at the ball and often prevented certain-looking boundaries. These diving tactics could be said to have given them their narrow victory in the Fourth Test.

Tayfield took the bowling honours and his almost perfect length was something the English batsmen found hard to counter. He spun the ball only a little, but made good use of the one which floated away and trapped several batsmen outside the off stump. His pace and flight were beautifully controlled and led to his great triumphs in the Third and Fourth Tests when he took eight and nine wickets in each second innings.

Adcock was the more effective of the two fast bowlers, but Heine always looked capable of producing the unplayable ball and his liberal use of the bumper caused plenty of concern to the England batsmen.

M.C.C. found a marked difference between the standard of play during the tour. Transvaal, Natal and perhaps Western Province were the only provincial sides capable of extending them. Most of the other teams were hopelessly outclassed. The chief criticisms of the tour were its length and the inadequate facilities for net practices. Long before the end of the tour the M.C.C. players were tired and jaded and it was said, with plenty of justification, that the return matches with the four leading provincial sides could have been eliminated. For their own benefit the South Africans should make every effort to improve the standard of their practice nets.

Also they probably learned that it is almost impossible to

prepare playing surfaces in two or three months. Twice, at Benoni and in the Fifth Test at Port Elizabeth, they relaid pitches shortly before matches and each time it failed, conditions deteriorating rapidly after the first few hours so that it was almost impossible for batsmen to make scoring strokes with safety.

The tour, capably managed by F. R. Brown, was the first run on a profit basis as far as a M.C.C. side in South Africa was concerned. Previously expenses only had been covered. Taking as their share approximately £60,000, representing a profit of £26,500, M.C.C. must have been well satisfied with the new arrangement.

SUMMARY OF THE TOUR

All Matches—Played 22, Won 13, Lost 3, Drawn 6

First-Class Matches—Played 20, Won 11, Lost 3, Drawn 6

Test Matches—Played 5, Won 2, Lost 2, Drawn 1

TEST MATCH AVERAGES

ENGLAND

BATTING

	Matches	Inns.	Not Outs	Runs	Highest Inns.	Average
D. J. Insole	5	10	2	312	110*	39.00
P. E. Richardson	5	10	0	369	117	36.90
M. C. Cowdrey	5	10	0	331	101	33.10
T. E. Bailey	5	10	0	259	80	25.90
D. C. S. Compton	5	10	0	242	64	24.20
T. G. Evans	5	10	0	164	62	16.40
P. B. H. May	5	10	0	153	61	15.30
F. H. Tyson	2	4	0	48	23	12.00
J. H. Wardle	4	7	1	68	22	11.33
J. B. Statham	4	7	3	35	12*	8.75
J. C. Laker	5	9	3	40	17	6.66
P. J. Loader	4	7	1	34	13	5.66

Also batted: G. A. R. Lock 14 and 12.

* *Signifies not out.*

BOWLING

	Overs	Maidens	Runs	Wickets	Average
T. E. Bailey	142.3	43	232	19	12.21
F. H. Tyson	49	14	100	8	12.50
J. H. Wardle	139.6	37	359	26	13.80
J. B. Statham	130.1	20	349	14	24.92
J. C. Laker	145.1	46	324	11	29.45
P. J. Loader	121	27	291	9	32.33

Also bowled: D. C. S. Compton 3—1—8—0; G. A. R. Lock 26—11—2—38.

SOUTH AFRICA

BATTING

	Matches	Inns.	Not Outs	Runs	Highest Inns.	Average
T. L. Goddard	5	10	0	333	69	33.30
R. A. McLean	5	10	0	309	100	30.90
K. J. Funston	3	6	0	133	44	22.16
J. H. B. Waite	5	10	2	169	61	21.12
C. B. Van Ryneveld....	5	10	2	166	36	20.75
W. R. Endean..........	5	10	0	158	70	15.80
H. J. Keith	3	6	0	90	42	15.00
H. Tayfield	5	9	2	91	24	13.00
A. J. Pithey..........	3	6	0	74	25	12.33
J. C. Watkins	2	4	1	24	9	8.00
C. A. R. Duckworth	2	4	0	28	13	7.00
P. Heine..............	5	9	2	45	17	6.42
N. A. T. Adcock	5	9	2	42	17	6.00

Also batted: D. J. McGlew 14 and 7; A. I. Taylor 12 and 6.

BOWLING

	Overs	Maidens	Runs	Wickets	Average
N. A. T. Adcock	142	31	313	21	14.90
H. Tayfield	285	105	636	37	17.18
T. L. Goddard	215.4	81	370	15	24.66
P. Heine...............	185	34	517	18	28.72
C. B. Van Ryneveld.......	44	8	166	4	41.50

Also bowled: J. C. Watkins 24—5—79—0.

M.C.C. TEAM BATTING AVERAGES

FIRST-CLASS MATCHES

	Matches	Inns.	Not Outs	Runs	Highest Inns.	Average
P. B. H. May	16	24	1	1270	206	55.21
D. J. Insole	18	25	4	996	192	47.42
M. C. Cowdrey	18	27	1	1035	173	39.80
D. C. S. Compton	14	22	1	792	131	37.71
T. E. Bailey	16	25	2	703	162	30.56
P. E. Richardson	17	26	0	789	117	30.34
A. S. M. Oakman	14	19	0	534	150	28.10
F. H. Tyson	13	17	5	294	55*	24.50
T. G. Evans	12	19	1	354	80	19.66
B. Taylor	11	13	0	249	65	19.15
G. A. R. Lock	14	18	4	229	39	16.35
J. H. Wardle	14	18	3	207	37	13.80
J. C. Laker	14	16	6	79	17	7.90
J. B. Statham	12	12	6	42	12*	7.00
P. J. Loader	15	16	2	81	13	5.78

Also batted: F. R. Brown 0; J. M. Parks 4.

* Signifies not out.

M.C.C. TEAM BOWLING AVERAGES
FIRST-CLASS MATCHES

	Overs	Maidens	Runs	Wickets	Average
J. H. Wardle	380.3	94	1103	90	12.25
G. A. R. Lock	352.7	120	833	56	14.87
T. E. Bailey	254.5	76	461	29	15.89
P. J. Loader	316	76	751	46	16.32
J. B. Statham	233.2	40	607	36	16.86
F. H. Tyson	254.3	65	636	37	17.18
J. C. Laker	387.7	122	875	50	17.50
D. C. S. Compton	16.2	1	73	3	24.33
A. S. M. Oakman	15	4	48	0	—

Also bowled: F. R. Brown 9—2—26—0; T. G. Evans 1—0—8—0.

The following nineteen three-figure innings, all first-class, were played for M.C.C. during the tour:—

P. B. H. May (6):
    206   v. Rhodesia at Salisbury.
    162   v. Western Province at Cape Town.
    124*   v. Rhodesia at Bulawayo.
    118   v. Eastern Province at Port Elizabeth.
    116   v. Western Province at Cape Town.
    107   v. Natal at Durban.
D. J. Insole (4):
    192   v. Transvaal at Johannesburg.
    110*   v. South Africa at Durban (Third Test).
    118   v. Eastern Province at Port Elizabeth.
    116   v. Natal at Durban.
T. E. Bailey (2):
    162   v. Border at East London.
    110   v. Rhodesia at Salisbury.
D. C. S. Compton (2):
    131   v. Transvaal at Johannesburg.
    101   v. Natal at Pietermaritzburg.
M. C. Cowdrey (2):
    173   v. Orange Free State at Bloemfontein.
    101   v. South Africa at Cape Town (Second Test).
P. E. Richardson (2):
    117   v. South Africa at Johannesburg (First Test).
    100   v. Rhodesia at Bulawayo.
A. S. M. Oakman (1):
    150   v. Orange Free State at Bloemfontein.

The following two three-figure innings were played against M.C.C.:—

R. Evans (1):
    110 for Griqualand West at Kimberley.
R. A. McLean (1):
    100 for South Africa at Durban (Third Test).

* Signifies not out.

M.C.C. FIELDING IN 20 FIRST-CLASS MATCHES

T. G. Evans 40 wickets (31 caught, 9 stumped), M. C. Cowdrey 28, D. J. Insole 24, A. S. M. Oakman 16, B. Taylor 18 wickets (12 caught, 6 stumped), G. A. R. Lock 11, J. H. Wardle 11, T. E. Bailey 10, D. C. S. Compton 7, P. J. Loader 5, J. B. Statham 5, P. B. H. May 4, F. H. Tyson 4, J. C. Laker 3, P. E. Richardson 2, Substitute 2 (Lock 2).

M.C.C. v. BOLAND AND SOUTH WESTERN DISTRICTS

At Paarl, October 23, 24. M.C.C. won by an innings and 127 runs, gaining an easy victory in a non-first-class match over an inexperienced, largely youthful side. M.C.C. batted freely and consistently and Wardle showed signs of things to come during the tour, baffling nearly all the batsmen. O. Wynne, a former South African Test player, showed good form in each innings.

M.C.C.

P. E. Richardson c Weinstein b Olivier 25	B. Taylor b Wellington 3
M. C. Cowdrey c A. Kennedy b Bezuidenhout 36	J. H. Wardle b Wellington 14
A. S. M. Oakman c and b Olivier. . 87	J. C. Laker not out 30
P. B. H. May c Olivier b Brett. . . . 68	F. H. Tyson not out 17
D. C. S. Compton c Sanvido b Wellington 75	B 14, l-b 4 18
D. J. Insole b Bezuidenhout 12	1/32 2/98 3/219 (8 wkts., dec.) 385
P. J. Loader did not bat.	4/229 5/263 6/314 7/315 8/336

Boland and South Western Districts

D. de Villiers c Taylor b Tyson	0	— lbw b Tyson	0
E. Sanvido c Taylor b Tyson	1	— b Loader	7
N. McGregor c Taylor b Loader	26	— lbw b Tyson	3
L. Weinstein c and b Wardle	18	— c Taylor b Wardle	2
A. Kennedy b Loader	0	— lbw b Wardle	29
O. Wynne run out	35	— c Oakman b Compton	27
J. Kennedy run out	10	— b Wardle	0
L. R. Wellington b Wardle	6	— c Oakman b Compton	14
J. Olivier b Wardle	22	— c Compton b Wardle	2
R. Brett c Compton b Wardle	8	— b Compton	7
D. Bezuidenhout not out	0	— not out	5
B 14, l-b 8, n-b 1	23	B 12, n-b 1	13

1/0 2/1 3/44 4/44 5/71 6/96 7/108   149   1/0 2/9 3/11 4/16 5/17   109
8/118 9/136   6/77 7/85 8/87 9/103

Boland and South Western Districts Bowling

	O.	M.	R.	W.	O.	M.	R.	W.
Olivier	17	0	98	2				
Wellington.	15	1	76	3				
Bezuidenhout . .	17	2	74	2				
Brett	15	0	63	1				
Wynne	4	0	22	0				
J. Kennedy	4	1	17	0				
McGregor	2	0	17	0				

M.C.C. Bowling

	O.	M.	R.	W.		O.	M.	R.	W.
Tyson	9	2	29	2	. . . .	5	1	11	2
Loader	9	0	23	2	. . . .	10	3	18	1
Wardle	16.4	2	48	4	. . . .	14	1	46	4
Laker	15	3	26	0					
Compton					. . . . .	4.6	0	21	3

Umpires: G. H. Eckhard and S. Collins.

M.C.C. v. WESTERN PROVINCE

At Cape Town, October 26, 27, 29, 30. M.C.C. won by an innings and 76 runs, being vastly superior in batting and bowling. Rain delayed the start until four o'clock on the first day, but the pitch had been completely covered and played easily. Splendid controlled fast bowling by Statham caused a collapse and in two hours Western Province scored only 39 for four, Statham taking all the wickets for ten runs. A little better resistance came next morning, but only Pfaff looked at ease. M.C.C. lost their opening pair for 22, but went ahead during a third wicket partnership of 115 between Oakman and May. May dominated the rest of the innings and played perfect cricket, scoring 162 (one 6, sixteen 4's) in just over five hours. Western Province, 205 behind, again broke down on a pitch taking spin slowly and on the final morning seven wickets went down in the first eighty-five minutes for 36 runs.

Western Province

A. Pithey lbw b Statham	10	—	lbw b Laker		34
J. Nel b Statham	1	—	lbw b Statham		0
G. Innes b Statham	1	—	lbw b Laker		14
C. B. van Ryneveld c Lock b Statham	27	—	b Laker		10
R. MacDonald c Taylor b Statham	0	—	lbw b Laker		28
J. Ferrandi c Statham b Laker	8	—	c Taylor b Statham		7
B. Pfaff b Bailey	46	—	b Laker		0
J. Pothecary b Laker	15	—	c Bailey b Lock		4
E. Fuller run out	7	—	lbw b Lock		0
J. Maile lbw b Bailey	4	—	b Laker		6
J. Liddle not out	6	—	not out		14
L-b 2, n-b 2	4		B 9, l-b 2, n-b 1		12
	129				**129**

1/1 2/4 3/33 4/33 5/46 6/50 7/67
8/93 9/111

1/1 2/54 3/59 4/78 5/98
6/98 7/107 8/109 9/109

M.C.C.

P. E. Richardson c Ferrandi b Fuller	15	B. Taylor c MacDonald b Fuller		18
M. C. Cowdrey b Fuller	63	J. C. Laker b Fuller		10
A. S. M. Oakman c Nel b Liddle	63	G. A. R. Lock not out		13
P. B. H. May c Ferrandi b Fuller	162	J. B. Statham b Fuller		0
J. M. Parks lbw b van Ryneveld	4	B 10, l-b 8, n-b 1		19
D. J. Insole lbw b van Ryneveld	18			
T. E. Bailey c Innes b Maile	12	1/15 2/22 3/137 4/152 5/182		**334**
		6/229 7/277 8/312 9/334		

M.C.C. Bowling

	O.	M.	R.	W.	O.	M.	R.	W.
Statham	16	5	26	5	10	2	28	2
Bailey	11.2	2	23	2	7	2	15	0
Laker	15	3	42	2	24	12	47	6
Lock	11	5	34	0	13	4	27	2

Western Province Bowling

	O.	M.	R.	W.
Fuller	22	4	83	6
Pothecary	11	1	38	0
Maile	21	9	58	1
Liddle	33	7	78	1
van Ryneveld	22	3	58	2
Innes	1	1	0	0

Umpires: D. Collins and V. Costello.

M.C.C. v. EASTERN PROVINCE

At Port Elizabeth, November 3, 5. M.C.C. won by an innings and 201 runs with a day to spare. Eastern Province provided weak opposition in batting and were outclassed. Heavy rain led to an agreement that the match should be postponed a day and another day added at the end. Put in to bat, Eastern Province were in trouble from the moment Wardle and Lock went on, even though the pitch took spin only slowly. M.C.C. struggled for a time against steady bowling, but Insole and May added 218 for the fourth wicket. May played another faultless innings, but Insole was not at his best. Eastern Province, 260 behind, were dismissed in an hour and forty minutes, the match ending in the last over of the second day. Again the spin bowlers were far too good for the batsmen, and Lock, on a pitch taking spin quicker than on the first day, was almost unplayable.

Eastern Province

G. Dakin b Wardle	9	—	lbw b Tyson		4
P. Jamieson b Tyson	6	—	lbw b Loader		4
B. Dold b Lock	31	—	c Bailey b Lock		22
H. Emslie c Insole b Lock	12	—	c Cowdrey b Lock		1
P. Copeland b Wardle	1	—	not out		1
A. Hicks b Wardle	24	—	c Cowdrey b Lock		8
B. Bradfield c Insole b Lock	3	—	c Richardson b Wardle		0
A. McKinnon c Insole b Lock	4	—	c Evans b Lock		0
I. Anderson c Compton b Wardle	5	—	b Lock		10
J. Ferrant c Lock b Wardle	4	—	c Evans b Lock		0
R. Forward not out	1	—	st Evans b Wardle		3
B 4, l-b 1	5		B 3, l-b 2, n-b 1		6

1/9 2/39 3/55 4/64 5/64 6/70 7/74   105   1/7 2/15 3/28 4/37 5/42   59
8/87 9/104   6/42 7/42 8/46 9/55

M.C.C.

P. E. Richardson c Bradfield b Anderson	11	G. A. R. Lock b Ferrant	5
M. C. Cowdrey run out	33	T. E. Bailey c Dakin b McKinnon	8
D. J. Insole c Forward b McKinnon	118	F. H. Tyson not out	16
D. C. S. Compton c Dold b McKinnon	7	P. J. Loader b McKinnon	7
P. B. H. May c Bradfield b Ferrant	118	B 3, l-b 3, n-b 9	15
T. G. Evans c Dold b Ferrant	8		
J. H. Wardle b McKinnon	19	1/23 2/58 3/75 4/293 5/307 365	
		6/313 7/332 8/332 9/357	

M.C.C. Bowling

	O.	M.	R.	W.		O.	M.	R.	W.
Tyson	4	0	10	1	....	5	2	10	1
Loader	6	2	9	0	....	4	0	6	1
Lock	19	2	51	4	....	7.4	2	14	6
Wardle	16.7	4	30	5	....	7	2	23	2

Eastern Province Bowling

	O.	M.	R.	W.
Anderson	15	0	45	1
Ferrant	32	12	75	3
McKinnon	41	4	159	5
Dakin	2	0	16	0
Hicks	1	0	2	0
Forward	7	0	36	0
Jamieson	2	0	17	0

Umpires: E. Howell and E. W. Prynn.

M.C.C. v. ORANGE FREE STATE

At Bloemfontein, November 9, 10. M.C.C. won by an innings and 168 runs, gaining another overwhelming success with a day to spare. Insole, who led the side for the first time, won the toss and M.C.C. batted on the fastest pitch they had met so far. Richardson soon fell to a catch at the wicket for the third time in succession, but Cowdrey and Oakman mastered a moderate attack and added 318 in 220 minutes, the highest partnership for the second wicket ever recorded in South Africa. Cowdrey hit twenty-one 4's while scoring 173 in four hours twelve minutes, and Oakman stayed three hours forty minutes for 150 which included one 6 and eighteen 4's. Insole declared first thing on the second morning and Orange Free State were dismissed twice in a day. Carlstein, an eighteen-year-old batsman, showed promise in each innings, and Johnstone, Fox and Kirby also made reasonable scores, but nearly everyone was baffled by the mixed spin of Wardle, who took 14 wickets for 96 runs. Insole claimed the extra half-hour and finished the match with nine minutes remaining. At the start of the O.F.S. second innings Statham tore the fibres under his right heel.

M.C.C.

P. E. Richardson c Kirby b Blenkinsop	9	T. E. Bailey not out	35
M. C. Cowdrey c Richardson b Blenkinsop	173	T. G. Evans not out	14
A. S. M. Oakman c Johnstone b Blenkinsop	150	B 1, l-b 5, n-b 1	7
D. C. S. Compton c Fox b Fairbairn	32		

1/19 2/337 3/339 4/400   (4 wkts., dec.) 420

D. J. Insole, J. H. Wardle, J. C. Laker, J. B. Statham and P. J. Loader did not bat.

Orange Free State

S. Hanson c Evans b Statham	0	— b Wardle	19
C. Richardson b Loader	0	— b Wardle	19
E. Johnstone c Oakman b Wardle	21	— c Oakman b Wardle	3
D. Schonegevel c Bailey b Loader	6	— lbw b Wardle	2
P. Carlstein c Wardle b Laker	25	— b Compton	41
S. Fox not out	17	— c and b Compton	29
I. Kirby c Evans b Wardle	0	— not out	47
G. Jackson c Bailey b Wardle	0	— b Wardle	7
I. Littleford st Evans b Wardle	1	— b Wardle	0
D. Fairbairn st Evans b Wardle	0	— st Evans b Wardle	8
A. Blenkinsop c Statham b Wardle	0	— c Loader b Wardle	6
L-b 1	1		

1/0 2/4 3/18 4/44 5/54 6/55 7/61 8/69 9/71   71

1/30 2/40 3/41 4/106 5/113 6/115 7/133 8/133 9/169   181

Orange Free State Bowling

	O.	M.	R.	W.
Littleford	15	3	68	0
Blenkinsop	20	2	97	3
Fairbairn	20	0	110	1
Hanson	10	1	30	0
Fox	7	0	47	0
Jackson	10	0	45	0
Carlstein	3	0	16	0

M.C.C. Bowling

	O.	M.	R.	W.		O.	M.	R.	W.
Statham	5	0	16	1	....	1	1	0	0
Loader	6	1	13	2	....	7	2	30	0
Bailey	3	1	7	0	....	4	2	8	0
Laker	9	3	18	1	....	13	5	20	0
Wardle	7.1	1	16	6	....	18.2	3	80	8
Compton					....	10	0	43	2

Umpires: J. Laupos and G. Niddrie.

M.C.C. v. RHODESIA

At Bulawayo, November 17, 18, 19. M.C.C. won by an innings and 86 runs with twenty-seven minutes to spare and continued their fine run of success. All five matches, four first-class, had been won with an innings to spare. This was the first victory by an official M.C.C. side over Rhodesia. On an easy pitch Rhodesia began steadily but collapsed after tea, taken at 133 for three. Bailey caused the breakdown with a spell of four wickets for three runs in 22 balls. Mansell hit the first fifty against the touring team. M.C.C. scored easily throughout Sunday when Richardson showed his best form for the first time, batting two and a half hours for 100. Oakman, Compton and Insole made useful contributions but May again dominated the cricket, scoring his third century in succession. In one hundred minutes after tea he made 102 and altogether batted just under three hours, hitting two 6's and seventeen 4's. May declared first thing on Monday and Rhodesia might have saved the game but for a downpour which affected the turf before the covers could be put into place. At the stoppage, five minutes after lunch, Rhodesia were 89 for two. Two hours remained when play resumed and Lock, spinning the ball quickly, was largely responsible for the rout of the remaining batsmen.

Rhodesia

D. O'Connell-Jones c Insole b Tyson	45	— run out	26
J. M. S. Baldwin c Oakman b Loader	7	— c Oakman b Loader	9
C. A. R. Duckworth b Wardle	19	— c Loader b Lock	40
D. J. Lewis c Taylor b Bailey	37	— c Taylor b Tyson	30
P. N. F. Mansell c Compton b Wardle	50	— c Loader b Lock	2
P. L. Winslow lbw b Bailey	0	— c Insole b Lock	2
D. B. Arnott b Bailey	3	— c Taylor b Tyson	0
R. W. Coventry b Bailey	0	— c Taylor b Lock	6
C. Wooler b Tyson	1	— c Insole b Wardle	1
H. Paton c and b Wardle	5	— not out	0
G. B. L. Lawrence not out	15	— c Insole b Lock	0
B 2, l-b 7, n-b 1	10	B 4, l-b 6, n-b 3	13
	192		129

1/28 2/58 3/92 4/136 5/144 6/148
7/148 8/151 9/165

1/17 2/48 3/102 4/105
5/107 6/119 7/121 8/129
9/129

M.C.C.

P. E. Richardson run out	100	B. Taylor c sub b Lawrence	2
A. S. M. Oakman c Mansell b Coventry	44	G. A. R. Lock c Lawrence b Paton	0
D. C. S. Compton c Lewis b Wooler	49	L-b 7, w 1, n-b 1	9
P. B. H. May not out	124		
D. J. Insole c and b Paton	67	1/99 2/178 3/219 (7 wkts., dec.) 407
T. E. Bailey c Arnott b Paton	12	4/333 5/372 6/399 7/407

F. H. Tyson, J. H. Wardle and P. J. Loader did not bat.

M.C.C. Bowling

	O.	M.	R.	W.		O.	M.	R.	W.
Tyson	13	2	29	2	....	8	1	28	2
Loader	10	1	34	1	....	7	1	13	1
Bailey	20	9	22	4	....	6	3	13	0
Wardle	19.6	3	68	3	....	15	5	50	1
Lock	9	2	29	0	....	14.2	11	12	5

Rhodesia Bowling

	O.	M.	R.	W.
Lawrence	19	3	61	1
Wooler	14	1	67	1
Coventry	20	0	121	1
Mansell	15	0	90	0
Paton	13.5	0	59	3

Umpires: A. Fox and M. Pengelly.

M.C.C. v. RHODESIA

At Salisbury, November 23, 24, 25. M.C.C. won by an innings and 292 runs with a day remaining, their biggest success of the tour. Rhodesia, who made three changes, were no match for M.C.C. on a pitch which gave fast bowlers a fair amount of help. After losing three wickets for 66, M.C.C. took control. May was again in tremendous form, playing his fourth three-figure innings in succession, and Bailey shared a stand of 301 in 245 minutes. May's 206, made in four and a half hours, included two 6's and thirty-three 4's. Evans hit 50 in three-quarters of an hour and was the first of three victims in an over to Lawrence, a tall, fast-medium bowler who alone troubled the batsmen. Rhodesia were helpless against the controlled swing of Loader, and after losing their first six wickets for 11, followed on 444 behind. Loader took two wickets in his first over before twisting a knee when losing the heel of a boot. A seventh wicket stand of 50 between a promising eighteen-year-old schoolboy, Bland, and Arnott delayed M.C.C.'s triumphant progress.

M.C.C.

M. C. Cowdrey c Coventry b Barber	20	J. C. Laker c Coventry b Lawrence	0
A. S. M. Oakman c Duckworth b Paton	26	G. A. R. Lock c O'Connell-Jones b Lawrence	0
T. E. Bailey b Lawrence	110	F. H. Tyson not out	19
D. J. Insole lbw b Lawrence	8	P. J. Loader c sub b Barber	0
P. B. H. May c Coventry b Barber	206	B 10, l-b 4, n-b 2	16
B. Taylor c Mansell b Lawrence	46		
T. G. Evans c and b Lawrence	50		501

1/42 2/48 3/66 4/367 5/393 6/465 7/465 8/465 9/500

Rhodesia

D. O'Connell-Jones lbw b Loader	2	— c Bailey b Loader	0
G. Barber lbw b Tyson	0	— lbw b Loader	2
C. A. R. Duckworth lbw b Tyson	7	— c Insole b Bailey	9
D. J. Lewis lbw b Loader	0	— lbw b Laker	4
P. N. F. Mansell c Evans b Loader	0	— c and b Tyson	12
M. Davies b Loader	0	— c Evans b Tyson	18
C. Bland c Evans b Lock	19	— c and b Lock	38
D. B. Arnott c Oakman b Lock	9	— run out	22
R. W. Coventry c Cowdrey b Loader	13	— b Laker	7
H. Paton b Loader	6	— c Oakman b Laker	21
G. B. L. Lawrence not out	0	— not out	12
N-b 1	1	B 3, l-b 3, n-b 1	7

1/1 2/7 3/7 4/7 5/7 6/11 7/34 8/51 9/57   57

1/4 2/6 3/13 4/23 5/47 6/48 7/98 8/105 9/127   152

Rhodesia Bowling

	O.	M.	R.	W.	O.	M.	R.	W.
Lawrence	35	11	104	6				
Coventry	30	4	138	0				
Barber	23.4	5	108	3				
Paton	24	4	98	1				
Mansell	9	0	37	0				

M.C.C. Bowling

	O.	M.	R.	W.	O.	M.	R.	W.
Tyson	8	2	16	2	11	4	23	2
Loader	13	3	28	7	3	1	3	2
Laker	4	2	3	0	19	6	63	3
Lock	2.4	1	9	1	12.3	4	31	1
Bailey					6	2	25	1

Umpires: H. Fox and A. Maddocks.

M.C.C. v. TRANSVAAL

At Johannesburg, November 30, December 1, 3, 4. M.C.C. won by three wickets but were given their first shock of the tour. Transvaal batted carefully but apart from Endean, who remained unbeaten after five hours twenty minutes, their caution did not pay. At the start of the second morning Statham did the hat-trick, clean bowling Ritchie, Charnas and Heine. Richardson and Cowdrey gave M.C.C. a useful start and Compton showed his best form so far, but the last five wickets fell for 50. Cowdrey spent six hours seven minutes over 84. M.C.C. looked to have an easy task in scoring 64 on a fast but good pitch in two and a half hours. Magnificent fast bowling by Heine and Adcock soon had them struggling, and when six wickets went for 36 Transvaal looked like winning. Compton and Tyson came to the rescue, but it took ten minutes to score the winning run and only ten minutes remained for play when Tyson won the game. Heine and Adcock in a fine feat of endurance bowled unchanged for two hours and twenty-five minutes with only the tea interval intervening.

Transvaal

A. I. Taylor b Laker	37	— b Tyson	1
A. Tayfield b Bailey	8	— c Wardle b Statham	38
W. R. Endean not out	81	— lbw b Tyson	0
K. J. Funston c Evans b Statham	13	— c Evans b Tyson	17
J. H. B. Waite c Wardle b Laker	15	— st Evans b Laker	15
R. Kimber c and b Wardle	23	— lbw b Statham	0
G. Ritchie b Statham	2	— c Evans b Tyson	19
M. Charnas b Statham	0	— b Laker	12
P. Heine b Statham	0	— c Bailey b Laker	10
K. Gibbs c Evans b Tyson	13	— b Laker	7
N. A. T. Adcock run out	6	— not out	2
B 6, l-b 5, n-b 3	14	B 4, l-b 4, n-b 1	9

1/38 2/57 3/76 4/105 5/150 6/163	212	1/5 2/5 3/51 4/74 5/74	130
7/163 8/163 9/204		6/87 7/101 8/112 9/121	

M.C.C.

P. E. Richardson b Gibbs	39	—	c Waite b Heine		9
M. C. Cowdrey lbw b Gibbs	84	—	c Tayfield b Adcock		1
A. S. M. Oakman c Charnas b Heine	16	—	c Waite b Adcock		8
P. B. H. May c Waite b Heine	0	—	c Waite b Heine		12
D. C. S. Compton b Heine	72	—	b Heine		13
T. E. Bailey b Adcock	11	—	c Waite b Adcock		1
T. G. Evans c Waite b Heine	25	—	c Waite b Heine		0
F. H. Tyson b Gibbs	10	—	not out		21
J. H. Wardle c Taylor b Heine	5	—	not out		0
J. C. Laker b Gibbs	4				
J. B. Statham not out	2				
B 5, l-b 4, n-b 2	11		L-b 1, n-b 1		2

1/63 2/95 3/95 4/207 5/229 6/233 　　279 　　1/10 2/10 3/29 (7 wkts.) 67
7/262 8/268 9/275 　　　　　　　　　　　　4/31 5/36 6/36 7/63

M.C.C. Bowling

	O.	M.	R.	W.		O.	M.	R.	W.
Statham	18	3	38	4	....	11	2	29	2
Tyson	15.2	3	62	1	....	15	4	44	4
Bailey	15	1	36	1					
Laker	19	3	41	2	....	17.3	6	40	4
Wardle	12	3	21	1	....	1	0	8	0

Transvaal Bowling

	O.	M.	R.	W.		O.	M.	R.	W.
Heine	24	2	86	5	....	11	2	39	4
Adcock	18	1	65	1	....	11	3	26	3
Gibbs	15.5	2	50	4					
Charnas	16	3	44	0					
Taylor	1	0	5	0					
Tayfield	6	1	18	0					

Umpires: A. Birkett and J. McMenamin.

M.C.C. v. SOUTH AFRICAN XI

At Pretoria, December 7, 8, 10, 11. South African XI won by 38 runs and ended M.C.C.'s one hundred per cent record. This was also the first time M.C.C. had lost on a turf pitch in South Africa; their first defeat in that country since 1930–31 and their first defeat outside a Test Match since 1913–14. The game was played on a football ground and the pitch had been laid only three months. It broke up on the first day and batsmen found it almost impossible to make a stroke. The South African side gained a big advantage in winning the toss, but the M.C.C. batting, even allowing for the conditions, disappointed. Spin bowlers were always in command, Tayfield and Wardle particularly enjoying themselves. A good innings by Funston turned the scales and M.C.C. were eventually set to get 148 to win. They lost half the side for 41, and although Bailey made a great effort, staying four hours five minutes for 26, they never looked like getting the runs. An unusual incident occurred at the end of the third day when McGlew ran off the field to see Insole about extra time, and Bailey and Lock, the not out batsmen, walked in with the umpires with the rest of the fieldsmen standing their ground. The batsmen had to return, having been under a misapprehension about the rules existing for extra time.

South African XI

D. J. McGlew st Taylor b Lock	41	— lbw b Wardle 15
A. I. Taylor b Wardle	34	— lbw b Loader 2
W. R. Endean b Wardle	11	— run out 3
K. J. Funston c Bailey b Loader	10	— c and b Lock 55
C. Burger b Lock	0	— b Wardle 0
J. Watkins b Wardle	8	— b Loader 2
P. Carlstein c Richardson b Lock	4	— b Wardle 9
R. Pearce lbw b Lock	0	— b Wardle 8
H. Tayfield st Taylor b Wardle	4	— b Wardle 7
K. Gibbs not out	2	— not out 0
G. B. L. Lawrence b Statham	12	— b Wardle 1
B 3, n-b 9	12	B 9, l-b 4, n-b 1 14

1/57 2/85 3/106 4/107 5/109 6/113   138   1/6 2/10 3/63 4/63 5/68   116
7/113 8/120 9/123   6/87 7/103 8/113 9/113

M.C.C.

P. E. Richardson c Lawrence b Tayfield .	23	— b Tayfield 4
A. S. M. Oakman b Lawrence..........	2	— run out 6
D. J. Insole lbw b Lawrence	7	— c Funston b Lawrence 0
D. C. S. Compton b Tayfield..........	15	— c Lawrence b Tayfield 2
M. C. Cowdrey c Burger b Tayfield	16	— b Gibbs 13
T. E. Bailey not out..................	20	— c Carlstein b Tayfield 26
B. Taylor lbw b Tayfield................	4	— lbw b Tayfield 6
G. A. R. Lock b Tayfield................	5	— c McGlew b Tayfield 0
J. H. Wardle b Watkins................	1	— lbw b Gibbs 21
P. J. Loader c McGlew b Tayfield	8	— c Watkins b Tayfield 10
J. B. Statham b Watkins................	0	— not out 3
L-b 4, n-b 2..........	6	B 10, l-b 8 18

1/10 2/37 3/37 4/62 5/69 6/73 7/81   107   1/16 2/16 3/16 4/21 5/41   109
8/82 9/93   6/79 7/88 8/90 9/106

M.C.C. Bowling

	O.	M.	R.	W.		O.	M.	R.	W.
Statham	10.1	1	17	1	....	4	1	9	0
Loader	11	3	18	1	....	6	1	14	2
Lock	24	8	63	4	....	15	5	49	1
Wardle	25	12	28	4	....	18.3	9	30	6

South African XI Bowling

Lawrence	13	4	26	2	....	24	9	24	1
Gibbs	6	2	13	0	....	12	5	19	2
Tayfield	16	4	36	6	....	36.5	18	47	6
Watkins	9.6	2	26	2	....	3	2	1	0

Umpires: G. I. Fitzpatrick and G. S. Hawkins.

M.C.C. v. NATAL

At Durban, December 14, 15, 17, 18. Drawn. M.C.C. took part in their first drawn game, but went close to winning. Batting first on a lively pitch they began badly, but May once more came to the rescue and Insole gave fine support. May, missed at 41, 73 and 94, was not quite at his best but, nevertheless, played many splendid strokes for four hours. Insole, slow but sure, completed his century on the second morning, batting over five and a half hours. McGlew and Goddard took three hours over their opening stand of 82 and the total reached 116 before the second wicket fell. Three wickets went at the same score in the last over before lunch and swung the game. Leading by 98, M.C.C. did not score quickly enough for an early declaration but looked to have a good chance of winning when Natal's seventh wicket fell with fifty minutes left. The soundness of Watkins saved Natal.

M.C.C.

P. E. Richardson c Pearce b Markham ..	7	—	b Smith	26
A. S. M. Oakman lbw b Goddard	14	—	lbw b Goddard	25
T. E. Bailey c Pearce b Markham	1	—	run out	4
P. B. H. May c Watkins b Goddard 107		—	c Pearce b Goddard	1
M. C. Cowdrey c and b Watkins	1	—	b Markham	32
D. J. Insole b Watkins	116	—	not out	33
T. G. Evans c McLean b Watkins	0	—	c Koch b Markham	2
F. H. Tyson c Keith b Markham	8	—	not out	2
G. A. R. Lock c Pearce b Markham	29	—	c Burger b Goddard	22
J. C. Laker not out	13			
P. J. Loader b Watkins	8			
L-b 2, n-b 1..................	3		B 2, l-b 1	3

1/8 2/10 3/50 4/55 5/191 6/194   307   1/51 2/55 (7 wkts., dec.) 150
7/218 8/269 9/299   3/55 4/89 5/94 6/131 7/135

Natal

D. J. McGlew c Evans b Tyson	27	—	c Cowdrey b Loader	5
T. L. Goddard st Evans b Laker........	89	—	b Loader	2
H. J. Keith lbw b Tyson	18	—	b Loader	35
J. C. Watkins b Laker........	8	—	not out	35
R. A. McLean b Laker	13	—	hit wkt b Lock	11
C. Burger run out	0	—	lbw b Loader	3
R. A. Pearce b Laker	0	—	b Tyson	1
L. Koch c Insole b Tyson........	21	—	c Cowdrey b Lock	14
N. Markham c Loader b Laker	6	—	not out	12
V. I. Smith not out	2	—	c Oakman b Tyson	0
P. Dodds b Tyson	3			
B 11, l-b 6, n-b 5	22		B 3, n-b 4	7

1/82 2/116 3/137 4/160 5/160 6/160   209   1/5 2/5 3/9 (7 wkts.) 90
7/186 8/196 9/201   4/18 5/25 6/53 7/55

Natal Bowling

	O.	M.	R.	W.		O.	M.	R.	W.
Markham	17	0	81	4	....	10.4	1	40	2
Goddard	35	11	60	2	....	15	4	26	3
Watkins	29.4	10	77	4	....	9	4	18	0
Dodds	11	1	38	0	....	6	1	24	0
Smith	14	3	48	0	....	16	4	39	1
			McGlew	......		1	1	0	0

M.C.C. Bowling

	O.	M.	R.	W.		O.	M.	R.	W.
Tyson	17.1	4	41	4		7	2	19	2
Loader	20	5	50	4		9	4	13	3
Bailey	10	2	20	0					
Laker........	27	8	53	5		14	5	30	0
Lock	9	3	23	0		12	4	21	2

Umpires: B. V. Malan and W. Marais.

M.C.C. v. NORTH-EASTERN TRANSVAAL

At Benoni, December 20. 21, 22. Drawn. Cricket was restricted to five hours twenty minutes. M.C.C. arrived late at the ground because of a train hold-up and play did not start until 3.40 p.m. Then bad light and rain stopped play for the day after ninety minutes with North-Eastern Transvaal 44 for four. Helfrich, who batted without gloves, made several fine drives in a stay of two and a half hours. Extras was the next best score. M.C.C. started steadily, but Compton, on the ground where he made 300 eight years earlier, showed dazzling form, scoring 71 in seventy minutes with the help of eleven 4's. He and Richardson put on 96 in forty-five minutes. Rain again curtailed play and not a ball could be bowled on the last day.

North-Eastern Transvaal

P. C. Davies b Wardle	10	H. Patterson st Taylor b Wardle..	0
J. Farham b Statham	0	B. McBride c Cowdrey b Wardle..	12
C. D. Abrams b Statham	0	G. Middlewick b Lock	1
P. R. Richardson c Taylor b Statham	3	R. Smith not out	4
K. Helfrich c Tyson b Wardle....	71	B 6, l-b 5, n-b 5	16
F. Seyfried lbw b Statham	1		—
S. F. Burke b Tyson	7		125

1/1 2/1 3/6 4/41 5/49 6/84 7/85 8/113 9/117

M.C.C.

P. E. Richardson b Helfrich	52	N-b 1	1
A. S. M. Oakman b Middlewick..	21		—
D. C. S. Compton not out	71		
M. C. Cowdrey not out	3	1/30 2/126 (2 wkts.)	148

D. J. Insole, B. Taylor, J. H. Wardle, F. H. Tyson, G. A. R. Lock, P. J. Loader and J. B. Statham did not bat.

M.C.C. Bowling	O.	M.	R.	W.	North-Eastern Transvaal Bowling	O.	M.	R.	W.
Statham	10	1	37	4	Middlewick ...	6	1	18	1
Tyson	10	3	25	1	McBride	6	0	23	0
Loader	6	0	18	0	Burke	7	0	51	0
Wardle	7.4	3	22	4	Abrams	3	0	31	0
Lock	2	0	7	1	Helfrich	3	0	24	1

Umpires: C. D. Coate and R. Haugh.

ENGLAND v. SOUTH AFRICA

First Test Match

At Johannesburg, December 24, 26, 27, 28, 29. England won by 131 runs in a slow-scoring match. The scoring rate averaged 28 runs an hour over the entire game and there were many periods when it dropped considerably lower. Admittedly the pitch did not encourage batsmen to make strokes, for the ball often lifted a little and much of the bowling was negative, but even so hardly any batsmen made the slightest effort to take the initiative. Although the match was saved as a spectacle by the frequent fall of wickets after the opening day, the first 100,000 crowd to attend a game in South Africa saw nothing of the charm of cricket.

This was the first Test Match to be played on the new Wanderers ground, and although the pitch showed no sign of wear it always helped the faster bowlers because of the lift and movement in the air and off the turf they were able to obtain. South Africa were unfortunate to lose their captain and most dependable batsman, McGlew, who dropped out the day before the match with a slightly dislocated left shoulder.

Still seeking a satisfactory opening partner for Richardson, May decided to give Bailey a further opportunity when he won the toss. Bailey had occasionally opened the innings in Test Matches, but he had not been tried there in earlier matches on the tour. The general pattern of the game was shown in the first hour when Richardson and Bailey scored only 20. In two hours twenty minutes to lunch England reached 45 while losing the wickets of Bailey and Compton, and when May left soon afterwards the situation looked bad for them.

Then occurred the one effective partnership of the game. Richardson and Cowdrey remained together for the rest of the day, England finishing with 157 for three after six hours. Richardson, who rarely attempted a scoring stroke unless absolutely safe, batted all day for 69.

The stand, which added 121 in three and a half hours, soon ended next day, but Richardson continued his stubborn defensive tactics and his century, after eight hours eight minutes, was the slowest in the history of Test cricket. In all he batted eight hours forty-six minutes for 117 and hit only six 4's.

At the end of the second day South Africa looked to be getting on top for they had lost only one wicket for 91. England's fight back began first thing on the third morning. Tyson developed tonsillitis overnight and could not bowl or field again in the match. Largely because of this Bailey was given more opportunity with the ball and it proved a telling factor. After Statham dismissed Goddard in the opening over, Bailey sent back Keith and McLean in one over and from these quick shocks South Africa failed to recover. The tail-end batsmen improved matters slightly, 74 being added for the last three wickets, but England gained a useful lead of 35 in what was obviously to be a low-scoring match.

They were forced to struggle again, and at the end of the third day three men were out for 42. Evans brought the only sparkle into the batting, everyone else having to fight desperately for runs. South Africa were set to get 204 to win, not an unreasonable task with plenty of time to spare, but their hopes quickly disappeared. Against good bowling by Bailey and Statham they lost seven wickets for 40 runs in one and three-quarter hours to the close, batting very poorly.

The match was over within eighty minutes on the last morning, South Africa being dismissed for their lowest total in a home Test since 1898–99 and the lowest score they had made against England since being dismissed for 30 at Birmingham in 1924.

Apart from the slow scoring, good bowling and weak batting, the match was notable for the excellent standard of catching. Bailey held a wonderful diving catch at slip to get rid of van Ryneveld in the first innings, and Endean, at square-leg, threw himself horizontally in the air to grasp a firm hit by May in England's second innings. Cowdrey, Insole, Goddard and Keith also held fine catches. South Africa's ground fielding was also of the highest class.

England

P. E. Richardson lbw b Goddard	117	—	lbw b Adcock	10
T. E. Bailey c Waite b Heine	16	—	c Endean b Heine	10
D. C. S. Compton c Keith b Goddard	5	—	c and b Tayfield	32
P. B. H. May c Goddard b Adcock	6	—	c Endean b Heine	14
M. C. Cowdrey c Goddard b Heine	59	—	c Goddard b Adcock	6
D. J. Insole c Waite b van Ryneveld	1	—	c Waite b Goddard	29
T. G. Evans c Keith b Adcock	20	—	c Heine b Tayfield	30
F. H. Tyson b Adcock	22	—	c Watkins b Adcock	2
J. H. Wardle not out	6	—	lbw b Heine	0
J. C. Laker c Goddard b Adcock	0	—	not out	3
J. B. Statham c Waite b Goddard	0	—	lbw b Tayfield	2
B 4, l-b 9, n-b 3	16		B 8, l-b 1, n-b 3	12

1/28 2/37 3/48 4/169 5/170 6/205   268   1/11 2/37 3/37 4/84   150
7/259 8/263 9/263   5/100 6/107 7/126 8/145
                                                9/147

South Africa

A. I. Taylor st Evans b Wardle	12	—	c Insole b Bailey	6
T. L. Goddard c Cowdrey b Statham	49	—	c Insole b Bailey	5
H. J. Keith c Cowdrey b Bailey	42	—	c Evans b Bailey	2
W. R. Endean c Cowdrey b Laker	18	—	b Statham	3
R. A. McLean lbw b Bailey	0	—	c Insole b Bailey	6
J. C. Watkins c Insole b Wardle	9	—	b Laker	8
C. B. van Ryneveld c Bailey b Statham	10	—	run out	16
J. H. B. Waite c Evans b Bailey	17	—	b Statham	0
H. J. Tayfield b Wardle	24	—	c Evans b Bailey	2
P. Heine not out	13	—	run out	17
N. A. T. Adcock b Statham	17	—	not out	0
B 1, l-b 3	4		B 2, l-b 3, n-b 2	7

1/54 2/92 3/112 4/112 5/126 6/141   215   1/6 2/10 3/11 4/20 5/25   72
7/141 8/176 9/194   6/36 7/40 8/44 9/71

South Africa Bowling

	O.	M.	R.	W.		O.	M.	R.	W.
Heine	31	5	89	2	....	19	7	41	3
Adcock	20	6	36	4	....	13	1	33	3
Goddard	28.5	9	51	3	....	14	7	14	1
Watkins	11	3	23	0	....	3	0	10	0
Tayfield	20	4	30	0	....	17.6	5	40	3
van Ryneveld	8	2	23	1					

M.C.C. Bowling

	O.	M.	R.	W.		O.	M.	R.	W.
Statham	24.1	4	71	3	....	13	4	22	2
Tyson	9	1	22	0					
Wardle	20	4	52	3	....	3	0	18	0
Laker	21	10	33	1	....	2	1	5	1
Bailey	15	5	33	3	....	15.4	6	20	5

Umpires: J. McMenamin and W. Marais.

ENGLAND v. SOUTH AFRICA

Second Test Match

At Cape Town, January 1, 2, 3, 4, 5. England won by 312 runs and placed themselves in a strong position to win the series. They took control almost from the start and never relaxed, finally racing to victory when South Africa collapsed badly for the second time in two Tests. Cricket history was made on the last day when the first handled ball dismissal occurred in a Test Match.

Tyson, because of tonsillitis, could not be considered for England, being replaced by Loader. McGlew, despite his shoulder trouble, captained South

Africa, displacing Taylor. May won the toss for the second time and it quickly became obvious that the pitch lacked pace which, with South Africa's type of attack, proved a big handicap to them. Richardson and Bailey gave England a sound start, but soon after lunch South Africa broke the stand and, in the space of seventy minutes, three wickets, including that of May, fell for the addition of 43 runs.

The situation changed when Cowdrey joined Compton. Neither took the slightest risk, but they rarely looked in trouble. They added 67 and by the close England, with a total of 214 for four, had recovered well. Tayfield, going on fifty minutes after the start of the match, bowled unchanged at one end until the close, sending down 41 successive overs and taking three of the four wickets for 69.

England lost Insole early next morning, but South Africa's hopes of finishing the innings quickly were dashed by Cowdrey and Evans, who put on 93 in eighty-five minutes. Evans, one of the few batsmen who attempted attacking strokes, scored 62 of the runs. The next three wickets fell for 20, but Cowdrey remained, and when Statham, the last man, joined him he needed 20 for his century. At last, departing from rigid defence, Cowdrey, after being missed at long-on off Tayfield when 85, promptly hit that bowler for 13 in an over and reached his century. One run later he was out, having batted six hours ten minutes and hit one 6 and nine 4's. His solid play helped considerably to give England their good total.

McGlew and Goddard looked safe enough when they opened the South Africa innings, but when the slow bowlers appeared the situation changed rapidly. McGlew, batting with his shoulder strapped, fell in Laker's fourth over, and although the fast-medium Loader took the next two wickets it was apparent that spin was going to decide the match. South Africa finished the second day at 51 for three and despite useful efforts from McLean and Waite they never really recovered. Laker could not get the ball to turn quickly, but Wardle, with his off-breaks and googlies, caused innumerable problems. He spun the ball a prodigious amount, although not quickly enough on the slow pitch to be really unplayable.

Although leading by 164, May did not enforce the follow-on and England built an impregnable position. When the third day ended Richardson and Bailey had scored 21 without loss and they carried their stand to 74. Adcock could not play on the fourth day because of a sore toe, and van Ryneveld, although fielding, could not bowl because of a slightly fractured little finger on his right hand.

McGlew endeavoured to keep down runs and did not employ a slip or close fieldsman for either Heine or Goddard, who bowled unchanged throughout the morning and for twenty minutes after lunch. The deep defensive field succeeded in restricting England's rate of progress, but steadily the lead mounted. Compton and Cowdrey again shared a good stand and this time Cowdrey showed his wide range of strokes, scoring 61 of the 87 added in eighty-six minutes.

May declared when Compton gave a return catch in the last over before tea and South Africa were set to get 385 to win in eight hours on a pitch which made quick scoring extremely difficult. Their task was almost hopeless and from the first they decided on defensive tactics in an effort to save the game. Again Wardle was England's trump card. He bowled McGlew round his legs in his second over and quickly followed by getting Keith caught at cover.

South Africa ended the fourth day at 41 for two, and although defeat looked inevitable it came much quicker than expected. Wardle, again making the ball spin considerably, did almost as he pleased and the match ended after ninety minutes on the last day. Four wickets fell at 67 and altogether the remaining eight wickets went down for the addition of 31 runs, South Africa being out for the same total as their second innings in the First Test.

Wardle's seven for 36 were his best Test figures and his beautifully controlled and varied spin left South Africa nonplussed.

The "handled ball" incident occurred when Endean pushed out his leg outside the off stump to Laker in the second innings. The ball rose high and might well have fallen on to the stumps had not Endean thrown up a hand and diverted it. On appeal the umpire had no option but to give him out. Endean, curiously, was concerned in the previous strange Test dismissal, being the wicket-keeper when Hutton was given out "obstructing the field" at The Oval in 1951. Endean might have made a catch had not Hutton knocked away the ball when trying to protect his wicket.

England

P. E. Richardson lbw b Heine	45	— c Endean b Goddard	44
T. E. Bailey c Waite b Tayfield	34	— b Heine	28
D. C. S. Compton c McLean b Tayfield	58	— c and b Goddard	64
P. B. H. May c Waite b Tayfield	8	— c Waite b Heine	15
M. C. Cowdrey lbw b Adcock	101	— c Waite b Tayfield	61
D. J. Insole c Goddard b Adcock	29	— not out	3
T. G. Evans c McGlew b Goddard	62	— c Endean b Goddard	1
J. H. Wardle st Waite b Tayfield	3		
J. C. Laker b Adcock	0		
P. J. Loader c Keith b Tayfield	10		
J. B. Statham not out	2		
B 6, l-b 6, n-b 5	17	L-b 2 n-b 2	4

1/76 2/88 3/116 4/183 5/233 6/326   **369**   1/74 2/74   (6 wkts., dec.) **220**
7/334 8/335 9/346   3/109 4/196 5/208 6/220

South Africa

D. J. McGlew c Cowdrey b Laker	14	— b Wardle	7
T. L. Goddard c Evans b Loader	18	— c Bailey b Wardle	26
H. J. Keith c Evans b Loader	14	— c May b Wardle	4
C. B. van Ryneveld b Wardle	25	— not out	0
H. J. Tayfield run out	5	— c Evans b Wardle	4
R. A. McLean c May b Statham	42	— lbw b Laker	22
J. H. B. Waite c Evans b Wardle	49	— c Cowdrey b Wardle	2
W. R. Endean b Wardle	17	— handled ball	3
J. C. Watkins not out	7	— c and b Wardle	0
P. Heine b Wardle	0	— b Wardle	0
N. A. T. Adcock c Evans b Wardle	11	— b Laker	1
B 1, l-b 1, n-b 1	3	L-b 2, n-b 1	3

1/23 2/39 3/48 4/63 5/110 6/126   **205**   1/21 2/28 3/42 4/56 5/67   **72**
7/178 8/191 9/191   6/67 7/67 8/67 9/71

South Africa Bowling

	O.	M.	R.	W.		O.	M.	R.	W.
Heine	19	0	78	1	....	21	1	67	2
Adcock	22.2	2	54	3	....	3	0	8	0
Tayfield	53	21	130	5	....	12	4	33	1
Goddard	38	12	74	1	....	17.5	1	62	3
van Ryneveld	3	0	16	0					
Watkins						10	2	46	0

England Bowling

	O.	M.	R.	W.		O.	M.	R.	W.
Statham	16	0	38	1	....	8	2	12	0
Loader	21	5	33	2	....	7	2	11	0
Laker	28	8	65	1	....	14.1	9	7	2
Bailey	11	5	13	0					
Wardle	23.6	9	53	5	....	19	3	36	7
Compton						2	1	3	0

Umpires: D. Collins and V. Costello.

M.C.C. v. COUNTRY DISTRICTS XI

At Queenstown January 8, 9. M.C.C. won by an innings and 110 runs. The second of the two non-first-class matches brought another overwhelming victory against a side containing a fair leavening of experienced players. Loader and Wardle were far too good for the batsmen and bright innings came from May, Insole and Compton. May took only seventy minutes over 91 and he and Compton put on 85 in thirty-five minutes. Good hitting by the Country Districts' middle batsmen in the second innings prevented a complete debacle.

Country Districts XI

G. Barber lbw b Loader	2	—	c Loader b Brown	14
H. S. Lacey st Taylor b Wardle	12	—	c Taylor b Tyson	0
L. Lund c Wardle b Loader	0	—	c Wardle b Loader	3
P. Tainton c Taylor b Tyson	2	—	b Tyson	4
E. Eaglestone b Lock	5	—	c Insole b Brown	5
M. Price-Moore b Loader	13	—	c Richardson b Wardle	27
R. Faasen c Taylor b Wardle	8	—	c Richardson b Wardle	21
L. W. Payn b Loader	1	—	c Lock b Wardle	26
J. Harty b Loader	0	—	c Taylor b Loader	9
P. Gallop not out	1	—	st Taylor b Wardle	2
J. Gush st Taylor b Wardle	0	—	not out	1
L-b 3, n-b 3	6		B 1, l-b 2	3
	50			**115**

1/5 2/8 3/14 4/21 5/38 6/40   1/1 2/4 3/13 4/27 5/40
7/45 8/45 9/50   6/77 7/82 8/112 9/114

M.C.C.

P. E. Richardson run out	8		F. R. Brown c Lacey b Gush	11
B. Taylor c and b Gush	41		F. H. Tyson not out	1
D. J. Insole lbw b Lund	70		B 5, l-b 2	7
P. B. H. May b Barber	91			
D. C. S. Compton not out	44		1/12 2/98 3/158 (6 wkts., dec.) 275	
T. G. Evans c Faasen b Barber	2		4/243 5/249 6/267	

G. A. R. Lock, J. H. Wardle and P. J. Loader did not bat.

M.C.C. Bowling

	O.	M.	R.	W.		O.	M.	R.	W.
Tyson	6	3	6	1	....	6	3	6	2
Loader	8	1	14	5	....	7	4	10	2
Lock	5	1	10	1	....	8	2	35	0
Wardle	2.3	0	14	3	....	8.3	1	37	4
Brown						6	1	24	2

Country Districts XI Bowling

	O.	M.	R.	W.
Gush	16	2	76	2
Gallop	7	0	35	0
Payn	14	0	79	0
Lund	3	0	36	1
Barber	6	0	42	2

Umpires: G. Jureidin and J. E. Roach.

M.C.C. v. BORDER

At East London, January 11, 12. M.C.C. won by an innings and 218 runs with a day to spare, once more outclassing weak opposition. Bailey and Oakman shared the first three-figure opening stand of the tour and Bailey also helped in century partnerships with May and Cowdrey. Batting five and three-quarter hours for 162 out of 356, Bailey hit fifteen 4's. He and Cowdrey added 102 in sixty-five minutes. May declared after an hour on the second morning and Border were dismissed the first time in two hours twenty minutes, their batsmen having little answer to pace or spin. In the Border first innings Statham dismissed both opening batsmen with the first ball each received. Border promised more resistance in the second innings but again failed.

M.C.C.

T. E. Bailey c Geach b Chalmers . .	162	F. H. Tyson c sub b Knott		0
A. S. M. Oakman c Dawson b		G. A. R. Lock c Wilson b Chalmers		6
Chalmers	49	J. H. Wardle c Wilson b Knott		9
B. Taylor c Price b Chalmers	12	B 2, l-b 5		7
P. B. H. May b Knott	79			
M. C. Cowdrey c Geach b Chalmers	62	1/103 2/121 3/254 (8 wkts., dec.)	400
D. J. Insole not out	14	4/356 5/370 6/370 7/381 8/400	

J. C. Laker and J. B. Statham did not bat.

Border

W. Wilson b Statham	0	— b Statham	20
R. Geach b Statham	0	— c Taylor b Tyson	12
O. Dawson c Wardle b Tyson	11	— b Lock	11
K. Kirton c Oakman b Laker	18	— b Laker	0
B. Crews c Cowdrey b Laker	5	— lbw b Wardle	9
R. Phillips c Cowdrey b Laker	25	— c Cowdrey b Wardle	9
R. Thorne c Insole b Laker	5	— c Statham b Lock	14
S. Knott c Oakman b Wardle	7	— c and b Lock	8
M. Price c Statham b Wardle	0	— not out	16
W. Chalmers not out	0	— c Cowdrey b Wardle	3
E. Schreiber absent hurt	0	— absent hurt	
B 5, l-b 1, n-b 1	7	B 2	2
1/0 2/1 3/16 4/33 5/59 6/66 7/71	78	1/32 2/32 3/33 4/45 5/58	104
8/72 9/78		6/77 7/77 8/101 9/104	

Border Bowling

	O.	M.	R.	W.		O.	M.	R.	W.
Knott	22.6	3	83	3					
Thorne	17	1	67	0					
Chalmers	43	7	133	5					
Schreiber	19	5	42	0					
Dawson	13	1	68	0					

M.C.C. Bowling

	O.	M.	R.	W.		O.	M.	R.	W.
Statham	7	1	23	2	. . . .	5	2	17	1
Tyson	7	1	10	1	. . . .	4	0	16	1
Laker	10	5	16	4	. . . .	2	0	10	1
Wardle	6.3	0	22	2	. . . .	6.2	0	45	3
			Lock	. . . .	8	1	14	3

Umpires: R. J. Capstick and R. Smith.

M.C.C. v. NATAL

At Pietermaritzburg, January 18, 19, 21, 22. Drawn. This was only the third drawn match of the tour and Natal were concerned in two. The game followed closely on the lines of the previous meeting at Durban, M.C.C. declaring but having insufficient time to win. M.C.C. began badly, but Compton and Cowdrey shared a fourth wicket stand of 147. Compton hit his first century of the tour. Wardle and Tyson put on a useful 56, but the side batted unevenly. Following an opening partnership of 61, Natal broke down before a varied attack, but going in again 130 ahead M.C.C. scored slowly and, setting Natal to get 253, left themselves only three hours to dismiss them on a good pitch. Rain on the first and second afternoons reduced play by just over four hours.

M.C.C.

T. E. Bailey c Pearce b Markham	0	— c McLean b Goddard	20
A. S. M. Oakman b Goddard	4	— c Smith b Goddard	29
B. Taylor c Burger b Watkins	15	— c Markham b Goddard	2
D. C. S. Compton c Eaglestone b Goddard	101	— c and b Markham	6
M. C. Cowdrey lbw b Smith	76		
D. J. Insole b Goddard	6	— b Dodds	6
J. H. Wardle c Koch b Markham	37	— not out	11
F. H. Tyson c Pearce b Goddard	35	— c Markham b Smith	19
G. A. R. Lock lbw b Goddard	10	— not out	21
J. C. Laker not out	2		
P. J. Loader c Keith b Markham	0		
L-b 2, n-b 5	7	B 8	8

1/0 2/93 3/31 4/178 5/199 6/219   293   1/49 2/50 (6 wkts., dec.) 122
7/275 8/281 9/292   3/57 4/57 5/77 6/89

Natal

T. L. Goddard c Compton b Lock	39	— lbw b Laker	41
J. C. Watkins b Lock	22	— b Lock	27
H. J. Keith c Oakman b Laker	19	— lbw b Laker	8
C. Burger c Wardle b Loader	0	— st Taylor b Wardle	14
R. A. McLean c Taylor b Loader	10	— b Tyson	45
E. Eaglestone c Compton b Wardle	10	— not out	20
L. Koch run out	24	— not out	22
R. A. Pearce c Compton b Wardle	21		
N. E. Markham c and b Wardle	4		
V. I. Smith c Insole b Lock	2		
P. M. Dodds not out	3		
L-b 7, n-b 2	9	B 5, l-b 3	8

1/61 2/73 3/86 4/96 5/107 6/113   163   1/56 2/76 3/89 (5 wkts.) 185
7/146 8/154 9/159   4/128 5/142

Natal Bowling

	O.	M.	R.	W.		O.	M.	R.	W.
Markham	21.4	2	94	3	....	11	3	23	1
Goddard	24	6	65	5	....	16	5	33	3
Watkins	6	2	31	1					
Dodds	13	3	35	0	....	5	1	23	1
Smith	20	3	61	1	....	11	3	35	1

M.C.C. Bowling

	O.	M.	R.	W.		O.	M.	R.	W.
Tyson	11	2	30	0	....	7	2	32	1
Loader	9	0	30	2	....	5	1	16	0
Bailey	5	1	9	0					
Lock	14.2	5	29	3	....	11	0	42	1
Laker	7	1	11	1	....	8	3	33	2
Wardle	8	1	45	3	....	6	0	36	1
					Compton	3	0	18	0

Umpires: D. Drew and A. N. McCabe.

ENGLAND v. SOUTH AFRICA

Third Test Match

At Durban, January 25, 26, 28, 29, 30. Drawn. South Africa gave a much improved display and at times seemed to be heading towards victory, but England never allowed the situation to get out of hand. For the most part the batting on both sides disappointed, but McLean for South Africa and Insole for England played praiseworthy innings.

England fielded an unchanged side which meant that Tyson, although fit, was omitted. South Africa made two alterations; Funston replaced Watkins and Pithey, a twenty-three-year-old opening batsman, made his Test debut in place of McGlew, who during the match announced that because of his injured shoulder and lack of practice he would not be available for the remaining Tests.

May again won the toss, the third time running in the series and for the eleventh time in thirteen Tests as captain of England. The start brought some of the brightest batting of the series, Richardson and Bailey scoring 103 together in two hours before lunch. Richardson, who broke the middle finger of his right hand at Queenstown a fortnight earlier, showed no signs of the injury in the first match on his return, maintaining his fine Test form with a delightful innings. When 20 he received a nasty blow on the left forearm from Heine which caused considerable pain, but even this did not upset him. The stand reached 115 in two hours twenty minutes before Richardson fell lbw for the fourth time in five Test innings.

From that moment England surprisingly lost the initiative. Between lunch and tea only 52 runs were added and three men left, the others being Compton and May, who again had an unhappy match. Meanwhile, Bailey went completely into his shell and when bad light ended play twenty-five minutes early on the first day he had batted five hours thirty-five minutes for 71 out of England's 184 for four.

Tayfield, between half-past two and five minutes to five, sent down fourteen consecutive maidens, nine to Bailey. England's complete lack of enterprise after such a good start was unexpected. Next morning the remaining six wickets fell in ninety minutes for 34. Bailey, seventh out, stayed six hours thirty-five minutes, making a valuable contribution in his own defensive way.

South Africa replied with their best opening stand of the series; Pithey showed a straight bat and plenty of promise and Goddard shaped splendidly. They lost the upper hand when Keith and Endean failed, but regained it during a fine fourth wicket stand between Goddard and McLean who put on 59 overnight when South Africa finished well placed—78 behind with six wickets left. The pair added only five more next morning, but South Africa went ahead with five wickets left.

England's bowlers did well to restrict the final lead to 65, but they could not disturb McLean who hit the first century of the tour against the Englishmen. Not so aggressive as usual, he showed extremely sound judgment in choosing the hittable ball and when he did go for his strokes they were clean and powerful. He drove and pulled particularly well, most of his fourteen 4's coming from these strokes. He batted for four hours twenty minutes.

South Africa scored only slightly faster than England and the two innings were not completed until tea time on the third day, despite the moderate totals. Wardle, bowling mostly orthodox leg-breaks, although slipping in the occasional chinaman and googly, was again England's leading bowler.

Richardson and Bailey gave England another useful start, but following a break for bad light, the third day running twenty-five minutes before the scheduled close, play was unexpectedly resumed and one run later Richardson was out. Shortly after England's innings began Bailey received a bad blow on the right hand from a short-pitched ball from Heine, and although he continued to the close when England were 48 for one, he was subsequently found to have cracked a bone at the back of his hand near the right knuckle.

Bailey did not resume his innings first thing next morning, Insole joining Compton. Rain restricted play to half an hour before lunch, at which point England had exactly cleared the arrears for the loss of one wicket. Once again they surrendered control, Compton and May being dismissed by the first and seventh balls of one over from Tayfield.

The situation then looked dangerous for England, for with Bailey injured and the last of the recognised batsmen, Insole and Cowdrey, together, they stood only 14 ahead. Insole looked like falling at any time, often being beaten by Adcock, but he gradually settled down and by careful methods the pair put on 65.

Bailey resumed at the fall of the fifth wicket with his bruised right hand in plaster and stayed fifty-five minutes, obtaining three runs before being out to the final ball of the day. Insole was then 77.

The last day began with South Africa in a satisfactory position, England being 127 on with only four wickets left. Nearly everything depended on how quickly South Africa could capture the remaining wickets. As it happened England's tail-end batsmen rose to the occasion in support of Insole and they stayed an hour and forty minutes, adding 62. Insole completed his maiden Test century with the last man in and took out his bat after a great-hearted display lasting six hours ten minutes. He played better and better the longer he remained and on the last morning was in complete control. As usual most of his runs came on the leg side, but he also cut well and occasionally produced a good cover drive.

Tayfield, floating the ball into the breeze, commanded considerable respect and finished with eight for 69, the best performance by a bowler in South Africa's Test history, beating the eight for 90 by S. J. Snooke against England in 1905–6. Tayfield was destined to improve the record still further in the next match.

South Africa needed 190 to win in four hours ten minutes, a rate of 45 an hour which, taking the series as a whole, was faster than average. They lost a wicket second ball and were so pegged back by accurate bowling that they fell farther and farther behind the clock.

Between lunch and tea they scored only 30 runs while losing three wickets and England then looked to have a chance of success. This was dashed by Funston and Endean who not only added 75 but gave their side an outside chance of victory. Funston, when 11, offered a low return catch to Wardle which, if accepted, might have won the game. South Africa needed 83 in the last hour, but when Funston and Endean left at the same total they gave up thoughts of victory and England could not capture the last four wickets in half an hour.

Bailey did not field in South Africa's second innings. The pitch gave little help to fast bowlers, getting slower as the match progressed, and the spinners were never able to turn the ball quickly enough to be dangerous.

The attendance on the first day was only 8,800, but as South Africa's hopes rose the public showed more interest, and on the last day 14,500 attended.

England

P. E. Richardson lbw b Adcock	68	— b van Ryneveld 32
T. E. Bailey c Keith b Adcock	80	— c van Ryneveld b Tayfield.. 18
D. C. S. Compton b Heine	16	— c Keith b Tayfield 19
P. B. H. May c Goddard b Tayfield	2	— lbw b Tayfield 2
M. C. Cowdrey lbw b Goddard	6	— lbw b Heine 24
D. J. Insole b van Ryneveld	13	— not out 110
T. G. Evans st Waite b van Ryneveld	0	— c Waite b Tayfield 10
J. H. Wardle b Heine	13	— c Waite b Tayfield 8
J. C. Laker not out	0	— c Goddard b Tayfield 6
P. J. Loader c Waite b Adcock	1	— lbw b Tayfield 3
J. B. Statham b Adcock	6	— c van Ryneveld b Tayfield.. 9
B 2, l-b 4, w 5, n-b 2	13	B 8, l-b 4, n-b 1....... 13
	218	254

1/115 2/148 3/151 4/163 5/186 6/186   1/45 2/77 3/79 4/144
7/202 8/210 9/212   5/167 6/192 7/203 8/220
                                               9/230

South Africa

A. Pithey st Evans b Wardle	25	— b Statham	0
T. L. Goddard lbw b Statham	69	— c Cowdrey b Wardle	18
H. J. Keith c Evans b Loader	6	— c sub b Laker	22
W. R. Endean c sub b Wardle	5	— c and b Laker	26
R. A. McLean c Insole b Bailey	100	— b Wardle	4
K. J. Funston b Wardle	19	— b Loader	44
J. H. B. Waite b Statham	12	— not out	1
C. B. van Ryneveld c Cowdrey b Loader	16	— not out	14
H. Tayfield not out	20		
P. S. Heine b Wardle	6		
N. A. T. Adcock lbw b Wardle	3		
L-b 2	2	B 5, l-b 6, n-b 2	42

1/65 2/76 3/81 4/145 5/199 6/225   283   1/0 2/39 3/45   (6 wkts.) 113
7/241 8/264 9/279   4/49 5/124 6/124

South Africa Bowling

	O.	M.	R.	W.		O.	M.	R.	W.
Heine	16	2	65	2	....	22	3	58	1
Adcock	15.3	3	39	4	....	21	7	39	0
Goddard	25	11	42	1	....	13	5	26	0
Tayfield	24	17	21	1	....	37.7	14	69	8
van Ryneveld	14	4	38	1	....	14	2	49	1

England Bowling

	O.	M.	R.	W.		O.	M.	R.	W.
Statham	22	4	56	2	....	11	0	32	1
Loader	25	6	79	2	....	8	2	21	1
Bailey	17	3	38	1					
Wardle	20.2	6	61	5	....	20	7	42	2
Laker	12	1	47	0	....	18	7	29	2
Compton					....	1	0	5	0

Umpires: W. Marais and B. V. Malan.

M.C.C. v. TRANSVAAL

At Johannesburg, February 1, 2, 4, 5. Drawn. The loss of nearly seven hours through rain and May's decision not to declare made a definite result out of the question. The start was delayed two hours. Transvaal were always struggling against good fast bowling but enjoyed considerable luck. Nearly every batsmen played and missed at the swinging ball on numerous occasions. Statham retired with a slightly torn abdomen muscle after three overs, but Tyson, Loader and Lock, the three regular bowlers left, did splendidly. Transvaal's innings extended into the third day. M.C.C. made the highest total ever recorded against a Transvaal side and Insole played the biggest innings by any M.C.C. touring player against them. Transvaal, who were without Adock and Waite, could not check the flow of runs. Taylor and May added 121 in an hour and fifty minutes; Compton and Insole put on 223 in three hours. Insole's 192 came in four and a half hours, including twenty 4's. With his attack limited, May did not consider it possible to win on a good pitch, so continued batting despite the big lead.

Transvaal

A. I. Taylor c Lock b Tyson	22	M. Charnas not out	13
A. Tayfield b Loader	21	K. Gibbs b Loader	11
W. R. Endean st Evans b Lock	25	P. S. Heine b Loader	8
K. J. Funston c Insole b Tyson	15	L-b 3, w 1, n-b 6	10
G. Ritchie lbw b Lock	42		
P. J. M. Gibb c Lock b Tyson	10		
D. Pistorius b Loader	19	1/36 2/51 3/81 4/98 5/122	232
H. J. Tayfield c Evans b Lock	36	6/146 7/199 8/199 9/220	

M.C.C.

P. E. Richardson c A. Tayfield b Pistorius 4	F. H. Tyson not out 55
A. S. M. Oakman run out........ 11	G. A. R. Lock c Ritchie b A. Tayfield 24
B. Taylor lbw b Gibbs 65	P. J. Loader not out 10
P. B. H. May c Pistorius b H. J. Tayfield 73	B 4, l-b 8, w 1, n-b 5 18
D. C. S. Compton b Heine 131	
D. J. Insole b Taylor 192	
T. G. Evans c H. J. Tayfield b Heine 11	1/5 2/22 3/143 4/180 (8 wkts.) 594
J. B. Statham did not bat.	5/403 6/444 7/542 8/575

M.C.C. Bowling

	O.	M.	R.	W.
Statham	3	0	10	0
Loader	25	3	68	4
Tyson	23	6	52	3
Lock	24	9	77	3
Oakman	3	1	15	0

Transvaal Bowling

	O.	M.	R.	W.
Heine	20	2	97	2
Pistorius	18	1	104	1
H. J. Tayfield..	23	3	102	1
K. Gibbs	19	0	98	1
Charnas	5	0	24	0
Ritchie	3	1	22	0
Taylor	12	1	52	1
A. Tayfield....	10	0	70	1
Endean	3	0	7	0

Umpires: J. McMenamin and L. Birkett.

M.C.C. v. GRIQUALAND WEST

At Kimberley, February 8, 9, 11. M.C.C. won by an innings and 47, gaining another easy victory against weak opposition early on the last day. Rain caused the loss of seventy-five minutes on the first day when M.C.C. scored at just over a run a minute. Richardson took only an hour and fifty minutes over 83. Insole also scored quickly and Cowdrey seized the opportunity to get useful practice after absence through stomach trouble. Griqualand West lost three wickets cheaply to the fast bowlers, but were even more helpless against Wardle who, despite being hit for 16 in one over, took seven for 20 in 41 balls. Following on 234 behind, they did better, thanks to their opening batsman, Evans, who obtained the second century of the tour against M.C.C. He was 99 not out on Saturday and took another hour getting the single for his hundred. He batted altogether four hours ten minutes and hit two 6's and eight 4's. On the last morning, against Loader and Laker, not a run was scored for fifty minutes; until the last ball of the thirteenth over.

M.C.C.

P. E. Richardson c Scurr b Waddington 83	G. A. R. Lock not out.......... 12
A. S. M. Oakman c Scurr b English 1	J. C. Laker c Scurr b Lee 6
B. Taylor c Evans b English...... 15	P. J. Loader c Waddington b Lee.. 4
M. C. Cowdrey b Waddington .. 52	B 9, l-b 8, n-b 1............. 18
P. B. H. May c and b Drury 15	
D. J. Insole c Drury b English.... 53	
F. H. Tyson run out............. 25	
J. H. Wardle c Gallagher b Waddington 26	1/17 2/55 3/133 4/172 5/196 310 6/258 7/276 8/292 9/306

Griqualand West

R. Evans b Loader	5	— c May b Loader	110
R. Gloak b Loader	0	— run out	5
D. Lee c Insole b Tyson	12	— b Wardle	0
E. Draper c Cowdrey b Wardle	11	— c Cowdrey b Lock	25
B. Goble b Wardle	5	— c Cowdrey b Wardle	1
T. Heale b Wardle	0	— c Cowdrey b Wardle	11
J. Waddington c Laker b Wardle	9	— c Lock b Laker	7
I. Drury lbw b Wardle	0	— b Loader	1
A. Gallagher c Oakman b Wardle	12	— c Loader b Laker	4
C. English b Wardle	8	— not out	0
R. Scurr not out	0	— b Loader	3
B 4, l-b 5, n-b 5	14	B 7, l-b 11, n-b 2	20

1/3 2/12 3/31 4/40 5/46 6/51 7/56   76
8/68 9/71

1/34 2/39 3/85 4/100   187
5/132 6/162 7/163 8/171
9/183

Griqualand West Bowling

	O.	M.	R.	W.	O.	M.	R.	W.
English	14	0	59	3				
Gallagher	10	0	64	0				
Waddington	25	1	91	3				
Drury	12	0	57	1				
Lee	3.7	0	21	2				

M.C.C. Bowling

	O.	M.	R.	W.	O.	M.	R.	W.
Tyson	7	3	19	1	3	1	3	0
Loader	6	2	7	2	16	9	33	3
Wardle	5.1	2	20	7	16	0	74	3
Laker	5	1	16	0	16.3	7	24	2
Lock					15	6	33	1

Umpires: A. Dunn and A. J. Minogue.

ENGLAND v. SOUTH AFRICA
Fourth Test Match

At Johannesburg, February 15, 16, 18, 19, 20. South Africa won by 17 runs and gained their first victory over England in their own country for 26 years. Never before had they beaten England in South Africa on a turf pitch. The match proved a personal triumph for Tayfield, although both sides deserve credit for making the game so exciting. The cricket followed the usual pattern of slow, cautious batting, but there was plenty of interest throughout.

Tayfield established a new record for a South African bowler in taking nine wickets in an innings of a Test Match. He also became the first South African to take 13 wickets in a Test against England.

England relied on the team which drew at Durban and South Africa made one change, Duckworth making his Test debut in place of Keith. The pitch, shorn of most of its grass in contrast to the previous game on the ground, looked ideal for batting and so it proved.

Winning the toss for the first time, South Africa quickly showed their intention of going boldly for victory. Pithey did not last long, but Goddard again revealed his skill and Waite, promoted to number three, helped in the first century stand of the tour against M.C.C., adding 112 for the second wicket. Both were a little fortunate with snicks, but they batted well and set South Africa on the road to their good total. Waite scored faster than Goddard, who, third out, stayed four hours ten minutes.

A miss at slip by Insole off Loader cost England dearly. Insole, usually so good in the field, had not dropped a catch the entire tour, but he allowed McLean to escape when three and the hard-hitting South African stayed almost four hours. He had plenty of luck early in his innings when he was right out of touch, but later played splendidly.

On the second morning England made a good effort to swing the game, turning the overnight score of 234 for four to 251 for six, but McLean found a steady partner in van Ryneveld, who helped to add 58.

McLean was run out when seven short of his second century in successive Tests. South Africa's 340 was easily the highest score against the touring team, being the first time a side had reached 300.

England began shakily, both the opening batsmen being out for 40, but Insole, promoted to number three, continued his fine form of recent weeks and May at last found something like his touch in Tests. They put on 91 before an unusual incident ended the stand. Tayfield unsuccessfully appealed against Insole for lbw. The ball went into the hands of Goddard at slip, but Insole, thinking it had gone through, started for a run. Goddard had time to run forward and remove the bails before Insole could regain his crease.

This proved an unfortunate blow for England, who never mastered the attack. May, although not at his best, stayed three hours ten minutes before playing on in the last over before lunch on the third day.

Compton played a remarkable innings, being so tied down by the accuracy of Tayfield that his score at the end of two and a half hours to tea was no more than 13. England at that point were 176 for seven and in danger of following on, but Compton improved after the interval and the tail again proved defiant. Compton remained altogether three and a half hours. The last pair, Loader and Statham, stayed forty-eight minutes and put on 24.

South Africa failed to add to their lead of 89 in the one over bowled in their innings on the third evening. The stage was set for quick scoring on the fourth day, but great-hearted accurate bowling not only prevented this but turned the game so much that England stood a reasonable chance of victory. In two hours to lunch only 51 were scored and the opening partnership of 62 by Pithey and Goddard lasted in all two hours twenty-five minutes.

Trying to make up for lost time the South Africans ran into trouble, losing five wickets for 48 in two hours between lunch and tea. Slight improvement came, but when England went in three-quarters of an hour before the close they needed 232 to win.

Bailey was out just before time and England started the last day requiring 213 at a rate of 34 an hour. This was the most exciting day of the series. England for a long time looked almost certain victors before finally collapsing. South Africa's chief hope was Tayfield. He spun the ball just enough to be difficult and, as in previous Tests, bowled most accurately to a well-placed field.

England decided on a bold policy which nearly succeeded. Richardson and Insole scored 55 in seventy-two minutes for the second wicket and Insole found another good partner in Cowdrey. Twenty-five minutes after lunch England were 147 for two and another 85 were needed, but once the stand of 82 in an hour and forty minutes ended the batting broke down.

Insole's second excellent innings of the game lasted just under three hours. The loss of May and Compton for a single between them was a blow from which England never recovered. Cowdrey made a fine, determined effort and good hitting by Wardle put England back in the picture.

At tea time the game was still open, England wanting 46 with four wickets left, but the end came fifty minutes later with Arthur Tayfield, fielding substitute for Funston, who hurt a leg, catching Loader on the long-on boundary off his brother's bowling.

Hugh Tayfield was deservedly chaired off the field. He bowled throughout the four hours fifty minutes on the final day, sending down 35 overs, and although heavily punished by the early batsmen he always looked menacing. Cowdrey, finding himself running out of partners, tried attacking him, but when he gave a return catch after staying three hours twenty minutes, the end was in sight.

After a closely fought and keen struggle South Africa went into the last Test with a chance of sharing the rubber—an excellent effort considering they were two down after two matches.

South Africa

A. Pithey c Wardle b Bailey	10	— b Laker		18
T. L. Goddard b Bailey	67	— c Evans b Bailey		49
J. H. B. Waite c Evans b Statham	61	— c Cowdrey b Statham		17
K. J. Funston c Evans b Bailey	20	— run out		23
R. A. McLean run out	93	— c Cowdrey b Statham		0
C. A. R. Duckworth c Wardle b Loader	13	— b Wardle		3
W. R. Endean b Statham	13	— c Insole b Bailey		2
C. B. van Ryneveld c Cowdrey b Laker	36	— c and b Statham		12
H. J. Tayfield c Bailey b Wardle	10	— not out		12
P. S. Heine not out	1	— c Insole b Wardle		0
N. A. T. Adcock lbw b Wardle	6	— run out		1
L-b 8, w 1, n-b 1	10	B 4, l-b 1		5

1/22 2/134 3/151 4/172 5/238 6/251　340
7/309 8/328 9/333

1/62 2/91 3/94 4/95 5/97　142
6/104 7/129 8/130 9/131

England

P. E. Richardson c Tayfield b Heine	11	— b Tayfield		39
T. E. Bailey c Waite b Adcock	13	— c Endean b Tayfield		1
D. J. Insole run out	47	— c Tayfield b Goddard		68
P. B. H. May b Adcock	61	— c Endean b Tayfield		0
D. C. S. Compton c Pithey b Heine	42	— c Goddard b Tayfield		1
M. C. Cowdrey c Goddard b Tayfield	8	— c and b Tayfield		55
T. G. Evans c Endean b Tayfield	7	— b Tayfield		8
J. H. Wardle c Goddard b Tayfield	16	— c Waite b Tayfield		22
J. C. Laker lbw b Tayfield	17	— c Duckworth b Tayfield		5
P. J. Loader c Endean b Goddard	13	— c sub b Tayfield		7
J. B. Statham not out	12	— not out		4
L-b 1, n-b 3	4	B 3, l-b 1		4

1/25 2/40 3/131 4/135 5/152 6/160　251
7/176 8/213 9/227

1/10 2/65 3/147 4/148　214
5/156 6/186 7/196 8/199
9/208

England Bowling

	O.	M.	R.	W.		O.	M.	R.	W.
Statham	23	5	81	2	....	13	1	37	3
Loader	23	3	78	1	....	13	3	33	0
Bailey	21	3	54	3	....	13	4	12	2
Wardle	19.6	4	68	2	....	14	4	29	2
Laker	15	3	49	1	....	7	1	26	1

South Africa Bowling

	O.	M.	R.	W.		O.	M.	R.	W.
Adcock	21	5	52	2	....	8	1	22	0
Heine	23	6	54	2	....	8	1	21	0
Goddard	25.2	15	22	1	....	25	5	54	1
Tayfield	37	15	79	4	....	37	11	113	9
van Ryneveld	8	0	40	0					

Umpires: J. McMenamin and B. V. Malan.

M.C.C. v. WESTERN PROVINCE

At Cape Town, February 22, 23, 25, 26. Drawn. M.C.C. were well below their best, particularly in the field, but even so should have won comfortably. May played two fine innings. His 116 took only three hours. Insole, Tyson and Lock also hit strongly. The deadest pitch encountered on the tour gave little help to bowlers although the spinners were able to turn the ball slowly. Western Province began well, Innes staying four hours and van Ryneveld three hours,

but Lock and Wardle caused a breakdown that was checked only by Ferrandi.
Leading by 78, M.C.C. went boldly for runs, May taking only an hour and a half
over 79 and adding, with Cowdrey, 103 in eighty-two minutes. Western Province
lost four wickets cheaply, but the remainder of the side, helped by dropped catches,
held out. Only three wickets fell in the last two and a half hours. Ferrandi gave
another good display and became the only player to score two separate fifties in
a match against the touring team.

M.C.C.

P. E. Richardson c Dumbrill b Fuller ...	11 —	lbw b Fuller 0
A. S. M. Oakman c Innes b van Ryneveld	36 —	c van Ryneveld b Dumbrill. 23
B. Taylor c and b Bromfield	7 —	c Dumbrill b Bromfield 8
P. B. H. May c Pothecary b van Ryneveld.	116 —	c van Ryneveld b Bromfield. 79
M. C. Cowdrey c and b Bromfield	18 —	b Fuller................ 48
D. J. Insole c Pothecary b Bromfield	45 —	b Fuller................ 1
T. E. Bailey lbw b Pothecary	22	
F. H. Tyson c Heldsinger b van Ryneveld	30 —	lbw b Fuller 6
G. A. R. Lock b McDonald b van Ryneveld	39 —	not out 9
J. H. Wardle b van Ryneveld	6 —	c and b Fuller 4
J. B. Statham not out	2	
L-b 3	3	B 6, l-b 1, n-b 1 8

1/16 2/43 3/79 4/171 5/198 6/230   335   1/6 2/28   (8 wkts., dec.) 186
7/280 8/310 9/331   3/58 4/161 5/165 6/169
                       7/180 8/186

Western Province

A. Pithey c Taylor b Lock	13 —	c Insole b Lock 30
G. Innes c Oakman b Lock	75 —	b Bailey 3
J. Siedle c Taylor b Bailey	25 —	lbw b Wardle 18
C. B. van Ryneveld c Oakman b Wardle..	50 —	c and b Lock 8
R. MacDonald c Insole b Lock.........	13 —	c Taylor b Lock 16
K. Heldsinger c Insole b Lock..........	8 —	st Taylor b Wardle 0
J. Ferrandi not out	52 —	c Tyson b Lock 60
J. Pothecary lbw b Lock	5 —	c Oakman b Lock 7
E. R. H. Fuller c Insole b Wardle	3 —	not out 20
J. Dumbrill lbw b Wardle	0 —	not out 2
H. Bromfield run out	0	
B 6, l-b 6, n-b 1	13	B 8, l-b 3, n-b 1 12

1/44 2/114 3/136 4/168 5/181 6/208   257   1/8 2/36 3/61   (8 wkts.) 176
7/216 8/233 9/248   4/61 5/62 6/107 7/125 8/169

Western Province Bowling

	O.	M.	R.	W.		O.	M.	R.	W.
Fuller	25	4	86	1	....	13.1	4	26	5
Pothecary	19	1	53	1	....	3	0	18	0
Bromfield.....	30	13	57	3	....	21	4	69	2
van Ryneveld ..	18.3	0	95	5	....	5	0	25	0
Dumbrill	18	6	41	0	....	10	1	40	1
					Innes	1	1	0	0

M.C.C. Bowling

	O.	M.	R.	W.		O.	M.	R.	W.
Statham	3	1	8	0					
Tyson	19	7	36	0	....	11	2	31	0
Bailey	17	5	40	1	....	8	3	11	1
Wardle	26	2	91	3	....	19	7	35	2
Lock	38	15	69	5	....	27	8	75	5
					Oakman	7	3	12	0

Umpires: A. Prowse and G. Eckard.

ENGLAND v. SOUTH AFRICA

Fifth Test Match

At Port Elizabeth, March 1, 2, 4, 5. South Africa won by 58 runs and shared the rubber. Considerable controversy arose over the condition of the pitch. In order to improve it the authorities imported special soil from the Durban area, but unfortunately they did not give it long enough to settle. They might have learned their lesson from Pretoria where similar efforts were made to re-lay a pitch in two months. This time three months were allowed, but it would have been a remarkable achievement to get a Test strip ready so quickly.

The result was a dead slow pitch from which the ball kept exceptionally low from the end of the first day onwards and the number of shooters was more than one sees in a full season. As a result batsmen had to adopt a new technique. Back players were at a severe disadvantage and those without power to hit strongly found that they could rarely penetrate the field. Usually, it also paid to lift the ball.

The faster bowlers, particularly from one end, were devastating. They produced many almost unplayable balls which hit one of the unusually wide, deep cracks in the ground, shot through and sometimes turned as well. Naturally winning the toss under such conditions was of paramount importance, for it meant batting before the pitch became really difficult.

South Africa played an unchanged side for the only time in the series, but England were without two of their leading bowlers because of injuries. Statham, who had not recovered from foot trouble suffered in the previous match, was badly missed; the pitch would have given his style of bowling considerable help. Two days before the Test began Wardle slipped a cartilage in the left knee which had been worrying him all the tour and a manipulative operation was necessary; it was too risky to include him.

With strokes so awkward to make and scoring in front of the wicket so difficult, it followed that run-getting would be unusually slow even for the slow-scoring series. South Africa batted all day except for the final fifteen minute when bad light intervened, scoring 138 for five, but even then it was fairly obvious that this total was satisfactory.

England did well to get down the first five wickets for 78, but South Africa's recovery came at that point and they were on top for the rest of the match. Endean played his only good innings of the series and he could not have timed it better. He stayed four hours fifty minutes and with van Ryneveld added 65 for the sixth wicket.

On the second day a record crowd for the ground, nearly 15,000, saw South Africa lose their last five wickets for 26 and England struggle to make 110 for nine. South Africa batted seven and a quarter hours in their first innings. England began by losing Richardson and Compton in the second over of the innings, but excellent batting from Bailey and May followed. Both realised that it was imperative to hit the half volley hard whenever possible and Bailey forsook his normal defensive methods and, considering the circumstances, played one of the best innings of his Test career.

One of the few balls that lifted in the match accounted for May, caught at cover off the edge of his bat when trying to play to leg. Bailey fell to a shooter just after lunch, having stayed two hours twenty-five minutes. The rest of the side did little, although Lock batted for an hour and three-quarters.

The third day's play was the slowest in Test history, 122 runs being scored in five hours fifty minutes. First England lost their remaining wicket without addition and South Africa, with a useful lead of 54, concentrated on increasing it as much as possible. Goddard and Funston took the score from 21 to 64 when Goddard swept a ball into his chin and had to retire. This gave the initiative back to bowlers and, despite determined efforts by van Ryneveld and McLean, batsmen never regained it. Goddard returned at the fall of the fifth wicket, but could not settle again. When going in a few minutes before the close of the second day Loader was struck on the instep first ball and could bowl only four overs on Monday before retiring.

He was one of several casualties in the match. Compton fell down a flight of stairs in his hotel and badly bruised his side; Tayfield developed knee trouble, but was able to continue, and Waite tore fibres in his left shoulder when diving for a shooter while keeping wicket, and so Endean took over shortly after the start of the second innings.

Tyson, bowling with a considerably shortened run, upset South Africa, who on the fourth morning lost their last three wickets for 12. Set to make 189, England never looked like succeeding. A spinner, Tayfield, was successful for the first time, but his wickets were mainly due to batsmen hitting out against him because it was nearly impossible to score off the faster bowlers at the other end. Tayfield brought his wickets in the Tests to 37, establishing a new South African record for one series.

Bailey and May again showed promise of staying, but once more the side collapsed when they were parted. Evans, Tyson and Lock hit powerfully whenever possible, but the almost inevitable victory came with a day and fifty-five minutes to spare. At the close the crowd swarmed to examine the unusual pitch and several people took away pieces of ground as souvenirs. Special praise was earned by Evans for his magnificent wicket-keeping under extremely difficult circumstances. He allowed only one bye—an extraordinary performance by an extraordinary man.

South Africa

A. Pithey c Evans b Bailey	15	— b Laker	6
T. L. Goddard lbw b Bailey	2	— c Evans b Tyson	30
J. H. B. Waite c Evans b Loader	3	— not out	7
K. J. Funston b Bailey	3	— b Lock	24
W. R. Endean lbw b Tyson	70	— b Tyson	1
R. A. McLean c Evans b Lock	23	— b Bailey	19
C. V. van Ryneveld c Tyson b Loader	24	— lbw b Tyson	13
C. A. R. Duckworth lbw b Laker	6	— b Tyson	6
H. Tayfield b Loader	4	— c Evans b Tyson	10
P. Heine b Tyson	4	— c Evans b Tyson	4
N. A. T. Adcock not out	0	— b Bailey	3
L-b 1, n-b 9	10	B 1, l-b 7, n-b 3	11

1/4 2/15 3/21 4/41 5/78 6/143 7/155　164　　1/20 2/21 3/65 4/98 5/99　134
8/155 9/163　　6/105 7/111 8/123 9/129

England

P. E. Richardson lbw b Adcock	0	— b Adcock	3
T. E. Bailey b Heine	41	— c McLean b Tayfield	18
D. C. S. Compton b Adcock	0	— c Endean b Tayfield	5
P. B. H. May c Duckworth b Goddard	24	— lbw b Goddard	21
D. J. Insole lbw b Heine	4	— c Duckworth b Tayfield	8
M. C. Cowdrey c Waite b Adcock	3	— c van Ryneveld b Tayfield	8
T. G. Evans b Heine	5	— c Endean b Heine	21
G. A. R. Lock b Adcock	14	— c Goddard b Tayfield	12
F. H. Tyson c and b Heine	1	— c Tayfield b Goddard	23
J. C. Laker b Goddard	6	— not out	3
P. J. Loader not out	0	— c McLean b Tayfield	0
B 8, l-b 4	12	B 5, l-b 3	8

1/1 2/1 3/55 4/77 5/78 6/86 7/89　110　　1/15 2/41 3/53 4/57 5/71　130
8/97 9/110　　6/72 7/99 8/127 9/129

England Bowling

	O.	M.	R.	W.		O.	M.	R.	W.
Loader	20	3	35	3	....	4	3	1	0
Bailey	25	12	23	3	....	24.7	5	39	2
Tyson	17	6	38	2	....	23	7	40	6
Laker	14	1	37	1	....	14	5	26	1
Lock	11	5	21	1	....	15	6	17	1

South Africa Bowling

	O.	M.	R.	W.	O.	M.	R.	W.
Heine	15	6	22	4	 11	3	22	1
Adcock	11.3	4	20	4	 7	2	10	1
Tayfield	22	8	43	0	.... 24.3	6	78	6
Goddard	13	8	13	2	 16	8	12	2

Umpires: V. Costello and W. Marais.

M.C.C. v. COMBINED UNIVERSITIES

At Cape Town, March 9, 11, 12. M.C.C. won by an innings and 28 runs, so finishing their tour in convincing manner. As Insole, Bailey, Wardle and Statham flew home before the match the team was reduced to eleven, and when Tyson developed a cold in his back on the morning of the match F. R. Brown, the manager, completed the side. Rain had seeped through the covers and the Universities were put in on a difficult pitch. They tried hard, but were always struggling. M.C.C. went ahead for the loss of two wickets and scored rapidly. Evans, Cowdrey and Compton played bright innings and Universities needed 193 to avoid an innings defeat. They lost their leading batsman, A. Pithey, the Test player, for the second time in the match without scoring, and only a good sixth wicket stand of 87 in eighty minutes between Varnals and Rushmere prevented a rout. The match ended before lunch on the last day.

Combined Universities

A. Pithey c Oakman b Loader	 0	— c Compton b Loader	 0
I. Morrison c Cowdrey b Laker	 14	— c Cowdrey b Loader.	 9
D. Varnals lbw b Loader	 12	— b Lock	 53
R. MacDonald c Lock b Laker	 18	— c Cowdrey b Laker	 7
C. Wesley c Oakman b Loader	 25	— b Laker	 4
D. Pithey c Cowdrey b Lock	 17	— c Lock b Laker	 0
C. Rushmere b Lock	 10	— run out	 46
P. van der Merwe lbw b Laker	 10	— lbw b Loader	 2
R. Cleaver c Laker b Lock	 4	— lbw b Lock	 9
C. Halse st Taylor b Lock	 10	— not out	 6
N. Ridgeway not out	 16	— c May b Compton	 14
B 3, l-b 3	6	B 6, l-b 8, n-b 1	 15

1/0 2/25 3/40 4/46 5/76 6/94 7/109   142   1/0 2/13 3/21 4/35 5/35   165
8/109 9/121   6/122 7/131 8/141 9/141

M.C.C.

P. E. Richardson c D. Pithey b Ridgeway	 27	G. A. R. Lock c Halse b van der Merwe 8
A. S. M. Oakman b Ridgeway	... 6	F. R. Brown b van der Merwe ... 0
B. Taylor b D. Pithey	 49	J. C. Laker not out 4
T. G. Evans c MacDonald b D. Pithey	 80	P. J. Loader c MacDonald b D. Pithey 0
M. C. Cowdrey b van der Merwe. .	72	B 4, l-b 8, n-b 1 13
D. C. S. Compton c Halse b D. Pithey	 51	
P. B. H. May c van der Merwe b D. Pithey	 25	1/9 2/55 3/151 4/196 5/274 335
		6/312 7/330 8/330 9/334

M.C.C. Bowling

	O.	M.	R.	W.	O.	M.	R.	W.
Loader	12	6	17	3	14	4	40	3
Brown	3	1	6	0	6	1	20	0
Laker	21	3	50	3	12	3	34	3
Lock	22	7	63	4	17	7	23	2
Oakman					5	0	21	0
Evans					1	0	8	0
Compton					0.2	0	4	1

Combined Universities Bowling

Ridgeway......	18	3	64	2
Halse	14	2	65	0
Rushmere	11	1	51	0
D. Pithey	20.6	0	100	5
van der Merwe.	16	5	42	3

Umpires: D. Collins and J. Malone.

BENEFITS IN 1958

A. Wharton—Lancashire v. Surrey at Old Trafford, May 28, 29, 30.

J. V. Wilson—Yorkshire v. Surrey at Sheffield, June 14, 16, 17.

A. Hamer—Derbyshire v. Yorkshire at Chesterfield, July 5, 7, 8.

E. A. Bedser—Surrey v. Yorkshire at The Oval, July 19, 21, 22.

D. Shackleton—Hampshire v. Lancashire at Bournemouth, July 19, 21, 22.

D. Brookes—Northamptonshire v. Worcestershire at Northampton, July 26, 28, 29.

F. C. Gardner—Warwickshire v. Lancashire at Edgbaston, July 26, 28, 29.

F. Ridgway—Kent v. Hampshire at Canterbury, August 2, 4, 5.

Testimonial: A. Jepson (Nottinghamshire).

AUSTRALIANS IN NEW ZEALAND 1957

The fourteen Australians who visited New Zealand in 1957 were one of the youngest sets of cricketers sent abroad by any country; they proved a strong combination and enjoyed a successful and popular tour under their 21-year-old captain, Ian Craig. Most of them were in their early twenties, with R. N. Harvey (28) the eldest, and N. O'Neill (19) the youngest. In contrast, the majority of the New Zealand players in the three representative games were over 30.

At first the Australians found some difficulty in attuning themselves to the slow-paced pitches of New Zealand, but they went through the tour unbeaten, gaining confidence throughout and finished with a convincing win in the third and last representative match, after drawing the first two. The remaining four first-class games also provided victories; never were the Australians in real danger of defeat.

The batting was especially strong, for only Watson had cause to be disappointed. Although making runs freely in minor games, he failed to find his best form in the first-class engagements. Favell, on the other hand, hit hard and true from the first ball of several innings, and his aggressive displays were both entertaining and valuable.

Harvey, much the most experienced Australian, batted well, as did Burge, and Craig found his best stroke-making form after a quiet start. Early on, few chances fell to the youthful O'Neill, but this forceful driver did splendidly later and justified his choice for the last representative match by hitting an excellent century. Simpson batted soundly in the first two games against New Zealand, and as usual he fielded brilliantly in the slips.

Undoubtedly Australia's best player was Benaud. He batted forcibly; took most wickets with his leg-breaks and in fielding, too, he stood out in a side which, becoming youth, displayed very good out-cricket. In view of Australia's need to find successors to Lindwall and Miller, the success of the pace bowlers, Meckiff (left-arm), Drennan and Gaunt was most pleasing. Of the two left-arm spin bowlers who supported Benaud, Martin proved the most effective. Kline, with his "chinamen," began well, but did not maintain his success.

The wicket-keeper, Jarman, failed to fufil expectations, for he missed quite a few chances and did not always take the ball cleanly.

The New Zealanders were led by Reid, whose bowling activities were restricted by a leg injury. Yet it was in their out-cricket that their main strength lay, with Cave a particularly accurate and effective medium-pace bowler. Blair gave him good support, but the spin of Alabaster and Rabone made little impression on the Australians.

Although Miller, Reid and Sutcliffe all played useful innings the batsmen generally showed a reluctance to make strokes which compared unfavourably with the enterprising cricket of their opponents.

RESULTS OF ALL MATCHES
Played 12, Won 7, Drawn 5
First-Class Matches—Played 7, Won 5, Drawn 2
Representative Matches—Played 3, Won 1, Drawn 2

AUSTRALIAN BATTING AVERAGES IN FIRST-CLASS MATCHES

	Matches	Inns.	Not Outs	Runs	Highest Inns.	Average
N. O'Neill	4	4	1	218	102*	72.66
R. Benaud	6	8	2	323	113	53.83
R. N. Harvey	6	10	1	448	161	49.77
R. Simpson	6	9	3	271	75	45.16
L. Favell	6	10	1	354	71	39.33
P. Burge	7	10	2	310	105	38.75
I. D. Craig	6	9	1	308	123*	38.50
J. Martin	4	5	1	88	30	22.00
J. Drennan	6	6	2	76	28*	19.00
R. Gaunt	5	5	1	49	19*	12.25
B. Jarman	7	7	0	72	33	10.28
L. Kline	6	6	1	37	13	7.40
W. Watson	4	7	0	23	12	3.28
I. Meckiff	4	3	1	2	1*	1.00

* Signifies not out.

AUSTRALIAN BOWLING AVERAGES IN FIRST-CLASS MATCHES

	Overs	Maidens	Runs	Wickets	Average
I. Meckiff	122.1	47	217	20	10.85
J. Drennan	148.3	57	275	22	12.50
J. Martin	96.5	29	214	15	14.26
R. Benaud	285.2	91	618	32	19.31
R. Gaunt	139.4	28	347	14	24.78
L. Kline	145.4	39	385	15	25.66
R. N. Harvey	24	9	44	1	44.00

The following five three-figure innings were played for the Australians in first-class matches:—

R. N. Harvey (1):
    161 v. Otago at Dunedin.

I. D. Craig (1):
    123* v. New Zealand at Christchurch (First Representative Match).

R. Benaud (1):
    113 v. Central Districts at New Plymouth.

P. J. Burge (1):
    105 v. Canterbury at Christchurch.

N. C. O'Neil (1):
    102* v. New Zealand at Auckland (Third Representative Match).

One three-figure innings was played against the Australians:—

B. Sutcliffe:
    107 for New Zealand at Wellington (Second Representative Match).

CANTERBURY v. AUSTRALIANS

At Christchurch, February 15, 16, 18. Australians won by five wickets. Canterbury 229 (R. Benaud four for 44) and 241 (M. E. Chapple 65, R. Gaunt four for 54); Australians 249 (P. Burge 105, M. B. Poore four for 27) and 223 for five (R. Benaud 75 not out, R. N. Harvey 68).

SOUTHLAND v. AUSTRALIANS

At Invercargill, February 20, 21. Drawn, no play being possible, because of rain, on second day. Southland 84 (R. Gaunt six for 23); Australians 237 for six (L. Favell 81, W. Watson 74, J. Hill four for 79).

OTAGO v. AUSTRALIANS

At Dunedin, February 22, 23. Australians won by an innings and 102 runs. Australians 344 (R. N. Harvey 161, R. Simpson 75, F. J. Cameron six for 95, A. M. Moir four for 89); Otago 187 (B. Sutcliffe 54, R. Benaud four for 46) and 55 (J. Drennan four for 7).

COMBINED MINOR ASSOCIATIONS v. AUSTRALIANS

At Timaru, February 27, 28. Australians won by an innings and 18 runs although no play was possible on the first day. Combined Minor Associations 43 (I. Meckiff eight for 19) and 76 (R. Gaunt four for 4, R. Benaud four for 7); Australians 137 for eight, declared (M. Sandri four for 36).

NEW ZEALAND v. AUSTRALIA
(First Representative Match)

At Christchurch, March 1, 2, 4. Drawn. When New Zealand gained a lead of 52, they raised hopes of victory, but the confident batting of Harvey, Craig and Burge enabled Australia to recover completely and they set New Zealand a task well beyond their powers. At first steady bowling, particularly by the medium-paced Cave, supported by keen fielding, caused five Australian wickets to fall for 77 before Simpson led a fine rally by the tail. New Zealand batted with admirable consistency, although finding some trouble with the spin of Benaud (leg-breaks) and Kline (left-arm), and they would have established a bigger lead but for misunderstandings in running. Cave again bowled well in Australia's second innings, but others made no impression on Harvey, who hit thirteen 4's in a classical display. Craig shared in two century partnerships and gradually attained his best stroke-play as the danger of defeat passed. Finally New Zealand were set to make 233 to win in two hours twenty minutes, and although Miller and Rabone began with a century stand, they made no serious attempt to get the runs.

Australia

L. Favell b Cave	23	—	b Cave	26
W. Watson run out	0	—	lbw b Cave	1
R. N. Harvey c Chapple b Alabaster	29	—	b Cave	84
I. D. Craig b Cave	3	—	not out	123
P. Burge b Rabone	17	—	not out	45
R. Simpson lbw b MacGibbon	47			
R. Benaud b Alabaster	28			
B. Jarman c Rabone b Cave	33			
I. Meckiff c and b Cave	0			
L. Kline c Guillen b Blair	13			
R. Gaunt not out	19			
Extras	4		Extras	5

1/7 2/52 3/52 4/65 5/77 6/115 7/175   216   1/15 2/41   (3 wkts., dec.) 284
8/178 9/184   3/146

New Zealand

L. S. M. Miller run out	38	— c Jarman b Kline	59
G. O. Rabone lbw b Benaud	22	— c Meckiff b Kline	37
B. Sutcliffe c Craig b Benaud	13		
J. R. Reid c Craig b Harvey	58		
D. D. Taylor c Simpson b Kline	37		
M. E. Chapple run out	19		
A. R. MacGibbon c Jarman b Kline	25	— not out	9
S. C. Guillen run out	11		
H. B. Cave not out	13		
J. C. Alabaster c Watson b Benaud	9		
R. W. Blair st Jarman b Kline	2		
Extras	21	Extras	7

1/46 2/86 3/86 4/178 5/196 6/274   268   1/101 2/112   (2 wkts.) 112
7/233 8/252 9/263

New Zealand Bowling

	O.	M.	R.	W.		O.	M.	R.	W.
Blair	12.5	0	52	1	....	18	6	44	0
Cave	27	10	57	4	....	31	12	74	3
MacGibbon	13	1	45	1	....	4	1	16	0
Alabaster	26	9	48	2	....	30	12	74	0
Rabone	7	3	10	1	....	19	4	57	0
					Chapple	2	0	14	0

Australia Bowling

	O.	M.	R.	W.		O.	M.	R.	W.
Meckiff	11	3	31	0	....	9	3	10	0
Gaunt	26	6	62	0	....	8	1	27	0
Benaud	36	12	83	3	....	17	6	32	0
Kline	23.2	5	62	3	....	11.2	4	32	2
Harvey	12	4	9	1	....	4	3	4	0

WAIRARAPA v. AUSTRALIANS

At Masterton, March 5, 6. Australians won by an innings and 217 runs. Australians 424 (W. Watson 136, L. Favell 67); Wairarapa 50 and 157.

NEW ZEALAND v. AUSTRALIA
(Second Representative Match)

At Wellington, March 8, 9, 11. Drawn. The match followed a similar course to the first representative game, New Zealand gaining a useful lead of 34, only for Australia to fight back. This time, however, Australia lost wickets more readily, and a definite result might have been reached had not rain caused the loss of three hours on the final day. When the match began, Cave bowled with tantalising accuracy, and his fellow opening bowler, Blair, though heavily punished at times, proved effective. Alabaster also bowled his leg-breaks well, and only punishing batting by Favell and another sound display from Simpson enabled Australia to reach a reasonable total. New Zealand depended heavily on Sutcliffe, the left-hander. He produced a wide range of strokes, and with the sound support of Rabone, Miller and Taylor put his team into a strong position. Benaud's leg-breaks were too much for most other batsmen and restricted the lead. Cave, a model of steadiness, again troubled the Australians on the rain-ruined final day.

Australia

W. Watson c Alabaster b Blair	1	—	b Cave	0
L. Favell c MacGibbon c Blair	62	—	b Cave	36
R. N. Harvey lbw b Cave	2	—	c and b Cave	3
I. D. Craig b Alabaster	9	—	c Chapple b Cave	32
P. Burge c Guillen b Blair	8	—	b Cave	14
R. Simpson b Cave	67	—	not out	26
R. Benaud c Chapple b Cave	5	—	not out	3
B. Jarman c Taylor b Alabaster	2	—	run out	19
J. Drennan not out	28			
L. Kline b Blair	0			
R. Gaunt b MacGibbon	17			
Extras	14		Extras	13

1/25 2/36 3/71 4/89 5/99 6/106   215   1/22 2/44 3/47   (6 wkts.) 146
7/128 8/183 9/184   4/75 5/106 6/135

New Zealand

G. O. Rabone lbw b Benaud	22	S. C. Guillen b Gaunt	6
L. S. M. Miller lbw b Drennan	41	H. B. Cave not out	17
B. Sutcliffe c Benaud b Gaunt	107	R. W. Blair b Gaunt	3
D. D. Taylor b Benaud	32	J. C. Alabaster c Harvey b Benaud	9
J. R. Reid c Simpson b Benaud	0	Extras	12
M. E. Chapple c Simpson b Benaud	0		
A. R. MacGibbon c Jarman b Benaud	0	1/55 2/83 3/175 4/175 5/175	249
		6/179 7/216 8/233 9/240	

New Zealand Bowling

	O.	M.	R.	W.	O.	M.	R.	W.
Blair	25	5	95	4	11	1	50	0
Cave	25	13	28	3	27	12	46	5
MacGibbon	12.4	4	34	1	17	5	37	0
Rabone	9	3	19	0				
Alabaster	15	7	25	2	3	3	0	0

Australia Bowling

	O.	M.	R.	W.
Gaunt	28	7	69	3
Drennan	26	10	33	1
Benaud	38	14	79	6
Harvey	1	0	10	0
Kline	15	5	46	0

POVERTY BAY v. AUSTRALIANS

At Gisborne, March 13, 14. Drawn. Australians 478 for nine wickets, declared (R. N. Harvey 112, R. Benaud 104, I. D. Craig 92, K. Hough five for 142); Poverty Bay 122 (J. Martin four for 37) and 58 for five wickets.

AUCKLAND v. AUSTRALIANS

At Auckland, March 16, 18, 19. Australians won by an innings and 54 runs. Auckland 128 (I. Meckiff four for 12) and 122 (Meckiff five for 48); Australians 304 (L. Favell 71, G. O. Rabone eight for 66).

WAIKATO v. AUSTRALIANS

At Hamilton, March 20, 21. Drawn. Australians 213 for five wickets, declared (W. Watson 75); Waikato 93 (J. Martin five for 30) and 30 for three wickets.

CENTRAL DISTRICTS v. AUSTRALIANS

At New Plymouth, March 23, 25, 26. Australians won by ten wickets. Central Districts 176 (D. D. Beard 57, D. McLeod 55, J. Martin four for 41, R. Benaud four for 47) and 153 (J. W. Guy 73, R. Benaud four for 75); Australians 272 (R. Benaud 113, N. O'Neill 63, D. R. Tarrant four for 65) and 58 for no wicket.

NEW ZEALAND v. AUSTRALIA

(Third Representative Match)

At Auckland, March 29, 30, April 1. Australia won by ten wickets, clearly asserting their superiority over the New Zealanders, who wasted their opportunity on the first day when they were fortunate to gain first use of a splendid pitch. Extreme caution led them into trouble against steady bowling, particularly by Meckiff (left-arm fast) and Benaud, who bowled his leg-breaks for long spells, but the Australians did not take all their chances, otherwise the New Zealand total would indeed have been modest. Maintaining a scoring rate of nearly one a minute, the tourists batted with sharply contrasting confidence. The aggressive Favell again gave them a good start; Craig produced elegant stroke-play and O'Neill played an excellent innings. Batting for two hours forty minutes, he displayed a wide range of strokes and hit thirteen 4's. Apart from a sound innings by Reid, the New Zealanders in their second venture could make little of the well-flighted left-arm slows of Martin, and Australia wanted only 10 runs when they batted again.

New Zealand

L. S. M. Miller c Benaud b Meckiff	....	18	— c and b Martin	37
G. O. Rabone c Jarman b Meckiff	.....	16	— c Favell b Meckiff.........	9
B. Sutcliffe c O'Neill b Drennan	....	33	— c O'Neill b Meckiff.........	0
D. D. Taylor c Burge b Benaud	....	0	— lbw b Benaud	1
J. R. Reid b Benaud		20	— hit wkt b Martin	54
M. E. Chapple c O'Neill b Meckiff	....	7	— hit wkt b Martin	19
A. R. MacGibbon b Martin		18	— c and b Martin	9
S. C. Guillen c Simpson b Benaud	....	23	— lbw b Benaud	0
H. B. Cave b Benaud		0	— c Simpson b Martin	0
R. W. Blair c Martin b Meckiff	.....	19	— not out	4
J. C. Alabaster not out		25	— c Meckiff b Martin	1
Extras...................		19	Extras	27

1/26 2/68 3/73 4/101 5/101 6/124   198   1/27 2/27 3/28 4/104   161
7/133 8/158 9/158   5/125 6/152 7/153 8/157
                                             9/161

Australia

L. Favell c Miller b Blair	65	— not out	1
R. Simpson c Rabone b MacGibbon	... 0	— not out	8
R. N. Harvey lbw b Blair	11		
I. D. Craig b Cave	57		
P. Burge lbw b MacGibbon	31		
N. O'Neill not out	102		
R. Benaud c Guillen b Cave	42		
J. Martin b Reid	30		
J. Drennan run out	0		
Extras..................	12	Extras	4

1/1 2/29 3/108 4/165   (8 wkts., dec.) 350   13
5/178 6/250 7/339 8/350

I. Meckiff and B. Jarman did not bat.

Australia Bowling

	O.	M.	R.	W.		O.	M.	R.	W.
Meckiff	27.2	16	28	4	....	11	5	17	2
Drennan	21	6	58	1	....	5	0	16	0
Benaud........	36	14	77	4	....	31	10	55	2
Martin	12	3	16	1	....	22	9	46	6

New Zealand Bowling

	O.	M.	R.	W.		O.	M.	R.	W.
Reid	15.5	8	25	1					
Blair	35	10	105	2	....	1.1	0	2	0
MacGibbon....	18	4	59	2	....	1	0	7	0
Cave ..,......	33	9	79	2					
Rabone	14	4	31	0					
Alabaster	8	2	39	0					

DUKE OF NORFOLK'S TEAM IN JAMAICA

The Duke of Norfolk took a party of 13 county cricketers on a six weeks' tour of Jamaica during February and March, 1957. Both from a playing and social standpoint the tour proved highly successful. The party, who were under the captaincy of E. D. R. Eagar, won two of their three first-class matches and remained unbeaten in all ten fixtures. Of the batsmen, R. E. Marshall, the Hampshire and West Indies player, was the most successful, scoring 929 runs. G. E. Tribe, the Northamptonshire and Australian left-arm spinner, who took 45 wickets at moderate cost, emerged as the best bowler.

All Matches—Played 10, Won 4, Lost 0, Drawn 6

DUKE OF NORFOLK'S XI v. ST. MARY

At Prospect St. Mary, February 22, 23. Duke of Norfolk's XI won by 97 runs. Duke of Norfolk's XI 168 (W. Watson 77, Hartley four for 27) and 214 for one wicket, declared (R. E. Marshall 106 not out, D. V. Smith 60); St. Mary 168 and 187 (Pottinger 61, D. V. P. Wright seven for 31).

DUKE OF NORFOLK'S XI v. COUNTRY DISTRICTS

At Chedwyn Park, February 25, 26. Drawn. Country Districts 232 for nine, declared (Greenhough four for 62). Duke of Norfolk's XI 363 for eight wickets (R. E. Marshall 87, W. Watson 76, G. E. Tribe 66).

DUKE OF NORFOLK'S XI v. JAMAICA NEXT XI

At Sabina Park, February 27, 28, March 1. Drawn. Duke of Norfolk's XI 334 for five wickets, declared (R. E. Marshall 95, T. W. Graveney 90, W. Watson 55 not out) and 185 for seven wickets, declared (D. V. Smith 72). Jamaica Next XI 222 for nine wickets, declared (J. J. Warr four for 46) and 185 for five wickets (Geo. Smith 64).

DUKE OF NORFOLK'S XI v. ALL JAMAICA

At Sabina Park, March 2, 4, 5. Drawn. Jamaica in their first innings owed much to N. Bonitto and J. K. Holt, Jnr., who between them scored 200 runs. Graveney made an attractive 92 for the Duke of Norfolk's team who led by 52. The Jamaican batsmen were never in difficulties on an easy-paced pitch and set the tourists to get 275 to win. A good fight developed, but neither side could claim an advantage at the close.

Jamaica

A. F. Rae c Graveney b Moss	2	— c Graveney b Wright	48
E. McMorris c Marshall b Moss	7	— lbw b Smith	114
J. K. Holt (jnr.) c Greenhough b Tribe	71	— b Tribe	44
O. G. Smith c Marshall b Tribe	29	— c Blake b Tribe	0
L. N. Bonitto lbw b Wright	129	— not out	49
A. Binns c Blake b Smith	47	— c Blake b Tribe	47
F. Lewis b Tribe	0		
Geo. Smith not out	26	— not out	8
T. Dewdney lbw b Tribe	2		
R. Maragh st Blake b Tribe	0		
R. Gilchrist b Wright	1		
B 5, l-b 1, w 1, n-b 6	13	B 12, l-b 3, n-b 1	16
	327	(5 wkts. dec.)	326

Duke of Norfolk's XI

R. E. Marshall lbw b Gilchrist	12	— b Smith	46
D. V. Smith c and b Smith	49	— c Binns b Dewdney	40
D. E. Blake c Bonitto b Gilchrist	62	— not out	26
T. W. Graveney c Maragh b Dewdney	92	— c Geo. Smith b Lewis	34
W. Watson b Gilchrist	36	— lbw b Dewdney	29
E. D. R. Eagar c Lewis b Smith	39	— c McMorris b Smith	0
G. E. Tribe c McMorris b Lewis	39	— lbw b Gilchrist	23
J. J. Warr c sub b Smith	9	— not out	2
A. E. Moss b Gilchrist	9	— b Smith	0
T. Greenhough b Gilchrist	2		
D. V. P. Wright not out	11		
B 9, l-b 6, w 4	19	B 4, l-b 10, w 8	22
	379	(7 wkts.)	222

Duke of Norfolk's XI Bowling

	O.	M.	R.	W.		O.	M.	R.	W.
Moss	15	0	61	2	....	16	1	52	0
Warr	11	3	41	0	....	19	3	70	0
Smith	9	3	28	1	....	14	4	51	1
Tribe	25	4	94	5	....	19	2	74	3
Wright	18.1	2	56	2	....	11	1	44	1
Greenhough	4	0	34	0	....	4	0	19	0

Jamaica Bowling

	O.	M.	R.	W.		O.	M.	R.	W.
Gilchrist	29.2	7	110	5	....	15	2	51	1
Dewdney	16	1	71	1	....	11	3	32	2
Holt	4	1	11	0	....	2	0	12	0
O. G. Smith	28	3	90	3	....	24	3	67	3
Maragh	9	3	35	0	....	3	0	17	0
Lewis	11	3	43	1	....	5	0	21	1

DUKE OF NORFOLK'S XI v. ST. ELIZABETH

At Unity Hall, Monymusk, March 7, 8. Drawn. St. Elizabeth 121 (G. E. Tribe four for 39) and 134 for five wickets. Duke of Norfolk's XI 248 for eight wickets, declared (R. E. Marshall 128).

DUKE OF NORFOLK'S XI v. CORNWALL

At Montego Bay, March 9, 11. Drawn. Cornwall 116 for thirteen wickets, declared (A. E. Moss six for 36) and 94 for ten wickets. Duke of Norfolk's XI 232 (D. V. Smith 55, A. C. D. Ingleby-McKenzie 53, Lord Cobham 50).

DUKE OF NORFOLK'S XI v. COMBINED ESTATES

At Frome, March 12, 13. Duke of Norfolk's XI won by an innings and 21 runs. Combined Estates 127 (G. E. Tribe six for 41) and 110 (G. E. Tribe five for 48). Duke of Norfolk's XI 258 for nine wickets, declared (R. E. Marshall 100, D. V. Smith 62).

DUKE OF NORFOLK'S XI v. JAMAICA

At Melbourne Park, March 15, 16, 18, 19. Duke of Norfolk's XI won by three wickets. The return match against Jamaica gave the Duke's team their first major win of the tour. Apart from Graveney (51) and Watson (71) the tourists offered little resistance to the accurate fast-medium bowling of Kentish in their first innings and finished 112 runs behind. The Jamaicans then collapsed against Smith, Moss and Tribe and the Duke's side were set to score 291 runs to win in four and a half hours. Marshall and Barrick both played excellently.

Jamaica

A. F. Rae c Ingleby-McKenzie b Moss	..	28	— c and b Smith	....	15
E. McMorris c Graveney b Moss	....	36	— lbw b Moss	....	0
J. K. Holt (jnr.) not out	....	36	— not out	....	93
O. G. Smith c Warr b Moss	....	118	— b Moss	....	23
A. P. Binns c Tribe b Smith	....	28	— lbw b Tribe	....	3
Geo. Smith lbw b Tribe	....	0	— lbw b Smith	....	21
F. Lewis lbw b Tribe	....	10	— b Tribe	....	0
F. C. Alexander b Warr	....	41	— st Ingleby-McKenzie b Tribe		4
R. Gilchrist b Moss	....	13	— b Warr	....	15
A. Valentine c and b Moss	....	2	— b Moss	....	0
E. S. Kentish (did not bat)	....		— run out	....	2
B 7, l-b 8, n-b 3	....	18	N-b 2		2
	(9 wkts., dec.)	—			—
		330			178

Duke of Norfolk's XI

D. V. Smith b Gilchrist	....	13	— c Alexander b Smith	....	35
R. E. Marshall lbw b Kentish	....	18	— c Binns b Valentine	....	97
A. C. D. Ingleby-McKenzie c Valentine b Kentish		6	— b Gilchrist	....	17
T. W. Graveney c Alexander b Smith	....	51	— c Alexander b Smith	....	22
D. Barrick lbw b Gilchrist	....	0	— st Alexander b Kentish	....	66
G. E. Tribe c Holt b Lewis	....	4	— not out	....	23
E. D. R. Eagar b Valentine	....	20	— b Holt	....	8
W. Watson not out	....	71	— run out	....	7
J. J. Warr b Kentish	....	7	— not out	....	2
D. V. P. Wright b Kentish	....	13			
A. E. Moss lbw b Kentish	....	0			
B 5, l-b 9, n-b 1	....	15	B 9, l-b 5		14
		—			—
		218		(7 wkts.)	291

Duke of Norfolk's XI Bowling

	O.	M.	R.	W.	O.	M.	R.	W.
Moss	27.4	5	84	5	14.3	2	36	3
Warr	22	4	66	1	16	5	43	1
Smith	11	2	37	1	14	3	41	2
Tribe	12	2	71	2	17	4	44	3
Wright	15	2	54	0	2	0	12	0

Jamaica Bowling

	O.	M.	R.	W.	O.	M.	R.	W.
Gilchrist	22	7	63	2	22	6	64	1
Kentish	12.2	2	36	5	18	1	69	1
Valentine	23	5	52	1	11	0	54	1
O. G. Smith	18	4	37	1	19	2	88	2
Lewis	7	3	15	1				
Holt					1	0	2	1

DUKE OF NORFOLK'S XI v. JAMAICA

At Sabina Park, March 21, 22, 23, 25, 26. Duke of Norfolk's XI won by seven wickets. The final colony match against Jamaica was a triumph for the touring batsmen. Although Jamaica experienced little difficulty in totalling 261 on a plumb pitch and then bowling themselves into a 26 runs lead, they showed little inclination to go for the runs in their second innings. They crawled to 321, leaving the Duke's XI to get 348 to win in seven and a half hours. This task was easily accomplished on a still perfect pitch. An opening stand of 148 by Marshall and Smith set the pace and victory came shortly after lunch on the fifth day.

Jamaica

A. F. Rae b Smith	7	—	b Smith		74
E. McMorris b Smith	58	—	b Marshall		33
J. K. Holt (jnr.) c Tribe b Moss	17	—	b Tribe		55
O. G. Smith c Graveney b Moss	118	—	c Ingleby-McKenzie b Warr		82
A. P. Binns b Tribe	10	—	b Tribe		0
Geo. Smith run out	18	—	c Watson b Tribe		17
F. C. Alexander b Wright	1	—	not out		41
H. Tullock lbw b Tribe	0	—	c Graveney b Tribe		0
R. Gilchrist lbw b Warr	16	—	b Wright		0
T. Dewdney c Eagar b Moss	5	—	lbw b Tribe		2
A. Valentine not out	2	—	b Tribe		5
B 4, l-b 5	9		B 6, l-b 2, n-b 4		12
	261				321

Duke of Norfolk's XI

R. E. Marshall lbw b Valentine	18	—	c Alexander b Dewdney		82
D. V. Smith c Tullock b Dewdney	38	—	c Alexander b Smith		68
T. W. Graveney c McMorris b Smith	47	—	not out		83
D. Barrick c Alexander b Dewdney	37	—	b Gilchrist		46
W. Watson lbw b Gilchrist	21	—	not out		54
A. C. D. Ingleby-McKenzie c Alexander b Dewdney	21				
G. E. Tribe c O. G. Smith b Dewdney	20				
E. D. R. Eagar c Alexander b Dewdney	12				
J. J. Warr c Alexander b Dewdney	8				
D. V. P. Wright c Rae b Dewdney	2				
A. Moss not out	0				
B 4, l-b 5, w 2	11		B 9, l-b 4, n-b 2		15
	235		(3 wkts.)		348

Duke of Norfolk's XI Bowling

	O.	M.	R.	W.	O.	M.	R.	W.
Moss	23	1	74	3	23	4	75	0
Warr	16.1	5	30	1	16	2	44	1
Smith	14	8	23	2	10	2	36	1
Tribe	29	5	83	2	23	2	83	6
Wright	15	1	42	1	14	4	39	1
Marshall					9	0	32	1

Jamaica Bowling

	O.	M.	R.	W.	O.	M.	R.	W.
Gilchrist	24	3	83	1	17	1	87	1
Dewdney	19.2	4	55	7	19	1	74	1
Holt	3	0	9	0	4	0	23	0
Valentine	5	0	21	1	29	5	82	0
O. G. Smith	14	0	37	1	23	6	67	1
Tullock	3	0	19	0				

DUKE OF NORFOLK'S XI v. COMBINED PARISHES

At St. Antonio, March 28. Drawn. Duke of Norfolk's XI 267 (R. E. Marshall 69). Combined Parishes 93 for four wickets.

AVERAGES (All Matches)
BATTING

	Innings	Not Outs	Runs	Highest Innings	Average
R. E. Marshall	14	1	929	128	71.45
W. Watson	13	5	527	77	65.12
T. W. Graveney	14	2	594	92	49.50
D. V. Smith	14	0	581	72	41.50
D. Barrick	9	0	255	66	28.33
D. E. Blake	6	1	130	62	26.00
G. E. Tribe	10	1	215	66	23.88
A. C. D. Ingleby-McKenzie	9	1	152	53	19.00
Lord Cobham	5	0	81	50	16.20
E. D. R. Eagar	10	1	130	39	14.44
D. V. P. Wright	6	3	38	13	12.66
T. Greenhough	5	1	36	11	9.00
A. E. Moss	9	2	63	13	9.00
J. J. Warr	10	4	49	9*	8.16
Duke of Norfolk	4	1	19	10	6.33

* Signifies not out.

BOWLING

	Overs	Maidens	Runs	Wickets	Average
G. Tribe	217.5	34	806	45	17.91
D. V. P. Wright	148.1	30	477	24	19.87
A. E. Moss	192	31	576	28	20.57
D. V. Smith	122	38	346	16	21.62
T. Greenhough	118	27	364	15	24.26
J. J. Warr	159.4	32	469	17	27.58

Also bowled: Duke of Norfolk 2.2—1—2—2; Lord Cobham 3—0—7—1; D. Barrick 8.3—1—30—3; W. Watson 3—0—13—1; R. E. Marshall 22—5—59—1; T. W. Graveney 15—1—48—1; E. D. R. Eagar 4—0—25—0.

BENGAL SILVER JUBILEE

A party of twelve players managed by Mr. C. G. Howard, the Lancashire secretary, flew to India on Boxing Day 1956 for two four-day festival matches as part of the Silver Jubilee celebrations of the Bengal Cricket Association. They lost their match against the West Bengal Chief Minister's XI but beat the India President's XI.

C. G. HOWARD'S XI v. CHIEF MINISTER'S XI

At Eden Gardens, Calcutta, December 30, 31, 1956, January 1 and 2, 1957. Chief Minister's XI won by 142 runs. After Trueman, Dooland and Tribe had dismissed the Minister's XI for 149, W. J. Edrich played a bright innings in helping the touring team to a first innings lead of 78. Attractive stroke-play by N. J. Contractor, who opened the Minister's second innings, soon wiped out the arrears. He defied the attack for nearly six and a half hours, scoring 157, and C. G. Howard's XI were left to make 301 to win. They were handicapped when Graveney and Livingston became ill and could not bat. Only Trueman, who hit a hurricane 46, and Watson offered much resistance to the clever spin bowling of Ghulam Ahmed and Mankad.

Chief Minister's XI

P. Roy c and b Tribe	21	— st Livingston b Tribe	43
N. J. Contractor st Livingston b Tribe	24	— c Edrich b Bedser	157
Mushtaq Ali b Trueman	17	— c and b Dooland	16
V. S. Hazare c Moss b Trueman	21	— c Livingston b Dooland	60
V. Mankad c Watson b Tribe	32	— run out	4
G. S. Ramchand c Edrich b Dooland	0	— b Trueman	0
C. S. Gopinath hit wkt b Trueman	5	— b Bedser	5
L. Amarnath b Dooland	11	— not out	59
P. Sen b Tribe	10	— c sub b Trueman	3
S. P. Gupte b Dooland	3		
Ghulam Ahmed not out	2	— not out	0
Extras	3	Extras	31
	149	**(8 wkts., dec.)**	**378**

C. G. Howard's XI

A. Wharton st Sen b Amarnath	13	— c Mankad b Ghulam Ahmed	16
W. Watson c Hazare b Ghulam Ahmed	24	— b Ghulam Ahmed	32
T. W. Graveney c Sen b Gupte	11	— absent ill	0
T. L. Livingston b Gupte	29	— absent ill	0
W. J. Edrich c Gopinath b Gupte	58	— c Ramchand b Mankad	5
G. Tribe c Ramchand b Ghulam Ahmed	25	— c Ramchand b Mankad	13
R. T. Simpson c and b Ghulam Ahmed	24	— c Sen b Mankad	9
B. Dooland lbw b Gupte	3	— c Hazare b Ghulam Ahmed	9
F. S. Trueman not out	11	— not out	46
A. V. Bedser b Ghulam Ahmed	0	— c Sen b Gupte	10
A. E. Moss not out	0	— b Ghulam Ahmed	13
Extras	29	Extras	5
(9 wkts., dec.)	**227**		**158**

C. G. Howard's XI Bowling

	O.	M.	R.	W.	O.	M.	R.	W.
Trueman	10	1	38	3	21	2	71	2
Bedser	4	1	8	0	27	6	66	2
Moss	2	0	7	0	12.5	2	33	0
Dooland	19	6	52	3	29	8	70	2
Tribe	12.2	2	41	4	15	3	70	1
Edrich					6	1	15	0
Wharton					7	0	22	0

Chief Minister's XI Bowling

	O.	M.	R.	W.		O.	M.	R.	W.
Ramchand	2	0	7	0	....	1	0	7	0
Amarnath	9	4	20	1	....	1	0	1	0
Hazare	5	1	15	0	....	2	1	2	0
Gupte	21	4	76	4	....	5	0	23	1
Ghulam Ahmed	21.4	6	68	4	....	17.3	4	38	4
Mankad	6	1	12	0	....	20	5	82	3

C. G. HOWARD'S XI v. CRICKET CLUB OF INDIA PRESIDENT'S XI

At Brabourne Stadium, Bombay, January 5, 6, 7, 8. C. G. Howard's XI won by 152 runs. Graveney dominated the match. In the first innings he scored 153, delighting the crowd with his majestic stroke-play. After Howard's team had gained a first innings lead of 148, Graveney obtained his second century of the match and the Indians were left to score 462 to win. They made a good effort but despite a punishing hundred by Umrigar, Howard's XI gained a comfortable victory over their opponents who were handicapped through an injury to Hazare.

C. G. Howard's XI

R. T. Simpson c Modi b Ramchand	27	— b Mankad	37
A. Wharton c Hazare b Gupte	25	— c Mushtaq Ali b Borde	47
C. McCool c and b Borde	23	— lbw b Gupte..................	1
T. W. Graveney c Hardikar b Nadkarni..	153	— c sub b Mankad	120
W. Watson c Mushtaq Ali b Mankad....	21	— b Gupte	25
W. J. Edrich b Gupte	4	— st Tamhane b Gupte	58
G. Tribe c Tamhane b Gupte	8	— not out	8
B. Dooland c Tamhane b Mankad	15	— not out	6
F. S. Trueman c Mushtaq Ali b Gupte..	33	— st Tamhane b Gupte	6
A. E. Moss b Nadkarni	0		
A. V. Bedser not out	0		
Extras.......................	10	Extras	5
	319	**(7 wkts., dec.)**	**313**

President's XI

Mushtaq Ali c Graveney b Trueman ..	13	— c Wharton b Trueman	8
V. Mankad st McCool b Dooland	27	— c Bedser b Tribe	28
P. R. Umrigar c and b Dooland	57	— b Moss	100
V. S. Hazare retired hurt	32	— absent ill	0
R. S. Modi b Moss	1	— c Moss b Trueman	39
G. S. Ramchand b Tribe	8	— c Bedser b Tribe	5
M. S. Hardikar lbw b Moss	0	— c Edrich b Tribe	38
R. Nadkarni c Watson b Tribe	4	— run out	35
C. G. Borde not out	6	— b Moss	21
N. S. Tamhane c and b Dooland	0	— run out	11
S. P. Gupte c Moss b Tribe	9	— not out	10
Extras.......................	14	Extras	14
	171		**309**

President's XI Bowling

	O.	M.	R.	W.		O.	M.	R.	W.
Umrigar	7	2	26	0					
Ramchand	18	4	50	1	....	6	0	14	0
Hazare	2	0	11	0					
Gupte	23.4	3	99	4	....	16	1	77	4
Nadkarni	11	1	33	2	....	15	2	43	0
Borde	5	0	18	1	....	9	0	59	1
Mankad	18	2	59	2	....	19	4	82	2
Hardikar	2	0	13	0	....	3	0	13	0
Modi						12	5	20	0

C. G. Howard's XI Bowling

	O.	M.	R.	W.		O.	M.	R.	W.
Trueman	13	4	29	1	....	17	2	66	2
Moss	13	5	13	2	....	16	1	48	2
Bedser	7	0	22	0	....	11	3	23	0
Dooland	17	3	38	3	....	20.1	1	65	0
Tribe	13.4	2	55	3	....	33	3	93	3

OVERSEAS CRICKET, 1956–57

AUSTRALIAN INTER-STATE MATCHES

By T. L. Goodman

SHEFFIELD SHIELD RESULTS

	Played	Won	Won on 1st Inns.	Tied	Lost on 1st Inns.	Lost	Points
Points awarded ...	—	5	3	2	1	—	—
New South Wales...	8	3	2	1	2	0	25
Queensland	8	2	4	0	2	0	24
Victoria	8	3	1	1	1	2	21
Western Australia..	8	1	1	0	3	3	11
South Australia....	8	0	2	0	2	4	8

As in the previous summer, Australia had a season devoted to domestic cricket. There was a record number of 20 matches in the Sheffield Shield inter-State competition. Western Australia, who since 1947–48 had been in the competition on a modified experimental basis, were admitted to full membership, and so each State had a full programme of home and away matches.

New South Wales won the competition for the fourth successive season, but by only one point from Queensland who have yet to win the Shield competition, which they entered in 1926–27.

The Shield series was supplemented by a testimonial match in Sydney tendered by the New South Wales Cricket Association to two former Test players, S. J. McCabe and W. J. O'Reilly. It was also approved by the Australian Board of Control as an official selection trial for the Australia team to tour New Zealand towards the end of the season, and also for the team chosen at the end of May to tour South Africa in 1957–58.

I. W. Johnson, captain, and K. R. Miller, vice-captain, of the Australian team that toured England in 1956, announced their retirements from first-class cricket. Johnson was succeeded as captain of Victoria by R. N. Harvey, and Miller as captain of New South Wales by I. D. Craig.

Queensland were without their Test all-rounder, R. G. Archer, because of a knee injury sustained in Pakistan.

Wicket-keeper G. R. Langley, 37, who had effected 98 dismissals in 26 Test matches, chose South Australia's game with New South Wales in Adelaide to mark his retirement. He was cheered from the field by New South Wales players after he had scored 100 runs in the last innings of the match. South Australia's captain, P. R. Ridings, announced that the season would be his last in first-class cricket.

Traditional rivals, New South Wales and Victoria, played two extraordinary matches. The first, in Melbourne, resulted in the first tie ever recorded in the 65-year-old Shield competition. New South Wales in the last innings needed 161 runs to win. Skipper Craig was in bed at the team's hotel, suffering from tonsilitis. J. W. Burke, who had batted through the first innings for 132 not out, had had the little finger of his right hand broken by a fast ball from I. Meckiff in the opening over of the second innings and he retired.

Craig was sent for when his team were 38 for four wickets. He could not call loud enough for his batting partner to hear when he joined R. Benaud at 70 for seven but scored 24 of a stubborn eighth-wicket stand of 75. Benaud made 63. Burke resumed at number ten, with 15 wanted to tie. Twelve were still wanted when the last man, A. Wyatt, joined him. Burke, batting under difficulties, and with Victoria applying full pressure, stole singles. The total reached 160. Then Burke snicked a ball from Meckiff and was caught behind the wicket by L. Maddocks.

A dogged fourth-wicket partnership by S. Carroll and Craig saved New South Wales from outright defeat by Victoria in Sydney. Their team was beaten on the first innings; but the point saved prevented the Shield being lost to Queensland, who would have won on averages had the teams finished the competition level.

Craig had put Victoria in to bat on a pitch that proved to be docile, and Victoria made 375 for three wickets on the first day. Harvey, who opened because C. C. McDonald had had his nose broken while practising before the match began, scored 209—his fourth Shield century of the season and the fifth double century of his career. New South Wales, routed in the first innings, were nearly 300 in arrears and 42 for three wickets in the second when Craig joined opener Carroll with ten and a half hours left for play. The fourth-wicket pair had to consume time; but Carroll was batting with a badly cut and painfully bruised right hand. With a full day's play remaining, they had taken the score to 198. Carroll had batted four and a half hours for 60 and Craig four hours for 88. Craig, 93, went early on the last day; but Carroll continued his memorable stand. He batted in all for six and a half hours and reached 86. The "tail" wagged and Victoria had only one over for batting. Victoria were without their fast bowler, Meckiff, who had hurt himself when bowling in New South Wales's second innings.

Prior to this match Queensland, led by R. R. Lindwall, had repeated their win of the previous season over New South Wales in Sydney. K. Mackay (169 runs in six hours twenty-one minutes) blunted the home attack, and wicket-keeper W. Grout, batting number nine, hit powerfully for 119 not out—his first Shield century. Queensland, in Melbourne, had beaten Victoria by an innings for the first time since 1939, and later the team beat Victoria

on the first innings in Brisbane. P. Burge showed outstanding
batting development.

Victoria, again playing their home games on St. Kilda Oval,
as Melbourne Cricket Ground was required for the Olympic
Games, began with two outright defeats; but their new captain,
Neil Harvey, soon got his team into better shape and put backbone
into the batting by his own consistent efforts.

Western Australia celebrated their "coming of age" by beating
South Australia in Adelaide and followed with their first outright
win over Victoria in Melbourne. But the team had no success in
home matches, despite impressive batting in Perth by R. Simpson,
who had been acquired from New South Wales, and a great stand
by K. Meuleman, whose 234 not out against South Australia was
a record individual score in a first-class match in Perth. Young
left-hander, B. Shepherd, had some prolific partnerships with
Meuleman. Fast bowler, R. Gaunt, and medium-pacer, R. Strauss,
achieved some fine bowling performances.

South Australia finished at the bottom of the Shield table.
Their opening batsman, L. Favell, scored a century in each innings
against New South Wales in Sydney (the second innings was a
brilliant one) and C. Pinch repeated the feat against Western
Australia in Perth.

R. N. Harvey (Victoria) scored 744 runs and headed the
Shield batting averages at 106.28. K. Meuleman (Western
Australia) scored most runs, 779; other leading run-makers were
C. Pinch (South Australia) 739, K. Mackay (Queensland) 676 and
P. Burge (Queensland) 675. Harvey, Meuleman, Burge, J. Burke
(N.S.W.) and W. Watson (N.S.W.) each scored a double century.

A notable innings was that of 127 played by Norman O'Neill
(N.S.W.), aged 19, against South Australia in Sydney. It was a
classical display of controlled power. Indeed, O'Neill outshone
Craig who made 102 in the same innings.

R. R. Lindwall (Queensland) was again prominent with 24
wickets at 22.25 each, but a happy feature of the season was the
development of new bowling talent and particularly the form
showed by the Victorian left-handers, I. Meckiff and L. Kline,
both aged 22. Meckiff, a tall fast bowler, who takes a comparatively short run, produced splendid speed and caused the ball
to lift. Kline, a left arm off-spinner who also bowled a googly,
took most wickets in the Shield, 37. Meckiff and Kline toured
New Zealand with the Australian team led by Craig and both
were subsequently chosen to tour South Africa in 1957–58.

There was ill-feeling on the last day of the Western Australia
v. Queensland match in Perth. Umpire O. Cooley intervened after
fast bowler Gaunt (W. A.) had bowled many "bumpers," with a
packed leg-side field. Left-arm spinner, Preen, had bowled outside
the leg stump with eight men on the leg side. The tactics were a

protest against Queensland not having closed their innings at the overnight score with a very big lead. Queensland captain, Lindwall, was ill in bed; some other Queensland players were indisposed.

Queensland's two members of the Australian Board of Control both died in 1957. Mr. J. T. Burge died in Brisbane in January, while his son, Peter, was batting in the selection trial match in Sydney. Mr. Burge was manager of the Australian team on tour of the West Indies in 1954–55.

Mr. J. S. Hutcheon, Q.C., C.B.E., died in Brisbane in June, at the age of 75. He had been president of Queensland Cricket Association for 30 years and a member of the Australian Board of Control for 38 years. He captained Queensland in 1910–11.

QUEENSLAND v. NEW SOUTH WALES

At Brisbane, October 26, 27, 29, 30. New South Wales won on first innings. Queensland received a good start, McLaughlin, driving splendidly, and Archer settling down after a shaky beginning. O'Neill, 19 years old and playing in only his second Shield match, hit attractively for New South Wales, who were also well served by Martin, a left-hander making his first appearance. With the pitch more responsive to spin on each succeeding day, Queensland were saved in their second innings by an eighth wicket stand of 72 between Walmsley and Muddle. Even so, New South Wales, with over four and a half hours in which to score 224 runs, would probably have won comfortably but for rain.

Queensland

C. Harvey c and b Martin	40	—	c Philpott b Treanor	28
R. Lyons c Martin b Philpott	66	—	b Fagan	0
J. McLaughlin c Martin b Philpott	52	—	c Watson b Livingston	11
K. Archer b Treanor	65	—	lbw b Livingston	5
J. Cooper c de Courcy b Martin	7	—	b Treanor	23
J. Bratchford c Martin b Livingston	27	—	b Martin	43
W. Grout c Lambert b Treanor	33	—	b Martin	19
W. Walmsley lbw b Treanor	4	—	lbw b Livingston	40
D. Muddle c Watson b Treanor	10	—	not out	37
V. N. Raymer c Watson b Martin	20	—	c Martin b Livingston	20
J. Freeman not out	0	—	lbw b Treanor	0
Extras	1		Extras	17
	325			**243**

New South Wales

W. Watson c Lyons b Bratchford	4	—	lbw b Raymer	35
S. Carroll c Raymer b Freeman	70	—	c Bratchford b Muddle	9
N. O'Neill c Grout b Walmsley	63	—	not out	60
J. H. de Courcy c Archer b Walmsley	52	—	c Grout b Archer	17
C. Johnston c Harvey b Freeman	68			
J. Martin c Grout b Freeman	47			
P. Philpott c Harvey b Freeman	6			
A. Fagan c Bratchford b Raymer	8			
J. Treanor c Raymer b Freeman	6			
O. Lambert not out	9	—	not out	4
B. Livingston b Raymer	4	—	run out	4
Extras	8		Extras	2
	345		**(4 wkts.)**	**131**

New South Wales Bowling

	O.	M.	R.	W.		O.	M.	R.	W.
Fagan	13	4	52	0	....	18	6	35	1
Livingston	12	3	42	1	....	17	5	43	4
Treanor	19	2	93	4	....	19.5	4	54	3
Martin	15.7	1	68	3	....	14	0	50	2
Philpott	23	3	63	2	....	18	3	44	0
O'Neill	1	0	6	0					

Queensland Bowling

	O.	M.	R.	W.		O.	M.	R.	W.
Bratchford	18	2	67	1	....	8	1	33	0
Muddle	11	1	50	0	....	6	0	36	1
Raymer	16	7	29	2	....	10	2	17	1
Walmsley	22	11	114	2					
Freeman	24	3	77	5	....	2	0	13	0
Archer						3	1	12	1
Cooper						3	0	18	0

SOUTH AUSTRALIA v. WESTERN AUSTRALIA

At Adelaide, November 2, 4, 5, 6. Western Australia won on first innings. Capital bowling by Strauss formed the feature of the first innings. Hole, Pinch and Ducker showed fight and prevented a rout. Strauss, moving the ball either way, bowled six of his seven victims. Western Australia suffered an early reverse, but solid batting by the middle men placed them in a strong position. Shepherd and Meuleman played particularly well, being severe on both pace and spin. South Australia's batting improved in the second innings, and centuries by Stevens, his first in Shield cricket, and Pinch made the game safe.

South Australia

L. Favell c Buggins b Gaunt	33	— b Strauss	16
C. Grant b Strauss	6	— c Gorringe b Simpson	42
G. Stevens b Strauss	0	— not out	125
C. Pinch c Shepherd b Gaunt	46	— st Buggins b Meuleman	116
G. B. Hole c Preen b Strauss	89	— not out	18
P. Ridings b Strauss	5		
J. Ducker not out	44		
J. Drennan b Strauss	10		
L. Weekley b Strauss	0		
J. Gregg b Strauss	0		
J. Bedford b Preen	19		
Extras	9	Extras	5
	261	(3 wkts., dec.)	322

Western Australia

B. Buggins b Drennan	1	— not out	38
L. Sawle c and b Bedford	46	— not out	39
R. L. Simpson lbw b Drennan	26		
B. Shepherd run out	94		
K. Meuleman c Grant b Bedford	140		
A. Edwards b Gregg	46		
M. Vernon b Gregg	11		
A. Preen not out	11		
R. Strauss b Gregg	16		
H. Gorringe b Gregg	0		
R. Gaunt b Gregg	3		
Extras	12	Extras	8
	406	(No wkt.)	85

Western Australia Bowling

	O.	M.	R.	W.		O.	M.	R.	W.
Gaunt	19	1	58	2	....	18	6	53	0
Gorringe	18	1	95	0	....	19	2	61	0
Strauss	18	3	59	7	....	23	6	55	1
Preen	14.3	5	32	1	....	21	4	65	0
Simpson	1	0	8	0	....	11	2	38	1
Meuleman					....	7	0	32	1
Edwards					....	2	0	13	0

South Australia Bowling

	O.	M.	R.	W.		O.	M.	R.	W.
Drennan	23	1	84	2					
Gregg	36.4	6	115	5	....	7	2	16	0
Bedford	37	8	108	2	....	6	3	11	0
Hole	11	3	23	0	....	5	1	10	0
Weekley	17	1	64	0	....	5	1	15	0
Pinch					....	3	0	9	0
Ridings					....	2	0	9	0
Stevens					....	1	0	4	0
Favell					....	1	0	3	0

VICTORIA v. WESTERN AUSTRALIA

At Melbourne, November 9, 10, 11, 12. Western Australia won by four wickets. Victoria started disastrously, losing six wickets for 34. A seventh wicket stand of 38 by Dick and Botham brought some recovery. Western Australia also began poorly but Meuleman and Hoare, who put on 69 for the ninth wicket, took them ahead. Victoria batted unevenly in the second innings, but Shaw shared two stands of 66 each with Loxton and Dick. Western Australia soon lost Buggins, but solid batting gave them a comfortable victory. Strauss bowled well, finishing with a match analysis of nine wickets for 85.

Victoria

W. Lawry c Rigg b Strauss	5	—	b Strauss	1
J. Cosgrave c Buggins b Strauss	3	—	c Rigg b Gaunt	4
J. Shaw b Gaunt	2	—	c Gaunt b Hoare	82
K. Kendall b Strauss	17	—	c Buggins b Hoare	10
L. Maddocks c Sawle b Hoare	5	—	run out	31
S. J. Loxton b Strauss	1	—	c Rigg b Gaunt	30
A. Dick c and b Hoare	20	—	b Strauss	34
L. Kline c Edwards b Hoare	11	—	c Simpson b Strauss	2
L. Botham c Buggins b Preen	21	—	not out	4
I. Meckiff not out	19	—	b Strauss	11
J. Salmon b Hoare	26	—	b Strauss	9
Extras	1		Extras	24
	131			**242**

Western Australia

L. Sawle c Shaw b Salmon	0	—	lbw b Kline c Shaw b Salmon	49
B. Buggins run out	15	—	b Salmon	2
R. L. Simpson c Maddocks b Meckiff	0	—	c Shaw b Dick	40
B. Shepherd c Salmon b Meckiff	8	—	c Kendall b Kline	19
A. Edwards c Shaw b Dick	15	—	not out	43
K. Meuleman c Kendall b Meckiff	65	—	b Kline	10
A. Preen lbw b Kline	4	—	lbw b Kline	0
B. Rigg c and b Dick	7	—	not out	42
R. Strauss c Salmon b Kline	4			
R. Gaunt run out	7			
D. Hoare not out	32			
Extras	8		Extras	4
	165			**(6 wkts.) 209**

Western Australia Bowling

	O.	M.	R.	W.		O.	M.	R.	W.
Gaunt	9	2	19	1	....	13	1	50	2
Strauss	14	3	38	4	....	22.7	8	47	5
Hoare	11.3	1	43	4	....	21	3	83	2
Preen	6	1	30	1	....	13	2	34	0
				Meuleman	....	2	0	4	0

Victoria Bowling

	O.	M.	R.	W.		O.	M.	R.	W.
Salmon	15	5	19	1	....	4	0	15	1
Meckiff	18.7	3	44	3	....	11	1	40	0
Kline	21	6	62	3	....	27.1	5	79	4
Dick	7	0	21	1	....	34	10	61	1
Loxton	5	3	11	0	....	4	0	10	0

QUEENSLAND v. WESTERN AUSTRALIA

At Brisbane, November 16, 18, 19, 20. Queensland won on first innings. Sound batting by Lyons, Mackay, McLaughlin and Burge enabled Queensland to score rapidly on the first day, and before the close Western Australia lost four wickets for 18 runs. Rain limited play to ninety minutes next day, when Shepherd and Meuleman advanced the score to 128 without being parted. Each went on to complete a century but when the partnership was broken the innings ended for 43 more runs. Freeman, with spin bowling, and the wicket-keeper, Grout, formed an effective combination for Queensland.

Queensland

C. Harvey c Hoare b Gaunt	2	— not out	?
R. Lyons c Shepherd b Preen	66	— c Edwards b Buggins	12
K. Mackay c Hoare b Gaunt	88		
J. McLaughlin b Meuleman	93		
D. Bull c Edwards b Meuleman	4		
J. Bratchford c and b Preen	0		
P. Burge c Preen b Shepherd	105		
R. R. Lindwall b Preen	10		
W. Grout c Edwards b Strauss	7		
W. Walmsley not out	0		
J. Freeman b Preen	0		
Extras	14	Extras	4
	389	(1 wkt.)	18

Western Australia

L. Sawle st Grout b Freeman	8	R. Strauss b Lindwall	6
B. Buggins st Grout b Freeman	8	A. Preen st Grout b Freeman	10
R. L. Simpson b Bratchford	0	D. Hoare c Grout b Freeman	0
B. Shepherd st Grout b Freeman	173	R. Gaunt not out	15
A. Edwards c Harvey b Freeman	0	Extras	9
K. Meuleman c Harvey b Lindwall	125		
B. Rigg lbw b Mackay	11		365

Western Australia Bowling

	O.	M.	R.	W.		O.	M.	R.	W.
Gaunt	24	9	58	2					
Strauss	38	13	74	1					
Hoare	12	4	37	0					
Preen	38.6	11	69	4	....	1	0	5	0
Meuleman	12	1	58	2					
Simpson	18	0	66	0					
Rigg	2	0	10	0	....	1	0	8	0
Shepherd	1	0	3	1					
			Buggins		....	3	2	1	1

Queensland Bowling

	O.	M.	R.	W.
Lindwall	22	7	43	2
Bratchford	28	6	68	1
Freeman	37.2	4	134	6
Walmsley	16	0	52	0
Mackay	18	0	58	1
Bull	1	0	1	0

SOUTH AUSTRALIA v. VICTORIA

At Adelaide, November 23, 25, 26, 27. Victoria won by an innings and 88 runs. South Australia's collapse in the first innings was not entirely due to poor batting. A sustained spell of medium-pace bowling by Salmon and a lively pitch did much toward the downfall. The turf was far less helpful to bowlers when Victoria batted and Lawry and Kendall gave them a good start by adding 109 for the second wicket. Loxton, who drove forcefully, and Shaw put on 180 runs in two hours. South Australia batted poorly in the second innings in perfect conditions, losing eight men for 139. Weekley added 52 with Ridings and 45 with Gregg, but first innings arrears of 324 proved too heavy.

South Australia

L. Favell c Longney b Salmon	16	— c Dick b Meckiff	0
C. Grant c Longney b Salmon	5	— st Longney b Dick	20
G. Stevens lbw b Salmon	14	— b Dick	63
C. Pinch c R. Maddocks b Loxton	3	— lbw b Dick	4
G. B. Hole b Salmon	17	— c Longney b Kline	23
P. Ridings b Kline	26	— b Salmon	48
B. Jarman c Longney b Loxton	14	— c and b Kline	2
J. Beagley c Loxton b Kline	10	— c Kendall b Kline	0
L. Weekley c Salmon b Kline	1	— b Dick	40
J. Wilson not out	0	— b Kline	0
J. Gregg run out	3	— not out	27
Extras	6	Extras	9
	115		**236**

Victoria

J. Cosgrave c Stevens b Beagley	0	D. Longney st Jarman b Weekley	0
W. Lawry c Favell b Beagley	38	L. Kline b Hole	0
K. Kendall c Jarman b Beagley	119	J. Salmon lbw b Beagley	0
R. Maddocks lbw b Wilson	16	I. Meckiff not out	0
J. Shaw lbw b Weekley	114	Extras	7
S. J. Loxton st Jarman b Weekley	134		
A. Dick c and b Weekley	11		**439**

Victoria Bowling

	O.	M.	R.	W.		O.	M.	R.	W.
Salmon	17	8	31	4	….	8	3	35	1
Meckiff	7	0	27	0	….	15	2	39	1
Dick	4	0	15	0	….	18.1	6	46	4
Kline	3.3	0	6	3	….	25	5	107	4
Loxton	11	2	30	2					

South Australia Bowling

	O.	M.	R.	W.			O.	M.	R.	W.
Beagley	28	5	115	4		Pinch	1	0	5	0
Gregg	20	2	57	0		Hole	8	0	30	1
Wilson	26	8	73	1		Stevens	1	0	11	0
Weekley	25.5	2	141	4						

NEW SOUTH WALES v. WESTERN AUSTRALIA

At Sydney, November 23, 25, 26, 27. New South Wales won by 80 runs after being 51 behind on the first innings. Benaud bowled particularly well. With Strauss in good form, New South Wales failed at the first attempt, only Craig and Benaud achieving much. A century by Carroll in the second innings laid the foundations of the win. He was well supported by Martin and Davidson. Western Australia never looked like scoring the 268 runs required to win. Simpson batted without chance, but his colleagues found runs hard to obtain, especially off Benaud.

New South Wales

I. W. Burke c Shepherd b Gaunt	0	— c Buggins b Gaunt	0
S. Carroll b Gaunt	17	— c Buggins b Gaunt	100
N. O'Neill c Simpson b Hoare	8	— b Gaunt	8
I. D. Craig b Strauss	53	— c Buggins b Gaunt	3
W. Watson run out	7	— b Gaunt	8
R. Benaud c Buggins b Strauss	24	— c Rigg b Gaunt	3
J. Martin lbw b Strauss	8	— b Strauss	71
A. K. Davidson lbw b Strauss	9	— c Shepherd b Gaunt	84
P. Crawford b Strauss	0	— c Simpson b Hoare	14
J. Treanor b Strauss	11	— not out	9
O. Lambert not out	1	— lbw b Simpson	0
Extras	7	Extras	18
	145		**318**

Western Australia

L. Sawle c Martin b Crawford	17	— b Davidson	16
R. Strauss c and b Treanor	1	— b Benaud	26
B. Rigg b Treanor	8	— lbw b Davidson	0
R. L. Simpson c Lambert b Treanor	27	— c Lambert b Benaud	75
B. Shepherd b Benaud	17	— c sub b Treanor	2
K. Meuleman b Crawford	14	— c Benaud b Treanor	24
A. Edwards c Martin b Benaud	52	— c and b Martin	7
A. Preen not out	27	— c Benaud b Treanor	1
B. Buggins b Crawford	0	— st Lambert b Benaud	25
D. Hoare run out	3	— not out	0
R. Gaunt c Carroll b Benaud	10	— c Davidson b Benaud	2
Extras	20	Extras	9
	196		**187**

Western Australia Bowling

	O.	M.	R.	W.	O.	M.	R.	W.
Gaunt	5	1	25	2	20	3	104	7
Hoare	6	1	12	1	9	0	33	1
Strauss	16.6	3	66	6	20	3	92	1
Preen	9	2	33	0	10	2	29	0
Simpson	1	0	2	0	5.6	0	32	1
Shepherd					3	0	10	0

New South Wales Bowling

	O.	M.	R.	W.	O.	M.	R.	W.
Crawford	16	4	31	3	4	0	22	0
Davidson	9	1	38	0	8	0	42	2
Treanor	13	4	21	3	20	4	39	3
Benaud	25.4	6	69	3	18.5	2	59	4
Martin	4	0	17	0	6	0	16	1

VICTORIA v. QUEENSLAND

At Melbourne, December 8, 10, 11, 12. Queensland won by an innings and 42 runs. Harvey, captaining Victoria for the first time, made a great effort, scoring 161 runs of their aggregate of 416, but he could not prevent Queensland from gaining their first victory in Melbourne. Lindwall moved the ball disconcertingly in the first innings, troubling all the Victoria batsmen. In the second innings Bratchford did most damage. Burge was the best batsman for Queensland, scoring a brilliant century.

Victoria

C. C. McDonald c Freeman b Lindwall	0	—	lbw b Bratchford	8
W. Lawry c Bratchford b Lindwall	15	—	lbw b Freeman	51
R. N. Harvey c Bull b Walmsley	108	—	b Mackay	53
J. Shaw run out	7	—	st Grout b Freeman	20
K. Kendall c Burge b Bratchford	2	—	lbw b Mackay	3
S. J. Loxton c and b Lindwall	4	—	c Burge b Bratchford	28
L. Maddocks c Grout b Freeman	10	—	b Walmsley	5
A. Dick c Mackay b Walmsley	45	—	not out	26
I. Meckiff b Lindwall	2	—	c and b Bratchford	0
L. Kline b Lindwall	0	—	lbw b Bratchford	1
J. Salmon not out	3	—	b Bratchford	0
Extras	11		Extras	14
	207			**209**

Queensland

R. Lyons lbw b Dick	30	W. Grout b Meckiff	44
R. Reynolds c Shaw b Kline	24	W. Walmsley not out	4
K. Mackay c Harvey b Salmon	66	J. Freeman c and b Dick	4
P. Burge b Loxton	135	Extras	23
J. McLaughlin run out	4		
D. Bull lbw b Loxton	24		
J. Bratchford b Loxton	30		
R. R. Lindwall c Maddocks b Meckiff	70		**458**

Queensland Bowling

	O.	M.	R.	W.		O.	M.	R.	W.
Lindwall	15.4	2	60	5		19	4	40	0
Bratchford	14	1	46	1		16.7	4	28	5
Freeman	8	1	33	1		19	6	52	2
Mackay	5	0	17	0		23	7	45	2
Walmsley	7	0	31	2		6	0	30	1
Bull	1	0	9	0					

Victoria Bowling

	O.	M.	R.	W.
Meckiff	34	6	83	2
Salmon	32	6	102	1
Loxton	20	3	58	3
Dick	22.3	5	71	2
Kline	30	6	121	1

WESTERN AUSTRALIA v. NEW SOUTH WALES

At Perth, December 8, 10, 11, 12. New South Wales won by an innings and 31 runs. Western Australia opened in fine style and a second wicket stand of 140 by Sawle and Simpson placed them in a strong position, but Edwards alone did much afterwards. Simpson was particularly severe on the spin bowlers. The pitch played well when New South Wales batted, and a fourth wicket partnership between Craig and Watson yielded 264 runs. Craig, fortunate to be dropped at 87, completed 155. When the pitch crumbled in Western Australia's second innings, Benaud took full advantage, and arrears of 229 never looked like being cleared.

Western Australia

J. Rutherford b Martin	18	— c Lambert b Martin	33
L. Sawle c Watson b Davidson	85	— c Carroll b Davidson	7
R. L. Simpson lbw b Benaud	97	— c O'Neill b Benaud	26
B. Shepherd run out	4	— c Watson b Benaud	20
K. Meuleman c Davidson b Treanor	18	— c and b Martin	3
A. Edwards c Lambert b Davidson	55	— b Benaud	30
A. Preen b Davidson	7	— c and b Benaud	26
B. Buggins run out	2	— c Martin b Treanor	0
R. Strauss c Benaud b Davidson	3	— retired hurt	2
D. Hoare st Lambert b Benaud	1	— not out	18
R. Gaunt not out	0	— b Wyatt	25
Extras	11	Extras	8
	301		**198**

New South Wales

J. W. Burke c Buggins b Strauss	2	A. K. Davidson lbw b Strauss	19
S. Carroll c Buggins b Gaunt	10	J. Treanor b Preen	11
N. O'Neill lbw b Strauss	63	O. Lambert not out	3
I. D. Craig c Simpson b Gaunt	155	A. Wyatt not out	0
W. Watson c Sawle b Strauss	206	Extras	13
R. Benaud c Shepherd b Hoare	25		
J. Martin b Preen	23	**(9 wkts., dec.) 530**	

New South Wales Bowling

	O.	M.	R.	W.		O.	M.	R.	W.
Wyatt	12	1	53	0		7.4	1	22	1
Davidson	23.6	4	69	4		10	3	23	1
Martin	15	1	52	1		10	2	45	2
Benaud	32	9	72	2		28	1	75	4
Treanor	10	2	44	1		13	5	24	1
					Burke	1	0	1	0

Western Australia Bowling

	O.	M.	R.	W.
Strauss	35	10	101	4
Gaunt	21	1	114	2
Hoare	15	0	91	1
Rutherford	12	2	44	0
Preen	26.6	4	99	2
Simpson	8	0	39	0
Meuleman	4	0	29	0

SOUTH AUSTRALIA v. NEW SOUTH WALES

At Adelaide, December 14, 15, 17, 18. New South Wales won by an innings and 62 runs. The leading features were the brilliant batting performances of Burke and Carroll for New South Wales and Stevens and Langley for South Australia. Burke, playing one of his finest attacking innings, scored brilliantly and laid the foundation for victory. He and O'Neill added a brisk 130. South Australia found the leg-break bowling of Treanor too much for them in the first innings. Stevens was last out, alone offering much resistance. When South Australia followed on 265 behind, Langley marked his last appearance in first-class cricket with a fighting hundred.

New South Wales

J. W. Burke c Weekley b Wilson..220	A. K. Davidson lbw b Beagley.... 3
S. Carroll c Ducker b Beagley....113	J. Treanor c Langley b Beagley... 5
N. O'Neill c Langley b Beagley... 62	O. Lambert b Beagley 1
I. D. Craig c Hole b Drennan 0	A. Wyatt not out 1
R. Benaud lbw b Drennan 0	Extras.................... 18
W. Watson c Favell b Drennan... 3	—
J. Martin lbw b Beagley......... 28	454

South Australia

L. Favell c Burke b Davidson 36	— lbw b Wyatt	9
J. Ducker lbw b Martin 30	— c Lambert b Davidson	1
C. Pinch lbw b Martin 1	— lbw b Wyatt	0
G. Stevens b Treanor 74	— lbw b Davidson	6
G. B. Hole c Lambert b Davidson 24	— c Benaud b Davidson	30
P. Ridings c Benaud b Treanor 7	— c Watson b Benaud	46
G. R. Langley b Treanor 4	— st Lambert b Benaud 100	
J. Drennan c Benaud b Treanor 0	— c Watson b Benaud	1
L. Weekley c Martin b Benaud 5	— b Martin	0
J. Beagley b Treanor 4	— b Martin	4
J. Wilson not out 0	— not out	0
Extras................... 4	Extras...............	6
189	203

South Australia Bowling

	O.	M.	R.	W.	O.	M.	R.	W.
Drennan	29	3	95	3				
Beagley	33	4	121	6				
Wilson	37.4	12	88	1				
Weekley	19	0	109	0				
Hole	4	0	23	0				
Pinch	1	1	0	0				

New South Wales Bowling

	O.	M.	R.	W.		O.	M.	R.	W.
Wyatt	6	1	30	0	....	13	1	53	2
Davidson	13	4	34	2	....	7	2	20	3
Treanor	19.6	3	58	5	....	10	1	38	0
Benaud........	17	3	25	1	....	16	6	31	3
Martin	8	2	38	2	....	14	0	55	2

WESTERN AUSTRALIA v. QUEENSLAND

At Perth, December 15, 17, 18, 19. Queensland won on first innings. This match drew considerable attention because one of the umpires, O. Cooley, warned Gaunt, Western Australia, for intimidating bowling, and advised his captain, Meuleman, to alter his field placing. The incident occurred when Queensland, with five players ill and leading by 402 with five and a half hours left for play, continued their second innings. As a further demonstration against this policy, the spin bowler, Preen, placed a leg-side field of eight men. Mackay, in the absence of Lindwall, made the decision to bat on, and the circumstances provided some excuse. The outstanding performance of the match was the splendid batting of Simpson, whose scores of 96 and 112 not out prevented Queensland from gaining an outright win.

Queensland

R. Lyons c Buggins b Bevan	23	— st Buggins b Meuleman	...	27
R. Reynolds b Gaunt	57	— b Preen		52
K. Mackay c Preen b Gaunt	41	— c Slater b Gaunt		83
P. Burge c Sawle b Gaunt	32	— b Slater		36
J. McLaughlin c Buggins b Slater	33	— not out		32
D. Bull c Buggins b Meuleman	2	— not out		53
J. Bratchford b Slater	30			
R. R. Lindwall b Slater	19			
W. Grout c Shepherd b Bevan	9			
W. Walmsley b Gaunt	15			
J. Freeman not out	12			
Extras	17	Extras		18
	290	(4 wkts., dec.)		301

Western Australia

J. Rutherford c Grout b Bratchford	25	— lbw b Walmsley		31
L. Sawle c Burge b Bratchford	1	— c Freeman b Walmsley	...	66
R. L. Simpson c Lindwall b Walmsley	96	— not out		112
B. Shepherd c Lyons b Freeman	1			
K. Meuleman c Grout b Lindwall	10	— not out		29
K. Slater b Walmsley	0			
A. Edwards c Walmsley b Freeman	7			
A. Preen c and b Freeman	12			
B. Buggins b Walmsley	7	— b Freeman		6
H. Bevan c Burge b Walmsley	0			
R. Gaunt not out	9			
Extras	7	Extras		11
	175	(3 wkts.)		255

Western Australia Bowling

	O.	M.	R.	W.	O.	M.	R.	W.
Gaunt	20.2	5	74	4	16	0	57	1
Bevan	20	2	80	2	9	2	33	0
Slater	26	8	73	3	21	5	67	1
Preen	16	7	27	0	24	12	37	1
Meuleman	3	0	13	1	6	0	43	1
Simpson	1	0	6	0				
Rutherford					13	6	31	0
Shepherd					2	0	14	0
Edwards					1	0	1	0

Queensland Bowling

	O.	M.	R.	W.	O.	M.	R.	W.
Walmsley	11	3	22	4	28	3	76	2
Bratchford	9	0	46	2	12	0	45	0
Freeman	15.7	5	51	3	26	2	76	1
Mackay	7	0	38	0	8	0	19	0
Lindwall	11	7	11	1				
Bull					7	2	11	0
McLaughlin					1	0	2	0
Reynolds					1	0	4	0
Lyons					3	1	10	0
Burge					1	0	1	0

SOUTH AUSTRALIA v. QUEENSLAND

At Adelaide, December 22, 24, 26, 27. South Australia won on first innings. Splendid batting by Pinch, Hole and Ridings laid the foundation of South Australia's total. Pinch batted with special brilliance. Hooking and off-driving beautifully, he added 122 for the fourth wicket in partnership with Hole. Of the Queensland batsmen, only Mackay mastered the bowling in the first innings. Following on, 175 behind, Queensland fared much better. Reynolds batted confidently, and though South Australia used ten bowlers they never looked like winning outright.

South Australia

L. Favell c McLaughlin b Walmsley	60	J. Drennan b Lindwall		9
G. Stevens b Lindwall	33	J. Bedford lbw b Freeman		28
J. Ducker lbw b Mackay	33	J. Beagley b Walmsley		0
C. Pinch lbw b Lindwall	84	J. Wilson c Grout b Lindwall		12
G. B. Hole c Lindwall b Mackay	72	Extras		15
P. Ridings not out	86			—
B. Jarman run out	1			433

Queensland

R. Lyons lbw b Drennan	19	— c Beagley b Pinch	34
R. Reynolds c Bedford b Beagley	14	— not out	110
K. Mackay lbw b Beagley	107	— lbw b Drennan	38
P. Burge lbw b Bedford	24	— c Beagley b Pinch	79
J. McLaughlin c and b Bedford	17	— not out	23
D. Bull c Jarman b Wilson	16		
J. Bratchford b Beagley	13		
R. R. Lindwall c Hole b Beagley	0		
W. Grout b Drennan	1		
W. Walmsley lbw b Wilson	26		
J. Freeman not out	17		
Extras	4	Extras	10
	—		—
	258	(3 wkts.)	294

Queensland Bowling

	O.	M.	R.	W.	O.	M.	R.	W.
Lindwall	27.3	4	85	4				
Bratchford	22	4	73	0				
Freeman	30	10	94	1				
Walmsley	31	7	116	2				
Mackay	22	7	50	2				

South Australia Bowling

	O.	M.	R.	W.	O.	M.	R.	W.
Drennan	23	4	48	2	13	2	40	1
Beagley	29	7	70	4	4	0	19	0
Wilson	40.4	16	76	2	19	3	62	0
Bedford	26	11	49	2	14	3	53	0
Hole	3	0	11	0	13	1	47	0
Pinch					9	1	34	2
Stevens					3	0	8	0
Ridings					3	0	13	0
Ducker					1	0	8	0
Favell					1	1	0	0

NEW SOUTH WALES v. VICTORIA

At Melbourne, December 22, 24, 26, 27. Tied. Craig, suffering from tonsillitis, and Burke, with a broken finger, batted for New South Wales in their second innings and helped in the first tie in the 100 years' history of inter-State cricket. On a drying pitch New South Wales needed 161 runs for victory. When seven wickets fell for 70 they seemed sure to be beaten, but Craig and Benaud shared a stand of 75 for the eighth wicket. Craig, pale and weak, batted for thirty minutes. Victoria's heroes were the 22-year-old Kline, slow left-arm bowler, and Meckiff, tall and fast, who also played a valuable first innings. For New South Wales, Burke carried his bat through the first innings and was well supported by the 19-year-old O'Neill.

Victoria

C. C. McDonald b Benaud	50	—	c Lambert b Wyatt	8
W. Lawry c Lambert b Davidson	1	—	lbw b Wyatt	7
R. N. Harvey c Lambert b Treanor	46	—	b Burke	22
J. Shaw lbw b Martin	26	—	st Lambert b Treanor	52
K. Kendall c Watson b Benaud	8	—	lbw b Treanor	21
S. J. Loxton b Benaud	26	—	c sub b Treanor	0
L. Maddocks c Craig b Martin	16	—	b Benaud	33
A. Dick b Benaud	0	—	b Benaud	29
I. Meckiff b Wyatt	55	—	b Treanor	8
L. Kline b Davidson	11	—	not out	9
J. Salmon not out	0	—	b Treanor	0
Extras	5		Extras	8
	244			**197**

New South Wales

S. Carroll c Dick b Meckiff	11	—	b Kline	14
J. W. Burke not out	132	—	c Maddocks b Meckiff	8
J. Treanor c Maddocks b Salmon	14	—	c Maddocks b Meckiff	0
N. O'Neill st Maddocks b Kline	69	—	c and b Kline	11
I. D. Craig lbw b Dick	3	—	c Lawry b Kline	24
W. Watson c Harvey b Meckiff	16	—	lbw b Kline	15
R. Benaud c Harvey b Meckiff	8	—	c Shaw b Kline	63
J. Martin b Loxton	1	—	c Maddocks b Meckiff	6
A. K. Davidson lbw b Kline	22	—	b Meckiff	0
O. Lambert b Kline	0	—	lbw b Kline	5
A. Wyatt run out	0	—	not out	2
Extras	5		Extras	12
	281			**160**

New South Wales Bowling

	O.	M.	R.	W.	O.	M.	R.	W.
Wyatt	9.3	0	38	1	4	2	14	2
Davidson	14	3	50	2	17	1	65	0
Treanor	16	5	50	1	10.4	2	36	5
Benaud	26	2	67	4	21	9	34	2
Martin	7	0	34	2				
Burke					13	1	40	1

Victoria Bowling

	O.	M.	R.	W.	O.	M.	R.	W.
Meckiff	21	6	65	3	21.1	6	56	4
Salmon	13	4	41	1				
Loxton	9	0	56	1	5	2	10	0
Kline	20	0	72	3	19	3	57	6
Dick	14	2	42	1	13	1	25	0

NEW SOUTH WALES v. QUEENSLAND

At Sydney, December 29, 31, January 1, 2. Queensland won on first innings, and would have won outright but for Watson. Though dropped three times while hitting 198, Watson alone of the New South Wales batsmen subdued the bowling of Walmsley and Bratchford. Davidson prevented a complete collapse in the first New South Wales innings, but he also profited from missed chances. For Queensland, Mackay scored a brilliant century, but this was overshadowed by a ninth wicket stand of 152, a Queensland record, between Grout, who scored his first century in first-class cricket, and Walmsley.

New South Wales

S. Carroll b Bratchford	36	— c Lyons b Walmsley 36
W. Watson c Burge b Walmsley	50	— c Burge b Freeman 198
N. O'Neill b Walmsley	16	— st Grout b Walmsley 0
I. D. Craig b Lindwall	28	— lbw b Walmsley 15
Ray Harvey lbw b Walmsley	3	— c Grout b Bratchford 24
R. Benaud c Burge b Lindwall	15	— c Grout b Bratchford 2
J. Martin lbw b Mackay	20	— c Bratchford b Walmsley .. 1
A. K. Davidson not out	72	— b Walmsley 29
J. Treanor c Grout b Lindwall	20	— not out 18
O. Lambert b Mackay	0	
A. Wyatt c Bratchford b Lindwall	2	
Extras	9	Extras 12
	271	**(8 wkts.) 335**

Queensland

R. Lyons c Lambert b Benaud.... 41	R. R. Lindwall c Davidson b Wyatt 16
R. Reynolds b Martin 11	W. Grout not out 119
K. Mackay c Benaud b Martin...169	W. Walmsley not out 41
P. Burge b Wyatt 31	Extras 23
J. McLaughlin c Harvey b Treanor 88	
D. Bull c Lambert b Treanor..... 16	
J. Bratchford b Martin 19	**(8 wkts., dec.) 574**

J. Freeman did not bat.

Queensland Bowling

	O.	M.	R.	W.	O.	M.	R.	W.
Lindwall	21.1	3	82	4	20	1	74	0
Bratchford	20	1	80	1	16	3	37	2
Walmsley	13	2	52	3	30	2	124	5
Freeman	6	1	13	0	20.3	2	86	1
Mackay	14	2	35	2	1	0	2	0

New South Wales Bowling

	O.	M.	R.	W.
Wyatt	20	5	34	2
Davidson	28	1	97	0
Benaud	24	10	139	1
Treanor	42	3	157	2
Martin	25	3	110	3
O'Neill	1	0	14	0

VICTORIA v. SOUTH AUSTRALIA

At Melbourne, December 29, 31, January 1, 2. Victoria won by 152 runs. The batting of McDonald and Harvey, and, in the second innings, of Lawry, and effective bowling by Kline and Edwards played big parts in the victory.

Pinch, the only South Australia batsman to succeed in both innings, found an able helper in Stevens when South Australia were set to score 400 to win on a pitch which afforded bowlers some help. A feature of the Victoria first innings was the excellent bowling of Drennan.

Victoria

C. C. McDonald st Jarman b Hole	46 —	c Stevens b Drennan 101
W. Lawry c Jarman b Drennan	12 —	c Stevens b Wilson 74
R. N. Harvey c Jarman b Drennan	....125 —	not out 66
J. Shaw c Ridings b Drennan	1 —	lbw b Gregg 13
K. Kendall lbw b Beagley	20 —	c Drennan b Gregg........ 5
L. Maddocks c Jarman b Drennan	4	
S. J. Loxton c Jarman b Drennan	11 —	not out 11
A. Dick b Beagley	26	
I. Meckiff c Jarman b Drennan	2	
L. Kline not out	15	
J. Edwards c Stevens b Beagley	4	
Extras	6	Extras 6
	272	**(4 wkts., dec.) 276**

South Australia

L. Favell lbw b Loxton	36 —	b Kline 37
G. Stevens b Meckiff	0 —	c and b Edwards 93
J. Ducker c Meckiff b Edwards	6 —	st Maddocks b Kline 11
C. Pinch c and b Kline	51 —	b Meckiff 61
G. B. Hole c Maddocks b Kline	0 —	b Meckiff 1
P. Ridings lbw b Dick	13 —	b Edwards 21
B. Jarman c Lawry b Kline	13 —	c Maddocks b Meckiff 0
J. Drennan c Kendall b Kline	11 —	b Edwards 4
J. Beagley b Dick	6 —	not out 9
J. Gregg b Kline	6 —	b Edwards 2
J. Wilson not out	2 —	b Edwards 0
Extras	5	Extras 8
	149	**247**

South Australia Bowling

	O.	M.	R.	W.	O.	M.	R.	W.
Drennan	24	1	69	6	13	1	41	1
Beagley	20.1	2	78	3	14	0	58	0
Wilson	17	2	60	0	19	2	58	1
Gregg	12	1	40	0	18	1	63	2
Hole	8	1	19	1	7	1	34	0
Pinch					1	0	6	0
Ridings					1	0	10	0

Victoria Bowling

	O.	M.	R.	W.	O.	M.	R.	W.
Meckiff	11	3	35	1	23	3	62	3
Edwards	5	0	12	1	18.6	1	51	5
Loxton	3	1	6	1	1	0	2	0
Kline	18	3	65	5	23	4	84	2
Dick	9.3	1	26	2	17	4	40	0

QUEENSLAND v. SOUTH AUSTRALIA

At Brisbane, January 11, 12, 14, 15. Queensland won by an innings and 75 runs. Rain curtailed play, and on the last day South Australia had four first innings wickets to fall, but, following on 180 behind, they collapsed against the medium-pace bowling of Mackay and Walmsley. Heartening for South Australia was the continued form of their young batsman, Pinch. Lindwall, Queensland's top scorer, also bowled well in the first innings.

Queensland

R. Lyons c Ducker b Drennan....	2	W. Grout not out	43
R. Reynolds c Hole b Wilson....	86	D. Muddle lbw b Beagley	14
K. Mackay lbw b Drennan	84	W. Walmsley run out	12
P. Burge c Favell b Drennan.....	23	J. Freeman not out	0
J. McLaughlin st Jarman b Ridings	91	Extras	7
J. Bratchford c Drennan b Gregg.	5		
R. R. Lindwall b Beagley	93	(9 wkts., dec.)	460

South Australia

L. Favell st Grout b Walmsley	46	— b Bratchford	4
G. Stevens lbw b Lindwall	7	— b Walmsley	29
C. Pinch st Grout b Freeman	41	— lbw b Mackay	42
J. Ducker lbw b Lindwall	26	— st Grout b Walmsley	0
G. B. Hole c Lyons b Lindwall	89	— c Grout b Mackay	9
P. Ridings c Lyons b Bratchford........	31	— b Mackay	3
B. Jarman b Lindwall	3	— c Grout b Mackay	9
J. Drennan c Burge b Bratchford	17	— st Grout b Walmsley	0
J. Beagley b Lindwall	2	— not out	7
J. Gregg c Grout b Bratchford	1	— b Mackay	0
J. Wilson not out	1	— st Grout b Walmsley	0
Extras......................	16	Extras	2
	280		105

South Australia Bowling

	O.	M.	R.	W.	O.	M.	R.	W.
Drennan	28	2	77	3				
Beagley	25	2	87	2				
Gregg	27	2	83	1				
Wilson	41	9	121	1				
Hole	15	1	50	0				
Pinch	10	2	27	0				
Ridings	4	0	8	1				

Queensland Bowling

	O.	M.	R.	W.		O.	M.	R.	W.
Lindwall	18	3	50	5	....	6	2	11	0
Bratchford	19.7	4	56	3	....	5	3	3	1
Muddle	10	2	14	0	....	1	0	1	0
Walmsley	19	1	79	1	....	16	6	51	4
Freeman	16	3	60	1	....	6	2	22	0
Mackay	2	0	5	0	....	9	2	15	5

QUEENSLAND v. VICTORIA

At Brisbane, January 18, 19, 21, 22. Queensland won on first innings. This victory, which assured Queensland of second place in the competition, was a tribute to the skill with which Lindwall handled the bowling. At lunch on the final day Victoria had only two wickets down and Harvey and Shaw together. Harvey left immediately afterwards and despite a good innings by Huntington, the last wicket fell twelve minutes from time. A double century by Burge overshadowed everything else in the Queensland innings.

Queensland

R. Lyons b Edwards 11	R. R. Lindwall lbw b Loxton..... 1
R. Reynolds c Huntington b Meckiff 17	W. Grout c Edwards b Meckiff... 79
K. Mackay c Harvey b Edwards.. 0	D. Muddle c Maddocks b Dick... 4
P. Burge b Maddocks b Harvey..210	W. Walmsley c McDonald b Dick. 58
J. McLaughlin c Maddocks b Edwards 6	J. Freeman not out 1
J. Bratchford c Harvey b Edwards. 13	Extras 11
	—
	411

Victoria

C. C. McDonald c Lindwall b Bratchford 18	A. Dick c Lindwall b Freeman... 9
W. Lawry c Grout b Bratchford.. 3	I. Meckiff b Lindwall 5
R. N. Harvey c Burge b Lindwall.115	L. Kline not out 6
J. Shaw lbw b Freeman 96	J. Edwards lbw b Walmsley 8
I. Huntington b Muddle 50	Extras 16
S. J. Loxton c Grout b Walmsley.. 11	—
L. Maddocks c Grout b Lindwall.. 29	366

Victoria Bowling

	O.	M.	R.	W.
Meckiff	34	9	68	2
Edwards	39	16	87	4
Loxton	19	2	51	1
Dick	22	2	77	2
Kline	18	0	93	0
Huntington ...	5	0	14	0
Harvey	1.6	1	10	1

Queensland Bowling

	O.	M.	R.	W.
Lindwall	29	7	78	3
Bratchford	22	3	71	2
Muddle	18	3	47	1
Mackay.......	14	0	34	0
Walmsley......	19.7	2	48	2
Freeman	25	1	72	2

NEW SOUTH WALES v. SOUTH AUSTRALIA

At Sydney, January 18, 20, 21, 22. New South Wales won on first innings. Rain checked their bid for outright victory on the last day when they needed 196 in a hundred and forty-three minutes. The feature of the match was the performance of the South Australia opening batsman, Favell, who equalled a 32-year-old record for his State by scoring a century in each innings. He was particularly strong in strokes off the back foot. Benaud was the only man to cause Favell much concern. For New South Wales O'Neill shared in big stands with Burke and Craig.

South Australia

L. Favell st Lambert b Benaud 112	—	run out 114
G. Stevens b Wyatt 0	—	run out 32
C. Pinch c Lambert b Davidson 0	—	b Davidson 80
J. Ducker c and b Benaud 13	—	st Lambert b Benaud 0
G. B. Hole c Lambert b Benaud 2	—	c O'Neill b Davidson 4
P. Ridings run out 0	—	b Benaud 51
A. Bedford b Davidson............... 15	—	c Treanor b Burke 25
B. Jarman b Wyatt 51	—	c and b Benaud 14
J. Drennan c Davidson b Wyatt 35	—	b Benaud 0
J. Beagley c Benaud b Davidson 12	—	b Benaud 0
J. Wilson not out 0	—	not out 0
Extras.................... 8		Extras 13
248		333

New South Wales

S. Carroll c Pinch b Drennan	0 — not out	4
J. W. Burke c and b Bedford	57	
W. Watson c Jarman b Drennan	0 — not out	2
N. O'Neill c Beagley b Wilson	127	
I. D. Craig c Stevens b Bedford	102	
R. Benaud c and b Bedford	0	
A. K. Davidson c Hole b Bedford	74	
J. Martin c and b Wilson	6	
J. Treanor c and b Wilson	3	
O. Lambert not out	0	
A. Wyatt c Stevens b Wilson	0	
Extras	17	
	386	(No wkt.) 6

New South Wales Bowling

	O.	M.	R.	W.		O.	M.	R.	W.
Wyatt	14	2	53	3	....	14	2	76	0
Davidson	18.6	3	59	3	....	20	3	61	2
Benaud	22	5	73	3	....	31	10	70	5
Martin	10	0	27	0	....	11	2	37	0
Treanor	6	0	21	0	....	9	2	46	0
Burke	1	0	7	0	....	11.1	1	30	1

South Australia Bowling

	O.	M.	R.	W.		O.	M.	R.	W.
Pinch	1	0	2	0					
Hole	7	0	52	0					
Bedford	20	5	80	4					
Wilson	29.3	9	78	4					
Drennan	17	4	65	2	....	1	0	4	0
Beagley	17	3	92	0	....	1	0	2	0

NEW SOUTH WALES v. VICTORIA

At Sydney, January 26, 28, 29, 30. Victoria won on first innings. New South Wales batted nearly eleven hours in their second innings and in averting outright defeat gained the one point needed to win the Sheffield Shield for the fourth consecutive year. Harvey, Shaw and Huntington were in fine form for Victoria, but Craig alone batted with confidence for New South Wales, who followed on 292 behind. Craig was again the mainstay of the second innings batting, and he, together with the cautious play of Carroll, Benaud and Martin, thwarted Victorian hopes.

Victoria

L. Maddocks lbw b Wyatt	33 — not out	2
R. N. Harvey b Davidson	209	
J. Shaw c Benaud b Wyatt	66	
I. Huntington c Lambert b Davidson	83	
G. Stevens lbw b Wyatt	19	
C. C. McDonald b Wyatt	1 — not out	3
A. Dick b Wyatt	0	
I. Meckiff run out	5	
S. J. Loxton not out	15	
L. Kline c Lambert b Davidson	5	
J. Edwards b Davidson	0	
Extras	5	
	441	(No wkt.) 5

New South Wales

J. W. Burke lbw b Meckiff	1	— lbw b Kline	24
S. Carroll c Kline b Loxton	21	— c Maddocks b Kline	86
W. Watson b Loxton	12	— c Loxton b Edwards	1
N. O'Neill run out	12	— c Maddocks b Kline	2
I. D. Craig c Loxton b Edwards	45	— c Maddocks b Loxton	93
R. Benaud c Maddocks b Loxton	8	— c Maddocks b Kline	47
A. K. Davidson c Maddocks b Loxton	0	— b Kline	21
J. Martin c Edwards b Meckiff	30	— c Harvey b Edwards	48
O. Lambert c Maddocks b Edwards	5	— c Loxton b Huntington	15
A. Wyatt b Kline	5	— st Maddocks b Dick	40
J. Treanor not out	0	— not out	7
Extras	10	Extras	16
	149		**400**

New South Wales Bowling

	O.	M.	R.	W.	O.	M.	R.	W.
Davidson	20	2	99	4				
Wyatt	23	2	100	5				
Burke	10	1	39	0				
Benaud	24	3	87	0				
Treanor	12	0	52	0				
Martin	12	0	59	0				
Lambert					1	0	5	0

Victoria Bowling

	O.	M.	R.	W.	O.	M.	R.	W.
Meckiff	11	1	27	2				
Edwards	13	3	19	2	37	14	66	2
Loxton	14	4	44	4	15	2	32	1
Kline	9	0	49	1	61	18	126	5
Dick					44.2	17	81	1
Huntington					12	2	41	1
Stevens					2	0	5	0
McDonald					2	1	2	0
Harvey					5	3	5	0
Shaw					3	0	26	0

WESTERN AUSTRALIA v. SOUTH AUSTRALIA

At Perth, January 26, 28, 29, 30. South Australia won on first innings. On a pitch that gave little help to bowlers, batsmen were generally masters. Noteworthy performances were those by Pinch, who scored two centuries for South Australia, and Meuleman, who took out his bat for 234, the highest Sheffield Shield innings of the season, and the biggest to be scored on the Perth ground.

South Australia

L. Favell c Strauss b Slater	73	— b Strauss	1
G. Stevens c Shepherd b Gaunt	2	— c Buggins b Meuleman	80
J. Lee c Slater b Bevan	11	— not out	19
C. Pinch c Sawle b Strauss	110	— c and b Edwards	100
G. B. Hole c Meuleman b Strauss	104	— not out	26
B. Jarman b Slater	53		
J. Drennan c Buggins b Rutherford	0		
J. Beagley b Rutherford	0		
P. Ridings st Buggins b Slater	75		
L. Weekley c Buggins b Rutherford	1		
J. Wilson not out	0		
Extras	18	Extras	13
	447	(3 wkts., dec.)	**239**

Western Australia

L. Sawle c Hole b Beagley	20	— c Ridings b Beagley	3
J. Rutherford b Beagley	15	— not out	71
R. L. Simpson lbw b Beagley	0	— not out	28
K. Meuleman not out	234		
A. Edwards c Jarman b Drennan	15		
B. Shepherd c Pinch b Drennan	0		
K. Slater c Drennan b Wilson	23		
B. Buggins lbw b Wilson	20		
R. Strauss c Favell b Wilson	43		
H. Bevan b Wilson	22		
R. Gaunt c Hole b Drennan	14		
Extras	6	Extras	3
	412	(1 wkt.)	105

Western Australia Bowling

	O.	M.	R.	W.		O.	M.	R.	W.
Gaunt	16	0	92	1	....	12	0	45	0
Bevan	18	2	98	1	....	9	1	40	0
Strauss	23	2	86	2	....	11	3	35	1
Slater	21	4	82	3	....	13	5	36	0
Rutherford	9	2	20	3	....	18	6	34	0
Meuleman	1	0	17	0	....	3	0	15	1
Simspon	4	0	32	0	....	4	0	10	0
Edwards	1	0	2	0	....	4	0	11	1

South Australia Bowling

	O.	M.	R.	W.		O.	M.	R.	W.
Drennan	24	1	92	3	....	3	0	13	0
Beagley	18	2	77	3	....	3	0	27	1
Hole	19	1	60	0					
Wilson	48	17	99	4					
Weekley	14	1	78	0	....	3	0	31	0
Ridings					....	2	0	21	0
Favell					....	1	0	10	0

WESTERN AUSTRALIA v. VICTORIA

At Perth, March 1, 2, 4, 5. Victoria won by nine wickets. Victoria included three young newcomers, and their form suggested that they will be of great value in future seasons. Potter, aged 17, played some excellent strokes, and the bowling feats of Day and Germaine helped substantially to bring about success. The Western Australia batsmen were never comfortable against the varied attack. Only Meuleman, in the first innings, and Rutherford and Shepherd, in the second, looked like staying for long. Maddocks and Stevens took the batting honours for Victoria.

Victoria

C. C. McDonald b Bevan	6	— not out	46
W. Lawry b Slater	19	— c Rutherford b Strauss	22
L. Maddocks b Bevan	109		
I. Huntington c Slater b Bevan	28	— not out	21
J. Shaw lbw b Slater	29		
J. Potter c Buggins b Bevan	21		
S. J. Loxton c Edwards b Bevan	12		
G. Stevens c Buggins b Vernon	76		
J. Edwards run out	16		
A. Day c Buggins b Bevan	16		
L. Germaine not out	2		
Extras	9	Extras	8
	343	(1 wkt.)	97

Western Australia

L. Sawle c Shaw b Loxton	11	— c Maddocks b Day	19
J. Rutherford c Maddocks b Day	2	— lbw b Edwards	50
B. Shepherd c Stevens b Day	25	— b Day	101
K. Meuleman c Edwards b Loxton	70	— lbw b Edwards	37
A. Edwards c McDonald b Day	0	— c Maddocks b Germaine	17
M. Vernon c Maddocks b Loxton	0	— run out	4
K. Slater c Lawry b Loxton	1	— c Maddocks b Germaine	21
B. Buggins c McDonald b Edwards	9	— c Huntington b Germaine	7
R. Strauss c Maddocks b Loxton	28	— lbw b Germaine	7
H. Bevan not out	16	— c Maddocks b Germaine	0
R. Stubbs c Maddocks b Loxton	4	— not out	0
		Extras	7
	166		270

Western Australia Bowling

	O.	M.	R.	W.		O.	M.	R.	W.
Bevan	22	2	106	6	....	7	1	25	0
Slater	19	2	55	2	....	5	0	19	0
Strauss	21	3	66	0	....	9	2	23	1
Stubbs	10	0	63	0	....	1.7	0	16	0
Rutherford	9	1	14	0	....	5	2	6	0
Vernon	3	0	27	1					
Meuleman	1	0	3	0					

Victoria Bowling

	O.	M.	R.	W.		O.	M.	R.	W.
Day	19	3	39	3	....	22	5	63	2
Edwards	18	3	40	1	....	34	14	74	2
Loxton	12.2	0	49	6	....	9	1	22	0
Germaine	7	0	38	0	....	16.1	1	69	5
				Huntington	...	8	1	35	0

SHEFFIELD SHIELD AVERAGES
SEASON 1956–57

NEW SOUTH WALES
BATTING

	Innings	Not Outs	Runs	100's	Highest Innings	Average
J. W. Burke	9	1	444	2	220	55.50
I. D. Craig	11	0	521	2	155	47.36
W. Watson	14	1	557	2	206	42.84
N. O'Neill	13	1	501	1	127	41.75
S. Carroll	14	1	527	2	113	40.53
A. K. Davidson	11	1	333	0	84	33.30
J. Martin	12	0	289	0	71	24.08
R. Benaud	11	0	195	0	63	17.72
J. Treanor	12	4	104	0	20	13.00
A. Wyatt	8	3	50	0	40	10.00
O. Lambert	12	5	43	0	15	6.14

Also batted: J. H. de Courcy, 52, 17; P. Crawford, 0, 14; A. Fagan, 8; R. Harvey, 3, 24; C. Johnston, 68; B. Livingston, 4, 4; P. Philpott, 6.

BOWLING

	Overs	Maidens	Runs	Wickets	Average
R. Benaud	285.1	66	801	32	25.03
J. Treanor	219.7	37	733	28	26.17
A. K. Davidson	188.4	27	657	23	28.56
A. Wyatt	122.7	17	473	16	29.56
J. Martin	151.7	11	608	18	33.77
J. W. Burke	36.1	3	117	2	58.50
N. O'Neill	2	0	20	0	—

Also bowled: A. Fagan 31—10—87—1; P. Crawford 20—4—53—3; O. Lambert 1—0—5—0; B. Livingston 29—8—85—5; P. Philpott 41—6—107—2.

QUEENSLAND

BATTING

	Innings	Not Outs	Runs	100's	Highest Innings	Average
K. Mackay	9	0	676	2	169	75.11
P. Burge	9	0	675	3	210	75.00
R. Reynolds	8	1	371	1	110	53.00
W. Grout	9	2	354	1	119*	50.57
J. McLaughlin	11	2	450	0	93	50.00
W. Walmsley	9	3	200	0	58	33.33
R. R. Lindwall	7	0	209	0	93	29.85
R. Lyons	12	0	331	0	66	27.58
C. Harvey	4	1	72	0	40	24.00
D. Bull	6	1	115	0	53*	23.00
D. Muddle	4	1	65	0	37*	21.66
J. Bratchford	9	0	180	0	43	20.00
J. Freeman	8	5	34	0	17*	11.33

Also batted: K. Archer 65, 5; J. Cooper 7, 23; V. N. Raymer 20, 20.

* Signifies not out.

BOWLING

	Overs	Maidens	Runs	Wickets	Average
R. R. Lindwall	189	40	534	24	22.25
K. Mackay	123	18	318	12	26.50
W. Walmsley	218.7	37	795	28	28.39
J. Freeman	235.4	40	783	23	34.04
J. Bratchford	210.6	32	653	19	34.36
D. Muddle	46	6	148	2	74.00
D. Bull	9	2	21	0	—

Also bowled: R. Archer 3—1—12—1; P. Burge 1—0—1—0; J. Cooper 3—0—18—0; R. Lyons 3—1—10—0; J. McLaughlin 1—0—2—0; V. N. Raymer 26—9—46—3; R. Reynolds 1—0—4—0.

VICTORIA

BATTING

	Innings	Not Outs	Runs	100's	Highest Innings	Average
R. N. Harvey	8	1	744	4	209	106.28
I. Huntington	4	1	182	0	83	60.66
G. Stevens	2	0	95	0	76	47.50
J. Shaw	12	0	508	1	114	42.33
C. C. McDonald	11	2	287	1	101	31.88
S. J. Loxton	12	2	283	1	134	28.30
L. Maddocks	11	1	277	1	109	27.70
K. Kendall	9	0	205	1	119	22.77
A. Dick	10	1	200	0	45	22.22
W. Lawry	12	0	248	0	74	20.66
I. Meckiff	10	2	107	0	55	13.37
L. Kline	10	3	60	0	15*	8.57
J. Salmon	7	2	38	0	26	7.60
J. Edwards	4	0	28	0	16	7.00
J. Cosgrave	3	0	7	0	4	2.33

Also batted: L. Botham 21, 4*; A. Day 16; L. Germaine 2*; D. Longney 0; R. Maddocks 16; J. Potter 21.

* Signifies not out.

BOWLING

	Overs	Maidens	Runs	Wickets	Average
S. J. Loxton	127.2	20	381	19	20.05
J. Edwards	164.6	51	349	17	20.52
L. Kline	274.4	50	921	37	24.89
I. Meckiff	207	40	546	21	26.00
J. Salmon	89	26	243	9	27.00
A. Dick	205.1	48	505	14	36.07
I. Huntington	25	3	90	1	90.00

Also bowled: A. Day 41—8—102—5; L. Germaine 23.1—1—107—5; R. N. Harvey 6.6—4—15—1; C. C. McDonald 2—1—2—0; J. Shaw 3—0—26—0; G. Stevens 2—0—5—0.

WESTERN AUSTRALIA

BATTING

	Innings	Not Outs	Runs	100's	Highest Innings	Average
K. Meuleman	13	2	779	3	234*	70.81
R. L. Simpson	12	2	527	1	112*	52.70
B. Shepherd	12	0	464	2	173	38.66
J. Rutherford	8	1	245	0	71*	35.00
L. Sawle	15	1	387	0	85	27.64
A. Edwards	12	1	287	0	55	26.09
D. Hoare	6	3	54	0	32*	18.00
R. Rigg	5	1	68	0	42*	17.00
R. Strauss	10	1	136	0	43	15.11
R. Gaunt	9	3	85	0	25	14.16
A. Preen	9	2	98	0	27*	14.00
H. Bevan	4	1	38	0	22	12.66
K. Slater	4	0	45	0	23	11.25
B. Buggins	14	1	140	0	38*	10.76
M. Vernon	3	0	15	0	11	5.00

Also batted: H. Gorringe 0; R. Stubbs 4, 0*.

* Signifies not out.

BOWLING

	Overs	Maidens	Runs	Wickets	Average
R. Strauss	251.1	59	742	33	22.48
A. Edwards	8	0	27	1	27.00
B. Shepherd	6	0	27	1	27.00
R. Gaunt	193.2	29	749	24	31.20
D. Hoare	74.3	9	299	9	33.22
K. Meuleman	39	1	214	6	35.66
K. Slater	105	24	332	9	36.88
H. Bevan	85	10	382	9	42.44
J. Rutherford	66	19	149	3	49.66
A. Preen	179.7	50	460	9	51.11
R. L. Simpson	53.6	2	233	2	116.50

Also bowled: B. Buggins 3—2—1—1; H. Gorringe 37—3—156—0; B. Rigg 3—0—18—0; R. Stubbs 11.7—0—79—0; M. Vernon 3—0—27—1.

SOUTH AUSTRALIA

BATTING

	Innings	Not Outs	Runs	100's	Highest Innings	Average
C. Pinch	15	0	739	3	116	49.26
G. Stevens	15	1	558	1	125*	39.85
L. Favell	15	0	593	2	114	39.53
G. B. Hole	15	2	508	1	104	39.07
P. Ridings	13	1	412	0	86*	34.33
J. Bedford	4	0	87	0	28	21.75
C. Grant	4	0	73	0	42	18.25
J. Ducker	10	1	164	0	44*	18.22
B. Jarman	10	0	160	0	53	16.00
J. Drennan	11	0	87	0	35	7.90
L. Weekley	6	0	47	0	40	7.83
J. Gregg	7	1	39	0	27*	6.50
J. Beagley	12	2	54	0	12	5.40
J. Wilson	12	8	15	0	12	3.75

Also batted: G. R. Langley 4, 100; J. Lee 11, 19*.

* Signifies not out.

BOWLING

	Overs	Maidens	Runs	Wickets	Average
J. Drennan	198	19	628	23	27.30
J. Beagley	192.1	25	746	23	32.43
J. Bedford	103	30	301	8	37.62
C. Pinch	26	4	83	2	42.50
J. Gregg	120.4	14	374	8	46.75
J. Wilson	277.3	78	715	14	51.07
P. Ridings	12	0	61	1	61.00
L. Weekley	83.5	5	438	4	109.50
G. B. Hole	100	9	359	2	179.50
L. Favell	3	1	13	0	—
G. Stevens	5	0	23	0	—

Also bowled: J. Ducker 1—0—8—0.

SHEFFIELD SHIELD HOLDERS

1892–93	Victoria	1924–25	Victoria
1893–94	South Australia	1925–26	New South Wales
1894–95	Victoria	1926–27	South Australia
1895–96	New South Wales	1927–28	Victoria
1896–97	New South Wales	1928–29	New South Wales
1897–98	Victoria	1929–30	Victoria
1898–99	Victoria	1930–31	Victoria
1899–1900	New South Wales	1931–32	New South Wales
1900–1	Victoria	1932–33	New South Wales
1901–2	New South Wales	1933–34	Victoria
1902–3	New South Wales	1934–35	Victoria
1903–4	New South Wales	1935–36	South Australia
1904–5	New South Wales	1936–37	Victoria
1905–6	New South Wales	1937–38	New South Wales
1906–7	New South Wales	1938–39	South Australia
1907–8	Victoria	1939–40	New South Wales
1908–9	New South Wales	1940–46	No competition
1909–10	South Australia	1946–47	Victoria
1910–11	New South Wales	1947–48	Western Australia
1911–12	New South Wales	1948–49	New South Wales
1912–13	South Australia	1949–50	New South Wales
1913–14	New South Wales	1950–51	Victoria
1914–15	Victoria	1951–52	New South Wales
1915–19	No competition	1952–53	South Australia
1919–20	New South Wales	1953–54	New South Wales
1920–21	New South Wales	1954–55	New South Wales
1921–22	Victoria	1955–56	New South Wales
1922–23	New South Wales	1956–57	New South Wales
1923–24	Victoria		

New South Wales have won the Shield 29 times, Victoria 18, South Australia 7, Western Australia 1, Queensland 0.

(Queensland participated for the first time in 1926–27. Western Australia entered the competition in 1947–48 and were made full members at the end of the 1955–56 season).

S. J. McCABE—W. J. O'REILLY TESTIMONIAL

R. R. Lindwall's XI v. R. N. Harvey's XI

At Sydney, January 5, 6, 8, 9. Harvey's XI won by seven wickets. This match was used by the Australian selectors as a trial game in view of the tour to New Zealand and South Africa. Several promising young cricketers were blended with eleven players of Test experience but Craig (ill) and Burke (injured) were not available. Meckiff, a left-arm pace bowler, did extremely well on his first appearance in Sydney, and though Kline and Gaunt did not achieve the same success, both bowled keenly on unhelpful turf. McDonald and Mackay batted soundly and O'Neill, before being struck on the head by a ball from Davidson, confirmed his earlier promise with some excellent stroke-play. Harvey's side, set to score 198 for victory, hit off the runs in two and a quarter hours. An unbroken fourth wicket partnership between Harvey and Benaud produced 90 in forty-five minutes. Over 35,000 people attended and each beneficiary received £A4,000, the testimonial fund being supplemented by other matches of an exhibition nature.

Ray Lindwall's XI

C. C. McDonald c Davidson b Freeman..	78	—	b Benaud		22
S. Carroll c Benaud b Davidson	42	—	c Shepherd b Davidson ...		13
K. Mackay c Grout b Meckiff............	99	—	c Harvey b Benaud		46
R. Simpson b Meckiff	35	—	b Benaud		10
G. B. Hole c Favell b Meckiff...........	13	—	c Benaud b Davidson		9
N. O'Neill lbw b Meckiff	43	—	retired hurt.		23
L. Maddocks c Davidson b Benaud	40	—	b Davidson		28
R. R. Lindwall c Meckiff b Davidson	14	—	c and b Benaud		19
J. Treanor not out	33	—	b Davidson		6
L. Kline b Meckiff	13	—	c Grout b Davidson		1
R. Gaunt b Meckiff	4	—	not out		3
Extras....................	14	—	Extras		8
	428				**188**

Neil Harvey's XI

L. Favell c O'Neill b Kline	64	—	lbw b Kline		42
W. Watson c Simpson b Gaunt..........	66	—	c Maddocks b Lindwall		41
R. N. Harvey c Simpson b Mackay	31	—	not out		61
P. Burge retired hurt	43				
B. Shepherd b Lindwall	44	—	c Lindwall b Treanor ...		3
R. Benaud lbw b Gaunt	8	—	not out		45
A. K. Davidson c Maddocks b Lindwall.	41				
W. Grout not out	49				
I. Meckiff c and b Mackay.............	47				
J. Freeman c Hole b Gaunt	12				
R. Strauss absent hurt................	0				
Extras................	14		Extras		6
	419		(3 wkts.)		**198**

Neil Harvey's XI Bowling

	O.	M.	R.	W.		O.	M.	R.	W.
Meckiff	24	6	75	6	....	3	0	18	0
Strauss	14	1	77	0					
Davidson	23	1	103	2	....	18	0	65	5
Benaud........	23	3	75	1	....	16.4	3	66	4
Freeman	21	1	84	1	....	7	0	31	0

Ray Lindwall's XI Bowling

	O.	M.	R.	W.		O.	M.	R.	W.
Gaunt........	21.2	1	83	3	....	4	0	37	0
Lindwall	18	3	68	2	....	9	0	39	1
Mackay	13	1	40	2	....	5	0	22	0
Hole	1	0	12	0					
Treanor	17	0	82	0	....	6	0	31	1
Kline	22	3	120	1	....	6	0	59	1
			McDonald	....	0.4	0	4	0	

CRICKET IN SOUTH AFRICA, 1956–57

In view of the M.C.C. tour, no Currie Cup tournament took place. There were eight inter-provincial first-class friendly matches.

At East London, October 19, 20, 22. Border 333 (K. N. Kirton 146, R. K. Thorne 77, O. C. Dawson 51) and 250 for four wickets, declared (O. C. Dawson 137 not out, K. N. Kirton 56); Eastern Province 269 (P. Jamieson 91, A. W. Hicks 52) and 232 (B. Dold 56, R. K. Thorne seven for 79). Border won by 82 runs.

At East London, October 26, 27, 29. Natal 307 (E. Eaglestone 126 not out, C. G. Burger 118, W. R. Chalmers five for 89) and 183 (A. L. Upton 69); Border 209 (T. J. Geach 74. T. L. Goddard five for 59) and 11. Natal won by 170 runs.

At Johannesburg, November 16, 17, 19. Natal 216 (H. J. Keith 113, R. A. McLean 85, P. S. Heine seven for 61) and 125 (J. C. Watkins 41, N. A. T. Adcock five for 47, P. S. Heine four for 29); Transvaal 71 (T. L. Goddard six for 35) and 271 for seven wickets (A. I. Taylor 85). Transvaal won by three wickets.

At East London, November 23, 24, 26. Border 212 (R. R. Phillips 73, K. N. Kirton 57) and 276 (R. I. Geach 97, W. D. Wilson 84); Western Province 166 (H. N. P. Roy 75, R. K. Thorne six for 60) and 324 for nine wickets (A. J. Pithey 133, G. A. S. Innes 72). Western Province won by one wicket.

At Durban, November 30, December 1, 2. Western Province 213 (J. H. Ferrandi 57, T. L. Goddard five for 36) and 199 for six wickets (G. A. S. Innes 59, A. J. Pithey 50); Natal 468 (T. L. Goddard 135, R. W. Pearce 95, C. G. Burger 85, R. A. McLean 53). Drawn.

At Port Elizabeth, December 31, January 1, 2. Border 215 (B. Crews 110, I. F. Anderson six for 46) and 284 (K. N. Kirton 60); Eastern Province 170 (W. R. Chalmers five for 42) and 330 for eight wickets (P. Jamieson 87, G. F. Dakin 70, C. Touhy 51 not out). Eastern Province won by two wickets.

At Johannesburg, January 18, 19, 21. Transvaal 417 (W. R. Endean 171, K. J. Funston 89, A. Tayfield 69, G. Lawrence five for 95); Rhodesia 212 (A. J. Pithey 90) and 252 for six wickets (C. A. R. Duckworth 105, A. J. Pithey 69). Drawn.

At Bloemfontein, February 7, 8. 9. Eastern Province 265 (G. D. Varnals 55, M. Wheals four for 58) and 325 for seven wickets, declared (G. D. Varnals 77, G. F. Dakin 65, C. Rushmere 55, B. Dold 53, M. Wheals five for 69); Orange Free State 228 (S. L. Hanson 65) and 219 for nine wickets (I. E. Kirby 54). Drawn.

CRICKET IN WEST INDIES, 1956–57

For the first time the four colonies contested the Quadrangular tournament on the same ground, at Bourda, Georgetown, British Guiana. The three games were scheduled to last five days each but an extra day was added to the first match and to the final because of rain.

British Guiana, for so long one of the weaker teams, won the competition and their improved form reflected credit on C. L. Walcott, who had a coaching assignment in the colony. R. J. Christiani, the former West Indies Test cricketer, also helped in the development of the side.

Rohan Kanhai, subsequently chosen for the tour of England, proved one of the big successes by hitting 129 against Jamaica and 195 against Barbados. J. Solomon, who also hit two centuries, helped Kanhai put on 251 for the fifth wicket in the final.

QUADRANGULAR TOURNAMENT DETAILS

At Georgetown, October 4, 5, 6, 8, 9, 10. Trinidad 115 (A. Holder seven for 38) and 170 (D. Ramsamooj 70, G. Sobers four for 24, D. Atkinson four for 43); Barbados 433 (C. De Peiza 65, N. Birket 57, E. Atkinson 54, E. D. Weekes 54, A. Holder 52). Barbados won by ani nnings and 148 runs.

At Georgetown, October 11, 12, 13, 15, 16. British Guiana 601 for five wickets, declared (B. Butcher 154 not out, Rohan Kanhai 129, J. Solomon 114 not out, B. H. Pairaudeau 111) and 60 for one wicket; Jamaica 469 (A. P. Binns 151, O. G. Smith 109, A. Rae 80, L. Gibbs four for 113, I. Madray four for 168). British Guiana won on first innings.

At Georgetown, October 19, 20. 22, 23, 24, 25. British Guiana 581 (Rohan Kanhai 195, J. Solomon 108, G. Gibbs 80, C. L. Walcott 64); Barbados 211 (G. Sobers 77, E. D. Weekes 63, I. Madray four for 61, L. Gibbs four for 68) and 67 for four wickets. British Guiana won on first innings.

TRIAL MATCHES

Two trial matches were played at Port of Spain to help the selectors in choosing their party for the tour of England. O. G. Smith, a hard-hitting batsman and off-spin bowler, proved a lively all-rounder in these games, hitting 252 runs and taking thirteen wickets for 281 runs. Rohan Kanhai followed his good batting in the Quadrangular tournament with scores of 62 and 90 in the first trial. He hit a century in the second match and with C. L. Walcott added 224 for the second wicket.

Summarised scores:

First Match: January 26 to 31. E. D. Weekes' XI 441 for eight wickets, declared (G. Sobers 129, E. D. Weekes 83, O. G. Smith 67, H. Furlonge 65) and 177 for five wickets, declared (H. Furlonge 75, E. D. Weekes 50); C. L. Walcott's XI 310 (B. Pairaudeau 91, Rohan Kanhai 62, A. Ganteaume 53, R. Gilchrist four for 78, G. Sobers three for 42) and 220 (Rohan Kanhai 90, C. L. Walcott 57, O. G. Smith six for 84). E. D. Weekes' XI won by 98 runs.

Second Match: February 2 to 7. E. D. Weekes' XI 507 (B. Pairaudeau 120, N. Asgarali 106, H. Furlonge 106, B. Butcher 76, R. Gilchrist three for 96) and 291 (W. Hall 77, B. Pairaudeau 57, A. Holder six for 60, O. G. Smith three for 72); C. L. Walcott's XI 412 (C. L. Walcott 132, Rohan Kanhai 117, O. G. Smith 102 not out, E. Atkinson four for 50, A. L. Valentine three for 85) and 389 for nine (A. Ganteaume 106, C. L. Walcott 90, O. G. Smith 67, W. Hall three for 63). C. L. Walcott's XI won by one wicket.

CRICKET IN NEW ZEALAND, 1956–57

PLUNKET SHIELD

(Won by Wellington)

FINAL PLACINGS

	Played	Won Outright	Won on 1st Inns.	Lost Outright	Lost on 1st Inns.	Points
Points awarded	—	8	4	—	2	—
Wellington...........	5	4	0	0	1	34
Otago	5	3	1	1	0	28
Central Districts	5	1	2	1	1	18
Canterbury	5	1	0	1	3	14
Auckland	5	0	2	2	1	10
Northern Districts	5	0	1	4	0	4

Plunket Shield Holders: Auckland 14 times; Canterbury 13, Wellington 11 Otago 5, Central Districts 1.

Four outright wins in five matches demonstrates the merit of Wellington's success in the Plunket Shield. They called on only 13 players throughout the season and showed great strength all round. Their batting was most reliable, with six of the team averaging over 30 runs per innings. L. S. M. Miller proved the most prolific. He led the final Shield averages with 366 runs in eight innings, three not out, an average of 73.20.

R. W. Blair, Wellington's right-arm fast bowler, who was more accurate than in previous years, took the greatest number of wickets in a Shield season; 46 at an average of 9.47. This was eight wickets more than the total of T. B. Burtt, of Canterbury, six years earlier. Blair twice took nine wickets in an innings, which also represented a Shield record. Twenty-seven years had elapsed since a bowler last took nine wickets in an innings in New Zealand cricket.

Northern Districts took part in the competition for the first time and although finishing last they showed promise of better results in the future.

PLUNKET SHIELD DETAILS

At Cook's Gardens, Wanganui, December 25, 26, 27. Wellington 290 (R. A. Vance 109, R. T. Barber 70, L. S. M. Miller 50); Central Districts 314 for six wickets (D. N. McLeod 117, J. W. Guy 50). Central Districts won on first innings.

At Lancaster Park, Christchurch, December 25, 26, 27. Canterbury 229 (J. W. D'Arcy 85, J. C. Alabaster five for 75) and 117 for two wickets; Otago 265 (B. Sutcliffe 73, G. N. Gearry four for 57). Otago won on first innings.

At Seddon Park, Hamilton, December 25, 26, 27. Northern Districts 258 (J. K. Everest 69, D. J. Gray 58) and 22 for no wicket; Auckland 144 (A. F. Lissette four for 35, D. Ferrow four for 50). Northern Districts won on first innings.

At Basin Reserve, Wellington, December 29, 31, January 1. Canterbury 228 (S. C. Guillen 96, M. B. Poore 59, R. W. Blair nine for 75) and 222 (P. G. Z. Harris 62, L. A. Clark five for 60, R. W. Blair five for 61); Wellington 380 for nine wickets, declared (E. W. Dempster 105, L. A. Clark 68 not out. J. E. F. Beck 56) and 71 for one. Wellington won by nine wickets.

At Pukekura Park, New Plymouth, December 29, 31, January 1. Central Districts 312 for eight wickets, declared (E. M. Meuli 100, N. S. Harford 51); Northern District 106 (H. B. Cave seven for 33) and 86 (R. Brown five for 29, D. D. Beard four for 27). Central Districts won by an innings and 120 runs.

At Eden Park, Auckland, December 29, 31, January 1. Otago 251 (J. R. Reid 79, G. D. Alabaster 51) and 137 (J. A. Hayes four for 23, E. Dunn four for 41); Auckland 135 (G. O. Rabone 50 not out, J. C. Alabaster five for 35) and 227 (D. D. Taylor 58, F. J. Cameron four for 53). Otago won by 26 runs.

At Seddon Park, Hamilton, January 3, 4, 5. Otago 377 for nine wickets, declared (B. Sutcliffe 152 not out, S. N. McGregor 50, K. Hough four for 101); Northern Districts 98 (J. C. Alabaster four for 37) and 217 (N. Puna 62, B. N. Graham 56, E. C. Petrie 55, B. Sutcliffe five for 102). Otago won by an innings and 62 runs.

At Eden Park, Auckland, January 3, 4, 5. Auckland 443 (D. L. Perry 104, S. G. Gedye 68, B. J. Postles 55, G. O. Rabone 54, M. B. Poore four for 72) and 74 for two wickets (B. J. Postles 53 not out); Canterbury 440 (M. E. Chapple 146, M. B. Poore 103, J. W. D'Arcy 60, B. C. Guillen 56, R. M. Harris four for 105, H. Moyle four for 110). Auckland won on first innings.

At Seddon Park, Hamilton, January 7, 8, 9. Northern Districts 102 and 305 (J. K. Everest 104); Canterbury 313 (M. E. Chapple 88, P. G. Z. Harris 83, K. Hough four for 101) and 95 for three wickets. Canterbury won by seven wickets.

At Trafalgar Park, Nelson, January 11, 12, 14. Central Districts 351 (J. W. Guy 89, G. Buist 51) and 164 for four wickets; Auckland 393 (G. O. Rabone 80, R. M. Harris 79, S. G. Gedye 50, H. B. Cave six for 81). Auckland won on first innings.

At Basin Reserve, Wellington, January 12, 14, 15. Wellington 379 (A. H. Preston 122, L. S. M. Miller 57, E. W. Dempster 52, D. B. Clarke four for 108) and 97 for one wicket; Northern Districts 195 (J. K. Everest 61, J. L. Wyatt 54, R. W. Blair five for 36, B. D. Morrison five for 58) and 280 (J. K. Everest 59, R. W. Blair five for 80). Wellington won by nine wickets.

At Basin Reserve, Wellington, January 18, 19. Wellington 332 (L. S. M. Miller 83, R. T. Barber 69, G. O. Rabone seven for 79); Auckland 163 (D. L. Perry 78, R. W. Blair nine for 72) and 131 (L. A. Clark four for 46). Wellington won by an innings and 38 runs.

At Carisbrook, Dunedin, January 18, 19, 21. Otago 264 (J. R. Reid 97, E. A. Watson 76, D. D. Beard seven for 56) and 176 (W. S. Haig 64, D. R. Tarrant four for 40, D. D. Beard four for 43); Central Districts 186 and 81 (J. R. Reid seven for 20). Otago won by 173 runs.

At Carisbrook, Dunedin, January 25, 26. Otago 34 (R. W. Blair six for 13, B. D. Morrison four for 19) and 144 (R. W. Blair four for 32); Wellington 154 (L. S. M. Miller 81 not out, W. S. Haig four for 12, J. C. Alabaster four for 60) and 25 for no wicket. Wellington won by ten wickets.

At Lancaster Park, Christchurch, January 25, 26, 28. Canterbury 234 and 247 for eight wickets, declared (M. B. Poore 70, J. W. D'Arcy 66); Central Districts 239 (H. B. Cave 65) and 182 for eight wickets (K. F. H. Smith 58). Central Districts won on first innings.

OTHER MATCH

J. H. Phillips, manager of the New Zealand team which toured England in 1949, selected a strong side from that party to play Wellington in a three-day benefit match for the Wellington Cricket Association's new stand at Basin Reserve. The New Zealand Cricket Board of Control ruled that it should not be recognised as a first-class fixture.

The presence of M. P. Donnelly, the attractive left-hand batsman, who has lived in Australia for several years, helped to make the game a great success.

Summarised score:

At Basin Reserve, Wellington, December 7, 8, 10. Wellington 281 (R. A. Vance 66, L. S. M. Miller 55, B. W. Sinclair 45, W. M. Curtis 45 not out, H. B. Cave five for 73) and 73 for four wickets; J. H. Phillips' XI 82 (L. A. Clark four for 16) and 350 for nine wickets, declared (G. O. Rabone 92, B. Sutcliffe 61, M. P. Donnelly 48). Drawn.

CRICKET IN INDIA, 1956–57

Apart from two brief tours, one consisting of three Test matches by Australia under Ian Johnson in October and the first week of November, India had a home season and the Ranji Trophy championship rightly occupied most attention. Bombay, for the ninth time in their career, claimed the handsome trophy, defeating the Services in the final.

This success was another proof of Bombay's capacity to produce a match-winning combination whatever the circumstances. In a year in which they lost the services of Mankad, Ramchand and Manjrekar, all of whom were engaged as professionals by other States, Bombay demonstrated that they still possessed sufficient reserve strength to win the championship. The young players seized their opportunities and supported splendidly the efforts of the more experienced members of the team. Mantri's leadership played no small part in the achievement. It was his third triumph as captain.

R. B. Kenny, a free-scoring batsman, had an excellent season with 139 *v.* Maharashtra, 132 *v.* Uttar Pradesh and 218 *v.* Madras in successive matches. Hardikar began the championship with a fine knock of 204 against Gujerat, and Y. K. Rele and P. K. Kamat, two other youngsters, ran into three figures. Rusi Modi showed that he was still a force by hitting two centuries, and Umrigar batted and bowled splendidly. Mantri was consistent. Desai, Amroliwalla and Guard displayed all-round excellence, and with most of these players striking form in every game, it was no small wonder that Bombay won all their matches with ease.

The Services reached the final for the first time in their career. They were somewhat lucky to do so, for in the semi-final with Bengal they were in danger of defeat on the first innings. Facing a total of 399, Bengal made 302 for four when rain intervened and a decision had to be taken by the spin of the coin which fell in favour of the Services. In the earlier rounds the Services had defeated Patiala and Delhi. Gadkari was a consistent scorer and Muddiah a steady wicket-taker.

Much was expected of the Rajasthan team who were greatly strengthened by the inclusion of Mankad, Ramchand, Nimbalkar and Dhanwade. They raised great hopes by hitting 594 for eight against Madhya Bharat, formerly Holkar. But despite a century by Ramchand, they lost to Uttar Pradesh, for whom Mushtaq Ali made a century and their captain, C. K. Nayudu, at the age of 62, hit a brilliant 84, including nine 4's and two successive 6's off Mankad!

From the South, Madras reached the semi-final through victories over Hyderabad and Mysore. They had a remarkable game with Mysore when after losing half the side for only 55 runs they scored 384, thanks mainly to a fighting partnership of 217 for the sixth wicket between C. D. Gopinath (133) and M. Balakrishnan (124).

P. Chatterjee, of Bengal, who took 15 wickets in the match against Madhya Pradesh the previous season and so became India's first bowler to achieve the feat, gained further distinction when he took all ten wickets in Assam's first innings, his figures being 19—11—20—10.

RANJI TROPHY DETAILS

At Bombay, December 8, 9, 10. Bombay 525 (M. S. Hardikar 204, R. S. Modi 146) and 49 for one; Gujerat 222 (R. Surti 72, B. P. Gupte seven for 109) and 366 (N. J. Contractor 176, A. H. Desai six for 108). Bombay won on first innings.

At New Delhi, December 8, 9, 10, 11. Punjab 166 (V. Mehra 72, B. Bhandari five for 60, M. Mehra four for 10) and 190 (R. Vaid four for 52); Delhi 271 (Y. M. Choudhry 95, P. Bhandari 56) and 87 for one. Delhi won by nine wickets.

At Salem, December 14, 15, 16, 17. Madras 431 (S. Balakrishnan 101, R. Raghavan 79, M. Balakrishnan 75, A. R. Sridhar 70, B. N. Krishnamurthy six for 137) and 329 for six wickets, declared (A. R. Sridhar 124 not out, C. D. Gopinath 68); Hyderabad 310 (Jaisimha 71, E. B. Aibara 64, V. V. Kumar five for 100) and 194 for seven (Afzal Ali 64, Jaisimha 50, M. K. Murugesh seven for 65). Madras won on first innings.

At Khadakwasla, November 24, 25, 26. Saurashtra 83 (V. R. Ranjane nine for 35) and 88 (Kudus Khan four for 25, V. R. Ranjane four for 36); Maharashtra 332 (R. G. Nadkarni, 125, Y. P. Sidlnaye 83, S. Nayalchand six for 83). Maharashtra won by an innings and 161 runs.

Banaras, December 15, 16, 17. Madhya Pradesh 116 (C. S. Nayudu seven for 53) and 177 (C. S. Nayudu five for 69); Uttar Pradesh 238 (K. M. Tiwari 55, M. S. Sathe six for 55) and 56 for one. Uttar Pradesh won by nine wickets.

Indore, December 22, 23, 24. Madhya Bharat 91 and 184 (Hanumanth Singh 61); Rajasthan 594 for eight (Arjun Singh 119, K. M. Rungta 113 not out, S. Durani 88, S. D. Dhanawade 62 not out, V. Mankad 56). Rajasthan won by an innings and 319 runs.

At Jamshedpur, December 22, 23, 24, 25. Orissa 196 (B. Patnaik 59) and 350 for seven wickets, declared (A. S. Rao 153, T. Ram Shastry 65); Bihar 217 (D. S. Murthi four for 49) and 254 for four (T. Dutta 91, S. Das 80). Bihar won on first innings.

At Guntur, January 12, 13, 14, 15. Travancore-Cochin 180 and 182; Andhra 171 (S. Aaron five for 77) and 201 for three (G. S. N. Raju 88). Andhra won by seven wickets.

At New Delhi, January 13, 14, 15, 16. Services 246 (Mohindra Singh 50, Malinder Singh five for 77) and 85 (L. Amarnath seven for 30); Patiala 164 (D. P. Azad 50, V. N. Swamy four for 52) and 121 (V. M. Muddiah five for 54, V. N. Swamy four for 31). Services won by 46 runs.

At Nasik, January 18, 19, 20, 21. Maharashtra 441 (Y. P. Sidhaye 135, R. G. Nadkarni 111); Baroda 226 (M. V. Mathe five for 58, V. R. Ranjane four for 66) and 358 for six (D. K. Gaekwad 128, C. G. Borde 100, R. D. Patel 54, V. J. Paranjpe 54). Maharashtra won on first innings.

At Jorhat, January 27, 28, 29. Bengal 505 (S. Shome 122, P. Sen 83, K. Biswas 69 not out, D. G. Phadkar 51, S. K. Girdhari seven for 157); Assam 54 (P. Chatterjee ten for 20) and 245 (S. K. Girdhari 100, D. G. Phadkar seven for 67). Bengal won by an innings and 206 runs.

At Guntur, January 30, 31, February 1, 2. Andhra 266 (G. S. N. Raju 66, V. Rajagopal 62, V. L. Manjrekar 55) and 234 for eight wickets, declared (G. S. N. Raju 94); Mysore 296 (L. T. Subbu 55, S. Narayan 51 not out, Naziruddin five for 88) and 205 for eight (A. S. Krishnaswamy 62, N. P. Kumar four for 52). Mysore won by two wickets.

At Banaras, February 2, 3, 4. Uttar Pradesh 310 (C. K. Nayudu 84, C. N. Bobjee 72, S. N. Nayudu 55) and 342 for five (S. Mushtaq Ali 101, K. M. Tiwari 76, C. S. Nayudu 61 not out); Rajasthan 256 (C. S. Ramchand 106, C. S. Nayudu six for 103). Rajasthan conceded victory to Uttar Pradesh.

At Calcutta, February 9, 10, 11. Bengal 356 (S. Bose 85, P. Sen 81); Bihar 124 (D. G. Phadkar seven for 37) and 83. Bengal won by an innings and 149 runs.

At New Delhi, February 9, 10, 11, 12. Services 289 (H. T. Dani 81, Atma Singh 62 not out, M. Mehra four for 41) and 269 (Mohindra Singh 85, C. V. Gadkari 82, M. Mehra five for 47); Delhi 221 (Y. M. Choudhry 50) and 218 for seven (P. Bhandari 105). Services won on first innings.

At Bombay, February 12, 13, 14, 15. Maharashtra 171 (S. R. Patil 69, A. K. Balooch 54, P. R. Umrigar six for 36) and 193 (Kuddus Khan 63, P. R. Umrigar six for 51); Bombay 657 for nine wickets, declared (R. B. Kenny 139, P. K. Kamat 158, P. R. Umrigar 92, M. K. Mantri 81, Y. K. Rele 71, R. G. Nadkarni five for 162). Bombay won by an innings and 293 runs.

At Madras, February 15, 16, 17, 18. Mysore 251 (L. T. Subbu 59, K. V. Anantaswami 52, J. C. Patel four for 17) and 254 for nine wickets, declared (A. S. Krishnaswamy 53); Madras 384 (C. D. Gopinath 133, M. Balakrishnan 124, C. M. Varadaraj four for 77) and 128 for three. Madras won by seven wickets.

At Banaras, March 2, 3, 4. Uttar Pradesh 147 (A. H. Desai four for 21, P. R. Umrigar four for 84) and 229 (C. K. Nayudu 52); Bombay 575 (P. R. Umrigar 153, R. B. Kenny 132, A. H. Desai 69, H. Amroliwala 64 not out, C. S. Nayudu five for 194, C. K. Nayudu three for 91). Bombay won by an innings and 199 runs.

SEMI-FINALS

At Calcutta, February 23, 24, 25, 26, 27. Services 399 (Atma Singh 126, H. R. Adhikari 74, Mohindra Singh 51 not out, P. Chatterjee four for 141); Bengal 302 for four (P. Roy 159 not out, B. Chanda 59). Services won by the spin of the coin.

At Bombay, March 16, 17, 18, 19. Bombay 634 for nine wickets, declared (R. B. Kenny 218, R. S. Modi 172, H. D. Amroliwala 77, K. R. Panjri 60 not out); Madras 150 (P. R. Umrigar six for 62, G. M. Guard four for 31) and 161 (K. R. Panjri six for 37). Bombay won by an innings and 323 runs.

FINAL

At New Delhi, March 29, 30, 31, April 1. Services 171 (C. V. Gadkari 53, G. N. Kunzru 50, P. R. Umrigar four for 65) and 150 (K. R. Panjri five for 57, P. R. Umrigar four for 57); Bombay 359 for seven wickets, declared (Y. K. Rele 162 not out, N. S. Tamhane 66, M. K. Mantri 62). Bombay won by an innings and 38 runs.

RANJI TROPHY HOLDERS

1934–35	Bombay	1946–47	Baroda
1935–36	Bombay	1947–48	Holkar
1936–37	Nawanagar	1948–49	Bombay
1937–38	Hyderabad	1949–50	Baroda
1938–39	Bengal	1950–51	Holkar
1939–40	Maharashtra	1951–52	Bombay
1940–41	Maharashtra	1952–53	Holkar
1941–42	Bombay	1953–54	Bombay
1942–43	Baroda	1954–55	Madras
1943–44	Western India	1955–56	Bombay
1944–45	Bombay	1956–57	Bombay
1945–46	Holkar		

CRICKET IN PAKISTAN, 1956–57

Punjab won the Quaid-i-Azam tournament for the first time mainly because of the good all-round form of Fazal Mahmood. In the semi-final against Services he took fifteen wickets for 78 runs and scored 91. Hanif Mohammad hit 228 for Karachi, the beaten finalists, in the semi-final and headed the batting averages. Fazal finished top of the bowling and also held an average of over 50 in batting.

QUAID-I-AZAM TROPHY DETAILS

At Peshawar, December 25, 26, 27. Punjab 309 (Fazal Mahmood 74, Allaf Nizami 74); Peshawar 64 (Fazal Mahmood eight for 21) and 74 (Shankah Ali four for 10). Punjab won by an innings and 171 runs.

At Karachi, December 28, 29, 30. Karachi (Greens) 150 (Ziaullah 77, M. Munaf four for 31) and 254 (Mahmood Hussain eight for 93); Karachi (Whites) 298 (Hanif Mohammad 62, Mohed 55, Ikram Quereshi 52, Taufig Lodhi four for 28) and 110 for two wickets. Karachi (Whites) won by eight wickets.

At Hyderabad, January 2, 3, 4. Hyderabad 44 (Mahmood Hussain five for 21) and 84 (Mushtaq Mohammad five for 28); Karachi (Whites) 396 (Mushtaq Mohammad 87, A. R. Dyer 77 not out, Ikram Quereshi 51). Karachi (Whites) won by an innings and 268 runs.

At Lahore, January 2, 3, 4. Punjab 262 (Gul Mohammad 175, Israr Ali five for 89); Bahawalpur 63 (Khalid Quereshi six for 18) and 174 (M. Ramzan 52, Khalid Quereshi six for 67). Punjab won by an innings and 25 runs.

At Lahore, January 4, 5, 6. Punjab "A" 56 (Abdul Wahab five for 15) and 276 (Salim Kazi 81, Ikram Elahi five for 71); Karachi (Blues) 265 (A. Rasheed 95, W. Mathias 53, A. Mustafa 51, A. Rehman seven for 68) and 73 for three wickets. Karachi (Blues) won by seven wickets.

At Rawalpindi, January 11, 12, 13. Punjab "B" 187 (K. A. Saeed 83 not out, Israr Ali four for 63); Bahawalpur five for no wicket. No result.

At Lahore, January 13, 14, 15. Punjab "A" 132 (Ghafoor Butt six for 56) and 112 (Ijaz Hussain six for 37); Pakistan Railways 231 (Ehsau-ul-Haq 69 not out, Saghir Mirza 52) and 14 for no wicket. Pakistan Railways won by ten wickets.

At Peshawar, January 17, 18, 19. Bahawalpur 148 (F. Salim 60, Sajjad Ahmed seven for 38) and 163 (Zulfiqar Ahmed 57, Sajjad Ahmed six for 51); Peshawar 66 (Zulfiqar Ahmed six for 17) and 101 (M. Ramzan four for 13). Bahawalpur won by 144 runs.

At Dacca, January 18, 19, 20. Services 171 (Ismail Gul five for 51) and 245 (Qaruai 80 not out); East Pakistan (Greens) 52 (Shuja-ud-Din five for 20) and 142 (Tahir 52 not out). Services won by 222 runs.

At Lahore, January 23, 24, 25. Punjab 174 (Munir Malik five for 19) and 187 for five wickets, declared; Punjab "B" 56 (Fazal Mahmood seven for 24) and 83 (Khalid Quereshi four for 24). Punjab won by an innings and 222 runs.

At Dacca, January 24, 25, 26. East Pakistan (Whites) 33 (Miran Bux six for 15) and 117 (Hatini five for 40); Services 220 for five wickets, declared. Services won by an innings and 70 runs.

At Karachi, January 25, 26, 27. Karachi (Greens) 171 (Illeat five for 82) and 208 for six wickets, declared (Aftab Alam 100 not out, Illeat four for 87); Hyderabad 116 and 125 (Iqbal Hussain 53, Salahuddin four for 68). Karachi (Greens) won by 138 runs.

At Karachi, January 25, 26, 27. Pakistan Railways 140 (Maqsood Ahmed five for 54) and 195 (M. Yusuf 88, Ikram Elahi six for 70); Karachi (Blues) 230 (Ismail Ibrahim 56 not out, Ghafoor Butt four for 68) and 107 for one wicket (Shahid Mahmood 51 not out); Karachi (Blues) won by nine wickets.

At Dacca, January 28, 29, 30. East Pakistan (Greens) 124 and 110; East Pakistan (Whites) 117 and 95 (Amirullah six for 33). East Pakistan (Greens) won by 22 runs.

At Peshawar, February 1, 2, 3. Peshawar 147 and 108 (Munir five for 40); Punjab "B" 217 (Salahuddin 76, Hasib eight for 72) and 42 for five wickets. Punjab "B" won by five wickets.

SEMI-FINALS

At Karachi, February 1, 2, 3, 5, 6. Karachi (Blues) 314 (Maqsood Ahmed 90, Ismail Ibrahim 59, Mahmood Hussain five for 117) and 316; Karachi (Whites) 762 (Hanif Mohammad 228, Mohammad Aslam 112 not out, Wazir Mohammad 110, Mobed 96, Alim-ud-Din 94). Karachi (Whites) won by an innings and 132 runs.

At Lahore, February 7, 8, 9, 11, 12. Services 112 (Shuja-ud-Din 56, Fazal Mahmood six for 35) and 99 (Fazal Mahmood nine for 43); Punjab 253 (Fazal Mahmood 91, Shankah Ali 65). Punjab won by an innings and 42 runs.

FINAL

At Lahore, March 8, 9, 10, 12. Punjab 418 (Ijar Butt 147, Shakoor Ahmed 73) and 182 (Agha Saadat 56, M. Munaf six for 67); Karachi 289 (Alim-ud-Din 105, Waqar Hassan 68, Yawar Saeed five for 89) and 268 (Waqar Hassan 51, Ehsau Elahi four for 62). Punjab won by 43 runs.

CRICKET IN CEYLON, 1956–57

The Ceylon Cricket Association won the M. J. Gopalan Trophy for the fourth successive year when they defeated Madras by five wickets in the annual match at the Colombo Oval.

Madras 56 (J. Arenhold six for 17) and 161 (J. Arenhold five for 26, K. M. T. Perera four for 45); Ceylon Cricket Association 140 (V. V. Kumar four for 38, Mohan Rai four for 43) and 78 for five wickets.

INDIANS IN CEYLON, 1956–57

A strong Indian team led by P. R. Umrigar toured Ceylon in November 1956. Ten of the side, P. R. Umrigar, Ghulam Ahmed, P. Roy, V. L. Manjrekar, Kripal Singh, G. S. Ramchand, S. P. Gupte, N. Contractor, P. Bhandari and N. Tamhand, had appeared just previously in the Tests against Australia. M. L. Apte, another member of the team, had played against Pakistan and West Indies.

India met Ceylon in two unofficial Tests and there was a two-day match at Kandy. G. Goonesena captained Ceylon in the second representative match; J. Arenhold, an Oxford Blue, also played for Ceylon.

With only one hour's cricket possible on the first day and the whole of the second day completely washed out, the first Representative match was drawn. Scores:

Ceylon 120 (A. C. M. Lafir 55, C. I. Gunersekera 37, S. P. Gupte five for 55); India 119 for three wickets (N. Contractor 65 not out).

The second Representative match also produced a tame draw. Goonesena accomplished a fine all-round performance and Contractor and Umrigar put on 116 for India's second wicket. Scores:
India 283 (N. Contractor 78, V. L. Manjrekar 77, P. R. Umrigar 61, G. Goonesena seven for 79) and 125 for two wickets, declared (N. Contractor 42, P. Roy 42, Kripal Singh 33 not out); Ceylon 150 (G. Goonesena 48, S. P. Gupte six for 64, Ghulam Ahmed three for 45) and 93 for five wickets (N. Contractor three for 12).

CRICKET IN UGANDA, 1956

Cricket in Uganda has made rapid strides in recent years. Besides European, Asian and Goan sides, there are several African teams, mainly from schools, taking part in competitions. W. R. Watkins, the former Middlesex player now senior coach to M.C.C., visits the Protectorate each year and his coaching has done much to improve the standard of play.

In 1956 a strong Pakistan side under the captaincy of A. H. Kardar visited Uganda. They beat Uganda by an innings and 60 runs in a two-day match at Kampala. Summarised score:

Uganda 121 (J. A. Boucher 51, Ikram Elahi five for 25, Zulfiqar Ahmed five for 43) and 150 (Ikram Elahi four for 21, Zulfiqar Ahmed four for 31); Pakistan 331 for eight wickets, declared (Alim-ud-Din 117, W. Mathias 75, Imtiaz Ahmed 62).

Inter-Territorial matches were played as follows:

At Zanzibar, August 23, 24. Uganda 210 for eight wickets, declared (Shashikant 53 not out, Narottam 50) and 153 for six wickets, declared (Ebrahim four for 81); Zanzibar 165 (Ahmed Himidi 50, Gandalal five for 30) and 106 for five wickets. Drawn.

At Dar-es-Salaam, August 25, 26, 27. Uganda 120 (M. Husein four for 23) and 260 (Salaudin 117, Meredew four for 64); Tanganyika 321 for six wickets, declared (K. R. Patel 133, Bresler 106) and 60 for three wickets. Tanganyika won by seven wickets.

At Kampala, December 8, 9, 10. Uganda 223 and 149 (Ranjit Singh seven for 56); Kenya 116 (Kishore four for 37) and 172 (Kishore five for 42). Uganda won by 84 runs.

CRICKET IN CANADA, 1957

The principal item of importance in the 1957 season was the initial tour of England by a representative Junior Canadian Team comprised of 17 boys between the ages of 17 and 20, all of whom had learned the game of cricket in Canada. Although marred by atrocious weather which affected all but four of the sixteen matches played against public schools, the tour was an outstanding success. The final record of one game won, five drawn, seven lost and three abandoned was creditable under the circumstances, especially in view of the fact that practically all the members of the Canadian side had had no previous experience of grass wickets, let alone such wickets affected by rain.

The players received coaching at Lord's and gained much valuable experience in matches against well-informed opponents. T. T. Gibson, of Toronto, who scored 337 runs in ten innings for an average of 42.12, secured 26 wickets for 373 runs (average 14.30) and topped both batting and bowling averages, proved himself an all-round player of the highest promise. His 101 not out against Marlborough was the highest score by a Canadian player on the tour. It is hoped that this experience can be repeated at regular intervals in the future as the interest evinced by junior players across Canada when the tour was first announced was adequate proof that here, at last, was something tangible to offer the junior player who would seek to learn the intricacies of cricket at home.

This summer (1958) the second Inter-Provincial Junior Tournament will be held in Winnipeg between June 29 and July 6. Teams from British Columbia, Alberta, Manitoba and Ontario will compete, each playing the other twice during the tournament. This is part of the Canadian Cricket Association's current programme for development and training of junior players.

Apart from the Junior Tour of England, 1957 saw more tours undertaken involving Canadian clubs than had been the case in any season previously. Bermuda toured Ontario with success in August, Haverford College returned to that Province for the first time since 1952, Ottawa and Montreal combined forces and flew to California where the newly formed Western Canadian Stragglers Club followed them later in the summer, Edmonton Sportsmen journeyed to the Okanagan Region of British Columbia, Ridley College repeated a previous visit to Bermuda, Milwaukee drove 1800 miles to play a day's cricket in Winnipeg, and the itinerant Toronto Ramblers played fourteen games against a variety of opposition in Philadelphia, Washington and New York. All told, more games were played in Canada in 1957 than had been the case in any previous season. Two new clubs commenced operations in Ontario and one in Manitoba and the future outlook continues to give justifiable grounds for discreet optimism.—DONALD KING.

SCOTTISH CRICKET IN 1957

Scotland played five International Matches, drawing with M.C.C., Lancashire and Yorkshire, and losing to Warwickshire and Gentlemen of Ireland. The defeat in Dublin was the first sustained at the hands of the Irish since 1949 and occurred on a rain-affected pitch in a low-scoring match where the side winning the toss, Ireland, appeared to gain a big advantage. The visit of M.C.C., captained by F. R. Brown, to Aberdeen coincided with one of the few fine spells of weather in what was otherwise a wetter season than usual. The Scottish XI included some useful players but no bowler good enough to trouble first-class opposition seriously, and this was the chief reason for their lack of success against County teams. The best bowler was A. D. Livingstone, whose 18 wickets included eleven for 51 against Ireland. The best batsmen were two of the more experienced, J. Aitchison and R. H. Chisholm, and the most promising of the younger players, D. Barr, though J. N. Kemsley, who made 103, and L. C. Dudman both batted well against M.C.C. J. Brown, a most capable wicket-keeper-batsman, scored 90 against Yorkshire and equalled a world wicket-keeping record of seven victims (caught 4, stumped 3) in a single innings of a first-class match against Ireland.

The new County Champions were Forfar who included *the* personality of the season, C. Depeiza. A member of the West Indies Touring Team to New

Zealand in 1955–56, it was expected that he would be a strong contender for one of the wicket-keeping places in the West Indies England touring side, but he surprised everyone by withdrawing in the midst of the Tour Trials to sign as professional for Forfar. He failed only once in County Matches, made the only century and displaying unexpected ability as a bowler, headed both batting and bowling averages. Aberdeenshire were runners-up in their Centenary Year with their captain and former International, G. W. Youngson, again proving himself the leading amateur bowler amongst the Counties. An interesting event was the visit in mid-September to Aberdeen of the full Surrey Championship XI captained by P. B. H. May to play an XI sponsored by Sir John Hay, President of the County. Perthshire, Champions for the last four years, finished third and were the strongest batting side with three batsmen in the first six places in the averages, the best being S. A. Hay. Fife were fourth, their professional, A. E. G. Rhodes (Derbyshire), having a successful season as a bowler.

The Western Union title was shared by Poloc, 1956 Champions, and Ferguslie, 1955 Champions, with Greenock, West of Scotland and Kelburne next in order. The issue was not decided until the last Saturday of the season, as happened the previous year, and so close was the struggle that any one of the first five clubs were in the running. The first four clubs were well served by their professionals, R. Halton (Staffs) of Poloc, Balan Pandit (Travancore-Cochin, India) of Ferguslie, W. R. Coldwell (Lord's staff) of Greenock and F. H. Vigar (Essex) of West of Scotland. The leading amateurs in the first three sides were A. D. Livingstone and E. L. Kirk (Poloc), E. M. Kirkwood, A. D. Baxter and J. Orr (Ferguslie), and D. W. Drummond (Greenock). Other professionals who had good seasons with their clubs were C. Oakes (Sussex) with Ayr and W. B. Morris (Essex) with Kilmarnock.

The East of Scotland League, now in its fifth year, was won by Edinburgh Academicals. Their success was due to the excellent batting of their former Internationals, A. I. S. Macpherson and J. A. Stevenson, ably supported by younger players who included T. McClung, their best bowler, who is also a Rugby International, and, in the latter part of the season, J. M. Allan (Oxford University, Kent and Scotland). Runners-up for the second time in three seasons were Kirkcaldy, the only club with a professional, W. J. Dennis from Cumberland, who was an effective all-rounder. Royal High School F.P., third, gained their highest position to date. They had two Internationals, D. A. R. Lawrence, who took most wickets in the competition, and F. O. Thomas, one of the most elegant stroke-players in Scotland. Stenhousemuir, Champions in 1955 and 1956, were fourth, and in R. S. Bell, who improved on his 1956 figures, they possessed one of the fastest bowlers in Scotland, whilst R. F. T. Paterson, former Essex Secretary, was again their leading batsman. Grange, for long one of the leading clubs in Scotland and twice winners of the league, fell away rather surprisingly to finish twelfth. Carlton, another famous club, were seventh despite the efforts of D. Tattersall, a Lancastrian student at Edinburgh University, who made the only League century and averaged 55. Other players to shine were G. Millar (Heriots F.P.), D. Barr (Melville F.P.), W. McNab, C. A. R. and D. Cowan (Watsonians), F. A. Jones (Grange) and K. D. Robinson (Edinburgh University).

The Border League was won by Gala for the eighth year in succession, during which period they have played very much the same team—dominated by the Nichol family; R. J. Nichol, the captain, was again a very steady bowler, D. Nichol, another International, a slow left-hander and opening batsman, and A. W. Nichol emerged as the highest run-getter. Gala were hard-pressed by the runners-up, Dumfries, both times they met but prevailed by eleven and two runs respectively. A fine personality who will be missed in Border cricket is F. Barkham, who has now retired. He came to Scotland in 1930 from Yorkshire and since then made over 20,000 runs including 54 centuries, and took over 800 wickets. Besides playing for Scotland in four Internationals he did much good work in the coaching field.

In the north-east the Strathmore Union was won by the Strathmore club, whose professional for the past three seasons has been N. Hazel, a Bermudian, who was formerly with Aberdeenshire. Meigle, who were second, were another club with a professional, A. Manville, who was the most effective bowler in the competition, the leading batsman being the former Northants player D. G. Greasley (Arbroath). Two other prominent players were amateurs—G. Campbell

(Gordonians), the best batsman, and G. Myles (Strathmore), the best bowler, the third year in succession in which he gained this honour.

The following gained International "Caps" during 1957: Captain, S. H. Cosh (Ayr); J. M. Allan (Edinburgh Academicals); J. Aitchison (Carlton); D. Barr (Melville F.P.); J. Brown, L. C. Dudman, M. Kerrigan (Perthshire); R. H. Chisholm (Stewarts F.P.); G. W. L. Courtenay (Grange); W. D. F. Dow, J. N. Kemsley, J. B. Roberts (Clydesdale); D. W. Drummond (Greenock); D. A. R. Lawrence (Royal High School F.P.); A. D. Livingstone (Poloc): and J. S. Wilson (Brechin).

IRISH CRICKET IN 1957

Ireland enjoyed their most successful season for ten years. Of five representative matches they won two, beating Scotland for the first time since 1949—by 38 runs—and Free Foresters with an innings to spare. When they drew with West Indies in Belfast the Irishmen performed very well as they did on the second day against M.C.C., but the game at Lord's was lost.

The bowling, as always, was particularly good. In the five games, F. Fee, the off-spinner from Queen's University, took 29 wickets for 272 runs, average 9.36. C. J. M. Kenny, the former Cambridge University and Essex bowler, took 16 wickets for 323 runs, average 20.18. Fee's success has been phenomenal. In seven matches for Ireland he has taken 43 wickets. Two of these which rank as first-class brought him 26 wickets for 160, an Irish record. Fee is tall, changes his pace well, has flight, spin and looks like a true successor to the great J. C. Boucher.

Kenny, who specialises in fastish off-cutters, has become more of an arm bowler since an operation on his left knee compelled him to point his left foot straight down the pitch when delivering. More accurate now than during his fast bowling days, he is indispensable to the Irish attack. S. S. J. Huey, left-arm slow, could play only in the two games against West Indies in which he took six wickets. Ireland would have liked him to play more often, and they also required a fast opening bowler.

When R. O'Brien, the Cambridge Blue of 1955–56, and M. A. Eagar, the present Oxford secretary, were both available, the batting bore a respectable appearance. If inelegant, the left-handed S. F. Bergin proved an effective opening partner for O'Brien. K. Quinn, the former Rugby International and the fourth brother of this family to receive a Cricket Cap, also opened in some games. L. Warke, the captain, became the second Irishman to score a hundred against M.C.C. at Lord's. A fine batsman, he was a trifle inconsistent. J. S. Pollock, the veteran of the team, had a reasonably good season with the bat, as did a young newcomer, A. Finlay.

The real find of the season was R. Hunter, of Lisburn Cricket Club. He hit a century in the Ulster Cup Final and was picked for Ireland in the last game of the season against Free Foresters when the total of 371 for six wickets was the highest for Ireland in Ireland since 1876. In this match Hunter made 74 not out in seventy-two minutes—a great debut. Of fine physique, he shaped most confidently and hit strongly off the back foot.

Ireland is very proud of its cricketing heritage and tradition and looks forward eagerly to the 1958 M.C.C. game which will be played in College Park, Dublin, in early September. This will be the centenary match, for it was in May 1858 that M.C.C. first played Ireland at Lord's, the first time an Irish XI ever played away from home.

All cricket in Ireland is on a competitive basis. There are Leagues and Cups in Derry, Dublin and Cork, but no professionalism. The famous North of Ireland Club won the Ulster Senior League, with Woodvale second. Lisburn beat Woodvale in the Ulster Senior Cup by an innings, the 19-year-old Ray Hunter contributing 133 to Lisburn's score of 336.

The Leinster Senior League (Dublin) was won by a very strong Pembroke team. Pembroke completed the double by winning the Cup, and the Leinster Cricket Club, who were founded in 1852, were runners-up in both competitions.

The Leinster experiment of commencing Senior League matches on Friday evenings at 6.30 and continuing at 2.30 on Saturdays, begun in 1956, was continued in 1957. This gives approximately eight hours' playing time and provides conditions more akin to a two-day match than does the usual five-hour rush and scramble of Saturday afternoons.—DEREK SCOTT.

BIRTHS AND DEATHS OF CRICKETERS

Details of Cricketers who died before 1936 are omitted although members of famous cricketing families and some personalities of special interest are retained. The qualification now is ten appearances in first-class cricket during one season in England, or the award of a County Cap or University Blue. Overseas cricketers are usually included only if they have represented their country in a tour of England.

University Players are given in the List of Blues on page 677.

a Beckett, Mr. E. L. (Victoria), b Aug 11, 1907

Abel, R. (Surrey), b Nov 30, 1857, d Dec 10, 1936

Abel, T. E. (Surrey and Glamorgan), b Sept 10, 1890, d Jan 23, 1937

Abel, W. J. (Surrey), b Aug 29, 1887, d March 23, 1934

Abell, Sir G. E. B. (Oxford Univ. and Worcestershire), b June 22, 1904

Aberdare, 3rd Lord (see Bruce, Hon. C. N.)

Achong, Mr. E. (West Indies), b Feb 16, 1904

Adam, Gen. Sir Ronald, 1st Bart., President M.C.C., b Oct 30, 1885

Adams, Mr. G. C. A. (Hampshire), b May 24, 1909

Adcock, Mr. N. A. T. (South Africa), b March 8, 1931

Adhikari, Mr. H. R. (India), b Aug 12, 1919

Ahl, F. D. (Worcestershire), b Nov 24, 1908

Ainsworth, Lt.-Cdr. M. L. Y. (Worcestershire), b May 13, 1922

Aird, Mr. R. (Camb. Univ. and Hampshire, Secretary M.C.C. from 1953), b May 4, 1902

Akers-Douglas, Mr. I. S. (Kent), b Nov 16, 1909, d Dec 16, 1952

Alcock, Mr. C. W. (Sec., Surrey C.C.C. 1872-1907), b Dec 2, 1842, d Feb 26, 1907

Alderman, A. E. (Derbyshire), b Oct 30, 1907

Aldridge, J. (Worcestershire), b March 13, 1935

Alexander, Mr. F. C. M. (Camb. Univ. and West Indies), b Nov 2, 1928

Alexander, Mr. H. (Victoria) b June 9, 1905

Alexander, Mr. W. C. (South Australia), b Sept 14, 1907

Alim-ud-Din (Pakistan), b April 15, 1928

Allcott, Mr. C. F. W. (New Zealand), b Oct 7, 1896

Allan, Mr. J. M. (Oxford U., Kent and Scotland), b April 2, 1932

Allen, Mr. A. W. (Camb. Univ., and Northamptonshire), b Dec 22, 1912

Allen, Mr. B. O. (Camb. Univ. and Gloucestershire), b Oct 13, 1911

Allen, D. A. (Gloucestershire), b Oct 29, 1935

Allen, Mr. G. O. (Camb. Univ. and Middlesex), b at Sydney, Australia, July 31, 1902

Allen, M. H. J. (Northamptonshire), b Jan 7, 1933

Allen, R. (Yorkshire), b April 1893, d Oct 14, 1950

Alletson, E. (Nottinghamshire), b March 6, 1884

Alley, W. E. (N.S.W. and Somerset), b March 3, 1919

Allom, Mr. M. J. C. (Camb. Univ. and Surrey), b March 23, 1906

Altham, Mr. H. S. (Oxford Univ., Surrey and Hampshire), b Nov 30, 1888

Amarnath, L. (India), b Sep 11, 1911

Amar Singh (India), b Dec 4, 1910, d May 20, 1940

Ames, L. E. G. (Kent), b Dec 3, 1905

Amir Elahi (India), b Sept 1, 1908

Andrew, K. V. (Northamptonshire), b Dec 15, 1929

Andrews, Mr. T. J. E. (New South Wales), b Aug 26, 1890

Andrews, W. H. R. (Somerset), b April 14, 1908

Angell, F. L. (Somerset), b June 29, 1922

Anson, Hon. Rupert (Middlesex), b Nov 7, 1889

Appleyard, Mr. F. (Essex), b Sept 9, 1906

Appleyard, R. (Yorkshire), b June 27, 1924

Archer, Mr. R. G. (Queensland), b Oct 25, 1933

Arenhold, Mr. J. A. (Oxford Univ.), b May 9, 1931

Arkwright, Mr. H. A. (Essex and Oxford Univ.), b Nov 10, 1872, d Dec 10, 1942

Arlington, Mr. G. H. A. (Sussex), b May 28, 1872, d 1944

Armstrong, Mr. E. K. (Queensland), b Feb 5, 1881

Armstrong, N. F. (Leicestershire), b Dec 22, 1894

Armstrong, T. R. (Derbyshire), b Oct 13, 1909

Armstrong, Mr. W. W. (Victoria), b May 22, 1879, d July 13, 1947

Arnold, E. G. (Worcestershire), b Nov 7, 1877, d Oct 25, 1942

Arnold, John (Oxfordshire and Hampshire), b Nov 30, 1907

Arnold, P. (Canterbury and Northamptonshire), b Oct 16, 1926

Arnott, Mr. T. (Glamorgan and Monmouthshire), b Feb 16, 1902

Asgarali, Mr. N. (West Indies), b Dec 28, 1922

Ashcroft, Dr. E. Maynard (Derbyshire), b Sept 27, 1875, d Feb 26, 1955

Ashdown, W. H. (Kent), b Dec 27, 1898

Ashman, J. R. (Yorkshire and Worcestershire), b May 20, 1926

Ashton, Sqdn.-Ldr. C.T. (Camb. Univ. and Essex), b Feb 19, 1901, d Oct 31, 1942

Ashton, Mr. G. (Camb. Univ. and Worcestershire), b Sept 27, 1896

Ashton, Mr. H. (Camb. Univ. and Essex), b Feb 13, 1898

Aspinall, R. (Yorkshire), b Nov 26, 1918

Astill, W. E. (Leicestershire), b Mar 1, 1888, d Feb 10, 1948

Astor, of Hever, Col. Lord J. (Eton, Buckinghamshire, President M.C.C., 1937), b May 20, 1886

Atfield, A. J. (Gloucestershire and Wiltshire), b Mar 3, 1868, d Jan 1, 1949

Atkins, Mr. F. M. (Kent), b Mar 28, 1864, d Jan 13, 1941

Atkinson, Mr. B. G. W. (Northamptonshire and Middlesex), b Sept 1900

Atkinson, Mr. D. (West Indies), b Feb 26, 1925

Atkinson, G. G. (Somerset), b March 29, 1938

Atkinson, Mr. J. A. (Victoria and Tasmania), b April 4, 1896, d June 11, 1956

Atkinson-Clark, Mr. J. C. (Middlesex), b July 9, 1912

Attewell, Thos. (Nottinghamshire), b Nov 7, 1869, d July 6, 1937

Attewell, W. (Nottinghamshire), b June 12, 1861, d June 11, 1927

Austin, Sir H. B. G. (Barbados), b July 15, 1877, d July 27, 1943

Austin, Mr. H. M. (Camb. Univ.), b March 8, 1903

Avery, A. V. (Essex), b Dec 19, 1914

Awdry, Mr. R. W. (Oxford Univ. and Wiltshire), b May 20, 1881, d Feb 3, 1949

Bacmeister, Mr. L. H. (Middlesex), b Nov 22, 1869

Badcock, Mr. C. L. (Tasmania and South Australia), b April 10, 1914

Badcock, Mr. F. T. (New Zealand), b Aug 9, 1898

Badcock, J. R. (Hampshire) b Oct 4, 1883

Baggallay, Mr. M. E. C. (Camb. Univ.), b Dec 7, 1887

Baggallay, Lt.-Col. R. R. C. (Derbyshire), b May 4, 1884

Bagguley, R. (Nottinghamshire), b July 10, 1873, d 1947

Bagnall, Mr. H. F. (Camb. Univ. and Northamptonshire), b Feb 18, 1904

Bailey, A. (Surrey and Somerset), b March 14, 1872

Bailey, Mr. B. T. R. (South Australia), b Dec 5, 1874

Bailey, Sir D. (Bart.) (Gloucestershire), b Aug 15, 1918

Bailey, J. (Hampshire), b April 6, 1908

Bailey, Mr. J. A. (Essex and Oxford Univ.), b June 22, 1930

Bailey, Mr. T. E. (Essex and Camb. Univ.), b Dec 3, 1923

Baily, Mr. E. P. (Camb. Univ., Somerset and Middlesex), b Jan 18, 1852, d Jan 21, 1941

Baily, Mr. R. E. H. (Camb. Univ. and Surrey), b June 6, 1885

Bainbridge, Mr. H. W. (Camb. Univ., Surrey and Warwickshire), b Assam, India, Oct 29, 1862, d Mar 3, 1940

Bairstow, A. L. (Yorkshire), b Aug 14, 1870, d Feb 21, 1948

Baiss, Mr. R. S. H. (Kent), b March 6, 1873, d May 2, 1955

Baker, A. (Surrey), b Nov 28, 1872, d April 29, 1948

Baker, C. S. (Warwickshire and Cornwall), b Jan 5, 1883

Baker, Mr. C. V. (Middlesex), b Nov 23, 1885, d Dec 7, 1947

Baker, Mr. E. C. (Camb. Univ., Sussex and Somerset), b Jan 7, 1892

Baker, Mr. E. S. (Worcestershire), b Nov 9, 1910

Baker, G. R. (Yorkshire & Lancashire), b April 18, 1862, d Feb 6, 1938

Baker, Mr. H. Z. (Kent), b Feb 7, 1880

Baker, Mr. P. C. (Kent), b May 2, 1874, d Dec 30, 1939

Bakewell, A. H. (Northamptonshire), b Nov 2, 1908

Balaskas, Mr. X. (South Africa), b Oct 15, 1910

Baldry, D. O. (Middlesex), b Dec 26, 1931

Baldwin, C. (Surrey and Suffolk), b Dec 29, 1865, d May 2, 1947

Baldwin, H. (Hampshire), b Nov 27, 1860, d Jan 12, 1935

Baldwin, H. G. (Surrey), b March 16, 1895

Baldwin of Bewdley, 1st Earl (President, M.C.C., 1938), b Aug 3, 1867, d Dec 14, 1947

Bale, E. (Surrey and Worcestershire), b Sept 18, 1878, d July 7, 1952

Bale, F. (Leicestershire), b Jan 9, 1893

Balfour-Melville, Mr. L. M. (Scotland), b March 9, 1854, d July 16, 1937

Ballance, Major T. G. L., M.C. (Oxford Univ.), b April 21, 1916, d Dec 4, 1943

Baloo, P (India), b March 19, 1876, d July 4, 1955

Bancroft, Mr. C. K. (West Indies), b Oct 30, 1885, d 1915

Banerjee, S. (India), b Oct 3, 1913

Bannerman, Mr. A. C. (New South Wales), b March 21, 1859, d Sept 19, 1924

Bannerman, Mr. Charles (New South Wales), b in Kent, July 3, 1851, d Aug 20, 1930

Bannister, A. F. (Worcestershire), b June 15, 1875

Bannister, Mr. H. M. (Leicestershire), b June 3, 1889

Bannister, J. D. (Warwickshire), b Aug 23, 1930

Bannon, Mr. B. D. (Oxford Univ. and Kent), b Dec 7, 1874, d Dec 18, 1938

Barber, Mr. A. T. (Oxford Univ. and Yorkshire), b June 17, 1905

Barber, Mr. R. W. (Lancashire and Camb. Univ.), b Sept 26, 1935

Barber, W. (Yorkshire) b April 18, 1902

Bardsley, Mr. R. V. (Oxford Univ. and Lancashire), b 1890, d July 26, 1952

Bardsley, Mr. W. (New South Wales), b Dec 7, 1883, d Jan 20, 1954

Baring, Mr. A. E. G. (Hampshire), b Jan 21, 1910

Barker, G. (Essex), b July 6, 1932

Barker, Mr. K. E. M. (Surrey), b Oct 27, 1877, d Aug 6, 1938

Barling, T. H. (Surrey), b Sept 1, 1906

Barlow, A. (Lancashire), b Aug 31, 1915

Barlow, Mr. E. A. (Oxford Univ., Lancashire and Denbighshire), b Feb 24, 1912

Barnard, Mr. F. H. (Oxford Univ.), b May 6, 1902

Barnard, H. M. (Hampshire), b July 18, 1933

Barnes, Mr. J. R. (Lancashire), b May 18, 1897, d July 22, 1945

Barnes, S. F. (Warwickshire, Lancashire and Staffordshire), b April 19, 1873

Barnes, Mr. S. G. (New South Wales), b June 5, 1916

Barnett, Mr. B. A. (Victoria and Buckinghamshire), b May 23, 1908

Barnett, C. J. (Gloucestershire), b July 3, 1910

Barnett, Mr. C. S. (Gloucestershire) b Feb 26, 1884

Barnett, Mr. E. P. (Gloucestershire), b March 22, 1885, d Jan 1, 1922

Barnwell, Mr. C. J. P. (Somerset), b June 23, 1914

Barratt, F. (Nottinghamshire), b April 12, 1894, d Jan 30, 1947

Barrett, Capt. E. I. M. (Hampshire), b June 22, 1879, d July 11, 1950

Barrick, D. (Northamptonshire), b April 28, 1926

Barrington, Mr. G. B. (Derbyshire), b April 20, 1857, d Feb 26, 1942

Barrington, K. F. (Surrey), b Nov 24, 1930

Barron, W. (Durham and Northamptonshire), b Oct 26, 1917

Barrow, Mr. I. (West Indies), b Jan 6, 1911

Bartholomew, Mr. A. C. (Oxford Univ.), b Feb 21, 1846, d March 29, 1940

Bartlett, Mr. E. L. (West Indies), b March 18, 1906

Bartlett, Mr. H. T. (Camb. Univ., Surrey and Sussex), b Oct 7, 1914

Bartlett, Mr. J. N. (Oxford Univ. and Sussex), b June 6, 1928

Barton, Mr. H. G. M. (Hampshire), b Oct 10, 1882

Barton, Mr. M. R. (Winchester, Oxford Univ., Norfolk and Surrey), b Oct 14, 1914

Bassett, Mr. H. (Oxford Univ., Oxfordshire and Suffolk), b Oct 5, 1868, d June 13, 1943

Bateman-Champain, Col. C. E. (Cheltenham and Gloucestershire), b March 30, 1875

Bateman-Champain, Mr. F. H. (Gloucestershire and Oxford Univ.), b June 17, 1877, d Dec 29, 1942

Bateman-Champain, Brig.-Gen. H. F. (Cheltenham and Gloucestershire), b April 6, 1869, d Oct 7, 1933

Bates, D. L. (Sussex), b May 10, 1933

Bates, L. A. (Warwickshire), b March 20, 1895

Bates, W. E. (Yorkshire, Glamorgan and Cheshire), b March 5, 1884, d Jan 17, 1957

Bathurst, Mr. L. C. V. (Oxford Univ., Middlesex and Norfolk), b June 4, 1871, d Feb 22, 1939

Baumgartner, Mr. H. V. (Orange Free State and South Africa), b Nov 17, 1882, d April 8, 1938

Baxter, Mr. A. D. (Devon, Lancashire, Middlesex and Scotland), b Jan 20, 1910

Baxter, Mr. A. G. (Nottinghamshire), b Sept 21, 1931

Bayes, G. (Yorkshire), b Feb 27, 1884

Bean, Mr. E. E. (Victoria), b April 17, 1866, d March 22, 1939

Bear, M. (Essex), b Feb 23, 1934

Beattie, Mr. F. D. (Lancashire), b Aug 18, 1909

Beaumont, H. (Yorkshire), b Oct 14, 1916

Beaumont, Mr. R. (South Africa), b Feb 4, 1884

Bedser, A. V. (Surrey), b July 4, 1918

Bedser, E. A. (Surrey), b July 4, 1918

Beet, G. (Derbyshire), b April 24, 1886, d Dec 13, 1946

Beet, G. H. (Derbyshire), b May 30, 1904, d Aug 22, 1949

Begbie, Mr. D. W. (South Africa), b Dec 12, 1914

Beldam, Mr. G. W. (Middlesex), b May 1, 1868, d Nov 23, 1937

Bell, Mr. A. J. (South Africa), b April 15, 1906

Bell, J. T. (Yorkshire and Glamorgan), b June 16, 1898

Bell, Mr. R. M. (London County and M.C.C.), b Jan 1, 1874, d June 11, 1953

Bell, R. V. (Middlesex and Sussex), b Jan 7, 1931

Bellamy, B. (Northamptonshire), b April 22, 1891

Belle, Mr. B. H. (Oxford Univ., Essex and Suffolk), b April 7, 1914

Beloe, Mr. G. H. (Gloucestershire), b Nov 21, 1877, d Oct 6, 1944

Benaud, Mr. R. (New South Wales), b Oct 6, 1930

Bencraft, Sir H. W. Russell (Hampshire), b March 4, 1858, d Dec 25, 1943

Benham, C. (Essex), b June 24, 1881

Benn, Mr. A. (Oxford Univ.), b Oct 7, 1912

Bennett, A. (Lancashire), b May 18, 1910

Bennett, Mr. C. T. (Camb. Univ., Surrey and Middlesex), b Aug 10, 1902

Bennett, D. (Middlesex), b Dec 18, 1933

Bennett Mr. G. M. (Somerset), b Dec 17, 1909

Bennett, J. W. (Derbyshire), b Feb 22, 1864, dead

Bennett, Mr. N. H. (Surrey), b Sept 23, 1912

Bennett, Mr. R. A. (Hampshire), b Dec 12, 1872, d July 16, 1951

Benskin, W. E. (Leicestershire and Scotland), b April 8, 1883

Benson, Mr. E. T. (Oxford Univ. and Gloucestershire), b Nov 20, 1907

Beresford, Mr. R. A. A. (Northamptonshire and Norfolk), b Aug 12, 1869, d July 12, 1941

Berkeley, Mr. G. F. H. (Oxford Univ.), b Jan 29, 1870, d Nov 14, 1955

Berkeley, Mr. M. (Essex), b Sept 6, 1872, d Aug 9, 1947

Bernard, Mr. C. A. (Somerset), b Feb 16, 1876, d 1953

Bernau, Mr. E. H. L. (New Zealand), b April 6, 1896

Berridge, Mr. W. C. M. (Leicestershire), b Dec 2, 1894

Berry, F. (Surrey), b Feb 13, 1911

Berry, L. G. (Leicestershire), b April 28, 1906

Berry, R. (Lancashire and Worcestershire), b Jan 29, 1926

Berwick, A. (Derbyshire), b July 30, 1865, dead

Bessant, J. G. (Gloucestershire), b Nov 11, 1895

Bestwick, W. (Derbyshire and Glamorgan), b Feb 24, 1876, d May 3, 1938

Betham, Mr. J. D. (Author of "Oxford and Camb. Cricket Scores and Biographies"), b Feb 13, 1874, d Jan 1, 1956

Beton, S. (Middlesex), b Nov 22, 1895

Bettington, Mr. R. H. B. (Oxford Univ., Middlesex and New South Wales), b Feb 24, 1900

Beveridge R. (Middlesex), b Sept 16, 1909

Bick, D. A. (Middlesex), b Feb 22, 1936

Bickmore, Mr. A. F. (Oxford Univ. and Kent), b May 19, 1899

Bignell, Lt.-Col. G. N. (Hampshire), b Dec 3, 1886

Binks, J. G. (Yorkshire), b Oct 5, 1935

Bird, Rev. F. N. (Buckinghamshire, Gloucestershire, Northamptonshire, Devon and Suffolk), b 1876

Bird, Mr. M. C. (Lancashire and Surrey) b March 25, 1888, d Dec 9, 1933

Bird, Mr. R. C. (Hampshire), b March 17, 1874, d Oct 18, 1936

Bird, Mr. R. E. (Worcestershire), b April 4, 1915

Birkett, Mr. L. S. (West Indies), b April 14, 1905

Birrell, Mr. H. B. (Oxford Univ.), b Dec 12, 1927

Birtles, T. J. (Yorkshire), b Oct 26, 1887

Birtwell, Mr. A. J. (Buckinghamshire and Lancashire), b Dec 17, 1910

Bisgood, Mr. B. L. (Somerset) b March 11, 1881

Bishop, Mr. F. A. (Essex), b June 11, 1862

Bisset, Mr. J. J. (Natal), b Dec, 1882

Bisset, Sir M. (South Africa), b April 14, 1876, d Oct 24, 1931

Blackham, Mr. J. McC. (Victoria), b May 11, 1853, d Dec 27, 1932

Blackie, Mr. D. J. (Victoria), b April 5, 1882, d April 21, 1955

Blagg, Mr. P. H.(Oxford Univ.), b Sept 11, 1918, d March 18, 1943

Blaikie, Mr. K. G. (Oxford Univ. and Somerset), b May 8, 1897

Blair, Brig.-Gen. E. M. (Kent), b July 26, 1866, d May 16, 1939

Blake, Mr. D. E. (Hampshire), b April 27, 1925

Blake, Capt. J. P. (Camb. Univ. and Hampshire), b Nov 17, 1917, d June 3, 1944

Blake, Rev. P. D. S. (Oxford Univ. and Sussex), b May 23, 1927

Blaker, Mr. R. N. R. (Camb. Univ. and Kent), b Oct 24, 1879, d Sept 11, 1950

Blanckenberg, Mr. J. M. (South Africa), b Dec 31, 1893

Bland, Cyril H. G. (Lincolnshire and Sussex), b May 23, 1872, d July 1, 1950

Bland, Mr. R. D. F. (Nottinghamshire), b May 16, 1911

Blaxland, Mr. L. B. (Derbyshire), b March 25, 1898

Bligh, Mr. A. S. (Somerset), b Oct 6, 1888, d Dec 27, 1952

Bligh, Hon. and Rev. E. V. (Oxford Univ. and Kent), b Feb 28, 1829, d April 22, 1908

Bligh, Hon. and Rev. Henry (Kent), b June 10, 1834, d March 4, 1905

Bligh, Hon. Ivo, see Darnley, 8th Earl

Bligh, Mr. L. E. (Kent), b Nov 24, 1854, d May 16, 1924

Block Mr. S. A. (Camb. Univ. and Surrey), b July 15, 1908

Blomley, B. (Lancashire), b Nov. 1885

Bloodworth, B. S. (Gloucestershire), b Dec, 1893

Bloy, Mr. N. C. F. (Oxford University), b Jan 2, 1923

Blundell, Mr. E. D. (Camb. Univ. and New Zealand), b May 29, 1907

Blunden, A. (Kent), b Sept 5, 1906

Blunt, Mr. R. C. (New Zealand). b Nov 3, 1900

Blythe, C. (Kent), b May 30, 1879, d Nov 1917

Boddington, Mr. R. A. (Lancashire), b June 30, 1892

Boden, Rev. C. A. (Leicestershire), b Dec 18, 1890

Bodkin, Mr. P. E. (Camb. Univ. and Hertfordshire), b Sep 15, 1924

Boger, Mr. A. J. (Oxford Univ. and Hertfordshire), b Aug 31, 1871, d June 3, 1940

Bohlen, Mr. F. H. (Philadelphia), b July 31, 1868, d Dec 9, 1942

Bolton, Capt. R. H. D. (Dorset and Hampshire), b Jan 13, 1893

Bolus, F. (Somerset), b Nov 2, 1864

Bond, Mr. G. E. (South Africa), b April 5, 1910

Bond, J. D. (Lancashire), b May 6, 1932

Bonham-Carter, Sir M. (Oxford Univ. and Kent), b Oct 11, 1880

Bonnor, Mr. G. J. (N.S.W. and Victoria), b Feb 22, 1855, d June 27, 1912

Boobbyer, Mr. B. (Oxford Univ.), b Feb. 25, 1928

Booth, A. (Yorkshire), b Nov 3, 1902

Booth, F. S. (Lancashire), b Feb 12, 1907

Booth, R. (Yorkshire and Worcestershire), b Oct 1, 1926

Bosanquet, Mr. B. J. T. (Middlesex and Oxford Univ.), b Oct 13, 1877, d Oct 12, 1936

Boshier, B. (Leicestershire), b March 6, 1932

Boswell, C. S. R. (Essex and Norfolk), b Jan 19, 1911

Bouch, Mr. H. E. (Kent), b April 15, 1868, dead

Boucher, Mr. J. C. (Ireland), b Dec 22, 1910

Boughton, Mr. W. A. (Gloucestershire), b Dec 23, 1854, d Nov 26, 1936

Bowden, J. (Derbyshire), b Oct 8, 1889

Bowell, A. (Hampshire), b April 27, 1881

Bower, W. (Nottinghamshire), b Jan 2, 1895

Bowes, W. E. (Yorkshire), b July 25, 1908

Bowles, J. J. (Worcestershire), b April 3, 1891

Bowley, E. H. (Sussex), b June 7, 1890

Bowley, F. J. (Leicestershire), b Feb 20, 1909

Bowley, F. L. (Worcestershire), b Nov 9, 1875, d May 31, 1943

Bowley, T. (Northamptonshire, Surrey and Dorset), b Feb 28, 1857, d Nov 9, 1939

Bowman, Mr. R. (Oxford Univ. and Lancashire), b Jan 26, 1934

Bowmer, Mr. H. E. (Derbyshire), b July 14, 1891

Boyes, G. S. (Hampshire), b March 31, 1899

Bracey, F. (Derbyshire), b July 20, 1887

Bracher, Mr. F. C. (Gloucestershire), b Oct 25, 1868

Brackley, Visct., 4th Earl of Ellesmere (Eton), b Nov 14, 1872, d Aug 24, 1944

Bradby, Mr. H. C. (Oxford Univ.), b Dec 28, 1868, d June 28, 1947

Braddell, Mr. R. L. L. (Oxford Univ. and Suffolk), b Dec 14, 1888

Bradley, J. (Nottinghamshire), b Oct 3, 1913

Bradley, Mr. W M. (Kent), b Jan 2, 1875, d June 19, 1944

Bradman, Sir D. G. (New South Wales and South Australia), b Aug 27, 1908

Bradshaw, J. C. (Leicestershire), b Jan 25, 1902

Brain, Mr. W. H. (Oxford Univ., Gloucestershire and Glamorgan), b July 21, 1870, d Nov 20, 1934

Brann, Mr. G. (Sussex), b April 23, 1865, d June 14, 1954

Branston, Mr. G. T. (Oxford Univ. and Nottinghamshire), b Sept 3, 1884

Braund, L. C. (Surrey and Somerset), b Oct 18, 1875, d Dec 22, 1955

Bray, Mr. C. (Essex), b April 6, 1898

Bray, Sir E. H. (Camb. Univ. and Middlesex), b April 15, 1874, d Nov 27, 1950

Brazier, A. F. (Surrey and Kent), b Dec 7, 1924

Brearley, Mr. W. (Lancashire and Cheshire), b March 11, 1876, d Jan 30, 1937

Brennan, Mr. D. V. (Yorkshire), b Feb 10, 1920

Brice, G. (Northamptonshire), b May 4, 1924

Brice, Mr. W. S. (New Zealand), b Nov 14, 1880

Bridgeman, 1st Visct. (Camb. Univ. and Staffordshire: President, M.C.C., 1931), b Dec 31, 1864, d Aug 14, 1935

Bridger, Rev. J. R. (Hampshire), b April 8, 1920

Bridges, Mr. J. J. (Somerset), b June 28, 1887

Bridgman, Mr. H. (South Australia), b Feb 1, 1890, d Dec 3, 1953

Brierley, T. L. (Glamorgan and Lancashire), b June 15, 1910

Briggs, John (Lancashire), b Oct 3, 1862, d Jan 11, 1902

Briggs, Canon R. (Oxford Univ.), b Dec 30, 1853, d Aug 21, 1936

Brinton, Mr. R. S. (Worcestershire), b Dec 15, 1869, d Feb 23, 1942

Briscoe, Mr. A. W. (South Africa), b Feb 6, 1911, d April 21, 1941

Bristowe, Mr. O. C. (Oxford Univ. and Essex), b April 12, 1895, d Dec 27, 1938

Broadbent, R. (Worcestershire), b June 21, 1924

Brocklebank, Mr. J. M. (Camb. Univ. and Lancashire), b Sept 3, 1915

Brocklehurst, Mr. B. G. (Somerset), b Feb 18, 1922

Brockwell, W. (Surrey), b Jan 21, 1866, d July 1, 1935

Broderick, V. (Northamptonshire), b Aug 17, 1920

Brodhurst, Mr. A. H. (Camb. Univ. and Gloucestershire), b July 21, 1916

Bromley, Mr. E. H. (Victoria), b Sept 2, 1912

Bromley, P. H. (Warwickshire), b July 30, 1930

Bromley-Davenport, Mr. H. R. (Camb. Univ., Cheshire and Middlesex), b Aug 18, 1870, d May 23, 1954

Bromley-Martin, Mr. E. G. (Worcestershire), b Oct 2, 1866, d Jan 23, 1946

Bromley-Martin, Mr. G. E. (Oxford Univ. and Worcestershire), b Oct 18, 1875, d May 31, 1941

Brook, G. W. (Worcestershire), b Aug 30, 1895

Brooke, Lt.-Col. F. R. R. (Lancashire), b Oct 2, 1884

Brooke, Mr. R. H. J. (Oxford Univ. and Bucks), b June 6, 1909

Brookes, D. (Northamptonshire), b Oct 29, 1915

Brookes, Mr. W. H. (Editor of *Wisden* 1936 to 1939), b Dec 5, 1894, d May 28, 1955

Brooke-Taylor, Mr. G. P. (Camb. Univ. and Derbyshire), b Oct 25, 1895

Brooks, E. W. J. (Surrey), b July 6, 1898

Brooks, Lt.-Gen. R. A. D. (Hampshire), b Aug 22, 1896

Broughton, Mr. E. A. (Leicestershire), b April 22, 1905

Brown, A. S. (Gloucestershire), b June 24, 1936

Brown, E. (Warwickshire), b Nov 27, 1911

Brown, Mr. F. R. (Camb. Univ., Surrey and Northamptonshire), b Lima, Dec 16, 1910.

Brown, G. (Hampshire), b Oct 6, 1887

Brown, Mr. G. R. R. (Essex), b Dec 8, 1905

Brown, J. T. (Yorkshire), b Aug 20, 1869, d Nov 4, 1904

Brown, J. T. (Yorkshire), b Nov 24, 1874, d April 12, 1950

Brown, L. (Leicestershire), b March 12, 1874, d Oct 14, 1951

Brown, Mr. L. S. (South Africa), b Nov 24, 1910

Brown, S. M. (Middlesex), b Dec 8, 1917

Brown, W. (Leicestershire), b April 11, 1888

Brown, Mr. W. A. (New South Wales and Queensland), b July 31, 1912

Brown, Mr. W. C. (Northamptonshire), b Nov 13, 1900

Brown, Mr. W. S. A. (Gloucestershire), b May 23, 1877, d Sept 12, 1952

Browne, Mr. C. R. (West Indies), b Oct 8, 1890

Browne, Rev. F. B. R. (Camb. Univ. and Sussex), b July 28, 1899

Browne, Mr. F. D. (Kent), b March 4, 1873, d Aug 12, 1946

Brownlee, Mr. L. D. (Oxford Univ., Gloucestershire and Somerset), b Dec 17, 1882, d Sept 22, 1955

Bruce, Hon. C. N. (3rd Lord Aberdare), (Oxford Univ. and Middlesex), b Aug 2, 1885, d Oct 4, 1957

Brunton, Rev. J. du V. (Camb. Univ.), b July 23, 1869

Brutton, Mr. C. P. (Hampshire and Denbighshire), b Jan 20, 1899

Bryan, Capt. G. J. (Kent), b Dec 29, 1902

Bryan, Mr J. L. (Camb. Univ. and Kent), b May 26, 1896

Bryan, Mr. R. T. (Rugby and Kent), b July 30, 1898

Bryant, Mr. H. W. (Middlesex), b June 30, 1867

Buccleuch, 7th Duke of (President, M.C.C., 1913, as Earl of Dalkeith), b May 30, 1864

Buchanan, Mr. J. N. (Camb. Univ. and Buckinghamshire), b in South Africa, May 30, 1887

Buckenham, C. P. (Essex), b Jan 16, 1876, d Feb 23, 1937

Buckingham, J. (Warwickshire), b Jan 21, 1904

Buckston, Mr. G. M. (Camb. Univ. and Derbyshire), b March 12, 1881, d Nov 24, 1942

Buckston, Mr. R. H. R. (Derbyshire), b Oct 10, 1908

Budd, W. L. (Hampshire), b Oct 25, 1913

Bull, Mr. A. H. (Northamptonshire), b Jan 23, 1892

Bull, C. H. (Kent and Worcestershire), b March 29, 1909, d May 28, 1939

Buller, J. S. (Yorkshire and Worcestershire), b Aug 23, 1909

Bulsara, Mr. M. D. (India), b Sept 2, 1877

Bunce, Mr. N. (Somerset), b April 17, 1911

Burchell, T. (Sussex), b April 26, 1876, d Feb, 1950

Burden, M. D. (Hampshire), b Oct 4, 1930

Burge, Mr. P. (Queensland), b May 17, 1932

Burgess, Mr. J. (Leicestershire), b Nov 22, 1880, d 1953

Burke, Mr. C. (New Zealand), b March 27, 1914

Burke, Mr. J. W. (New South Wales), b June 12, 1930

Burn, Mr. K. E. (Tasmania), b Sept 17, 1863, d July 20, 1956

Burn, Mr. R. C. W. (Oxford Univ.), b Oct 29, 1882, d May 8, 1955

Burnett, Mr. A. C. (Camb. Univ.), b Oct 26, 1923

Burns, James (Essex), b June 20, 1865, d Sept 11, 1957

Burnup, Mr. C. J. (Camb. Univ. and Kent), b Nov 21, 1875

Burrough, Mr. H. D. (Somerset), b Feb 6, 1909

Burrows, R. D. (Worcestershire), b June 6, 1872, d Feb 1943

Burton, Mr. D. C. F. (Yorkshire), b Sept 13, 1887

Burton, J. (Derbyshire), b Dec 10, 1874 d Jan 25, 1940

Burton, Mr. R. C. (Yorkshire), b April 11, 1891

Burton, T. (West Indies), b Jan 31, 1878

Burtt, Mr. T. B. (New Zealand), b Jan 22, 1915

Buse, H. T. F. (Somerset), b Aug 5, 1910

Bush, Col. H. S. (Surrey), b Oct 7, 1871, d March 18, 1942

Bush, Mr. J. E. (Oxford Univ.), b Aug 28, 1928

Bush, Mr. R. E. (Gloucestershire), b Oct 11, 1855, d Dec 9, 1939

Bushby, Mr. M. H. (Camb. Univ.), b July 29, 1931

Buswell, J. (Northamptonshire), b July 3, 1911

Buswell, W. A. (Northamptonshire), b Jan 12, 1875, d April 24, 1950

Butler, Mr. E. M. (Camb. Univ. and Middlesex), b Dec 31, 1866, d Feb 11, 1948

Butler, H. J. (Nottinghamshire), b March 12, 1913

Butterworth, Mr. H. R. W. (Camb. Univ., Denbighshire and Lancashire), b Feb 4, 1909

Buxton, J. H. (Nottinghamshire), b Nov 20, 1914

Buxton, Mr. R. V. (Oxford Univ. and Middlesex), b April 29, 1883, d Oct 1, 1953

Byrne, Mr. J. F. (Warwickshire), b June 19, 1871, d May 10, 1954

Cadman, S. (Derbyshire), b Jan 29, 1880, d May 6, 1952

Cahn, Sir Julien, 1st Bart. (Nottinghamshire C.C.C.), b Oct 21, 1882, d Sept 26, 1944

Caine, Mr. C. Stewart (Editor of *Wisden* 1926 to 1933), b Oct 28, 1861, d April 15, 1933

Calthorpe, Hon. F. S. G. (Camb. Univ., Sussex and Warwickshire), b May 27, 1892, d Nov 19, 1935

Cameron, Mr. H. B. (South Africa), b July 5, 1905, d Nov 2, 1935

Cameron, Mr. J. H. (Camb. Univ., Somerset and West Indies), b April 8, 1914

Cameron, Dr. J. J. (West Indies), b May, 1882

Campbell, Mr. I. P. (Oxford Univ. and Kent), b Feb 5, 1928

Campbell, Mr. I. P. F. (Oxford Univ. and Surrey), b Nov 25, 1890

Campbell, Mr. P. (Essex), b Dec 26, 1887

Cangley, Mr. B. G. (Camb. Univ. and Cambridgeshire), b Sept 12, 1922

Cannings, V. H. D. (Warwickshire and Hampshire), b April 3, 1920

Cardus, Mr. Neville (Cricket Writer), b April 2, 1890

Carey, P. A. D. (Sussex), b May 21, 1920

Carkeek, Mr. W. (Victoria), b Oct 17, 1878, d Feb 21, 1937

Carlin, J. (Nottinghamshire), b Nov 3, 1861

Carlisle, Mr. K. M. (Oxford Univ.), b Aug 7, 1882

Carpenter, D. (Gloucestershire), b Sept 12, 1935

Carr, Mr. A. W. (Nottinghamshire), b May 18, 1893

Carr, Mr. D. B. (Oxford Univ. and Derbyshire), b Dec 28, 1926

Carr, Mr. D. W. (Kent), b March 17, 1872, d March 23, 1950

Carrington, E. (Derbyshire), b March 25, 1914

Carris Mr. B. D. (Camb. Univ. and Middlesex), b Oct 23, 1917

Carris, Mr. H. E. (Camb. Univ. and Middlesex), b July 7, 1909

Carrol, Mr. E. V. (Victoria), b Jan 16, 1885

Carson, Mr. W. N. (New Zealand), b July 16, 1916, d Oct 1944

Carter, Mr. C. P. (South Africa and Cornwall), b April 23, 1881, d Nov 8, 1952

Carter, Mr. H. (New South Wales), b in Yorkshire, March 15, 1878, d June 8, 1948

Carter, R. (Derbyshire), b Nov 7, 1933

Carter, R. G. (Warwickshire), b April 14, 1933

Cartwright, Mr. Philip (Sussex) b at Gibraltar, Sept 26, 1880, d Nov 21, 1955

Cartwright, T. W. (Warwickshire), b July 22, 1935

Carty, R. A. (Hampshire), b July 28, 1922

Case, Mr. C. C. (Somerset), b Sept 7, 1895

Case, Mr. T. B. (Oxford Univ. and Oxfordshire), b Feb 19, 1871, d Nov 10, 1941

Castle, Mr. F. (Somerset), b April 9, 1909

Castledine, S. W. T. (Nottinghamshire), b April 10, 1912

Catterall, Mr. R. H. (South Africa), b July 10, 1900

Cave, Mr. H. B. (New Zealand), b Oct 10, 1922

Cave, W. (Hampshire), b Aug 4, 1867

Cawston, Mr. E. (Camb. Univ., Sussex and Berkshire), b Jan 16, 1911

Chalk, Mr. F. G. H. (Oxford Univ. and Kent), b Sept 7, 1910, d Feb 1943

Challen, Mr. J. B. (Somerset), b March 26, 1863, d June 5, 1937

Challenor, Mr. G. (West Indies), b June 28, 1888, d July 30, 1947

Chamberlain, Mr. L. W. (South Australia), b Jan 15, 1889

Chandler, Mr. A. (Surrey), b Dec 5, 1849, d Dec 25, 1926

Chaplin, Mr. H. P. (Sussex), b March 1, 1883

Chapman, Mr. A. P. F. (Camb. Univ., Berkshire and Kent), b Sept 3, 1900

Chapman, Mr. J. (Derbyshire), b March 11, 1877, d Aug 12, 1956

Chapman, T. A. (Leicestershire), b May 14, 1919

Charlesworth, C. (Warwickshire), b Feb 12, 1877, d June 15, 1953

Charlton, Mr. P. C. (New South Wales), b April 9, 1867, d Sept 30, 1954

Cheetham, Mr. A. G. (Australia), b Dec 7, 1915

Cheetham, Mr. J. E. (South Africa), b May 26, 1920

Chester F. (Worcestershire. Umpire), b Jan 20, 1896, d April 8, 1957

Chesterfield, 10th Earl of (President, M.C.C., 1909), b March 15, 1854, d Jan 24, 1933

Chesterton, Mr. G. H. (Oxford Univ. and Worcestershire), b July 15, 1922

Chidgey, H. (Somerset), b July 25, 1879, d Nov 30, 1941

Chignell, Mr. T. A. (Hampshire), b Oct 31, 1880

Childs-Clarke, Mr. A. W. (Middlesex and Northamptonshire), b May 13, 1905

Chipperfield, Mr. A. G. (New South Wales), b Nov 17, 1905

Chowdhury, Mr. N. R. (India), b 1923

Christiani, Mr. C. M. (West Indies), b Oct 28, 1913, d April 4, 1938

Christiani, Mr. R. J. (West Indies), b July 19, 1920

Christopherson, Mr. J. C. (Camb. Univ. and Kent), b June 1, 1909

Christopherson, Mr. P. (Kent and Berkshire), b March 31, 1866, d May 4, 1921

Christopherson, Mr. Stanley (Kent, President M.C.C. 1939–46), b Nov 11, 1861, d April 6, 1949

Christy, Mr. J. A. J. (South Africa and Queensland), b Dec 12, 1904

Chubb, Mr. G. W. A. (South Africa), b April 12, 1911

Clapp, A. E. (Somerset), b May 3, 1867

Clark, Mr. D. G. (Kent), b Jan 27, 1919

Clark, E. W. (Northamptonshire), b Aug. 9, 1902

Clark, Mr. L. S. (Essex), b March 6, 1914

Clark, T. H. (Surrey), b Oct 5, 1924

Clarke, Lt.-Col. B. F. (Gloucestershire and Leicestershire), b Sept 26, 1885, d May, 1940

Clarke, Dr. C. B. (West Indies and Northamptonshire), b April 7, 1918

Clarke, Mr. C. C. (Derbyshire, Staffordshire and Sussex), b Dec 22, 1910

Clarke, R. W. (Northamptonshire), b April 22, 1924

Clarke, W. (Nottinghamshire), b March 17, 1850, d May 29, 1935

Clay, Mr. J. C. (Glamorgan), b March 18, 1898

Clay, J. D. (Nottinghamshire), b Oct 15, 1924

Clift, P. (Glamorgan), b Sept 3, 1919

Clode, H. (Surrey and Durham), b Sept 7, 1878

Close, D. B. (Yorkshire), b Feb. 24, 1931

Clube, Mr. S. V. M. (Oxford Univ.), b Oct 22, 1931

Clugston, D. L. (Warwickshire), b Feb 5, 1908

Cobb, Mr. Humphry H. (Middlesex), b July 12, 1876, d Dec 13, 1949

Cobbold, Mr. P. W. (Camb. Univ., and Suffolk), b Jan 5, 1875, d Dec 28, 1945

Cobbold, Mr. R. H. (Camb. Univ.), b May 22, 1906

Cobbold, Mr. W. N. (Kent), b Feb 4, 1863, d April 8, 1922

Cobcroft, Mr. L. T. (New South Wales and New Zealand), b Feb 12, 1869, d March 9, 1938

Cobden, Mr. F. C. (Camb. Univ.), b Oct 14, 1849, d Dec 7, 1932

Cobham, 8th Visct. (5th Baron Lyttelton) (Camb. Univ., President, M.C.C., 1886), b Oct 27, 1842, d June 9, 1922

Cobham, 9th Visct. (Hon. J. C. Lyttelton), (Worcestershire; President, M.C.C., 1935), b Oct 23, 1881, d July 31, 1949

Cobham, 10th Visct. (Hon. C. J. Lyttelton) (Worcestershire), b Aug 8, 1909

Cobley, A. (Leicestershire), b Oct 5, 1875

Cochrane, Mr. A. H. J. (Oxford Univ. and Derbyshire), b Jan 26, 1865, d Dec 14, 1948

Cochrane, Mr. R. S. T. (Sec., Derbyshire C.C.C. 1907–8), b Aug 27, 1877

Cock, Mr. D. F. (Essex), b Oct 22, 1914

Cockett, Mr. J. A. (Camb. Univ.), b Dec 23, 1927

Coe, F. (Northamptonshire), b May 26, 1867

Coe, S. (Leicestershire), b June 3, 1873, d Nov 4, 1955

Coen, Mr. S. K. (South Africa), b Oct 14, 1902

Colah, S. H. M. (India), b Sept 22 1902, d Sept 11, 1950

Coldwell, L. (Worcestershire), b Jan 10, 1933

Cole, C. G. (Kent), b July 7, 1916

Cole, Mr. F. L. (Gloucestershire), b Oct 4, 1856, d July 1, 1941

Cole, Mr. T. G. O. (Derbyshire, Lancashire, Somerset and Denbighshire), b Nov 14, 1877, d Dec 15, 1944

Colebrooke, Rev. E. L. (Oxford Univ.), b Oct 29, 1858, d Aug 10, 1939

Coleman, C. A. (Leicestershire), b July 7, 1906

Collett, Mr. G. F. (Gloucestershire), b July 18, 1879 d Feb 26, 1945

Collin, T. (Warwickshire and Durham), b April 17, 1911

Collins, Mr. A. (Sussex), b 1872, d July 1945

Collins, Mr. D. C. (Camb. Univ.), b Oct 1, 1887

Collins, G. (Kent), b Sept 21, 1889, d Jan 23, 1949

Collins, Mr. G. A. K. (Sussex), b May 16, 1909

Collins, Mr. H. L. (New South Wales), b Jan 21, 1889

Collins, Brig.-Gen. L. P. (Oxford Univ., Berkshire and India). b Nov 27, 1878, d Sept 27, 1957

Collins, R. (Lancashire), b March 10, 1934

Collishaw, W. F. (Warwickshire), b Oct 2, 1860, d Feb 1, 1936

Colman, Sir Jeremiah, 1st Bt. (President, Surrey C.C.C., 1916 to 1923), b April 24, 1859, d Jan 15, 1942

Colman, Mr. S. (Surrey), b Jan 6, 1862, d Feb 27, 1942

Colson, G. H. (Northamptonshire), b Jan 21, 1868

Comber, Mr. J. T. H. (Camb. Univ.), b Feb 26, 1911

Compton, D. C. S. (Middlesex), b May 23, 1918

Compton, L. H. (Middlesex), b Sept 12, 1912

Coningham, Mr. A. (Queensland and New South Wales), b July 14, 1866, d June 13, 1939

Conradi, Mr. E. R. (Camb. Univ.), b July 25, 1920

Considine, Mr. S. G. U. (Somerset), b Aug 11, 1901, d Aug 31, 1950

Constable, B. (Surrey), b Feb 19, 1921

Constantine, L. N. (West Indies), b Sept 21, 1902

Constantine, Mr. L. S. (Trinidad), b May 25, 1874, d Jan 5, 1942

Conway, A. J. (Worcestershire), b April 1, 1886, d Nov 1, 1954

Coode, Mr. A. T. (Camb. Univ. and Middlesex), b Feb 5, 1876, d Dec 28, 1940

Cook, C. (Gloucestershire), b Aug 8, 1921

Cook, Mr. G. W. (Camb. Univ. and Kent), b Feb 9, 1936

Cook, L. (Lancashire), b March 28, 1885, d Dec 2, 1933

Cook, T. E. (Sussex), b Feb 5, 1901, d Jan 15, 1950

Cook, W. (Lancashire), b Jan 16, 1882, d Dec 18, 1947

Cook, Mr. W. T. (Surrey), b Dec 6, 1891

Cooke, R. (Warwickshire), b May 25, 1900

Coope, M. (Somerset), b Nov 28, 1917

Cooper, E. (Worcestershire), b Nov 30, 1915

Cooper, F. (Worcestershire), b April 18, 1921

Cooper, H. (Derbyshire), b Dec 23, 1883

Cooper, Mr. W. H. (Victoria), b Sept 11, 1849, d April 5, 1939

Copley, S. H. (Nottinghamshire), b Nov 1, 1906

Copson, W. H. (Derbyshire), b April 27, 1909

Corbett, Mr. L. J. (Gloucestershire), b May 12, 1897

Cording, Mr. G. E. (Glamorgan), b Jan 1, 1878, d Feb 2, 1946

Cornford, J. H. (Sussex), b Dec 9, 1911

Cornford, W. (Sussex), b Dec 25, 1900

Cornwallis, Capt. Hon. W. S., 2nd Lord Cornwallis (Kent), b March 14, 1892

Corrall, P. (Leicestershire), b July 16, 1906

Cotter, Mr. A. (New South Wales), b Dec 3, 1883, d Oct 20, 1917

Coulson, S. S. (Leicestershire), b Oct 17, 1898

Coupe, E. (Derbyshire), b June 9, 1863

Court, R. C. (Hampshire), b Oct 23, 1916

Cousens, P. (Essex), b May 15, 1932

Coutts, Mr. I. D. F. (Oxford Univ.), b April 27, 1928

Coventry, Hon. J. B. (Worcestershire), b Jan 9, 1903

Coverdale, W. W. (Northamptonshire), b May 30, 1912

Cowan, Capt. C. F. R. (Warwickshire), b Sept, 1883

Cowan, M. J. (Yorkshire), b June 10, 1933

Cowdrey, Mr. M. C. (Kent and Oxford Univ.), b Dec 24, 1932

Cowie, Mr. J. (New Zealand) b March 30, 1912

Cox, A. L. (Northamptonshire), b July 22, 1908

Cox, G., jun. (Sussex), b Aug 23, 1911

Cox, Mr. G. C. (Worcestershire), b July 5, 1908

Cox, G. R. (Sussex), b Nov 29, 1873, d March 24, 1949

Cox, Mr. H. R. (Nottinghamshire), b May 19, 1911

Cox, Mr. J. L. (South Africa), b June 28, 1886

Cox, M. (Northamptonshire), b May 10, 1881

Coxon, A. (Yorkshire), b Jan 18, 1917

Coxon, Mr. A. J. (Oxford Univ.), b March 18, 1930

Crabtree, Mr. H. P. (Essex), b April 30, 1906

Craig, Mr. I. D. (New South Wales), b June 12, 1935

Cranfield, L. M. (Gloucestershire), b Aug 29, 1910

Crankshaw, Major Sir E. N. S. (Gloucestershire), b July 1, 1885

Cranmer, Mr. P. (Warwickshire), b Sept 10, 1914

Cranston, Mr. K. (Lancashire), b Oct 20, 1917

Crapp, J. F. (Gloucestershire), b Oct 14, 1912

Crawford, Mr. J. N. (Surrey and South Australia), b Dec 1, 1886

Crawford, Mr. P. (New South Wales), b Aug 3, 1933

Crawford, Mr. R. T. (Leicestershire), b June 11, 1882, d Nov 15, 1945

Crawford, Mr. V. F. S. (Surrey and Leicestershire), b April 11, 1879, d Aug 21, 1922

Crawfurd, Mr. J. W. F. (Oxford Univ., Surrey and Ireland), b Nov 14, 1878, d June 22, 1939

Crawley, Mr. A. M. (Oxford Univ. and Kent), b April 10, 1908

Crawley, Mr. L. G. (Camb. Univ., Durham, Worcestershire and Essex), b July 26, 1903

Cray, S. J. (Essex), b May 29, 1921

Creber, H. (Glamorgan), b April 30, 1874, d March 27, 1939

Creese, W. L. (Hampshire), b Dec 28, 1907

Cresswell, Mr. G. F. (New Zealand), b March 22, 1915

Crisp, Mr. R. J. (South Africa and Worcestershire), b May 28, 1911

Critchley-Salmonson, Mr. H. S. (Somerset), b Jan 19, 1894

Crockford, Mr. E. B. (Warwickshire), b Oct 13, 1888

Croft, Mr. P. D. (Camb. Univ.), b July 7, 1933

Cromb, Mr. I. B. (New Zealand), b June 25, 1905

Cromer, 2nd Earl of (President, M.C.C., 1934), b Nov 29, 1877

Crookes, Mr. D. V. (Camb. Univ.), b June 18, 1931

Croom, A. J. (Warwickshire), b May 23, 1897, d Aug 16, 1947

Cropper, M. (Derbyshire), b July 16, 1864

Crosse, Mr. E. M. (Northamptonshire), b Dec 11, 1882

Crossland, Mr. A. P. (Yorkshire), b Dec 10, 1863

Crow, John (Kent Scorer 1874–96), b July 19, 1847, d Jan 22, 1939

Crowe, Mr. G. L. (Worcestershire), b Jan 8, 1885

Crush, Mr. E. (Kent), b April 25, 1917

Crutchley, Mr. G. E. V. (Oxford Univ. and Middlesex), b Nov 19, 1890

Cuff, Mr. L. A. (New Zealand and Tasmania), b March 28, 1866, d Oct 9, 1954

Cullen, L. (Northamptonshire), b Nov 23, 1914

Cumberlege, Mr. B. S. (Camb. Univ., Northumberland and Kent), b June 5, 1891

Cumming, Mr. D. L. (Sussex), b July 11, 1916

Cunningham, Mr. W. (New Zealand), b Jan 23, 1900

Curgenven, Mr. H. G. (Derbyshire), b Dec 22, 1875

Curnow, Mr. S. H. (South Africa), b Dec. 16, 1907

Currie, Mr. C. E. (Hampshire), b April 4, 1861, d Jan 2, 1937

Curtis, J. S. (Leicestershire), b Dec 21, 1887

Curzon, Viscount (Eton). See Howe, 4th Earl

Cuthbertson, Mr. G. B. (Middlesex and Northamptonshire), b March 28, 1901

Cutmore, J. A. (Essex), b Dec 28, 1900

Da Costa, Mr. O. C. (West Indies), b Sept 11, 1907, d Oct 1, 1936

Dacre, C. C. (New Zealand and Gloucestershire), b May 21, 1900

Daer, Mr. A. G. (Essex), b Nov 20, 1906

Daer, H. (Essex), b Dec 10, 1918

Daffen, Mr. A. (Kent and Berkshire), b Dec 30, 1862

Daft, H. B. (Nottinghamshire), b April 5, 1866, d Jan 12, 1945

Daily, C. (Surrey), b April 28, 1900

Dales, Mr. H. L. (Middlesex), b May 18, 1888

Daley, J. V. (Norfolk, Surrey and Suffolk), b Feb 1, 1907

Dalkeith, Earl of (President, M.C.C., 1913), *see* Buccleuch, 7th Duke of

Dalmeny, Lord (6th Earl of Rosebery), (Bucks, Middlesex and Surrey), b Jan 8, 1882

Dalton, Mr. E. L. (South Africa), b Dec 2, 1906

Daniell, Mr. J. (Camb. Univ. and Somerset), b Dec 12, 1878

Dare, R. (Hampshire), b Nov 26, 1921

Darling, Mr. J. (South Australia), b Nov 21, 1870, d Jan 2, 1946

Darling, Mr. L. S. (Victoria), b Aug 14, 1909

Darnley, 8th Earl of (Hon. Ivo Bligh), (Camb. Univ., Kent, and President, M.C.C., 1900), b March 13, 1859, d April 10, 1927

Dartmouth, 6th Earl of (President, M.C.C., 1893), b May 6, 1851, d March 11, 1936

Dartmouth, 7th Earl of (President, M.C.C., 1932), b Feb 22, 1881

Darwall-Smith, Mr. R. F. H. (Oxford Univ. and Sussex), b July 11, 1914

Datta, Mr. P. B. (Camb. Univ.), b 1925

David, Mr. R. F. A. (Glamorgan), b June 19, 1907

Davidson, Mr. A. K. (New South Wales), b June 14, 1929

Davidson, Mr. K. R. (Yorkshire), b Dec 24, 1905, d Dec 25, 1954

Davidson, Mr. W. W. (Oxford Univ. and Sussex), b March 20, 1920

Davies, Dai (Glamorgan), b Aug 26, 1896

Davies, D. A. (Glamorgan), b July 11, 1915

Davies, Emrys (Glamorgan), b June 27, 1904

Davies, Mr. E. Q. (South Africa), b Aug 26, 1909

Davies, Mr. G. A. (Manager Australia in England, 1953), b March 19, 1895, d Nov 27, 1957

Davies, H. D. (Glamorgan), b July 23, 1932

Davies, H. G. (Glamorgan), b April 23, 1913

Davies, Mr. J. G. W. (Camb. Univ. and Kent), b Sept 10, 1911

Davies, W. (Glamorgan), b July 3, 1936

Davis, E. (Northamptonshire), b March 8, 1922

Davis, P. (Northamptonshire), b May 24, 1916

Davis, P. (Kent), b April 4, 1922

Davis, Mr. R. A. (Tasmania), b Oct 22, 1892

Davis, W. E. (Surrey), b Nov 26, 1880

Dawkes, G. (Leicestershire and Derbyshire), b July 19, 1920

Dawson, Mr. E. W. (Camb. Univ. and Leicestershire), b Feb 13, 1904

Dawson, G. (Hampshire), b Dec 9, 1916

Dawson, Mr. O. C. (South Africa), b Sept 1, 1919

Day, Mr. A. P. (Kent), b April 10, 1885

Day, Mr. H. L. V. (Bedfordshire and Hampshire), b Aug 12, 1898

Day, J. W. (Nottinghamshire and Lincolnshire), b Sept 16, 1882

Day, Mr. S. H. (Camb. Univ. and Kent), b Dec 29, 1878, d Feb 20, 1950

Dean, H. (Lancashire and Cheshire). b Aug 13, 1885, d March 12, 1957

Dean, T. A. (Hampshire), b Nov 21, 1920

Deane, Mr. H. G. (South Africa), b July 21, 1895, d Oct 21, 1939

de Caires, Mr. C. (Joint Manager with T. Pierce West Indies in England 1957), b Nov 25, 1917

De Caires, Mr. F. I. (West Indies), b May 12, 1909

de Courcy, Mr. J. H. (New South Wales), b April 18, 1927

Deed, Mr. J. A. (Kent), b Sept 12, 1901

Deighton, Major J. H. G. (Lancashire), b April 5, 1920

Delisle, Mr. G. P. S. (Middlesex and Oxford Univ.), b Dec 25, 1934

de Lisle, Mr. J. A. (Leicestershire), b Sept 27, 1891

Delme-Radcliffe, Mr. A. H. (Hampshire and Berkshire), b Nov 23, 1870, d June 30. 1950

Dempster, Mr. C. S. (New Zealand, Scotland, Leicestershire and Warwickshire), b Nov 15, 1903

Dench, C. E. (Nottinghamshire), b Sept 6, 1873

Dennett, George (Gloucestershire), b April 27, 1880, d Sept 14, 1937

Dennis, F. (Yorkshire and Cheshire), b June 11, 1907

Dennis, Mr. J. N (Essex), b Jan 4, 1913

Denton, David (Yorkshire), b July 4, 1874, d Feb 17, 1950

Denton, J. (Yorkshire), b Feb 3, 1865, d July 19, 1946

Denton, Mr. J. S. (Northamptonshire), b Nov 2, 1890

Denton, Mr. W. H. (Northamptonshire), b Nov 2, 1890

De Saram, Mr. F. C. (Oxford Univ. and Hertfordshire), b Sept, 1912

Desborough, 1st Lord (President, M.C.C., 1911), b Oct 30, 1855, d Jan 9, 1945 de Trafford, The Hon. C. E. (Lancashire and Leicestershire), b May 21, 1864, d Nov 12, 1951

Devereux, L. N. (Worcestershire and Glamorgan), b October 20, 1931

Devey, John (Warwickshire), b Dec 26, 1866, d Oct 13, 1940

Devonshire, 9th Duke of (President, M.C.C., 1912), b May 31, 1868, d May 6, 1938

Dewdney, Mr. T. (West Indies), b Oct 23, 1933

Dewes, Mr. J. G. (Camb. Univ. and Middlesex), b Oct 11, 1926

De Winton, Mr. S. (Gloucestershire), b Sept 5, 1869

Dews, G. (Worcestershire), b June 5, 1921

Dexter, Mr. E. R. (Camb. Univ. and Sussex), b May 15, 1935

Deyes, G. (Yorkshire and Staffordshire), b Feb 11, 1879

de Zoete, Mr. H. W. (Camb. Univ. and Essex), b Feb 14, 1877, d March 1957

Dickinson, Mr. D. C. (Camb. Univ.), b Dec 11, 1929

Dickinson, Mr. P. J. (Camb. Univ. and Surrey), b Aug 18, 1919

Dickson, Mr. M. R. (Scotland), b Jan 2, 1882, d Jan 10, 1940

Difford, Mr. I. D. (Transvaal, Sec., S. African Cricket Assn., 1903–14), b Jan 29, 1873, d Feb 5, 1949

Dillon, Mr. E. W. (Oxford Univ. and Kent), b Feb 15, 1881, d April 25, 1941

Diment, Mr. R. A. (Gloucestershire and Leicestershire), b Feb 9, 1927

Dines, W. J. (Essex), b Sept 14, 1916

Dipper, A. E. (Gloucestershire), b Nov 9, 1887, d Nov 9, 1945

Divecha, R. V. (Oxford Univ. and India), b Oct 18, 1927

Dixon, A. L. (Kent), b Nov 27, 1933

Dixon, Mr. E. J. H. (Oxford Univ. and Northamptonshire), b Sept 22, 1915, d April 20, 1941

Dixon, Mr. J. A. (Nottinghamshire), b May 27, 1861, d June 8, 1931

Dixon, Mr. J. G. (Essex), b Sept 3, 1895, d Nov 19, 1954

Docker, Mr. C. T. (Australian Imperial Forces Team), b March 3, 1884

Docker, Mr. L. C. (Derbyshire and Warwickshire, President, Warwickshire C.C.C.), b Nov 26, 1860, d Aug 1, 1940

Dodd, W. T. F. (Hampshire), b March 9, 1908

Dodds, T. C. (Essex), b May 29, 1919

Doggart, Mr. A. G. (Camb. Univ., Durham and Middlesex), b June 2, 1897

Doggart, Mr. G. H. G. (Camb. Univ. and Sussex), b July 18, 1925

Doll, Mr. M. H. C. (Hertfordshire and Middlesex), b April 5, 1888

Dollery, H. E. (Warwickshire), b Oct 14, 1914

Dollery, K. R. (Warwickshire), b Dec 9, 1924

Dolling, Mr. C. E. (South Australia), b Sept 4, 1886, d June 11, 1936

Dolphin, A. (Yorkshire), b Dec 24, 1886, d Oct 24, 1942

Donnan, Mr. H. (New South Wales), b Nov 12, 1864

Donnelly, Mr. M. P. (New Zealand, Oxford Univ., Middlesex and Warwickshire), b Oct 17, 1917

Dooland, B. (South Australia and Nottinghamshire), b Nov 1, 1923

Douglas Col. A. P. (Surrey and Middlesex), b June 7, 1867, d Jan 24, 1953

Douglas, Mr. C. H. (Essex), b June 28, 1866, d Sept, 1954

Douglas, Mr. J. (Camb. Univ. and Middlesex), b Jan 8, 1870

Douglas, Mr. J. W. H. T. (Essex), b Sept 3, 1882, d Dec 19, 1930

Douglas, Rev. R. N. (Camb. Univ., Surrey and Middlesex), b Nov 9, 1868, d Feb 27, 1957

Douglas, S. (Yorkshire), b April 4, 1903

Dovey, R. R. (Kent), b July 18, 1920

Dowding, Mr. A. L. (Oxford Univ.), b April 4, 1929

Dowling, Mr. W. J. (Manager Australia in England, 1956), b Sept 23, 1904

Downes, Mr. K. D. (Camb. Univ.), b June 12, 1917

Dowson, Mr. E. M. (Camb. Univ. and Surrey), b June 21, 1880, d July 22, 1933

Drake, E. J. (Hampshire), b Aug 16, 1912

Druce, Mr. N. F. (Camb. Univ. and Surrey), b Jan 1, 1875, d Oct 27, 1954

Druce, Mr. W. G. (Camb. Univ.), b Sept 16, 1872

Ducat, A. (Surrey), b Feb 16, 1886, d July 23, 1942

Duckfield, R. (Glamorgan), b July 2, 1906

Duckworth, Mr. C. A. R. (South Africa), b March 22, 1933

Duckworth, G. (Lancashire), b May 9, 1901

Duleepsinhji, K. S. (Camb. Univ. and Sussex), b June 13, 1905

Dunglass, Lord (Middlesex), b July 2, 1903

Dunkley, F. (Middlesex), b Sept 9, 1863

Dunkley, M. E. F. (Northamptonshire), b Feb 19, 1914

Dunning, Mr. J. A. (New Zealand), b Feb 6, 1903

Durnell, Mr. T. W. (Warwickshire), b June 17, 1901

Durston, T. J. (Middlesex), b July 11, 1894

Dyer, Mr. D. V. (South Africa), b May 2, 1914

Dyson, A. H. (Glamorgan), b July 10, 1905

Dyson, J. (Lancashire), b July 8, 1934

Dyson, Mr. J. H. (Oxford Univ.), b Sept 26, 1913

Eady, Mr. C. J. (Tasmania), b Oct 29, 1870, d Dec 23, 1945

Eagar, Mr. E. D. R. (Oxford Univ., Gloucestershire and Hampshire), b Dec 8, 1917

Eagar, Mr. M. A. (Oxford Univ., Gloucestershire and Ireland), b March 20, 1934

Eaglestone, J. T. (Middlesex and Glamorgan), b July 24, 1923

Earle, Mr. G. F. (Surrey and Somerset), b Aug 24, 1891

Eastman, G. (Essex), b April 7, 1903

Eastman, L. C. (Essex), b June 3, 1897, d April 17, 1941

Eaton, J. (Sussex), b June 19, 1904

Ebbisham, First Baron (George Rowland Blades) (Surrey Club, captain Lords and Commons), b April 15, 1868, d May 24, 1953

Ebden, Mr. C. H. M. (Camb. Univ., Sussex and Middlesex), b June 29, 1880, d May 24, 1949

Ebeling, Mr. H. I. (Victoria), b Jan 1, 1905

Eckersley, Lt. P. T., R.N.V.R., M.P. (Lancashire), b July 2, 1904, d Aug 13, 1940

Ede, Mr. E. M. C. (Hampshire), b April 24, 1881

Edrich, B. R. (Norfolk, Kent and Glamorgan), b Aug 18, 1922

Edrich, E. H. (Norfolk and Lancashire), b March 27, 1914

Edrich, G. A. (Norfolk and Lancashire), b July 13, 1918

Edrich, Mr. W. J. (Norfolk and Middlesex), b March 26, 1916

Eggar, Mr. J. D. (Oxford Univ. and Derbyshire), b Dec 1, 1916

Eglington, Mr. R. (Surrey), b April 1, 1908

Elam, Mr. F. W. (Yorkshire), b Sept 13, 1871, d March 19, 1943

Elgood, Mr. B. C. (Camb. Univ. and Berkshire), b March 10, 1922

Ellesmere, 4th Earl of (President, M.C.C., 1920) (see Brackley, Lord)

Elliott, C. S. (Derbyshire), b April 24, 1912

Elliott, H. (Derbyshire), b Nov 2, 1895

Ellis, H. (Northamptonshire), b March 13, 1885

Ellis, Mr. J. L. (Victoria), b May 9, 1891

Ellis, W. (Derbyshire), b Aug 28, 1876

Emery, Mr. S. H. (New South Wales), b Oct 16, 1886

Emmett, G. M. (Gloucestershire) b Dec 2, 1912

Endean, Mr. W. R. (South Africa), b May 31, 1924

English, Mr. E. A. (Hampshire), b Jan 1, 1864

Enthoven, Mr. H. J. (Camb. Univ. and Middlesex), b June 4, 1903

Ernle, 1st Lord (see Prothero)

Estcourt, Mr. N. S. D. (Camb. Univ.), b Jan 7, 1929

Etheridge, R. J. (Gloucestershire), b March 25, 1934

Etheridge, Mr. S. G. (Middlesex and Hertfordshire), b Nov 3, 1882, d Sept 3, 1945

Evans, Mr. A. J. (Oxford Univ., Hampshire and Kent), b May 1, 1889

Evans, Col. D. MacN. (Hampshire), b Dec 12, 1886

Evans, Mr. E. N. (Oxford Univ.), b Dec 7, 1911

Evans, Mr. G. (Oxford Univ. and Leicestershire), b Aug 13, 1915

Evans, Mr. J. (Hampshire), b July 14, 1891

Evans, Mr. R. G. (Camb. Univ.), b Aug 20, 1899

Evans, T. G. (Kent), b Aug 18, 1920

Evans, V. J. (Essex), b March 4, 1912

Evans, Mr. W. T. (Queensland), b April 9, 1876

Eve, Mr. S. C. (Essex), b Dec 8, 1925

Everett, Mr. S. C. (New South Wales), b June 17, 1901

Evers, Mr. H. A. (New South Wales and West Australia), b Feb 28, 1876

Evers, Mr. R. D. M. (Worcestershire), b Aug 11, 1913

Evershed, Sir S. H. (Derbyshire), b Jan 13, 1861, d March 7, 1937

Every, T. (Glamorgan), b Dec 19, 1909

Evetts, Mr. W. (Oxford Univ.), b June 30, 1847, d April 7, 1936

Fabian, Mr. A. H. (Camb. Univ.), b March 20, 1909

Fagg, A. E. (Kent), b June 18, 1915

Fairbairn, Mr. A. (Middlesex), b Jan 25, 1923

Fairbairn, Capt. G. A. (Camb. Univ. and Middlesex), b June 26, 1892

Fairfax, Mr. A. G. (New South Wales), b June 16, 1906, d May 17, 1955

Fairservice, C. (Kent and Middlesex), b Aug 21, 1909

Fairservice, W. J. (Kent and Northumberland), b May 16, 1881

Falcon, Mr. M. (Camb. Univ. and Norfolk), b July 21, 1888

Fallows, Mr. J. A. (Lancashire), b July 25, 1907

Fane, Mr. F. L. (Oxford Univ. and Essex), b April 27, 1875

Fantham, W. E. (Warwickshire), b May 14, 1918

Farnes, P/O K. (Camb. Univ. and Essex), b July 8, 1911, d Oct 20, 1941

Farquhar, Mr. J. F. (Queensland), b Jan 1, 1887

Farrimond, W. (Lancashire), b May 23, 1903

Fasken, Mr. D. K. (Oxford Univ.), b March 23, 1932

Faulkner, Mr. G. A. (Transvaal), b Dec 17, 1881, d Sept 10, 1930

Faviell, Lt.-Col. W. F. O. (Essex and India), b June 5, 1882, d Feb 14, 1950

Fazal Mahmood (Pakistan), b Feb 18, 1927

Fellows-Smith, Mr. J. P. (Oxford Univ. and Northants), b Feb. 3, 1932

Felton, Mr. R. (Middlesex), b Dec 27, 1909

Fender, Mr. P. G. H. (Sussex and Surrey), b Aug 22, 1892

Fenley, S. (Surrey and Hampshire), b Jan 4, 1896

Fereday, J. (Worcestershire and Staffordshire), b Nov 24, 1875

Ferguson, Mr. V. (Hampshire), b Jan 10, 1866

Fernandes, Mr. M. P. (West Indies), b Aug 12, 1897

Fernie, Mr. A. E. (Camb. Univ. and Staffordshire), b April 9, 1877

Fida Hussain (Manager Pakistan in England, 1954), b Dec 4, 1908

Fiddian-Green, Mr. C. A. (Camb. Univ., Warwickshire and Worcestershire), b Dec 22, 1898

Fiddling, K. (Yorkshire and Northamptonshire), b Oct 13, 1917

Field, Mr. E. (Middlesex and Camb Univ.), b Dec 18, 1871, d Jan 9, 1947

Field, F. E. (Warwickshire), b Sept 23, 1875, d Aug 25, 1934

Fielder, Arthur (Kent), b July 19, 1878, d Aug 30, 1949

Findlay, Mr. A. P. (Tasmania), b March 17, 1892

Findlay, Mr. W. (Oxford Univ. and Lancashire; Sec. Surrey C.C.C.; Sec., M.C.C., 1926 to 1936), b June 22, 1880, d June 19, 1953

Fingleton, Mr. J. H. (New South Wales), b April 28, 1908

Firth, J. (Yorkshire and Leicestershire), b June 27, 1918

Fisher, H. (Yorkshire), b Aug 2, 1902

Fishlock, L. B. (Surrey), b Jan 2, 1907

Fishwick, Mr. T. S. (Warwickshire), b July 24, 1876, d Feb 21, 1950

Flamson, W. H. (Leicestershire), b Aug 12, 1905, d Jan 9 1945

Flavell, J. (Worcestershire), b May 15, 1929

Fleetwood-Smith, Mr. L. O'B (Victoria), b March 30, 1910

Fletcher, D. G. W. (Surrey), b July 6, 1924

Flint, B. (Nottinghamshire), b Jan 12, 1893

Flint, W. A. (Nottinghamshire), b March 21, 1890, d Feb 5, 1955

Foenander, Mr. S. P. (Colombo), b April 11, 1883

Foley, Lt.-Col. C. P. (Camb. Univ., Worcestershire and Middlesex), b Nov. 1, 1868, d March 9, 1936

Foord, C. W. (Yorkshire), b June 11, 1924

Ford, Mr. A. F. J. (Camb. Univ. and Middlesex), b Sept 12, 1858, d May 20, 1931

Ford, Mr. F. G. J. (Camb. Univ. and Middlesex), b Dec 14, 1866, d Feb 7, 1940

Ford, Mr. F. W. J. (Repton), b Oct 14, 1854, d Sept 11, 1920

Ford, Mr. H. J. (Repton), b Feb 5, 1860, d Nov 19, 1941

Ford, Mr. R. (Gloucestershire), b March 3, 1907

Ford, Very Rev. L. G. B. J. (Repton), b Sept 3, 1865, d March 27, 1932

Ford, Mr. N. M. (Oxford Univ., Derbyshire and Middlesex), b Nov 18, 1906

Ford, Mr. W. A. J. (Repton), b March 20 1861, d Aug 21, 1938

Foreman, D. J. (Sussex), b Feb 1, 1933

Forster, 1st Lord (Oxford Univ. and Hampshire; President, M.C.C., 1919), b Jan 31, 1866, d Jan 15, 1936

Foster, Mr. B. S. (Middlesex and Worcestershire), b Feb 12, 1882

Foster, Mr. D. G. (Warwickshire), b March 19, 1907

Foster, Mr. F. R. (Warwickshire), b Jan 31, 1889

Foster, Mr. G. N. (Oxford Univ., Worcestershire and Kent), b Oct 16, 1884

Foster, Mr. H. K. (Oxford Univ. and Worcestershire), b Oct 30, 1873, d June 23, 1950

Foster, Mr. M. K. (Worcestershire), b Jan 1, 1889, d Dec 3, 1940

Foster, Mr. N. J. A. (Worcestershire), b Sept 28 1890

Foster, Mr. N. K. (Queensland), b Jan 19, 1878

Foster, Mr. P. G. (Kent), b 1916

Foster, Mr. R. E. (Oxford Univ. and Worcestershire), b April 16, 1878, d May 13, 1914

Foster, Major W. L. (Worcestershire), b Dec 2, 1874

Fowke, Major G. H. S. (Leicestershire), b Oct 18, 1880, d June 24, 1946

Fowler, Mr. W. H. (Essex and Somerset), b May 28, 1856, d April 13, 1941

Fox, J. (Warwickshire and Worcestershire), b Sept 7, 1904, d April 13, 1941

Fox, Lt.-Col. R. W. (Oxford Univ. and Sussex), b July 11, 1873, d Aug 21, 1948

Fox, W. V. (Worcestershire), b Jan 8, 1898, d Feb 18, 1949

Foy, F. G. (Kent), b April 11, 1915

Foy, Mr. P. A. (Somerset and Argentine), b Oct 16, 1891, d Feb 12, 1957

Frames, Mr. A. S. (Manager South Africa team in England 1947), b Jan 7, 1891

Francis, Mr. Guy (Gloucestershire), b Aug 16, 1860, d May 1948

Francis, G. N. (West Indies), b Dec 7, 1897, d Jan 1942

Francis, H. H. (Gloucestershire and South Africa), d Jan 7, 1936, aged 65

Francis, Mr. T. E. S. (Camb. Univ. and Somerset), b Nov 21, 1902

Frank, Mr. R. W. (Yorkshire), b May 29, 1864, d Sept 9, 1950

Franklin, Mr. H. W. F. (Oxford Univ., Surrey and Essex), b June 30, 1901

Franklin, Mr. W. B. (Camb. Univ. and Buckinghamshire), b Aug 16, 1891

Fraser, Mr. J. N. (Oxford Univ.), b Aug 6, 1890

Fraser, Mr. T. W. (Camb. Univ.), b June 26, 1912

Freeman, A. P. (Kent), b May 17, 1889

Freeman, E. C. (Essex), b Dec 7, 1860, d Oct 16, 1939

Freeman, E. J. (Essex and Dorset), b Oct 16, 1880

Freeman, J. R. (Essex), b Sept 3, 1883

Freeman-Thomas, Mr. F., 1st Marquess of Willingdon (Camb. Univ. and Sussex), b Sept 12, 1866, d Aug 12, 1941

Fry, Mr. C. B. (Oxford Univ., Surrey, Sussex and Hampshire), b in Surrey, April 25, 1872, d Sept 7, 1956

Fry, Mr. K. R. B. (Camb. Univ. and Sussex), b March 15, 1883, d June 21, 1949

Fry, Mr. Stephen (Hampshire), b May 23, 1900

Fuller, Mr. F. R. H. (South Africa), b Aug 2, 1931

Fullerton, Mr. G. M. (South Africa), b Dec 8, 1922

Fynn, Mr. C. G. (Hampshire), b April 24, 1898

Gaekwad, Mr. D. K. (India), b Oct 27, 1928

Gaekwad, Mr. H. G. (India), b Aug 29, 1928

Gale, Mr. Norman (Cricket Poet), b March 4, 1862, d Oct 7, 1942

Gale, Mr. P. G. (London County), b May 22, 1865, d Sept 7, 1940

Gale, R. A. (Middlesex), b Dec 10, 1933

Gallichan, Mr. N. (New Zealand), b June 3, 1906

Gamble, F. C. (Surrey and Devon), b May 29, 1906

Gange, T. H. (Gloucestershire), b April 15, 1891, d March 19, 1949

Ganteaume, Mr. A. G. (West Indies), b Jan 22, 1921

Gardner, F. C. (Warwickshire), b June 4, 1922

Gardner, L. R. (Leicestershire), b Feb 23, 1934

Garland-Wells, Mr. H. M. (Oxford Univ. and Surrey), b Nov 14, 1907

Garlick, R. G. (Lancashire and Northamptonshire), b April 11, 1917

Garnier, Canon E. S. (Oxford Univ.), b April 5, 1850, d Aug 8, 1938

Garnsey, Mr. G. L. (New South Wales), b Feb 10, 1881, d April 18, 1951

Garrett, Mr. T. W. (New South Wales), b July 26, 1858, d Aug 6, 1943

Garrett, Mr. W. T. (Essex), b Jan 9, 1877, d Feb 17, 1953

Garthwaite, Mr. P. F. (Oxford Univ.), b Oct 22, 1909

Gauld, Dr. G. O. (Nottinghamshire), b June 21, 1873, d June 16, 1950

Gay, Mr. L. H. (Camb. Univ., Hampshire and Somerset), b March 24, 1871, d Nov 1, 1949

Geary, A. C. T. (Surrey), b Sept 11, 1900

Geary, G. (Leicestershire), b July 9, 1893

Gehrs, Mr. D. R. A. (South Australia), b Nov 29, 1880, d June, 1953

Gentry, Mr. J. S. B. (Hampshire, Surrey and Essex), b Oct 4, 1899

Gerrard, Major R. A. (Somerset), b Jan 18, 1912, d Jan 22. 1943

Ghazali, M. E. Z. (Pakistan), b June 15, 1924

Ghulam Ahmed (India), b July 4, 1922

Ghulam Mahomed (India), b July 12, 1898

Gibb, Mr. P. A. (Camb. Univ., Scotland, Yorkshire and Essex), b July 11, 1913

Gibbons, H. H. I. H. (Worcestershire), b Oct 10, 1904

Gibson, Mr. A. L. (Essex), b Sept 4, 1877, d July 29, 1943

Gibson, Mr. C. H. (Camb. Univ., Sussex and Argentine), b Aug 23, 1900

Gibson, Mr. I. M. (Oxford Univ. and Derbyshire), b Aug 15, 1936

Gibson, Mr. K. L. (Essex), b May, 1888

Giffen, Mr. George (South Australia), b March 27, 1859, d Nov 29, 1927

Giffen, Mr. Walter F. (South Australia), b Sept 10, 1863, d June 29, 1949

Gilbert, Mr. H. A. (Monmouthshire, Oxford Univ., Worcestershire and Radnorshire), b June 2, 1886

Gilchrist, Mr. R. (West Indies), b June 28, 1934

Giles, R. J. (Nottinghamshire), b Oct 17, 1919

Gill, G. C. (Somerset & Leicestershire), b April 18, 1876, d Aug 21, 1937

Giller, Mr. J. F. (Victoria), b May 1, 1870, d Jan 13, 1947

Gillespie, Mr. D. W. (Camb. Univ.), b April 26, 1917

Gilliat, Mr. I. A. W. (Oxford Univ.), b Jan 8, 1903

Gilligan, Mr. A. E. R. (Camb. Univ., Surrey and Sussex), b Dec 23, 1894

Gilligan, Mr. A. H. H. (Sussex), b June 29, 1896

Gilligan, Mr. F. W. (Oxford Univ. and Essex), b Sept 20, 1893

Gillingham, Canon F. H. (Essex), b Sept 6, 1875, d April 1, 1953

Gilman, Mr. J. (Camb. Univ., London County, Middlesex and Northumberland), b March 17, 1879

Gimblett, H. (Somerset), b Oct 19, 1914

Gladwin, C. (Derbyshire), b April 3, 1917

Glover, Mr. A. C. S. (Warwickshire), b April 19, 1872, d May 22, 1949

Glover, Mr. E. R. K. (Glamorgan), b July 19, 1911

Goatly, E. G. (Surrey), b Dec 3, 1882

Godambe, S. R. (India), b March 1, 1899

Goddard, Mr. J. D. (West Indies), b April 21, 1919

Goddard, Mr. T. L. (South Africa), b Aug 1, 1931

Goddard, T. W. (Gloucestershire), b Oct 1, 1900

Godfrey, Rev. C. J. M. (Sussex), b Nov 24, 1862, d Sept 28, 1941

Godsell, Mr. R. T. (Camb. Univ. and Gloucestershire), b Jan 9, 1880, d March, 1954

Goldie, Major K. O. (Sussex), b Sept 19, 1882, d Jan 14, 1938

Gomez, Mr. G. E. (West Indies), b Oct 10, 1919

Goodacre, Mr. W. B. (Nottinghamshire), b Feb 26, 1873, d 1950

Gooder, L. (Surrey), b Feb 11, 1876

Goodway, Mr. C. C. (Staffordshire and Warwickshire), b July 10, 1909

Goodwin, Mr. H. S. (Gloucestershire), b Sept 30, 1870, d Nov 13, 1955

Goodwin, J. (Leicestershire), b Jan 22, 1929

Goonesena, Mr. G. (Ceylon, Nottinghamshire and Camb. Univ.), b Feb 16, 1931

Gopalan, M. J. (India), b June 6, 1909

Gopinath, Mr. C. D. (India), b March 1, 1930

Gordon, Sir Home, 12th Bart. (Author of "Cricket Form at a Glance," etc.), b Sept 30, 1871, d Sept 9, 1956

Gordon, Mr. N. (South Africa), b Aug 6, 1911

Gorell-Barnes, Mr. R., 3rd Lord Gorell (Oxford Univ. and Suffolk), b April 16, 1884

Gothard, Mr. E. J. (Derbyshire), b Oct 1, 1904

Gouldsworthy, Mr. W. R. (Gloucestershire), b May 20, 1892

Gover, A. R. (Surrey), b Feb 29, 1908

Gowans, Lt.-Col. J. (Harrow), b April 23, 1872, d April 27, 1936

Graburn, Mr. W. T. (Surrey), b March 14, 1865, d Dec 13, 1944

Grace, Dr. Alfred, b May 17, 1840, d May 24, 1916

Grace, Dr. Alfred H. (Gloucestershire), b March 10, 1866, d Sept 16, 1929

Grace, Mr. C. B. (Clifton), b March 1882, d June 6, 1938

Grace, Dr. E. M. (Gloucestershire), b Nov 28, 1841, d May 20, 1911

Grace, Dr. Edgar M. (M.C.C.), son of E. M. Grace, b Oct 6, 1886

Grace, Mr. G. F. (Gloucestershire), b Dec 13, 1850, d Sept 22, 1880

Grace, Dr. H. M. (Father of W. G., E. M., G. F.), b Feb 21, 1808, d Dec 23, 1871

Grace, Mrs. H. M. (Mother of W. G., E. M., G. F.), b July 18, 1812, d July 25, 1884

Grace, Dr. Henry, b Jan 31, 1833, d Nov 15, 1895

Grace, Dr. W. G. (Gloucestershire), b July 18, 1848, d Oct 23, 1915

Grace, Mr. W. G., jun. (Camb. Univ. and Gloucestershire), b July 6, 1874, d March 2, 1905

Graham, H. C. (Leicestershire), b May 31, 1914

Grant, Mr. G. C. (West Indies and Camb. Univ.), b May 9, 1907

Grant, Mr. R. S. (West Indies and Camb. Univ.), b Dec 15, 1909

Graveney, J. K. (Gloucestershire), b Dec 16, 1924

Graveney, T. W. (Gloucestershire), b June 16, 1927

Gray, Mr. C. D. (Middlesex), b April 26, 1895

Gray, Rev. Horace (Camb. Univ. and Cambridgeshire), b Nov 29, 1874, d Jan 20, 1938

Gray, J. R. (Hampshire), b May 19, 1926

Gray, L. H. (Middlesex), b Dec 16, 1915

Greasley, D. G. (Northamptonshire), b Jan 20, 1926

Green, Mr. D. J. (Derbyshire and Camb. Univ.), b Dec 18, 1935

Green, Col. Leonard (Lancashire), b Feb 1, 1890

Green, Brig. M. A. (Gloucestershire and Essex and Manager M.C.C. Team South Africa, 1948–49, Australia, 1950–51), b Oct 3, 1891

Greenhalgh, E. (Lancashire), b May 18, 1910

Greenhough, T. (Lancashire), b Nov 9, 1931

Greensmith, W. T. (Essex), b Aug 16, 1930

Greenstock, Mr. J. W. (Oxford Univ. and Worcestershire), b May 15, 1905

Greenwood, Mr. F. E. (Yorkshire), b Sept 28, 1905

Greenwood, H. W. (Sussex and Northamptonshire), b Sept 4, 1909

Greenwood, P. (Lancashire), b Sept 11, 1924

Gregory, Mr. G. R. (Derbyshire), b Aug 27, 1878

Gregory, Mr. J. M. (New South Wales), b Aug 14, 1895

Gregory, Sgt.-Obsr. R. G. (Victoria), b Feb 28, 1916, d June 1942

Gregory, R. J. (Surrey), b Aug 26, 1902

Gregory, Mr. S. E. (New South Wales), b April 14, 1870, d Aug 1, 1929

Gregson, W. R. (Lancashire), b Aug 5, 1878

Greig, Rev. J. G., formerly Colonel (Hampshire), b Oct 24, 1871

Gresson, Mr. F. H. (Oxford Univ. and Sussex), b Feb 18, 1868, d Jan 31, 1949

Greswell, Mr. E. A. (Somerset), b June 6, 1885

Greswell, Mr. W. T. (Somerset), b Oct 15, 1889

Gribble, Mr. H. W. R. (Gloucestershire), b Dec 23, 1860, d June 12, 1943

Grierson, Mr. H. (Bedfordshire and Camb. Univ.), b Aug 26, 1891

Grieves, K. (New South Wales and Lancashire), b Aug 27, 1925

Grieveson, Mr. R. E. (South Africa), b Aug 24, 1909

Griffith, Mr. H. C. (West Indies), b Dec 1, 1893

Griffith, Mr. S. C. (Camb. Univ., Surrey and Sussex), b June 16, 1914

Griffiths, Mr. C. (Essex), b Dec 9, 1930

Griffiths, J. V. C. (Gloucestershire), b Jan 19, 1931

Griffiths, S. S. (Warwickshire), b July 11, 1930

Griffiths, Mr. W. H. (Camb. Univ. and Glamorgan), b Sept 26, 1922

Grimmett, Mr. C. V. (Victoria and South Australia), b Dec 25, 1892

Grimshaw, C. H. (Yorkshire and Worcestershire), b May 12, 1880, d Sept 25, 1947

Grimshaw, V. (Worcestershire), b April 15, 1916

Grimshaw, B/S/M J. W. T. (Camb. Univ. and Kent), b Feb 17, 1912, d Sept 26, 1944

Grimshaw, N. (Northamptonshire), b May 5, 1912

Grimston, Mr. George S. (Sussex), b April 2, 1905

Grinter, Mr. T. G. (Essex), b Dec 12, 1888

Gross, Mr. F. A. (Hampshire), b Sept 17, 1902

Grove, C. W. (Warwickshire and Worcestershire), b Dec 12, 1912

Grover, Mr. J. N. (Oxford Univ. and Northumberland), b Oct 15, 1915

Groves, Mr. G. J. (Nottinghamshire), b Oct 19, 1868, d Feb 18, 1941

Guise, Mr. J. D. (India and M.C.C.), b Oct 31, 1872, d July 3, 1953

Guise, Mr. J. L (Oxford Univ. and Middlesex), b Nov 25, 1903

Gunasekara, Dr. C. H. (Middlesex and Ceylon), b July 27, 1894

Gunn, G. (Nottinghamshire), b June 13, 1879

Gunn, G. V. (Nottinghamshire), b June 21, 1905, d Oct 14, 1957

Gunn, J. (Nottinghamshire), b July 19, 1876

Gunn, W. (Nottinghamshire), b Dec 4, 1858, d Jan 29, 1921

Gupta, Mr. P. (India) (Manager teams in England), b Oct. 10, 1899

Hadingham, Mr. A. W. G. (Camb. Univ. and Surrey), b March 1, 1913

Hadlee, Mr. W. A. (New Zealand), b June 4, 1915

Hadow, Mr. P. F. (Middlesex), b Jan 24, 1855, d June 29, 1946

Hafeez, A. (India) (now A. H. Kardar), b Jan 17, 1925

Haig, Mr. N. E. (Middlesex), b Dec 12, 1887

Haigh, Schofield (Yorkshire), b March 19, 1871, d Feb 27, 1921

Haigh Smith, Mr. H. A. (Hampshire), b Oct 21, 1884, d Oct 28, 1955

Hailsham, 1st Visct. (President, M.C.C., 1933), b Feb 28, 1872

Haines, Mr. A. H. (Gloucestershire), b Aug 27, 1877

Haines, Mr. C. V. G. (Glamorgan), b Jan 17, 1906

Hake, Mr. H. D. (Hampshire), b Nov 8, 1894

Hale, W. H. (Somerset and Gloucestershire), b March 6, 1870, d Aug 12, 1956

Halfyard, D. J. (Surrey and Kent), b April 3, 1931

Hall, A. E. (South Africa and Lancashire), b Jan 23, 1896

Hall, C. H. (Yorkshire), b April 5, 1906

Hall, Mr. P. J. (Camb. Univ.), b Dec 4, 1927

Hall, Mr. P. M. (Hampshire), b March 19, 1894, d Dec 11, 1945

Hall, Mr. T. A. (Derbyshire and Somerset), b Aug 19, 1930

Hall, Mr. W. (West Indies), b Sept 12, 1937

Hallam, A. W. (Lancashire, Nottinghamshire and Leicestershire), b Nov 12, 1872, d 1940

Hallam, H. (Derbyshire), b April 12, 1882

Hallam, M. R. (Leicestershire), b Sept 10, 1931

Halliday, H. (Yorkshire), b Feb 9, 1920

Halliday, Mr. J. G. (Oxford Univ. and Oxfordshire), b July 4, 1915, d Dec 3, 1945

Hallows, C. (Lancashire), b April 4, 1895

Hambling, Mr. M. L. (Somerset), b Dec 6, 1893

Hamence, Mr. R. A. (South Australia), b Nov 25, 1915

Hamer, A. (Yorkshire and Derbyshire), b Dec 8, 1916

Hamilton, Col. L. A. H. (Kent), b Dec 23, 1862

Hammond, H. E. (Sussex), b Nov 7, 1907

Hammond, Mr. W. R. (Gloucestershire), b in Kent, June 19, 1903

Hampden, 3rd Visct. (President, M.C.C., 1926), b Jan 29, 1869

Hampton, Mr. W. M. (Warwickshire and Worcestershire), b Jan 20, 1903

Hancock, J. W. (Derbyshire), b Nov 26, 1877, d May 23, 1939

Handford, A. (Nottinghamshire), b May 3, 1869, d Oct 15, 1935

Handford, J. (Derbyshire), b Feb 1, 1890

Handley, G. (Nottinghamshire), b Jan 10, 1876

Hands, Mr. P. A. M. (Oxford Authentics and South Africa), b March 18, 1890, d April 27, 1951

Hands, Mr. W. C. (Warwickshire), b Dec 20, 1886

Hanif Mohammad (Pakistan), b Dec 24, 1934

Harbinson, Mr. W. K. (Camb. Univ.), b July 11, 1906

Harbord, Mr. W. E. (Yorkshire), b Dec 15, 1908

Harding, N. W. (Kent), b March 19, 1916, d Sept 25, 1947

Hardinge, H. T. W. (Kent), b Feb 25, 1886

Hardisty, C. H. (Yorkshire and Northumberland), b Dec 10, 1885

Hardstaff, J. (Nottinghamshire), b Nov 9, 1882, d April 2, 1947

Hardstaff, J., jun. (Nottinghamshire), b July 3, 1911

Hardstaff, R. G. (Nottinghamshire), b Jan 12, 1863, d April 18, 1932

Harfield, L. (Hampshire), b Aug 16, 1905

Hargreaves, H. S. (Yorkshire), b March 22, 1913

Harkness, D. (Worcestershire), b Feb 13, 1931

Harragin, Mr. A. E. A. (Trinidad), b May 4, 1877, d May 21, 1941

Harris, 4th Lord (Oxford Univ. and Kent, President, M.C.C., 1895), b West Indies, Feb 3, 1851, d March 24, 1932

Harris, C. B. (Nottinghamshire), b Dec 6, 1908, d Aug 8, 1954

Harris, Mr. G. W. (South Australia), b Dec 11, 1898

Harris, Mr. T. A. (South Africa), b Aug 27, 1916

Harrison, Mr. C. S. (Worcestershire), b Nov 11, 1915

Harrison, Mr. E. W. (Tasmania), b July 21, 1874

Harrison, Rear-Adml. G. C. (Hampshire), b Oct 8, 1883, d Aug 10, 1943

Harrison, G. P. (Yorkshire), b Feb 11, 1862, d Sept 14, 1940

Harrison, H. S. (Surrey), b April 12, 1883

Harrison, L. (Hampshire), b June 8, 1922

Harrison, Mr. W. P.(Kent,Camb. Univ. and Middlesex), b Nov 13, 1885

Harron, D. G. (Leicestershire), b Sept 12, 1921

Hart, G. E. (Middlesex), b Jan 13, 1902

Hart, Mr. T. M. (Oxford Univ. and Scotland), b March 1, 1909

Hartigan, Mr. G. P. D. (South Africa), b Dec 30, 1884, d Jan 7, 1955

Hartigan, Mr. R. J. (New South Wales and Queensland), b Dec 12, 1879

Hartkopf, Dr. A. E. V. (Victoria), b Dec 28, 1889

Hartley, Lt.-Col. J. C. (Oxford Univ. and Sussex), b Nov 15, 1874

Harvey, P. F. (Nottinghamshire), b Jan 15, 1923

Harvey, Mr. R. L. (South Africa), b Sept 14, 1911

Harvey, Mr. R. N. (Victoria), b Oct 8, 1928

Hassett, Mr. A. L. (Victoria), b Aug 28, 1913

Hawke, 7th Lord (Camb. Univ. and Yorkshire; President, M.C.C. 1914–1918), b Aug 16, 1860, d Oct 10, 1938

Hawkins, D. (Gloucestershire), b May 18, 1935

Hawkwood, C. (Lancashire), b Nov 16, 1909

Hawtin, Mr. A. P. R. (Northamptonshire), b Feb 1, 1883

Hay, Mr. Douglas (New Zealand), b Aug 31, 1876

Hayes, E. G. (Surrey and Leicestershire), b Nov 6, 1876, d Dec 2, 1953

Hayes, Mr. J. A. (New Zealand), b Jan 11, 1927

Haynes, R. W. (Gloucestershire), b Aug 27, 1913

Hayter, E. (Hampshire), b Sept 8, 1913

Hayward, T. W. (Surrey), b March 29, 1871, d July 19, 1939

Hayward, Mr. W. I. D. (Cambridge Univ.), b April 15, 1930

Haywood, R. A. (Northamptonshire), b Sept 16, 1887, d June 1, 1942

Hazare, V. S. (India), b March 11, 1915

Hazell, H. L. (Somerset), b Sept 30, 1909

Hazlerigg, Lord, formerly Sir Arthur Grey, 13th Bart. (Leicestershire), b Nov 17, 1878, d May 25, 1949

Hazlerigg, Lord, 14th Bart., formerly the Hon. A. G. (Camb. Univ. and Leicestershire), b Feb 24, 1910

Headley, Mr. G. (West Indies), b May 30, 1909

Heane, Mr. G. F. H. (Nottinghamshire and Lincolnshire), b Jan 2, 1904

Heap, J. S. (Lancashire), b Aug 12, 1883, d Jan 30, 1951

Hearn, P. (Kent), b Nov 18, 1925

Hearne, Alec (Kent), b July 22, 1863, d May 16, 1952

Hearne, Frank (Kent and South Africa), b Nov 23, 1858, d July 14, 1949

Hearne, G. (Buckinghamshire and Middlesex), b May 15, 1829, d Dec 9, 1904

Hearne, Mr. G. A. L. (South Africa), b March 27, 1888

Hearne, George F. (Middlesex, Pavilion Clerk, Lord's), b Oct 18, 1851, d May 29, 1931

Hearne, George G. (Kent), b July 7, 1856, d Feb 13, 1932

Hearne, Herbert (Kent), b March 15, 1862, d June 13, 1906

Hearne, J. T. (Middlesex), b May 3, 1867, d April 17, 1944

Hearne, J. W. (Middlesex), b Feb 11, 1891

Hearne, Thomas (Buckinghamshire and Middlesex), b Sept 4, 1826, d May 13, 1900

Hearne, Thomas, jun. (Middlesex and Ground Superintendent at Lord's), b Dec 29, 1849, d Jan 29, 1910

Hearne, Walter (Kent), b Jan 15, 1864, d April 2, 1925

Hearne, Wm. (Buckinghamshire), b July 15, 1828, d July 17, 1908

Heath, Mr. A. B. (Hampshire), b Jan 19, 1865

Heath, D. M. W. (Warwickshire), b Dec 4, 1931

Heath, G. E. M. (Hampshire), b Feb 20, 1913

Heath, M. (Hampshire), b March 9, 1934

Hedges, B. (Glamorgan), b Nov 10, 1927

Hedges, Mr. L. P. (Oxford Univ., Kent and Gloucestershire), b July 13, 1900, d Jan 12, 1933

Hedley, Col. Sir W. C. (Kent, Somerset, Devon and Hampshire), b Dec 12, 1865, d Dec 27, 1937

Heffernan, Mr. F. W. (Queensland), b May 25. 1901

Heine, Mr. P. (South Africa), b June 28, 1929

Hemingway, Mr. W. M'G. (Camb. Univ. and Gloucestershire), b Nov 12, 1873

Henderson, Mr. D. (Oxford Univ.), b March 9, 1926

Henderson, Mr. M. (New Zealand), b Aug 2, 1895

Hendren, D. (Middlesex and Durham), b Sept 25, 1882

Hendren, E. (Middlesex), b Feb 5, 1889

Hendry, Mr. H. L. (New South Wales and Victoria), b May 24, 1895

Henery, Mr. P. J. T. (Camb. Univ. and Middlesex), b June 6, 1859, d Aug 10, 1938

Henley, Mr. D. F. (Oxford Univ.), b July 21, 1923

Henley, Mr. F. A. H. (Oxford Univ., Suffolk and Middlesex), b Feb 11, 1884

Henson, W. (Nottinghamshire), b Dec 7, 1874

Herman, O. W. (Hampshire), b Sept 18, 1907

Heseltine, Lt.-Col. C., O.B.E., D.L. (Hampshire), b Nov 26, 1869, d June 13, 1944

Hever, N. (Middlesex and Glamorgan), b Dec 17, 1924

Hewan, Mr. G. E. (Camb. Univ. and Berkshire), b Dec 23, 1916

Hewetson, Mr. E. P. (Oxford Univ. and Warwickshire), b May 27, 1902

Heygate, Mr. R. B. (Sussex), b May 13, 1883

Hibbert, W. J. (Lancashire), b July 11, 1874

Hiddleston, Mr. J. S. (New Zealand), b Dec 10, 1890, d Oct 30, 1940

Hide, Mr. A. E. (Sussex), b May 7, 1860, d Nov. 5. 1933

Higgins, Mr. H. L. (Worcestershire), b Feb 24, 1894

Higgins, Mr. J. B. (Worcestershire), b Dec 31, 1885

Higgs, Mr. K. A. (Sussex), b Oct 5, 1886

Higson, Mr. T. A. (Derbyshire, Cheshire and Lancashire), b Nov 18, 1873, d Aug 3, 1949

Higson, Mr. T. A., jun. (Derbyshire and Lancashire), b March 25, 1911

Hilder, Mr. A. L. (Kent), b Oct 8, 1901

Hill, Allen (Yorkshire), b Nov 14, 1845, d Aug 29, 1910

Hill, Mr. A. E. L. (Hampshire), b July 14, 1901

Hill, Mr. A. J. L. (Camb Univ. and Hampshire), b July 26, 1871, d Sept 6, 1950

Hill, Mr. Clement (South Australia), b March 18, 1877, d Sept 5, 1945

Hill, Capt. D. V. (Worcestershire), b April 13, 1896

Hill, E. (Somerset), b July 9, 1923

Hill, G. (Hampshire), b April 15, 1913

Hill, Mr. J. C. (Victoria), b June 25, 1923

Hill, Mr. J. E. (Warwickshire), b Sept 27, 1867

Hill, M. (Nottinghamshire), b Sept 14, 1935

Hill, Mr. M. Ll. (Somerset and Glamorgan), b June 23, 1902, d Feb 28. 1948

Hill, N. (Nottinghamshire), b Aug 22, 1935

Hill, W. A. (Warwickshire), b April 27, 1910

Hills, H. M. (Essex), b Sept 28, 1886

Hills, J. (Glamorgan), b Oct 14, 1897

Hill-Wood, Sir B. S. (Derbyshire), b Feb 5, 1900, d July 3, 1954

Hill-Wood, Mr. C. K. (Oxford Univ. and Derbyshire), b June 5, 1907

Hill-Wood, Mr. D. J. (Oxford Univ. and Derbyshire), b June 25, 1906

Hill-Wood, Sir S. H. (Derbyshire and Suffolk), b March 21, 1872, d Jan 4, 1949

Hill-Wood, Mr. W. W. (Camb. Univ. and Derbyshire), b Sept 8, 1901

Hillyard, Cmdr. G. W., R.N. (Middlesex, Hertfordshire and Leicestershire), b Feb 6, 1864, d March 24, 1943

Hilton, J. (Lancashire and Somerset), b Dec 29, 1930

Hilton, M. J. (Lancashire), b Aug 2, 1928

Hind, Mr. A. E. (Camb. Univ. and Nottinghamshire), b April 7, 1878, d March 22, 1947

Hindlekar, D. D. (India), b Jan 1, 1909, d March 30, 1949

Hinds, Mr. S. A. (West Indies), b June 1, 1880

Hine-Haycock, Rev. T. R. (Oxford Univ. and Kent), b Dec 3, 1861, d Nov 2, 1953

Hipkin, A. B. (Essex), b Aug 8, 1900, d Feb 11, 1957

Hirst, G. H. (Yorkshire), b Sept 7, 1871, d May 10, 1954

Hitch, J. W. (Surrey), b May 7, 1886

Hitchcock, R. E. (Canterbury and Warwickshire), b Nov 28, 1929

Hoad, Mr. E. L. G. (West Indies), b Jan 29, 1896

Hobbs, Mr. J. A. D. (Oxford Univ.), b Nov 30, 1935

Hobbs, Sir J. B. (Cambridgeshire and Surrey), b Dec 16, 1882

Hobson, Mr. B. S. (Camb. Univ.), b Nov 22, 1925

Hodgkinson, Mr. G. F. (Derbyshire), b Feb 19, 1914

Hodgkinson, Mr. G. W. (Somerset), b Feb 19, 1883

Hodgson, G. (Lancashire), b April 16, 1904, d June 14, 1951

Hofmeyr, Mr. M. B. (Oxford Univ.), b Dec. 9, 1925

Holdsworth, Mr. R. L. (Oxford Univ., Warwickshire and Sussex), b Feb 25, 1899

Holdsworth, W. E. N. (Yorkshire), b Sept 17, 1928

Hole, Mr. G. B. (South Australia), b Jan 6, 1931

Holland, F. C. (Surrey), b Feb 10, 1876, d Feb 5, 1957

Hollies, W. E. (Warwickshire), b June 5, 1912

Hollingdale, R. A. (Sussex), b March 6, 1906

Hollins, Sir A. M., 2nd Bart. (Oxford Univ.), b July 16, 1876, d July 30, 1938

Hollins, Sir F. H., 3rd Bart. (Oxford Univ., Cumberland and Lancashire), b Oct 31, 1877

Holloway, Mr. G. W. (Gloucestershire), b April 26, 1884

Holloway, Mr. N. J. (Camb. Univ. and Sussex), b Nov 11, 1889

Holmes, Gr. Capt. A. J. (Sussex), b June 30, 1899, d May 21, 1950

Holmes, Mr. E. R. T. (Oxford Univ. and Surrey), b Aug 21, 1905

Holmes, Percy (Yorkshire), b Nov 25, 1886

Holroyd,J.(Lancashire),b April 15,1907

Holt, A. (Hampshire), b April 8, 1912

Hone, Mr. B. W. (South Australia, Oxford Univ. and Wiltshire), b July 1, 1907

Hooker, Mr. H. (New South Wales), b March 6, 1898

Hooker, R. W. (Middlesex), b Feb 22, 1935

Hooman, Mr. C. V. L. (Oxford Univ., Devon and Kent), b Oct 3, 1887

Hopkins, Mr. A. J. (New South Wales), b May 3, 1876, d April 25, 1931

Hopkins, Mr. H. O. (Oxford Univ. and Worcestershire), b July 6, 1895

Hopkins, V. (Gloucestershire), b Jan 21, 1913

Hopley, Mr. F. J. V. (Camb. Univ. and Western Province), b Aug 27, 1883, d Aug 16, 1951

Hopwood, J. L. (Lancashire), b Oct 30, 1903

Hordern, Dr. H. V. (New South Wales and Philadelphians), b Feb 10, 1884, d June 17, 1938

Hornby, Mr. A. H. (Lancashire), b July 29, 1877, d Sept 9, 1952

Horner, N. F. (Yorkshire and Warwickshire), b May 10, 1926

Hornibrook, Mr. P. M. (Queensland), b July 27, 1899

Horrocks, W. J. (Lancashire), b June 18, 1905

Horsfall, R. (Essex and Glamorgan), b June 26, 1920

Horton, H. (Worcestershire and Hampshire), b April 18, 1924

Horton, J. (Worcestershire), b Aug 12, 1916

Horton, M. J. (Worcestershire), b April 21, 1934

Horwood, Mr. S. E. (Western Province), b July 22, 1877

Hosie, Mr. A. L. (Hampshire), b Aug 6, 1890, d June 11, 1957

Hossell, Mr. J. J., junior (Warwickshire), b May 25, 1914

Hotchkin, Mr. N. S. (Camb. Univ., Lincolnshire and Middlesex), b Feb 4, 1914

Hough, Mr. G. de L. (Kent), b May 14, 1894

Houldsworth, Mr. W. H. (Lancashire), b April 6, 1873, dead

Hounsfield, Mr. T. D. (Derbyshire), b April 28, 1911

Howard, A. H. (Glamorgan), b Dec 11, 1910

Howard, Mr. B. J. (Lancashire), b May 21, 1926

Howard, J. (Leicestershire), b Nov. 24, 1917

Howard, Mr. N. D. (Lancashire), b May 18, 1925

Howard, Major R. (Lancashire and Sec. Lancashire C.C.C.), b April 17,

Howell, H. (Warwickshire), b Nov 29, 1890, d July 9, 1932

Howell, Mr. M. (Oxford Univ. and Surrey), b Sept 9, 1893

Howell, Mr. R. G. D. (Sussex), b Jan 23, 1877, d Sept 27, 1942

Howell, Mr. W. P. (New South Wales), b Dec 29, 1869, d July 14, 1940

Howitt, Mr. R. H. (Nottinghamshire), b July 21, 1864, d Jan 10, 1951

Howlett, Brigadier B. (Kent), b Dec 18, 1898, d Nov 1943

Howorth, R. (Worcestershire), b April 26, 1909

Hubble, J. C. (Kent), b Feb 10, 1881

Huddleston, W. (Lancashire), b Feb 27, 1875

Huggins, H. J. (Gloucestershire), b March 15, 1877, d Nov 19, 1942

Hughes, Mr. D. W. (Glamorgan), b July 12, 1910

Hughes, N. (Worcestershire), b Apr 6, 1929

Hughes, Mr. O. (Camb. Univ.), b July 7, 1889

Hughes, R. (Worcestershire), b Sept 30, 1926

Hughes-Hallett, Mr. N. M. (Derbyshire), b April 1895

Huish, F. H. (Kent), b Nov 15, 1872, d March 16, 1957

Hulme, J. J. (Derbyshire), b June 30, 1862, d July 11, 1940

Hulme, J. H. A. (Middlesex), b Aug 26, 1904

Human, Mr. J. H. (Camb. Univ., Berkshire and Middlesex), b Jan 13, 1912

Human, Capt. R. H. C. (Camb. Univ., Berkshire and Worcestershire), b May 11, 1909, d Nov 1942

Humphreys, E. (Kent), b Aug 24, 1881, d Nov 6, 1949

Humphries, J. (Derbyshire), b May 18, 1876, d May 8, 1946

Hunt, F. (Kent and Worcestershire), b Sept 13, 1875

Hunt, G. (Somerset), b Sept 30, 1896

Hunt, H. (Somerset), b Nov 18, 1911

Hunt, Mr. R. G. (Camb. Univ. and Sussex), b April 13, 1915

Hunte, Mr. E. (West Indies), b Oct 3, 1905

Hunter, David (Yorkshire), b March 23, 1860, d Jan 11, 1927

Hunter, Mr. F. C. (Derbyshire and Cheshire), b Aug 23, 1886

Hurst, Mr. C. S. (Oxford Univ. and Kent), b July 20, 1886

Hurst, R. J. (Middlesex), b Dec 29, 1933

Hurwood, Mr. A. (Queensland), b June 17, 1902

Husain, Shafquat (India), b July 17, 1885

Hussain, Dilawar (India), b March 19, 1907

Hutcheon, Mr. J. S. (Queensland), b April 5, 1882, d June 18, 1957

Hutchings, Mr. F. V. (Kent), b June 3, 1880, d Aug 6, 1934

Hutchings, Mr. K. L. (Kent), b Dec 7, 1882, d Sept 3, 1916

Hutchings, Mr. W. E. C. (Kent and Worcestershire), b May 31, 1879, d March 8, 1948

Hutchinson, J. M. (Derbyshire), b Nov 29, 1897

Hutton, Sir L. (Yorkshire), b June 23, 1916

Hylton, Mr. L. G. (West Indies), b March 29, 1905, d May 17, 1955

Hylton-Stewart, Mr. B. D. (Somerset and Hertfordshire), b Nov 27, 1891

Hyman, Mr. W. (Somerset), b March 7, 1875

I'Anson, J. (Lancashire), b Oct 26, 1869, d Sept 16, 1936

Ibadulla, K. (Warwickshire), b Dec 20, 1935

Iddon, J. (Lancashire), b Jan 8, 1903, d April 17, 1946

Ikin, J. T. (Lancashire), b March 7, 1918

Ikram Elahi (Pakistan), b March 3, 1934

Illingworth, R. (Yorkshire), b June 8, 1932

Imlay, Mr. A. D. (Camb. Univ. and Gloucestershire), b Feb 14, 1885

Imtiaz Ahmed (Pakistan), b Jan 5, 1928

Ineson, P. (Yorkshire), b May 5, 1867, d Oct 10, 1939

Ingle, Mr. R. A. (Somerset), b Nov 5, 1903

Ingleby-Mackenzie, Mr. A. C. D. (Hampshire), b Sept 15, 1933

Ingram, Mr. E. A. (Middlesex and Ireland), b Aug 14, 1910

Ingram, I. (Kent), b May 14, 1855

Insole, Mr. D. J. (Camb. Univ. and Essex), b April 18, 1926

Ireland, Mr. J. F. (Camb. Univ. and Suffolk), b Aug 12, 1888

Iremonger, A. (Nottinghamshire), b June 15, 1884

Iremonger, J. (Nottinghamshire), b March 5, 1876, d March 25, 1956

Irish, A. F. (Somerset), b Nov 23, 1918

Ironmonger, H. (Queensland and Victoria), b April 7, 1887

Irvine, Mr. L. G. (Camb. Univ. and Kent), b Jan 11, 1906

Isherwood, Capt. L. C. R. (Hampshire and Sussex), b April 13, 1891

Jackson, Mr. A. A. (New South Wales) b Sept 5, 1909, d Feb 16, 1933

Jackson, Mr. A. H. M. (Derbyshire), b Nov 9, 1899

Jackson, Rt. Hon. Sir F. S. (Camb. Univ. and Yorkshire; President, M.C.C., 1921), b Nov 21, 1870, d March 9, 1947

Jackson, Mr. G. R. (Derbyshire), b June 23, 1896

Jackson, Mr. K. L. T. (Oxford Univ. and Berkshire), b Nov, 1913

Jackson, F. M'I. (Surrey), b May 24, 1882, dead

Jackson, L. (Derbyshire), b April 5, 1921

Jackson, P. F. (Worcestershire), b May 11, 1911

Jackson, V. E. (Leicestershire), b Oct 25, 1916

Jacques, Mr. T. A. (Yorkshire), b Feb 19, 1905

Jagger, Mr. S. T. (Camb. Univ., Worcestershire, Denbighshire and Sussex), b June 30, 1904

Jahangir Khan, M. (India and Camb. Univ.), b Feb 1, 1910

Jai, L. P. (India), b April 1, 1902

Jakeman, F. (Yorkshire and Northamptonshire), b Jan 10, 1921

James, A. E. (Sussex), b Aug 7, 1924

James, C. E. (Nottinghamshire), b Sept 14, 1885

James, K. C. (New Zealand and Northamptonshire), b March 12, 1905

James, Mr. R. M. (Camb. Univ.), b Oct 2 1934

Jameson, Capt. T. O. (Hampshire), b April 4, 1892

Jardine, Mr. D. R. (Oxford Univ. and Surrey), b Oct 23, 1900

Jardine, Mr. M. R. (Oxford Univ. and Middlesex), b June 8, 1869, d Jan 16, 1947

Jarrett, H. (Warwickshire), b Sept 23, 1907

Jarvis, Mr. L. K. (Camb. Univ. and Norfolk), b Aug 3, 1857, d May 16 1938

Jaya Ram, Mr. B. (India and London County), b April 23, 1872

Jeacocke, Mr. A. (Surrey), b Dec 1, 1892

Jeanes, Mr. W. H. (Secretary, Australian Board of Control), b May 19, 1883

Jellicoe, Rev. F. G. G. (Oxford Univ. and Hampshire), b Feb 24, 1858, d July 29, 1927

Jenkins, R. O. (Worcestershire), b Nov 24, 1918

Jenkins, Mr. V. G. J. (Oxford Univ. and Glamorgan), b Nov 2, 1911

Jenkins, Mr. W. L. T. (Glamorgan), b Aug 26, 1898

Jenner, F. D. (Sussex), b Nov 15, 1893, d March 31, 1953

Jennings, Mr. C. B. (South Australia and Queensland), b June 5, 1884, d June 25, 1950

Jennings, T. S. (Surrey), b Nov 3, 1896

Jephson, Mr. W. V. (Hampshire), b Oct 6, 1873

Jepson, A. (Nottinghamshire), b July 12, 1915

Jessop, Mr. G. L. (Gloucestershire and Camb. Univ.), b May 19, 1874, d May 11, 1955

Jewell, Mr. M. F. S. (Sussex and Worcestershire), b Sept 15, 1885

Jilani, M. Baqa (India), b July 20, 1911, d July 2, 1941

Joginder Singh (India), b July 7, 1904

Johnson, Mr. G. H. (Northamptonshire), b Dec 16, 1894

Johnson, Mr. H. H. (West Indies), b July 17, 1910

Johnson, H. L. (Derbyshire), b Nov 8, 1927

Johnson, Mr. I. W. (Victoria), b Dec 8, 1918

Johnson, Mr. P. R. (New Zealand, Camb. Univ., Devon and Somerset), b Aug 5, 1880

Johnston, Col. A. C. (Hampshire), b Jan 26, 1884, d Dec 27, 1952

Johnston, Mr. W. A. (Victoria), b Feb 26, 1922

Johnstone, Mr. C. P. (Camb. Univ. and Kent), b Aug 19, 1895

Jones, Mr. A. O. (Nottinghamshire and Camb. Univ.), b Aug 16, 1872, d Dec 21, 1914

Jones, D. (Nottinghamshire), b April 9, 1914

Jones, Mr. E. (South Australia), b Sept 30, 1869, d Nov 23, 1943

Jones, E. C. (Glamorgan), b Dec 14, 1912

Jones, Mr. G. L. (Hampshire), b Feb 11, 1909

Jones, Mr. P. E. (West Indies), b June 6, 1917

Jones, Mr. R. T. (Oxford Univ. and Shropshire), b June 27, 1871, d Aug 30, 1940

Jones, Mr. S. P. (New South Wales), b Aug 1, 1861, d July 14, 1951

Jones, W. E. (Glamorgan), b Oct 31, 1916

Jordan, J. (Lancashire), b Feb 7, 1932

Jose, Mr. A. D. (Oxford Univ. and Kent), b Feb 17, 1929

Jowett, Mr. D. C. P. R. (Oxford Univ.), b Jan 24, 1931

Jowett, Mr. R. L. (Oxford Univ.), b April 29, 1937

Joy, Mr. F. D. H. (Somerset), b Sept 26, 1880

Joyce, Mr. F. M. (Leicestershire), b Dec 16, 1886

Joynt, Mr. H. W. (Oxford Univ.), b Jan 7, 1931

Judd, Mr. A. K. (Camb. Univ. and Hampshire), b Jan 1, 1904

Judge, P. F. (Middlesex and Glamorgan), b May 23, 1916

Jupp, Mr. V. W. C. (Sussex and Northamptonshire), b March 27, 1891

Kamm, Mr. A. (Oxford Univ.), b March 2, 1931

Kanga, Dr. H.D. (India), b April 9, 1880, d Dec 29, 1945

Kanhai, Mr. Rohan (West Indies), b Dec 26, 1935

Kapadia, B. E. (India), b April 9, 1900

Kardar, A. H. (formerly Abdul Hafeez) (India, Oxford Univ., Warwickshire and Pakistan), b Jan 17, 1925

Kaye, Lt.-Col. H. S. (Yorkshire), b Aug 9, 1882, d Nov 6, 1953

Kaye, Mr. M. A. C. P. (Camb. Univ.), b Jan 11, 1916

Keeton, W. W. (Nottinghamshire), b April 30, 1905

Keighley, Mr. W. G. (Oxford Univ. and Yorkshire), b Jan 10, 1925

Keigwin, Mr. R. P. (Camb. Univ. Essex and Gloucestershire), b April 8, 1883

Keith, Mr. H. J. (South Africa), b Oct 25, 1927

Kelland, Mr. P. A. (Cambridge Univ.), b Sept 20, 1926

Kelleher, H. R. A. (Surrey and Northamptonshire), b March 3, 1929

Kelleway, Mr. C. (New South Wales), b April 25, 1889, d Nov 16, 1944

Kelly, Mr. G. W. F. (Oxford Univ. and Ireland), b April 2, 1877, d Aug 16, 1951

Kelly, J. (Lancashire and Derbyshire), b March 19, 1922

Kelly, J. (Nottinghamshire), b Sept 15, 1930

Kelly, Mr. J. J. (New South Wales), b May 10, 1867, d Aug 14, 1938

Kemp, Lt.-Col. Sir G., 1st Lord Rochdale (Camb. Univ. and Lancashire), b June 9, 1866, d March 24, 1945

Kemp, Mr. M. C. (Oxford Univ. and Kent), b Sept 7, 1861, d June 30, 1951

Kempis, Mr. G. S. (South Africa), b. Nov 26, 1871, d March 1948

Kemp-Welch, Capt. G. D. (Camb. Univ. and Warwickshire), b Aug 4, 1907, d June 18, 1944

Kennedy, A. S. (Hampshire) b Jan 24, 1891

Kenny, Mr. C. J. M. (Camb. Univ. Essex and Ireland), b May 19, 1929

Kent, Mr. K. G. (Warwickshire), b Dec 10, 1901

Kentish, Mr. E. S. M. (West Indies and Oxford Univ.), b Feb 21, 1916

Kenward, Mr. R. (Derbyshire and Sussex), b May 23, 1875

Kenyon, D. (Worcestershire), b May 15, 1924

Kenyon, Mr. M. N. (Lancashire), b Dec. 25, 1886

Kermode, A. (New South Wales and Lancashire), b May 15, 1876, d July 17, 1934

Kerr, Mr. J. L. (New Zealand), b Dec 28, 1910

Kerr, Mr. J. R. (Scotland), b Dec 4, 1883

Kerr, Mr. J. (Scotland), b April 8, 1885

Key, Sir K. J., 4th Bart (Oxford Univ. and Surrey), b Oct 11, 1864, d Aug 9, 1932

Khalid Hassan (Pakistan), b July 14, 1937

Khalid Wazir (Pakistan) b April 27, 1936

Khan Mohammad (Pakistan), b Jan 1, 1928

Khanna, Mr. B. C. (Camb. Univ.), b June 22, 1914

Kidd, Mr. E. L. (Camb. Univ. and Middlesex), b Oct 18, 1889

Kidney, Mr. J. M. (Manager West Indies team in England, 1933, 1939, 1950), b Oct 29, 1888

Killick, Ernest Harry (Sussex), b Jan 17, 1875, d Sept 29, 1948

Killick, Rev. E. T. (Camb. Univ. and Middlesex), b May 9, 1907, d May 18. 1953

Kilner, N. (Yorkshire and Warwickshire), b July 21, 1896

Kilner, R. (Yorkshire), b Oct 17, 1890, d April 5, 1928

Kimmins, Mr. S. E. A. (Kent), b May 26, 1930

Kimpton, Mr. R. C. M. (Oxford Univ. and Worcestershire), b Sept 21, 1916

King, B. P. (Worcestershire and Lancashire), b April 22, 1915

King, Mr. F. (Camb. Univ.), b April 6, 1911

King, I. M. (Warwickshire and Essex), b Nov 10, 1931

King, Mr. J. B. (Philadelphia), b Oct 19, 1873

King, J. H. (Leicestershire), b April 16, 1871, d Nov 20, 1946

King, J. W. (Worcestershire and Leicestershire), b Jan 21, 1908

King, K. C. W. (Surrey), b Dec 4, 1915

Kingsley, Mr. P. G. T. (Oxford Univ. and Hertfordshire), b May 26, 1908

Kingston, Mr. C. A. (Northamptonshire), b Dec 5, 1865, d Oct 14, 1917

Kingston, Rev. F. W. (Camb. Univ. and Northamptonshire), b Dec 24, 1855, d Jan 30, 1933

Kingston, Rev. G. H. (Northamptonshire), b Feb 22, 1864

Kingston, Mr. H. E. (Northamptonshire), b Aug 15, 1876, d June 9, 1955

Kingston, Mr. H. J. (Northamptonshire), b June 26, 1862, d April 14, 1944

Kingston, Mr. J. P. (Northamptonshire and Warwickshire), b July 8, 1857, d March, 1929

Kingston, Mr. W. H. (Northamptonshire), b Aug 12, 1874, d March 28, 1956

Kingston, Rev. W. P. (Northamptonshire), b 1867, d April 15, 1937

Kippax, Mr. A. F. (New South Wales), b May 25, 1897

Kirk, Mr. L. (Nottinghamshire), b Nov 1, 1884, d Feb 27, 1953

Kitcat, Mr. S. A. P. (Gloucestershire), b July 20, 1868, d June 17, 1942

Kitchener, F. (Hampshire), b July 2, 1871

Kitson, D. L. (Somerset), b Sept 13, 1925

Knight, Albert E. (Leicestershire), b Oct 8, 1873, d April 1946

Knight, B. (Essex), b Feb 18, 1938

Knight, Mr. D. J. (Oxford Univ. and Surrey), b May 12, 1894

Knight, Mr. N. S. (Oxford Univ.), b March, 1914

Knight, Mr. R. F. (Northamptonshire), b Aug 10, 1879, d Jan 9, 1955

Knight, Mr. R. L. (Oxford Univ.), b April 21, 1858, d May 22, 1938

Knightley-Smith, Mr. W. (Middlesex, Camb. Univ. and Gloucestershire), b Aug 1, 1932

Knott, Mr. C. (Hampshire), b Nov 26, 1914

Knott, Mr. C. H. (Oxford Univ. and Kent), b March 20, 1901

Knott, Mr. F. H. (Oxford Univ., Kent and Sussex), b Oct 30, 1891

Knowles, J. (Nottinghamshire), b March 25, 1910

Knowles, Mr. W. L. (Kent and Sussex, Sec. Sussex Co. Club 1919 to 1943), b Nov 27, 1871, d Dec 1, 1943

Knox, Mr. F. P. (Oxford Univ. and Surrey), b Jan 23, 1880

Knox, Major N. A. (Surrey), b Oct 10, 1884, d March 3, 1935

Knutton, H. J. (Warwickshire), b 1867

Kortright, Mr. C. J. (M.C.C. and Essex), b Jan 9, 1871, d Dec 12, 1952

Kotze, Mr. J. J. (South Africa), b Aug 7, 1879, d July 8, 1931

Lacey, Sir F. E. (Camb. Univ. and Hampshire; Secretary, M.C.C., 1898–1926), b Oct 19, 1859, d May 26, 1946

Lacy-Scott, Mr. D. G. (Camb. Univ. and Kent), b Aug 18, 1920

Lagden, Mr. R. B. (Camb. Univ. and Surrey), b April 15, 1893, d Oct 20, 1944

Laing, Mr. J. M. (Canada), b March 3, 1874, d Nov 1, 1947

Lake, G. J. (Gloucestershire), b May 15, 1935

Laker, J. C. (Surrey), b Feb 9, 1922

Lall Singh (India), b Dec 16, 1909

Lamason, Mr. J. R. (New Zealand), b Oct 29, 1905

Lamb, Mr. H. J. H. (Northamptonshire), b May 3, 1912

Lambert, G. E. (Gloucestershire), b May 5, 1919

Lampard, Mr. A. W. (Australian Imperial Forces Team), b July 3, 1885

Lancashire, Mr. W. (Hampshire and Dorset), b Oct 28, 1903

Lancaster, Mr. A. J. (Sec. Kent C.C.C., 1885-1936), b April 25, 1859, d Nov 16, 1936

Lancaster, T. (Yorkshire and Lancashire), b Feb 11, 1863, d Dec 12, 1935

Lane, Mr. W. W. Claypon (Surrey), b Aug 1, 1845, d March 31, 1939

Langdale, Mr. G. R. (Norfolk, Derbyshire, Somerset and Berkshire), b March 11, 1916

Langdon, T. (Gloucestershire), b Jan 8, 1879, d Nov 30, 1944

Langford, B. (Somerset), b Dec 17, 1935

Langford, W. (Hampshire), b Oct 5, 1875, d Feb 20, 1957

Langley, Mr. C. K. (Warwickshire), b July 11, 1888, d June 26, 1948

Langley, Mr. G. R. (South Australia), b Sept 19, 1919

Langley, Mr. J. D. A. (Camb. Univ.), b April 25, 1918

Langridge, Jas. (Sussex), b July 10, 1906

Langridge, John (Sussex), b Feb 10, 1910

Langton, Mr. A. B. C. (South Africa), b March 2, 1912, d Nov 1942

Large, J. (Surrey), b March 26, 1866

Larwood, H. (Nottinghamshire), b Nov 14, 1904

Lavers, Mr. A. B. (Essex), b Sept 6, 1918

Lavis, G. (Glamorgan), b Aug 17, 1908 d July 29, 1956

Lawrence, A. A. K. (Sussex), b Nov 3, 1930

Lawrence, Mr. A. S. (Camb. Univ.), b March 25, 1911, d March 17, 1939

Lawrence, C. (Surrey, Middlesex, New South Wales and Australian Aboriginal Team, 1868), b Dec 16, 1828, d Jan 6, 1917

Lawrence, J. (Somerset), b March 29, 1914

Lawrence, Mr. T. P. (Essex), b April 26, 1910

Lawrie, Mr. P. E. (Hampshire), b Dec 12, 1902

Lawson, H. M. (Hampshire), b May 22, 1924

Lawton, Mr. A. E. (Derbyshire, Lancashire and Cheshire), b March 31, 1879, d Dec 25, 1955

Lawton, C. G. (Warwickshire), b April 4, 1863

Lawton, Thomas (Warwickshire), b Jan 31, 1865

Leach, Cecil (Lancashire and Somerset), b Nov 28, 1897

Leach, C. W. (Warwickshire), b Dec 4, 1934

Leach, G. (Sussex), b at Malta, July 18, 1881, d Jan 10, 1945

Leadbeater, E. (Yorkshire and Warwickshire), b Aug 15, 1927

Leaf, Mr. H. (Surrey), b Oct 10, 1854, d Feb 13, 1936

Learmond, Mr. G. C. (Trinidad), b July 4, 1875

Leary, S. E. (Kent), b April 30, 1933

Leatham, Mr. A. E. (Gloucestershire), b Aug 9, 1859, d July 13, 1948

Leconfield, 3rd Lord (President, M.C.C., 1927), b Feb 17 1872, d April 16, 1952

Le Couteur, Mr. P. R. (Oxford Univ.), b June 26, 1885

Lee, C. (Yorkshire and Derbyshire), b March 17, 1924

Lee, Mr. E. C. (Hampshire and Oxford Univ.), b June 18, 1877, d June 16, 1942

Lee, Mr. F. M. (Kent and Somerset), b Jan 8, 1871

Lee, F. S. (Somerset), b July 24, 1907

Lee, G. M. (Nottinghamshire and Derbyshire), b June 7, 1887

Lee, H. W. (Middlesex), b Oct 26, 1890

Lee, J. W. (Middlesex and Somerset), b Feb 1, 1904, d July 1944

Lee, Mr. P. K. (South Australia), b Sept 14, 1904

Lees, Walter S. (Surrey), b Dec 25, 1876, d Sept 10, 1924

Leese, Mr. C. P. (Lancashire and Oxford Univ.), b May 22, 1889, d Jan 19, 1947

Le Fleming, Mr. H. (Kent), b Aug 17, 1870, d Sept 5, 1949

Le Fleming, Mr. J. (Kent), b Oct 23, 1865, d Oct 9, 1942

Legard, Mr. A. R. (Oxford Univ. and Worcestershire), b Jan 17, 1912

Legge, Lt.-Cmdr. G. B., R.N.V.R., F.A.A. (Oxford Univ. and Kent), b Jan 26, 1903, d Nov 21, 1940

Lenham, L. J. (Sussex), b April 24, 1936

Le Roy, Mr. P. N. (Philadelphia), b Sept 25, 1881, d 1950

Lester, E. (Yorkshire), b Feb 18, 1923

Lester, G. (Leicestershire), b Dec 27, 1915

Leveson Gower, Sir H. D. G. (Oxford Univ. and Surrey), b May 8, 1873, d Feb 1, 1954

Levett, Mr. W. H. V. (Kent), b Jan 25, 1909

Lewis, A. E. (Somerset), b Jan 20, 1877, d March 1956

Lewis, C. (Kent), b July 27, 1910

Lewis, Mr. D. J. (Oxford Univ.), b July 27, 1927

Lewis, Mr. E. B. (Warwickshire), b Jan 5, 1918

Lewis, K. H. (Glamorgan), b Nov 10, 1928

Lewis, Mr. L. K. (Camb. Univ.) b Sept 25, 1929

Lewis, Mr. P. T. (Oxford Authentics and South Africa), b Oct 2, 1884

Lewisham, Viscount, *see* Dartmouth

Leyland, M. (Yorkshire), b July 20, 1900

Liddell, A. G. (Northamptonshire), b May 2, 1907

Liddicut, Mr. A. E. (Victoria), b Oct 17, 1891

Light, E. (Hampshire) b Sept, 1, 1874

Lightfoot, A. (Northamptonshire), b Jan 8, 1936

Lilford, 5th Lord (Northamptonshire), b Jan 12, 1863, d Dec 17, 1945

Lilley, A. A. (Warwickshire), b Nov 18, 1867, d Nov 17, 1929

Lilley, B. (Nottinghamshire), b Feb 11, 1895, d Aug 4, 1950

Lillywhite, James (Sussex), b Feb 23, 1842, d Oct 25, 1929

Lincoln, Earl of (Nottinghamshire), b April 8, 1907

Lindley, Mr. Tinsley (Nottinghamshire), b Oct 27, 1865, d March 30, 1940

Lindsay, Mr. J. D. (South Africa), b Sept 8, 1909

Lindsay, Mr. N. V. (Transvaal), b July 30, 1887

Lindwall, Mr. R. R. (New South Wales and Queensland), b Oct 3, 1921

Ling, Mr. W. V. (Griqualand West), b Oct 3, 1891

Linney, Mr. C. K. (Somerset), b Aug 26, 1912

Lipscomb, Mr. F. (Kent), b March 13, 1864, d 1952

Lister, Mr. J. (Yorkshire and Worcestershire), b May 14, 1930

Lister, Mr. W. H. L. (Lancashire), b Oct 7, 1911

Litteljohn, Mr. E. S. (Middlesex), b Sept 24, 1878

Livesay, Brig.-Gen. R. O'H. (Kent), b June 27, 1876, d March 23, 1946

Livingston, L. (N.S.W. and Northants), b May 3, 1920

Livsey, W. H. (Hampshire), b Sept 23, 1894

Llewellyn, G. C. B. (Natal and Hampshire), b Sept 26, 1876

Loader, P. J. (Surrey), b Oct 25, 1929

Lobb, B. (Warwickshire and Somerset), b Jan 11, 1931

Lock, G. A. R. (Surrey), b July 5, 1929

Lock, H. (Surrey and Devon), b May 8, 1903

Locker, W. (Derbyshire), b Feb 16, 1867, d Aug 14. 1952

Lockhart, Mr. J. H. Bruce (Berkshire and Camb Univ.), b March 4, 1889, d June 4, 1956

Lockton, Mr. J. H. (Surrey), b May 22, 1892

Lockwood, W. H. (Nottinghamshire and Surrey), b March 25, 1868, d April 26, 1932

Lohmann, G. A. (Surrey), b June 2, 1865, d Dec 1, 1901

Lomas, Mr. J. M. (Oxford Univ.), b Dec 12, 1917, d Dec 4, 1945

Lomax, J. G. (Lancashire and Somerset), b May 5, 1925

Longfield, Mr. T. C. (Camb. Univ. and Kent), b May 12, 1906

Longman, Mr. G. H. (Camb. Univ. and Hampshire), b Aug 3, 1852, d Aug 19, 1938

Longman, Lt.-Col. H. K. (Camb. Univ., Surrey and Middlesex), b March 8, 1881

Longrigg, Mr. E. F. (Camb. Univ. and Somerset), b April 16, 1906

Lord, A. (Leicestershire), b Aug 28, 1888

Lord, W. A. (Warwickshire), b Aug 8, 1874

Louden, Mr. G. M. (Essex), b Sept 6, 1885

Loughnan, Mr. Austin (Victoria), d Oct 1926

Love, Mr. H. S. B. (New South Wales and Victoria), b Aug 10, 1895

Loveday, F. (Essex), b Sept 14, 1894

Loveitt, Mr. F. R. (Warwickshire), b April 24, 1871, d Sept 1, 1939

Lowe, Wing-Cmdr. J. C. M. (Oxford Univ. and Warwickshire), b Feb 21, 1888

Lowe, R. F. (Surrey), b July 28, 1905

Lowe, Mr. R. G. H. (Camb. Univ. and Kent), b June 11, 1904

Lowe, Mr. W. W. (Camb. Univ. and Worcestershire), b Nov 17, 1873, d May 26, 1945

Lowndes, Mr. W. G. L. F. (Oxford Univ. and Hampshire), b Jan 24, 1898

Lowry, Mr. T. C. (Camb. Univ., Somerset and New Zealand), b Feb 17. 1898

Lowson, F.A. (Yorkshire), b July 1, 1925

Loxton, Mr. S. J. (Victoria), b March 29, 1921

Luard, Col. A. J. H. (Gloucestershire and Hampshire), b Sept 3, 1861, d May 22, 1944

Lucan Brig.-Gen., 5th Earl of (President, M.C.C., 1928), b Dec 21 1860, d April 20, 1949

Lucas, Mr. A. P. (Camb. Univ., Surrey, Middlesex and Essex), b Feb 20, 1857, d Oct 12, 1923

Lucas, Mr. E. V. (Sussex and M.C.C.), b June 12, 1868, d June 26, 1938

Lucas, Mr. M. P. (Sussex and Warwickshire), b Nov 24, 1856, d July 9, 1921

Lucas, Mr. R. S. (Middlesex), b July 17, 1867, d Jan 5, 1942

Luce, Mr. F. M. (Gloucestershire), b April 26, 1878

Luckes, W. T. (Somerset), b Jan 1, 1901

Lumsden, Mr. V. R. (Jamaica and Camb. Univ.), b July 19, 1930

Lupton, Major A. W. (Yorkshire), b Feb 23, 1879, d April 14, 1944

Luther, Major A. C. G. (Sussex and Berkshire), b Sept 17, 1880

Lynes, J. (Warwickshire), b June 6, 1872

Lyon, Mr. B. H. (Oxford Univ., Wiltshire and Gloucestershire), b Jan 19, 1902

Lyon, Mr. G. W. F. (Oxford Univ.), b May 22, 1905, d Dec 1932

Lyon, Mr. M. D. (Camb. Univ., Wiltshire and Somerset), b April 22, 1898

Lyons, Mr. J. J. (South Australia), b May 21, 1863, d July 21, 1927

Lyttelton, 4th Lord (Camb. Univ), b March 31, 1817, d April 18, 1876

Lyttelton, Rt. Hon. Alfred, M.P. (Camb. Univ., Middlesex and President, M.C.C., 1898), b Feb 7, 1857, d July 5, 1913

Lyttelton, Rt. Rev. the Hon. A. T. (Eton), b Jan 7, 1852, d Feb 19, 1903

Lyttelton, Hon. and Rev. A. V. (Worcestershire), b June 29, 1844, d April 4, 1928

Lyttelton, Hon. and Rev. C. F. (Camb. Univ. and Worcestershire), b Jan 26, 1887, d Oct 3, 1931

Lyttelton, Hon. C. G. (*see* 8th Visct. Cobham)

Lyttelton, Hon. C. J. (*see* 10th Visct. Cobham)

Lyttelton, Canon the Hon. Edward (Camb. Univ. and Middlesex), b July 23, 1855, d Jan 26, 1942

Lyttelton, Hon. G. W. (Eton), b Jan 6, 1883

Lyttelton, Hon. G. W. Spencer (Camb. Univ.), b June 12, 1847, d Dec 5, 1913

Lyttelton, Hon. J. C. (*see* 9th Visct. Cobham)

Lyttelton, Gen. the Rt. Hon. Sir N. G. (Eton), b Oct 28, 1845, d July 6, 1931

Lyttelton, Hon. R. H. (Eton), b Jan 18, 1854, d Nov 7, 1939

Maartenoz, Mr. G. A. (Hampshire), b April 14, 1882

McAlister, Mr. P. A. (Victoria), b July 11, 1869, d May 10, 1938

Macan, Mr. G. (Camb. Univ.), b Sept 9, 1853, d Nov 2, 1943

Macartney, Mr. C. G. (New South Wales), b June 27, 1886

Macaulay, P/O, G. G. (Yorkshire), b Dec 7, 1897, d Dec 14, 1940

McBride, Mr. W. N. (Oxford Univ. and Hampshire), b Nov 27, 1904

MacBryan, Mr. J. C. W. (Camb. Univ. and Somerset), b July 22, 1892

McCabe, Mr. S. J. (New South Wales), b July 16, 1910

McCanlis, Mr. M. A. (Oxford Univ., Surrey and Gloucestershire), b June 17, 1906

McCarthy, Mr. C. N. (South Africa and Camb. Univ.), b March 24, 1929

McConnon, J. E. (Glamorgan), b June 21, 1923

McCool, C. L. (Queensland and Somerset), b Dec 9, 1915

McCorkell, N. (Hampshire), b March 23, 1912

McCormick, Mr. E. J. (Sussex), b Nov 1, 1862, d Jan 1942

McCormick, Mr. E. L. (Victoria), b May 16, 1906

McDonald, Mr. C. C. (Victoria), b Nov 17, 1928

McDonald, E. A. (Victoria and Lancashire), b in Tasmania, Jan 6, 1892, d July 22, 1937

MacDonald, Dr. R. (Queensland and Leicestershire), b Feb 28, 1872, d May 1945

McDonell, Mr. H. C. (Camb. Univ., Surrey and Hampshire), b Sept 19, 1882

McElhone, Mr. W. P. (Australian Board of Control), b Dec 22, 1870, d April 21, 1932

McGahey, Mr. C. P. (Essex), b Feb 12, 1871, d Jan 10, 1935

McGirr, Mr. H. M. (New Zealand), b Nov 5, 1891

McGlew, Mr. D. J. (South Africa), b March 11, 1929

McGlinchy, Mr. W. W. (New South Wales and Queensland), b Jan 31, 1866, d July 1, 1946

Machin, Mr. R. S. (Camb. Univ. and Surrey), b April 16, 1904

McHugh, F. P. (Yorkshire and Glos.), b Nov 15, 1925

McIlwraith, Mr. J. (Victoria), b 1857, d July 13, 1938

Macindoe, Mr. D. H. (Oxford Univ. and Buckinghamshire), b Sept 1, 1917

McIntosh, Mr. R. I. F. (Oxford Univ.), b Aug 19, 1907

McIntyre, A. J. (Surrey), b May 14, 1918

McIntyre, A. S. (Hampshire), b May 29, 1889

McIver, Mr. C. D. (Oxford Univ. and Essex), b Jan 23, 1881, d May 13, 1954

Mackay, Mr. J. R. M. (New South Wales), b Sept 9, 1881, d June 13, 1953

Mackay, Mr. K. (Queensland), b Oct 24, 1925

Mackenzie, Mr. A. C. K. (New South Wales), b Dec 10, 1870, d April 11, 1947

Mackenzie, P. A. (Hampshire), b Oct 5, 1918

McKibbin, Mr. T. R. (New South Wales), b Dec 10, 1870, d Dec 15, 1939

McKinna, Mr. G. H. (Oxford Univ.), b Aug 2, 1930

Mackinnon, Mr. F. A. (Camb. Univ. and Kent), b April 9, 1848, d Feb 27, 1947

McLachlan, Mr. I. M. (Camb. Univ.), b Oct 2, 1936

MacLaren, Mr. A. C. (Lancashire), b Dec 1, 1871, d Nov 17, 1944

McLean, Mr. R. A. (South Africa), b July 9, 1930

MacLeod, Mr. K. G. (Camb. Univ. and Lancashire), b Feb 2, 1888

McLeod, Mr. A. (Hampshire), b Nov 12, 1894

McMahon, J. W. (Surrey and Somerset), b Dec 28, 1919

McMillan, Mr. Q. (South Africa), b June 23, 1904, d July 3, 1948

McMurray, T. (Surrey), b July 24, 1911

McNamee, Mr. R. J. A. (New South Wales), b Aug 26, 1899, d Sept 18, 1949

McRae, Mr. F. M. (Somerset), b Feb 12, 1916, d Feb 25, 1944

Maddocks, Mr. L. (Victoria), b May 24, 1926

Mahmood Hussain (Pakistan), b April 2, 1932

Mahomed, Gul (India), b Oct 15, 1921

Mailey, Mr. A. A. (New South Wales), b Jan 3, 1888

Mainprice, Mr. H. (Camb. Univ. and Gloucestershire), b Nov. 27, 1882

Maitland, Mr. W. Fuller (Essex and Oxford Univ.), b May 6, 1844, d Nov 15, 1932

Makepeace, H. (Lancashire), b Aug 22 1881 d Dec 19, 1952

Makin, Mr. J. (Victoria), b Feb 11, 1904

Malden, Mr. Ernest (Kent), b Oct 10, 1870

Malden, Rev. Eustace (Kent), b Aug 19, 1863, d Dec 3, 1947

Malik, Mr. H. S. (Sussex), b Nov 30, 1894

Mallett, Mr. A. W. H. (Kent and Oxford Univ.), b Aug. 29, 1924

Mallett, Mr. R. H. (Durham), (Secretary Minor Counties), b Oct 14, 1858, d Nov 29, 1939

Manjrekar, Mr. V. L. (India), b Sept 26, 1931

Mankad, M. "Vinoo" (India), b April 12, 1917

Mann, Mr. E. W. (Camb. Univ. and Kent), b March 4, 1882, d Feb 15, 1954

Mann, Mr. F. G. (Camb. Univ. and Middlesex), b Sept 6, 1917

Mann, Mr. F. T. (Camb. Univ. and Middlesex), b March 3, 1888

Mann, Mr. J. E. F. (Camb. Univ.), b Dec 2, 1903

Mann, Mr. J. P. (Middlesex), b June 13, 1919

Mann, Mr. N. B. F. (South Africa), b Dec 28, 1921, d July 31. 1952

Manning, J. S. (South Australia and Northants), b June 11, 1924

Manning, Mr. T. E. (Northamptonshire), b Sept 2, 1884

Mansell, Mr. P. N. F. (South Africa) b March 16, 1920

Mantell, D. N. (Sussex), b July 22,1934

Mantri, Mr. M. K. (India), b Sept 1, 1921

Maqsood Ahmed (Pakistan), b March 26, 1925

Marchant, Mr. F. (Camb. Univ. and Kent), b May 22, 1864, d April 13, 1946

Marks, Mr. A. (New South Wales), b Dec 10, 1919

Marlar, Mr. R. G. (Camb. Univ. and Sussex), b Jan 2, 1931

Marlow, F. W. (Staffordshire and Sussex), b Oct 8, 1867, d Aug 7, 1952

Marlow, W. H. (Leicestershire), b Feb 13, 1900

Marner, P. (Lancashire), b March 31, 1936

Marriott, Mr. C. (Oxford Univ. and Leicestershire), b Oct 18, 1848, d July 9, 1918

Marriott, Mr. C. S. (Camb. Univ., Lancashire and Kent), b Sept 14, 1895

Marriott, Rev. G. S. (Oxford Univ. and Leicestershire), b Oct 7, 1855, d Oct 21, 1905

Marriott, Mr. H. H. (Camb. Univ. and Leicestershire), b Jan 20, 1875, d November 15, 1949

Marriott, Mr. J. M. (Leicestershire), b March 6, 1853, d Oct 21, 1910

Marsh, E. (Derbyshire), b July 7, 1920

Marshall, Mr. A. G. (Somerset), b April 17, 1895

Marshall, B. (Nottinghamshire), b May 5, 1902

Marshall, Charles (Surrey and Leicestershire), b Oct 1, 1866, d Nov 25, 1948

Marshall, Mr. H. M. (Camb. Univ.), b Aug 1, 1841, d March 2, 1913

Marshall, Mr. J. C. (Oxford Univ), b Jan 30, 1929

Marshall, J. M. A. (Warwickshire), b Oct 26, 1916

Marshall, N. D. (India), b Jan 3, 1905

Marshall, Mr. R. E. (West Indies and Hampshire), b April 25, 1930

Marsham, Mr. A. J. B. (Oxford Univ. and Kent), b Aug 14, 1919

Marsham, Rev. C. D. (Oxford Univ.), b Jan 30, 1835, d March 2, 1915

Marsham, Mr. C. H. B. (Oxford Univ. and Kent), b Feb 10, 1879, d July 18, 1928

Marsham, Mr. C. J. B. (Oxford Univ.) b Jan 10, 1829, d Aug 20, 1901

Marsham, Brig. F. W. B. (Kent), b July 13, 1883

Marsham, Mr. George (Kent), b April 10, 1849, d Dec 2, 1927

Marsham, the Hon. and Rev. John (Kent), b July 25, 1842, d Sept 16, 1926

Marsham, Mr. R. H. B. (Oxford Univ.), b Sept 3, 1833, d April 5, 1913

Marsland, Mr. G. P. (Oxford Univ.), b May 17, 1932

Martin, E. J. (Nottinghamshire), b Aug 17, 1925

Martin, Mr. E. G. (Oxford Univ. and Worcestershire), b March 22, 1881, d April 27, 1945

Martin, Mr. F. R. (West Indies) b Oct 12, 1893

Martin, Mr. J. W. (Kent), b Feb 16, 1917

Martin, S. H. (Worcestershire), b Jan 11, 1909

Martindale, Mr. E. A. (West Indies), b Nov 25, 1909

Mason, A. (Yorkshire), b May 2, 1921

Mason, Mr. J. R. (Kent), b March 26, 1874

Mason, Percy (Nottinghamshire), b Nov 19, 1874

Massie, Mr. Hugh H. (New South Wales), b April 11, 1855, d Oct 12, 1938

Matheson, Mr. A. M. (New Zealand), b Feb 27, 1906

Mathews, Mr. J. K. (Sussex), b Feb 6, 1884

Mathews, Mr. K. P. A. (Camb. Univ. and Sussex), b May 10, 1926

Matthews, A. (Gloucestershire), b May 3, 1913

Matthews, Mr. A. D. G. (Northamptonshire and Glamorgan), b May 3, 1905

Matthews, C. S. (Notts), b Oct 17, 1931

Matthews, F. C. L. (Nottinghamshire), b Aug 15, 1893

Matthews, Mr. M. H. (Oxford Univ.), b April 26, 1914, d May, 1940

Matthews, Hon. R. C. (Sponsor, Canadian Cricket Tour in England, 1936), b June 14, 1871, d Sept 20, 1952

Matthews Mr. T. J. (Victoria), b April 3, 1884, d Oct 14, 1943

Maudsley, Mr. R. H. (Oxford Univ. and Warwickshire), b April 8, 1918

Maul, Mr. H. C. (Warwickshire), b Oct 6, 1850, d Oct 10, 1940

Maxwell, Mr. C. R. (Nottinghamshire, Middlesex and Worcestershire), b May 21, 1913

Maxwell, J. (Somerset and Glamorgan), b Jan. 13, 1884

May, Mr. P. B. H. (Cambridge Univ. and Surrey), b Dec 31, 1929

May, Mr. P. R. (Camb. Univ., London County and Surrey), b March 13, 1884

Mayer, J. H. (Warwickshire), b March 2, 1902

Mayes, R. (Kent), b Oct 7, 1921

Mayne, Mr. E. R. (South Australia and Victoria), b July 4, 1883

Mead, C. P. (Hampshire and Suffolk), b March 9, 1887

Mead, Walter (Essex), b March 25, 1869, d March 18, 1954

Meads, E. A. (Nottinghamshire), b Aug 17, 1916

Medlicott, Mr. W. S. (Oxford Univ. and Wiltshire), b Aug. 28, 1879

Mee, R. J. (Nottinghamshire and Staffordshire), b Sept 25, 1867

Meherhomji, R. P. (India), b March 4, 1877

Meherhomji, K. R. (India), b Aug 9, 1911

Mehta, A. H. (Parsees), b April 8, 1876

Melle, Mr. B. G. von B. (South Africa, Oxford Univ. and Hampshire), b March 31, 1891

Melle, Mr. M. G. (South Africa), b June 3, 1930

Melluish, Mr. M. E. L. (Camb. Univ. and Middlesex), b June 13, 1932

Melsome, Capt. R. G. W. (Gloucestershire), b Jan 16, 1906

Melville, Mr. A. (Oxford Univ., Sussex and South Africa), b May 19, 1910

Melville, Mr. C. D. (Oxford Univ.), b Oct 4, 1935

Mercer, J. (Sussex, Glamorgan and Northamptonshire), b April 22, 1895

Merchant, V. M. (India), b Oct 12, 1911

Merrick, Mr. H. (Gloucestershire), b Dec 21, 1887

Merritt, W. E. (New Zealand and Northamptonshire), b Aug 18, 1908

Merry, Mr. C. A. (West Indies), b Jan 20, 1911

Meston, Mr. S. P. (Gloucestershire and Essex), b Nov 19, 1882

Metcalfe, Mr. E. J. (Hertfordshire and Queensland), b Sept 29, 1865, d June 14, 1951

Metcalfe, Mr. S. G. (Oxford Univ.) b, June 20, 1932

Meyer, Mr. R. J. O. (Camb. Univ. and Somerset), b March 15, 1905

Meyer, Mr. W. E. (Gloucestershire), b Jan 12, 1883, d Oct 1, 1953

Meyrick-Jones, Rev. F. (Camb. Univ., Hampshire, Kent and Norfolk), b Jan 14, 1867, d Oct 25, 1950

Miller, Mr. K. R. (Victoria and N.S.W.), b Nov 28, 1919

Miller, Mr. Neville (Surrey), b Aug 27, 1874

Miller, Mr. R. A. T. (Sussex), b Nov 12, 1896, d July 1941

Miles-Lade, Hon. H. A. (Kent), b Nov 24, 1867, d July 30, 1937

Millman, G. (Nottinghamshire), b Oct 2, 1934

Mills, Mr. J. E. (New Zealand), b Sept 3, 1905

Mills, Mr. J. M. (Camb. Univ. and Warwickshire). b July 27, 1921

Mills, P. T. (Gloucestershire), b May 7, 1883, d Dec 8, 1950

Milton, C. A. (Gloucestershire), b March 10, 1928

Minnett, Mr. R.B. (New South Wales), b June 13, 1888

Minnett, Mr. R. V. (New South Wales), b Sept 2, 1884

Mischler, Mr. N. M. (Camb. Univ.), b Oct 9, 1920

Mistri, Col. K. M. (India), b Nov 7, 1874

Mitchell, A. (Yorkshire), b Sept 13, 1902

Mitchell, Mr. B. (South Africa), b Jan 8, 1909

Mitchell, Mr. C. (Kent), b Feb 20, 1862, d Oct, 1937

Mitchell, Mr. C. G. (Somerset), b Jan 27, 1929

Mitchell, Mr. Frank (Camb. Univ., Yorkshire and South Africa), b Aug 13, 1872, d Oct 11, 1935

Mitchell, F. R. (Warwickshire), b June 3, 1922

Mitchell, T. B. (Derbyshire), b Sept 4, 1902

Mitchell, Mr. T. F. (Kent), b Oct 22, 1907

Mitchell, Mr. W. M. (Oxford Univ.), b Aug 15, 1929

Mitchell-Innes, Mr. N. S. (Oxford Univ. and Somerset), b Sept 7, 1914

Mobey, G. S. (Surrey), b March 5, 1904

Modi, R. S. (India), b Nov 11, 1924

Mohammad Aslam (Pakistan), b Jan 5, 1920

Moloney, Mr. D. A. R. (New Zealand), b Aug 11, 1910, d 1943

Monks, Mr. C. (Gloucestershire), b March 4, 1912

Montezuma, Mr. L. de (Sussex), b April 16, 1870

Montgomery, S. (Essex and Glamorgan), b July 7, 1920

Montgomery, W. (Surrey, Somerset, Wiltshire, Cheshire and Hertfordshire), b March 4, 1882

Montmorency, Mr. R. H. de (Oxford Univ., Herts and Bucks), b Oct 6, 1871, d Dec 19, 1938

Moody, Mr. C. P. (Author of *Australian Cricket and Cricketers*, etc.), b Aug 11, 1867, d Nov 29, 1937

Moon, Sir Cecil E., 2nd Bart. (London County and Wanderers, Chairman New Zealand Cricket Council, 1914–17), b Sept 2, 1867, d Feb 22, 1951

Moon, Mr. W. R. (Middlesex), b June 27, 1868, d Jan 9, 1943

Mooney, Mr. F. L. H. (New Zealand), b May 26, 1921

Moore, Mr. D. N. (Oxford Univ. and Gloucestershire), b Sept 26. 1910

Moore, F. W. (Lancashire), b Jan 17, 1931

Moore, J. (Hampshire), b April 29, 1891

Moore, Mr. R. H. (Hampshire), b Nov 14, 1913

Moorhouse, F. (Warwickshire and Cheshire), b March 25, 1880, dead

Morcom, Mr. A. F. (Camb. Univ. and Bedfordshire), b Feb 16, 1885, d Feb 12, 1952

Mordaunt, Mr. E. C. (Middlesex, Kent and Hampshire), b Sept 6, 1870, d June 21, 1938

Mordaunt, Mr. G. J. (Oxford Univ. and Kent), b Jan. 20, 1873

Mordaunt, Sir H. J., 12th Bart. (Camb. Univ., Middlesex and Hampshire), b July 12, 1867, d Jan 15, 1939

Mordaunt, Lt.-Col. O. C. (Somerset), b May 26, 1876, dead

More, Mr. R. E. (Oxford Univ. and Middlesex), b Jan 3, 1879, d Nov 24, 1936

Morfee, P. E. (Kent and Scotland), b May 2, 1887, dead

Morgan, Mr. C. L. (Surrey), b May 27, 1867

Morgan, D. C. (Derbyshire), b Feb 26, 1929

Morgan, Mr. J. T. (Camb. Univ. and Glamorgan), b May 7, 1907

Morgan, M. (Nottinghamshire), b May 21, 1936

Morgan, Mr. M. N. (Camb. Univ.), b May 15, 1932

Morgan, Mr. W. G. (Glamorgan), b Dec 26, 1907

Morkel, Mr. D. P. B. (South Africa), b Jan 25, 1906

Morley, W. L. (Essex), b Aug 26, 1894

Morris, Mr. A. R. (New South Wales), b Jan 19, 1922

Morris, Mr. H. M. (Essex), b April 16, 1898

Morris, Mr. P. E. (Essex), b Nov 26, 1877, d July 10, 1945

Morris Mr. R. J. (Camb. Univ. and Kent), b Nov 27, 1926

Morris, W. B. (Essex), b May 28, 1917

Morrison, Mr. J. S. F. (Camb. Univ., Northumberland and Somerset), b April 17, 1892

Mortimer, Sir R. G. E. (Lancashire), b July 7, 1869, d May 3, 1955

Mortimore, J. (Gloucestershire), b June 14, 1933

Morton, A. (Derbyshire), b May 7, 1884, d Dec 19, 1935

Morton, Mr. F. L. (South Australia and Victoria), b Dec 21, 1901

Morton, Mr. H. G. S. (Queensland), b Oct 14, 1881

Moses, Mr. H. (New South Wales), b Feb 13, 1858, d Dec 7, 1938

Moss, A. E. (Middlesex), b Nov 14, 1930

Moss, J. (Nottinghamshire), b Feb 7, 1864, d July 10, 1950

Moss, Rev. R. H. (Oxford Univ., Lancashire, Bedfordshire and Worcestershire), b Feb 24, 1868

Moule, Mr. W. H. (Victoria), b Jan 21, 1858, d Sept, 1939

Mounsey, Joseph T. (Yorkshire), b Aug 30, 1871, d April 6, 1949

Mounteney, A. (Leicestershire), b Feb 11, 1883, d June 1, 1933

Moyes, Mr. A. G. (South Australia and Victoria), b Jan 2, 1893

Muir, Mr. G. H. (Hon. Sec. Hampshire C.C.), b Sept 23, 1869, d March 29, 1939

Mulholland, Right Hon. Sir H. G. H., 1st Bart. (Camb. Univ.), b Dec 20, 1888

Mulla, H. F. (India), b May 4, 1885

Muncer, B. L. (Middlesex and Glamorgan), b Oct 23, 1913

Munden, V. (Leicestershire), b Jan 2, 1928

Murdin, J. V. (Northamptonshire), b Aug 16, 1891

Murdoch, Mr. W. L. (New South Wales and Sussex), b Oct 18, 1855, d Feb 18, 1911

Murray, Mr. A. L. (Warwickshire), b June 29, 1901

Murray, Mr. A. R. A. (South Africa), b April 30, 1922

Murray, J. T. (Middlesex), b April 1, 1935

Murray Willis, Mr. P. E. (Worcestershire and Northamptonshire), b July 14, 1910

Murray Wood, Mr. W. (Oxford Univ. and Kent), b June 30, 1917

Murrell, H. R. (Kent and Middlesex), b Nov 19, 1880, d Aug 15, 1952

Mushtaq Ali (India), b Dec 17, 1914

Musson, Mr. F. W. (Lancashire), b May 31, 1894

Myers, H. (Yorkshire and Tasmania), b Jan 2, 1877, d June 12, 1944

Nagel, Mr. L. E. (Victoria), b March 6, 1905

Naoomal Jeoomal (India), b April 17, 1904

Napier, Rev. J. R. (Marlborough and Lancashire), b Jan 5, 1859, d March 12, 1939

Nash, A. J. (Glamorgan), b Sept 18, 1873, d Dec 6, 1956

Nash, Mr. L. J. (Tasmania and Victoria), b May 2, 1910

Naumann, Mr. F. C. G. (Oxford Univ. and Surrey), b April 9, 1892, d Oct 30, 1947

Naumann Mr. J. H. (Camb. Univ. and Sussex), b Sept 9, 1893

Navle, J. G. (India), b Dec 7, 1902

Nayudu, C. K. (India), b Oct 31, 1895

Nayudu, C. S. (India), b April 18, 1914

Nazir Ali, S. (India and Sussex), b June 8, 1906

Neale, W. L. (Gloucestershire), b March 3, 1904, d Oct 26, 1955

Neblett, Mr. J. M. (West Indies), b Nov 13, 1901

Needham, E. (Derbyshire), b Jan 21, 1873, d March 7, 1936

Nelson, Mr. R. P., Lieut. R.M. (Camb. Univ., Middlesex and Northamptonshire), b Aug 7, 1912, d Oct 29, 1940

Neser, Mr. V. H. (Oxford Univ.), b June 16, 1894, d Dec 22, 1956

Nevell, W. T. (Middlesex, Surrey and Northamptonshire), b June 13, 1916

Newham, Mr. W. (Sussex), b Dec 12, 1860, d June 26, 1944

Newman, Mr. G. C. (Oxford Univ. and Middlesex), b April 26, 1904

Newman, J. (Hampshire), b Nov 12, 1887

Newnham, Lt.-Col. A. T. H. (Gloucestershire), b Jan 17, 1861, d Dec 29, 1941

Newson, Mr. E. S. (South Africa), b Dec 2, 1910

Newstead, J. T. (Yorkshire), b Sept 8, 1879, d March 25, 1952

Newton, Mr. A. E. (Oxford Univ. and Somerset), b Sept 12, 1862, d Sept 15, 1952

Newton-Thompson, Mr. J. O. (Oxford Univ.), b Dec 2, 1920

Nice, E. H. L. (Surrey), b Aug 1, 1875, d June 6, 1946

Nichol, M. (Worcestershire), b Sept 10, 1905, d May 21, 1934

Nicholas, Capt. F. W. H. (Essex and Bedfordshire), b July 25, 1893

Nicholls, Mr. B. E. (Oxford Univ. and Sussex), b Oct 4, 1864, d June 5, 1945

Nicholls, Mr. C. O. (New South Wales), b Dec 5, 1901

Nicholls, J. E. (Worcestershire and Staffordshire), b April 20, 1878

Nicholls, R. B. (Gloucestershire), b Dec 4, 1933

Nicholls, Mr. R. W. (Middlesex), b July 23, 1875, d Jan 22, 1948

Nichols, M. S. (Essex), b Oct 6, 1900

Nicol, Mr. D. J. (South Africa), b Dec 11, 1887

Nicolson, Mr. J. F. W. (South Africa), b July 19, 1899, d Dec 18, 1935

Nimbalkar, R. B. (India), b Dec 1, 1915

Nissar, Mahomed (India), b Aug 1, 1910

Nitschke, Mr. H. C. (South Australia), b April 14, 1906

Noble, Mr. M. A. (New South Wales), b Jan 28, 1873, d June 21, 1940

Noel, Mr. J. (South Australia), b March 28, 1858, d Jan 9, 1938

Norbury, V. (Hampshire and Lancashire), b Aug 3. 1887

Norman, M. (Northamptonshire), b Jan 19, 1933

Norman, Mr. N. F. (Northamptonshire), b Feb 2, 1884

North, E. J. (Middlesex), b Sept 23, 1896

Northway, Mr. R. P. (Somerset and Northamptonshire), b Aug 14, 1906, d Aug 26, 1936

Nothling, Dr. O. E. (Queensland and N.S.W.), b Aug 1, 1900

Nourse, Mr. A. D. (South Africa), b at Croydon, Jan 26, 1878, d July 8, 1948

Nourse, Mr. A. D., jun. (South Africa), b Nov 12, 1910

Nunes, Mr. R. K. (West Indies), b June, 7, 1894

Nunn, Mr. J. A. (Oxford Univ. and Middlesex), b March 19, 1906

Nupen, Mr. E. P. (South Africa), b Jan 1, 1902

Nutter, A. E. (Lancashire and Northamptonshire), b June 28, 1913

Nye, J. K. (Sussex), b May 23, 1914

Oakes, C. (Sussex), b Aug 10, 1912

Oakes, J. (Sussex), b March 3, 1916

Oakley, L. (Worcestershire), b Jan 11, 1916

Oakley, William (Lancashire and Shropshire), b May 6, 1861

Oakman, A. S. M. (Sussex), b April 20, 1930

Oates, A. W. (Nottinghamshire), b Dec 9, 1908

Oates, T. W. (Nottinghamshire), b Aug 9, 1875, d June 18, 1949

Oates, W. F. (Yorkshire), b June 11, 1925

O'Brien, Mr. L. P. J. (Victoria), b July 2, 1908

O'Brien, Mr. R. (Camb. Univ. and Ireland), b Nov 20, 1932

O'Brien, Sir T. C., 3rd Bart. (Oxford Univ., Middlesex and Ireland), b Nov 5, 1861, d Dec 9, 1948

O'Byrne, Mr. W. F. T. (Sussex), b April 30, 1908, d Oct 23, 1951

Ochse, Mr. A. L. (South Africa), b Oct 11, 1899, d May 6, 1949

O'Connor, J. (Essex and Buckinghamshire), b Nov 5, 1899

O'Connor, Mr. J. A. (New South Wales and South Australia), b Sept 9, 1875, d Aug 23, 1941

O'Connor, Mr. L. P. D. (Queensland), b April 11, 1891

O'Halloran, J. (Victoria and Southland, N.Z.), b Jan 12, 1872

Oldfield, N. (Lancashire and Northamptonshire), b April 30, 1911

Oldfield, Mr. P. C. (Oxford Univ.), b Feb 27, 1911

Oldfield, Mr. W. A. (New South Wales), b Sept 9, 1897

Oldroyd, E. (Yorkshire), b Oct 1, 1888

O'Linn, S. (Kent), b May 5, 1927

Oliver, Mr. C. (New Zealand), b Nov 1. 1905

Oliver, Mr. L. (Derbyshire), b Oct 18, 1886, d Jan 26, 1948

Ollivierre, Mr. C. A. (West Indies and Derbyshire), b July 20, 1876, d March 25, 1949

Ollivierre, Mr. R. C. (West Indies), b 1880, d June 5, 1937

Ord, J. S. (Warwickshire), b July 12, 1912

O'Reilly, Mr. W. J. (New South Wales), b Dec 20, 1905

Orford, Mr. L. A. (Camb. Univ.), b March 12, 1865, d Jan 18, 1948

Orlebar, Rev. A. ("Arthur," of "Tom Brown's Schooldays") (Bedfordshire), d Sept 30, 1912, aged 88

Orr, Cmdr. H. J. (Hampshire), b Jan 21, 1878

Orr, Mr. J. H. (Scotland), b Oct 18, 1878

Osman, J. (Surrey), b Dec 14, 1868

Outschoorn, L. (Worcestershire), b Sept 26, 1918

Ovenstone, Mr. D. M. (South Africa), b July 31, 1921

Owen, J. G. (Surrey and Bedfordshire), b Jan 23, 1909

Owen-Smith, Mr. H. G. O. (South Africa, Oxford Univ. and Middlesex), b Feb 18, 1909

Oxenham, Mr. R. K. (Queensland), b July 28, 1891, d Aug 16, 1939

Oyston, C. (Yorkshire), b May 12, 1869, d July 15, 1942

Packe, Major C. W. C. (Leicestershire), b May 2, 1909, d July 1, 1944

Packe, Mr. M. St. J. (Leicestershire), b Aug 21, 1916

Padgett, D. E. V. (Yorkshire), b July 20, 1934

Page, Mr. D. A. C. (Gloucestershire), b April 11, 1911, d Sept 2, 1936

Page, J. C. T. (Kent), b May 20, 1930

Page, Mr. M. L. (New Zealand), b May 8, 1902

Pai, M. D. (India), b June 21, 1883

Paine, G. A. E. (Middlesex and Warwickshire), b June 11, 1908

Pairaudeau, Mr. B. H. (West Indies), b April 14, 1931

Paish, A. (Gloucestershire), b April 5, 1874, d Aug 15, 1948

Palairet, Mr. L. C. H. (Oxford Univ. and Somerset), b May 27, 1870, d March 27, 1933

Palairet, Mr. R. C. N. (Oxford Univ. and Somerset), b June 25, 1871, d Feb 11, 1955

Palia, P. E. (India), b Sept 5, 1910

Palm, Mr. A. W. (South Africa), b June 8, 1901

Palmer, Mr. C. (Camb. Univ. and Middlesex), b July 14, 1885

Palmer, Mr. C. H. (Worcestershire and Leicestershire), b May 15, 1919

Palmer, Mr. H. J. (Essex), b Aug. 30, 1890

Palmer, K. E. (Somerset), b April 22, 1937

Papillon, Mr. G. K. (Northamptonshire), b Sept 24, 1867, d Aug 14, 1942

Pardon, Mr. Charles Frederick (five years Editor of *Wisden*), b March 28, 1850, d April 18, 1890

Pardon, Mr. Edgar S. (for twelve years associated with *Wisden*), b Sept 28, 1859, d July 16, 1898

Pardon, Mr. S. H. (Editor of *Wisden* from 1891 to 1925), b Sept 23, 1855, d Nov 20, 1925

Parfitt, P. H. (Middlesex), b Dec 8, 1936

Paris, Mr. C. G. A. (Hampshire), b Aug 20, 1911

Park, Dr. R. L. (Victoria), b July 30 1892, d Jan 24, 1947

Parker, C. W. L. (Gloucestershire), b Oct 14, 1884

Parker, Mr. G. M. (South Africa), b May 27, 1899

Parker, Mr. G. W. (Camb. Univ. and Gloucestershire), b Feb 11, 1912

Parker, J. F. (Surrey), b April 23, 1913

Parker, Mr. J. P. (Hampshire), b Nov 29, 1902

Parkhouse, W. G. A. (Glamorgan), b Oct 12, 1925

Parkin, C. H. (Durham, Yorkshire and Lancashire), b Feb 18, 1886, d June 15, 1943

Parkin, R. (Lancashire), b March 17, 1908

Parkinson, L. W. (Lancashire), b Sept 15, 1908

Parks, H. W. (Sussex), b July 18, 1906

Parks, James H. (Sussex), b May 12, 1903

Parks, J. M. (Sussex), b Oct 21, 1931

Parr, F. D. (Lancs), b June 1, 1928

Parris, F. (Sussex), b Sept 20, 1867, d Jan 17, 1941

Parry, Mr. D. M. (Camb. Univ.), b Feb 8, 1911

Parsons, Mr. A. B. D. (Camb. Univ.), b Sept 20, 1933

Parsons, Mr. H. F. (Victoria), b May 21, 1875, d Dec 20, 1937

Parsons, Rev. J. H. (Warwickshire), b May 30, 1890

Partridge, Mr. N. E. (Camb. Univ. and Warwickshire), b Aug 10, 1900

Partridge, R. J. (Northamptonshire), b Feb 11, 1912

Pataudi, Nawab of (Oxford Univ., Worcestershire and India), b March 16, 1910, d Jan 5, 1952

Paterson, Mr. R. F. T. (Essex), b Sept 8, 1916

Patiala, H.H. the Maharaja of (India), b Oct 12, 1891, d March 23, 1938

Patten, Mr. M. (Oxford Univ. and Scotland), b July 28, 1901

Patterson, Rev. J. I. (Oxford Univ. and Kent), b March 11, 1860, d Sept 22, 1943

Patterson, Mr. W. H. (Oxford Univ. and Kent), b March 11, 1859, d May 3, 1946

Patterson, Mr. W. S. (Camb. Univ. and Lancashire), b March 19, 1854, d Oct 20, 1939

Paul, A. G. (Lancashire), b July 24, 1864, d Jan 14, 1947

Pavri, Dr. M. E. (Parsees and Middlesex), b Oct 10, 1866, d April 19, 1946

Pawle, Mr. J. H. (Camb. Univ. and Essex), b May 18, 1915

Pawson, Mr. A. C. (Oxford Univ.), b Jan 5, 1882

Pawson, Mr. A. G. (Oxford Univ. and Worcestershire), b May 30, 1888

Pawson, Mr. H. A. (Kent and Oxford Univ.), b Aug 22, 1921

Payn, Mr. L. W. (South Africa), b May 6, 1915

Payne, A. (Sussex), b April 28, 1858, d July 23, 1943

Payne, Mr. A. U. (Camb. Univ. and Buckinghamshire), b Jan 28, 1903

Payne, Mr. C. A. L. (Oxford Univ. and Middlesex), b Aug 30, 1885

Payne, Mr. J. H. (Lancashire), b March 19, 1858, d Jan 24, 1942

Payne, Mr. M. W. (Camb. Univ. and Middlesex), b May 10, 1885

Paynter, E. (Lancashire), b Nov 5, 1901

Payton, Rev. W. E. G. (Camb. Univ. Nottinghamshire and Derbyshire), b Dec. 27, 1913

Payton, W. R. D. (Nottinghamshire), b Feb 13, 1882, d May 21, 1943

Peach, C. W. (Kent), b Jan 3, 1900

Peach, H. A. (Surrey and Berkshire), b Oct 6, 1890

Peake, Rev. E. (Oxford Univ., Gloucestershire and Berkshire), b March 29, 1860, d Jan 3, 1945

Pearce, G. (Sussex), b Oct 27, 1908

Pearce, Mr. T. A. (Kent), b Dec 18, 1910

Pearce, Mr. T. N. (Essex), b Nov 3, 1905

Pearse, Mr. A. (Somerset), b April 22, 1915

Pearse, Mr. G. V. (Natal and Oxford Univ.), b Sept 7, 1891

Pearse, Mr. C. O. C. (South Africa), b Oct 10, 1884, d May 28, 1953

Pearson, F. (Worcestershire), b Sept 23, 1880

Peat, Mr. C. U. (Oxford Univ. and Middlesex), b Feb 28, 1892

Peebles, Mr. I. A. R. (Oxford Univ. and Middlesex), b Jan 20, 1908

Peel, R. (Yorkshire), b Feb 12, 1857, d Aug 12, 1941

Pegler, Mr. S. J. (South Africa and Manager South African Team in England, 1951), b July 28, 1889

Pelham, Mr. A. G. (Camb. Univ., Sussex and Somerset), b Sept 4, 1911

Pellew, Mr. C. E. (South Australia), b Sept 21, 1893

Pennington, J. (Nottinghamshire), b June 24, 1881

Pepall, G. (Gloucestershire), b Feb 29, 1876, d Jan 8, 1953

Pepper, Mr. J. (Camb. Univ.), b Oct 21, 1922

Perkins, C. (Northamptonshire and Suffolk), b June 4, 1911

Perkins, Mr. T. T. N. (Camb. Univ , Essex, Kent and Wiltshire), b Dec 19, 1870, d July 20, 1946

Perks, R. T. D. (Monmouthshire and Worcestershire), b Oct 4, 1911

Perrin, Mr. P. A. (Essex), b May 26, 1876, d Nov 20, 1945

Perry, Mr. E. H. (Worcestershire), b Jan 16, 1908

Pether, Mr. S. (Oxford Univ. and Oxfordshire), b Oct 15, 1916

Pettiford, J. (New South Wales and Kent), b Nov 29, 1919

Pewtress, Mr. A. W. (Lancashire), b Aug 27, 1891

Phadkar, Mr. D. G. (India), b Dec 12, 1925

Phebey, A. H. (Kent), b Oct 1, 1924

Phillipps, Mr. J. H. (Manager New Zealand team in England, 1949), b Jan 1, 1898

Phillips, Mr. F. A. (Essex, Somerset and Oxford Univ.), b April 11, 1873, d March 5, 1955

Phillips, Mr. J. B. (Oxford Univ. and Kent), b Nov 19, 1933

Phillipson, W. E. (Lancashire), b Dec 3, 1910

Pickles, D. (Yorkshire), b Nov 16, 1935

Pickles, L. (Somerset), b Sept 17, 1932

Pierce, Mr. T. (Joint Manager with C. de Caires, West Indies in England 1957), b Dec. 26, 1916

Pieris, Mr. P. I. (Camb. Univ.), b March 14, 1933

Pierpoint, F. G. (Surrey and Norfolk), b April 24, 1915

Pierre, Mr. L. R. (West Indies), b June 5, 1921

Pilkington, Mr. C. C. (Oxford Univ., Lancashire and Middlesex), b Dec 13, 1876, d Jan 8, 1950

Pilkington, Mr. H. C. (Oxford Univ. and Middlesex), b Oct 25, 1879, d June 17, 1942

Pinch, Mr. F. B. (Glamorgan), b Feb 24, 1891

Pitchford, L.(Glamorgan),b Dec 4,1900

Pitman R. W. C. (Hampshire), b Feb, 21, 1933

Piton, Mr. J. H. (Western Province, Natal and Transvaal), b April 20, 1865, d July 20, 1942

Place, W. (Lancashire), b Dec 7, 1914

Platt, G. J. W. (Surrey), b June 9, 1882, d April 14, 1955

Platt, R. K. (Yorkshire), b Dec 21, 1932

Pleass, J. (Glamorgan), b May 21, 1923

Plimsoll, Mr. J. B. (South Africa), b Oct 27, 1917

Plumer, Field-Marshal, 1st Visct. (President, M.C.C., 1929), b March 13, 1857, d July 16, 1932

Podmore, Mr. A. (Haileybury) (Cricket Writer), b Sept 14, 1861, d Oct 17, 1937

Poidevin, Mr. L. O. S. (New South Wales, London County and Lancashire), b Nov 5, 1876, d Nov 18, 1931

Pollard, R. (Lancashire), b June 19, 1912

Ponsford, Mr. W. H. (Victoria), b Oct 19, 1900

Pool, Mr. C. J. T. (Northamptonshire), b Jan 21, 1876, d Oct 13, 1954

Poole, C. J. (Nottinghamshire), b March 13, 1921

Poole, K. J. (Nottinghamshire), b April 27, 1934

Poore, Brig.-Gen. Robert M.(Wiltshire, Hampshire and South Africa), b March 20, 1866, d July 14, 1938

Pope, A. V. (Derbyshire), b Aug 15, 1909

Pope, Mr. C. G. (Camb. Univ. and Bedfordshire), b Jan 21, 1872

Pope, D. F. (Gloucestershire and Essex), b Oct 28, 1908, d Sept 8, 1934

Pope, G. H. (Derbyshire), b Jan 27, 1911

Pope, Dr. R. J. (New South Wales and M.C.C.), b Feb 18, 1864, d July 27, 1952

Popplewell, Mr. O. B. (Camb. Univ.), b Aug 15, 1927

Porch, Mr. R. B. (Somerset), b April 3, 1875

Porter, Mr. A. (Glamorgan), b March 25, 1914

Posthuma, Mr. C. J. (Holland and London County), b Jan 11, 1868, d Dec 21, 1939

Pothecary, E. A. (Hampshire), b March 1, 1906

Pothecary, S. (Hampshire), b May 6, 1890

Potter, Mr. G. (Lancashire and Cheshire), b Oct 3, 1878

Potter, G. (Sussex), b Oct 26, 1931

Potts, Mr. H. J. (Oxford Univ.), b Jan 23, 1925

Powell, Mr. A. G. (Camb. Univ., Essex and Suffolk), b Aug 17, 1912

Powell, Mr. W. A. (Kent), b May 19, 1885, d Jan 1, 1954

Poynton, Dr. F. J. (Somerset), b June 26, 1869, d Oct 29, 1943

Poyntz, Mr. E. S. M. (Somerset), b Oct 27, 1883, d Dec 26, 1934

Poyntz, Col. H. S. (Somerset), b Sept 17, 1877, d June 22, 1955

Pratt, R. C. E. (Surrey), b May 5, 1928

Preece, C. R. (Worcestershire), b Dec 15, 1888

Prentice, F. T. (Leicestershire), b April 22, 1912

Pressdee, J. (Glamorgan), b June 19, 1933

Prest, Mr. H. E. W. (Camb. Univ. and Kent), b Jan 9, 1890, d Jan 5, 1955

Preston, Mr. Hubert (Editor of *Wisden* 1944 to 1951), b Dec 16, 1868

Preston, H. J. (Kent), b Oct 25, 1886

Preston, K. C. (Essex), b Aug 22, 1925

Pretlove, Mr. J. F. (Camb. Univ. and Kent), b Nov 23, 1932

Pretty, Dr. Harold C. (Surrey and Northamptonshire), b Oct 23, 1875, d May 31, 1952

Price, E. (Lancashire and Essex), b Oct 27, 1918

Price, Mr. V. R. (Oxford Univ. and Surrey), b May 22, 1895

Price, W. F. (Middlesex), b April 25, 1902

Pritchard, T. L. (New Zealand, Warwickshire and Kent) b March 10, 1917

Proffitt, S. (Essex), b Oct 8, 1911

Prothero, Mr. R. E., 1st Lord Ernle (Marlborough, Hampshire and President, M.C.C., 1924), b Sept 6, 1852, d July 1, 1937

Proud, Mr. R. B. (Oxford Univ. and Hampshire and Durham), b Sept 19, 1919

Prouton, R. (Hampshire), b March 1, 1926

Pryer, Mr. B. J. K. (Camb. Univ. and Kent), b Feb 1, 1925

Pullar, G. (Lancashire), b Aug 1, 1935

Pullen, Mr. W. W. F. (Gloucestershire, Somerset and Glamorgan), b June 24, 1866, d Aug 9, 1937

Pullin, Mr. A. W. (Cricket Writer under non-de-plume of "Old Ebor"), b July 30, 1860, d June 23, 1934

Pullinger, Mr. G. R. (Essex), b March 14, 1920

Pulman, Rev. W. W. (Oxford Univ.), b Nov. 14, 1852, d Aug 22, 1936

Purdy, H. (Derbyshire), b Jan 17, 1884, dead

Purdy, T. (Derbyshire), b July 3, 1864, d 1944

Putner, F. W. (Middlesex), b Sept 26, 1912

Quaife, Mr. B. W. (Warwickshire and Worcestershire), b Nov 24, 1899

Quaife, Walter (Sussex, Warwickshire and Suffolk), b April 1, 1864, d Jan 18, 1943

Quaife, W. G. (Sussex and Warwickshire), b March 17, 1872, d Oct 13, 1951

Quick, Mr. A. B. (Essex), b Feb 10, 1915

Quinn, Mr. N. A. (South Africa), b Feb 21, 1908, d Aug 5, 1934

Quist, Mr. K. H. (New South Wales, Western Australia and South Australia), b Aug 18, 1875

Rabone, Mr. G. O. (New Zealand), b Nov 6, 1921

Radcliffe, Mr. E. J. R. H. (Yorkshire), b Jan 27, 1884

Radcliffe, George (Lancashire), b Sept 25, 1877, d Oct 27, 1951

Radcliffe, Lees (Lancashire and Durham), b Nov 23, 1871

Radcliffe, Mr. O. G. (Somerset, Gloucestershire and Wiltshire), b Oct 20, 1859, d April 13, 1940

Rae, Mr. A. F. (West Indies), b Sept 30, 1922

Rae, Mr. E. A. (West Indies), b Nov 8, 1897

Raikes, Rev. G. B. (Oxford Univ., Hampshire and Norfolk), b March 14, 1873

Raikes, Mr. T. B. (Oxford Univ. and Norfolk), b Dec 16, 1902

Rait Kerr, Col. R. S. (Rugby and R.M.A., Woolwich, Secretary, M.C.C. 1936–52, b April 13, 1891

Ralph, Mr. R. (Essex), b May 22, 1920

Ramadhin, Mr. S. (West Indies), b May 1, 1930

Ramaswami, C. (India), b June 18, 1896

Ramchand, Mr. G. S. (India), b July 26, 1927

Ramsay, Mr. R. C. (Camb. Univ. and Somerset), b Dec 20, 1861

Ranjitsinhji, Kumar Shri, afterwards H.H. The Jam Saheb of Nawanagar (India, Camb. Univ., Cambridgeshire and Sussex), b Sept 10, 1872, d April 2, 1933

Ransford, Mr. V. S. (Victoria), b March 20, 1885

Ransom, Mr. V. J. (Hampshire), b March 17, 1918

Raphael, Mr. F. C. (Hon. Sec., New Zealand Council), b Dec 29, 1866, d June, 1940

Rashleigh, Canon W. (Oxford Univ. and Kent), b March 7, 1867, d Feb 13, 1937

Ratcliffe, Mr. A. (Camb. Univ., Denbighshire, Surrey and Buckinghamshire), b March 31, 1909

Raven, Mr. R. O. (Northamptonshire), b Nov 26, 1884, d April 4, 1936

Rawlin, E. R. (Yorkshire), b Oct 4, 1899, d Jan 11, 1943

Rayment, A. W. H. (Hampshire), b May 29, 1928

Read, Mr. A. H. (Essex), b Jan 24, 1880

Read, Mr. H. D. (Surrey and Essex), b Jan 28, 1910

Read, J. Maurice (Surrey), b Feb 9, 1859, d Feb 17, 1929

Reay, Mr. G. M. (Surrey), b Jan 24, 1887

Reddick, Mr. T. B. (Middlesex and Nottinghamshire), b Feb 17, 1912

Reddish, J. (Nottinghamshire), b Dec 22, 1906

Redgrave, Mr. S. J. (New South Wales and Queensland), b Aug 5, 1878

Redman, J. (Somerset), b March 1, 1926

Rees-Davies, Mr. W. R. (Camb. Univ.), b Nov 19, 1916

Reese, Mr. D. (New Zealand and Essex), b Jan 26, 1879, d June 12, 1953

Reeves, W. (Essex), b June 22, 1876, d March 22, 1944

Reid, Mr. J. R. (New Zealand), b June 3, 1928

Relf, A. E. (Norfolk and Sussex), b June 26, 1874, d March 26, 1937

Relf, R. R. (Berkshire and Sussex), b Sept 1, 1883

Remnant, E. R. (Hampshire), b May 1, 1884

Revill, A. C. (Derbyshire), b March 27, 1923

Reynolds, B. L. (Northamptonshire), b June 10, 1932

Rhodes, A. C. (Yorkshire) b Oct 14, 1906, d May 2, 1957

Rhodes, A. E. (Derbyshire), b Oct 10, 1916

Rhodes, Mr. S. D. (Nottinghamshire), b March 24, 1910

Rhodes, Wilfred (Yorkshire), b Oct 29, 1877

Rice, Mr. R. W. (Gloucestershire, Oxford Univ. and Bedfordshire), b Nov 14, 1868, d Feb 11, 1938

Richards, R. (Sussex), b Sept 10, 1908

Richardson, A. (Nottinghamshire), b Oct 28, 1926

Richardson, Arthur J. (South Australia and Western Australia), b July 24, 1888

Richardson, Mr. A. W. (Derbyshire), b June, 1907

Richardson, B. II. (Derbyshire), b March 12, 1932

Richardson, Mr. C. A. (New South Wales and Wellington, N.Z.), b Feb 22, 1864, d Aug 17, 1949

Richardson, D. W. (Worcestershire), b Nov 3, 1934

Richardson, H. (Nottinghamshire), b Oct 4, 1856, d March, 1940

Richardson, Mr. H. B. (Surrey and California), b March 10, 1873

Richardson, Mr. J. V. (Oxford Univ. and Essex), b Dec 16, 1903

Richardson, Mr, P. E. (Worcestershire), b July 4, 1931

Richardson, S. (Derbyshire), b May 22, 1844, d March 1938

Richardson, T. (Surrey and Somerset), b Aug 11, 1870, d July 2, 1912

Richardson, Mr. V. Y. (South Australia), b Sept 7, 1894

Riches, Mr. N. V. H. (Glamorgan), b June 9, 1883

Richmond, T. L. (Nottinghamshire), b June 23, 1892, d Dec 30, 1957

Rickman, Mr. R. B. (Derbyshire), b May 6, 1881, d 1940

Riddell, Mr. V. H. (Camb. Univ.), b July 23, 1905

Riddington, A. (Leicestershire), b Dec 22, 1911

Ridgway, F. (Kent), b Aug 10, 1923

Rigg, Mr. K. E. (Victoria), b May 21, 1906

Riley, H. (Leicestershire), b Oct 3, 1903

Riley, Mr. W. N. (Camb. Univ. and Leicestershire), b Nov 24, 1892, d Nov 20, 1955

Rimell, Mr. A. G. J. (Camb. Univ. and Hampshire), b Aug 29, 1928

Ring, Mr. D. (Victoria), b Oct 14, 1918

Ringrose, W. (Yorkshire and Scotland), b Sept 2, 1871, d Sept 14, 1943

Rippon, Mr. A. D. E. (Somerset), b April 29, 1892

Rippon, Mr. A. E. S. (Somerset), b April 29, 1892

Rist, F. (Essex), b March 30, 1914

Roach, Mr. C. A. (West Indies), b March 13, 1904

Roberts, Mr. A. W. (New Zealand), b Aug. 20, 1909

Roberts, Mr. A. W. (Gloucestershire), b Sept 23, 1874

Roberts, Mr. D. (M.C.C. and Surrey), b Feb 5, 1894

Roberts, F. G. (Gloucestershire), b April 1, 1862, d April 7, 1936

Roberts, H. E. (Sussex), b Feb 8, 1890

Roberts, H. J. (Warwickshire), b May 5, 1912

Roberts, W. B. (Lancashire), b Sept 27, 1914, d Aug 24, 1951

Roberts, W. C. (Hampshire), b June 15, 1861

Robertson, J. D. (Middlesex), b Feb 22, 1917

Robertson, Mr. W. P. (Camb. Univ. and Middlesex), b Sept 5, 1879, d May 7, 1950

Robertson-Glasgow, Mr. R. C. (Oxford Univ. and Somerset), b July 15, 1901

Robins, Mr. R. V. C. (Middlesex), b March 13, 1935

Robins, Mr. R. W. V. (Camb. Univ. and Middlesex), b June 3, 1906

Robinson, A. G. (Northamptonshire), b March 22, 1917

Robinson, Canon C. D. (Natal and Buckinghamshire), b July 18, 1873, d Aug 26, 1948

Robinson, Mr. C. J. (Somerset), b May 21, 1864, d June 8, 1941

Robinson, Lt.-Col. D. C. (Essex and Gloucestershire), b April 20, 1883

Robinson, E. (Yorkshire), b Nov 16, 1884

Robinson, E. P. (Yorkshire and Somerset), b Aug 10, 1911

Robinson, Mr. F. G. (Gloucestershire), b Sept 19, 1880

Robinson, Mr. G. E. (Oxford Univ.), b March 13, 1861, d Nov 30, 1944

Robinson, G. W. (Nottinghamshire), b Feb 15, 1908

Robinson, Mr. H. B. (Oxford Univ.), b March 3, 1919

Robinson, Mr. J. J. (Camb. Univ.), b June 28, 1872

Robinson, Mr. M. (Glamorgan and Warwickshire), b July 16, 1921

Robinson, Mr. P. G. (Gloucestershire), b Nov 2, 1882, d Jan 30, 1951

Robinson, Sir R. L., 1st Lord Robinson (Oxford Univ.), b May 8, 1883, d Sept 5, 1952

Robinson, Mr. Theo (Somerset), b Feb. 16, 1866

Robson, Mr. C. (Middlesex and Hampshire), b June 20, 1859, d Sept 27, 1943

Rochdale, 1st Lord, C.B. (George Kemp) (Cambridge, Lancashire), b June 9, 1866, d March 24, 1945

Rochford, P. (Gloucestershire), b Aug 27, 1928

Rock, Mr. C. W. (Warwickshire, Camb. Univ. and Tasmania), b June 9 1863, d July 27, 1950

Roe, Mr. W. N. (Camb. Univ. and Somerset), b March 21, 1861, d Oct 11, 1937

Rogers, A. (Gloucestershire), b Feb 1, 1908

Rogers, Lt.-Col. F. G. (Gloucestershire), b April 7, 1897

Rogers, H. O. (Worcestershire), b Jan 21, 1891

Rogers, N. H. (Hampshire), b March 9, 1918

Rogers, Mr. S. S. (Somerset), b March 18, 1923

Roller, Mr. W. E. (Surrey), b Feb 1, 1858, d Aug 27, 1949

Romans, Mr. G. (Gloucestershire), b Nov 30, 1876, d Jan 2, 1946

Root, C. F. (Derbyshire and Worcestershire), b April 16, 1890, d Jan 20, 1954

Rosebery, 5th Earl of (Vice-President, Surrey C.C.C.), b May 7, 1847, d May 21, 1929

Rosebery, 6th Earl of (see Dalmeny, Lord)

Rotherham, Mr. G. A. (Camb. Univ. and Warwickshire), b May 28, 1899

Rotherham, Mr. Hugh (Warwickshire), b March 16, 1861, d Feb 24, 1939

Rought-Rought, Mr. D. C. (Camb. Univ. and Norfolk), b May 3, 1912

Rought-Rought, Mr. R. C. (Camb. Univ. and Norfolk), b Feb 17, 1908

Routledge, R. (Middlesex), b July 7, 1920

Rowan, Mr. A. M. B. (South Africa), b Feb 7, 1921

Rowan, Mr. E. A. B. (South Africa), b July 20, 1909

Rowe, E. J. (Nottinghamshire), b July 21, 1920

Rowe, Mr. W. (Queensland), b Jan 10, 1892

Rowlands, Mr. W. H. (Gloucestershire), b July 30, 1883, d July 30, 1948

Rowley, Mr. Ernest (Lancashire), b Jan 15, 1870

Roy, Mr. P. (India), b May 31, 1928

Rucker, Mr. C. E. S. (Oxford Univ.), b Sept 4, 1894

Rucker, Capt. P. W. (Oxford Univ.), b May 5, 1900, d May 1940

Rudd, Mr. C. R. D. (Oxford Univ.), b March 25, 1929

Rudd, Mr. G. B. F. (Leicestershire), b July 3, 1894

Rudston, H. (Yorkshire), b Nov 22, 1879

Ruffell, R. (Hampshire), b Oct 3, 1869, d. 1944

Rumbold, Mr. J. S. (Oxford Univ.), b March 5, 1920

Rundell, Mr. P. D. (South Australia), b Nov 20, 1890

Rushby, T. (Surrey), b Sept 6, 1881

Rushton, F. (Lancashire), b April 21, 1906

Russell, A. C. (Essex), b Oct 7, 1887

Russell, Mr. A. I. (Hampshire), b Feb 21, 1867

Rutherford, Mr. J. (Western Australia), b Sept 25, 1929

Ryan, F. (Hampshire and Glamorgan), b Nov 14, 1888, d Jan 6, 1954

Ryder, Mr. J. (Victoria), b Aug 8, 1889

Ryder, Mr. R. V. (Staffordshire and Sec., Warwickshire C.C.C.), b March 11, 1873, d Sept. 1, 1949

Rye, G. J. (Norfolk and Minor Counties Umpire), b Nov 2, 1857, d Jan 6, 1943

Rymill, Mr. J. W. (South Australia), b March 20, 1901

Sadler, W. C. H. (Surrey and Durham), b Sept 24, 1896

Saggers, Mr. R. A. (New South Wales), b May 15, 1917

Sainsbury, P. J. (Hampshire), b June 13, 1934

St. Hill, Mr. A. B. (West Indies), d Aug. 23, 1911

St Hill, Mr. E. L. (West Indies), b March 9, 1904, d May 21, 1957

St. Hill, Mr. W. H. (West Indies), b July 6, 1893

Salam-ud-din, K. (India), b Oct 16, 1888

Sale, Mr. R. (Oxford Univ. and Derbyshire), b June 21, 1889

Sale, Mr. R., jun. (Oxford Univ, Warwickshire and Derbyshire), b Oct 4, 1919

Salmon, Mr. G. H. (Leicestershire), b Aug. 1, 1894

Salter, Mr. M. G. (Oxford Univ. and Gloucestershire), b May 10, 1887

Samuel, Mr. G. N. T. W. (Glamorgan), b Oct 26, 1917

Sanders, W. (Warwickshire), b April 4, 1910

Sandham, A. (Surrey), b July 6, 1890

Santall, F. R. (Warwickshire), b July 12, 1903, d Nov 3, 1950

Santall, J. F. E. (Worcestershire), b Dec 3, 1907

Santall, S. (Northamptonshire and Warwickshire), b June 10, 1873, d March 19, 1957

Sarel, Major W. G. M. (Surrey, Trinidad, Northumberland, Kent and Sussex, late Sec. Sussex C.C.C.), b Dec 11, 1875, d April 5, 1950

Sargent, M. A. J. (Leicestershire), b Aug 23, 1928

Sarwate, C. T. (India), b June 22, 1920

Saunders, Sir A. A. (Sussex), b Dec. 15, 1892, d Feb 26, 1957

Saunders, Mr. J. V. (Victoria), b Feb 3, 1876, d Dec 21, 1927

Savage, J. S. (Leicestershire), b March 15, 1929

Savill, L. (Essex), b June 30, 1935

Saville, Mr. S. H. (Camb. Univ. and Middlesex), b Nov 21, 1889

Scaife, Mr. J. A. (Victoria), b Nov 14, 1909

Schultz (afterwards Storey), Mr. S. S. (Camb. Univ. and Lancashire), b Aug 29, 1857, d Dec 18, 1937

Scorer, Col. R. I. (Warwickshire), b Jan 6, 1892

Scott, Canon A. T. (Camb. Univ.), b July 18, 1848, d June 18, 1925

Scott, C. J. (Gloucestershire), b May 1, 1919

Scott, Capt. Lord George W. Montagu-Douglas (Oxford Univ. and Middlesex), b Aug 21, 1866, d Feb 23, 1947

Scott, Mr. J. D. (New South Wales and South Australia), b Jan 24, 1890

Scott, Major K. B. (Oxford Univ. and Sussex), b Aug 17, 1915, d Aug 9, 1943

Scott, Mr. M. D. (Oxford Univ.), b Nov 14, 1933

Scott, Mr. O. C. (West Indies), b Aug 25, 1893

Scott, Mr. R. S. G. (Oxford Univ. and Sussex), b April 26, 1909, d Aug 26, 1957

Scott, Mr. V. J. (New Zealand), b July 31, 1916

Seabrook, Mr. F. J. (Camb. Univ. and Gloucestershire), b Jan 9, 1899

Sealey, Mr. B. J. (West Indies), b Aug 12, 1899

Sealy, Mr. J. E. D. (West Indies), b Sept 11, 1912

Seamer, Mr. J. W. (Somerset and Oxford Univ.), b June 23, 1913

Searle, Mr. Jas. (New South Wales), b Aug 28, 1863, d Dec 28, 1936

Seitz, Mr. J. A. (Oxford Univ. and Victoria), b Sept 19, 1883

Sellar, Lt.-Cmdr. K. A. (Royal Navy and Sussex), b Aug 11, 1906

Sellers, Mr. A. (Yorkshire), b May 30, 1870, d Sept 25, 1941

Sellers, Mr. A. B. (Yorkshire), b March 5, 1907

Semmence, D. J. (Sussex), b April 20, 1938

Sen, Mr. P. (India), b May 31, 1926

Sohan Chari, K. (India), b Jan. 2, 1875

Sewell, Mr. C. O. H. (Natal and Gloucestershire), b Dec 19, 1874, d Aug 19, 1951

Sewell, Mr. E. H. D. (Bedfordshire, India, Essex and Buckinghamshire), b Sept 30, 1872, d Sept 20, 1947

Seymour, James (Kent), b Oct 25, 1879, d Sept 30, 1930

Seymour, John (Sussex and Northamptonshire), b Aug 24, 1883

Shackleton, D. (Hampshire), b Aug 12, 1924

Shacklock, F. (Derbyshire, Nottinghamshire and Otago), b Sept 22, 1861, d May 3, 1937

Shakespeare, Mr. W. H. N. (Worcestershire), b Aug 24, 1893

Shakoor Ahmed (Pakistan), b Sept 15, 1928

Shardlow, W. (Derbyshire), b Sept 30, 1902

Sharp, Mr. A. T. (Leicestershire), b March 23, 1889

Sharp, H. P. (Middlesex), b Oct 6, 1917

Sharp, Mr. J. (Lancashire), b Feb 15, 1878, d Jan 27, 1938

Sharp, Capt. R. H. (Essex), b June 11, 1893

Sharpe, J. W. (Surrey and Nottinghamshire), b Dec 9, 1866, d June 19, 1936

Shaw, Alfred (Nottinghamshire and Sussex), b Aug 29, 1842, d Jan 16, 1907

Shaw, Rt. Rev. E. D. (Oxford Univ., Hertfordshire, Middlesex and Buckinghamshire), b Oct 5, 1860, d Nov 5, 1937

Sheffield, E. J. (Surrey and Kent), b June 20, 1908

Sheffield, J. R. (Essex), b Nov 19, 1906

Sheldrake, Mr. E. F. T. (Hampshire), b Jan 18, 1864

Shelmerdine, Mr. G. O. (Camb. Univ. and Lancashire), b Sept 7, 1899

Shelton, Mr. A. W. (Nottinghamshire C.C.C.), b Nov 14, 1862, d Sept 10, 1938

Shepherd, D. J. (Glamorgan), b Aug 8, 1927

Shepherd, T. F. (Surrey), b Dec 5, 1890, d Feb 13, 1957

Sheppard, Rev. D. S. (Sussex and Cambridge Univ.), b March 6, 1929

Sheppard, Mr. R. A. (Surrey), b Aug 24, 1879, d Jan 28, 1953

Sherwell, Mr. N. B. (Camb. Univ. and Middlesex), b March 16, 1904

Sherwell, Mr. P. W. (Cornwall and South Africa), b Aug 17, 1880, d April 17, 1948

Shields, Mr. J. (Leicestershire), b Feb 1, 1882

Shinde, S. G. (India), b Aug 18, 1923, d June 22, 1955

Shine, Mr. E. B. (Camb. Univ. and Kent), b July 9, 1873, d Nov 11, 1952

Shipman, A. (Leicestershire), b March 7, 1901

Shipman, W. (Leicestershire), b March 1, 1886, d Aug 26, 1943

Shipston, F. W. (Nottinghamshire), b July 29, 1906

Shirley, Mr. W. R. de la C. (Camb. Univ. and Hampshire), b Oct 13, 1900

Shirreff, Mr. A. C. (Camb. Univ., Hampshire and Kent), b Feb 12, 1919

Shivram, P. (India), b March 6, 1878

Shortland, Mr. N. A. (Warwickshire), b July 16, 1916

Shrewsbury, A. (Nottinghamshire), b April 11, 1856, d May 19, 1903

Shuja-ud-Din (Pakistan), b April 10, 1930

Shuter, Mr. L. A. (Surrey), b May 15, 1852, d July 13, 1928

Shuttleworth, Mr. G. M. (Camb. Univ.), b Nov 6, 1926

Sibbles, F. M. (Lancashire), b March 15, 1904

Sidwell, T. E. (Leicestershire), b Jan 30, 1888

Siedle, Mr. I. J. (South Africa), b Jan 11, 1903

Sievers, Mr. M. W. S. (Victoria), b April 13, 1912

Silk, Mr. D. R. W. (Camb. Univ. and Somerset), b Oct 8, 1931

Sime, Mr. W. A. (Bedfordshire and Nottinghamshire), b Feb 8, 1909

Simms, Mr. H. L. (Sussex and Warwickshire), b Jan 31, 1888, d June 9, 1942

Simpson, Mr. E. T. B. (Oxford Univ. and Yorkshire), b March 5, 1867, d March 20, 1944

Simpson, Mr. R. T. (Nottinghamshire), b Feb 27, 1920

Simpson-Hayward, Mr. G. H. (Worcestershire), b June 7, 1875, d Oct 2, 1936

Sims, J. M. (Middlesex), b May 13, 1904

Sinclair, Mr. E. H. L. G. (Oxford Univ.), b Sept 10, 1904

Sinclair, Mr. J. H. (South Africa), b Oct 16, 1876, d Feb 23, 1913

Sinfield, R. A. (Gloucestershire), b Dec 24, 1901

Singh, S. (E. Punjab, Camb. Univ. and Warwickshire), b Aug 18, 1931

Singleton, Mr. A. P. (Oxford Univ. and Worcestershire), b Aug 5, 1914

Skeet, Mr. C. H. L. (Oxford Univ. and Middlesex), b Aug 17, 1895

Skelding, Alec (Leicestershire), b Sept 5, 1886

Skene, Mr. R. W. (Oxford Univ.), b May 20, 1908

Skinner, Mr. A. F. (Derbyshire and Northamptonshire), b April 22, 1913

Skinner, Mr. D. A. (Derbyshire), b March 22, 1920

Skinner, I. J. (Essex), b April 1, 1928

Slack, Mr. J. K. E. (Camb. Univ.), b Dec 23, 1930

Slater, A. G. (Derbyshire), b Nov 22, 1890, d July 22, 1949

Smailes, T. F. (Yorkshire), b March 27, 1910

Smales, K. (Yorkshire and Nottinghamshire), b Sept 15, 1927

Small, Mr. J. A. (West Indies), b Nov 3, 1892

Smart, C. C. (Glamorgan and Warwickshire), b July 23, 1898

Smart, Jack (Warwickshire), b April 12, 1894

Smith, Mr. A. F. (Camb. Univ. and Middlesex), b May 13, 1853, d Jan 18, 1936

Smith, Mr. B. C. (Northamptonshire and First Class Umpire), b July 10, 1859, d Nov 29, 1942

Smith, Sir C. A. (Camb. Univ., Transvaal and Sussex), b July 21, 1863, d Dec 20, 1948

Smith, C. I. J. (Wiltshire and Middlesex), b Aug 25, 1906

Smith, Mr. C. L. A. (Sussex), b Jan 2, 1879, d Nov 22, 1949

Smith, Mr. C. S. (Lancashire and Camb. Univ.), b Oct 1, 1932

Smith, Denis (Derbyshire), b Jan 24, 1907

Smith, Douglas (Somerset, Glamorgan and Worcestershire), b May 29, 1874, d Aug 16, 1949

Smith, Mr. D. (Victoria), b Sept 14, 1884

Smith, Mr. D. J. (Camb. Univ.), b Oct 19, 1933

Smith, D. R. (Gloucestershire), b Oct 5, 1934

Smith, D. V. (Sussex), b June 14, 1923

Smith, Mr. Ernest (Oxford Univ. and Yorkshire), b Oct 19, 1869, d April 11, 1945

Smith, E. (Derbyshire), b Jan 2, 1934

Smith, E. J. (Warwickshire), b Feb 6, 1887

Smith, Mr. F. B. (New Zealand), b March 13, 1922

Smith, F. E. (Suffolk and Surrey), b May 13, 1872, d Dec 3, 1943

Smith, Mr. G. (Kent), b Nov 30, 1925

Smith, G. (Essex), b April 2, 1935

Smith, Mr. G. O. (Oxford Univ. and Surrey), b Nov 25, 1872, d Dec 6, 1943

Smith, H. (Gloucestershire), b May 21, 1891, d Nov 12, 1937

Smith, H. A. (Leicestershire), b March 29, 1901, d Aug 7, 1948

Smith, Mr. H. E. (Transvaal), b April 21, 1884

Smith, Mr. H. T. O. (Essex), b March 5, 1906

Smith, I. W. (Worcestershire), b Oct 26, 1880

Smith, J. C. (Worcestershire), b Sept 26, 1894

Smith, K. D. (Leicestershire), b April 29, 1922

Smith, Mr. M. J. K. (Leicestershire, Oxford Univ. and Warwickshire), b June 30, 1933

Smith, Mr. O. G. (West Indies), b May 5, 1933

Smith, P. (Leicestershire), b Oct 5, 1934

Smith, Mr. R. (Lancashire), b May 1, 1868

Smith, R. (Essex), b Aug 10, 1914

Smith, R. (Somerset), b April 14, 1930

Smith, R. C. (Leicestershire), b Aug 3, 1935

Smith, Mr. S. (Manager, Australian Teams, 1921 and 1926), b March 1, 1880

Smith, S. (Lancashire), b Jan 14, 1929

Smith, Mr. S. G. (West Indies, Northamptonshire and New Zealand), b Jan 15, 1881

Smith, Mr. T. M. (Hampshire), b June 15, 1899

Smith, T. P. B. (Essex), b Oct 30, 1908

Smith, Mr. V. I. (South Africa), b Feb 23, 1925

Smith, Mr. W. A. (Leicestershire), b Feb 23, 1913

Smith, W. C. (Oxfordshire and Surrey), b Oct 4, 1877, d July 15, 1946

Smithson, G. A. (Yorkshire and Leicestershire), b Nov 1, 1926

Smoker, H. G. (Hampshire and Cheshire), b March 1, 1881

Snary, H. C. (Leicestershire), b Sept 22, 1898

Snedden, Mr. N. C. (New Zealand), b April 3, 1892

Snell, Mr. A. P. (Essex), b March 17, 1870, d July 26, 1937

Snooke, Mr. S. D. (South Africa), b Nov. 11, 1878

Snooke, Mr. S. J. (South Africa), b Feb 1, 1881

Snowden, Mr. A. W. (Northamptonshire), b Aug 15, 1913

Soar, T. (Hampshire and Carmarthen), b Sept 3, 1865, d May 17, 1939

Sobers, Mr. G. (West Indies), b July 28, 1936

Sohoni, S. W. (India), b March 5, 1918

Solbé, Mr. E. P. (Kent), b May 10, 1902

Somers, 6th Lord (Worcestershire, President, M.C.C., 1936), b March 19, 1887, d July 14, 1944

Somerset, Mr. A. P. F. C. (Sussex), b Sept 28, 1889

Southerton, Mr. S. J. (Editor of *Wisden* 1934–1935), b July 7, 1874, d March 12, 1935

Spanswick, J. (Kent), b Sept 30, 1933

Spence, L. A. (Leicestershire), b Jan 14, 1932

Spencer, C. T. (Leicestershire), b Aug 18, 1931

Spencer, T. W. (Kent), b Mar 22, 1914

Sperry, J. (Leicestershire), b March 19, 1910

Spiers, Mr. F. W. (Promoter of first English Team to Australia), d May 31, 1911, aged 79

Spiller, Mr. W. (Glamorgan), b July 8, 1886

Spofforth, Mr. F. R. (New South Wales, Victoria and Derbyshire), b Sept 9, 1853, d June 4, 1926

Spooner, Mr. A. F. (Lancashire), b May 21, 1886

Spooner, Mr. R. H. (Lancashire), b Oct 21, 1880

Spooner, R. T. (Warwickshire), b Dec 30, 1919

Spring, A. W. (Surrey), b May 17, 1881

Springall, J. P. (Nottinghamshire), b Sept 19, 1932

Sprinks, Mr. H. S. (Hampshire), b Aug 19, 1905

Sprot, Mr. E. M. (Hampshire), b Feb 4, 1872, d Oct 8, 1945

Spry, E. (Gloucestershire), b July 31, 1881

Squires, H. S. (Surrey), b Feb 22, 1909, d Jan 24, 1950

Stacey, F. C. (Surrey), b April 27, 1878

Stainton, Mr. R. G. (Oxford Univ. and Sussex), b May 23, 1910

Stannard, G. (Sussex), b July 9, 1894

Stanning, Mr. H. D. (Lancashire), b Nov 14, 1881, d March 5, 1946

Stanton, Mr. H. V. L. ("Wanderer" of the *Sportsman*), b Nov 10, 1859, d May 30, 1933

Stanyforth, Major R. T. (Army, Capt. of M.C.C. in South Africa, 1927–28, and Yorkshire), b May 30, 1892

Staples, A. (Nottinghamshire), b Feb 4, 1899

Staples, S. J. (Nottinghamshire), b Sept 18, 1892, d June 4, 1950

Stapleton, J. (Nottinghamshire and Derbyshire), b Aug 8, 1880, d July 10, 1944

Starkie, S. (Northamptonshire), b April 4, 1926

Statham, J. B. (Lancashire), b June 17, 1930

Steel, Mr. A. G. (Camb. Univ. and Lancashire, President, M.C.C., 1902), b Sept 24, 1858, d June 5, 1914

Steel, Mr. D. Q. (Camb. Univ. and Lancashire), b June 19, 1856, d Dec 2, 1933

Steel, Mr. E. E. (Lancashire), b June 25, 1864, d July 14, 1941

Steel, Mr. H. B. (Lancashire), b April 9, 1862, d June 29, 1911

Steele, Dr. D. M. (South Australia), b Aug 17, 1893

Steele, Rev. J. W. J. (Hampshire), b July 30, 1905

Steeples, A. (Derbyshire), b July 28, 1870, d Aug 14, 1945

Steeples, R. (Derbyshire and Monmouthshire), b April 30, 1873, d Aug 2, 1946

Stephens, E. J. (Gloucestershire), b March 23, 1910

Stephens, Mr. F. G. (Warwickshire), b April 26, 1889

Stephens, Mr. G. W. (Warwickshire), b April 26, 1889, d 1950

Stephenson, H. W. (Somerset), b July 18, 1920

Stephenson, Mr. J. S. (Oxford Univ. and Yorkshire), b Nov 10, 1903

Stephenson, Lt.-Col. J. W. A. (Essex and Worcestershire), b Aug 1, 1907

Stevens, Mr. G. T. S. (Oxford Univ. and Middlesex), b Jan 7, 1901

Stevenson, Mr. M. H. (Camb. Univ. and Derbyshire), b June 13, 1927

Stewart, Mr. H. C. (Kent), b Feb 28, 1868, d June 16, 1942

Stewart, M. J. (Surrey), b Sept 16, 1932

Stewart, W. J. (Warwickshire), b Aug 31, 1934

Stewart-Brown, Mr. P. H. (Oxford Univ.), b April 30, 1904

Steyn, Mr. S. S. L. (South Africa), b March 11, 1905

Stirling, Mr. W. S. (South Australia and Australian Imperial Forces Team), b March 20, 1891

Stocks, Mr. F. W. (Leicestershire and Oxford Univ.), b Dec 10, 1873, d May 21, 1929

Stocks, F. W. (Nottinghamshire), b Nov 6, 1918

Stoddart, Mr. A. E. (Middlesex), b March 11, 1863, d April 3, 1915

Stogdon, Mr. J. H. (Camb. Univ. and Middlesex), b April 25, 1876, d Dec 17, 1944

Stollmeyer, Mr. J. B. (West Indies), b March 11, 1921

Stollmeyer, Mr. V. H. (West Indies), b Jan 24, 1916

Stone, Mr. C. C. (Leicestershire and Oxfordshire), b June 13, 1865, d Nov 11, 1951

Stone, James (Hampshire and Glamorgan), b Nov 29, 1878, d Nov 15, 1942

Storer, H. (Derbyshire), b Feb 2, 1898

Stork, Mr. J. B. (Northamptonshire), b March 21, 1867, d Aug 26, 1944

Stott, W. B. (Yorkshire), b July 18, 1934

Straw, T. (Worcestershire), b Sept 2, 1872

Street, A. E. (Surrey), b July 7, 1871, d Feb 18, 1951

Stricker, Mr. L. A. (South Africa), b May 26, 1884

Strudwick, H. (Surrey), b Jan 28, 1880

Studd, Mr. A. H. (Hampshire), b Nov 19, 1863, d Jan 26, 1919

Studd, Mr. C. T. (Camb. Univ. and Middlesex), b Dec 2, 1860, d July 16, 1931

Studd, Mr. E. J. C. (Cheltenham and M.C.C.), b Feb 13, 1849, d March 9, 1909

Studd, Mr. G. B. (Camb. Univ. and Middlesex), b Oct 20, 1859, d Feb 13, 1945

Studd, Brig.-Gen. H. W. (Middlesex and Hampshire), b Dec 26, 1870, d Aug 8, 1947

Studd, Sir J. E. K., 1st Bart. (Camb. Univ. and Middlesex, President, M.C.C., 1930), b July 26, 1858, d Jan 14, 1944

Studd, Mr. P. M. (Camb. Univ.), b Sept 15, 1916

Studd, Mr. R. A. (Camb. Univ. and Hampshire), b Dec 18, 1873, d Feb 3, 1948

Sturman, W. (Leicestershire), b Aug 29, 1883

Sturt, Mr. M. A. S. (Somerset), b Nov 11, 1876

Styler, S. W. (Worcestershire), b Aug 26, 1909

Subba Row, Mr. R. (Camb. Univ., Surrey and Northamptonshire), b Jan 29, 1932

Sugg, F. H. (Yorkshire, Derbyshire and Lancashire), b Jan 11, 1862, d May 29, 1933

Sugg, W. (Yorkshire and Derbyshire), b May 21, 1860, d May 21, 1933

Sullivan, D. (Surrey and Glamorgan), b Jan 28, 1887

Summers, D. W. L. (Worcestershire), b Oct 12, 1911

Summers, F. T. (Worcestershire), b Jan 25, 1887

Sunnucks, P. R. (Kent), b June 22, 1916

Surridge, Mr. W. S. (Surrey), b Sept 3, 1917

Susskind, Mr. M. J. (Middlesex and South Africa), b June 8, 1891, d July 9, 1957

Sutcliffe, Mr. B. (New Zealand), b Nov 17, 1923

Sutcliffe, H. (Yorkshire), b Nov 24, 1894

Sutcliffe, Mr. W. H. H. (Yorkshire), b Oct 10, 1926

Sutherland, T. (Hampshire), b Feb 17, 1880

Sutthery, Mr. A. M. (Camb. Univ. and Devon), b March 25, 1864, d May 15, 1937

Suttle, K. G. (Sussex), b Aug 25, 1928

Sutton, Mr. M. A. (Oxford Univ.), b March 29, 1921

Swan, Mr. H. D. (President, Essex C.C.), b July 28, 1879, d Dec 21, 1941

Swanton, Mr. E. W. (Cricket Writer) (Middlesex), b Feb 11, 1907

Swetman, R. (Surrey), b Oct 25, 1933

Swift, Mr. B. T. (Camb. Univ.), b Sept 9, 1937

Symington, Mr. S. J. (Leicestershire), b Sept 16, 1926

Symonds, Mr. H. G. (Glamorgan), b June 24, 1889, d Jan 1, 1945

Tabart, Mr. T. A. (Tasmania), b Aug 10, 1879

Tait, Mr. J. R. (Glamorgan), b Nov 20, 1886, d April 13, 1945

Talbot, Mr. R. O. (New Zealand), b Nov 26, 1904

Tallon, Mr. D. (Queensland), b Feb 17, 1916

Tancred, Mr. L. J. (South Africa), b Oct 7, 1876, d July 30, 1934

Tanner, Mr. A. R. (Middlesex), b Dec 25, 1889

Tapscott, Mr. G. L. (South Africa), b Nov 7, 1889, d Dec 13, 1940

Tapscott, Mr. L. D. (Griqualand West), b March 18, 1894, d July 7, 1934

Tarbox, C. V. (Worcestershire and Hertfordshire), b July 2, 1893

Tarrant, F. A. (Victoria and Middlesex), b Dec 11, 1881, d Jan 29, 1951

Tasker, Mr. J. (Yorkshire), b Feb 4, 1887

Tate, C. F. (Derbyshire and Warwickshire), b May 1, 1908

Tate, E. (Hampshire), b Aug 30, 1877, d Jan 4, 1953

Tate, F. W. (Sussex), b July 24, 1867, d Feb 24, 1943

Tate, M. W. (Sussex), b April 29, 1895, d May 18, 1956

Tattersall, R. (Lancashire), b Aug 17, 1922

Tayfield, Mr. H. J. (South Africa), b Jan 30, 1928

Taylor, B. (Essex), b June 19, 1932

Taylor, B. (Nottinghamshire), b June 16, 1875

Taylor, Mr. C. H. (Oxford Univ., Leicestershire and Buckinghamshire), b Feb 6, 1904

Taylor, D. (Warwickshire), b 1918

Taylor, Don. (Warwickshire), b March 2, 1923

Taylor, Mr. E. J. (Gloucestershire), b Dec 31, 1854, d Dec 25, 1936

Taylor, Mr. Frank (Gloucestershire and Lancashire), b May 4, 1855, d Aug 16, 1936

Taylor, Mr. F. H. (Derbyshire), b June 14, 1890

Taylor, Mr. G. R. (Hampshire), b Nov 25, 1912

Taylor, H. (Kent), b April 5, 1908

Taylor, Mr. H. W. (South Africa), b May 5, 1889

Taylor, Mr. J. M. (New South Wales), b Oct 10, 1895

Taylor, K. (Yorkshire), b Aug 21, 1935

Taylor, K. A. (Warwickshire), b Sept 29, 1916

Taylor, M. L. (Lancashire and Dorset), b July 16, 1904

Taylor, R. A. (Nottinghamshire), b March 25, 1909

Taylor, R. M. (Essex), b Nov 30, 1909

Taylor, Mr. T. L. (Camb. Univ. and Yorkshire), b May 25, 1878

Taylor, Mr. W. H. (Worcestershire), b June 23, 1885

Taylor, Mr. W. T. (Derbyshire, Secretary, Derbyshire C.C.), b April 14, 1885

Tebay, H. (Sussex), b Oct 5, 1866

Teesdale, Mr. H. (Oxford Univ. and Surrey), b Feb 12, 1886

Tennyson, 3rd Lord (Hon. L. H.) (Hampshire), b Nov 7, 1889, d June 6, 1951

Thomas, A. E. (Northamptonshire), b June 7. 1893

Thomas, R. (Lancashire), b July 15. 1871

Thompson, A. (Middlesex), b April 17, 1916

Thompson, Mr. A. R. (Northamptonshire), b Dec 1, 1876, d Feb 1951

Thompson, E. C. (Essex), b Feb 27, 1907

Thompson, Mr. F. C. (Queensland), b Aug 1, 1890

Thompson, G. J. (Northamptonshire), b Oct 27, 1877, d March 3, 1943

Thompson, H. (Surrey), b Dec 6, 1870

Thompson, Mr. H. (Leicestershire), b May 14, 1886, d Aug 8, 1941

Thompson, Mr. J. R. (Camb. Univ. and Warwickshire), b May 10, 1918

Thompson, R. G. (Warwickshire), b Sept 26, 1932.

Thomson, N. I. (Sussex), b Jan 23, 1930

Thornton, Mr. C. I. (Camb. Univ., Kent and Middlesex), b March 20, 1850, d Dec 10, 1929

Thornton, Dr. G. (Yorkshire, Middlesex and South Africa), b Dec 24, 1867, d Jan 31, 1939

Thorp, P. (Worcestershire), b May 6, 1911

Thorpe, Mr. C. (Northamptonshire), b Aug 11, 1882, d May 5, 1953

Thursting, L. D. (Leicestershire), b Sept 9, 1916

Tillard, Mr. C. (Camb. Univ., Surrey and Norfolk), b April 18, 1851, d March 7, 1944

Timms, J. E. (Northamptonshire), b Nov 3, 1907

Timms, Mr. W. W. (Northamptonshire), b Sept 28, 1902

Tindall, Mr. M. (Camb. Univ. and Middlesex), b March 31, 1914

Tindall, Capt. R. G. (Oxford Univ. and Dorset), b Feb 20, 1912, d Jan 29, 1942

Tindill, Mr. E. W. (New Zealand), b Dec 18, 1910

Tinsley, H. J. (Yorkshire and Lancashire), b Feb 20, 1865

Titchmarsh, Mr. C. H. (Herts), b Feb 18, 1881, d May 23, 1930

Titmus, F. J. (Middlesex), b Nov 24, 1932

Todd, L. J. (Kent), b June 19, 1907

Tomlinson, Mr. D. S. (South Africa), b Sept 4, 1910

Tomlinson, Mr. W. J. V. (Camb. Univ. and Derbyshire), b Aug 10, 1901

Tompkin. M. (Leicestershire), b Feb 17, 1919, d Sept 27, 1956

Toone, Sir F. C. (Sec., Yorkshire), b June 25, 1868, d June 10, 1930

Toppin, Mr. C. (Camb. Univ., Cumberland and Worcestershire), b Aug 9, 1864. d June 8. 1928

Toppin, Mr. C. G. (Worcestershire), b April 17, 1906

Tordoff, Mr. G. G. (Camb. Univ. and Somerset), b Dec 6, 1929

Toshack, Mr. E. R. H. (New South Wales), b Dec 15, 1917

Towell, Mr. E. F. (Northamptonshire), b July 5, 1901

Towler, W. (Yorkshire), b Nov 12, 1866

Townsend, A. F. (Derbyshire), b March 29, 1912

Townsend, A. (Warwickshire), b Aug 26, 1921

Townsend, Mr. A. F. M. (Gloucestershire and Essex), b Aug 1, 1885, d 1950

Townsend, Mr. C. L. (Gloucestershire), b Nov 7, 1876

Townsend, Mr. D. C. H. (Oxford Univ. and Durham), b April 20, 1912

Townsend, L. F. (Derbyshire and Northumberland), b June 8, 1903

Trapnell, Mr. B. M. W. (Camb. Univ. and Middlesex), b May 18, 1924

Trask, Mr. W. (Somerset), b July 15, 1859, d June 24, 1949

Travers, Mr. B. H. (Oxford Univ. and Oxfordshire), b July 7, 1919

Treglown, Mr. C. J. H. (Essex), b Feb 13, 1893

Tremlett, M. F. (Somerset), b July 5, 1923

Tremlin, B. (Essex), b Sept 18, 1877 d April 12, 1936

Trestrail, Mr. K. B. (West Indies), b Nov 26, 1927

Tribe, G. E. (Victoria and Northants), b Oct 4, 1920

Tripp, G. M. (Somerset), b June 29, 1932

Troup, Mr. W. (Gloucestershire), b Oct 16, 1869, d Jan 1941

Trueman, F. S. (Yorkshire), b Feb 6, 1931

Trumble, Mr. Hugh (Victoria), b May 12, 1867, d Aug 14, 1938

Trumble, Mr. J. W. (Victoria), b Sept 16, 1863, d Aug 17, 1944

Trumper, Mr. V. T. (New South Wales), b Nov 2, 1877, d June 28, 1915

Tuckett, Mr. L. (South Africa), b Feb 2, 1919

Tufnell, Mr. N. C. (Camb. Univ. and Surrey), b June 13, 1887, d Aug 3, 1951

Tutton, Hon. J. S. R., 2nd Lord Hothfield (Kent), b Nov 8, 1873, d Dec 21, 1952

Tumilty, Mr. L. R. (Tasmania), b June 12, 1884

Tunnicliffe, John (Yorkshire), b Aug 26, 1866, d July 11, 1948

Tuppin, A. G. (Sussex), b 17, Dec 1911

Turnbull, Major M. J. (Camb. Univ. and Glamorgan), b March 16, 1906, d Aug 5, 1944

Turner, A. (Yorkshire), b Sept 2, 1885, d Aug 29, 1951

Turner, Brig.-Gen. Arthur Jervois (Essex), b July 10, 1878, d Sept 8, 1952

Turner, C. (Yorkshire), b Jan 11, 1902

Turner, Mr. C. T. B. (New South Wales), b Nov 16, 1862, d Jan 1, 1944

Turner, Mr. N. V. C. (Nottinghamshire), b May 12, 1887, d June 13, 1941

Turner, R. E. (Worcestershire), b May 4, 1888

Turner, Mr. R. H. T. (Nottinghamshire), b Oct. 26, 1888, d Sept 13, 1947

Turner, Lt.-Col. W. M. F. (Essex), b April 4, 1881, d Feb 1, 1948

Twining, Mr. R. H. (Oxford Univ. and Middlesex), b Nov 3, 1889

Tyldesley, E. (Lancashire), b Feb 5, 1889

Tyldesley, Harry (Lancashire), b 1893, d Aug 30, 1935

Tyldesley, Jas. D. (Lancashire), b Aug 10, 1889, d Jan 31, 1923

Tyldesley, J. T. (Lancashire), b Nov 22, 1873, d Nov 27, 1930

Tyldesley, Richard Knowles (Lancashire), b March 11, 1898, d Sept 17, 1943

Tylecote, Mr. E. F. S. (Oxford Univ., Bedfordshire and Kent), b June 23, 1849, d March 15, 1938

Tylecote, Mr. H. G. (Oxford Univ., Bedfordshire and Hertfordshire), b July 24, 1853, d March 8, 1935

Tyler, Mr. C. (Gloucestershire), b Jan 26, 1911

Tyler, Mr. C. H. (Northamptonshire), b Sept 13, 1887

Tyson, C. (Yorkshire), b Jan 24, 1889, d April 4, 1940

Tyson, F. H. (Northamptonshire), b June 6, 1930

Udal, Mr. N. R. (Oxford Univ., Dorset and Devon), b Oct 16, 1883

Ufton, D. G. (Kent), b May 31, 1928

Ullswater, 1st Viscount (President M.C.C., 1923), b April 1, 1855, d March 27, 1949

Umrigar, Mr. P. R. (India), b March 28, 1926

Unwin, Mr. St. F. G. (Essex), b April 23, 1911

Urquhart, Mr. J. R. (Camb. Univ. and Essex), b May 29, 1921

Utley, Pilot-Officer R. T. H. (R.A.F. and Hampshire), b Feb 11, 1906

Valentine, Mr A. L. (West Indies), b April 28, 1930

Valentine, Mr. B. H. (Camb. Univ. and Kent) b Jan 17, 1908

Valentine, V. A. (West Indies), b April 4, 1908

Van der Bijl, Mr. P. G. (Oxford Univ. and South Africa), b Oct 21, 1907

Van der Merwe, Mr. E. A. (South Africa), b Nov 9, 1904

Van Geloven, J. (Yorkshire and Leicestershire), b Jan 4, 1934

Van Ryneveld, Mr. C. B. (Oxford Univ. and South Africa), b March 19, 1928

Vann, Mr. D. W. A. (Northamptonshire), b Nov 21, 1916

Vassall, Mr. G. C. (Somerset), b April 5, 1876, d Sept 19, 1941

Vaulkhard, Mr. P. (Nottinghamshire, Northumberland and Derbyshire), b Sept 15, 1911

Venn, W. H. (Warwickshire), b July 4, 1892, d Nov 23, 1953

Vere Hodge, Mr. N. (Essex), b Oct 31, 1912

Verity, Capt. Hedley (Yorkshire), b May 18, 1905, d July 31, 1943

Vials, Mr. G. A. T. (Northamptonshire), b March 18, 1887

Vidler, Mr. J. L. S. (Oxford Univ., Sussex and Oxfordshire), b March 30, 1890

Vigar, F. H. (Essex), b July 7, 1917

Vigar, H. E. (Surrey), b Nov 29, 1883

Viljoen, Mr. K. G. (South Africa, Manager South Africa in England, 1955), b May 14, 1910

Vincent, Mr. C. L. (South Africa), b Feb 16, 1902

Vincent, Mr. H. G. (Camb. Univ.), b Nov 13, 1891

Vincett, J. H. (Sussex and Surrey), b May 24, 1883

Vine, J. (Sussex), b May 15, 1875, d April 25, 1946

Vivian, Mr. H. G. (New Zealand), b Nov 4, 1912

Vizianagram, Maharaj Kumar, Sir Vijaya of (India), b Dec 28, 1905

Voce, W. (Nottinghamshre), b Aug 8, 1909

Vogler, A. E. E. (South Africa), b Nov 28, 1876, d Aug 10, 1946

Waddington, A. (Yorkshire), b Feb 4, 1893

Waddy, Rev. E. F. (New South Wales and Warwickshire), b Oct 5, 1880

Waddy, Mr. E. L. (New South Wales), b Dec 3, 1878

Waddy, Canon P. S. (New South Wales and Oxford Univ.), b Jan 8, 1875, d Feb 8, 1937

Wade, Mr. H. F. (South Africa), b Sept 14, 1905

Wade, T. H. (Essex), b Nov 24, 1911

Wade, Mr. W. W. (South Afrca), b June 18, 1914

Wainwright, W. (Yorkshire), b Jan 9, 1882

Wait, Mr. O. J. (Camb. Univ. and Surrey), b Aug 2, 1926

Waite, Mr. J. H. B. (South Africa), b Jan 19, 1930

Waite, Mr. M. G. (South Australia), b Jan 7, 1911

Walcott, Mr. C. L. (West Indies), b Jan 17, 1926

Walden, F. (Northamptonshire), b March 1, 1888, d May 3, 1949

Waldock, Mr. F. A. (Oxford Univ. and Somerset), b March 16, 1898

Walford, Mr. M. M. (Oxford Univ., Durham and Somerset), b Nov 27, 1915

Walker, A. K. (New South Wales and Nottinghamshire), b Oct 4, 1925

Walker, C. (Yorkshire and Hampshire), b June 27, 1920

Walker, F/O C. W. (South Australia), b Feb 19, 1909, d Dec 21 1942

Walker, Flt.-Lt. D. F. (Oxford Univ. and Norfolk), b May 31, 1913, d Feb 6, 1942

Walker, Flt.-Lt. D. F. (Hampshire), b Aug 15, 1912, d June 18, 1941

Walker, G. A. (Nottinghamshire), b Jan 25, 1919

Walker, Mr. J. G. (Oxford Univ. and Middlesex), b Oct 9, 1859, d March 24, 1923

Walker, Mr. L. (Surrey), b June 13, 1879 d Oct 10, 1940

Walker, M. (Somerset), b Oct 14, 1933

Walker, P. (Glamorgan), b Feb 7, 1936

Walker, Mr. R. D. (Oxford Univ. and Middlesex), b Feb 13, 1842, d March 29, 1922

Walker, Willis (Nottinghamshire), b Nov 24, 1894

Wall, Mr. T. W. (South Australia), b May 13, 1904

Wallace, Mr. W. M. (New Zealand), b Dec 19, 1916

Wallroth, Mr. C. A. (Oxford Univ., Kent and Derbyshire), b May 17, 1851, d Feb 22, 1926

Walsh, J. E. (Leicestershire) b Dec 4, 1912

Walshe, Mr. A. P. (Oxford Univ.) b Jan 1, 1934

Walters, Mr. C. F. (Glamorgan and Worcestershire), b Aug 28, 1905

Walton, Mr. A. C. (Oxford Univ. and Middlesex), b Sept 26, 1933

Walton, Mr. H. (Yorkshire), b May 21, 1868

Waqar Hassan (Pakistan), b Sept 12, 1932

Ward, A. (Yorkshire and Lancashire), b Nov 21, 1865, d Jan 6, 1939

Ward, Rev. C. G. (Hampshire, Lincolnshire and Hertfordshire), b Sept 23, 1875, d June 27, 1954

Ward, D. J. (Glamorgan), b Aug 30, 1934

Ward, Rev. E. E. Harrison (Camb. Univ. and Suffolk), b July 16, 1847, d March 25, 1940

Ward, F. (Lancashire), b Jan 9, 1865

Ward, Mr. F. A. (South Australia), b Feb 23, 1909

Ward, Mr. H. P. (Oxford Univ.), b Jan 20, 1899, d Dec 16, 1946

Ward, Mr. T. A. (South Africa), b Aug 2, 1887, d Feb 16, 1936

Ward, W. (Warwickshire), b May 24, 1874

Wardle, J. H. (Yorkshire), b Jan 8, 1923

Warne, F. (Victoria and Worcestershire), b Oct 3, 1908

Warner, Sir Pelham F. (Oxford Univ. and Middlesex), b in West Indies, Oct 2, 1873

Warr, Mr. J. J. (Camb. Univ. and Middlesex), b July 16, 1927

Warren, A. R. (Derbyshire), b April 2, 1875, d Sept 3, 1951

Washbrook, C. (Lancashire), b Dec 6, 1914

Wass, T. (Nottinghamshire), b Dec 26 1873, d Oct 27, 1953

Waterman, Mr. A. G. (Essex), b May 13, 1911

Waters, Mr. A. E. (Gloucestershire), b May 8, 1902

Wathen, Mr. A. C. (Kent), b March 27, 1841, d March 14, 1937

Watkin, D. (Nottinghamshire), b June 28, 1914

Watkins, A. J. (Glamorgan), b April 21, 1922

Watkins, B. T. L. (Gloucestershire), b June 25, 1907

Watson, Lt.-Col. A. C. (Essex and Sussex), b March 17, 1884, d Jan 16, 1952

Watson, Mr. A. K. (Oxford Univ., Middlesex, Suffolk and Norfolk), b March 23, 1867, d Jan 2, 1947

Watson, Mr. A. L. (Hampshire), b Aug 27, 1866

Watson, F. (Lancashire), b Sept 17, 1899

Watson, G. S. (Leicestershire and Kent), b April 10, 1909

Watson, H. (Yorkshire), b Sept 26, 1884

Watson, Mr. H. D. (Oxford Univ.), b Dec 31, 1869, d Oct 9, 1947

Watson, W. (Yorkshire), b March 7, 1920

Watt, A. E. (Kent), b June 19, 1907

Watt, Mr. K. E. (Tasmania), b Dec 12, 1891

Watts, E. A. (Surrey), b Aug 1, 1911

Watts, G. (Surrey and Cambridgeshire), b Feb 18, 1867, d April 22, 1949

Watts, Mr. H. E. (Somerset and Camb. Univ.), b March 4, 1922

Wauchope, Mr. A. R. Don (Scotland), b April 29, 1861, d Jan 16, 1948

Wazir Ali, S. (India), b Sept 15, 1903, d June 17, 1950

Wazir Mohammad (Pakistan), b Dec 12, 1929

Webb, A. (Hampshire), b Aug 6, 1869

Webb, R. T. (Sussex), b July 11, 1922

Webbe, Mr. A. J. (Oxford Univ. and Middlesex), b Jan 16, 1855, d Feb 19, 1941

Webster, Mr. H. (South Australia), b Feb 17, 1889, d Oct 7, 1949

Webster, Mr. J. (Camb. Univ. and Northamptonshire), b Oct 28, 1917

Webster, Mr. W. H. (Camb. Univ. and Middlesex), b Feb 22, 1910

Wedel, Mr. G. A. (Gloucestershire), b May 18, 1900

Weekes, Mr. E. (West Indies), b Feb 26, 1925

Weekes, Mr. K. H. (West Indies), b Jan 24, 1912

Weeks, R. T. (Warwickshire), b April 30, 1930

Weigall, Mr. G. J. V. (Camb. Univ. and Kent), b Oct 19, 1870, d May 17, 1944

Weir, Mr. G. L. (New Zealand), b June 2, 1908

Welch, T. B. G. (Northamptonshire), b July 31, 1906

Welford, J. W. (Warwickshire), b March 27, 1869, d Jan 17, 1945

Wellard, A. W. (Somerset), b April 8, 1903

Wellings, Mr. E. M. (Oxford Univ. and Surrey), b April 6, 1909

Wells, B. D. (Gloucestershire), b July 27, 1930

Wells, Mr. C. M. (Camb. Univ., Surrey and Middlesex), b March 21, 1871

Wells, Mr. T. U. (Cambridge Univ. and Sussex), b Feb 6, 1927

Wells, W. (Northamptonshire), b Mar 14, 1881, d March 18, 1939

Wensley, A. F. (Sussex), b May 24, 1898

West, W. A. J. (Northamptonshire and Warwickshire, Umpire), b Nov 17, 1862, d Feb 22, 1938

Westcott, A. H. (Somerset), b Nov 6, 1870

Weston, Mr. H. W. (Middlesex), b Jan 2, 1888, d 1914

Wetherall, Mr. C. R. (Northamptonshire), b Aug 24, 1878, d April 22, 1955

Wharmby, G. E. (Nottinghamshire, Lancashire and Bedfordshire), b Dec 7, 1870, d 1951

Wharton, A. (Lancashire), b April 30, 1923

Whately, Mr. E. G. (Somerset and Hertfordshire), b July 27, 1882

Wheat, A. B. (Nottinghamshire), b May 13, 1898

Wheatley, Mr. G. A. (Oxford Univ. and Surrey), b May 28, 1923

Wheatley, Mr. O. S. (Camb. Univ. and Warwickshire), b May 28, 1935

Whitcombe, Mr. P. A. (Oxford Univ. and Middlesex), b April 23, 1923

Whitcombe, Mr. P. J. (Oxford Univ. and Worcestershire), b Nov 11, 1928

White, Mr. A. F. T. (Camb. Univ., Warwickshire and Worcestershire), b Sept 5, 1915

White, Mr. A. H. (Camb. Univ.), b Oct 18, 1901

White, Sir A. W., 4th Bart. (Yorkshire), b Oct 11, 1877, d Dec 16, 1945

White, Mr. E. S. (New South Wales), b April 17, 1913

White, Rev. H. (Northumberland and Oxford Univ.), b June 16, 1876

White, Mr. J. C. (Somerset), b Feb 19, 1891

White, M. E. (Worcestershire), b Jan 21, 1908

White, Brig.-Gen. W. N. (Hampshire), b Sept 10, 1879, d Dec 27, 1951

Whitehead, H. (Leicestershire), b Sept 19, 1875, d Sept 16, 1944

Whitehead, J. P. (Yorkshire and Worcestershire), b Sept 3, 1925

Whitehead, Ralph (Lancashire), b Oct 16, 1883

Whiteside, J. P. (Lancashire and Leicestershire), b June 11, 1861, d March 8, 1946

Whitfield, E. W. (Surrey and Northamptonshire), b May 31, 1911

Whiting, C. P. (Yorkshire), b April 19, 1890

Whiting, N. H. (Worcestershire), b Oct 2, 1920

Whitington, Mr. R. S. (Adelaide Univ. and South Australia), b June 30, 1912

Whittaker, G. J. (Surrey), b May 29, 1916

Whitting, Mr. E. J. (Somerset), b Sept 1, 1872, d March 8, 1938

Whittington, Mr. T. A. L. (Glamorgan), b July 29, 1881, d July 19, 1944

Whittle, A. E. (Warwickshire and Somerset), b Sept 16, 1877, dead

Whitty, Mr. W. J. (South Australia), b Aug 15, 1886

Whitwell, Mr. W. F. (Yorkshire and Durham), b Dec 12, 1867, d April 12, 1942

Whysall, W. W. (Nottinghamshire), b Oct 31, 1887, d Nov 11, 1930

Wickham, Preb. A. P. (Oxford Univ., Norfolk and Somerset), b Nov 9, 1855, d Oct 13, 1935

Wigginton, S. H. (Leicestershire), b March 26, 1909

Wight, Mr. C. V. (West Indies), b July 28, 1902

Wight, Mr. O. S. (West Indies), b Aug 10, 1906

Wight, P. B. (British Guiana and Somerset), b June 25, 1930

Wilcox, Mr. A. G. S. (Gloucestershire), b July 7, 1920

Wilcox, Mr. D. R. (Camb. Univ. and Essex), b June 4, 1910, d Feb 6, 1953

Wild, Mr. J. (Northamptonshire), b Feb 24, 1935

Wild, Mr. J. V. (Camb. Univ.), b April 26, 1915

Wilenkin, Mr. B. C. G. (Camb. Univ.), b June 20, 1933

Wiles, Mr. C. A. (West Indies), b Aug 11, 1892

Wiley, Mr. W. G. A. (Oxford Univ.), b Nov 7, 1931

Wilkinson, Mr. C. T. A. (London County and Surrey), b Oct 4, 1884

Wilkinson, F. (Yorkshire), b May 23, 1914

Wilkinson, Mr. H. (Yorkshire), b Dec 11, 1877

Wilkinson, John (Gloucestershire), b July 16, 1876, d 1948

Wilkinson, L. L. (Lancashire), b Nov 5, 1916

Wilkinson, W. (Nottinghamshire), b July 5, 18 69

Wilkinson, Major W. A. C. (Oxford Univ.), b Dec 6, 18 92

Wilkinson, W. H. (Yorkshire), b March 12, 1881

Willatt, Mr. G. L. (Camb. Univ., Nottinghamshire and Derbyshire), b May 7, 1918

Williams, Mr. C. B. (West Indies), b March 8, 1926

Williams, Mr. C. C. P. (Oxford Univ. and Essex), b Feb 9, 1933

Williams, Mr. E. A. V. (West Indies), b April 10, 1914

Williams, Mr. Leo (Sussex), b May 15, 1900

Williams, Sir P. F. C., 2nd Bart. (Gloucestershire), b July 6, 1884

Williams, Mr. P. V. (Sussex), b July 10, 1897

Williams, Mr. R. A. (Oxford Univ., Oxfordshire and Berkshire), b Feb 2, 1879

Williams, Mr. R. H. (Worcestershire), b April 23, 1901

Williams, Mr. R. J. (South Africa), b April 12, 1912

Williams, Mr. W. (Middlesex), b April 12, 1861, d April 14, 1951

Willingdon, 1st Marquis of (*see* Freeman-Thomas), d Aug 12, 1941

Willoughby, F. G. (Hampshire), b April 25, 1862

Willson, R. H. (Sussex), b July 14, 1933

Wilmot, K. (Warwickshire), b April 3, 1911

Wilmot, W. (Derbyshire), b Dec 25, 1872, d May 19, 1957

Wilson, A. (Lancashire), b April 24, 1921

Wilson, A. E. (Gloucestershire), b May 5, 1912

Wilson, B. B. (Yorkshire), b Dec 11, 1879, d Sept 14, 1957

Wilson, Bishop C. (Kent), b Sept 9, 1860, d Jan 20, 1941

Wilson, Prebendary C. E. M. (Camb. Univ. and Yorkshire), b May 15, 1875, d Feb 8, 1944

Wilson, Mr. C. P. (Camb. Univ. and Norfolk), b May 12, 1859, d March 9, 1938

Wilson, E. F. (Surrey), b June 24, 1907

Wilson, Mr E. R. (Camb. Univ. and Yorkshire), b March 25, 1879, d June 21, 1957

Wilson. Mr. F. B. (Camb. Univ.), b Sept 21, 1881, d Jan 19, 1932

Wilson, Mr. G. (Camb. Univ. and Yorkshire), b Aug 21, 1895

Wilson, Mr. G. (Worcestershire), b April 9, 1932

Wilson, Mr. G. A. (Yorkshire) b Feb 2, 1916

Wilson, G. A. (Worcestershire), b April 5, 1877

Wilson, Mr. H. L. (Suffolk and Sussex), b June 27, 1881, d March 14, 1937

Wilson, Mr. J. (South Australia), b Aug. 20, 1922

Wilson, Mr. John (Yorkshire), b June 20, 1858, d Nov 13, 1931

Wilson, Mr. J. P. (Yorkshire), b April 3, 1889

Wilson, J. V. (Yorkshire), b Jan 17, 1921

Wilson, Mr. Leslie (Kent), b March 16, 1859, d April 15, 1944

Wilson, Canon R. A. (Rugby and M.C.C.; senior brother of C. E. M. and E. R.), b July 18, 1868

Wilson, R. C. (Kent), b Feb 18, 1928

Wilson, Mr. R. W. (Oxford Univ.), b July 15, 1934

Wilson, Mr. T. S. B. (Oxford Univ.), b Aug 15, 1870, d May 19, 1941

Winfield, H. M. (Nottinghamshire), b June 13, 1933

Winlaw Sqdn.-Ldr. R. de W. K. (Camb. Univ., Bedfordshire and Surrey), b March 28, 1912, d Oct 31, 1942

Winn, Mr. C. E. (Oxford Univ. and Sussex), b Nov 13, 1926

Winning, Mr. C. S. (Australian Imperial Forces Team), b July 17, 1889

Winrow, H. (Nottinghamshire), b Jan 17, 1916

Winrow, R. (Nottinghamshire), b Dec 30, 1910

Winslow, Mr. P. L. (South Africa), b May 21, 1929

Winter, Rev. A. H. (Camb. Univ. and Middlesex), b Dec 4, 1844, d Dec 31, 1937

Winter, Mr. C. E. (Camb. Univ.), b Sept 1, 1879

Wisden, John (Sussex), Founder of John Wisden & Co. and *Wisden's Cricketers' Almanack*, b Sept 5, 1826, d April 5, 1884

Witherden, E. G. (Kent), b May 1, 1922

Wolton, A. V. (Berkshire and Warwickshire), b June 12, 1919

Womersley, Mr. D. (Essex), b July 28, 1860, d Aug 22, 1942

Wood, A. (Yorkshire), b Aug 25, 1898

Wood, Mr. A. M. (Nottinghamshire, Derbyshire and Philadelphia), b Feb 21, 1861, d Aug 25, 1947

Wood, Mr. C. J. B. (Leicestershire), b Nov 21, 1875

Wood, D. J. (Sussex), b May 19, 1914

Wood, Mr. G. E. C. (Camb. Univ. and Kent), b Aug 22, 1893

Wood, Rev. H. (Yorkshire and Camb. Univ.), b March 22, 1855, d July 31, 1941

Woodcock, Mr. R. G. (Oxford Univ.), b Nov 26, 1934

Woodfull, Mr. W. M. (Victoria), b Aug 22, 1897

Woodhead, Mr. F. E. (Yorkshire), b May 29, 1868, d Aug 25, 1943

Woodhead, F. G. (Nottinghamshire), b Oct 30, 1912

Woodhouse, Mr. G. E. S. (Somerset), b Feb 15, 1924

Woodhouse, Mr. W. H. (Yorkshire), b April 16, 1857, d March 4, 1938

Woods, Mr. S. M. J. (Somerset and Camb. Univ.), b April 14, 1868, d April 30, 1931

Woof, W. A. (Gloucestershire), b July 9, 1859, d April 4, 1937

Wooler, C. (Leicestershire), b June 30, 1930

Wooller, Mr. W. (Camb. Univ. and Glamorgan), b Nov 20, 1912

Woollett, A. F. (Kent), b Sept 20, 1927

Woolley, C. N. (Gloucestershire and Northamptonshire), b May 5, 1886

Woolley, F. E. (Kent), b May 27, 1887

Wootton, James (Kent and Hampshire), b Mar 9, 1860, d Feb 1941

Wormald, Mr. J. (Middlesex), b Feb 23, 1882

Worrall, Mr. J. (Victoria), b May 12, 1863, d Nov 17, 1937

Worrell, Mr. F. M. (West Indies), b Aug 1, 1924

Worsley, Capt. Sir W. A., 4th Bart. (Yorkshire), b April 5, 1890

Worthington, Mr. C. R. (Camb. Univ. and Kent), b Feb 28, 1877, d Dec 7, 1950

Worthington, T. S. (Derbyshire), b Aug 21, 1905

Wrathall, H. (Gloucestershire and Northumberland), b Feb 1, 1869

Wreford-Brown, Mr. A. J. (Sussex), b Oct 26, 1912

Wreford-Brown, Mr. C. (Gloucestershire), b Oct 9, 1866, d Nov 26, 1951

Wright, A. C. (Kent), b April 6, 1896

Wright, Mr. C. C. G. (Camb. Univ.), b March 7, 1887

Wright, Mr. C. W. (Camb. Univ. and Nottinghamshire), b May 27, 1863, d Jan 10, 1936

Wright, D. V. P. (Kent), b Aug 21, 1914

Wright, Mr. E. C. (Gloucestershire, Oxford Univ. and Kent), b April 23, 1874, d July 28, 1947

Wright, Mr. H. F. (Derbyshire), b Oct 9 1870, d Feb 23, 1947

Wright, L. (Worcestershire), b Jan 20, 1903, d Jan 6, 1956

Wright, Mr. L. G. (Derbyshire), b Jan 15, 1862, d Jan 11, 1953

Wright, Mr. P. A. (Camb. Univ. and Northamptonshire), b May 16, 1903

Wright, Walter (Nottinghamshire and Kent), b Feb 29, 1856, d March 22, 1940

Wrigley, Mr. M. H. (Oxford Univ.), b July 30, 1924

Wyatt, Mr. R. E. S. (Warwickshire and Worcestershire), b May 2, 1901

Wykes, Mr. N. G. (Camb. Univ. and Essex), b March 19, 1906

Wyld, Mr. H. J. (Oxford Univ. and Middlesex), b April 16, 1880

Wynyard, Major E. G. (Hampshire), b April 1, 1861, d Oct 30, 1936

Yardley, Mr. N. W. D. (Camb. Univ. and Yorkshire), b March 19, 1915

Yarnold, H. (Worcestershire), b July 6, 1917

Yates, Major H. W. M. (Hampshire), b March 25, 1883, d Aug 21, 1956

Yates, W. G. (Nottinghamshire), b June 18, 1919

Yawar Saeed (Somerset), b Jan 22, 1935

Young, A. (Somerset), b 1890, d April 2, 1936

Young, D. M. (Worcestershire and Gloucestershire), b April 15, 1924

Young, H. (Essex), b Feb 5, 1876

Young, J. A. (Middlesex), b Oct 14, 1912

Young, Mr. R. A. (Camb. Univ. and Sussex), b Sept 16, 1885

Zulfiqar Ahmed (Pakistan), b Nov 22, 1926

OBITUARY, 1957

ABERDARE, THE THIRD BARON (Clarence Napier Bruce), who died on October 4, aged 72, was one of the best all-round sportsmen of his time. His death was caused by drowning after his car fell over a precipice in Yugoslavia into three feet of water in a river bed. As the Hon. C. N. Bruce, he was in the Winchester XI of 1904 and would have gained his Blue at Oxford as a Freshman but for illness. Against Cambridge at Lord's in 1907 he scored only five runs, but the following year his 46 in the Dark Blues' first innings was second top score. A fine batsman who hit the ball hard with perfect timing, due mainly to splendid wristwork, he first appeared for Middlesex in 1908 and played his last match for them in 1929. In all first-class games he scored 4,316 runs, average 28.96. Against Lancashire at Lord's in 1919 he hit 149 in two hours twenty-five minutes and two seasons later again trounced the Lancashire bowling on the same ground, scoring 82 not out and helping Hendren add 50 in quarter of an hour. In 1921 he also scored 144 against Warwickshire and 127 for Gentlemen v. Players at The Oval.

He won most honours at rackets, for he was the Winchester first string in 1903–4; won the Public Schools championship in 1904; played for Oxford v. Cambridge in 1905–8; won the Oxford University Silver Racket in 1907; won the Amateur Championship in 1922 and 1931; was ten times Doubles Champion; was Champion of the U.S.A. in 1928 and 1930; Singles Champion of Canada in 1928 and 1930 and Doubles Champion also in 1930. At tennis, Bruce was U.S.A. Amateur Champion in 1930 and of the British Isles in 1932 and 1938. He played eighteen times for Great Britain in the Bathurst Cup and six times won the Coupe de Paris. He carried off the M.C.C. Gold Prize on five occasions and nine times won the Silver Prize. He also excelled at golf, playing for Oxford against Cambridge from 1905 to 1908, was a good footballer and a capital shot.

In 1937 he was appointed chairman of the National Advisory Council in connection with the Government scheme for improving the physical fitness of the nation. For twenty years he was a member of the International Olympic Executive and he played a big part in organising the 1948 Games in London. In his later years he devoted himself closely to work for the Order of St. John of Jerusalem and the St. John Ambulance Association, and was a member of the executive committee of the National Playing Fields Association. He succeeded to the title in 1929.

ARNOLD, MR. WELLER, who died in Hobart on October 28, aged 75, was Vice-President of the Tasmanian Cricket Association. He was one of the most prominent sportsmen in Tasmania during this century, his interests including cricket, Australian Rules football and horse racing. A useful right-handed batsman, he played for Tasmania against Victoria in 1915, scoring 5 and 30, and in 1909–10 season headed the Tasmanian averages with 75.33, his aggregate being 453. In 1954 he received the O.B.E. for services to sport.

BATES, WILLIAM EDRIC, who died in a Belfast hospital on January 17, aged 72, did much fine work as a batsman for Glamorgan in their first eleven years as a first-class county. He could not secure a regular place in the side for Yorkshire, as did his more famous father, "Billy" Bates, and after seven seasons with the county of his birth he joined Glamorgan. A consistent batsman with a variety of strokes and watchful defence, he in six summers exceeded 1,000 runs in Championship matches for the Welsh county, scoring ten centuries. His best season was that of 1927 when his aggregate reached 1,575, average 45.00, and he reached three figures on four occasions, including 200 not out against Worcestershire at Kidderminster and 105 and 111 in the game with Essex at Leyton. Following his retirement from first-class cricket in 1931, he held several coaching engagements in Ireland.

BENNETT, LORD PETER, OF EDGBASTON, who died at his home at Four Oaks, Warwickshire, on September 27, aged 77, was chairman of Warwickshire C.C.C. From 1951 to 1952 he was Parliamentary Secretary to the Ministry of Labour and National Service, was Knighted in 1941 and elevated to the Peerage twelve years later.

BEOKU-BETTS, SIR ERNEST, who died at Freetown, Sierra Leone, on September 11, aged 62, was Speaker of the Sierra Leone House of Representatives. For many years he was a member of the Council of the Sierra Leone Cricket League.

BOOTH, MR. ALBERT, who died in February, aged 69, was for over 40 years well known as a cricketer and Association football journalist. For 23 years he was Sports Editor of the Manchester edition of the *Daily Herald*.

BOWELL, ALEC, who died at Oxford on August 28, aged 76, played for Hampshire from 1902 till 1927. An opening batsman sound in defence and specially skilled in cutting, he scored 18,510 runs, average 24.13, and was a splendid fieldsman at cover-point. His highest innings was 204 out of a total of 377 for Hampshire against Lancashire at Bournemouth, to which venue the match was transferred from Portsmouth owing to the outbreak of the First World War. He took part in the celebrated match with Warwickshire at Birmingham in 1922 when Hampshire, after being dismissed by H. Howell and the Hon. F. S. G. Calthorpe for 15 and following-on 208 behind, put together a total of 521 and triumphed by 155 runs. Bowell was one of eight men dismissed without scoring in the first innings.

BURGE, MR. THOMAS JOHN, who died at his home in Brisbane on January 7, aged 53, while listening to a radio commentary on a cricket match in which his son was batting, had been a member of the Australian Board of Control since 1952. He suffered a heart attack while his son was touring England in 1956. He was a life-member of the Queensland C.A. and managed the first Australian team to tour the West Indies in 1955.

BURNS, JAMES, who died at Hampstead on September 11, aged 92, played as a batsman for Essex from 1890 to 1895. He was in the side when the county acquired first-class status in 1894. The following season, when Essex were admitted to the Championship competition, he hit 114 against Warwickshire at Birmingham.

CARROLL, MR. THOMAS DAVIS, who died at Hobart on June 3 following a road accident, aged 73, was one of the best-known cricketers and cricket administrators in Tasmania in the early part of the century. He played in ten matches for the State as a fast-medium right-arm bowler between 1908 and 1922, taking 16 wickets for 48.3 runs each. He was Tasmanian member of the Australian Board of Control for two years after 1929, and was, in 1930, appointed an Australian Selector, a position he was compelled to relinquish within a year because his employment was transferred to Western Australia. Carroll was opening bowler for Tasmania in 1912 when M.C.C. scored 574 for four wickets in four and a half hours, of which F. E. Woolley made 305 not out.

CHESTER, FRANK, who died at his home at Bushey, Hertfordshire, on April 8, aged 61, will be remembered as the man who raised umpiring to a higher level than had ever been known in the history of cricket. For some years he had suffered from stomach ulcers. Often he stood as umpire when in considerable pain, which unfortunately caused him to become somewhat irascible at times, and at the end of the 1955 season he retired, terminating a career in which he officiated in over 1,000 first-class fixtures, including 48 Test matches.

The First World War cut short his ambitions as an all-rounder for Worcestershire. In 1912, at the age of 16, he joined that county's staff and in the following season he scored 703 runs, including three centuries, average 28.12, and took with off-breaks 44 wickets, average 26.88. *Wisden* said of him that year: "Nothing stood out more prominently than the remarkable development of Chester, the youngest professional regularly engaged in first-class cricket. . . . Very few players in the history of cricket have shown such form at the age of seventeen and a half. Playing with a beautifully straight bat, he depended to a large extent on his watchfulness in defence. Increased hitting power will naturally come with time. He bowls with a high, easy action and, commanding an accurate length, can get plenty of spin on the ball. Having begun so well, Chester should continue to improve and it seems only reasonable to expect that when he has filled out and gained more strength, he will be an England cricketer."

In 1914 he put together an aggregate of 924 runs, average 27.17, with an innings of 178 not out—including four 6's from the bowling of J. W. H. T. Douglas—against Essex at Worcester, his highest. Then came the war and, in the course of service with the Army in Salonika, he lost his right arm just below the elbow. That, of course, meant no more cricket as a player for Chester; but in 1922 he became a first-class umpire and, with the advantage of youth when the majority of his colleagues were men who had retired as cricketers on the score of *Anno Domini*, he swiftly gained a big reputation. His lack of years caused him difficulty on one occasion at Northampton for a gate-man refused him admission, declining to believe that one so young could be an umpire, and suggested that he should try the ground of a neighbouring works team!

From the very beginning of his career as an umpire, he gave his decisions without fear or favour. In an article, "Thirty Years an Umpire," in the 1954 *Wisden*, Vivian Jenkins told how, when standing in his first county match, Essex v. Somerset at Leyton, Chester was called on to give decisions against both captains, J. W. H. T. Douglas and J. Daniell, and did his duty according to his lights—Douglas lbw, Daniell stumped. "You'll be signing your death warrant if you go on like that," he was warned by his venerable colleague, but he went on undeterred.

Chester began the custom, now prevalent among umpires, of bending low over the wicket when the bowler delivered the ball, and his decisions were both prompt and rarely questioned. Yet the ruling which probably caused most discussion was one in which Chester was wrong. This occurred during the England v. West Indies Test match at Trent Bridge in 1950, when S. Ramadhin bowled D. J. Insole off his pads. Chester contended that the batsman was leg before wicket, because he (Chester) gave his decision in the brief time before the ball hit the stumps, and as "lbw" Insole remained in the score. Soon after this, M.C.C. added a Note to Law 34 which made it clear beyond dispute that, where a batsman is dismissed in such circumstances, he is out "bowled."

Chester had some brushes with Australian touring players, whose demonstrative methods of appealing annoyed him, but nevertheless Sir Donald Bradman termed him "the greatest umpire under whom I played." Chester, for his part, rated Bradman "the greatest run-making machine I have ever known," and considered Sir John Hobbs the greatest batsman of all time on all pitches.

Throughout his long spell as an umpire Chester used, for counting the balls per over, six small pebbles which he picked up from his mother's garden at Bushey before he "stood" in his first match.

Tributes included:—

Mr. R. Aird, Secretary of M.C.C.: "He was an inspiration to other umpires. He seemed to have a flair for the job and did the right thing by instinct. He was outstanding among umpires for a very long time."

Sir John Hobbs: "I played against him in his brief career and am sure he would have been a great England all-rounder. As an umpire, he was right on top. I class him with that great Australian, Bob Crockett."

F. S. Lee, the Test match umpire: "Frank was unquestionably the greatest umpire I have known. His decisions were fearless, whether the batsman to be given out was captain or not. There is a great deal for which umpires have to thank him."

COLEY, MR. ERIC, who died at Northampton on May 3, aged 53, was at one time honorary secretary to Northamptonshire. Better known as a Rugby footballer for Northampton, he represented England as a forward against France in 1929 and Wales in 1932 and also played for the Barbarians. From 1937 to 1947 he was a member of the International Selection Committee.

COLLINS, BRIGADIER LIONEL PETER, who died at his home at Fleet, Hampshire, on September 27, aged 78, was an excellent hard-hitting batsman for Marlborough and Oxford University. In his second year in the Marlborough XI, 1897, when *Wisden* described him as "a batsman second to none among schoolboys," he headed the batting averages with 670 runs, highest innings 203, for 55.10 per innings. He also represented the school at hockey, for which he gained his Blue from 1898 to 1900 besides playing cricket against Cambridge in 1899. He did

good service for Berkshire from 1897 to 1899. He joined the Indian Army in
1901 and while on tour with a Ghurka Brigade team hit three double centuries
in the course of ten days. During the First World War he was three times
mentioned in dispatches and awarded the D.S.O.; in 1934 he became a C.B.
and he also held the C.S.I. and the O.B.E. From 1934 to 1936, when he retired,
he was A.D.C. to King George V.

COOKE, ERNEST J., who died at Nottingham on October 22, aged 58, was a
first-class umpire from 1936 to 1956. In 1948 he officiated in the England v.
Australia Test match at Trent Bridge. He was at one time a member of the
Nottinghamshire ground staff.

DAVIES, MR. GEORGE A., who died in Melbourne on November 27, aged 66,
was manager of the Australian team who toured England under A. L. Hassett
in 1953. In a few appearances for Victoria in the early 1920's, Davies scored
143 runs, average 20.42, and took five wickets for nearly 18 runs each. He was a
member of the executive committee of the Victorian Cricket Association.

DAVISON, ROBERT WATSON JAMES, who died in June, aged 78, played as a
slow-medium left-arm bowler for Yorkshire Second XI while professional to
Dewsbury.

DEAN, HARRY, who died at his home at Garstang, near Blackpool, on March
12, aged 71, was one of the most successful bowlers who ever played for Lancashire.
He first appeared for the county in 1906 and before he left them at the end of the
1921 season he took, with left-arm bowling, 1,301 wickets in all first-class matches
for 18.14 runs apiece. He suited his methods to the conditions, bowling fast-
medium with deceptive swerve or slow according to the state of the pitch. He
made an auspicious start, for in his first season he dismissed 60 batsmen, and in
each of the next seven summers he took over 100 wickets, as he did also in 1920.
Six times he obtained nine wickets in an innings, his best analysis being 15.1 overs,
8 maidens, 31 runs, 9 wickets against Somerset at Old Trafford in 1909.

The performance which afforded Dean most satisfaction, however, was
against Yorkshire at Aigburth in 1913 in an extra match arranged to mark the
visit to Liverpool of King George V. He took nine wickets for 62 in the first
innings and eight for 29 in the second, bringing his match figures to 17 for 91.
There is no recorded instance of greater success by a bowler in a "Roses" match.
In his best season, 1911, Dean secured 183 wickets, average 17.43. He played for
England in two Test matches against Australia and one against South Africa in
the 1912 Triangular Tournament, his 11 wickets in these three games costing
153 runs. After the end of his first-class career, he played for some years for
Cheshire and from 1926 to 1932 was coach at Rossall School.

DE ZOETE, MR. HERMAN WALTER, who died in March, aged 80, played for
Cambridge against Oxford in 1897 and 1898. He bore a big share in victory by
179 runs in the first of these University matches, helping C. E. M. Wilson in an
eighth wicket stand of 56 and, with medium-pace bowling, dismissing four men
for 26 runs in the Oxford second innings. He also represented Cambridge at golf
in 1896, 1897 and 1898. He was in the Eton XI of 1895 and in 1898 appeared once
for Essex.

DOUGLAS, THE REV. ROBERT NOEL, who died at Colyton, Devon, on
February 27, aged 88, played both cricket and Rugby football for Cambridge.
He went to the University from Dulwich College in 1889 and for the three following
years appeared against Oxford at Lord's, scoring as opening batsman an aggregate
of 97 runs in the six innings. Twice he assisted Gentlemen against Players and
he later turned out first for Surrey and then for Middlesex. Altogether he hit
2,661 runs in first-class cricket, average 23.13. He played as a forward in the
University Rugby match of 1891 and also helped the Harlequins. He was a master
at Uppingham before serving as headmaster of Giggleswick from 1910 to 1931.

EVERSHED, MR. EDWARD, who died in Birmingham on February 18, aged 89, played with his brother for Derbyshire from 1888 to 1892 when they were a second-class county. At one time captain of Rosslyn Park R.F.C. and of Handsworth Golf Club, he was also a member of the Committee of Warwickshire C.C.C.

FERGUSON, MR. WILLIAM HENRY, who died at Bath on September 22, aged 77, was the best-known cricket scorer in the world. For 52 years, from the time he first visited England with Joe Darling's Australian side of 1905, he acted as scorer and baggage-master for England, South Africa, West Indies, New Zealand and, naturally, Australia, in no fewer than 43 tours. In all that time his boast was that he never lost a bag. "Fergie," as he was affectionately known in the cricket world, scored in no fewer than 208 Test matches in every country where big cricket is played. He liked to relate how he first took up the job. The office in Sydney, his birthplace, where he was employed as a clerk, overlooked the harbour and he often felt the urge to travel. So in 1905 he "thought up a nice toothache," went to see his dentist, M. A. Noble, the Test batsman, and brought up the question of scoring. Amused at the ingenious method of approach, Noble put forward "Fergie's" name to the authorities, with the result that this short, slightly-built man began his travels which totalled well over half a million miles. His salary for the 1905 tour was £2 per week, from which he defrayed his expenses, and he paid his own passage.

For all his long connection with it, "Fergie" never took much active part in the game, but figures, for which he always had a passion, fascinated him, and he loved to travel. Besides actual scoring, he kept diagrams of every stroke played, with their value, by every batsman in the matches in which he was concerned, and could account for every ball bowled—and who fielded it. Touring captains, including D. G. Bradman and D. R. Jardine, employed his charts to study the strength and weaknesses of opposing batsmen.

When in England with the Australian team of 1948, "Fergie" was presented to King George VI. That summer Bradman scored 2,428 runs. Said the King: "Mr. Ferguson, do you use an adding-machine when the Don is in?"

"Fergie," who received the British Empire Medal in 1951 for his services to cricket, emerged from two years' retirement to score for the West Indies last summer. A fall at an hotel in August prevented him from finishing the tour, and he spent some time in hospital, returning home only two days before his death. His autobiography, titled *Mr. Cricket*, was published in May, 1957.

FIRTH, CANON JOHN D'EWES EVELYN, who died at Winchester on September 21, aged 57, was Master of the Temple and Canon Emeritus of Winchester Cathedral. A scholar of Winchester and Christ Church, he later became a master at the school. "Budge" Firth was in the Winchester XI of 1917, when heading the bowling averages with 29 wickets, average 6.55, and captained the side the following year. A leg-break bowler who cleverly varied pace and flight, he set up a Winchester record in a one-day "unofficial" match with Eton at Winchester in 1917 by taking all ten Eton wickets for 41 runs. Even so, Eton won by seven runs. Nine days earlier he dismissed eight Harrow batsmen for 48 runs. Only once previously had the feat of taking all ten wickets been achieved in an Eton v. Winchester match. That was in 1902 when G. A. C. Sandeman, of Eton, did so at a cost of 22 runs. At Oxford, Firth played in two matches for the University in 1919 and 1920, but did not get his Blue. He also appeared for Nottinghamshire in 1919.

FOWLER, CAPTAIN R. H., who died in May, aged 99 years and 11 months, played in two matches for Ireland in 1888. He was the father of R. St. L. Fowler, who in 1910 was the hero of the Eton v. Harrow match—known ever since as "Fowler's Match." Eton followed on 165 behind and, despite an innings of 64 by Fowler, Harrow needed only 55 to win; but Fowler, with off-breaks, bowled in deadly form, taking eight wickets for 23 runs, and Eton snatched victory by nine runs.

Foy, Mr. Philip Arnold, who died in the British Hospital, Buenos Aires, on February 12, aged 65, was for many years prominent as a bowler in Argentine cricket. He distinguished himself against the M.C.C. touring side captained by Lord Hawke in 1912. Educated at Bedford School, Foy played for Bedfordshire and when on leave assisted Somerset, for whom, in 1920, he took 31 wickets, average 22.48, and scored 352 runs, with 72 against Essex at Leyton his highest innings in first-class cricket.

Freeman, Mr. Eric Howard, who died suddenly at his home at Sedgley, Wolverhampton, on July 12, was a qualified M.C.C. coach who did much work in training boys and old boys of King Edward's School. He played on occasion for the Warwickshire Club and Ground side and was also a keen golfer and Rugby footballer.

Gunn, George Vernon, who died in hospital at Shrewsbury on October 15, aged 52, as the result of injuries received in a motor-cycle accident, played for Nottinghamshire from 1928 to 1939, scoring in that time just over 10,000 runs and taking close upon 300 wickets. In 1931 he scored 100 not out—his first century—against Warwickshire at Edgbaston and in the same innings his father, George Gunn, then 53, hit 183. This, it is believed, is the only instance of a father and son each reaching three figures in the same first-class match. G. V. Gunn's best season as an all-rounder was that of 1934 when he obtained 922 runs and, with slow leg-breaks, dismissed 77 batsmen. In that summer he achieved his best bowling performance, taking 10 wickets for 120 in the game with Hampshire at Trent Bridge. He exceeded 1,000 runs in each of his last five seasons with the county, his highest aggregate being 1,765, average 44.07, in 1937. His biggest innings was 184 against Leicestershire at Nottingham the following year a display featured by brilliant driving. After giving up county cricket, he coached in the north of England and later at Wrekin College and for Worcestershire C.C.C.

Harris, Lieut.-Colonel Frank, who died at Tunbridge Wells on July 2, aged 91, was for thirty-five years captain of Southborough C.C., for whom he first played when 16. In his younger days an enthusiastic runner, he walked from Bidborough to London on his 70th birthday because his father did the same thing and had told him that he would not be able to do so when he was 70. The journey occupied him just over thirteen hours. He served in the Royal Engineers during the First World War, being mentioned in dispatches.

Hipkin, Augustus Bernard, who died in a Lanarkshire hospital on February 11, aged 56, did much excellent work as a slow left-arm bowler for Essex from 1923 to 1931. A "discovery" of J. W. H. T. Douglas, then Essex captain, "Joe" Hipkin took in all first-class matches 528 wickets at an average of 25.56. He flighted the ball cleverly with a high action and spun it considerably. His best season was that of 1924 when, in dismissing 109 batsmen for 20.34 runs each, he headed the Essex averages. That year he performed the "hat-trick" against Lancashire at Blackpool. He was also a capital fieldsman and a useful batsman, scoring 4,446 runs, average 16.40. When Essex did not renew his contract, he went to Scotland, meeting with marked success as professional with the Uddingstone and West of Scotland clubs.

Holland, Frederick Charles, who died on February 5, five days before his 81st birthday, played as a batsman for Surrey from 1894 to 1908, scoring 10,384 runs, including twelve centuries, average 25.57. Four times he exceeded 1,000 runs in a season. Encouraged by his seven elder brothers, he played cricket from the early age of three, and when 17 joined The Oval ground staff. Of graceful style, he showed to special advantage in cutting and hitting to leg, and he was also a very good short slip. His highest innings was 171 against Cambridge University at The Oval in 1895, when he and R. Abel (165) added 306 for the third Surrey wicket. Next season he hit 153 from the Warwickshire bowling at Edgbaston. Following his retirement from first-class cricket, he became coach at Oundle.

HOSIE, MR. ALEC L., who died on June 11, aged 66, played periodically for Hampshire between 1913 and 1935 when on leave from India. He was educated at St. Lawrence College, Ramsgate, and Magdalen College, Oxford, where he gained Blues for hockey, lawn tennis and Association football. A quick-footed, hard-hitting batsman, he scored 4,176 runs in first-class cricket, average 26.10. His best season for the county was that of 1928, when, with 1,187 runs, average 31.23, he stood third in the Hampshire averages. That summer he made his highest score, 155 against Yorkshire at Southampton, and he also hit two centuries against Middlesex—132 at Portsmouth and 106 at Lord's.

HUISH, FREDERICK HENRY, who died at Northiam, Sussex, on March 16, aged 87, was the first of a line of exceptional Kent wicket-keepers which L. E. G. Ames and T. G. Evans continued. First appearing for the county in 1895, he continued until the outbreak of war in 1914, accounting in the meantime for no fewer than 1,328 batsmen—952 caught and 376 stumped. Yet, unlike Ames and Evans, he was never chosen to play for England and only once, at Lord's in 1902, for Players against Gentlemen.

It was a curious fact that while Huish, born at Clapham, was a Surrey man who played for Kent, H. Wood, from whom he learned much of his skill, was Kentish by birth and assisted Surrey. One of the ablest and least demonstrative wicket-keepers of his generation, Huish was among the few to assist in the taking of 100 wickets in a season. This performance he achieved twice, for in 1911 he obtained 100 victims (62 caught, 38 stumped) and in 1913 raised his tally to 102 (70 caught, 32 stumped). In 1911 he enjoyed his greatest triumph in a single match when, against Surrey at The Oval, he caught one batsman and stumped nine, thus dismissing ten in the two innings. On five other occasions he disposed of eight men in a game. Four times he helped Kent to carry off the County Championship, in 1906, 1909, 1910 and 1913.

Huish showed his readiness and resource in memorable if lucky fashion in a match between Kent and the Australians at Canterbury in 1902. He was standing far back to W. M. Bradley, the famous amateur fast bowler, when R. A. Duff played a ball a few yards behind the wicket and the Australian's partner called for a run. To get to the ball, Huish had to move so far that he realised that he would not have time to gather it before the batsmen got home. Accordingly he attempted to kick it on to the stumps at his end. The ball missed its immediate objective, but Huish put so much power into his effort that the ball went on and hit the wicket at the other end before Duff could make the necessary ground.

Though not generally successful as a batsman, Huish scored 562 runs in 1906, his best innings being 93 against Somerset at Gravesend. When Huish became the Kent senior professional, he was reputed to exercise remarkable control over his colleagues. Indeed, it used to be alleged that, unless he appealed, no brother professional dared to ask for a catch at the wicket!

HUTCHEON, MR. JOHN SILVESTER, C.B.E., Q.C., who died at Brisbane on June 18, aged 75, represented Queensland at cricket and lacrosse. He was a member of the Australian Board of Control for International Cricket from 1919 onwards and at one time chairman. He was called to the Bar by Lincoln's Inn in 1914 and became a member of the Queensland Bar in 1916.

JONES, MR. W. E., who died in hospital at Chester on December 13, aged 69, was in his younger days a prominent all-rounder for Cheshire, whom he often captained. His brother, two sons and two nephews all played for the county. When he gave up active participation in the game, he bore a leading part in administrative affairs, being one of the sponsors of the county scheme for coaching young players. He was a Chester City magistrate.

KEMPTON, MR. ANDREW, who died in a London hospital on November 17, aged 72, did much good work over nearly 50 years for Surrey. He was the "Father" of the Surrey Colts team, whom he captained up to last season. In his younger days he played as an excellent wicket-keeper-batsman for Catford and Richmond. It was while he was President of Catford that J. C. Laker, now the England off-break bowler, returning from military service overseas, turned out for the club, and Kempton brought him to the notice of the Surrey authorities. A great friend of Sir John Hobbs, Kempton was a founder-director of his sports-outfitters firm in 1919.

HH

LANGFORD, W., who died in Faversham Hospital on February 20, aged 81, played as a fast-medium bowler for Hampshire between 1902 and 1908, taking during that time 215 wickets, average 26.88. He headed his county's averages in 1904 with 42 wickets at a cost of 13.95 runs each, his most successful match being against Warwickshire at Southampton that season. In the first innings he dismissed five men for 30 runs and in the second six for 41. After retiring from first-class cricket, he served for some years as coach at Tonbridge School.

LEVICK, CAPTAIN THOMAS HENRY CARLTON, who died at Bournemouth on October 19, aged 90, was a member of M.C.C. for over forty years. He was honorary manager of the M.C.C. touring teams who visited West Indies in 1925–26 and 1934–35, South Africa in 1930–31 and Canada in 1937. He was a member of the Southgate Club for 58 years.

LEWIS, MAJOR NORMAN ALLEN, who died at his home at Blackheath on December 22, aged 78, played in his younger days for Lancashire Second XI. Rising from private to major in the Sportsmen's Battalion of the Royal Fusiliers during the First World War, he was awarded the D.S.O. and the M.C. with bar. For long services to the boys of London, and the Boys' Brigade in particular, he received the O.B.E. in 1950.

PITT, MR. THOMAS ALFRED, who died at Northampton on April 23, aged 63, played for Northamptonshire in 1934 and 1935, taking 43 wickets for just over 26 runs each. Of medium-pace, he kept a good length and made the ball turn a little either way. A pilot in the R.F.C. during the First World War, he served with the R.A.F. in the Second.

RHODES, ARTHUR CECIL, who died on May 21, aged 50, played for Yorkshire from 1932 to 1934, taking 107 wickets, average 28.28, with fast-medium bowling and, by forcing methods, scoring 917 runs, average 17.93. Among his performances was the taking of nine Gloucestershire wickets for 117 runs in the match at Sheffield in 1933, in which season he hit his highest first-class score, 64 not out against Leicestershire at Leicester. He was well known in Yorkshire and Lancashire League cricket.

RICH, MR. ARTHUR, who died on December 14, aged 90, often played as a hard-hitting batsman for Cambridgeshire during a cricket career extending over more than thirty years. He was in the county side when Sir John Hobbs appeared as an amateur in 1901.

RICHMOND, THOMAS LEONARD, who died on December 30, aged 65, was a prominent slow bowler for Nottinghamshire between 1912 and 1928. During his career in first-class cricket he took 1,158 wickets, average 21.24. The number of runs he scored exceeded his total of wickets by no more than 406, so that when he scored 70 in a last wicket partnership of 140 in sixty-five minutes with S. J. Staples against Derbyshire at Worksop in 1922 the general surprise may readily be imagined. The batting skill he displayed in this his highest innings was not repeated and it is as a skilful leg-break bowler who did not allow occasional heavy punishment to upset him that he will be remembered.

In one or two appearances in the county side before the First World War he accomplished little, but afterwards he became one of the best bowlers of his type in the country. He dismissed more than 100 batsmen in each of eight seasons, his best being that of 1922 when his 169 wickets cost him 13.48 runs each and exceeded the Nottinghamshire record of 163 set up by T. Wass in 1907. Among his most notable performances were: nine wickets for 21 in Hampshire's second innings at Nottingham in 1922; nine for 19 (three for 9 and six for 10) in the match with Leicestershire at Trent Bridge and fourteen for 83 (seven for 30 and seven for 53)—all in one day—against Gloucestershire at Cheltenham in 1925; thirteen for 76 v. Leicestershire at Nottingham in 1920; thirteen for 107 v. Essex at Leyton in 1922, and thirteen for 165, including a hat-trick, v. Lancashire at Nottingham in 1926. For Pudsey St. Lawrence in 1920 he disposed of all ten Lowmoor batsmen in an innings for 39 runs. "Tich" Richmond played in one Test match for England, against Australia at Trent Bridge in 1921, taking two wickets for 86 runs.

ROBINSON, MR. LAURENCE MILNER, who died in a nursing home at Dorking on September 15, aged 72, was in the Marlborough XI of 1904, heading the bowling averages with 24 wickets for 16.20 runs each. He also represented the school at hockey and Rugby football. Going up to Cambridge, he played at centre half-back in the University hockey match from 1906 to 1908, being captain in the last year. In each of these games his twin brother, J. Y. Robinson, played for the Dark Blues against him. The brothers also figured in the England half-back line on three occasions. For services in the Consular service, he was made C.M.G. in 1944.

ST. HILL, EDWIN LLOYD, who died at Withington, Lancs., on May 21, aged 51, played as a medium-paced bowler for Trinidad and for the West Indies against the Hon. F. S. G. Calthorpe's M.C.C. touring team in 1930. On the occasion of St. Hill's second representative match appearance, George Headley set up a record by scoring a century in each innings. From 1943 to 1951, St. Hill played in Central Lancashire League cricket.

SANTALL, SYDNEY, who died at his home at Bournemouth on March 19, aged 83, rendered valuable service to Warwickshire as a right-arm medium-pace bowler from 1892 to 1914. From 1894, when the county attained first-class status, till the outbreak of the First World War he took 1,219 wickets, average 24.41, and held 150 catches. He appeared for Northamptonshire as an amateur before going on trial to Warwickshire in 1892 and he remained, first as player and then as coach, till 1920.

He was also a useful batsman, and in his first-class career he scored 6,561 runs, average 15.58. His best season as an all-rounder was probably that of 1905, when he dismissed 94 batsmen at a cost of 24.59 runs each and obtained 685 runs, including his highest score—67 against Hampshire at Southampton—average 22.83. On four occasions he headed the Warwickshire bowling figures, his greatest success with the ball occurring in 1907 when he took 100 wickets, average 16.79. In that season he numbered among his performances seven wickets for 38 runs v. Leicestershire at Coventry; eight for 72 v. Yorkshire at Sheffield and seven for 77 v. P. W. Sherwell's South African team at Edgbaston. Other good analyses were seven for 39 v. Lancashire at Liverpool and eight for 32 v. Essex at Edgbaston in 1898; eight for 23 v. Leicestershire at Edgbaston in 1900 and eight for 44 v. Somerset at Leamington in 1908, when Warwickshire, after being 86 behind on the first innings, dismissed their opponents for 93 and won by 161 runs. His son, F. R. Santall, who died in 1950, played for many years as a batsman for Warwickshire.

SARAVANAMUTTU, LIEUT.-COLONEL S., who died suddenly at Colombo on July 17, aged 59, was President of the Board of Control for Cricket in Ceylon. While a schoolboy at St. Thomas's, he hit 121 against St. Anthony's, Kandy, in thirty-eight minutes, the fastest century scored in Ceylon. He captained the Tamil Union Club for eight years, played in the European-Ceylonese Test series and for Ceylon against New Zealand, M.C.C. and Australia, being captain on two occasions. He figured with some success in the University trials at Cambridge from 1921 to 1923 without getting a Blue. He held the M.B.E.

SCOTT, MR. ROBERT STRICKLAND GILBERT, who died after an operation at Peasmarsh, Sussex, on August 26, aged 48, was a former Oxford Blue. After three seasons from 1926 to 1928 in the eleven at Winchester, where he was captain in the last year, he went up to Oxford, appearing with much success against Cambridge in 1931. In that game A. T. Ratcliffe set up a record for the University match by hitting 201 in the Cambridge first innings—a record which lasted only one day, for in the Oxford reply the Nawab of Pataudi scored 238. Despite Ratcliffe's big innings, Scott, bowling above medium-pace, took six wickets for 64 runs in a total of 385 and in the second innings helped further towards victory by eight wickets when dismissing two men for 23. He played in one game for Sussex that season and for the next two years was a regular member of the county side. In 1932, when the health of K. S. Duleepsinhji broke down and Scott captained the team in several games, he hit 559 runs, average 20.70, including 116 out of 169 (seven 6's, eleven 4's) in a hundred minutes, and took 54 wickets, average 20.31. He also played in a Test Trial match. The following summer he took 113 from the Hampshire bowling at Horsham. The end of his first-class career came when his father died in 1933. He figured prominently in Sussex affairs and became High Sheriff of the county.

SHEPHERD, THOMAS F., who died in Kingston Hospital on February 13, aged 66, was one of Surrey's great batsmen at a period after the First World War when the county were richly endowed with run-getters and a place in the side was extremely difficult to command. Between 1919 and 1932, when he retired and became head groundsman and coach to Wandgas C.C.—a post he held till his death—Shepherd hit 18,719 runs, including 42 centuries, average 39.82, in first-class cricket, took 441 wickets, average 30.81, with medium-pace bowling, and, generally fielding in the slips, held 268 catches.

His rise to fame was sensational. In 1920 he provided almost the entire batting strength of the Second XI. He hit 236 from the Essex Second XI bowling at Leyton and altogether scored 709 runs, average 101.28. As he also took 38 wickets, average 15.50, he headed both sets of averages. These performances literally forced Surrey to give him a regular position in the Championship team, and he seized his opportunity with such avidity that in each of eleven successive seasons he exceeded 1,000 runs. In 1921 he distinguished himself by hitting 212 against Lancashire at The Oval and 210 not out against Kent at Blackheath—then known as "The Surrey Graveyard"—in following innings and he obtained 1,658 runs, including six centuries, in Championship fixtures, average 51.81. He did even better in 1927, putting together eight scores of three figures, with 277 not out against Gloucestershire at The Oval the highest. In the course of this innings which, the biggest of his career, occupied four and three-quarter hours, he and A. Ducat put on 289 in two and three-quarter hours for the fourth wicket. Shepherd's aggregate that summer reached 2,145, average 55.00, of which 1,681 were registered in competition matches. The previous season he hit two separate centuries in a match—121 and 101 not out from the Leicestershire attack at The Oval.

Born at Headington Quarry, near Oxford, Shepherd played for his village team at the early age of eleven. A player of imperturbable temperament, he suited his methods to the conditions and the state of the game, for while he could pull and hit to the off with exhilarating power, he was capable of considerable patience. He appeared in Test Trial matches and for Players against Gentlemen, but, so great was the competition during his time, he never played for England.

SIMPSON, MR. GERALD AMYATT, who died on February 22, aged 70, took part in a few first-class matches for Kent in 1929 and 1930 after spending his early manhood in the Argentine. For many years he captained Kent Second XI; he led the Club and Ground team till he was 63, and he played for the Band of Brothers and the St. Lawrence clubs. A hard-hitting batsman, he was also a splendid fieldsman close to the wicket. As a member of the Committee, he rendered long service to Kent. During the First World War he served in the Royal Artillery and was wounded in France.

SKIMMING, MR. EDWARD HUGH BOWRING, who died at Taplow, Bucks, on October 20, aged 82, was in the Marlborough XI of 1893. He dismissed four batsmen in 45 overs for 89 runs in the match with Rugby at Lord's and headed the bowling averages with 45 wickets for 11.20 runs each. Rheumatic fever contracted while at school ended his athletic career. He was a well-known figure in London shipping circles.

SPENCER, MR. GEORGE ALFRED, who died in hospital at Nottingham on November 21, aged 84, was President of Nottinghamshire in 1949. When Socialist M.P. for the Broxtowe Division in 1918–29 he played for the House of Commons cricket team. One of a family of eighteen, he was a past-President of the Notts and District Miners Federated Union and vice-chairman of the North Midlands Coal Board.

STEVENS, GEORGE, who died at his home at Gaywood, Norfolk, on March 28, aged 89, played cricket with and against the brothers E. M. and W. G. Grace. In fifteen matches for Norfolk from 1905 to 1911, "Pro" Stevens scored 257 runs and, with left-arm medium-pace bowling, took 27 wickets. His best performance with the ball was six wickets for 56 runs against Suffolk in 1909. Born at Bognor, Sussex, he served as professional to Lynn Town C.C. before becoming groundsman at King Edward VII School, King's Lynn, a post he held for 41 years. Dr. E. M. Grace once wrote of Stevens: "No one knows better how to prepare a first-class cricket pitch," and also praised him as an all-rounder.

SUSSKIND, MR. MANFRED J., collapsed and died on July 9, aged 66, at the Johannesburg Stock Exchange, of which he was a member for thirty years. Educated at University College School and Cambridge University, he played in a few games for Middlesex before returning home and assisting Transvaal, for whom he obtained 2,595 runs, average 49.90, in Currie Cup matches, hitting six centuries. He and H. B. Cameron set up a Transvaal record when adding 207 for the sixth wicket against Eastern Province in 1926–27. In 1924 "Fred" Susskind, as he was always known, was one of H. W. Taylor's South African team in England, playing in all five Test matches. He was second in the Test batting averages with 268 runs, average 33.50, and in all games scored 1,469 runs, including two centuries, average 32.64. A tall batsman, he was often cramped in style and his proneness to pad-play caused a good deal of criticism during the tour.

SYED HASSAN SHAH, who died on September 28, aged 67, following a car accident at Multon, played for about nine years in the Bombay Quadrangular Tournament, captaining the Muslims on two occasions. Educated at Government College, Lahore, and M.A.O. College, Alligarh, he later took the Civil Engineering course in England.

THWAITE, DR. HAROLD, who died at his home at Lower Kingswood, Surrey, on October 26, aged 74, was President of Warwickshire C.C.C. from 1942 to 1955. He had been in poor health during the previous year. A prominent figure in Midlands medical circles for nearly fifty years, Thwaite began his association with Warwickshire when a medical student at Birmingham University in 1900. He became a member of the Committee in 1926 and served as honorary treasurer from 1930 till he was elected President.

WILMOT, WILLIAM, who died on May 19, aged 84, played occasionally for Derbyshire between 1897 and 1901. An excellent wicket-keeper, he was unfortunate to be contemporary with W. Storer and J. Humphries.

WILSON, BENJAMIN B., who died on September 17, aged 77, played as opening batsman for Yorkshire between 1906 and 1914 and later coached at St. Peter's School, York, and at Harrow. During his first-class career he scored 6,454 runs, including fifteen centuries, for an average of 27.69. His highest innings was 208 against Sussex at Bradford in 1914, when he put together an aggregate of 1,605 runs—his best—and altogether he exceeded 1,000 runs in a season five times. Yet, as illustrated by references to him in *Wisden* by that excellent judge Sydney H. Pardon, he rarely showed his real capabilities and this led to his services being dispensed with by the county following the First World War. Of him in 1909 Mr. Pardon wrote: "Playing in excellent style, he had everything in his favour, but for some reason that one is quite unable to explain, his success made him unduly cautious"; next year: "If he would only give free play to his natural ability, he might soon be first-rate"; and the following season: "Possessing every physical advantage, he is at his best a very fine hitter, but he is apt for no reason whatever to subside into laborious slowness. He ought by this time to have been Tunnicliffe's successor, but he cannot be considered as more than a partial success." Had Wilson given full rein to his natural skill in driving and cutting, he might well have earned himself a place among the great men of Yorkshire cricket.

WILSON, MR. EVELYN ROCKLEY, who died at Winchester on July 21, aged 78, was one of the best amateur slow right-arm bowlers of his time. Educated at Rugby, he was in the XI for three years from 1895, heading both batting and bowling figures when captain in 1897. With a highest innings of 206 not out, he averaged 51.11 in batting and he took 31 wickets for 14.93 runs each. Before he gained his Blue at Cambridge, whom he represented against Oxford in four matches from 1899 to 1902, he scored a century against his University for A. J. Webbe's XI. In the University match of 1901 he hit 118 and 27 and took five wickets for 71 runs and two for 38, and in that of 1902, when captain, he played a noteworthy part in victory by five wickets for the Light Blues by taking five wickets for 23 and three for 66.

He made a brief appearance for Yorkshire in 1899, but when, on going down from Cambridge, he became a master at Winchester, a position he held for forty years, he preferred to engage in club cricket during the school holidays, his stated reason being that he preferred to play in three matches a week rather than two. He did, however, go to America with B. J. T. Bosanquet's side in 1901; with the team of English amateurs who visited the West Indies in 1902, when he stood first in the bowling averages with 78 wickets for less than 11 runs each, and with the M.C.C. to Argentina in 1912.

A suggestion that Wilson might use his residential qualification for Hampshire led to him being pressed into service once again by Yorkshire when over forty years of age, but, whatever the reason, there could be no doubt as to his immense value to the county during the closing weeks of each season. In 1913 he made his only century for Yorkshire, 104 not out against Essex at Bradford, in the course of which he claimed to have hit the only six obtained by skying a ball directly over the wicket-keeper's head, but it was as a bowler that he achieved his best work. He met with such success in 1920 that he took 64 wickets for 13.84 runs apiece, being fourth in the English averages. This brought him a place in J. W. H. T. Douglas's M.C.C. team who, the following winter, toured Australia. Wilson played in his only Test match during that tour, of which *Wisden* of the time reported: "A good deal of friction was caused by cable messages sent home to the *Daily Express* by Mr. E. R. Wilson. This led to a resolution passed at the annual meeting of the Marylebone Club in May deprecating the reporting of matches by players concerned in them."

Among Wilson's best performances was that in the match with Middlesex at Bradford in 1922 when, in the second innings, he sent down 44 overs, 22 of them maidens, for 62 runs and six wickets. He and A. Waddington shared in a last wicket stand of 53 for Yorkshire, but all the same Middlesex won an exciting struggle by four runs. Wilson was the first bowler to perform the hat-trick for Gentlemen against Players, which he did at Scarborough in 1919. Altogether in first-class cricket he took 385 wickets, average 21.66, and scored 3,033 runs, average 18.94.

Immaculate length and cleverly-disguised variation of pace made Wilson difficult to punish. His own explanation of his success was typically whimsical. "I have always been a lucky bowler," he said, "as my best ball has been the ball which broke from the off when I meant to break from leg. I bowled far more of these as a man of forty than as a young man." Another example of this slightly-built, diffident cricketer's sense of humour was provided at the nets at Winchester when to a somewhat inept boy batsman he said: "My dear boy, you must hit one ball in the middle of your bat before you meet your Maker." He will always be remembered by the vast number of Wykehamists who enjoyed the benefit of his advice and of whom several gained cricket fame. His elder brother, C. E. M. Wilson, also captained Cambridge.

WORMALD, MAJOR JOHN, who died on November 14, aged 75, was in the Eton XI, in 1899 and the following year. A sound batsman, he scored 326 runs in 1899, average 29.63. From 1910 to 1912 he played in a few matches for Middlesex and subsequently he assisted Norfolk. He hit 61 against Yorkshire at Lord's in 1910 and he equalled that score against Sussex on the same ground the following season. He was awarded the M.C. while serving with the King's Royal Rifle Corps in France during the First World War.

OBITUARY, 1956

GARRARD, MR. WILSON ROZIERE, who died at Auckland on June 2, 1956, aged 56, played as wicket-keeper for New Zealand in 1924–25. Unfortunate to be contemporary with R. W. Rountree, who kept wicket for New Zealand, he made only eleven appearances for Auckland. A member of the legal profession, he was compelled by business claims to end his representative cricket career at the age of 26.

LAMBERT, MR. ROBERT H., who died on March 24, 1956, aged 81, was the best all-rounder produced by Ireland, for whom he played 52 times between 1893 and 1930, scoring 1,995 runs, including four centuries, average 27.70, taking 179 wickets for 18.35 runs each and holding 41 catches. He captained his country on thirteen occasions. He enjoyed his greatest success towards the close of last century when in each of three successive seasons he scored over 2,000 runs and took more than 200 wickets. He hit his 100th three-figure innings at the age of 59. At the invitation of Dr. W. G. Grace he made several appearances for London County. After his playing days ended, Lambert served for many years as an Irish selector and was twice President of the Irish Cricket Union. He was also an International badminton player and held the Irish Championship in 1911.

MILLS, MR. ISAAC who, died at Auckland on August 16, 1956, aged 87, was a member of the first New Zealand representative team to tour Australia in 1898–99. Born in Kent, he was taken to New Zealand in his sixth year. He and three of his brothers played for Auckland and he and his brother, George, for New Zealand.

NESER, MR. JUSTICE V. H. Regarding the obituary which appeared in the 1957 *Almanack*, Mr. A. S. Frames, Secretary of the South African Cricket Association, writes: "The late Mr. Neser captained South Africa in all five Test matches in 1924–25 against Mr. S. B. Joel's touring side. Colours were not granted, but this was probably the most outstanding feature of Mr. Neser's cricket career in South Africa."

CRICKETERS OF THE YEAR

Following is a complete alphabetical list of cricketers whose portraits and biographies have appeared in *Wisden* since, in the issue for 1889, the idea of publishing photographs of prominent players was first adopted. The number of cricketers selected for this feature has varied from time to time. Six bowlers of the year were chosen for the 1889 issue and in the following edition portraits of nine batsmen were given in the Almanack. A group of five representative wicket-keepers formed the subject of illustration for 1891 and photographs of five all-round cricketers were published in a subsequent issue.

Apart from a few exceptions, most recently during the war years in the issues from 1941 to 1946, each successive *Wisden* has included portraits and biographical details of five players who, in the opinion of the Editor, most deserved the honour by reason of their accomplishments, especially during the previous season.

Abel, R. (Surrey), 1890
Adams, P. W. (Cheltenham), 1919
Ames, L. E. G. (Kent), 1929
Appleyard, R. (Yorks.), 1952
Armstrong, W. W. (Aust.), 1903
Ashton, H. (Winchester, Camb. U. and Essex), 1922
Astill, W. E. (Leics.), 1933
Attewell, W. (Notts.), 1892

Bailey, T. E. (Dulwich, Camb. U. and Essex), 1950
Bakewell, A. H. (Northants), 1934
Bardsley, W. (Aust.), 1910
Barnes, S. F. (War., Lancs. and Staffs.), 1910
Barnes, William (Notts.), 1890
Barnett, C. J. (Glos.), 1937
Bartlett, H. T. (Dulwich, Camb. U., Surrey and Sussex), 1939
Bedser, A. V. (Surrey), 1947
Blackham, J. McC. (Aust.), 1891
Blunt, R. C. (N.Z.), 1928
Blythe, C. (Kent), 1904
Booth, M. W. (Yorks.), 1914
Bosanquet, B. J. T. (Middx.), 1905
Bowes, W. E. (Yorks.), 1932
Bowley, E. H. (Sussex), 1930
Bradman, Sir Donald G. (Aust.), 1931
Braund, L. C. (Surrey and Som.), 1902
Brearley, W. (Lancs.), 1909
Briggs, John (Lancs.), 1889
Brockwell, W. (Surrey), 1895
Brookes, D. (Northants), 1957
Brown, F. R. (Leys, Camb. U. and Surrey), 1933
Brown, J. T. (Yorks), 1895
Brown, W. A. (Aust.), 1939
Bryan, J. L. (Rugby, Camb. U. and Kent), 1922
Bull, F. G. (Essex), 1898
Burke, J. W. (Australia), 1957

Burnup, C. J. (Malvern, Camb. U. and Kent), 1903
Calder, H. L. (Cranleigh School), 1918
Cameron, H. B. (S.A.), 1936
Carr, A. W. (Notts.), 1923
Carr, D. W. (Kent), 1910
Catterall, R. H. (S.A.), 1925
Chapman, A. P. F. (Uppingham), 1919
Compton, D. C. S. (Middx.) 1939
Constantine, L. N. (W.I.), 1940
Copson, W. H. (Derby.), 1937
Cowdrey, M. C. (Tonbridge, Oxford U. and Kent), 1956
Crawford, J. N. (Repton and Surrey), 1907
Cuttell, W. R. (Yorks. and Lancs.), 1898

Darling, J. (Aust.), 1900
Day, A. P. (Malvern and Kent), 1910
Dempster, C. S (N.Z.), 1932
Denton, David (Yorks.), 1906
Dollery, H. E. (War.), 1952
Donnelly, M. P. (N.Z. and Oxf. U.), 1948
Dooland, B. (Aust. and Notts.), 1955
Douglas, J. W. H. T. (Felsted School and Essex), 1915
Druce, N. F. (Marlborough, Camb. U. and Surrey), 1898
Ducat, A. (Surrey), 1920
Duckworth, G. (Lancs.), 1929
Duleepsinhji, K. S. (Camb. U. and Sussex), 1930

Edrich, W. J. (Middx.), 1940
Evans, T. G. (Kent), 1951

Farnes, K. (Camb. U. and Essex), 1939
Fazal Mahmood (Pakistan), 1955
Fender, P. G. H. (St. Paul's School, Sussex and Surrey), 1915
Ferris, J. J. (Aust. and Glos.), 1889

Tyldesley, R. (Lancs.), 1925
Tyson, F. H. (Durham U. and Northants), 1956

Valentine, A. L. (W.I.), 1951
Verity, H. (Yorks.), 1932
Vine, J. (Sussex), 1906
Voce, W. (Notts.), 1933
Vogler, A. E. (S.A.), 1908

Wainwright, E. (Yorks.), 1894
Walcott, C. L. (W.I.), 1958
Walters, C. F. (Glam. and Worcs.) 1934
Ward, A. (Yorks. and Lancs.), 1890
Wardle, J. H. (Yorks.), 1954
Warner, Sir Pelham (Rugby, Oxf. U. and Middx.), 1904 and special portrait, 1921
Washbrook, C. (Lancs.), 1947
Wass, T. (Notts.), 1908

Watson, W. (Yorks.), 1954
Weekes, E. D. (W.I.), 1951
Wellard, A. W. (Som.), 1936
White, J. C. (Som.), 1929
Whysall, W. (Notts.), 1925
Wisden, John (Sussex). Special memoir and portrait, 1913
Wood, A. (Yorks.), 1939
Wood, H. (Surrey), 1891
Woodfull, W. M. (Aust.), 1927
Woods, S. M. J. (Camb. U., Som. and Aust.), 1889
Woolley, F. E. (Kent), 1911
Worrell, F. M. (W.I.), 1951
Worthington, T. S. (Derby.), 1937
Wright, D. V. P. (Kent), 1940
Wright, L. G. (Derby.), 1906
Wyatt, R. E. S. (War.), 1930

Yardley, N. W. D. (St. Peter's, Camb. U. and Yorks.), 1948

ADDRESSES OF REPRESENTATIVE BODIES

ENGLAND: M.C.C., Lord's Cricket Ground, St. John's Wood, London, N.W.8.
AUSTRALIA: Australian Cricket Board of Control, V.C.A. Rooms, 1, Collins Place, Melbourne, C.1, Victoria.
SOUTH AFRICA: South African Cricket Association, P.O. Box 19, P.O. Northlands, Johannesburg.
WEST INDIES: West Indies Board of Control, P.O. Box 286, Port of Spain, Trinidad.
INDIA: India Cricket Board of Control, Ranji Stadium, Eden Gardens, Calcutta.
NEW ZEALAND: New Zealand Cricket Council, P.O. Box 958, Christchurch, N.Z.
PAKISTAN: Board of Control for Cricket in Pakistan, Group Capt. M. M. A. Cheema, R.P.A.F. Station, Drigh Road, Karachi, 8.
FIJI: Fiji Cricket Association, Government Buildings, Suva, Fiji Islands.
CANADA: Candian Cricket Association, Donald King, 534A, Eglington Avenue West, Toronto 12, Ontario.

The addresses of the First-Class Counties, Universities and Minor Counties are given at the head of each separate section.

MISCELLANEOUS ADDRESSES

BIRMINGHAM LEAGUE: K. Spooner, 34, Chestnut Road, Birmingham, 13.
BRADFORD LEAGUE: W. W. Snowden, 226, Westfield Lane, Shipley, Yorks.
CLUB CRICKET CONFERENCE: Major S. W. Woods, 64A, Hill Road, London, S.W.19.
COMBINED SERVICES CRICKET ASSOCIATION, c/o Army Sports Control Board, Stanmore, Middlesex.
CRICKET SOCIETY: C. V. P. Airey, 71, Lincoln's Inn Fields, London, W.C.2.
CRICKET SOCIETY OF SCOTLAND: J. M. Fleming, 31, Murrayfield Gardens, Edinburgh, 12.
HASTINGS FESTIVAL: G. L. Lay, 77, Lower Park Road, Hastings, Sussex.
LANCASHIRE CRICKET LEAGUE: J. Isherwood, 118, Manor Street, Accrington.
NATIONAL CLUB CRICKET ASSOCIATION: T. R. Kent, 28A, Lawrence Road, Hove 3, Sussex.
NORTHERN CRICKET SOCIETY: C. R. YEOMANS, 88, Church Lane, Cross Gates, Leeds.
SCARBOROUGH FESTIVAL: A. Rutherford, North Marine Road, Scarborough, Yorks.
TORQUAY FESTIVAL: D. L. Haines, Kathleen Court Cottage, Lower Warberry Road, Torquay, Devon.
WOMEN'S CRICKET ASSOCIATION: Miss N. Rheinberg, 9, Birkdale Avenue, Pinner, Middlesex.
YORKSHIRE COUNCIL: N. Stead, 337, Leeds Road, Scholes, Leeds.

THE LAWS OF CRICKET

(1947 Code—2nd Edition)

(A)—THE PLAYERS, UMPIRES, AND SCORERS

SIDES

1.—A match is played between two sides of eleven players each, unless otherwise agreed. Each side shall play under a Captain who before the toss for innings shall nominate his players who may not thereafter be changed without the consent of the opposing Captain.

NOTES

1.—If a Captain is not available at any time, a Deputy must act for him to deal promptly with any points arising from this and other laws.

2.—No match in which more than eleven players a side take part can be regarded as First-class, and in any case no side should field with more than eleven players.

SUBSTITUTES

2.—A Substitute shall be allowed to field or run between the wickets for any player who may during the match be incapacitated from illness or injury, but not for any other reason without the consent of the opposing Captain; no Substitute shall be allowed to bat or to bowl. Consent as to the person to act as substitute in the field shall be obtained from the opposing Captain, who may indicate positions in which the Substitute shall not field.

NOTES

1.—A player may bat, bowl or field even though a substitute has acted for him previously.

2.—An injured batsman may be "Out" should his runner infringe Laws 36, 40 or 41. As *Striker* he remains himself subject to the Laws: should he be out of his ground for any purpose he may be "Out" under Laws 41 and 42 at the wicket-keeper's end, irrespective of the position of the other batsman or the substitute when the wicket is put down. When *not the Striker* the injured batsman is out of the game and stands where he does not interfere with the play.

THE APPOINTMENT OF UMPIRES

3.—Before the toss for innings two Umpires shall be appointed; one for each end to control the game as required by the Laws with absolute impartiality. No Umpire shall be changed during a match without the consent of both Captains.

NOTE

1.—The umpires should report themselves to the executive of the ground 30 minutes before the start of each day's play.

THE SCORERS

4.—All runs scored shall be recorded by Scorers appointed for the purpose, the Scorers shall accept and acknowledge all instructions and signals given to them by the Umpires.

NOTE

1.—The umpires should wait until a signal has been answered by a scorer before allowing the game to proceed. Mutual consultation between the scorers and the umpires to clear up doubtful points is at all times permissible.

(B)—THE IMPLEMENTS OF THE GAME, AND THE GROUND

THE BALL

5.—The Ball shall weigh not less than 5½ ounces, nor more than 5¾ ounces. It shall measure not less than 8 13/16 inches, nor more than 9 inches in circumference. Subject to agreement to the contrary, either Captain may demand a new ball at the start of each innings. In the event of a ball being lost or becoming unfit for play, the Umpires shall allow another ball to be taken into use. They shall inform the Batsmen whenever a ball is to be changed.

NOTES

1.—All cricket balls used in First-class matches should be approved before the start of a match by the umpires and captains. The latter may demand a new ball at the start of each innings.

2.—Except in the United Kingdom, or if local regulations provide otherwise, after 200 runs have been made off a ball in First-class matches, the captain of the fielding side may demand a new one. In First-class matches in the United Kingdom the fielding side may demand a new ball after 65 (6 ball) overs have been bowled with the old one. In other grades of cricket these regulations will not apply unless agreed before the toss for innings.

3.—Any ball substituted for one lost or becoming unfit for play should have had similar wear or use as that of the one discarded.

THE BAT

6.—The Bat shall not exceed 4¼ inches in the widest part. It shall not be more than 38 inches in length.

THE PITCH

7.—The Pitch is deemed to be the area of ground between the bowling creases, 5 feet in width on either side of the line joining the centre of the wickets. Before the toss for innings, the executive of the ground shall be responsible for the selection and preparation of the Pitch; thereafter the Umpires shall control its use and maintenance. The Pitch shall not be changed during a match unless it becomes unfit for play, and then only with the consent of both Captains.

THE WICKETS

8.—The Wickets shall be pitched opposite and parallel to each other at a distance of 22 yards from stump to stump. Each Wicket shall be 9 inches in width and consist of three stumps with two bails upon the top. The stumps shall be of equal and of sufficient size to prevent the ball from passing through, with their tops 28 inches above the ground. The bails shall be each 4 3/8 inches in length, and, when in position on the top of the stumps, shall not project more than ½ inch above them.

NOTES

1.—Except for the bail grooves the tops of the stumps shall be dome-shaped.

2.—In a high wind the captains may agree, with the approval of the umpires, to dispense with the use of bails (*see* Law 31, Note 3).

THE BOWLING AND POPPING CREASES

9.—The Bowling crease shall be in line with the stumps; 8 feet 8 inches in length; the stumps in the centre; with a Return crease at each end at right angles behind the wicket. The Popping crease shall be marked 4 feet in front of and parallel with the Bowling crease. Both the Return and Popping creases shall be deemed unlimited in length.

NOTE

1.—The distance of the Popping Crease from the wicket is measured from a line running through the centre of the stumps to the inside edge of the crease.

(C) – THE CARE AND MAINTENANCE OF THE PITCH

ROLLING, MOWING AND WATERING

10.—Unless permitted by special regulations, the Pitch shall not be rolled during a match except before the start of each innings and of each day's play, when, if the Captain of the batting side so elect, it may be swept and rolled for not more than 7 minutes. The Pitch shall not be mown during a match unless special regulations so provide. Under no circumstances shall the Pitch be watered during a match.

NOTES

1.—"Special Regulations," within the framework of the Laws, referred to in this and subsequent Laws, are those authorised by M.C.C. in respect of County cricket, or by Overseas Governing Bodies in respect of cricket in the countries concerned. Such Regulations do not apply to matches played by touring teams unless included in these Notes and Interpretations of the Official Laws, or unless agreed to by both parties before the visiting team arrives.

2.—The umpires are responsible that any rolling permitted by this Law and carried out at the request of the captain of the batting side, is in accordance with the regulations laid down and that it is completed so as to allow play to start at the stipulated time. The normal rolling before the start of each day's play shall take place not earlier than half an hour before the start of play, but the captain of the batting side may delay such rolling until 10 minutes before the start of play should he so desire.

3.—The time allowed for rolling shall be taken out of the normal playing time if a captain declare an innings closed either, (a) before play starts on any day so late that the other captain is prevented from exercising his option in regard to rolling under this Law, or (b) during the luncheon interval later than 15 minutes after the start of such interval.

4.—In Australia, South Africa, the West Indies and New Zealand, if at any time a rain affected pitch is damaged by play thereon, it shall be swept and rolled for a period of not more than ten consecutive minutes at any time between the close of play on the day on which it was damaged and the next resumption of play, provided that:—

(i) The umpires shall instruct the groundsman to sweep and roll the pitch only after they have agreed that damage caused to it as a result of play after rain has fallen warrants such rolling additional to that provided for in Law 10.

(ii) Such rolling shall in all cases be done under the personal supervision of both umpires and shall take place at such time and with such roller as the groundsman shall consider best calculated to repair the damage to the pitch.

(iii) Not more than one such additional rolling shall be permitted as a result of rain on any particular day.

(iv) The rolling provided for in Law 10 to take place before the start of play shall not be permitted on any day on which the rolling herein provided for takes place within two hours of the time appointed for commencement of play on that day.

5.—The pitch shall be mown under the supervision of the umpires before play begins on alternate days after the start of a match, but should the pitch not be so mown on any day on account of play not taking place, it shall be mown on the first day on which the match is resumed and thereafter on alternate days. (For the purpose of this rule a rest day counts as a day.)

COVERING THE PITCH

11.—The Pitch shall not be completely covered during a match unless special regulations so provide; covers used to protect the bowlers' run up shall not extend to a greater distance than 3½ feet in front of the Popping creases.

NOTE

1.—It is usual under this Law to protect the bowlers' run up, before and during a match both at night and, when necessary, during the day. The covers should be removed early each morning, if fine.

MAINTENANCE OF THE PITCH

12.—The Batsman may beat the Pitch with his bat, and Players may secure their footholds by the use of sawdust, provided Law 46 be not thereby contravened. In wet weather the Umpires shall see that the holes made by the Bowlers and Batsmen are cleaned out and dried whenever necessary to facilitate play.

(D)—THE CONDUCT OF THE GAME

INNINGS

13.—Each side has two innings, taken alternately, except in the case provided for in Law 14. The choice of innings shall be decided by tossing on the field of play.

NOTES

1.—The captains should toss for innings not later than 15 minutes before the time agreed upon for play to start. The winner of the toss may not alter his decision to bat or field once it has been notified to the opposing captain.

2.—This Law also governs a One-day match in which play continues after the completion of the first innings of both sides. (*See also* Law 22.)

FOLLOWING INNINGS

14.—The side which bats first and leads by 150 runs in a match of three days or more, by 100 runs in a two-day match, or by 75 runs in a one-day match, shall have the option of requiring the other side to follow their innings.

DECLARATIONS

15.—The captain of the batting side may declare an innings closed at any time during a match irrespective of its duration.

16.—When the start of play is delayed by weather, Law 14 shall apply in accordance with the number of days' play remaining from the actual start of the match.

START AND CLOSE OF PLAY AND INTERVALS

17.—The Umpires shall allow such intervals as have been agreed upon for meals, 10 minutes between each innings and not more than 2 minutes for each fresh batsman to come in. At the start of each innings and of each day's play and at the end of any interval the Umpire at the Bowler's end shall call "Play," when the side refusing to play shall lose the match. After "Play" has been called no trial ball shall be allowed to any player, and when one of the Batsmen is out the use of the bat shall not be allowed to any player until the next Batsman shall come in.

NOTES

1.—The umpires shall not award a match under this Law unless (i) "Play" has been called in such a manner that both sides can clearly understand that play is to start, (ii) an appeal has been made, and (iii) they are satisfied that a side will not, or cannot, continue play.

2.—It is an essential duty of the captains to ensure that the "in-going" batsman passes the "out-going" one before the latter leaves the field of play. This is all the more important in view of the responsibility resting on the umpires for deciding whether or not the delay of the individual amounts to a refusal of the batting side to continue play.

3.—The interval for luncheon should not exceed 45 minutes unless otherwise agreed (but *see* Law 10, Note 3). In the event of the last wicket falling within 2 minutes of the time arranged for luncheon or tea, the game shall be resumed at the usual hour, no allowance being made for the 10 minutes between the innings.

4.—Bowling practice *on the pitch* is forbidden at any time during the game.

18.—The Umpires shall call "Time," and at the same time remove the bails from both wickets, on the cessation of play before any arranged interval, at the end of each day's play, and at the conclusion of the match. An "Over" shall always be started if "Time" has not been reached, and shall be completed unless a batsman is "Out" or "Retires" within 2 minutes of the completion of any period of play, but the "Over" in progress at the close of play on the final day of a match shall be completed at the request of either Captain even if a wicket fall after "Time" has been reached. If, during the completion of this last over of the match, the players leave the field owing to weather or bad light, there shall be no resumption of play, and the match shall be at an end.

SCORING

19.—The score shall be reckoned by runs. A run is scored:—

1st.—So often as the Batsmen after a hit, or at any time while the ball is in play, shall have crossed and made good their ground from end to end; but if either Batsman run a short run, the Umpire shall call and signal "One short" and that run shall not be scored. The Striker being caught, no run shall be scored; a Batsman being run out, that run which was being attempted shall not be scored.

2nd.—For penalties under Laws 21, 27, 29, 44, and boundary allowances under Law 20.

NOTES

1.—If while the ball is in play, the batsmen have crossed in running, neither returns to the wicket he has left except in the case of a boundary hit, or under Laws 30, Note 1, and 46, Note 4 (vii). This rule applies even should a short run have been called, or should no run be reckoned as in the case of a catch.

2.—A run is "short" if either, or both, batsmen fail to make good their ground in turning for a further run. Although such a "short" run shortens the succeeding one, the latter, if completed, counts. Similarly a batsman taking stance in front of his popping crease may run from that point without penalty.

3 (1).—One run only is deducted if both batsmen are short in one and the same run.

(2).—Only if three or more runs are attempted can more than one run be "short" and then subject to (1) above, all runs so called shall be disallowed.

4.—An umpire signals "short" runs when the ball becomes "Dead" by bending his arm upwards to touch the shoulder with the tips of his fingers. If there has been more than one "short" run, the umpires must instruct the scorers as to the number of runs disallowed. (*See* Note 1 to Law 4.)

BOUNDARIES

20.—Before the toss for innings the Umpires shall agree with both sides on the Boundaries for play, and on the allowances to be made for them. An Umpire shall call or signal "Boundary" whenever, in his opinion, a ball in play hits, crosses or is carried over the Boundary. The runs completed at the instant the ball reaches the Boundary shall count only should they exceed the allowance, but if the "Boundary" result from an overthrow or from the wilful act of a fieldsman, any runs already made and the allowance shall be added to the score.

NOTES

1.—If flags or posts are used to mark a boundary, the real or imaginary line joining such points shall be regarded as the boundary, which should be marked by a white line if possible.

2.—In deciding on the allowances to be made for boundaries the umpires will be guided by the prevailing custom of the ground.

3.—It is a "Boundary" if the ball touches any boundary line or if a fieldsman with the ball in hand grounds any part of his person on or over that line. A fieldsman, however, standing within the playing area may lean against or touch a boundary fence in fielding a ball (*see also* Law 35, Note 5).

4.—An obstacle, or person, within the playing area is not regarded as a boundary unless so arranged by the umpires. The umpire is not a boundary, but sight screens within the playing area shall be so regarded.

5.—The customary allowance for a boundary is 4 runs, but it is usual to allow 6 runs for all hits pitching over and clear of the boundary line or fence (even though the ball has been previously touched by a fieldsman). It is not usual to allow 6 runs when a ball hits a sight screen full pitch, if the latter is on or inside the boundary.

6.—In the case of a boundary resulting from either an over-throw or the wilful act of a fieldsman, the run in progress counts provided that the batsmen have crossed at the instant of the throw or act.

7.—The umpire signals "Boundary" by waving an arm from side to side, or a boundary "6" by raising both arms above the head.

LOST BALL

21.—If a ball in play cannot be found or recovered any Fieldsman may call "Lost Ball," when 6 runs shall be added to the score; but if more than 6 have been run before "Lost Ball" be called, as many runs as have been run shall be scored.

THE RESULT

22.—A match is won by the side which shall have scored a total of runs in excess of that scored by the opposing side in its two completed innings, one-day matches, unless thus played out, shall be decided by the first innings. A match may also be determined by being given up as lost by one of the sides, or in the case governed by Law 17. A match not determined in any of these ways shall count as a "Draw."

NOTES

1.—It is the responsibility of the captains to satisfy themselves on the correctness of the scores on the conclusion of play.

2.—Neither side can be compelled to continue after a match is finished; a one-day match shall not be regarded as finished on the result of the first innings if the umpires consider there is a prospect of carrying the game to a further issue in the time remaining.

3.—The result of a finished match is stated as a win by runs, except in the case of a win by the side batting last, when it is by the number of wickets still then to fall. In a one-day match which is not played out on the second innings, this rule applies to the position at the time when a result on the first innings was reached.

4.—A "Draw" is regarded as a "Tie" when the scores are equal at the conclusion of play but only if the match has been played out. If the scores of the completed first innings of a one-day match are equal, it is a "Tie," but only if the match has not been played out to a further conclusion.

THE OVER

23.—The ball shall be bowled from each wicket alternately in Overs of either 8 or 6 balls according to the agreed conditions of play. When the agreed number have been bowled and it has become clear to the Umpire at the Bowler's wicket that both sides have ceased to regard the ball as in play, the Umpire shall call "Over" in a distinct manner before leaving the wicket. Neither a "No Ball" nor a "Wide Ball" shall be reckoned as one of the "Over."

NOTE

1.—In default of any agreement to the contrary, in the United Kingdom the "over" shall be 6 balls.

24.—A Bowler shall finish an "Over" in progress unless he be incapacitated or be suspended for unfair play. He shall be allowed to change ends as often as desired, provided only that he shall not bowl two "Overs" consecutively in one innings. A Bowler may require the Batsman at the wicket from which he is bowling to stand on whichever side of it he may direct.

DEAD BALL

25.—The ball shall be held to be "dead"—on being in the opinion of the Umpire finally settled in the hands of the Wicket-keeper or of the Bowler; or on reaching or pitching over the boundary; or, whether played or not, on lodging in the dress of either a Batsman or Umpire; or on the call of "Over" or "Time" by the Umpire; or on a Batsman being out from any cause; or on any penalty being awarded under Laws 21 or 44. The Umpire shall call "Dead Ball" should he decide to intervene under Law 46 in a case of unfair play or in the event of a serious injury to a player; or should he require to suspend play prior to the Striker receiving a delivery. The ball shall cease to be "Dead" on the Bowler starting his run or bowling action.

NOTES

1.—Whether the ball is "finally settled" is a question of fact for the umpire alone to decide.

2.—An umpire is justified in suspending play prior to the striker receiving a delivery in any of the following circumstances:—

 (i) If satisfied that, for an *adequate* reason, the striker is not ready to receive the ball, and makes no attempt to play it.

 (ii) If the bowler drops the ball accidentally before delivery, or if the ball does not leave his hand for any reason.

 (iii) If one or both bails fall from the striker's wicket before he receives the delivery.

In such cases the ball is regarded as "Dead" from the time it last came into play.

3.—A ball does not become "Dead" when it strikes an umpire (unless it lodges in his dress), when the wicket is broken or struck down (unless a batsman is out thereby), or when an unsuccessful appeal is made.

4.—For the purpose of this and other Laws, the term "dress" includes the equipment and clothing of players and umpires as normally worn.

NO BALL

26.—For a delivery to be fair the ball must be bowled, not thrown or jerked: if either Umpire be not entirely satisfied of the absolute fairness of a delivery in this respect, he shall call and signal "No Ball" instantly upon delivery. The Umpire at the Bowler's wicket shall call and signal "No Ball" if he is not satisfied that at the instant of delivery the Bowler has at least some part of one foot behind the Bowling crease and within the Return crease, and not touching or grounded over either crease.

NOTES

1.—Subject to the provisions of the Law being complied with a bowler in not debarred from delivering the ball with both feet behind the bowling crease.

2.—The striker is entitled to know whether the bowler intends to bowl over or round the wicket, overarm or underarm, right or left handed. An umpire may regard any failure to notify a change in the mode of delivery as "unfair," if so, he should call "No ball."

3.—It is a "No Ball" if the bowler before delivering a ball throws it at the striker's wicket even in an attempt to run him out (*see* Law 46, Note 4 (vii).)

4.—If a bowler break the near wicket with any part of his person during the delivery, such act in itself does not constitute a "No Ball."

5.—The umpire signals "No Ball" by extending one arm horizontally.

6.—An umpire should revoke the call "No Ball" if the ball does not leave the bowler's hand for any reason.

27.—The ball does not become "Dead" on the call of "No Ball." The Striker may hit a "No Ball" and whatever runs result shall be added to his score, but runs made otherwise from a "No Ball" shall be scored "No Balls," and if no runs be made one run shall be so scored. The Striker shall be out from a "No Ball" if he break Law 37, and either Batsman may be run out, or given out if he break Laws 36 or 40.

NOTES

1.—The penalty for a "No Ball" is only scored if no runs result otherwise.

2.—Law 46, Note 4 (vii), covers attempts to run before the ball is delivered, but should the non-striker unfairly leave his ground too soon, the fielding side may run out the batsman at the bowler's end by any recognised method. If the bowler throws at the near wicket, the umpire does not call "No Ball," though any runs resulting are so scored. The throw does not count in the "Over."

WIDE BALL

28.—If the Bowler shall bowl the ball so high over or so wide of the wicket that in the opinion of the Umpire it passes out of reach of the Striker, and would not have been within his reach when taking guard in the normal position, the Umpire shall call and signal "Wide Ball" as soon as it shall have passed the Striker.

NOTES

1.—If a ball which the umpire considers to have been delivered comes to rest in front of the striker "Wide" should not be called, and no runs should be added to the score unless they result from the striker hitting the ball which he has a right to do without interference by the fielding side.

2.—The umpire signals "Wide" by extending both arms horizontally.

3.—An umpire should revoke the call if the striker hits a ball which has been called "Wide."

29.—The ball does not become "Dead" on the call of "Wide Ball." All runs that are run from a "Wide Ball" shall be scored "Wide Balls," or if no runs be made one run shall be so scored. The Striker may be out from a "Wide Ball" if he break Laws 38 or 42, and either Batsman may be run out, or given out if he break Laws 36 or 40.

BYE AND LEG BYE

30.—If the ball, not having been called "Wide" or "No Ball," pass the Striker without touching his bat or person, and any runs be obtained, the Umpire shall call or signal "Bye"; but if the ball touch any part of the Striker's dress or person except his hand holding the bat, and any run be obtained, the Umpire shall call or signal "Leg Bye"; such runs to be scored "Byes" and "Leg Byes" respectively.

NOTES

1.—Leg byes which result from the unintentional deflection of the ball by any part of the striker's person, other than the hand holding the bat, whether he has played at the ball or not, are fair. If the umpire is not entirely satisfied that the act was unintentional he shall call "Dead Ball" as soon as he sees that the fielding side have no chance of dismissing either batsman as an immediate result of such deflection.

2.—The umpire signals "Bye" by raising an open hand above the head, and "Leg Bye" by touching a raised knee with the hand.

THE WICKET IS DOWN

31.—The wicket shall be held to be "Down" if either the ball or the Striker's bat or person completely removes either bail from the top of the stumps, or, if both bails be off, strikes a stump out of the ground. Any player may use his hand or arm to put the wicket down or, even should the bails be previously off, may pull up a stump provided always that the ball is held in the hand or hands so used.

NOTES

1.—A wicket is not "down" merely on account of the disturbance of a bail, but it is "down" if a bail in falling from the wicket lodges between two of the stumps.

2.—If one bail is off, it is sufficient for the purpose of this Law to dislodge the remaining one in any of the ways stated or to strike any of the three stumps out of the ground.

3.—If, owing to the strength of the wind, the captains have agreed to dispense with the use of bails (*see* Law 8, Note 2), the decision as to when a wicket is "down" is one for the umpires to decide on the facts before them. In such circumstances the wicket would be held to be "down" even though a stump has not been struck out of the ground.

4.—If the wicket is broken while the ball is in play, it is not the umpire's duty to remake the wicket until the ball has become "dead." A fieldsman, however, may remake the wicket in such circumstances.

5.—For the purpose of this and other Laws, the term "person" includes a player's dress as defined in Law 25, Note 4.

OUT OF HIS GROUND

32.—A Batsman shall be held to be "Out of his ground" unless some part of his bat in hand or of his person be grounded behind the line of the Popping Crease.

BATSMAN RETIRING

33.—A Batsman may retire at any time, but may not resume his innings without the consent of the opposing Captain, and then only on the fall of a wicket.

NOTE

1.—When a batsman has retired owing to illness, injury, or some other unavoidable cause, his innings is recorded as "Retired, Not Out," but otherwise as a completed innings to be recorded as "Retired, Out."

BOWLED

34.—The Striker is out "Bowled"—If the wicket be bowled down, even if the ball first touch his bat or person.

NOTE

1.—The striker, after playing the ball, is out "Bowled" if he then kicks or hits it on to his wicket before the completion of his stroke

2.—The striker is out "Bowled" under this Law when the ball is deflected on to his wicket off his person, even though a decision against him might be justified under Law 39 L.B.W.

CAUGHT

35.—The Striker is out "Caught"—If the ball, from a stroke of the bat or of the hand holding the bat, but not the wrist, be held by a Fieldsman before it touch the ground, although it be hugged to the body of the catcher, or be accidentally lodged in his dress. The Fieldsman must have both his feet entirely within the playing area at the instant the catch is completed.

NOTES

1.—Provided the ball does not touch the ground, the hand holding it may do so in effecting a catch.

2.—The umpire is justified in disregarding the fact that the ball has touched the ground, or has been carried over the boundary provided that a catch has in fact been completed prior to such occurrence.

3.—The fact that a ball has touched the striker's person before or after touching his bat does not invalidate a catch.

4.—The striker may be "Caught" even if the fieldsman has not touched the ball with his hands, including the case of a ball lodging in the wicket-keeper's pads.

5.—A fieldsman standing within the playing area may lean against the boundary to catch a ball, and this may be done even if the ball has passed over the boundary.

6.—If the striker lawfully plays the ball a second time he may be out under this Law, but only if the ball has not touched the ground since being first struck.

7.—The striker may be caught off any obstruction within the playing area provided it has not previously been decided on as a boundary.

HANDLED THE BALL

36.—Either Batsman is out "Handled the ball"—If he touch it while in play with his hands, unless it be done at the request of the opposite side.

NOTES

1.—A hand holding the bat is regarded as part of it for the purposes of Laws 36, 37 and 39.

2. The correct entry in the score book when a batsman is given out under this Law is "Handled the Ball," and the bowler does not get credit for the wicket.

HIT THE BALL TWICE

37.—The Striker is out "Hit the ball twice"—If the ball be struck or be stopped by any part of his person, and he wilfully strike it again, except for the sole purpose of guarding his wicket, which he may do with his bat or any part of his person, other than his hands. No runs except those which result from an overthrow shall be scored from a ball lawfully struck twice.

NOTES

1.—It is for the umpire to decide whether the ball has been so struck a second time legitimately or not. The umpire may regard the fact that a run is attempted as evidence of the batsmen's intention to take advantage of the second stroke, but it is not conclusive.

2.—A batsman may not attempt to hit the ball twice, if in so doing he baulk the wicket-keeper or any fieldsman attempting to make a catch.

3.—This Law is infringed if the striker, after playing the ball and without any request from the opposite side, uses his bat to return the ball to a fieldsman.

4.—The correct entry in the score book when the striker is given out under this Law is "Hit the ball twice," and the bowler does not get credit for the wicket.

HIT WICKET

38.—The Striker is out "Hit wicket"—If in playing at the ball he hit down his wicket with his bat or any part of his person.

NOTES

1.—The striker is "Out" under this Law if:—

(i) In making a second stroke to keep the ball out of his wicket he hits it down.

(ii) While playing at the ball, but not otherwise, his wicket is broken by his cap or hat falling, or by part of his bat.

2.—A batsman is not out for breaking the wicket with his bat or person while in the act of running.

L.B.W.

39.—The Striker is out "Leg before wicket"—If with any part of his person **except his hand,** which is in a straight line between wicket and wicket, **even though the point of impact** be above the level of the bails, he intercept a ball which has not first touched his bat or hand, and which, in the opinion of the Umpire, shall have, or would have, pitched on a straight line from the Bowler's wicket to the Striker's wicket, or shall have pitched on the off-side of the Striker's wicket, provided always that the ball would have hit the wicket.

NOTES

1.—The word "hand" used in this Law should be interpreted as the hand holding the bat.

2.—A batsman is only "Out" under this Law if *all* the four following questions are answered in the affirmative.

  (i) Would the ball have hit the wicket?

  (ii) Did the ball pitch on a straight line between wicket and wicket (and this case includes a ball intercepted full pitch by the striker), or did it pitch on the off-side of the striker's wicket?

  (iii) Was it part of the striker's person other than the hand which first intercepted the ball?

  (iv) Was that part of the striker's person in a straight line between wicket and wicket at the moment of impact, irrespective of the height of the point of impact?

OBSTRUCTING THE FIELD

40.—Either Batsman is out "Obstructing the field"—If he wilfully obstruct the opposite side; should such wilful obstruction by either Batsman prevent a ball from being caught it is the Striker who is out.

NOTES

1.—The umpire must decide whether the obstruction was "wilful" or not. The involuntary interception by a batsman while running of a throw in is not in itself an offence.

2.—The correct entry in the score book when a batsman is given out under this Law is "Obstructing the field," and the bowler does not get credit for the wicket.

RUN OUT

41.—Either Batsman is out "Run out"—If in running or at any time, while the ball is in play, he be out of his ground, and his wicket be put down by the opposite side. If the batsmen have crossed each other, he that runs for the wicket which is put down is out; if they have not crossed, he that has left the wicket which is put down is out. But unless he attempt to run, the Striker shall not be given "Run out" in the circumstances stated in Law 42, even should "No Ball" have been called.

NOTE

1.—If the ball is played on to the opposite wicket, neither batsman is liable to be "Run out" unless the ball has been touched by a fieldsman before the wicket is put down.

STUMPED

42.—The Striker is out "Stumped"—If in receiving a ball, not being a "No Ball," delivered by the Bowler, he be out of his ground otherwise than in attempting a run, and the wicket be put down by the Wicket-keeper without the intervention of another fieldsman. Only when the ball has touched the bat or person of the Striker may the Wicket-keeper take it in front of the wicket for this purpose.

NOTE

1.—The striker may be "Stumped" if the wicket is broken by a ball rebounding from the wicket-keeper's person.

THE WICKET-KEEPER

43.—The Wicket-keeper shall remain wholly behind the wicket until a ball delivered by the Bowler touches the bat or person of the Striker, or passes the wicket, or until the Striker attempts a run. Should the Wicket-keeper contravene this Law, the Striker shall not be out except under Laws 36, 37, 40 and 41 and then only subject to Law 46.

NOTE

1.—This Law is provided to secure to the striker his right to play the ball and to guard his wicket without interference from the wicket-keeper. The striker may not be penalised if in the legitimate defence of his wicket he interferes with the wicket-keeper except as provided for in Law 37, Note 2.

THE FIELDSMAN

44.—The Fieldsman may stop the ball with any part of his person, but if he wilfully stop it otherwise five runs shall be added to the run or runs already made; if no run has been made five runs shall be scored. The penalty shall be added to the score of the Striker if the ball has been struck, but otherwise to the score of Byes, Leg Byes, No Balls or Wides as the case may be.

NOTES

1.—A fieldsman must not use his cap, etc., for the purpose of fielding a ball.

2.—The five runs are a penalty and the batsmen do not change ends.

(E)—DUTIES OF THE UMPIRES

45.—Before the toss for innings, the Umpires shall acquaint themselves with any special regulations, and shall agree with both Captains on any other conditions affecting the conduct of the match; shall satisfy themselves that the wickets are properly pitched; and shall agree between themselves on the watch or clock to be followed during play.

NOTES

1.—Apart from "Special Regulations" (*see* Law 10, Note 1), other conditions of play within the framework of the Laws are frequently necessary, *e.g.* Hours of play, Intervals, etc.

2.—The captains are entitled to know which clock or watch will be followed during play.

46.—Before and during a match the Umpires shall ensure that the conduct of the game and the implements used are strictly in accordance with the Laws; they are the sole judges of fair and unfair play, and the final judges of the fitness of the ground, the weather and the light for play in the event of the decision being left to them; all disputes shall be determined by them, and if they disagree the actual state of things shall continue. The Umpires shall change ends after each side has had one innings.

NOTES

1.—An umpire should stand where he can best see any act upon which his decision may be required. Subject to this over-riding consideration the umpire at the bowler's end should stand where he does not interfere with either the bowler's run up or the striker's view. If the other umpire wishes to stand on the off instead of the leg side of the pitch, he should obtain the permission of the captain of the fielding side and inform the batsman.

2.—The umpires must not allow the attitude of the players or spectators to influence their decisions under the Laws.

3.—A code of signals for umpires is laid down in the Notes to the relevant Laws; but an umpire must call as well as signal, if necessary, to inform the players and scorers.

4.—FAIR AND UNFAIR PLAY.

(i) The umpires are entitled to intervene without appeal in the case of unfair play, but should not otherwise interfere with the progress of the game, except as required to do so by the Laws.

(ii) In the event of a player failing to comply with the instructions of an umpire or criticising his decisions, the umpires should in the first place request the captains to take action, and if this proves ineffective, report the incident forthwith to the executives of the teams taking part in the match.

(iii) It is illegal for a player to lift the seam of the ball in order to obtain a better hold. In such a case the umpire will if necessary change the ball for one which has had similar wear, and will warn the captain that the practice is unfair. The use of resin, wax, etc., by bowlers is also unfair, but a bowler may dry the ball when wet on a towel or with sawdust.

(iv) An umpire is justified in intervening under this Law should any player of the fielding side incommode the striker by any noise or motion while he is receiving a ball.

(v) The umpires are justified in preventing players from causing damage to the pitch which may assist the bowlers.

(vi) The persistent bowling of fast short-pitched balls at the batsman is unfair if, in the opinion of the umpire at the bowler's end, it constitutes a systematic attempt at intimidation. In such event he must adopt the following procedure:—

    (a) When he decides that such bowling is becoming persistent he forthwith "cautions" the bowler.

    (b) If this "caution" is ineffective, he informs the captain of the fielding side and the other umpire of what has occurred.

    (c) Should the above prove ineffective, the umpire at the bowler's end must:—

        (i) At the first repetition call "Dead Ball," when the over is regarded as completed.

        (ii) Request the captain of the fielding side to take the bowler off forthwith.

        (iii) Report the occurrence to the captain of the batting side as soon as an interval of play takes place.

    A bowler who has been "taken off" as above may not bowl again during the same innings.

(vii) Any attempt by the batsmen to *steal a run* during the bowler's run up is unfair. Unless the bowler throws the ball at either wicket (*see* Laws 26, Note 3, and 27, Note 2), the umpire should call "Dead Ball" as soon as the batsmen cross in any such attempt to run, after which they return to their original wickets.

(viii) No player shall leave the field for the purpose of having a rub down or shower while play is actually in progress.

5.—GROUND, WEATHER AND LIGHT.

(i) Unless agreement to the contrary is made before the start of a match, the captains (during actual play the batsmen at the wickets may deputise for their captain) may elect to decide in regard to the fitness of the ground, weather or light for play; otherwise or in the event of disagreement, the Umpires are required to decide.

(ii) Play should only be suspended when the conditions are so bad that it is unreasonable or dangerous for it to continue. The ground is unfit for play when water stands on the surface or when it is so wet or slippery as to deprive the batsmen or bowlers of a reasonable foothold, or the fieldsmen of the power of free movement. Play should *not* be suspended merely because the grass is wet and the ball slippery.

(iii) After any suspension of play, the captains, or, if the decision has been left to them, the Umpires, unaccompanied by any of the players, will without further instruction carry out an inspection immediately the conditions improve, and will continue to inspect at intervals. Immediately the responsible parties decide that play is possible, they must call upon the players to resume the game.

APPEALS

47.—The Umpires shall not order a Batsman out unless appealed to by the other side which shall be done prior to the delivery of the next ball, and before "Time" is called under Law 18. The Umpire at the Bowler's wicket shall answer appeals before the other Umpire in all cases except those arising out of Laws 38 or 42 and out of Law 41 for run out at the Striker's wicket. In any case in which an Umpire is unable to give a decision, he shall appeal to the other Umpire whose decision shall be final.

NOTES

1.—An appeal, "How's that?" covers all ways of being out (within the jurisdiction of the umpire appealed to), unless a specific way of getting out is stated by the person asking. When either umpire has given a batsman "Not out" the other umpire may answer any appeal within his jurisdiction, provided it is made in time.

2.—The umpires signal "Out" by raising the index finger above the head. If the batsman is not out, the umpire calls "Not out."

3.—An umpire may alter his decision provided that such alteration is made promptly.

4.—Nothing in this Law prevents an umpire before giving a decision from consulting the other umpire on a point of fact which the latter may have been in a better position to observe. An umpire should not appeal to the other umpire in cases on which he could give a decision, merely because he is unwilling to give that decision. If after consultation he is still in any doubt, the principle laid down in Law 46 applies and the decision will be in favour of the batsman.

5.—The umpires should intervene if satisfied that a batsman, not having been given out, has left his wicket under a misapprehension.

6.—Under Law 25 the ball is "Dead" on "Over" being called; this does not invalidate an appeal made prior to the first ball of the following "Over," provided the bails have not been removed by both umpires after "Time" has been called.

NOTES FOR SCORERS AND UMPIRES

1. (a) Law 4 explains the status of the scorers in relation to the umpires.

(b) During the progress of the game, if two scorers have been appointed, they should frequently check the total to ensure that the score sheets agree.

(c) The following method of entering "No Balls" and "Wides" (Laws 27 and 29) in the score sheet is recommended: —

(i) If no run is scored from the bat off a "No Ball," the latter should be entered as an "Extra," and a dot placed in the bowling analysis with a circle round it to show that the ball does not count in the over.

(ii) If runs are scored from the bat off a "No Ball," they should be credited to the striker, and entered in the bowling analysis with a circle round the figure. Such runs count against the bowler in his analysis even though the ball does not count in the over.

(iii) All runs scored from "Wide Balls" are entered as "Extras," and inserted in the bowler's analysis with a cross to indicate that the ball does not count in the over.

2. The following code of signalling between the umpires and the scorers has been approved:—

> Boundaries—by waving the hand from side to side.
> A boundary six—by raising both arms above the head.
> Byes—by raising the open hand above the head.
> Leg Byes—by touching a raised knee with the hand.
> Wides—by extending both arms horizontally.
> No Balls—by extending one arm horizontally.
> The decision "Out"—by raising the index finger above the head.
> "One Short"—by bending the arm upwards and by touching the top of the nearest shoulder with the tips of the fingers of one hand.

3. If the above instructions are properly carried out, cases of disagreement as regards the scores and the results of matches should not occur.

It is, however, important that the captains should satisfy themselves of the correctness of the scores on the conclusion of play, as errors cannot subsequently be corrected.

It should be noted that, in general, by accepting the result notified by the scorers, the captain of the losing side has thereby acquiesced in the "playing out or giving up" of the match as stated in Law 22.

SPECIAL INSTRUCTIONS FOR UMPIRES IN FIRST-CLASS MATCHES, 1957

1. THE CONDUCT OF THE GAME

(a) The conduct of the game will be governed by the official Laws of Cricket 1947 Code—Second Edition 1952.

(b) The attention of Umpires is particularly drawn to the provisions of Law 45. Should there be more than one clock on the ground, the Umpires must notify the Ground Authority (who in turn may inform the Press) which clock they propose to follow.

(c) The attention of Umpires is also particularly drawn to the provisions of Law 46.

In addition to reporting as laid down in Note 4 (vi) to Law 46, they will make a report to the Secretary of M.C.C. and to the Secretary of the Club to which the offending player belongs in the event of their having to intervene in any case of unfair play.

Umpires are reminded that any waste of time—a bowler wasting time, the fielders crossing over slowly between the overs and for left-handed batsmen; captains being unduly deliberate in field placing and not starting such field placing until a new batsman has reached the wicket; incoming batsmen taking too long to reach the wicket—constitutes unfair play, and after consultation together and, where possible, after warning the captain concerned, they shall report such occurrences as above.

In the event of a bowler taking unnecessarily long to bowl an over, the Umpire at the bowler's end, after consultation with the other Umpire, shall take the following immediate action:—

(i) Caution the bowler and inform the captain of the fielding side that he has done so.

(ii) Should this caution prove ineffective:—

(a) Request the captain of the fielding side to take the bowler off at the end of the over in progress.

(b) Report the occurrence to the captain of the batting side as soon as an interval of play takes place.

(c) Send a written report of the occurrence to the Secretary of M.C.C. and to the Secretary of the Club to which the offending player belongs.

A bowler who has been "taken off" as above may not bowl again during the same innings.

((c) (i) and (ii) will apply to Inter-County Matches only.)

2. APPEALS AGAINST THE LIGHT

(a) Law 46 will apply in respect of bad light in the following sense: Appeals against the light, in any form whatever, may not be made by the players of either side. If, however, either Umpire considers that the light is so bad that to continue play would be dangerous to the striker, he will consult his fellow Umpire, and, if both are agreed, the game will be suspended. Should conditions improve later, the Umpires shall, without waiting for instructions, call upon the players to resume the game. Umpires will note that it is the light as it affects the striker which is the deciding factor, therefore it may sometimes be necessary for both of them to observe the conditions from each end of the pitch. The Umpires must make their decision and act upon it without conferring with the Captain of the fielding side or any of the players. (b) The above shall not operate in any first-class match with the West Indies, except the Test Matches, when the following Rule will apply:—

"The Umpires on appeal shall decide the fitness of the light for play. Only one appeal per batting side per session shall be allowed. If an interruption takes place on appeal in any period of play and play restarts before the next adjournment, the fitness of the light for play shall be in the Umpires' hands until play commences after such adjournment."

After play has been suspended, should conditions improve, the Umpires shall, without waiting for instructions, call upon the players to resume the game.

3. NEW BALL RULE. LAW 5, NOTE 2

Law 5, Note 2, as applicable to first-class matches in the United Kingdom, will be in abeyance and the captain of the fielding side shall have the choice of taking the new ball after 200 runs have been scored off, or 75 overs bowled with the old one. (After the 65th over, the scorers shall display a small white flag or signal, which shall be replaced by a yellow signal after the 70th over. At the commencement of the 75th over both signals shall be exposed, and left exposed until the new ball is taken. Alternatively some counties may prefer to display numbers indicating the overs bowled, commencing from the end of the 65th over up to and including the 75th over.)

4. DECLARATIONS

(a) If under Law 16 a match becomes a one-day one no side shall declare its first innings closed until it has batted for at least sixty minutes.

(b) Law 15 provides an option to the captain of a batting side only, and it is not the intention that any declaration should become the subject of an agreement between the captains. If the umpires have grounds for thinking that any such agreement has taken place, they shall report accordingly to the M.C.C., and if the M.C.C. Committee is satisfied that agreement is proved, any points scored shall not be counted in the Championship table.

5. LAW 30—NOTE 1

In 1957 the following experimental Note 1 to Law 30 shall apply:—

"The Umpire shall regard the deliberate deflection of the ball by any part of the striker's person, except the hand holding the bat, as unfair, and as soon as he is satisfied that the fielding side have no chance of dismissing either batsman as an immediate result of such action, he shall without delay, call 'Dead Ball.' In deciding whether such deflection is deliberate the criterion shall be whether or not the batsman has attempted to play the ball with his bat."

6. MOWING THE PITCH.   See Law 10, Note 5.

7. ROLLING THE PITCH.   See Law 10, Note 2.

8. DRYING THE PITCH

The attention of Umpires is drawn to the regulations on pp. 23 and 24 of the 1947 code—2nd Edition, 1952 of the Official Laws of Cricket.

9. COVERING THE PITCH

Law 11 shall apply.

The whole pitch may be covered only:—

(i) At any time before the start of a match and until the first ball is bowled, provided no match is actually in progress on the ground.

(ii) In the case of a week-end match, provided it is the rule of the ground, when, if necessary, the pitch may be wholly covered from the cessation of play on Saturday until the restart of play. Such covering, however, is permissible only if the pitch has already been wholly covered as provided in (i) above.

(iii) If both Captains and Umpires are in agreement that, during the course of a match, the pitch has become so saturated that further rain will considerably delay the restart. In this event the Umpires shall decide when the covers will be removed. (The Umpires may, if they consider it necessary, issue instructions to the groundsman overnight regarding the removal of the covers early next day.)

10. RENOVATION OF BOWLERS' FOOTHOLDS

In 1957, the following experimental addition to Law 12 will be used:—

"After consultation with the Ground Authority, the Umpires shall see that wherever possible and whenever it is considered necessary, action is taken at the end of a day's play to do whatever is practicable to improve the bowlers' footholds." (This instruction shall not apply to Test Matches.)

11. STANDARDISATION OF BOUNDARIES—LAW 20

The boundaries should be limited to a maximum of 75 yards in any direction from the centre of the pitch in use. (Where circumstances make it undesirable to keep within the maximum, a certain latitude will be allowed and in such cases the Ground Authority will inform the Umpires and Captains before the start of the match that the maximum has been exceeded.)

(To apply in Inter-County Matches only.)

12. LIMITATION OF THE NUMBER OF ON-SIDE FIELDERS—EXPERIMENTAL NOTE 3 TO LAW 44

The number of on-side fieldsmen shall not exceed five, of whom not more than two may be behind the popping crease at the instant of the bowler's delivery.

In the event of an infringement of this Rule by the fielding side the square-leg Umpire should call "No Ball."

NOTE.—It is anticipated that the Umpire would, by permission of the fielding Captain, often elect to stand on the off-side.

(To apply to Inter-County Matches only.)

13. ATTENDANCE OF UMPIRES

Umpires shall report themselves to the management of the ground one hour before the commencement of play on the first day and at 9 a.m. on succeeding days. They must remain on the ground for half an hour after "Time" on each day, if required to by the management.

(In the event of Counties experimenting with Late Evening play up till 8.15 or 8.30 p.m., this Instruction will be relaxed. A special rule applies for Test Matches.)

REGULATIONS FOR DRYING THE PITCH AND GROUND IN FIRST-CLASS MATCHES IN THE UNITED KINGDOM

N.B.—*These regulations are primarily designed for First-class Cricket, and their application in whole or in part in other grades of Cricket in the United Kingdom is at the discretion of the ground, etc., authorities.*

1. Except as provided below, the existing regulations in regard to the rolling of the wicket and the fitness of the ground for play shall apply. (*See* Laws 10, 12 and 46.)

2. (i) To enable play to proceed with the least possible delay after rain, the groundsman shall adopt every practical means to protect or rid the surface of the ground, *other than the pitch*, of water or dampness at any time except while play is in progress.

(ii) Prior to tossing for choice of innings, the artificial drying of the pitch shall be at the discretion of the groundsman, but thereafter, and throughout the match, the drying process shall be carried out only on the instructions and under the supervision of the umpires, who shall be empowered to have the pitch dried, without reference to the captains, at any time they are of opinion that it is unfit for play.

(iii) In wet weather, the umpires shall see that the foot-holes made by the bowlers and batsmen are cleaned, dried and filled up with sawdust at any time during the match, although the game is not actually in progress.

The groundsman, without instructions from the umpires, may also clean out in this way foot-holes, provided they are not on any part of the pitch, more than 3 ft. 6 ins. in front of the Popping creases.

The *drying* of foot-holes on the pitch itself shall be supervised by the umpires, but, in the interval between close of play on any day and its further resumption, the groundsman may *protect* against further rain, marks made by the bowlers, even though they be more than 3 ft. 6 ins. in front of the Popping creases, provided they are not between wicket and wicket, with loose sawdust, which, however, shall be removed prior to the resumption of play.

(iv) The umpires shall ascertain from the groundsman before the commencement of a match what equipment is available for drying the pitch artificially.

Before drying the pitch the umpires shall have regard to the condition of the outfield and the prospects of its fitness for play. The drier shall be removed when they are satisfied that the pitch is fit for play, or as they may direct.

Any roller may be used, if the umpires think desirable but only (except as laid down in paragraph (2) (v)) for the purpose of drying the pitch and making it fit for play, and not otherwise. This would allow umpires to roll the pitch after drying it, say with a light roller, for a minute or two, should they consider it desirable.

(v) When the artificial drying of the pitch, under the supervision of the umpires, coincides with any interval during the match, after the toss for choice of innings, the umpires, and not the captain of the batting side, shall select the roller to be used.

(vi) The fact that the umpires may have dried the pitch artificially does not take the decision as regards the fitness of the pitch and ground for play out of the hands of the captains, even though the umpires may have selected the roller to be used for the drying process. Law 46, Note 5 (i) is applicable in such cases.

IMPERIAL CRICKET CONFERENCE

CONSTITUTION

The governing bodies of cricket in countries within the British Commonwealth, having been duly elected, shall be entitled to send not more than two representatives to a meeting of the Conference. The M.C.C., on its own initiative, may, or on the request of any two members, summon a meeting of the Imperial Cricket Conference.

RULES FOR TEST MATCHES

Test Matches are matches played between sides duly selected by Governing Bodies of cricket who are members of the Imperial Cricket Conference.

A cricketer can be qualified to play in a Test Match either by birth or residence.

(a) QUALIFICATION BY BIRTH.—A cricketer unless debarred by the Imperial Cricket Conference is always eligible to play for the country of his birth.

(b) QUALIFICATION BY RESIDENCE.—A cricketer unless debarred by the Imperial Cricket Conference shall be entitled to play for any country in which he is residing and has been residing during the four immediately preceding years provided that he has not played for the country of his birth during that period.

(c) Notwithstanding anything hereinbefore contained, any player who has once played in a Test Match for any country shall not afterwards be eligible to play in a Test Match against that country without the consent of its Governing Body.

(d) Members shall be responsible for submitting, in reasonable time for the approval of the Conference, the names of any cricketers whose qualifications are in doubt, and who are likely to be selected to play in any approaching series of Test Matches, furnishing their qualifications and stating if any player has during the four immediately preceding years played for the country of his birth. In the case of cricketers qualified by residence, they shall further state the periods of residence upon which such qualifications are founded.

RULES FOR APPOINTMENT OF TEST UMPIRES

The following rules for the selection and appointment of Test Match umpires shall be followed as far as it is practicable to do so:—

(a) The Home authority to nominate a group of umpires considered qualified to officiate in Test Matches.

(b) All umpires in this group should be considered as equally qualified for the purpose of appointment in accordance with the policy of the Home authority in this matter.

(c) While a captain is entitled to submit objections to a particular umpire being appointed for a Test Match, he may not ask for a particular umpire to be given precedence for appointment over any other umpire in the group.

(d) Previous to any Test Match the visiting captain whenever possible should be given an opportunity of judging the umpires being considered for appointment, and the names of the umpires to be appointed to officiate in a Test Match shall not be made public until the captains have had reasonable opportunity to submit objections.

(e) During each series of Test Matches a Committee should be appointed by the Home authority to adjudicate on matters arising from (c) and (d) and their decisions shall be regarded as final.

(f) The sole authority for handling Press enquiries shall be the official representative appointed by the Home authority for the purpose, and not the captains or any of the players.

FIRST-CLASS MATCH DEFINED

A match of three or more days duration between two sides of eleven players officially adjudged First-class shall be regarded as a First-class fixture.

The following matches by this definition shall not be regarded as First-class: If either team has more than 11 players. If the duration of the match is shorter than three days.

The Governing body in each country shall decide the status of teams.

Any question arising under these rules shall be submitted to the Imperial Cricket Conference, and their decision shall be final.

DURATION OF TEST MATCHES

Beginning with the M.C.C. 1946–47 tour, the duration of Test matches between England and Australia has been standardised at 30 hours' play spread over six days in Australia and five days in England, without prejudice to the final Test which may be played to a finish in certain circumstances.

FUTURE TOURS

Visits to U.K.		*Tours Abroad*	
1958	New Zealand	1957–58	Australia to South Africa.
1959	India.	1957–58	Pakistan to West Indies.
1960	South Africa.	1958–59	M.C.C. to Australia and New Zealand.
1961	Australia.		
1962	Pakistan.	1959–60	M.C.C. to West Indies.
1963	West Indies.	1960–61	West Indies to Australia.
1964	Australia.	1961–62	M.C.C. to India, Pakistan and Ceylon.
		1962–63	M.C.C. to Australia and New Zealand.
		1963–64	South Africa to Australia.
		1964–65	M.C.C. to South Africa.

BOARD OF CONTROL OF "TEST" MATCHES AT HOME
(Formed at the request of the Counties by the M.C.C., 1898)

To consist of the President of M.C.C. or his nominee, and not more than five of its Club Committee, one representative from each of the first ten Counties of the previous season's First-class Championship table, and one representative from each County on whose ground a Test Match is to be played subject to such County not already being represented, whenever matters affecting such Test Matches are to be discussed.

The Board shall be responsible for the organisation and administration of all Test and Trial matches in England.

N.B.1.—The Agenda for the Board of Control meetings will be issued to all Counties and the Minor Counties' Cricket Association.

N.B.2.—Counties not represented on the Board of Control may send one representative to the meetings of the Board. In addition, the Minor Counties' Cricket Association may appoint one of their members to attend meetings of the Board. Such representatives shall not be entitled to vote on any resolution, but, provided not less than three days' previous notice has been given to the Secretary of the M.C.C. of the wish of a County Committee, their representative shall be permitted to take part in the discussion upon specifically stated Agenda items

Rules for 1957

(TEST MATCHES WITH WEST INDIES)

FINANCIAL CONDITIONS

The Manager of the visiting team will receive on behalf of his Governing Body from each ground authority, 50 per cent of the net revenue, after deduction of Entertainment Tax, received in respect of admission of spectators at the outer gate.

The charge for admission at the outer gate in Test Matches at all grounds shall be 5/- per day.

No collections shall be allowed on the ground during any Test Match.

PLAYING CONDITIONS

Except as specially provided for, the current Official Laws of Cricket shall apply in all Test Matches.

The attention of umpires is called to the Special Instructions issued for 1955, which shall apply in all Test Matches, except so far as they are not varied by the following playing conditions.

UMPIRES

The Chairman of the Selection Committee and the Captain of the visiting team shall be notified confidentially in advance of Test Matches of the names of the umpires appointed to stand. Any objection lodged against either umpire must be received within three days of the notice being issued, and will be dealt with by the Umpires' Committee whose decision shall be final.

No member of either team will make any statement to the Press in connection with the appointment of umpires.

DURATION OF MATCHES AND HOURS OF PLAY

The Test Matches shall be of five days' duration. In all Test Matches play shall begin at 11.30 a.m. on each day. Stumps shall be drawn at 6.30 each day. Luncheon Interval 1.30–2.10. A Tea Interval shall be allowed as provided for in Match Regulation No. 3.

Drinks shall not be taken on the field to the same team more than once in each period of play.

EXCHANGING TEAMS

The two captains before tossing shall give each other a list of the eleven selected to play together with the emergency fieldsman. Afterwards no alteration shall be made in either eleven or emergency fieldsman without the consent of the opposing captain.

PLAYERS LEAVING THE FIELD

No player on the fielding side shall leave the field for the purpose of having a rub down or shower whilst a Test Match is actually in progress.

BOUNDARIES

The boundary lines shall be in accordance with the custom of the ground for Test Matches except when agreement to the contrary has been reached between the parties concerned not less that 14 days before the start of any match.

SCREENS

The matter of providing screens behind the bowler's arm at each end of the ground shall be left to the discretion of the ground authority on which a Test Match is played, the usual custom on such ground to prevail.

COVERING THE PITCH

The pitch shall be completely protected against rain if necessary and as far as practicable twenty-four hours before the time advertised for the start of a Test Match or until play begins. After the first ball has been bowled the covers shall not protect more than 3 ft. 6 in. in front of the popping crease at each end.

MOWING AND ROLLING THE PITCH

The grass on the pitch shall be mown as laid down in Law 10, Note 5 of the Official Laws of Cricket.

Except as provided for in the Regulations for drying the pitch, Law 10 of the Official Laws of Cricket shall govern the rolling of the pitch.

FITNESS OF PITCH AND GROUND

Except as provided for in the Official Laws of Cricket the two captains shall decide as to the fitness of the pitch and ground for play, unless they disagree or prefer to leave the decision to the umpires. If the decision is left to the umpires the captains shall forthwith advise them accordingly.

In wet weather the pitch may be dried artificially in accordance with the Regulations in the Official Laws of Cricket.

TRAVELLING EXPENSES

A player or umpire will be paid the cost of a first-class railway fare from the ground on which he was last engaged or from his home, if he has not been immediately engaged prior to the Test Match. He will similarly be paid the cost of a first-class railway fare to the ground on which he is next engaged or to his home if he is not so engaged.

Selectors may claim an allowance of 6d. per mile for the use of their private car in the course of their duties.

If a player or umpire travels by car he may claim the equivalent railway fare as stipulated above, but may not claim garage charges in addition.

HOTEL AND INCIDENTAL EXPENSES

The ground authority, when so requested, will arrange for hotel accommodation, and will pay the hotel account excluding expenses for guests, drinks, tobacco and other personal items.

Players who do not use the accommodation so provided will not be entitled to claim hotel or lodging charges. Umpires and Selectors may however do so.

All professionals and umpires will be allowed 10/- per day for the actual duration of any match for incidental expenses. This allowance does not apply to amateurs who will be entitled to claim an allowance of 10/- a meal for meals taken away from the hotel and during journeys to and from the match.

A match allowance of £7 10s. 0d. for a five-day Test Match (the allowance to be £6 and £4 10s. 0d. respectively for a four-day and three-day Test Match) to cover travelling expenses not otherwise provided for, fares to and from the ground and hotel, tips, upkeep of equipment and clothing and the cost of laundry.

REMUNERATION OF PLAYERS, ETC.

					Test Match
Professionals playing	..	..	..	..	£100 per match
12th man (on duty through Test)	..	..	..	£60 per match
12th man (1st and 2nd days)	..	..	..	£30
12th man (3rd, 4th and 5th days)	..	..	..	£30
Reserves	..	..	..	..	£25 per match
Umpires	..	..	..	..	£65 per match
Scorer for match of over 3 days' duration	..	..	£25 per match

An emergency fieldsman will be paid a fee to be agreed on by the Ground authority and the Chairman of the Selection Committee.

INSURANCE OF PLAYERS

The Secretary M.C.C. will take out an insurance policy to cover the risk of accidents to professionals (including 12th man and reserves) playing in Test or Trial Matches.

DISTRIBUTION OF PROFITS

All monies taken at Stands and Enclosures at all Test Matches together with gate money in respect thereof, less the opponents' 50 per cent share for each person paying admission at the outer gate, less tax and expenses, shall be distributed as follows: 40 per cent between each first-class county on whose ground the Test Match is played; 50 per cent between the remaining first-class counties (Oxford and Cambridge Universities together to count as one first-class county); 10 per cent between each Minor County with Combined Services to receive one-half of the amount given to a Minor County club. M.C.C. to rank as a first-class county for the purpose of the foregoing.

SELECTION COMMITTEE

The Selection Committee shall consist of a Chairman and three members with the power to call into consultation at any meeting any cricketer, past or present. The Committee shall select a captain who shall be an *ex-officio* member of the Committee. The Committee, with the captain, shall select the team. In the event of no majority agreement, the captain's wish in regard to the selection of a player shall prevail.

ADVISORY COUNTY CRICKET COMMITTEE

In 1904, with the approval of the Counties, the M.C.C. formed an Advisory County Cricket Committee to consider cases arising out of County and other Cricket.

RULES

1.—The Advisory County Cricket Committee shall consist of a representative of each First-Class County, appointed by his Committee, and three members representing and appointed by the Minor Counties' Cricket Association, and at least one member of the M.C.C.

2.—The Chairman of this Committee shall be the President of the M.C.C. or some other member of the Committee of the M.C.C. nominated by him or in default of such nomination, by the Committee of the M.C.C.

3.—All resolutions passed by this Committee shall be submitted to the M.C.C. Committee for confirmation.

4.—A meeting may be convened either by five or more First-Class Counties or by the Minor Counties' Cricket Association and two, or more, First-Class Counties or by the M.C.C., and notice shall be sent to all parties interested at least 21 days before the day of meeting.

5.—When submitting any item for inclusion in the Agenda, it shall be incumbent on the proposer to forward a memorandum on the subject.

6.—The notice shall contain an agenda of the meeting. Notice of an amendment to a resolution on the agenda must be given at least 14 days before the day of meeting.

THE COUNTY CRICKET COMPETITIONS AND CLASSIFICATION

1. Cricketing Counties may be classified either as First-class or Minor; included in the latter category are the second XI's of First-class Counties who have joined the Minor Counties' Cricket Association.

2. First-class Counties are as defined in Appendix III to the Rules of the Imperial Cricket Conference. Minor Counties are as defined in the Rules of the Minor Counties' Cricket Association.

3. There shall be no limit to the number of First-class Counties. The M.C.C. Committee may bring new Counties into the list, may remove existing Counties from it, or may do both.

4. The First-class County competition shall be competed for by the First-class Counties. To qualify a county shall be required to play as many matches as may be decided from time to time by the Advisory County Cricket Committee.

5. After the close of each cricket season, the Committee of the M.C.C. shall, if necessary, decide the First-class County Championship.

6. The Rules for the Minor County competition are laid down in the Minor Counties' Cricket Association's handbook.

REGULATIONS FOR A.C.C.C. FIXTURES SUB-COMMITTEE

1. A Sub-Committee shall be appointed annually to arrange provisionally the County fixtures for the year next but one.

2. The Sub-Committee shall consist of four members:—One County Secretary, who will be eligible for re-election; One member of the M.C.C., not a County Secretary, who shall be nominated annually by the M.C.C. The Secretaries of two Counties who shall be elected annually by ballot at the meeting referred to in paragraph 4, who shall serve for one year and shall not be eligible for re-election until all other Counties have (by their Secretaries) served on the Sub-Committee.

3. The Secretary of each County shall submit before 1st January for the consideration of the Sub-Committee a draft programme of matches to be played by his County calling attention to particular dates, "weeks," etc. Provisional programmes shall then be arranged by the Sub-Committee and circulated to the Secretaries by the middle of February.

4. A meeting of County Secretaries shall be held annually at The Oval during the first week in March, for the purpose of revising the provisional lists referred to in paragraph 3, and to elect the fixtures Sub-Committee for the following year.

5. The Sub-Committee shall have power at the meeting of Secretaries referred to in paragraph 4 (March) to revise any list and that no alterations in the provisional lists shall be made before that meeting except with the approval of the Fixtures Sub-Committee and no alterations after that meeting except by mutual consent.

6. Every County shall play every other County each season; twelve of the opponents to be played twice and the remainder once.

Each County shall have eight opponents who will remain "Permanent" subject to alteration as is provided for below, and who will be played twice in each season. Not more than four of such permanent opponents may be selected by mutual agreement, and the remainder shall be allotted by the Fixtures Sub-Committee.

Of the remaining Counties, four shall be played once each season (List A) for two consecutive seasons and the remaining four (List B) shall be played twice; at the end of the two-year cycle, Lists A and B shall be reversed.

In the case of the four Counties played once each season two matches shall be "Home" and two "Away"; these shall be reversed in the following season.

The division of the eight non-permanent opponents into List A and B shall be made by the Fixtures Sub-Committee on the principle of equalising as closely as possible the distribution of matches between the two lists.

Counties may, by mutual agreement, make changes in their permanent fixtures to take effect at the end of each four-year cycle; any changes must be made in time to conform to paragraph 3 of these Regulations.

7. That the Annual Meeting of Secretaries at Lord's be held in December.

8. No alteration in these rules shall be adopted for recommendation to the A.C.C.C. unless notice of such proposed alteration is given to the Chairman of the Fixtures Sub-Committee in time to be included by him in the notice convening the Annual Meeting of the County Secretaries at The Oval. (March.)

MATCH REGULATIONS
FIRST-CLASS MATCHES, 1957.

REGULATION 1. HOURS OF PLAY.

The "Standard" hours of play in Inter-County Matches are as under:—

1st and 2nd days   11.30 a.m. to 6.30 p.m.
3rd day   11.30 a.m. to 6 p.m. with an extra 30 minutes on this day on the demand of either Captain for the purpose of securing a result in the match or on the first innings.

Alterations in the above "Standard" hours shall only be permitted in the following circumstances and within the limits stated:—

(*a*) The total hours (including all intervals, stoppages and extra time) shall not exceed 21 hours, or be less than 20 hours in any match, and shall not exceed 7 hours (including extra time) on the third day, or 8 hours (excluding extra time) on any other day.

(*b*) On no day shall play commence earlier than 11 a.m. or end later than 7.30 p.m. (including extra time) on either of the first two days, or 6.30 p.m (including extra time) on the third day.

(*c*) Subject to (*a*) and (*b*) above, the executive of the Home County may modify the "Standard" hours of play in order to meet the requirements of evening play on the first and second days, and, if essential, to facilitate travelling on the third day in those cases only in which a team will be unable to reach its next destination before midnight, in which case a match must not be scheduled to end earlier than 4.30 p.m. (including extra time) on the third day.

The "Standard" hours of play shall be adhered to as closely as possible, and any departure from them, mutually agreed between the two Counties will be notified to all concerned including the Press, before the commencement of the season and thereafter no alternative will be permitted, except to meet exceptional travelling difficulties of either team or the umpires. In the latter case the County requiring departure from the "Standard" hours, shall notify its opponents within 7 days of the match, and the Home County will be responsible for giving notice of such alterations to the Umpires and the Press.

(*d*) If, in the opinion of both Captains, 30 minutes extra time at the end of the first and/or second day's play would bring about a definite result on that day the umpires shall order the same. If, however, the Captains disagree the decision shall be left to the umpires. Any time so claimed will not preclude either side demanding an extra 30 minutes on the third day for the purpose of securing a result in the match or on the first innings, provided the maximum of 21 hours allowed by sub-para. (*a*) is not exceeded.

(*e*) Should counties agree to experiment with late evening play up to 8.15 or 8.30 p.m. the foregoing regulations except paragraph (*a*) shall be relaxed.

REGULATION 2. INTERVALS.

The first bell shall be rung 15 minutes before the time appointed for the start of play on each day. The second bell shall be rung 10 minutes later, when the umpires shall go to the wickets. Luncheon shall take place at 1.30 p.m., or at such hour as may be mutually agreed in advance of the match, unless an alteration owing to the weather or the state of the ground has been agreed upon by the Captains or ordered by the umpires. The first bell shall be rung at 1.55 p.m. and the ground cleared. The second bell shall be rung 10 minutes later, when the umpires shall go to the wickets. Play shall commence at 2.10 p.m. unless the above-mentioned alteration has been made, when corresponding intervals shall be observed. Five minutes before the termination of an interval, between innings or for tea, the bell shall be rung, when the ground shall be cleared and the umpires shall go to the wickets.

REGULATION 3. TEA INTERVAL.

1. Subject to the provisions in sub-paras. (2) and (3)—
   (a) A tea interval of 20 minutes shall be taken to START not earlier than 3.45 p.m. or later than 4.45 p.m.
   (b) Tea shall be taken at 4.15 p.m. except in the following circumstances—
       (i) If nine wickets are then down, play shall continue for a period not exceeding 30 minutes after which tea will be taken.
       (ii) If at or after 3.45 p.m. an innings closes or play is suspended—this includes a suspension which may have begun before 3.45 p.m.—the tea interval of 20 minutes (to include the interval between innings) shall then be taken.
       (iii) If before 3.45 p.m. an innings closes or the game is resumed after a stoppage, tea shall be taken at 4.15 p.m. or after 50 minutes' play, whichever is the later.

2. There shall be no tea interval on any day—
   (i) If both Captains agree to forgo it.
   (ii) If the close of play on any day (excluding any extra time permitted by Regulation 1) has been fixed at or before 5.30 p.m.
   (iii) If there has been no play at all between 2.45 p.m. and 3.45 p.m.

3. The above timings shall apply in all cases, except when the close of play on any day has been fixed for 7 p.m. or later (excluding any extra time permitted by Regulation 1). In such cases all the timings in this Regulation shall be 15 minutes later.

REGULATION 4. REPORT BY UMPIRES, ETC.

The umpires and the executive of the Home Ground shall report any breach of Regulations 1 to 3 inclusive to the Secretary of M.C.C. Before submitting a report the umpires will inform the Secretary of the Home County of the points on which they are reporting.

REGULATION 5. SCORING OF POINTS IN THE COUNTY CHAMPIONSHIP

The scheme for scoring in the County Championship is as follows:—
(a) In cases (b) to (f) below, if the side leading on the first innings has scored the faster in the first innings (to be judged by runs per over), it shall score a further 2 points.
(b) Should a match be finished the winning side to score 12 points.
(c) Should a match be finished and the scores be equal (a "Tie") each side to score 6 points.
(d) Should the scores be equal in a drawn match the side batting in the fourth innings to score 6 points in all (whether or not it has first innings lead) and the opponents to score no points, except they will retain such first innings points as they may already have gained.
(e) Should a match be finished, the side which leads on the first innings, if it loses the match, to score 2 points. If the scores on the first innings are equal, the side which loses the match to score 1 point.
(f) Should a match not be finished the side which leads on the first innings to score 2 points (subject to (c) above).
(g) Should a match not be finished and the scores of the first innings be equal, each side to score 1 point (subject to (c) above).
(h) Even should there be no play for any reason, or no result obtained on the first innings, every match shall be included in the table of results as a "match played"; in these cases neither side to score points.
(i) If there is no play in the first two-thirds (measured by playing hours) of a match, and it is not carried to a further conclusion than that of the first innings, the side which leads on the first innings shall score 8 points.
(j) The side which has the highest aggregate on points gained at the end of the season shall be the Champion County.

RULES OF COUNTY CRICKET
FIRST- AND SECOND-CLASS COUNTY COMPETITIONS

(As amended by the Advisory County Cricket Committee on March 9, 1954,
and to become operative as from April 1, 1954)

GENERAL ARRANGEMENT	RULES
General Rules	1 to 5.
Qualifications	6 to 7.
Special Registration	8.
Engagement of Players	9.
Appeals and Decisions	10 to 11.

DEFINITIONS

(*a*) The term "Cricket Dominion" unless otherwise stated shall include only those countries, other than the United Kingdom, who are members or associate members of the Imperial Cricket Conference.

(*b*) An "Overseas First-Class Cricketer" is a cricketer not having been born in the United Kingdom who has played at any time in a first-class competition, organised by the Governing Body of a Cricket Dominion.

(*c*) The term "Residence" as used in these Rules shall mean a bona fide home, and not a mere acquirement or hiring of a tenement during a cricket season only.

(*d*) For the purpose of County Cricket, geographical County Boundaries are those applying at the time of a player's birth, or at the time of his qualification by residence or by any other means. The County of London is not to be regarded as a separate County.

GENERAL RULES

RULE 1. ALTERATIONS TO RULES

No alteration in, or addition to, the Rules of County Cricket shall be made except at a Meeting of the Advisory County Cricket Committee duly convened for the purpose; and no such alteration or addition shall be made except by a vote of two-thirds of the representatives present at such Meeting.

RULE 2. REGISTRATION OF PLAYERS

Before the beginning of each cricket season, each County Cricket Club shall send to the M.C.C. and to every other County Cricket Club, a list of the cricketers, with their respective qualifications, who are expected to play for the County during that season; and if, in the course of the season, a County wishes to play a cricketer not included in that list, his name and qualification shall be circulated in a similar manner forthwith.

Cricketers who have been specially registered for any County will continue to be shown as qualified under Rule 8, so long as they are on the playing strength of that County.

RULE 3. CRICKETER REFUSING RENEWAL OF ENGAGEMENT

A Cricketer who has refused the offer of a renewal of his engagement with a County by whom he has been previously employed, provided this offer did not involve pecuniary loss to the player, shall not be re-registered under any form of qualification.

RULE 4. CRICKETER NOT TO PLAY FOR MORE THAN ONE COUNTY IN A SEASON

A cricketer may not play for more than one County in either competition within the Calendar Year. The penalty for an infringement of this Rule shall be disqualification for two years. A Cricket Dominion shall for the purpose of this Rule be regarded as a County in respect of an Overseas First-class cricketer.

RULE 5. NOTICE TO COUNTIES

Correspondence on all matters which concerns a County Cricket Club will be addressed to the Secretary, and any notice sent to the Secretary of a County Cricket Club shall be regarded as notice to that County.

QUALIFICATIONS

RULE 6. BIRTH AND RESIDENCE

Subject to the provisions of Rules 4 and 9, a cricketer shall be qualified to play:—

(a) For the County of his birth.

(b) If born in the United Kingdom—for the County in which he is residing and has resided continually for not less than 12 months. The residence of a Master at a School shall count as a residence for this purpose.

(c) For the County in which his boarding School is situated:—

(i) Whilst at School.

(ii) For the 12 months thereafter.

If a cricketer has so played and provided that, at any time during the period referred to in (ii) above, he elects to continue to play for that County, his qualification under this Rule shall remain unbroken until he plays for another County.

(d) If born out of the United Kingdom, but not having played previously as an Overseas First-class cricketer—for the County in which he has resided for the previous 24 consecutive months and in which he is still residing.

(e) If born out of the United Kingdom, and having played as an Overseas First-class cricketer—for the County in which he has resided for the previous 36 consecutive months, and in which he is still residing. During this residential qualifying period he shall not engage in a cricket contract outside the County for which he is qualifying.

NOTE.—The County for which an Overseas cricketer is qualifying by residence shall notify M.C.C. of the date on which this player starts his residential qualification.

(f) If he has no qualifications for any County and is resident or was born in a County in which no First or Second-class cricket is played—for the County, the capital of which is nearest to the place of his birth or residence.

(g) For the County for which he has been Specially Registered.

(h) For the County for which his father has played regularly for at least three years.

RULE 7. CONTINUANCE AND CESSATION

(a) A cricketer qualified by residence for one County who then plays for the County of his birth loses the residential qualification for the first named. If he wishes to play again for the County for which he originally played under a residential qualification, he must be re-qualified or be Specially Registered.

(b) A cricketer may play for the County for which he has played and for which he is qualified by residence or by Special Registration, or if he has so played under Rule 6, para. (c) (i) and (ii) above—always provided he has elected to continue to play for that County within one year of the date of his leaving School—for the rest of his cricketing career.

(c) A cricketer, in the course of qualifying by residence for a County, breaks his qualification for that County if he plays for another, or if he engages in a regular cricket contract outside the County for which he is qualifying.

(d) A cricketer acquiring residential qualification for a County does not interrupt that qualifying period by undertaking Government Service or occasional winter work for business reasons outside the County in which his bona fide residence is situated.

SPECIAL REGISTRATION

RULE 8. PROCEDURE

(a) Notwithstanding the provisions of Rule 6, a Registration Committee, appointed by M.C.C. for the purpose, may specially register cricketers of the categories stated in this Rule, always provided that:—

(i) The County applying for a Special Registration has not, during any cricket season, more than 10 players, of whom not more than 8 may be Professionals, shown as qualified under this Rule on their list of players circulated in accordance with Rule 2. (This number shall include any cricketers who, since their Special Registration, may have become qualified by residence under Rule 6.)

(ii) Not more than two applications for Special Registration for any County shall be approved in any Calendar Year, beginning on 1st January.

(iii) The County applying for a Special Registration shall offer a Professional cricketer an engagement for a minimum of 3 years, exclusive of any period of National Service.

(In the case of an amateur cricketer, the County shall undertake to make reasonable use of the player's services, as far as these may be available for at least 2 seasons.)

(b) A cricketer shall be eligible for Special Registration if he is not required by the County (or Counties) for which he is qualified, or in which he is residing.

(c) The following shall not be eligible for Special Registration:—

(i) A cricketer born outside the United Kingdom, unless he has been resident in the United Kingdom for 10 consecutive years.

(ii) A cricketer who has been specially registered for another County within the previous 5 years, unless the Registration has been cancelled. (Vide paragraph (f).)

(d) Applications for Special Registration shall be made to M.C.C. on the form provided for the purpose and shall contain a full statement of the case with the written consent of the County (or Counties), for which the cricketer is qualified, or in which he is residing. Each such County shall, in addition, certify that:—

(i) The formalities laid down in Rule 9 have been completely complied with by the applying County.

(ii) They have no evidence that valuable consideration of any nature has passed in order to bring about the engagement or move.

The County applying for the Special Registration shall further guarantee that reasonable use is to be made of the services of the cricketer, and it shall be the duty of the Registration Committee to withhold approval to any application unless absolutely satisfied that the engagement or move is in the interests of the cricketer.

In considering an application for Special Registration, it shall be open either to the County (or Counties) asked to release the cricketer or to the Registration Committee:—

(i) to withhold consent, or

(ii) to agree to qualification under Rule 6 (b), or

(iii) to defer agreement, or

(iv) to agree to the cricketer's immediate Special Registration for the County applying.

(e) Subject to Rule 4, a cricketer shall be eligible to play for a County as soon as, but not until the Special Registration has been approved, and on receipt of the approval of a registration by the Registration Committee, the County concerned shall immediately carry out the provisions of Rule 2.

(f) M.C.C. shall be empowered to cancel a Special Registration, in any case in which a County has failed to carry out its obligations to make reasonable use of a player, or has been prevented from doing so, but only if such a course is shown to be in the interests of the cricketer.

(g) *Infringement of Rule 8 (above)*.—Should the attention of the M.C.C. be called to any unreasonable advantage being taken of the provisions of Rule 8, they shall be empowered to cancel the Special Registration of any cricketer, granted under that Rule. The penalty in Rule 4 shall apply in such cases.

ENGAGEMENT OF PLAYERS

RULE 9. PROCEDURE

(a) Cricketer NOT previously engaged by, or having played for, any County

A County wishing to offer a trial to, to engage or play a cricketer who has not previously been engaged by, Specially Registered for, or played for another County, must obtain the written consent of the County (or Counties) for which the cricketer is qualified, before starting negotiations with him. Such consent shall not be unreasonably withheld.

(b) Cricketers engaged by, or having played for, a County within the previous 24 months

Should a cricketer who has been engaged by, Specially Registered for, or played for a County within the previous 24 months, wish to qualify by residence for another County, he must obtain a written consent, which must not be antedated from the former County. His residential qualification shall not begin to run until he has obtained this consent, which shall not be unreasonably withheld.

A County wishing to engage or play a cricketer who is engaged by, Specially Registered for, or has played for another County within the previous 24 months, must give written notice to the latter County before starting negotiations with the cricketer.

(c) Overseas First-class Cricketers

The provisions of Paras. (a) and (b) above, apply to an Overseas First-class cricketer, except that in such cases written consent must be obtained from the State, Province, Colony, or other Cricket Authority concerned, before such a cricketer's residential qualification begins to run.

(d) Cricketer wishing to play for the County of his birth

A cricketer who wishes to play for the County of his birth (see Rule 6) must give written notice to any other County for which he has played within the previous 24 months.

(e) Infringement of Rule 9 (above)

In the event of the infringement of Rule 9, M.C.C. shall have special authority to fix the date when the cricketer shall become qualified by residence, or even bar him from qualifying.

APPEALS AND DECISIONS

RULE 10. DOUBTFUL CASES OF QUALIFICATION

If required to do so, it is obligatory on the County for which a cricketer wishes to play to prove his qualifications to the satisfaction of M.C.C.

RULE 11. APPEALS

Any question arising under these Rules shall be left to the decision of M.C.C. which shall be final.

MINOR COUNTIES' CRICKET ASSOCIATION RULES

1. The Association shall be called "The Minor Counties' Cricket Association."

2. All Counties not in the first-class (as classified by the M.C.C.) and the second elevens of first-class Counties shall be eligible to join the Association upon payment of an annual subscription of three guineas or such other sum as the Association shall from time to time determine, and shall be entitled to compete in the Second Division of the County Championship (the Minor Counties' Competition).

3. The Officers of the Association shall consist of President, Chairman, Hon. Secretary, Hon. Treasurer and the representatives of the Minor Counties on the Advisory County Cricket Committee, all of whom shall be *ex-officio* members of the Committee.

4. The Committee shall consist of the *ex-officio* members and one representative each from ten Counties, together with any duly elected Life Member.

5. The officers of the Association shall be elected and the Counties forming the Committee chosen annually at the Annual Meeting.

6. The Association shall have power to elect Life Members to the Committee.

7. The Annual Meeting shall be held at Lord's on the same day as the Annual Meeting of County Secretaries. A Special Meeting shall be called by the Hon. Secretary at the request of four or more Counties. One month's notice of every such Meeting shall be sent to each County, and the notice shall contain the agenda of the Meeting.

8. Only one representative from each County shall be entitled to vote at General Meetings of the Association.

9. Notices of motions to be brought forward at the Annual Meeting shall be sent to the Hon. Secretary before the end of October.

10. A County desirous of entering the Competition for the first time shall give notice to the Hon. Secretary before the end of the previous August.

11. Every County shall play out and home two-day matches with at least four other Counties. In cases of emergency and in order to enable all counties to obtain the necessary number of qualifying matches, prior to the Annual Meeting in each year, the Committee may, after consultation with County Secretaries, re-arrange fixtures for this purpose.

12. A County shall give twelve months' previous notice in writing to the Hon. Secretary and to their opponents of their intention to leave the Competition, such notice to expire on the 30th day of September in any one year.

13. The County which shall have obtained the greatest average points shall (in the absence of a challenge under Rule 16) be reckoned Champion County of the Second Division.

14. If two or more Counties shall have obtained the same average points, preference shall be given to that County which shall have won the greatest number of completed matches.

15. If two or more Counties shall have obtained the same average points and also won the same number of completed matches, their priority shall be decided according to the net batting averages.

* 16. If the two top Counties shall not have played each other, the second County shall have the right to challenge the first to a three-day match. which shall decide the Championship, and shall be played on a ground chosen by the challenged County. In the event of a challenge match, the winners shall be the Champion County, but in the event of a decision on the first innings only (the match not being played as a one-day match) the points for a result on the first innings shall be added in the table of results to those already gained by the respective Counties, and their average re-calculated accordingly. If no result shall have been attained in this match, the Championship shall be decided as if there had been no challenge.

17. In every challenge match under Rule 16 the hours of play shall be those in force for matches played in the First-Class Competition. Each County shall bear its own expenses and shall receive half the gross gate-money, after deducting the fees paid to the umpires and Entertainment Tax. Gross gate-money shall be regarded as the total sum paid for admission to the Ground by spectators as distinct from admission to Stands.

18. Points in the Competition shall be reckoned as follows:—Ten points shall be scored for a win in a completed two-day match and for a win on the first innings when there is no play on the first day of a two-day match, provided the match is not played out, when the match shall be played under the Rules of Cricket for one-day matches. Should a two-day match not be completed the side leading

on the first innings shall score three points and its opponents one point. In the event of a tie on the first innings in an unfinished match each side shall be awarded two points. In matches in which no result shall have been attained each side will be awarded two points. In the event of a tie,* the ten points shall be equally divided.

    * A tied match is one in which the scores are equal at the conclusion of play, but only if the match has been played out.

    First innings qualifying points (3) gained shall be retained irrespective of the final result of a match, provided that a county shall receive not more than ten points in such match.

    In a one-day match, there having been no play on the first day, a tie is recorded if the scores of the completed first innings are equal, providing only if the match has not been played out to a further conclusion.

    19. Neutral umpires shall be provided for all matches in the Competition, and the arrangements for the selection and appointment of such umpires shall be left to the Secretary of the M.C.C.

    20. The normal hours of play in the Competition shall be from 11.30 a.m. to 7 p.m. on the first day, and from 11 a.m. to 6 p.m. on the second day except only that, by agreement between the captains and when it is necessary to leave the ground for luncheon, the luncheon interval may be extended and the additional time made up at the end of the day. The umpires shall be informed of such extension before the luncheon interval. The interval for luncheon shall not exceed 40 minutes, unless a captain shall declare an innings closed during the luncheon interval later than 15 minutes after the start of such interval, in which case the time allowed for rolling the wicket (viz. 7 minutes) shall be added to the 40 minutes interval. The time for the luncheon interval shall be left to the home captain to decide before the day's play commences. An extra half hour shall be allowed on the second day of a match, if necessary, on the demand of either side.

    21. Before and after the actual commencement of play the wicket may be protected when necessary, and shall be protected every night if possible during the continuance of a match, but the covering must not protect more than 3 ft. 6 ins. in front of the popping crease. In the case of matches played on First-Class County Grounds, the wicket shall be covered in accordance with the rules in force on that ground.

    22. The result of each match in the Competition shall be telegraphed, and the full score (with bowling analysis) shall be posted to the Hon. Secretary by the home county immediately after its conclusion. This score shall for all purposes be deemed the official score.

    23. All disputes arising out of the Laws of the Game shall be referred to the M.C.C., whose decision shall be final.

    †24. Should any matter arise not provided for in these Rules, the Committee shall have power to deal with it.

    25. Except where they are inconsistent with the foregoing, the Rules governing the matches of the First Division of the County Championship shall apply.

    26. These Rules shall not be altered except at a General Meeting of the Association.

    At their Annual Meeting at Lord's on December 7, 1954, the Minor Counties' Cricket Association revised the following rules which take effect from the 1955 season:

    *Rule 16. If the two top Counties shall not have played each other, the second County shall have the right to challenge the first to a three-day match which shall decide the Championship and shall be played on a ground chosen by the challenged County. If no result shall have been attained in this match, the Championship shall be decided as if there had been no challenge. A lead on the first innings or a tie shall not be a "result" within the meaning of this Rule.

    †Rule 24. Should any matter arise not provided for in these rules or in the case of any dispute or difference as to the interpretation or application thereof, such questions shall be referred to the Committee whose decision on all matters shall be final and conclusive.

MEETINGS IN 1957

EXPERIMENTAL LAWS APPROVED

The Advisory County Cricket Committee met at Lord's on March 26 and 27 to consider the report of the M.C.C. Special Committee on the future welfare of first-class cricket. (*This report was given in full in Wisden 1957, pages 73–78.*)

Limitation of On-side Fielders

They accepted the proposal to limit the number of on-side fielders to five, of whom not more than two may be behind the popping crease at the instant of the bowler's delivery. The only variation they made from the original recommendation was the substitution of the words "popping crease" for "behind the wicket."

Standard Boundaries

The Committee agreed to adopt proposals for reducing time wasting and giving increased powers to umpires. They also approved the standardisation of boundaries with a maximum of 75 yards from the centre of the pitch.

Bonus Points

The Advisory Committee turned down the proposal to limit overs in first innings to 85. Instead they accepted a suggestion from Middlesex. This reduced the first innings points in Championship matches from four to two and provided for an additional two points for the side which led on first innings and scored at a faster rate per over. By this system a side could score a maximum of 14 points, 12 for a win plus two "bonus" points.

L.B.W. Law Unchanged

It was agreed that no change should be made to the existing lbw law, rejecting a proposal that there should be a return to the law obtaining before 1937. (This decision was reiterated later in the year. See paragraph farther on.)

Overseas Players

A proposal that no county should have more than two first-class players from overseas was accepted and a proviso added that those players with existing contracts should be allowed to continue after the starting date of the new rule in 1962.

TEST SELECTORS

The Board of Control for Test Matches at Home met at Lord's on March 27 and appointed the following Selection Committee for 1957: G. O. Allen (Cambridge University and Middlesex (chairman), W. Wooller (Glamorgan), C. Washbrook (Lancashire), H. E. Dollery (Warwickshire). Dollery replaced L. E. G. Ames (Kent) who stood down in order to concentrate on his new duties as team manager of Kent.

KNOCK-OUT COMPETITION SHELVED

The Advisory County Committee decided to abandon the proposed Knock-Out competition at their annual meeting on November 12 at Lord's.

Reasons given for shelving yet again a cricket cup were that no practical solution had been found for rain-ruined and other drawn matches and that difficulties abounded in fitting such a competition into the present frame-work of the County Championship. Doubts also existed as to whether a knock-out cup would be a financial success.

Experimental Laws Continued

Experiments introduced in 1957 for the County Championship were considered successful by the Advisory Committee and it was decided to continue them in 1958.

Standardisation of Boundaries to 75 yards from the middle of the pitch met with universal approval and in the opinion of the captains was a huge success.

Limitation of On-Side Fielders to five with only two behind the popping crease had not met with the same measure of approval, but the Counties decided that this experiment should continue for at least another year. It was agreed that this rule had proved severe on off-spin bowlers and that it was not the original intention to handicap them.

First Innings Points

A proposal to reorganise the points system in the County Championship, discarding the award of points for first innings, was defeated mainly because of the problem of the rain-spoiled match which prevents any chance of a definite result. It was agreed that the experiment of awarding two bonus points to the side which leads on the first innings and has scored faster than the opposition should be continued, but that in 1958 this would be decided not necessarily at the end of the innings but at the moment the question of the lead was settled. This was the only notable change.

Pre-1935 L.B.W. Law Not Wanted

Any likelihood of the old lbw law being reintroduced was ruled out by the Advisory Committee. This had one proposer but no seconder could be found.

Precedence in Championship Table

Emphasis on the importance of striving for victory and fast scoring was given impetus by the following decision: When two Counties stand equal on points in the Championship table the team with most wins to take the higher place; if the position still remains equal then the team with most bonus points to take precedence. The actual Championship could be decided this way.

Bowler's Drag

The question of the bowler's drag still remained a big problem. It was not considered likely that any solution would be forthcoming in time for M.C.C.'s tour of Australia in 1958–59. It was stated that M.C.C. admit that the Law (Number 26) as it stands is impossible for umpires to interpret. The relevant part reads: "The umpire at the bowler's wicket shall call and signal 'No-ball' if he is not satisfied that at the instant of delivery the bowler has at least some part of one foot behind the Bowling crease and within the Return crease, and not touching or grounded over either crease."

M.C.C. have conducted experiments on the position of the front foot in relation to the popping crease, but while these showed it was simple for young cricketers to atune themselves, older ones found it virtually impossible to change. Umpires too experienced difficulty in refocusing after looking at the front foot and then looking upwards at the bowler's arm.

Opinion of cricketers in England was that if the position of the back foot in the delivery stride was allowed to continue to be the guiding factor this would merely legalise drag and not solve the problem. Australia support this method. The system generally adopted in England of making offending bowlers bring down the back foot well behind the bowling crease also was not in line with the present law.

Fewer Overs per Hour

Umpires were again urged to hurry up county sides which dawdle over the matter of the number of overs sent down per hour. Returns sent to M.C.C. by scorers on this subject showed no improvement compared with 1956. The Advisory Committee empowered M.C.C. to write to any county falling below a certain rate.

EDICT ON PITCHES

Advisory Committee and the newly reconstituted Board of Control—on which all the seventeen first-class counties are now represented—agreed that it was essential that fast, true pitches be prepared for all first-class matches. The Board of Control decided to issue an edict to this effect to all ground authorities in England where Test matches are played.

Exhibition Matches

The Board of Control decided in principle, providing touring teams agreed, to hold exhibition matches on the day a Test ends provided at least three hours remained for play and reserved accommodation had been booked. This would not apply to a match ending on the fifth day. Accommodation would continue to be booked for the fourth day, and as hitherto there would be no refund of money if any days were blank through a premature finish.

(*It was estimated that in* 1957 £17,000 *was taken at Lord's, Leeds and The Oval for the fourth day but in each case the match was completed on the third day.*)

Test Match Profits

A total of £102,847 was distributed from the profits of the England–West Indies Tests. Six Test match grounds each received £7,542. Other first-class counties £3,639. Nineteen Minor Counties £526 each; Oxford and Cambridge Universities £1,819 each. Combined Services £263. In addition each first-class county received £1,500 as their share of £30,000 received from T.V. and sound radio.

County Attendances Improve

County Championship attendances, amounting to 1,197,979, showed an increase of 23,900 compared with 1956. Eight counties reported better gates; nine counties decreased.

Champion County v. The Rest Venue

The Champion County v. The Rest match at Scarborough which produced a profit of £543 for the Umpires Benevolent Fund may in future be held over until the beginning of the following season and take place at Lord's.

Protecting the Outfield

The counties agreed to follow a practice already in force in South Africa and cover any saturated parts of the outfield with blankets or coconut matting. Play would continue with these covers in use provided both captains agree. Umpires would not override the captains in this case.

TEST MATCH ARRANGEMENTS

The Board of Control announce the following provisional dates for the five Test Matches against India in 1959:—

First Test, at Trent Bridge, June 4–9.
Second Test, at Lord's, June 18–23.
Third Test, at Headingley, July 2–7.
Fourth Test, at Old Trafford, July 23–28.
Fifth Test, at The Oval, August 20–25.

MINOR COUNTIES' ASSOCIATION

The Minor Counties' Association, at their 53rd annual meeting at Lord's on December 10, re-elected Mr. W. B. Franklin as President. Mr. H. R. Neate became chairman of the Association in succession to Mr. Franklin. Mr. Frank Crompton was re-elected Hon. Secretary and Mr. S. A. Swift was appointed Hon. Treasurer in succession to Mr. Neate.

The meeting decided to press for an increase from five per cent to ten per cent of the share of receipts by M.C.C. from Television. Secretaries heard officially that Middlesex, Surrey, Kent and Derbyshire were withdrawing from the Competition in 1959. It was notified that M.C.C. had written to first-class counties pointing out that Rule 9 of the Rules of County Cricket, dealing with the approach to players only through the county concerned, applied also to Minor Counties.

A profit of £557 was made from the Minor Counties and West Indies match at Newcastle in 1957. Newcastle was also chosen as the venue for the game with New Zealand in 1958 and Stoke for the game with India on June 10, 11, 12, 1959.

COUNTY SECRETARIES' MEETING

Mr. R. Aird, Secretary of M.C.C., did not make his customary speech at the Annual Meeting of County Secretaries at Lord's on December 10. Secretaries heard a suggestion that a team from Fiji might make a short tour of England in 1959.

UMPIRES FOR 1957

Captains of the first-class counties chose the following twenty-three umpires to stand in first-class matches in 1958:—

H. G. Baldwin (Surrey), T. J. Bartley (Cheshire), J. B. Bowes (Lancashire), J. S. Buller (Worcestershire), P. Corrall (Leicestershire), W. H. Copson (Derbyshire), J. F. Crapp (Gloucestershire), D. Davies (Glamorgan), E. Davies (Glamorgan), C. S. Elliott (Derbyshire), Harry Elliott (Derbyshire), P. A. Gibb (Essex), L. H. Gray (Middlesex), John Langridge (Sussex), R. S. Lay (Northamptonshire), F. S. Lee (Somerset), N. Oldfield (Northamptonshire), W. E. Phillipson (Lancashire), E. A. Pothecary (Hampshire), W. F. Price (Middlesex), A. Skelding (Leicestershire), T. W. Spencer (Kent), D. J. Wood (Sussex).

Newcomers are J. B. Bowes and W. H. Copson. D. J. Wood came into the list before the beginning of the 1957 season when E. A. Roberts withdrew.

MINOR COUNTIES' UMPIRES FOR 1958

Representatives of the Minor Counties chose the following thirty-seven umpires to officiate in 1958:—

R. Aspinall, A. Barrett, F. Berry, A. E. Bradford, W. V. Brown, J. Buckingham, C. A. Cassie, W. D. Cory, S. Cox, L. D'Arcy, G. Downs, T. Drinkwater, C. E. Dunn, J. H. Elliss, C. Fairservice, C. I. Haines, G. E. Hart, W. J. Hucker, T. S. Jennings, P. C. Kellaway, J. H. Lichfield, Horace W. Lee, L. W. K. Martin, T. McMurray, S. H. Moore, H. W. Parks, R. O. Prouton, G. W. F. Reeves, D. S. Richards, R. E. Rushworth, W. F. Simpson, A. E. D. Smith, W. Stephens, H. C. Turner, J. Waddington, W. R. Watts, G. A. West.

CRICKET BOOKS, 1957

By John Arlott

The fact that only sixty-two titles have been submitted for review in this notice emphasises the trend of the past few years towards the publication of fewer cricket books than was the case in the "boom" period shortly after the war. Indeed, only twenty-three of these are of appreciable bulk; but they include several of considerable merit, entitled to a place in any selective library of the game.

Happily in the year of a West Indian touring team's visit, there appeared the first major works on the history of the game in the Caribbean. *West Indian Cricket*, by Christopher Nicole (Phoenix House: 30s.), is an ambitious record of the growth of inter-colonial cricket related to touring teams in and from the West Indies. Authoritative, impressively free from bias, and with useful appendices of records and a good index, it contains much information not previously available, and must take its place among the major histories of the game. Its appearance emphasises, once more, the sad lack of a history of cricket in Australia.

England v. The West Indies, by Canynge Caple (Littlebury & Co., Worcester: 15s.), is a record of Tests, compiled with the author's characteristic care and detail. Representative matches between the two countries began in 1928 and therefore the preceding period, not strictly relevant to the theme, is only briefly treated. From 1928 onwards, however, each tour is outlined, the full scores of the Tests are reproduced, and there are ample statistics.

The Valiant Stumper, by G. D. Martineau (Stanley Paul: 15s.), is sub-titled "A History of Wicket-Keeping" and it is, surprisingly enough, the first attempt to deal at any length with this remarkably neglected phase of the game. Mr. Martineau, as usual, marshals his material conscientiously and sets it down in orderly, and easily readable, prose. His book is, in fact, a series of sketches of wicket-keepers, through whom are traced the major developments in the history of wicket-keeping. Welcome as this study is in filling so important a gap in cricket literature, it cannot be called the definitive work on its subject. Mr. Martineau himself seems conscious of this fact, for, in his preface, he refers to the demands of wicket-keeping having "almost brought forth a separate race type." His book emphasises cricket literature's lack of a detailed history of the technique of wicket-keeping such as exists in respect of every other department of the game. It is to be regretted that C. B. Fry and G. W. Beldam, in their technical examinations of cricket, dealt much less fully with wicket-keeping than with batting, bowling and fielding. It is the most separate and specialist part of the game, yet one which even the best critics often overlook. It seems that only an experienced wicket-keeper is capable of writing the complementary book now demanded by Mr. Martineau's study.

Village Cricket, by A. J. Forrest (Hale: 16s.), is a pleasantly readable mixture of history, reminiscence, anecdote and conversation on the subject of village cricket. A book with such a vast subject is likely to fall between any number of stools. An author with such a theme must be discursive, unless he sets out to write a strict history, such as would show the development and, most important, the varying importance of village cricket within the game as a whole. Dr. Squire in his Henfield researches and, in fiction, Hugh de Selincourt with *The Cricket Match*, based their writing on single clubs: Mr. Forrest has no such limits. A rounded history of village cricket has yet to be written: Mr. Forrest points the way, and his book will be of value to the eventual chronicler of this happy facet of English life.

In *County Cricket Championships* (Phoenix House: 15s.) Roy Webber provides a body of reference not available within a single volume since the Rev. R. S. Holmes' work of the same title published in 1896. Marshalling his many facts skilfully, he gives complete County Championship tables from 1873 to 1956, traces the changes in the method of deciding the Championship, lists the captains of every county, record performances for each of the counties, the "caps" awarded since 1946, and, finally, short historic

sketches of the county clubs. Thus Mr. Webber adds to his already impressive list of authoritative reference books on cricket.

The Surrey Story, by Gordon Ross (Stanley Paul: 15s.), is the third book-length history of the county club, following the Alverstone and Alcock *Surrey Cricket* of 1902 and Louis Palgrave's *Story of the Oval* (1949). Thus, in devoting a quarter of the book to the remarkable Surrey seasons 1951–56, the author sets it shrewdly within the pattern of his subject. He writes with a pleasantly human touch, maintaining a nice balance between personality, figures and anecdote to provide a book which is readable, well arranged and—with its statistical appendices and good index—valuable reference.

The Lancashire County Cricket Club celebrated the centenary of its Headquarters with a 32-page pamphlet, *One Hundred Years of Old Trafford*, containing messages and appreciations from H.M. The Queen, officers of the club and various of its well-wishers.

Another anniversary was marked by the publication in Trinidad of *Diamond Jubilee: The Queen's Park Cricket Club; 1896–1956*, a symposium issued by the Club. It deals mainly with cricket—not only that of the Club but also inter-colonial and Test matches played on its Oval. Some personal memories provide useful reference to cricket in Trinidad not available elsewhere.

Lloyd's Register Cricket Club 1882–1956, by D. H. O. Kidd (printed by the Club for private circulation only), is a pleasantly produced contribution to the steadily growing chronicles of our clubs. Informally written, with due reference to persons as well as scores and results, it reviews each season and sets out Club records in an appendix.

A Century of Cricket, by Louis Cranfield, is a 16-page souvenir issued by the Heidelberg Cricket Club—originally the Yarra-Yarra Club—of Melbourne. It contains some worthwhile research into the Club's history.

Cricket Match History: Surrey v. Middlesex is a 22-page pamphlet similar to the series of *John Wisden's Cricket Match Histories* compiled by F. S. Ashley-Cooper in the early 'twenties. It bears no author's name, but was written by J. D. Lane: 100 copies were printed; a number were given to the author's friends and the remainder sold in aid of D. G. Fletcher's Benefit Fund.

Sportsman's Who's Who, by Raymond Glendenning and Robert Bateman (Museum Press: 16s.), is a reference book in which some 1,500 entries give the ages, short career histories and addresses of prominent present-day sportsmen, including the regular players of the first-class cricketing counties.

Short History of the Lancashire Schools' Cricket Association, by H. F. B. Thomas, and *Lancashire Schools' Cricket Association Handbook, 1957* (both available from H. F. B. Thomas, 24 Carill Drive, Manchester, 14; 6d. each), mark the work of a flourishing organisation. Founded in 1922, the Association has 44 member-clubs, runs eight leagues, and organises its North Lancashire v. South Lancashire match as well as matches with the Schools Associations of other counties. Already it can point to a number of its former players playing in the Lancashire County eleven.

Aberdeenshire Cricket Club Centenary 1857–1957: a Historical Survey (6s. 6d. plus 1s. postage and packing, from the Secretary, 375 Union Street, Aberdeen), edited by R. C. Kelman, is a solid 92-page account of one of Scotland's two most successful county clubs. Well illustrated and documented, and carefully written, it fits well into the small, but growing and valuable, documentation of Scottish cricket.

Repton 1557–1957, edited by Bernard Thomas (Batsford: 25s.), a history of the public school, contains a 23-page section, including a full-page photograph, on the subject of Repton cricket and the Repton Pilgrims. This chapter is by several hands, but is outstanding for the history of the school's cricket to 1908 by H. S. Altham, including his memories of J. N. Crawford—surely the greatest of all schoolboy cricketers—and of the great Repton teams in the first decade of this century.

Pakistan Cricket on the March (published by the author, Ministry of Interior, Government of Pakistan, Karachi: Rs. 4/8), by Qamaruddin Butt deals with the visits to Pakistan of the New Zealanders in 1955, the M.C.C. "A" team in 1955–56 and the

Australians, for a single match in October 1956; and with Pakistan's domestic competition—the Quaid-e-Azam Trophy of 1956–57. Pakistan's four "Tests" with the M.C.C. "A" team were classed as "unofficial," but Mr. Butt includes them in stating that Pakistan in this period played eight representative matches, won five, drew two and lost one: an impressive record. This 258-page book contains 21 illustrations, full tour scores and averages, plus averages of the Pakistani tour in India 1954–55. There is a foreword by A. H. Kardar, an introduction by Ray Robinson, and Mr. Butt, in his preface, writes: "No apology is needed for bringing out my third book on the subject on which there is a paucity of literature especially in Pakistan."

Cape Summer and the Australians in England, by Alan Ross (Hamish Hamilton: 18s.), as its title suggests, is divided into two parts, and deals mainly with the Test series of 1956 and 1956–57. Mr. Ross was an established poet and critic as well as a war-time "Blue" before he turned to cricket writing. He writes with sensitive care and here achieves greater distinction than usually is the case with sports books. He deals, indeed, with the facts and the story of the cricket, but also he relishes the characters of the players, conjures ideas and images out of the play and reacts to the topography of places on the way to the matches. Mr. Ross is the first outstanding cricket writer of recent years whose work appears uninfluenced by that of Mr. Neville Cardus.

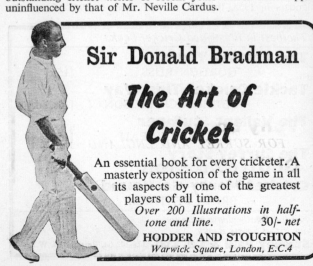

The M.C.C. Tour of South Africa 1956–57, by Charles Fortune (Harrap: 15s.), is one of three books on that tour, and the first by the well-known wireless commentator who has covered cricket tours in South Africa, England and Australia. The full score is given of every match on the tour, as well as an appendix of statistics and some interesting action illustrations. The author's close watching of the play is as apparent as the thought he has given to it, and the result is a book in which the focus is frequently and valuably varied. Mr. Fortune is not merely a reporter but also a critic, concerned with the wider aspects of cricket as with the details of play. Of the M.C.C. match with Natal at Pietermaritzburg he writes: "This game followed the line that to ensure success in Tests all else in cricket may be sacrificed. It is, I suppose, a natural belief for a generation that has been brought up in class rooms where the only thing that matters is success in the final examination."

It is surprising that no one had used for a cricket title *Pitch and Toss* (Hodder and Stoughton: 16s. 6d.) until it was chosen by Roy McLean, the South African Test player, for his account of the 1956–57 Test series. A personal book which reads like recorded conversation, it brings the reader close to the players and their reactions to the play, particularly to Mr. McLean's straightforward criticism: "There is nothing easy even in a game of cricket in these times. It is all sheer hard work."

Report from South Africa (Hale: 16s.), by E. W. Swanton, is a rounded account of the tour with full match scores, illustrations of play and a section of Tour Statistics by Arthur Wrigley. Mr. Swanton has reported over 120 Test matches in various countries and, out of this long experience, his cricket writing is always considered, and always influenced by his concern for the game as a whole. "In South Africa no less than in England the problem of the moment is to re-infuse cricket with that spice of virility and adventurous challenge which has always been at the root of its character."

The only book so far published on the Test series of 1957 is *West Indies Cricket Challenge* (Stanley Paul: 15s.), the ninth of Bruce Harris's books on major tours. "Frankness compels me to say that the 'challenge' was not as powerful, as enthralling, as we had hoped. . . ." he writes in his opening. Yet Edgbaston gave him "the most astonishing Test Match I have ever known among the hundred and more I have watched," and he records its surprising course faithfully and carefully. Full match scores—with details of times and boundary strokes in the Test batting—full averages, and a list of outstanding performances round off this solitary permanent record of an important Test series.

Two souvenirs of the tour were issued. As usual, the "Official Souvenir" *Cricketers From The West Indies* (Playfair Books: 1s.) was edited by Gordon Ross. It contains essays on West Indian cricket by E. W. Swanton and—with special reference to selection—Jack Anderson, in addition to the now familiar layout of photographs and biographical details of the players; statistics are by Roy Webber. Well-planned printing made possible the inclusion of photographs of "Early Days of the 1957 Tour in England."

They Live for Cricket (Edited and published by W. A. S. Hardy, 86 Porchester Terrace North, London, W.3: 1s. 6d.) follows the souvenir pamphlet of the same title issued in 1950. Its essays on West Indies cricket are by O. C. Mathurin, Pat Landsberg and the editor; it, too, includes portraits and pen-pictures of the players, a photo supplement and records—with a broadsheet of a calypso tipped in for good measure.

Two other publications have been received, marking a tour that has had little attention—the visit of the Kenya Asian cricketers to South Africa. Their hosts are generally known as the "Non-European cricketers" of the Union, whose governing body is called The South African Board of Cricket Control—a title which can lead to confusion. The Kenya team, containing the Pakistani Test player Shakoor Ahmed and three others who have played first-class cricket in Pakistan, made a seven weeks' tour, playing matches against provincial Non-European teams and three Tests.

The two publications are *The Official Souvenir Brochure of the Kenya Asian Cricket Tour of South Africa* (post free 1s. 3d.), a 12-page illustrated pamphlet published by the Eastern Province Cricket Federation, and *Kenya Tour Souvenir Programme* (post free 3s. 6d.), issued by South African Cricket Board of Control (both obtainable in Britain from E. K. Brown, Bevois Mount, Liskeard, Cornwall). The latter is a more substantial booklet of 72 pages with "messages" from various civic and cricketing personalities, biographical sketches of the tourists and a brief but valuable history of Non-European cricket in South Africa.

Seventeen books of varying sizes by or about W. G. Grace represents a bibliography large enough to suggest that A. A. Thomson's biography, *The Great Cricketer* (Hale: 16s.), could add little to the subject. This, however, proved an ideal theme for the writer who, in recent years, has established himself among the best of all sporting story-tellers. Here are the old stories and many which will be new to most readers, set in a study which is also a history and a pattern of pleasant reading. Mr. Thomson has the touch of a sensitive enthusiast. He writes of W. G. Grace's goodness—"It was like Wycliffe's Bible, 'understanded of simple men' "—that quality, too, is at the root of Mr. Thomson's writing about cricket.

Flannelled Foolishness (Hollis and Carter: 18s.) is the autobiography of E. R. T. Holmes, the Malvern School, Oxford

University and Surrey all-rounder and a tireless worker in the interests of cricket and cricketers. Engagingly, and in the lively, friendly, humorous language of his conversation, he tells a happy story of public school, university and county cricket played by an amateur of great enthusiasm and no mean skill.

Cricket at the Crossroads (Cassell: 16s.), by Ian Johnson, the Australian captain and off-spin bowler, is unusual among the books of famous players, in that it is only incidentally a personal account óf his cricket career. He sets out to write objectively of Australian Test cricket in the years since the end of war and, for a man who played in many of the matches and did so with full enthusiasm, he succeeds to an unusual degree. So, his book is one of observation and experience, rather than of experiences. It traces briefly Australia's rise to the top of the cricket world, then concentrates on the Test series of 1956 and finishes with illuminating examinations of contemporary cricket problems and cricketers—notably Keith Miller, Ray Lindwall and W. J. O'Reilly. The seven chapters on the Australian defeat in 1956 are expositions, footnotes and critical judgements, rather than reports. Read in conjunction with one of the detailed factual accounts of the series, they give a most valuable, unusual and illuminating picture of the play.

In *Spinning Round the World* (Muller: 16s.) Jim Laker has the magnificent cricket story of Surrey's sequence of Championships and of his own amazing career crowned by taking all ten Australian wickets twice in a summer. The book begins with his boyhood in Yorkshire, continues to his great successes and goes on to survey the social pattern of cricket and to look to the future of the game.

The autobiography of Laker's colleague, Tony Lock, is called *For Surrey and England* (Hodder and Stoughton: 12s. 6d.). To a far greater extent than Laker's book, this one deals, in season-to-season sequence, with Lock's cricket from the day when he became "A Pro at Sixteen," down to "Wardle and I" and "Where Do We Go From Here?" Considerable attention is devoted to county cricket and comments on players from a technical viewpoint.

Happy-Go-Johnny (Hale: 15s.) is the book of John Wardle, probably unique among cricketers for his ability to bowl to Test standard in two different techniques. It is sub-titled "by J. H. Wardle as told to A. A. Thomson." Both player and amanuensis are Yorkshiremen, immersed in that county's cricket; both, too, are raconteurs with humorous bents, and their joint book recounts Wardle's varied cricket career in an easy yet lively conversational style, missing nothing of effect, humour or excitement.

Cricket Umpiring and Scoring (Phoenix House: 9s. 6d.) is by R. S. Rait Kerr, former Secretary of M.C.C. and author of the definitive study, *The Laws of Cricket*. This book is the official handbook of The Association of Cricket Umpires and is intended as a complete reference for all umpires and, by the addition of a final section, for scorers also. With model precision and concentration, Colonel Rait Kerr has incorporated into a single volume the general and detailed duties of umpiring, the laws and the decisions and guidance of the Association and the Lord's secretariat on them. The Laws are printed in full with not merely the official notes but also a "Points for Umpires" section on each Law. The questions of no-ball and lbw are most valuably elucidated, while the instructions to scorers should produce accurate and uniform score-books. Many cricketers and followers will have recourse to this handbook which should be kept up to date as one of the game's standard works of reference.

Your Book of Cricket (Faber & Faber: 8s. 6d.) is a book of instruction written largely for schoolboy players by Michael Parker. It contains much careful advice, sound common sense, pleasant thought about the game and some helpful action photographs, among which those of Laker and Bedser bowling are also exciting.

Wisden Cricketers' Almanack 1957 (Sporting Handbooks: linen covers 16s., boards 18s. 6d.), edited by Norman Preston, was the 94th annual issue, so that the game's major work of reference stands within five editions of its centenary. Much of it is now taken for granted—even the unique service which keeps up to date the records of Births and Deaths, Test players, records, reviews of

County, Minor Counties and School cricket, and gives full scores and reports of major play all over the world. There has been, however, in recent years, an admirable effort to provide material for reading and thought about the game in an increase of essays. In this issue the Editor is critical of the move to legislate for brighter cricket, preferring the onus to be placed on the players; he is supported in his arguments by W. E. Bowes. D. R. Jardine contributes an appreciation of Stuart Surridge and Learie Constantine a study of the growth of West Indian cricket; Neville Cardus has written both a review of "Laker's Wonderful Year" and an obituary essay on C. B. Fry, while A. W. Ledbrooke celebrates the Old Trafford Centenary. A long essay, "Great Men of Gloucestershire," by H. F. Hutt, builds a history of the county's cricket round its outstanding players. Thus, the 1,051 pages contain their innovations as well as their solid, established and essential references.

Playfair Cricket Annual 1957 (Playfair Books: 5s.), edited by Gordon Ross, with statistics by the ubiquitous Roy Webber, appeared for the tenth year and is now almost the only survival from the number of cricket annuals which began publication directly after the war. In an attractive format, it continues to blend personal notes, generous illustration, records and comment with its valuable "Career Records" and "Who's Who" sections.

The News Chronicle and Daily Dispatch Cricket Annual for 1957 (News Chronicle: 1s. 6d.), edited by Crawford White, continues in its familiar and sound way to give records and biographical notes in a pocket-sized volume.

Flagstaff Cricket Annual 1957 (Flagstaff Press: 2s.) is edited by Roy Lester. As it has done since its first appearance in 1953, it contains general articles and review of each county, and continues with notes on women's cricket and current cricket books.

1957 Cricket Spotlight (edited and published by Robert Baker, 2 Aynho Walk, Sunnyside, Northampton: 1s.) is the second issue of an annual symposium of which "the proceeds are devoted to the English Schools Cricket Association." There is an admirable series of action photographs of the West Indian cricketers and the contributors include H. S. Altham, Peter May, John Goddard, Sir Leonard Hutton, Jack Cheetham, Frank Tyson and leading cricket writers.

Cricket Fixtures 1957 (The Times: 1s.) is the familiar list of firstclass and Minor Counties fixtures, followed by the averages for 1956.

The M.C.C. Diary 1958 (Playfair Books: 5s.) has now settled to a January–December dating and contains 62 pages of excellently chosen references of value to cricketers.

The Club Cricket Conference Official Handbook 1957 (C.C.C.: 3s.), within its 265 pages, provides secretaries with concise reference to all its clubs and activities. Simultaneously it demonstrates the extent of the Conference's growth and service to club cricket through the south and west of England since it started in 1915.

The Indian Cricket Almanack for 1955–56 (obtainable in Britain from *The Hindu*, 2 and 3 Salisbury Court, Fleet Street, E.C.4: 5s. 6d.), following its own particular dating system, deals with play which took place in the season of its title. Deriving, like most of the national annuals, from *Wisden*, it covers first-class, university and schools cricket in India, maintains an up-to-date record section, includes a photographic supplement and gives as its Three Cricketers of the Year, two of the touring New Zealanders —Sutcliffe and Reid—and N. J. Contractor.

South African Cricket Annual 1957, edited by Geoffrey Chettle (obtainable in Britain from E. K. Brown, Bevois Mount, Liskeard, Cornwall: 8s. 6d.), is now well established. Its photographic section is impressive, and so are the two compilations of career records, one of current players and the other of all South African Test cricketers. The Currie Cup and the M.C.C. tour, of course, are fully covered and it also treats of women's cricket and, at some length, the "Nuffield Week" which serves South African school cricket so generously.

The Cricket Almanack of New Zealand, edited by A. H. Carman and N. S. MacDonald (obtainable in Britain from E. K. Brown, Bevois Mount, Liskeard, Cornwall: 10s. 6d.), is the 10th issue of the third in this group of overseas annuals essential to the full reference library of cricket. It is less concerned than many of its kind with history and statistics but gives full coverage to the Plunket Shield matches and to colts, universities and minor association cricket in New Zealand.

Sports and Recreation in the Royal Navy 1957–58 (R.N. & R.M. Sports Control Board: 7s. 6d.) is published "In order to provide the Royal Navy with up-to-date information on the ever-changing laws of the various games and the rules governing naval competitions." The 30-page section on cricket lists results and players in the Royal Navy's inter-service matches and those of the Royal Navy Women's Cricket Association and quotes the laws in full.

During the last ten years the annual publications of the county clubs have sunk many of their differences until most of them now conform to a pattern which seems to combine the best points of all their different earlier forms. For economy's sake, they tend to be stiff-paper-covered. Their contents are invariably based on reports and full scores of the county team—and sometimes of the 2nd XI—for the previous season, a photographic section, the county's records, the captain's or committee's report, and a list of officers. In general, too, they have feature articles bearing on the county's cricket and sometimes with wider interest. The ten annuals received are listed here, with notes of items of special interest, or differences from the pattern outlined above.

Derbyshire County Cricket Year Book (Derbyshire C.C. Supporters' Club: 1s., 176 pp.), edited by F. G. Peach and A. F. Dawn, carries a list of all Derbyshire players.

Essex County Cricket Club 1957 Annual (Essex C.C.C.: 2s., 132 pp.), edited by Trevor Bailey, contains illuminating balance sheets of the county's various "weeks": pleasant use of colour in printing.

Glamorgan County Cricket Club Year Book 1957 (Glamorgan C.C.C.: 1s., 72 pp.): essays by Wilfred Wooller—on Gilbert Park-house—and by James D. Coldham, on the early South Wales club.

Hampshire County Cricket Club Handbook for 1957 (Hampshire C.C.C.: 2s., 136 pp.). Has seven substantial feature articles and the first instalment of an exhaustive statistical record of Hampshire cricket by Roy Webber.

Kent County Cricket Club Annual, 1957 (Kent C.C.C.: 2s., 188 pp.): very well produced photographic section.

Leicestershire County Cricket Club Year Book 1957 (Leicestershire C.C.C.: 1s., 100 pp.), edited by C. H. Palmer: appreciations of Jack Walsh and the late Maurice Tompkin.

Northamptonshire County Cricket Club Year Book 1957 (Northants C.C.C.: 2s. 6d., 140 pp.), edited by Lt.-Col. A. St. G. Coldwell, includes a sound historical article by J. B. Coldham on "The Kingston Family."

Nottinghamshire County Cricket Club Handbook 1957 (Nottinghamshire C.C.C.: 2s., 92 pp.): essays on James Iremonger and Bruce Dooland.

Sussex Cricket Handbook 1957 (Sussex C.C.C. and Sussex Cricket Association: 1s., 124 pp.) contains obituary essays on C. B. Fry by H. S. Altham, and Sir Home Gordon by A. W. T. Langford.

Warwickshire County Cricket Club Annual 1957 (Warwickshire C.C.C.: 1s., 118 pp.), edited by W. G. Wanklyn and E. A. Davies, has a profile of Warwickshire's new captain, M. J. K. Smith and, rather less expectedly, another of "Chloe."

Yorkshire County Cricket Club 1957 (Yorkshire C.C.C.: free to members) remains unique. In board covers, it now runs to 416 pages; a compendium reference to every facet of Yorkshire cricket and a list of the club's members.

The Friendly Game (Michael Joseph: 13s. 6d.) is the second cricket novel of William Godfrey, author of *Malleson at Melbourne*: Malleson, incidentally, is a character in this book also. Here is a good novel indeed: that is to say, although cricket provides its setting and most of its action, it is essentially a story, satisfying in plot, character and characters. Its climax is as ingenious, as surprising, and yet as unexceptionable as any cricket writer has achieved in fiction.

Volume 38 of *The Cricketer*, under the editorship of Sir Pelham

Warner, who founded it in 1921, appeared in its established post-war form of ten fortnightly numbers, with the pleasantly solid Spring and Winter Annuals. W. E. Bowes contributes critical reports of the season's Test matches.

The South African Cricket Review (The Editor, 206 Star Building, 33 Waterkant Street, Cape Town, South Africa: subscription 21s. p.a.), edited by Norman Howell, completed a happy first year in a country which, until recently, gave little encouragement to cricket periodicals. The magazine has nine issues a year, monthly during the South African season, two-monthly for April–May, June–July and August–September. Volume I covered the M.C.C. tour in generous detail and included a varied scope of criticism, history and feature articles.

The dictates of literary criticism preclude Mr. Arlott from noticing his own books. He has been responsible for a share of one book and the complete writing of another, published in 1957.

Hampshire County Cricket (Phoenix House: 30s.), which the Hampshire Club has adopted as its official history, makes good one of the gaps in county histories. It is composed of four sections: in the first, H. S. Altham, the leading cricket historian, treats of cricket from the days of the Hambledon men whose deeds "inspired an appreciation of their skill unrivalled in cricket literature," up to 1914. In the second, John Arlott deals with the inter-war period with pen pictures of some of Hampshire's greatest cricketers, The Hon. H. L. Tennyson, Mead, Brown, Kennedy and Newman. Then Desmond Eagar covers the post-war years in which he captained the county team; a modest story of improvement: as on the cricket field, he is completely self-effacing. Finally, Roy Webber contributes an exhaustive section of statistics. It is an enjoyable, sound book.

Alletson's Innings (Epworth Press: edition limited to 200 copies: £1.1s.), by John Arlott, is a short biography of the player and a detailed examination of his score of 189 in ninety minutes for Notts against Sussex in 1911, the greatest big hitting innings in the history of the game. The player's story is a surprising one, but even more remarkable is the research which shows that almost all the details of the innings given at the time—and repeated in the record books ever since—were incorrect. *Alletson's Innings* is a first-class piece of cricket research, and it also recaptures some of the thrill of that remarkable day. "Five balls at one time on the roof of the Skating Rink outside the ground." "Time was wasted trying to prise one ball out of the stand into whose soft wood Alletson had driven it—no chisel being available."—W. E. B.

FIXTURES FOR 1958

Saturday, April 26

Cambridge	Univ. v. Surrey

Wednesday, April 30

Cambridge	Univ. v. Sussex
Worcester	Worcs. v. New Zealand
Lord's	M.C.C. v. Yorkshire

Thursday, May 1

Taunton	Somerset v. Hampshire (2 days)

Saturday, May 3

Leicester (Grace Rd.)	Leics. v. New Zealand
Lord's	M.C.C. v. Surrey
Oxford	Univ. v. Gloucs.
Cambridge	Univ. v. Yorkshire

Monday, May 5

Southampton	Hampshire v. Royal Navy (2 days)

Tuesday, May 6

Ilkeston	Derby v. Northants (2 days)

Wednesday, May 7

Cardiff	Glamorgan v. Somerset
Bristol	Gloucs. v. Essex
Lord's	Middlesex v. Notts
Oval	Surrey v. New Zealand
Oxford	Univ. v. Yorkshire
Cambridge	Univ. v. Kent
Edgbaston	Warwick. v. Comb. Serv.
Manchester	Lancashire v. Worcs. (2 days)
Southampton	Hampshire v. Sussex (2 days)

Saturday, May 10

Ilford	Essex v. New Zealand
Dartford	Kent v. Somerset
Lord's	Middlesex v. Leics.
Trent Bridge	Notts v. Glamorgan
Oval	Surrey v. Gloucs.
Edgbaston	Warwick. v. Sussex
Bradford	Yorkshire v. Hampshire
Oxford	Univ. v. Derbyshire
Cambridge	Univ. v. Lancashire
Worcester	Worcs. v. R.A.F.

Wednesday, May 14

Derby	Derby v. Glamorgan
Ilford	Essex v. Somerset
Gloucester	Gloucs. v. Worcs.

Trent Bridge	Notts v. Hampshire
Hove	Sussex v. Leicestershire
Harrogate	Yorkshire v. Warwick.
Oxford	Univ. v. Lancashire
Cambridge	Univ. v. New Zealand

Saturday, May 17

Lord's	M.C.C. v. New Zealand
Chesterfield	Derbyshire v. Leics.
Bristol	Gloucs. v. Yorkshire
Gravesend	Kent v. Essex
Old Trafford	Lancs. v. Hampshire
Northampton	Northants v. Glamorgan
Oval	Surrey v. Warwick.
Hove	Sussex v. Notts
Worcester	Worcs. v. Middlesex

Wednesday, May 21

Portsmouth	Hampshire v. Worcs.
Gravesend	Kent v. Lancashire
Northampton	Northants v. Middlesex
Trent Bridge	Notts v. Essex
Bath	Somerset v. Yorkshire
Oval	Surrey v. Leicestershire
Edgbaston	Warwick. v. Gloucs.
Oxford	Univ. v. New Zealand
Lord's	M.C.C. v. Club Con. (2 days)
Hove	Sussex v. Royal Navy (2 days)

Saturday, May 24

Derby	Derbyshire v. Warwick.
Romford	Essex v. Worcs.
Cardiff	Glamorgan v. New Zealand
Southampton	Hampshire v. Kent
Leicester (Grace Rd.)	Leics. v. Northants
Lord's	Middlesex v. Sussex
Trent Bridge	Notts v. Surrey
Bath	Somerset v. Gloucs.
Leeds	Yorkshire v. Lancs.
Oxford	Univ. v. Free Foresters

Wednesday, May 28

Chesterfield	Derbyshire v. Gloucs.
Romford	Essex v. Yorkshire
Swansea	Glamorgan v. Kent
Old Trafford	Lancashire v. Surrey (A. Wharton's Benefit)
Leicester (Grace Rd.)	Leics. v. Hampshire
Peterborough	Northants v. Warwick.
Taunton	Somerset v. N. Zealand
Worcester	Worcs. v. Sussex
Oxford	Univ. v. The Army
Cambridge	Univ. v. Middlesex

Saturday, May 31

Bristol	Gloucs. v. Kent
Southampton	Hants v. New Zealand
Old Trafford	Lancs. v. Notts
Lord's	Middlesex v. Yorkshire
Northampton	Northants v. Derbyshire
Taunton	Somerset v. Sussex
Oval	Surrey v. Essex
Dudley	Worcs. v. Glamorgan
Cambridge	Univ. v. Cambridgeshire

Wednesday, June 4

Newport	Glamorgan v. Leics.
Bristol	Gloucs. v. Derbyshire
Lord's	Middlesex v. Hants
Oval	Surrey v. Northants
Hove	Sussex v. Lancashire
Oxford	Univ. v. Kent
Cambridge	Univ. v. Warwickshire
Middlesbro'	Yorkshire v. Scotland

Thursday, June 5

Edgbaston	ENGLAND v. NEW ZEALAND (First Test, 5 days)

Saturday, June 7

Buxton	Derbyshire v. Essex
Swansea	Glamorgan v. Warwick.
Cowes (IOW)	Hampshire v. Leics.
Tunbridge W.	Kent v. Sussex
Old Trafford	Lancs. v. Middlesex
Trent Bridge	Notts v. Worcs.
Taunton	Somerset v. Surrey
Bradford	Yorks. v. Northants
Cambridge	Univ. v. Free Foresters
Lord's	Beaumont v. Oratory (1 day)

Monday, June 9

Lord's	M.C.C. v. Scotland (2 days)

Wednesday, June 11

Derby	Derby. v. New Zealand
Brentwood	Essex v. Sussex
Tunbridge W.	Kent v. Gloucs.
Leicester (Grace Rd.)	Leics. v. Worcs.
Yeovil	Somerset v. Hampshire
Oval	Surrey v. Lancashire
Hull	Yorkshire v. Notts
Lord's	M.C.C. v. Camb. Univ.
Oxford	Oxford U. v. Middlesex
Eastbourne	Col. L. C. Stevens' XI v. R.A.F. (2 days)

Saturday, June 14

Brentwood	Essex v. Cambridge U.
Blackheath	Kent v. Notts

Leicester (Grace Rd.)	Leics. v. Lancashire
Lord's	Middlesex v. Gloucs.
Rushden	Northants v. Somerset
Hove	Sussex v. New Zealand
Coventry (Courtaulds)	Warwick. v. Glamorgan
Kidderminster	Worcs. v. Derbyshire
Sheffield	Yorkshire v. Surrey (J. V. Wilson's Benefit)
Oxford	Univ. v. Hampshire

Wednesday, June 18

Llanelly	Glamorgan v. Essex
Bournemouth	Hampshire v. Somerset
Northampton	Northants v. Camb. U.
Trent Bridge	Notts v. Lancashire
Edgbaston	Warwickshire v. Kent
Worcester	Worcs. v. Leics.
Leeds	Yorkshire v. Gloucs.
Oxford	Univ. v. Sussex

Thursday, June 19

Lord's	ENGLAND v. NEW ZEALAND (Second Test, 5 days)

Saturday, June 21

Chesterfield	Derbyshire v. Surrey
Cardiff	Glamorgan v. Middx.
Bristol	Gloucs. v. Hampshire
Old Trafford	Lancs. v. Northants
Hinckley	Leics. v. Warwick.
Trent Bridge	Notts v. Yorkshire
Taunton	Somerset v. Worcs.
Hastings	Sussex v. Kent
Woolwich	Army v. Cambridge U.

Monday, June 23

Chiswick	Civil Service v. R.A.F. (2 days)

Wednesday, June 25

Colchester	Essex v. Leicestershire
Neath	Glamorgan v. Hants
Old Trafford	Lancs. v. New Zealand
Lord's	Middlesex v. Kent
Northampton	Northants v. Gloucs.
Guildford	Surrey v. Cambridge U.
Hastings	Sussex v. Derbyshire
Edgbaston	Warwick. v. Oxford U.
Taunton	Somerset v. R.A.F.
Torquay	A Torquay XI v. Worcs. (2 days)

Saturday, June 28

Colchester	Essex v. Notts
Swansea	Glamorgan v. Derby.
Stroud	Gloucs. v. Oxford U.
Lord's	Middlesex v. Somerset

KK

Kettering	Northants v. Sussex
Guildford	Surrey v. Hampshire
Edgbaston	Warwick. v. Leics.
Worcester	Worcs. v. Cambridge U.
Sheffield	Yorks. v. New Zealand
Southampton	Hants v. Army (2 days)

Wednesday, July 2

Stroud	Gloucs. v. Cambridge U.
Southampton	Hants v. Glamorgan
Gillingham	Kent v. Leicestershire
Liverpool	Lancashire v. Sussex
Northampton	Northants v. Yorkshire
Bath	Somerset v. Derbyshire
Oval	Surrey v. Oxford U.
Edgbaston	Warwick. v. Middlesex
Trent Bridge	Notts v. R.A.F.

Thursday, July 3

Leeds	ENGLAND v. NEW ZEALAND (Third Test, 5 days)

Friday, July 4

Lord's	Eton v. Harrow (2 days)

Saturday, July 5

Chesterfield	Derbyshire v. Yorks. (A. Hamer's Benefit)
Cardiff	Glamorgan v. Gloucs.
Portsmouth	Hants v. Cambridge U.
Old Trafford	Lancs. v. Leics.
Trent Bridge	Notts v. Northants
Bath	Somerset v. Middlesex
Oval	Surrey v. Kent
Hove	Sussex v. Essex
Worcester	Worcs. v. Warwick.
Eastbourne	D. R. Jardine's XI v. Oxford U.

Monday, July 7

Lord's	Royal Artillery v. Royal Engineers (2 days)

Wednesday, July 9

Derby	Derbyshire v. Lancs.
Swansea	Glamorgan v. Surrey
Gloucester	Gloucs. v. Northants
Trent Bridge	Notts v. Kent
Edgbaston	Warwick. v. Essex
Stourbridge	Worcs. v. Somerset
Bradford	Yorkshire v. Sussex
Lord's	M.C.C. v. Oxford U.
Eastbourne	D. R. Jardine's XI v. Cambridge U.

Thursday, July 10

Selkirk	Scotland v. New Zealand (1 day)

Friday, July 11

Glasgow	Scotland v. New Zealand (3 days)

Saturday, July 12

Lord's	Oxford v. Cambridge
Westcliff	Essex v. Glamorgan
Gloucester	Gloucs. v. Notts
Portsmouth	Hampshire v. Sussex
Blackheath	Kent v. Surrey
Ashby	Leics. v. Derbyshire
Glastonbury	Somerset v. Northants
Edgbaston	Warwick. v. Worcs.
Sheffield	Yorkshire v. Middlesex
Old Trafford	Lancs. v. Comb. Serv.

Wednesday, July 16

Lord's	Gentlemen v. Players
Westcliff	Essex v. Derbyshire
Southampton	Hampshire v. Gloucs.
Old Trafford	Lancs. v. Warwick.
Leicester (Grace Rd.)	Leics. v. Middlesex
Northampton	Northants v. Notts
Oval	Surrey v. Glamorgan
Worcester	Worcs. v. Kent
Belfast	Ireland v. New Zealand (2 days)
Sunderland	Durham v. Yorkshire (2 days)
Torquay	Torquay C.C. v. Sussex (2 days)

Friday, July 18

Dublin	Ireland v. New Zealand (1 day)

Saturday, July 19

Bournemouth	Hampshire v. Lancs. (D. Shackleton's Benefit)
Lord's	Middx. v. New Zealand
Northampton	Northants v. Kent
Trent Bridge	Notts v. Derbyshire
Taunton	Somerset v. Warwick.
Oval	Surrey v. Yorkshire (E. A. Bedser's Benefit)
Worthing	Sussex v. Glamorgan
Worcester	Worcs. v. Gloucs.

Wednesday, July 23

Bristol	Gloucs. v. Surrey
Bournemouth	Hampshire v. Notts
Maidstone	Kent v. Worcs.
Coalville	Leicestershire v. Essex
Lord's	Middlesex v. Lancs.
Worthing	Sussex v. Yorkshire
Coventry (Courtaulds)	Warwick. v. Northants

Thursday July, 24

Old Trafford	ENGLAND v. NEW ZEALAND (Fourth Test, 5 days)

Saturday, July 26

Ilkeston	Derbyshire v. Notts
Leyton	Essex v. Surrey
Bristol	Gloucs. v. Sussex
Maidstone	Kent v. Yorkshire
Leicester (Grace Rd.)	Leics. v. Somerset
Lord's	Middlesex v. Glamorgan
Northampton	Northants v. Worcs. (D. Brookes's Benefit)
Edgbaston	Warwick. v. Lancs. (F. C. Gardner's Benefit)

Wednesday, July 30

Chesterfield	Derby. v. Middlesex
Leyton	Essex v. Northants
Pontypridd	Glamorgan v. Sussex
Blackpool	Lancs. v. Gloucs.
Leicester (Grace Rd.)	Leicestershire v. Kent
Trent Bridge	Notts v. Warwickshire
Oval	Surrey v. New Zealand
Worcester	Worcs. v. Hampshire
Sheffield	Yorkshire v. Somerset
Lord's	Rugby v. Marlborough (2 days)
Torquay	Devon v. R.A.F. (2 days)

Friday, August 1

Lord's	Cheltenham v. Haileybury & I.S.C (2 days)

Saturday, August 2

Swansea	Glamorgan v. New Zealand
Bristol	Gloucs. v. Somerset
Canterbury	Kent v. Hampshire (F. Ridgway's Benefit)
Old Trafford	Lancs. v. Yorkshire
Northampton	Northants v. Leics.
Oval	Surrey v. Notts
Hove	Sussex v. Middlesex
Edgbaston	Warwick. v. Derbyshire
Worcester	Worcestershire v. Essex

Monday, August 4

Lord's	Clifton v. Tonbridge (2 days)

Wednesday, August 6

Cardiff	Glamorgan v. Lancs.
Portsmouth	Hants v. Middlesex
Canterbury	Kent v. Derbyshire
Leicester (Grace Rd.)	Leics. v. Surrey
Weston	Somerset v. Notts
Hove	Sussex v. Gloucs.
Edgbaston	Warwick. v. N. Zealand
Worcester	Worcs. v. Northants
Middlesbro'	Yorkshire v. Essex
Lord's	Southern Schools v. The Rest (2 days)

Friday, August 8

Lord's	Comb. Serv. v. Public Schools (2 days)

Saturday, August 9

Derby	Derbyshire v. Sussex
Cheltenham	Gloucs. v. New Zealand
Portsmouth	Hampshire v. Warwick.
Old Trafford	Lancashire v. Kent
Wellingboro'	Northants v. Essex
Trent Bridge	Notts v. Leics.
Weston	Somerset v. Glamorgan
Oval	Surrey v. Middlesex
Bradford	Yorkshire v. Worcs.

Monday, August 11

Lord's	Royal Navy v. Army (2 days)

Wednesday, August 13

Burton	Derbyshire v. Hants
Clacton	Essex v. Kent
Cheltenham	Gloucs. v. Glamorgan
Lord's	Middlesex v. Worcs.
Northampton	Northants v. N. Zealand
Weston	Somerset v. Lancs.
Edgbaston	Warwick. v. Notts
Scarborough	Yorkshire v. Leics.
Hove	Sussex v. R.A.F.

Saturday, August 16

Clacton	Essex v. Hampshire
Cheltenham	Gloucs. v. Warwick.
Dover	Kent. v. Northants
Loughboro'	Leics. v. Glamorgan
Lord's	Middlesex v. Surrey
Trent Bridge	Notts v. New Zealand
Eastbourne	Sussex v. Somerset
Worcester	Worcs. v. Lancashire
Leeds	Yorkshire v. Derbyshire

Monday, August 18

Halton	Army v. R.A.F. (2 days)

Wednesday, August 20

Chesterfield	Derbyshire v. Worcs.
Dover	Kent v. Middlesex
Old Trafford	Lancs. v. Glamorgan
Northampton	Northants v. Surrey

Taunton	Somerset v. Essex
Eastbourne	Sussex v. Hampshire
Edgbaston	Warwick. v. Yorkshire
Leicester (Grace Rd.)	Leics. v. Notts
Lord's	Royal Navy v. R.A.F. (2 days)

Thursday, August 21

| Oval | ENGLAND v. NEW ZEALAND (Fifth Test, 5 days) |

Friday, August 22

| Lord's | M.C.C. Young Pros. v. English Schools C.A. (1 day) |

Saturday, August 23

Derby	Derbyshire v. Kent
Southend	Essex v. Middlesex
Swansea	Glamorgan v. Yorks.
Bristol	Gloucs. v. Lancashire
Southampton	Hants v. Northants
Trent Bridge	Notts v. Sussex
Edgbaston	Warwick. v. Somerset
Worcester	Worcs. v. Surrey

Tuesday, August 26

| Lord's | M.C.C. Young Pros. v. Ldn. Boys' Clubs (1 day) |

Wednesday, August 27

Southend	Essex v. Warwickshire
Bournemouth	Hampshire v. Yorkshire
Canterbury	Kent v. New Zealand
Old Trafford	Lancs. v. Derbyshire
Leicester (Grace Rd.)	Leics. v. Gloucs.

Lord's	Middlesex v. Northants
Oval	Surrey v. Somerset
Hove	Sussex v. Worcs.

Saturday, August 30

Ebbw Vale	Glamorgan v. Northants
Bournemouth	Hants v. Derbyshire
Trent Bridge	Notts v. Somerset
Lord's	Middlesex v. Warwick.
Hove	Sussex v. Surrey
Liverpool	Lancs. v. Yorkshire (Friendly)
Dublin	Ireland v. Worcs. (2 days)

Wednesday, September 3

Blackpool	Lancashire v. Essex
Oval	Surrey v. Worcs.
Scarborough	Yorkshire v. M.C.C.
Hastings	A. E. R. Gilligan's XI v. New Zealand

Saturday, September 6

Blackpool	Lancs. v. New Zealand
Hastings	An England XI v. A Commonwealth XI
Scarborough	Gentlemen v. Players
Torquay	North v. South

Wednesday, September 10

| Scarborough | T. N. Pearce's XI v. New Zealand |
| Torquay | England XI v. Commonwealth XI |

Saturday, September 13

| Newcastle | Minor Counties v. New Zealand (2 days) |

NEW ZEALAND TOUR 1958

APRIL

| 30 | Worcester | v. Worcestershire |

MAY

3	Leicester	v. Leicestershire
7	Oval	v. Surrey
10	Ilford	v. Essex
14	Cambridge	v. Cambridge Univ.
17	Lord's	v. M.C.C.
21	Oxford	v. Oxford Univ.
24	Cardiff	v. Glamorgan
28	Taunton	v. Somerset
31	Southampton	v. Hampshire

JUNE

5	Edgbaston	v. ENGLAND (First Test, 5 days)
11	Derby	v. Derbyshire
14	Hove	v. Sussex
19	Lord's	v. ENGLAND (Second Test, 5 days)
25	Old Trafford	v. Lancashire
28	Sheffield	v. Yorkshire

JULY

| 3 | Leeds | v. ENGLAND (Third Test, 5 days) |

10	Selkirk	v. Scotland (1 day)	13	Northampton	v. Northants
11	Glasgow	v. Scotland (3 days)	16	Trent Bridge	v. Nottinghamshire
16	Belfast	v. Ireland (2 days)	21	Oval	v. ENGLAND
18	Dublin	v. Ireland (1 day)			(Fifth Test, 5 days)
19	Lord's	v. Middlesex	27	Canterbury	v. Kent
24	Old Trafford	v. ENGLAND			
		(Fourth Test, 5 days)			
30	Oval	v. Surrey			

AUGUST

2	Swansea	v. Glamorgan
6	Edgbaston	v. Warwickshire
9	Cheltenham	v. Gloucestershire

SEPTEMBER

3	Hastings	v. A. E. R. Gilligan's XI
6	Blackpool	v. Lancashire
10	Scarborough	v. T. N. Pearce's XI
13	Newcastle	v. Minor Counties (2 days)

MINOR COUNTIES

Monday, May 12

| Bristol | Gloucs. II v. Lancs. II |
| Oakham | Leics. II v. Northants II |

Wednesday, May 14

Shrewsbury	Shropshire v. Staffs.
Coalville	Leics. II v. Notts II
Old Trafford	Lancs. II v. Warwick. II
Lord's	Middlesex II v. Kent II

Monday, May 19

Edgbaston	Warwick. II v. Cheshire
Barnsley	Yorks II v. Northants II
Taunton	Somerset II v. Essex II

Wednesday, May 21

Ilkeston	Derbyshire II v. Notts II
Blackburn	Lancs. II v. Cumberland
Chingford	Essex II v. Kent II

Friday, May 23

| Camborne | Cornwall v. Devon |

Saturday, May 24

| Oval | Surrey II v. Kent II |

Monday, May 26

Boston	Lincs. v. Bedford
Edgbaston	Warwick. II v. Derby. II
Old Trafford	Lancs. II v. Yorks II
Taunton	Somerset II v. Gloucs. II
Chester-le-Street	Durham v. Northmbld.

Wednesday, May 28

| Norton | Staffs. v. Shropshire |
| Leamington | Warwick. II v Surrey II |

Monday, June 2

Derby	Derby. II v. Lancs. II
Saltaire	Yorkshire II v. Lincs.
Rothwell	Northants II v. War. II
Sevenoaks	Kent II v. Middlesex II
Leicester	Leics. II v. Somerset II

Wednesday, June 4

| Oxton | Cheshire v. Staffordshire |
| Worksop | Notts II v. Lancs. II |

Thursday, June 5

| Harlow | Essex II v. Somerset II |
| Northampton | Northants II v. Derby. II |

Monday, June 9

| Northampton | Northants II v. Leics. II |
| Oval | Surrey II v. Lancs. II |

Wednesday, June 11

Macclesfield	Cheshire v. Yorks II
Birmingham (Mitchell and Butler's)	Warwick II v. Notts II
Wisbech	Cambs. v. Lincolnshire
Carlisle	Cumbld. v. Northmbld.

Thursday, June 12

| Old Trafford | Lancs. II v. Northants II |

Monday, June 16

Loughboro'	Leics. II v. Warwick. II
Wollaton	Notts II v. Northants II
Old Trafford	Lancs. II v. Durham
Aylesford	Kent II v. Somerset II

Tuesday, June 17

| March | Cambs. v. Bedfordshire |

Wednesday, June 18

Melton Mowbray	Leics. II v. Derby. II
Old Trafford	Lancs. II v. Cheshire
Bristol	Gloucs. II v. War. II
Braintree	Essex II v. Middlesex II
Whitehaven	Cumberland v. Durham

Monday, June 23

Blackhill	Durham v. Staffordshire
Jesmond	Northmbld. v. Yorks II
Oval	Surrey II v. Wiltshire
Penrith	Cumberland v. Lancs. II

Wednesday, June 25

Newcastle	Northmbld. v. Staffs.
Retford	Notts II v. Derby. II
Ealing	Middx. II v. Northants II
Lutterworth	Leics. II v. Lincs.
Gravesend	Kent II v. Essex II

Friday, June 27

Falmouth	Cornwall v. Somerset II

Monday, June 30

Derby	Derby. II v. Northants II
Bristol	Gloucs. II v. Somerset II
Jesmond	Northmbld. v. Lancs. II

Wednesday, July 2

Letchworth	Herts v. Beds
Bp. Auckland	Durham v. Lancs. II
Grimsby	Lincs. v. Cambs.
Market Drayton	Shropshire v. War. II

Friday, July 4

Canterbury	Kent II v. Surrey II
Mistley	Essex II v. Suffolk

Monday, July 7

Hornsey	Middlesex II v. Norfolk
Corby	Northants II v. Lancs. II
Mitcham	Surrey II v. Essex II
Edgbaston	Warwick. II v. Durham

Wednesday, July 9

Longton	Staffs. v. Durham
Hertford	Herts v. Norfolk
Neston	Cheshire v. War. II
Bourne	Lincs. v. Yorkshire II
Old Trafford	Lancs. II v. Notts II
Frinton	Essex II v. Cambs.

Monday, July 14

Northampton	Northants II v. Yorks. II
Oval	Surrey II v. Gloucs. II
Highton, Lpl.	Lancs. II v. Northmbld.

Wednesday, July 16

Wardown Pk., Luton	Bedfordshire v. Staffs.
Ely	Cambs. v. Norfolk
Derby	Derby. II v. Shropshire
Macclesfield	Cheshire v. Lancs. II
Middlesbro'	Yorks. II v. Northmbld.
Nottingham (Police Grd.)	Notts II v. Leics. II
Enfield	Middlesex II v. Essex II

Thursday, July 17

Penzance	Cornwall v. Gloucs. II

Monday, July 21

Jesmond	Northmbld. v. Cheshire
Bridlington	Yorkshire II v. Durham
Southport	Lancs. II v. Surrey II
Newark	Notts II v. Warwick. II

Wednesday, July 23

Wardown Pk., Luton	Beds v. Cambs.
Chesterfield	Derby. II v. Leics. II
York	Yorks II v. Cheshire
Northampton	Northants II v. Middx. II

Thursday, July 24

Edgbaston	Warwick. II v. Gloucs. II

Friday, July 25

Norwich	Norfolk v. Bucks

Monday, July 28

Norwich	Norfolk v. Middlesex II
H. Wycombe	Bucks v. Oxfordshire
Harrogate	Yorks II v. Cumberland
Stroud	Gloucs. II v. Surrey II
Nuneaton	Warwick. II v. Leics. II

Wednesday, July 30

Cambridge	Cambs. v. Herts
Torquay	Devon v. Somerset II
Northampton	Northants II v. Notts II
Camborne	Cornwall v. Berkshire
Bridgnorth	Shropshire v. Derby. II
Darlington	Durham v. Yorkshire II
Lincoln	Lincs. v. Leics. II

Friday, August 1

Oxford	Oxfordshire v. Bucks
Exeter	Devon v. Berkshire
Trowbridge	Wiltshire v. Somerset II

Monday, August 4

Bedford Schl.	Beds v. Shropshire
Norwich	Norfolk v. Herts
Seaton	Devon v. Cornwall

Derby	Derby. II v. War. II
Scarborough	Yorks. II v. Lancs. II
Swindon	Wiltshire v. Surrey II
Trent Bridge	Notts II v. Lincolnshire
Weymouth	Dorset v. Somerset II
Felixstowe	Suffolk v. Essex II
Jesmond	Northmbld. v. Durham
Slough	Bucks v. Berkshire

Wednesday, August 6

Bedford Schl.	Bedfordshire v. Lincs.
Leek	Staffordshire v. Cheshire
Norwich	Norfolk v. Suffolk
Burnham-on-Sea	Somerset II v. Cornwall
Reading	Berkshire v. Oxfordshire
Keswick	Cumberland v. Yorks. II
Old Trafford	Lancs. II v. Gloucs. II
Weymouth	Dorset v. Wiltshire
Sawston	Cambs. v. Essex II
South Shields	Durham v. Warwick. II
H. Wycombe	Bucks v. Herts

Friday, August 8

Bedford Sch.	Beds v. Herts
Norwich	Norfolk v. Notts II
Blandford	Dorset v. Cornwall
Trowbridge	Wiltshire v. Oxfordshire
Lowestoft	Suffolk v. Middlesex II
Newbury Sch.	Berks v. Bucks

Monday, August 11

Porthill	Staffs. v. Yorkshire II
Reading Sch.	Berkshire v. Cornwall
Edgbaston	War. II v. Shropshire
Oxford (Sports Club)	Oxfordshire v. Wiltshire
Brooklands	Cheshire v. Northmbld.
Chelmsford	Essex II v. Surrey II
Wimborne	Dorset v. Devon
Felixstowe	Suffolk v. Hertfordshire
Chesham	Bucks v. Kent II

Wednesday, August 13

Stockton-on-Tees	Durham v. Cumberland
Uttoxeter	Staffs. v. Northmbld.
Norwich	Norfolk v. Cambs.
Bristol	Gloucs. II v. Cornwall
Banbury	Oxfordshire v. Devon
Oval	Surrey II v. Warwick. II
Scunthorpe	Lincs. v. Notts II
Bemerton, Salisbury	Wiltshire v. Dorset

Friday, August 15

Felixstowe	Suffolk v. Norfolk
Oxford (Sports Grd.)	Oxfordshire v. Dorset

Folkestone	Kent II v. Bucks
Reading	Berkshire v. Devon
Frome	Somerset II v. Wiltshire

Monday, August 18

Wellington	Shropshire v. Beds.
Coventry (G.E.C. Grd.)	War. II v. Northants II
Reading	Berkshire v Dorset
Bristol (Imperial)	Somerset II v. Kent II
Croxley Green	Herts v. Bucks

Wednesday, August 20

Longton	Staffs. v Beds
Steetley (Shireoaks Gd.)	Notts II v. Yorkshire II
Yeovil	Somerset II v. Dorset
Winchmore Hill	Middlesex II v. Suffolk
Hitchin	Herts v. Cambs.
Jesmond	Northmbld. v. Cumbld.

Friday, August 22

St. Albans	Herts v. Suffolk
Ascott Park, Wing	Bucks v. Norfolk
Liskeard	Cornwall v. Dorset
Oxford (Christ Ch.)	Oxford. v. Berkshire

Saturday, August 23

Lord's	Middlesex II v. Surrey II

Monday, August 25

Old Trafford	Lancs. II v. Derby. II
Huddersfield	Yorks II v. Notts II
Plymouth	Devon v. Dorset
Weston	Somerset II v. Leics. II

Wednesday, August 27

Redcar	Yorks II v. Staffs.
Trent Bridge	Notts II v. Norfolk
Torquay	Devon v. Oxfordshire
Dorchester	Dorset v. Berkshire
Edgbaston	Warwick. II v. Lancs. II

Thursday, August 28

Beddington	Surrey II v. Middlesex II

Friday, August 29

Taunton	Somerset II v. Devon
Sherborne	Dorset v. Oxfordshire

Saturday, September 13

Newcastle	Minor Counties v. New Zealand